PUBLIC MANAGEMENT OF SOCIETY

# Public Management of Society

Rediscovering French Institutional Engineering in the European Context

Ton van der Eyden

IOS Press

Ohmsha

Amsterdam • Berlin • Oxford • Tokyo • Washington, DC

© 2003, The author

All rights reserved. No part of this book may be reproduced, stored in a retrieval system, or transmitted, in any form or by any means, without prior written permission from the publisher.

ISBN 1 58603 291 7 (IOS Press)
ISBN 4 274 90583 7 C3034 (Ohmsha)
Library of Congress Control Number: 2003102051

*Publisher*
IOS Press
Nieuwe Hemweg 6B
1013 BG Amsterdam
The Netherlands
fax: +31 20 620 3419
e-mail: order@iospress.nl

*Distributor in the UK and Ireland*
IOS Press/Lavis Marketing
73 Lime Walk
Headington
Oxford OX3 7AD
England
fax: +44 1865 75 0079

*Distributor in the USA and Canada*
IOS Press, Inc.
5795-G Burke Centre Parkway
Burke, VA 22015
USA
fax: +1 703 323 3668
e-mail: iosbooks@iospress.com

*Distributor in Germany, Austria and Switzerland*
IOS Press/LSL.de
Gerichtsweg 28
D-04103 Leipzig
Germany
fax: +49 341 995 4255

*Distributor in Japan*
Ohmsha, Ltd.
3-1 Kanda Nishiki-cho
Chiyoda-ku, Tokyo 101-8460
Japan
fax: +81 3 3233 2426

LEGAL NOTICE
The publisher is not responsible for the use which might be made of the following information.

PRINTED IN THE NETHERLANDS

# Preface by Christopher Pollitt

This is a daring and unusual book. It is also an overdue contribution to what has been, in the Anglo-Saxon world, a neglected topic, namely French institutions. During the last thirty years there has been a flowering of academic studies of public administration and public management in British and American universities, but very little of this effort has been focussed on France. Few Anglophone students of 'public management' study France or read French texts on public administration, politics or public law. Yet – as we Anglophones are vaguely aware, and as this book makes crystal clear – the French have made a huge contribution to these subjects, both in theory and in practice. Love it or hate it, the French state has been, and remains, a formidable assemblage of laws, traditions, capacities and practices. What is more, it has profoundly influenced many other countries and, most recently, has extensively shaped the institutions of the European Union. Yet as little as 30 kilometres away, in England, we largely ignore this rich heritage or (possibly even worse) we caricature and stereotype it, in order to reduce its significance. Even in continental states such as the Netherlands (which has certainly had its own historical connections with France!) and the Nordic countries, it seems that Anglo-American-Australasian materials take precedence in the study of public affairs, and French texts are the taste of a small minority.

Of course, for the English and Americans – often language laggards – the fact that most French scholarship is (unsurprisingly) in French has provided an excuse for ignoring it. Ton van der Eyden has totally removed this last, feeble excuse. He has provided the English-speaking world with a comprehensive and up-to-date overview of the 'public management of society' in France, going right back to the time of the Romans. So it has taken a Dutchman, writing in English about France, to overcome the Anglo-American mixture of suspicion, neglect and linguistic incompetence. [Of course there have been some honourable exceptions to this criticism of British and American scholars – and they are fully referenced in this book – but it seems that there were actually not all that many of them.]

In my first sentence I suggested that this was a daring and unusual work. I said this because of the scope of the book, its ambitious approach to theory, and the boldness of its historical interpretations. Its scope – two thousand years of French history, fully set in an international context – is very broad. Few writers would have the courage or the knowledge even to begin such an enterprise. I suspect that, like me, many who already know something of French institutions or French history will be able to take this text and use it in a satisfying way to locate their own fragments of knowledge in a much wider and deeper picture. As far as theory is concerned, Ton van der Eyden adopts a multi-disciplinary, generic treatment, using Luhmann's social systems theory and attempting to relate this to many other theoretical models in several disciplines. It is, in other words, an attempt at a massive synthesis and integration. Whilst I may have my own doubts about the eventual success of this treatment, I certainly admire the attempt to get beyond the usual, careful but narrow approach of the professional academic – to devise a theoretical apparatus which is equal in scope to the broad historical canvas that the book sets out to cover. As for historical interpretation, the book is challenging. In general it avoids the 'on the one hand, on the other hand' minuet of much academic history and offers, instead, clear, sharp and sometimes controversial renderings of key processes, institutions and events. All in all, therefore, it is an exciting read, in which the author's stance is abundantly clear and the reader is free to agree or disagree with the interpretation.

Most of all, however, it is obvious that this book is a labour of love. It is the product of many years of study, and of a straightforward fascination with and respect for French public life and letters. This, I suggest, is what gives the text its greatest appeal. It is not an apologia by an insider, but rather a sympathetic, yet critical appraisal by an extremely well-informed outsider. I hope that many other 'outsiders', throughout the Anglophone world, will read and enjoy it.

Christopher Pollitt
Professor of Public Management
Erasmus University Rotterdam
September 2002

# Acknowledgements

This book is dedicated to my beloved Lidwien (deceased), who waited for this book for so long. As a librarian this was the publication she missed in her book collection. I appreciate the sympathetic involvement of my sons Hans, Joost and Rob, who asked me weekly (for years) about the progress of the book, and especially thank them for solving my computer headaches. The author thanks Einar Fredriksson and his staff of IOS Press for their enthusiastic professionalism. A special word of gratitude goes to my daughter-in-law, Nicoline van der Eyden-Welsch, for time spent on making this manuscript camera-ready, and also to my sister-in-law, Wies Oldenziel-Werner, for her creativity in designing the cover. This book owes a great deal to Professor Arthur Ringeling of the Erasmus University in Rotterdam, as he made useful comments about versions of the manuscript. Peggy Birch is praised for her talented language upgrading. "Chapeau" for Professor Christopher Pollitt, British guru of Public Management, who wrote an original and stimulating preface. The author would like to pay tribute to all authors who activated him with thoughtprovoking ideas for this research project about that "eternal France" and the issue of Public Management of Society. With a research project like this, it is inevitable that there are shortcomings. The author would be glad to receive comments and suggestions for corrections. May this book contribute to a better understanding of the French way of Public Management of Society and its "esprit". I look forward to a critical and professional debate about a culturally intelligent Public Management of Society.

# Contents

**Preface by Christopher Pollitt** v
**Acknowledgements** vii

## Part 1. The Issue of Public Management of Society

1. Introduction 3
1.1. Public Management of Society 3
1.2. Alternative notions (public administration, state, government, politics, governance) 8
1.3. Plan of this research project 11
1.4. Summary 13

2. France, Unique Laboratory for Public Management of Society 24
2.1. French experiences during many centuries 24
2.2. Before the French Revolution 31
2.3. From French Revolution to Bonaparte 36
2.4. From Napoleon Bonaparte to Emperor Napoleon III 43
2.5. From Third Republic to Second World War 52
2.6. From Liberation to the start of the 21st century 56

## Part 2. The Fifth Republic

3. The Fifth Republic survived the 20th Century 69
3.1. De Gaulle, the first president of the Fifth Republic 69
3.1.1. Birth of the Fifth Republic: "République gaullienne" 69
3.1.2. De Gaulle fighting for the "grandeur de France" 71
3.1.3. De Gaulle as 20th century Napoleon 75
3.1.4. From "Gaullisme gaullien" to "Gaullisme gaulliste" 78
3.2. The Constitution of 1958 and the Fifth Republic 81
3.2.1. Historical developments 81
3.2.2. The Constitution of 1958 for the Fifth Republic 88
3.3. The Gaullist philosophy of Public Management of Society 94
3.3.1. De Gaulle's contribution to French specificity 94
3.3.2. De Gaulle and his ideas 99
3.3.3. The Gaullist movement 102
3.3.4. Independent, sovereign "grandeur" of France as central theme 103
3.3.5. Several interpretations of Gaullism 107
3.4. Public authorities and organisations 110
3.4.1. Public authorities and organisations with a national scope 110
3.4.2. Public Administration 116
3.4.3. Specific public authorities and organisations 121
3.4.4. Public Management in territorially subdivided France 125
3.4.5. Organisation of the French judiciary ("Justice") 129

## Part 3. Public Policymaking, Politics and Public Management of Society

| | |
|---|---|
| 4. Justice, Police and Penal System | 141 |
| 4.1. Specific French principles of jurisdiction | 141 |
| 4.2. Since 1958 judiciary authority instead of judiciary power | 147 |
| 4.3. From "Police" as public affairs to Police properly | 150 |
| 4.4. Some features of the French police model | 153 |
| 4.5. Juridical regime of the French police | 157 |
| 4.6. Police as qualified public service | 163 |
| 4.7. Prison system. Structural crisis in the penitentiary system | 166 |
| 4.8. Reforming justice and jurisdiction | 169 |
| 5. From Socio-economic Steering to Cultural Engineering | 194 |
| 5.1. French public management of the economy | 194 |
| 5.2. Managing reconstruction of devastated France since 1945 | 197 |
| 5.3. Construction of the Fifth Republic: modernisation | 200 |
| 5.4. Original French planning, "planification à la française" | 206 |
| 5.5. From centralist interventionism to sophisticated public management of society | 212 |
| 5.6. Some specific public policies | 218 |
| 5.7. Social security | 222 |
| 5.8. Health care | 226 |
| 5.9. Environmental policies | 229 |
| 5.10. Educational and cultural policies | 230 |
| 5.11. Cultural engineering and "Francophonie" | 236 |
| 5.12. Concluding remarks | 238 |
| 6. Politics and Public Management of Society | 251 |
| 6.1. The two births of French political science | 251 |
| 6.2. French institutionalist paradigm. Emergence of empirical social science | 254 |
| 6.3. The second birth of French political science | 258 |
| 6.4. German influences, Marxism and Communism | 259 |
| 6.5. From State to Public Management of Society | 262 |
| 6.6. Political parties and politicians, trying to kidnap public authority | 269 |
| 6.7. Party-politics in the first half of the 20th century | 272 |
| 6.8. Party-politics as a kind of "power-capitalism" | 274 |
| 6.9. Specifics of the French political system | 278 |
| 6.10. Socialist and other leftist movements | 281 |
| 6.11. Conservative, rightist movements and leftist reactions | 286 |
| 6.12. Political life after Liberation | 289 |
| 6.13. The Fourth Republic (1946-1958) | 292 |
| 6.14. From "Gaullist Republic" to post-De Gaulle Fifth Republic | 298 |
| 6.15. "Double Septennat-Mitterrand" (1981-1995); Chirac Era (1995-2002; 2002-2007) | 304 |

## Part 4. France in the International and Co-national Arena

### 7. International Relations: Military Management, Peace Management and Diplomacy — 329
7.1. Military management and peace management — 329
7.1.1 War and peace as institutions. French historical experiences — 329
7.1.2 French position as dominant power lost in the First World War — 336
7.1.3 Versailles Treaty, crisis and collaborative Vichy Regime (1940-1944) — 340
7.1.4 After the Second World War, changing geopolitical conditions — 347
7.2. Nuclear weapon heart of French strategy for military independence — 352
7.2.1 Nuclear diplomacy: keeping up with the superpowers — 352
7.2.2 France attached to an independent role — 359
7.3. Secret services — 363
7.3.1 A long tradition of French secret services — 363
7.3.2 After the First World War — 366
7.4. International relations and diplomacy — 372
7.4.1 Territorial obsession — 372
7.4.2 International law is broader than interstate law — 376
7.4.3 French preference for law as tool of diplomacy — 380
7.4.4 Collective security, common defence: NATO and NEO-NATO logics — 383

### 8. Public Management of Society in the European Union, in the Neo-European Age — 416
8.1. A short history of European integration — 416
8.2. Social and economic conditions of a Common Market — 419
8.3. French politicking as a structural phenomenon — 424
8.4. Treaty of Maastricht: European Union — 426
8.5. Juridical institutionalising from Rome (1957) to Amsterdam (1997) — 428
8.6. Institutionalising a new architecture of decision-making — 435
8.7. Treaty of Amsterdam (1997) — 440
8.8. Convergence between "Rule of Law" and "État de droit" in the European Union — 446
8.9. Beyond the Treaty of Amsterdam. Towards a European Constitution — 454

## Part 5. A Dialogue in the Framework of Theoretical Perspectives

### 9. Public Management of Society in Co-disciplinary Perspective — 479
9.1. Cultural specificity of French Public Management of Society — 479
9.2. Construction of social reality, (new) institutionalism and French institutionalists — 487
9.3. Public Management of Society beyond the modernism/postmodernism debate — 499
9.4. From governance to professional Public Management of Society — 512
9.5. Working-hypotheses for a co-disciplinary focus on public management of society — 527

### 10. Rule of Law, Idea of Public Authority and Cultural Intelligence — 549
10.1. From the vicious circle of vengeance to Roman law — 550
10.2. Rule of law in gestation — 554

10.3. French Revolution, impact of revolutions in Great-Britain and Northern America     560
10.4. Institutional outburst of the French Revolution     565
10.5. Confrontation of French doctrine with German ideas     569
10.6. Important French theoreticians of law     574
10.7. Ongoing debate about the state     579
10.8. The principle of sovereignty     586
10.9. "All-is-politics" thesis. Institutionalising of the state (Burdeau)     593
10.10. "Zero-State" thesis (De Bodinat)     600
10.11. "Law-without-the-State" thesis (Cohen-Tanugi)     602
10.12. Cultural mindset base for constitutional government     608
10.13. Cultural mapping of public authority     616
10.14. Cultural intelligence necessary condition for adequate Public Management of Society     620

**Epilogue**     639

**Appendix** (on CD-ROM)

I. The Relevance of History for Contemporary French Public Management of Society (I-XX Centuries)
II. Bibliography Public Management of Society

# Part One

# The Issue of Public Management of Society

# 1. Introduction

## 1.1. Public Management of Society

Good Public Management of Society is one of the most fundamental human needs, but it is not yet explicitly or formally recognised as one of the Human Rights. At best it is an implicit part of Human Rights. A Declaration of Human Rights is one thing, guaranteeing that these rights are realised and implemented is another issue, so Public Management of Society is a crucial phenomenon. One might argue that this is a phenomenon universal to all parts of the world, and in all historical periods. Studies often deal with parts or aspects of Public Management of Society, seeking to formulate generalisations supposed to have validity worldwide. In this research project it is shown that generalisations about Public Management of Society have to reckon with two basic axes: the dimension of universalism and the cultural specificity of regions, countries and nation-states. This study is concentrated on Public Management of Society in France, cradle of human rights, explicitly and in comparative perspective. In the last chapters Public Management of Society is dealt with in a more theoretical way. The object of study, Public Management of Society, is so multi-faceted that co-disciplinary research is needed. It is argued that the Rule of Law and the Idea of Public Authority are crucial for Public Management of Society. "The better the society, the less law there will be. The worse the society, the more law there will be." (Sitkin/Bies, 1994, p.X). The spectacular terrorist attacks on the Twin Towers of the World Trade Center in New York and the building of the Pentagon on 11 September 2001 make it evident again that law and order is a crucial, structural task of Public Management of Society. To understand this kind of violence better it is necessary to dive repeatedly into history's lessons (Kepel, 2001; Lewis, 1985). In a sense, history always hits back. When cultural aspects play a dominant role, as in Ben Laden's call for a "Jihad" against the infidel West (Jacquard, 2001) it is especially desirable to acquaint oneself with aspects of culturally different dimensions. France is a unique laboratory of Public Management of Society, so it is worth knowing more about French ideas and practices in historical perspective. Such knowledge is a useful antidote to the dominance of American theorising and practices in mainstream literature about Public Administration. Reckoning with cultural dimensions is necessary for adequate Public Management of Society in theory and in practice (Reynolds, 2001). We have to act and think with cultural intelligence in Public Management of Society.

Public Management of Society, the field of knowledge about the activities of public authorities in society, has to be distinguished from public management as it is understood in mainstream literature. Public Management of Society is defined as the primary social system regulating the processes of society using specific instruments to fulfil this task: legislation, jurisdiction, taking care of 'the general interest', legal monopoly of legitimised use of force. Society, the notion for groups of men and women living together in communities, is seen as the whole of sense-related social interactions between human beings. Society is the existential living world of human beings, with all social reality interpretations of groups and individuals as they experience them. Managing a Nation-State or parts of it is different from running a business or organisation, private or public. Managing the French Nation-State was and is different. In the competition of Nation-States (Porter, 1990), France can be seen as the long standing world-champion in developing arrangements for institutional engineering with regard to Public Management of Society (Coulborn, 1959; Greigueuil, 1999; McNeill, 1963). In the world history of institutional engineering, French Public Management of Society is prominent (Bagby, 1958; Braudel,

1994). Understanding contemporary Public Management of Society in France, in national and international perspective, is only possible with intensive knowledge of its historical dimensions and cultural roots (Bozeman, 1994). Historical dimensions are an integral part of actual realities, especially in France. The path dependent evolution of Public Management of Society is a crucial dimension of contemporary thinking and practices. One might think, that history is interesting in so far as it produces solutions for contemporary problems. If this is the case so much the better but there is much more that is relevant about historically based knowledge. Polybius (201-120 BC) wrote that studying history is the best preparation for public management practices. Public Management of Society is interconnected with all dimensions of society, with all aspects of human rivalries, ambitions, and other human passions. This interconnectedness makes it necessary to take a French style broad view of societal dimensions when considering Public Management of Society.

Cultural mapping, the analysis of cultural dimensions, proves to be a necessary adjunct to adequate theorising about Public Management of Society, but practitioners also need an adequate idea of the cultural context of their activities in order to be effective. A popular bias has it that circumstances are now so different from earlier times that a completely new situation has developed with globalisation, informatics and technology making earlier developments useless (Featherstone, 1990). The market is in, government is out. It is quite amazing that Osborne and Gaebler (1992) had such an echo in circles concerned with reforming government. More businesslike government on the basis of lessons learned from some of the best companies (Gore, 1997), is, with the exception of a few specific cases, the wrong answer to an incorrectly stated problem (Le Goff, 1995; 2000). They have an inadequate recipe for an ineffective medicine. The issue is how to improve public management broadly, on the basis of lessons learned from the most effective public managers (Pollitt/Bouckaert, 2000). Recognising the nature of changed circumstances nowadays one has to admit that historical knowledge is also crucial to a better understanding of how and why human beings act, react and think in different situations. Digressing on historical developments is necessary (Raadschelders, 1998) because Public Management of Society is an important part of the history of civilisation and evolution (Duby/Mandrou, 1984; Melko, 1969). Many publications deal with aspects of French culture, so dwelling on cultural and historical dimensions of French Public Management of Society, and that "eternal France" (Konopnicki, 2001), is justified, as is calling attention to French (re-)constructions of the past in comparative perspective (Revel/ Hunt, 1995). As has been said, re-reading history is the sole philosophy.

In April 2002 not only the French public but people everywhere were shocked by the near election of extreme-rightist Le Pen as President of the French Republic. This shock was understandable in view of both his program and his antecedents (Bresson/Lionet, 1994; Perrineau, 1997; Winock, 1994). He once said that the Holocaust was only a detail. A stubborn adherent of French Algeria and Vichy-Pétain, Poujadist, and since De Gaulle's choice for an independent Algeria a fierce anti-gaullist, he founded the extreme-rightist party "Le Front National"in 1973, opposing the Fifth Republic. Since 1983 Le Pen has achieved about 10%-15% of the votes. His 16.95% in the first round of the presidential elections (21 April 2002) was only 233,196 votes more than the Socialist Prime-Minister Jospin (16.22%), who, by denying his former membership of a trotskyite movement, had lost his credibility (Pingaud, 2002). Because on 5 May 2002 both left and right voted for neo-gaullist Chirac to rescue France from Le Pen, Chirac got the largest majority in the history of the Fifth Republic, 82.21% against 17.79% for Le Pen (Haziza, 2002). To understand this important event fully one has to acquaint oneself with French history. There are a number of reasons for the debacle of the left (Amar/Chemin, 2002) including dissension and the widely criticised policies of theJospin government (with Socialists,

Communists and Greens). Leftist France was forced to vote for Chirac, hoping to get as many votes as possible in the parliamentary elections (9-16 June 2002) to form a countervailing power in a new "cohabitation". Premier Jospin resigned and Jean-Pierre Raffarin (2002), writing a book with a plea for new governance, was nominated as Prime-Minister until 16 June 2002. Chirac, overcoming traditional rightist dissension by forming a new electoral cartel, "Union pour la Majorité Présidentielle" (UMP), got a record majority with 369 members out of a total 577 in the "Assemblée Nationale". Extreme-rightist Le Pen got no seat in parliament. Government-Raffarin-II was promptly installed. The future looks bright for the rightists in the period 2002-2007, with all power positions in their hands: Presidency, government and majorities in National Assembly and Senate.

When French Public Management of Society is discussed in Anglo-American media or in most of mainstream Anglo-American literature, it is often – with the exception of some excellent studies – played down or even ridiculed ("See the high unemployment in France, they cannot manage adequately with their State-obsession!" and the like). "The Economist" in June 1999 asserted that the French became ever more Anglo-Saxon or American. This may appear to be so with a standard Anglo-Saxon reflex and an Anglo-Saxon myopia about the specificity of French culture, but this is not the proper diagnostic. On the contrary, the French do take their culture seriously, and, what is more, France is a cultural superpower with a very positive surplus on its cultural import-export balance. When there is debate about some aspect of French Public Management of Society in mainstream Anglo-American literature it is often handled in a too anecdotal way, or references to French experiences and insights are reduced to short indications of the rich French cultural patrimony, or worse, put aside with one-liners. French public authorities, and especially French politicians, are to blame for many policy failures and malpractice, this is true, as it is in other countries. Several French authors criticise contemporary French Public Management of Society: Barreau (1997); Baverez (1997); Bébéar (2002); Crozier (1997); Fauroux/Spitz (2001); Joxe (1998); Montbrial (2002); Peyrefitte (1976); Pontaut/ Szpiner (1989); Revel (1992); Todd (1998); and Touraine (1996). It is however a blunder to use examples of mismanagement in the French public sphere to argue that American public management is superior, or to think that one can dismiss knowledge of French Public Management of Society which is far more sophisticated than often asserted or supposed (Gordon/Meunier, 2002). For French insiders, it is a serious annoyance that they are repeatedly confronted with so-called Anglo-American ideas, inventions or practices, when these are disguised emanations of the authentic French cultural patrimony. This is a two – way interaction of the Atlantic-European area and developments in France must be placed in the context of its primary environment, Europe as cultural challenge (Carbonell, 1999; Domenach, 1990).

"Europe has been much, much more protean, changeful, and innovative than any other part of the globe. It has moved from Roman imperial autocracy and law, through a Dark Ages, into feudalism, thence into absolutist and territorial states, finally into representative democracy, and then, beyond that, into the socialist collective autocracies until 1989 of the eastern part of the continent." (Finer, 1997, p.14). In his excellent history of government from the earliest times Finer deals with the French contribution in the development of institutional engineering, but on closer investigation, the conclusion is that Finer underestimates the French impact. That becomes obvious when investigations are concentrated on the many dimensions of French Public Management of Society, as in this study. 1999 marked the bicentenary of the institutional zenith of the first decade after the French Revolution (1789-1799). In this decade, as throughout the last two centuries, and in the period from the start of our era, France was a prominent institutional laboratory with an emanation worldwide. France remains a creative institutional laboratory. There was and is specific French institutional engineering. There has been a special relationship of rivalries and affections between France and Great Britain, and between France and Germany (Keiger, 2001). Walter (2001) told the love-story between English and French languages and the French can read Buruma's book about Anglomania in their language: "Anglomanie. Une fascination européenne" (2001). Misunderstandings between the French and the English have been a more or less continuous theme of the "mésentente cordiale" of their intercultural communication (Geoffroy, 2001). When one tries to be as objective as possible, one has to reckon with these dimensions and sensibilities, it is not always possible to translate expressions adequately with all the needed nuance. Intellectual histories of France and England have an impact upon matters in contemporary society. There is a British way and a French way of Public Management of Society.

Public Management of Society is the subject of this study, but an adequate "accessus ad materiam" for this field of study is quite complex. Public Management of Society (PMS) is chosen as the central concept as opposed to politics, state, government, governance or public administration. The notion of Public Management of Society as used here, differs from mainstream conceptualisation about public management, which is more or less an application of business management ideation to the field of public affairs. The PMS concept has to be interpreted as a more or less all-encompassing framework for studying the Public Management of Society phenomenon as such. The PMS phenomenon is so multidimensional, that for pragmatic reasons mostly a reductionist approach is followed, defining parts or dimensions out. In the framework of a reasonable division of labour, this is good practice, if only when seen as provisional. Complementary to this, building-blocks have to be brought together in the framework of an overarching, synthesising architecture. It is not adequate to think, as is sometimes done, that a more scientific approach for the study of PMS started with the official recognition of the discipline within the university framework of disciplines, or to date the PMS phenomenon back to the take-off period of the State. Long before that there were prominent thinkers and practitioners with professional knowledge and know-how about PMS and their work sometimes has a surprising actuality from which valuable insights can be gained. An adequate approach is to go back to the earliest times, as Finer (1997) did, reconstructing pre-history (Bell, 1994; Cohen, 1999), and history is rewarding (Greigueuil, 1999) for, from the earliest times on, human beings organised society giving some persons responsibilities as representatives of public authorities.

A number of dimensions, aspects and parts of the PMS phenomenon are entrusted to several disciplines, sub-disciplines and specialisations. The political part of PMS is for political science; juridical aspects are only partially tackled in this field, and for the rest, one is referred to the juridical discipline(s), sub-disciplines and specialisations. The international position of national public authorities is often forgotten in administrative science studies, or thought to be part of the international relations discipline. Transnational developments as in the European Union do create problems for the compartmentalisation of disciplines. Economic aspects are generally only partially handled and so it is with sociological, geographical, psychological, social-cultural anthropological, technological, historical, philosophical and other dimensions of the cultural side of this phenomenon. This is quite understandable in a pragmatic perspective. A synthesis of all relevant dimensions of PMS is probably a mission impossible, but it seems possible to come nearer to the ideal by consistently trying to realise a project, not only along disciplinary paths, but also in a co-disciplinary social science perspective, with due respect for the authentic and specific identity and contribution of various disciplines. For this objective, the social systems conceptualisation of Luhmann (1995) seems to give an adequate theoretical framework. In the 19th century, the PMS phenomenon was heavily in the grip of the juridical approach: juridical imperialism ("Rechtsstaat", "État de droit", "Rule of Law"). In the 20th century, the PMS phenomenon was the realm of political science following the axiom "all-is-politics", a sort of political science imperialism. In the last part of the 20th century, economic imperialism prevailed with the "all-is-market" approach and globalisation. It is obvious that public authorities still have an important function in contemporary society. In the 21st century, the PMS phenomenon should be recognised as an object of co-disciplinary, inclusive research, beyond specialisations and imperialisms (Thompson Klein, 1990). The relevance of a more institutional approach to social phenomena, often vilified earlier, is now recognised, so an institutional, historical and cultural approach of Public Management of Society is to the point.

Often "Science administrative" is seen as French discipline of Public Administration (Auby, 1966; Debbasch, 1989). "Science administrative" is about administration in general and public administration. When it deals with public administration, Public Management of Society is only partially treated. Analysis of relevant French literature shows that this applies also for several disciplines in France: "Science administrative", "Science politique", "Droit public", "Relations internationales", "Histoire de l'administration française". Development of Public Management of Society is a universal phenomenon, developing in the course of time for all peoples in different historical periods around the globe (universalism), so a comparative perspective is needed. The task which Finer (1997) performed with his study of government from earliest times in a comparative perspective is especially valuable. Nevertheless, a study concentrated on French PMS (in a comparative perspective), can be seen as a useful addition. There are a number of reasons to give French PMS study and practice a central place, especially when it is seen in a historical perspective. Public Management of Society as a key-issue of human culture and civilisation is crucial for the survival of mankind (Huntington, 1998). In different historical periods, cultures and civilisations, a variety of answers, methods and practices has been found. Developments in the field of knowledge and know-how about Public Management of Society must be seen in the framework of the history of thought (Jerphagnon/Dumas 1989/1990) and philosophy (Châtelet, 1999). Generalising about various approaches is not at all easy, if admissible, and one has to recognise that developments are mostly highly idiosyncratic. What makes French developments especially relevant is that these had a tremendous impact on many other countries, both in Europe and elsewhere.

As elaborated by Jacques Chevallier (1996), the development of administrative science in France is related to a specific French model of the State. In his view the uniqueness of the State in France is based on two phenomena: the social autonomy and the social supremacy of the State. The social autonomy is accentuated by its organic autonomy, legal autonomy (specific rules for the State apparatus which are exceptions to common law), and symbolic autonomy (the State as incarnation of the general interest transcending the particularist interests of the private sphere). The social supremacy of the State is related to the long tradition of interventionism in France. Differentiation between State and society helped to further the idea that a specific body of knowledge about public administration had to be developed. The notion "police" in earlier times was used to denote what we call public administration and management, as in the "Traité de police" (1705/1710) by De la Mare. Bonnin, with his "Principe d'Administration publique" (1812), was a pioneer, arguing for a more scientific study of public administration by developing general principles. In the first half of the 19th century a kind of administrative science as social science was started. With a pragmatic background and the intention to improve State effectiveness by grooming future civil servants, it tended to encompass a broad field of knowledge (economic science, political science, sociology, law). In the 19th century, the idea was that the crucial invention of the "État de droit" had to be implemented fully. So law was more or less seen as the sole relevant and decisive knowledge about the State (legalism). In 1849, an "École d'Administration" was created, but this had a short life and was replaced in 1872 by the "École Libre des Sciences Politiques". The dominance of law and the expansion of administration law blocked a more mature development of public administration as social science until the 20th century.

The field of study of French Public Management of Society is so broad, the richness of ideas and experiences so abundant, the historical dimensions so many-sided, the ways of thinking, theories and methods so impressive, that it would take more than a life's work, and even more than the teamwork of many scholars from diverse disciplines, to give even a meagre sketch of this phenomenon. This study aims to give an outline, intended as an invitation to further study, and forms a hypothesis that can be falsified by eventual better materials. Not unjustly Braudel (1990, p.10), writing about the identity of France, wrote that it is useful and even necessary for French writers to distance themselves from the typical French passions. H. Taine in his "Les Origines de la France contemporaine" (1875/1893) could not realise this. Ardagh (2000) and Fenby (1999), pretending to give an adequate overview of French society, could not analyse French society with a reasonable degree of objectivity either. French-English misunderstandings, prejudices and mental rigidities often caused an amazing "mésentente cordiale" (Geoffroy, 2001). This study must allow ample room for historical material and analyses, but these cannot be a match for the excellent historical guides available: Burguière/Revel, 1989; Carpentier/Lebrun, 1987; Duby, 1999; Ferro, 2001; Lavisse, 1903/1911; Madaule, 1943/1966; Michelet, 1833-1867; Philippe, 1970-1973. to name but a few. There are many studies such as the "Nouvelle histoire de la France contemporaine" (1972/1999), some dealing with the 20th century like the "Histoire de la France au XXe siècle" (1995) by Berstein/Milza, and "Notre siècle" (1991) by Rémond. For the Anglo-American audience excellent studies about French Public Management are available: "Governing France: The One and Indivisible Republic" (1983) by Hayward; "A History of France" (1990) by Cobban; "The Government and Politics of France" (1989) by Wright; and "The Government and Politics of France" (1993) by Stevens. F. Gallouedec-Genuys (1998) and D. Maus et al. (1996) all give an introduction to French administration. Chagnollaud/Quermonne (2000) is an actual overview.

## 1.2. Alternative notions (public administration, state, government, politics, governance)

If one does not know the names, there is no knowledge of things: "nomina si nescis, perit et cognitio rerum". This research project starts with the proposition that a stipulative definition denotes the field of inquiry: Public Management of Society as a field of knowledge about the activities of public authorities in society. A definition can be understood as an "explanation of the meaning or meanings of a word" (Webster's dictionary) and contains two components: a definiendum (the word to be defined) and a definiens (its characterisation). The definiendum is "Public Management of Society", and the definiens is "field of knowledge about the activities of public authorities in society". This definition might be qualified as intersubjectively adequate and capable of communicating contents reasonably unambiguously. According to Halpin (1997, pp.14-15): "A stipulative definition may be regarded as virtuous if it possesses an appropriate combination of the following features: i. Avoidance of incoherence, and/or ii. Avoidance of inconsistency; iii. Breadth of coverage; iv. Depth of coverage; v. Correlation with current usage..; vi. Fit with other schemes...; vii. Any intelligible issue can be discussed...". In the perspective of this research project it is asserted that Public Management of Society can comply with these conditions. Sartori (1975, p.12): "In any process of understanding, at least three elements are involved: i. concepts; ii. words; iii. phenomena. ...we may distinguish between i. concepts, conceptions and meanings, ii. words and terms, iii. phenomena and data. These distinctions are based on the following stipulations: 1. Idea is a mental image, a meaning. 2. Conception is a set of ideas associated with, or elicited by, a given word. 3. Concept is a conception treated according to logical rules. 4. Terms are words which unambiguously refer to concepts. The above stipulations sort out two levels of discourse common (ordinary) and scientific. In common discourse the three elements are: a. meanings, b. words, c. phenomena-or-facts. In scientific discourse the three elements become: a. concepts, b. terms, c. data." Words are the means to identify objects. They intervene in our perception of objects, convey interpretations and attach significance to their referents. "Public Management of Society" is broad enough as an adequate unit of thinking and data container. It encloses all activities of public authorities in society, while excluding activities of social actors behaving as private persons or organisations. Luhmann's "Theorie der Verwaltungswissenschaft" (1966), chosen here as theoretical framework, is theory rich. French Public Management of Society is theory and data rich.

Some argumentation is presented on behalf of "Public Management of Society" instead of the usual notions of "state", "public administration", "government", "politics" or "governance". As will be elaborated further on these notions have serious handicaps. Adequate terminology is essential. Whole libraries can be filled with books about the State. The State is circumscribed as a territorially defined population with recognised public authorities, disposing of specialised personnel (civil service, military service). This State, having sovereignty, is recognised by other States as independent. A drawback is that other public authorities than those functioning as part of the State do not fall within this term, and can only be added by an extending interpretation. Besides, State is an overburdened term. This concept, properly speaking, cannot be used with regard to public authorities in pre-State periods. A debate is going on in contemporary literature about bypassing the State, followed by a "bringing-the-State-back-in" discussion, and there are all kinds of constats about the obsolete nature of the State in the perspective of the seemingly overpowering impact of the (world) market and de-territorialisation. Nevertheless, the State (meant as system of public authorities) and/or a system of States as an international public management system, is a "conditio-sine-qua-non" for society. In the perspective of growing interpenetration of countries by communication technologies and massive social traffic State frontiers seem completely outdated. This argumentation seems decisive with respect to the end of the State as vital phenomenon of relevant public authority in society (Guéhenno, 1999; Habermas, 1999), but it is possible to place recent developments in a different perspective. National States in Europe lose basic, exclusive, sovereign competencies within the integration process of the European Union. This means that institutional engineering to realise adequate Public Management of Society is taking another form. The national State is instrumental with regard to adequate Public Management of Society. Contemporary circumstances are more or less comparable with the situation in the Middle Ages, when a greater socio-economic-cultural space developed, opening the closed frontiers of cities and towns with "in natura" economies and resulting in an inevitable. reshuffling of competencies of public authorities. Now it is more or less the same with regard to Nation-States within the European Union (mutatis mutandis).

The notion "Public Administration" seems to have won an unassailable position as the term to denote the field of administration of public affairs. More than a century after the call for independence for this field of study by Woodrow Wilson in his "The Study of Administration" (1887) this notion has become current, and perhaps even sacrosanct, in the Anglo-American world. Later developments in the French scientific community tended in the same direction with the "Science administrative" ("le fait administratif"). A demarcation between political science and administrative science was accepted; it was taken for granted that a significant part of the functioning of public authorities was entrusted to political science: political institutions. This meant that administrative science had to accept, or accepted, that the functioning of political institutions was not or not fully treated. Often the term (public) administration obfuscated the dilemma. One could interpret this term freely within the bandwidth between "administration is all human activity or organisation in the broadest sense of the word", and "administration is the execution of policy as decided upon by others, the decision-makers". That is obvious when one tries to clear up the notion policy. Policy might be defined as all one does and decides oneself and what all persons higher up in the hierarchy are doing and deciding. What is important is policy. What other people are doing lower in the hierarchy is administration or execution. Policy becomes a very relative notion: the same activity might be policy for one group, and execution or administration for another group. Dunsire (1973) took on the task of defining administration, noting a great many different notions. Administration as notion is not clear, it misses the demarcating precision which a term in the language of science should have.

Another term is government. It is confusing that Americans call "the Administration" what in England is called "the Government". Government is taken as notion to deal with the whole field of activities of public authorities. Finer (1997, p.1) subsumes tribes and states under his concept "government". This term government has serious drawbacks, however. When one tries to give an idea of the different public authorities in a political community or State, it is common to denote government as the competent national organ that has the national leadership over public affairs, but in a democracy this government does not have the last say, because it has to answer to an elected parliament for its policies. So government, composed of a number of ministers, has a clear-cut meaning as a specific organ with public authority. It is therefore quite artificial to denote the whole of public authorities in a Nation-State as government; this "pars-pro-toto" qualification is overburdening the notion of government, besides, it is nearly impossible to encompass all public authorities (e.g. judiciary, military, international public authorities) under this heading of government. This also applies to parliament, because it would be quite strange to bring the parliament under the term government. One may find this discussion to be quite useless, because we have the term politics. When you use the term "political system" to encompass all aspects of power-laden relations in society it seems logical to use the term politics. Many authors work with this all-encompassing term. In France, political science scholar Georges Burdeau elaborated an impressive conception, based upon an "all-is-politics" approach ("Traité de Science Politique", 1986). This approach obscures the specificity of the "Public Management of Society" phenomenon though; it is fundamentally ambivalent. When the decisive differentiating dimension of politics is seen in the power aspects of social life it is inconsistent to deal with "Public Management of Society" as an exclusively political phenomenon. Unless one follows Burdeau on his "all-is-politics" path it is evident that the "Public Management of Society" phenomenon is related also to law, economics, social psychology, cultural anthropology etc. Taking the Burdeau approach seriously, it is inevitable that political is made identical with social: political science would be the same as social science.

It is more fruitful to recognise the relevance of differentiated disciplinary activities to get a grip upon the varied social reality. Political science is about power aspects in society, but then it is inconsistent to see Public Management of Society only from the viewpoint of the power-dimension and not also from other relevant dimensions. Holden (1999), inquiring into the competence of political science in public administration, can be answered that political science as analytical discipline is not competent to handle Public Management of Society fully and adequately. Public Management of Society is a more consistent term to denote functioning and all-encompassing activities of public authorities. Public Management of Society seems the better notion, also in comparison with the modish term "governance", which is popular in the business world ("corporate governance"), and is not promptly and exclusively associated with the activities of public authorities. The term "public" is stretched out to encompass all kinds of social agents in society (Frederickson,

1997, pp.41-52). In public/private partnerships blurring of responsibilities is even seen as an asset: "hybrid governance" (Hupe/Meijs, 2000). Often the genuine public interest is secondary to private interests in the framework of "Private Interest Government" (Streeck/Schmitter, 1985). Globalisation and "the market is all" are popular, current, with the implication that Public Management of Society withers away (Higgott/Payne, 2001). Here the relevance of actualising the "Idea of Public Authority", also in the 21st century, is accentuated. World-systems theory, developed by Wallerstein (1974/1989), Denemark (1999) and Sanderson (1995), is adequate for handling Public Management of Society, especially in its actualised form, as tool for comparative study of cultures (Kardulias, 1999; Robertson, 1992).

The relatively unknown theoretical conception as developed by Niklas Luhmann (1995) is a promising perspective, and is chosen as theoretical framework for this research project. His social systems theory presents itself as integrating nucleus of a general theory of administration and management. Luhmann's concept of social systems refers to the real, existential world of experience of social actors, not to conceptions in theory (as in Parsons' theory). To ascertain the relationship with the reality of empirical processes, social systems are seen as systems of factual activity that are treated by actors themselves as distinct units. A system of human actions as Public Management of Society is a sense-directed coherence, held relatively constant towards a complex, changing environment. In "Theorie der Verwaltungswissenschaft" (1966), Luhmann had seven working-hypotheses for an integrated social science with Public Management of Society as subject matter: 1. Social systems theory; 2. Realisation of binding decisions; 3. Public management system and its environment; 4. Juridical structure of public management; 5. Rationalising public management by systems-rationality; 6. Functional-comparative method; 7. Bridging the gap between rationalising-normative and empirical-explanatory social science disciplines. His conceptualisation meets requirements for concept analysis by Sartori (1984).

## 1.3. Plan of this research project

The plan for this research project can be summarised. It seems a good opportunity to give a broad idea of the relevance of considering France as unique laboratory for Public Management of Society (PMS). This study is about development of thought and practice of Public Management of Society in France, embedded in a specific culture. A survey of French PMS in historical perspective can be consulted in the appendix "The Relevance of History for Contemporary French Public Management of Society (I-XX Centuries)". An impression is given of more than 40 years of experiences (1958-1998) in the Fifth Republic (Blanquer et al., 1998; Chagnollaud/Quermonne, 2000). Some issues are selected which have specific relevance in relation to the study of PMS. In comparative studies, similarities in different countries are generally compared (law with law, politics with politics, etc.; or parts of these dimensions), but law, (party-political) power, economics and social-psychological interaction can be seen as functionally equivalent with regard to Public Management of Society. Although these are different and seemingly cannot be compared with each other, they can be compared adequately with each other as functional equivalents, as is done in this study. To orientate French Public Management of Society in different historical periods and circumstances the following periods are marked out: Antiquity and the Gallo-Roman period; Middle Ages; Ancien Régime; French Revolution; the Napoleonic period up to the Third Republic (1799-1870); Third Republic (1870-1940); Vichy-France (1940-1944); Liberation, Fourth Republic (1946-1958); and Fifth Republic (1958-).With regard to a more thematic handling of relevant dimensions, this study deals later with justice, police and the penal system; socio-economic steering and cultural engineering;

politics and Public Management of Society; international relations (military and peace management, diplomacy); Public Management of Society in the European Union, in the Neo-European Age. Then follows some argument for analysis of PMS in a co-disciplinary perspective. And a sketch is given of the Rule of Law and the Idea of Public Authority. Studies are generally concentrated upon a specific sector or dimension of a social phenomenon, or part of it. An attempt, as in this research project, to try and overcome these kinds of specialisations, with a more or less artificial carving out of some part of social reality, might be an advantage, because of the fundamental coherence of social reality.

One conclusion of this study is that French Public Management of Society is specific ("l'exception française"); also that generally, one must reckon with the specific cultural dimensions of the environment in which Public Management of Society has to function. Every country, nation or region has to try to realise its own optimal mixture of universalism and cultural specificity by adequate Public Management of Society,so, cultural intelligence is required. Public Management of Society is positioned in the perspective of co-disciplinary co-operation. Otherwise than suggested in mainstream literature (Godfrey, 1998), public management is not an American invention. Public Management of Society is certainly, in quite a significant way, a French invention, as is shown in this study. This study is intended for a broad audience and for specialists from different disciplines (scholars and practitioners). Literature encompasses an inexhaustible and rich source of empirical experiences, theories and intellectual challenges. All chapters dispose of an elaborated list of literature as a broad data-base and research tool, split between French and English literature, about many relevant aspects and items of Public Management of Society (including experiences and ideas in Anglo-American literature ). The bibliography of literature is structured on the basis of a French-English language dichotomy, so overcoming the weakness of mainstream literature which has only incidental citations from books in the alternative language (English or French). This book is especially relevant for all those having to do professionally with representatives of French public authorities or with parts of the French public sector, indeed it might be seen as obligatory for all who communicate regularly with French officials, for example: public functionaries from other Member-States of the European Union and representatives from other countries. It is supposed to be interesting for all who like to have an overview of the French way of doing and seeing things in the public sphere. This book is written as a work of synthesis with the aim of giving readers a useful instrument for a better understanding of French ideas and practices. It is a good companion for all who feel themselves to be poorly informed about French literature and history.

In a study like this the richness of French literature cannot be adequately reproduced or summarised. The majority of French literature pre-supposes a familiarity with French history. French historical education in school and colleges may be among the best in the world. Historical permanent education via the media is taken for granted in France; an issue of a review, "Histoires d'Europe. De Jules César à l'euro." (1998), is one example out of many popularised communications relating contemporary life with French history. In a large proportion of French literature references to the inexhaustible cultural and historical patrimony of France are frequent, but mostly reduced, as French historical knowledge is supposed to be well known. For this reason substantial room is given here to historical recapitulations. For reasons of presentation reiterations are inevitable. The chapters, seen as parts of a coherent whole, are constructed so that it is possible to read them independently from their succession in this book. When one wants to have a specialised insight into a particular period, topic or aspect, consultation of the abundant literature is needed. This study is presented in English, although with regard to the specificity of the object of study, French Public Management of Society, English language is probably second best to reading original French texts. This study is perhaps only a meaningful footnote in the framework of the overwhelming abundance of French literature. It can function as eye-opener for all who try to give answers to "Big Questions for a Significant Public Administration" (Kirlin, 2001) in the all too American debate about Public Administration, as if any Public Administration would be more or less the same as American Public Administration. "It is wholly unclear whether the re-inventors know what they are reinventing." (Rosenbloom, 2001, p.164). Indeed it is the task of all scholarly work to raise doubts about existing fields of knowledge, so with this research project it is tried to test the self-confidence of the bastions of dominant American Public Administration. French ideation and practices have an impressive impact on the intellectual history of American Public Administration. This study is a welcome complement and companion for all who wish to understand better the French way of thinking, doing and living with culturally specific Public Management of Society. It is a useful guide for all who like to keep up with the French. Genius and "esprit" of French institutional engineering, as evident from abundant literature, are inviting us to dispatch the well-provided table with an appetising banquet, especially all who are insatiable about French culture. Culturally intelligent Public Management of Society is the real issue, also in the 21st century.

## 1.4. Summary

As bookmarker, indications are given about the ten chapters, classified in five parts (The Issue of Public Management of Society; The Fifth Republic; Public policy-making, Politics and Public Management of Society; France in the International and Co-national Arena; A Dialogue in the Framework of Theoretical Perspectives).

Part one: The Issue of Public Management of Society. Chapter 1. Introduction. This book is a reasoned plea for using the concept "Public Management of Society" (PMS), defined as the field of knowledge about the activities of public authorities, as key notion. This approach differs from most scholarly work about this specific societal phenomenon. In this research project the PMS concept is preferred to the usual notions like public administration, state, government, politics and governance. American Public Administration is said to be in an ongoing crisis. This can be solved by recognising that the object of Public Management of Society has to be handled in a broader field of study than Public Administration instead of trying to make it fit into the Procrustean bed of Public Administration. Public Management of Society has to be distinguished from public management, as it is understood in mainstream literature (as running organisations of public authorities like business organisations). The specific character of public organisations is misunderstood and underexposed, to make it more concrete the development of the French PMS is made the central object of research. France has long been characterised as the world-champion in developing arrangements for institutional engineering in the field of PMS. Historical dimensions are an integral part of actual realities, so historical knowledge is valuable to understand better how and why human beings act, react and think in different situations. A serious misunderstanding is that circumstances are now so fundamentally different (globalisation, informatics, technology), that most historical knowledge is obsolete and useless. In most Anglo-American literature an underlying idea is that Anglo-American ideation has more or less a universalist character applicable worldwide. That idea is wrong. Americans thus make the same mistake as the French since the 19th century with their assertion that French values are universal for the whole of mankind. On the basis of extensive materials about France it is made plausible that PMS must be placed in between universalism and historical-cultural specificity. Every country, nation or region has to be understood as trying to reach its optimum balance between universalism and existential, historical-cultural specificity. Cultural intelligence is a necessary adjunct for adequate theorising about Public Management of Society and practitioners need an adequate idea about the cultural context of their activities to be effective.

Chapter 2. France, unique laboratory for Public Management of Society. Here it is attempted to make the hypothesis that France has an unique character as laboratory of PMS during 20 centuries more plausible. Summarily the story of the development of PMS is told with factual, historical information in the context of society as a whole in France. Readers who are not familiar with this historical information can easily brush up historical knowledge in an appendix ("The Relevance of History for Contemporary French Public Management of Society") containing information about the period from the start of our era to the start of the Fifth Republic, others can continue elsewhere in this book secure in the knowledge that they can cast a glance at these pages any moment. Several periods are dealt with: before the French Revolution; from French Revolution to Bonaparte; from Napoleon Bonaparte to Napoleon III; from Third Republic to the Second World War; from Liberation to end 20th century. Aspects of French Public Management of Society are touched upon.

Part two. The Fifth Republic. Chapter 3. The Fifth Republic survived the 20th century. The fight between adherents of "Algérie française", opposing an independent Algeria, and others caused a civil war in France. After 12 years in the "desert", De Gaulle was invited to solve the Algerian crisis, which reached its apex with the military putsch of 13 May 1958. On 3 June 1958, parliament adopted a constitutional law. Preparing a new constitution was a high priority. De Gaulle had given his ideas about the necessary institutions for the new regime long before, so it was possible to work fast. Under the strict supervision of De Gaulle (like Napoleon!) and his right-hand Debré the draft constitution was finished. This was adopted by a referendum with an overwhelming majority on 28 September 1958. The Constitution of 1958 reinforced the powers of the executive, while the powers of the legislative body were substantially curtailed. The domain of the law was reduced. This was thought to give France the needed antidote ("parliamentarisme rationalisé") to the proverbial weaknesses of French parliamentarism. A constitutional reform of 1962 reinforced the position of the President of the Republic with the introduction of his direct election by the electorate.

When De Gaulle retired in 1969, after a negative referendum, the crucial constitutional issue was: would the Fifth Republic outlive its creator? Initially De Gaulle's legacy seemed to be in the safe hands of his loyal right-hand, Gaullist Pompidou ("pompidolisme"). When Pompidou died in officio (1974), the burning question was, who could ensure the continuity of the Fifth Republic. Liberal Giscard d'Estaing (1974-1981), not a Gaullist, was the next president ("giscardisme"). In 1981, the Socialists of Mitterrand got their chance. Mitterrand, one of the most severe critics of De Gaulle's institutional set-up, was now President ("mitterrandisme"). Mitterrand was loyal to the Constitution of 1958. His contribution was essential for making the political left accept the institutional arrangements of the Fifth Republic. Even during the periods of "cohabitation" (1986-1988, 1993-1995, and 1997-2002), – with a President of one political party and government in the hands of an opposing party or coalition – the institutions of the Fifth Republic were fire-proof. The last twenty years of the two thousand years of institutional engineering in France, with the "Double-Septennat-Mitterrand" (1981-1995) and the Era-Chirac (1995-2007), were a new experience with Public Management of Society. Surely the "Quinquennat-Chirac" (2002-2007) will also produce interesting experiences.

Part three. Public policymaking, Politics and Public Management of Society. Chapter 4. Justice, Police and the Penal System. Justice, police and the penal system are crucial public authority institutions, so in this chapter some specifics of the French manner of Public Management of Society in these fields are sketched. Because during the Ancien Régime the whole system was pervaded with privileges, a complete new structure was set up after the

French Revolution. In the course of time adaptations took place, while maintaining the basics. The Constitution of 1958 replaced "pouvoir judiciaire" by "autorité judiciaire", which emphasised that judges do not and should not have political power. Constitutional guarantees for independent jurisdiction were diminished in comparison with the Constitution of 1946 though, and the position of the executive power, in casu the head of State, was strengthened in relation to judges. Generally, it is necessary to know which jurisdiction has to be asked to judge, and what law is applicable. It is impossible to know the whole collection of legal texts, even for professionals (they are supposed to know where to find it). To avoid the creation of a structural pretext, exculpating everyone on the grounds that he did not know, a simple premise is used. Everybody is supposed to know the law, all the laws! There is an estimate that there are at least some 8,000 laws and 400,000 decrees or by-laws. It is a substantial task of public authorities that information about prevailing laws is easily available for all. Popularised codes of law are available for consultation in libraries, etc. The juridical-technical character of legal texts makes it nearly impossible to understand their real meaning. Reforms and reorganisations took place, but discontent about jurisdiction remains widespread.

There is a specific French police model: police as a public, professional and specialised organisation began in France with the royal edict of 15 March 1667. In contrast to Anglo-Saxon tradition, the French police were a creation of the State and the police developed as a specific institution within the system of public management, profiling itself especially with regard to the armed forces and the judiciary. During the Ancien Régime police forces had a military character, the "maréchaussée" was the national police. Revolutionaries wanted to abolish the existing police organisation, part of the hated Ancien Régime. In the revolutionary conception the notion of police was redefined as an organisation to maintain public order necessary to guarantee the rights and public liberties of citizens. Following the principle of separation of powers the police and judiciary became distinct institutions. Administrative police were charged with maintaining public order (prevention of delicts). Judiciary police were in charge of inquiring delicts, assembling evidence and presenting authors of delicts to judicial authorities. Legislative authorities charged them with decisions about sanctions. Police were seen as an essentially municipal function for which elected mayors became responsible. State police soon replaced municipal police, but during a long period of the Third Republic State police were juridically more the exception than the rule. The apparent need for reorganisation of municipal police could not overcome the stubborn opposition of locally elected authorities. At last the Vichy regime imposed State police. French police, different from English police, were considered as political police, due to the frequency of political conflicts and social upheavals. The police force is seen as a qualified public service with a specific objective, to maintain public order.

In a constitutional State there must be preceding legislation to decide eventual penalties for activities against the juridical order. Napoleonic legislation in the period 1799-1815 marked a historic apex. It has since then become the standard worldwide. The "Code pénal" formulated an elaborated system of crimes, delicts and contraventions. Procedures regarding prosecution, accusation and determination of penalties were regulated painstakingly. In France the penal procedure has an inquisitory character. The "ultimum remedium" of the system of jurisdiction and police is detention in prison. Without this instrument jurisdiction and police would lose an important part of their efficacy. The French prison system is going through a crisis of long duration. The total prison population rose from more than 26,000 in 1975 to more than 50,000 in the nineties, mostly in obsolete buildings, heavily overpopulated. Reform of the judiciary system, police and penitentiary system is a regular feature of the ongoing debate.

Chapter 5. From Socio-Economic Steering to Cultural Engineering. Etatist France has a long tradition of systematic public management of the economy going back to Richelieu and Colbert and centuries before them. The economic crisis of the 1930s, with its massive social problems, made interventionism a logical step. Just after Liberation, there was a wide consensus for a broad program of nationalisation. A specific kind of planning was made operational. Since the 1980s and 1990s France has been in the grip of privatisation. These historical and more recent experiences still have their impact. French experiences and theorising about economics produce a welcome complement to Anglo-American economic literature. French economic ideas and practices are a pioneering experience of institutional economics during a long historical period. In mainstream Anglo-American economic literature it was traditionally quite normal to discredit French theorising and practices for an excess of (juridical) institutionalism. Recently, the so-called New Institutionalism is in vogue. This can be seen as a belated reaction to a development in which institutionalising is seen as crucial. Analysis of French literature and economic history is paying dividends. In the 21st century, the French methods of Public Management of Society (more sophisticated than supposed) have an important contribution to make, also in the field of social-economic policies. A sketch is given of the superhuman task of managing the reconstruction of devastated France after 1945; modernisation with the Fifth Republic; changed circumstances in a transformed France; specific French planning; development of sophisticated public management and a summary sketch of public policies (social security, health care, environmental policies, educational and cultural policies).

Chapter 6. Politics and Public Management of Society. In the years around 1880 the most common meaning of the term politics in France was "ce qui est relatif au gouvernement de l'État, ni plus ni moins" (what is relative to the government of the State, no more, no less), in fact, more public management than politics. The term was extensively interpreted, and variously interpretable at that. It was by no means easy to determine the object of political science; it's about politics, but what is politics? Up to the 1880s the word "politique" was more general than "social" (mostly related to the labour movement). Later "social" was used as a more encompassing term, while "politique" got a more restricted meaning. French political science was born twice: in the years 1871-1913, and it was definitely institutionalised in the period 1943-1956. In the 19th century many prominent French jurists contributed to the theory of the State and public law. For Duguit there is no distinct political science, as "political phenomena are about the origin and functioning of the State". Invention of the "État de droit" was seen as so fundamental that public law was the dominant sphere of knowledge concerning public authorities. Many jurists had the view that political science is the science of law by definition. Since about 1890 social sciences, using an empirical methodology, were more the vogue than political science.

A prominent jurist, A. Esmein, was a pioneer of elaborating the object and method of study about "droit constitutionnel et institutions politiques": constitutional law and political institutions. This was an overlapping borderland between public law and political science. It founded "le paradigme institutionnaliste". This field of study analysed social and political questions in the framework of public law and political science. There is a confusing use of the term "political institutions", often not defined properly and, for example, encompassing courts (genuine public organisations) and political parties (private organisations). The notion of public institutions can better be reserved for all institutions having a task as public authority. Often political is used as catch-all-notion, encompassing all social phenomena and so becoming identical with social. What is called politics is often largely an arena of partisan activities. When political science is claiming more or less the whole field of activities of public authorities as its own it is stretching the span-of-control of political science too far. Formulating more precisely, it seems correct to define political science analytically as social science studying politics, the power aspect of human life. Demarcation of the non-political part of the public authority phenomenon (public administration) as a branch of political science is artificial and inconsistent. It is more appropriate to take the public authority phenomenon as an object of social science in full: as Public Management of Society. Politics has a huge impact on Public Management of Society. Political dimensions have to be reckoned with extensively. A sketch is given of the French system of political parties in a historical context (party-politics as power-capitalism). One of the causes of structural crises in French society is that political parties and politicians kidnapped the powers and competencies exclusively meant for public authorities and legitimised to serve the general interests of society.

Part four. France in the international and co-national arena. Chapter 7. International Relations: Military Management, Peace Management and Diplomacy. International relations (military management, peace management and diplomacy) are important in Public Management of Society. The field of study of military management was fertile in producing innovative ideas, methods and techniques, also for civilian public management and private management. Military management is a very special part of the whole of management, with specific rationalities and a sectoral logic. There have been private armies at various times and, worldwide, there are private armies now, but, in general, armies in modern countries are part of the public management sphere. In representative democracies armed forces are normally placed under the control of civilian authorities within a legal framework. Armed forces, disposing of a terrible war-machine, do their job under the umbrella of the public authorities' responsibility for the legitimised use of violence. Especially in modern times the military machine, with nuclear and biological-chemical weapons and sophisticated electronics for long-distance accurate rocket-systems, is a very complex structure. During the whole of recorded history war has been a nasty part of life. In view of the horrors of warfare it might be asserted that war should be forbidden, but this ideal seems to be unattainable for mankind.

If you want peace, prepare for war.: "Si vis pacem, para bellum." Warfare demands an extended division of labour and role differentiation, so war is to be seen as an institution with a large number of constituent roles: politicians, civil public functionaries, generals, officers, soldiers, and all kinds of professionals. Modern warfare is unthinkable without an institutionalised set of structured institutions. Peace is an institution as well, building up institutions for peace management is crucial. The French generally have a high consciousness of what warfare means. This is due to experiences on French soil (French-Prussian War, and two World Wars), and to their historical consciousness of many centuries' experiences of warfare. French history of warfare and conceptualisation about warfare has a paradigmatic significance. The French have their specific contribution to conceptualisation of military management and international relations. France has long been a prominent agent in international relations. Its diplomacy became the standard worldwide. In the 19th century, up to the First World War, France was a dominant power with interests in all five continents of the world. Since the Versailles Treaty the United States has taken over as superpower.

More than ever the threat of a new war in Europe was top of the agenda. The brutish activities of Hitler made war inevitable after the Nazi-invasion of Poland (1 September 1939). France and Great Britain reacted promptly by declaring war on Germany. It was May 1940 before military operations materialised in the French region ("silly war"), but then a sudden collapse was a fact. On 16 June 1940, Pétain sought an armistice. France had its loathed Vichy regime (1940-1944) collaborating with Nazis and its freedom-fighter De Gaulle, leading resistance with his appeal from London since 18 June 1940. At last Nazi-Germany was defeated, thanks to the combined efforts of the Allies (US, Great Britain, France) and the Soviet-Union. Managing the aftermath of this war was a new experience, with changed geopolitical conditions. The use of nuclear weapons for the first time in Hiroshima and Nagasaki (1945) produced a shock; a new era in the history of military technology. Because of the threat of Soviet aggression and a Communist take-over in

Western Europe, NATO was formed. Attached to an independent position of "grandeur", France played its role. The activity to build up French nuclear weapons is quite a story. French nuclear diplomacy aimed at keeping up with the superpowers. The Fall of the Berlin Wall (1989) caused a European revolution two centuries after the French Revolution (1789). The collapse of the Soviet-Union and the Communist system in Eastern Europe brought about a completely new situation, especially in the sphere of collective security and common defence activities (Neo-Nato logics). Special attention must be given to the secret services, a specific part of Public Management of Society. France has a long tradition of secret services. In international relations France was a prominent actor of old. Development of international law is seen as a preferred tool of diplomacy.

Chapter 8. Public Management of Society in the European Union, in the Neo-European Age. Historical and contemporary developments in France have to be placed in the context of its primary environment; Europe as cultural challenge. Europe has deep roots in history. The more recent history of European integration has to be considered in the perspective of many centuries of experiences, especially with regard to relations with neighbouring countries and regions. Since the end of the First World War, the European idea has had a new appeal. Co-operation in Western Europe became more urgent after 1945, especially in the field of common security: WEU (1948) and NATO (1949). The US gave financial aid for reconstruction, the Marshall Plan (1947), furthering co-operation in the economic field. Jean Monnet inspired the French Minister of foreign affairs, Robert Schuman, and on 9 May 1950 he proposed to place French and West-German production of steel and coal under a Common High Authority, so creating factual solidarity, with possibilities for other European countries to join. France, Italy, West Germany and the three Benelux countries formed the ECSC (1951). This was the start of European integration with a common market, EEC, treaty (1957). So the European Economic Community of the Six was formed on 1 January 1958. France, using its legal expertise, had a central role in the institutionalising of the EEC. Great Britain, although invited to join, refused membership. The EEC, despite several crises, had promising results.

In due course other countries joined: Great Britain, Ireland, Denmark (1973); Greece (1981); Spain, Portugal (1986); Sweden, Finland and Austria (1995). Institutional adaptations became ever more urgent resulting in the Treaty of Maastricht (1992) which created the European Union (EU). So the EU of the 15 became reality, and in 1997 the Treaty of Amsterdam followed. Other countries wanted to join the EU, making new institutional adaptations necessary. In Helsinki (1999), 13 countries were recognised as official candidates for membership: Poland, Estonia, Latvia, Lithuania, Czech Republic, Slovakia, Hungary, Slovenia, Romania, Bulgaria, Cyprus, Malta and Turkey. To become Member-States they must comply with many criteria. As f.e. accepting the "acquis communautaire" (basic institutional arrangements). France had a key-role from the beginning in institutionalising. Some items are discussed: institutional agenda, European law and national law, EMU and euro, chances of convergence between English Rule of Law and French "État de droit" towards a European Constitution. Co-national Public Management of Society, with interpenetration of European and national law and public policies, became a crucial issue.

Part five. A Dialogue in the framework of theoretical perspectives. Chapter 9. Public Management of Society in co-disciplinary perspective. As shown in this research project, French Public Management of Society must be qualified by its cultural specificity. In mainstream Anglo-American Public Administration literature there is a bias, due to its specific historical development, to keep American Public Administration at a distance from French and European law-based institutionalising. And from political science as well (politics-administration dichotomy). French institutional engineering since the French Revolution (Idea of Law, codification, etc.) was presented as part of universalist knowledge valid for the whole world. French ideas were seen as having a universalist character: the French legacy to humanity. Recently, there has been a structural tendency to consider Anglo-American Public Administration literature as dominantly relevant for the globe as a whole, especially since 1945, but without taking sufficient account of fundamental cultural differences in countries, nations and regions, as sophisticated comparative analysis should do. In an adequate approach, the specificity of culture(s) has to be recognised. This is made clear when so-called universalist ideas (also the French ideas) are confronted with specific cultures all over the world. So, it is a mixture of universalism and cultural specificity. Studies in the framework of world-systems theory show that it is necessary to study the historical circumstances of specific cultures. France could not and cannot escape from its cultural-path dependence, no nation, region or community can. Every Nation-State must find its own optimal mixture of universalism and cultural specificity. With contemporary thinking myopic in its "market is all" approach and globalisation euphoria, it is timely to accentuate the relevance of the Idea of Public Authority.

Adequate Public Management of Society is also necessary in the 21st century. The search for mature theorising demands a framework, including and going beyond approaches in mainstream literature. Recent discussions about Constructivism, "New Institutionalism", and Modernism/Postmodernism are dealt with, also the "governance" movement, professionalism of public functionaries, ethics and restoration of the Public Interest concept. A striking feature of contemporary social sciences is the fragmentation of social knowledge in so-called epistemological communities. With regard to Public Management of Society probably the most advanced theoretical conceptualisation was realised by Niklas Luhmann. He formulated seven working hypotheses for development of an integrated theory of Public Management of Society: social systems theory; binding decisions for society as specific function of public authorities; public management and environment; law as structure of public management; rationalising of public management; functional-comparative method; and bridging the gap between empirical and normative sciences. It seems possible to abstract away the cultural factor in universalised conceptualisation, but social reality and social inquiry are fundamentally interconnected with cultural and moral values and experiences. It seems appropriate to formulate a complementary working hypothesis. This study argues for an eighth working hypothesis about the cultural-existential dimension of Public Management of Society: cultural intelligence as a necessary condition of Public Management of Society in theory and practice.

Chapter 10. Rule of Law, Idea of Public Authority and Cultural Intelligence. The State or Nation-State, a brilliant combination of power and law for a nation, was not always a blessing, as the 20th century has shown. When the State breaks away from the Rule of Law it can be an instrument of massive disaster (Levene/Roberts, 1999). A crucial issue is how to organise effective discipline for powerful ruling persons and organs. The Rule of Law implies the Idea of Public Authority: public authorities must realise and guarantee the Rule of Law for all citizens. In prehistoric times and after, jurisdiction and solution of serious conflicts mostly had the form of private acts of vengeance. Breaking the vicious circle of vengeance was crucial. The need for vengeance was replaced by an independent judiciary. A higher level of civilisation was reached with public authority organising jurisdiction. Roman law was a major, qualitative jump, with an imposing impact on Gallo-Roman and later developments. The period of pregnancy for the Rule of Law opened interesting perspectives.

The English cradle of law and the Common Law tradition had a dominant influence. The "Magna Carta' (1215) functioned as an exemplary model for what was called a "pactum subiectionis", remote predecessor of the "contrat social". Due to excessive abuses of public authority and appalling mismanagement and violation of elementary human rights by the French monarchy, the French Revolution was an overreaction to a too long pent up rage of the common people, who lived in misery while the extravagant monarchy flaunted its luxury. One of the most vital energies of the people was activated by the widespread conviction that representatives of public authority systematically violated the Rule of Law. These public authorities outraged the Idea of Public Authority. The French Revolution was an institutional outburst of the recognition of human rights and making France a constitutional State. Pioneering philosophers of Public Management of Society developed the necessary concepts (Locke, Montesquieu, etc). In this context, the French doctrine is confronted with German ideas, and prominent French theoreticians of law pass in revue. The cultural mindset proves to be an essential base for the Constitutional State. Cultural mapping of public authority, reckoning with specific historical-cultural contexts, is seen as crucial. The ongoing debate about the State and the principle of sovereignty is discussed: the "All-is-Politics", "Zero-State" and "Law-without-the-State" theses are sketched. All in all, the Rule of Law is a necessary condition of the Idea of Public Authority as a basis for constitutional government. This study is concluded with an epilogue, inviting further studies in the field of Public Management of Society, with cultural intelligence.

**References**

French
Agulhon, M., La République. De Jules Ferry à François Mitterrand. (Paris, Hachette, 1990).
Agulhon, M., Les Métamorphoses de Marianne. (Paris, 2001).
Amar, C., Chemin, A., Jospin & Cie. Histoire de la Gauche Plurielle 1993-2002. (Paris, Seuil, 2002).
Auby, J.M., et al., Traité de Science Administrative. (Paris, Mouton, 1966).
Babu-Leyser, D., Faure, P., dir., Nouvelles technologies, nouvel État. (Paris, DF, 1999).
Barreau, J.C., La France va-t-elle disparaître? (Paris, Grasset, 1997).
Baverez, N., Les Trente piteuses. (Paris, Flammarion, 1997).
Bébéar, C., dir., Le Courage de Réformer. (Paris, Odille Jacob, 2002)
Berstein, S., Milza, P., Histoire de la France au XXe siècle. (Paris, Complexe, 1995).
Blanquer, J.M., et al., Les 40 ans de la Cinquième République. (Paris, LGDJ, 1998).
Bonnin, C.J., Principe d'administration publique. (Paris, Renaudière, 1812).
Brachet, P., L'étatisme à la française. (Paris, Publisud, 1999).
Braudel, F., L'Identité de la France. (Paris, Flammarion, 1990).
Bresson, G., Lionet, C., Le Pen. (Paris, Seuil, 1994).
Brosse, C., L'État Dinosaure. (Paris, A.Michel, 2000).
Burdeau, F., Histoire de l'administration française, du XVIIIe au XXe siècle. (Paris, Montchrestien, 1989).
Burdeau, G., Traité de science politique. (Paris, LGDJ, 1986).
Burguière, A., Revel, J., dir., La France dans son Histoire. (Paris, Seuil, 1989).
Buruma, I., L'Anglomanie. Une fascination européenne. (Paris, Bartillat, 2001).
Carbonell, C.O., dir., Une histoire européenne de l'Europe. (Paris, Privat, 1999).
Carpentier, J., Lebrun, F., dir., Histoire de France. (Paris, Seuil, 1987).
Carpentier, J., Lebrun, F., dir., Histoire de l'Europe. (Paris, Seuil, 1990).
Chagnollaud, D., Quermonne, J.L., La Ve République. (Paris, Flammarion, 2000).
Châtelet, F., dir., Histoire de la philosophie, idées, doctrines. (Paris, Hachette, 1999).
Chevallier, J., Science administrative. (Paris, PUF, 1996).
Cogan, C., Alliés éternels, amis ombrageux. Les Etats-Unis et la France depuis 1940. (Paris, LGDJ, 1999).
Cohen, C., L'Homme des origines. Savoirs et fictions en préhistoire. (Paris, Seuil, 1999).
Crozier, M., État moderne, État modeste. Stratégies pour un autre changement. (Paris, Fayard, 1997).
Debbasch, C., Science administrative. Administration publique. (Paris, Dalloz, 1989).
Devedjian, P., Le Temps des juges. (Paris, Flammarion, 1996).
Domenach, J.M., Europe: le défi culturel. (Paris, Découverte, 1990).
Domenach, J.M., Regarder la France: essais sur le malaise français. (Paris, Perrin, 1996).
Duby, G., dir., Histoire de la France. (Paris, Larousse, 1970/1971; 1999).
Duby, G., Mandrou, R., Histoire de la civilisation française. (Paris, A.Colin, 1968/1984).
Ellul, J., Histoire des institutions. (Paris, PUF, 1992-1994).
Fauroux, R., Spitz, B., dir., Notre État. Le livre vérité de la fonction publique. (Paris, Laffont, 2001).
Ferro, M., Histoire de France. (Paris, Odile Jacob, 2001).
François, B., Misère de la Ve République. (Paris, Denoël, 2001).

Geoffroy, C., La Mésentente cordiale. Voyage au coeur de l'espace interculturel franco-anglais. (Paris, Grasset, 2001).
Gordon, P.H., Meunier, S., Le Nouveau Défi Français. La France face à la Mondialisation. (Paris, Odile Jacob, 2002).
Greigueil, P. de, 2000 ans d'histoire de France. (Paris, Assouline, 1999).
Guéhenno, J.M., L'Avenir de la liberté. La démocratie dans la mondialisation. (Paris, Flammarion, 1999).
Habermas, J., L'Intégration républicaine. (Paris, Fayard, 1999).
Haziza, F., Chirac ou la Victoire en pleurant. (Paris, Ramsay, 2002).
Jack, A., Sur la France. Vive la différence! (Paris, Odile Jacob, 2000).
Jacquard, R., Au nom d'Ousama Ben Laden...Dossier secret sur le terroriste le plus recherché du monde. (Paris, Picollec, 2001).
Jacquard, R., Les Archives secrètes d'Al-Qaida. (Paris, Picollec, 2002).
Jerphagnon, L., Dumas, J.L., Histoire de la pensée. (Paris, Tallandier, 1989/1990).
Joxe, P., A propos de la France. (Paris, Flammarion, 1998).
Kepel, G., Jihad. Expansion et Déclin de l'Islamisme. (Paris, Gallimard, 2001).
Konopnicki, G., Pour en finir avec la France éternelle. (Paris, Grasset, 2001).
Laïdi, A., Salam, A., Le Jihad en Europe. Les filières du terrorisme islamiste. (Paris, Seuil, 2002).
Lavisse, E., Histoire de France depuis les origines jusqu'à la Révolution. (Paris, Hachette, 1903/1911).
Lavroff, D.G., Le système politique français. (Paris, Dalloz, 1991).
Le Goff, J.P., Le Mythe de l'entreprise. Critique de l'idéologie managériale. (Paris, Découverte, 1995).
Le Goff, J.P., Les Illusions du management. Pour le retour du bon sens. (Paris, Découverte, 2000).
Lesourne, J., Le Modèle français. Grandeur et décadence. (Paris, Odile Jacob, 1998).
Lewis, B., Le Retour de l'Islam. (Paris, Gallimard, 1985).
Madaule, J., Histoire de France. (Paris, 1943/1966).
Mayeur, N., Perrineau, P., dir., Le Front National à découvert. (Paris, FNSP, 1989).
Mendras, H., La Seconde Révolution française. (Paris, Gallimard, 1994).
Michelet, J., Histoire de France, 1833-1867. (Paris, Flammarion, 1893-1898).
Minc, A., La France de l'an 2000. (Paris, Odile Jacob, 1994).
Montbrial, T. de, La France du Nouveau Siècle. (Paris, PUF, 2002)
Muller, P., dir., L'Administration française est-elle en crise? (Paris, Harmattan, 1992).
Perrineau, P., Le Symptôme Le Pen. Radiographie des électeurs du Front National. (Paris, Fayard, 1997).
Peyrefitte, A., Le Mal français. (Paris, Plon, 1976).
Philippe, R., dir., Histoire de la France. (Paris, 1970-1973).
Pingaud, D., L'Impossible Défaite. (Paris, Seuil, 2002).
Pontaut, J.M., Szpiner, F., L'État hors la loi. (Paris, Fayard, 1989).
Raffarin, J.P., Pour une Nouvelle Gouvernance. (Paris, Archipel, 2002).
Rémond, R., Notre Siècle. (Paris, Fayard, 1991).
Revel, J.F., L'Absolutisme inefficace. (Paris, Plon, 1992).
Rosanvallon, P., L'État en France de 1789 à nos jours. (Paris, Seuil, 1990).
Roy, O., L'Islam mondialisé. (Paris, Seuil, 2002).
Roy, O., Les Illusions du 11 septembre. Le Débat stratégique face au terrorisme. (Paris, Altadis, 2002).
Sadran, P., Le système administratif français. (Paris, Montchrestien, 1992).
Sorman, G., Le Bonheur français. (Paris, Fayard, 1996).
Stiglitz, J.E., La Grande Désillusion. (Paris, Fayard, 2002).
Tacel, M., La France et le monde au XXe siècle. (Paris, Masson, 1989).
Taine, H., Les origines de la France contemporaine. (Paris, Laffont, 1875/1893; 1986).
Thuillier, G., Tulard, J., Histoire de l'administration française. (Paris, PUF, 1984).
Todd, E., L'Illusion économique. Essai sur la stagnation des sociétérs développées. (Paris, Gallimard, 1998).
Touchard, J., Histoire des idées politiques. (Paris, PUF, 1993).
Touraine, A., Le Grand refus. (Paris, Fayard, 1996).
Walter, H., Honni soit qui mal y pense. L'incroyable histoire d'amour entre le français et l'anglais. (Paris, Laffont, 2001).
Weil, P., Le droit administratif. (Paris, PUF, 1994).
Winock, M., La France politique: XIXe-XXe siècles. (Paris, Seuil, 1999).
Winock, M., dir., Histoire de l'extrême droite en France. (Paris, Seuil, 1994).

English
Aldrich, R., Greater France: A History of French Overseas Expansion. (London, Macmillan, 1996).
Aldrich, R., Connell, J., eds., France in World Politics. (London, Routledge, 1989).
Ardagh, J., France in the New Century. Portrait of a Changing Society. (London, Penguin, 2000).
Audretsch, D.B., Bonser, C.F., eds., Globalization and Regionalization. (London, Kluwer, 2001).

Bagby, P., Culture and History. Prolegomena to the Comparative Study of Civilisations. (London, Longmans/Green, 1958).
Bell, J.A., Reconstructing Prehistory. Scientific Method in Archaeology. (Philadelphia, Temple UP, 1994).
Blondel, J., ed., Comparative Government. (New York, Allen, 1990).
Bozeman, A.B., Politics and Culture in International History. From the Ancient Near East to the Opening of the Modern Age. (New Brunswick, NJ, Transaction, 1994).
Braudel, F., History of Civilisations. (New York, Lane/Penguin, 1994).
Brown, L.N., Garner, J.F., French Administrative Law. (Oxford, Clarendon, 1993).
Cobban, A., A History of France. (London, Penguin, 1990).
Coulborn, R., The Origin of Civilized Societes. (Princeton, Princeton UP, 1959).
Daemen, H., Schaap, L., eds., Citizen and City. Developments in fifteen Local Democracies in Europe. (Delft, Eburon, 2000).
Denemark, R., et al., eds., World System History: Social Science of Long Term Change. (Thousand Oaks, CA, Altamira Press, 1999).
Dunsire, A., Administration: the word and the science. (London, Robertson, 1973).
Easton, D., The Political System. An Inquiry into the State of Politcal Science. (New York, Knopf, 1953).
Easton, D., A Systems Analysis of Political Life. (New York, Wiley, 1965).
Featherstone, M., ed., Global Culture: Nationalism, Globalization and Modernity. (Newbury Park, Sage, 1990).
Fenby, J., On the Brink. The Trouble with France. (London, Little Brown/Warner, 1999).
Finer, S.E., Comparative Government. (Harmondsworth, Penguin, 1984).
Finer, S.E., The History of Government From the Earliest Times. (Oxford, OUP, 1997).
Flinders, M.V., Smith, M.J., eds., Quangos, Accountability and Reform. The Politics of Quasi-Government. (London, Macmillan, 1999).
Frederickson, H.G., The Spirit of Public Administration. (San Francisco, Jossey-Bass, 1997).
Gallouedec-Genuys, F., About French Administration. (Paris, DF, 1998).
Gildea, R., France since 1945. (Oxford, OUP, 1996).
Gladden, E.N., A History of Public Administration. (London, Cass, 1972).
Godfrey, P.C., ed., The Philosophical Roots of Management Thought. (In: International Journal of Public Administration, 1998).
Gordon, P.H., Meunier, S., The French Challenge. Adapting to Globalization. (Washington DC, Brookings Institution, 2001).
Gore, A., Businesslike Government: Lessons learned from America's best companies. (Pittsburgh, National Performance Review, 1997).
Greenwood, J., ed., Serving the State. Global Public Administration Education and Training. (Aldershot, Ashgate, 2000).
Hall, J.A., ed., States in History. (Oxford, Blackwell, 1986).
Halpin, A., Rights and Law Analysis and Theory. (Oxford, Hart, 1997).
Hayward, J.E.S., Governing France: The One and Indivisible Republic. (London, Norton, 1983).
Heady, F., Public Administration. A Comparative Perspective. (Englewood Cliffs, Prentice Hall, 1966; Basel, Dekker, 1991).
Heffen, O. van, Kickert, W.J.M., Thomassen, J., eds., Governance in Modern Society. (Dordrecht, Kluwer, 2000).
Higgott, R., Payne, A., eds., The New Political Economy of Globalisation. (Cheltenham, Elgar, 2001).
Hoff, J., Horrocks, J., Tops, P., eds., Democratic Governance and New Technology. (London, Routledge, 2000).
Holden, M., The Competence of Political Science: "Progress in Political Research" Revisited. (In: American Political Science Review, pp.1-19, 1999).
Huntington, S.P., The Clash of Civilizations and the Remaking of World Order. (London, Touchstone, 1998).
Hupe, P.L., Meijs, L., Hybrid Governance. (The Hague, Social and Cultural Planning Office, 2000).
IIAS, New Challenges for Public Administration in the 21st Century. (Amsterdam, IOS Press/International Institute of Administrative Sciences, 1997).
IISS, Iraq's weapons of mass destruction. A net assessment. (London, International Institute of Strategic Studies, 2002).
Johnson, D., et al., eds., France and Britain: Ten Centuries. (Folkestone, Dawson, 1980).
Kardulias, P.N., ed., World-Systems Theory in Practice. Leadership, Production and Exchange. (Lanham, Rowman/Littlefield, 1999).
Keiger, J.F.V., France and the World since 1870. (London, Arnold, 2001).
Kickert, W.J.M., ed., Public Management and Administrative Reform in Western Europe. (Cheltenham, Elgar, 1997).
Kickert, W.J.M., et al., eds., Managing Complex Networks. (London, Sage, 1997).

Kickert, W.J.M., Stillmar, R., eds., The Modern State and its Study. The New Administrative Sciences in a Changing Europe and United States. (Cheltenham, Elgar, 1999).
Kirlin, J.J., Big Questions for a Significant Public Administration. (In: Public Administration Review, pp.140-143, 2001).
Levene, M., Roberts, P., The Massacre in History. (London, 1999).
Luhmann, N., Social Systems. (Stanford, Stanford UP, 1995).
Lynn, N.B., Wildavsky, A., eds., Public Administration. The State of the Discipline. (Chatham, Chatham House, 1990).
Maus, D., ed., An Introduction to French Administration. (Paris, DF/IIAP, 1996).
McNeill, W.H., The Rise of the West. A History of the Human Community. (Chicago, University of Chicago Press, 1963).
Melko, M., The Nature of Civilizations. (Boston, Porter Sargent, 1969).
Mettam, R., Government and Society in Louis XIV's France. (London, Macmillan, 1977).
Osborne, D., Gaebler, T., Reinventing Government. How the Entrepreneurial Spirit is Transforming the Public Sector. (Reading, MA, Addison-Wesley, 1992).
Osborne, S.P., ed., Public-Private Partnerships. Theory and Practice in International Perspective. (London, Routledge, 2000).
Perry, J., ed., Research in Public Administration. (Stanford, JAI, 1999).
Peters, B.G., Savoie, D., eds., Governance in the 21st Century. Revitalizing the Public Service. (Montreal/Kingston, McGill/Queens UP, 2000).
Pickles, D., The Government and Politics of France. (London, Methuen, 1973).
Pollitt, C., Modernising Government. Four Points and Four Proposals. (London, Public Administration Committee, 2000).
Pollitt, C., Bouckaert, G., Public Management Reform: A Comparative Analysis. (Oxford, OUP, 2000).
Pollitt, C., Bouckaert, G., Evaluating Public Management Reforms. An International Perspective. (In: International Journal of Political Studies, pp.141-166, 2001).
Porter, M., The Competitive Advantages of Nations. (London, Weidenfeld & Nicolson, 1990).
Raadschelders, J.C.N., Handbook of Administrative History. (New Brunswick, Transaction, 1998).
Raadschelders, J.C.N., Government: A Public Administration Perspective. (Armonk, NY, Sharpe, 2003).
Revel, J., Hunt, L., eds., Histories: French Constructions of the Past. (New York, New Press, 1995).
Reynolds, D., One World Divisible. A Global History since 1945. (New York, Norton, 2001).
Robertson, R., Globalization: Social Theory and Global Culture. (Newbury Park, Sage, 1992).
Robson, W.A., The Civil Service in Britain and France. (London, Hoggart, 1975).
Rohr, J.A., Founding Republics in France and America; a Study in Constitutional Governance. (Lawrence, Kansas, University Press of Kansas, 1995).
Rosenbloom, D.H., History Lessons for Reinventors. (In: Public Administration Review, pp.161-165, 2001).
Rosenblum, M., Mission to Civilize: The French Way. (San Diego, Harcourt etc., 1986).
Rouban, L., ed., Citizens and the New Governance. Beyond New Public Management. (Amsterdam, IOS Press, 1999).
Sanderson, S., ed., Civilizations and World-Systems. (Thousand Oaks, Altamira Press, 1995).
Sartori, G., The Tower of Babel. In: Sartori, G., Riggs, F.W., Teune, H., Tower of Babel. On the Definition and Analysis of Concepts in the Social Sciences. (New York, International Studies Association, pp.7-37, 1975).
Sartori, G., ed., Social Science Concepts. A Systematic Analysis. (London, Sage, 1984).
Sitkin, S., Bies, R., eds., The Legalistic Organization. (London, Sage, 1994).
Snellen, I.T.M., Van der Donk, W.B.H.J., eds., Public Administration in an Information Age. A Handbook. (Amsterdam, IOS Press, 1998).
Streeck, W., Schmitter, P.C., Private Interest Government: Beyond Market and State. (London, 1985).
Stevens, A., The Government and Politics of France. (London, Macmillan, 1993).
Thompson Klein, J., Interdisciplinarity. History, Theory and Practice. (Detroit, Wayne State UP, 1990).
Tombs, R., France 1814-1914. (London, Longman, 1996).
Wallerstein, I., The Modern World-System. (New York, Academic Press, 1974/1989).
Wallerstein, I., Geopolitics and Geoculture: Essays on the Changing World-System. (Cambridge, CUP, 1992).
Wright, V., The Government and Politics of France. (London, Routledge, 1989).
Wunder, B., ed., The Influences of the Napoleonic "Model" of Administration on the Administrative Organisation of Other Countries. (Brussels, IIAS, 1995).
Young, R.J., France and the Origins of the Second World War. (London, Macmillan, 1996).
Zeldin, T., The French. (London, Harvill, 1997)

# 2. France, Unique Laboratory for Public Management of Society

## 2.1. French experiences during many centuries

This chapter tries to make the hypothesis that France has an unique character as a laboratory of Public Management of Society more plausible. Public Management of Society as specific cultural phenomenon is an extraordinary dynamical process of inventions, in which crucial aspects have to be invented again and again (Dawson, 1978; Sorokin, 1985). Peyrefitte (1995) argued that trust is the crucial factor to build society. When a human community entrusts promotion of common interests to one person or a restricted group of persons with specific competencies, there is public management and public authority. Public authority and public management are characterised by a mixture of more or less universal features and specific cultural-historical dimensions. These are normally determined by a particular conception and mindset of a concrete population and its leadership in a specific time-space environment. Public Management of Society is crucial for civilisation. This is shown in excellent studies (Braudel, 1994; Melko, 1969). As Finer (1997, p.2) confirmed, government (or Public Management of Society) is coeval with history, and may have antedated writing. Conceptualisation about public management of society is strongly influenced by historical developments, especially in France with a population living on a demarcated territory for a long period. Western Europe is known as the cradle of the European-Atlantic model for Public Management of Society. There is a wide consensus about the historical impact of Western Europe on developments worldwide (Domenach, 1990; Grosser, 1981; Spengler, 1926/1928). In all periods since our era started France has had a crucial role (Greigueuil, 1999; Martin, 1982).

Time and again, French authors had innovative ideas about Public Management of Society. Only the notion of the thoroughly historical character of Public Management of Society can protect against a narrowing of mind when contemporary public management is at stake. At the start of the 21st century authors write that society has changed so drastically (informatics, globalisation, etc.) that historical insight is rendered largely useless. That is a serious misunderstanding. Public Management of Society now and in the future will remain the result of a long historical process of inventing the best way of managing societal developments in constantly changing circumstances. Worldwide, France has an unique position in this process of ongoing inventions and innovations in the field of Public Management of Society. Because of the general emanation of French inventions and innovations all over the world France has a central place in the process of civilisation of Europe and the world (Duby/Mandrou, 1984), especially with Public Management of Society as institutional nucleus of civilisation. Pre-history started in this area with the Iron Age, since about 1000 BC. People living in the territory of contemporary France in the year 2000 and later can draw on the experiences of three millennia. When one starts with the beginning of our era, France from the year 2000 on is leaving behind two millennia. France stands at the start of the third millennium in the 21st century, so it is a good time to analyse developments of French Public Management of Society in the light of the previous two millennia as a cultural-historical framework.

Public Management of Society in contemporary France, with regard to underlying conceptions, structure and dimensions is substantially formed in dynamic interaction with French historical developments. Analysis of the French Revolution and its aftermath is a "conditio sine qua non" for adequate interpretation of later historical periods and events like "les Trois Glorieuses" (July 1830); revolution of 1848; parliamentarism of the Third Republic (1870-1940); Liberation on 25 August 1944; start of the Fourth Republic; and Fifth Republic from 1958 on. The official celebration in 1996 of the baptism of Frankish king Clovis in 496, with a ceremonial mass by Pope John Paul II and all political passions relating to this, is only one example of many (Rouche, 1996; Theis, 1996). It cost the French dearly, with painful tribulations, to write a universal history of mankind. Perhaps more than elsewhere, historical aspects of societal dimensions play a major role in the French mindset. Their education encourages them to associate life with earlier aspects of French society. They know about the "Grande Peste" (1347), "Grande Révolution" (1789), "Grande Peur" (1789), "Grande Guerre" (1914-1918), "Grande Dépression Economique" (1930-). The French generally act and think while using historical examples in daily life.

Formerly in the practice of public management, as today, historical examples are always present as possible indications for an approach to problems. To give a primary idea of French history, a short sketch is given. Elsewhere, it will be possible to consult an overview in depth. Many publications do not go further back in history than the French Revolution (1789) and what immediately preceded it. It will become obvious that it is not adequate to reduce the conceptual universe to the period of the French Revolution and after. In 1856, Tocqueville (1953) was one of the first authors who accentuated the combination of renewal and continuity in revolutionary France. He was not the last (Furet/Ozouf, 1989). Tocqueville argued that there had been for centuries in France a lasting conspiracy of ever more centralisation. Legists in the Middle Ages and during the French monarchy, professionally trained in Roman law, elaborated a centralised concept of public authority, with historical examples in mind (Alexander the Great; Greek city-state management; Roman Empire). Archaeological findings showed that there were people in the area of contemporary France centuries before our era. After Stone and Bronze Ages came the Iron Age, starting prehistory in this area about 1000 years BC. In that period, groups travelled along rivers (Seine, Garonne, Loire) and from the Mediterranean to the Atlantic Ocean. Along with Celtic invaders from Central Europe and Franks, they largely formed the ancestors of the authentic population of France. In the Roman period with Julius Caesar (110-44 BC), the area of contemporary France was inhabited by Aquitanians and Basques (Iberian race) and Celts. Gauls inhabited an area encompassing France, northern Italy, Switzerland, Luxemburg and Belgium. Brühl (1995) produced an outstanding analysis of the birth of the French nation.

In Antiquity, Greeks and Romans used several terms to denote a group of people living together and having common institutions for public management: ethnos, polis, gens, natio, patria, populus, res publica, and status rei publicae. The Greeks laid foundations for a democratic organisation of society, they opposed two terms: "aristoï-cratès" (power of the "polis" in the hands of the best, an elite) and "démos-cratès" (power of the "polis" in the hands of the population). Aristocracy in the authentic interpretation is government by the best (not the nobles), from above. Democracy means government by many, from below. In 600 BC, Massilia (contemporary Marseilles) was founded by Greek colonists. For a long period, the region around this settlement was part of the Roman Empire. In the area of contemporary France, from the beginning of our era, there was public management, as we know from the works of Julius Caesar ("De Bello Gallico"). The Roman Empire controlled this area, until the West-Roman Empire collapsed in 476. In the Middle Ages (476-1492), the territory of contemporary France was part of a larger empire, later it became a monarchy. Starting with Frankish king Clovis (481-511), the Merovingian dynasty ruled the "regnum Francorum" up to 751. Charlemagne (768-814) founded the Carolingian Empire, including an important part of Western Europe. The last Carolingian monarch died in 987.

Hugues Capet (947-996) was made king and the rule of the third dynasty began. Capetians ruled in direct line in the period 987-1328, and via sidelines Valois (1328-1589), Bourbon and Orléans up to 1792 and 1814-1848. In the Renaissance (1450-1600) Italy and France were the cultural centre of Europe.

Often, there is an overlap between political and public management discussions. According to Badie (1986), the modern period in the West is dominated by the idea and practice of the State. The State previously had a dominant place in political reflections. As Badie pointed out, Roman Christianity had a determining role in inventing modern political theory. Augustine (354-430) elaborated his "De civitate Dei" in the year that Rome was pillaged by Alaric (410). He is seen as inventor of the "linear" conception of history, starting with the Creation and ending with the Resurrection. This was a break with dominant theories in the Middle East about the recurring cycle of civilisations. In a decisive way, during centuries the religious dimension was distinguished ever more from the political dimension to organise an independent sphere for the Christian Church: religious domain versus political domain. The concept of politics was redefined, political power and/or public authority was seen as a necessity because of human perversity. In the Middle Ages, the Church had a dominant position in West-European society, with a different impact in several countries during various periods. The feudal system with its fragmented political powers enabled the Church to practise a divide and rule strategy, giving some princes religious support (divine legitimacy). The position of free men was recognised in royal assemblies. Their consent was thought to be a constitutive element of public authority. The Investiture Conflict in the second half of the 11th century between Pope Gregory VII (1073-1085) and the German Emperor was decisive in demarcating their domains of competence. The duality of competencies was recognised. The Church claimed superiority of the spiritual domain above the temporal domain and Popes interfered in worldly affairs, pretending to act "ratione peccati": a prince would have sinned. Pope Gelasius I (492-496) introduced the formula: "auctoritas" for the pope, and "potestas" for the prince. Later, the two-swords metaphor was used: spiritual sword and temporal sword. The Church proclaimed that potestas of political leaders could not be used arbitrarily, as public authority is a divine mission. The political domain was a matter for the human community.

In the 13th century, Greek conceptions of Antiquity such as those of Plato and Aristotle were rediscovered. Public power was seen as part of a natural order, its rational character would guarantee that it was in conformity with justice. Rediscovery of Greek conceptions, stimulated by monasteries as centres of culture, reactivated the natural law concept. Thomas Aquinas (1225-1274), professor in Paris, synthesised Greek conceptions with the Christian legacy in his "Summa theologica". Human beings are seen as members of "humanitas" (the temporal, natural city, domain of reason) and of "christianitas" (the spiritual, supernatural city, domain of faith on the basis of Revelation). Aquinas gave reason and natural law a position in the history of ideas in the West. He argued that it was legitimate to obey even a pagan prince, when he ruled with justice, in conformity with reason. So at the end of the Middle Ages the prehistory of the Rule of Law and the secular State was taking form. John of Salisbury (1110-1180) wrote "Policratius" (1159), seeing the human community as social organism. The conception of Aquinas was partially contested by Franciscan friars Duns Scot (1266-1308) and William of Ockham (1290-1349). They asserted that only the individual could reach knowledge. Association of individuals replaced political community as idea (Baudry, 1949; Landry, 1922). They objected to the axiom of the pre-ordained rational order (Gilson, 1976; Guelluy, 1947). They argued that the idea of human reason and nature as sole criterion encroached on God's sovereignty. Human beings would be alienated from their nature when specific justice, law and legitimacy loosened from Revelation were imputed to them. Duns Scot and Ockham, pioneering in voluntarism, stressed the will instead of reason. God's will determines possibilities; the wills of human beings influence the temporal order.

This temporal order, therefore, could not be based on an idea of nature, but on contractual solidarity, creating positive law (and not natural law). The modern idea of organisation of society was present in three elements of their conceptualisation: the idea of contract (prefiguring the social contract); the idea of the individual as emancipated from communitairian tutelage; and the idea of positive law. Positive law implied a normative system, obligating for its conformity to the will of a sovereign, and not on behalf of its conformity to a natural order. Marsilius of Padova in "Defensor Pacis" (1324) systematised the individualist and positivist principles of Duns Scot and Ockham on the political level. He elaborated the idea of the will and of political power to analyse relations between human actors. During the Middle Ages, customs had a dominant role. Customs were seen as being outside the competence of the monarch. In the 15th century, the debate about political conceptions began to concentrate around the notion of the State. Some authors had elaborated conceptions giving the prince as comprehensive a public authority and autonomy as possible. Especially professional jurists and legists, argued in favour of this approach. The competence to legislate was laid ever more in the hands of the monarch. A useful method was that the monarch confirmed customs as customary law by recognising it as legislation. The monarch as legislator was seen by legists as having no superior above him, except God and law.

The position of the French monarchy was reinforced by the necessity of ending enduring private wars between feudal lords. Centralised power in the hands of a divinely ordained monarch was propagated as a formula to bring peace to a bitterly torn society. When England claimed parts of contemporary France the Hundred Years War (1338-1453) devastated all chances of a peaceful, prosperous country. Macchiavelli (1469-1527) was a major innovator with his famous, thought-provoking work "Il Principe" (1513). On the basis of empirical experience, he developed the idea of the "reason of State". To realise objectives of the State all methods were seen as legitimate. About half a century later Bodin (1530-1596), in "Six livres de la République" (1576), gave the theoretical argument for absolutist monarchy within the framework of divine law in France. Bodin recognised that divine law and natural law were superior with regard to the monarch also, but for the rest the monarch had absolute sovereignty ("majestas"). The idea of representation with assemblies gave some counter-balance. Assemblies acquired some rights: controlling taxation, participating in the process of legislation. Philip Le Bel convened the first "États généraux" in 1302.

A major event was the Protestant Reformation as started by Luther (1483-1546) and Calvin (1509-1564). From then on there was no longer a formal Christian unitary society in Western Europe. Calvin in "Institutio christiani religionis" (1536) argued that there is justice and legitimacy only within the domain of divine Revelation. In that period the ideas of the Dutch humanist philosopher Erasmus (1467-1536) attracted attention. He argued for humanism and religious tolerance. France was torn by eight religious wars (1562-1594). These wars and civil wars created a general atmosphere of insecurity, requiring public management. Part of the Catholic/Protestant "war" was about the Catholic character of the monarchy, seen as fundamental law. The theoretically most harnessed opponents of this idea of Catholic monarchy were Protestant "Monarchomaques", active from the beginning of the religious wars: Hotman, Bèze and Mornay. They argued, that there should be participation in political power on the basis of a contract between monarch and subjects (Vautier, 1947). And that rebellion against oppressive monarchical power was legitimate. King Henry III (1574-1589) was murdered. He was succeeded by Huguenot Henry IV (1589-1610). Henry IV solved problems by becoming Catholic in 1593 ("Paris vaut bien une messe!"). He gave Protestants religious freedom with the "Édict de Nantes" (1598). Bodin experienced eight religious wars between Catholics and Protestants. Therefore Bodin argued for effective public management, a strong State.

After terrible religious civil wars between Catholics and Protestants – with activities of the Catholic "Sainte Ligue" (1576) and the murdering of Henry III in 1598 ànd Henry IV in 1610 –, tensions in French society remained. Religious conflicts and a series of wars between European countries caused a general feeling of insecurity. Managing international relations became an important part of public management of society. The Dutch Hugo Grotius (1583-1645) elaborated an innovative, encompassing law conception to rule international relations in his "Mare Liberum" (1609) and "De iure belli ac pacis" (1625). King Louis XIII (1610-1643) ruled France through his genial minister, Cardinal Richelieu in the period 1624-1642 (Wedgwood, 1962), and by another strategic manager, Cardinal Mazarin who dominated public management of France from 1642 to 1661 (during Louis XIV's minority his mother, Anna of Austria, was regent). They made monarchy a mighty institution, surviving Louis XIV's minority and the "Fronde" rebellion. After frustrations (loss of power and prestige), parts of the aristocracy organised uprisings against the monarchy, making use of the power vacuum during the regency: the "Fronde" (1648-1653). France was the dominant power on the continent of Europe. This was for an important part due to Richelieu and Mazarin.

In June 1648 the parliament of Paris decided an "arrêt de la chambre Saint-Louis", proclaiming that all public functionaries had to be recalled; that the vote of the parliament was needed for new taxes and creation of offices and that nobody could be held in custody for more than 48 hours without being heard by a judge. At first, the regent gave way, but on 26 August 1648, three members of the parliament were arrested. Paris reacted by building up barricades. Mazarin was criticised in hateful pamphlets, "Mazarinades" (Jouhaud, 1985). Mazarin had a diplomatic victory with the Treaty of Westphalia, ending war with Austria (October 1648). This Treaty, making the Protestant Dutch United Republic independent from Catholic Spain after the Eighty Years War (1568-1648), was a stimulus for all who wanted to rebel against French monarchy. Negotiations of Mazarin with representatives of the Parisian parliament finally produced the "paix de Rueil" (March 1649). This ended the civil war, which was given the name of a child's play, "Fronde" (Carrier, 1982). After this "Fronde parlementaire" discontent with Mazarin's rule remained. Information about rebellious activities in England was inspiring (Knachel, 1967). Condé, member of a branch of the House of Bourbon, made reckless by his victory over the Spanish armies, tried in 1649 to eliminate Mazarin: "Fronde des princes". Mazarin had him arrested. There was a fusion of the two Frondes in 1651. Later Mazarin released Condé. He pursued rebellious activities: "Fronde condéenne" (September 1651/August 1653) but, in spite of regional uprisings, public order was restored. This abortive coup reinforced absolutist monarchy. Aristocracy and the parliament of Paris could not realise effective public management (Kossman, 1954). When Mazarin died in 1661, King Louis XIV (1643-1715) assumed all powers. He chose able ministers such as Colbert. Under later monarchs, French monarchy was undermined by blatant mismanagement.

The French Revolution (1789) overthrew absolutist monarchy. Since 1792, France has been a Republic. King Louis XVI was murdered and France experienced a very difficult period in the years 1789-1799. In 1799 Napoleon Bonaparte took over as Consul and from 1804 ruled as Emperor. Napoleon was an autocratic despot, fighting a series of wars in Europe. In 1814, Napoleon was defeated, and banished to Elba. In March 1815, Napoleon escaped from Elba after which he ruled again. This "Hundred Days Regime" ended when on 18 June 1815 Napoleon was defeated at Waterloo. Constitutional monarchy (1814-1830) and July Monarchy (1830-1848) were responsible for a Restoration. The Socialist

Revolution of 24 February 1848 brought the Second Republic (1848-1851), then, with a coup (2 December 1851), Louis-Napoleon Bonaparte made himself emperor in the Second Empire (1852-1870). After his defeat at Sedan (1870), in the Franco-Prussian War, the Third Republic (1870-1940) was proclaimed. This longest regime (so far) was characterised by governmental instability. Following the First World War (1914-1918), France lost its hegemony and the Third Republic collapsed after the swift defeat by German troops in May 1940. The collaborating Vichy-regime (1940-1944) took over, while De Gaulle, from 18 June 1940 on, continued to fight in the name of "France libre". With the help of its Allies, France was liberated in 1944 and The Fourth Republic (1946-1958) was established. This was broken down by the Algerian War and a threat of civil war. De Gaulle came into power again in 1958. He brought Algerian independence and founded the Fifth Republic (1958-), the institutional foundation of contemporary France. France still has a prominent position as a world power, although it is surpassed by superpower United States, in the European Union France is one of the most important Member-States.

Reading this thumbnail historical sketch (Crucifix, 1997), it is a valid supposition that France is quite an interesting framework for analysing Public Management of Society, but there are several other aspects which make France a very interesting country for research about developments in Public Management of Society. The legacy of the French Revolution and its effect on the history of Public Management of Society is tremendous, as Finer (1997, pp. 1517-1566) pointed out. The modern nation probably emerged for the first time with the French Revolution (1789), as there is, strictly speaking, a nation only when public power (sovereignty) is identified with the mass of citizens in their union. The notion of citizen was reinvented then also. Before the French Revolution, there were antecedents and proto-nations (as in the French monarchy), and in former centuries there was public management but in 1789 a rupture formed the French nation by breaking with the previous Ancien Régime through an act of self-determination. In 1789, the "États Généraux" declared itself to be the National Assembly. In the "Déclaration des droits de l'homme et du citoyen" it was proclaimed that the principle of all sovereignty is based in the nation. By proclaiming their revolution to be a national revolution the revolutionaries constituted France as sovereign nation, legitimate basis of all power in society (Best, 1989; Furet/Ozouf, 1989; Kohn, 1967).

According to Singer (1986), the first French nation was conceived in a contractual way, but soon it had cultural dimensions too. While revolutionaries wanted to break with all historic deviations from what they saw as their ideal, they defined the nation in a rationalistic-contractual way. Revolutionaries wanted to create something lasting, infinite in a societal process, liable to temporal decline. They denied the relevance of historical developments up to their act of foundation, though later they saw history in a reinterpreted universe. They tried to nationalise the past and protect national patrimony against future usurpation. Revolutionaries defined concepts in universalistic terms, but wanted to connect the sovereign French nation with a specific territory. Organisation of the nation demanded clear distinctions of "in" and "out", national boundaries (Foucher, 1986; Sahlins, 1989). A favoured dispute of old centred around the natural frontiers of France. France now has more or less the same territory as during the revolutionary period. Related to a specific territory and history, it has an identity as nation longer than most (or all?) other countries. Before the invention of the concept "citoyen" (citizen) in 1789, inhabitants could not, unless they were French, inherit or leave behind property (property of foreigners after their death reverted to the French monarch). After the Revolution one had citizen's rights in France only if one was French. Foreigners were originally seen as standing outside society, as constituted by law. The big difference from the Ancien Régime was that all citizens were proclaimed as having equal rights under the law, all privileges being abolished. Citizenship, membership of the nation, meant that one had to accept being subordinate to the laws (Brubaker, 1992). In the contractualist conception of the nation, society was defined as association, formed by a contract between individuals willing to establish a common institution for the fulfilment of common ends. It was quite logical that the French Republic (The One and Indivisible Republic) was jealous of its unique character as representing the French nation. When one accepts a contractual conception of the nation, society is made dependent on the political constitution of the nation. The nation in a circle of self-determination was seen as the constituent power.

Once the nation was constituted, society seemed to have been there already. Political divisions and partiality did not threaten the existence of society. Public institutions could no longer claim to include society and civil society had to be differentiated from political society. This differentiation was crucial to the forming of the nation-state, while the nation in this context was the civil society. The state represented political society or polity. Cultural discourse about nation building defines the nation via society (the common relation to a combination of historical memory, geography, kinship, tradition, mores, religion and language). Contractual discourse defines nation via its political and/or public institutions. Contractual discourse tended to assimilate societal totality to its political and/or public institutions. Later society was "discovered" beneath the modes of political regulation. The notion of "state" as institutional entity separate from society came forward ever more from the late 18th and early 19th century on. Nation and state can exist separately. There are nations without states, and states without nations. A nation without a state seems to have an "ontological deficit". A state without a nation is seen as an artificial construct. Only about 10% of existing states are candidate for the title of "nation-state" in a strict sense (states with a homogeneous ethnic community), said Hall (1986). From 1900 to 2000, more than 150 States were formed, bringing the total of States up to some 200. More than two-thirds of contemporary States were formed after 1945 and many of them since 1960, following the liquidation of British, French, Dutch, Belgian, and Portuguese colonial empires. For Singer, contractual and cultural discourses seen separately tend to efface the division between politics and society, but taken together they sustain the division. Both are found in functioning modern democracies. The hyphen "nation-state" is complex (Singer, 1986).

France, now one of the most important of some 200 States in the world, was and is a remarkable Nation-State, and a prominent Member-State of the European Union, with its 15 Member-States encompassing more than 370 million inhabitants in 2000. In the 15th century, France was a national State, but not yet a Nation-State. When sovereignty is democratically exercised by the Nation, a national State is becoming a Nation-State. As Braudel (1990) and others confirmed, France has an emanation with a reach much wider than most descriptions. France is a large country in Western Europe with a territory of 547,026 square kilometres, only about 0.4% of the land-area in the whole world. This country is located between the 42nd and 51st northern latitude and between the 4th eastern and 8th western degree of longitude. It has a favourable location in the transit-area between Iberian peninsula and Central Europe, with openings to the sea in three directions: Mediterranean, Atlantic Ocean and North Sea. This is emphasized, as geographical circumstances do matter. Montesquieu said, mastery of the climate is the most powerful of all mastery. In the 19th century France was the basis of a world empire with territories on five continents. After a painful process of decolonisation, France is now reduced to its boundaries in Western Europe and some areas elsewhere. There are some small French overseas territories left in Central America and the Pacific. In 1990 France (population in West-Europe and overseas territories taken together) had about 58 million inhabitants. According to the data of a 1999 census the population had grown to more than 60 million inhabitants (about 58.4 million in France itself). In 2002 France has 61.1 million inhabitants (of which 1.7 million are in overseas territories). France still has a prominent global position at the start of the 21st century. Throughout the centuries, France built up a unique position as cultural centre of a worldwide process of civilisation, its favourable geographic position enabled it to function as meeting-place and focus of different cultures. Via the Mediterranean, this area was in contact with several cultures from earliest times. One can mention Greek culture and the cultures of the Middle East, cradle of religions such as Judaism, Christianity and Islam. The Romans left their mark on developments in this part of Western Europe, so France is an interesting field of research, especially when that research is concentrated upon Public Management of Society. We can convince ourselves by reading the "Journal de la France et des Français. Chronologie politique, culturelle et religieuse de Clovis à 2000" (Cibiel, 2001). Historical experiences with Public Management of Society are relevant in contemporary institutionalising. Guizot (1822): "One does not fight with social facts having roots where human beings cannot touch, and when they have occupied the soil, one has to live with them." So, it is opportune to look at French history specifically (Greigueuil, 1999). French history is reproduced summarily as an aid to memory.

## 2.2. Before the French Revolution

After the military operations of the Romans in 121 BC, southern Gaul was made a Roman province. German invasions proved the weakness of Gaul and its boundaries. A Roman army under Gaius Marius liberated the region, crushing in 102 BC the Teutons near Aquae Sextiae (Aix-en-Provence). The conquest of Gaul by Julius Caesar in the years 57-52 BC, described in his "De Bello Gallico", was made easier by internal discord. The Celtic population during the leadership of Vercingetorix (72-46 BC) was brought under control by Romans, and Gauls adopted many aspects of Roman culture, with Latin as language, Roman law and administration: Gallo-Roman civilisation. Roman Emperor Augustus (63 BC/14 AD) divided his territory in provinces under the leadership of Roman governors. In view of ongoing attacks by Teutons along the eastern boundaries of the Roman Empire the Romans tried to move the boundary to the Elbe, but they were defeated in the Teuton Wood (9 AD) and had to withdraw to the Rhine. An invasion in the German area (83 AD) led to the decision to construct a fortified wall from Cologne to Regensburg, but this wall was destroyed. In the third century, Romans withdrew to the Rhine again. Meanwhile massive migrations were going on, Salic Franks settled in the north of the Roman Empire, Ripuarian Franks settled outside Roman territory. Within the Roman Empire Christianity, after a period of repression, gained more adherents. The Edict of Milan (313) gave Christians religious freedom and under Emperor Theodosius I (379-395) Christianity was made the state-religion. The Roman Emperor was honoured as God's chosen representative on earth. Romans lost their grip on the extensive territory of the Roman Empire and Franks penetrated into the Gallo-Roman territory. Causes for the Roman Empire's decay were a slackening of military strength and weakening of control from the centre over extended parts of the Roman Empire.

In the year 395, the Roman Empire was split into the West-Roman Empire (395-476) and the East-Roman Empire (395-1453). Emperor Constantine the Great transferred his centre of public management from Rome to Byzantium, latterly Constantinople. From 31 December 406 on Vandals and other tribes, chased by aggressive Huns from Eastern Europe, crossed the Rhine westwards. In Gaul, Romans had Visigoths and Burgundians as allies. Shortly before the fall of the West-Roman Empire Euric, king of the Visigoths, defied the sovereignty of Rome. In 475, he brought Gaul south of the Loire under his control. In the course of time, Franks penetrated here also. East-Goths and West-Goths had settled in the south, Franks in the north, Burgundians and Alemans in the east and Bretons (on the run for Angles and Saxons) in the west. Around the year 480 powerful Euric had the best chance to gain control over the whole of Gaul, but Visigoths and Burgundians were Arians, they had the bishops of Gaul as powerful opponents. Arians, followers of Arius (256-336), denied the divinity of Christ. Some Roman Emperors adhered to this doctrine, which had many adherents under Goths, Longobards and Vandals. The Council of Nicea (325) condemned this as a heresy and so the bishops of Gaul supported the Salic Franks when their king Clovis converted to Christianity.

The Frankish kingdom, under Clovis (481-511) of the Merovingian dynasty (481-751), encompassed the whole of Gaul. In the last years of king Clovis, the "Lex Salica" was drawn up. This was a Latin text with Salic rules of customary law. Although Clovis consolidated a large kingdom in Gaul ("regnum Francorum") Roman law, organisational genius and Christianity were not strong enough to maintain his kingdom after his death. The Frankish custom of dividing the territory between male heirs, as if the royal territory were private land, caused wars time and again. The Frankish kingdom between 558 and 561 was united by one of Clovis' sons, Lotharius I. When he died, the area was divided up into Austrasia in the North, Neustria in the Southwest and Burgundy. In the East-Roman Empire Roman law was codified by order of Emperor Justinian I (484-565), "Codex Justinianus" (534). This was a decisive measure because in that period Roman law was fragmented and disintegrated. Justinian I was responsible for charging collection of the "Digesta" (533), an anthology of writings of important Roman jurists. A legal handbook, "Institutiones" (533), was based on "Institutiones" of Gaius (2nd century). Justinian I wanted to put an end to the fragmentation of legal rules by prohibiting working on authorised legal texts, but he authorised new rules later than 534, "Novellae", with "Codex", "Digesta", and "Institutiones" known as "Corpus iuris civilis".

Within the territory of France, the authority of kings was weakened as the kings did nothing ("rois fainéants"). Actual power came into the hands of major-domo's (Lemarignier, 1981). In the 7th century, the kingdom was in disarray. Pepin the Short, son of major-domo Charles Martel (714-741) who defeated the Arabs near Poitiers (732), dethroned the last Merovingian king. In 751 he had himself anointed as king in a religious ceremony, legitimising his coup with the support of the Church. With Old Testament kingship as framework, kingship got a sacral foundation. The basis was laid for a close tie between Church and Frankish kingdom. This created a solid foundation for the Carolingian Empire to extend all over Western Europe, led by his son Charlemagne (768-814). At Christmas 800, Charlemagne was crowned by the Pope, with obvious reminiscences to Roman Emperors. In the first half of the 8th century, the feudal system was a public management system resting on a personal bond between king and vassal, on the basis of landed property (Anderson, 1977; Ganshof, 1957). The feudal lord gave vassals as free men a feudal tenure to have a living; generally a piece of land or an office. The vassal promised loyal military service to his feudal lord (personal feudal bond). Delegating administration of the feudal area to vassals, the king could maintain his authority over a more extended territory without being forced to do it himself. When a feudal lord died, the fief reverted to the king. Later the grip of the king weakened as Feudal lords, seeing their fiefs more as their own property, appropriated yields, or enfeoffed parts of their fiefs.

Factual protection of goods and chattels became a top-priority after the end of the 8th century, with practically continuous pillages by Northmen and Arabs. When Charlemagne died in 814, Louis the Pious (814-840) succeeded him. To end repetitious problems with the succession, he ordained in 817 that his empire be divided up between his three sons, and that his eldest son would become emperor with superior authority, but things went wrong when the Emperor fathered another son from a second marriage for whom a part was also reserved in 829. There followed a battle for succession between the sons of Louis the Pious and when he died in 840 the cold war between the three sons became a hot war. They eventually divided the Empire with the Treaty of Verdun (843). Charles the Bold (840-877) took West-Francia (more or less the territory of contemporary France), Louis the German (840-876) obtained East-Francia and the eldest son, Lotharius I (840-855), had the title of emperor and the territory between the two other areas. When Lotharius I died in 855, his empire was divided up between his sons. Louis II became emperor of Italy, Lotharius II obtained the northern part, Lorraine. Charles of Burgundy had the part in between. As Lotharius II died in 869 without a legal heir, his empire was divided in 870 between Charles the Bold and Louis the German. When Louis the German died in 875 the Pope crowned Charles the Bold Emperor. After his demise in 877 West-Francia, for lack of descendants, came under the king of East-Francia, Charles the Fat, in 884. His nobles dethroned him in 887 and Carolingian Arnulf of Carinthia was made king (887-899). In West-Francia it was not a Carolingian, but Odo of Paris (888-898) who was chosen as king. The Frankish Empire fell apart, while feudal lords and counts had de-facto power, with competencies over army and jurisdiction, and the function of count as administrative authority became hereditary.

After the 9th century the king lost his monopoly of public authority. Local potentates took over responsibilities for army and jurisdiction as if these were private matters. In their seigniories they fulfilled functions of general administration, while the Church had important administrative power. When Odo of Paris died in 898, Carolingian Charles III the Simple (898-922) became king in West-Francia. This was at the instigation of the bishops, who thought to realise the ideal of a Christian Roman Empire. Charles III gave Rollo, the leader of the Northmen, Normandy as fief. In 922, Charles III was dethroned. His brother and son-in-law of Odo became king. When the last Carolingian died Odo's great-nephew Hugues Capet (947-996) was made king. Capetians, after Merovingians and Carolingians, were the third French dynasty. In spite of reduced powers, Capetians promoted systematic centralisation. As the kings gave counts and dukes ample policy room Capetians were recognised formally as king for centuries. Tradition going back to Carolingians was cherished. The Church promoted this, reinforcing the idea that the king had public authority in the name of God and celebrating the coronation with a Church ritual. Capetians ruled France in a direct line for the period 987-1328, and indirectly via sidelines Valois (1328-1589), Bourbon and Orléans up to 1792 and 1814-1848.

A short digression is appropriate to take into consideration the administrative-governing situation in England, which had been brought under Danish control in 1016. Duke William of Normandy conquered England in 1066 (Howarth, 1981) and so, as William the Conqueror, he became king of England (1066-1087). After his death in 1087, his son Robert obtained the duchy of Normandy. His son William II (1087-1100) became king of England and his son Henry was given some landed property in Normandy. In Francia, kings Louis VI (1108-1137) and Louis VII (1137-1180) made progress with solving territorial conflicts between feudal lords and local potentates who recognised the king's superior authority. A new concept was used: feudal lords could engage themselves no longer in feudal bonds with counts and dukes of other areas in France, as the king of France was the sole, superior, feudal lord. Counts and dukes did not agree with this, and in 1151 the duke of Normandy, Henry Plantagenet (1131-1189), became count of Anjou. In 1153, he married Eleonora of Aquitaria. His power was considerable, particularly when he became king of England as Henry II in 1154 and Plantagenets gained control over an important part of West-Francia. The French king, Louis VII, irritated by this power concentration, formed a counter-coalition (Francia, Flanders, Burgundy and Champagne). His successor, Philip II Augustus (1180-1223), expanded his influence in the area of Plantagenets by conspiring with landed gentry. He overruled English kings Henry II and Richard the Lionheart, and John Lackland (1199-1216), forced by his barons to sign the "Magna Carta" (1215). In 1204, Philip II Augustus took his chance when John Lackland married the betrothed of a vassal in Aquitania. He shirked his formal obligations as vassal in not answering a summons to appear for a jurisdiction and all his French fiefs were declared to have expired. With one stroke of the pen Normandy, Maine, Anjou, Touraine and Brittany were in the royal demesne of the French kings.

The French king Louis IX, Louis the Saint (1226-1270) had, as the greatest Christian monarch, the direction of the Last Crusade in 1270. The First Crusade, the battle of the united Christian world to liberate the "Holy Land" from Islam, took place in the years 1096-1099 under the leadership of Godfrey of Bouillon. This followed the appeal by Pope Urbanus II during the Synod of Clermont (1095). Capetian Philippe Le Bel (1285-1314) is known for his grim fight against the Tempeliers, the oldest order of knighthood, established to protect pilgrims to the "Holy Land". Their very rich possessions were too attractive for the insatiable greed of the French monarchs to resist. Philippe Le Bel made his fame in his power-struggle with the Pope, and by his decision to force the Exile of the Popes to Avignon. Against claims of worldly sovereignty of the Popes with regard to French territory he was unrelenting. He preferred the unity of France above the unity of Christianity. When the French dynasty of the Capetians died out in 1328, both the French pretender to the throne, Philippe de Valois, and the English king, Edward III (1327-1377), claimed the French crown. The nobles chose Philippe de Valois, who was made king of France as Philippe VI (1328-1350). In 1340, France had more than 28% of Europe's population and about 5% of the population of the world (as known at that time). France was demographically the third world power. In the 14th century, there was a prolonged economic crisis, while in 1348, about one-third of the European population died of the plague. One and a half centuries after the last crusade, France was confronted with warfare in its own territory due to English power aspirations, which had to be contested in the Hundred Years War (1338-1453). The motive for this war was that the English king, Edward III, claimed the French throne. The French victory over England was partly due to Jeanne d'Arc, who rescued Orléans, and brought Charles VII to Reims, where he was crowned. Jeanne d'Arc was burnt at the stake in 1413. In the line of Capetians, Louis XI (1461-1483) is known for his fight against important feudal lords under the leadership of Charles the Bold of Burgundy.

After the conquest of Constantinople (1453) by the Turks, the East-Roman Empire fell to pieces. Thereafter, more than before, Byzantine scholars with extensive knowledge of Greek manuscripts, came to Western Europe. This caused a strong upswing of interest in the Greco-Roman civilisation of Antiquity. Italy was the cultural centre then. Early Renaissance in the 15th century is distinguished from the Late Renaissance in the first half of the 16th century. The Reformation, the 16th century attempt to renovate the Christian Church and to purge it from all abuses, also had tremendous effects in France. On 31 October 1517 Luther nailed 95 theses to the churchdoor in the German town of Wittenberg and in 1534 Cauvin, better known as Calvin (1509-1564), fled from Paris to Basle because of his dissenting theological doctrine. Calvin made Geneva the base for the spread of the Calvinist doctrine, as elaborated in his "Institutio religionis christianae" (1536). Reformation and reactions caused grim religious wars, which threatened the official unity of the Christian Church and put the unity of France under extreme pressure. The Contra-Reformation, the counter-movement within the Roman-Catholic Church against the Protestant-Christian Reformation, took time to organise. The Council of Trent (1545-1563) established official doctrine against Protestant ideas. In the sphere of politics one can mention the idle attempt of King François I (1515-1547) to obtain the throne of the German emperor in 1519. At the Treaty of Crépy (1544) he had to abandon all claims on Italian territory. In 1550 France, with its 21 million inhabitants had the largest population in Europe (35.6% of a total of 59 million). Under King Henri III (1574-1589), there were grim religious wars in France. François d'Anjou died in 1584 and Henri de Navarre, a Huguenot, was the closest heir to the throne. There was strong opposition against a Huguenot upon the throne in Catholic France: the "Three Henri's War" broke out. The Catholic "Ligue" under Henri de Guise expelled Henri III from Paris on the "Journée des Barricades" (1588). Henri III murdered Henri de Guise, and was murdered himself.

Central power of the French kings was substantially reinforced by Henri IV (1589-1610), the first king from the House of Bourbon. He was Protestant, but was converted to Catholicism ("A Holy Mass for Paris is worthwhile"). With his Edict of Nantes (1598), he proclaimed freedom of religion for Protestants. This brought civil war about religious matters to an end and stimulated the unity of France. The Bourbon regime was absolutist and centralist. It was very eager to expand its territory. During two centuries (1589-1789), absolutist France under the Bourbons built up a huge and powerful empire. France inspired other countries in Europe and elsewhere with awe. It was fascinating especially for its unrivalled cultural emanation. At the time of Louis XIII (1610-1643) Corneille created a furore with plays for the theatre, Réné Descartes (1596-1650) laid innovating foundations for modern philosophy with his "Discours de la méthode." (1637), he had the insight that there was one thing sure: I think therefore I am. From this "Cogito, ergo sum", Descartes developed his renovating, rationalistic method, based solely upon human reason. King Louis XIII as governing authority was in the shadow of his genial first minister, Cardinal Richelieu, who enriched world literature about public management with his rather actual "Testament politique" (1642). When Louis XIII died in 1643 Cardinal-Minister Mazarin became the de-facto ruler of France (Dulong, 1999). After his death in 1661, King Louis XIV (1643-1715) assumed all powers. The "Roi Soleil" painstakingly controlled all, so that he as the Sun King was the absolute centre of all that happened, as the sun is. He ordered the rebuilding of the pompous Chateau of Versailles, and made his court the most glorious and extravagant court of all royal courts (Sabatier, 1999). Louis XIV had the assistance of professionals, but the direction of all was in his hands.

Under the outstanding leadership of Minister Colbert (1619-1683) with his French Mercantilist policy, named "Colbertisme", prosperity in France was growing. Mercantilism was an economic-political doctrine to promote national economic potency with regard to other countries by intensified intervention of public authorities in the productive system. Its target was to create a positive trade balance by organising exports, which would have to outdo imports in value as much as possible. To realise this, a varied set of policy instruments was used. Protection of national production with import tariffs, embargos on imports, export premiums, establishment of state-enterprises and enterprises with subsidies, acquisition of colonial territories. With the English East-Indian Company (from 1600) and the Dutch East-Indian Company (1602) in mind, Colbert established large French commercial West Indian and East-Indian Companies. Colbert promoted the build-up of important industries, such as the glass factory of Saint-Gobain and carpet-weaving in the "Maison des Gobelins" in Paris. The period of Louis XIV saw a flowering of literature, arts and other expressions of culture, "le grand siècle". Creating academies for painting, sculpture, architecture and sciences, Louis XIV was a Maecenas, making sponsoring of cultural activities operational in a modern way. Molière and Racine (theatre), Madame de Lafayette (novels), La Fontaine (fables) and others excelled in literature. In the field of architecture Mansard was admired, Le Brun and others were famous painters. Imposing buildings and infrastructural projects were realised ("Canal du Midi", connecting Atlantic Ocean with the Mediterranean). Another aspect of the regime of Louis XIV was his many military adventures, such as the Devolution War (1665-1668), Dutch War (1672-1678), Nine Years War (1688-1697) and Spanish Succession War (1700-1713). Many French were killed and wounded on battlefields, not to forget the countless victims from other countries. Louis XIV prosecuted Protestants and in 1685 the Edict of Nantes (1598) was abolished. The ostentatious monarch provoked widespread opposition by his military activities, persecution of Protestants and disgusting waste.

The mass of the population lived in bitter poverty, an absolute contrast with the exuberant luxury of the royal court, which financed its expenditure and the costs of many wars by constantly increasing the tax burden. In 17th century France the state was central, with the personal regime of absolutist despot Louis XIV, to whom the saying is ascribed: "The State, that's me!" This absolutist monarchy provoked discussions about its negative aspects. Representatives of Enlightenment produced innovative ideas (Hampson, 1972). François-Marie Arouet, better known as Voltaire (1694-1778), wrote bitter and sharp criticisms about existing institutions of power (Church, monarchy etc.) in his "Lettres anglaises" (introducing England as example of an enlightened country), and "Essai sur les moeurs et l'esprit des nations". Jean-Jacques Rousseau (1712-1778) started from the axiom that the individual human being is good, but that men are contaminated by a wicked society. He argued in "Émile, ou sur l'éducation" for a return to the natural situation of former times, when human beings were still good and happy. Because every human being is born as a free individual, the power of the state can be based only upon the common will of all, sovereignty of the people ("Contrat Social"). The project of Diderot and d'Alembert, the "Encyclopédie. Dictionnaire raisonné des sciences, des arts et des métiers" (1751-1772, 28 volumes), was important. It was an overview of all then available knowledge. The time was overripe for sweeping changes and there was a highly dynamic process of fermentation in society. The governing-administrative system of the Ancien Régime was not susceptible for necessary changes in society. Institutional arrangements systematically favoured a small group of privileged persons, while the masses had a bitter life, often without bread to eat. Institutions of the monarchy, which had forged the unity of France, were not in harmony with new needs of society. A violent revolution was necessary to demonstrate to the elite that institutions had to be changed. That was the French Revolution of 1789, known worldwide as the Revolution, although France had more revolutions, and there were revolutions in other countries as well.

## 2.3. From French Revolution to Bonaparte

Prévost-Paradol said in "la France nouvelle" (1868): The French Revolution founded a society, but it sought yet its public management system. A modern regime replaced the Ancien Régime. France's social structure was fundamentally different from the previous period as a consequence of French Revolution and First Empire, heir of this Revolution "under benefit of inventory" (Chevallier, 1967, p.113). French society was no longer built on the same principles, concept of man, philosophy of life and worldview (Tocqueville). Usually revolution is interpreted as a violent event or a series of violent activities by which a political regime or government is overthrown. Then a reduced term of regime is used. It is necessary to operate a more complete notion of regime. A regime is the whole of social, administrative, civil, religious, economic, governmental, political and constitutional institutions (Chevallier, 1967, p.7-8). Chevallier, whose excellent analysis is summarised here (o.c., pp.10-18), differentiated minor politics (running government) from major politics (policies about organisation of society). And between constitutional in a narrower sense (organisation of public authorities, constitution of public management), and constitutional in the widest sense (all of what constitutes society), with numerous mutual interconnections. The French Revolution was essential for the institutional set-up of public management, which also developed from this time. The French Revolution was in the minds of the people long before it happened (Mathiez, 1959). Victor Hugo made the masses in "Les Misérables" sing: "It's the fault of Voltaire", "It's the fault of Rousseau". Some authors saw the French Revolution as caused by Voltaire, Rousseau, Montesquieu and the Encyclopedists, but the real causes went deeper. The spirit of the age was sparkling with new ideas. Circumstances changed substantially. Authors disputed the dominant concepts of the 17th century. It was then seen as a duty to accept the limitations of human condition. Conscious acceptance of obedience on the basis of the Christian, supernatural conception of man: prefer eternal happiness to earthly fortune.

In the 18th century the spirit of the age was focused on sweeping away prejudices, which opposed reason, human nature and happiness. Rules or institutions, which could not be explained rationally by critical reasoning were seen as prejudices. This applied to all for whom it was necessary to invoke supernatural, mystic notions or traditions and customs, part of the field of irrationality. A prejudice is against nature, as human nature according to the postulate of Rousseau and Diderot is fundamentally good, but is perverted by traditional society. A prejudice was seen as against human happiness. Saint-Just proclaimed a new conception of happiness, disassociated from religious roots. Not happiness of the individual was the central theme, but common happiness of all human beings. "Philanthropy", happiness of the greatest number, as it later inspired Saint-Simon, a pioneer of socialism. "Philanthropy" implicated a social, humanitarian moral. Individual and common happiness were thought interconnected. Noble motives make people invest a considerable part of personal happiness in the happiness of others. The spirit of the time, in the name of reason (rationalism), nature (naturalism) and human happiness (hedonism) had to fight all prejudices and the legacy of an absurd past. All prejudices had to be eradicated to build up reasonable society producing continuous progress, directed by an independent moral, separate from religious roots. Progress as quintessence of modern consciousness was put forward as innovation. Turgot wrote "Tableau philosophique des progrès de l'esprit humain." (1750). Condorcet wrote in the revolutionary period his "Esquisse d'une tableau historique des progrès de l'esprit humain." (1795). It was primarily a revolt against religious prejudices, especially Catholic prejudices, as French society was based on prejudices of the dominant Catholic Church. Catholicism was the foundation of the whole fabric of political-administrative institutions. Louis XIV, legitimising his superior position by claiming its foundation in divine law, wrote in his memoirs: "Our submission to God is the rule, and also the model for the submission of all my subjects to me. Armies, governing councils and all human energies would be weak instruments to keep me on the throne when everybody thought to have the same right on the throne. And when they would not respect superior authority, of which my own authority is a part". Elimination of religious prejudices implied that prejudices of the whole political system were questioned.

That was dangerous for the existing institutional bases of society. It was part of the rationalistic state of mind that sciences had to play a decisive role, especially natural sciences, realising an astonishing progress in the 18th century. The basic idea was that human sciences could be transformed with scientific methods, which produced such formidable results in natural sciences: exactness, pure logic, abstraction. A new ideal according to Cournot (1872). For this spirit of the time there could be no "mystery of government". The veil over the mysteries of government had to be eliminated. Two fundamental notions buttressed monarchist society: the mysterious marriage between King and Nation and societal hierarchy based on three orders: clergy, aristocracy, and the third order (Olivier-Martin, 1948). The concept of public management of society was that the interests of King and Nation were made indissolubly intertwined by the mysterious marriage between King and Nation, with the character of a sacrament during a religious ceremony. In a rational analysis it was clear that this sacred foundation of the French monarchy was a medieval anachronism. When monarchy abused its position, while forsaking its duties and gulping in luxury and waste at the cost of the masses, it lost legitimacy. Rational analysis of the intellectual elite made the monarch fall from his august position. It was shown that interests of the Nation could be contrary to that of the King. The King was an exponent of the feudal structure with orders and guilds and this was not concordant with real societal conditions and needs, and opposed to reason, natural equality and common human happiness. It was against reason, natural equality and natural law that the dynamic bourgeoisie was the third order with only limited competencies.

For the bourgeoisie, natural equality was claimed as a right. The third order had some 24 million people out of a population of 25 million. Abbé Siéyès in his pamphlet "Qu'est-ce que le Tiers État?" (1788) could demonstrate that there was no reasonable representation of the common people. There were tensions within the order of nobility too. "Noblesse de robe" (toga-nobility) was jealous of "noblesse d'épée" (military nobility), nobility of the countryside looked up to court nobility, old nobility looked down on freshmade nobility and all nobles were jealous of the money-nobility. The time was gone when nobility had a societal function in defending population against violence from gangs of robbers, so legitimising their privileges. Chateaubriand: "time of service, time of privileges, time of vanities". Legists had the conception that there was in a monarchist state only a king and his subjects, all being equal under the laws of the king. They worked for the destruction of intermediary institutions between king and individual, which in their vision swallowed the State. They elaborated, contrary to the conception in England, absolute monarchy; the opposite of what Montesquieu wanted to realise. The French had an aristocratic conception of freedom. Tocqueville described this as the will to be free, as one has a special right to be, with a privilege corresponding with the position in society. In the 18th century, a democratic concept of freedom developed. Tocqueville: Everybody, supposed to have received insight to behave, when born, has an equal right to live independently for what concerns him, ruling his own destiny.

Against the background of this "bouillon des idées", the French Revolution was settled within two months (Chevallier, 1967, pp. 19-35). From 5 May 1789 (opening of the "États-Généraux") to the Fall of the Bastille on 14 July 1789 ("Quatorze Juillet"). In two months, the "États-Généraux", based on the three orders, were transformed into the new "Assemblée Nationale Constituante" with the task of adopting a Constitution; the fundamental coup of the third order. Two years earlier, in 1787, the "Assemblée des Notables" was convoked, to discuss the bankruptcy of the monarchy and to adopt new taxes. This meeting was a failure as Louis XVI and Minister Necker indulged a claim to convoke an antique institution, the "États-Généraux", not convoked since 1614. On 5 May 1789 the opening session took place in the "Hôtel des Menus Plaisirs" in Versailles in a room full of monarchist symbolism, with the King sitting on the throne, Queen Marie-Antoinette on an arm-chair lower than the throne, the clergy left, the aristocracy right, and the third order opposite to the throne. The third order got the right of "doublement": two representatives of the bourgeoisie, one of the clergy and one of the aristocracy. This right made sense for the bourgeoisie only if voting was per person, it had no fair meaning if voting was per order (then the bourgeoisie would lose). Some of the clergy and aristocracy were on the side of the third order. Each responsible public authority would have decided this crucial procedural question beforehand, but not Louis XVI and Necker, both the personification of indecision. The general expectation was that a decision would be taken about this issue on 5 May 1789 but there was no decision, the meeting was suspended. This acted as a proverbial spark to the tinder.

That evening on 5 May 1789 the third order met with 650 representatives of whom 300 were jurists. The agreement was that all would meet in the "Salle commune" and wait without saying anything and without forming a specific order. By no means, the impression might be that the third order met as such formally, meaning that they recognised the split-up in orders. They agreed to wait for representatives of clergy and aristocracy to come to them to discuss matters and determine competencies. This tactic was applied from 5 May to 10 June 1789. On the morning of 10 June 1789, Siéyès said that it was now time and for the last time representatives of the clergy and aristocracy were invited to join them, otherwise they would decide in the name of the French nation without them. As there was no response to this summons the meeting of third order representatives and factions of the other orders determined competencies. After passionate discussions on 15-16 June 1789, the "Assemblée Nationale" was formed as representation for the whole French nation. This was a very serious rebellion, a declaration of war to clergy and aristocracy and to the King and his public authority system. The vote for the motion-Siéyès was adopted with 491 votes to 90 (Mirabeau abstained). There was an unequalled enthusiasm: "Vive le Roi! Vive l'Assemblée Nationale!" This was a coup, a formidable institutional break. An institutional vacuum followed. The positive law of old times, based upon the hierarchy of orders, was denied and infringed.

The new conception, supported by this "fait accompli", was not legitimised by the sole legitimate authority, the King. With foresight, the National Assembly decided that all taxes, adopted by the National Assembly, could no longer be imposed, when the National Assembly for one reason or another had to finish its work. On 20 June 1789, the "Serment du Jeu de Paume" took place. Representatives of the self-chosen National Assembly pledged with this "Oath of the Tennis Court" that they would not stop working as National Assembly before having given France a Constitution. This was a precautionary measure against the expected coercive measures of the formal public authorities. At the royal meeting on 23 June 1789, the King took the side of clergy and aristocracy. He annulled what had happened since 5 May 1789, ordering representatives to go home. When representatives of clergy and aristocracy obeyed, after the departure of the King, the others remained sitting. This was the famous disobedience to the King. Mirabeau said: Say to those who sent you that we are here by the will of the people, and that we are not leaving, except by the force of bayonets (Chevallier, 1947, p.62). The formal public authorities capitulated and convoked a meeting of the three orders. Deputies were intimidated with troop movements, masses from Paris and suburbs supported their deputies. The Bastille was occupied on 14 July 1789, mother of future revolutions (Tocqueville). Some days later the King capitulated. This happened, because the formal public authorities did not react adequately to new circumstances and the spirit of the age.

The revolt of the American colonies against England, inspired by Locke, Montesquieu and others, in the American War of Independence (1776-1783) brought independence for the United States of America. Rebellion against existing structures of public authority proved to be possible, and even successful. Without any doubt this stimulated groups in France. The French National Assembly, using ideas circulating in France and abroad, adopted the "Déclaration des droits de l'homme et du citoyen" on 26 August 1789. In this declaration, a number of human rights were proclaimed in a metaphysical, abstract and universalistic style. This Human Rights Declaration was a philosophical catechism with principles and condemnation of abuses and privileges. The revolutionary catechism proclaimed: men are born and remain free and with equal rights (art.1). The objective of each political community is to maintain the natural and inviolable human rights (art.2):

freedom, property, security and the right of resistance against oppression. Not society is central, but the individual (individualistic postulate). Individual freedom is the basic axiom. Freedom means that one can do anything that does not damage others. Natural rights may only be restricted to guarantee natural rights of others. In this concept humans are seen as individuals living apart. Sovereignty was recognised as residing in the Nation (article 3). The Nation was not the population as living during a specific time in France, but the indivisible, "eternal" collectivity. The Constitution of 1791 defined this in a more Jacobin way as "one, indivisible and inviolable". The American principle "no taxation without representation" was borrowed in stating that taxes would be spread evenly amongst citizens, with the consent of their representatives (article 4). Article 6 said that the law was equal for all (against existing privileges). Arbitrary arrests and punishments, usual in the Ancien Régime, were prohibited in the same way as with the law of "Habeas Corpus" in England (articles 7-9). Freedom of speech and press replaced the Ancien Régime censorship. Religious liberty was recognised. The monopoly of public offices for the privileged was abolished with equal access to public offices according to talents (article 6). Citizens had the right to participate in legislation personally or via representatives, an interpretation of the "volonté générale" (article 6). The separation of powers ("trias politica") was recognised. Monarchical regimes were apprehensive of the risk of contagion with this revolutionary virus, exported by French universalism as an exemple for the whole world. Tocqueville argued: the French Revolution was a political revolution developing into a religious revolution. He concluded: important religions, especially Christianity, generally have a message without any indication of what could be specific for a period, a race, a population, a society or culture.

The French Revolution worked with regard to the terrestrial world in the same way as religious revolutions concerning the other world (the world to come). The question was not only which rights French citizens had, but also, which were the universal, political rights of human beings as such. In an abstract way human rights were defined, without a relation with any specific society. This made the French Human Rights Declaration clearly understandable for everybody, and inspiring for many abroad. The preamble proclaimed that man is good of nature, that ignorance, oblivion and contempt concerning human rights are the sole cause of public disasters, corruption of governments and other calamities for humanity, so a solemn declaration about the natural, inalienable and holy rights of man was needed to change the constitution of society for mankind. A kind of messianic message based on the premise that the social regime is responsible for what is going on in society. Of course, there was a big gap between principles and reality. In the revolutionary euphoria, the problem was how to fulfil the tasks of public management. Priority was given to a draft for the Constitution. There were opposing views about the organisation of public authorities. Everybody discussed passionately the American revolt and "L'Esprit des Lois" (Montesquieu) and "Contrat Social" (Rousseau) without having read these books. The American revolt was an example of a Republic with rigid separation of powers. The "American School" (La Fayette) could accept a monarchy only with as many republican dimensions as possible. The republican "Contrat Social" was a Bible of popular sovereignty. Robespierre made himself mouthpiece of this interpretation. The "English School" (Mounier), named "Anglo-maniacs" or "Monarchiens", followed Montesquieu's ideas; moderate citizens, royalists, liberals and liberal aristocrats were devoted to civil freedom. Montesquieu had warned: Abolish in a monarchy prerogatives for lords, clergy, nobility, cities, and you will soon have a popular State or a despotic State. They looked for a solution in between a state of the people and a despotic state. They supported a system similar to that of England (Ferrero, 1951). Against this well-balanced conception stood the abstract-doctrinarian school of Siéyès. As engineer of constitutions, he wanted to apply a kind of rational mechanics to the world of politics. Adherents of the English School lost the battle of constitutional conceptions. King Louis XVI, scared to death of revolutionaries, tried to flee the country on 21 June 1791 ("Fuite de Varennes"). He was intercepted and brought back to Paris. The monarch's position was undermined. On 27 August 1791, a coalition of Austria and Prussia declared war on France to rescue the French monarchy. After a vote of the National Assembly about the Constitution and the oath of King Louis XVI, recognising this Constitution on 14 September 1791, the "Constituante" was succeeding by the "Législative" with a constitutional monarchy as regime. This was short-lived.

Tensions piled up throughout French society. "Powers of the street" dominated ever more. Clubs, associations and popular masses in Paris organised continuous physical pressures on the Assembly who were trying to manage the country by gathering (Bastid, 1965). There were uprisings against the high cost of living for the common people (pillaging masses, guarded transports of cereals). The Assembly's decision to abolish feudal rights was reduced when rules were made operational. Opposition grew against "émigrés" and aristocrats (ransacking of their chateaux, to force them to accept the abolition of feudal rights). The slogan was: Rescue the Revolution. The masses were sensitive to the supposed treachery of monarchists and aristocrats working with foreigners to attempt to restore the Ancien Régime. A basic characteristic of society was a generalised distrust of everybody for everybody. The Assembly adopted decrees to deport priests refusing an oath of loyalty to revolutionary ideas. When King Louis XVI vetoed these decrees the fury of the Parisian masses was stirred up. On 20 June 1792, "Sansculottes" occupied the Tuileries, where King Louis XVI was in custody. On 11 July 1792 the Assembly declared the country to be in danger. Brunswick, commander-in-chief of the Austrian-Prussian coalition against France, arrogantly provoked Parisians on 25 July 1792, threatening dire consequences if they did not accept their King. On 10 August 1792 "Sansculottes" occupied the Tuileries again, with more violence. King Louis XVI and his family went to the building of the Assembly. On 11 August 1792, the King was suspended. Violations of the Constitution piled up. Property rights were declared inviolable, but emigrants' possessions were nationalised. There were numerous executions in September 1792. On 21 September 1792, the "Convention" proclaimed the abolition of kingship. On 22 September 1792, the First French Republic was a fact, "an I de la République française". After a vote on the guilt of Louis XVI in the National Assembly he was executed by the guillotine on 21 January 1793 (Lossky, 1994). Many tried to wash their hands of all blood for this regicide (Dunn, 1994).

The atmosphere in the group of leading revolutionaries became ever more grim. Now that the common enemy, the King and his following, were eliminated they sought enemies in their own circles. Purges followed purges. Robespierre, the most ruthless of all, purged all his enemies and friends away. Robespierre had an obsession, thinking that he was the sole true Jacobin. After one of those Parisian days with massive violence, 31 May 1793, there was an uprising against the "Convention" (21 September 1792/26 October 1795), followed soon by uprisings in Bordeaux and Normandy. On 24 June 1793, the "Convention" adopted a new Constitution, seeing the people as the sole source of public authority. Legislative power was subordinate to the people, and executive power was subordinate to legislative power. This "Constitution montagnarde" of 1793, adopted by a referendum, was never put into operation due to dangers threatening France from within and from abroad. It was thought necessary to concentrate powers in the hands of some committees of the "Convention", especially the "Comité du salut public", sharing power with the "Comité de sûreté générale". Terror ruled arbitrarily, with dictator Robespierre on top. The Assembly agreed to it all, paralysed by fright. Those men, after being ruthless for fear of their enemies, became more ruthless for fear of their friends. Exercising terror, murdering to avoid being murdered (Tocqueville). Absolute dictatorship of the "Convention" was transformed into dictatorship of the "Comité du Salut Public", with the personal dictatorship of Robespierre (April 1794/July 1794). On 27 July 1794 ("9 thermidor"), the "Convention" voted for the arrest of Robespierre. He, along with Saint-Just, Couthon and a hundred companions, was executed: the Thermidorean Reaction.

On 1 April 1795 ("12 germinal"), there was a leftist uprising, workers crying for bread and the Constitution of 1793. General Pichegru restored order. On 20 May 1795 ("1 prairal"), the "Convention" was occupied by leftist masses. A provisional government was formed with "députés robespierristes", surviving three days. Generals Menou and Murat restored order. The basic means of the people to realise a people's democracy was eliminated. The result of these "leftist days" was that the Constitution of 1793 (a maximum of democracy) was thrown away. The "Constitution de l'an III, anti-montagnarde" (1795), was adopted and Thermidoreans ruled the "décrets des deux tiers". In this institutional masterpiece, they ordained that 2/3 of the seats of the new Assembly had to be given to members of the "Convention". Royalist agitation against these decrees developed in Paris. Barras was asked to crush this royalist uprising on 5 October 1795 ("13 vendémiaire"). He chose Bonaparte as assistant. After his coup in December 1793 at Toulon, where Bonaparte defeated the English, he was made general, but later he was suspect as "robespierriste". This uprising of 1795 was ruthlessly crushed. Tocqueville (1856) concluded: It is interesting to follow, during the several phases of this long Revolution, the march of the army to sovereign power. Since "13 vendémiaire", it was not possible to govern without the army. After military intervention, it was possible to govern with the "Constitution de l'an III" (1795). This Constitution restored separation of powers by fragmentation of public organs with a part of public authority. Constituents wanted to prevent a new "Convention", a new 1793, a new Terror, a new "Comité du Salut Public", a new "Commune de Paris", and above all a new Robespierre (Chevallier, 1967, p. 96). For the first time, France had a real people's representation: "Conseil des Cinq Cents"; and "Conseil des Anciens". Executive power was divided between five directors in the "Directoire". This construction, based on supposed prudence, mutual respect and respect for Constitution and laws in legislative and executive powers, could not work. There was no conflict regulation between legislative and executive powers. And no politically responsible ministry. The sole safety valve was a coup!

This stabilised Republic with a Constitution survived 4 years, during the "Directoire" (26 October 1795/9 November 1799). A revolt of the poor directed by Gracchus Babeuf ("complot babouviste"), was oppressed brutally. They claimed common happiness as promised them by the Constitution of 1793: not only formal, but also factual equality. The real danger came from royalists, in contact with the future Louis XVIII and Charles X. They could not choose between elections and a coup. Elections in 1796 were not favourable for members of the "Convention". The two-thirds rule meant that only a minority was elected. Each year one-third of representatives had to be elected. The second election was shortly after the "mouvement babouviste", which alarmed landed proprietors. Catholics were angry, as there was no freedom of religion, guaranteed by a law of 1795. They were not allowed to ring church bells! Elections were a disaster for the Thermidorean "eternal" representatives: from 216 members of the "Convention", only 13 were re-elected. This was a real jerk to the right. When Bonaparte was in Italy, he was asked to restore order in Paris again, but he sent Augereau. The next year, there was a Jacobin conspiracy in April 1798. Elections of 1798 resulted in a jerk to the left. Election of 98 newly elected persons was declared invalid: coup of "Floréal an VI" (April 1798). The "Directoire" lost popularity, French armies had defeats abroad and the parliament replaced members of the "Directoire" (except "eternal" Barras) on 18 June 1799: "30 Prairal de l'an VII", Coup of Prairal. Siéyès, hating babouvists and royalists (he voted for regicide), came into the "Directoire". He got a new chance to manipulate. The most logical intellect of France and incarnate spirit of the time saw but one real source of power, the army. Siéyès concocted a plot to bring Bonaparte into power. The sole problem was that he and Bonaparte were too important to take the first step: "Querelle d'étiquette qui faillit mal finir!" This was a nice job for Talleyrand. Under the pretext of an anarchist plot, the "Conseil des Anciens" would move its seat to Saint Cloud, appointing Bonaparte military commander of Paris. Siéyès and Roger-Ducos would retire from the "Directoire" and ask Barras to do the same. With no functioning "Directoire", the two Councils would nominate three Consuls to govern: Bonaparte, Siéyès and Roger-Ducos. The legislative organ would get "support" by sending troops. All went well with this "Coup de 18 Brumaire" (9 November 1799) in Paris, although it nearly failed in Saint Cloud.

## 2.4. From Napoleon Bonaparte to Emperor Napoleon III

From 1789 to 1815, there were three different regimes: limited monarchy (1789/1792), Republic (1792/1799) and Bonapartist regime (1799/1814-1815). From 1814-1815 to 1870, there was a comparable succession: limited monarchy (1814-1815/1848), Republic (1848/1851) and Bonapartist regime (1851/1870). Bonaparte finished the work which was started with the French Revolution, which might be said to have ended provisionally in 1799. Different from the working-method used before of discussing texts in an assembly, now the French Solon, Siéyès, and Bonaparte determined the text of a new Constitution. There were two committees for the sake of appearances. To place this crucial phase in institutional engineering in a long term perspective Duverger (1996) marked the period 1799/1870 as a "waltz of constitutions". In this period there were several regimes with different constitutions. Consulate (4 years), First Empire (less than 15 years), Hundred Days Regime (less than 3 months), Restoration (16 years), July Monarchy (less than 18 years), Second Republic (3 years), and Second Empire (less than 19 years). There were, broadly speaking, three political systems in this period: parliamentary monarchy, republican monarchy of the Bonapartes, and presidential republic. Siéyès, superior engineer of constitutional constructions, wanted to build up the eternal model-constitution for the universe (Bastid, 1970; Bredin, 1988) and democracy under leadership of an autocrat, an authoritarian state supported by the masses (caesarism). Bonaparte rewrote the concepts of Siéyès and so, within 11 days, there was the text of the "Constitution du 22 Frimaire de l'an VIII". Article 95 said that this text would be presented to the French people in a plebiscite. The text ended with the words of Bonaparte: Citizens, the Revolution was determined in principles it developed, the Revolution is finished now. This Constitution was adopted. It had a façade of general suffrage and assemblies (Senate, Tribunate, and Legislative Corps), and a government of three Consuls. No country in the world had general suffrage then. Its effect was marginal due to the Siéyès invention of "listes de confiance", a cascade which dampened democratic influence by making a restricted group elect an electoral college electing an electoral college. He used the formula "authority comes from above, confidence from below". Real power was in the hands of the First Consul. The referendum over a constitutional text was transformed in a plebiscite over a man. The question in the streets of Paris about the contents of the constitution was answered with: Bonaparte. After "18 Brumaire" Bonaparte had the power, but he had to manoeuvre. Bonaparte and Siéyès used terms of Roman law (consules, senatus-consultus, etc.). In 1802, he had himself appointed by plebiscite (3.5 million yes, less than 8,400 no) as Consul-for-life.

After 1802 the "listes de confiance" were replaced by electoral assemblies, which could be easily manipulated. Conscious of the fragility of his power-base, Bonaparte was seeking sources for his legitimacy. He thought to reorganise the mystical marriage between Bourbon dynasty and French nation. The "Sénatus-consulte de l'an XII" (1804) transformed consulate-for-life into hereditary Empire, approved massively by plebiscite. He had himself installed as Emperor Napoleon with all pomp and rituals in a meeting in "Notre Dame". He set his crown on his own head, with the Pope in attendance. The "cérémonie du sacre" was invented by former usurpator Pépin le Bref, to legitimise his theft of the throne. Napoleon so realised a double legitimacy: by plebiscite and by the "sacre". Napoleon I, Emperor of the French Republic, imitating Roman Emperor Augustus, created an imperial court, which also imitated Louis XIV. He formed a new aristocracy, creating new privileges. When Napoleon received some flags, captured by French troops in the war with Spain near Estramadura, he sent these to the Legislative Body as a gesture. Empress Josephine remarked that it was nice that this first gesture of the Emperor was for the Legislative Body, "representing the Nation". Napoleon was upset and placed a famous erratum in the "Moniteur" of 1808. He argued that the Emperor was the sole representative of the Nation. This was Napoleon's theory of the French Empire. He wrote that assemblies during the Revolution appropriated the primacy of the people's representation, so creating all calamities for the French Nation. Napoleon made himself a revolving door between revolutionary legitimacy and monarchist legacy. His most real power-base was his military victories. When these were absent he was lost. After his defeat in 1814 he was forced to abdicate. This brought the First Restoration with a Bourbon King. King Louis XVIII benevolently accepted a new constitution, the "Charte de 1814". After his escape from his place of exile on Elba, Napoleon ruled again for a hundred days.

To profile himself with regard to the Bourbon King, Napoleon threw off his mask of hereditary Emperor, positioning himself as heir of the Revolution (Chevallier, 1967, pp. 119-128). He appealed to national sovereignty and revolutionary legitimacy. Apprehensive for the spirit of Paris, he did not want to make himself dependent on the Jacobin card. He thought that he could better try to join with the spirit of liberalism in society and asked former opponent Benjamin Constant to organise a parliamentary compromise. It was a curious meeting between Napoleon and Constant, who had compared Napoleon earlier with Attila and Ghengis Khan. He described him also as a cowardly deserter, because he had left his troops three times: in Egypt, Spain and Russia. Napoleon said that a minority wanted a Constitution above all, while the majority asked only for Napoleon as saviour of the country against the aristocracy. People were ready for a slaughter of aristocracy. He didn't like to be emperor on this basis and, comparing himself with Alexander the Great (356-323 BC), was outspoken: "I did want the empire of the whole world. So it was necessary to have unlimited power. To govern France, a constitution is better. Now I have one mission left, organising the take-off of France and giving it effective public management." Constant made an "Acte additionnel aux Constitutions de l'Empire". According to Bastid, this was probably the best-written, well-considered French constitution ever. Napoleon was forced to make the same concessions as Louis XVIII, heir of absolutist monarchs, in his "Charte" (1814). Neither republican plebiscitary dictatorship, nor imperial plebiscitary dictatorship or plebiscitary parliamentarism with constitutional monarchy in 1814 gave lasting institutions. Historical circumstances meant that Napoleon's institutional genius could not give public institutions their definitive form. He had considerable influence in the institutional engineering of public authority and public management in France (Chevallier, 1967, p.127). Napoleon was defeated at Waterloo (18 June 1815) where in a sense the French Revolution really came to its end. Napoleon wrote memoirs in St. Helena. On 6 July 1815, Louis XVIII was back in Paris.

The administrative-organisational heritage of Napoleon is impressive (Chevallier, 1967, pp. 129-134)). He left his mark upon numerous dimensions of the organisation of society;

public authority and public management; the juridical institutionalising of civil society and public institutions; military strategy and organisation; financial aspects; the relation between State and Church; universities and nearly all other parts of public management. Napoleon once said that the Revolution had left him with a country in ruins, without any coherent system: "Loose grains of sand. We can't build up the Republic definitively without bringing some masses of granite upon the soil of France." It is obvious now that Napoleon's institutional genius left behind institutions with the lasting characteristics of granite. Centralised public management in monarchical France was built up by successive monarchs, supported by the conception of legists. Against opposition by local potentates, guilds, Church, and aristocracy. This centralisation was encountered in the Ancien Régime by numerous hindrances in French society, stiff with privileges. The French Revolution made tabula rasa of numerous obstacles on the road to modern society, while reinforcing the centralist character of public management. It gave the floor to Napoleon to reconstruct society. The "Constituante" blew up the structures built up during centuries: ecclesiastical dioceses with civil-administrative functions; military structures; feudal powers; and private organisations usurping public authority (jurisdiction etc.).

The institutional set-up of the Ancien Régime was replaced by one uniform organisation with departments, demarcated regions with precise governing-administrative competencies. Departments were divided into districts, cantons and municipalities. Fragmented administrative structures and provinces, soaked in privileges, particularisms and traditional abuses, were abolished. The new regime was characterised by uniformity. Overreacting with regard to hated royal agents, usurping competencies of monarchs, the "Constituante" had constructed a rather confusing decentralisation. Power was entrusted to elected organs and functionaries. Each part became a semi-autonomous, self-governing republic. The 44,000 municipalities considered central executive authorities more as opponent than as co-responsible authorities. Public authorities after the "Constituante" had to restore centralisation. Revolutionaries abolished decentralisation by giving all powers in the hands of one party, the "Parti montagnard". The "Convention" had as objective a uniform republic, where citizens had everywhere the same, uniform laws and regulations, against remnants of the local spirit. After the Thermidorean Reaction, Girondins tried vainly to realise decentralisation, as they had their power-base in the provinces. During the "Directoire", there was in every departmental organ a "commissaire du Directoire", getting its instructions from central authorities. To prevent larger towns and cities from becoming "a state within the state", these were split-up into separate administrative units. Smaller municipalities were combined in cantons. Napoleon's authoritarian approach, fed by dreams about the Roman Empire, realised this institutional engineering. In his first year as Consul, Bonaparte issued his "Constitution du 22 frimaire an VIII". Administrative organisation was ruled in his "Loi du 28 pluviôse an VIII", "Constitution administrative Française", accentuating centralisation. A hierarchy with the prefect taking instructions from central government, as highest authority in his department. He gave instructions to sub-prefects in arrondissements, mayors and adjuncts in municipalities (military command model).

Napoleon did not shrink from any hindrance on his ambitious road. He managed to eliminate a serious stumbling block for the revolutionaries. The "Constituante" could not place religion and Church outside the State with one stroke (Cournot, 1872). As it was not possible for revolutionaries to abolish monarchy right away they had to deal with the other powerful institution, the Catholic Church, as well. They did not want to have a separation of State and Church, on the contrary; they wanted to make the bond between State and Church more intensive and structural: both had become business of the nation and should be governed by principles of liberty, equality and progress. The ministers of this renewed, democratic and Gallican Church had to be committed as propagandists for the new democratic order and State religion. That the Church should be outside the State must be avoided: "The Church is in the State!" Controversies caused passionate debates. The National Assembly had confiscated the possessions of the Church on 2 November 1789. On 19 November 1789, financial needs of the revolutionary regime were covered by the creation of "assignats", giving 5% interest and guaranteed by confiscated possessions of the Church, On 15 January 1790 France was divided into 83 departments. The number of bishoprics was therefore reduced from 135 to 83. A new procedure was instituted for the appointment of bishops and the whole clergy. They would be elected by general suffrage, as was the revolutionary objective with judges also. To make the "institution canonique" a pure French matter, the French archbishop had to invest all French bishops instead of the Pope. Priests were forced to take an oath of loyalty to the civil constitution of the clergy. This and other changes were totally contrary to existing laws of the Catholic Church, on the basis of which the bishop was the sole authority, responsible to God concerning his supervision in his diocese. From now on the bishop, recognising the unity of the Catholic Church, had to inform the Pope that he was appointed. Constituents expected that the Pope would accept this. The Pope, fearing a schism, hesitated. A schism would result in a French Constitutional Church as Church of the political party in power (Chevallier, 1967, pp. 135-152).

In the years of the "Convention" (1792-1795), there was a majority for followers of Voltaire ("Écrasez l'Infâme!") and the "philosophes". The "Constitution civile du clergé", formal instrument to nationalise the clergy, was maintained. Although it proved to be a failure, as the majority of Catholics did not accept it. On 27 June 1793, it was confirmed that the clergy would be paid, like public functionaries, from the public budget. From the provinces, a movement for de-christianisation was organised. The "Commune de Paris" thought it opportune to organise a counter-cult, "Culte de la Raison", combined with anti-religious manifestatos. The Gregorian calendar was replaced by the Republican calendar. Many churches were closed. Robespierre forced the issue, replacing Christianity by a religion with a credo, a cult and a moral, the cult of the "Supreme Being". On 7 May 1794, the "Convention" decreed: "art. I. The French population recognises the existence of the Supreme Being, and the immortality of the soul. Art. II. It recognises that the cult of this Supreme Being is practising the duties of man...Art. IV. Feasts are organised to make men remember divinity and the dignity of men." After Robespierre's execution, it was not possible to integrate the Catholic Church in a Jacobinist State. It was also impossible to eliminate this Church (Chevallier, 1967). A banal, materialist issue brought the separation of State and Church closer. The constitutional clergy, working in accordance with instructions of the revolutionary regime, claimed its salary. The "Convention" issued a new decree on 18 September 1794 declaring that the French Republic didn't pay the salaries of religious cults any more. The proclaimed freedom of religion was not guaranteed in practice. Activists for de-christianisation provoked a counter-movement of Catholics, claiming restoration of their cult. The "Rapport-Boissy d'Anglas" saw religion as product of ignorance. Its mistakes would finally be eliminated when philosophy illuminated humanity. Awaiting this, violent persecution would be a fault, stimulating fanaticism. Liberty of religious cults was the best method, with a guardian state more hostile than neutral. Religion was a private matter. After nationalising the Catholic religion, it was now re-privatised This report was the basis for the "décret du 3 Ventôse an III" (February 1795) adopting the freedom of the Catholic cult.

A more tolerant climate followed. Those who had bought nationalised ecclesiastical possessions became alarmed. Barras, member of the "Directoire", was worried, writing in January 1797: "..they get hungry while eating. We allow them with tolerance and generosity the possession of the Kingdom of Heaven, but it is not enough for them. They want to control the earth also, while they are challenging the temporal government." Elections of April 1797 were a success for opposition groups. Camille Jordan ("Jordan-Carillon") stirred up his election campaign, claiming the right to ring church bells (forbidden as a disturbance of public order). Then came the violent "coup de Fructidor" (4 September 1797), under leadership of members of the "Directoire", which became very hostile with regard to the Catholic Church. French troops in Italy even got the order to take Pope Pius VI, "le citoyen-pape" (84 years old) as a prisoner along the Alps to Valence where he died. It seemed as if the last Pope had died and that the Papacy as principle of the unity of the Catholic Church had been eliminated also. There was a Catholic restoration in that period however. A number of independent intellectuals argued for a Free Church, and others for a Free Church in a Free State. That would mean separation of State and Church. Bonaparte, with more foresight than most, knew that he had to settle the question of the relationship between State and Church. Advisers suggested the proclamation of the secular State. Napoleon thought that in France, drenched by centuries of Catholicism, a long period of secular education was needed first. He wanted to win time for pacification, convinced that otherwise a series of issues would create repeated tensions in French society as the power of the Pope, a foreign power, over French citizens was a very old issue already along with questions about the riches of the Church and its privileges, the uncontrolled return of forbidden religious congregations, the laborious position of the Constitutional Church and claims that confiscated ecclesiastical possessions would be restored. With strategic foresight, he knew as military general that he had to make a deal with the commander-in-chief of the Catholic Church, the Pope (Chevallier, 1967, pp. 143-152).

A "Concordat" was devised, integrating the Catholic Church again into French society, within a more modern institutional framework. His intuition taught him that he could use this source of power with authority over many people for his own purposes by making all priests "State apostles" or "spiritual policemen". Portalis, an outstanding jurist, wrote a report about the Concordat: "Public order doesn't allow that these religious institutions be allowed to take their own course. The system of a reasonable surveillance over cults is possible only on the basis of a legal organisation of the cults. This is part of the higher State police." Negotiations with the Vatican were laborious. With three issues: Catholicism State religion or not; renewal of personnel in the corps of French bishops and: recognition of nationalised ecclesiastical possessions. Bonaparte's representative Bernier came back from Rome, where he accepted the status of State religion for Catholicism. This caused a row in Paris. Talleyrand, former bishop of Autun (sic), said that State religion was against the spirit of the Revolution with its principle of equality for all cults. He had a lucky strike, suggesting Catholicism as religion of the majority. This became religion of the great majority of French citizens in the final text. Renewal of the corps of the bishops was also a tricky problem. Bonaparte wanted a complete renewal, otherwise the schism would persist. Bishops, appointed by the State, would be fired, but how about bishops appointed by the Pope? Never before had the Pope invited his bishops to withdraw in this way. Cardinal Consalvi exclaimed: "A massacre of 100 bishops is not done! The Catholic religion cannot be established in France on the ruins of 100 cadavers murdered with the sword of Peter who had to make them get up again." This operation took five months after signing the Concordat (1802).

Then there was the money-issue, always tricky for human beings. For former ecclesiastical possessions a formula had to be invented which would give new proprietors guarantees, without forcing the Pope to recognise a juridical cession. That was unthinkable for these ecclesiastical possessions during a long period. What could be the compensation? An indemnity for the value of the confiscated possessions, about one million francs, would have given the French national Catholic Church financial autonomy. This was not what

Bonaparte liked. He preferred to give priests salaries, so that he could control them as functionaries. Representatives of the Vatican had concessions, fearing that a new wave of Gallicanism would prevail. As the Concordat said nothing about religious congregations, these could develop again. Later, the absence of such a clause in the Concordat would provoke problems in the Third Republic. With this Concordat, the Pope wanted to put an end to the old Gallicanism. Napoleon wanted to make the French Catholic Church an institution, supporting the stability of the State. The solution was the guarantee that the State would pay the salaries of the priests, as compensation for the factual, not the juridical recognition by the Catholic Church that its possessions were confiscated (article 13 Concordat). The Concordat of 10 September 1801 was adopted with the law of "18 Germinal de l'an X" (8 April 1802). The Concordat was announced simultaneously with the Peace Treaty of Amiens (1802). Chateaubriand came with his "Génie du Christianisme" for a Catholic réveil.

One of the most sensitive areas for the confrontation between the new revolutionary, republican regime and the Catholic Church remained education. In the Ancien Régime, education was practically a monopoly of the Catholic Church, with some exceptions. It was a new idea that education was a matter for the State: "Only since the Revolution, the State, later than the Church, understood that it had a task in educating children so it was possible to develop in them, at an age which is not yet an age of discussion, a solid foundation of crucial ideas which would resist all assaults during the rest of their lives." (Hauriou). Talleyrand, asked by the "Constituante" to make a report, argued for liberty of education. The "Constituante" had the following phrase in the fundamental constitutional guarantees: "There will be created a common public instruction for all citizens, gratis for those parts of education which are indispensable for all." Because of the disruption of the structures of the Catholic Church, the education system was also disrupted. A Report-Condorcet argued for a-political education. After "Thermidor", there was a reorganisation ("loi du 3 brumaire an IV"), 83 "écoles centrales, purement laïques" (pure secular schools) were created for secondary education to replace existing "collèges" with a dominant religious character. Relations were poisoned between adherents of these anti-clerical schools and those of Catholic education. Napoleon's reorganisation adapted secondary education and introduced a militarily, disciplined university system. Primary education did not interest Napoleon; this was entrusted to religious brethren. As an essential part of Napoleon's conception, the law of 1 May 1802, created "lycées", replacing the "écoles centrales". Here the cadres for the Nation had to be formed in a strict discipline. The law of 10 May 1802 ruled that the "Université impériale" was established, on top of the education system, with competencies about the way all institutions of education had to work.

A crucial part of Napoleon's institutional engineering was what he could realise in the sphere of legislation. The Constitution of 1791 proclaimed: "There will be realised a Code of all laws for the whole of the Kingdom." Bonaparte in power was impatient about the hesitant and inactive work of jurists trying to codify existing law. Napoleon, knowing that not only military successes, but also realisation of codification would make his fame, put his energetic authority to the codification process. A committee of experts, excellent professional jurists formed in the Ancien Régime, was created with Bigot de Préameneu, Tronchet and Portalis. Its draft and comments were intensively discussed in 102 sessions of the "Conseil d'État". There was a highly creative process, in which excellent jurists were forced by Napoleon to go to the limits of their expertise and mental capacities. Napoleon with his ready wit, common sense and overactive energy proved to be an institutional genius, going to the heart of the matter within the verbal world of jurists. Napoleon pushed through his conceptions, cleaving difficult problems and dilemmas. The draft was discussed in Senate, Tribunat and Legislative Corps. It was criticised for having too many legal concepts from the Ancien Régime and was qualified as counter-revolutionary. Napoleon withdrew the draft, and decided to purge the legislative organs first: "l'élimination de l'an X" (1802). The "Code civil" was proclaimed in March 1804. This world-famous project of codification was a demonstration of the efficiency and willpower with which he realised his program, against all hindrances and opposition (Chevallier, 1967, pp. 159-163).

This "Code civil' proved that Napoleon was heir to the French Revolution: the national unity of France had to be guaranteed by codifying uniform rules based on crucial principles, but he was heir also to the Ancien Régime with numerous valuable legal constructions. The "Code civil" was a brilliant reconciling synthesis and although fundamentally anti-feminine, it maintained the bond with Roman law. The juridical spirit had won the battle against the philosophical spirit. Abolition of the feudal system and realised nationalisations were confirmed, while the free property right was proclaimed. For the right of succession, the texts were reactionary. This was cancelled by saying: "The new theories are mere maxims of some individuals, the old maxims are the spirit of centuries". Respect for authority was given priority over proclaimed liberties. Paternal power was made the crux of family law, "for the sake of maintaining the customs and public calm". The man was made the master everywhere in society. Women were treated as minors. Natural children were no longer legal heirs. Boys needed the consent of their parents for marriage until 25 years, girls until 21 years. All in all the "Code civil", as the civil constitution of France, can be seen as the codification of the rules for a conservative, bourgeois society. Basic innovations of the revolutionary period were combined with valuable elements of the Ancien Régime. As a genius of strategic management, Napoleon with personal interventions realised a modern institutional universe, with far-reaching consequences for the future. After Napoleon's abrupt abdication, the Senate, recognising Louis XVIII as King and trying to bind him with a constitution, made the "Constitution sénatoriale" (1814), with more or less the same contents as the "Charte" (1814). Coming back from Elba, Napoleon made a new constitutional text in his "Hundred Days Regime": "Acte additionnel aux Constitutions de l'Empire" (1815).

The period from 1815 to 1870 can be seen as a period of restorations. Mostly this term restoration is reserved for the monarchy of Louis XVIII and Charles X ("Le Roi ultra"), restoring the regime of Louis XVI, ending in 1792. The Second Republic and the Second Empire can be qualified as restorations also. These regimes imitated a lot of former regimes. Louis-Napoleon, as Emperor Napoleon III, helped the French, having their phantom-pains, because they missed the authoritarian authority of Napoleon. Napoleon III could remedy these phantom-pains temporarily by imitating the model of Napoleon I, hiding behind the ghost of Napoleon I (Lucas-Dubreton, 1960). Parliamentary characteristics were developing during the Restoration of Louis XVIII and Charles X. Louis-Philippe gave an impulse for parliamentarism (Rosanvallon, 1995). From 1814 to 1848, not limited monarchy, but a semi-parliamentary monarchy resembling the English system. The democratic base was very small. During the Restoration one had to be above 30 years and pay 300 francs direct taxes to be "électeur". To be eligible, one had to be 40 years or more, and pay 1,000 francs or more direct taxes. From 1817 to 1827, the number of persons entitled to vote diminished from 110,000 to 89,000, due to tax reliefs by which government wanted to reduce the electorate. Under the Restoration, some 100,000 persons could vote. Under the July Monarchy, this number was 200,000, while France had 30 million inhabitants. With the "Charte constitutionnelle" (4 June 1814), Louis XVIII (1814-1824) proclaimed himself as King "par la grâce de Dieu". This "Charte" was based on divine law, and did not refer to national sovereignty. Catholicism was made State religion, suffrage was reduced. Charles X (1824-1830) tried to restore the Ancien Régime.

The July revolution (1830) overthrew King Charles X, and brought Louis-Philippe d'Orléans to the throne (Thureau-Dangin, 1884/1892; Vigier, 1962). Orleanist parliamentarism implied that government needed the confidence of King and Parliament. Louis-Philippe had royal blood, and he was the closest legitimate heir after Charles X and his heirs, so he had the advantage of a double legitimacy: King on the basis of the sovereignty of the Nation. He was brought to the throne by a people's revolution, recognised by the "Chambre des députés", but this double legitimacy had its problems. For monarchists he was a false king, and for republicans he was a false incarnation of the national sovereignty. During the Restoration, monarchists had two wings: "ultras" and moderates, both recognising the King. Since 1830, supporters of Charles X, the former "ultras", did call themselves "légitimistes". They wanted the legitimate King to be recognised within the framework of traditional monarchist principles. Moderate monarchists accepted the new regime; they were called "orléanistes". The "Charte de 1830" was adopted by the "Chambre des députés" and accepted by the King as "Roi des Français". By his oath "citizen-king", Louis-Philippe concluded a pact with representatives of the French nation, so both King and Nation were incarnations of national sovereignty: the relation with divine law was cut through. During the July Monarchy of Louis-Philippe (1830-1848) the number of persons entitled to vote was enlarged, in 1846 their number was 240,983. Recruiting of deputies for Parliament was corrupted by a system of "députés-fonctionnaires" (Julien-Lafferrière, 1970). Government could put pressure on them because otherwise government would fire them as functionaries (like the "Walpole-system" in Great Britain).

The revolution of 1848 brought the Second Republic (1848-1851), using ideas from the system in the United States of America, making it different from the First Republic. The revolutionaries wanted to create a kind of limited monarchy. The American model not only inspired the Second Republic (Curtis, 1918), but also the Fifth Republic since 1958. Especially in 1962, when the system of presidential elections was changed (Brown, 1994; Gilson, 1968; Toinet, 1990). Tocqueville (1978) participated in the work on the Constitution of 1848. In fact, the revolution of 1848 consisted of two revolutions: the Republican revolution of February 1848 (which succeeded), and the Social revolution of June 1848 (which was crushed). The revolution of 24 February 1848 overthrew the July Monarchy by creating a Republic which had a broad adherence (Agulhon, 1973; Vigier, 1967). Universal direct suffrage was adopted with a rather modern electoral system (secrecy of voting, etc.). As leftist groups feared, the new universal direct suffrage was good for the more conservative, moderate movements. The first elections on 23 April 1848 brought a majority for moderates. Out of 900 deputies, 450 were moderate republicans, 200 "Orléanistes", 50 "Légitimistes" and 200 "Républicains avancés" or "Démocrates Socialistes". Legislative power was entrusted to the "Assemblée Nationale" (one house only) and executive power was in the hands of the President of the Republic, directly elected by the electorate for 4 years, (re-eligible after a break). Frustrated by the results of the elections, workers and adherents rose up in June 1848. Bourgeois republicans, fearing that the proletariat ("the reds") would provoke a situation like the Terror of Robespierre, reacted with a terrible repression by general Cavaignac. The regime at once became dictatorial and the liberty of press and liberty to form associations and organise meetings were abolished. This repression was one of the reasons that French Socialism was more violent than elsewhere in the 19th century ("Blanquisme") as well as in the 20th century, with French variations of Communism. Extreme leftists took over the estafette after the Jacobins. For moderate French, legitimacy since "48" was based upon universal suffrage (Duveau, 1965).

There was a strong movement to restore the monarchist principle, that throne and altar would be the base as under the Restoration. The "Loi Falloux" (1850) brought free education, meaning Catholic education. Since the second half of the 19th century the Catholic clergy in majority argued against the republican idea. This provoked an anticlerical reaction, virulent long into the 20th century. The Constitution of 4 November 1848 confirmed the Declaration of Human Rights, proclaiming national sovereignty, liberty and equality as in 1789 (Cohen, 1935) but there were supplements as "fraternité" (brotherhood), and God were invoked while social rights were added: the rights of work, social assistance, and education. The Second Republic was a Republic without republicans when on 10/11 December 1848 Louis-Napoléon Bonaparte was elected President (Tudesq, 1965). Legislative elections on 13/14 May 1849 brought a victory for the right with more than 53% of the votes. Due to the electoral system, the right got 3/4 of the seats (Genique, 1921). Moderate republicans got 12%, while the left had nearly 35% of the vote. French society in the years 1814-1870 changed considerably, inter alia by the Industrial Revolution and the emergence of Socialism (Duverger, 1996). The Industrial Revolution brought the masses a lot of social miseries. Their sole method of survival seemed to be to become a hard-worker for a very low salary, on the brink of starvation, with the daily risk of dismissal (Villermé, 1840). It was the Malthusian perspective for many. The concept of Marx with exploitation of the proletariat was actual. Already during the "Directoire" (1795-1799) Babeuf developed socialist ideas. His attempt to take power, to improve conditions for workers, failed. The February Revolution (1848), a revolution of workers, was a conflict between socialists and capitalists, not a conflict between aristocracy and bourgeoisie.

Louis-Napoléon used the paths of the Second Republic to have himself elected President and then made a coup on 2 December 1851. The mandate of Louis-Napoléon would end in March 1852. The National Assembly refused to change the clause which prevented direct re-election of the President. A monarchist majority wanted the opportunity to get rid of the President and restore the monarchy, so, three months before this date on 2 December 1851, Louis-Napoléon preferred the certain to the uncertain by organising his coup. After this coup a decree asked the electorate to authorise Louis-Napoléon to make a constitution on the basis of five elements as proclaimed on 2 December 1851: election of the president for ten years; government chosen by the president; a "Conseil d'État" to prepare laws; a legislative corps elected by universal suffrage; and a Senate. The plebiscite accepted this with 7.5 million voting yes. The Constitution of 14 January 1852 was proclaimed. Institutions of the First Empire were copied as much as possible. With a "sénatus-consulte" of 7 December 1852 a hereditary Empire was proclaimed. Emperor Napoleon III had all powers, executive power and legislative power. Formally there were organs with legislative competencies, but Napoleon III alone had the initiative of legislation and could refuse to make laws operative even when voted. A difference to the First Empire was that after 1852 there was universal direct suffrage of deputies for the legislative organ. The First Empire became ever more autocratic, but Napoleon III made the regime less autocratic after 1860. The regime of the Second Empire was like a dictatorship; universal direct suffrage was marginalised by "candidature officielle", prefects selected "good" candidates, elected after support with facilities of propaganda etc. It was made impossible for "bad" candidates to campaign. From 1860 on the Second Empire developed in the direction of a parliamentary system. In the years 1860-1861, competencies of the legislative organ were extended and in the years 1867-1869 it got the right of interpellation and the rights of initiating and amendment of legislation. The Senate was a second legislative house.

## 2.5. From Third Republic to Second World War

The Second Empire collapsed because on 4 September 1870 Napoleon III was defeated by Prussians at Sedan in the Franco-Prussian War. The Republic was proclaimed again and, apart from the Vichy-regime (1940-1944), France has had a Republic since then (Mayeur, 1973). Before 1875 the parliamentary system functioned within a monarchist framework. Between 1789 and 1875 no regime endured longer than 19 years, but the Third Republic (1875-1940) lasted 65 years, while the Fourth Republic (1945-1958), after the Vichy-regime, in fact continued the regime of the Third Republic. This remarkable continuity of regime was allied to the proverbial instability of French governments, due to "parlementarisme à la française" (Soulier, 1938). This instability of French governments is often explained as an effect of the institutions, but the real cause was, above all, the system of political parties in relation to the electoral system (Duverger, 1996). It is amazing that the Third Republic was established by a majority in the Assembly of one vote only, with the "amendement Wallon" (30 January 1875), and that, while properly speaking the Assembly, with about 400 monarchists out of 600 deputies, wanted a different regime, a monarch, but the monarchists wasted this unique opportunity by dissension. When "Légitimistes" (adherents of descendants of Charles X) and "Orléanistes" (adherents of descendants of Louis-Philippe) had a deal, the claimant to the throne failed this by intransigence about a detail (Mayeur, 1984). Most monarchists in Parliament were "Orléanistes". They wanted a parliamentary monarchy. When they could not realise this, they preferred a parliamentary republic. For the time being, they thought, because it would be easy to transform their president into a hereditary monarch (Halévy, 1930; 1937; Hanotaux, 1925). The Third Republic had no authentic Constitution, only three constitutional laws. Laws about Senate (24 February 1875), organisation of public authorities (25 February 1875), and relations between public authorities (16 July 1875). As the monarchist majority wanted to have their hands free for a monarchist coup, proclaiming a Constitution was not opportune. To make "Orléanistes" accept a republican regime, they acheived a conservative Senate with 75 senators (40 years old or more), indirectly elected for 9 years, and who were unremovable (abolished in 1884). Recruiting senators with an electoral college guaranteed a conservative Senate. The "Chambre des députés" was elected for four years with direct universal suffrage. Election was a "scrutin majoritaire à deux tours, uninominal".

The two houses of parliament had more or less the same powers (voting laws and budget), and could overthrow government. Executive power was divided between President of the Republic (elected by the two houses in one meeting, "Congrès") and the government. Ministers had to be appointed by the President, but they needed support of the parliamentary majority. Government, having no confidence in parliament, could dissolve the house of deputies. When this produced a majority against a government, the government had to resign. This fell into disuse after 1877, as the Senate had to produce a conform advice. An odd arrangement, because such an indirectly chosen college could veto the decisions of directly elected representatives (Barthélemy, 1938; Duguit, 1921/1925). The constitutional laws of 1875 were adopted by a coalition of moderate monarchists, who wanted a strong and powerful President, and moderate republicans, who wanted a parliamentary system in which parliament had the power and the president was as ceremonial as possible (Rudelle, 1982). This controversy became acute in the crisis of 16 May 1877. President Mac-Mahon (monarchist) dismissed a government, which had the confidence of the "Chambre des députés", and appointed a minority government. When elections produced the same majority as before, Mac-Mahon gave way and appointed a government which had the confidence of the majority. In 1879, Mac-Mahon resigned. From 1877 on, institutional practice was that the majority in the "Chambre des députés" had all powers: "parlementarisme à la française" (Goualt, 1954). It made French governmental instability proverbial. In the Third Republic, governments could not survive, on average, for longer than eight months. Surprisingly, because of a more than average stability of the same politicians in succeeding governments, there was a stability in ministers (Ollé-Laprune, 1962). The right to dissolve the "Chambre des députés" fell into desuetude. Deputies could overthrow government without the risk of new elections. Combined with many weakly organised political parties without discipline in their voting behaviour, this produced structural governmental instability.

The existing French system of Public Management of Society is unfathomable without some insight into the historical developments which influenced the institutional, political and administrative organisation deeply. Roman law and the administrative model which Romans used before and after the beginning of our era, have had a lasting impact on European and French administrative concepts (Lintott, 1993). Centuries of Gallo-Roman experiences with public management had significant influence on French public management (Ellul, 1994; Gladden, 1972). The French model of public management has through the centuries been very centralist. Political and administrative centralisation was the work of French Kings and their assistants, using the Roman law model as a framework. They used the concept of divine law as basis for the absolute monarchy of Kings. French Kings fought systematically against all local feudal powers, aristocracy and the powerful Church. They expanded their territory by all means (war, marriage, purchase, tricks). The unity of France (territory, military organisation, culture, language, jurisdiction, legislation, money system) was forced around the King as absolute monarch. With a policy of cultural centralisation, people had to accept the language of the French King as sole language, and Paris as centre of French culture ("parisinianisme"). "Intendants du roi", predecessors of prefects in Empire and Republic, in the Ancien Régime until 1789 saw to it that the will of the French King was law in all parts of the kingdom. Local authorities, "notables", could maintain a certain local autonomy and policy leeway. In former periods the time-consuming communications over long distances with Paris left ample room for autonomy. The French Revolution was a tremendous institutional earthquake, which upset societal order in all its parts. Privileges were abolished on 4 August 1789. Human rights were proclaimed in the "Déclaration des Droits de l'Homme et du Citoyen" of 27 August 1789. The people got representation and a constitution as the basis of the constitutional state. The conquest of the hated state prison "La Bastille" on the 14th of July 1789 was the catalyst for many violent actions. An uprising caused by long pent-up rage, over the many necessary societal changes which had not come about. The commemoration of the first anniversary on 14 July 1790 seemed a festival of a federal state, when provinces presented themselves as autonomous authorities. Parisian revolutionaries saw this as a contra-revolution. "Jacobins" with all violence forced centralisation from Paris to "rescue the Revolution". Then started the cruel "Terror" of Robespierre. Jacobins did not hesitate to break resistance against centralisation coming from former friends ("Girondins") with mass murder and brutal violence.

Since then, Jacobin centralisation attracted many in France. In spite of strong Jacobin centralism, revolutionaries also laid the foundations for local public authorities. "Communes" replaced the existing variety of local communities with the same administrative statute. To break the power constructions and institutions of the Ancien Régime (diseased by aristocratic privileges), the country was administratively reorganised on the basis of "départements". Napoleon consolidated central authority over local authorities. In 1800, he created the function of "préfets", functionaries after the example of the former "intendants du roi", who got their instructions directly from the head of state. With the military model in mind, Napoleon laid lasting foundations for the build-up of French administration and stimulated establishment of the "grandes écoles" for professional training of military and civilian functionaries. Napoleon made his fame with his program of codification, the standard worldwide since then. After the constitutional monarchy (1815-1830) on the basis of the "Charte constitutionnelle" of Louis XVIII, and the July-revolution as reaction against anti-democratic ordinances of King Charles X, citizen-king Louis-Philippe d'Orléans was exponent of the July-Monarchy (1830-1848). The "Charte de 1830" replaced "souveraineté de droit divin" by sovereignty of the Nation. Louis-Philippe was King of the French who ruled by the will of the people. This July-Monarchy was overthrown by the February-Revolution of 24 February 1848. Closing of the "ateliers nationaux" (provision of work for unemployed) was taken as a motive by the left ("babouvistes, blanquistes, réformateurs, démocrates-sociaux") to realise a democratic system. After this coup, general direct elections were organised to elect an "Assemblée nationale constituante" to establish a new constitution. Elections of 23 April 1848 brought a conservative majority; out of 900 representatives 450 were moderate republicans (many royalists), 200 Orléanists, 50 "Légitimists" (wanting the Bourbon monarchy restored) and 200 "républicains avancés" and "démocrates socialistes". The "Constitution du 4 novembre 1848" was the base for the Second Republic (1848-1851).

Strong individualised executive power was given to the president of the Republic. On 10 December 1848, Louis-Napoléon Bonaparte was chosen as president. On 13 May 1849, a monarchist majority chose the Assembly. As this Assembly was not co-operative in changing the constitution, Louis-Napoléon came with his coup of 2 December 1851, giving him all powers. The Second Republic changed into an autocratic regime, as the First Republic before had been followed by an autocratic regime. Louis-Napoléon needed six weeks for the presentation of a new constitution. He had an innovation: the people would previously decide parts of the new constitution. Louis-Napoléon wanted to get approbation by the people for his coup. The plebiscite gave massive support: 92% voted pro, 8% contra (only 17.2% abstentions). The Constitution of 14 January 1852 gave him power for ten years; he was responsible only to the people. The "senatus-consulte" of 7 November 1852 transmuted this to hereditary emperorship. This Second Empire (1852-1870) with its democratic caesarism came to an end in the Franco-Prussian war (1870/1871), started by Napoleon III with an arrogant declaration of war. In the chaos after the humiliating debacle of Napoleon III, the "Commune de Paris" activated political agitation for a free federation of free municipalities. This caused a next phase in centralisation. The Third Republic (1870-1940) was a new experience. The 1871 law for departments and the 1884 law for municipalities brought some local democracy, but the French State got strong powers over these administrative units. Prefects used their powers for all parts of local administration. After 1875 it was necessary to organise voters and political parties were established mostly grouped around a famous personality or a journal. In the last part of the 19th century, Socialists had a well organised mass party. Political parties had a far reaching influence in parliament. Mostly, there were only minorities and coalition building was necessary. When a coalition-partner did not agree with some part of government policy, it withdrew its ministers and a new government had to be formed. Instability of governments (combined with stability of the same politicians as ministers) was a typical feature of the Third and Fourth Republic. "Parlementarisme à la française" had some elements: an anarchist system of many parties; absolute adherence to sovereignty of parliament; degradation of the function of the head of state to a honorary post; dropping of the president's power to dissolve the Assembly. It caused instability (101 governments from 1875 to 1940) and governmental immobilism. Governments were entirely dependent on (fractions of) the majority.

During the First World War, a law giving government full powers was invented as a precedent. Criticised for structural governmental weakness, the houses of parliament from

1926 onwards authorised government to rule with "décrets-lois", governmental decrees with force of laws. Formally, these decrees would have been ratified afterwards, but parliamentarians did not like to make themselves responsible for unpopular measures. These institutional practices were in defiance of constitutional laws: parliament was not allowed to delegate its legislative powers (Barthélemy, 1938). A law of 8 December 1939 made ruling with these "décrets-lois" a normal procedure for government in time of war. Before 1914, political practices were characterised by weakly organised political movements, with some exceptions. There was in practice a big gap between electoral alliances and their parliamentary counterparts. From 1877 to 1914, electoral alliances were organised around the axis right against left, order against change, conservatives against republicans, or "cléricaux" against "républicains". Republicans by preference referred to the French Revolution of 1789, while the right was opposed to all revolutionary ideas. In 1879, leftist republicans, winning elections with their catchword "défense de la République", came into government, with conservatives and "cléricaux" in the opposition. From 1881 on, "Radicaux" were discontented with colonial policies of government. As Socialism had been handicapped since the repression of the 1870 "Commune", Socialism got more adherence only after the nineties in the 19th century (Ligou, 1962). Jean Jaurès was leader of reformist Socialism. When Pope Leo XIII in an encyclical letter of 1892 asked French Catholics to accept the Republic, a small number of them did so ("ralliement"). The Dreyfus Affair (1898-1899) showed that the right and Catholics in majority were against the Republic (Reberioux, 1975). Socialists had the tactics of support without participation in government. So, from 1899 to 1909, a leftist coalition could govern. In the years 1910-1914, moderate republicans formed alliances with centre-right. After the First World War, the situation changed, due to the Russian Revolution (1917) and the upsurge of Communism (Courtois/Lazar, 1995; Robrieux, 1980). There was a crisis of the regime (Bernard, 1975), with arguments for reforming institutions (Chardon, 1921; Leroy, 1918).

The First World War (1914-1918) was concluded with the Treaty of Versailles (1919). This brought retrocession of Alsace-Lorraine and reparations from the Germans for the damages. After the centre-right "Bloc National" (1919-1924), the "Cartel des gauches" (1924-1926) formed a government. A coalition of right and radicals governed in a "Union nationale" (1926-1929). In 1930, the economic world crisis caused a lot of problems. France had the Popular Front (1936-1938), with Socialists and Communists in government. Internationally, relations became strained, especially by the brutal agitation of Adolph Hitler, with his violent Nazi-movement coming to power in Germany. Shortly after the First World War, Alexandre Millerand tried in vain to introduce a Presidential Orleanism. The Leftist Cartel (1924-1932) could govern (Siegfried, 1930). After electoral victories, Radicals formed a government several times, and later changed the composition of the coalition by replacing Socialists with Ministers of the centre-right (Dubief, 1976). In 1926, Radicals left the government to form a new one with Poincaré ("Union nationale"). In 1934, they did the same, while Radicals left the "Front populaire" in 1938 (Berstein, 1980/1982; Nicolet, -1994; Nordmann, 1974). This undermined the confidence of the people in the parliamentary system. Authors presented ideas about reforming institutions (Bardoux, 1936; Barthélemy, 1934; Capitant, 1934). Tardieu (1934; 1936) proposed institutional arrangements from the US as a solution. Since 1922 (Italy) and 1933 (Germany), Fascism was on the rise. France came into the grip of Fascist ideas (Plumyène/Lasierra, 1963). The extra-parliamentary violence of "Ligues" caused the Fascist uprising of 6 February 1934, which tried to create an authoritarian dictatorship (Gicquel/Sfez, 1965). This met a strong reaction from the "Front populaire" (1936-1938) of Radicals, Socialists and Communists. This Popular Front had a short life, as did nearly all governments in the Third Republic. Especially since Munich (1938), the possibility of war had been the central issue (Azéma, 1979).

As were the First Empire and Second Empire, the Third Republic was overthrown by a military defeat. France and Great Britain declared war on Germany on 3 September 1939, as a reaction to the German invasion of Poland on 1 September 1939 (Azéma, 1979). German troops invaded France in May 1940, French troops were outclassed. On 16 June 1940 the Reynaud Government made it known in Bordeaux that it resigned, as it refused to accept an armistice with the invading Nazis. The President of the Republic appointed Pétain as premier. On 17 June 1940 Premier Pétain said on radio: "Fighting has to be stopped" De Gaulle left for London, from where he appealed to the French on 18 June 1940 to continue fighting. Because Pétain thought that Great Britain would soon have to capitulate too, he had chosen for rapid capitulation. He signed an armistice on 22 June 1940 (Durand, 1972). After the armistice, the Parliament went to Bordeaux and then to Vichy. France was split up into an occupied zone and an unoccupied zone from 2 July 1940, with Vichy as the centre of government (Aron, 1973; Paxton, 1973). Pétain had not asked parliament to agree to an armistice. The Assembly accepted this afterwards. On 10 July 1940, a constitutional law was adopted with 569 to 80 votes. It gave government authority to proclaim a new constitution in the form of constitutional acts, when adopted by Pétain and ratified by the nation. The next day "actes constitutionnels" formed an authoritarian regime with Petain as autocrat. There was no ratification by the nation. This Vichy-regime was an anti-constitutional coup (Duverger, 1996). De Gaulle, subsecretary of state in the Reynaud government, refused to recognise the Pétain government, armistice and Vichy-regime. As "man of 18 June 1940" he appealed in a broadcast from London to his compatriots to persevere as "France libre" in the fight against the Nazis (Amouroux, 1976/1993). In August 1940, French Equatorial Africa and Cameroon came under authority of De Gaulle. In 1941 he established the "Comité national français", and in France several resistance movements were unified in the "Conseil national de la Résistance". From June 1940 until the Liberation (August 1944), there were two public authorities: Vichy-government and "France libre" of De Gaulle. The collaborationist Vichy-regime will remain one of the most shameful memories for the French, not least because French authorities and functionaries systematically collaborated with Nazi Jew baiting. De Gaulle organised the armed "Free French", who continued to fight the Nazis, together with the Allies. Germans occupied the unoccupied zone from 11 November 1942 on. After the disembarkation of November 1942 at Algiers, Darlan and Giraud (adherents of Pétain) had public authority in Algiers. In 1943, it was united with the "Comité national français", creating the "Comité français de la Libération nationale" with De Gaulle and Giraud as co-presidents. De Gaulle could kick Giraud out of this position. On 3 June 1944, this "Comité" was the provisional government: "Gouvernement provisoire de la République française" (GPRF).

## 2.6. From Liberation to the start of the 21st century

This GPRF, with the dominant leadership of De Gaulle as Head of State and Prime Minister, had all powers and made ordinances and decrees. On 14 June 1944 De Gaulle was in Normandy. The Anglo-American Allies had recognised him only since 11 July 1944 as the French head of state. De Gaulle refused the Allied proposal to administer France provisionally by the "Allied Military Government Occupied Territories". After 1943, there was an "Assemblée consultative" in Algiers. The ordinance of 21 April 1944, proclaimed in Algiers, functioned as a provisional "Charte" from Liberation (August 1944) to the referendum of 21 October 1945. This ordinance concluded that legally the Republic had never ceased to exist, denying the collaborationist Vichy-regime any legitimacy. The "Assemblée consultative" was reorganised in October 1944. It included former parliamentarians of the Third Republic and members of resistance movements. In the GPRF, opinions differed about the way forward institutionally (back to the Constitution of 1875 or a new Constitution?). De Gaulle cut the knot, proposing a referendum which would adopt a sort of pre-constitution. After his glorious entry in Paris with "Libération", De Gaulle became head of the provisional government. Organisation of a combination of referendum and legislative elections encompassed a number of institutional innovations. Women, for the first time got the right to vote, as was decided with the ordinance of 21 April 1944 in Algiers. The electorate was also enlarged with the inhabitants of French overseas territories, and with the military. The electoral system would be based on proportional representation with separate electoral lists, and distribution of remaining votes according to the best average per department. On 21 October 1945, French citizens could elect their representatives and determine their powers in a referendum about two questions: Do you want the newly elected assembly to prepare a new constitution? And, if the electorate in majority has said yes to the first question: Do you agree with the powers for public authorities as circumscribed, until the new constitution is proclaimed? With a negative answer to the first question, the assembly had to organise itself as a "Chambre des députés" (Constitution of 1875). A negative answer to the second question would give the assembly unlimited powers for an unlimited period. A positive answer would limit the powers of this assembly, giving it 7 months to prepare a new constitution. In France itself, nearly 18 million voters said yes to the first question, and a mere 670,672 said no. The second answer was positive, more than 12.3 million said yes although more than 6.2 million said no. The text accepted by the referendum became the "loi supra-constitutionnelle" of 2 November 1945. This gave a special parliamentary regime with a strong president, appointed by the "Assemblée constituante" and also premier. Differing from other constituent assemblies in French history so far, this Constituent Assembly did not incarnate national sovereignty, as it was limited in powers by the referendum (Duverger, 1996). The "Assemblée constituante" of 1945 was the most leftist assembly ever. Socialists and Communists had together more than 51% of votes.

On 21 November 1945, elections were held, the "Constitution of 1875" was rejected by a referendum and the Assembly was invited to make a new constitution. The second provisional government. De Gaulle got the unanimous support of all 555 deputies of the Assembly, but this government had a short life. In the beginning of January 1946 Socialists forced a reduction of the military budget by 20%. De Gaulle resigned on 19 January 1946. On 29 September 1946 the three large political parties adopted a concept-constitution, criticised by De Gaulle. "Tripartisme" started with three dominant political parties in government: Communists, Socialists and Christian-Democrats (MRP). The first draft for a new constitution on which the left had put its mark resembled the traditional system of the Third Republic, with a dominant parliament and a rather powerless president. It was rejected by the referendum of 5 May 1946 with about 10.2 million against about 9.1 million votes. As ordained by the supra-constitutional law of 2 November 1945, a provisional assembly came into force on 2 June 1946 for a maximum of 7 months, the second "Assemblée constituante". This assembly adapted the first draft, giving the president more powers and creating a second house in parliament. This second draft was adopted by the referendum of 13 October 1946. A marginal electorate supported it (7.8 million abstentions, some 9 million voting yes, about 7.8 million voting no). This Constitution had the support of only 35% of the vote. With this Constitution of 27 October 1946, modified on 7 December 1954, the basis was laid for the institutions of the Fourth Republic (1946-1958). De Gaulle gave his ideas about the Constitution in his famous speech of Bayeux (16 June 1946). The concept-constitution was supported by half of 36% of the electorate (massive abstention). On 27 October 1946, the Constitution of the Fourth Republic (1947-1958) was proclaimed. The Fourth Republic had similar features to the Third Republic including governmental instability.

The Constitution of 1946 had a preamble, confirming the Declaration of Human Rights (1789) and fundamental principles as recognised by laws of the Republic. It proclaimed new principles, especially those with regard to economic and social rights. The 1946 Constitution changed "Chambre des députés" to "Assemblée nationale", and "Sénat" to "Conseil de la République" (since 1948 again "Sénat"). Following a law of 9 May 1951 proportional representation was adapted with a majoritarian correction. When electoral lists were combined at least 8 days before elections, a combined list getting the majority of votes would win all seats (proportionally distributed over the lists). Otherwise, seats would be distributed proportionally over all lists. This electoral manoeuvring was intended to further the Socialists, MRP and Moderate parties, while blocking Communists and Gaullists. Both houses of parliament elected the President of the Republic for 7 years. Government was responsible for the Assembly. The constitutional reform of 7 December 1954 was not substantial (it was called "la réformette"). It concerned the way the government was installed and the powers of the Senate. By this modification the Premier could choose ministers before the "vote d'investiture". The condition that government needed the support of the absolute majority in the Assembly was abolished. During the Third Republic concept-texts for laws travelled to and fro between the two houses of parliament like a shuttle and senators could paralyse law making indefinitely. In 1954, the Assembly restored this so-called "navette" between the two houses of parliament in second reading, but only for a period of a hundred days after the adoption of a text. These minor adaptations were part of a movement to restore gradually the situation as in the Third Republic and so the Fourth Republic ever more resembled the Third Republic with its governmental instability and immobilism, but there were differences; "Suffrage majoritaire à deux tours" was replaced by proportional representation, preventing electoral alliances, though these reappeared later. The relevant change in political power relations was the dominant position of the Communists.

In the years 1945-1947 the Communists were good administrators. Their participation in government brought social stability (less strikes). After 4 May 1947 Communist Ministers were forced to retire; the "Cold War" between Western Allies and Soviet-Union began and the Communist coup in Prague (1948) and other practices of hard Stalinist Communism lost French Communists a lot of their goodwill as built up in the Resistance. Communist votes in the Assembly were not needed to form a government, but were important to overthrow government. Opposition of Communists and Gaullists (an amazing negative coalition) furthered an atmosphere of governmental instability. France had difficult problems with the process of decolonisation, especially with regard to Algeria. From 1947 to 1958 the average lifetime of governments was only 6 months A number of French colonels destroyed the Fourth Republic by their coup of 13 May 1958 in Algiers (Lentin, 1958). The Algerian war tore French society to pieces. The fight between adherents of "L'Algérie française" and others caused civil war, with a prominent role for the military. With his penetrating criticisms, De Gaulle continued to urge the need for a fundamental reorganisation of public institutions, but governments had other problems: the war in Indochina since October 1950 (on 7 May 1954 the fall of Dien Bien Phu). And since 1 November 1954, the Algerian war, causing permanent drama and violence, even in France. Civil war could break out at any time in France. It was a confrontation between adherents of "Algérie française" and adherents of an independent Algeria. It was evident that government could not handle the Algerian problem; government had no authority. In addition to the three big parties (Communists, Socialists, MRP) there were ten small parties, forming and breaking coalitions. Since 1947 Communists and Gaullists opposed government. In the twelve years of the Fourth Republic (1946-1958), there were 28 governments often falling apart over internal conflicts. A leading group of the military, behaving as politicians, opposed with all means the development of an independent Algeria.

On 13 May 1958 the military putsch at Algiers put the spark to the tinder. Because of real risks of civil war De Gaulle was asked to take up leadership. He had some conditions, which were accepted. in In June 1958 parliament adopted the law giving him full powers for six months. De Gaulle suppressed the mutiny vigorously and restored order. He stimulated the making of a draft for a new constitution. After 12 years in the "desert" De Gaulle was asked to solve the fundamental crises of the Fourth Republic. On 3 June 1958 parliament adopted a constitutional law with 350 votes to 160, and 70 abstentions. The procedure for a revision of the 1946 Constitution (article 90) was adapted. Constituent power was given to government on 1 June 1958. The new Constitution had to fulfil at least five principles. Universal suffrage had to be the sole source of power; legislative and executive powers had to be derived from it. Legislative and executive powers had to be separate institutions. Government was politically responsible to the Assembly. Judiciary power had to be independent. The Constitution had to organise relations of the French Republic and associated peoples. When De Gaulle was invested with the necessary powers and competencies, he left for Algiers to restore law and order. Promptly after his return to Paris, he asked Minister of Justice Debré to work out a draft for the new constitution. De Gaulle had given his ideas about the required institutions for the new regime long before (his speech at Bayeux, 1946). So it was possible to work fast. The "Comité consultatif constitutionnel" between 29 July and 14 August 1958 produced an elaborated text. Michel Debré was president of the commission for a new constitution with De Gaulle actively participating in its work. De Gaulle wanted the new constitution to be ready by 4 September 1958, anniversary of the proclamation of the Republic in 1870. On 4 September 1958, De Gaulle proclaimed the new constitution. Apart from the Communists, all parties declared their support for the new constitution. When the concept on 28 September 1958 was put to test in a referendum, nearly 80% of the vote supported the constitution. On 1 October 1958 a new Gaullist party was formed to challenge the old political parties, the "Union pour la Nouvelle République" (UNR). On 21 December 1958, an electoral college chose De Gaulle, according to the procedure of the new Constitution of 1958, as the first President of the Fifth Republic. France had this archaic system of an electoral college until 1962, archaic because the President is not elected by the people. De Gaulle could push towards a more modern system in France.

Under the supervision of De Gaulle and his right-hand Debré, the draft for a constitution was finished. This draft was adopted by referendum with an overwhelming majority on 28 September 1958. De Gaulle got massive support for his constitution. In France itself 17,668,790 voted yes, and 4,624,511 voted no, while there were 4,016,614 abstentions. In French overseas territories, the positive majority was more imposing yet (except in Guinée). The Constitution of 1958 reinforced the powers of the executive, while powers of the legislative body were restrained by the framework of the "parlementarisme rationalisé". The domain of the law was reduced. The position of the President of the Republic was substantially reinforced. The constitutional reform of 6 November 1962 made it possible for the President of the Republic to be elected directly by universal suffrage. In the presidential elections, elements from American and English systems were incorporated. De Gaulle based this constitutional reform of 1962 on article 11 of the Constitution. This was disputed, as this article was not meant for constitutional reforms: it was unconstitutional. This was overruled by referendum of 28 October 1962, adopting the reform with 12,809,363 votes against 7,942,695 votes; 6,280,297 abstentions. By now, direct election of the President of the Republic was widely accepted. When President De Gaulle retired after the negative referendum of 1969, the crucial institutional issue was whether the Fifth Republic would outlive its creator. Elections made former Premier Pompidou the first President (1969-1974) after De Gaulle himself. De Gaulle's legacy seemed safe in the hands of this loyal right-hand of De Gaulle. Pompidou transformed Gaullism pragmatically ("pompidolisme"). He abolished De Gaulle's veto of Great Britain's entry in the European Community. It was a real drawback when Pompidou died in officio in 1974. Now again the burning question was, who as president could ensure the Fifth Republic's continuity. Presidential elections made a non-Gaullist President of the Fifth Republic, liberal Independent Republican Giscard d'Estaing (1974-1981). This was a new experience; he gave the regime some liberal accents.

As economic conditions deteriorated Socialists exploited widespread dissatisfaction and Mitterrand became the first Socialist President of the Fifth Republic (1981-1995). A curious experience ("mitterrandisme"), because Mitterrand more than anybody else was an opponent of De Gaulle and his institutional arrangements, especially the Constitution of 1958. Mitterrand proved to be loyal to the Constitution of 1958 taking it very seriously indeed. The contribution of Mitterrand was essential in making the political left accept the institutional arrangements of the Fifth Republic. In 1986-1988, 1993-1995, and 1997-2002, periods of "cohabitation" (a President of the Republic of one political party and government of an opposing political party or coalition), institutions of the Fifth Republic proved fireproof. In 1995 President Chirac could succeed Mitterrand. Since 1995, with the political power-positions (Presidency of the Republic, Government and majority in the National Assembly), in the hands of Gaullists, the Fifth Republic seemed to be safe. The Fifth Republic with the "septennat-Chirac" (1995-2002) survived into the 21st century. Because of serious economic problems (unemployment) and political problems (dissension on the political right), President Chirac decided in 1997 to advance legislative elections, formally to be held in 1998. The electorate did not repay this manoeuvre. The Gaullist majority in the Assembly was crushed and after the electoral victory of Socialists, Jospin became Premier. Again France had its "cohabitation". The last twenty years of two thousand years of institutional engineering in France, with the "Double-Septennat-Mitterrand" (1981-1995) and "Septennat-Chirac" (1995-2002), form an interesting new experience, especially in historical perspective. The perspective of France as European Republic will give new institutional innovations, as shown in "La France et l'Europe d'ici 2010" (Foucauld, 1993). The situation at the end of the 20th century was quite different from that half a century ago with the terrible reminiscences of the Second World War, not only because of technological breakthroughs such as nuclear energy and phenomena like informatics, making "virtual reality" often look more relevant than real reality. The world seems to be more knit together by new possibilities of communication technologies than ever: "Global Village", The Cold War (1947-1991), after "Fall of the Berlin Wall (1989) and the disintegration of the Soviet Union (1991) is history, but this phenomenon continues to have its consequences.

The collapse of the Communist regimes in Eastern Europe opened new perspectives and threats for Europe. Civil wars in former Yugoslavia between Croats, Serbs and Muslims with disgusting aspects of "ethnic cleansing", made it clear that the lessons of the Second World War had not been taken to heart. The European Union (EU) could not prevent this drama and was not able to have a credible common policy. The EU had a catharsis due to the new situation: former enemies now trying to become members of EU and NATO. The geopolitical situation had to be rethought completely (US, China, Japan and European Union as important players, not to forget the former "Third World", from developing countries becoming partly developed countries) but national problems also demanded adequate policies. Massive unemployment, fiscal crises due to the unaffordable welfare state (Rosanvallon, 1995), retrenchment policies, growing insecurity (criminality, drugs etc.), insights about environmental threats, problems with growing immigration, especially because of the new composition of immigrants (masses of poor people often in the grip of fundamentalist Islam). It is an economic crisis with new dimensions, but also a cultural crisis demanding adequate responses. The last word has not been written about "The Clash of Civilisations and the Remaking of World Order" (1998) of S. Huntington. France, in the heart of Western Europe, is vulnerable in the new situation. Cannac, in "Juste Pouvoir" (1984) pleading for a prominent role of law in public management of society, rightly questioned the prevailing dominance of party-politics in public policies. Well-balanced public policies for a reasonable society are a necessary condition. After the collapse of Communism, the situation in the world seems dominated by the international market (globalisation), making nation-states look like completely outdated phenomena, which they are not. The World Bank Report about "The State in a Changing World" (1997) makes this crystal clear. Every Nation-State has co-responsibilities for global Public Management of Society. "Non-Governmental Organisations" (NGO) have a role (Weiss/Gordenker, 1996). Is it possible to maintain democracy? (Felden, 1996). There is a lot to do and to think, "Getting to the 21st Century" (Korten, 1990). Especially to realise reasonable life in the 21st century.

The overview given so far makes it obvious that French Public Management of Society is quite interesting as a unique phenomenon. In the rest of this research study, this is emphasised even more. Contemporary French Public Management of Society encloses a complex of organs, instances and organisations (Chagnollaud/Quermonne, 2000). On behalf of these institutions, numerous functionaries are active. Millions of public functionaries, a quarter of the total active professional population. Trying to end debates and to deprive regional independence movements of all illusions, the Constitution after the French Revolution had embedded as a principle that France is a Republic, one and indivisible. So it was made obvious that there is only one national legislator, while the French State determines the competencies of all other public organs. Several processes of decentralisation took place in the whole nation, and also of international and even supranational institutionalising of competencies, but the French State can be qualified as a unitary State, a unitary State with unity of legislation, jurisdiction and administration for the French Nation within its territory in Western Europe, which forms a community of French people on the basis of common history, language and culture. To function as a State it is necessary that a State is recognised as such by the national and international community and that three conditions are fulfilled. There has to be a population, a geographically determined territory and a public authority. Since 1789, France has had a constitution. France can be qualified as a constitutional State since then (Vichy regime excluded). Public authorities are bound by laws, formally expressing the "volonté générale". At the start of the 21st century, the prevailing constitution is the somewhat changed Constitution of 1958, on the basis of which the Fifth Republic began. The 1958 Constitution is the 16th constitution since 27 June 1789, but differs fundamentally from the constitution of the Fourth Republic and institutions in the 1946-1958 period (Crucifix, 1997). The French system is a parliamentary-presidential democracy. A parliamentary democracy: parliament can force government to resign, and a presidential democracy because the president as head of state has wide powers and cannot be discharged. The president was elected for seven years by general direct elections and could be re-elected unrestrained. In the year 2000, the decision was taken to shorten this period to 5 years, "quinquennat" (Duhamel, 2000). The Fifth Republic has had five presidents so far: Charles De Gaulle (1958-1969); Georges Pompidou (1969-1974); Valéry Giscard d'Estaing (1974-1981); François Mitterrand (1981-1995); and, elected on 7 May 1995, president Jacques Chirac (1995-2002). With the elections of 2002, Chirac was re-elected as President for the period 2002-2007.

Meanwhile, France had experienced this new regime of the Fifth Republic for more than 40 years. In this period France's membership of the European Community (European Union) and the completely new geopolitical circumstances since the breakdown of the Communist system in Eastern Europe threw up new challenges. In the last two decennia, the French political system has changed in a number of aspects (West European Politics, 1999). New creativity is needed to make the "Public Good" a reality in the 21st century. Part of this new creativity is an adequate digesting of historic lessons about the way human beings act and react upon actual circumstances, ideas and practices. After this short survey it is reasonably plausible that France has been an unique laboratory for the Public Management of Society throughout 20 centuries (See also the appendix "The Relevance of History for Contemporary French Public Management of Society"). There is debate about the crisis of State and public administration in the framework of modernisation (Lesourne, 1998). Debates are fed with intellectual, intelligent and passionate contributions about the "exception française" (Petot, 1998) or "spécificité française" related to the French identity (Muller, 1992). It's called a crisis because of uncertainties about the choices to be made on behalf of structural perspectives. There are many factors which confront other countries as well, and which make adaptations necessary. Technological revolutions, informatics, globalisation, market forces to name but a few. Modernisation is complicated by a rather unique and dominant factor: the overly centralist system of public management with a high grade of penetration in societal processes. So it is not only a reform of public administration, but a reform of the State. Modernisation of the State in all its dimensions requires the education of many agents to make professional public service a reality. This is possible with adequate concepts. Traditional methods of administrative reform are not enough. Contributions of social sciences for intelligent empowerment of Public Management of Society are needed to make it fit for the 21st century.

France is one of the most centralised states in the world. Legislation since 1981 has brought some moderation. Authors tried to find the key to unlock the black box with analyses and explanations about the specific nature of French Public Management of Society as it developed historically and in contemporary France. There are publications such as "Histoire de l'Administration en France (1843-1852) by A.Costaz, and "Études administratives" (1852) by A. Vivien. Most studies about the history of French public management are recent: "Les institutions de la France de 1814 à 1870." (1966) by F. Ponteil; "Histoire de l'Administration de 1750 à nos jours" (1968) by P.Legendre; "Histoire de l'Administration française" (1984) by G. Thuillier/J. Tulard; "Histoire des institutions publiques depuis la Révolution française." (1985) by G. Sautel; "Les institutions de la France sous la Révolution et l'Empire" (1985) by J. Godechot; "Histoire des institutions publiques de la France de 1789 à nos jours." (1989) by P. Villard; "Histoire de l'administration française." (1989) by F.Burdeau; and "Histoire des institutions de l'époque franque à la Révolution" (1994) by J.C. Harouel and others. And the outstanding "Histoire des institutions" (1992/1994) by J. Ellul. J.L. Bodiguel (1978) and M.C. Kessler (1986) stressed the impact of the structure of the public function and the role of the "grands corps". S. Hoffman (1976) accentuated the closed structure of decision-making on the basis of a top-down logic. M. Crozier (1964) with "Le phénomène bureaucratique" caused a furore, and stressed the societal "blocage". Crozier (1997) pleaded in favour of strategies to realise a slender State. Studies argued that the character of the Fifth Republic is different from former French Republics (Chagnollaud/Quermonne, 2000; Duverger, 1996). J.L. Quermonne (1987) argued that executive power was constitutionally corroborated, especially central government. G. Timsit (1987) accentuated the integrative method of administration in the Fifth Republic. P. Rosanvallon (1990) realised an analysis of specific State intervention with the indicative "Plan" and its key role in modernisation.

## References

French
Agulhon, M, 1848 ou l'apprentissage de la République (1848-1852). (Paris, Seuil, 1973).
Agulhon, M., La République. De Jules Ferry à François Mitterrand. (Paris, Hachette, 1990).
Agulhon, M., Marianne au Combat. (Paris, 1979).
Agulhon, M., Marianne au Pouvoir. (Paris, 1989).
Agulhon, M., Les Métamorphoses de Marianne. (Paris, 2001).
Amouroux, H., La Grande Histoire des Français sous l'Occupation. (Paris, 1976/1993).
Amson, D., La République floue. (Paris, Odile Jacob, 2002).
Aron, R., Histoire de Vichy, 1940-1944. (Paris, Fayard, 1973; 1974).
Azéma, J.P., De Munich à la Libération (1938-1944). (Paris, Seuil, 1979).
Azouvi, F., Descartes et la France. Histoire d'une passion nationale. (Paris, Fyard, 2002).
Badie, B., Les deux États. Pouvoir et société en Occident et en terre de l'Islam. (Paris, Fayard, 1986).
Bardoux, J., La France de demain. (Paris, 1936).
Barthélemy, J., Essai sur le travail parlementaire et le système des commissions. (Paris, 1934).
Barthélemy, J., Précis de droit constitutionnel. (Paris, 1938).
Bastid, P., Le gouvernement d'assemblée. (Paris, 1965).
Bastid, P., Siéyès et sa pensée. (Paris, 1970).
Baudry, L., Guilleaume d'Occam, sa vie, son oeuvre, ses idées sociales et politiques. (Paris, Vrin, 1949).
Becker, J.J., Crises et alternances 1774-2000. (Paris, Seuil, 2002).
Bernard, P., La Fin d'un monde (1914-1929). (Paris, Seuil, 1975).
Berstein, S., Histoire du Parti radical. (Paris, 1980/1982).
Bodiguel, J.L., Les Anciens Élèves de l'ENA. (Paris, FNSP, 1978).
Braudel, F., L'Identité de la France. (Paris, Flammarion, 1986; 1990).
Bredin, J.D., Siéyès, la clef de la Révolution française. (Paris, 1988).
Brown, B.E., L'État et la politique aux États-Unis. (Paris, PUF, 1994).
Brühl, C., Naissance de deux peuples. (Paris, Fayard, 1995).
Burdeau, F., Histoire de l'administration française du XVIIIe au XXe siècle. (Paris, Montchrestien, 1989).
Cannac, Y., Juste Pouvoir. (Faris, 1984).
Capitant, R., La Réforme du parlementarisme. (Paris, 1934).
Carrier, H., La Fronde. Contestation démocratique et misère paysanne. (Paris, EDHIS, 1982).
Chagnollaud, D., Quermonne J.L., La Ve République. (Paris, Flammarion, 2000).
Chardon, H., Le nombre et l'élite. (Paris, 1921).
Chevallier, J.J., Mirabeau. (Paris, 1947).
Chevallier, J.J., Les grandes oeuvres politiques. (Paris, 1949).
Chevallier, J.J., Histoire des institutions et des régimes politiques de la France contemporaine (1789-1958). (Paris, Dalloz, 1967; A.Colin, 2001).
Cibiel, F., dir., Journal de la France et des Français. Chronologie politique, culturelle et religieuse de Clovis à 2000. (Paris, Gallimard, 2001).
Cohen, J., La Préparation de la Constitution de 1848. (Paris, Université, 1935).
Comor, J.C., Beyeler, O., Zéro politique. (Paris, Éd. Mille et une nuits, 2002).
Condorcet, A., Esquisse d'une tableau historique des progrès de l'esprit human. (Paris, 1795).
Costaz, A., Histoire de l'Administration en France. (Paris, 1843/1852).
Cournot, A.A., Considérations sur le marche des idées et des événements dans les temps modernes. (Paris, 1872).
Courtois, S., Lazar, M., Histoire du Parti communiste français (1920-1994). (Paris, PUF, 1995).
Crozier, M., Le Phénomène Bureaucratique. (Paris, Seuil, 1964).
Crozier, M., État Moderne, État Modeste. (Paris, Fayard, 1997).
Crucifix, I., dir., Institutions et vie politique. (Paris, DF, 1997).
Domenach, J.M., Europe: le Défi culturel. (Paris, Découverte, 1990).
Dubief, H., Le Déclin de la IIIe République (1929-1938). (Paris, Seuil, 1976).
Duby, G., Mandrou, R., Histoire de la Civilisation française. (Paris, A.Colin, 1984).
Duguit, L., Traité de droit constitutionnel. (Paris, 1921/1925; 1929).
Duhamel, O., Le Quinquennat. (Paris, Presses de Sciences Po, 2000).
Dulong, C., Mazarin. (Paris, Perrin, 1999).
Duquesne, J., Pour comprendre la guerre d'Algérie. (Paris, Perrin, 2002).
Durand, Y., Vichy 1940-1944. (Paris, Bordas, 1972).
Duveau, G., 1848. (Paris, 1965).
Duverger, M., Le Système politique français. (Paris, PUF, 1996).

Ellul, J., Histoire des Institutions. (Paris, PUF, 1994).
Fauroux, R., Spitz, B., Notre État. Le livre vérité de la fonction publique. (Paris, Laffont, 2002).
Felden, M., La Démocratie au XXIe siècle. (Paris, Lattès, 1996).
Ferrero, G., Les Deux Révolutions françaises. (Neuchâtel, 1951).
Foucauld, J.B. de, La France et l'Europe d'ici 2010. (Paris, DF, 1993).
Foucher, M., L'Invention des frontières. (Paris, 1986).
Furet, F., Ozouf, M., Dictionnaire critique de la Révolution française. (Paris, Flammarion, 1989).
Ganshof, F.L., Qu'est-ce que la féodalité? (Bruxelles, 1957).
Gauchet, M., La Démocratie contre elle-même. (Paris, 2002).
Génique, G., L'élection de l'Assemblée législative de 1849. (Paris, Université, 1921).
Gicquel, J., Sfez, L., Problèmes de la réforme de l'État en France depuis 1934. (Paris, 1965).
Gilson, B., La Découverte du régime présidentiel. (Paris, 1968).
Gilson, E., La Philosophie au Moyen Âge. (Paris, Payot, 1976).
Godechot, J., Les Institutions de la France sous la Révolution et l'Empire. (Paris, PUF, 1985).
Goualt, J., Comment la France est devenue républicaine. Les élections générales et partielles à l'Assemblée nationale, 1870-1875. (Paris, A.Colin, 1954).
Greigueuil, P. de, 2.000 Ans d'Histoire de France. (Paris, Assouline, 1999).
Grosser, A., Les Occidentaux. (Paris, Fayard, 1981).
Guelluy, R., Philosophie et théologie chez Guilleaume d'Occam. (Louvain, 1947).
Guénaire, M., Déclin et Renaissance du Pouvoir. (Paris, Gallimard, 2002).
Guizot, F., De la peine du mort en matière politique. (Paris, 1822).
Halévy, D., La Fin des notables. (Paris, 1930; Grasset, 1972).
Halévy, D., La République des Ducs. (Paris, 1937).
Hampson, N., Le Siècle des Lumières. (Paris, Seuil, 1972).
Hanotaux, G., Histoire de la fondation de la IIIe République. (Paris, 1925).
Harouel, J.L., et al., Histoire des Institutions de l'Époque Franque à la Révolution. (Paris, PUF, 1987; 1994).
Héritier, P., Gouverner sans le peuple. (Paris, Éd. de l'Atelier, 2002).
Hoffmann, S., Sur la France. (Paris, Seuil, 1976).
Joffrin, L., Le Gouvernement invisible. (Paris, Arléa, 2002).
Jouhaud, C., Mazarinades: la Fronde des mots. (Paris, Aubier, 1985).
Julien-Lafferrière, F., Les députés fonctionnaires sous la Monarchie de Juillet. (Paris, 1970).
Kessler, M.C., Les Grands Corps de l'État. (Paris, FNSP, 1986; 1994).
Kossmann, E.H., La Fronde. (Leyde, Presses Universitaires, 1954).
Landry, B., La Philosophie de Duns Scot. (Paris, Firmin-Didot, 1922).
Legendre, P., Histoire de l'Administration de 1750 à nos jours. (Paris, PUF, 1968).
Lemarignier, J.F., La France médiévale. Institutions & société. (Paris, A.Colin, 1981).
Lentin, A.P., L'Algérie des colonels. (Paris, 1958).
Leroy, M., Pour gouverner. (Paris, 1918).
Lesourne, J., Le Modèle Français. Grandeur et Déclin. (Paris, Odile Jacob, 1998).
Ligou, D., Histoire du socialisme en France (1871-1961). (Paris, PUF, 1962).
Lucas-Dubreton, J., Le Culte de Napoléon (1815-1848). (Paris, 1960).
Marseille, J., dir., France et Algérie. Journal d'une passion. (Paris, Larousse, 2002).
Martin, M.M., Histoire de l'unité française, l'idée de patrie en France des origines à nos jours. (Paris, PUF, 1982).
Mathiez, A., La Révolution française. (Paris, 1959).
Mayeur, J.M., Les Débuts de la IIIe République (1871-1898). (Paris, Seuil, 1973).
Mayeur, J.M., La Vie politique sous la Troisième République (1870-1940). (Paris, Seuil, 1984).
Montesquieu, C.L. de Secondat baron de, De L'Esprit des Lois. (Paris, 1734).
Muller, P., dir., L'Administration Française, est-elle en Crise? (Paris, Harmattan, 1992).
Nicolet, C., L'Idée Républicaine en France (1789-1924). (Paris, Gallimard, 1994).
Nordmann, J.T., Histoire des radicaux (1820-1973). (Paris, La Table Ronde, 1974).
Olivier-Martin, F., Histoire du droit français. (Paris, Domat, 1948).
Ollé-Laprune, J., La Stabilité des ministres sous la IIIe République. (Paris, 1962).
Orléans, J. d', Les Ténébreuses Affaires du Comte de Paris. (Paris, A.Michel, 1999).
Paxton, R.O., La France de Vichy, 1940-1944. (Paris, Seuil, 1973).
Perrot, M., Les Ombres de l'Histoire. (Paris, Flammarion, 2001).
Perrot, M., Duby, G., dir., Histoire des Femmes. (Paris, Perrin, 2002).
Petot, J., L'Exception Française. (Dans: Revue du droit public, pp.1057-1088, 1998).
Peyrefitte, A., Le Mal français. (Paris, Odile Jacob, 1976).
Peyrefitte, A., La Société de confiance. (Paris, Odile Jacob, 1995).

Plumyène, J., Lasierra, R., Les Fascismes français (1923-1963). (Paris, Seuil, 1963).
Ponteil, F., Les Institutions de la France de 1814 à 1870. (Paris, PUF, 1966).
Prévost-Paradol, L., La France nouvelle. (Paris, 1868).
Puech, J., La Démocratie confisquée. Paris gouverne, la France étouffe. (Paris, Archipel, 2002).
Quermonne, J.L., Le Gouvernement de la France sous la Ve République. (Paris, Dalloz, 1987).
Rebérioux, M., La République radicale? (1898-1914). (Paris, Seuil, 1975).
Rivet, D., Le Maghreb à l'épreuve de la colonisation. (Paris, Hachette, 2002).
Robrieux, P., Histoire interieure du Parti communiste. (Paris, 1980).
Rosanvallon, P., L'État en France de 1789 à nos jours. (Paris, Seuil, 1990).
Rosanvallon, P., La Monarchie impossible: les Chartes de 1814 et 1830. (Paris, 1995).
Rosanvallon, P., La Nouvelle question sociale. (Paris, Seuil, 1995).
Rouche, M., Clovis. (Paris, Fayard, 1996).
Rudelle, O., La République absolue. Aux origines de l'instabilité constitutionnelle de la France républicaine, 1870-1889. (Paris, Sorbonne, 1982).
Sabatier, G., Versailles, ou la Figure du Roi. (Paris, A.Michel, 1999).
Sautel, G., Histoire des Institutions Publiques depuis la Révolution Française. (Paris, Dalloz, 1985).
Schnapper, D., La Démocratie providentielle. (Paris, Gallimard, 2002).
Siegfried, A., Tableau des partis en France. (Paris, 1930).
Siéyès, E.J., Qu'est-ce que le Tiers État? (Paris, 1788).
Simonnot, P., Vingt et Un Siècles d'Économie. (Paris, Belles Lettres, 2002).
Sirinelli, J.F., dir., La Culture de Masse de France de la Belle Époque à Aujourd'hui. (Paris, Fayard, 2002).
Soulier, A., L'Instabilité ministérielle sous la IIIe République. (Paris, 1938).
Tardieu, A., L'heure de la décision. (Paris, 1934).
Tardieu, A., La profession parlementaire. (Paris, 1936).
Theis, L., Clovis. De l'Histoire au mythe. (Bruxelles, Complexe, 1996).
Thuillier, G., Tulard, J., Histoire de l'Administration Française. (Paris, PUF, 1984).
Thureau-Dangin, P., Histoire de la Monarchie de Juillet. (Paris, 1884/1892).
Timsit, G., Administrations et États. Étude comparée. (Paris, PUF, 1987).
Tocqueville, A. de, L'Ancien Régime et la Révolution (1835-1840). (Dans: Oeuvres complètes. Paris, Gallimard, 1953; 1964).
Tocqueville, A. de, Souvenirs. (Paris, coll. Folio, 1978).
Toinet, M.F., Le Système politique aux États-Unis. (Paris, 1990).
Tudesq, A., L'Élection présidentielle de Louis-Napoléon Bonaparte. (Paris, 1965).
Turgot, R., Tableau philosophique des progrès de l'esprit humain. (Paris, 1750).
Vautier, C., Les théories relatives à la souveraineté et à la résistance chez l'auteur des "Vindiciae contra tyrannos". (Lausanne, 1947).
Verdès-Leroux, J., Les Français d'Algérie de 1830 à nos jours. (Paris, Fayard, 2002).
Vidal-Naquet, P., La Raison d'État. (Paris, Découverte, 2002).
Vigier, P., La Monarchie de Juillet. (Paris, PUF, 1962).
Vigier, P., La Seconde République. (Paris, PUF, 1967).
Villard, P., Histoire des Institutions Publiques de la France de 1789 à nos jours. (Paris, Dalloz, 1989).
Villermé, L.R., Tableau de l'état physique et moral des ouvriers employés dans les manufactures de coton, de laine et de soie. (Paris, 1840; 1971).
Vivien, A., Études administratives. (Paris, 1852; Cujas, 1974).
Weil, P., Qu'est-ce qu'un Français? Histoire de la nationalité française depuis la Révolution. (Paris, Grasset, 2002).

English
Anderson, P., Passages from Antiquity to Feudalism. (London, NLB, 1977).
Best, G., ed., The Permanent Revolution: The French Revolution and its Legacy. (Chicago, 1989).
Braudel, F., History of Civilizations. (New York, Lane/Penguin, 1994).
Brubaker, R., Citizenship and Nationhood in France and Germany. (Cambridge, MA, 1992).
Curtis, H.N., American constitutional doctrine and the French assembly of 1848. (New York, 1918).
Dawson, C., Dynamics of World History. (LaSalle, IL, Sherwood Sugden, 1978).
Dunn, S., The Deaths of Louis XVI: Regicide and the French Political Imagination. (Princeton, Princeton UP, 1994).
Edwards, A.R., Hupe, P.L., France. A Strong State, towards a Stronger Local Democracy? (In: Daemen, H., Schaap, L., eds., Citizen and City. Developments in fifteen Local Democracies in Europe. Delft, Eburon, 2000).
Finer, S.E., The History of Government from the Earliest Times. (Oxford, OUP, 1997).

Gladden, E.N., A History of Public Administration. (London, Cass, 1972).
Hall, J., ed., The State in History. (Oxford, Blakwell, 1986).
Howarth, D., 1066. The Year of the Conquest. (Harmondsworth, Penguin, 1981).
Huntington, S., The Clash of Civilisations and the Remaking of World Order. (New York, Simon & Schuster, 1957).
Knachel, P.H., England and the Fronde. The Impact of the English War and Revolution on France. (Ithaca/New York, 1967).
Kohn, H., Prelude to Nation-States: The French and German Experience, 1789-1815. (Princeton, Princeton UP, 1967).
Korten, D.C., Getting to the 21st Century. (West Hartford, Kuwarian Press, 1990).
Lintott, A.W., Imperium Romanum. Politics and Administration. (London, 1993).
Lossky, A., Louis XVI and the French Monarchy. (New Brunswick, Rutgers UP, 1994).
Melko, M., The Nature of Civilizations. (Boston, Porter Sargent, 1969).
Sahlins, P., Boundaries. The Making of France and Spain in the Pyrenees. (Berkeley, University of California Press, 1989).
Singer, B., Society, Theory and the French Revolution. (New York, 1986).
Sorokin, P., Social and Cultural Dynamics. (New York, American Book Co., 1985).
Spengler, O., Decline of the West. (New York, Knopf, 1926/1928).
Wedgwood, C.V., Richelieu and the French Monarchy. (New York, Macmillan, 1962).
Weis, T.G., Gordenker, L., eds., NGO's, the United Nations and Global Governance. (London, Rienner, 1996).
West European Politics (Review), The Changing French Political System. (October, 1999).
World Bank, The State in a Changing World. (Washington DC, World Bank, 1997).

# Part Two

# The Fifth Republic

# 3. The Fifth Republic survived the 20th Century

## 3.1. De Gaulle, the first president of the Fifth Republic

*3.1.1. Birth of the Fifth Republic: "République gaullienne"*

Circumstances in 1958 were so critical in France that no regime could have escaped without serious scars. The smashing defeat at Dien Bien Phu on 7 May 1954, ending French hegemony in Indo-China, left deep traces of frustration in collective consciousness, especially for the French military. The Assembly agreed with the Accords of Geneva (20 July 1954). In the first week of August 1954, there was an armistice in Vietnam, Cambodia and Laos. After this humiliating experience, many felt that the defence of Algeria, the closest colony, against rebels and independence fighters would be a glorious affair, especially for the French military, but the Algerian war, which started on the first of November 1954, had all the ingredients to deteriorate into a civil war in France. "Algérie française" fanatically opposed Algerian independence (Favrod, 1959). In spite of changing governments, accepted as a fact of life, the political situation seemed tenable, with one exception: the Algerian question. The Common Market had started In January 1958 and on the 31st of January 1958, a "loi-cadre" concerning Algeria was adopted. When events became more violent, social republicans invoked De Gaulle to take up leadership of France again (Hamon, 1958). Government-Gaillard was overthrown on 15 April 1958 and a manifestation "pour l'Algérie française" took place in Algiers on 26 April 1958. Government-Pflimlin was installed on 13 May 1958. This date was chosen by generals for a military putsch in Algiers, a desperate offensive to keep Algeria French (Lentin, 1958). This putsch was enough to explode the Fourth Republic (Bromberger, 1959). De Gaulle was asked to take up leadership and on 15 May 1958 he said that he was ready when called upon; he would agree to take over only in a legal way.

On 19 May 1958, De Gaulle said that he was disposed to take up State leadership if some conditions were fulfilled. All legal procedures should be followed. He announced the preparation of a draft for a new constitution, which would be presented to the people by way of referendum. When chaos grew with a Corsican uprising, Pflimlin resigned. De Gaulle was appointed premier on 29 May by president Coty and was installed on the first of June 1958. The Assembly, with a majority of about 100, gave De Gaulle full powers and adjourned till October. He could rule with "ordonnances", regulations comparable to laws, not requiring acceptance by the Assembly. During his stay in Algeria (4-7 June 1958), De Gaulle said: "I understand you." With the referendum on 28 September 1958 an overwhelming majority supported the new constitution. On 8 January 1959, his function as last premier of the Fourth Republic was transformed into the function of first president of the Fifth Republic. Michel Debré became premier. For the dominant impact of De Gaulle on the institutional build-up of the Fifth Republic and his irreversible marks on French politics and government, his presidency is called "République gaullienne". Less than four months passed between the authorisation to make a draft for a new constitution and a successful referendum on the new constitution, a record. The work was not done by an Assembly, as was the case for the Third and the Fourth Republic, but by a small committee under Michel Debré, trusted supporter of De Gaulle. This committee took the constitutional ideas of De Gaulle as the premise for its work. The constitution had to end the weaknesses of public management, organising rationalised parliamentarism.

There were the useful ideas of authoritative authors like G. Vedel and M. Duverger for rationalised parliamentarism. De Gaulle, with a biting criticism of the whole show of political parties, had a rather complete conception of a new constitutional framework. His famed speech of Bayeux (16 June 1946) was a summary of this conception. A working group with experts from the "Conseil d'État" made a first draft for the constitution between 12 June and the middle of July 1958. The committee-Debré had amendments. The draft was presented to the Council of Ministers and "Comité consultatif constitutionnel", with parliamentarians (16 from both Assembly and Senate, representing political parties, Communists excepted) and 13 experts designated by government. This committee presented its advice on 15 August 1958. The "Conseil d'État" had criticisms. The draft was ready with a final examination by the Council of Ministers on 3 September 1958. De Gaulle announced the new constitution on 4 September 1958, anniversary of the proclamation of the Third Republic. Adherents of "Algérie française" relied on De Gaulle, whilst others thought he could find a peaceful solution for the Algerian war which had France under the threat hold of imminent civil war. The position of political parties on the referendum was relevant. MRP and a majority of Radicals were pro, but an important minority of Radicals (with Mendès France) opposed plebiscites, the "mendèsistes". The Socialist party SFIO, overcoming divisions about European Defence Community and Guy Mollet's policy towards Algeria, now broke into two parts. One group split off as "Parti socialiste autonome". Two years later its name was "Parti socialiste unifié" (PSU). Halfway through September 1958, there was a majority for the referendum: MRP, nearly the entire right, and a majority of Socialists and Radicals.

De Gaulle was overactive to win people for the new constitution. For the first time television played a penetrating role in the consultation of the people. After 4 September 1958 De Gaulle visited several cities, French Africa, Madegascar and Oceania. The poll on 28 September 1958 was remarkably high with a participation of nearly 85%. The result was not the expected two pro and one against, but 4-1. In France itself nearly 80% was pro, and in all departments the majority voted affirmatively. No-voters got no more than 900,000 votes (the total of votes for Communists in 1956). The crisis of 1958 and De Gaulle's charismatic personality caused a political earthquake. The widening damburst since 13 May 1958 in the base of legitimacy of the regime was filled. De Gaulle was authorised to solve the Algerian problem. Compared with the Third Republic, without a general vote of the people, and the Fourth Republic, supported by 1/3 of the electorate, support for the Fifth Republic was high. The Constitution of 1958 was officially proclaimed on 4 October 1958. The mandate given by the Assembly to De Gaulle was expired. Institutions had to get their base in the new constitution. The Constitution said nothing about the voting system for the Assembly. There was no legislative parliament, so government had to determine the voting system, De Gaulle himself. In 1945, he refused pre-war "scrutin majoritaire d'arrondissement à deux tours". His provisional government chose the proportional system. In 1958, De Gaulle, fearing for a proportional system, which could make a workable majority impossible, came up with a different idea: "scrutin majoritaire uninominal à deux tours". The French territory was divided into as many constituencies as there were seats in the Assembly, for France itself 465. It was a complicated operation. The distribution of the population on the basis of the 1954 census was used.

This comeback of the adapted electoral system of 1936, in a country thoroughly changed, required organisational skill. De Gaulle announced his decision on 10 October 1958. On 13 and 14 October 1958, election lists were published. The first election round was on 23 November 1958. On the first of October 1958, five Gaullist movements fused into the "Union pour la nouvelle République" (UNR), with a directorate of "barons", historic fathers of Gaullism: Chaban-Delmas, Debré, Frey, Michelet, Soustelle etc. UNR did not have the monopoly of Gaullism; there was also a "Centre de la réforme républicaine". Elections in November and December 1958 affirmed the success of the referendum about the constitution. Parties of the "yes" vote got a clear majority. Gaullists with their 3.6 million votes got 17.6%, Independents nearly 20%. Communists, who during the Fourth Republic had a stable electorate and never had less than 25%, lost a third of their followers (from 5.5 million to 3 850 000 votes). De Gaulle, by virtue of his charisma, was responsible for this falling back of the Communist electorate. In the second round of the election this was apparent, also because there was no list-combination between Socialists and Communists. Communists got only 10% of the 465 seats, while since 1945 they had taken about 160 seats (except for 1951). Socialists got 44 seats. With 23 Radicals and several elected representatives for the UDSR the left had less than 80 seats. The Assembly was, at the end of 1958, the most radically renewed since 1945. Only 131 deputies had already been members of parliament. Gaullists (198 seats) and Independents (133 seats) had the power. A "Chambre introuvable" again, more rightist than in 1919. Not since 8 February 1871 had the Assembly been so rightist. After 1962, the Gaullist estafette baton was taken over by the "UNR-UDT". In 1967 by the "UDVe". After the 1968 crisis, by the "Union pour la défense de la République" (UDR). In 1976 by the "Rassemblement pour la République" (RPR).

*3.1.2. De Gaulle fighting for the "grandeur de France"*

Adherents of the European Community worried about the effects of De Gaulle's comeback in 1958. De Gaulle was known as an opponent of all supranational constructions, especially with regard to the European Defence Community. Convinced that international relations could be built upon nation-states only, he was an adherent of "l'Europe des États-nations". But De Gaulle participated in building up European institutions. He forced through a common agricultural policy, because this was favourable for French farmers. De Gaulle had reservations towards the European Coal and Steel Community (ECSC) but he completed the inspired work of Schuman with the French-German treaty of January 1963. De Gaulle insisted on deciding unanimously about the future European build-up, no interference with French sovereignty was allowed. The Fouchet plan was not supranational enough for France's partners. In the negotiations about Great Britain's eventual entrance into the common market, De Gaulle was playing his cards. In 1957, London refused the invitation to join the EEC, as it had in 1950 with the ECSC. When the EEC proved to be a success, Great Britain formed the European Free Trade Area (EFTA) in 1959 with Austria and the Scandinavian countries. EEC-partners of France were willing to make concessions to have Great Britain as a member-state, but De Gaulle refused. Great Britain would be a Trojan horse and sally port for American interests in Europe. It would always let l its privileged relation with the US prevai above relations with the European continent. De Gaulle got proof of his suspicions in November 1962. The British nuclear weapon was integrated into the American weapons system, the end of autonomous British production of nuclear weapons (Nassau agreement).

De Gaulle had a counter-strike. On 15 January 1963, he declared that France would accept Great Britain's entry into the common market if it accepted all normal conditions without any derogation. Political parties reacted differently after several examples of De Gaulle's intransigence. Communists applauded the cooling off of relations with Americans and improved relations with Soviets, the UNR supported De Gaulle whilst other parties opposed De Gaulle's foreign policy even more. After "solving" the Algerian problem, De Gaulle put his stamp on other policy fields. Premier Debré used the policy room created by the Constitution, relieving government from excessive parliamentary control. According to article 34, everything not explicitly enumerated in the Constitution belonged to the sphere of "règlements". Important policy fields were organised with "lois-programmes":

agriculture, social security, health care, economic structure etc. De Gaulle was not particularly interested in economics, but saw economics as a means to strengthen the French position. The State in his vision has a crucial role in economics. De Gaulle saw the Plan as a must. Pierre Massé laid foundations for strong State intervention on the basis of the Plan, "planification à la française". In 1963, DATAR ("Délégation à l'aménagement du territoire et à l'action régionale") was created as an instrument for regional social-economic policies. Many players in the political arena had to change their attitudes and political parties had to reorient themselves. Many thought developments were due to necessary depoliticising. Parliamentarians were not happy with their experience of lost power. Politicians without power thought writing books was a therapy. Mitterrand published his "Le coup d'État permanent" (1964), an attack upon De Gaulle's institutional revolution with the new Constitution. Criticisms were abundant about De Gaulle acting as an authoritarian despot, an absolutist monarch (historical examples!). Support for De Gaulle was withering.

Education politics was widening the cleavage between De Gaulle and the political parties. From the start of the Fifth Republic, Catholic leaders claimed revision of the "loi Barangé". De Gaulle thought education too loaded with principles to use the easy way of "ordonnances". As was the case in 1945 (Philip-committee) and in 1950 (Boncour-committee), a Lapie-committee was asked to come up with propositions. The idea was to let public and private education converge. Private schools had four options: complete liberty without obligations or advantages (subsidies etc.); complete integration as part of the "service public"; a simple contract; or a contract of association. In the last two options the State would pay more or less, when private schools accepted more or less obligations. This project was strongly opposed. The political right felt that Catholic education had a right to be aided. The proposal was seen as too compelling. For the political left the principle of "laïcité" (secularisation) would be impaired. SFIO expelled the minister of education, Boulloche. Premier Debré took his place during discussions in parliament, and the law got the name "loi-Debré", adopted on 31 December 1959. "Cartel national d'action laïque" (CNAL) had a petition to withdraw the law: ten million signatures and a mass-demonstration at Vincennes in March 1960, with some hundreds of thousands. Candidates promised to withdraw the law when the left came into power. The "loi-Debré" contributed to a reconciliation between public and private education though.

The majority of the population was convinced that there was no contradiction in respecting secularity of the State and public financial aid to school establishments, accepting minimum standards and co-operation with the "service public de l'enseignement", but with the Debré-law, De Gaulle lost support on the political left In 1962, he no longer had a majority in the Assembly. Many politicians waited for the end of the Algerian war to release France from De Gaulle and his regime, and to play the parliamentary games as before. Premier Pompidou at his 24 April 1962 debut in parliament said: "Nominated by the Head of State, so having in him its source of power, Government is responsible before the Assembly." The Pompidou Government was supported by 259 deputies. Three fourths of Independents did not support a confidence vote. Three weeks later, MRP ministers left government after De Gaulle's chaffing remarks about Europeans. In June 1962, a "motion des Européens", rejecting the foreign policy of government and De Gaulle, was supported by a majority from all parts of the Assembly except UNR. Opposition to De Gaulle was growing; murderous assaults included (8 September 1961). Intellectuals argued that it is right to kill an authority when it is not fulfilling its task. Fanatic adherents of "Algérie française" were furious about De Gaulle's "treachery". On 22 August 1962, De Gaulle left "Élysée" by car to go to the airfield of Villacoublay. Near Petit-Clamart, his group fell into an ambush. More than 150 bullets were fired, but De Gaulle survived. This was a serious warning for De Gaulle. It made him aware of the fact that the regime and its institutions were very vulnerable. If he had been killed, the constitutional electoral college would have elected a respectable parliamentarian and the risk was great that practices of the Fourth Republic would start again. De Gaulle felt that the president had to be elected directly by the people. De Gaulle came up with another example of his strategic genius. On 12 September 1962, he announced a referendum, substituting the existing presidential election system by direct general election of the president. Politicians were confused by this surprise.

On 20 September 1962, he gave more information, activating a controversial debate. The constitutional referendum had some remarkable aspects. The first issue was De Gaulle's choice to present the proposal (as he said on the basis of article 11 of the Constitution), directly to the people, without first presenting it to the Assembly. This was a modification of the Constitution, which according to article 89 had to be presented to the parliament. In that case the President had the choice, only after adoption of the same text in both houses of Parliament, of presenting it to a congress (a meeting of both houses of parliament) or let a referendum adopt it. De Gaulle purposely chose article 11, because Parliament never would adopt a modification involving loss of parliamentary influence on the presidential election. Nearly all prominent jurists disapproved this misuse of constitutional procedure. The chairman of the Senate said it was misfeasance. Two fundamentally contradictory conceptions clashed here. The idea of democracy as majority in parliament, and the conception about sovereignty of the people combined with strong public authority. Both political right (except UNR) and left denounced it as personalised power politics. An old friend of De Gaulle, Paul Reynaud, sharply passed sentence over this "faux pas". He suggested that the premier: "Tell the Élysée..For us the Republic is here in the Palais-Bourbon, and not elsewhere. The representatives of the people together form the nation. There is no expression higher than the vote of the people after public debate." This referendum was a vote of confidence in De Gaulle. He asked for a clear and massive yes. If there was only a meagre majority, he must leave the floor. Opponents saw this as a proof that the regime was becoming more monarchical. After the recess of parliament, all parliamentary groups except UNR presented a motion of no confidence in government. So the campaign of the "Cartel des non" started. The motion was supported by 280 votes (the absolute majority being 241). The Pompidou Government was overthrown. De Gaulle waited to appoint a new government until after the referendum, and dissolved parliament. Parliamentary elections were announced for 18 and 25 November 1962. At the referendum of 28 October 1962, out of 77% of the electorate more than 13 million votes were pro (62%), less than 8 million votes against. Political parties prepared themselves more than ever for parliamentary elections.

Political parties attacked the General's party with a new name ("Association pour la Ve République") which combined the majority of the UNR, Independents of Giscard d'Estaing and MRP dissidents. UNR got 32% of the votes; its 233 seats were only some seats short of absolute majority. Independents got 36 seats, so the majority was secure. For Independents who at the referendum had chosen for the "Cartel des non", it was a drama. They fell back from 106 to 26 seats. Communists had some 21%. With the SFIO left had no more than 35%. The General had won this political war on all fronts. De Gaulle appointed Pompidou as premier who replaced some ministers. Pompidou, presenting his government on 3 December 1962, was supported with 268 votes against 116. With years without elections ahead (1963/1965), the Algerian war ended and with the institutional crisis solved and political parties licking their wounds, the future seemed shining. Pompidou profiled himself as a leading moderniser of France, which must become a prominent industrialised country. The "Traité de l'Élysée" (January 1963) tightened relations with West Germany. In 1964, De Gaulle elaborated his theory of supreme power: on top of a State there should not be a double management. All State power should come from the president, chosen by the nation. De Gaulle could now concentrate his energies upon international relations. Ever more he kept aloof from the US, criticising US policies (Vietnam), following an independent course (Paxton/Wahl, 1994). He refused to join the US-Soviet Moscow agreement, prohibiting nuclear tests in the air, in water and underground. De Gaulle was also defying his EEC partners. To benefit farmers, De Gaulle increased tensions over EEC agricultural policy.

After July 1965 De Gaulle played the trick of the "chaise vide" (empty chair), withdrawing French representatives from decision-making meetings, to show that it was not possible to run the EEC without unanimous agreement of governments. To end this institutional war the EEC partners of France, agreeing that they not agreed, accepted the Luxemburg Agreement (January 1966). Each member-state could use its veto to an agreement when it felt that vital interests were stake. France could benefit from economic growth, for an important part due to opening frontiers in the EEC. French industry was forced to modernise without protection. Agriculture was revolutionised and achieved rising productivity, producing more with fewer people. The number of farmers in active professions went from 36% in 1946 to 12% in 1972, and 6% in 1986. Society was changing rapidly. After the failure of the "Cartel des non" political parties speculated over the future. The system of presidential elections, with in the second round only the two candidates with most votes, forced political parties in a bipolar system. The crucial question was who would be the next president. What about De Gaulle himself? In 1964 he had a prostate operation and he was 75 years old in 1965. Would De Gaulle present himself as candidate or not? It was very tricky for possible candidates to know if and when they would stand. On 19 September 1963, Servan-Schreiber sketched a portrait of the candidate ("Monsieur X") for the presidency in the weekly "Express" to start the debate. In November 1963, Defferre, mayor of Marseilles and SFIO member, was mentioned. On 18 December 1963, he declared he would run for president. SFIO leader Mollet aimed at co-operation with Communists (21% of the electorate), but Defferre wanted to form a coalition with the centre. The choice for the left was between a kind of Popular Front or centre left. The SFIO at the 2 February 1964 congress supported Defferre. The MRP congress in May 1964 opted for a centre coalition, but could not make a choice between rightist Independents or Socialists. "Convention des institutions républicaines" and "Club des Jacobins" wanted a reorganisation of political parties. With Defferre, a coalition in between Communists and Gaullists seemed possible.

Municipal elections on 14 and 21 March 1965, some months before presidential elections, were an interesting test. Results for Gaullists were disappointing. Communists won, Socialists lost and Defferre was stimulated to pursue efforts to form a centrist coalition. In May 1965, he launched the "Fédération démocrate-socialiste", a coalition of SFIO, Radicals, MRP and the clubs. MRP and SFIO decided to join. SFIO did not want to break with Communists. MRP maintained links with Independents. The meeting on 18 June 1965 to get together was a failure. SFIO played the secularisation question hard. MRP declined socialism in the name of the coalition. On 25 June 1965, Defferre announced he would no longer be a presidential candidate, probably a premature decision. Now the path was free for a coalition with Communists. The day that De Gaulle hedged about his candidacy, 9 September 1965, Mitterrand (civil servant of the Vichy regime, 11 times minister) declared his. In 1958, Mitterrand was one of the most vigorous opponents of De Gaulle, accused by him of misusing power. In "Le Coup d'État permanent" (1964) he wrote about the permanent "coup" of De Gaulle. Shrewd Mitterrand knew that Communists would not put forward a candidate and had no conditions for their support. SFIO decided on 15 September 1965 to support Mitterrand and on 23 September 1965 Communists announced their support for Mitterrand. The left could make a fist against De Gaulle. On the 4th of November 1965, one month before the first round of presidential elections, De Gaulle broke his silence, announcing his candidacy. He had to rescue the Republic from the old political parties.

In the first round, six candidates were running for president. Everybody expected De Gaulle to win in the first round. De Gaulle thought it beneath him to use the TV-time given him, an equal time for all candidates. Gaullist support came from nearly 80% (28 September 1958) and 62% (28 October 1962) to 45% on 5 December 1965. Mitterrand got 32%, only 13% less than the founder of the Fifth Republic, and Lecanuet nearly 16%. Mitterrand and Lecanuet together had more than 11 million votes, more than the 10.3 million votes for De Gaulle. De Gaulle decided to hit back after this dishonourable need to pass "ballotage" of the second round and now used TV. In the second round, Mitterrand came from 32% in the first round to 45%, De Gaulle from 45% to 55%. The difference between them was 2.3 million votes upon nearly 24 million votes. The republican monarch was leader of a democratically chosen majority only. "De Gaulle was not the same idol any more. He had to behave as a candidate, and participate in the partisan universe, with a party-political team and program. He was desecrated, degraded from the level of mysticism to that of politics." (Viansson-Ponté, 1971). This was disappointing for De Gaulle. Only 7 years ago 80% of the electorate supported him. The electoral revolving door from one elections to the next was a crucial political fact. Mitterrand had created a very good position for the next presidential elections. De Gaulle appointed Pompidou as premier again. Giscard d'Estaing, blamed for the poor results in the first election round, lost his ministerial post. Because of his unpopular stabilisation policy, although De Gaulle himself was responsible for that. Giscard d'Estaing would brand this injustice from now on. He reinforced the party of Independent Republicans, opposing Gaullism ever more. The attitude of Independent Republicans changed from co-operation, loyal alliance, and critical support, to open opposition. Above personal rivalries, there were two different State conceptions. De Gaulle wanted a direct, authoritarian democracy, with primary responsibility for the State. Independent Republicans wanted a more liberal conception, with restricted State intervention, room for private initiatives and respect for the rights of parliament.

The 45% Mitterrand built up his "Fédération de la Gauche Démocratique et Socialiste" (FGDS). He organised that FGDS had one candidate for the parliamentary elections of Spring 1967. FGDS and PCF agreed on 20 December 1966 that the best placed candidate after the first round would get all support. Later the PSU joined this electoral arrangement. In February 1966, Lecanuet had established the "Centre Démocrate" (CD), a coalition from MRP, farmers and a part of the Independents. Gaullists appropriated the Fifth Republic as their own performance, reducing elections to pro or contra the Fifth Republic. Giscard d'Estaing formed the "Fédération des républicains indépendents" (FRI), profiling with reservations to Gaullist policy and the slogan "oui, mais" (yes, but). De Gaulle reacted acrimoniously: "One cannot govern by repeating: yes, but.". So the electoral fight was between three coalitions: left (FGDS and PCF); governmental majority (Gaullists and Giscardians); and "Le Centre Démocrate". After the first round on 5 March 1967, the "Union pour la Ve République" got 38% (2% more), PCF 22.5% (0.5% more) and the FGDS stabilised its position. After the second round, it seemed that the governmental coalition was losing, but overseas territories guaranteed a majority (247 out of a total of 487). This was a real surprise for the left. It was proven that it was possible to reach governmental power and to have Mitterrand as president. Premier Pompidou, with a marginal majority in parliament, was given authorisation up to 31 October 1967 to legislate with "ordonnances". Opposition needed ten votes to overthrow the government.

*3.1.3. De Gaulle as 20th century Napoleon*

Foreign policy remained the favoured playing field for De Gaulle. On 7 March 1966 he withdrew France from the integrated commanding structure of NATO, which implied that NATO headquarters had to leave France. This decision bewildered NATO partners and

French political parties. Only Communists applauded this US-bashing. To promote French independence, De Gaulle pushed development of a "force de dissuasion nucléaire" (nuclear weapon). The first nuclear propelled French submarine was launched in March 1967. During his visit to Cambodia, De Gaulle sharply criticised the US for escalating involvement in the Vietnamese war (Paxton/Wahl, 1994). He perplexed Western partners with a trip to the Soviet Union resulting in hot telephone communications between Moscow and Paris. In 1967, De Gaulle affirmed his veto against Great Britain's entry in the Common Market. When the Six Days War (June 1967) broke out between Israel and the Arab countries, he ordered an embargo on delivering weaponry. This hit Israel most. The jews of France were furious. De Gaulle made it worse, saying that Israel was a dominant elitist nation. This caused a deep rift between Gaullism and Jews. During a trip to Canada, De Gaulle had his next provocation, to stir up French separatism he said in a mass meeting in Montreal: "Vive le Quebec...libre!". to be rewarded with deafening applause. Due to this provocation the official trip was abruptly terminated, and the shock waves of this action were felt long afterwards. In their 1995 elections separatists in Canada just lost their campaign for separatism. De Gaulle made himself highly controversial.

In 1968 the future for France looked bright. The process of decolonisation was finished, the French State was stabilised with new institutions. France reinforced its international prestige with an independent defence and the "force de frappe nucléaire". Prosperity reached an unprecedented level. But in 1968, all of a sudden, France had a new revolutionary crisis. This was qualified by Aron as "Révolution introuvable" (1968) which started with student revolts (Schnapp/Vidal-Naquet, 1968). People under 21 years then represented more than one third of the population (Hamon/Rotman, 1987-1988). In less than ten years the number of students had been quadrupled by a policy of mass education. All proposals to reform universities were received with distrust, They were seen as disguised measures to subordinate university education to economics, market forces and capitalism. The education reform (1966) of minister Fouchet aroused passions. Althusser defined universities as ideological "state apparatus". Bourdieu said, that university supported the heirs of the well to do, it meant social reproduction. Shocking disclosures about the Soviet regime and a Russian invasion in Hungary undermined Marxist and left movements. Students also opposed American bombing of North Vietnam, albeit a minority of the mass of students. On 22 March 1968, students (Trotskyites, Maoists, anarchists) occupied the administration of the faculty of arts at Nanterre. This was solved by closing the university for some days before Easter, but then actions started again. The faculty was closed 2 May 1968 sine die. The revolt spreaded from Nanterre to the Quartier Latin in Paris. On 3 May 1968 the rector of the Sorbonne asked the police to intervene. The police carried off some 500 students. This caused thousands of youngsters to join. The authorities didn't know how to handle this. Drastic action shocked the public and attempts to reconcile were seen as weakness. During the night of 10/11 May 1968 barricades at the Sorbonne were removed, with massive damage and 400 wounded. There were protests all over France, trade unions joined the movement (Morin, et al., 1988). Many tried to understand "La Pensée 68" (Ferry/Renaut, 1985).

On 13 May 1968 a mass demonstration was organised reminiscent of 13 May 1958 (the putsch of Algeria).. Sit-in strikes started in enterprises, railways and public services also went on strike, which made many enterprises close. There were some 9 or 10 million strikers. On 24 May 1968 De Gaulle, back from a visit to Romania, thought to put down the crisis by announcing a referendum about participation. This failed to impress. The Communist trade union C.G.T. was afraid of a take-over by unorganised movements. Minister Jeanneney, secretary of state Chirac and Balladur started negotiations with trade unions and employers' organisations in the ministry. This brought a general social agreement (27 May 1968), "Accord de Matignon": the minimum wage was raised by 35%;

wages were raised 10% in two tranches; the position of trade unions within enterprises was recognised; hours of work were shortened; the position of elderly employees improved; etc. Strikers reacted with shouting. In the last week of May 1968 the government appeared about to fall, all efforts had failed. A student crisis was followed by a social crisis, causing a political crisis. De Gaulle said: "The situation is untenable." Mendès France seemed justified in his prediction, that the new regime would be a failure. Mitterrand thought the time ripe to attack. On 28 May 1968 he organised a press conference ande said that there seemed to be no State. He proposed the formation of a provisional government to prepare presidential elections. He declared his candidacy. He got what he deserved (bitter blame), with his unconstitutional bending for street-power (Joffrin, 1988). In the morning of 29 May 1968, the Council of Ministers heard that the normal session on Wednesday was postponed. De Gaulle said to Pompidou that he needed more time. Later it became known that De Gaulle had visited Massu in Baden-Baden. Everybody was asking what for? Many thought that De Gaulle would resign. That evening Pompidou was asked to convene a meeting next day. Before the meeting, De Gaulle contacted Pompidou. Pompidou advised him to give up the referendum, dissolve the Assembly and organise elections.

De Gaulle adapted his speech (there was a TV strike), the French were glued to their radio at 16.30 p.m. when De Gaulle spoke. The referendum was postponed, the Assembly was dissolved and new elections were announced. Pompidou replaced ministers held responsible for "Mai '68". In the elections of 23 and 30 June 1968, the political right won. The most conservative Assembly since 1919 was chosen. For the first time in the Fifth Republic, one party had the absolute majority. The UDR had 293 out of 487 seats, 38% of the electorate. The Independent Republicans of Giscard d'Estaing came from 42 to 61 seats. These two parts of the majority held 3/4 of the seats in the Assembly. PCF fell from 73 to 34 seats, Socialists from 121 to 57 seats. Revenge for De Gaulle was complete after Mitterrand's blow below the belt, but "68" became a symbol of the movement of "soixante-huitards" with new ideals and opposition to authorities. De Gaulle produced his next surprise. He had praised Pompidou recently and elections could be seen as a victory for Pompidou, but De Gaulle dismissed Pompidou: the duel De Gaulle-Pompidou came to the fore (Alexandre, 1970). Couve de Murville, "eternal" minister of foreign affairs, became premier. Edgar Faure was minister of education. On 12 November 1968, he managed to make the Assembly adopt the "Loi Edgar Faure", creating participation for teaching staff and students. Universities became autonomous organisations, freed from tutelage of the State. Multidisciplinary universities were substituted for mono-disciplinary faculties. The societal peat-moor fire smouldered, causing sudden fires in diverse sectors of society. Damage from "68" to the economy was tremendous (production losses, raised wages, social costs). On 23 November 1968, the Council of Ministers joined. Astonishment was widespread: the franc was not devaluated.

De Gaulle saw the participation of citizens as the new answer to social turbulence. After the education law of Faure, in December 1968, a law was adopted to strengthen the position of trade unions within enterprises. Political decentralisation came ever more to the fore. From the French Revolution on the left had stubbornly clung to the unitary state model to realise centralisation and equality everywhere in France. The political right was more in favour of provincial diversity. After the sixties this changed. The left, seeing that the central State was an instrument for the political right, took initiatives for decentralisation. This made the left popular. Leftist parties criticised Jacobin over-centralisation, the Napoleonic model of administration and the rigid-republican scheme, they were now champions for the identity of regions. Proletarian leftist groups favoured more radical changes, if necessary with the use of violence. De Gaulle (78 years old) wanted to further participation. He made it his last battle by linking the referendum about participation with his own existence as president. He combined this with a fusion of Senate and "Conseil économique et social", and creation of regions as administrative units. The Senate would lose important powers (no participation in legislation any more; no control of government). As the opposition of the Senate was to be expected, this was combined with the referendum. The date for the referendum was planned for April 1969. On 19 March 1969 the Council of Ministers adopted the proposal (15 pages with abolition of the Senate, forming of regions, and a speech of De Gaulle). Senators were enraged, campaigning for a "Cartel des non". Giscard d'Estaing tried in vain to mitigate the proposal, he did not support the referendum. Pompidou said that he was available for president. Public opinion saw him as an alternative if De Gaulle were to lose the referendum and quit (chaos was turned aside). De Gaulle reacted, saying that his mandate ended in 1972.

More than 80% of the electorate used its right to vote on 27 April 1969. Some 53% voted "non". The difference was only 1.4 million out of 23 million votes. Only 700.000 voters could have changed the result by voting otherwise. Some minutes after midnight a communiqué came from Colombey-des-deux-Églises: "I resign as President of the Republic. This decision is effective from twelve o'clock today." The regime-De Gaulle ended, the "République gaullienne" (1958-1969) was history. De Gaulle started retired life, writing his memoirs: "Mémoires d'espoir". On the 9th of November 1970, De Gaulle, – "l'homme du 18 juin 1940", "l'homme du 26 août 1944", "l'homme du 13 mai 1958", "l'homme du 27 avril 1969" – died. "Napoleon of the 20th century" was gone. De Gaulle was one of the greatest statesmen France ever had (Williams, 1997). After deep humiliations by Nazi-Germany, De Gaulle defended the French honour till France was liberated from the Hitler terror. He organised that France participated in fighting for the victory on the side of the Allied victors. He stimulated modernisation of the French economy. On 13 May 1958 France's appeal to him was not in vain when France was on the verge of civil war by the military putsch in Algeria. Under the presidency of De Gaulle, France completed decolonisation. Indefatigable, De Gaulle was always fighting for the "grandeur de la France". He organised a lasting new constitutional regime, overcoming manifest weaknesses of the Third and Fourth Republics. He gave France the Fifth Republic, still doing service into the 21st century.

*3.1.4. From "Gaullisme gaullien" to "Gaullisme gaulliste"*

With the grandmaster of "Gaullisme gaullien" gone, presidential elections again had some suspense. Was it possible to continue the institutions of the Fifth Republic without its pioneer? At the first round (1 June 1969), Pompidou got 44%. At the second round (15 June 1969), he defeated the exponent of traditional parliamentarism, Poher (58% against 42%). The "Gaullisme pompidolienne" proved that it was possible to have Gaullism without the grandmaster himself as steersman (Bredin, 1974). President Pompidou, "dauphin du régime" tried to realise some changes. He made a gesture to the political centre ("Centre Démocrate et Progrès", CDP) by appointing some centrist ministers. He distinguished himself from his illustrious predecessor by bringing international policy objectives closer to real possibilities. He decided that devaluation of the franc was inescapable. He concentrated his energies upon modernising France economically. Pompidou with a moderate attitude, shifting to rightist policies, lost the support of the left of the political spectrum. He also had bitter critics such as Vallon (1969) who qualified Pompidou as "L'Anti-de Gaulle". Without the charismatic leader, traditional dissension between Gaullists intensified. In December 1972 Fouchet started his split off, "Mouvement pour l'avenir du peuple français". Premier Chaban-Delmas (20 June 1969/5 July 1972) formulated a program for a new society, a mixture of Gaullist participation and social-democratic policies. When this threatened to produce too many social reforms, Pompidou replaced Chaban Delmas, although on 24 May 1972 he got the confidence of the Assembly. Designation of premier Messmer was seen as a victory for orthodox Gaullists.

Three parts of the parliamentary majority – Gaullists, Independent Republicans, and Centrists – were united under the umbrella of the "Union des Républicains de Progrès pour le soutien au président de la République" (URP), to improve chances for parliamentary elections of 4 March 1973. At the first round, the URP got only some 35% of the votes. The common government program of Socialists and Communists had its impact. At the second round Gaullists fell back from 273 to 184 seats, Independent Republicans from 61 to 54 seats, and CDP from 26 to 23 seats. The sudden death of President Pompidou on 2 April 1974 caused a shock, especially as there was no explicit shadow president. Rivalries and ambitions abruptly came to the fore, causing sensitive scars long since then. When it seemed to become a fight between Giscard d'Estaing and Chaban-Delmas, Jacques Chirac pleaded in favour of nominating only one candidate (meant to block Chaban-Delmas). Results at the first round (5 May 1974) disappointed Chaban-Delmas. The second round (19 May 1974) was between Giscard d'Estaing (50.8%) and Mitterrand (49.2%). After this narrow escape, President Giscard d'Estaing (May 1974/May 1981) started a new phase in the Fifth Republic (Duhamel, 1980). For the first time, the President was not a Gaullist. By designating Chirac as premier on 27 May 1974, Giscard d'Estaing repaid the support Chirac gave him in elections. Chirac transformed the Gaullist voting machine for his own purposes. After playing up his conflict with President Giscard d'Estaing, Premier Chirac resigned in August 1976. In December 1976 he had the lead of the UDR, transforming UDR to the RPR ("Rassemblement pour la République"). Due to elections in 1978, opposition against the Barre government (25 August 1976/13 May 1981) was fierce. This contributed to the victory of Mitterrand in 1981.

Over the years the institutional system had undergone a transformation in a silent revolution (Avril, 1987; Cohen-Tanugi, 1989). The "Conseil Constitutionnel" (CC), with its decision in principle of 17 July 1971 about freedom of association, constructed the foundation for testing laws and administration on the principles in the preamble of the Constitution of 1958. Since 1974, an oppositional minority (60 deputies or 60 senators) got the chance by a revision of the Constitution of asking the CC to test the constitutionality of laws adopted by the Assembly. Giscard d'Estaing promoted a more liberal interpretation of majority politics. The "alternance" since election (10 May 1981) of president Mitterrand (51.8%), defeating his predecessor Giscard d'Estaing (48.2%), was an important new phase in the Fifth Republic. Because for the first time, a president was chosen from the opposition of Gaullism. This was important as the societal basis for institutions of the Fifth Republic was broadened now. Although denied by oppositional political parties, so vehemently stultified by De Gaulle, it is a fact that De Gaulle caused a fundamental transformation of the institutional system. There is an ongoing debate about the relevance of revising the Constitution (Duhamel, 1993; Vedel c.s., 1993). Three major interpretations of the nature of Gaullism and its changes in State institutions are: Marxist analysis; Gaullist phenomenon; Gaullism/Bonapartism (Petitfils, 1994, p.83). For a long time Communists railed at Gaullism as Fascism. Demonstrations against the come-back of De Gaulle in 1958 had slogans such as "Fascism does not go by." Since their congress of June 1959, Communists changed their attitude towards the Fifth Republic. It was thought to be time to combat the new phase of the monopoly-capitalism of the State. Gaullism was seen as an instrument in the hands of the moneyed interests (Claude, 1960). For Mallet (1965), Gaullism is a political transformation of neo-capitalist economics characterised by technocracy, consumption society and planning, subordinated to interests of large capitalistic companies. This cannot explain why elsewhere there was nothing comparable with Gaullism.

Charlot (1970) elaborated a different interpretation. For him, Gaullism goes further than the charismatic personality of De Gaulle and his influence upon the masses. It coincided with changes in the political system. Political parties became electoral associations. A strong president supported by a dominant mass party, which can provide for a majority, determines the balance of power. Gaullist parties resembled other political parties. There is a crucial role for parliamentarians (Borella, 1973). Gaullism, instead of continuing the unstable system of parties, enforced bi-polarisation concentrated on the parliamentary majority. Historians accentuate similarities between Gaullism and former Bonapartism (Choisel, 1987). Gaullist Seguin (1990) showed that there is strong congeniality between the two. Without restoring France to its former Ancien Régime, Napoleon wanted to complete the French Revolution maintaining its essential innovations, building up a new autocratic system of administration. The authoritarian regime of the First Empire (1804-1814) was a plebiscitary democracy. Louis-Napoleon knew that his ideas did not conform to ideas of the Orleanists and Liberals who brought him to power. After his coup of 2 December 1851, Louis-Napoleon restored universal suffrage for men, which had been abolished. With his authoritarian leadership, his regime made a shift to the right (order, progress, authority and democracy). Louis-Napoleon could be said to have progressive ideas. He wrote a brochure about the eradication of poverty, he promoted free trade and modernising of the economy, he was inspired by the ideas of Saint-Simon. After the downfall of the Second Empire, the nationalist authoritarian right had a revitalisation by "général Revanche" Boulanger. In 1887, the "Parti républicain national" (PRN) was established. Before 1940, La Rocque promoted a rightist-authoritarian anti-parliamentarism. In 1937 there was a "Parti social français" (PSF), coming from an association of military veterans, "Les Croix de Feu". The war of 1940 prevented this PSF with some 2 million adherents from organising itself. Resemblance of the RPF ("Rassemblement du Peuple Français") of 1947, to the PRN of 1887, and PSF of 1937, is striking: "The same mixture of appeal to the people and soldiers. The same combination of nationalism and direct democracy. The same passion to reconcile the national idea with social justice." (Petitfils, 1994, p.91).

Gaullism is an ideology of a people's movement surpassing the right-left dichotomy. Plebiscites of the Second Empire and referenda of the Fifth Republic are focused upon the relationship of confidence between "monarch" and his people. Gaullism took full account of different circumstances between the agrarian 19th century France and urbanised 20th century France. Gaullism might be seen as a contemporary version of a tradition, which had the face of Bonapartism, when it showed itself for the first time. After the Sedan debacle of Louis-Napoleon, Bonapartism crumbled. That can't be said about Gaullism after the resignation of De Gaulle, with neo-Gaullist president Chirac leading France into the 21st century. During the last decades systematic work was made of de Gaulle's legacy, so that others could take over the torch of Gaullism. Gaullism could maintain its position only by incorporating very different movements. The Gaullist "rassemblement" as people's movement gave a political roof to a wide variety of movements, which by their controversies contribute time and again to the typical and characteristic sphere of conflict inside Gaullism. President Chirac, having the three power positions in his hands (presidency, government and majority in Parliament) but losing popularity with the governments Juppé-I and Juppé-II, thought that by shrewdly anticipating legislative elections from 1998 to 1997, he would have a comforting majority in the future. The bitter consequences of this misjudged gamble of President Chirac were manifest. Government-Jospin (1997-2002), with Socialists, Communists and Greens, got a strong position in Parliament, because Neo-Gaullists and allies lost an important part of their seats. In the presidential elections of 2002, Neo-Gaullist Chirac had a huge victory over extreme-rightist Le Pen. So President Chirac (2002-2007) can give Neo-Gaullism a new impulse. Whatever can be said about the new institutions, inherited from De Gaulle, political parties still have a dominant impact. For Suleiman (1995) the Fifth Republic is a "régime des partis".

## 3.2. The Constitution of 1958 and the Fifth Republic

*3.2.1. Historical developments*

The prevailing (revised) Constitution of 1958, crucial for the rights of citizens, competencies of public authorities and the functioning of representative democracy, is profoundly influenced by historical developments (Chevallier, 1991; Duhamel, 1995; Guchet, 1993). Meanwhile, there is empirical experience with the 1958 Constitution for more than 40 years (Revue du droit public, 1998). The most important dimension of a Constitution is its potency as fundamental law to guarantee the Rule of Law in the future. A Constitution, once adopted, is not an absolutely secure possession, but a vulnerable asset, which has to be revitalised constantly by practices, adapted to societal dynamics. Before dealing with the institutional foundation of the Fifth Republic (1958-), a summary historical sketch is well timed. It is not adequate just to go back to the French Revolution, as Morabito/Bourmaud (1993) and others seem to suggest. In this study there is ample evidence about the historical roots of contemporary French Public Management of Society. Excellent work of Ellul (1993) and Finer (1997) can be used as permanent frame of reference. The notion of constitution before the Constitution of the United States (1787), as system of government, is distinguished from constitutional law as fundamental law. For centuries France had a monarchical regime. At the end of the Ancien Régime this was overthrown by the French Revolution (1789). The "États Généraux" (clergy, nobility, third estate) was replaced by the "Assemblée nationale" as representation of the population. Article 3 of the "Déclaration des droits de l'homme et du citoyen" (27 August 1789) of this National Assembly proclaimed that sovereignty, supreme authority in the country, no longer belonged to the King, but to the Nation (Rials, 1988). The Nation delegated its powers to representatives of the population, the "Assemblée générale" (Bacot, 1985). The French Revolution brought a transformation into constitutional monarchy, constrained by a constitution (Duclos, 1932).

The "Assemblée nationale constituante" (June 1789/September 1791) adopted the Constitution of 1791 on 3/14 September 1791 (Bart, 1993). "Assemblée législative" (October 1791/September 1792) succeeded "Assemblée constituante". Meanwhile, there were terrorist activities, also against the royal family (Aulard, 1989). The position of the terrified King Louis XVI, weakened by his failed attempt to escape abroad, the "Fuite de Varennes" (21 June 1791), was undermined further by his clumsy confrontations with the Assembly. This had its apex with the "Commune de Paris" (9/10 August 1792). After the storming of the "Tuileries", constitutional monarchy came to its end and France became a Republic. "Assemblée législative" was succeeded by the "Convention nationale" (September 1792/October 1795). King Louis XVI was executed on 21 January 1793 by the "guillotine". A new constitution was adopted, the "Constitution du 24 juin 1793 (an I)", but this was not implemented. From 1789 to 1875, France had 13 written constitutions, while the number of different regimes exceeded this figure (there were regimes without a constitution). From 1875 to 1958 only three new constitutions were adopted. In spite of several regimes, there was continuity due to legal legacy and institutions, with civil servants and political functionaries going from one regime to another. Setting aside periods of personal ruling and dictatorship, there was an ongoing evolution to democracy (Petot, 1970). France had experiences with several regimes: absolutist monarchy, constitutional monarchy (1789-1792), Republic (1792-1793), "Terreur" (1793-1794), "Directoire" (1795-1799), "Consulate" (1799-1804), First Empire (1804-1814/1815), "Restauration" (1815-1830), "Monarchie de juillet" (1830-1848), Second Republic (1848-1851), Second Empire (1852-1870).

After the "waltz" of Constitutions (1799-1870) came the "waltz" of governments (1870-1958), before the Fifth Republic started (Duverger, 1996). There was a period of more than a century with a Republican regime (except for the loathed Vichy Regime with Nazi occupation). The Third Republic (1875-1940) started with constitutional laws, considered as a Constitution. The Fourth Republic (1946-1958) was seen by De Gaulle as successor of the Third Republic. The Vichy Regime, as vassal of Nazis, was not recognised as French State as De Gaulle from 18 June 1940 represented the Free French. De Gaulle cherished the strategic fiction that he was personally the incarnation of the French Republic until after Liberation. After the Second World War, De Gaulle took leadership of provisional governments before adoption of the Constitution of 1946, but not accepting parliamentarism-as-before, De Gaulle as first Prime Minister of the Fourth Republic resigned. This meant twelve years in the political desert (1946-1958) before his comeback in May 1958 (Rémond, 1985). De Gaulle, after rescuing France from civil war over Algeria, put his mark upon the Constitution of 1958, birth certificate of the Fifth Republic (1958-). To analyse the 1958 Constitution, former constitutions must be sketched (Burdeau c.s, 1997).

The threatening bankruptcy of the French monarchy, caused by French military support for North-American colonies fighting for independence against Great Britain and also by the disgustingly extravagant royal court, made King Louis XVI convoke the "États Généraux" (clergy, nobility and third estate) on 5 May 1789 at Versailles. This was quite a move. This institution was convoked in 1614 for the last time. A royal decree of 24 January 1789 doubled the number of representatives of the third estate. That was not conforming widespread ideas about a reasonable representation of French population. When the voting mechanism in the "États Généraux" was based upon an equal vote for each of the three orders, this meant that two privileged orders (clergy, nobility) could overrule every proposal for renewal. Representatives got "cahiers de doléances" with complaints and proposals, collected in the whole country. Representatives of the third estate, when their claims were not taken seriously, declared that they were representatives of the population. With a part of representatives of the two other orders they proclaimed themselves as "Assemblée nationale constituante" on 27 June 1789.

This "Constituante" on 26 August 1789 adopted the "Declaration des droits de l'homme et du citoyen" (17 articles). Inspired by conceptions, deduced also from Greek and Roman Antiquity, Christianity, Renaissance and Enlightenment, this Declaration centred around fundamental rights of all human beings (liberty, equality, property rights). These implied fundamental political rights of citizens. The American Declaration of Independence (4 July 1776) and the Constitution of the United States (1787) had their impact (Lacorne, 1991; Wood, 1992). The "Déclaration" of 1789 proclaimed that public authorities and others had to recognise national sovereignty (articles 3 and 6), separation of powers (art. 16), accountability of public functionaries (art. 15) and approval of taxes by the representatives of the people (art. 14). The first Constitution of 1791 was result of bargaining between groups with several ideas. Especially three political movements presented themselves: "Monarchiens" (adherents of limited monarchy), "Girondins" (adherents of a liberal, democratic republic) and "Jacobins" (adherents of direct, egalitarian democracy). "Monarchiens" won the first battle, France became a constitutional monarchy. Others got their share of revolutionary spoils as parts of liberal democracy were accepted. In the footsteps of Montesquieu, it was ordained that public authorities had to be organised so that individual liberties were not impaired. Separation of powers, decentralisation, and formal proclamation of individual liberties were seen as techniques to realise this. The Jacobin conception, inspired by Rousseau's "Contrat Social" ("volonté générale"), had direct democracy by the people as objective (no separation of powers). The Nation, recognised as sovereign, could not rule, so competencies to exercise sovereignty were delegated to representatives. This was ruled in the Constitution of 1791 (and of 1795). The Constitution of 1793 had the Jacobin principle of sovereignty of the people. Jacobins wanted universal elections. Others, fearing this would bring aristocratic elites to power, restricted the right to vote to the about 4.3 million "citoyens actifs" paying taxes, out of a population of 24 million.

According to the Constitution of 1791, the King, assisted by ministers, incarnated executive power in a republican monarchy (Furet/Halevy, 1996). Legislative power was in the hands of one assembly, with 745 representatives, elected for two years. Separation between legislative and executive powers was rigid. There was no adequate institutional mechanism for solving the many conflicts between them. On 21 September 1792, the monarchy was abolished and France became a Republic for the first time. To accentuate the demarcation with the former regime, steeped in Christian traditions, the beginning of the era was changed. There now began a new era with "an I" (1792). The Jacobins could later push through their conception, the "régime d'assemblée". The totality of all powers (legislative, executive, and jurisdictional) was placed in the hands of elected representatives of the people. The Constitution of 1793, never applied due to civil war developing in the country (uprisings in Vendée) and war with other nations, was a model for the "Convention". This "Convention" (April 1793/Juillet 1794), having all the powers concentrated in this assembly, created an absolutist Republic. The assembly of this "Convention" was divided in "comités", elected for one month, dominating the Assembly. The Jacobin upsurge led to the "Terreur" of Robespierre, overthrown in the Thermidorian Revolution of 27 July 1794 ("9 thermidor an II"). After these terrible experiences, the "Directoire" (1795-1799) restored public order more or less as an interregnum before the Napoleonic regime. Then came a new constitution, proclaiming separation between legislative power and executive power (Dupuy/Morabito, 1996). This "Constitution du 5 fructidor an III (22 août 1795)" proclaimed two assemblies of elected representatives ("Conseil des Cinq-cents"; "Conseil des Anciens") as legislative power, and the "Directoire" (5 members) as executive power. In this context there was no procedure whatsoever (a coup excluded) to solve conflicts between legislative and executive powers. General Bonaparte, thanks to manipulations of Siéyès, member of the "Directoire", could organise a coup: the "coup d'État du 18 brumaire".

By this coup, he could organise public order after ten years of revolutionary uprisings. Bonaparte adapted the draft of Siéyès for a constitution. To strengthen its legitimacy, article 95 ruled that the constitution would be decided by a plebiscite. This "Constitution de l'an VIII" (13 December 1799) entrusted government to three "Consuls", appointed for ten years (Bonaparte, Cambacéres, Lebrun), while the First Consul had all powers. Ministers (without autonomy) and their functionaries, and "Conseil d'État", preparing laws, assisted them. Legislative power was divided between three organs ("Tribunat", "Corps législatif", "Sénat"). The first, composed of 100 members elected by the Senate, could only discuss bills of the government. The second ("Corps de muets"), composed of 300 members elected by the Senate, could adopt or reject bills without the right of amendment. The Senate, 80 members nominated for life, had to control if adopted laws were conform the Constitution and had to decide interpretation and revision of the Constitution. The Senate had to appoint Consuls, legislators, judges, etc. This ingenious construction had the objective of preventing real opposition and guaranteeing the dominance of executive power by the First Consul (Bourdon, 1942). Bonaparte's lust for power was not satisfied, however, as it never would be. He thought it opportune to formalise his personalised power position in the "Constitution de l'an X" (4 August 1802). With references to the Roman Empire, this Constitution was proclaimed as "Senatus-consulte" of the Senate. Bonaparte was made First Consul for life. Powers of legislative assemblies were reduced. "Senatus-consultes" were used as legal instrument. So the "senatus-consulte du 28 floréal de l'an XII" (18 May 1804) established the French Empire for Emperor Napoleon and his (and his brothers') hereditary descendants. Emperor Napoleon Bonaparte could interpret and abolish each law, as he saw fit. There were some limits. Formally, Napoleon could not declare war without intervention of the "Corps législatif" (this was used by the Senate against Napoleon in 1814).

Military defeats forced Napoleon to abdicate. He was held in custody on Elba from 1814. In the first Restoration, King Louis XVIII granted his "Charte" (4 June 1814) to accentuate the constitutional character of his monarchy. The Senate proclaimed on 6 April 1814 that the French people called Louis XVIII to the throne, if he accepted the constitution as made by the Senate. This Louis XVIII refused, as he could not give up the principle of royal legitimacy. With his "Déclaration de Saint-Ouen" (2 May 1814), he made it clear that he would make his own constitution. On 4 June 1814, Louis XVIII granted his constitution to the people, known as "Charte de 1814". This recognised liberties and rights, not as natural rights, but as concessions of the King. The position of the nobility was restored. Catholicism became the religion of the French nation again. There came an electoral system based upon a very restrictive census giving rights to the very rich. The "Charte de 1814" was inspired by the English model of a monarchy with aspects of representative democracy (Bagehot, 1993; Gough, 1992). Legislative initiative according to the "Charte" was exclusively for the King, who could refuse to accept a law as adopted by the Parliament. Parliament was composed of "Chambre des Pairs" (appointed by the King) and "Chambre des Députés", elected by citizens paying at least 300 francs as direct taxes. For Barthélémy (1904), the "Charte" introduced parliamentarism in France. Government needed the majority of the "Chambre des Députés" to continue. A crucial part of it was the political responsibility of ministers, which the "Charte" didn't mention, but which was practised in this period. At first the government waited for a repetition of negative votes before it resigned

Napoleon escaped from Elba, the "Hundred Days Regime" brought him back to power. He pretended to restore revolutionary liberties eliminated by the Bourbon monarchy, although the "Charte de 1814" was more liberal than Napoleonic constitutions. Napoleon used the "Acte additionnel aux constitutions de l'Empire" (22 April 1815) to introduce a new regime (Radiguet, 1911). Maintaining a dominant executive power, legislative power got more impact. The "Acte additionnel" can even be given credit for the start of parliamentarism. This "Acte additionnel" was put in force on 1 June 1815. But on 18 June 1815, Napoleon had his defeat at Waterloo. He had to abdicate on 22 June 1815 (Godechot, 1985). It was like a mission impossible to find a synthesis of monarchical legitimacy of the Ancien Régime and new "acquis révolutionnaire" (Rosanvallon, 1994). The "Restauration" realised this in a period of parliamentary monarchy (Bastid, 1954). From 1830 on, one vote (on a vital issue) was enough to overthrow the government. Louis XVIII died in 1824, he was succeeded by Charles X (1824-1830), the "Roi ultra". He tried to cancel innovations, to restore the Ancien Régime. He was overthrown in the revolution of July 1830, bringing the "Monarchie de Juillet" (1830-1848). The oldest branch of the royal family (Bourbons) was succeeded on the throne by someone of the youngest branch (Orléans), Louis-Philippe. Citizen-king Louis-Philippe had to accept the "Charte du 4 août 1830" to become king. When he did, France had its "orléanist" parliamentarism (1830-1848). This "Charte de 1830" replaced sovereignty based on divine law by sovereignty of the Nation. Monarchy was accepted as contractual monarchy on the basis of a pact between representatives of the people and the King. The election system was extended, but remained reserved for the rich. Restoration was a match between aristocracy and bourgeoisie (Bagge, 1952). To those who criticised this parliamentarism of the rich, Guizot said: "Enrich yourselves!".

The gap between the few haves and the many have-nots was too manifest. On 24 February 1848, there was a Socialist Revolution, in which several leftist groups tried to force real democracy. It started as protest against the closedown of "ateliers nationaux", where poor unemployed could earn a meagre salary. A provisional government was set up (Agulhon, 1992). Monarchy was abolished. With a decree of 5 March 1848, universal suffrage (for all of 21 years or more) was adopted for a national assembly with the task of making a new constitution. What leftist groups feared (a victory for conservatives, due to the situation in the countryside) was exactly what happened. After elections of 23 April 1848, upon the total of 900 representatives, "Républicains modérés" got 450 seats, "Orléanistes" 200 seats, "Légitimistes" 50 seats, and "Républicains avancés" ("Démocrates socialistes") 200 seats. This influenced the "Constitution du 4 novembre 1848" of the Second French Republic (1848-1851). The constituent National Assembly confirmed the proclamation of the Republic. When the Constitution was adopted by the shortly elected National Assembly, it was thought redundant to ask the people its acceptance (Cohen, 1935). The new National Assembly (750 members) as legislative power was elected for three years. Executive power was entrusted to the President of the Republic, with extensive competencies, elected directly by the people for four years (Bastid, 1945). On 10 December 1848, Louis-Napoleon Bonaparte, nephew of Emperor Napoleon, was elected with a large majority as President of the Second French Republic (Vigier, 1996). The Prince-President wanted to guarantee his re-election before expiration of the four years term. This was not accepted by the National Assembly with the needed 2/3 majority. Then Louis-Napoleon organised his coup on 2 December 1851 (Guillemin, 1951). He disbanded the National Assembly and organised a plebiscite about elements of the future constitution. To further his popularity, he restored universal suffrage. It worked, Louis-Napoleon got more powers than before, his coup was legitimised by a spectacular majority of 92%.

The new Constitution of 14 January 1852 was inspired by the "Constitution de l'an VIII" (1799) of his uncle Napoleon. It combined sovereignty of the people and personal power of one man. Executive power was for ten years entrusted to President Louis-Napoleon (Séguin, 1990). He could nominate and fire ministers at any moment. The President was only accountable to the people. Legislative powers were divided between "Conseil d'État" (preparing bills); "Corps législatif" (for six years elected by universal suffrage, but to be disbanded by the President at will; adopting bills without the right of amendment); and "Sénat" (appointed by the Emperor for life, controlling the constitutionality of laws). With a "senatus-consulte" of 7 November 1852, the hereditary Empire was established. The authoritarian regime gradually became more liberal, especially after 1860. This trend towards a more liberal Empire and parliamentarism was ruled with "senatus-consultes" (Berton, 1902). At the end of the Second Empire (1852-1870), there was a new Constitution of 21 May 1870. This had the form of a "senatus-consulte", adopted by plebiscite. It established a parliamentary regime, making ministers accountable to the "Corps législatif". The Senate was a second house, with the same legislative competencies as the "Corps législatif". The Second Empire collapsed soon after the naive declaration of war to Prussia by Emperor Napoleon III, who had his shameful defeat at Sedan. On 4 September 1870 again a Parisian day. Street riots produced a government with Gambetta, Ferry, Simon and Favre. They called elections on 16 October 1870 and later on 8 February 1871.

Monarchist partisans of peace (under conditions of the French-Prussian armistice) got the majority in the National Assembly. Republicans became a minority (Azéma/ Winock, 1991). This National Assembly, awaiting restoration of the monarchy, in the "Pacte de Bordeaux" on 17 February 1871 chose M. Thiers as head of executive power in the French Republic: "He will exercise his functions under authority of the National Assembly, with the help of ministers, chosen by him." (Chastenet, 1952/1963). Monarchists could not push through their will. They were divided about succession to the throne between "Légitimistes" (adherents of the comte de Chambord, grandson of Charles X) and "Orléanistes" (adherents of the comte de Paris, grandson of Louis-Philippe). Anticipating the death of the comte de Chambord (childless), they had a wait-and-see attitude. Clumsily quarrelling, they missed the historical momentum, contributing to adoption of a conservative republican constitution (Gouault, 1954). With a law of 31 August 1871 ("constitution Rivet"), an attempt was made to diminish the influence of Thiers upon parliament, while naming him president (Dreyfus, 1930). Thiers was so dominant, that a law of 13 March 1873 ("constitution de Broglie") ruled that he could not impress parliament by his eloquence. He could send a message, requesting the chance to speak (without debate).

After an interpellation of duc de Broglie, Thiers resigned on 24 May 1873. Monarchist Mac Mahon was elected President of the Republic. Meanwhile, royalist expectations were reduced to zero by the intransigence of the comte de Chambord. In August 1873, he refused to accept the "drapeau tricolore" (symbol of revolutionary republicanism). President Mac Mahon was nominated for 7 years with the law of 20 November 1873 which made only his ministers accountable to parliament. This law ruled that a commission would work on constitutional laws. The "Constitution of 1875", operational since 8 March 1875, was not a genuine Constitution. The National Assembly adopted three "lois constitutionnelles" about Senate (24 February 1875), public powers (25 February 1875) and the relation between public powers (16 July 1875). These 34 articles of occasional legislation produced a flexible institutional framework, giving ample room for constitutional customs (DF, 1992). The president of the Republic was elected for 7 years by "Sénat" and "Chambre des Députés", and had extensive competencies. He was a non-hereditary monarch. Monarchists thought it to be easy to make their candidate president, and, with a simple constitutional law, monarch (Hanotaux, 1925). The "Chambre des Députés" was elected by universal suffrage for 4 years. The Senate, chosen for 9 years by the cadre of rural, conservative France, was seen as countervailing power for the "Chambre des Députés".

Two important mechanisms of parliamentarism were introduced. The President of the Republic got the right to disband the "Chambre des Députés", after "avis conforme" of the Senate and with "contreseign ministériel" (art. 5), while government would issue writs for new elections within three months. Political accountability of government was embedded in article 6: "ministers are together responsible for general government policies, and individually for their personal activities." Parliamentarism had free play, supported by universal suffrage (since 1875 more extended than in 1848). The organisation of modern political mass parties was coming up since this period. Mac-Mahon, after elections of March 1876 (good for Republicans), entrusted government to moderate Republicans. He forced its resignation (against the parliamentary majority) in May 1877, appointing a rightist government. Before the parliament could oppose, the parliament was disbanded. Mac Mahon thought to get control of the crisis of 16 May 1877 by new elections, but the same Republican majority came back. After this rebuff, there was no presidential disbanding of the parliament in the Third Republic. Mac Mahon, according to the Gambetta-formula, could "se soumettre ou se démettre" (bow or quit). He did both, appointing a Republican government-Dufaure, and resigning himself in January 1879. Successor Grévy, in his presidential message, promised to do nothing against the majority of parliament. This "Constitution Grévy" abolished the presidential right to disband parliament, as all succeeding presidents accepted it. The parliamentary majority was the dominant power.

So the leadership of political parties could usurp the power and competencies of public authorities. Sovereignty of the people (Nation) was replaced by sovereignty of the parliament and sovereignty of the parliament was replaced by sovereignty of political parties. Thanks to an anarchical multi-party system and absence of one dominant political party, there was mostly a fragmented parliament, which could form only vulnerable coalition governments. This caused the proverbial "parlementarisme à la française" and governmental instability: 101 governments in the period from 1876 to 1940 (Goguel,

1981), and governmental immobility, because government was totally dependent on the floating vote of the parliamentary majority, itself kidnapped by circumstantial coalitions falling apart upon partisan issues. The position of the President of the Republic was reduced to a symbol; executive power was eroded and those ruling didn't feel responsibility for what they did. When governments fell they would probably participate in the next government again (Soulier, 1938). This generalised feeling of irresponsibility spread through the whole sphere of public authorities and public functionaries. Representatives, mostly only concerned about re-election, often sold their democratic soul to the devil of private interests. Vital interests of the Nation were fundamentally impaired by a widely abused set of institutions (Mayeur, 1984). Although the "Constitution de 1875" was meant to be short-lived, it prevailed with some modifications until 1940 (65 years). Thanks to its flexibility, it could survive national (Panama-affair, Boulangism, Dreyfus-affair, Stavisky-affair) and international (Fachoda-crisis, First World War) crises. One might say that France lived for 65 years without a Constitution. There was consciousness that an institutional renovation was necessary for effective executive power to handle growing societal problems (Capitant, 1934; Tardieu, 1937), especially since the financial crises, political crisis of 1934, social crisis of 1936, and crisis since 1938 due to the provocations of Hitler (Dubief, 1976). The Vichy Regime (1940-1944) and Second World War were needed to give France a new Constitution.

Confronted with a total military defeat in May/June 1940, Premier Reynaud resigned on 16 June 1940. President Lebrun appointed Pétain as Premier. Pétain made known, on 17 June 1940, that France accepted an armistice, not knowing the conditions of the Nazis. De Gaulle, hearing this, promptly went to London, where he broadcast an appeal to the French people to continue the fight against the Nazis (18 June 1940). After the signing of the armistice the parliament moved its seat from Bordeaux to Vichy in unoccupied France. Following the procedure for a revision of the Constitution in art. 8 of the constitutional law of 25 February 1875, both houses of parliament adopted a resolution with a vast majority. Both houses together adopted the next day a constitutional law with 569 against 80 votes (18 abstentions). This 'loi constitutionnelle du 10 juillet 1940" had only one article: "The National Assembly gives the government of the Republic all powers, under the authority and signature of Marshall Pétain. So with some formal acts a new constitution was proclaimed of the "État français". This constitution would guarantee the rights of work, family and fatherland. It was to be ratified by the nation, and applied by the assemblies created. This was not a Constitution, but rather a transfer of constituent competence to government, to Marshall Pétain. He enacted 13 constitutional laws from 10 July 1940 to 27 September 1943 (Bonnard, 1942). The constitutional law of 11 July 1940 proclaimed that the head of state had all powers (executive, legislative, constituent). This personal dictatorship changed from 18 April 1942 on, when Nazi-zealot Pierre Laval was appointed premier with actual power in his hands, under strict control of the Nazis (Aron, 1954).

After his broadcast appeal from London, "the man of 18 June 1940", De Gaulle, taking decisions and issuing "ordonnances" (as laws), created the "Conseil de défense de l'Empire" on 27 October 1940. With the "ordonnance" of 24 September 1941, the "Comité national français" was established with "Commissaires" under presidency of De Gaulle who appointed them. This "Comité" exercised legislative power (as soon as possible ordinances would be ratified by a national representation). A new situation developed after the Allied disembarkation in Northern Africa. The "Comité Français de Libération Nationale" (CFLN) was created at Algiers. Exercise of sovereignty of the French people was said to be suspended by the Nazi occupation. The CFLN would exercise this sovereignty as parts of French territory became liberated, then a provisional government would be established. After outmanoeuvring Giraud, De Gaulle alone had the presidency of the CFLN. The CFLN, became "Gouvernement Provisoire de la République Française" (GPRF) shortly before the Normandy raid (3 June 1944), and functioned up to 2 November 1945 (Chapsal/Lancelot, 1984). The First GPRF was a government of fact. The Second GPRF had a basis in the constitutional law of 2 November 1945, adopted by the French people on 21 October 1945. The electorate could answer two questions: 1. Do you want the Assembly elected today to be constituent?; 2. Do you agree that public authority is exercised in accordance with enclosed law proposal until the new Constitution is established? The first question got 96% of the votes, the second question 2/3 of the votes. This referendum had special features. For the first time there was universal suffrage not only for men, but also for women. The French people could give its opinion about restoring the regime of the Third Republic or not on the basis of the constitutional laws of 1875. After this answer from the electorate the Assembly had 7 months to make a Constitution. The Assembly adopted a draft on 19 April 1946. This was rejected by the French people in the referendum of 5 May 1946 with 53% of votes (Dujardin, 1977). A new National Assembly was elected on 2 June 1946. A new draft for a constitution was adopted on 29 September 1946. This draft was accepted at the referendum of 13 October 1946. With a marginal majority (1/3 abstentions, 1/3 positive, 1/3 against). Until 28 November 1946, there were three provisional governments: government-De Gaulle (up to 23 January 1946); government-Gouin (up to 26 June 1946) and government-Bidault (up to 28 November 1946). The Fourth Republic (1946-1958) could start.

On 27 October 1946 the new Constitution was proclaimed. Its preamble confirmed the "Déclaration des droits de l'homme et du citoyen" (1789) and recognised principles of social and economic democracy. The Fourth Republic had a parliamentary character with a dominant Assembly, elected by universal suffrage (Rioux, 1980). The President of the Republic had a position comparable to that in the Third Republic, with fewer competencies. He was elected by parliament, not being accountable. His acts needed countersignature by the president of the Council of Ministers, Premier (chosen by the President) and one minister. The Premier, choosing ministers, was leader of government, in leading-strings of the Assembly's majority. The Council of Ministers could decide the dissolution of the Assembly only after the first 18 months of a newly (for 5 years) elected Assembly, and only when there were two governmental crises in a period of 18 months. The Assembly, voting laws and closely checking government, had control of the Council of Ministers by its investiture procedure, and permanently afterwards. The Fourth Republic by its institutional arrangements and practices resembled the Third Republic, with its "parlementarisme à la française", governmental instability and immobilism (Avril/Vincent, 1988). The Fourth Republic had 28 governments in 12 years, and two presidents: Auriol (1947-1954) and Coty (1954-1958). Three political parties dominated the political theatre (Communists, Socialists, MRP). There were many minor parties (Julliard, 1981). After 1947, there was fierce opposition from left (Communists) and right (Gaullists). The Fourth Republic collapsed, unable to solve the Algerian question (Elgey, 1968).

### 3.2.2. The Constitution of 1958 for the Fifth Republic

The Constitution of 1958 was a formidable innovation. A crucial aspect is the power shift from legislative to executive power. The since 1877 ("Constitution Grévy") weakened position of executive authorities, governing in uncertain dependency on the precarious parliament, was ended. The president of the Republic, head of state, was given a dominant position as leader of executive power. In the reinforced position of the president (article 16), one saw the nucleus of a "monarchist" regime. According to the Constitution of 1958, in the original version, the president was chosen by a college of 80.000 "grands électeurs" composed of mayors and parliamentarians. After 1962 this indirect election by way of an electoral college was substituted by direct election of the president in general elections in two rounds. The second round is only between the two candidates with the highest score. The head of state designates the premier. The position of the president became dominant, but the regime kept its parliamentarian character. Government is responsible to the National Assembly, which has the power to overthrow government. Several articles were incorporated in the Constitution to reduce chances of government crises. The original election method was criticised as causing an oligarchy of notables. One can ask whose heir the Fifth Republic really is: the authoritarian Second Republic, July Monarchy, Bonapartism or Orleanism? Many thought the legitimacy of the take-over of power on 13 May 1958 crucial for the character of the regime. As the people approved the referendum overwhelmingly, the take-over was sanctioned. A complex period was closed. De Gaulle had spared the country the shame of a military coup. He gave France a new constitution.

De Gaulle's ideas about the Constitution that France needed were no surprise in 1958 (Debré, 1975). After his resignation as first Premier of the Fourth Republic in January 1946, utterly disgusted by the same party-political games as under the Third Republic, De Gaulle used his time well. He gave his constitutional conception in his famous "Discours de Bayeux" (16 June 1946): "All principles and experiences demand that public authorities (legislative, executive, judiciary) are adequately separated and equilibrated. That, over and above all political contingencies, there will come a national arbitration, guaranteeing continuity in all circumstances...It is evident that executive power cannot proceed from parliament, composed of two houses and exercising legislative power. Otherwise there would be confusion, while government would be only an assemblage of delegations. It is from the Head of State, placed above political parties, and elected by a college (with representatives from the parliament) that executive power has to emanate. It is up to the Head of State to represent the general interest with the choice of functionaries, in relation to orientations in parliament...The Head of State has to function as arbiter, above all political contingencies, in circumstances of serious confusion, by inviting the nation to make its sovereign decision known in elections." He pursued a strong State, in a position to unite all the French, independent from partisan factions. The French State needed one person, responsible for promotion of the general interests of the Nation, the President of the Republic. Executive, legislative and judiciary authorities would have to be subordinate to him. The Assembly, elected by universal suffrage, would adopt laws and control activities of government, appointed by the President. A second house of parliament had to represent local communities and societal organisations, a countervailing power against the Assembly.

Promptly after his investiture in the Assembly (329 against 224 votes) on 1 June 1958, De Gaulle made Parliament accept three texts: a resolution in which both houses decided not to convene again; a law giving full powers to the government-De Gaulle; and a constitutional law changing the procedure to review the Constitution of 1946. The "loi des pleins pouvoirs" (3 June 1958) ruled that government could rule for six months by means of all legislative measures needed for public order. With this constitutional law constituent competence was transferred from parliament to government, respecting some principles (universal suffrage, separation of powers, accountability of government to the parliament). Under the direction of Michel Debré, Minister of Justice, experts made a draft for the constitution. Clusters of articles were presented to a "Comité interministériel" with Houphouët-Boigny, Cassin, Mollet, Pflimlin and Pompidou, under presidency of De Gaulle. The government on 23-25 July 1958 adopted a draft. This was presented to the "Comité consultatif constitutionnel" (16 members of both houses of Parliament, and 13 representatives of government). This amended the concept. An adapted text went to the "Conseil d'État" for advice. Government could adopt a draft on 3 September 1958. On 4 September 1958, anniversary of the proclamation of the Third Republic, De Gaulle presented the new Constitution on the "Place de la République" (Luchaire/Maus, 1987-1988). The Constitution, the first that had not been discussed before in Parliament, was adopted by referendum of 28 September 1958. In France with 17,668,790 positive votes (79.2%) and 4,624,511 negative votes (20.7%); 22,596,850 of 26,603,464 voters voted. With voters in Algeria, overseas departments and territories, and the French abroad, the electorate was composed of 47,249,142, of which 38,097,853 voted: of them 31,123,483 positive (82.6%), and 6,556,073 negative (17.4%). A majority accepted the Constitution in all departments. With this acceptance (Communists opposed), its legitimacy was ensured. It was more of a choice between chaos or De Gaulle than about the Constitution.

The Constitution was proclaimed on 4 October 1958. Legislative elections in November 1958 produced a new National Assembly, with a prominent position for the Gaullist party UNR ("Union pour la nouvelle République") newly created on 1 October 1958. An electoral college, as foreseen in the Constitution, elected De Gaulle as first President of the Fifth Republic on 21 December1958. The Constitution of 1958, with De Gaulle's mark on it, had 92 articles, and after the revision of 1996, 89 articles. It was preceded by a preamble: "The French people solemnly proclaims its attachment to Human Rights and the principles of national sovereignty as defined in the Declaration of 1789, confirmed and completed by the preamble of the Constitution of 1946. On the basis of these principles and that of the free determination of peoples, the Republic offers to the overseas territories, manifesting the will to adhere, the new institutions founded on the common ideal of liberty, equality and fraternity, and developed in view of their democratic evolution." The Constitution of 1958, during the more than forty years of its validity, provoked an impressive series of scholarly comments. This is understandable for its specific characteristics, a mixture of Jacobinist and liberal-democratic elements. The Fifth Republic was explicitly placed in the tradition of human rights, republicanism and parliamentary democracy. Adapted to the conception of De Gaulle and Michel Debré (1958) to guarantee effective functioning of public authorities. In the first article, French Republic and the peoples of overseas territories (in free determination) declared to form a "Communauté", based upon equality and solidarity.

The first paragraph is about sovereignty. Article 2 copied the formula of the 1946 Constitution, proclaiming that the Republic is one and indivisible, secular, democratic and social: "La France est une République indivisible, laïque, démocratique et sociale." Important constitutional elements were proclaimed. Guarantees for the equality of all citizens under the law, without distinction of origin, race or religion (respect for all religions), and some specifics: the language is French; the "tricolore" flag is the national emblem; "Marseillaise" the national hymn; the motto of the Republic is "Liberté, Égalité, Fraternité"; and its principle: government of the people, by the people and for the people. To exclude other sources of sovereignty, article 3 declares the national sovereignty to belong to the people, exercising its sovereignty by means of representatives (indirectly), or referendum (directly). Representatives are directly or indirectly elected by universal, equal and secret suffrage, in the conditions of the Constitution. All adult French nationals of both sexes, having their civil and political rights, form the electorate, within conditions of the law. Article 4 deals with political parties as organisations preparing elections, proclaiming that they are free in their activities only if they respect the principles of national sovereignty and democracy. Debate is possible about democracy. Often it is seen as dominance of parliamentary majority, but that is incorrect, a remnant of primitive customs in war circumstances (winner takes all). Full-grown democracy in a civilised society requires much more than that. As respect for human rights and (the rights of) minorities; an open, pluralist society with participation for all groups; etc. Article 3 has an explicit constitutional interdiction of usurpation of exercise of national sovereignty by any part of the people or any individual. In relation to contended or factual usurpations this is a passionately debated issue: political parties ("État-RPR", État-PS"), regions (Corsica), and presidents (De Gaulle; Mitterrand; Chirac).

Before the paragraph about Parliament (IV), the Constitution deals with President of the Republic (II) and Government (III). It was accentuated that the first place in the Republic was not for Parliament as in the Third Republic with the malaise of "parlementarisme à la française". In spite of the parliamentary character of the Fifth Republic, it can be seen as semi-presidential/semi-parliamentary due to the prominent position of the President of the Republic, and the constitutionally reduced powers of Parliament ("parlementarisme rationalisé"). Legislative power was entrusted to the Parliament with two houses (art. 24): "Assemblée nationale" (577 members elected by direct universal suffrage for 5 years, except in case of dissolution) and "Sénat" (321 members elected indirectly by universal suffrage for 9 years, as representation of territorial public organisations and the French living abroad). Parliamentarians have an independent, irrevocable and representative mandate which is general (for the whole country; not for their constituency, as happened more than once). Each imperative mandate is forbidden (art. 27). Parliamentarians are not bound by engagements to electors (or political parties!!). To be candidate for the National Assembly one has to be 23 years (compulsory military service fulfilled). To be a deputy, one has to be elected by the absolute majority and by at least 1/4 of the registered electorate (first round) or by a relative majority (second round). Since the law of 9 July 1976, one has to get 12.5% of the registered electorate (in 1958 5%, since 1966 10%), to participate in the second round. To become a senator one has to be 35 years or older. Incompatibilities do not imply ineligibility, but make a choice needed between mandate and some public (minister, public functionary – professors in higher education excluded), or private functions (board of national enterprises, national public establishments, and private enterprises being subsidised by the State). A law of 24 January 1972 ruled, that an elected parliamentarian has to decide within 14 days about these functions, and to make known to the bureau of Parliament which other functions he or she has. A law of 30 December 1985 restricted combination of mandates ("cumul des mandats"), forbidding parliamentarians to be: member of the European Parliament; "conseiller régional"; conseiller général; "conseiller de Paris"; or other functions, but France, in comparison with other democracies, has a broad view about combination of political functions. Former Premier Juppé was also mayor of Bordeaux. Government-Jospin intended to reduce the "cumul".

During their mandate, parliamentarians get a financial compensation, support (since 1995 three co-workers), material benefits, and some protections: "irresponsibility" (freedom of giving opinions or voting without the risk of being sued) and "inviolability" as immunities (art. 26). Except in the case of "flagrant délit", parliamentarians cannot be arrested during the parliamentary session without authorisation of the house of which they are a member. Outside this period they cannot be arrested except in case of "flagrant délit", authorised persecutions or definite condemnation (also with authorisation). Affairs about financial influencing of parliamentarians and financing of political parties poisoned the political scene. Members of Parliament were obligated to make their private capital known at the start and the end of their mandate. Since laws of 11 March 1988, 15 January 1990 and 29 January 1993, expenditures for elections are strictly regulated. For the legislative elections of 1993, these expenditures were bound to a maximum of 500,000 francs per candidate. Political affairs continued though. Several political parties used disguised forms of financing to evade legal restrictions. Abuses in the sphere of influence by (leadership of) political parties upon the functioning of Parliament and public authorities in general have been criticised, but not enough to produce essential improvements. Setting aside constitutional restrictions for the functioning of the Parliament ("parlementarisme rationalisé") in the Constitution of 1958, there was also a dominant impact from the phenomenon of the parliamentary majority. Periods of "cohabitation" – a President of the Republic, coming from one political party, and a Government, or Government and majority in the National Assembly in the hands of another political party or coalition – contributed to the revitalisation of parliamentary democracy.

The role of the Parliament (art. 24-33) is relevant in the sphere of legislation, making laws a prerogative of the Parliament, and with its task of controlling Government, having (within constraints of the Constitution, giving prerogatives to the President of the Republic), the leadership over the executive apparatus of public functionaries. Since the Constitution of 1958, the domain of the law, formerly nearly all-encompassing, was restricted to a limited number of subjects (art. 34). The domain of "règlements", legal rules issued by government, was extended (art. 37) so that the position of the Parliament was structurally weakened in relation to the empowered position of executive power. The Parliament before 1958 had near autonomy in organising its work. This changed with the "parlementarisme rationalisé" (articles 28/30 Constitution). To diminish the Parliament's hegemony and give Government more latitude, the (modified in 1963) system provided for two normal sessions yearly: 90 days in Spring, 80 days in Autumn. Since the constitutional revision of 4 August 1995, there are three categories of sessions: "ordinaire unique", "extraordinaire", "de plein droit". The Parliament sits for 9 months from October to June (120 days, sometimes more).

At the request of the Premier or the majority of the National Assembly, an extraordinary session can arise (opened and closed by the President of the Republic, who can decide if there is an extraordinary session, and about what). On 30 June 1993, President Mitterrand wanted to consent, but not with regard to the disputed bill about revision of the "Loi Falloux". There is a session according to the law in the case of general elections, and during the period of application of art. 16 of the Constitution (national emergency). Government can largely force the agenda and the sequence of subjects to be handled. This has been disputed often. Since revision of the Constitution on 4 August 1995 at least one session weekly is reserved by priority for answering the questions of parliament, and one session per month. Sessions of Parliament are held in public. After a specific procedure a closed session is possible (art. 33 Constitution). To rationalise the functioning of the Parliament, so that Government can push through its program, there is a set procedural rules favouring the position of Government (an overreaction to abuses in the Third and Fourth Republics). For example; reduction of the number of permanent commissions (6), to prevent them from becoming counter-ministries. The President of the Republic, may, on the basis of a proposal from Government or two houses of Parliament, subject a bill about organisation of public authorities or ratification of a treaty to the procedure of a referendum (art. 11).

In conceptualising the position of the President of the Republic, De Gaulle did not have the powerless presidents of the Fourth Republic in mind, but strong executive personalities like Napoleon and Louis-Napoleon. The result is not wholly consistent, due to the fact that De Gaulle had to bargain with representatives of Parliament. That is explicitly the case with regard to competencies of President of the Republic and Premier or Government in relation to each other: in the cockpit of national French public management. The President of the Republic has far-reaching competencies. He has to guard respect for the Constitution, guaranteeing by his "arbitrage" regular functioning of public powers and continuity of the French Republic. He warrants national independence, integrity of the national territory, and respect for accords of the French "Communauté" and treaties (art. 5). Elected directly by the electorate for 7 years (since 2002 for 5 years), the President appoints and fires the Premier (formally after resignation of the Government) and other ministers upon a proposition of the Premier (art. 8). To maximise possibilities for influencing the work of Government, the President has to preside at the Council of Ministers (art. 9). The President has to sign ordinances and decrees as deliberated in the Council of Ministers (art. 13) but the Premier according to the Constitution (art. 20/21) is put in general charge of the work of Government, which "determines and directs the policy of the nation", disposing of administration and armed forces. The Premier is made responsible for National Defence (art. 21). The President is supreme commander of armed forces, presiding at higher councils and committees of National Defence (art. 15). The President appoints (higher) military and civil functionaries (art. 13). The Premier nominates military and civil functionaries, reckoning with art. 13 (art. 21). A dual command in the cockpit of the French nation, competencies are not clearly divided.

The powers of President of the Republic and Government with regard to the Parliament are striking. It is crucial that the domain of the law is substantially reduced, while the executive can issue rules with the quality of laws, "règlements". In the framework of the "parlementarisme rationalisé", procedural rules are established to reduce possibilities for the Parliament to hinder Government. The President of the Republic has the power to proclaim laws. He can request, within 14 days after their adoption in Parliament, a new debate in Parliament about adopted laws or articles of these laws (art. 10). The President may, after consulting Premier and presidents of both parliamentary houses, dissolve the Parliament (art. 12). When the President communicates with the Parliament, he does this with messages, which are read in Parliament, but not discussed (art. 18). To emphasise the curtailing of Parliament, there is a paragraph V about the relation between Parliament and Government (art. 34-51). Legislative initiative (art. 39) is in the hands of Premier ("projets de loi") and members of Parliament ("propositions de loi"). Bills from Parliament are rejected formally by the Constitution (art. 40), if adoption implies reduction of public resources or augmentation of public debt.

Government and members of Parliament may amend bills. Asked by Government, each house of Parliament has to vote once about a text, only including amendments proposed or accepted by Government. The famous "vote bloqué". Each bill is examined in both houses of Parliament with the objective of reaching an identical text, and when this is not realised following a specific procedure (a committee with equal representation of both houses), Government has the right to force a decision by the National Assembly (art. 45). Budget laws are an important instrument to control Government activities. When the Assembly does not decide upon a bill about the "projet de loi de finances" within 40 days after presentation by Government, Government can force the Senate to take a decision within 14 days. Then the procedure of art. 45 is followed. When Parliament does not take a decision within 70 days, the budget bill may be issued as "ordonnance" (art. 47). When the budget bill is not decided upon before the start of the budget year, Government can ask Parliament to authorise urgent measures (taxes, credits etc). The Premier can ask the Assembly to take a vote of confidence on his program or a general political declaration, or about a text (art. 49). A "motion de censure", supported by 10% of members of the National Assembly, and adopted 48 hours after its presentation by a majority, can test whether the Government has the support of the Assembly. When the (majority of the) Assembly adopts a "motion de censure", or does not accept the Government program or its general political statement, the Premier has to present the resignation of his Government to the President of the Republic (art. 50).

The prominent position of the President is also emphasised in the Constitution by competencies given him in the sphere of international relations (art. 52-55), the military field and in case of a national emergency. The President of the Republic is competent to negotiate and ratify treaties (art. 52). He has to be informed about all negotiations that can lead to the conclusion of an international agreement, which is not subject to ratification. The President of the Republic accredits ambassadors and special envoys (art. 14). A crucial part of his prestige is due to the fact that the President of the Republic, warrant of international independence and territorial integrity (art. 5), is supreme commander of the armies (art. 15). In this nuclear age this means, that he alone is competent to "push the nuclear button". The President of the Republic, on the basis of art. 16 (national emergency), has ample, even total and unchecked powers, while he can define the circumstances in which art. 16 is at stake. This power of the President was only used between 23 April and 30 September 1961 after a military putsch in Algeria. The intertwined functions of the President of the Republic can be summarised as: head of state; warrant of the national interest; head of the executive, boss of important public functionaries in civil and military jobs; and prominent politician. This Constitution seemed to be written for De Gaulle, presenting himself as standing above all parties. His successors used the powers of this position fully, often with a party-political attitude. There were enduring criticisms of "État gaulliste", "État giscardiste", "État mitterrandiste", "État chiracquiste". Disqualifications of the regime in public opinion are manifest in terms "État-RPR", and "État-PS", suggesting that public authorities are in the grip of political parties.

For the first time in French history the 1958 Constitution introduced a jurisdictional organ with real powers to check legislative power: the "Conseil constitutionnel" (CC). This proved to be one of the most important innovations of the 1958 Constitution. This instrument for a constitutional check on legislation was originally met with a lot of scepticism but 40 years on the CC is widely accepted and praised. Paragraph VII of the Constitution deals exclusively with the "Conseil constitutionnel" (art. 56-63). Before 1958, the idea of the inviolable position of the law (and of the maker of the laws: the (majority of) Parliament) was nearly sacrosanct. To give a new content to the principle of separation of powers, a new balance of powers was sought. The position of the executive power had to be reinforced by all means, so the reach of the domain of the law was restricted to a limited number of policy fields. Executive power, interfering in the field of legislative power, could make "règlements" with the character of laws. The President of the Republic appoints the president of the CC, having 9 members chosen for 9 years. The CC has tasks in the sphere of controlling elections and procedures with a referendum (art. 58-61). More important is its competence to check the constitutionality of organic laws (art. 46), and other laws.

Since the constitutional revision of 29 October 1974 not only the President of the Republic, Premier, presidents of the houses of Parliament, but also 60 deputies or 60 senators can ask the "Conseil constitutionnel" to check bills before they are proclaimed (art. 61). This "saisine" had a growing popularity, inter alia as weapon of the opposition in Parliament. Especially since 1971, the CC has been prominent as a guardian of fundamental freedoms. In the "French Marbury v. Madison case", the CC based its decision on 16 July 1971 regarding the freedom of association not on the Constitution itself, but on its Preamble. The CC thus raised the Preamble, and therefore its component texts (the Preamble of the Constitution of 1946 and the Declaration of Human Rights of 1789), to full constitutional status. This caused new jurisprudence on civil rights. According to art. 62 a text declared unconstitutional by the CC cannot be proclaimed or implemented, and there is no appeal against decisions of the CC. To exclude interpretations this article established that decisions of the CC are imposed upon all public authorities and all administrative and jurisdictional authorities. The Constitution of 1958 has rulings about jurisdictional authorities (art. 64-66), "Haute Cour de justice" (art. 67-68), penal responsibility of members of Government (art. 68-1, 68-2), "Conseil économique et social" (art. 69-71), "collectivités territoriales" (art. 72-76), "Communauté" (art. 77-87), "accords d'association" (art. 88), European Communities/European Union (art. 88-1/art. 88-4). Finally the Constitution deals with its revision (art. 89) and transitory rules (art. 90-93).

## 3.3. The Gaullist philosophy of Public Management of Society

*3.3.1. De Gaulle's contribution to French specificity*

Charles De Gaulle (1890-1970) has been a statesman with lasting influence on the institutional structure of the French Republic. He started his "Mémoires de guerre" (1954) with the words: My whole life I had a certain idea about France. After beginning his training in 1910 at the famed Saint-Cyr, he became a career officer. At this time there were strong feelings of "revanche" against Germany (in 1911 the crisis of Agadir). De Gaulle adhered to the ideas about republican nationalism of Maurice Barrès. During the First World War (1914-1918) he fought in Poland. In "La discorde chez l'ennemi" (1924) he analysed, as a 34-year old captain with experiences in trench-warfare and German prisons, the causes of the German defeat and anticipated a German revenge. In 1924 the issue was implementation of the Versailles Treaty (1919). In 1934 Adolph Hitler was in power. De Gaulle argued for the reinforcing of national defence ("Le Fil de l'Épée", 1932). In his book "L'armée de l'avenir" (1934) De Gaulle argued with foresight for a regular army, something the French government only got around to from 1996 on. On 15 May 1940, De Gaulle was brigadier-general and on 5 June 1940 a member of government as secretary of state. He disagreed with Pétain, adhering to prompt capitulation. De Gaulle went to London, addressing himself on 18 June 1940 to the French and the armed forces to continue fighting. He had leadership over the "Free French" fighting Vichy-collaborators. After the armistice, Pétain decided to collaborate with the Nazis. France was split into occupied and unoccupied zones. After De Gaulle's insubordination Pétain demoted him to colonel. In August 1940 he was sentenced to death. De Gaulle laid thenfoundations of the liberation of France and the Fifth Republic.

Before this however France had to endure serious tribulations. To encourage his compatriots De Gaulle said in March 1941 in London: "There is a contract which has lasted twenty centuries between the grandeur of France and the liberty of the world." After June 1943 he took the leadership of the "Comité de la Libération Nationale" at Algiers. After D-Day and the Liberation of France the "Journal officiel" of 9 August 1944, in the ordinance about the restoration of Republican legality, said: "The first act of this restoration of Republican legality is the observation that the form of government remains the Republic. According to law the Republic has existed without a break. The next observation is that laws and regulations of the actual authority (Nazis and collaborators), imposed upon France, do not have any obligatory character. All after the fall of the last legitimate government of the Republic on 16 June 1940 is rendered null." De Gaulle was received as liberator in Paris on 26 August 1944. On 13 November 1945 he was chosen Premier (unanimously). His government was short-lived. When Socialists refused to support his defence budget, De Gaulle resigned in January 1946. With his speech at Bayeux (16 June 1946), he started his strategic campaign to win the French over to his constitutional ideas. The National Assembly on 27 September 1946 adopted the second draft for a new constitution. Criticised by De Gaulle, this draft was approved in a referendum on 13 October 1946. In Epinal, De Gaulle elaborated his vision on 28 September 1946. "It seems to me necessary that the Head of State is elected and chosen to really represent France and the French Union. That in our divided, weakened and threatened country, this Head of State should guarantee, above the political parties, the regular functioning of institutions, and, amidst political contingencies, also the permanent interests of the nation. To ensure that the President of the Republic can fulfil these tasks it is necessary that he has the competence to invest successive governments, to preside at its councils, and to sign decrees, and also that he is able to dissolve the Assembly, elected with universal suffrage, when there is no coherent majority to fulfil its role as legislator or support of any government normally.

Whatever the circumstances, he has the task to be the guarantee of national independence and the integrity of the territory and the treaties as signed by France."

In April 1947, De Gaulle established a new political movement; "Rassemblement du Peuple Français" (RPF). It lasted until the military putsch in Algeria in May 1958 when De Gaulle came back to power. All of a sudden De Gaulle had a chance of realising his constitutional ideas. He had a grand idea of the "grandeur de la France" (Cerny, 1986). He was disposed to take leadership, refusing to force his way with illegal methods. When Government-Pflimlin announced its resignation on 28 May 1958, President Coty asked De Gaulle to form a government on 29 May 1958. Preparation of a draft for a new constitution was entrusted to Michel Debré, with De Gaulle actively participating in this work. Resistance to the constitutional ideas of De Gaulle was strong. Because De Gaulle wanted to end the kidnapping of State institutions by political parties, and he wanted to break the dominant position of parliament. De Gaulle proclaimed the new Constitution on 4 September 1958. The new Constitution was approved in a referendum by nearly 80% of the voters. According to the procedure of the new Constitution, De Gaulle was elected as first President of the Fifth Republic on 21 December 1958. The Constitution of 1958 is fundamentally different from the model of the Third Republic. The Third Republic was inspired by a vision on human beings and humanity which reaches back to the rationalistic conception of the 18th century. This conception, rejecting values of Christian revelation, was based upon positivism, belief in progress by science and Neo-Kantian ethics. The "IIIe République laïque" wanted to be anticlerical (Rémond, 1985). The republican model of the Third Republic excluded all who did not accept the philosophical roots of the regime.

It is difficult to find comparable philosophical roots in the foundations of the Fifth Republic (Berstein/Rudelle, 1992). Ideological and religious opinions are seen as belonging to the private sphere. The State does not interfere in the philosophical choices of citizens. The ambition to unite all French in a national community is decisive, over all party-political, philosophical or religious dissension. For the first time in French history consensus is seen as an important criterion. Absence of specified philosophical roots in the Constitution of 1958 is the result of a purposeful endeavour to base the republican, impartial State on behalf of all French inhabitants, and to prevent exclusion of any groups or conceptions. So the relation between regime and citizens in the Fifth Republic is more detached, less passionate and emotional than in the Third Republic. The republican model in the first thirty years of the 20th century was dominantly influenced by the framework of the French Revolution and the principle of sovereignty of the nation. After 1958, the French Revolution was no longer the sole key for each historical reflection, although it is an important part of French national history. Henceforth, the period of the Second World War is accentuated. The legitimacy of the Fifth Republic is not based on circumstances of 13 May 1958 in Algeria, but upon the legitimacy won during the Second World War by the "man of 18 June 1940", De Gaulle, and upon the need for a powerful and independent France with a strong executive power, not hindered by manipulating political parties. The underlying political culture is also different. Individuals and their rights are not in the centre as in the Third Republic, but the French State. De Gaulle used the term republic differently from what it had meant before. For him the republic is a powerful French State guaranteeing national unity, with a position above political parties, that had compromised the State.

De Gaulle stressed the function of the French State to represent the nation and to warrant stability of its institutions in view of continuity. A constitutional State guaranteeing fundamental liberties and rights of French society. An institutional break was realised by giving primacy to the State, which, according to article 16 of the Constitution, under specific circumstances has priority over individual liberties. In the first half of the 20th century, the political-institutional centre of gravity was in parliament at the expense of government and executive power. The Constitution of 1958 changed this. Parliament maintained an important function, but now parliament is subsidiary to the nation as embodied in the head of executive power, the President of the Republic. Since 1958 the President of the Republic is not, as in the previous regime, elected by the meeting of Senate and Assembly in congress. The President gets his legitimacy from his election, since 1962 directly from election by the French people. In view of the painful experiences of the Second World War, the former principal pacifism is transformed into the necessity of having autonomous French armed forces to guarantee lasting independence. This implied independence with regard to nuclear weaponry (Doise/Vaïsse, 1987). Reinforcing the international position of France was a constant factor in De Gaulle's foreign policy. All was subordinated to the "grandeur de la France" (Cerny, 1986). De Gaulle tried to create an independent position for France in between the superpowers, United States and Soviet-Union.

Although both, Third Republic and Fifth Republic, can be characterised by participation of the sovereign nation in public affairs, the differences are remarkable. During the Third Republic, sovereignty of the people in accordance with republican tradition was interpreted as "parlementarisme à la française". Elected deputies saw themselves as sole representatives of the sovereign nation. They (mis-)used their powers (legislation, adoption of the budget, control of government) so that the institutional equilibrium was in structural imbalance with unstable and powerless governments. The Fifth Republic caused an institutional break, deviating from republican traditions. Models were used: the strong American presidency and Bonapartist tradition of direct democracy with plebiscitary referenda. This resulted in an ambivalent institutional complex. The republican model since 1877 gave ultimate power to a majority in Parliament. In a presidential regime the centre of political-institutional gravity is in the hands of the Head of State. De Gaulle did not choose for one of these principles. The result is an institutional mixture with sui-generis character, a "régime semi-présidentiel". This was also a consequence of strong political movements in the Fourth Republic, which wanted to maintain the parliamentary character of the regime as much as possible. The Constitution of 1958, and institutional practices also, have promoted presidential preponderance. Although the Fifth Republic in the beginning was severely criticised by Communists and Socialists, now the Fifth Republic is not generally contested but extreme-rightist Le Pen, losing the presidential elections of 2002 from Chirac, did contest it. The crucial question was whether institutional innovations of the Fifth Republic would survive its founder. With Gaullist Pompidou (1969-1974), progressive-liberal Giscard d'Estaing (1974-1981) and socialist Mitterrand (1981-1995) as successive presidents, the regime of the Fifth Republic developed broad acceptance and legitimacy in society. Neo-gaullist Chirac (1995-2002) as president brought France over the threshold of the 21st century, and was elected president for the first "quinquennat" (2002-2007).

For Berstein (1992, pp. 416-419), the 1958 Constitution brought at least four institutional innovations: a reinforced position of the Head of State; reduction of powers for Parliament; dual influence on Government via President and Parliament; and the "Conseil Constitutionnel". The wording of the presidential functions seems not so different: guaranteeing the continuity of the State, national independence and integrity of the French territory; guaranteeing respect for the Constitution; and taking care of the regularly functioning public authorities with his "arbitrage". New to the Constitution of 1958 was the authority of the Head of State as a result of the procedure for his appointment and his constitutional competencies. The Constitution of 1958 made the President the elected by 80,000 notables, not by parliamentarians as before. The revision of the Constitution in 1962 reinforced the position of the Head of State. By election in general direct elections he got a direct base of legitimacy straight from the people. The President of the Republic became the sole person who is elected by the sovereign people as a whole. The Constitution of 1958 gave the President more power. The President can address himself to the people with referenda about organisation of public authorities. He can dissolve the National Assembly (article 12). Article 16 gives him extraordinary competencies when institutions of the Republic, national independence, integrity of French territory or observance of its international obligations are threatened. To protect liberties of citizens and in relation to a historical distrust in executive authorities and personalised power, republican tradition reduced the position of the Head of State to a decorative role according to protocol, while Government was subordinated to Parliament. Now the Head of State's position was reinforced spectacularly.

In the Third and Fourth Republic, the Parliament was the institutional centre of power. In the Fifth Republic, the role of Parliament is reduced to legislative and budget-controlling tasks. Possibilities for legislative initiatives and for control of Government activities are strictly regulated. Members of Parliament are not allowed to present proposals which reduce revenues or raise the expenditure of the State. The formerly frequently used interpellations about any subject to overthrow Government are now constitutionally excluded. Parliament can force Government to resign in strictly defined circumstances. During the Third and Fourth Republic Government was only dependent on the parliamentary majority. In the Fifth Republic Government is appointed and fired by the President, and Government is responsible to the National Assembly: a "dual drive" of Government. The role of Government can be important. Article 20 of the Constitution rules that Government determines and directs the policies of the nation. This might unjustly be read as if the Premier, with a majority in the Assembly, determines policy without the need of approval by the Head of State. This is what is called the risky "dyarchie" in the heart of the institutional power complex of the Fifth Republic. The first "cohabitation" (a Socialist Head of State and a non-Socialist majority in Parliament) in 1986-1988, second "cohabitation" (1993-1995) and third "cohabitation" (1997-2002) proved that the Head of State can fulfil his functions well in such circumstances. Institutional practices showed that Government is dependent on the Head of State. The "Conseil Constitutionnel" (CC) was a huge innovation. The example of the American Supreme Court (watching over fair procedures at elections; competent to test the constitutional character of laws) is followed partially with this CC. In the Third and Fourth Republic there was no institution above Parliament. Now ultimate authority is vested in constitutional laws, as it should be in a constitutional state. Laws apply to everybody, also to public authorities and national representatives.

The years 1958-1962 were decisive for the institutional build-up of contemporary institutions of the French State. The national drama of the Algerian crisis hit French individuals in their daily lives. A military coup, chaos and civil war threatened France. These fundamental problems could not be solved because of fundamental dissension. The vast majority of the people were convinced that only De Gaulle had the necessary prestige to restore order. De Gaulle did what they wanted him to do and he used these critical circumstances to give France other public institutions based upon his matured conception of the State. He fulfilled his task as strategic manager by putting his institutional conception into the Constitution of 1958. He gave this constitutional text its legitimacy with the acceptance of the French people. De Gaulle put his seal on this Constitution, sometimes going too far. The Constitution of 1958 was accepted by the people, and he said that the institutions could be adapted. In his "Mémoires d'espoir" (t.1, Le renouveau, p.341, 1970), he wrote: "The new institutions are in place. From the top of the State, how will I adapt them? Largely, it's up to me to do this." He thought that he could reinterpret presidential competencies, if that was useful for his idea of the State.

Presidents after De Gaulle used the presidential powers exhaustively; even Mitterrand, one of the most fierce critics of De Gaulle and his institutional innovations. As opposition leader without any chance whatsoever of becoming President himself, Mitterrand in his book "Le Coup d'État permanent" (1964), could not find a positive point in the Constitution of 1958, of which De Gaulle was the "auctor intellectualis". Once President himself Mitterrand used all the powers given him. This contributed to Socialist acceptance of the Constitution of 1958. Mitterrand and others rightly criticised De Gaulle's personalised autocratic way of exercising power. De Gaulle, as a sovereign, forced his interpretation of the Constitution. He determined the reach of his power and he imposed his will on Government and humiliated Parliament time and again. Once elected by general direct elections, he thought it redundant to be accountable to anybody, except to the nation, by preference in a theatrical performance on TV. The "domaine réservé", policy domain reserved for the President (international politics, defence, European Community) was extended ever more. Every Minister had to co-ordinate his policy with an expert from the President's staff. The French President's "arbitrage" caused a "présidentialisation de l'exécutif". President Mitterrand controlled Government policy dominantly in 1981-1988 and 1988-1993, relying on a parliamentary majority. From 1993 on, President Mitterrand was less interventionist. It was the "cohabitation douce" with Balladur as Premier (Balladur, 1995). Practice deviated from the "bicephalous" executive intended by the Constitution, the Premier played second fiddle (an "orleanist" position). For the Constitution, the Premier is accountable to the Assembly, in practice, he is accountable to the Head of State. In a controversy, the Premier can bow or quit (the Gambetta-formula).

*3.3.2. De Gaulle and his ideas*

It is necessary to distinguish the views of De Gaulle himself from those of his followers, some of whom have very different ideas about what Gaullism means (Petitfils, 1994). Due to these different interpretations of Gaullism, less significance can be given to the phrase ascribed to De Gaulle: Everybody has been, is or will be Gaullist. Shortly after the Second World War, the following of De Gaulle in French population was extraordinarily massive, the stubborn collaborationist adherents of Pétain excepted. This was due to De Gaulle's prestige during the war (War Gaullism). After his resignation in January 1946 Gaullism was more ideological, due to his indefatigable campaign against the "old political parties". His constitutional ideas (Bayeux speech, 16 June 1946) were opposed to conceptions of most important political movements (Communists, Socialists, Republicans). Many remained aloof from De Gaulle's opinions, while an important minority followed De Gaulle (Political Gaullism). Over the years many named themselves Gaullist on very different grounds. Those who were enthusiast followers, since "the man of 18 June 1940" spoke about freeing France form Nazi-terror, those who were grateful for his role as liberator of France, those who joined him in his constitutional convictions, those who supported him coming back to power in 1958, those who approved the "Accords d'Évian" about the Algerian question (1962), those who stood behind his foreign policy and those who were members or voters of one of the Gaullist parties. Petitfils differentiates between three levels of Gaullism: conceptions; transformation of conceptions in institutions; and political movement.

The axis around which all ideas of De Gaulle rotate is formed by the objective of making France a strong nation. Therefore "grandeur" is the target, independence of France the condition, and power the instrument. Although striving for the "grandeur" of France to the utmost, De Gaulle diagnosed that the former position of France as one of the superpowers was over and done with. In his conception, based on ideals such as humanitarian solidarity and Christian humanism, France has a task to propagate in the world the values it has developed in its history. Values such as freedom, human dignity and other ideals to enlighten the world with the universalism of French culture (moral leadership). France has a special mission, as defined by De Gaulle on 31 July 1964: "The character of its genius has made of France a ferment and a champion of human liberation." For De Gaulle, there was a real possibility to act as a superpower in the theatre of the world but this meant sacrifices. Internal policy had to be subordinated to foreign policy in a "politique de grandeur". During the Cold War this meant that France had to build up an independent position with regard to United States and Soviet-Union. With this conceptualisation, De Gaulle continued to build upon time-honoured conceptions of the sovereign nation-state. To be a free nation, independence is necessary. Therefore, De Gaulle fought passionately against all sorts of external dependence. By accepting the armistice in June 1940, Pétain had lost in his eyes every legitimacy. Since 18 June 1940, De Gaulle had seen himself as representative of the real, free and independent France. Although he had not the tools to fulfil expectations. During the war the "Anglo-Americans" time and again did not take De Gaulle very seriously when he insisted on being acknowledged as a complete ally. This confirmed De Gaulle in his refusal to accept the Yalta-division in two blocks (Tourette, 2000). In his decision to withdraw France from the integrated command structure of NATO and in his resistance to the supra-nationality of European institutions. For De Gaulle international and supranational concepts had to recognise nations and peoples as ultimate, hard realities. Peace in the world could be based on co-operation of nation-states only. De Gaulle argued for a united Europe from Atlantic Ocean to the Urals, but a "Europe des États-nations", a confederation of sovereign states with a leading role for France in a European Europe (without American hegemony).

Independence and "grandeur" cannot reach far without sufficient power. In the 19th century protectionism, agriculture and the colonial empire had given France a position of power. In the 20th century, it was evident that economics and technology were decisive therefore France had to concentrate on modernisation. De Gaulle's strategy was focused on the modernisation of French industry. France had to attain a prominent position in the world with prestigious technological projects ("Concorde, Secam, plan calcul, énergie atomique"). Next to economics and technology, military strength is seen as an essential power base. Promptly after his comeback in 1958 De Gaulle suggested in a memorandum that France form with the United States and Great Britain a military directorate of the three countries with nuclear weapons. De Gaulle reacted to the expected refusal by building up independent French nuclear weaponry. France was withdrawn from the integrated command structure of NATO. The "force de frappe", the French nuclear weapon system, had strategic objectives. France had autonomy for decisions about the use of nuclear weapons in European and mondial armed conflicts, not only as part of NATO. Independent nuclear weaponry had to guarantee that France as nuclear power could participate on an equal footing in the international game of diplomacy, based upon deterrents.

A penetrating analysis of French history convinced De Gaulle that a countervailing power had to be created, despite the natural inclination of the French for mutual discord: "le vieil esprit gaulois de sectes et de factions". A strong and just State was the answer. De Gaulle was a declared opponent of the Marxist concept of class society, which would split up the national community. Uniting citizens, above all sorts of differences between political parties, interest groups, religions and societal classes, was the issue. Referring to attempts in French history – "Union des patriotes" (1793); "Union sacré" (1914); "La Victoire" (1918); and "La Libération" (1945) –, De Gaulle formulated the central objective: assemble the French for France. Gaullism, especially in the conception of De Gaulle, was not so much the doctrine of a political party. He saw political parties as interest groups for a section of the people, not as representative of the population as a whole. Political parties could not free themselves from political games. De Gaulle had no confidence in intermediary structures between citizens and public authorities ("corporatisme"). When De Gaulle took the initiative to establish the "Rassemblement pour la France" (RPF), he did not see the RPF as a party like other political parties. Unlike Communism and Fascism (totalitarian one-party state), Gaullism accepts pluralism of political parties. Gaullism claims that it stands for the higher options of the nation being superior to all ideological values. Fighting Gaullism was seen as fighting France itself, as separatism or as an anti-French attitude. Gaullism was meant to free the French from traditional discord, but it provoked deep controversies. "Parlementarisme à la française" reduced the French State to a powerless symbol of immobility. Gaullism wanted to restore order and create a strong regime, not dependent on factions and political parties.

To organise a strong State it was seen as a necessity to give one person ultimate responsibility for the interests of the French State. The President as "the man of the Nation, above all political combinations, who as a referee guarantees the regular functioning of public authorities, and the continuity of the State under all circumstances." Because the President has to represent the French Nation, he should not present himself as representative of a specific political party. He has to derive his power and legitimacy not from the (majority of) Parliament, but directly from the people. De Gaulle thought the influence of political parties could be mitigated by a system of electing the President by a college of respected personalities, as was the original arrangement in the Constitution of 1958. Direct election of the President, as was made the rule with the modification of the Constitution in 1962, conformed more to the conception of De Gaulle. De Gaulle was partisan for a strong President, but he rejected the American system of a strong president (the function of Premier abolished, and executive powers for legislative authorities). In the Constitution of 1958, the President as Head of State assumed extensive powers formally, outside the "domaine réservé" of the President (defence, foreign policy), the leadership is given to Government. The principle of separation of powers was met in the Constitution of 1958, but the centre of gravity was shifted from Parliament to executive power, with the President as executive head.

An important part of the Gaullist unitary logic is societal reconciliation. On Labour Day, 1 May 1950, De Gaulle said in Paris that the sterile class struggle should be ended, as it poisons human relations, disrupts States, wrecks the unity of nations and causes wars. The spirit of reconciliation had to change the approach of employers and employees A third way in between capitalism and state socialism, as used by other movements, should be the guideline. Gaullism favoured association between capital and labour, and participation. A more specific characteristic of Gaullism can be seen in its voluntarism, its "philosophie de la volonté" (Petitfils, 1994, p.28). This philosophy implies that circumstances are not accepted as definite even when the situation is, in reality, hopeless, as with the defeat of 1940. When Pétain chose for an armistice, De Gaulle decided to go to London and to continue the fight against the Nazis. De Gaulle was deeply influenced by the ideas and circumstances of his time as well as by history. Some authors assert that there is a resemblance between conceptions of De Gaulle and Charles Maurras, leader of the "Action Française". In "Enquête sur la monarchie", Maurras pleaded in favour of a hereditary, anti-parliamentary and decentralised monarchy. Both detested French parliamentarism and had a desire for "grandeur de la France", but there were substantial differences. Maurras wanted to restore privileges of the Ancien Régime after restoration of French unity around the king. He adhered to a corporative society with an important position for intermediate structures.

De Gaulle, however, disliked intermediate structures between citizens and State which reduced the power of the State. De Gaulle was a "Jacobin" centraliser. He took the attainments of Revolution and Republic as realities. De Gaulle kept himself aloof from the extreme-rightist conservative ideas of Maurras. He took his inspiration from christian-democratic and social-catholic concepts. Although in the beginning De Gaulle was positive about the Christian-democratic MRP, later he had reservations because of his ideas about all political parties. There were important differences between Gaullism and Christian-

Democratic ideas. Christian Democracy is inspired by a Christian concept with pluralism, autonomy for natural communities, parliamentary democracy and the organic construct of democracy. The living tissue of society with families, organisations, natural and spiritual communities is starting-point. De Gaulle, as a real Jacobin, did not like intermediary structures between the people and the State. Christian-Democrats in Western Europe were in favour of European integration. De Gaulle was an adherent of solid ties with other European countries only when France had the lead and without supra-nationality. "Fédéraliste à l'extérieur, le général est jacobin à l'intérieur." (Petitfils, 1994, p.40). Gaullism cannot be reduced to one other doctrine, it is a result of nationalist traditions in France (Touchard, 1978).

*3.3.3. The Gaullist movement*

Gaullism is not only an intellectual construct, but also a movement in political practice. When De Gaulle resigned as Premier on 20 January 1946 because his objective of an adequate military budget was not supported, he thought to be back soon in the political theatre with more powers. At the end of 1945 his Government had the unanimous support of the National Assembly. Controversies between the leading political parties were so fierce, that an appeal to De Gaulle seemed inevitable, but political parties did their best to prevent a comeback of De Gaulle, who was known to hate their traditional practices. On 16 June 1946, he presented his ideas on necessary constitutional reforms. Capitant and others established the "Union gaulliste" in July 1946. This yielded ten deputies in the November 1946 elections. After adoption on 27 September 1946 of the second draft for a constitution by the Assembly, De Gaulle criticised this draft and made his ideas about the strong State known. The draft of the new constitution was adopted in a referendum by 1/3 of the electorate (massive abstention). According to De Gaulle, this constitution, supported by a minority, gave too much power to political parties and National Assembly. The authority of the State was unacceptably weakened. De Gaulle appealed to the French people to rally around his person in the interest of France. On 7 April 1947, he announced the establishment of the "Rassemblement du Peuple Français" (RPF). The RPF tried to profile itself not as a new political party, but as a "rassemblement", a movement bypassing all social, political and religious discords. It was possible to be a member of a political party and of the RPF as well. Soon the RPF became a common political party with some themes: criticism of the Fourth Republic; reforms of State institutions; association of capital and labour; maintenance of French overseas territories; resistance to German rearmament; and fierce anti-Communism. De Gaulle had stigmatised French Communists on 27 July 1947 as separatists, as they put themselves outside the French community by behaving as subordinates of the Communist party in Moscow. At municipal elections of October 1947, the RPF scored a remarkable success with 40% of the votes in municipalities of more than 9,000 inhabitants. The greatest municipalities chose a Gaullist majority. The general's brother, Pierre de Gaulle, became president of the Parisian municipal council. The RPF campaigned for dissolution of the Assembly and new elections.

In spite of De Gaulle's campaigning himself in every part of France this project failed. Other political parties organised a counterattack. They rejected the double membership (of a political party and of RPF). In the electoral law a complex mechanism was inserted by which Communists and RPF could be isolated. In the elections of June 1951, Gaullists got 16.5% of the votes and 117 deputies, second after Communists. This was less than De Gaulle expected: with 200 deputies the system could be blocked. De Gaulle started using the methods of the political parties he'd always hated, systematic opposition. Dissidents of RPF voted once for Premier Pinay. This group was then expelled. They formed the "Action républicaine et sociale", in 1953 part of "Centre national des Indépendants". When more politicians kept aloof from RPF, De Gaulle sneered about people who don't want to fight and take their soup. It became worse, when RPF supported Government-Mayer in January 1953. When RPF got fewer votes than before in the elections of April 1953 De Gaulle decided to give parliamentarians more room by mitigating voting discipline. Gaullist deputies formed the "Union des Républicains d'Action Sociale" (URAS). On 20 June 1953, Gaullists voted for Government-Laniel with three URAS ministers. Gaullists participated in Government-Mendès France. On 2 July 1955, the second time in the wilderness began for De Gaulle, who announced his intention to remain aloof from politics. Once freed from De Gaulle's control, Gaullists identified themselves more with the Fourth Republic. In the January 1956 elections the "Républicains Sociaux" (successors of RPF) had a huge loss. They got 800,000 votes against 4.3 million votes in 1951. They missed the charisma of De Gaulle. If there had been no Algerian crisis Gaullism would have been extinguished. With the Algerian crisis, the "République gaullienne" (1958-1969) developed. A totally different Gaullism came on the political theatre.

André Malraux's dictum is pregnant: Gaullism is like the metro, one does meet everybody there. For more than half a century, Gaullism showed a remarkable continuity of ideas and people. Publications of contemporary personalities during De Gaulle's years such as Debré, Michelet, Fouchet, Noël, Soustelle and others proved intensive involvement in Gaullism. A fertile soil for Gaullism developed during the "Résistance". The idea was that it was possible to bridge the gap between French individuals with their political, religious and social discords, and to unite them in a passionate fight for France. After common tribulations as comrades in arms many wanted to continue the fight in politics. The staff of the RPF was largely recruited from "Résistance" and "France libre" (Charlot, 1970). The first generation of Gaullists had such common experiences as the collapse of France in June 1940, the betrayal of Pétain with his sudden armistice, De Gaulle's appeal on 18 June 1940 to continue the fight of the Free French, the dramatic war, resistance against Nazi terror, and Liberation. These "historical Gaullists" were welded together by strong ties of comradeship. Since 1962, a new generation of Gaullists came to the fore. At the UNR-UDT congress in November 1967, modern Gaullists defeated the old guard. To ensure that after the resignation of De Gaulle in 1969 leadership did not fall into the wrong hands, "Présence du gaullisme" was created. In June-July 1969, the parliamentary club "Présence et action du gaullisme" was formed. The third generation of Gaullists came up at the beginning of Pompidou's "septennat", "jeunes loups" (young wolves) Chirac and others. Chirac revitalised the movement with the new RPR in 1976. A fourth generation of Gaullists (Juppé, Toubon, Séguin) are named "Chiracquistes". They have come to the forefront since Chirac was Premier (1986-1988). Neo-Gaullists won legislative elections (1993) and Chirac won the presidential election in 1995, so Neo-Gaullists had all power positions in their hands (Presidency, government, parliamentary majority). Chirac called parliamentary elections in 1997 (instead of 1998). This caused a huge loss for his party. Socialists won, and Socialist Jospin formed a government with Communists and Greens. Chirac fought back, and by beating extreme-rightist Le Pen in 2002 became president again for the years 2002-2007. In the parliamentary elections of June 2002, Chirac's "Union pour la Majorité Présidentielle" (UMP) got a majority. So, Neo-Gaullists had all power positions in their hands again.

*3.3.4. Independent, sovereign "grandeur" of France as central theme*

The field in which De Gaulle had the most adherents, from left to right in all political parties and movements, was foreign affairs. This was especially because De Gaulle always, consistently and uncompromisingly, defended the national independence and sovereignty of France. In the Cold War, French authorities allowed some concessions by making France a member of alliances to further Western European security, but at all times and in all circumstances France had been very keen to defend national sovereignty. De Gaulle sneered at that "régime des partis" which had given away part of French sovereignty to NATO and the European Community. At the height of his power in the "République Gaullienne" (1958-1969) he was actively trying to restore the position of France in the world. He radicalised with his "politique de grandeur", trying to challenge the position of the superpowers US and Soviet-Union. De Gaulle came far by creating an autonomous position for France. He knew that France had lost its dominant position since the First World War, but De Gaulle wanted to give France the first position among nations in the second range after the superpowers. All his activities in the military, economic, social and cultural fields were secondary to that sole objective: making France a powerful, independent and self-conscious nation-state deciding as much of its own fate as possible.

The Constitution of 1958 replaced "Union française" for the French Empire in the Constitution of the Fourth Republic by "Communauté", formed by France and its overseas territories. This institutional arrangement implied that organs of this "Communauté" had competencies in the field of defence, foreign affairs, monetary matters and economic policy. At the head of it was an executive with the French President of the Republic, Premier and competent Minister, and the Premiers of member-states. The consultative Senate of the "Communauté" had 186 French delegates and 98 delegates representing the other 13 States. In a referendum of 28 September 1958, electorates in overseas territories could choose for membership. Only Guinea chose for independence. The "Communauté", intended to be the French Commonwealth, survived two years. Senegal and Sudan, forming the Republic of Mali since January 1959, asked for independence, while continuing membership of the "Communauté". When other member-states asked for the same status the law of 4 June 1960 institutionalised this. All member-states chose this formula. In 1961, the common institutions of the "Communauté" went out of use. While French-speaking former colonies of France were independent states now, France kept an overwhelming influence in these countries. This was made operational by a huge program of helping these young States with financial aid, technical assistance and military support. The African policy of De Gaulle, in spite of the failure with the "Communauté", was successful for the time being. It achieved stability south from the Sahara, and mostly gave French enterprises continuation of markets in this region. It was part of a policy for emanation of French culture, a basis for a global role for France.

A crucial feature of De Gaulle's legacy is the imperishable memory of his attitude to the US (Paxton/Wahl, 1994). After the experiences with his Anglo-American allies during the Second World War and its aftermath, De Gaulle, back in power since 1958, was convinced that the 1949 arrangements in NATO were outdated. It was obvious to him, that it was no longer necessary to make French security dependent on the American nuclear umbrella. Since Kennedy became President in 1961, American military strategy had changed. Under the leadership of Robert McNamara, the idea of massive reprisals in the case of Soviet aggression against the US or its allies, was backed up by the strategy of flexible response. The US, before using nuclear weapons with a long distance range, would employ the conventional arsenal of NATO and then nuclear weapons with a short and medium-distance range. This escalation system could be interrupted any moment. A hot telephone line between presidents of the two superpowers was installed in 1963. Europe seemed to be the privileged battlefield for a war between the superpowers. For De Gaulle, it was obvious that France had to be involved in decision-making when its security was at stake. An agreement between the US and Great Britain was signed on 3 July 1958 concerning confidential information in the nuclear field and the selling of atomic submarines and uranium to Great Britain. Dulles refused De Gaulle the required nuclear support unless De Gaulle would accept the installation of strategic intercontinental ballistic missiles (ICBM) under NATO control. Confronted with the build-up of an Anglo-American directorate, De Gaulle sent a memo to President Eisenhower and Premier Macmillan on 17 September 1958, proposing to form a tripartite directorate of NATO (US, Great-Britain, France). This would be responsible for deciding common military strategy, control of atomic weapons and nuclear secret information and in this way France could veto any nuclear decision of the US. The answer of the American president was negative, of course. In February 1959, De Gaulle decided to withdraw the French Mediterranean fleet from the integrated command structure of NATO. De Gaulle: "The defence of France has to be French!"

When in 1962 France was at last free from its Algerian problem it had built up a nucleus of a French nuclear weapons. In July 1962, Kennedy proposed a "grand design". American leadership would be replaced by Atlantic partnership with Western Europe, based on two equal pillars. There was only one exception. US would maintain the nuclear monopoly ("one trigger only"). American nuclear potency would be integrated with the British nuclear program and French "Force de frappe". At the end of 1962, Kennedy made it concrete with the project of a multilateral force. This implicated bi-national warships with American nuclear weapons. Premier Macmillan accepted this in Nassau (Bahamas). The US proposed to make Polaris missiles available for European allies within the NATO framework. Only the American president would have competence to decide on implementation. De Gaulle rejected this on 14 January 1963. De Gaulle developed a military strategy which was essentially different from the Pentagon approach. In June 1963 De Gaulle withdrew his Atlantic fleet from the integrated command structure of NATO, and he brought French air forces under national control again. He forbade Americans to introduce atomic bombs to France, and in September 1964, he refused French participation in naval manoeuvres of NATO. In May 1965, he prevented French participation in the "Fallex" war game. These actions could be seen as pinpricks, but were part of a carefully prepared long-term strategy. On 7 March 1966, this became clear in a personal message of De Gaulle to President Johnson. De Gaulle announced that France would remain member of NATO and would not use the possibility of article 13 of the Atlantic Pact to withdraw from the alliance within three years. France would fight with its allies against aggression as before, but was restoring its sovereignty, which was injured by the permanent presence of allied military organisations on French territory. He said he had decided to withdraw France from the integrated military command structure of NATO. After all his earlier pinpricks America was warned. At a press conference of 21 February 1966, he argued that a new definition of French military strategy was needed. De Gaulle said that each time the US is militarily active somewhere in the world (Korea, Cuba, Vietnam) there is a risk that Europe will become involved also by NATO Even if Europe does not want involvement. On 9 March 1966 The French Council of Ministers approved this, on 1 July 1966 French representatives in military organisations of NATO were withdrawn. On 1 April 1967 all North-American military bases on French soil were dismantled. With these actions France provoked the US and its other allies. France continued to fulfil engagements in the Atlantic alliance though.

De Gaulle knew better than anyone that the position of France as second-class world power depended upon its economic production, technology and military potency. Therefore, modernisation of French industry was a vital part of his strategy. Public opinion in France was shocked by Servan-Schreiber's "Le Défi Américain" (1967). He argued that within 15 years the third industrial power in the world after the US and Soviet-Union would be American industry in Europe. De Gaulle promoted advanced industrial projects: supersonic aeroplane "Concorde" (with Great Britain); "SECAM" (television); nuclear submarine "Redoutable" (since March 1967); "Plan Calcul" (informatics); etc. With regard to the military potency of France, De Gaulle's impulses were all the more decisive, while building upon foundations laid during the Fourth Republic. Since March 1952, Ailleret had argued that France needed nuclear strategic weapons (Doise/Vaïsse, 1987). In 1954, government-Mendès France decided to stimulate research and production of nuclear weapons and submarines. The debacle of Dien Bien Phu (Americans refused to rescue trapped French with aeroplanes and nuclear weapons) made decisions easier. France was dependent with regard to atomic weapons. Rearmament of West Germany and its membership of NATO helped the development of a French nuclear weapon. France could have superiority in this field, forbidden to Germans.

During the Suez-crisis (1956), the Soviets threatened to use their nuclear weapons. To avoid this kind of atomic blackmail Government-Mollet decided in 1956 to accelerate the nuclear program. A committee-Ély was asked to develop a project "force de frappe aérienne". In 1957 the construction of experimental nuclear sites was started near Reggane in the Sahara. The first explosion of a French nuclear bomb was planned for spring 1960. When De Gaulle came into power in 1958 he reorganised fragmented activities so far. He made the "force de frappe nucléaire" a coherent key-project. On 13 February 1960 the first French nuclear bomb was exploded at Reggane. "Hourra pour la France!" said De Gaulle's wire message. It took 8 years to produce the first French H-bomb at Mururoa in the South Pacific (August 1968). For De Gaulle, the French nuclear weapon had not only a military objective. The "Force de frappe" gave France a prominent position as semi-superpower. So France could challenge American hegemony, claiming a position equivalent to that of Great Britain. Credibility was a crucial aspect of the nuclear weapon: was it able to discourage a potential enemy? This meant availability of nuclear material and transport facilities to hit an aggressor at home.

For De Gaulle the "Force de frappe" was the instrument to confirm the position of France as independent nation-state. In 1967, the "Force de frappe" was formed by 62 "Mirage IV" built in Dassault plants. These were divided over 9 airports and could transport A-bombs of 60 kilotons. In 1964 "Forces Aériennes Stratégiques" (FAS) were operational. The French nuclear weapon was ridiculed as "bombinette" but its credibility became stronger year by year. Transport systems, with a limited range of some 3,000 kilometres, were vulnerable. From 1960, the "Missile sol-sol-ballistique-stratégique" (SSBS) was developed, operational from 1971. Construction was prepared of nuclear submarines in 1960, with 16 "Missiles mer-sol" (MMS), containing a nuclear warhead of 500 kilotons and with a range of 2,500 to 3,000 kilometres. "Le Redoutable", the first, was launched in March 1967, followed by others like "Terrible" and "Foudroyant". All were advanced weapons for nuclear deterrence and practically undetectable. From the seventies onwards France had a credible strategic nuclear weapon making France the third nuclear power. It was composed of the "Mirages IV", "SSBS" at the plateau d'Albion, and "MSBS" on operational nuclear submarines. After the experiences of military revolts and kidnapping of public authority the Constitution of 1958 ruled that armed forces were subordinate to civil public authorities. The President of the Republic was made "chef des Armées". A decree of 14 January 1964 ruled that the President of the Republic had supreme power over the strategic nuclear weapon. He was to be the sole eventual implementor of the nuclear deterrent by "pressing the button", so making the concept of nuclear deterrents concrete. Up to the middle of the seventies, the French doctrine of military strategy was based on "dissuasion" (discouraging). The objective was not winning a nuclear war, but making a war between nuclear powers impossible. The perception was that a nuclear war between the US and Soviet-Union would imply total destruction of Europe. The French strategic concept rejected the American flexible response. It was based on "dissuasion du faible au fort" (discouraging of the strong by the weak). De Gaulle argued (23 July 1964): "From a certain nuclear capacity on, the proportion of means has no absolute value." After De Gaulle withdrew France from the integrated command structure of NATO in 1966 the character of French nuclear strategy changed. This was built on "sanctuarisation absolue" of its territory with massive reprisals. No nuclear reaction as long as an enemy did not enter French territory. When an enemy crossed the threshold there would be a total nuclear reaction. In principle the French nuclear weapon could hit anywhere; this was the "stratégie tous azimuts".

French sovereignty was for De Gaulle the criterion to evaluate the process of European integration. Before his coming to power in 1958, France signed the Treaty of Rome (1957), creating EEC and Euratom. The ECSC was in function earlier (1951). Founding fathers of the European Community were inspired by ideals of growing European integration with supranational European institutions. They thought it useful to start with economic integration, forming a Common Market, supplemented by political integration. De Gaulle launched his idea of "Europe des nations", accentuating the sovereignty of nation-states. He criticised supranational constructions led by "technocrates apatrides" (European Commission; majority vote in the European Council of Ministers). De Gaulle made EEC partners accept the formation of a committee-Fouchet, elaborating ideas about political co-operation. The "Plan Fouchet" (October 1961) proposed a "Union des États" with common foreign policy, defence policy and cultural policy. Heads of State would form the Council, deciding with unanimity. This would imply forming of a classic international organisation (Gerbet, 1983). The "Plan Fouchet" was buried after May 1962.

De Gaulle had another chance of blocking European integration by refusing to accept the entrance of Great Britain in the Common Market. Since 2 August 1961, British government had been asking for membership of European Communities. De Gaulle was adamant; he saw Great Britain, orientated always towards big brother US, as a kind of Trojan horse in the EEC. De Gaulle made his unilateral decision known on 14 January 1963, despite the fact that the other member-states of the EEC were in favour of Britain's membership. This provoked a crisis in the EEC, coming to the fore in 1965. Negotiations about the common agricultural policy did not give the French enough results. They wanted more subsidies for farmers, a mighty pressure group in France. De Gaulle withdrew French representatives in the European Communities on 1 July 1965: the politics of the empty chair, which paralysed the EEC for six months. The other EEC member-states complied though the "compromis de Luxembourg" was no compromise at all, it was an agreement that the five EEC partners disagreed with France. This was a blow for EEC decision-making. As it stood unanimity prevailed. Each member-state got a right of veto, when one member-state said that its vital interests were at stake it could block proceedings, contrary to the spirit of the Treaty of Rome. Europe was interesting for De Gaulle as it gave France opportunities to play a role in the world. After a conversation with De Gaulle in 1961, Premier MacMillan said: "He speaks about Europe, in fact it's about France." (MacMillan, 1972). A steady part of De Gaulle's activities in Europe was building up good relations with West Germany. In 1963, De Gaulle and Adenauer signed a French-German treaty for regular conversations between the two heads of state. When Adenauer left office (end 1963), relations cooled off.

### 3.3.5. Several interpretations of Gaullism

The political thinking of De Gaulle himself forms a part of Gaullist ideology. In all Gaullist movements, favourite themes of De Gaulle recur: national independence, authority of the State, economic progress, and social participation. There are several interpretations of Gaullism, due to the vagueness of parts of the doctrine of De Gaulle and different gradations and dosages are used. One might say that there are as many gaullisms as there are societal groups: "Gaullisme d'affaires", "Gaullisme jacobin", "Gaullisme technocratique et mendésiste", "Gaullisme activiste" etc. Despite this variation of interpretations, according to Petitfils (1994, p.102) there are three major Gaullist movements: orthodox Gaullism; liberal-opportunistic Gaullism; and leftist Gaullism. Orthodox Gaullism sticks rigidly to the ideas of De Gaulle. In this movement, we find Michel Debré, who put his mark on the Constitution of 1958; Couve de Murville and Messmer, one of the driving forces for the "force de dissuasion nucléaire". Sanguinetti, Lefranc, de Saint-Robert, Pasqua and Séguin can also be mentioned. These orthodox Gaullists, a minority with regard to the Gaullist liberal majority, are impassioned opponents of European integration, especially of supranational interference with national sovereignty. The more liberal and pragmatic Gaullists handle the range of De Gaulle's ideas more flexibly. They think it necessary to stick to the basic ideas of De Gaulle but they are convinced that they have to adapt to circumstances. These pragmatists have found their political ideal in "Pompidolisme", because of the fact that neo-gaullist President Pompidou proved the significance of pragmatism in political practice. Édouard Balladur, Premier in the 1993-1995 period, was an exponent of liberal Gaullism. Most Gaullists since 1981 keep aloof from De Gaulle's ideas about economic interventionism. It might seem contradictory since Gaullism rejects a right-left dichotomy, but leftist Gaullism is another movement. Leftist Gaullists prefer to take as policy targets: independence (non-alignment with American and Russian imperialism) and participative society.

De Gaulle and Gaullism deny political parties the right to represent the national interest. A central paradox of Gaullism is that, after the resignation of its founder, it was not possible to continue this movement without becoming a political party. De Gaulle always denigrated political parties. The difference between "Gaullisme Gaullien", based on absolute loyalty to De Gaulle, and partisan Gaullism was manifest. There was continuity between RPF, UNR and contemporary RPR. Around this political party system of Gaullists many clubs, associations and networks have been functioning, all claiming to act according to De Gaulle's ideas. The "Rassemblement du Peuple Français" (RPF), established in 1947, was a success. In October 1947, RPF had some 1.5 million members. So RPF even surpassed the Communists. Gaullism in the regions had a different set of adherents. It was strongly represented in the Parisian region, northern France, Gironde, Finistère, Alsace, Lorraine, and urbanised regions like Marseilles and Lyon. Over the whole territory of France an organisation was built up. Next to this territorially based organisation, there came a professional network of organisations, which penetrated in all professions and groups. "Action ouvrière" mobilised several hundreds of enterprises. There was a "service d'ordre". The movement did not have a strong position in the press. The organisation of the RPF was authoritarian and centralised. This party required that representatives behaved with a kind of blind obedience to the party, causing many to leave. In January 1954 the "Centre national des Républicains Sociaux" was created under the dominant influence of parliamentarians.

Because RPF did not have the expected success at elections, with the start of the new Republic the "Union pour la Nouvelle République" (UNR) was established on 1 October 1958 with a collective leadership. At first, the UNR was more or less a committee to select candidates for elections. These had to be absolutely loyal to De Gaulle. As Chaban-Delmas said: "The UNR has to be the party which can govern at the left and at the right, guaranteeing equilibrium, the party in power." On 14 April 1959 a group of leftist Gaullists with Capitant and others formed the "Union démocratique du Travail" (UDT). Under pressure from De Gaulle the UDT decided to connect the electoral lists of UNR and UDT after the legislative elections of November 1962. The UNR-UDT became an electoral party. Results at elections in March 1967 were disappointing. With the leadership of Pompidou, a national directorate of five members was formed, regularly discussing political claims of parliamentarians with the Premier. At the congress at Lille (24/26 November 1967) Pompidou won a victory over historical Gaullists. He could modernise the party organisation. The party got the name "Union des Démocrates pour la Ve République"

(UDVe). After May 1968, the name became: "Union des Démocrates pour la République" (UDR). In the elections of 1974 the UDR had some 250,000 members, the second largest membership after the Communists (PC).

The Gaullist movement was passing through a crisis since De Gaulle's resignation in 1969. After the defeat of Chaban-Delmas at the presidential elections in 1974, caused by Chirac, the Gaullist movement seemed to fall to pieces but the coup of Chirac in December 1974 gave new hope. There was a spectacular revitalisation. On 5 December 1976, the "Rassemblement pour la République" (RPR) was created. The RPR became a real political party, with some 850,000 members in 1986. It had a centralist structure; party president Chirac had the power. Gaullism became "mouvement chiracquien", "Gaullisme chiracquiste". Over the years different Gaullist organisations have been active. The orthodox "Association nationale d'action pour la fidélité au général de Gaulle" became a centre of documentation. The "Service d'Action" (SAC), established in 1958 by militant Gaullists from the "service d'ordre" of the RPF, was dissolved in July 1982. The most right wing faction of Gaullism formed "Comités de Défense de la République" (CDR) with more than 100,000 adherents in 1969 after the crisis of May 1968. The "Union des Jeunes pour le Progrès" (UJP) represented "Gaullisme intégriste". Leftist Gaullists attempted to form a countervailing power against rightist movements in Gaullism but mutual conflicts, personal rivalries and few adherents meant that leftist Gaullism had only little influence. In October 1966, a regrouping was tried with the "Convention de la gauche Ve République", but this failed. In 1971, Grandval tried a new regrouping with the "Union travailliste". Leftist Gaullists supporting Pompidou formed the "Mouvement pour le Socialisme par la Participation" (MSP), a federation of "Union de la gauche Ve République", "Démocratie et Travail" and "Front travailliste".

The composition of the Gaullist electorate was analysed regularly (IFOP, 1971). For Petifils (1994, p.117) three main aspects characterise the Gaullist electorate after 13 May 1958: two different Gaullisms (Gaullism of De Gaulle; partisan Gaullism); Gaullism becoming a national party; and the shift to the political right. The "Gaullisme gaullien" was unapproachable when De Gaulle in "la belle époque du gaullisme charismatique" (1958-1962) had an unprecedented popularity. At the first three referenda the yes-voters were not less than 75% of the vote, although the UNR got less than 20%. After 1963, De Gaulle's popularity diminished, reaching its lowest point with the miners' strike. Then came a recovery, but the former level was not reached, because the heroic leader of all the French seemed to have become merely the partisan leader of a political majority. Partisan Gaullism was a success: 4.1 million votes in November 1958; 6.5 million in November 1962; 7 million in 1967; and 9.6 million in 1968, then adherence to Gaullism declined: 5.6 million in 1973; and 6.3 million in 1978 (the electorate had grown from 24 to 28.5 million). In 1951, Gaullism was a typical phenomenon of industrial northern France, after 1967 penetration of Gaullism in central and southern France was stronger. Gaullism spread more over the whole nation. In 1973, adherence to Gaullism fell back at the elections. The elections of 1981 were lost, but Gaullism had a remarkable comeback. This caused two periods of "cohabitation" (1986-1988, 1993-1995) with a strong position in the National Assembly. In May 1995, Chirac was elected President. A third aspect of Gaullism is the shift to the political right. Gaullism in 1958 attracted more than 1.5 million votes from Socialists and Communists, but the electorate underwent a shift to centre-right. Extreme-right of Le Pen with his xenophobia gained adherents, as the right wing of Gaullism was thought to be too moderate. The RPR deviated from the intentions of De Gaulle to break the traditional left-right dichotomy by forming a "rassemblement" for all French. The ideas of founding father De Gaulle have gone through a process of wear and tear, or became more or less the common property of several political parties. Since 1977 Communists have supported the "force de frappe nucléaire". Since 1978 Socialists have done the same.

In forming his ideas, De Gaulle could draw from the inexhaustible history of France, so he could appeal to many French by corroborating their self-confidence. The ideas of De Gaulle are not the property of one political party or group. According to Petitfils (1994, p.125) the French absorbed Gaullist ideas as a common heritage for all French in their collective consciousness. De Gaulle's concepts will influence institutions of the French State far into the 21st century. More than De Gaulle planned, political parties have a prominent position in the Fifth Republic. According to Suleiman (1995, p.144), the Fifth Republic is even more a party-politicial regime than the Fourth Republic. The instability of the Fourth Republic was caused by weakness of party-politically dominated structures. In the Fifth Republic, the party-political majority can dominate the regime. Two crucial factors are the presidential and the electoral systems. It remains to be seen if and in what way "Gaullisme chiracquiste" will realise deviating arrangements. When Neo-Gaullists lost the majority in the National Assembly after the decision of President Chirac to change the date of the legislative elections to May 1997 (instead of 1998), frustrations were deep. The fighting spirit of the Neo-Gaullists was vital as always. Pasqua in his "Adresse à mes compagnons" (Le Monde, 21-10-1997): "Around those basic principles of our community – national sovereignty, values of the Republic, authority of the State – the Gaullist movement appeals again to all French, and not to some social class, category or corporation. It will reconquer its base in the population." Since the spectacular victory for Chirac at the presidential elections in 2002, his newly formed electoral cartel, "Union pour la Majorité Présidentielle" has the majority in the Assembly. The Neo-Gaullists have all power positions in their hands.

## 3.4. Public authorities and organisations

*3.4.1. Public authorities and organisations with a national scope*

Following the historical sketch of French Public Management of Society, it is time now to give a sketch of public authorities and organisations. It is necessary to distinguish right from the start between public authorities and organisations on the one hand, and private organisations on the other. Of course, there is also a wide variety of public-private arrangements, and in contemporary society hybrids are a popular phenomenon (Hupe et al., 2000). In a number of studies, the concept of a political system is taken as starting-point, making all kinds of organisations part of it: political institutions (parliament, government), political parties, mass media, business organisations, other private organisations, interest groups. In an often inadequate and inconsistent way, even jurisdiction and the whole body of public functionaries are considered to be part of the political system. Insofar as these studies are concerned with the power-related interrelatedness of all kinds of societal organisations and groups, so far so good. When the specific position and responsibility of public authorities is at stake, this approach of politics-as-all-encompassing is inadequate. This approach is currently popular. Many authors emphasise the fading away of differences between public and private organisations.

Authors writing specifically and exclusively about institutions in the sphere of public authority often use the term "political institutions". They define these institutions as political, using the notion political in at least a double sense: as power-related phenomenon and as exclusively related to public authority. That is inconsistent and inconsequent. Either the specific characteristic of public authorities is qualified as political, in which case all phenomena, not related to public authorities are not political, or all power-related phenomena are called political (also those of public authorities), but then qualifying public authorities as political institutions is incorrect. If this is made plausible, the term Public

Management of Society (the sphere of public authorities) is adequate as distinct from private management. Another approach makes the notion of politics subordinate to the notion of human organisation: not public administration versus business administration, but administration or organisation as such. Administration or organisation is thought to enclose political organisations. Whatever can be said about these terms, we should use the term Public Management of Society, as more adequate than political institutions, when we deal with the functioning of public authorities. Political institutions (parliament, government) and not-political institutions (jurisdiction, offices, police, army etc.) are both part of Public Management of Society.

In a State, public authorities representing the Nation-State are as necessary as a territory and people. Bonds of nationality interconnect all citizens in a Nation-State, the people. The Nation-State encompasses all inhabitants of the State territory and all who have nationality. In a constitutional State, competencies of public authorities are defined precisely, legitimising these as specific representatives of national community, the Nation-State. In constitutional logic, public authorities have the right and duty to act as public authorities in so far as they function within the reach of their constitutional competencies. Philosophers have questioned the right of human beings towards their fellows to enforce obedience to their decisions and regulations. A constitution is a recognised institution to provide legitimacy for persons acting in the name of the Nation-State, as public authorities. In French monarchy, public authority of the Kings was based upon divine law. They purported to act in the name of God. After the French Revolution, public authorities had to be accepted by representatives of the people. Public authority was subjected to law, expression of the "volonté générale" (Rousseau). Since then, France has had several regimes with different levels of power for public authorities. In the Third Republic, the dominant concept resulted in a kind of dictatorship of parliament, provoking governmental instability. The Fourth Republic resembled this with comparable French parliamentarism. The 1958 Constitution laid foundations for a different regime reinforcing the executive branch, especially for the President. Public authorities with a constitutional base have a specific status. A sketch of these public authorities is useful.

The Head of the French State according to the 1958 Constitution (articles 5-19), is the President of the Republic, residing in "Palais de l'Élysée, 55 rue du Faubourg-Saint Honoré in Paris. With more powers than presidents in the Third and Fourth Republic (Masso:, 1986; Pouvoirs, 1987). Since constitutional reform after the referendum of 1962, the president has been elected directly for a seven-year term ("septennat"), until in 2000 the decision was taken to change this to a five-year term ("quinquennat"). In his function as Head of State, the President of the Republic has the tasks of all heads of state, but more than elsewhere he determines foreign policy and defence matters ("domaine réservé"). The President is commander-in-chief of the armed forces and has far-reaching powers to guarantee independence of France as well as the primary role in diplomacy. He alone decides the use of French nuclear weaponry ("force de frappe"). He alone can push the button (decree of 14 January 1964). The President is the guardian of the national interest and has to guarantee that the Constitution is respected. The President presides over the Council of Ministers. He is competent to proclaim laws, which have to be signed by him. The President also signs "ordonnances" (legal regulations of government which do not need to pass through Parliament), and decrees of the Council of Ministers. When he thinks a law, accepted by Parliament, fails to respect the Constitution, he may present this law to the "Conseil Constitutionnel" with the constitutional competence to test laws on their constitutionality. The President appoints the Premier and, on proposal of the Premier, other ministers. He can also fire them. He has the power of appointment to key positions in the Government, armed forces, civil service and judiciary. He can dissolve the Assembly and may call a referendum. When he thinks the French territory or French institutions threatened, he can use extraordinary powers (art. 16 Constitution).

The "Premier Ministre", appointed and dismissed by the President, resides at "Hôtel Matignon", 57 rue de Varenne in Paris. The President chooses the Premier freely, but usually appoints a Premier who is politically trusted by a parliamentary majority. After the defeat of the Socialists at the 1986 elections, President Mitterrand chose Chirac, leader of the largest party, as Premier: the first "cohabitation". According to the Constitution, the President dismisses the Premier, who presents the resignation of his government. In practice, the President dismisses the Premier as he chooses. The Premier presents candidates for his ministers, but the President has the last say. The Premier directs government as "chef de l'Administration" (article 21 of the 1958 Constitution). Apart from the President's "domaine réservé", he is responsible for national defence. On behalf of the government, the Premier can present bills to the Assembly. He ensures implementation of laws and has "pouvoir réglementaire" (to issue legal decrees). The Premier appoints civilian functionaries, excluding appointments which are for the President. He can delegate competencies to ministers and he can propose a revision of the Constitution to the President. By putting the vote of confidence in the Assembly, he can engage the responsibility of his government. Before the President can use extraordinary powers in case of emergency he must consult the Premier. Government has a "cabinet", with politically sympathetic assistants who come and go with their Ministers.

The "Gouvernement" according to article 20 of the Constitution formally determines and directs the policies of the nation. The government is composed of Premier, Ministers and Secretaries of State (only participating ad hoc in the Council of Ministers). The President appoints members of government. Unlike the Third and Fourth Republic, there is no investiture of government by Parliament. When the Premier presents the resignation of government to the President, government is substituted. When the President ends the appointment of a Minister ("révocation"), there is only a ministerial reshuffle. A Minister can resign, as Alain Savary did in 1984 when his bill for a public service of education was a failure. Alain Devaquet, a Minister in the Chirac government, resigned after mass demonstrations against his proposals to reform universities. Formally the Assembly cannot, as in the Fourth Republic, force a Minister to resign, but it can make his political life so unbearable that the Minister may as well resign. Members of government get a "lettre de mission" with a definition of their responsibilities. The number of Ministers and Secretaries of State can vary. Article 23 of the 1958 Constitution rules that the function of a member of government is incompatible with "every parliamentary mandate, each function of national professional representative, and each public office or professional activity." It is not possible to combine the function of member of the Assembly and that of Minister. Strangely enough another "cumul des mandats" was popular: being a Minister and a Mayor. Former Premier Juppé (1995-1997) could combine this function with his position as mayor of Bordeaux (not a small town!). The government-Jospin (1997-) lived up to electoral promises (for this part) by not using this kind of cumulation of political functions. Government can meet in "Conseil de cabinet" (Premier as president) while the "Conseil des Ministres" (every Wednesday) is normally presided over by the President of the Republic. A "Comité interministériel", presided over by the Premier, brings together members of government involved in a specific policy area. Each member of government is responsible under civil law and can during the exercise of his function be condemned to pay compensation to private persons. They are also responsible under criminal law for crimes and offences committed during the exercise of their function. The "Cour de justice de la République" acting as judge.

The "Assemblée Nationale", meeting in Palais-Bourbon, is according to the 1958 Constitution (articles 24-33) the most important house of Parliament, the "Sénat" being the upper house. Since 1985 there are in France 555 polling-districts. The National Assembly has 577 "députés", 555 for France itself ("métropole"). Members of the Assembly (minimum age 23 years) are elected normally for a five-year term at direct universal elections. This period can be shortened when the President dissolves the Assembly, as President Chirac did in 1997. He gave away his parliamentary majority to the Socialists, who formed government-Jospin with the Communists. To reduce elections between times, according to the "système de suppléant" a substitute takes the place of a deputy who ends his function. The election system is called "scrutin uninominal majoritaire à deux tours" (one deputy chosen per constituency in elections with two rounds). Candidates participate in the second round only if they score at least 12.5% of the total entitled to vote. So large political parties are favoured and bi-polarisation is promoted. The forming of a "troisième force" is made difficult (parties are forced to make voting arrangements to combine their lists). Smaller political parties are therefore in favour of a proportional voting system. The Assembly, legislative authority, votes "projets de loi" (law proposals of Government), or "propositions de lois" (proposals from Parliament). The Assembly has to control the activities of Government, by voting the budget ("projet de loi des finances"), asking questions etc. The Assembly can force Government to resign with a motion of censure. The Assembly has two sessions. In Spring starting 2 April, lasting 90 days. And in Autumn starting 2 October, lasting 80 days. The premier or a majority of the Assembly can ask for an extraordinary session, opened and closed by presidential decree (Ameller, 1994).

The "Sénat" is the upper house of the Parliament as "chambre de réflexion", meeting in "Palais du Luxembourg" (Pouvoirs, 1988). Political and societal pressures on the Senate are less than for the National Assembly and the President cannot dissolve the Senate. Senators (minimum age 35 years), as elected by the elected, are elected indirectly for nine years. Every three years there are elections for a third of the Senate. The Senate has 322 senators: 296 for France; 8 for overseas departments; 4 for TOM; 2 for Mayotte and St. Pierre-et-Miquélon; and 12 who represent the French living outside France. In each department, a "collège des électeurs de sénateurs" is formed, composed of members of National Assembly, regional, departmental and municipal councils. The election system is different in proportion to the number of senators a department can elect. With 1-4 senators in a department, there is the "scrutin majoritaire à deux tours". For departments with more than 4 senators it is the "scrutin de liste à représentation proportionnelle". Splitting up of administration with more than 36,500 municipalities (33,000 less than 2,000 inhabitants), favours smaller municipalities. Towns and cities with more than 30,000 inhabitants, 22.5% of total population, have 10% of the electors. This election system is seen as the explanation for the rightist composition of the Senate. The Senate presents amendments and "propositions de loi", and votes on the "projets de loi" of Government, it controls the activities of Government, but it cannot overthrow Government. Both houses of Parliament have six permanent commissions, which fulfil preparatory work in the legislative process. Chapter V of the 1958 Constitution (articles 34-51) shows that executive power, not legislative power, is the dominant power in the Fifth Republic.

A specific public organ with a constitutional base is the "Conseil Constitutionnel", or CC (articles 56-63 of the 1958 Constitution), residing in the "Palais-Royal", 2 rue de Montpensier in Paris. Its task is to take care of respect for the Constitution and for the regular course of elections and referenda (Avril/Gicquel, 1995; Pouvoirs, 1980). The CC is composed of the former Presidents of the Republic and of nine other members (1/3 appointed by the President of the Republic; 1/3 by the president of the National Assembly; and 1/3 by the president of the Senate). Every three years one-third of the CC is renewed. Members are appointed for a non-renewable 9-year term. Before the proclamation of organic laws, qualified laws completing the Constitution, the Constitutional Council has to test constitutionality. The head of state, premier, presidents of National Assembly and

Senate may ask that the CC tests the constitutionality of laws decided upon in Parliament before their proclamation ("saisie du CC" postpones proclamation). Since the constitutional reform of 29 October 1974, either 60 deputies or 60 senators may ask the same. The CC has to take a decision within a month. In case of urgency the Government may ask for a decision within 8 days. A CC decision is definitive, there is no appeal. A text declared unconstitutional by the CC cannot be proclaimed or implemented. The CC can mediate between Government and Parliament to determine boundaries between "domaine de la loi" and "domaine réglementaire", it also has a function in exceptional situations; the CC ascertains a vacancy of the Presidency and has to advise before the President of the Republic uses the extraordinary powers of article 16 of the 1958 Constitution.

The "Haute Cour de Justice" (art. 67 of the 1958 Constitution), since a constitutional revision of 1993, has 24 members appointed by and from both houses of Parliament. Until 1987 this jurisdiction had no cases. Since then, a series of grim debates have been going on over several affairs. In December 1987 the affair of Nucci, former Minister, concerning fraud with public funds (amnesty). In December 1992 the "affaire du sang contaminé" (contaminated blood) in which former Premier Fabius and Ministers Dufoix and Hervé were involved. The parliamentary majority made it impossible for this case to be decided by the "Haute Cour de Justice". Public opinion interpreted this as an indication that Ministers cannot be prosecuted according to penal law. This resulted in pleas for reforming the "Haute Cour de Justice". On the basis of a report-Vedel a constitutional reform was prepared. Since the constitutional modification of 27 July 1993 the President can be judged by this court for serious offences when a majority of both parliamentary houses requests this with a resolution signed by at least 10% of parliament. Discussions before this court are in public. There is no appeal against a decision of this court. Since a law of 23 November 1993 Ministers are judged for serious offences by the "Cour de Justice de la République".

With the constitutional revision of 27 July 1993, the "Conseil Supérieur de la Magistrature" (CSM), residing at 15 quai Branly in Paris, was given the function of taking care of the independence of jurisdictional authority. Originally the head of state appointed members of the CSM, as De Gaulle wished (article 65). This was criticised, because such an independence of the judicial authority might be compromised under political pressure. Public opinion polls showed that a majority of the French doubt the independence of judicial authorities. Amnesty for former politicians was seen as an improper intervention of the (politicised) executive in the competencies of judicial authorities. The position of judges with respect to citizens was thus undermined. In some cases there was obvious pressure from political parties to start legal procedures against some persons, or to drop cases against specific persons. Article 64 of the Constitution rules that the President of the Republic has to guarantee the independence of jurisdictional authority. The President of the Republic is president of the CSM, the Minister of Justice is vice-president. The CSM advises on the appointment of "magistrats du siège" (judging judges) and "magistrats du parquet" (public prosecutors) and is disciplinary council for these functionaries. "Conseil d'État" (CE), residing in the "Palais-Royal" in Paris, has jurisdictional and advisory functions (Robineau/Truchet, 1994). The CE was formed by the Constitution of the year VII (1800). According to the 1958 Constitution, Government is obliged to ask the advice of the CE for "projets de lois" (article 39), drafts for "ordonnances" (article 38), and "projets de décrets" with modifications of legislation ante-dating the 1958 Constitution, now falling in the "domaine réglementaire" (article 37). The jurisdictional role of the CE is to judge important cases and as court of appeal for decisions of "Tribunaux administratifs"; and to be "Cour de Cassation" for special administrative courts.

The "Conseil économique et social" (CES), residing at 1 avenue d'Iéna in Paris, with a constitutional base in articles 69/71 of the 1958 Constitution, participates in elaboration of socio-economic policies and advises Government. The CES is formed according to ideas developed during the "Résistance" against the Nazi occupation: all living socio-professional forces in society should participate in national policy. Government is obliged to ask their advice on all bills and programs, and preparation of the "Plan". Government. The CES presents an analysis each half year of the past semester and an advice for the coming semester. The CES can take the initiative to advise Government over diverse matters. Since the 1984 reform, it has been composed of 231 members, appointed or designated for a five-year term. 70% of members are designated by organisations (trade unions, associations) and 30% appointed by Government. The CES has nine specialised sections: finance; regional economics and planning; social matters; labour; agriculture and food; foreign relations; general economics and conjuncture; production, research and technology and living conditions. Sections prepare advices for plenary sessions.

Following the Swedish example of the Ombudsman, in 1973 "Le médiateur" became a French institution. The French Ombudsman is independent and doesn't get instructions from any public authority. He is appointed for a 6-year term (not renewable) by decision of the Council of Ministers. He has an apparatus, with professionals, which analyses all complaints against any part of the French administration. The Ombudsman has correspondents in departments, working permanently in prefectures. He is free to present recommendations to Government and every part of administration. Publication of recommendations and criticisms in the "Journal Officiel" is his most effective instrument. The "Médiateur" has "pouvoir d'injonction": when the sentence of a court is not (adequately) implemented he can invite the authority involved to implement the sentence within a fixed term. If this does not have the intended effect, a report can be published in the "Journal Officiel". This threat is generally enough. Every person, and since 1992 every corporate body, can go to the Ombudsman in the case of (supposed) damage by a public organisation. This must be done via a member of the Assembly. Yearly more than 35,000 files are examined. The annual report is published in the "Journal Officiel".

In the French centralised structure, the "Grands Corps de l'État" have a prominent role: "Cour des Comptes", "Inspection Générale des Finances", "Contrôle Général des Armées", "Diplomatie". The "Cour des Comptes", residing at 23 rue Cambon in Paris, has the task of verifying the legality and appropriateness of public expenditure (Raynaud, 1988). It also examines the organisations of social security, public enterprises and affiliations. Under specific conditions, even private organisations using public finance (subsidies etc.) and organisations invoking "public generosity". Since a law of 10 July 1982, amended by a law of 5 January 1988, "Chambres régionales et territoriales des comptes" verify the expenditure of municipalities, departments and regions and their "établissements publics". Appeal against the decisions of this audit office to the "Cour des Comptes" is open. For (a cluster of) municipalities with less than 2,000 inhabitants and no more than 2 million francs as revenue, the audit ("apurement administratif") is done by "trésoriers-payeurs généraux" or "receveurs particuliers des finances". The annual report of the "Cour des Comptes" to the President is published. Recommendations are published in the "Journal Official". Since 1991, the "Cour des Comptes" has published the reports of audits. It supports Parliament by auditing implementation of the "loi des finances". Responsible functionaries committing budgetary irregularities can be punished with sanctions of the "Cour de discipline budgétaire". At the same address reside "Conseil des impôts" and "Comité central d'enquête sur le coût et le rendement des services publics". The "Inspection Générale des Finances" (IGF), residing in the Ministry of Finance, must verify the financial management of public authorities and organisations and of all "comptables publiques et de la comptabilité administrative des ordonnateurs secondaires", "établissements publics", semi-public organisations and enterprises under the economic or financial control of the State. Mostly inspectors are detached to the organisations they have to inspect. Another inspection is the

"Inspection Générale de l'Administration", residing at 15 rue Cambarécès in Paris. This has 22 general inspectors, 15 inspectors and 19 adjunct-inspectors. It has the task of examining the general course of events in public organisations of the State and territorial administrations and in public enterprises. There is also the "Contrôle Générale des Armées", residing at 14 rue St. Dominique in Paris. They check all parts of the armed forces.

"Diplomatie" as "Grand Corps de l'État" has a crucial role in the relations of France with other countries. Since 1945 the career of French diplomats starts at the "ENA". In 1726 diplomacy meant study of international treaties and since 1774, the art of negotiating these treaties. In former times personal relations between monarchs and heads of state dominated international relations. Heads of State, Premiers and Ministers of foreign affairs did not formerly travel frequently, so negotiations between representatives of countries took place via "missions diplomatiques". As missions were expensive in the XVth-XVIth centuries, permanent representation by a lower level came into use. Representation of the French State in foreign countries is at three levels: "ambassadeur", "consul" and "attaché". In 1993, France had 147 embassies, 16 permanent representations, 4 delegations and 124 consular posts in other countries. Diplomatic personnel, family and domestic personnel included, enjoy diplomatic immunity on the basis of the Convention of Vienna (18 April 1961). "Exterritorialité" implies "inviolation personnelle" (arrest or deprivation of liberty is forbidden); "inviolabilité de la correspondence diplomatique" (opening or seizing "valises diplomatiques" is not allowed); "inviolabilité de l'hôtel" (immunity of residence of "chef de mission"); "inviolabilité des archives diplomatiques" (inviolability of archives). Personnel have diplomatic passports.

A specific organisation is the "Commissariat Général du Plan" (CGP). On the basis of a note from Jean Monnet (4 December 1945) Premier De Gaulle, after a decision of the Council of Ministers, signed the decree of 3 January 1946 establishing the CGP. Monnet was appointed the first "Commissaire au Plan". The CGP became the centre of the "planification à la française", a specific kind of indicative planning in a mixed polity combining State interventionism and market ("économie orientée"). Since the first Plan (1947-1953), there were succeeding plans up to the XIth Plan (1993-1997). Plans were made to steer socio-economic development in France. Mostly study groups were formed to analyse important issues. They came with prominent reports as guidelines for policy. A good overview is found in "Le Xe Plan 1989-1992" by P.Y. Cosse (1989). After the tenth Plan, preparations started for the eleventh plan (1993-1997) resulting in a series of important reports. The working-group Charpin published the report "L'économie française en perspective" (1993). The objectives of the eleventh plan were: "Réussir l'Union européenne" (Making the European Union a success); "Lutter contre le chômage" (Fighting unemployment); "Favoriser une société plus soucieuse de l'homme et de la nature (politique de la ville intensifiée et lutte contre l'exclusion)" (Promoting a more caring society); "Rénover l'action publique" (Renewal of public action).

*3.4.2. Public Administration*

(Party) politics has a primary role in the functions of the President of the Republic, Government and Parliament (political administration). It is different with the bureaucratic part of public authorities and organisations (public administration), but (party) politics can and does play a role here also. Differentiation between political administration and public administration is not a vehicle for an absolute politics-administration dichotomy. The administrative apparatus of the French State, "L'Administration", comprises the central and de-concentrated administrations, spread throughout the territory of France (and abroad). Central administration is under hierarchical authority of Government and has national tasks. The Premier is supported by the secretary-general and his staff, co-ordinating the activities of ministries. Each Minister has authority over the personnel of his ministry (central offices in Paris, and de-concentrated field organisations) for the preparation and implementation of policies. De-concentrated field organisations have the task of implementing the laws and regulations of all ministries in the whole of France. They have relations with "collectivités territoriales" (regions, departments, municipalities). Each territorial administration disposes of its own services to implement decisions of elected local representatives: "conseil régional" (regions), "conseil général" (departments) and "conseil municipal" (municipalities). A crucial distinction is made between decentralisation and de-concentration. The strongly centralised French State finds its structure in concentrating power in a centralised, political decision centre as executive power (President and Government) and in central administrations in Paris under the authority of Ministers. To mitigate the centralist character there are two principally different methods: decentralisation and de-concentration. By way of decentralisation, competencies of the State are transferred to local, politically autonomous institutions (the State loses competencies). With de-concentration competencies of central administrations are transferred to de-concentrated organisations, under the hierarchical authority of the Government.

France has a centralised, concentrated, structure of power and administration. Since 1970, it has been evident that this over-centralisation and over-concentration reduced the efficacy of Government and administration. Central administrations were structurally overburdened, often with less important questions and this contributed to the slackening of decision-making. Many ten thousands dossiers were transported to Paris and back and decisions had to be taken often without adequate knowledge of local circumstances. Decisions were frequently made in a stereotyped bureaucratic and uniform way, while circumstances were very different. By taking the same decisions for fundamentally different situations, application of the principle of equality (treating equal cases equally) was perverted (unequal cases treated equally), but there is room for intelligent and creative interpretation of regulations, to find solutions in a pragmatic way, on the margins of the rigid-legalistic system. In the French constitutional system, de-concentration can take place, with "règlements' of Government, as it is about the internal organisation of the State. Decentralisation asks for legislation, because the relation between public authorities is changed with regard to competencies and finances. Implementation of administration can be more effective when competencies are transferred to the functionaries who are more directly confronted with the problems.

In the case of de-concentration, competencies are given to dependent de-concentrated authorities. De-concentrated services of the State are subordinate to prefects; they are subordinate to State administrations. In the case of decentralisation, the power to decide, competencies and responsibilities are transferred to autonomous, decentralised authorities, local public authorities without a-priori tutelage. Locally elected authorities are accountable to their voters, while they are submitted to an a posteriori control of legality. In the last decennia, various forms of partnerships were developed to make it possible for de-concentrated services of the State to function as real partners with local authorities within the same administrative territory, so it is not necessary to ask for permanent instructions from central administrations before they can act or decide. There are various policy areas where it is not possible to act without co-operation between a de-concentrated authority and a decentralised authority, as with the "Revenu Minimum d'Insertion", decided upon by the State and giving people the rights to a minimum income, while the departmental "Conseil général" is responsible for "insertion" (trying to give them work etc.). Simultaneous decision-making by de-concentrated and de-centralised authorities is needed to reach consensus.

Up until 1992, concentration was the rule and de-concentration the exception in the administrative system. Nearly all competencies were concentrated in the hierarchical top, the central administrations of the State. Decrees had to be very detailed about de-concentrated tasks. A push to change this came from the Chirac government in 1975 with the "décrets anti-remontées". These were meant to give more responsibilities to local representatives of the State. And also to relieve the overburdened State bureaucracy: "Le mal français", defined by Peyrefitte (1976) as follows: "France is expiring from a stroke, because all the blood has gone to the head." Over the years, various methods were practised to reduce centrifugal tendencies in administration, such as "évocation" and "parapluie". With "évocation", central administrations of the State can always deprive de-concentrated services of a dossier and handle it. Politicians can realise their preference for having a dossier handled by the ministry of a politically friendly Minister. Politically sensitive dossiers are lifted in the administrative hierarchy, eventually by the request of pressure groups. With the "parapluie", a local functionary passes a politically delicate and technically complicated dossier to a higher echelon in the hierarchy. With the argument that it is not obvious which of several possible norms have to be applied the general centralised sphere promoted this kind of abdication of responsibilities.

Concentration manifests itself in the regime of circulars, often degenerating into "pseudo-legislation". Circulars with specified, detailed regulations are sent to de-concentrated services, to give indications for the application of laws, regulations and decrees. Many thousands of circulars from Paris flood the offices of de-concentrated services. Detailed circulars often don't give any room for practical application or adaptation to local circumstances. In the heydays of over-concentration (1962-1974) circulars frequently had an imperative character towards local authorities, adding new regulations for the interpretation of laws. Administrative jurisdiction reduced this in a number of cases. Local authorities and functionaries were often so legally docile that they cultivated the "régime des circulaires" cult rigidly. The inefficiency of over-concentration was demonstrated in studies, but the reform and modernisation of public administration habits are longwinded. Functionaries kept asking for detailed circulars, otherwise they didn't know how to handle matters ("orphelins de la circulaire"). Local functionaries had to learn to use the latitude given them. Decentralisation since 1982, and the de-concentration started later on, gave the impulse for modernisation. A law of 6 February 1992 concerning "l'administration territoriale de la République" was intended to start a Copernican revolution with systematic de-concentration: "To central administrations are entrusted only tasks of a national character, or those which, on the basis of the law, cannot be delegated to a lower, territorial level, other tasks, especially those which involve relations between State and territorial public organisations, are entrusted to de-concentrated services." (Article 1). At the request of a local authority, de-concentrated services have to give all professional help on the basis of conventions, so there is an explicit relationship between decentralisation and de-concentration.

The administrative organisation of the State over the whole territory of France is structured. Important administrative bases for State activities are the Regions, Departments and Arrondissements. The State organisation also adapts itself to Cantons and Municipalities. The notion "département" is used in different meanings. As "collectivité locale, le Conseil général et ses services", and as "circonscription administrative de l'État (le Préfet et ses services)". The ministries of old organised their own subdivisions, using the departmental framework. More recent ministries (Environment etc.) opted for a regional administrative structure. Geographical boundaries of a ministry coincide with the framework of Region or Department. For "Éducation Nationale", the "Recteur" is the de-concentrated authority over a specific geographic area ("l'académie"), encompassing some Departments, not necessarily coinciding with the Region. Jurisdiction and armed forces have specific geographical areas. Before the decentralisation legislation (1981) cumulation of functions for de-concentrated services of the State was normal. "Direction départementale des affaires sanitaires et sociales" (DDASS) was the de-concentrated departmental administration of the State, and the apparatus under the authority of the departmental "Conseil général" due to the fact that the prefect is State representative in the department, and head of the executive branch of local authorities. The first law of decentralisation of 2 March 1982 proclaimed separation of State authorities and services, and authorities and services of "collectivités territoriales". Field organisations of the State don't have competencies in administrations falling under local authorities.

The local apparatus of the State comprises "institution préfectorale" and the de-concentrated services of ministries. "Préfets de département", created by the law of "28 pluviôse an VIII" (1800) of Napoleon, resemble the "Intendants de l'Ancien Régime". "Préfets" represent the State in the departments. With the establishment of regions in 1964 "Préfets de région" were installed. At the "arrondissement" level, the "Sous-préfets d'arrondissement" have the same competencies as Prefects, on the basis of delegation. Prefects of Regions and Departments and sub-prefects have ample competencies, they represent Government and have authority over functionaries of field organisations of the State working in their area (except in some cases). The Prefect has to take care that laws, regulations and the decisions of Government are implemented. In addition to Prefects with general competencies there are "Préfets de Police" in Paris, Marseilles, Lyon and Bordeaux. Decentralisation legislation (law of 2 March 1982, decree of 10 May 1982) changed the position of Prefects fundamentally. Before this legislation, the Prefect was the representative of the State and head of the department, since then, the Prefect is representative of the State, Government and Ministers in his department. His competencies are less far-reaching than before. The president of the departmental council got his role as executive head of the departmental council.

Prefects are appointed as "autorité interministérielle déconcentrée", with a decree from the Council of Ministers, on the recommendation of the Minister of the Interior, the superior of Prefects, who can terminate their function at any time. Prefects generally continue their function for 4 years in the same Region or Department. Experience showed that they often behaved as feudal lords, or developed too close a relationship with local authorities (neglecting their national responsibilities). Such a relationship between Prefect and local authorities would threaten the central authority of the State. The Prefect is the representative of the State, politically loyal to the Government, so changes in national political relative power ("alternances") induce substitution of Prefects. Gaullists had the power in the period 1958-1974, and they appointed practically only adherents as Prefects. This was an aspect of the defamed "État-RPR". In 1974, a number of RPR-prefects were substituted by "préfets giscardiens", contributing to the rupture between Giscard d'Estaing and Chirac. After the Socialist victory in 1981 rightist Prefects were substituted by leftists ("État-PS"). Shifts in political power also caused the substitution of prefects in 1986, 1988, 1993, 1995, 1997 and 2002. Like other functionaries, Prefects have a grade and a function When they lose their function, they keep their grade. Shifts in political power on the national level have produced a number of "Préfets hors cadre". Recruitment of Prefects has latterly taken place less on the basis of party adherence and more for professionalism, with some consideration of political affinities. Prefects must be top functionaries with a full awareness of their function as State representative. The "Préfet de région" is Prefect of the Department where the chief town of the Region is located. He is president of the "Conférence administrative régionale" (CAR). As primus inter pares with other Prefects, he co-ordinates administration. De-concentrated State services don't have authority over the services of the department.

Official functionaries, "fonctionnaires publiques", have functions in administrations of the State, a territorial administration or an "établissement public" (hospitals etc). France has millions of official functionaries, more than a quarter of the active professional population. They have a "fonction publique" a specific status. The "Statut Général des fonctionnaires" has two "concours" to get a job as an official functionary. A "concours externe" for candidates with specific certificates, and a "concours interne" for functionaries with seniority. Functionaries belong to a "corps" with some grades composed of echelons. Figures from the 1990s give an idea of numbers of functionaries in several ministries: "Éducation nationale" 1,058,300; Defence (without conscripts) 405,200; Economics, finance and budget 177,900; Interior 163,100; Equipment and transport 113,100; Justice 57,200; Agriculture 29,700; Social affairs 26,200; Culture 12,100; remaining ministries 41,800. There are alternatives for employment as public functionaries. Public tasks can be contracted out to individuals (as to the "Fermiers généraux" for tax collection in the Ancien Régime) or to corporations: concessions, delegations etc. It is possible to have elections for functions (judges, members of a jury). There are two concepts. The Left, in solidarity with unions of functionaries, adheres to "service publique en régie directe" and enlargement of the number of functionaries (after the Second World War by nationalisations). Rightist movements are in favour of reducing the number of public functionaries. Recently privatisation has taken place with the support of both right and left.

Before the decentralisation movement of 1981, there were two different "statuts de la fonction publique": "statut général des fonctionnaires de l'État" (1946, 1959) and "statut de la fonction publique communale". Functionaries employed by Regions and Departments had no statute, but there were regulations. The statute for State functionaries had some principles; protection of liberties; the right to form unions; guarantee of the job; democratisation by equal entry on the basis of examinations. This statute did not apply to a growing number, because administrations tried to bypass the rigid statute by contracting auxiliary personnel with short-term contracts ("contractuels"). Decentralisation changed the statute. For the "fonction publique territoriale" a statute was made for functionaries of municipalities, departments, regions and their public organisations. Napoleon in his time ordered that, in the case of comparable function and seniority, a functionary of the State should earn 20-25% more than local functionaries. He did this to guarantee the recruitment of elites for the State. Unions, conservatively defending the privileges of State functionaries, were opposed to equal pay for functionaries in local administrations, but equal pay was needed for a flexible transfer from functionaries of the State to territorial administrations and vice versa. Functionaries with a contract, some 340,000 in 1988, had to be integrated and the increased part-time work had to be regulated. The ordinance of 31 March 1982 was for all employees, as was the Decree of 20 July 1982, with general regulations for all functionaries.

A law of 13 July 1983 regulated the rights and duties of all public functionaries (State and territorial administrations). The law of 11 January 1984 established the personnel statute for State functionaries. The "loi-Anicet Lepors" of 26 January 1984 contained the statute for personnel of local authorities. For public health organisations, the law of 9 January 1986 had a personnel statute. In addition to the general statute there are several specific statutes. For territorial administrations these are called "cadre de l'emploi". A law of 30 July 1987 brought some more liberal modifications, especially for local administrations. Regulation of the employer/employee relationship in the framework of the "fonction publique" was delicate. The existing statute prohibited public "patrons" to appoint or fire their personnel, or to motivate some with special premiums, although they were expected to manage with the logic of business. Government-Rocard (May 1988 / May 1991) tried to introduce payment for performance in the "fonction publique", but this caused a lot of commotion. The traditionally high grade of union organisation forced

Government into difficult bargaining for the modernisation of public administration. To eliminate privileges and abuses of the Ancien Régime, the "Déclaration des Droits de l'Homme et du Citoyen" (1789) stated: "All citizens have equal entitlement to all public positions and jobs." The constitutional equal access to public functions is made operational by a system of "concours" and guarantees (equality between men and women, no discrimination on the basis of religion or race) but it is necessary to fulfil several criteria: French nationality, full capacity to exercise civil rights, certificate of health, and professional capabilities. Application of the Treaty of Maastricht (1991) meant that France had to open all public functions (except functions related to the "puissance publique" and sovereignty) to inhabitants coming from a member-state of the European Union.

Official functionaries are classified in "corps" (subdivided in categories A, B, C and D corresponding to a specific level) with the same conditions of access and the same statute. A-functionaries have a diploma of higher education and fulfil functions of management and policy determination. B-functionaries (with a certificate of a higher technical school or a "baccalauréat") have functions with room for policymaking. C-functionaries (professional training corresponding with BEPC) have specialised tasks for implementation, and D-functionaries (with lower or no certificates) carry out the more "simple" executive work. Functionaries, maintaining their salary in one administration, can be temporarily seconded to another administration. In case of "détachement", the functionary, maintaining his rights of promotion and pension, is paid by the administration he is working for. "Disponibilité" means that a functionary who has temporarily finished his work, has to be at the disposal of his employer. When one loses a function, one is "hors cadre", as is the case with prefects at a change of the political majority. Since 1983 parenthood leave is possible for a maximum of two years (no job, no salary). Functionaries are assessed yearly by their principal, on the basis of which promotion is possible for some of them, otherwise seniority is applied. Promotions are registered on a conduct-roll. Functionaries get as salary a "traitement", based upon index numbers, each "corps" having its own indicative salary-scale, mostly with eleven scales.

*3.4.3. Specific public authorities and organisations*

Under the authority of the Minister of the Interior, responsible for maintaining "Republican order" and security of State and citizens, internal security management and security for citizens is entrusted to the "Police Nationale" (for towns/cities with more than 10,000 inhabitants) and the "Gendarmerie" (other municipalities). In the Ministry of the Interior, the "Direction de la sécurité civile" (DSC) has the task of internal security management, including prevention and organisation of operational services (as "Plan ORSEC", help for calamities). "Commissaries de police" have the command, while Inspectors of police, under the authority of a "commissaire de police", are charged with "enquêtes judiciaires" (prosecution) and other inquiries. "Officiers de la paix" command guarding police units; "Gardiens de la paix", which are charged with guarding services. Functionaries of the police, recruited with an examination (concours), work in one of the following directions and services: "Inspection générale de la police nationale" (IGPN) or "Police des Polices" (controlling the police itself), "Service central des polices urbaines" (SCPU), "Direction centrale de la police judiciaire" (DCPJ) fighting criminality, "Direction centrale des renseignements généraux" (DCRG) organising information for Government, "Service central des compagnies républicaines de sécurité" (CRS) for maintaining public order and organising guarding services. Then there are the "Service central de la police de l'air et des frontières" (PAF) the border police (2,875 kilometres land and 3,035 kilometres sea borders; 116 airports), the "Service des voyages officiels" which organises visits of official persons, the "Direction de la surveillance du territoire" (DST) which is charged with combating activities which undermine security and "Service de la coopération technique internationale de la police" which co-ordinates international technical cooperation.

The "Défense Nationale" (DN), charged with external security management, has a special position within the State organisation (Pouvoirs, 1986). National Defence has the task of protecting the country, at any moment and under all circumstances, against all forms of aggression, and taking care of the population's security and guaranteeing the security and integrity of French territory. The President of the Republic, head of state according to the Constitution, is guarantor for national independence, integrity of French territory and the observance of international treaties. He is also commander-in-chief of the armed forces, and competent for decisions regarding the use of nuclear weaponry. The Parliament, by way of legislation, determines organisation and finance of the armed forces. Government is responsible for implementation of decisions taken during meetings under the presidency of the head of state. The Premier is charged with National Defence, and co-ordinaes activities related to National Defence, which fall under several ministries, but the Minister of Defence is in charge of implementation of military policies. Assisted by "chefs d'état-major", he has authority over the armed forces. The French territory in Europe is divided up into three identical "Régions Militaires de Défense" (RMD) for land armies, air force and gendarmerie: "Atlantique, Nord-Est, Méditerranée". These RMD's are subdivided into eight "Circonscriptions Militaires de Défense" (CMD) and a military command for the "Ile-de-France" (the region around Paris). For naval forces, the area is subdivided into two "régions maritimes": "Atlantique" (base Brest) and "Méditerranée" (base Toulon). Overseas departments and territories are organised into five "zones de défense": "Antilles, Guyane, Sud de l'Océan Indien, Polynésie et Nouvelle-Caledonie". Each CMD has a "préfet de zone de défense", charged with civil and economic defence.

In 1995 French armed forces (land forces, air force, naval forces, gendarmerie) comprised some 500,000 men and women. Land forces, organised in "force d'action rapide, force militaire terrestre and forces d'outre-mer", had some 275,000 military, of which 138,000 were conscripts and 34,000 civilians. The air force had some 96,000 military: 34,700 conscripts and 5,000 civilians. "Forces Aériennes Stratégiques" (FAS), with Mirages IV and SSBS-rockets, form the "Force Nucléaire Stratégique" (FNS). The air force could deploy "intercepteurs" Mirage 2000 and Mirage F1 for the defence of French airspace. "Force Aérienne Tactique" (FATAC) had Mirage 2000 and Jaguar. Military transport had at its disposal "Transall, DC 8, Hercules, Mystère 20" and the helicopters "Alouette, Puma, Écureuil, Fennec". The national navy had some 72,000 military: 18,770 conscripts and 6,900 civilians. It is subdivided into the "Force Océanique Stratégique" (FOS) with 5 submarines with launchers at its disposal; "Forces Classiques de Surface" (FCS); "Forces Sous-Marines" (FSM); and "Aéronautique navale". The fourth unit of the armed forces is the "Gendarmerie" with more than 92,000 gendarmes, of which 11,000 conscripts and 1,000 civilians. "Maréchaussée" was renamed "Gendarmerie Nationale" in 1791. "Gendarmerie", charged with public order, security and respect for the law, participates in the military defence of the country. The "Gendarmerie" had 3,642 "brigades territoriales" (50,800 gendarmes); "gendarmerie mobile" (128 squadrons); "Groupement de Sécurité et d'Intervention de la Gendarmerie Nationale"; "Garde Républicaine"; specialised units such as "Gendarmerie Maritime", "Gendarmerie de l'air" etc. In 1996, President Chirac decided on a reorganisation of the armed forces: with the abolition of conscription and a reduction of the regular armed force by some 140,000. A decree of 27 June 2001 abolished conscription.

A specific prerogative of public authorities is the capacity to compel citizens, enterprises and corporations to pay taxes. Fiscal and financial public authorities have to be considered in their specific character. Various forms of taxation were already known in ancient times. In the Middle Ages, there was hardly a public organisation, which could be distinguished from the private household of monarchs. Thomas Aquinas (1224-1274) and others accentuated the legal ground for taxation. They saw taxation as an extraordinary, additional source of resources ("ultimum remedium") to fulfil public functions, when normal income from the royal fortune was insufficient. In the 13th century, the money necessary for public expenses was in the "sac du roi, le budjet". Jean Bodin (1530-1596) in his pioneering "Six livres de la République" (1576-1577), conceived taxation as an extraordinary source of resources, to use only in extreme circumstances (war etc.). Prominent French mercantilist S. de Vauban (1663-1707), in his famous memorandum for Louis XIV of 1695 ("La Dîme Royale"), criticised the existing system of taxation. He argued for the introduction of a general tax on all sources of income. Later, "Physiocrates" had the (wrong) idea that land was the sole real source of riches. They advocated taxation of the net yield of land as sole tax ("impôt unique"), because other taxes would finally devolve onto owners of land. Jean Baptiste Say had his "Law of the market": products are bought with products. In "Traité d'Économie Politique" (1803), Say's thesis was that the best public budget is the smallest budget because of the non-productive character of public expenses. Under influence of English writers on classical economics, P. Leroy-Beaulieu wrote his often used "Traité des Finances" (1877). In the 19th century, the budget was the result of the financial control of Parliament on activities of Government. At the end of the 19th century, law faculties had a chair for "Finances Publiques". Jèze's "Traité de la science financière" was published in 1927 and later, French concepts of taxation and public expenses were influenced by J.M. Keynes and the international discussion.

The "Ministère de l'Économie et des Finances" is one of the most important parts of the French system, because public finances play a crucial role (Pouvoirs, 1990). The "Budget de l'État" is a central tool of public management and administration (Cotteret/Emeri, 1984; Maigret, 1993). The "Direction de la Prévision" of the Ministry prepares macroeconomic prospects: "les budgets économiques d'hiver" (Winter) and "les budgets économiques d'été" (Summer). Preparation of the State budget is a long, continuous process. At the beginning of the calendar year the first phase is started up with preparations for the budget of calendar year + 1. In February the "direction du budget" presents "Perspectives" with detailed data per budget chapter. In March the Minister gets an outline, a three-year projection and an analysis of social funds. Then the Government decides the main points of budgetary policy and the Premier, with his "lettre de cadrage", starts negotiations between "le Ministre du Budget" and other Ministers. If necessary the "Ministre du Budget" or the Premier takes decisions. Budget proposals have to be ready in May and halfway through May Ministers go to "Bercy" to defend their sectoral interests. This produces a list of points agreed upon and a list of points of conflict. In early July Ministers meet the Minister of the Budget to try to resolve remaining problems. Only the most important points are submitted to the Premier, who gives each Minister the budget ceiling in "lettres-plafonds". The parliamentary debate about the bill for the "loi des finances" takes most of the Autumn session. Parliament has the budget power to control Government.

The second phase of the budget process takes place in August and September. In each Ministry documents are drawn up for discussion in Parliament ("les bleus") and the resources for the State budget are determined. When the "bleu général de la loi des finances" has been fixed the bill is sent to the "Conseil d'État". At the end of September the bill is decided upon by the Council of Ministers and presented to Parliament. The bill of the "loi des finances" has to be deposited, at the latest, on the first of October before the budget year. To avoid a system of provisional approval of one-twelfth of the budget for each month, the Constitution ruled that Parliament has to adopt the "loi des finances" before 1 January of the budget year. When Parliament disregards the maximum available term (70 days), Government can decide the budget with an ordinance. In this way executive power can break into the sphere of legislative power. Government has up till now not used this power. After examinations in the first lecture, "navettes" (negotiating contacts) between the two houses of Parliament start to try to reach identical texts. For parts where it has not been possible to reach identical texts a "commission mixte paritaire" (7 deputies and 7 senators) tries to formulate identical texts. Texts of this committee can be presented to Parliament for adoption, but when this committee is also unable to present an identical text, Government, after debate in both houses of Parliament, can ask the National Assembly to take the decision. As with all bills, voting over the "loi des finances" takes place over every article separately. With the "parlementarisme rationalisé", a 1959 organic ordinance reduced the number of votes to some 200 (in comparison with 3,000 votes in the Third and 5,000 votes in the Fourth Republic). The Government can postpone voting over an article until the end of the debate, and request voting over the whole text: "procédure du vote bloqué" (article 44 Constitution). Government can link a vote of confidence to some text (article 49, paragraph 3) and Parliament can force changes in the budget with a majority.

Separate discussion is needed about the "Autorités monétaires". The money system is an essential of the institutional build-up of society. Historically seen, the invention of money was a breakthrough enabling a more effective system than barter. Trust in the money system, based upon control by public authorities, proved to be essential. Originally the mark of the public authorities was the guarantee that coins had the indicated weight. The money system is now seen as a collective good, guaranteeing a reliable societal system of transactions. Three functions of money are distinguished: unit of calculation, means of payment and instrument of saving. During the 17th and 18th centuries metal money was introduced (gold, silver). To create monetary order in the time of the French monarchs coins received, after certification, a mark as a guarantee of legal value. When the concept of French mercantilism was dominant policy was concentrated upon foreign trade yielding as much gold as possible. The law of "Germinal an XI" (1803) defined the value of the franc by relating it to a weight in gold: one gram of gold was declared equivalent with 15.5 gram money. When mutual shifts in the relative value of gold and silver were causing uncertainty, France chose in 1876 for one metal. As long as paper money was at any time completely convertible into gold, nothing went wrong. Before the First World War the gold standard prevailed in the international transfer of payments. Because all currencies were related to gold, physical relations in gold-content determined mutual value relations. During the war this system began to stagger. In 1928, convertibility of the French franc in gold was restored with the "franc Poincaré", equal in weight to one-fifth of the "franc Germinal". So the franc was devalued. Economic crisis forced countries to release convertibility in gold. Paper money meant that mutual value relations were determined in the market. After the Second World War, international money traffic was based on the American dollar, up to 1971 the sole currency related to gold.

In addition to metal and paper money, fiduciary and deposit money came into use. In ancient times the Greeks, Romans and other peoples used some system of written debentures as means of payment. Bills of exchange came into use, especially via Italian and other trade circles, and gradually some banks began to specialise in payments and credit. In exchange for debentures banks gave money. They needed adequate reserves in gold. These banks had the experience that the relation between their gold and the issued money did not need to be 1 to 1. On the basis of a fixed quantity of gold, they could issue a much larger amount of paper money and deposits. A complex money system is functioning at the start of the 21st century, with several sorts of money (cheques, bankcards, electronic money etc.). Whatever the form of the money, trust is a basic necessity in the money system. When this trust fails, everybody flies into real goods. Public authorities stated that paper money and bankcards are legal tender and have to be accepted. Public authorities must defend the monopoly of the "Institut d'émission" ("Trésor Public") to issue legal tender against all endeavours to counterfeit money. Not only public authorities can create money. Within legal conditions, private banks can create money (giving more credit than they have legal tender). Monetary authorities have to guarantee an adequate money system.

All modern states have a Central Bank as "Banque des banques", guarantor for a good money system. The "Banque de France" (BdF), has, since 1848, had the "monopole d'émission". It had the power to issue paper money and to create money as normal banks do (giving more credit than the legal tender they have). The Central Bank can also create money, enlarging the money mass, by giving the Treasury advances and exchanging foreign currencies (a surplus of the trade balance causes exporters to exchange foreign currencies for French francs). Banks, according to their legal permit, are obliged to give clients paper money for deposits, so these banks need to have enough money in reserve. In order to fulfil this obligation these banks, under specific conditions, can get money from the Central Bank with the task of regulating the money mass to guarantee the stable value of the money. In this way the Central Bank transforms the money, created by the second echelon, into officially recognised money. Banks must have an interest-free cash reserve with the Central Bank, fixed in relation to their deposits. When a bank does not have enough cash reserve it has to borrow it. The bank of the French State is the "Trésor Public". By issuing "bons du Trésor" it creates money to finance budget deficits.

The institutional basis of the French banking system was most recently stated in the "loi bancaire" of 24 January 1984 (replacing legislation of the period 1941-1945). Important changes were: participation of France in the European Monetary System from March 1979; reorganisation of the French capital market in the eighties; abolition of controls of rates of exchange in January 1990; more independence of the French Central Bank; and preparations for Economic and Monetary Union (EMU). According to the Treaty of Maastricht (1991) EMU in the third phase (not later than 1999) would lead to a common European currency for member-states fulfilling the convergence criteria: the "euro". A law of 4 August 1993 brought changes. The "Conseil de la politique monétaire" was established, and the "Conseil national du crédit", "Comité de la réglementation bancaire", "Comité des établissements de crédit" and "Commission bancaire". The most important innovation was the new statute for the "Banque de France": "The Banque de France defines and implements monetary policy, with the objective of guaranteeing stability of prices." While French Government determined earlier monetary policy, the French Central Bank has only had a really independent position since the beginning of 1994. In other modern industrial states this had been the case for a long time. It has been proved sufficiently that inflation in countries with an independent Central Bank is significantly lower than in other countries where this is not the case (Schaling, 1995). France at last eliminated its arrears which brought this country disadvantages, because risk premiums had to be paid for the French franc. In money and capital markets one always had to reckon with the real possibility that the French Government, forced by pressure groups, would loosen inflationary control. Since 1983 the Government had adhered to a courageous anti-inflationary policy allowing France to "import German credibility". While France was pioneering in institutionalising separation of legislative, executive and jurisdictional powers, she has had an independent monetary power only since 1994. European institutionalising will reduce national freedom of monetary policy. Since 1 January 1999 the common currency, the euro, was a huge innovation for 11 (12 since 2001) Member-States of the European Union. The European Central Bank took over important functions of the national Central Banks.

*3.4.4. Public Management in territorially subdivided France*

The National territory of France encompasses "La France métropolitaine" (continental France and Corsica), 4 overseas departments and 4 overseas territories (Auby, 1985). Continental France is divided up into 22 Regions enclosing some Departments. There are 4 overseas Regions (Corsica has a special statute). Departments are subdivided into "arrondissements" and "cantons". Continental France has 327 "arrondissements" with 3,715 "cantons", and 12 overseas "arrondissements" (124 "cantons"). French specificity in administrative geography is striking: France has 36,763 municipalities (114 overseas). Municipalities with less than 10,000 inhabitants, with in total 48% of population, form 98% of all municipalities. More than 25,000 municipalities have less than 700 inhabitants. Functional administrative areas often do not coincide with general administrations: social security regions, military regions etc.

Since the decentralisation law of 2 March 1982, "Régions" have become general territorial administrative units, with an elected "Conseil général" composed of "conseillers régionaux" (Turpin, 1986). Previously the regions were only social-economic advisory bodies. Regional councillors are elected for six years, with lists ("représentation proportionnelle, la plus forte moyenne, sans panache ni vote préférentiel"). The president of the regional council is elected for six years by the absolute majority of the regional council. He presides over meetings of the regional council, at least once quarterly, in the "hôtel de région". Since 1982, the president of the regional council replaced the Prefect as head of regional administration. He can seek advice from the "Comité économique et social régional" (CESR). The law of 2 March 1982 states: The "Conseil regional" rules the affairs of the Region after deliberations. The Region is privileged partner of the State for elaborating and implementing the national "Plan". Regions have "contrats de plan" with the State, to mobilise financial means for realisation of common objectives. Regions also participate in infrastructure projects. In the framework of "aménagament du territoire", the Region has as task to take care of the harmonious development of the area (environment, infrastructure, communications). An important task of the Region is secondary education. The Region is responsible for buildings, equipment and exploitation of the "lycées", and takes care of their functioning (security, maintenance, renovation etc.). The Region makes a plan for professional schooling. The Region can interfere in the sphere of culture, environment, research, communications, transport, and tourism. In addition to financial contributions of the State, loans and several sources of income from activities, Regions get income from taxation: "la taxe régionale", surcharges on local taxes; "la taxe sur les droits de mutation" on all real estate transactions; "la taxe sur les permis de conduire" on driver's licences; and "la taxe sur les cartes grises des véhicules automobiles" on registration certificates for motor cars.

The 100 "Départements" (96 in France) and 4 overseas Departments (Guadeloupe, Guyane, Martinique, Réunion), are subdivided into "cantons": 79 in "Département du Nord", 15 in the "Territoire de Belfort" (Auby/Pontier, 1988). Departments were created after the French Revolution to end the organisation of the Ancien Régime with all its privileges and power structures. Napoleon made Departments an effective administration, with the leadership of Prefects representing the State, in all parts of the country. Since the law of 2 March 1982 Departments are "collectivités territoriales". To reduce the "tutélage de l'État" via the Prefect the president of the departmental council, chosen by the absolute majority of this council, became head of the departmental apparatus. A member of the departmental council per "canton" is elected. Departments have several tasks: social affairs and public health (prevention, social services), infrastructure: maintenance and construction of motorways, agrarian infrastructure, construction of buildings (libraries, museums, bureaux for the gendarmerie etc.), fire-brigade, protection of the environment and promotion of tourism. The departmental council is responsible for construction, equipment and exploitation of the "collèges" (secondary schools) and the free transport of scholars in non-urban areas. Departments support financially weak municipalities and can promote economic development of their area. In addition to the financial contributions of the State, Departments get resources from: "taxe différentielle sur les véhicules à moteur (la vignette)", tax for motor cars; registration fees; "taxes espaces verts, d'urbanisme et d'environnement"; "taxe sur les droits de mutation" (each transaction in real estate); departmental surcharges on local taxes. More than half of departmental expenses is for obligatory social outlays.

The 36,763 "Communes" are the geographically smallest general administrative units (Lachaume, 1994; Richard/ Cotten, 1986). In addition to the 25,000 municipalities with less than 700 inhabitants, there are cities and large cities with specific administrative structures (Paris, Lyon, Marseilles). The number of municipal councillors, elected for a six-year term and not paid for their work, varies with the size of the municipalities. Mayors and aldermen get financial compensation. For municipalities with less than 3,500 inhabitants election takes place on the basis of absolute majority in two rounds. Councillors in municipalities of more than 3,500 inhabitants are elected by lists with a mixed system, partly proportional and partly by majority, in two rounds. To be eligible to vote one has to be 18 years old, of French nationality or, under specific conditions, be an inhabitant from a Member-State of the European Union, dispose of civil and political rights and be registered on an electoral list. In the first meeting of the newly elected council (at the latest on the Sunday after elections), the mayor (minimum age 21 years) is chosen for a six-year term by an absolute majority (maximum three rounds). The number of aldermen cannot be higher than 30% of the number of councillors. When the mayor is chosen he presides over the council, which chooses aldermen.

The "Maire" is responsible for his municipality: "seul chargé de l'administration de la commune". Aldermen, councillors and officials assist him. The mayor has a prominent position, sometimes in combination with a national function; Premier Juppé was chosen as mayor of Bordeaux on 11 June 1995. This "cumul des mandats" is a conspicuous part of French specificity. This combination of functions is regularly debated. Politicians are attached to it, as the function of mayor is an ideal springboard for national ambitions. The mayor decides whether to delegate some competencies to aldermen. This is done with an "arrêtée", determining the nature and conditions of this delegation. He cannot delegate competencies to councillors, though an alderman can do so. The law of 3 February 1992 has some guarantees for councillors fulfilling their mandate. To emphasise his authority the mayor has a blue white and red sash, an official badge and an identity card. The mayor can make his authority felt in all parts of municipal policy. His decisions have legal effect for all inhabitants. The mayor represents the municipality to citizens, enterprises and public instances, he is the official representative of the French State in the municipality and has authority over the municipal police, or over a "police rurale", to guarantee public order, security and public health. This is done with "arrêtés de police" (for traffic regulation etc.). As president of the municipal council he prepares meetings and implements decisions of the council. He manages the municipal budget and is responsible for paying bills and receiving resources for the municipality. The mayor represents the municipality when the council gives him the mandate, as for signing contracts. As head of the municipality he appoints personnel and organises municipal services. On the basis of a fixed destination plan, a "Plan Occupation des Sols" (POS), the mayor issues licences for construction. As the subordinate of the prefect he is representative of the State and has to take care of publishing laws and regulations, organising elections, etc.

The "Conseil Municipal", after deliberations, rules the affairs of the municipality. It votes the budget, necessary for all activities decided upon. The municipal council is the local representation, meeting at least four times yearly to debate and decide in public (adoption of the budget). Municipalities must take care of legally obligatory services (registration service; elections; social and medical help; maintenance of roads; primary education; municipal police). Besides these there are municipal services for which users have to pay: energy; water; funerals; refuse disposal; nurseries; swimming pools; libraries;

museums; transportation; parking; markets; etc. Municipalities have competencies in the sphere of town and country planning, development planning, social housing, protection of architectural inheritance and environment, and industrial development. The municipal council takes decisions about maintenance of its own buildings, and eventually about subsidising enterprises to maintain local facilities. The budget year of the municipality has three phases. In January and February the "budget primitif" is established (main lines; level local tax tariffs), from April to October accounts for the previous year are made ("compte administratif"). Promptly after adopting this the municipal council vote on the "budget supplémentaire". Unlike the State budget, the municipal budget has to be balanced. There are four municipal taxes. "Taxe foncière sur les propriétés bâties" (real estate with buildings). "Taxe foncière sur propriétés non bâties" (real estate without buildings). "Taxe d'habitation", paid by owner/user of furnished apartments, and "taxe professionnelle", paid by corporations or individuals without salaried professions (shopkeepers etc.). By paying surcharges, one contributes to finance the "communauté urbaine", district, department and region. Municipal tariffs vary per municipality and can change every year. Municipalities get income from "Dotation Globale de Fonctionnement" (DGF) of the State, several taxes (for household refuse; tax for staying in the municipality etc), subsidies and loans.

Institutionalised co-operation between territorial administrative units can take several forms: "<u>Groupement des collectivités territoriales</u>". "Coopération intercommunale" implies that municipalities decide to establish an "établissement public". For one service: some 14,350 "Syndicats Intercommunales à Vocation Unique", and for several services: there are some 2,372 "Syndicats Intercommunales à Vocation Multiple". Co-operation can take the form of a district for fire-brigades etc. (some 315 districts), and as "communauté des villes" for common activities in the sphere of development planning and economic development. There are 9 "communautés urbaines" for common development planning, infrastructure and economic development: Bordeaux, Brest, Cherbourg, Le Creusot, Dunkerque, Lille, Lyon, Le Mans and Strasbourg. Fusion of two (or more) municipalities is possible, but rarely realised. There are also 9 "Syndicats d'Agglomérations Nouvelles". The "<u>Organisation administrative de Paris</u>" is a special case. The French capital is the only one which is simultaneously a municipality and a department. The agglomeration of Paris has some 9.3 million inhabitants, and Paris itself more than 2 million. The "Ile-de-France" region has some 10.7 million inhabitants. There are in France 58 cities with more than 100,000 inhabitants and having an agglomeration administration. After Paris come ten cities: Marseilles-Aix-en-Provence (800,550); Lyon (415,500); Toulouse (358,700); Nice (342,450); Strasbourg (252,350); Nantes (245,000); Bordeaux (210,300); Montpellier (208,000); St.Etienne (200,000) and Rennes (197,500). Formerly Paris did not fall under the legislation for municipalities and had a specific charter. Since the law of 31 December 1975 Paris became a municipality, falling under the "Code des communes". The municipality of Paris has a mayor and a "Conseil de Paris" with 163 elected councillors. Paris is subdivided into twenty "arrondissements" each electing a number of councillors for the "Conseil de Paris". The mayor of Paris is chosen by this council for a six-year term. He cannot also be president of the "Conseil Régional d'Ile-de-France", but can be a member of Government While in other cities and municipalities the mayor has authority over municipal police, in Paris the "préfet de police" has that authority. The geographical area of Paris has two territorial administrations: the municipality Paris and the department Paris.

"<u>Départements d'outre-mer</u>" (DOM), parts of the French Republic and of the European Union, have a special position in the French State (Ziller, 1991). Guadeloupe (with capital Basse-Terre) in the French Antilles in the Caribbean, an area of 1,780 square kilometres, has some 386,000 inhabitants. Martinique (capital Fort-de-France), also in the Caribbean, an area of 1,100 square kilometres, has some 359,800 inhabitants. Guyane (capital Cayenne) on the north-east coast of South-America, an area of some 90,000 square kilometres, has about 114,900 inhabitants, and Réunion (capital Saint-Denis), an area of 2,510 square kilometres east of Madagascar in the Indian Ocean, has some 596,000 inhabitants. French laws and rulings are in force here, and the organisation of public administration is the same. Each overseas Department has a regional council elected by general direct elections. The four "Territoires d'outre-mer" (TOM) are part of the French Republic, but not of the European Union. Island "Nouvelle-Calédonie" in the Pacific, an area of 19,100 square kilometres, has about 164,200 inhabitants. Here administrative organisation is based upon the law of 9 November 1988. In the eastern part of the Pacific there are 150 islands cf "Polynésie française" with some 188,800 inhabitants; since a law of 12 July 1990 it has internal autonomy. "Wallis et Futuna" are archipelagos, some 200 kilometres from Tahiti, with about 13,700 inhabitants on an area of 274 square kilometres. The fourth TOM are the "Terres australes et antarctiques françaises" (TAAF), with districts "îles Saint-Paul et Amsterdam, îles des Crozet, îles des Kerguelen, Terre Adélie", under a high official, resorting under the ministry of "DOM-TOM". "Collectivités territoriales" Saint-Pierre-et-Miquelon (about 6,300 inhabitants) in the Atlantic Ocean near the Saint-Laurent gulf, and Mayotte (Comores archipelago, with some 94,400 inhabitants) are administered by a "conseil général", Government is represented by a Prefect.

*3.4.5. Organisation of the French judiciary ("Justice")*

After the French Revolution it was forbidden for judges to interfere in the activities of the executive branch. Two autonomous jurisdictions were established: "juridictions judiciaires" and "juridictions administratives". "Juridictions administratives" judge conflicts within public administration and conflicts between citizens and public administration organs. "Juridictions judiciaires" apply civil law ("juridictions civiles") and criminal law ("juridictions pénales"), with specific legislation, competencies and procedures. When it is not clear if a "juridiction administrative" or a "juridiction judiciaire" applies, the "Tribunal des Conflits" can decide. "Magistrature" has "magistrats amovibles du parquet (magistrature dite debout: ils requièrent debout"), public prosecutors, and "magistrats du siège inamovibles (magistrature dite assise: ils rendent leurs jugements assis"), judges (Vincent, c.s., 1985). In 1993 the French judiciary had a budget of some 20 billion francs. The "Conseil d'État" is the highest administrative judicial body. Lawsuits between citizens and public administration are judged in the first instance by one of the 33 "Tribunaux administratifs" (more than 70,000 cases yearly). Citizens can ask for a TA cancellation of the decision of a public organ on grounds of "recours en excès de pouvoir", or seek compensation ("réparation"). Judges of the "Tribunaux administratifs" (TA) are former ENA disciples. They are appointed by decree and come under the Ministry of the Interior. The TA are competent for decisions of public authorities and organs; most cases of damage caused by activities of public administration; contracts with a public organ as party; and conflicts about the value added tax. "Juridictions judiciaires", are competent for conflicts about traffic accidents (also when a car of a public organisation is involved); indirect taxes (except value added tax); and conflicts about public enterprises. When there is a decision of a public organ, one has two months to contest this decision before a TA. When there is no decision of a public organ, one has to request a decision of this organ. If there is an answer, one has two months to contest this before a TA. When there is no answer within four months, one can bring it to a TA within two months.

Before presenting a case to a TA one can use "recours gracieux" (trying to settle the question with the public organ) or "recours hiérarchique" (bringing it to a hierarchically higher echelon). The competent TA is the tribunal which resides in the place where the conflict is centred or where the public organ has its seat. The only way to present a case before a TA is with a "requête", a registered letter with a factual description of complaints and claims. The procedure is in writing. The "commissaire du gouvernement", a judge, presents facts and arguments for both sides and comes to a conclusion. Defending the public organ is not his task. He has to inform the TA adequately, if necessary passing sentence on the public organ. Three judges set a date for their decision ("mise en délibéré"), then the decision is announced by registered letter. It is possible to appeal against this decision to a "Cour administrative d'appel", or the "Conseil d'État". The "Conseil d'État" (CE) was established by the Constitution of the year VIII (1800) and has several functions: advising over bills and decrees; deciding conflicts between public organs; and the highest level of appeal. Members of the CE are not magistrates, as functionaries they can be removed from their function. There are four grades. "Auditeurs de seconde classe", coming from ENA, they can get promotion to the category "auditeurs de première classe"; "Maîtres de requêtes" (3/4 from "auditeurs" and 1/4 from public administration); "Conseillers d'État" (2/3 from the "maîtres de requêtes" and 1/3 from public administration) and "conseillers d'État en service extraordinaire", appointed for a term, due to their expertise, by Government. The Premier is president of the CE, the Minister of Justice his deputy. The CE functions as judicial organ: in the appeal of decisions of administrative tribunals, as a judge of cassation for decisions of some special administrative courts and as judge in the first and last instance for some, nationally important, cases. The CE resides in the "Palais-Royal" in Paris.

In the category of the "juridictions judiciaires", the 473 "Tribunaux d'instance" (TI), which since 1958 replaced the 2,918 "justices de paix", are competent for the more straightforward cases (in 1992 537,360 cases). One judge decides alone ("juge unique"). He is competent for houserents; guardianship over minors and the elderly; attachment of wages; cases involving an amount of money less than 30,000 francs; and arrears of payments. Mostly an attempt is made to reach a compromise. When this does not succeed, parties are invited and, after hearing both sides, the judge decides. When the dispute is about arrears of payment, the judge is asked to give a warrant to pay, eventually with a registered letter or summons. There are four ways to appeal against a decision of this judge: when the not-present and not-represented party is resisting the decision, when the not represented third party thinks he is damaged by the decision, in the case of an appeal for cases involving more than 30,000 francs and cassation, when one party thinks the procedure was not correct and an appeal is not possible (amount of money involved is less than 13,000 francs). One can appear in person or be represented.

More complicated cases are handled by one of the 181 "Tribunaux de Grande Instance" (TGI). Sessions take place in public, except for family affairs. The TGI are competent for family law (adoption, law of succession, divorce, nationality, civil status etc.), and material law (property, expropriation etc.) for cases involving more than 30,000 francs. The TGI of the defending party is Competent, unless the issue is about real estate, inheritances or contracts (then the TGI of the place where these are, or are sold in an executory sale, is competent). One is obligated to use an advocate. The TGI handles cases with a college of three judges and the same possibilities of appeal are open ("opposition, tierce opposition, appel, pourvoi en cassation") against the decision of a TGI. A case before a TGI starts with the "assignation"; announcing to the defending party the exact contents of the dispute and the claims by way of "exploit d'huissier" (summons). A copy goes to the office of the clerk where it is registered and gets a number. The defending party then calls in an advocate. Advocates exchange their conclusions. At the session, advocates present conclusions orally. Then the court decides.

There are also several "Juridictions spécialisées". The 229 "Tribunaux de Commerce" handled some 500,000 cases in 1992. The 280 "Conseils de prud'hommes" in 1992 had to decide 172,585 new cases about labour contracts. The 437 "Tribunaux paritaires des baux ruraux" decide conflicts between proprietors and lease-holders. The 110 "Commissions techniques de Sécurité sociale" have the task of determining the grade of invalidity for those who have rights regarding social and medical care (some 110,000 cases yearly). The "Juge des loyers commerciaux" is competent for conflicts about the level of commercial rents. The "Juge des référés" decides over provisional urgent measures, which do not prejudice. Since 10 February 1994, the "Juge aux affaires familiales" is the judge of family matters. The "Juge de l'exécution", established by the law of 9 July 1991 and decree of 31 July 1992, handles cases of executorial sales of things of people who cannot pay their debts. The "Juge de l'expropriation" is competent for expropriations and decisions about compensations.

In the sphere of criminal law there are 453 "Juridictions de 1er degré. Tribunaux de police". They judge offences ("contraventions") for which penalties are a maximum of 2 months imprisonment or a maximum fine of 10,000 francs. In 1992, this meant 10,945,326 decisions. Appeal is possible when the penalty is more than 5 days imprisonment or a fine of more than 1,300 francs. The "Tribunaux correctionnels" are competent for delicts involving penalties of more than 2 months imprisonment or a fine of more than 10,000 francs. In 1992, they had to decide over 434,678 cases. The 33 "Juridictions d'appel", "Cours d'appel" are not competent to impose more heavy penalties and for that reason have a lot of appeals by condemned. When an appeal comes from the public prosecutor the courts can give heavier or lower penalties. The 102 "Cours d'Assises" judge crimes, after "instruction préalable à 2 degrés: le juge d'instruction et la chambre d'accusation". Against the decisions of these courts, only cassation is possible (judging law, facts are definite). In 1992, there were 2,293 condemnations. "Cours d'Assises" have a specific composition: three professional judges ("la cour") and nine citizens assigned by lot ("le jury"). Conditions for becoming member of the jury are: age above 23 years, able to read and write, no criminal record, no incompatible function (policeman etc.). The Prefect announces 15 days before the opening session who the appointed members of the jury are. One has to be present under penalty of a fine, though dispensations are possible (age, sickness, travel, already having been a member of a jury). The maximum penalty is life imprisonment, the death penalty having been abolished in 1981. The "Cour de Cassation" judges criminal law (offences and crimes) and civil law cases in the event of a cassation appeal. When the possibilities of appeal are exhausted, in exceptional circumstances, one can request a "procès en révision".

One is confronted with a judge for criminal law after an "enquête" (an examination after which one suspects the identity of the offender) and "instruction" (an enquiry into the circumstances of the offender), and when a "procureur" starts the procedure, after a complaint or in the case of "flagrant délit" (person taken in the very act). The instruction phase is obligatory for crimes and facultative for transgressions. The "juge d'instruction" examines the evidence, and can issue decrees for arrest and custody. When the instruction phase is finished, the case is presented to the competent jurisdiction. After instruction for "Cours d'assises", the case is presented to the "Chambre des mises en accusation". If there is enough evidence, the "arrêt de mise en accusation" follows. The "Code pénal" describes acts which the criminal law can penalise. In criminal law there is "l'action publique" (penalisation) and "l'action civile" (compensation or recuperation). The public prosecutor requests a penalty, the judge decides. Sentences are registered in the "cashier judiciaire". Part one lists all sentences (available for some public authorities only). Part two has only some sentences (for public administration), and part three lists all sentences for more than two years imprisonment (the person himself gets a copy). To get a copy of one's own 'cashier judiciaire", one has to send a request (with a birth certificate) to the "Casier judiciaire national", 44079 Nantes, cedex 01. It is possible to see one's own complete "casier judiciaire" at the "Procureur de la République" in the place of residence. One does not get a copy. In the sphere of criminal law there are also "Juridictions spécialisés", as in the sphere of the law for children. "Juridictions pour enfants" ("Juges des enfants"), for minors under 18 year, are competent for civil and criminal law. The 138 "Tribunaux pour enfants" can take measures for minors under 18 years having committed an offence. Minors between 16 and 18 years, having committed a crime, are judged by the "Cours d'assises des mineurs". Children above 13 years can be obliged to follow programs of re-education until their 18th year. For minors between 16 and 18 years, they can decide "mise sous protection judiciaire" for a maximum of 5 years. For appeal there are "Chambre spéciale des mineurs de la cour d'appel" and "Juge d'application des peines."

**References**

French
Ageron, C.R., Les Algériens musulmans et la France. (Paris, PUF, 1968).
Agulhon, M., La République, 1880 à nos jours. (Paris, Hachette, 1990).
Agulhon, M., 1848 ou l'apprentissage de la République (1848-1852). (Paris, Seuil, 1992).
Alexandre, A., Le Duel De Gaulle-Pompidou. (Paris, Grasset, 1970).
Ameller, M., L'Assemblée nationale. (Paris, PUF, 1994).
Amouroux, H., La Vie des Français sous l'Occupation. (Paris, Fayard, 1983).
Antonetti, J., Histoire Contemporaine Politique et Sociale. (Paris, PUF, 1989).
Aron, R., Histoire de Vichy. (Paris, Fayard, 1954).
Aron, R., La Tragédie Algérienne. (Paris, Plon, 1957).
Aron, R., L'Algérie et la République. (Paris, Plon, 1958).
Aron, R., Histoire de la Libération de la France. (Paris, Fayard, 1959).
Aron, R., Immuable et Changeante. De la IVe à la Ve République. (Paris, Calmann-Lévy, 1959).
Aron, R., La Révolution Introuvable. Réflexions sur la Révolution de Mai. (Paris, Julliard, 1968).
Aron, R., De Gaulle. (Paris, Perrin, 1972).
Association française de Science Politique, La Constitution de la Cinquième République. (Paris, FNSP, 1985).
Auby, J.B. et J.F., Droit des Collectivités Locales. (Paris, PUF, 1998).
Auby, J.F., Les Services Publics Locaux. (Paris, PUF, 1982).
Auby, J.F., Organisation Administrative du Territoire. (Paris, Sirey, 1985).
Auby, J.F., Pontier, J.M., Le Département. (Paris, Economica, 1988).
Auby, J.M., dir., Droit Public. (Paris, Economica, 1985).
Auby, J.M. et J.B., Institutions Administratives. (Paris, Dalloz, 1996).
Auby, J.M. et J.B., Droit de la Fonction Publique. État, Collectivités Locales, Hôpitaux. (Paris, Dalloz, 1997).
Aulard, A., Histoire politique de la Révolution française (1789-1804). (Paris, 1901; A.Colin, 1989).
Avril, P., Le Régime Politique de la Ve République. (Paris, LGDJ, 1975).
Avril, P., La Ve République. Histoire Politique et Constitutionnelle. (Paris, PUF, 1987; 1994).
Avril, P., Essai sur les Partis Politiques. (Paris, LGDJ, 1991).
Avril, P., Gicquel, J., Le Conseil Constitutionnel. (Paris, Montchrestien, 1995).
Avril, P., Vincent, G., La IVe République. Histoire et Société. (Paris, Fayard, 1988).
Azéma, J.P., De Munich à la Libération. (Paris, Seuil, 1979).
Azéma, J.P., Winock, M., La IIIe République: 1870-1940. (Paris, Hachette, 1991).
Bahu-Leyser, D., De Gaulle, les Français et l'Europe. (Paris, PUF, 1981).
Bacot, P., Carré de Malberg et l'origine de la distinction souveraineté du peuple – souveraineté nationale. (Paris, CNRS, 1985).
Baecque, F. de, Qui Gouverne la France? (Paris, PUF, 1976).
Baecque, F. de, Quermonne, J.L., dir., Administration et Politique sous la Ve République. (Paris, FNSP, 1982).
Bagge, D., Les idées politiques en France. (Paris, PUF, 1952).
Bahu-Leyser, D., De Gaulle, les Français et l'Europe. (Paris, PUF, 1981).
Balladur, É., Je crois en l'Homme plus qu'en l'État. (Paris, Flammarion, 1987).
Balladur, É., Deux ans à Matignon. (Paris, Plon, 1995).
Balladur, É., Caractère de la France. (Paris, Plon, 1997).
Bart, J., dir., La constitution française de 1791. Colloque Dijon. (Paris, Economica, 1993).
Barrillon, R., et al., Dictionnaire de la Constitution. (Paris, Cujas, 1980).
Barthélemy, J., Le régime parlementaire en France sous Louis XVIII et Charles X. (Paris, 1904).

Barthélemy, J., Duez, P., Traité de droit constitutionnel. (Paris, Dalloz, 1933; Economica, 1985).
Bastid, P., Institutions politiques de la Seconde République. (Paris, Hachette, 1945).
Bastid, P., Les institutions politiques de la monarchie parlementaire française (1814-1848). (Paris, Sirey, 1954).
Bastid, P., L'Idée de Constitution. (Paris, Economica, 1985).
Baumel, J., De Gaulle, l'exile intérieur. (Paris, A. Michel, 2002).
Berstein, S., La Ve République: un nouveau modèle républicain? Dans: Berstein, S., Rudelle, O., dir., Le modèle républicain. (Paris, PUF, pp.407-432, 1992).
Berstein, S., Histoire du Gaullisme. (Paris, Perrin, 2002).
Berstein, S., Rudelle, O., dir., Le Modèle républicain. (Paris, PUF, 1992).
Berton, J., L'évolution constitutionnelle du Second Empire. (Paris, Université, 1902).
Blanquer, J.M., et al., Les 40 ans de la Cinquième République. (Paris, LGDJ, 1998).
Boissieu, A. de, Pour combattre avec De Gaulle. (Paris, Plon, 1981).
Boissieu, A. de, Pour servir le Général, 1946-1970. (Paris, Plon, 1982)
Bonnard, R., Les actes constitutionnelles de 1940. (Paris, 1942).
Borella, F., Les partis politiques dans la France d'aujourd'hui. (Paris, Seuil, 1973; 1990).
Bourdieu, P., Noblesse d'État. (Paris, Minuit, 1962).
Bourdon, J., La Constitution de l'an VIII. (Paris, Université, 1942).
Bouthillier, Y., Le Drame de Vichy. (Paris, Plon, 1950).
Bredin, J.D., La République de M. Pompidou. (Paris, 1974).
Bromberger, M. et S., Les 13 complots du 13 mai. (Paris, Fayard, 1959).
Burdeau, F., Histoire de l'Administration Française, du XVIIIe au XXe siècles. (Paris, Montchrestien, 1989).
Burdeau, G., Hamon, F., Troper, M., Droit constitutionnel. (Paris, LGDJ, 1997).
Burin des Roziers, E., Retour aux sources: 1962, l'année décisive. (Paris, Plon, 1986).
Capitant, R., La réforme du parlementarisme. (Paris, Sirey, 1934).
Cerny, P.C., Une politique de grandeur: aspects idéologiques de la politique extérieure de De Gaulle. (Paris, Flammarion, 1986).
Chagnollaud, D., Quermonne, J.L., La Ve République. (Paris, Flammarion, 2000).
Chantebout, B., Droit Constitutionnel et Institutions Politiques. (Paris, Economica, 1980).
Chapsal, J., La Vie politique sous la Ve République. (Paris, PUF, 1987).
Chapsal, J., Lancelot, A., La vie politique en France depuis 1940. (Paris, PUF, 1984).
Charlot, J., Le Gaullisme. (Paris, A.Colin, 1970).
Charlot, J., Le Phénomène gaulliste. (Paris, Fayard, 1970).
Charpin, J.M., dir., L'économie française en perspective. (Paris, DF/CGP, 1993).
Chastenet, J., Histoire de la IIIe République. (Paris, Hachette, 1952/1963).
Chevallier, J.J., Histoire de la Pensée Politique. (Paris, Payot, 1979/1984).
Chevallier, J.J., Histoire des institutions et des régimes politiques de la France de 1789 à nos jours. (Paris, Dalloz, 1991).
Choisel, F., Bonapartisme et Gaullisme. (Paris, Albatros, 1987).
Claude, H., Gaullisme et grand capital. (Paris, Éditions sociales, 1960).
Cohen, J., La préparation de la Constitution de 1848. (Paris, Éditios sociales, 1935).
Cohen, S., Les Conseillers du Président: de Charles de Gaulle à Valéry Giscard d'Estaing. (Paris, PUF, 1980).
Cohen-Tanugi, L., La Métamorphose et la Démocratie. (Paris, Odile Jacob, 1989).
Cosse, P.Y., Le Xe Plan 1989-1992. (Paris, DF, 1989).
Cotteret, J.M., Emeri, C., Le Budget de l'État. (Paris, PUF, 1984).
Danan, Y.M., La Vie Politique à Alger 1940-1944. (Paris, LGDJ, 1963).
Debré, J.L., Les idées constitutionnelles du général de Gaulle. (Paris, LGDJ, 1974).
Debré, J.L., La Constitution de la Ve République. (Paris, PUF, 1975).
Debré, M., Refaire une Démocratie, un Pouvoir, un État. (Paris, 1958).
Decaumont, F., dir., Le Discours de Bayeux, hier et aujourd'hui. (Paris, Economica, 1991).
De Gaulle, C., La discorde chez l'ennemi. (Paris, 1924; Plon, 1972).
De Gaulle, C., Le Fil de l'Épée. (Paris, Plon, 1932; 1971).
De Gaulle, C., Vers l'armée de métier. L'Armée de la future. (Paris, 1934; Plon, 1971).
De Gaulle, C., La France et son armée. (Paris, Plon, 1938; 1971).
De Gaulle, C., Mémoires de guerre. I. L'appel, 1940-1942. II. L'unité, 1942-1944. III. Le salut, 1944-1946. (Paris, Plon, 1954/1959).
De Gaulle, C., Mémoires d'espoir. I. Le renouveau, 1958-1962. II. L'effort, 1962-. (Paris, Plon, 1970/1971).
De Gaulle, C., Discours et messages. (Paris, Plon, 1970).

De Gaulle, C., Articles et Écrits. (Paris, Plon, 1982).
De Gaulle, C., Oeuvres. (Paris, Plon, 1994).
De Gaulle, C., Mémoires. (Paris, Gallimard, 2000).
De La Gorce, P.M., De Gaulle entre deux mondes. (Paris, Fayard, 1964).
Deslandres, M., Histoire Constitutionnelle de la France depuis 1789. (Paris, 1933/1937; Duchemin, 1977).
Devedjian, P., Le Temps des Juges. (Paris, Flammarion, 1996).
Documentation française (DF), Répertoire de l'administration française. (Paris, DF, 1990).
DF, Documents pour servir á l'histoire de l'élaboration de la Constitution du 4 octobre 1958. (Paris, DF, 1991).
DF, Les Institutions de la IIIe République. (Paris, DF, 1992).
DF, Les Institutions de la IVe République. (Paris, DF, 1994).
DF, Le Controle de constitutionnalité. (Paris, DF, 1994).
DF, Constitution française du 4 octobre 1958. (Paris, DF, 1996).
DF, Les Révisions de la Constitution de 1958. (Paris, DF, 1996).
DF, Institutions et vie politique. (Paris, DF, 1997).
DF, La Justice administrative en pratique. (Paris, DF, 1997).
DF, Les institutions locales en France. (Paris, DF, 2001).
Doise, J., Vaïsse, M., Diplomatie et outil militaire 1871-1969. (Paris, Imprimerie nationale, 1987; Seuil, 1991).
Domenach, J.M., Regarder la France. Essais sur le Malaise Français. (Paris, Perrin, 1996).
Dreyfus, A., La République de M. Thiers. (Paris, 1930).
Dubief, H., Le Déclin de la IIIe République, 1929-1939. (Paris, 1976).
Duclos, P., La notion de constitution dans l'oeuvre de l'Assemblée constituante de 1789. (Paris, Université, 1932).
Duhamel, A., La République giscardienne. (Paris, 1980).
Duhamel, O., Droit constitutionnel et politique. (Paris, Seuil, 1993).
Duhamel, O., Histoire constitutionnelle de la France. (Paris, Seuil, 1995).
Duhamel, O., Parodi, J.L., dir., La Constitution de la Ve République. (Paris, FNSP, 1965).
Dujardin, P., Le Discours constituant du 7 mars-19 avril 1946. (Lyon, Université, 1977).
Dupuy, R., Morabito, M., dir., 1795: Pour une République sans Revolution. (Rennes, PU, 1996).
Duverger, M., Les Constitutions de la France. (Paris, PUF, 1996).
Elgey, G., La République des illusions. (Paris, Fayard, 1968).
Elgey, G., Histoire de la IVe République. (Paris, Fayard, 1993).
Ellul, J., Histoire des institutions. (Paris, PUF, 1993).
Favier, P., Martin-Roland, M., La Décennie Mitterrand. (Paris, Seuil, 1990).
Favrod, C., La Révolution algérienne. (Paris, 1959).
Ferry, L., Renaut, A., La Pensée 68. Essai sur l'antihumanisme contemporain. (Paris, Gallimard, 1985).
Feuilloley, P., La France du General De Gaulle. De l'acte de foi à l'ingratitude. (Paris, Harmattan, 2002).
Fondation Charles de Gaulle, Charles de Gaulle, la jeunesse et la guerre, 1890-1920. (Paris, Plon, 2002).
Fouchet, C., Mémoires d'hier et de demain. (Paris, Plon, 1971/1973).
François, B., Misère de la Ve République. (Paris, Denoël, 2001).
Furet, F., Halevy, R., La Monarchie républicaine. La Constitution de 1791. (Paris, Fayard, 1996).
Gerbet, P., La Construction de l'Europe. (Paris, Imprimerie nationale, 1983).
Gicquel, J., Essai sur la pratique de la Ve Republique. (Paris, LGDJ, 1968).
Gicquel, Droit Constitutionnel et Institutions Politiques. (Paris, Montchrestien, 1985).
Gillois, A., Histoire secrète des Français à Londres. (Paris, Cercle du nouveau livre, 1973).
Godechot, J., Les Constitutions en France de 1789 à nos jours. (Paris, Flammarion, 1982).
Godechot, J., Les Institutions de la France sous la Révolution et l'Empire. (Paris, PUF, 1985; 1989).
Goguel, F., La politique des partis sous la IIIe République. (Paris, Seuil, 1981).
Gouault, J., Comment la France est devenue républicaine. (Paris, A.Colin, 1954).
Gough, J.W., L'idée de loi fondamentale dans l'histoire constitutionnelle anglaise (1955). (Paris, PUF, 1992).
Guchet, Y., Histoire constitutionnelle française. (Paris, A.Colin, 1993).
Guillemin, H., Le Coup du 2 décembre 1851. (Paris, Gallimard, 1951).
Gun, N., Les Secrets des Archives Américaines. (Paris, A.Michel, 1979).
Hamon, L., De Gaulle dans la République. (Paris, Plon, 1958).
Hamon, L., Delcros, X., Une République Présidentielle. (Paris, Bordas, 1977).
Hamon, L., Rotman, P., Génération. T.1. Les Années de rêve. T.2. Les Années de poudre. (Paris, Seuil, 1987/1988).
Hanotaux, G., Histoire de la France contemporaine (1871-1900). (Paris, Combet, 1908).

Hanotaux, G., Histoire de la fondation de la IIIe République. (Paris, 1925).
IFOP, Les Français et de Gaulle. (Paris, Plon, 1971).
Isoart, P., Bidegaray, C., dir., Des Républiques Françaises. (Paris, Economica, 1988).
Joffrin, L., Mai 68. Histoire des événements. (Paris, Seuil, 1988).
Julliard, J., La IVe République: 1947-1958. (Paris, Livre de poche, 1981).
Kriegel-Valrimont, M., La Libération. (Paris, Minuit, 1964).
Lachaume, J.F., L'Administration Communale. (Paris, LGDJ, 1994).
Lacorne, D., L'Invention de la République. Le Modèle américain. (Paris, 1991).
La Gorce, P.M. de, Moschetto, B., La Cinquième République. (Paris, PUF, 1996).
Lacouture, J., De Gaulle. (Paris, Seuil, 1984/1986).
Laferrière, J., Manuel de Droit Constitutionnel. (Paris, 1947).
Langer, W., Le Jeu Américain à Vichy. (Paris, Plon, 1948).
Lapierre, D., Collins, L., Paris brûle-t-il? (Paris, Laffont, 1964).
Lavisse, E., Histoire de France contemporaine depuis la Révolution française jusqu'à la paix de 1919. (Paris, 1921).
Lavroff, D.G., Le Système Politique Français. (Paris, Dalloz, 1982).
Leca, D., La Rupture de 1940. (Paris, Fayard, 1978).
Lech, J.M., Les Secrets de l'élection présidentielle. (Paris, Stock, 2001).
Lentin, A.P., L'Algérie des colonels. (Paris, 1958).
Lévêque, P., Histoire des Forces Politiques en France de 1789 à nos jours. (Paris, A.Colin, 1994/1997).
L'Histoire (revue), Les Années de Gaulle, 1958-1974. (Paris, juillet-août, 1987).
Luchaire, F., Maus, D., Documents pour servir à l'histoire de l'élaboration de la Constitution du 4 octobre 1958. (Paris, DF, 1987/1988).
Madelin, P., Les Gaullistes et l'argent. (Paris, L'Archipel, 2002).
Madiot, Y., Institutions politiques de la France. (Paris, Dalloz, 1994).
Maigret, E., dir., Le Budget de l'État. (Paris, DF, 1993).
Malafosse, J. de, Histoire des Institutions et des Régimes Politiques, de la Révolution à la IVe République. (Montchrestien, 1975).
Mallet, S., Le Gaullisme et la Gauche. (Paris, Seuil, 1965).
Massot, J., La Présidence de la République en France. (Paris, DF, 1986).
Massot, J., Chef de l'État et Chef de Gouvernement. Dyarchie et hiérarchie. (Paris, DF, 1993).
Massot, J., Girardot, T., Le Conseil d'État. (Paris, DF, 1999).
Maurras, C., Enquête sur la monarchie. (Paris, 1900/1903).
Maus, D., Les grands textes de la pratique institutionnelle de la Ve République. (Paris, DF, 1995).
Maus, D., Favoreu, L., Parodi, J.L., L'ecriture de la Constitution de 1958. (Paris, Economica, 1992).
Mayeur, J.M., La vie politique sous la IIIe République. (Paris, Seuil, 1984).
Mendras, H., La Seconde Révolution Française. (Paris, Gallimard, 1994).
Mény, Y., Le Système Politique Français. (Paris, Montchrestien, 1993).
Mengin, R., De Gaulle à Londres. (Paris, Table Ronde, 1965).
Minc, A., La France de l'An 2000. (Paris, Odile Jacob, 1994).
Minc, A., Au Nom de la Loi. (Paris, Gallimard, 1998).
Mitterrand, F., Le Coup d'état permanent. (Paris, Plon, 1964; Julliard, 1984).
Monneron, J.C., Rowley, A., Les 25 ans qui ont transformé la France. (Paris, Nouvelle Librairie de France, 1986).
Morabito, M., Bourmaud, D., Histoire constitutionnelle et politique de la France (1789-1958). (Paris, Montchrestien, 1993).
Moreau, J., Administration Régionale, Départementale et Municipale. (Paris, Dalloz, 1995).
Morin, E., et al., Mai 68. La Brèche, suivi de vingt ans après. (Bruxelles, Complexe, 1988).
Nallet, H., Tempête sur la Justice. (Paris, Plon, 1992).
Nicolet, C., L'Idée Républicaine en France (1789-1924). (Paris, Gallimard, 1982; 1994).
Noël, L., La Traversée du Désert. (Paris, Plon, 1972).
Pactet, P., Institutions politiques. Droit constitutionnel. (Paris, Masson, 1994).
Petitfils, J.C., La Démocratie giscardienne. (Paris, PUF, 1981).
Petitfils, J.C., Le Gaullisme. (Paris, PUF, 1994).
Petot, J., Les grandes érapes du régime républicain français (1792-1969). (Paris, 1970).
Peyrefitte, A., Le Mal français. (Paris, Plon, 1976).
Picht, R., Leenhardt, J., dir., Au Jardin des Malentendus. Le Commerce Franco-Allemand des Idées. (Paris, Babel, 1997).
Pilleul, G., dir., L'Entourage et de Gaulle. (Paris, Plon, 1979).

Pognon, E., De Gaulle et l'Armée. (Paris, Plon, 1976).
Portelli, H., La Politique en France sous la Ve République. (Paris, Grasset, 1987).
Pouvoirs (Revue), Le Conseil constitutionnel. (Paris, Seuil, 1980).
Pouvoirs, L'Armée. (Paris, Seuil, 1986).
Pouvoirs, Le Président. (Paris, Seuil, 1987).
Pouvoirs, Le Sénat. (Paris, Seuil, 1988).
Pouvoirs, Le Ministère des Finances. (Paris, Seuil, 1990).
Pouvoirs, La Décentralisation. (Paris, Seuil, 1992).
Pouvoirs, La République. (Paris, Seuil, 2002).
Prenant, M., Vie et Mort des Français, 1934-1945. (Paris, Hachette, 1971).
Quermonne, J.L., Le Gouvernement de la France sous la Ve République. (Paris, Dalloz, 1987).
Quermonne, J.L., L'Appareil Administratif de l'État. (Paris, Seuil, 1991).
Quermonne, J.L., Chagnollaud, D., Le Gouvernement de la France sous la Ve République. (Paris, Dalloz, 1991).
Radiguet, L., L'Acte additionnel aux constitutions de l'Empire. (Caen, Université, 1911).
Raynaud, J., La Cour des comptes. (Paris, PUF, 1988).
Rémond, R., La Vie Politique en France. (Paris, A.Colin, 1965).
Rémond, R., Le Retour de De Gaulle. (Bruxelles, Complexe, 1984; 1985).
Rémond, R., Les Droites en France. (Paris, Aubier-Montaigu, 1985).
Revue du droit public, Les 40 ans de la Ve République. (Paris, LGDJ, 1998).
Rials, S., La Déclaration des droits de l'homme et du citoyen. (Paris, Hachette, 1988).
Richard, P., Cotten, M., Les Communes Françaises d'Aujourd'hui. (Paris, PUF, 1986).
Rioux, J.P., La France de la IVe République (1944-1958). (Paris, Seuil, 1980).
Robineau, Y., Truchet, D., Le Conseil d'État. (Paris, PUF, 1994).
Rochefort, R., La Société des Consommateurs. (Paris, Odile Jacob, 1995).
Rosanvallon, P., Le Sacre du Citoyen. (Paris, Gallimard, 1992).
Rosanvallon, P., La Monarchie impossible. Les Chartes de 1814 et de 1830. (Paris, Fayard, 1994).
Roussel, É., Charles de Gaulle. (Paris, Gallimard, 2002).
Rouvillois, F., Les Origines de la République. (Paris, PUF, 1998).
Rudelle, O., Mai 58, de Gaulle et la République. (Paris, Plon, 1988).
Sadran, P., Le Système Administratif Français. (Paris, Montchrestien, 1992).
Sautel, G., Harouel, J.L., Histoire des Institutions Publiques depuis la Révolution. (Paris, Dalloz, 1997).
Schnapp, A., Vidal-Naquet, P., Journal de la Commune étudiante. Novembre 67 – juin 68. (Paris, Seuil, 1968).
Séguin, P., Louis-Napoléon le Grand. (Paris, Grasset, 1990).
Servan-Schreiber, J.J., Le Défi Américain. (Paris, Denoël, 1967).
Sirinelli, J.F., Histoire des Droites en France. (Paris, Gallimard, 1992).
Soulier, A., L'instabilité ministérielle sous la IIIe République. (Paris, Sirey, 1938).
Suleiman, E.N., Les Ressorts cachées de la Réussite française. (Paris, Seuil, 1995).
Sur, S., La Vie politique en France sous la Ve République. (Paris, Montchrestien, 1987).
Szramkiewicz, R., Bouineau, J., Histoire des Institutions, 1750-1914. (Paris, Litec, 1989).
Tardieu, A., La Révolution à refaire. (Paris, Flammarion, 1937).
Tillinac, D., Chirac le Gaulois. (Paris, La Table Ronde, 2002).
Touchard, J., Le Gaullisme. (Paris, Seuil, 1978).
Tourette, F., Yalta et ses Mythes. (Dans: Revue d'Histoire Diplomatique, pp.101-114, 2000).
Tournoux, J.R., Pétain et de Gaulle. (Paris, Plon, 1964).
Turpin, D., La Région. (Paris, Economica, 1986).
Turpin, D., Droit constitutionnel. (Paris, PUF, 1992).
Vallon, L., L'Anti-De Gaulle. (Paris, Seuil, 1969).
Vedel, G., dir., Comité consultatif pour la révision de la Constitution. (Paris, DF, 1993).
Viansson-Ponté, P., Histoire de la République Gaullienne. (Paris, Fayard, 1970/1971).
Vigier, P., La Seconde République. (Paris, Fayard, 1996).
Vincent, J., Montagne, G., Varinard, A., La Justice et ses institutions. (Paris, Dalloz, 1985).
Viorst, M., Les Alliés Ennemis: FDR et De Gaulle. (Paris, Denoël, 1965).
Vovelle, M., et al., Nouvelle Histoire de la France Contemporaine. (Paris, Seuil, 1972/1999).
Zemmour, E., L'Homme qui ne s'aimait pas. (Paris, Balland, 2002).
Ziller, J., Les "Dom-Tom". (Paris, LGDJ, 1991).

English
Adamthwaite, A., Grandeur and Misery. France's Bid for Power in Europe, 1914-1940. (London, Arnold, 1995).
Alexander, M., The Republic in Danger. General Maurice Gamelin and the Politics of French Defence, 1933-1940. (Cambridge, CUP, 1992).
Andrew, C., Mitrokhin, V , The Mitrokhin Archive. The KGB in Europe and the West. (London, Lane/Penguin, 1999).
Bagehot, W., The English Constitution. (London, 1867; Collins, 1993).
Bell, P.M.H., France and Britain, 1900-1940. Entente and Estrangement. (London, Longman, 1996).
De Gaulle, C., Vers l'armée de métier. The Army of the Future. (London, Hutchinson, 1940).
De Gaulle, C., L'Histoire de l'Armée française. France and her Army. (London, Hutchinson, 1945).
De Gaulle, C., Mémoires de Guerre. War Memoirs. (London, Collins/Weidenfeld & Nicolson, 1955/1959).
De Gaulle, C., Le Fil del'Épée. The Edge of the Sword. (London, Faber and Faber, 1960).
Duroselle, J.B., et al., France. Change and Tradition. (Cambridge, MA, Harvard UP, 1963).
Finer, S.E., The History of Government from the Earliest Times. (Oxford, OUP, 1997).
Gildea, R., France since 1945. (Oxford, OUP, 1997).
Hayward, J.E.S., Governing France. The One and Indivisible French Republic. (London, Weidenfeld & Nicolson, 1983).
Hayward, J.E.S., ed., De Gaulle to Mitterrand. Presidential Power in France. (New York, New York UP, 1993).
Horne, A., The French Army and Politics 1870-1970. (London, Macmillan, 1984).
Hupe, P.L., et al., Hybrid Governance. (The Hague, Social and Cultural Planning Office, 2000).
Kersaudy, F., Churchill and De Gaulle. (New York, Athenaeum, 1981).
Macmillan, H., Memoirs. (London, 1972).
Mendl, W., Deterrence and Persuasion. French Nuclear Armament in the Context of National Policy, 1945-1969. (London, Faber, 1970).
Morris, P., Williams, S., eds., France in the World. (London, Association for the Study of Modern and Contemporary France, 1985).
Paxton, R.O., Wahl, N., eds., De Gaulle and the United States. A Centennial Reappraisal. (Oxford, Berg, 1994).
Pickles, D., The Uneasy Entente. French Foreign Policy and Franco-British Misunderstandings. (Oxford, OUP, 1966).
Pickles, D., The Government and Politics of France. (London, Methuen, 1973).
Rosenblum, M., Mission to Civilize: The French Way. (San Diego, Harcourt Brace Jovanovich, 1986).
Schaling, E., Institutions and Monetary Policy. Credibility, Flexibility and Central Bank Independence. (Tilburg, Netherlands, University of Tilburg, 1995).
Servan-Schreiber, J.J., The American Challenge. (London, Hamish Hamilton, 1968).
Spears, E., Assignment to Catastrophe. (London, Heinemann, 1954).
Spears, E., Two Men who Saved France. (London, Eyre and Spottiswoode, 1966).
Werth, A., De Gaulle. (London, Penguin, 1965).
Williams, C., The Last Great Frenchman. A Life of General De Gaulle. (London, Wiley, 1997).
Wood, G., The Creation of the American Republic, 1776-1787. (Chapel Hill, University of North Carolina Press, 1992).
Woodward, L.L., British Foreign Policy in the Second World War. (London, 1970).
Wright, V., The Government and Politics of France. (London, Routledge, 1992).
Young, R.J., France, the Cold War and the Western Alliance., 1944-1949. (Leicester, Leicester UP, 1990).
Zeldin, T., The French. (London, Collins, 1983).

# Part Three

# Public Policymaking, Politics and Public Management of Society

# 4. Justice, Police and Penal System

## 4.1. Specific French principles of jurisdiction

Law has an essential role in society; it is important for citizens and public authorities to know what law prevails. Justice, police and a penal system belong to the crucial parts of public authority institutionalising, in the context of general law development (constitution, legislation, jurisprudence, law creation in society). French jurisdiction is based on some basic principles (Rassat, 1994). In comparison with the Anglo-Saxon system of the single judge, advantages are mentioned of collegial jurisdiction in France, dominant in previous times. Such as protection against political dependency and corruption; reduction of failures as a consequence of discussion; training of younger judges; a sentence decided by more judges would have more authority; the responsibility for unpleasant decisions does not fall to one person; and doctrine could be developed more freely, because criticisms would not be personal. In spite of this, there are now more single judges in contemporary French jurisdiction, as this system costs less and works faster. In the Ancien Régime, judges had no fixed seat and travelled around. Since 1789 jurisdictions have a permanent seat on behalf of continuous service. With some exceptions, for instance the 30 "Cours d'assises", appeal instances for the 95 departments. The principle of professionalism, dating from feudal times, is maintained. The technical character of law makes professionalism necessary. There is assistance of non-jurists with other expertise, especially in case of judging by participation of equals: for the military in the "jury criminel", for businessmen in the "tribunal de commerce", for politicians, in "Haute Cour de Justice" and "Cour de justice de la République". Sometimes non-jurists function as judges or assessors.

The independence of judges is meant to protect them against interference in their work by political authorities, other jurisdictions, politicians, pressure groups, citizens and mass media. Independence of judges with regard to political authorities is generally supported, but the dominant idea in French public opinion is that politicians can and do influence the career of judges and exercise undue pressure on their decisions. Time and again, newspapers inform the public about dubious politicking with regard to the functioning of jurisdictions. Article 64, par. 1 of the Constitution of 1958 proclaimed "inamovibilité" (irremovability). This is not convincing however as a rule guaranteeing the independence of judges. Executive power, the top of which is in the hands of party-political persons, has ample possibilities to influence judges with disciplinary measures and promotions. To avoid this, the "Conseil supérieur de la magistrature" (CSM) was created, whose members are appointed by the President of the Republic, but this was seen as unsatisfactory (the Head of State is a party-politician). Since 27 July 1993, members of CSM are elected or appointed by others than the President of the Republic. The CSM has to give an "avis conforme" for appointment of "magistrats du siège", and it presents proposals for important nominations. The statute for judges of the "juridiction judiciaire" has five career-scales. Promotion is possible only by a government decision on the basis of a CSM advice. There are guarantees for eventual sanctions and disciplinary measures. Until recently there were no guarantees for the independence of judges in the administrative jurisdiction. For the "Conseil d'État" there is factual irremovability. To prevent political pressures promotion takes place on the basis of seniority. A law of 6 January 1986 did not give judges of administrative tribunals (7 ranks) and administrative courts (7 ranks) the right of irremovability. Their career is supervised by a "Conseil supérieur des tribunaux administratifs et des cours administratives d'appel".

Several principles of good jurisdiction have been formulated, such as the accessibility of jurisdiction, inter alia by a judicial process, for free. Up till 1970 the costs of a judicial process had to be paid by the losing party, which had to pay its own costs and the costs of the other party. A law of 1977 introduced "gratuité de la justice" for civil and administrative procedures, costs were paid by the State. In the penal procedure, the condemned has to pay the costs himself though this is often a symbolic issue due to insolvency. One has to pay the costs of defending oneself (solicitors etc.). It was thought to be unfair that somebody whose rights were damaged could not have access to jurisdiction, with the help of a solicitor, for lack of financial means, so laws of 1851, 1972 and 1991 had a State-funded arrangement for free legal aid on behalf of those who didn't have enough finances. Judges can distribute process costs between parties for civil procedures since 1976, and for penal procedures since 1981. The principle of equal jurisdiction implies that cases of all inhabitants are treated by the same jurisdictions. This principle was realised by the revolutionaries in 1789 to end the abuses and privileges of the Ancien Régime (aristocracy had its own judges). In the course of time this was limited with specialised jurisdictions and a more reduced interpretation of this principle became the vogue: equal treatment in the same cases. In civil procedures there is equality of process parties. In administrative law procedures public authorities, and in penal procedures the public prosecutor, have process advantages. Due to socio-economic conditions and differences between citizens, juridical equality of citizens is in fact a juridical fiction. The well to do can afford to pay the best and most expensive solicitors. A judge can only reach a good judgement after hearing the arguments of both sides, and if he has all relevant information. Besides, there are the "principe du contradictoire" for civil procedures, and "droits de la défense" for penal procedures. Detailed rules try to regulate the information admitted to the procedure, and the way it can be used. The presence of both parties at the process is supposed, but only in the penal procedure can one be forced to appear before the jurisdiction personally.

The objective of jurisdiction is to restore harmony in disturbed social relations, so jurisdictions have to function reasonably to further acceptance of sentences, and sentences have to be effectuated. It has to be guaranteed that sentences can be implemented, if necessary by force ("principe de la force exécutoire"). In the sphere of penal law, the public prosecutor takes care that sentences are executed. In civil procedures, the party, who has won the case has to initiate an action. He has to persuade the other party to carry the decision of the judge into effect, eventually supported by the risk of a fine. Execution of decisions of administrative jurisdictions is quite simple, when addressed to private individuals, it becomes more complicated if an organ of public authority is asked by a judge to do something. Often the State does not comply (promptly) with the decisions of judges. Government can initiate a law with retroactive effect for administrative decisions, annulled by a judge. An arrangement meant that one could ask a judge that a sentence be executed ("recours pour excès de pouvoir") or could call in an ombudsman and a law of 16 July 1980 gave rules to prevent abuses by public authorities.

Recently, the "principe de responsabilité publique pour défaillance du système" was introduced. This principle enables process parties to ask for compensation when the administration of justice has failed. Before 1972 it was accepted that the administration of justice could not be made responsible for its bad functioning. A law of 1972, transforming administration of justice from "pouvoir" into "service publique", changed this. The State is held responsible in the person of the "agent judiciaire de Trésor". When condemned, the State has to compensate for the damage done. Eventually the loss is recovered from the functionary involved. In penal law there are some situations where the State can be made responsible. When an innocent person is condemned (Dreyfus was perhaps the most famous tragic example), compensation can be given, but all those of whom it is concluded that they cannot be prosecuted and who are released, don't get compensation, because in these cases the innocence of the persons concerned cannot be proved. A law of 1970 ruled that compensation can be paid if somebody has been held in provisional custody unjustly and has suffered considerable damage as a result. The question of whether the State can be held responsible when the State did not protect victims of penal infringements is only partially answered. In administrative jurisprudence responsibility of the State for damages caused by persons, condemned and escaped from custody or a flexible regime is recognised. There are rulings to award compensation to victims of penal infringements.

Systematically understaffed jurisdictions are a fundamental shortcoming with regard to the proclaimed principles of good jurisdiction. This applies to "juridiction judiciaire" (civil and penal law procedures) and "justice administrative" (administrative jurisdiction). "Magistrature debout" (magistracy standing up), with instructions from Ministry of Justice and formulating the claim ("le parquet", "le ministère public"), is distinguished from "magistrature assise" (seated magistracy of judges), which has the task of judging. Although their work and competencies have been extended markedly, the number of magistrates in 1992 at about 6,000 was only 40% higher than in 1968 (the level of 1914). In this period, the number of civil cases rose by 150%, and of penal cases by 87%. In 1993, common "juridiction judiciaire" encompassed a "Cours de cassation"; 33 "Cours d'appel"; 102 "Cours d'assises"; 181 "Tribunaux de grande instance"; 473 "Tribunaux d'instance"; 133 "Tribunaux pour enfants"; 229 "Tribunaux de commerce"; 270 "Conseils de prud'hommes"; 437 "Tribunaux paritaires"; and 113 "Tribunaux des affaires de sécurité sociale". "Conseils de prud'hommes", competent exclusively for conflicts of labour law (equal representation from employers and employees), are subdivided into sections (industry, agriculture etc). The "Activité principale de l'entreprise" on the wage-sheet, determines the competence of the section. Appeal is possible against decisions concerning cases involving more than 18,900 francs.

The "Tribunal d'instance" (TI), judging with a single judge, is competent for simple cases (rents, debts, etc.) involving less than 30,000 francs. These TI's handle more than 300,000 cases yearly. Decisions of a TI can be challenged in four ways: opposition by a person not present, and not represented; "tierce opposition", opposition by a third party; appeal for an amount of more than 13,000 francs and cassation. The "Tribunal de grande instance" (TGI), judging with a panel of three judges, handles more complicated cases (divorce, adoption, succession, property, expropriation etc.) and when more than 30,000 francs is involved. The "Tribunal de commerce"(TC), competent only for commercial cases, is judged by two businessmen who are elected for two years (yearly some 240,000 cases). Up to 13,000 francs the TC decides as a last resort, only cassation is available thereafter. For cases above 13,000 francs appeal upon the civilian chamber of the "Cour d'appel" is possible. The "juge de l'expropriation" (seat in the capital of the department), is competent for fixing indemnities for expropriations and measures in the sphere of spatial planning. The "Tribunal paritaire des baux ruraux", established at every TI, is competent for conflicts between owners and tenants of agrarian real estate. "Tribunaux des affaires de sécurité sociale" (since 1945), are ruled by the "Nouveau code de sécurité sociale" (21-12-1985). The "Commission d'indemnisation de certaines victimes d'infractions", established at every TGI since 1977, decides indemnities to be paid by the State. A law of 6 July 1990 ruled integral compensation.

According to the "principe de l'unité de la justice civile et répressive", there are no sepatate civil judges and penal judges, all judges in the "ordre judiciaire" can fulfil functions in civil and penal procedures simultaneously and successively. In the penal procedure, the first level is entrusted to two kinds of tribunals and some specialised jurisdictions. "Tribunaux de police", normally with the same resort as the TI's and judging with one judge more than 8 million cases yearly, are competent for infractions, more serious infringments, offences qualified by the "Code pénal" with two months of imprisonment as sanction, are handled by the "Chambre correctionnelle" (three judges). The "Tribunal correctionnel", the penal chamber of the TGI, is competent for offences only (about 600,000 cases yearly). The public prosecutor, represented by "Procureur de la République" or substitute, formulates the sentence with regard to the sanction. To investigate facts and circumstances, the "Juge d'instruction" (JI), selected from judges of the TGI and appointed by decree of the President of the Republic for three years, has ample competencies. The calling in of the JI is obligatory for crimes, and facultative for offences. He may do all he thinks necessary to recover the truth, "à charge et à décharge", his work can also be on behalf of the suspect. The JI can order "comparition" (presentation of a person); "mandat d'amener" (arrest for interrogation); "dépôt" (custody in a house of detention); and arrest. The JI has a double function, investigator and judge. The penal function of the TGI encompasses an investigator-judge, a penal chamber, a criminal judge for children, and the "juge de l'application des peines", created in 1958. The "Cour d'assises", with a seat in every department, has three professional judges ("la cour") and 9 members of a jury (assigned by lot). It is competent for judging crimes and offences in the first and last instance. Members of the jury are assigned in three steps. Yearly by lot on the basis of electoral lists per department. On the basis of this selection there is an assignment by lot for each session, and for each case (some refusals are possible). If one does not attend, despite assignment by lot, as member of the jury, one can be fined. The "Cour d'assises" has a session of 15 days each quarter, sometimes there are more sessions.

For the principle of the "double degré de juridiction" there is no good jurisdiction if there is no possibility of appeal, to re-evaluate the decision of a judge integrally (factually and with regard to the application of the law), or when only cassation is allowed (then only the application of the law is evaluated). For all civil or penal procedures ("de droit commun ou spécialisées"), about which there is a decision in first instance, appeal is possible to one of the 35 "Cours d'appel" for complete re-judging. The "Cour de Cassation" is on top of the organisation of jurisdiction. It has to guarantee the legally established juridical order and the unity of jurisprudence. This "Cour de Cassation" reviews only the application of laws, not facts so it is not a third instance. The "Cour de Cassation" was introduced in 1790. Revolutionaries had a deep distrust with regard to judges which was understandable because of abuses of the jurisdiction system during the Ancien Régime, so they ruled that judges were not allowed to issue general rules (the exclusive task of the legislator), their task was to judge individual cases by literally applying the law. A court of cassation was seen as an arrangement to correct the faulty decisions of judges. When this Court of Cassation thinks that the law has been applied unjustly the case is remitted to another judge of the same instance, with a different personal composure ("juridiction de renvoi"). The "Cour de Cassation" has the task to guarantee that the same rules of written or unwritten law are applied everywhere in France. The law of 15 May 1991 created the possibility for jurisdictions to ask advice of the Court of Cassation concerning questions of new law. Because of the two different forms of jurisdiction, common jurisdiction and administrative jurisdiction, distribution of competencies is a crucial issue. To prevent situations of refusal of jurisdiction due to problems with competencies, the "Tribunal des conflits" was established. Boundaries of competence are not completely determined, so an instance has to decide about competencies, preventing the possibility of no decision at all.

Administrative jurisdiction is an original French innovation. "Justice administrative" is composed of "Conseil d'État"; 5 "Cours administratives d'appel"; and 33 "Tribunaux administratifs" (of which 7 in overseas territories). Some organs have a specific function: "Cour des comptes"; "Chambres régionales des comptes"; and "Cour de discipline budgétaire et financière". With some exceptions, administrative jurisdictions are subordinate to the "Conseil d'État" via appeal on one of the "Cours administratives" or on the basis of cassation, so the unity of administrative jurisdiction is guaranteed. Since the law of 31 December 1987 administrative jurisdictions can ask the advice of the "Conseil d'État" about any new, serious problem of law. "Tribunaux administratifs" (TA) replaced "conseils de préfecture" (created in the year VIII) after 1953. Procedures for the TA have been governed by the "Code des tribunaux administratifs et des cours administratifs d'appel" since 7 September 1989. The TA are the normal judges for cases of administrative law. Since 1 January 1989 five "Cours administratives d'appel" (CAA) have been created to relieve the "Conseil d'État", in Paris, Lyon, Nancy, Nantes and Bordeaux, as courts of appeal for decisions of the TA. Only cassation is possible against decisions of CAA. "Cour des comptes" is competent for checking the accounts of public organs, if no irregularity is found it discharges with "arrêt de décharge" ("quitus"), otherwise it issues an "arrêt de débet".

Decentralisation legislation (law of 10 July 1982, and a decree of 22 March 1983) created "chambres régionales des comptes" to control the accounts of local public authorities and their organs. The "Cours de discipline budgétaire et financière" (law of 25 September 1948) was established to assess "ordonnateurs", responsible for ordering specific expenditures. Unlike magistrates of common jurisdiction, administrative judges don't form one corps. In earlier times, distribution of competencies between common jurisdiction and administrative jurisdiction was fairly clear. The decree of "16 fructidor an III" simply forbade the common judge to interfere in activities of administration. Conflicts over these activities had to be handled by administrative judges. As the content of the administrative decree was not clear, legislator and "Conseil d'État" had to clarify this. Issuing of one-sided decrees and individual measures was seen as the specific prerogative of public organs. When legal texts did not rule competencies exactly judges developed criteria to determine competencies. Up till 1872 the "Conseil d'État" used criteria like "State-debtor" (the State could be condemned to pay), distinction between "actes d'autorité" and "actes de gestion" (comparable to acts of private persons), and "gestion publique" (only the State can have this task).

The "Tribunal des conflits", with its Blanco-judgment (8 February 1872), created a juridical breach of this trend by stating that administrative law is an autonomous sphere of law, and by launching a new notion; "service public". This jurisdiction had to decide the question of which judge was competent to determine responsibility for an accident in a tobacco factory at Bordeaux. The decision was that this was not covered by civil law, as damage had been caused by a "service public". For the "école du service public", this criterion of the public service was decisive to determine the competence of the administrative judge. Even when there is a public service, the administrative judge is not always competent. A public organ can perform civil law activities (contracts) for which the civil judge is competent. The "Conseil d'État" uses "service publique" and "prérogatives de puissance publique" as criteria. To ascertain if the administrative judge can judge contractual relations, a public person (corporation) has to be party. This is a necessary, not a sufficient condition. When an administrative judge is confronted with questions of civil and administrative law, these are presented to common jurisdiction as prejudicial questions. Questions of administrative law in a procedure for common jurisdiction can be presented to the administrative judge.

The premise is that government administration in a constitutional state is subordinate to law: there is no space without law. Efficacy of this principle depends on the sanction with which a decree of government administration is hit, when this does not conform to prevailing juridical norms. In French jurisprudence the principle was developed that everybody can ask the administrative judge to annul an illegal decree on the basis of "recours pour excès de pouvoir". The "Conseil d'État" has extended the conditions needed for this basis for appeal. The person involved has to have an interest. While during the 19th century only a personal interest was accepted as such, jurisprudence later gave a wider interpretation to this. After the beginning of the 20th century the interest of an association was recognised ("C.E., 28 décembre 1906, Syndicat des patrons coiffeurs de Limoges"). Not only a material interest, but also an immaterial interest was recognised and both individuals and public corporations could use this basis for an appeal. With the new possibilities of control over government administration (law of 2 March 1982), "recours pour excès de pouvoir" became the normal procedure to decide the legality of decisions of public authorities. Decrees of public organs "faisant grief" (one-sided decisions with detrimental effects) can be attacked by this kind of appeal (within two months of publication of the decree). When somebody asks a public organ to rule otherwise ("recours gracieux ou hiérarchique") this term starts later. Appealing the decree of a public organ normally has no suspending effect; it is valid until annulled by a judge.

Several reasons can lead to the annulment of the decree of a public organ ("éléments constitutifs de l'illegalité"). Only incompetence could cause annulment, until the "Conseil d'État", distinguishing between "légalité externe" and "légalité interne", enlarged the number of possible causes. External lawfulness is about the formal conditions of decisions and measures of public organs. Judges must determine their formal conditions and the (in)competency of the public organ ex officio (even if it has not been requested). "Vices de forme et de procédure" are about the formal and procedural defects of decisions and measures. Internal lawfulness is about the contents of decisions and measures: respect for the law, objectives for which competencies were given, etc. A judge has to verify several aspects. He examines whether a decision has a legal basis and whether the legal text has been interpreted correctly ("erreur de droit") and if the facts which are the foundation of the decision are correct ("exactitude matérielle des faits"). The juridical qualification of facts is tested. Can the facts justify the measure taken? When a public organ made a decision using the competences for another objective, it is nullified for "détournement de pouvoir". Other grounds for appeal are: "l'erreur manifeste d'appréciation" and "théorie du bilan".

A decision of a public organ, nullified by an administrative judge, is annulled for everybody. It is as though the nullified decision never existed. The retroactive effect of an annulment means that the public organ has to restore the original situation. There are exceptions, such as when there has been a long period between the issuing and annulment of a decision. When annulment is difficult in circumstances as they have developed, a public organ sometimes uses the disputed procedure of "validation législative". The sentence of a judge is then cancelled by a later law. This practice violates the principles of "l'autorité de la chose jugée" and the separation of executive and jurisdictional powers. The risk of nullification for unlawful administrative decrees means that juridical conditions are observed more strictly. There are limits to the competence of the administrative judge due to the nature of decrees; Actes du "gouvernement" are withdrawn from his control. A decision of the President of the Republic to apply article 16 of the Constitution cannot be attacked by a "recours pour excès de pouvoir". The administrative judge may not interfere in common jurisdiction. The administrative judge has to abstain from interventions in the activities of government administration concerning civil registration, individual liberties and private property. Common jurisdiction is seen as the natural protector of liberties, limited only by the legislator.

The function of common jurisdiction is the protection of rights, goods and the liberties of persons by adjudicating conflicts between private persons ("juridictions civiles"; "justice civile"), and to oppose actions against law and public order ("juridictions pénales"; "justice pénale"). Competencies of civil judges are ruled by civil law in the broadest sense ("droit civil, droit commercial, droit du travail, droit de la sécurité sociale"). They are competent concerning "voie de fait" (decisions of public authorities which impair fundamental liberties of persons or property right, when public authority is not competent or trespasses competence), and about the "emprise", an unlawful encroaching upon property right which comes near to expropriation. Penal jurisdiction has to maintain public order, inter alia by undoing "actes délicteux". The initiative is taken by the public prosecutor, the magistrates of the "parquet", who claims the application of law and oversees the implementation of judicial sentences. Sometimes this function is fulfilled by government administration itself, as with infringements of the laws of indirect taxation and customs. The public prosecutor, as guard of public order, has the power to decide opportunity of prosecution. In the penal procedure, the public prosecutor claims the sanction asked by law, but the judge decides about the sanction. Public order is maintained inter alia by prosecuting and penalising crimes and offences. Personal rights and liberties have to be protected against arbitrariness.

Several texts have proclaimed these rights and liberties. The most fundamental being the "Déclaration des droits de l'homme et du citoyen" (1789) which is an integral part of the preamble of the Constitution of 1958. There is the principle of "légalité des délits et des peines", and the non-retroactive effect of laws. To effect a prosecution it must be ascertained that the prosecuted person is guilty according to the facts which are constituent components of the circumscription of the offences or crime. The penalty must have a basis in the law. Only a later law, which is more favourable for the person involved, can be applied upon preceding facts. Another guarantee is proclaimed in article 66 of the Constitution, elaboration of article 9 of the Human Rights Declaration: "Nobody may be detained arbitrarily. The judiciary, guarantor of individual liberty, has to guarantee respect for this principle, according to the conditions of the law." This is supposed to guarantee that nobody is detained by the police without a legal basis. The code of penal procedure rules which grounds can be used to hold somebody in provisional custody: 24 hours custody, with extention for another 24 hours on the basis of an authorisation from an attorney or "juge d'instruction". After provisional custody, provisional detention for four months is possible, further extended by two months (in the case of previous detention within the last 5 years this extention can be unlimited, with 4 months every time). Measures of deprivation of liberty preceding the sentence of a judge are overseen by a penal judge. With a law of 17 July 1970, indemnity can be requested when provisional measures of deprivation of liberty are unjustified. If the sentence is a fine or detention penalties must be implemented, if necessary by force, by the public prosecutor with the "force publique".

## 4.2. Since 1958 judiciary authority instead of judiciary power

The Constitution of 1958 replaced "pouvoir judiciaire" by "autorité judiciaire", to emphasize that judges do not, and should not, have political power, but constitutional guarantees for independent jurisdiction were less than in the Constitution of 1946. The position of executive power, in casu the Head of State, was reinforced in relation to judges. It is necessary to know which jurisdiction has to be asked to judge, and what law is applicable. It is quite impossible, even for professionals, to know the whole collection of legal texts. To prevent this causing a structural pretext, exculpating anyone saying that he did not know that this or that was the legal ruling, a basic and simple premise is used. Everybody is supposed to know the law, all laws! There are some 8,000 laws and 400,000 decrees or by-laws, so public authorities have to arrange for information about prevailing laws to be easily available to all. Popularised codes of law are available for consultation in many public places (libraries etc.). Accessibility of laws is reduced by the juridical-technical character of legal texts making it nearly impossible to understand their meaning. Professional assistance is nearly always needed. In reaction to the complexity of the collection of laws, lawyers are organised into a series of specialisations and sub-specialisations.

After 1958, reforms took place (Taisne, 1994). In "jurisdictions judiciaires", "justices de paix" and "tribunaux civils" were replaced by "tribunaux d'instance" (TI) and "tribunaux de grande instance" (TGI). The "cours d'appel" retained only jurisdiction in the second instance. The "Code d'instruction criminelle" (1808) was replaced by the "Nouveau Code de procédure pénale" (NCPP). All legal texts concerning judges were collected in the "Code de l'organisation judiciaire" (COJ). Statute and career perspectives for judges were renewed. A new "Centre national d'études judiciaires" was started, transformed into "École nationale de la magistrature". Much work was done in the field of codification: "Code de Justice Militaire" (CJM, 1965); "Code des Tribunaux Administratifs" (CTA, 1973); "Nouveau code de procédure civile" (NCPC, 1975); "Code de l'organisation judiciaire" (COJ, 1978). Specialised jurisdictions were reformed: "Conseils des prud'hommes" (labour legislation), "Tribunaux des affaires de sécurité sociale" (TASS, 1985) and "Tribunaux de commerce" (1987). To relieve the "Conseil d'État", in 1987 "Cours administratives d'appel" (CAA) were established. Guarantees for the independence of administrative judges were improved (1986/1987) and the penal law procedure was changed. The profession of barristers came under new legislation. A law of 1990 was the framework for a fusion of barristers and juridical advisers. "Procédures d'exécution" about seizures etc. were revised with the law of 9 July 1991. After revision of juridical assistance in 1972 and free juridical assistance in 1977, a new revision came in with the law of 1992. The Constitution was revised with the constitutional law of 27 July 1993. Political jurisdictions were renewed. "Haute cour de justice" (HCJ) for judging eventual high-treachery by the President of the Republic. "Cour de justice de la République" (CJR) to judge eventual crimes and offences of ministers committed in execution of their functions (article 68, subsections 1 and 2). "Conseil supérieur de la magistrature". Laws of 1992, 1993 and 1994 renewed the statute of "magistrature judiciaire", reinforcing their independence and improving their performance, but widespread discontent about jurisdiction in France remains. Budgetary neglect is a structural phenomenon. The budget is in total some 4.5 billion euro; per head of population this is half of what is spent on justice in Germany.

Outside the structure of common and administrative jurisdictions there are two specific organs of the judiciary authority: "Tribunal des conflits" (TC), and "Conseil Constitutionnel" (CC). When a case, in which government administration is involved, is brought before the common judge the prefect, with a "déclatoire de compétence", asks him to declare himself incompetent (positive conflict of competence). When he does, the process party is remitted to the administrative jurisdiction. If he does not, the prefect can start an "arrêté de conflit" to put the case before the TC, having three months to take a decision. There is a negative conflict of competence if the common judge rules that the earlier approached administrative judge was competent anyhow, and then the TC decides which judge is competent. With a "conflit du renvoi" a judge can ask TC to prevent a negative conflict of competence (common judge and administrative judge declare themselves incompetent concerning the same case). The TC can be asked to fulfil a "saisie au fond", when two sentences (of common judge and administrative judge) in a case are contradictory, causing "déni de justice" (denial of justice).

A vital aspect of jurisdiction is its accessibility for citizens. Often representation by solicitors is obligatory, as in procedures before "Tribunal de grande instance", "Cours d'appel" and "Cour de cassation". Professional help is thought to be needed for the quality of the procedure, but representation is not always possible. A judge must have the opportunity to speak to a suspect in privatet. In several phases free juridical help is possible. The French Revolution eliminated the payments by process parties to judges. Judges from then on were paid as functionaries by the State. Since 1851, solicitors have worked without asking to be paid by those who had no money ("assistance judiciaire"). The law of 3 January 1972 introduced a scheme whereby the State pays solicitors working for those with a minimal income ("l'aide judiciaire"). Since then, the system of free juridical assistance has been reformed. A law of 10 July 1991, modified with the law of 24 August 1993, distinguishes three variants: assistance for the jurisdictional procedure; help to get adequate access to law; and assistance of a solicitor. "Aide juridictionnelle", paid by the State, replaced "aide judiciaire", and is available for all who have no more than a fixed minimum income. This was an income of 4,400 francs monthly for all-encompassing jurisdictional help, and 6,600 francs monthly for partial help (combined with a contribution to be paid by the process party). Since 1 January 1993, these amounts have been reviewed annually. Juridical assistance now has the form of the modernised "aide juridique". This help does not mean that in the case of a loss at the procedure and a condemnation to pay process costs, these costs are paid by the State. A law of 10 July 1991 brought renewal of the "aide à l'accès au droit" for simple juridical advice. In a penal process the condemned person has to pay all costs. When the verdict is acquittal, the suspect does not pay the costs of prosecution, but gets no compensation for the costs of defence either.

According to principles of the good juridical process, several conditions must be fulfilled, such as "droits de la défense". A process party must be summoned betimes with a "notification par le greffe" (registered letter) or "signification par voie d'huissier" (summons). In civil cases, "nullités de fond" (as unqualified representation) and "nullités de forme" (formal nullities like a wrong date) are distinguished. In the penal process, there is nullity when a "formalité substantielle" is violated. In administrative process, there are "formalités substantielles" (when not fulfilled, automatic nullity) and "formalités non substantielles" (only nullity when invoked). Terms are relevant. A judge must ascertain if he is competent, if not, he does not try the case ("non-recevabilité"). Nobody may be sentenced without being heard according to the principle "audi et alteram partem" and nobody can be judged without hearing what he is accused of. One has to make one's identity known to the other party. The process party who has taken the initiative for a process has to make clear to the other party "l'objet du procès" (what it's all about), and the grounds for starting the procedure. Process parties have to inform one another betimes about facts and legal remedies, and available evidence. To preclude suggestions of possible unlawful practices, a juridical process must normally take place in public but publicity about juridical processes may not further scandal. Some fundamental rights may not be violated, like the right of privacy and the presumption of innocence. The judicial investigation takes place secretly, in the interest of prosecution, suspect and public (prevention of abuses). For civil cases, hearing of the parties can take place in a closed chamber. In penal cases, it is possible to opt for a trial in a closed chamber, as with the prosecution of minors. The trial can take place in administrative cases in a closed "chambre du conseil". The procedure is partially oral ("verba volant") and partially on paper ("scripta manent"). In penal procedure, investigation ("instruction") is mainly with written material ("dossier"), and trial is mostly verbal. In civil procedure, traditionally chiefly verbal, ever more documents are used. Administrative process is mainly in writing. In civil cases, the initiative is for the parties; the judge has a more passive role. He may consider only what the parties have communicated ("interdiction de statuer ultra petita"). In penal procedure, the judge is active. He has to be critical towards the public prosecutor, in spite of all evidence.

When a judge has decided the sentence, this decision (setting aside appeal and cassation), according to the principle "res judicata pro veritate habetur", has authority: "l'autorité de la chose jugée". No new juridical procedure is possible concerning this case ("exception de chose jugée"). Normally sentences are directly executable, if necessary forced by the strong arm of the law ("force exécutoire du jugement"). Appeal and cassation are justified as it is possible that, factually or in application of the law, mistakes were made or there is an injustice. Appeal, in principle, has a suspending effect. There are terms within which appeal must be invoked. For penal law procedures it is normally 10 days after the sentence, for civil law procedures, one month after notification of the judgement, for administrative law procedures, normally two months after notification. Setting aside some exceptions, in civil and administrative law procedures cassation does not suspend. In penal law, cassation normally suspends, depending on the gravity of the case. With "pourvoi dans l'intérêt de la loi", cassation is started to ask for a decision in principle for the future, without effects for the process parties. Extraordinary appeal is directed on revision of a judgement: "pourvoi en révision". To prevent misuse, revision in penal procedures is possible in the case of indications that somebody is condemned while innocent, for example due to new evidence (law of 23 June 1989).

Execution of judgements normally takes place on the initiative of the most involved party. It is necessary to obtain a copy of the judgement with executory effect ("lever la grosse"), in exceptional cases, on the basis of the judgement itself ("exécution sur minute"). When the judgement is not notified to the other process party it must be notified by summons. When the terms for appeal are expired, one has to ask the office of the clerk for a "certificat de non-recours". For decisions of arbiters as private persons, and of judges abroad, the strong arm of the law cannot be invoked. Then the "procédure d'exéquatur" has to be started before the "Tribunal de grande instance". There are several methods for "exécution forcée". Seizure of effects is ruled anew with the law of 9 July 1991, operative since 1 January 1993. To prepare for seizure some form of garnishee can be used. Different kinds of execution are possible: "saisie-attribution" (seizure of possessions of a third party); "saisie des rémunérations" (seizure upon the salary); and "saisie-vente" (the creditor can sell the possessions of his debtor). For real estate there is a procedure of long duration. When there are several creditors, the procedure for the "distribution des deniers" (law of 9 July 1991; decree of 31 July 1992, articles 283/293) must be followed. Setting aside execution of sentences for civil interests, execution of penal law sentences is up to the public prosecutor, who can decide detention or release. Fines are collected by the treasury, the sole organ that can force payment of debts by detention. Private persons can try to get their rights by invoking a bailiff ("huissier"). The position of private persons towards public authorities has been reinforced with the introduction of "médiateur" (ombudsman) since 24 December 1976, and some other measures (law of 16 July 1980). Public functionaries are responsible when refusing to execute a judgement of a jurisdiction.

### 4.3. From "Police" as public affairs to Police properly

Each society needs social order. Organising, protecting and restoring social order and implementation of sanctions against persons who disturb social order form the "raison d'être" of public authorities. The objective of social order is that people may live in some harmony, with peace, security and protection against aggression. In this task, the police have a central position. When Romans occupied territory they appointed a proconsul in each province, charged with administration, jurisdiction and police. The proconsul delegated police tasks to "curatores". In Roman law, the prefect was charged with civil and military functions. After the fourth century, civil authority and military power were distinguished in Gallia. The notion "police" underwent several reinterpretations in the course of time. Originally going back to the Greek "polis", the term police in former times was used to indicate the whole of the activities of public authorities. This term was used in royal ordinances from the 15th century onwards in France. Then it was practically identical with public affairs. Since the 11th century, the "prévot de Paris", appointed by the King, was charged with jurisdiction, regulation and police. Elsewhere, similar functionaries were appointed mostly with different rulings. For King Charles V in the 14th century, "bonne police" encompassed the whole task of public authorities. Since the 15th century the notion "police" was used to denote maintaining public order. Under the authority of King François I (1494-1547), the "Ordonnance de Villers-Cotterêts sur le fait de justice, police, finances" was issued (192 articles). This was in force up until the French Revolution (1789). To fight criminality in the countryside, François I charged military "prévots des maréchaux" with jurisdictional tasks also. In the 17th century, police meant administrative regulation. Domat (1625-1696) in his "Traité des Loix" used the concept of "police universelle de la société". For De la Mare in his "Traité de la police" (1748), French Kings were wise to adopt the Roman law system, administration and "police". For him, police encompassed the most varied activities of public authorities, but he was aware of the ambiguity of identifying police with the whole of public law. He preferred a restricted interpretation of maintaining public order. In the Ancien Régime, police formed the domain of the law. Since the French Revolution, police has been more strictly defined.

During the Ancien Régime, the Kings, trying to find finances for rising expenditures, increasingly sold offices, including those of jurisdiction and police. At the end of the 17th century, the monarchy was confronted with serious political, religious and social problems, provoking disturbances of societal order. Criminality became a growing societal nuisance. The rebellious noble movement of the "Fronde" (1648-1653) threatened royal authority and disorganised society. Minister Colbert formed a "Conseil de police" to make suggestions for taking control of public order problems. Several (purchased or inherited) functions of public authorities were mixed up. King Louis XIV (1661-1715), with the royal edict of 15 March 1667, established the function of "lieutenants de police", charged with regulation, jurisdiction and policing. Before 1667 policing was a fragmented whole of rival functionaries, with interference of "parlements" and feudal traditions. Since the end of the 17th century it is seen as a function specifically of the State. At the end of the 17th century, police was centralised, under royal authority, working via "intendants" in provinces and via "lieutenants de police" in towns. The "Grande ordonnance criminelle" (1670) divided jurisdiction into three phases: information-gathering, preparing investigation and judging. This regulation and a "Déclaration royale" of 5 February 1731 ruled that only judges were competent to investigate and judge (setting aside cases of "flagrant délit"). In practice, it was different. Often military armed forces (with mercenaries) restored public order, if police functionaries could not do this. In the countryside there was confusion. Due to ongoing conflicts over the question of which law was applicable, and regarding division of competencies (Municipal authorities, feudal lords, representatives of Church or King). Conflicts were sharpened by provocatively operating "parlements" with jurisdictional and ruling competencies.

According to Alexis de Tocqueville, the place for the notion of law in the human mind was vacant at the end of the Ancien Régime. The system of the "droit ancien" had then already changed, but the French Revolution had the most decisive impact. Revolutionaries wanted to abolish the existing police organisation as part of the hated Ancien Régime. The sale and inheritance of offices were eliminated. The "maréchaussée" was transformed into the "gendarmerie nationale". The "Déclaration des droits de l'homme et du citoyen" (1789) made the notion of constitutional state operational with the proclamation of principles of law. Like separation of powers; innocence had to be supposed until guilt was proven; no retroactive effect of laws; etc. Guaranteeing human rights made armed forces necessary, on behalf of all citizens (not only for those who possessed offices, as before). After 1789 policing became a task of local authorities. The mayor got competencies to order the use of force to end disturbances of public order, with the help of the "Garde nationale", composed of citizens. With the decree of 19/22 July 1791 the competencies of the mayor were extended. State police and police organisation soon replaced this municipal police for Paris (as in the Ancien Régime). In 1790, "commissaires de police" were elected functionaries. After the "Terreur" (1793/1794), the police was reorganised, election of police commissioners was abolished. Danton's dictum was: "Let us be terrible to forestall the people to become terrible"

An important principle of the Republican order was proclaimed. Only civil public authorities got competencies in the field of maintaining and restoring public order, so military authorities could take action for restoring public order only when asked by civil public authorities. A law of 1789 gave "officiers municipaux" the competence to dispose of armed public forces in case of disturbances of public order. The police commissioner was now under the authority of the mayor. The "Code des délits et des peines du 3 brumaire an IV" ruled that police maintain public order, freedom, property, and individual security. To end abuses of former "parlements" it was ruled that "police administrative" (maintaining public order) and "police judiciaire" (investigation of transgressions; bringing offenders before jurisdictions) had to be divided. Police was made competent before and after but not during the penal procedure (without authorisation of judges). According to the law of 17 April 1798, the "Gendarmerie Nationale" was made a force to ensure public order and the implementation of laws. The foundation was laid for the function of the police in the sphere of internal, national security management. With the law of 2 January 1796, a Ministry of Police was created. The first ministers of police succeeded each other at a rapid pace until the notorious Joseph Fouché, seen as founder of the modern police, was appointed on 20 July 1799. He had this function, with some breaks, until September 1815, under quite different regimes. Fouché discovered the importance of information about the opinions of groups in society, to repress intrigues and attacks on State security.

On the basis of the law of 17 February 1800, the administrative organisation of the police was reorganised. This was the first attempt to organise national police on a rational basis. The police prefect of Paris, succeeding the "lieutenant général de police" of the Ancien Régime, was charged with everything concerning the police. In other cities, and in the provinces, police commissioners were appointed under the authority of prefect and Minister of police. The "Code d'instruction criminelle" (1808) formulated the task of the judicial police, including tracing crimes, offences and transgressions; collecting evidence; and bringing offenders before judges. Police functionaries fulfil their functions having several tasks as delegated to them. Until 1940 the institutional situation of the police did not change very much. With an imperial decree of 22 February 1855, a special railway police was established. It also had the task of informing government about political and social developments. In November 1871 there came a "Direction de la sûreté générale et de la presse" in the Ministry of the Interior. The "Charte municipale" of 5 April 1884 confirmed the extended police competencies of mayors, while Paris maintained its police prefect. This law made municipal authorities a decentralised part of the State, with the emphasis on its administrative function. Police in the Third Republic was the object of controversies (Berlière, 1991). Seen as an executive part of the State to maintain public order, Municipal police had strong defenders, but centralisation of police was needed to handle problems with public order due to urbanisation and industrialisation.

Because opposition against State police was strong, State police was more the exception than the rule throughout a long period of the Third Republic. Generally municipal police had too little capacity (materially and concerning human resources), and often there were conflicts between mayors and prefects (Journès, 1988). More and more the efficacy of police activities was impeded by lack of unity. Rivalries abounded; there were even police wars. Counter-espionage was, until the end of the 19th century, the role of the armed forces. The row about the "Affaire Dreyfus" meant that counter-espionage was withdrawn from the Ministries of War and the Navy. The Ministry of the Interior was responsible for counter-espionage aftere May 1899. Government charged the police organisation "Sûreté générale" with this task. A decree of 20 May 1903 about the gendarmerie gave non-commissioned officers of the army, who could not then become "Officier de police judiciaire", competencies in the field of judiciary police. With a decree (30 December 1907) "brigades mobiles" for quick jurisdiction were established to fight growing criminality. The "Police judiciaire" was formed with a decree of 30 October 1917. The "Rapport-Plytas" (1934) demonstrated that the reorganisation of the police was urgent. With a decree of 28 April 1934 "Sûreté générale" became "Sûreté nationale", meant to give the State more grip on the organisation of police in the country. The reorganisation did not have the expected results. The objective was to improve co-ordination and to finish conflicts of competencies between prefects, mayors and magistrates. Formalised relations between "Préfecture de police" of Paris and "Sureté" existed on paper.

The Vichy regime (1940-1944) has left behind some traces in contemporary police organisation. A law of 23 April 1941 established the "Police National" (PN) with specialised central directions. The police in cities with more than 10,000 inhabitants was incorporated in the PN. There came a regional structure of police services. "École nationale de police" was a "grande école de l'État". It had an "École supérieure" for the training of police commissioners, and an "École pratique" for inspectors. After Liberation, PN was "Sécurité Nationale" (SN). "Code d'instruction criminelle" was replaced by "Code de procédure pénale" (laws of 1957, 1958 and 1959). "Officiers de police judiciaire" were extended. Gendarmes and police-inspectors got "compétence d'attribution", becoming "Agents de police judiciaire". The authority of judges over judiciary police was confirmed. Reorganisations followed. A law of 9 July 1966 incorporated functionaries of "Sûreté nationale" and "préfecture de la police" into "Police Nationale". A decree of 29 September 1969 abolished "Sûreté nationale" and "Sécretariat générale pour la police". "Direction générale de la police nationale" came under the Minister of the Interior, national gendarmerie under the Ministry of Defence.

### 4.4. Some features of the French police model

Police as a public, professional and specialised organisation began in France with the royal edict of 15 March 1667. This established the function of "lieutenant général de police" representing royal authority and independent from "parlements". The start of a police structure is related to the establishment of the French State. It was quite logical to have a specialised organisation in charge of maintaining public order. In contrast with Anglo-Saxon tradition, the French police was in essence a creation of the State. Gradually, the police developed itself as a specific institution within public management, profiling itself with regard to armed forces and judiciary. Traditionally the armed forces had an important task in defending national public order. In the Ancien Régime, police forces had a military character; "maréchaussée" was the national police. Revolutionaries wanted to abolish the existing police as part of the hated Ancien Régime. The function of the "lieutenant générale de police" was abrogated on 4 August 1789. In the revolutionary conception, the notion police was redefined as an organisation to maintain public order to guarantee rights and public liberties of citizens. The "Code des délits et des peines du 3 brumaire an IV" stated: police has to maintain public order, freedom, property and individual security. It was split into administrative police and judiciary police.

To follow the principle of separation of powers, police and judiciary were separate institutions. Administrative police was charged with maintaining public order (prevention of offences). Judiciary police had to inquire offences, assemble evidence and present authors of offences to judicial authorities, by the legislative authority charged with deciding sanctions. Police functionaries generally have both administrative and judicial competencies. One has to take account of the fact, that the same operation may change its character as a result of circumstances. The difference between administrative police and judiciary police has its practical significance above all in different juridical regimes. Administrative police are placed directly under the authority of administrative authorities. Judiciary police function in each resort of a "Cours d'appel", under surveillance of the "procureur général" and under supervision of the "Chambre d'accusation". The judiciary police was the first specialised police. Police was seen as an essentially municipal function, based upon two principles of public law. Election of locally responsible authorities, and recognition of the municipality as natural and private association. Elected mayors became responsible for policing. They had to fulfil this task with the help of the "Garde nationale", composed of citizens. The law of 14 December 1789 and other regulations charged municipal police to ensure that citizens can enjoy the advantages of good policing and public management with regard to possessions, health, and security. This municipal police was replaced by State police and a specific police organisation for Paris (as under the Ancien Régime). To decrease the use of armed forces, a specific military organisation was mobilised, "gendarmerie", created in 1790, under the authority of the Minister of Defence it was committed to maintaining public order in the countryside. The "gendarmerie" was not effective at first. For revolutionaries, this organisation should not be too strong. Since reorganisation of the year VI this changed. The "gendarmerie" became an essential part of public forces.

"Directoire", "Consulat" and "Empire" made the police an administrative apparatus at the disposal of central State power. But local police were maintained. With a law of 2 January 1796, a Ministry of Police was created, abolished in 1818 and restored under the Second Empire, but finally abolished in 1853. Police was made part of the Ministry of the Interior. Developments in the 19th century were characterised by the duality between State police and municipal police. Up to the municipal law of 1884, the police was seen as a specific function of the local community. The bill for the reform of municipal councils of 18 July 1837 was based on the idea that the competencies of municipal police were delegated by the State. Vivien (1859) criticised this. In his view, the mayor did not exercise his functions under the authority of the prefect, but under his surveillance. After the beginning of the Third Republic municipal police lost its specific position as part of the local community in an administrative reorganisation of the national territory. Revolutionary days in 1830 and 1848 showed that police forces had to handle specific problems during mass movements in the narrow streets of Paris. To make repression effective, barracks were built at strategic points. The municipal law (1884) made municipal authority a decentralised part of the State structure, emphasising its administrative function. Article 97 stated that municipal police had to ensure public order, security and health. The mayor was made responsible for public order in his municipality. He became the authority for the police, while the police force was at his disposal. In towns with 5,000 or more inhabitants there was a "commissaire", appointed by decree of central government. The mayor appointed policemen and inspectors. The municipal law stated that the mayor for towns with more than 40,000 inhabitants could appoint policemen only when approved by the prefect.

Napoleon appointed Joseph Fouché minister of police (1804-1810), who made political police a seemingly effective instrument to control society. This shadow police, working in secret, caused myths about its efficacy (Brunet, 1990). Authors like Bayley (1975) argued that French police is a political police. It has the reputation of operationalising an intensified surveillance over public opinion and the activities of societal groups and political parties. This was the case during the Ancien Régime, but more professionalised since Fouché. Fouché preferred systematic collection of information, via omnipresent police, to control the situation and prevent eventual upheavals. This secret police survived a sequence of regimes. After being more or less abandoned at the beginning of the 19th century it was re-intensified after 1855 with a "service spécial de surveillance des chemins de fer". Since the Second Empire secret police had been institutionalised. In spite of critics, political police was reinforced in the Third Republic. After 1911, a functionary was charged with political police. The head of archives was "contrôleur général des services de police administrative". In 1937, government created a director of the "services des renseignements généraux et de la police administrative". The Vichy regime made this a national directorate. It has maintained this form since then. The French police encompassed a political police but also police as "une force de dissuasion politique" (Gleizal c.s., 1993, p.78). Public authorities reacted to (perceived) disorder with legislation and legally based activities, reducing liberties relative to press, the right to form associations and unions, strikes, and mass demonstrations Governments used exceptional measures such as legislation against subversive activities ("état de siège", "état d'urgence"), some of them going further than Anglo-Saxon tradition. The "Garde nationale", composed of citizens, played a role in guarding public order during the period 1789-1871. It functioned more or less as a "nation armée" against the nation itself (Girard, 1964). One may ask if arming the people increases the risk of civil war. Efforts were undertaken, since the beginning of the 19th century, to give government professional intervention forces, but they failed. Since 1870 governments have preferred specialised units within gendarmerie and police to maintain public order, to the use of military force. A proposal was presented in 1905 to introduce mobile police units, but this did not succeed. In 1941, "groupes mobiles de réserve" were established. The provisional government after Liberation took up this idea, creating "compagnies républicaines de sécurité" by decree of 8 December 1944, to mobilise some 15,000 men in 18 regions. This was confirmed with an ordinance of 7 March 1945.

Armed forces played an important role during the 19th century in the defence of the established order. After the Napoleonic period, the army was from 1815 to 1872 a regular army. Armed forces restored order in revolts under the Restoration and July Monarchy. They were also active after 1870 and during social upheavals. Ever more authorities became conscious of the disadvantages of using armed forces to restore public order. With a law of 27 July 1872, obligatory military service, conscription, was introduced. In 1883, a police school was established in Paris. The police gradually profiled itself as a specific institution. Armed forces traditionally had the important task of defending national public order. In the Ancien Régime, police forces had in essence a military character; the "maréchaussée" was the national police. Some 19,000 gendarmes, spread over the national territory, worked in the Third Republic. After the First World War, the gendarmerie was modernised. The position of the "commissaires" was ambiguous: head of the municipal police under the authority of the mayor, and functionary under the authority of the prefect. Generally, the municipal police had too little capacity (personally and materially). Conflicts between mayors and prefects abounded (Journès, 1989). The clearly apparent need for the reorganisation of the municipal police could not overcome stubborn opposition of locally elected authorities. At last the Vichy regime imposed the State police on 10 April 1941, after which municipal police did play a subsidiary role. Efficacy of police activities was impeded by lack of unity. After the First World War, the gendarmerie was modernised. Counter-espionage was up to the end of the 19th century part of the armed forces but the Dreyfus affair resulted in the abolition of the "deuxième bureau". From May 1899 the Minister of the Interior was responsible for counter-espionage. Minister Clémenceau created "police judiciaire with a decree of 30 October 1917", the "police des renseignements" was a separate service. In the Third Republic some measures furthered the unity of the police.

After Liberation the national police were abolished. The "Sûreté nationale" encompassed administrative directions, "police judiciaire", "renseignements généraux", "sécurité publique" and "surveillance du territoire". Directors lost their territorial networks, efficacy suffered. The Constitution of 1946 announced the municipalisation of police, but a rise in the number of social conflicts led to more centralisation. Unity of police had to wait for the Fifth Republic. A law of 1948 brought a statute for all police personnel; a "lex specialis" with regard to the general statute, giving police functionaries the right to form unions, but forbidding them to strike. A law of 10 July 1964 brought a transitional solution, making the Paris "prefecture de police" part of the State personal. In 1964, the gendarmerie was reorganised again, taking more account of the situation in the regions. A new "ordre gendarmique" (Lafont/Meyer, 1980) was created, to adapt better to changing circumstances. Police changed by differentiation and specialisation. This was attended with rivalries and "police wars". The law of 3 July 1966 brought juridical unity with the "Police nationale". But the Paris prefecture of police maintained its powers. Rivalries abounded as before. Municipal police and gendarmerie were not integrated in the national police. Professionalisation of the police was realised gradually. French police, different from the English police, were from the start seen as political police, due to the frequency of political conflicts and social upheavals. "Police du renseignement" were given ample competencies to control public opinion. Police, influenced by politics, were used by central authorities as an instrument to influence partisan politics. Several efforts to make police more of a service for citizens, as in the Anglo-Saxon model, mostly failed. Since the 17th century the monarchy had been endangered by resistance movements against centralisation, religious tensions and social movements against taxes. French society has continued to have its conflicts since then. This partially explains the over-accentuation of the central role of the State (Julliard, 1990). For Bayley (1975) an explanation for political police in France can be found in the role of the inquisition of the Church, interfering in private life.

In the Ancien Régime, political police were active in royal censorship, controlling press, books and correspondence (breaking privacy of letters). In 1789, revolutionaries understandably saw the police as an instrument to fight the spread of new ideas, but their critics of traditional practices did not end this political police, in the regimes which followed this police conception continued. A special service was created, "service des renseignements généraux". In 1913 the "contrôleur général des services de police administrative" was established to organise political police activities, in 1934 the "Direction de la surveillance du territoire" (DST) came in, and in 1937 the "Renseignements généraux" (RG). During the Third Republic the police actively penetrated and infiltrated movements from within (Machelon, 1981). Political police got a nasty reputation especially after the Vichy-Regime. After Liberation RG remained a disputed part of police activities. Secret policing is a very sensitive part of public management, in contemporary France also (Brunet, 1990; Porch, 1995). Relations between politics and police are structurally in a vulnerable position (Journès, 1988). According to Loubet del Bayle (1981, p.509), the police as a specific, intermediary institution is functioning on the intersection between political organisation and the whole of the societal system. Public opinion generally sees the police as an instrument of the State and far less as an institution to protect the people. In fact, the creation of municipal police was an endeavour to bring police and society closer to each other, but municipal police proved to be too close to local political power.

The disadvantages of municipal police were a consequence of too short a distance between police functionaries and local potentates, listening to family, partisan and private interests more than working for the common good. Another method was to make police more visible. In 1829, prefect Debelleyme created in Paris a "corps de sergents de ville", the first uniformed police in Europe. This reform was meant to depoliticise police and to improve their relations with the people. Originally this "corps de sergents de ville" was meant to be a police of individual surveillance as in the London model, but was soon made a repressive instrument for the prefecture of police. This corps discredited itself in public opinion. After the 1870 defeat, the "corps de sergents de ville" was disbanded. "Gardiens de la paix" were formed, charged with maintaining public order and the security of persons and goods. The police are more or less constantly criticised by public opinion. Law and public necessity seem to be deficient as a basis for legitimacy. Especially via "gardiens de la paix", unionism penetrated into the police and in 1901 the "Fédération des sociétés amicales de police de France et des colonies" was created, joined in 1912 by the "Association générale professionelle du personnel de la Préfecture de la Police". Police syndicalism contributed to professionalisation and modernisation.

## 4.5. Juridical regime of the French police

Traditionally, knowledge about the police is more juridical in France, while in Anglo-Saxon countries the sociological approach dominated. Meanwhile this situation has changed. In France research activities have deepened insight into the police phenomenon. The establishment of the "Institut des hautes études de la sécurité intérieure" (IHESI) in 1989 marked a definite reorientation in the form of interdisciplinary research. In Europe, development of the police concept was directly related to the forming of modern States. The French police model has specific characteristics. This makes it necessary to analyse police in the perspective of historical developments (the logic of history). The juridical regime of the French police is significantly different from that in England, as Gleizal c.s. (1993, pp. 133-177) showed. Aspects such as the French concept of constitutional state, the duality of public/private law, historical development of the police system and the political-administrative organisation are relevant. In a democratic society, it is nowhere and never easy to organise an optimising balance between public order and liberties. One objective of the "loi Sécurité et Liberté" of February 1981 was, to improve the protection of liberties in the face of growing police powers. The French model, with the inquisitory procedure, makes the police a crucial agent in penal procedure, above all in the "instruction préparatoire". There are differences between police practice and regulations of the "Code de procédure pénale". The history of French penal procedure can be seen as a series of reforms to protect public liberties, while guaranteeing the efficacy of police repression if necessary. Due to the specific function of the police, there is a separate police law. A specific aspect of police law is that legal rules are subordinated to the needs of maintaining public order. In qualifying the juridical regime of the French police some distinctions play a role: between general police and specialised police; "autorités de police" and "forces de police"; "police administrative" and "police judiciaire".

Police activities have their own features, which make it necessary to distinguish them from the rest of the public management system. The police function is a specific, autonomous State function. As "fonction d'ordre" the police are charged with the maintenance of public order. This activity is of necessity a primary function of the State (Picard, 1984). The notion of guaranteeing public order on the basis of legal norms by itself is open-ended. It is used as criterion to demarcate police from other activities in public management. Administrative judges have to state precisely the contents of this notion, and the relation of police activities to law. French administrative doctrine distinguishes two essential State functions. "Le service public" with the objective of "l'intérêt général", and police with the specific objective of maintaining public order (a specific qualification of the general interest). In administrative jurisprudence, police is a "service fonctionnel", "services publics" are "services organiques". The "Conseil Constitutionnel" in its decision of 27 July 1982, declared maintaining public order as an objective with a constitutional character. Public order is seen as the basis of legitimacy for police activities. Therefore the police disposes of a large "pouvoir d'appréciation", policy room. As the police function of the State is directly related to the necessities of social order, only law is conditioning the application of police activities. It is up to police authorities to qualify circumstances, justify interventions and determine measures. No law text can a priori specify the exact conditions of police intervention. The Rule of Law defines the competencies of police authorities and functionaries. Administrative judges are thus enabled to control police interventions a-posteriori, judging whether the relation between the measures taken and concrete circumstances is justified. Because of the function of the police in maintaining public order, the French administrative law distinguishes between the police and other parts of public administration. The national police authority does not get its competencies from some special juridical arrangement, but on the basis of "necessity". On 8 August 1919, the administrative judge ordained that it is the task of the Head of State, outside all legislative delegation, on the basis of his competencies, to take police measures for the national territory.

The distinction between "police générale" and "polices spéciales" in doctrine and jurisprudence is seen as a relevant, intrinsic criterion. General policing is founded on the necessity of public order as such. Specialised policing needs a legislative base conditioning the exercise of police powers. There are law texts, which do not give competencies to specialised police activities, but just recognise a general police competence. So it is with the competence of the mayor to prescribe measures when circumstances make these necessary in the presence of (imminent) serious danger. Legislative texts defining specific competencies for specialised police authorities are meant to legitimise the application of a law regime, which derogates the normal police law. The distinction between "autorités de police" and "forces de police" is thought to be essential to assure primacy of law over the use of force, by differentiating the functions of issuing norms (by civilian authorities) and material execution of norms (by civilian and military authorities). On the national level, the Premier is the most important police authority. The Minister of the Interior, without competencies for issuing norms (except in case of the policing of foreigners) has directing authority over the police. On the territorial level the prefect has normative authority of police and directing authority. Relations between civil authorities and military police forces are more complicated because of the (in practice only partially effective) principle of separation of civil and military competencies. This principle leads to subordination of armed forces to civil public authorities. The "réquisition" procedure then replaces the giving of orders. Requisition consists of a written order, fulfilling some legal conditions, determining the objective, while leaving the choice of means to the executors.

The distinction between "police administrative" and "police judiciaire", resulting from the French conception of the State, separation of powers and public/private law, has a number of consequences. A law of 16/24 August 1790 made a distinction between "police administrative" and "police judiciaire" operational, elaborating the split between "autorités administratives" and "autorités judiciaires". The "Conseil d'État" developed the difference between them as criterion, necessary as there was no organic separation between these functions. The criterion was found in the nature of activities. The necessity to maintain public order characterises "police administrative". "Police judiciaire" is related to handling of infractions against public order. Until 1951 the administrative judge used some criteria, preferring formal to material criteria. Since then, the administrative judge has simplified matters by using one criterion only, the "finalité de l'action", the objective of actions. In the "arrêt Baud" of 11 May 1951, the "Conseil d'État" followed conclusions of "commissaire du gouvernement", Pierre Devolve. The operation is judiciary once there is a clear-cut case for prosecution, or when research is directed upon a precise transgression. When a police functionary is fulfilling tasks of control or surveillance, and his inquiry is not directed on a precise transgression or offence, this activity belongs to "police administrative". The nature of police activities is related to the existence of penal transgressions. The distinction "police administrative"/"police judiciaire" conditions the prerogatives of police and determines jurisdictional competencies.

Applicable law for police activities also depends on the distinction between "police administrative" and "police judiciaire". "Police judiciaire" is regulated more strictly, "Police administrative" is ruled more by principles and limits to its actions, determined a posteriori by the administrative judge. Law is relevant in defining the notion of public order and the legality of police activities. Due to the lack of a precise ruling, the administrative judge has to do this. The notion of public order has no a priori contents, it depends on circumstances and several rather vague qualifications. To prevent the necessity of restoring public order from becoming arbitrariness, the law has a double function: delimiting objectives and interventions of administrative police and determining possibilities of the administrative judge to assess a posteriori police interventions. The law of administrative police is jurisprudence law. The Premier is the national authority charged with police. Other authorities act on the basis of delegation, except in case of specific legislation.

As administrative police is based on necessity, it is ruled by specific regulations. The general opportunity principle of administrative action is not applicable for police activities. When there is necessity, the police must act. The necessity principle overrules the opportunity principle. This obligation is neither general nor absolute. An administrative judge must specify the conditions for police intervention. The "Conseil d'État" in its "arrêt Doublet" of 14 December 1959 decided that the obligation exists, when the following three conditions prevail: the measure has to be indispensable to end serious danger which is the result of a situation that is very risky for public order. When, in the case of abstention of police action, the administrative judge a posteriori determines that police authorities had to intervene, authorities can be made responsible, if abstention caused damage. Administrative police has a public authority function, which is indispensable for society. Administrative police has to be exercised directly by competent authorities and cannot be delegated to other public authorities or private persons and organisations. This has not been an obstacle to private militia and guard services. Since 1983 legislation allowed these, but forbids intervention in the public domain or substitution of police. The administrative judge implements law to concrete police activities, applying the principle of adaptation of measures to circumstances. He starts with the qualifying of facts, verifying that there was a serious threat to public order. He substitutes his appreciation for that of authorities involved and verifies if measures were adequate in view of the facts, which police authorities thought necessary to react upon. This approach was developed by the "Conseil d'État" in the ' arrêt Benjamin" of 19 May 1933.

Normal police law, based on the necessity of public order, can be replaced in specific circumstances by the "droit de l'exception". Exceptional laws can take the form of "l'état de siège" or "l'état d'urgence". The administrative judge also developed the theory of exceptional circumstances. The "Conseil d'État" used this theory as "théorie des pouvoirs de guerre" for the first time in 1918. This legislation and jurisprudence are based upon the idea that normal legality can be overruled in exceptional circumstances. Article 16 of the 1958 Constitution authorises the President of the Republic to take all the measures needed in a crisis. Several legislative texts extend the normal competencies for police when there are specific circumstances. So the prefect has extensive competencies in case of catastrophes, plan ORSEC ("Organisation des Secours") or plan POLMAR (maritime disasters). The law of 22 July 1987 gave the prefect competencies for organising civil security, protection of woods against fires and prevention of serious threats. There is legislation for the most important risks to society. The second exceptional regime is "état d'urgence", ruled by the modified law of 3 April 1955, applied during the Algerian war and after the troubles in "Nouvelle-Calédonie" in 1985. Circumstances can justify the calling in of armed forces by civilian authorities. Mobilising the army for maintaining or restoring public order is part of French history. Since the end of the 19th century, the role of the army has been more reduced in this field. If necessary, the army is used for maintaining public order on the basis of a specific procedure, the "réquisition". In some cases military authorities replace civilian police authorities (not the special police authorities). A law of 9 August 1949 about the "état de siège" had this solution. Now this regime is ruled by article 36 of the 1958 Constitution.

In France, penal procedure has an inquisitory character, while the English system is based upon the accusatory character, which can guarantee the interests of the accused person better. The accusatory model is public, oral and contradictory. A striking handicap of the inquisitory system (secret, written and not contradictory) is the reduced place of the rights of the defence in juridical procedures. In spite of enlargement of guarantees for individual liberty and mitigation of inquisitorial dimensions since the start of the Third Republic, the procedure nowadays maintains largely the initial inquisitorial character. The phase of the "instruction préparatoire", nearly non-existent in the accusatory model, has a strong impact. The rights of the defence are partially guaranteed in this phase. In this system an important role is given to the police during the penal procedure. The role given to the public prosecutor by the "Code de procédure pénale" is closely related to police intervention. Justice has to check police activities in respect of liberties. There is a difference between police practices and the Rule of Law. In the penal procedure there are two different situations: when the information phase has started, the police executes delegated tasks or orders of the "juridiction d'instruction", and before the information phase has started, the police are charged with finding transgressions, collection of evidence and the search for offenders.

Police competencies are different in the case of "enquête de flagrance", "enquête préliminaire" or "commission rogatoire". Judiciary police is subordinated to judicial authorities and under the direction of the "procureur de la République", and in every resort of the "Cour d'appel" under surveillance of the attorney general and under control of the "Chambre d'accusation". Since the reform of 1966, members of national police or gendarmerie, who are qualified "officiers de la police judiciaire", are only allowed to use their competencies when they are working in a corresponding job and are authorised by the "procureur général près la cour d'appel". Police authorities must inform the "procureur" promptly about transgressions, especially about crimes and "délit flagrant". All in all, the role of the defence in this first phase of the penal procedure is non-existent in French procedure. At the end of the 1970s there was debate about several dimensions of security. The President of the Republic charged a commission to analyse violence and criminality in 1976. The Peyrefitte-report "Réponses à la violence" (1977) concluded that there had been an increase of minor criminality and argued for preventive action against violence. Government chose to reinforce repression and enlarge the means of intervention for the police. This was operational in "loi Sécurité et liberté" (2 February 1981).

The commission "Justice pénale et droits de l'homme", analysing the difficulties of combining efficacy of police activities with fundamental liberties, published the report-Delmas-Marty (1991) with a number of propositions. In the framework of modernisation of the police, a better form of regulating police activities is seen in developing a "déontologie de la police" (code of behaviour). Belorgey (1981) argued for furthering confidence in the relationship between police and citizens. The research of Gleizal (1988) into police culture and of Monjardet (1984) concerning the daily activities of the police gives more accurate information about police practices. The "Code de déontologie" (decree of 18 March 1986), stated that police have to apply respect for individuals and Republican legality, and necessary moderation in the use of force. It was a new endeavour to define the rights and obligations of police personnel, with notions such as integrity, impartiality and dignity. Article 17 of the "Code déontologie" is meant to corroborate an attitude of responsibility of police. Subordinate functionaries have to comply with instructions of the competent authority. Except when the order is clearly illegal, or is seriously compromising a public interest. The subordinate, having objections, must inform the person giving instructions, if necessary mentioning that he thinks the activities are illegal.

A contribution to a better understanding between police and citizens can be achieved by more transparency of police activities. The secrecy of police activities has been a dominant feature of police bureaucracy for a long time, and still is to some extent now (principle of professional discretion). In French tradition, it was thought quite normal that bureaucracy should maintain a distance in its relations with the public, especially police bureaucracy. Since the 1960s, efforts have been made to change this attitude. The pre-report of Belorgey (1981) argued for transparency in relations between police and citizens as a means to further confidence. Police bureaux should be more open and hospitable places, legislation about administrative documents should be changed to make its access easier and more police procedures should be legalised to make them more open to control. The establishment of an independent commission charged with publicly testing the legality of police activities and their conformity to republican traditions was proposed. This complemented the work of "Commission nationale de l'informatique et des libertés" (CNIL) and "Commission d'accès aux documents administratifs" (CADA). On 31 October 1990, the Minister of the Interior announced the creation of a "Conseil supérieur de l'activité policière", part of "loi sur la sécurité intérieure" (1991).

In the "arrêt Bertin" of 19 May 1983, the administrative judge decided that the CADA had to declare itself incompetent with regard to the "fichiers" related to public security. There was no legislation with regard to the tapping of telephone conversations. Illegal practices proliferated and it was necessary to comply with European law. Between 1973 and 1980, five bills dealing with the tapping of telephone calls brought no results. The European Court for human rights in Strasbourg condemned France in two cases. Article 8 of the European Convention for Human Rights rules that each individual has a right to respect for private life, home and correspondence. It authorises competent public authorities to interfere with these rights only when certain conditions are fulfilled. It has to be ruled by national law and the measure must be necessary for national security, public order, or economic well-being of the country, to defend public order, prevent penal transgressions, and protect health, morals, and the rights and liberties of others. The law of 10 July 1991 about the confidentiality of correspondence by way of telecommunication gave a legal framework. This law distinguishes between interceptions for security reasons and those ordained by judiciary police. The competent public authority may tap in cases of necessity, defined by the law. An independent "Commission nationale de contrôle des interceptions de sécurité" was created to verify legality of tapping, making recommendations.

The information revolution had a tremendous impact upon police organisation. To fulfil its tasks, police had always been strongly dependent on adequate information. At the end of the 19th century Bertillon revolutionalised the technical means of identification of persons. Since then, methods have been perfected, with new possibilities of computerised informatics since the 1970s as zenith. The unlimited possibilities have enlarged the risks of invasion of privacy, therefore rulings were adapted with the law "Informatique et Libertés" of 7 January 1978. This resulted from reactions to the automated information system used by the police ("Safari"). It is not permitted to use this information to damage human identity, human rights, individual or public liberties. In the domain of the police only the "fichiers de la DST" are not made public. A new, independent commission was created: "Commission nationale de l'informatique et des libertés" (CNIL), having "pouvoir réglementaire" to make law-like rules. Article 31 of the law of 7 January 1978 stated: It is forbidden, except with the consent of persons involved, to produce or store data that informs about the race, political, philosophical or religious opinions, or membership of trade unions of persons. The law has exceptions for the sake of public interest. Respect of article 31 depends on the CNIL doctrine.

The nature of the data assembled is the relevant criterion. The changed rulings restrict several traditional practices of "RG" and "DST", in the collecting of data about political, philosophical and religious opinions of citizens. Negotiations between government and CNIL have been difficult. In 1980 government presented the draft for a decree, which encompassed some thirty exceptions to article 31 for the Ministries of Defence and of the Interior. In 1981, however, CNIL rejected this text. After eight years CNIL realised that the RG data had been published. The rulings involved were published on the first of March 1990. After public turmoil these texts were withdrawn two days later. Finally, the decree of 14 October 1991 was adopted. The establishment of the "fichier central du terrorisme" gave CNIL the opportunity to define one of the "critères de fichage". This concerned persons with direct and regular relations with those known to practise terrorist activities. Police services are free to establish tailor-made data collections. When CNIL is analysing automated data related to man-made data these are also examined. The law of 1978 made it possible for citizens to realise their "droit d'accès", and to have access to information. It is possible for individuals to claim that data about themselves be rectified, completed, clarified, actualised or removed, if that data are inaccurate, incomplete, ambivalent, superannuated, or when collection or use, communication or storage of the data is forbidden. Data about the security of the State, Defence or public security are not directly accessible. A request for information has to be addressed to the CNIL, examining the data and if necessary the contents eventually.

Development of a Europe-without-frontiers had new challenges for public authorities, especially the police. The "Single European Act" (signed in 1986) and in force since July 1987, had its consequences. It created the internal market for Member-States of the EEC on the first of January 1993. A new European space was created with free circulation of persons, goods and capital. This made it necessary to have new agreements with regard to police activities and the control of migration: the "Schengen Agreement" (14 June 1985). In the short term there was an agreement between France, West Germany and Benelux about abolishing existing control at internal frontiers and replacing it with simplified surveillance. For the long run, Schengen was meant to realise a "European space" (control at external frontiers; harmonisation of legislation on internal security and illegal migration from outside the European Community etc.). An additional convention about the application of the Schengen Agreement was signed on 19 June 1990 when Italy, Spain, Portugal and Greece also adhered to these Schengen accords. Co-ordination of police activities between Member States was intensified.

Experiences with Interpol were found to be inadequate. Therefore in 1976 the group "TREVI" was formed to help Member-States to improve their co-ordination in the bitter fight against terrorism and organised crime. It had the long term objective of a European police organisation. The base for co-operation of police activities was laid in article 39, subsection 1 of the additional convention of Schengen. Contracting parties pledged that their police services would comply with assistance, for reasons of prevention and inquiry of penal activities, within the framework of national law and the limits of their competencies. This meant organising new structures, defining new competencies and elaborating an information system at European level. Ratification of the additional Schengen convention raised discussions about the relation between the principles of Schengen, national sovereignty and the protection of liberties. The "Conseil Constitutionnel" in its decision of 25 July 1991 declared that the law approving the additional convention was in conformity with the 1958 Constitution. The build-up of the "système d'information Schengen" (SIS) as databank is one of the more concrete parts of the co-ordination of police activities. The Maastricht treaty, signed on 7 February 1992, obliged Member-States to intensify police, customs and judiciary co-operation. Not all Member-States of the EU signed the Schengen Agreements because of fear of organised crime. Criminals can make use of easy crossing of internal EU boundaries (Leteur, 1991). Implementation of the Schengen Agreements is full of problems (Pauly, 1994). The terrorist attack with hi-jacked planes against the Twin Towers of the World Trade Center in New York and the Pentagon building on 11 September 2001 re-opened the debate on improved security and checks at the external frontiers of the European Union against terrorism.

## 4.6. Police as qualified public service

The notion of public order in itself is open-ended (Picard, 1984), but it is used as a criterion to demarcate police activities from other activities in public management. Administrative judges have to state precisely the contents of this notion and the relation of police activities to the law. French administrative doctrine distinguishes two essential state functions. "Le service public", with the objective of "l'intérêt général", and police with the specific objective of maintaining "l'ordre public". Lépine, prefect at the "préfecture de police" in Paris from 1893 up to 1913, was a pioneer of the French concept of maintenance of public order. In "Mes Souvenirs" (1929), he developed advanced methods to prevent uprisings and reduce the number of killed and wounded persons. He preferred the police to the armed forces. For Picard, public order is a general and abstract norm within the Idea of Law, with the same title as the primacy of liberty. Public order is founded upon legality and necessity (consubstantiality).

The "Conseil Constitutionnel" in its decision of 27 July 1982 declared maintainance of public order to be an objective with a constitutional character, so public order is seen as the foundation and base of legitimacy for police activities. Therefore police have ample policy room and discretionary powers. As the police function of the State is directly related to the necessities of social order, the law regulated only the application of police activities. Police activities emphasize, in a fundamental sense, the critical relationship between factual circumstances and the law, provoking dilemmas and contradictions. Police normally have to operate within the limits and conditions of the law. A distinction is made between "autorités de police" (Premier, prefect and mayor), with competencies in the field of formulating orders and norms to ensure respect for public order, and "forces de police", who in fact have to maintain public order. Police authorities are competent to qualify circumstances, justify interventions, and determine concrete measures. No law text can specify a priori the exact conditions of police intervention. According to the Rule of Law the competencies of police authorities and functionaries are conditional. The unilateral acts of police are administrative acts, which have to respect the law, and as such can be checked by administrative judges. Administrative judges are thus able to have a posteriori control of police interventions, judging whether the relation between the measures taken and the concrete circumstances was justified ("Conseil d'État" in the Benjamin-case of 19 May 1933). Police must take action, when necessities of public order require this (the measure is necessary to end a serious danger resulting from a dangerous situation for public order ("Conseil d'État" in the Doublet-case of 23 October 1959). The Police includes "police judiciaire", under the responsibility of the Minister of Justice; national police (124,960 functionaries in 1990), under responsibility of the Minister of the Interior; and gendarmerie (nearly 90,000 functionaries in 1990), composed of military police functionaries, under responsibility of the Minister of the armed forces. These three parts of policing are distinguished as "police d'ordre ou administrative", "police judiciaire" and "police d'information politique". The police are regulated by the law "informatique et libertés" (6 January 1978) which created the "Commission nationale de l'informatique et des Libertés" (CNIL). A law of 28 September 1948 gave police functionaries a special statute. In the pre-report of Belorgey

(1981) this special statute was questioned. It was not thought opportune to abolish the ban on strike action for police functionaries, functionaries like others, but nevertheless different.

When Socialists took over the government in 1981 they tried to reorganise the police, introducing a new concept. The "Rapport-Peyrefitte" (1977) made the diagnosis that France lived in fear, the feeling of insecurity was widespread, due to the growth of criminality, but its reasonable propositions were not followed. The rightist government voted in the law "Sécurité et Liberté" (2 February 1981) choosing for more repression. In May 1982 the Socialist government, criticising the policing policies of former governments, formed a committee of mayors under the presidency of Bonnemaison to launch a new conept of policing, but its Report-Bonnemaison (1983) largely proposed the same approach as the Report-Peyrefitte. The Socialist leadership now recognised that the growth in criminality was a cause of widespread feelings of insecurity and the police were reorganised. It started with "Pré-Rapport Belorgey"(1981), proposing to make the police a "service public", and restoring the confidence of the people in the police by a series of measures like prevention, neighbourhood police, training, a new code for police functionaries ("Déontologie policière") etc. This pre-report had an important role in reconciling the political left and the police. Minister of the Interior Joxe made the National Assembly adopt the "loi de modernisation de la police nationale". In the "Xe Plan" (1989) security was presented as an important objective of society. "Délégation interministérielle à la Ville" (DIV) and "Institut des Hautes Études de la Sécurité Intérieure" (IHESI), established in 1989, made the notion security more operational with "Diagnostics locaux de sécurité" (DLS), locally adapted security diagnoses, in 1990/1992. The "Rapport Clauzel" (1990) had proposals to improve municipal police. A new police model developed with key-issues such as professionalism, territorialisation, transparency, autonomy and Europe. Police co-ordination in the framework of Europe became an ever more important aspect of police activities.

Historical developments offer a partial explanation for the complexity of the French police system and some of its incoherencies. The reform of 1966 reorganised this system by putting the "Préfecture de police de Paris" and the provincial police (under the authority of the "Sûreté nationale") together in the "Police nationale". This unification led to the creation of the "Direction générale de la police nationale" within the Ministry of the Interior. In spite of this juridical unification, the police of Paris preserved its specific position and autonomy. In addition to the national police there are the municipal police (under the authority of the mayor) and the gendarmerie (a military corps falling under the authority of the Ministry of Defence). This fragmentation of police administration, due also to specialisation, is a continuous characteristic. Relations between "police judiciaire" (PJ) and jurisdiction are intense, while the double hierarchy (Interior and Justice) causes problems. The PJ partly fulfils the function of the judiciary police as "sûretés urbaines" and "brigades spécialisés de la gendarmerie" also have functions in this area. On the local level the police are organised in deconcentrated services. The prefect, the most important police authority in the department, is charged with co-ordination. Territorial administrative divisions (regions, departments, municipalities) are not the same for different specialised police organisations. There is a difference between police and gendarmerie. Apart from gendarmes and municipal policemen there are more than 120,000 agents, 70% of them member of a union.

On the national level, the Premier is "autorité de police". He can issue instructions for the national police in the whole territory of France. Following principles of the constitutional state, (civil) authorities of police, issuing rulings, are distinguished from (military and civil) police forces, materially executing activities. The Minister of the Interior, responsible for the maintenance of public order and security in the whole territory of France, is charged with management of the national police and can order all the measures he thinks appropriate. He has authority over police forces and gendarmes, and is hierarchical boss. With regard to "police judicaire" he is co-responsible with the Minister of

Justice but apart from specific missions (police of foreigners) the Minister of the Interior does not have the quality of "autorité de police". To avoid an excessively repressive character when the police were placed under an autonomous Minister of Police, as a result of a long discussion in history, policing was entrusted to the Minister of the Interior. After the unification of police in 1966, a decree of 29 September 1969 created the "Direction générale de la police nationale" (DGPN), subordinate to one functionary reporting directly to the Minister of the Interior. The director-general of the national police has wide-ranging powers. He is chosen from higher functionaries (prefects).

The "cabinet du directeur" has "service de sécurité"; "service centrale automobile"; "unité de recherche, assistance, intervention et dissuasion" (RAID, since 1985); "unité de coordination et de lutte anti-terroriste" (since 1984); and "département prévention". The DGPN, reorganised in 1985, traditionally encompassed two administrative directions, four active directions, four central services and the "Inspection générale de la police nationale" (IGPN). A decree of 2 October 1985 created the "direction des libertés publiques et des affaires juridiques". One objective was to take more account of international and European law. This direction has subsections: "libertés publiques et la police administrative"; "les étrangers et la circulation transfrontalière"; "la circulation et la sécurité routière"; "le contentieux et les affaires juridiques". Personnel and material resources are entrusted to two separate directorates: "direction du personnel et de la formation", and "direction de la logistique". In 1982 the "Charte de la formation" was adopted. According to article 14 of the "Code de procédure pénale", PJ has the task to discover and establish crimes and offences, search for authors and proof, and bring suspects before the competent authorities. Other police services also gather information, but PJ is specialised in the fighting of organised crime. Local organisation of police activities has specific dimensions. An important aspect of local policing is that hierarchical police units have a territorial logic of their own. The national gendarmerie is part of the army, the Minister of Defence is responsible. Territorial organisation of the gendarmerie follows geographical military organisation. A circular of 30 January 1990 include measures to improve co-operation between police and gendarmerie.

In a constitutional state, there must be prior legislation governing eventual penalties for activities against the juridical order. The Napoleonic legislation of the period 1799-1815 marked a historic apex. It has been used as the standard worldwide since then. The "Code pénal" had an elaborated system of crimes, offences and contraventions. Procedures regarding prosecution, accusation and determination of penalties were regulated painstakingly. In France, the penal process has an inquisitory character. There are several relations between justice and police. In the framework of penal law an apparatus is needed to detect and investigate offences. Citizens are obliged to report to the police when they know that an offence or crime has been committed, and to bear witness when they know that a suspected person is not guilty. Every citizen is obliged to sit in a jury when assigned (a fine as sanction). Within narrow conditions a citizen may temporarily hold a delinquent taken in the very act. Detecting and investigating offences and crimes is generally in the hands of professionals (police), however. The police has at least three tasks: prevention of disturbances by the protection of persons, goods and activities; assistance to people in trouble; and preventing infractions of public order and juridical order.

The first two tasks are entrusted to the "police administrative". The third has to be looked after by the "police judiciaire". When police functionaries fulfil tasks of this judiciary police they are working as "policiers auxiliaires du juge répressif". Competencies of the judiciary police differ in several phases of the investigation. Before a judicial action is undertaken, the police have to fulfil several roles. Judicial authorities must be informed and although citizens, as witnesses or victims, can go directly to the judicial authorities, in practice they go to the police. The "rôle d'information" implies that statements have to be registered and made known to judicial authorities. The police do not wait for citizens to make statements, but investigates on its own initiative ("rôle de constatation"). Before the police reports its findings these must be verified. The police has the right to arrest, when persons are caught in the act. When action of the judicial authorities begins the initiative of the police ends. Thereafter the police does only what is ordered by the judicial authorities. Police make arrests by order of "juge d'instruction', or a penal judge. The police have to do what is ordered by the investigating judge, circumscribing in detail the transgressions for which the investigation is held.

Within the sphere of the judiciary police there are "officiers de police judiciaire" (OPJ), "agents de police judiciaire" (APJ), and "agents de police adjoints" (APA). Local public authorities and police functionaries have, according to the law, the quality of OPJ. This makes them competent for the investigation, with the help of coercive measures, of serious crimes; warrants for detention; implementation of investigations ordered by judges and calling in the assistance of public authorities, police or gendarmerie. Gendarmes, police inspectors and investigating police functionaries ex officio, have the right to make preliminary investigations and to make up an official report. Judicial police, under leadership of a "procureur de la République", is overseen by judiciary authorities. The "procureur de la République" has to be warned in the case of offences. He decides the actions to be taken; he has to authorise specific actions. He can go to the place involved to take up the leadership of operations. Disciplinary competencies concerning police functionaries are given to the "Chambre d'accusation" of the court of appeal. Sanctions can vary from a simple warning to a definite interdiction to fulfil a function in judiciary police. When a failure of an OPJ produces an act of punishment (as for example an unjustified arrest, which causes the offence of arbitrary detention), the police functionary involved can be prosecuted in a penal procedure. The victims of such arbitrary activities can get compensation by requesting it from the penal judge.

### 4.7. Prison system. Structural crisis in the penitentiary system.

The "ultimum remedium" of the system of jurisdiction and police is detention in a prison, because without this instrument jurisdiction and police would lose an important part of their efficacy. Before 1981 the death penalty could be issued. The last time a death penalty was issued was in 1978. The death penalty was abolished in 1981. It is a sweeping competence for public authorities that they can incarcerate persons against their wills, even when these are criminals. Imprisonment is a reaction on behalf of society against those persons who have seriously violated the juridical order. Foucault (1975), in his book about the birth of the prison, has analysed the penal system quite originally. The French prison system with its specific characteristics is going through a crisis of long duration (Faugeron/Tournier, 1991). The total population of the penitentiary system rose from more than 26,000 in 1975 to more than 50,000 in the nineties. It is nearly impossible for the management of prisons to determine adequately the number of prisoners. All those condemned by penal law judges have to be lodged. Judges could condemn fewer people or decrease the duration of the detention to reduce structural pressure upon prisons. The President of the Republic can issue a collective amnesty, either when he is elected or on "Quatorze Juillet". The penitentiary system in the 1990s had about 50 establishments, more than 120 houses of custody and 10 centres of semi-liberty. Thus 180 buildings for some 52,000 detainees, while normal capacity is only 40,300 places: a grade of occupation of 125%. To reduce deficiency of capacity in the penitentiary system Minister Chaladon, foreseeing a shortage of about 20,000 places, proposed in 1987 the privatised construction and exploitation of 25,000 prison places. The "Conseil Constitutionnel" rejected this, arguing that the equality of treatment for citizens would be affected. Privatisation of more neutral services (food catering, laundry, maintenance of buildings) was allowed.

Roughly speaking, one can distinguish two prison models in France (Delteil, 1990; Favard, 1987). The first model is concerned with short-stay detention for a regularly rotating population (provisional detention, less serious infractions against the law). The second model of prisons is for detention of long duration. Several ideas were elaborated about the policies for prisons (Badinter, 2000). It is thought necessary for imprisonment to be unpleasant if it is to have a deterrent effect. Another point of view is that the sole relevant objective is incarceration, so society is protected against criminals. Prisoners have to be re-educated according to the "doctrine de la défense sociale". It is emphasized that detainees have to be prepared as well as possible for their return to society. Social handicaps should be reduced if possible. There is also a point of view stating that prisons have to be abolished as they are thought to be an inadequate instrument against criminality. Since the 1960s, public opinion became ever more convinced that the penitentiary system had serious deficiencies. This view was stimulated by reports and books by former prisoners telling about their experiences, like Knobelspiess (1981) and Bauer (1990). Between the end of 1971 and the summer of 1974, there was an acute crisis. Uprisings in prisons brought problems of the penitentiary system onto the societal agenda. Liberalising measures were taken and alternative sanctions were introduced. These involved less than 2% of the condemned. Reduction of overpopulation in prisons did not materialise (Robert, 1984). After 1975, this liberal policy was criticised, and policies on prisons were ever more politicised.

Statistics of judicial policy proved irrefutably that criminality was rising continually. Mild penalties as given by penal jurisdictions were seen as one of the causes. The accent was ever more on the maintenance of public order. A law of 1978 created penalties for security reasons. A "loi sécurité et liberté" of 2 February 1981 made more robust penalties possible, as well as faster procedures (quick justice). Special problems are caused by the delinquencies of minors and young adults. The "Protection judiciaire de la jeunesse" in 1991 had at its disposal about 1,500 establishments and services for difficult youth. The number of minors who had contact with the police rose to 170,000 in 1992, young delinquents form about 1% of the imprisoned. When the Socialists took over 1981, the "alternance" was coupled with a search for a new doctrine for the penitentiary system. A partial return to the "défense sociale" philosophy of the fifties (Ancel, 1989). A legislative innovation was the law of 10 June 1983. It introduced three sanctions as a substitute for detention: "immobilisation des véhicules" (immobilising cars); "jour-amende" (if the fine is not paid, detention follows for half of the unpaid days); and "travail d'intérêt général" (TIG), some work in the general interest. With this TIG judges had an alternative for detention in penitentiary establishments. Penalised persons could be made to work for local public authorities under the responsibility of a "Juge de l'application des peines", assisted by a "Comité de probation et d'assistance aux libérés". In the framework of decentralisation legislation (1982/1983) the "Conseil national de prévention de la délinquance" (CNPD) was created. This CNPD promoted consensus creation at the local level; a pragmatic combination of prevention and repression; intensifying social control and reinforcing social relations in neighbourhoods (Dubet, 1985). Departmental networks were created and "Comités de communes pour prévention de la délinquance" for co-operation of all instances. Since the 1986 "alternance", policy has been more repressive. In September 1986, laws brought sentences for some crimes from 20 to 30 years; reductions of penalties were diminished.

When Socialists came back into government in 1988, policies as previously formed by the political right were partially cancelled. The accent was on preparing the return to society, penalties outside the prison, reduction of provisional detention, and prevention by departments and municipalities under the umbrella of the "Délégation interministérielle des villes". With the law of 9 July 1989 rapid social inquiries were reintroduced; shorter periods of provisional detention, especially for minors; etc. The situation in the overpopulated penitentiary system remained critical. The growth of the prison population ("inflation carcérale") with more than 7% yearly was alarming (Kensey, 1990). Compared with the situation in 1975, the prison population in the 1990s has more people older than 30, more women (now 4.1% of the total) and more foreigners (30% of the total). The growth of the prison population was almost 50% due to foreigners. Dangerous criminals (more than 6,000), of whom 415 had life sentences, were incarcerated in special jails ("réclusion criminelle"). For about 80% of the penitentiary establishments, built before 1914, renovation was urgent. A number of prisons which would have to be closed were held open because of the alarming shortage of places. There are several forms of control over the penitentiary system, a general inspection, and regional directions within the penitentiary system itself, and in the framework of the jurisdictional organisation, by attorneys in every resort of the "Cours d'appel". "Juges de l'application des peines" (JAP) have to report regularly about the situation of detainees. In every establishment there is a "commission de surveillance" reporting to the prefect. The last parliamentary inquiry of prisons was in 1872, causing a row then and since. Following scandals, the Ministry of social affairs has controlled medical care and hygiene since 1983.

After research into the facts, the "Inspection générale des affaires sociales" published a report (1984) about the deplorable situation. Since then some improvements have been made (Prescrire, 1997), especially since the law of 18 January 1994, as shown in the report (1997) of the "Direction des Hôpitaux". Penitentiary establishments are self regulating; there is hardly any external control. In periods of relatively liberalising policies there was some extension of the "droit de regard" of the JAP, despite fierce opposition from prison managers. After the repeated protests of prison personnel against their work situation, the "Rapport-Bonnemaison" (1989) was issued. The guard personnel in France forms about 80% of the total personnel, which is relatively high compared with other countries. In spite of this, the ratio of guards to detainees in France is low. This means a high pressure of work (Conseil de l'Europe, 1990). Newly recruited personnel, mostly better trained, are less willing to accept obsolete circumstances. Newly built prisons are urgently needed. Alternative sanctions for detention like TIG (nearly 13,000 in 1992) have reached their limits (Rugo, 1988). The composition of the prison population has made work more complex (many foreigners, drugs etc.). The "Rapport-Bonnemaison" had some relevant propositions: less centralised management of prisons; more responsibilities for the cadre; involvement of local authorities with penitentiary systems; professionalisation of personnel; and reorganisation of the social formation services to improve return to society. Inquiries of the Council of Europe showed that the hygiene in police-cells was still seriously deficient, as it had been in 1967 (Mathiesen, 1967). A central objective of penitentiary policy is the target to return imprisoned persons to society in a better condition, recognising human rights in prisons and in society (King/Morgan, 1980). The New Guide for Prisoners (Dindo c.s., 2000) is quite informative.

Penal law legislation, after futile attempts in 1892, 1934 and 1976, was adapted with the "Nouveau Code Pénale" of 1994 (Leclerc, 1994). This is overstated as the end of the Code Napoléon. "Juridictions spécialisées" (especially for minors) are distinguished from "Juridictions de droit commun": "Tribunal de Police" for contraventions; "Tribunal Correctionnel" for offences; and "Cour d'Assises" for crimes. Classification is on the basis of the gravity of the infractions. In the sphere of penal law, 13,980,445 decisions were taken in 1995 (Ministry of Justice, 1995). "Cours d'Assises" was responsible for 2,127, Tribunaux Correctionnels" for 418,924 and "Tribunaux de Police" for 1,235,833 decisions. "Cour de Cassation" realised 5,839 and "Cours d'appel" 43,167 decisions. "Tribunal de Police" as single judge handles contraventions in five classes. For the first four classes, fines were not more than 250-5,000 francs, for the fifth class the maximum was 10,000 francs (20,000 in case of recidivism). Penalties decided upon by the "Tribunal Correctionnel" carry a maximum betwee 6 months and 10 years imprisonment. Other penalties here are: fines, "jour-amende" (a fine, and detention follows if this fine is not paid), or work for the general interest. The "Juridiction d'instruction" with its seat at the "Tribunal de Grande Instance" has to investigate the most serious offences and crimes, ordering provisional detention as necessary (Robert, 1992). The "Cour d'Assises" can decide on penalties for the most serious crimes: 15, 20 or 30 years imprisonment or more, and even life-long. This court has a special composition, and the verdict is determined by a jury of three professional judges and 9 jury members, assigned by lot from citizens on the basis of electoral lists. Once the decision about the penalty is taken the "Juge d'application des peines" controls execution of penalties, and can decide mitigation. A special institution is the "Juge pour enfants", deciding penalties for minors (44,256 in 1995). Since 1987, provisional detention for minors under 13 years has been forbidden. In 1990 guarded education was organised as "Protection judiciaire de la jeunesse".

## 4.8. Reforming justice and jurisdiction

Several components and dimensions of justice and the penal system are continually criticised. The position of victims is often neglected (Collard, 1997; Damiani, 1997; Lopez, 1997). There is an "un-civil society" with petty violence becoming normal (Roché, 1996). Mass demonstrations, like those of strikers in December 1995, cause police functionaries a series of problems in maintaining public order (Touraine, 1996). Vagabonds and beggars not only confront the general public but can also prove a problem for police functionaries, not least because of the psychiatrist patients and drugs addicts among them (Damon, 1996). The Committee Delmas-Marty (1991) had radical propositions, inspired by the Anglo-Saxon accusatory system. These were too revolutionary for the Socialist government. In a law of 4 January 1993 improvements were realised for the rights of the defence. The European Court of Human Rights has a crucial role in the development of norms. Since 1981 France has been condemned 63 times by this European Court. The July 1999 decision of this Court to condemn France for the torture by policemen of a person suspected of drugs trafficking in 1991, was shocking. France, the Nation-State that invented the legal protection of human rights!

In the last ten years public outrage has been aroused regularly by a whole series of affairs: contaminated blood (Beaud, 1999; Casteret, 1992; Hermitte, 1996); corruption; fraud; etc. (Lascoumes, 2000). A number of these undermined general confidence in the impartial position of judges. On 30 October 1995 the "Tribunal Administratif" of Paris refused to authorise a taxpayer to proceed in a juridical process against Chirac, suspected for having abused his position as mayor of Paris to enrich his family by renting an expensive apartment belonging to the City of Paris below its price. This caused an ongoing debate about the penal immunity of the President of the Republic. On 22 January 2000, the "Conseil constitutionnel" decided that the President of the Republic enjoys immunity during his mandate for activities carried out before he started his function. This decision, seen as a deal between president of the CC, Dumas and Chirac, was criticised sharply. On 10 October 2000, the CC specified this: The President of the Republic is not exonerated from penal responsibility during his mandate, but enjoys a privilege until the end of his mandate. A judicial procedure was started against Premier Juppé by the "Association pour la défense des contribuables parisiens" for the offence of "prise illégale d'intérêt". As deputy-mayor of Paris, he ordered a reduction in the rent of an apartment for his son of

1,000 francs per month. The administrative tribunal refused to authorise this juridical action. Illegal financing of political parties shocked the public. An anonymous writer ("corbeau"), has since 1996 sent documents to judge Halphen, charged with the "Affaire des HLM", about illegal financing of the RPR. The office of "Renseignements Généraux" (RG), charged with the collection of information for the government, has often been connected with a series of scandals (Rougelet, 1997) and France was shocked by disclosures about the dubious role of Mitterrand's son, who was charged by his father, in his function as President of the Republic, to handle African affairs (Lethier, 2000).

Polls made clear that the confidence of the public in the independence of French justice was regularly in question, so it was quite logical for President Chirac to launch a great reform program for the judiciary system in January 1997. A committee-Truche was installed to prepare this. A poll by "SOFRES" concluded that 82% of the French think that the justice authorities are subject to party-political pressure (Le Monde, 31-1-1997). In April 1997, the "Affaire des écoutes" shook the political world in France. The archives were found in a garage, on 19 February 1997, of Prouteau, chef of the "cellule d'Élysée". They showed that this organisation had been eavesdropping illegally on a large scale. In 1993 judge Valat was charged with a special investigation about illegal spying by the "cellule antiterroriste de l'Élysée". Because former Socialist President Mitterrand (deceased) was directly involved in this, his friends qualified this affair as a "Watergate posthume". From 1982 to 1988, there was a "cabinet noir", directly instructed by President Mitterrand, spying upon numerous persons (his political opponents etc.) under cover of the "defence secret". Former "directeur de cabinet" of Mitterrand for eleven years, Ménage, decided to divulge all he knew. Premier Juppé ordered an investigation. Much has to be done to reduce the gap between "État de droit" and reality. A serious aspect of practices in France is the widespread conviction that judges decide under party-political pressures. Reforming the judiciary system is a regular subject of debate in France, but this talking about changing the rules of justice is also criticised: the rules of justice only have to be applied (Montgolfier, Le Monde 6-2-1997). Commissions published impressive reports to improve the judicial system, like the "Commission Delmas-Marty (1991), but generally these did not materialise in a change of institutional arrangements. In spite of all attempts to cover up fraud, corruption and abuse of public resources, a never-ending series of scandals became public. Years of scandals about the functioning of the administration of Justice and Jurisdiction have been undermining the crucial institutions whose task is to bring the Rule of Law nearby in French society.

From his TV-speech of 12 December 1996 on, President Chirac urged for a reform of Justice and Jurisdiction: priority of his "septennat" (1995-2002). He brought the question of making the Office for prosecution independent from the Minister to the fore. He announced that he would ask Government to install a commission to present reform proposals. Just before the installation of the Commission-Truche, Chirac sketched his ideas on TV again (20 January 1997). He claimed that for the good administration of justice, uncontested and respected, the bonds between Minister and the Office for the prosecution should be modified or abolished. A judiciary authority, independent of executive and legislative powers, in the framework of necessary responsibilities. Respect for the presumption of innocence. The Report-Truche, without revolutionary proposals, was presented to Chirac on 10 July 1997. The report wanted to respect the rich French judiciary heritage. It sought a compromise between the politicising of justice and judiciary corporatism. The legitimacy of the judiciary is based not only upon professionalism, it has its source particularly in the crucial function of justice in the heart of the "État de droit", and in its direct or indirect relation with politics. It is thought imperative to prevent justice, essential to the State with its necessary link with politics, from being perverted by partisan interference in the normal course of its application. The report was against total autonomy of the Public Prosecutor:

For constitutional reasons, the judiciary policy of the nation in a democracy has to be the responsibility of government (Minister of Justice). This public policy, based on the law, requires responsibility of the Minister of Justice on the national level, and co-ordination by "procureurs généraux' on the regional, and "procureurs de la République" on the local level.

The Commission-Truche came up with several proposals to improve the situation, and to restore confidence in the judiciary system. The Minister should present a yearly report about judiciary policy to Parliament. Application of the opportunity principle for prosecution with general and public directives from the Minister should be controlled. Introduction of appeal for each person, who can't be a civil party in a juridical case, against decisions of the Prosecutor to refuse (further) prosecution. Interdiction of instructions of the Minister for individual dossiers, especially in cases of conflict of interests for the executive. Maintaining "concertation" between "chancellerie" (Ministry) and "parquet" concerning the application of general policy directives in individual cases. Statutory independence of all "magistrats du parquet" is consolidated by concordant advice of the "Conseil supérieur de la magistrature" (CSM). To strengthen the legitimacy of this CSM, its composition should be changed, so that magistrates no longer have a majority. It was proposed to give CSM disciplinary competencies towards magistrates, and to reinforce the grip of the judiciary authority upon the judiciary police, also to reorganise the "carte judiciaire", the spread of judiciaries over the country. The Commission-Truche had proposals to protect the presumption of innocence of suspects.

After the political earthquake of the Socialist victory in the brought-forward legislative elections, Minister Guigou of the Socialist Government-Jospin (1997-2002) was actively trying to give her name to an ambitious reform program. Reforming Justice and Jurisdiction became a sensitive issue in the party-political "cohabitation". Socialists and their coalition, with a majority in the National Assembly, could not realise reforms on their own because a constitutional law needs approval of an identical text in both houses of Parliament. Neo-Gaullists (RPR) and rightist Liberals (UDF), with a majority in the Senate, announced fierce opposition against reform proposals. There was obstinate resistance in circles of magistrates, as shown during manifestations on 5 May 1998. The reform program of Minister Guigou, – a justice to serve the citizens and to protect liberties, and an independent and impartial justice –, was presented on 29 October 1997. It encompassed reforming of CSM; adaptation of the Code for the penal procedure, especially with regard to the criticised "instruction" phase; regulation of the relation between judiciary authorities and press; and reform of the office of the prosecution, with more instructions from the Minister about the general penal policies, and abolition of his instructions in individual cases. It proposed trusting decision-making about provisional detention (average 4 months) to a specific judge (not "juge d'instruction" any more) so that abusive detentions could be reduced (Robert, 1992; Tournier, 1995).

The reform program of the government started with proposals for reforming the CSM, established in 1947. This institution became crucial to the further independence of judges. Whoever wants to change the subtle equilibrium between judiciary authority and (party-politically dominated) legislative and executive powers, must reform the CSM. The nomination of 6,000 magistrates, 181 "procureurs" and 33 "procureurs généraux" would need, according to the proposals, the concordant advice of CSM, whose composition, with a majority of magistrates, would also be changed to prevent "corporatisme" (dominance of the pressure group of professionals) and in order that nominations which were manifestly party-politically influenced.could be stopped. In 1946 Coste-Floret, reporting to the National Assembly, already said that the CSM had to be at equidistant from subordination towards the "pouvoir politique" and an inadmissible corporatism. Due to the institutional logic of De Gaulle ("The President is the sole source of legitimacy.") all members of the CSM had been appointed by the President since the Constitution of 1958. Since 1993 magistrates have had a majority in the CSM, with extended competencies. Reforming the judiciary system, making it more independent from party-political vicissitudes, is urgent (Soulez/Larivière, 1997). This was part of the "Appel des 103 magistrats" (11-5-1997), claiming restoration of the Republican pact: Impartiality of justice is a kernel of real progress of democracy. The public prosecutor now is doubly limited in his discretionary competencies. The Minister can appoint "procureurs" and "procureurs généraux" and he can give instructions to the "parquet", so interfering in each individual case.

Of all the European countries with a judiciary system based upon a hierarchical bond between executive (Minister) and office for prosecution ("parquet"), France had the most rigid system, with a nearly complete dependency of the officers for prosecution on behalf of the (party-political) Minister. The "juge d'instruction" pursued inquiries as long as permitted by the (party-) political authorities. This was also the experience in the "Urba dossier" (1991) of Jean-Pierre, who discovered the use of illegal methods to finance the "Parti Socialiste", for which its president Emmanuelli was sentenced. When Jean-Pierre came too near to the secret financial sources of Mitterrand's political power in 1994, planning a search in the "Élysée" itself, he was blocked and switched to a sidetrack. Not for nothing are arguments put forward for a radical split-up between the "parquet" and the Minister, and also for a separation of "parquet" and magistrates. In practice, there is an interpenetration of careers for magistrates and officers of the prosecution. This is questionable because of the risks to the genuine independence of judges. The French Minister of Justice, Elisabeth Guigou, sketched her reform program: "Justice: from the Ministry of Affairs to the Ministry of Justice" (Le Monde, 1-9-1999). She ascertained that the budget for justice had been far too low for decades. More fundamentally, the people's trust in justice is undermined by scandals, while the political cronies of those in power could get anything done that they wanted. Impartiality of judges was not practised. She claimed that her program should realise equal and impartial justice for all.

At last, France has a modernised system, operational since 1 January 2001. Due to a series of activities opposing reform, like strikes of barristers, fierce protests of magistrates and pressure in the media, part of this reform only took effect in June 2001. The "loi renforçant la protection de la présomption d'innocence et les droits des victimes" is a mini-revolution. This reform was necessary to adapt French national legislation and practices to the European Convention for the Protection of Human Rights and Fundamental Freedoms (3 September 1953). This reform is about custody, provisional detention, research phase for assembling information about crimes and offences ("instruction"), appeal for the "cours d'assises", and measures in the sphere of application of penalties. Barristers (without perusal of files), in a meeting of half an hour with the suspect, can be involved from the first hour of custody (not from the 20th hour as before). Police must inform the suspect of the nature of the offence with which he is charged, and about his right to remain silent. Video records are made of the interrogations of minors. The law creates a specific "juge des libertés et de la détention" to decide about provisional detention (instead of the "juge d'instruction"). The duration of provisional detention is reduced to a maximum of 2 years (offences) or 4 years (crimes). The rights of suspects are extended for the "instruction" phase. One can be interrogated in presence of a barrister without being taken in official examination. When there are indications against individuals, they can be "témoins assistés", they can be taken into official examination only when there are serious indications. The law creates the possibility of appeal against decisions of the "jurys d'assises" in case of condemnation, and also against the way penalties are applied (conditional release, semi-liberty, workplaces outside prison). The Minister of Justice can no longer decide conditional release for long term prisoners, instead regional jurisdictions are made competent to decide these, while appeal on a national jurisdiction is possible.

The myth in the prevailing dogma of democracy about the legitimacy based upon elections might be seen in relative perspective. In historical perspective one might conclude that the basis for legitimising public authority was found earlier in God, Nature, the People, or the Nation. In the course of time the notion of the People or Nation was replaced by the Parliament, elected by the people, or by the parliamentary majority. This denaturalised the original idea of democracy, as political parties practised the "winner takes all" philosophy. They in fact kidnapped public authority which is meant to work for the common good of all, and not for a partisan group. What is, mutatis mutandis, the difference between the partisan group, dominating in the Ancien Régime (aristocracy) and the leadership of the party-political group with the majority nowadays? There is an ongoing series of wars between several cliques having power. Often the illusion of representative democracy on the basis of elections is (ab)used to push party-political and partisan interests, so undermining confidence in public authorities. Former Minister of Justice, Badinter said: In the Republic government is politically responsible for the acts of public functionaries. Magistrates, although having a specific statute, remain public functionaries. Government is responsible for their functioning also (Le Monde, 29-10-1997). The interview of Minister Guigou, presenting her proposals for reforming justice, is instructive: "'pouvoir' (power) comes from universal suffrage, so power is in the hands of Parliament, of which Government is an emanation." (Le Monde, 30-10-1997). A clear example of semantic problems for the French using the notion "pouvoir". This can mean (party-political) power and public authority, but these must be distinguished. It is serious that authentic responsibility of public functionaries ex officio is denied: power for all public authorities is in the hands of the Parliament alone.

In the Ancien Régime, a whole army of legists had constructed the idea that French Kings were representatives of God (rituals of unction), so all public authority, and all law, was proclaimed to come from the King (and God). The institution of the public prosecutor was developed from the end of the Middle Ages. Contemporary "magistrats du parquet" are the functional heirs of the "gens du Roi", and of institutional ideas of the Revolution as well. Revolutionaries argued that the legitimising basis, also for the public prosecutor, had to be the elections of functionaries by the people. This was reduced to the elected representatives of the people. The King was replaced by the parliamentary majority as power base and foundation of legitimacy (the function of the unction was fulfilled by elections). Magistrates also have democratic legitimacy from the Constitution, as other public authorities have. Election is by no means the exclusive canal for producing legitimacy. The more magistrates, fulfilling their mission to produce equal law for all, can function independently, the greater their legitimacy. Judges and officers for the prosecution are limited by their duty to apply the law. According to J.F. Kriegk (Le Monde, 23-1-1997), there is no risk of government by judges. When power and control of public authority is in the hands of the (party-)political majority, a countervailing judiciary power is an asset for genuine democracy. The Idea of Democracy, as developing in France, should be enriched by the idea that each functionary with a public function has a specific authority and responsibility "ex officio", professionally. This is fundamentally different from the mainstream conception that party-politicians, once elected or nominated, are the boss of public functionaries, thought to have no competencies of their own. Public functionaries derive their competencies largely directly from accepting their public job, not only indirectly via the instructions of (party-political) bosses. Public functionaries owe their legitimacy to the statute of their public function as circumscribed on the basis of laws. It is obvious that public functionaries are crucial for the implementation of law and public policies. It is crucial that the Rule of Law prevails, especially in practice: Ubi ius, ibi societas.

Cohen-Tanugi (1985, 1993)) compared two conceptions of societal regulation. A model of State-regulation (State law) and a model of a self-regulating society (contractual society). In the framework of an underdeveloped "Idea of Law", law in France is above all the production of norms by the State, dominating prevailing law, so creation of law by civil society itself is obstructed. Partners in society lost the habit of making mutual arrangements to organise reasonable societal relations themselves. It was seen as normal that these were organised via, and under control of the State ("tutelle"). It is commonly recognised that France is living under the yoke of a rigid-dirigist model of State-regulation developed since the French Revolution. The ideology of the French State robbed French society of fundamental law. Cohen-Tanugi pleaded in favour of more sophisticated self-regulation in a society with adequately functioning public authorities. France seems to evolve into a more contractual society (Cannac, 1983; Prévost, 1983; Minc, 1984). According to Karpik (2000) the position of Justice became more central in French society during the last two decades, not so much at the instigation of judges, although judges have had a crucial role in the new constellation, recognising the newly diversified position of interactive citizenry ("citoyenneté judiciaire"). Several aspects created a different situation: prominence of the market; weakening of the State; ubiquitous media; democratic individualism and a new public spirit. Karpik's thesis is that transformations in penal and civil judiciary are so spectacular, that the unfortunate history with regard to the French judiciary, which began with the French Revolution, seems to have made a crucial turn. These transformations were realised without appreciable modifications of structure, but with diversification of functions and growing contractualisation of societal relations. In a sense, France is catching up with other European countries with regard to the societal position of the judiciary. Karpik signals a return of personal responsibility in penalisation of political and bureaucratic public functionaries (Engel, 1995; Massot, 1999). French society is witnessing invisible revolutions especially in the sphere of societal law creation (Cohen c.s, 1998). The French judiciary system created a surprise in the case of Maurice Papon, condemned in 1998 for crimes as functionary of the Vichy Regime. The "Conseil d'État" on 12 April 2002 ordered the State to pay half of the indemnity which Papon had to pay, and on 9 July 2002 the "Tribunal Administratif" of Paris ordered the State to pay a symbolic euro for its responsibility in crimes committed by Papon under the Vichy Regime. The Papon case had more surprises. On the basis of a recent amendment in the law concerning the rights of sick people, the Court of Paris decided on 18 September 2002 to release Papon, causing public indignation. The Minister of Justice said that he would try to cancel this decision in a cassation procedure. All in all, France is very interesting with its juridical institutionalising of society.

**References**

French
Abraham, R., Droit international, droit communautaire et droit français. (Paris, Hachette, 1989).
Aldeeb Abu-Salieh, S., Les Musulmans face aux Droits de l'Homme. Religion, Droit, Politique. (Bochum, Winkler, 1994).
Allix, D., Le Droit Pénal. (Paris, LGDJ, 2000).
Alt, E., Luc, I., La Lutte contre la Corruption. (Paris, PUF, 1997).
Ancel, M., La Défense sociale. (Paris, PUF, 1989).
Ardant, P., Institutions Politiques et Droit Constitutionnel. (Paris, LGDJ, 1997).
Arnaud, A.J., Les Juristes face à la Société. Du XIXe siècle à nos jours. (Paris, PUF, 1975).
Arnaud, A.J., Pour une Pensée Juridique Européenne. (Paris, PUF, 1991).
Assemblée nationale, Les pouvoirs publics. Textes essentiels. (Paris, DF, 2002).
Association française pour l'histoire de la justice, Juger les Juges. Du Moyen Age au Conseil Supérieur de la Magistrature. (Paris, DF, 2000).
Association française pour l'histoire de la justice, La Cour d'Assises. (Paris, DF, 2001).

Association internationale des hautes juridictions administratives, Receuil de décisions des hautes juridictions administratives 2000. (Paris, DF, 2000).
Aubert, J., Petit, M., La Police en France. Service Public. (Paris, Berger-Levrault, 1981).
Aubusson de Cavarlay, B., Godefroy, T., Condemnations et Condamnés. Qui condamne-t-on? A quoi? Pourquoi? (Paris, SEPC, 1981).
Auby, J.M. et J.B., Institutions Administratives. (Paris, Dalloz, 1997).
Auby, J.M. et J.B., Droit de la Fonction Publique. État, Collectivités locales, Hôpitaux. (Paris, Dalloz, 1997).
Auby, J.M., Drago, R., Traité de Contentieux Administratif. (Paris, LGDJ, 1984).
Avril, P., Les Conventions de la Constitution. Normes non écrites du droit politique. (Paris, PUF, 1997).
Babès, L., Oubrou, T., Loi d'Allah, Loi des Hommes. (Paris, A.Michel, 2002).
Badinter, R., La Prison républicaine. (Paris, Fayard, 1992; 2000).
Baecque, A. de, Schmale, W., Vovelle, M., L'An I des Droits de l'Homme. (Paris, CNRS, 1989).
Barret-Kriegel, B., Les Droits de l'Homme et le Droit Naturel. (Paris, PUF, 1989).
Basdevant-Gaudemet, B., Goutal-Arnal, V., Histoire du Droit et des Institutions. (Paris, LGDJ, 1997).
Bauer, A. et X., Violences et Insécurité Urbaines. (Paris, PUF, 2001).
Bauer, A., Ventre, A.M., Les Polices en France. (Paris, PUF, 2001).
Bauer, C., Fracture d'une vie. (Paris, Seuil, 1990).
Beaud, O., Le Sang contaminé. (Paris, PUF, 1999).
Beaud, O., Blansquer, J.M., dir., La Responsabilité des Gouvernants. (Paris, Descartes, 1999).
Beaud, O., Wachsmann, P., dir., La Science Juridique Française et la Science Juridique Allemande de 1870 à 1918. (Strasbourg, PU, 1997).
Beccaria, C. de, Des délits et des peines (1764). (Paris, Garnier/Flammarion, 1991).
Béchillon, D. de, Qu'est-ce qu'une Règle de Droit? (Paris, Odile Jacob, 1997).
Belaid, S., Essai sur le Pouvoir Créateur et Normatif du Juge. (Paris, LGDJ, 1974).
Bellefonds, X.L. de, L'Informatique et le Droit. (Paris, PUF, 1992).
Belorgey, J.M., Pré-rapport. (Paris, 1981).
Belorgey, J.M., La Police au rapport. (Nancy, PU, 1991).
Belorgey, J.M., Lutter contre les discriminations. Rapport. (Paris, 1999).
Benkheira, M.H., L'Amour de la Loi. Essai sur la Normativité en Islam. (Paris, PUF, 1997).
Bensadon, N., Les Droits de la Femme. (Paris, PUF, 1990).
Ben Salah, T., Droit de la Fonction Publique. (Paris, Masson, 1992).
Benyon, J., La Coopération de la Police en Europe. (Dans: Cahiers de la sécurité intérieure, pp.137-166, 1992).
Bergougnoux, J., Romeuf, J.P., dir., Criminalité et Délinquance Apparentes. Une Approche Territoriale. (Paris, DF, 2000).
Berlière, J.M., L'Institution Policière en France sous la IIIe République. (Dijon, Université, 1991).
Berlière, J.M., La Police des Moeurs sous la IIIe République. (Paris, Seuil, 1992).
Berlière, J.M., Le Monde des Polices en France. (Bruxelles, Complexe, 1996).
Berlière, J.M., Peschanski, D., dir., La Police Française (1930-1950). (Paris, DF, 2000).
Bernard, C., La Justice. (Paris, Le Monde/Marabout, 1996).
Berthélémy, H., Traité élémentaire de droit administratif. (Paris, Rousseau, 1901).
Bertrand, D., La Protection Sociale. (Paris, PUF, 1987).
Bertrand, M., Renoux, T., Roux, A., La Cour de Justice de la République. (Paris, PUF, 1995).
Bettati, M., Droit Humanitaire. (Paris, Seuil, 2000).
Bigaut, C., La Responsabilité Pénale des Hommes Politiques. (Paris, LGDJ, 1996).
Bigaut, C., Les Révisions de la Constitution de 1958. (Paris, DF, 2000).
Bigaut, C., Le Réformisme Constitutionnel en France (1789-2000). (Paris, DF, 2001).
Bigo, D., Polices en Réseaux. L'Expérience Européenne. (Paris, FNSP, 1996).
Bigo, D., dir., L'Europe des Polices et de la Sécurité Intérieure. (Bruxelles, Complexe, 1992).
Bodineau, P., Verpeaux, M., Histoire Constitutionnelle de la France. (Paris, PUF, 2000).
Body-Gendrot, S., Les Villes: La Fin de la Violence? (Paris, FNSP, 2001).
Body-Gendrot, S., Le Guennec, N., Rapport sur les Violences Urbaines. (Paris, FNSP, 1998).
Boëtsch, G., Dupret, B., Ferrié, J.N., dir., Droits et Sociétés dans le Monde Arabe. Perspectives Socio-anthropologiques. (Aix-Marseille, PU, 1997).
Boneface-Schmitt, J.P., La Médiation. (Paris, DF, 2002).
Bonnemaison, G., Face à la délinquance: prévention, répression, solidarité. (Paris, DF, 1983).
Bonnemaison, G., dir., La Modernisation du Service Pénitentiaire. Rapport. (Paris, Ministère de la Justice, 1989).
Bossard, A., La Criminalité Internationale. (Paris, PUF, 1988).
Boucheron, J.M., Carnets de Prison. (Paris, Arlea, 2001).

Bouloc, B., Pénologie. (Paris, Dalloz, 1991).
Bouloc, B., L'Influence du Droit Communautaire sur le Droit Pénal Interne. Dans: Mélanges Levasseur. (Paris, Litec, 1992).
Boulouis, J., Chapuissat, J., Le Mire, P., dir., Le Droit Administratif. (Paris, AJDA, 1995).
Bourdon, W., La Cour Pénale Internationale. (Paris, Seuil, 2000).
Boutet, D., Vers l'État de Droit. La Théorie de l'État et du Droit. (Paris, Harmattan, 1991).
Boyer-Chammard, G., Les Magistrats. (Paris, PUF, 1985).
Braibant,, G., Stirn, B., Le Droit Administratif Français. (Paris, FNSP, 1999).
Bredin, J.D., Un Coupable. (Paris, Gallimard, 1985).
Brunel, A., Justice, l'Autorité sans Pouvoir. (Paris, Félin, 1991).
Brunet, J.P., La police de l'ombre, indicateurs et provocateurs dans la France contemporaine. (Paris, Seuil, 1990).
Bruneteau, P., Maintenir l'Odre. (Paris, FNSP, 1996).
Bruron, J., Droit Pénal Fiscal. (Paris, LGDJ, 1993).
Buisson, H., La Police, son Histoire. (Paris, Nouvelles éditions latines, 1958).
Buisson, H., L'Acte de Police. (Lyon, Université, 1988).
Bullier, A., Pansier, F.J., Proof and Evidence: La Preuve Pénale en Droit Français et Anglais. (Dans: Gazette du Palais, juillet 1993).
Burdeau, F., Histoire de l'Administration Française du XVIIIe au XXe siècles. (Paris, Montchrestien, 1989).
Burdeau, F., Histoire du Droit Administratif. (Paris, PUF, 1995).
Burdeau, F., dir., Administration et Droit. (Paris, LGDJ, 1996).
Burdeau, G., Traité de Science Politique. (Paris, LGDJ, 1950/1957; 1986).
Burdeau, G., Droit Constitutionnel et Institutions Politiques. (Paris, LGDJ, 1980).
Burdeau, G., Hamon, F., Troper, M., Droit Constitutionnel. (Paris, LGDJ, 1997).
Cahm, E., L'Affaire Dreyfus. (Paris, Hachette, 1994).
Callé, B., La Détention Provisoire. (Paris, PUF, 1992).
Camus, A., Koestler, A., Réflexions sur la Peine Capitale. (Paris, Gallimard, 2002).
Canivet, G., dir., Amélioration du controle extérieur des établissements pénitentiaires. (Paris, DF, 2000).
Cannac, Y., Le Juste Pouvoir. (Paris, Lattès, 1983).
Cappeletti, M., dir., Accès à la Justice et État-Providence. (Paris, Economica, 1984).
Capul, J.Y., dir., La Justice. (Paris, DF, 1991).
Carbajo, J., Droit des Services Publics. (Paris, Dalloz, 1997).
Carbasse, J., Introduction historique au Droit Pénal. (Paris, PUF, 1990).
Carbasse, J., La Peine de Mort. (Paris, PUF, 2000).
Carbonnier, J., Droit et Passion du Droit sous la Ve République. (Paris, Flammarion, 1996).
Caresche-Pandraud (Rapport-), Les chiffres de la délinquance depuis un demi-siècle. (Paris, DF, 2002).
Cartuyvels, Y., et al., dir., Politique, Police et Justice du Futur. (Paris, Harmattan, 1998).
Casamayor, J.M. de, (pseud. de Serge Fuster), Le Bras Séculier. (Paris, Seuil, 1960).
Casamayor, J.M. de, La Police. (Paris, Gallimard, 1973).
Casteret, A.M., L'Affaire du Sang. (Paris, Découverte, 1992).
Cathala, F., Pratiques et réactions policières. (Paris, Champ-de-Mars, 1977).
Cedras, J., Le Droit Pénale Américain. (Paris, PUF, 1997).
Cespedes, V., La Cerise sur le Béton. Violences Urbaines et Libéralisme Sauvage. (Paris, Flammarion, 2002).
Chabanol, D., La Pratique du Contentieux Administratif. (Paris, Litec, 1991).
Chabanol, D., Le Juge Administratif. (Paris, LGDJ, 1993).
Chagnollaud, D., Le Conseil Constitutionnel et la Corse. (Dans: Pouvoirs locaux, no.53, 2002).
Chagnollaud, D., Quermonne, J.L., La Ve République. 1. Le Régime Politique; 2. Le Pouvoir Politique et l'Administration; 3. Le Pouvoir Législatif et le Système des Partis; 4. L'État de Droit et la Justice. (Paris, Flammarion, 2000).
Chaladon, S., Nivelle, P., Crimes contre l'Humanité. (Paris, Plon, 1998).
Chalom, M., Le Policier et le Citoyen. Pour une Police de Proximité. (Montréal, Liber, 1998).
Chantebout, B., Droit Constitutionnel et Science Politique. (Paris, A.Colin, 1982).
Chapus, R., Droit du Contentieux Administratif. (Paris, Montchrestien, 1993).
Chapus, R., Droit Administratif Général. (Paris, Montchrestien, 1997).
Charon, J.M., Furet, C., Un Secret si bien violé. La Loi, le Juge, le Journaliste. (Paris, Seuil, 2000).
Charvin, R., Sueur, J.J., Droits de l'Homme et Libertés de la Personne. (Paris, Litec, 1997).
Chauvaud, F., Les Experts de Crime. La Médécine Légale en France au XIXe siècle. (Paris, Aubier, 2000).
Chevallier, J., L'Élaboration Historique du Principe de Séparation de la Juridiction Administrative et l'Administration Active. (Paris, LGDJ, 1970).
Chevallier, J., L'État de Droit. (Paris, Montchrestien, 1994).

Chevallier, J., dir., Droit et Politique. (Paris, PUF, 1993).
Chevallier, J.J., Histoire des Institutions et des Régimes Politiques de la France de 1789 à nos jours. (Paris, Dalloz, 1967; 2001).
Chiaverini, P., Mardesson, D., Tribunaux Administratifs et Cours Administratives d'Appel. (Paris, LGDJ, 1996).
Clauzel, J., Rapport au Ministre de l'Intérieur sur les Polices Municipales. (Paris, DF, 1990).
Cligman, O., Gratiot, L., Hanoteau, J.C., Le Droit en Prison. (Paris, Dalloz, 2001).
Cliquennois, M., dir., La Convention Européenne des Droits de l'Homme et le Juge Français. Vademecum de Pratique Professionnelle. (Paris, Harmattan, 1997).
Cohen, D., et al., dir., France: Les Révolutions invisibles. (Paris, Calmann-Lévy, 1998).
Cohen-Jonathan, G., Aspects Européens des Droits de l'Homme. (Paris, DF, 1999).
Cohen-Jonathan, G., La Protection Internationale des Droits de l'Homme. (Paris, DF, 1999).
Cohen-Tanugi, L., Le Droit sans État. (Paris, PUF, 1985).
Cohen-Tanugi, L., Les Métamorphoses de la Démocratie. (Paris, Odile Jacob, 1993).
Collard, J., Victimes. Les Oubliés de la Justice. (Paris, Stock, 1997).
Collectif, La Crise des Prisons. (Paris, Le Monde, 1992).
Collectif, La Justice Déboussolée. (Paris, Le Monde, 1993).
Collectif, La Peine de Mort de Voltaire à Badinter. (Paris, Flammarion, 2001).
Collectif, La Peine de Mort. (Paris, Le Monde, 2002).
Colloque du Nouvel Observateur, La Corruption Internationale. (Paris, Maisonneuve et Larose, 1999).
Colloque de Royaumont, Quelle Politique Pénale pour l'Europe? (Paris, Economica, 1993).
Combessy, P., Sociologie de la Prison. (Paris, Découverte, 2001).
Commissariat général du Plan (CGP), La Loi relatve à la lutte contre le tabagisme et l'alcoolisme. (Paris, DF, 2000).
Commission européenne pour la démocratie par le dsroit, Intégration européenne et droit constitutionnel. (Paris, DF/Conseil de l'Europe, 2002).
Commission nationale consultative des droits de l'homme, La Lutte contre le Racisme et la Xénophobie. (Paris, DF, 2001).
Commission nationale de controle des interceptions de sécurité, Rapport. (Paris, DF, 2002).
Commission nationale de déontologie de la sécurité, Rapport. (Paris, DF, 2002).
Commission nationale de l'informatique et des libertés, Rapport d'activité 2001. (Paris, DF, 2002).
Commission nationale de l'informatique et des libertés, 23$^e$ Conférence internationale des commissaires à la protection des données personnelles. (Paris, DF, 2002).
Conan, E., Le Procès Papon. (Paris, Gallimard, 1998).
Conseil d'État, L'Aide juridique pour un meilleur accès au droit et à la justice. (Paris, DF, 1991).
Conseil d'État, Jurisprudence et avis de 2001. Collectivités publiques et concurrence. (Paris, DF, 2002).
Conseil d'État, EDCE (Études et Documents du Conseil d'État). Collection.
Conseil de l'Europe, Enquête sur les systèmes pénitentiaires dans les États-membres du Conseil de l'Europe (Strasbourg, 1990).
Conseil de l'Europe, Le Code Européen d'Éthique de la Police. (Paris, DF, 2002).
Conseil de l'Europe, Combattre la torture en Europe. (Paris, DF, 2002).
Conseil de l'Europe, Droits de l'homme en droit international. (Paris, DF, 2002).
Costa, J.P., Della Cananea, G., dir., Droits de l'Homme et Administrations Publiques. (Bruxelles, IIAS, 1997).
Cour de Cassation, Le Droit des Preuves au Défi de la Modernité. Colloque 24 mars 2000. (Paris, DF, 2000).
Cour de Cassation, La Protection de la Personne. (Paris, DF, 2001).
Cour de Cassation, Les Libertés. (Paris, DF, 2002).
Crenner, E., Insécurité et Sentiment d'Insécurité. (Paris, INSEE, 1996).
CURAPP (Centre universitaire de recherches administratives et politiques de Picardie), Le Droit en Procès. (Paris, PUF, 1984).
CURAPP, Droit et Politique. (Paris, PUF, 1993).
Damiani, C., Les Victimes. (Paris, Bayard, 1997).
Damon, J., Des hommes en trop. Essai sur le vagabondage et la mendicité. (Paris, Éd. de l'Aube, 1996).
Danet, J., Défendre, pour une Défense Pénale Critique. (Paris, Dalloz, 2001).
David, R., Les Grands Systèmes de Droit Contemporain. (Paris, LGDJ, 1992).
Debbasch, C., Science administrative. Administration publique. (Paris, Dalloz, 1989).
Decock, A., Montreuil, J., Buisson, J., Le droit de la police. (Paris, Litec, 1992).
Dejours, C., Souffrance en France. La Banalisation d'Injustice Sociale. (Paris, Seuil, 2000).
Delamare, N., Traité de la police. (Paris, 1748).
Delarue, J., OAS contre De Gaulle. (Paris, Fayard, 1981).
Delay, A.F., La Formation Professionnelle dans l'Institution Policière, 1870-1941. (Lyon, Université, 1989).

Dellis, G., Droit Pénal et Droit Administratif. L'Influence des Principes du Droit Pénal sur le Droit Administratif Répressif. (Paris, LGDJ, 1997).
Delmas-Marty, M., Les Chemins de la Répression. (Paris, PUF, 1980).
Delmas-Marty, M., Droit Pénal des Affaires. (Paris, PUF, 1981; 1990).
Delmas-Marty, M., Modèles et Mouvements de Politique Criminelle. (Paris, Economica, 1983).
Delmas-Marty, M., Face à l'Inflation Pénale. Une Exigence Nouvelle, la Qualité de la Loi. (Paris, 1986).
Delmas-Marty, M., Les Grands Systèmes de Politique Criminelle. (Paris, PUF, 1992).
Delmas-Marty, M., dir., La mise en état des affaires pénales. Rapport. (Paris, DF, 1991).
Delmas-Marty, M., Teitgen-Colly, C., Punir sans Juger? De la Répression Administrative vers un Droit Administratif Pénal. (Paris, Economica, 1992).
Delpérée, F., Les Droits Politiques des Étrangers. (Paris, PUF, 1995).
Delpérée, F., Foucher, P., dir., La Saisine du Juge Constitutionnel. Aspects de Droit Comparé. (Bruxelles, Bruylant, 1998).
Delteil, G., Prisons: la marmite infernale. (Paris, Syros, 1990).
Demonque, P., Les Policiers. (Paris, Découverte, 1983).
Desportes, F., Le Gunéhec, F., Le Nouveau Droit Pénal. (Paris, Economica, 1994).
DF (Documentation française), La Justice Administrative en Pratique. (Paris, DF, 1998).
DF, Les Droits de l'Homme à l'Aube du XXIe siècle. (Paris, DF, 1999).
DF, Guide Pratique de la Police de Proximité. (Paris, DF, 2000).
DF, L'Autre Europe des Drogues. (Paris, DF, 2000).
DF, La Constitution face à l'Europe. (Paris, DF, 2000).
DF, L'Univers Pénitentiaire. (Paris, DF, 2001).
DF, Jurisprudence des cours administratives d'appel 2000. (Paris, DF, 2002).
DF, Les Traités de Rome, Maastricht, Amsterdam et Nice. (Paris, DF, 2002).
Dindo, S., et al., dir., Le Nouveau Guide du Prisonier. (Paris, Éd. de l'Atelier, 2000).
Direction des Hôpitaux, Bilan de la Réforme de la Santé en Prison. (Paris, 1997).
Domat, J., Le droit public suivi des lois civiles dans leur ordre naturel. (Paris, Coignard, 1697).
Dominicé, C., L'Ordre Juridique International entre Tradition et Innovation. (Genève, PUF, 1997).
Drouin, M., dir., L'Affaire Dreyfus de A à Z. (Paris, Flammarion, 1994).
Dubet, F., et al., Les opérations "été-jeunes". (Paris, CTNERHI, 1985).
Dubouis, L., dir., Progrès Medical et Droit Européen. (Paris, DF, 1999).
Dubourg-Lavroff, S., Pantélis, A., Les Décisions Essentielles du Conseil Constitutionnel. Des Origines à nos jours. (Paris, Harmattan, 1994).
Duchaine, C., Juge à Monaco. (Paris, Lafon, 2002).
Dufourg, J.M., Section Manipulation, de l'Antiterrorisme à l'Affaire Doucé. (Paris, Lafon, 1991).
Duguit, L., Traité de Droit Constitutionnel. (Paris, Fontemoing, 1927/1930).
Duguit, L., Monnier, H., Bonnard, R., Les Constitutions et les Principales Lois Politiques de la France depuis 1789. (Paris, LGDJ, 1952).
Duhamel, O., Histoire Constitutionnelle de la France. (Paris, Seuil, 1995).
Dumas, A., Histoire du Droit Francais. (Aix-en-Provence, Université, 1978).
Dumas, R., Les Avocats. (Paris, Grasset, 1977).
Dumay, J.M., Le Procès de Maurice Papon. (Paris, Le Monde, 1998).
Dupont Delestraint, P., Droit Pénal des Affaires et des Sociétés Commerciales. (Paris, Dalloz, 1980).
Duprez, D., Leclerc-Olive, M., Pinet, M., Vivre Ensemble. La Diversité des Quartiers "sensibles" à l'Epreuve de la Vie Quotidienne. (Lille, Laboratoire de Sociologie du Travail, de l'Éducation et de l'Emploi, 1996).
Dupuis, G. (Études en l'honneur de), Droit Public. (Paris, LGDJ, 1997).
Duran, P., Penser l'Action Publique. (Paris, LGDJ, 1999).
Durupt, B., La Police Judiciaire, la Scène de Crime. (Paris, Gallimard, 2000).
Duverger, M., Institutions politiques et Droit Constitutionnel. (Paris, PUF, 1980).
Duverger, M., Éléments de Droit Public. (Paris, PUF, 1981).
Dworkin, R., L'Empire du Droit. (Paris, PUF, trad., 1993).
Dworkin, R., Prendre les Droits au sérieux. (Paris, PUF, trad., 1995).
Dye, V., La Sécurité Civile. (Paris, PUF, 1995).
Ebel, E., Les Préfets et le Maintien de l'Ordre Public, en France au XIXe siècle. (Paris, DF, 2000).
Ecole Nationale d'Administration, Administration et politiques pénitentiaires. (Paris, Revue française d'administration publique, no.99, 2002).
Eisenmann, C., La Justice Constitutionnelle et la Haute Cour Constitutionnelle d'Autriche. (Paris, Economica, 1928).
Ellul, J., Histoire des Institutions. (Paris, PUF, 1993; 1998).
Engel, L., La Responsabilité en Crise. (Paris, Hachette, 1995).

Erbès, J.M., et al., Polices d'Europe. (Paris, Harmattan/IHESI, 1992).
Esmein, A., Histoire de la Procédure Criminelle en France. (Paris, Sirey, 1882).
Esmein, A., Éléments de Droit Constitutionnel Français et Comparé. (Paris, Sirey, 1906; 1921).
Estoup, P., La Justice Française. (Paris, Litec, 1989).
Fabre, M.H., Principes Républicains de Droit Constitutionnel. (Paris, LGDJ, 1970; 1984).
Fanachi, P., Le Procès Administratif. (Paris, PUF, 1993).
Fanachi, P., La Justice Administrative. (Paris, PUF, 1995).
Farcie, J.C., Guide des Archives Judiciaires et Pénitentiaires, 1800-1958. (Paris, CNRS, 1992).
Farcie, J.C., Deux Siècles d'Histoire de la Justice (1789-1999). (Paris, CNRS, 1996).
Farcie, J.C., Magistrats en Majesté. Les Discours de rentrée aux audiences solennelles des cours d'appel. XIXe-XXe siècles. (Paris, CNRS, 1998).
Faugeron, C., Tournier, P., La Crise des Prisons françaises. Dans: Léonard, Y., dir., La Justice. (Paris, DF, pp.128-136, 1991).
Favard, J., Des Prisons. (Paris, Gallimard, 1987).
Favoreu, L., Les Cours Constitutionelles. (Paris, PUF, 1986).
Favoreu, L., dir., Le Domaine de la Loi et du Règlement. (Paris, Economica, 1978).
Favoreu, J., dir., Cours Constitutionnelles Européennes et Droits Fondamentaux. (Paris, Economica, 1982).
Favoreu, J., dir., Le Pouvoir des Juges. (Paris, Economica, 1990).
Favoreu, J., Philip, L., Les Grandes Décisions du Conseil Constitutionnel. (Paris, Dalloz, 1995).
Favoreu, J., Philip, L., Le Conseil Constitutionnel. (Paris, PUF, 1995).
Favre, P., Filleule, O., Manifestations Pacifiques et Manifestations Violentes dans la France Contemporaine, 1982-1990. (Paris, IHESI, 1992).
Ferret, J., Ocqueteau, F., dir., Évaluer la Police de Proximité? Problèmes, Concepts, Méthodes. (Paris, DF, 1999).
Fleury, C., Histoire du Droit Français. (Paris, Le Petit, 1674).
Fleury, C., Droit Public. (Paris, Pierre, 1769).
Foll, O., L'Insécurité en France. Un Grand Flic Accuse. (Paris, Flammarion, 2002).
Fontanaud, D., La Criminalité organisée. (Paris, DF, 2002).
Foucault, M., Surveiller et Punir. Naissance de la Prison. (Paris, Gallimard, 1975).
Franck, C., Les Fonctions Juridictionnelles du Conseil Constitutionnel et du Conseil d'État dans l'Ordre Constitutionnel. (Paris. LGDJ, 1974).
Frison, D., Introduction au Droit Anglais. Institutions Britanniques. (Paris, Ellipses, 2000).
Fromont, M., Introduction au Droit Allemand. (Paris, Cujas, 1979/1984).
Gaetner, G., Paringaux, R.P., Un Juge face au Pouvoir (de la gauche à la droite, les secrets de Renaud Van Ruymbeke). (Paris, Grasset, 1994).
Garapon, A., Bien Juger. Essai sur le Rituel Judiciaire. (Paris, Odile Jacob, 1997).
Garapon, A., La Démocratie à l'épreuve de la Justice. (Dans: Justice, no.1, 1999).
Garapon, A., Gros, F., Pech, T., Et ce sera Justice. Punir en Démocratie. (Paris, Odile Jacob, 2001).
Garapon, A., Salas, D., dir., La Justice et le Mal. (Paris, Odile Jacob, 1997).
Garbar, C., Le Droit applicable au Personnel des Entreprises Publiques. (Paris, LGDJ, 1996).
Garisson, F., Histoire du Droit et des Institutions. (Paris, Montchrestien, 1983).
Garnot, B., dir., Histoire et Criminalité de l'Antiquité au XXe siècle. (Dijon, Université, 1998).
Garrigue, P., La Gendarmerie française. (Paris, Éd. Hologramme, 1989).
Gaudemet, J., Les Naissances du Droit. Le Temps, le Pouvoir et la Science au Service du Droit. (Paris, Montchrestien, 1997).
Genthial, J., Audit sur la Qualité des Relations entre la Police et la Population. (Paris, Ministère de l'Intérieur, 1995).
Gentot, M., Oberdorff, H., Les Cours Administratives d'Appel. (Paris, PUF, 1991).
Georges, P., Droit Public. (Paris, Dalloz, 1999).
Ghestin, J., Goubeaux, G., Traité de Droit Civil. (Paris, LGDJ, 1983).
Gicquel, J., Droit Constitutionnel et Institutions Politiques. (Paris, Montchrestien, 1987; 1995).
Gilbert, C., Le Pouvoir en Situation Extrême. (Paris, Harmattan, 1992).
Girard, L., La Garde nationale, 1814-1871. (Paris, Plon, 1964).
Girard, R., La Violence et le Sacré. (Paris, Grasset, 1972).
Giudicelli-Delage, G., Institutions Judiciaires et Juridictionnelles. (Paris, PUF, 1986).
Gleizal, J.J., Le Désordre Policier. (Paris, PUF, 1985).
Gleizal, J.J., Police et Culture. (Paris, PUF, 1988).
Gleizal, J.J., La Police en France. (Paris, PUF, 1993).
Gleizal, J.J., Les Référents Juridiques dans l'Action Policière. (Grenoble, CERAT, 1987).
Gleizal, J.J., Gatti-Domenach, J., Journès, C., La Police. Le cas des démocraties libérales. (Paris, PUF, 1993).

Godechot, J., Les Constitutions de la France depuis 1789. (Paris, Garnier-Flammarion, 1970).
Golfier, C., Poisson-Harduin, M.H., Droit Pénal et Procédure Pénal. (Paris, Ellipses, 2000).
Golfier, C., Poisson-Harduin, M.H., Droit du Contentieux. (Paris, Ellipses, 2000).
Gomien, D., Harris, D., Swaak, L., Convention Européen des Droits de l'Homme et Charte Sociale Européenne. Droit et Pratique. (Strasbourg, Conseil de l'Europe, 1998).
Gonod, P., Edouard Laferrière. Un Juriste au Service de la République. (Paris, LGDJ, 1997).
Greilsamer, L., Interpol. (Paris, Fayard, 1997).
Greilsamer, L., Schneidermann, Les Juges Parlent. (Paris, Fayard, 1992).
Greilsamer, L., Schneidermann, Où vont les Juges? (Paris, Fayard, 2002).
Guéno, J.P., dir., Paroles de Détenus. (Paris, Librio, 2000).
Guettier, C., Droit Administrtatif. (Paris, Montchrestien, 2000).
Guigon, L., Les Statuts Spéciaux des Personnels de Police. (Paris, Université, thèse, 1962).
Guigou, E., et al., Le Service Public de la Justice. (Paris, Odile Jacob, 1998).
Guillot, R., La Liberté. (Paris, PUF, 1993).
Guinzburg, C., Le Juge et l'Historien. (Lagrasse, Verdier, 1997).
Gunten, B. de, Martin, A., Niogret, M., Les Institutions de la France. (Paris, Nathan, 1994).
Gurvitch, G., L'Idée de Droit Social. (Paris, 1932).
Haarscher, G., Philosophie des Droits de l'Homme. (Paris, 1993).
Habermas, J., Droit et Démocratie. Entre Faits et Normes. (Paris, Gallimard, trad., 1997).
Haenel, H., Arthuis, J., Rapport de la Commission de Controle sur les Conditions de Fonctionnement des Services Relevant de l'Autorité Judiciaire. (Paris, Imprimerie du Sénat, 1991).
Haenel, H., Arthuis, J., Rapport de la Commission Sénatoriale sur le Fonxctionnement des Juridictions de l'Ordre Administratif. (Paris, Imprimerie du Sénat, 1992).
Haenel, H., Frison-Roche, M.A., Le Juge et le Politique. (Paris, PUF, 1998).
Haenel, H., Pichon, R., La Gendarmerie. (Paris, PUF, 1983).
Halévy, D., Regards sur l'Affaire Dreyfus. (Paris, Fallois, 1994).
Hamon, A., Marchand, J.C., P....comme Police. (Paris, A.Moreau, 1983).
Hamon, F., Wiener, C., Le Controle de Constitutionnalité. (Paris, DF, 1994).
Hamon, F., Wiener, C., La Loi sous Surveillance. (Paris, Odile Jacob, 1999).
Hamon, F., Wiener, C., La Justice Constitutionnelle. Présentation Générale, France, États-Unis. (Paris, DF, 2001).
Harouel, J.L., Histoire de l'Expropriation. (Paris, PUF, 2000).
Harouel, J.L., et al., Histoire des Institutions de l'Époque Franque à la Révolution. (Paris, PUF, 1992).
Harouel, V., Grands Texts du Droit Humanitaire. (Paris, PUF, 2001).
Harstrich, J., Calvi, F., R.G., 20 ans de Police Politique. (Paris, Calmann-Lévy, 1991).
Hart, H.L.A., Le Concept de Droit. (Bruxelles, Université, trad., 1976).
Hauriou, A., Gicquel, J., Droit Constitutionnel et Institutions Politiques. (Paris, Montchrestien, 1980).
Hauriou, M., Précis de Droit Administratif. (Paris, Larose, 1897).
Hauriou, M., Principes de Droit Public. (Paris, Sirey, 1916).
Hauriou, M., Précis de Droit Constitutionnel. (Paris, Sirey, 1929).
Hauterive, E. d', Napoléon et sa Police. (Paris, 1943).
Hayek, F.A., Droit, Législation et Liberté. (Paris, PUF, trad., 1983).
Hazan, P., La Justice face à la Guerre. (Paris, Stock, 2000).
Hebberecht, P., Sack, F., dir., La Prévention de la Délinquance en Europe. Nouvelles Stratégies. (Paris, Harmattan, 1997).
Heilmann, E., Des Herbiers aux Fichiers Informatiques. L'Évolution du Traitement de l'Information dans la Police. (Strasbourg, Université, thèse, 1991).
Hennion, C., Chronique des Flagrants Délits. (Paris, Stock, 1976).
Herblay, V., la Police Judiciaire. (Paris, PUF, 1988).
Hermitte, M.A., Le Sang et le Droit. Essai sur la transfusion sanguine. (Paris, Seuil, 1996).
Heymann-Doat, A., Libertés Publques et Droits de l'Homme. (Paris, LGDJ, 1992).
Howard, J., État des Prisons, des Hôpitaux et des Maisons de Fous. (Paris, 1788).
Hreblay, V., La Police Judiciaire. (Paris, PUF, 1988).
Hubert, P., dir., Quels Avenirs pour l'Europe de la Justice et de la Police? (Paris, DF, 2000).
Huerre, P., Ni Anges Ni Sauvages. Les Jeunes et la Violence. (Paris, Éd. Carrière, 2002).
Huglo, C., Lepage-Jessua, C., Code des Procédures Administratives Contentieuses. (Paris, Litec, 1990).
Hulsman, L., Bernat de Celis, J., Peines Perdues. Le Système Pénal en Question. (Paris, Centurion, 1982).
IHESI (Institut des hautes études de la sécurité intérieure), Diagnostics Locaux de Sécurité. (Paris, IHESI, 1990).
IHESI, État de la Recherche. (Paris, IHESI, 1999).

IHESI, Risque et Démocratie. Paris, Cahiers de la sécurité intérieure. (Paris, DF, 2000).
IHESI, Police et recherches. (Paris, DF, 2002).
Imbert, J., La Peine de Mort. (Paris, PUF, 1993).
Institut international d'administration publique, L'Administration de la Sécurité. (Paris, Revue française d'administration publique, 2000).
Jadot, B., Ost, F., dir., Élaborer la Loi Aujourd'hui, Mission Impossible? Colloque 22-10-1998. (Bruxelles, Saint-Louis, 1999).
Jeanneu, B., Droit Constitutionnel et Institutions Politiques. (Paris, Dalloz, 1987).
Jeanneney, J.N., Le Passé dans le Prétoire. L'Historien, le Juge et le Journaliste. (Paris, Seuil, 1998).
Jean-Pierre, D., Crime et Blanchissement. (Paris, 1993).
Jean-Pierre, D., Livre Noir de la Corruption. (Paris, 1994).
Jèze, G., Les Principes Généraux du Droit Administratif. (Paris, Berger-Levrault, 1904).
Jobard, F., L'Usage de la Force par la Police dans les Pays Anglo-Saxons. (Paris, IHESI, 1994).
Jobard, F., L'Usage de la Force par la Police. Sur quelques aspects de la mise en oeuvre du Monopole de la Violence Légitime par la Police Nationale dans la France Contemporaine. (Paris, IEP, 1998).
Jolowicz, J.A., Le Droit Anglais. (Paris, Dalloz, 1986).
Journal Officiel, Constitution, Lois Organiques et Ordonnances relatives aux Pouvoirs Publics. (Paris, J.O., 1974).
Journès, C., dir., Police et Politique. (Lyon, PUL, 1988).
Journès, C., dir., La Formation Professionnelle dans l'Institution Policière, 1870-1941. (Lyon, Université-II, 1989).
Julliard, J., dir., L'État et ses conflits. (Paris, Seuil, 1990).
Kaftani, C., La Formation du Concept de Fonction Publique en France. (Paris, LGDJ, 1998).
Kalck, P., Tribunaux Administratifs et Cours Administratives d'Appel. (Paris, Berger-Levrault, 1990).
Kalifa, D., Naissance de la Police Privée. Détectives et Agences de Recherches en France, 1832-1942. (Paris, Plon, 2000).
Kant, I., Doctrine du Droit. (Paris, Vrin, trad., 1988).
Kant, I., Critique de la Raison Pure. (Paris, Aubier, trad., 1997).
Karli, P., Les Racines de la Violence. Réflexions d'un Neurobiologiste. (Paris, Odile Jacob, 2002).
Karpik, L., Les Avocats. Entre l'État, le Public et le Marché: XVIIIe-XXe siècle. (Paris, Gallimard, 1995).
Karpik, L., L'Avancée de la Justice menace-t-elle la République? (Dans: Le Débat, pp.238-257, 2000).
Kdhir, M., Dictionnaire Juridique de la Cour Internationale de la Justice. (Bruxelles, Bruylant, 1997).
Kelsen, H., Théorie Pure du Droit (1934). (Paris, Dalloz, trad., 1962; Neuchâtel, Baconnière, 1988).
Kelsen, H., Théorie Générale du Droit et de l'État. Suivi de la doctrine du droit naturel, et le positivisme juridique. (Bruxelles, Bruylant/LGDJ, trad., 1997).
Kensey, A., Note sur les perspectives d'évolution de la population carcérale. (Paris, Direction de l'administration pénitentiaire, 1990).
Killias, M., Précis de Criminologie. (Bern, Staempfli, 1991).
Kinder-Gest, P., Droit Anglais, Institutions Politiques et Judiciaires. (Paris, LGDJ, 1993).
Kinder-Gest, P., Les Institutions Britanniques. (Paris, PUF, 1995).
Kis, J., L'Égale Dignité. Essai sur les Fondements des Droits de l'Homme. (Paris, Seuil, 1989).
Klarsfeld, A., Papon, un Verdict Français. (Paris, Ramsay, 1998).
Knobelspiess, R., L'Acharnement ou la volonté d'erreur judiciaire. (Paris, Stock, 1981).
Kourisky-Augeven, C., dir., Socialisation Juridique et Conscience du Droit. Attitudes Individuelles, Modèles Culturels et Changement Social. (Paris, LGDJ, 1997).
Kriegel, B., Le Sang, la Justice, la Politique. (Paris, Plon, 1999).
Kriegel, B., Réflexions sur la Justice. (Paris, Plon, 2001).
Laband, P., Le Droit Public de l'Empire Allemand. (Paris, trad., 1876; 1904).
Labbee, P., Introduction au Droit Processuel. (Lille, PUL, 1994).
Labbée, X., Les Critères de la Norme Juridique. (Lille, PUL, 1994).
Laclère, M., La Police. (Paris, PUF, 1972).
Laé, J.F., L'Ogre du Jugement. (Paris, Stock, 2001).
Laferrière, J., Manuel de Droit Constitutionnel. (Paris, Domat/Montchrestien, 1947).
Laferrière, M.F., Cours théorique et pratique de droit public et administratif. (Paris, 1854).
Lafont, H., Meyer, P., Le Nouvel Ordre Gendarmique. (Paris, Seuil, 1980).
Lagrange, H., La Civilité à l'Épreuve. Crime et Sentiment d'Insécurité. (Paris, PUF, 1995).
Lagrange, H., et al., Perceptions de la Violence et Sentiment d'Insécurité. (Grenoble, IEP, 1983).
Lajoye, A., Jugements de Valeur. Le Discours Judiciaire et le Droit. (Paris, PUF, 1997).
Lambert, E., Le Gouvernement des Juges et la Lutte contre la Législation Sociale aux États-Unis. (Paris, 1921).
Lameyre, X., La Criminalité Sexuelle. (Paris, Flammarion, 2000).

Langlois, D., Le Guide du Militant. (Paris, Seuil, 1972).
Langui, A., Histoire du Droit Pénal. (Paris, PUF, 1993).
Lantéri-Laura, G., Histoire de la Phrénologie. (Paris, PUF, 1970).
Larguier, J., Le Droit Pénal. (Paris, PUF, 1994; 2000).
Larguier, J., La Procédure Pénale. (Paris, PUF, 1994).
Laroque, P., Au Service de l'Homme et du Droit. (Paris, DF, 2000).
Lascoumes, P., Corruptions. (Paris, FNSP, 2000).
Lascoumes, P., Poncela, P., Lenoël, P., Au Nom de l'Ordre. Une Histoire Politique du Code Pénal. (Paris, Hachette, 1989).
Lascoumes, P., Poncela, P., Lenoël, P., Les Grands Phases d'Incrimination. Les Mouvements de la Législation Pénale 1815-1940. (Paris, 1992).
Lazare, B., Une Erreur Judiciaire. L'Affaire Dreyfus. (Paris, Allia, 1993).
Lazerges, C., La Politique Criminelle. (Paris, PUF, 1987).
Léauté, J., Criminologie et Science Pénitentiaire. (Paris, PUF, 1972).
Léauté, J., Les Prisons. (Paris, PUF, 1990).
Lebigre, A., La Justice du Roi. La Vie Judiciaire dans l'Ancienne France. (Paris, A.Michel, 1988; Bruxelles, Complexe, 1995).
Lebigre, A., Histoire de la Police. (Paris, Ministère de l'Intérieur).
Lebon, A., Migrations et nationalité en France en 2000. (Paris, DF, 2002).
Lebreton, G., Libertés Publiques et Droits de l'Homme. (Paris, A.Colin, 1999).
Le Caisne, L., Prison. Une Ethnologue en Centrale. (Paris, Odile Jacob, 2001).
Leclerc, D., Institutions Politiques et Droit Constitutionnel. (Paris, LGDJ, 1977).
Leclerc, H., Le Nouveau Code Pénal. (Paris, Seuil, 1994).
Le Clère, M., La Police. (Paris, PUF, 1972; 1986).
Le Clère, M., Manuel de Police Technique. (Paris, Éd. Police Revue, 1974).
Le Clère, M., Histoire de la Police. (Paris, PUF, 1975).
Legohérel, H., Histoire du Droit Public Français. (Paris, PUF, 1994).
Legohérel, H., Histoire du Droit International Public. (Paris, PUF, 1996).
Le Hardy de Beaulieu, L., L'Union Européenne. Introduction à l'Étude de l'Ordre Juridique et des Institutions Communautaires. (Namur, PU de Namur, 1998).
Lemaire, T., La Justice jusqu'à l'Absurde. (Paris, Fayard, 2001).
Lemaître, A., Assurance et Criminalité. Gérer et Prévenir. Étude Criminologique de l'Assurance-Vol. (Liège, Université, 1992/1993).
Lemeunier, F., Litiges et Procès. (Paris, Masson, 1980).
Le Mire, P., La Loi et le Règlement. (Paris, DF, 1994).
Lemonde, M., Police et Justice. (Lyon, Lyon-III, thèse, 1975).
Le Monde, La Crise des Prisons. (Paris, Le Monde, 1992).
Le Monde, La Justice Déboussolée. (Paris, Le Monde, 1993.
Lenaerts, K., Le Juge et la Constitution aux États-Unis d'Amérique et dans l'Ordre Juridique Européen. (Bruxelles, Bruylant, 1988).
Lenoble, J., dir., La Crise du Juge. (Paris, LGDJ, 1990).
Léonard, Y., dir., La Justice. (Paris, DF, 1991).
Lépine, L., Mes Souvenirs. (Paris, Payot, 1929).
Leruez, J., Les Institutions du Royaume-Uni. (Paris, DF, 1999).
Leteur, S., La Coopération Policière Européenne. (Paris, École nationale supérieure de police, 1991).
Lethier, P., L'Argent Secret. L'Espion de l'Affaire Elf Parle. (Paris, A.Michel, 2000).
Letourneur, M., Bauchet, J., Méric, J., Le Conseil d'État et les Tribunaux Administratifs. (Paris, A.Colin, 1970).
Levasseur, A.A., Le Droit des États-Unis. (Paris, Dalloz, 1990).
Levasseur, G., Chavanne, A., Montreuil, J., Droit Pénal et Procédure Pénale. (Paris, Sirey, 1983).
Lévi-Bruhl, H., Sociologie du Droit. (Paris, 1961).
Lévy, R., Du Suspect au Coupable. Le Travail de Police Judiciaire. (Paris, Méridiens-Klincksieck, 1987).
Leyrit, C., Les partis politiques et l'argent. (Paris, Le Monde, 1995).
L'Heuillet, H., Basse Politique, Haute Police. Une Approche Historique et Philosophique de la Police. (Paris, Fayard, 2001).
Lhuillier, D., Les Policiers au Quotidien. Une Psychologue dans la Police. (Paris, Harmattan, 1987).
Lhuillier, D., Lemiszewska, A., Le Choc Carcéral. (Paris, Bayard, 2001).
Loiselle, M., La Résurgence du Discours de l'État de Droit. (Amiens, Université, 1991).
Lombard, M., Droit Administratif. (Paris, Dalloz, 1997).
Lombois, C., Droit Pénal International. (Paris, Dalloz, 1979).

Long, M., et al., Les Grands Arrêts de la Jurisprudence Administrative. (Paris, Dalloz, 1996).
Lopez, G., Victimologie. (Paris, Dalloz, 1997).
Lopez, G., Bornstein, S., Les Comportements Criminels. (Paris, PUF, 1994).
Loschak, D., La Justice Administrative. (Paris, Montchrestien, 1994).
Loschak, D., dir., Les Usages Sociales du Droit. (Paris, PUF, 1989).
Loubet del Bayle, J.L., La Police dans le Système Politique. (Dans: Revue française de science politique, pp.509-534, 1981).
Loubet del Bayle, J.L., La Police. Approche Sociopolitique. (Paris, Montchrestien, 1992).
Loubet del Bayle, J.L., dir., Police et Société. (Toulouse, IEP, 1988).
MacCormick, N., Raisonnement Juridique et Théorie du Droit. (Paris, PUF, trad., 1996).
Machelon, J.P., La République contre les libertés? (Paris, FNSP, 1981).
Madelin, L., Fouché. (Paris, Plon, 1955).
Mahiou, A., dir., L'État de Droit dans le Monde Arabe. (Paris, CNRS, 1997).
Maillard, J. de, L'Avenir du Crime. (Paris, Flammarion, 1997).
Maisl, H., Le Droit des Données Publiques. (Paris, LGDJ, 1996).
Marchetti, A.M., Perpétuités. Le Temps Infini des Longues Peines. (Paris, Plon, 2001).
Marcou, J., Justice Constitutionnelle et Systèmes Politiques. États-Unis, Europe, France. (Saint-Martin-d'Hères, PU de Grenoble, 1997).
Marguénaud, J.P., CEDH et Droit Privé. L'Influence de la Jurisprudence de la Cour Européenne des Droits de l'Homme sur le Droit Privé Français. (Paris, DF, 2001).
Marty, F., dir., Le Jeune Délinquant. (Paris, Payot, 2002).
Mary, F.L., Femmes, Délinquants et Controle Penal. (Paris, Centre de Recherche Sociologique sur le Droit et les Institutions Pénales, 1996).
Masclet, J.C., Textes sur les Libertés Publiques. (Paris, PUF, 1988).
Massot, J., dir., La Responsabilité Pénale des Décideurs Publics. (Paris, DF, 2000).
Massot, J., Fouquet, O., Le Conseil d'État, Juge de Cassation. (Paris, Berger-Levrault, 1993).
Massot, J., Girardot, T., Le Conseil d'État. (Paris, DF, 1999).
Mathiesen, M.T., Résistances au changement dans les institutions pénitentiaires. (Strasbourg, Conseil de l'Europe. 1967).
Mathieu, J.L., La Défense Internationale des Droits de l'Homme. (Paris, PUF, 1993).
Mathieu, J.L., L'Insécurité. (Paris, PUF, 1995).
Matscher, F., Petzold, H., dir., Protection des Droits de l'Homme. La Dimension Européenne. (Paris, 1990).
Maurer, B., Le Principe de Respect de la Dignité Humaine et la Convention Européenne des Droits de l'Homme. (Paris, DF, 1999).
Maurin, A., Droit Administratif. (Paris, Sirey, 1999).
Maus, D., Mathieu, B., dir., La Cour de Justice de la République et après? (Paris, DF, 2000).
Mayer, O., Le Droit Administratif Allemand. (Paris, 1903).
Mélin-Soucramanien, F., Le Principe d'Égalité dans la Jurisprudence du Conseil Constitutionnel. (Aix-Marseille, PU, 1997).
Merle, R., Droit Pénal Général Complémentaire. (Paris, PUF, 1957).
Merle, R., La Pénitence et la Peine. (Paris, Cujas, 1985).
Merle, R., Vitu, A., Traité de Droit Criminel. (Paris, Cujas, 1989).
Messner, F. de, Les "Sectes" et le Droit en France. (Paris, PUF, 1999).
Mestre, J.L., Introduction Historique au Droit Administratif Français. (Paris, PUF, 1985).
Meulders-Klein, M.T., dir., Familles et Justice. Justice Civile et Évolution du Contentieux Familial en Droit Comparé. (Bruxelles, Bruylant/LGDJ, 1997).
Meunier, J., Le Pouvoir du Conseil Constitutionnel. Essai d'Analyse Stratégique. (Paris, LGDJ, 1994).
Meyzonnier, P., Les Forces de Police dans l'Union Européenne. (Paris, Harmattan/IHESI, 1994).
Miall, H., dir., Les Droits des Minorités en Europe. Vers un Régime Transnational. (Paris, Harmattan, 1997).
Michaud, Y., La Violence. (Paris, PUF, 1992).
Michaud, Y., Changements dans la Violence. Essai sur la Bienveillance Universelle et la Peur. (Paris, Odile Jacob, 2002).
Michaut, F., L'École de la Sociological Jurisprudence et le Mouvement Réaliste Américain. (Lille, Université de Lille, 1985).
Midol, A., Réseau Banlieue SNCF. Quelle Police? Quels Policiers? (Paris, IHESI, 1990).
Mignard, J.P., Vogelweith, A., Justice pour Tous. (Paris, Découverte, 2001).
Minc, A., L'Avenir en faqce. (Paris, Seuil, 1984).
Minc, A., Au nom de la Loi. (Paris, Gallimard, 1998).
Ministère de l'Économie, des Finances et de l'Industrie, Les Droits de l'Homme et de l'Enfant face à la Mondialisation. (Paris, DF, 2000).

Ministère de l'Éducation Nationale, Receuil de textes et documents à l'occasion du Bicentenaire de la Révolution. (Paris, DF, 1989).
Ministère de l'Emploi et de la Solidarité, L'Acceuil des Demandeurs d'Asile et des Réfugiés. (Paris, DF, 1998).
Ministère de l'Emploi et de la Solidarité, Femmes. Pour une Réelle Égalité des Chances et des Droits. (Paris, DF, 1999).
Ministère de l'Intérieur, Les Policiers, leurs Métiers, leur Formation. (Paris, DF, 1983).
Ministère de l'Intérieur, Présentation des Services de la Police Nationale. (Paris, 1989).
Ministère de l'Intérieur, Projet de Contrat pluriannuel de la Formation pour la Police Nationale. (Paris, 1989).
Ministère de l'Intérieur, Aspects de Criminalité et de Délinquance Constatées en France par les Services de Police et de Gendarmerie d'après les Statistiques de Police Judiciaire. (Paris, DF, 2000/2001).
Ministère de l'Intérieur, Guide Pratique de la Police de Proximité. (Paris, DF, 2000).
Ministère de la Justice, Les Chiffres-clés de la Justice. (Paris, 1995).
Ministère de la Justice, Les 200 Mots-clés de la Justice. (Paris, 1995).
Ministère de la Justice, Administration Pénitentiaire. (Paris, DF, 1999).
Ministère de la Justice, Annuaire Statistique de la Justice. (Paris, DF, 2000).
Ministère de la Justice, Eurojustice. Actes de la Conférence de Rouen 1999. (Paris, DF, 2000).
Ministère de la Justice, Quel Droit, Pour Quelles Familles? (Paris, DF, 2001).
Ministère de la Justice, La Nationalité Française. (Paris, DF, 2001).
Ministère de la Justice, Annuaire statistique de la Justice. (Paris, DF, 2002)
Ministère de la Justice, Administration pénitentiaire. Rapport annuel d'activité. (Paris, DF, 2002).
Miquel, P., Les Gendarmes. (Paris, Orban, 1990).
Miquel, P., L'Affaire Dreyfus. (Paris, PUF, 1996).
Moch, J., L'État de la Police en France (1789-1914). (Paris, Droz, 1979).
Moderne, F., Les Quasi-Contrats Administratifs. (Paris, Dalloz, 1995).
Molfessis, N., Le Conseil Constitutionnel et le Droit Privé. (Paris, LGDJ, 1997).
Mommsen, T., Le Droit Public Romain. (Paris, Boccard, 1892, 1984).
Monjardet, D., Les Policiers. (Paris, Découverte, 1983).
Monjardet, D., La Police au quotidien. (Paris, CNRS, 1984).
Monjardet, D., Formation et Recherche dans les Polices Nord-Américaines. Rapport de Mission. (Paris, 1986).
Monjardet, D., Le Modèle Français de Police. Dans: Les Cahiers de la Sécurité Intérieure. (Paris, 1993).
Monjardet, D., Ce que fait la Police. Sociologie de la Force Politique. (Paris, Découverte, 1996).
Monjardet, D., Chauvenet, A., Orlic, F., Sociologie du Travail Policier. (Paris, CNRS, 1995).
Montesquieu, C. de, De l'Esprit des Lois. (Genève, 1748).
Moor, P., Droit Administratif. (Berne, Staempfli, 1994).
Morabito, M., Bourmaud, D., Histoire Constitutionnelle et Politique de la France. (Paris, Montchrestien, 1992).
Morange, J., Les Libertés Publiques. (Paris, PUF, 1993).
Morange, J., La Liberté d'Expression. (Paris, PUF, 1993).
Morange, J., La Déclaration des Droits de l'Homme et du Citoyen, 26 août 1789. (Paris, PUF, 1993).
Moreau, J., Police Administrative et Police Judiciaire. Recherches d'un Critère de Distinction. (Dans: AJDA, 1963).
Moreau, J., Droit Administratif. (Paris, PUF, 1989).
Morin, J.Y., L'État de Droit. Émergence d'un Principe du Droit International. (La Haye, Nijhoff, 1996).
Mouhanna, C., Ackerman, W., Une Affaire de Confiance. Les Relations OP/Magistrats dans le Processus Pénal. (Paris, IHESI, 1995).
Mouhanna, C., Ackerman, W., Polices Judiciaires et Magistrats. (Paris, DF, 2001).
Mourgeon, J., les Droits de l'Homme. (Paris, PUF, 1990).
Mucchielli, L., Transformations de la Famille et Délinquance Juvénile. (Paris, DF, 2001).
Mucchielli, L., Violences et Insécurité. Fantasmes et Réalités dans le Débat Français. (Paris, Découverte, 2001).
Mucchielli, L., dir., Histoire de la Criminologie Française. (Paris, Harmattan, 1994).
Mucchielli, L., Robert, P., dir., Crime et Sécurité. L'État des Savoirs. (Paris, Découverte, 2002).
Muchenbled, R., La Société Policée. Politique et Politesse en France du XVIe au XXe siècle. (Paris, Seuil, 1998).
Munoz-Dardé, V., La Justice Sociale. (Paris, Nathan, 2000).
Nallet, H., Tempête sur la Justice. (Paris, Plon, 1992).
Nations Unies, Les Nations Unies et les Droits de l'Homme, 1945-1995. (New York, 1995).
Nicod, B., Les Voies d'Exécution. (Paris, PUF, 1994).

Nizard, L., La Jurisprudence Administrative des Circonstances Exceptionnelles et la Légalité. (Paris, LGDJ, 1962).
Noiriel, G., Réfugiés et Sans-papiers. La République face au Droit d'Asile, XIXe-XXe siècles. (Paris, LGF, 1998).
Noiriel, L., La Tyrannie du National. Le Droit d'Asile en Europe, 1793-1993. (Paris, Calmann-Lévy, 1991).
Norek, C., Doumic-Doublet, F., Le Droit d'Asile en France. (Paris, PUF, 1989).
Noyer, A., La Sûreté de l'État (1789-1965). (Paris, LGDJ, 1966).
Obrien, P., Correction ou Châtiment. (Paris, PUF, 1988).
Observatoire Géopolitique des Drogues, Rapport Annuel. (Paris).
Ocqueteau, F., Les Marchés de la Sécurité Privée. Développement et Implications. Dans: Le Marché de la Sécurité Privée. (Paris, Cahiers de la sécurité intérieure, pp.81-112, 1990/1991).
Odent, R., Contentieux Administratif. (Paris, Les cours de droit, 1981).
Olivier, S., Roland, G., Environnement et Contentieux Administratif. (Paris, Juris, 1996).
Olivier-Martin, F., Histoire du Droit Français des Origines à la Révolution. (Paris, CNRS, 1992).
Onorio, J.B. d', dir., Le Respect de la Vie en Droit Français. (Paris, Téqui, 1997).
Oppetit, B., Philosophie du Droit. (Paris, Dalloz, 1999).
Oriol, P., J'Accuse! Emile Zola et l'Affaire Dreyfus. (Paris, Librio, 1998).
Ortolland, A., La Justice. Ses Moyens Financiers, ses Actions. (Paris, DF, 1985).
Ost, F., Gutwirth, S., dir., Quel Avenir pour le Droit de l'Environnement? (Bruxelles, VUB, 1996).
Pacteau, B., Contentieux Administratif. (Paris, PUF, 1994).
Padoa-Schioffa, A., dir., Justice et Législation. (Paris, PUF, 2001).
Paléologue, M., Journal de l'Affaire Dreyfus. (Paris, Plon, 1955).
Pallard, H., Tzitzis, S., dir., Droits Fondamentaux et Spécificités Culturelles. (Paris, Harmattan, 1997).
Palle, C., Godefroy, T., Les Dépenses de Sécurité, 1992-1996. (Guyancourt, CESDIP, 1998).
Pansier, F.J., Le Droit Pénal des Affaires. (Paris, PUF, 1992).
Pansier, F.J., La Peine et le Droit. (Paris, PUF, 1994).
Pansier, F.J., Guellaty, K., Le Droit Musulman. (Paris, PUF, 2000).
Pansier, F.J., Jez, E., La Criminalité sur Internet. (Paris, PUF, 2000).
Papanicolaïdes, D., Introduction Générale à la Théorie de la Police Administrative. (Paris, LGDJ, 1960).
Paperman, P., Vision en Sous-Sol. La Vie Quotidienne des Policiers dans le Métro. (Paris, IHESI, 1992).
Paravicini, W., Werner, K.F., dir., Histoire Comparée de l'Administration (IVe-XVIIIe siècles). (München, Artemis, 1980).
Parra, C., Montreuil, J., Traité de Procédure Pénale Policière. (Paris, Quillet, 1981).
Paul, C., Du Droit et des Libertés sur Internet. (Paris, DF, 2001).
Pauly, A., dir., Les Accords de Schengen. (Maastricht, 1993).
Pauly, A., dir., Schengen en panne. (Maastricht, 1994).
Peiser, G., Contentieux Administratif. (Paris, Dalloz, 1985; 1995).
Peiser, G., Droit Administratif. (Paris, Dalloz, 1998).
Pellissier, G., Le Principe d'Égalité en Droit Public. (Paris, LGDJ, 1996).
Perrot, M., L'Impossible Prison. Recherche sur le Système Pénitentiaire au XIXe siècle. (Paris, Seuil, 1980).
Perrot, M., Introduction aux "Écrits sur le système pénitentiaire en France et à l'étranger" d'A. de Tocqueville. (Paris, Gallimard, 1984).
Perrot, M., Les Ombres de l'Histoire. Crime et Châtiment au XIXe siècle. (Paris, Flammarion, 2001).
Perrot, R., Droit Judiciaire Privé. (Paris, Cours de droit, 1977/1981).
Perrot, R., Institutions Judiciaires. (Paris, Domat, 1993).
Petit, J., dir., La Prison, le Bagne et l'Histoire. (Paris, 1984).
Petit, J.G., Ces Peines Obscures. La Prison Pénale en France (1780-1875). (Paris, Fayard, 1990).
Petit, J.G., et al., Histoire des Galères, Bagnes et Prisons, XIIIe-XXe siècles. (Toulouse, Privat, 1991).
Peyrefitte, A., Réponses à la Violence. Rapport. (Paris, DF, 1977).
Peyrical, J.M., Droit Administratif. (Paris, Montchrestien, 1997).
Peyrat, D., La Justice de proximité, (Paris, DF, 2002).
Philip, C., La Cour de Justice des Communautés Européennes. (Paris, PUF, 1983).
Philip, C., Textes Institutionnels des Communautés Européennes. (Paris, PUF, 1993).
Picard, E., La Notion de Police Administrative. (Paris, LGDJ, 1984).
Picca, G., La Criminologie. (Paris, PUF, 1993).
Picca, G., Cobert, L., La Cour de Cassation. (Paris, PUF, 1986).
Pinseau, H., L'Organisation Judiciaire en France. (Paris, DF, 1985).
Poirmeur, Y., Bernard, B., dir., La Doctrine en Droit. (Paris, PUF, 1993).
Pontaut, J.M., Les Secrets des Écoutes Téléphoniques. (Paris, Presses de la Cité, 1978).
Ponteil, F., Les Institutions de la France de 1814 à 1870. (Paris, PUF, 1966).

Ponton, L., Philosophie et Droits de l'Homme. (Paris, 1990).
Porra, S., Paoli, C., Code Annoté de Déontologie Policière. (Paris, LGDJ, 1991).
Poughon, J.M., Le Code Civil. (Paris, PUF, 1992).
Pouille, A., Le Pouvoir Judiciaire et les Tribunaux. (Paris, Masson, 1985).
Poujade, B., Textes de Contentieux Administratif. (Paris, PUF, 1991).
Poullet, P., Les Institutions Françaises, 1795-1815. (Paris, 1907).
Pouvoirs (Revue), Droit Administratif. Bilan Critique. (Paris, Seuil, 1988).
Pouvoirs, Le Conseil Constitutionnel. (Paris, Seuil, 1991).
Pouvoirs, Les Cours Européens. Luxembourg et Strasbourg. (Paris, Seuil, 2001).
Pradel, J., Droit Pénal. (Paris, Cujas, 1980/1981).
Pradel, J., Histoire des Doctrines Pénales. (Paris, PUF, 1991).
Prélot, M., Boulouis, J., Institutions Politiques et Droit Constitutionnel. (Paris, Dalloz, 1981).
Prescrire (Revue médicale), Santé et Prisons en France. (Paris, Éd. Mieux prescrire, 1997).
Prétot, X., Le Droit Social Européen. (Paris, PUF, 1990).
Prévost, J.F., Le Peuple et son Maître. (Paris, Plon, 1983).
Puech, M., Labbé, B., Le Bien et le Mal. (Milan, Les goûtiers philo, 2001).
Puech, M., Labbé, B., La Justice et l'Injustice. (Milan, Les goûtiers philo, 2001).
Racine, P.F., et al., Jurisprudence des Cours Administratives d'Appel 1999. (Paris, DF, 2001).
Rainaud, J.M., La Crise du Service Public Français. (Paris, PUF, 1999).
Rassat, M.L., Pour une Politique Criminelle du Bon Sens. (Paris, Vrin, 1978).
Rassat, M.L., Le Ministère Public entre son Passé et son Avenir. (Paris, LGDJ, 1985).
Rassat, M.L., Droit Pénal Général et Procédure Pénale. (Paris, PUF, 1986).
Rassat, M.L., Institutions Judiciaires. (Paris, PUF, 1993).
Rassat, M.L., La Justice en France. (Paris, PUF, 1994).
Rassat, M.L., Rapport sur la Réforme de la Procédure Pénale. (Paris, PUF, 1996).
Rassat, M.L., Vouin, R., Droit Pénal Spécial. (Paris, Dalloz, 1988).
Rawls, J., Théorie de la Justice. (Paris, Seuil, trad., 1997).
Redor, M.J., De l'État Légal à l'État de Droit. L'Évolution des Conceptions de la Doctrine Publiciste Française 1879-1914. (Paris, Economica, 1992).
Regards sur l'actualité (revue), L'Univers Pénitentiaire. (Paris, DF, 2000).
Renard, G., Théorie de l'Institution. Essai d'Ontologie Juridique. (Paris, 1930).
Renaut, A., Kant Aujourd'hui. (Paris, Aubier, 1997).
Renneville, M., Le Langage des Crânes. Une Histoire de la Phrénologie. (Paris, Ed. Synthélabo, 2000).
Renoux, T., Les Conseils Supérieurs de la Magistrature en Europe. (Paris, DF, 2000).
Renoux, T., De Villiers, M., Code Constitutionnel. (Paris, Dalloz, 1996).
Renucci, J.F., Le Droit Pénal des Mineurs. (Paris, PUF, 1991).
Revue Administrative, Évolutions et Révolution du Contentieux Administratif. (Paris, PUF, 1999).
Revue française d'administration publique, L'Administration de la Justice. (Paris, janv.-mars 1991).
Revue française de sociologie, Mesurer le Crime. Entre Statistiques de Police et Enquêtes de Victimation (1985-1995). (Paris, 1999).
Rey, H., La Peur des Banlieues. (Paris, Presses de Sciences Po, 1996).
Rials, A., L'Accès à la Justice. (Paris, PUF, 1993).
Ricard, T., Le Conseil Supérieur de la Magistrature. (Paris, PUF, 1990).
Richer, D., Les Procédures Fiscales. (Paris, PUF, 1991).
Richer, L., Le Droit de l'Immigration. (Paris, PUF, 1986).
Richer, L., Droit des Contrats Administratifs. (Paris, LGDJ, 1995).
Richet, D., La France Moderne. L'Esprit des Institutions. (Paris, Flammarion, 1973).
Rideau, J., Droit Institutionnel de l'Union et des Communautés Européennes. (Paris, LGDJ, 1996).
Rigaud, F., La Loi des Juges. (Paris, Odile Jacob, 1997).
Rivéro, J., Waline, J., Droit Administratif. (Paris, Dalloz, 1996).
Robert, P., La Question Pénale. (Genève, Droz, 1984).
Robert, P., Le Citoyen, le Crime et l'État. (Paris, Droz, 1999).
Robert, P., dir., Les Politiques de Prévention de la Délinquance à l'Aune de la Recherche. (Paris, Harmattan, 1991).
Robert, P., dir., Entre l'Ordre et la Liberté, la détention provisoire. Deux siècles de débats. (Paris, Harmattan, 1992).
Robert, P., dir., La Justice ou le Chaos. (Paris, Stock, 1996).
Robert, P., et al., Les Comptes de Crime. (Paris, Harmattan, 1994).
Robert, P., Faugeron, C., Les Forces Cachées de la Justice. (Paris, Centurion, 1980).

Robert, P., Zauberman, R., Pottier, M.L., Mesurer le Crime. Entre Statistiques de Police et Enquêtes de Victimation (1985-1995). (Paris, Revue française de sociologie, 1999).
Roché, S., Le Sentiment d'Insécurité en France. (Grenoble, IEP, thèse, 1991).
Roché, S., Insécurité et Libertés. (Paris, Seuil, 1994).
Roché, S., La Société incvile. Qu'est-ce que l'insécurité? (Paris, Seuil, 1996).
Roché, S., Tolérance Zéro? Incivilités et Insécurités. (Paris, Odile Jacob, 2002).
Rojzman, C., Savoir vivre ensemble. Agir autrement contre la violence. (Paris, Découverte, 2001).
Rolland, P., La Protection des Libertés en France. (Paris, Dalloz, 1995).
Rolland, P., Tavernier, P., La Protection Internationale des Droits de l'Homme. (Paris, PUF, 1989).
Romain, V.W.P., Dossier de la Police. (Paris, Perrin, 1966).
Romano, S., L'Ordre Juridique (1946). (Paris, Dalloz, trad., 1975).
Romilly, J. de, La Loi dans la Pensée Grecque. (Paris, Belles Lettres, 2001).
Rossi, M., Dix-sept Ans dans le Couloir de la Mort. (Paris, Fayard, 2001).
Roubier, P., Théorie Générale du Droit. (Paris, 1951).
Rouet, G., Justice et Justiciables aux XIXe et XXe siècles. (Paris, Belin, 2000).
Rougelet, P., RG, la machine à scandales. (Paris, A.Michel, 1997).
Rougeot, A., Verne, J.M., L'Affaire Péat. Des Assassins au Coeur du Pouvoir. (Paris, Flammarion, 1997).
Rousseau, D., Droit du Contentieux Constitutionnel. (Paris, Montchrestien, 1995).
Rousseau, D., La Justice Constitutionnelle en Europe. (Paris, Montchrestien, 1992).
Rousseau, J.J., Politique du contrat social ou principes du droit politique. (Paris, 1762; UGE, 1966).
Rousseau, J.J., Discours sur l'origine et les fondements de l'inégalité parmi les hommes. (Paris, 1765; UGE, 1966).
Roussel, V., Les Magistrats dans les Scandales Politiques. (Dans: Revue française de science politique, pp.245-273, 1998).
Rousset, M., Droit Administratif. (Grenoble, PUG, 1994).
Roussillon, H., Le Conseil Constitutionnel. (Paris, Dalloz, 1996).
Royer, J.P., La Société Judiciaire depuis la XVIIIe siècle. (Paris, PUF, 1979).
Roter, J.P., Histoire de la Justice en France, de la Monarchie à la République. (Paris, PUF, 1996; 2001).
Royer, J.P., et al., Juges et Notables aux XIXe siècle. (Paris, PUF, 1982).
Rozès, S., dir., L'Administration de la Justice. (Dans; Revue fr. d'administration publique, janv./mars 1991).
Rugo, A., Le milieu ouvert. Le tournant 1983-1988. (Lyon, AREPS, 1988).
Ruymbeke, R. van, Le Juge d'Instruction. (Paris, PUF, 1992).
Ruzie, D., Droit International Public. (Paris, Dalloz, 1997).
Salas, D., Le Tiers Pouvoir. Vers une Autre Justice. (Paris, Hachette, 1998; 2000).
Salas, D., La Délinquance des Mineurs. (Paris, DF, 1998).
Salas, D., Garapon, A., La Justice et le Mal. (Paris, Odile Jacob, 1995).
Salon, S., La Fonction Publique. (Paris, DF, 1998).
Samet, C., dir., Violence et Délinquance des Jeunes. (Paris, DF, 2001).
Santoni, F., Contre-enquête sur trois assassinats. (Paris, Denoël, 2001).
Santucci, M.R., Délinquance et Répression au XIXe siècle. (Paris, Economica, 1986).
Sauron, J.L., L'Application du Droit de l'Union Européenne en France. (Paris, DF, 1995; 2000).
Sauron, J.L., Droit et Pratique du Contentieux Communautaire. (Paris, DF, 1998).
Sautel, G., Histoire des Institutions Publiques depuis la Révolution française: Administration, Justice, Finance. (Paris, Dalloz, 1982).
Sautel, G., Harouel, J.L., Histoire des Institutions Publiques depuis la Révolution Française. (Paris, Dalloz, 1997).
Sazarin, J., Le Système Marcellin. La Police en Miettes. (Paris, Calmann-Lévy, 1974).
Scelle, G., Précis de droit des gens. (Paris, Sirey, 1932).
Schapira, J., Le Droit Européen des Affaires. (Paris, PUF, 1992).
Schmitt, C., Théorie de la Constitution (1927). (Paris, PUF, trad., 1993).
Schnapper, B., Les Peines Arbitraires du XIIIe au XVIIIe siècles. (Paris, LGDJ, 1973).
Schwarz-Liebermann von Wahlendorf, H.A., Introduction à l'Esprit et à l'Histoire du Droit Anglais. (Paris, LGDJ, 1977).
Servier, J., Le Terrorisme. (Paris, PUF, 1992).
Seurin, J.L., dir., Le Constitutionalisme aujourd'hui. (Paris, Economica, 1984).
Seyler, M., La Prison Immobile. (Paris, desclée de Brouwer, 2001).
Shâfi'i, La Risâla. Les Fondements du Droit Musulman. (Paris, Actes-Sud, trad., 1997).
Simon, D., Le Système Juridique Communautaire. (Paris, PUF, 1997).
Sicot, M., Servitude et Grandeur Policières. Quarante Ans à la Sûreté. (Paris, Production de Paris, 1959).
Société d'histoire de la révolution de 1848, Maintien de l'Ordre et Polices. (Paris, Créaphis, 1987).

Solé, L'Âge d'Or de la Prostitution, de 1870 à nos jours. (Paris, Plon, 1993).
Solus, H., Perrot, R., Traité de Droit Judiciaire Privé. (Paris, Sirey, 1962/1973).
Sommier, I., Le Terrorisme. (Paris, Flammarion, 2000).
Souchon, H., Admonester, du Pouvoir Discrétionnaire des Organes de Police. (Lyon, CNRS, 1982).
Soulez Larivière, D., Justice pour la Justice. (Paris, Seuil, 1990).
Soulez Larivière, D., Grand Soir pour la Justice. (Paris, Seuil, 1997).
Soulez Larivière, D., Dalle, H., dir., Notre Justice. Le Livre Vérité de la Justice Française. (Paris, Laffont, 2002).
Soulier, G., Nos Droits face à l'État. (Paris, Seuil, 1981).
Soulier, G., L'Europe, Histoire, Civilisation, Institutions. (Paris, A.Colin, 1994).
Soullez, C., Rudolph, L., La Police en France. (Milan, Les Essentiels, 2000).
Soyer, J.C., Droit Pénal et Procédure Pénal. (Paris, LGDJ, 1997).
Stéfani, G., Levasseur, G., Bouloc, B., Procédure Pénale. (Paris, Dalloz, 1990).
Stéfani, G., Levasseur, G., Jambu-Merlin, R., Criminologie et Science Pénitentiaire. (Paris, Dallloz, 1982).
Stirn, B., Le Conseil d'État. Son Rôle, sa Jurisprudence. (Paris, Hachette, 1994).
Stirn, B., Les Sources Constitutionnelles du Droit Administratif. (Paris, LGDJ, 1995).
Stirn, B., les Libertés en Question. (Paris, Montchrestien, 1996).
Stolleis, M., Histoire du Droit Public en Allemagne. La Théorie du Droit Impérial et la Science de la Police, 1600-1800. (Paris, PUF, 1999).
Storme, M., éd., Rapprochement du Droit Judiciaire de l'Union Européenne/ Approximation of Judiciary Law in the European Union. (Boston, Kluwer, 1994).
Sudre, F., La Convention Européenne des Droits de l'Homme. (Paris, PUF, 1992).
Sudre, F., Droit International et Européen des Droits de l'Homme. (Paris, PUF, 1995).
Sudre, F., Les Grands Arrêts de la Cour Européenne des Droits de l'Homme. (Paris, PUF, 1997).
Sueur, P., Histoire du Droit Public Français (XVe-XVIIIe siècle). (Paris, PUF, 1989/1993).
Susini, J., La Police. Pour une Approche Nouvelle. (Toulouse, IEP, 1983).
Taisne, J.J., Institutions Judiciaires. (Paris, Dalloz, 1994).
Tanguy, J.F., Maintien de l'Ordre et Police en France et en Europe aux XIXe siècle. (Paris, Créaphis, 1987).
Terré, F., Introduction Générale au Droit. (Paris, Dalloz, 1991; 1998).
Terré, F. (Mélanges en l'honneur de), L'Avenir du Droit. (Paris, Dalloz, 1999).
Terson, H., Origines et Évolution du Ministère de l'Intérieur. (Montpellier, 1913).
Theolleyre, J.M., L'Accusée (45 ans de Justice en France, 1945-1990). (Paris, Laffont, 1991).
Thireau, J.L., dir., Le Droit entre Laïcisation et Néo-Sacralisation. (Paris, PUF, 1997).
Thomas, B., Les Provocations Policières. (Paris, Fayard, 1972).
Thomas, M., Esterhazy ou l'Envers de l'Affaire Dreyfus. (Paris, Vernal/Lebaud, 1989).
Thomasset, C., Bourcier, D., dir., Interpréter le Droit. Le Sens, l'Interprète, la Machine. (Bruxelles, Bruylant, 1996).
Thué, L., Porcher, R., Trois Administrations en Fiche: Police, Gendarmerie, Douanes. (Dans: Cahiers de la Sécurité Intérieure, pp.167-176, 1990).
Thuillier, F., L'Europe du Secret. Mythes et Réalités du Renseignement Politique Interne. (Paris, DF, 2001).
Thuillier, G., Tulard, J., Histoire de l'Administration Française. (Paris, IEP, 1982).
Tiberghien, F., Le Droit des Réfugiés en France. (Paris, DF, 2000).
Tiévant, S., et al., La Mission Sécurisation. Étude du Dispositif des Patrouilles CRS en Renfort de la PU. (Paris, IHESI, 1990).
Timbal, P.C., Histoire des Institutions Publiques et des Faits Sociaux. (Paris, Dalloz, 1990).
Timsit, G., Archipel de la Norme. (Paris, PUF, 1997).
Tixier, G., Droit Fiscal International. (Paris, PUF, 1986).
Tixier, G., Robert, J.M., Droit Pénal Fiscal. (Paris, Dalloz, 1980).
Tocqueville, A. de, L'Ancien Régime et la Révolution. (Paris, Gallimard, 1965).
Tocqueville, A. de, De la Démocratie en Amérique (1835-1840). (Paris, Gallimard, 1981).
Touchard, J., Histoire des Idées Politiques. (Paris, PUF, 1993).
Touraine, A., et al., Le Grand Refus. Réflexions sur la grève de décembre 1995. (Paris, Fayard, 1996).
Tournier, P., La Détention provisoire et sa mesure. (Paris, Criminologie, 1995).
Tournier, P., Barré, M.D., Enquête sur les Systèmes Pénitentiaires dans les États-Membres du Conseil de l'Europe. (Dans: Bulletin d'informations pénitentiaires du Conseil de l'Europe. Strasbourg, 1990).
Touscoz, J., Droit International. (Paris, PUF, 1993).
Toutin, T., Le Profilage Criminel. (Paris, DF, 2000).
Trémeau, J., La Réserve de la Loi. Compétence Législative et Constitution. (Aix-Marseille, PU, 1997).
Trigeaud, J.M., Essais de Philosophie du Droit. (Paris, 1987).
Tronquoy, P., Le Droit dans la Société. (Paris, DF, 1998).

Tronquoy, P., dir., Les Libertés Publiques. (Paris, DF, 2000).
Tronquoy, P., dir., Etat, société et délinquance. (Paris, DF, 2002).
Troper, M., La Séparation des Pouvoirs et l'Histoire Constitutionnelle Française. (Paris, LGDJ, 1980).
Troper, M., Pour une Théorie Juridique de l'État. (Paris, PUF, 1994).
Trosa, S., Quand l'État s'engage: La Démarche Contractuelle. (Paris, Éd. d'organisation, 1999).
Trotabas, L., Isoart, P., Droit Public. (Paris, LGDJ, 1996).
Truche, P., Justice et Institutions Judiciaires. (Paris, DF, 2001).
Truche, P., Juger, être jugé. Le Magistrat face aux autres et à lui-même. (Paris, Fayard, 2001).
Truche, P., dir., Rapport de la Commission de réflexion sur la Justice. (Paris, DF, 1997).
Tunc, A., Le Droit des États-Unis. (Paris, PUF, 1989).
Turpin, D., Droit Constitutionnel. (Paris, PUF, 1992).
Turpin, D., Contentieux Constitutionnel. (Paris, PUF, 1994).
Turpin, D., Le Conseil Constitutionnel. Son Rôle, sa Jurisprudence. (Paris, Hachette, 1995).
Turpin, D., Mémento de la Jurisprudence du Conseil Constitutionnel. (Paris, Hachette, 1997).
Unesco, Le Droit à l'Assistance Humanitaire. (Paris, Unesco, 1996).
Vailhé, J., La France face aux Exigences de la Convention Européenne des Droits de l'Homme. (Paris, DF, 2001).
Vallée, C., Le Droit des Communautés Européennes. (Paris, PUF, 1986).
Valkeneer, C. de, Police et Public. Un Rendez-vous Manqué? (Bruxelles, La Charte, 1988).
Van Lang, A., Juge Judiciaire et Droit Administratif. (Paris, LGDJ, 1996).
Vareilles-Sommières, P. de, La Compétence Internationale de l'État en matière de Droit Privé. Droit International Public et Droit International Privé. (Paris, LGDJ, 1997).
Veaujour, J., La Sécurité du Citoyen. (Paris, PUF, 1980).
Vedel, G., Droit Constitutionnel. (Paris, Sirey, 1949).
Vedel, G., Delvolvé, P., Droit Administratif. (Paris, PUF, 1992).
Venezia, J.C., Gaudemet, Y, Laubadère, A. de, Traité de Droit Administratif. (Paris, LGDJ, 1999).
Verdier, R., Thomas, Y., Courtois, G., La Vengeance. Études d'Ethnologie, d'Histoire et de Philosophie. (Paris, Cujas, 1980).
Vernier, D., La Justice en France. (Paris, Découverte, 1993).
Vernier, D., Peyrot, M., La Cour d'Assises. (Paris, PUF, 1989).
Vernis, J.M., Le Syndicalisme dans la Police Nationale. (Toulouse, CERP, 1980).
Verpeaux, M., La Naissance du Pouvoir Réglementaire, 1789-1799. (Paris, PUF, 1991).
Verpraet, G., Le Juge. Cet Inconnu. (Paris, Ministère de la Justice, 1975).
Vichnievsky, L., Sans Instructions. (Paris, Stock, 2002).
Vidal-Naquet, P., La Torture dans la République. (Paris, Minuit, 1972).
Vigarello, G., Histoire du Viol, XVe-XXe siècle. (Paris, Seuil, 1998).
Vilain, J.P., Les Victimes. Entre Disculpation de Soi et Accusation de l'État. (Dans: Justices, no.2, 2000).
Villey, M., Le Droit Romain. (Paris, PUF, 1993).
Vimont, J.C., La Prison Politique en France (XVIIIe-XIXe siècle). (Paris, Anthropos, 1993).
Vincent, J., Voies d'Exécution et procédures de distribution. (Paris, Dalloz, 1981).
Vincent, J., Guinchard, S., Procédure Civile. (Paris, Dalloz, 1991).
Vincent, J., et al., La Justice et ses Institutions. (Paris, Dalloz, 1996).
Vivien, A., Raunet, M., Les Français de l'Étranger. (Paris, PUF, 1997).
Vivien, A.F., Études administratives (1859). (Paris, Guillaumin; Cujas, 1974).
Vlachos, G., Principes Généraux du Droit Administratif. (Paris, Ellipses, 1994).
Vouin, R., Léauté, J., Droit Pénal et Procédure Pénal. (Paris, PUF, 1969).
Wagnard, J.F., Le Vagabond à la Fin du XIXe Siècle. (Paris, Belin, 1999).
Weil, P., Le Droit Administratif. (Paris, PUF, 1994).
Weil, P., Rapport Mission d'étude des législations de la nationalité et de l'immigration. Des conditions d'application du principe du droit du sol pour l'attribution de la nationalité française. (Paris, DF, 1997).
Wicquefort, A. de, Chronique discontinue de la Fronde (1648-1652). (Paris, Fayard, 1978).
Wolton, T., Le KGB en France. (Paris, Grasset, 1986).
Xynopoulos, G., Le Contrôle de Proportionalité dans le Contentieux de la Constitutionnalité et de la Légalité. (Paris, LGDJ, 1995).
Yannakopoulos, C., La Notion des Droits Acquis en Droit Administratif Français. (Paris, LGDJ, 1997).
Yolka, P., La Propiété Publique. Éléments pour une Théorie. (Paris, LGDJ, 1997).
Zauberman, R., Robert, P., Du Côté des Victimes. Un Autre Regard sur la Délinquance. (Paris, Harmattan, 1995).
Zauberman, R., et al., Les Victimes, Comportements et Attitudes. Enquête Nationale de Victimation. (Paris, CESDIP, 1990).

Zemmour, E., Le Coup d'État des Juges. (Paris, Grasset, 1997).

English
Abraham, H.J., The Judicial Process. An introductory analysis of the courts of the United States, England and France. (New York, OUP, 1998).
Ackroyd, S., et al., New Technology and Practical Police Work. (Buckingham, Open UP, 1993).
Adams, J., The Financing of Terror. (New York, Simon & Schuster, 1986).
Alexander, Y., Carlton, D., Wilkinson, P., eds., Terrorism. Theory and Practice. (Boulder, CO, Westview, 1979).
Alexander, Y., Finger, S.M., eds., Terrorism. Interdisciplinary Perspectives. (New York, John Jay Press, 1977).
Amos and Walton, Introduction to French Law. (Oxford, Lawson/Brown, 1967).
Anderson, F.M., The Constitutions and other select documents illustrative of the history of France, 1789-1907. (Minneapolis, Wilson, 1908; Darby, Arden, 1978).
Arnold, E.A., Fouché, Napoléon and the General Police. (Washington DC, University Press of America, 1979).
Bartlett, R., Trial by Fire and Water. The Medieval Judicial Order. (Oxford, Clarendon, 1988).
Bayley, D.H., The police and political development in Europe. In: Tilly, C., ed., The formation of the national State in Western Europe. (Princeton, Princeton UP, 1975).
Bayley, D.H., ed., Patterns of Policing. A Comparative International Analysis. (New Brunswick, Rutgers UP, 1985).
Beatson, J., Tridimas, T., New Directions in European Public Law. (Oxford, Hart, 1988).
Bell, J., French Constitutional Law. (Oxford, Clarendon, 1992).
Bennett, C.J., Regulating Privacy. Data Protection and Public Policy in Europe and the United States. (Ithaca, Cornell UP, 1992).
Berman, H.J., Law and Revolution. The Formation of the Western Legal Tradition. (Boston, Harvard UP, 1983).
Bittner, E., The Functions of the Police in Modern Society. A Review of Background Factors. Current Practice and Possible Role Models. (Cambridge, MA, Gunn & Hain, 1980).
Body-Gendrot, S., The Social Control of Cities. (Oxford, Blackwell, 2000).
Braithwaite, J., Pettit, P., Not Just Deserts. A Republican Theory of Criminal Justice. (Oxford, OUP, 1990).
Brogden, M., The Police: Autonomy and Consent. (London, Academic Press, 1982).
Brown, L.N., Garner, J.F., French Administrative Law. (Oxford, Clarendon, 1993).
Cann, S.J., Administrative Law. (London, Sage, 1998).
Carlen, P., Magistrate's Justice. (London, Robertson, 1976).
Cohen, S., Visions of Social Control: Crime, Punishment and Classification. (Cambridge, Polity, 1985).
Coleman, C., Moynihan, J., Understanding Crime Data. (Buckingham, Open UP, 1996).
Cope, S., a.o., Police Professionalisation. (Cardiff, Business School, 1997).
Craig, P.P., Administrative Law. (London, Sweet & Maxwell, 1994).
Critchley, T.A., A History of Police in England and Wales, 900-1966. (London, Constable, 1967).
Cross, R., English Sentencing System. (London, Butterworths, 1981).
Dadomo, C., Farran, S., The French Legal System. (London, Sweet & Maxwell, 1993).
David, R., French Law. Its Structures, Sources and Methodology. (Baton Rouge, Louisiana State UP, 1972).
David, R., English and French Law. (London, Stevens, 1980).
Davis, K.C., Police Discretion. (St.Paul, West, 1975).
Den Boer, M., ed., Undercover Policing and Accountability from an International Perspective. (Maastricht, IEAP, 1997).
Den Boer, M., ed., Schengen, Judicial Cooperation and Policy Coordination. (Maastricht, IEAP, 1997).
Dillon, M., Politics of Security. Towards a Political Philosophy of Continental Thought. (London, Routledge, 1996).
Ducloux, L., From Blackmail to Treason. Political Crime and Corruption in France, 1920-1940. (London, Deutsch, 1958).
Duxbury, N., Patterns of American Jurisprudence. (Oxford, OUP, 1995).
Dworkin, R., Taking Rights Seriously. (London, Duckworth, 1978).
Dworkin, R., A Matter of Principle. (Boston, Harvard UP, 1985).
Dworkin, R., Law's Empire. (Boston, Harvard UP, 1986).
Dworkin, R., Freedom's Law. (Oxford, OUP, 1996).
Emsley, C., Policing and its Context, 1750-1870. (London, Macmillan, 1983).
Emsley, C., The English Police. (London, Harvester Wheatsheaf, St.Martin's, 1991).

Emsley, C., Weinberger, B., eds., Policing Western Europe. Politics, Professionalism and Public Order, 1850-1940. (London, Greenwood, 1991).
European Annual of Public Administration, Administration and Police in Europe. (Paris, PU d'Aix-Marseille, 1999).
Farrell, A., Crime, Class and Corruption. The Politics of the Police. (London, Bookmarks, 1993).
Fattah, E.A., Criminology. Past, Present and Future. (London, Macmillan, 1997).
Fijnaut, C., Marx, G.T., eds., Undercover. Police Surveillance in Comparative Perspective. (The Hague, Kluwer, 1995).
Forstenzer, T.R., French Provincial Police and the Fall of the Second Republic. (Princeton, Princeton UP, 1981).
Gal-Or, N., International Cooperation to Suppress Terrorism. (New York, St.Martin's, 1985).
Galtier-Boissière, J., Mysteries of the French Secret Police. (Plymouth, Stanley Paul, 1938).
Garland, D., Punishment and Welfare. A History of Penal Strategies. (Aldershot, Hants, 1985).
Garland, D., Punishment and Modern Society. (Chicago, University of Chicago Press, 1990).
Gaucher, R., The Terrorists. (London, Secker & Warburg, 1968).
Glendon, M.A., A Nation under Lawyers. How the Crisis in the Legal Profession is Transforming American Society. (New York, Farr-Straus-Giroux, 1994).
Gordon, R., Judicial Review: Law and Procedure. (London, Sweet and Maxwell, 1996).
Harris, D., Tallon, D., Contract Law Today. Anglo-French Comparisons. (Oxford, Clarendon, 1989).
Hart, H.L.A., Punishment and Responsibility. (Oxford, OUP, 1968).
Hart, H.L.A., The Concept of Law. (Oxford, Clarendon, 1972).
Hart, H.L.A., Essays in Jurisprudence and Philosophy. (Oxford, Clarendon, 1983).
Hart, H.M., Sacks, A.M., The Legal Process. (New York, Eskridge, 1994).
Hayek, F., Law, Legislation and Liberty. (Chicago, University of Chcago Press, 1973/1979).
Heidensohn, F., Farrell, M., eds., Crime in Europe. (London, Routledge, 1991).
Hewitt, C., The Effectiveness of Anti-Terrorist Policies. (New York, University Press of America, 1984).
Heydon, J.H., Ockelton, M., Evidence, cases & materials. (London, Butterworths, 1996).
HMSO, Audit Commission. Streetwise. Effective Police Patrol. (London, HMSO, 1996).
Holdaway, S., Inside the British Police. A Force at Work. (London, Blackwell, 1983).
Hutchinson, C.M., Revolutionary Terrorism. (Stanford, Hoover Institution, 1978).
Ingraham, B.L., Political Crime in Europe. A Comparative Study of France, Germany and England. (Berkeley, University of California Press, 1979).
Jay, S., Most Humble Servants. The Advisory Role of Early Judges. (New Haven, Yale UP, 1997).
Jenkins, B.M., International Terrorism. A New Mode of Conflict. (Los Angeles, Crescent, 1975).
Juviller, P., Gross, B., eds., Human Rights in the 21st Century. (New York, Sage, 1993).
Kagan, R., Adversial Legalism. The American Way of Law. (Harvard, Harvard UP, 2000).
Kahn, P.W., The Reign of Law. Marbury v. Madison and the Constitution of America. (New Haven, Yale UP, 1997).
Kahn-Freund, O., et al., A Source-Book on French Law. System, Methods, Outlines of Contract. (Oxford, OUP, 1979).
King, R.D., Morgan, R., The Future of the Prison System. (Aldershot, Gowers, 1980).
Kley, D. van der, ed., The French Idea of Freedom. The Old Regime and the Declaration of Rights of 1789. (Cambridge, CUP, 1997).
Kochler, H., ed., Terrorism and National Liberation. (Frankfurt, Lang, 1988).
Kupperman, R., Trent, D., eds., Terrorism, Threat, Reality, Response. (Stanford, Hoover, 1979).
Laqueur, W., The Age of Terrorism. (Boston, Little-Brown, 1987).
Lewis, B., The Assassins. A Radical Sect in Islam. (Oxford, OUP, 1967).
Livington, N., Arnold, T., eds., Fighting Back. Winning the War Against Terrorism. (Lexington, MA, Lexington Books, 1986).
Lodge, J., ed., Terrorism. A Challenge to the State. (New York, St.Martin's, 1981).
Loveday, B., The Police Service. In: Laffe, M., ed., Beyond Bureaucracy. The Professions of the Contemporary Public Sector. (Aldershot, Ashgate, 1998).
Luhmann, N., A Sociological Theory of Law. (London, Routledge & Kegan Paul, 1985).
MacCormick, N., Legal Reasoning and Legal Theory. (Oxford, OUP, 1978).
MacCormick, N., Weinberger, O., An Institutional Theory of Law. (Dordrecht, Reidel, 1986).
Maitland, F.W., Pollock, F., The History of English Law. (Cambridge, CUP, 1968).
Mény, Y., The French Political System. (Paris, DF, 1998).
Merkl, P., ed., Political Violence and Terror. (Berkeley, University of California Press, 1986).
Miller, A., ed., Terrorism, the Media and the Law. (Dobbs Ferry, NY, Transnational, 1982).

Mommsen, W., Hirschfeld, G., eds., Social Protest, Violence and Terror in Nineteenth and Twentieth Century Europe. (New York, St. Martin's, 1982).
Morgan, R., Newburn, T., eds., The Future of Policing. (Oxford, Clarendon, 1997).
Morgan, R., Smith, D., eds., Coming to Terms with Policing. (London, Routledge, 1989).
Morris, N., Tonry, M., eds., Modern Policing. (Chicago, University of Chicago Press, 1992).
Mouly, C., ed., The Legal System of France. In: Redden, K.R., ed., Modern Legal Systems Cyclopedia. (New York, Hein, 1987).
Neville Brown, L., Garner, J.F., French Administrative Law. (London, Butterworths, 1983).
Nye, R.A., Crime, Madness and Politics in Modern France. The Medical Concept of National Decline. (Princeton, Princeton UP, 1984).
O'Brien, P., The Promise of Punishment. Prisons in 19th century France. (Princeton, Princeton UP, 1982).
O'Neill, A., Decisions of the European Court of Justice and their Constitutional Implications. (London, Butterworths, 1994).
Paxton, R.O., Vichy France. Old Guard and New Order. (London, Barrie & Jenkins, 1972).
Payne, H.C., The Police State of Louis-Napoléon Bonaparte (1851-1860). (Washington, Washington UP, 1966).
Pearl, J., The Crime of Crimes. Demonology and Politics in France, 1560-1620. (Waterloo, Ontario, Wilfrid Laurier UP, 1999).
Peretti, T., In Defense of a Political Court. (Princeton, Princeton UP, 1999).
Petitfer, E.W., Punishments of Former Days. (London, Waterside Press, 1992).
Porch, D., The French Secret Services. From the Dreyfus Affair to the Gulf War. (New York, Farrar/Straus/Giroux, 1995).
Possony, S.T., Bouchay, L.F., International Terrorism, the Communist Connection. With a Case Study of West Germany Terrorist Ulrike Meinhoff. (Washington DC, American Council for World Freedom, 1978).
Pound, R., Criminal Justice in America. (New Brunswick, Transaction, 1998).
Pugsley, D., Lawyers and Precedents. (Exeter, University of Exeter, 1989).
Radzinowicz, L., A History of English Criminal Law and its Administration. (London, Macmillan, 1948).
Rapoport, D.C., Inside Terrorist Organizations. (New York, Columbia UP, 1988).
Rapoport, D.C., ed., Assassination and Terrorism. (Toronto, CBC, 1971).
Rapoport, D.C., Alexander, Y., eds., The Morality of Terrorism. (New York, Columbia UP, 1988).
Rawls, J., A Theory of Justice. (New York, OUP, 1972).
Raz, J., The Concept of a Legal System. (Oxford, OUP, 1970).
Reich, W., ed., The Origins of Terrorism. Psychologies, Ideologies, Theologies, States of Mind. (Cambridge, CUP, 1990).
Reiner, R., Chief Constables, Bobbies, Bosses or Bureaucrats? (Oxford, OUP, 1991).
Reiss, A.J., The Police and the Public. (New Haven, Yale UP, 1971).
Reith, C., A Short History of the British Police. (London, OUP, 1948).
Renteln, A.D., International Human Rights. (Newbury Park, Sage, 1990).
Richardson, N., The French Prefectoral Corps, 1814-1830. (Cambridge, CUP, 1966).
Robinson, P.H., Dartley, J.M., Justice, Blame and the Criminal Law. (Boulder, Westview, 1995).
Rossi, P.H., Berk, R.A., Just Punishments. Sentencing Guidelines and Public Opinion Compared. (Hawthorne, 1997).
Schmid, A.P., et al., Political Terrorism. (New York, North-Holland Press, 1988).
Schneider, H.J., ed., The Victims in International Perspective. (New York, De Gruyter, 1982).
Schwartz, B., French Administrative Law and the Common-Law World. (New York, New York UP, 1954).
Schwartz, B., ed., The Code Napoléon and the Common-Law World. (New York, New York UP, 1956).
Scott, H., Scotland Yard. (Harmondsworth, Penguin, 1957).
Shearing, C., Stenning, P., eds., Private Policing. (Newbury Park, Sage, 1987).
Sherman, L.W., Scandal and Reform. Controlling Police Corruption. (Berkeley, University of California Press, 1978).
Simon, J.D., Terrorists and the Potential Use of Biological Weapons. (Santa Monica, Rand, 1989).
Sinclair, I., Miller, C., Measures of Police Effectiveness and Efficiency. (London, Home Office, 1984).
Singh, R., The Future of Human Rights in the United Kingdom. (Oxford, Hart, 1997).
Sitkin, S.B., Bies, R.J., The Legalistic Organization. (London, Sage, 1994).
Slapper, G., Kelley, D., Principles of the English Legal System. (London, Cavendish, 1997).
Smit-van Zijl, D., Dunkel, F., Imprisonment Today and Tomorrow. (Deventer, Kluwer, 1991).
Smith, G., et al., eds., Criminal Justice in the Old World and the New. (Toronto, Centre of Criminology, 1998).
Stead, P.J., The Police of France. (London, Macmillan, 1983).
Sterling, C., The Terror Network. (New York, Holt Rinehart, 1981).

Stohl, M., Lopez, G., eds., The State as Terrorist. (Westport, Greenwood, 1984).
Stone, A., The Birth of Judicial Politics in France. The Constitutional Council in Comparative Perspective. (Oxford, OUP, 1992).
Stone, A., Judicialization and the Construction of Governance. (Florence, European University, 1996).
Szladits, C., German, C.M., Guide to Foreign Legal Materials: French. (New York, Dobbs Ferry, 1985).
Taheri, A., Holy Terror: Inside the World of Islamic Terrorism. (Bethesda, MD, Adler & Adler, 1987).
Taylor, M., The Terrorist. (London, Pergamon Brassey, 1988).
Teubner, G., Law as an Autopoietic System. (New York, Bankowski, 1993).
UK Home Office, Police Reform. (London, HMSO, 1993).
Vries, H. de, et al., Materials for the French Legal System. (New York, Columbia UP, 1979).
Walker, N., Crime and Criminality. (Oxford, OUP, 1987).
Walker and Walker, English Legal System. (London, Butterworths, 1994).
Walter, E.V., Terror and Resistance. (Oxford, OUP, 1969).
Wardlaw, G., Political Terrorism. Theory, Tactics and Counter-Measures. (Cambridge, CUP, 1982).
Watson, M., An English Reader's Guide to the French Legal System. (Oxford, Berg, 1991).
Weinberg, I.B., Davis, P.B., Introduction to Political Terrorism. (New York, McGraw-Hill, 1989).
Wheatheritt, M., Innovations in Policing. (London, Croom Helm, 1986).
Wheatheritt, M., ed., Police Research. Some Future Prospects. (Aldershot, Avebury, 1989).
Williams, A., The Police of Paris, 1718-1789. (Baton Rouge, Louisiana State UP, 1979).
Wilkinson, P., Terrorism and the Liberal State. (London, Macmillan, 1979).
Wilkinson, P., The New Fascists. (London, Pan, 1983).
Willmott, P., ed., Policing and the Community. (London, Policy Studies Institute, 1987).
Wright, G., Between the Guillotine and Liberty: Two Centuries of the Crime Problem in France. (New York, OUP, 1983).
Wright, R., Sacred Rage: The Wrath of Militant Islam. (New York, Simon & Schuster, 1986).
Wunder, B., ed., The Influences of the Napoleonic "Model" of Administration on the Administrative Organization of Other Countries. (Brussels, IIAS, 1995).
Wynen T.A., Thomas, A.J , A World Rule of Law. (Dallas, SMU, 1975).
Young, M., An Inside Job. Policing and Police Culture in Britain. (Oxford, Clarendon, 1991).
Zander, M., The Law-Making Process. (London, Butterworths, 1994).
Zyl-Smit, D. van, Dunkel, F., The Future of the Prison System. (Deventer, Kluwer, 1991).

# 5. From Socio-economic Steering to Cultural Engineering

## 5.1. French public management of the economy

Mono-disciplinary analyses often deal only with aspects of Public Management of Society. Dimensions not treated in this mono-disciplinary approach are abstracted away. A minority of authors handle this complex phenomenon from different, mono-disciplinary perspectives simultaneously or consecutively. Economists are often focused on the market, secondarily on economic policies influencing the free play of market forces. Jurists emphasize the relevance of juridical instruments (contracts, law). Sociologists make empirical analyses of interactions in processes of societal regulation. Political scientists treat aspects of Public Management of Society (PMS) from the perspective of political power. One has to recognise that PMS is possible with (combinations of) tools for societal regulation: law (legislation, contracts), (party-)political power, economics (market, State intervention) and social interactions. For Public Management of Society, law, (party-)political power, economics and social interaction are functionally equivalent, and although they differ, comparison is possible. From the economic point of view, there are several approaches to economic regulation. Abstinence of intervention, giving free play to the market (Hayek), or total State control of the economy can be pursued, as in the Soviet Union (1917-1990). Mostly, there is a mixed economy, with market mechanism and some State intervention. Primacy of politically based public management of the economy is more or less a structural feature of French society. Since end 20th century, the balance has been shifting towards primacy of the market worldwide (globalisation).

Privatisation has become a popular instrument of public policy (Bailey/Pack, 1995; Ott/Hartley, 1991). Public management of the economy remains important, while new styles are coming up (public-private osmosis, hybrid organisations) and new methods are used. Here a concept of Public Management of Society is used which is broader than management of the public sector. Worldwide there is a re-evaluation of the role of public authorities, as shown in a World Bank report, "The State in a Changing World" (1997). Knowledge of society is needed for adequate management of society. Understanding and shaping society is difficult (Lindblom, 1990). Knowledge of the specific cultural-historical environment proves to be a necessary condition for adequate Public Management of Society. France has a long tradition of systematic public management of the economy, going back to Richelieu and Colbert, and centuries before them (Minard, 1998). The "Manufactures royales" are seen as the first public industrial enterprises in France. In the 17th century, public enterprises were established in the glass-, textile and pottery-industries (Saint-Gobain, Gobelins, Sèvres). In Saint-Etienne a weapons industry was established, and from 1816 the tobacco industry was made a sector of public enterprise. Other sectors also had public enterprises ("Banque de France", "Caisse des Dépôts", "Journal Officiel", etc.). In the 20th century the four phases of nationalisation were: after "Versailles" (1919); during the crisis of the thirties; after Liberation and as part of the program of Socialist government from 1981. After "Versailles", German plants became French public enterprises and financial institutions supported reconstruction. The Alsace potassium industry (1921), "Office National de l'Azote" (1924) and "Compagnie Française des Pétroles" (1924) began.

The crisis of the thirties with its massive social problems made a more interventionist approach a logical step. Just after Liberation there was a wide consensus for a broad program of nationalisation. Many of these public enterprises have built up a prominent position in the French economy since then. When the Socialists took over government for the first time in decades in 1981, they satisfied ideological priorities by expanding the nationalised sector further. The total of exploitation subsidies in 1982 was 24.7 billion francs. Privatisation was more en vogue (Wright, 1993) and the sector of public enterprises remained extended. French interventionism in the economy encompasses much more than public enterprises alone; there is a wide range of institutional arrangements. These historical and more recent experiences still have their impact today (Carsalade, 1998). Insight into the historical development of economic circumstances and ideas is a conditio-sine-qua-non for understanding contemporary institutions and practices. In the course of time economic circumstances changed drastically. They had an impact on changing economic conceptions and policies. Hafsi (1984) developed a theory about the relation between government and public enterprises in the framework of French industrial policy. At the establishment of a new public enterprise it will identify nearly completely with government objectives. The ministry has a representative to issue orders for a public enterprise with a bureaucratic structure. After some time, co-operation by execution of bureaucratic orders turns into confrontation. The management of a public enterprise identifies increasingly with commercial interests of the enterprise, fighting for as much autonomy as possible. It is busy not only with efficient realisation of externally determined targets (economic strategy), but also especially with enlarging its autonomy (institutional strategy). In this phase of confrontation, a growing number of issues are ruled in contracts. When public enterprises dispose of specific expertise and financial means, and the environment for public enterprises is complex, it is costly for government to control them adequately (and not only formally).

Empirical data show that in France relations between members of the "Corps d'État" dominantly influence relations between government and public enterprises. According to Hafsi public enterprises pass the phases co-operation, confrontation and autonomy nearly paradigmatically. For reasons of efficacy (avoidance of power struggles), planning contracts are used. French authors developed conceptualisation about Public Management of Society further. This was more sophisticated than original "planification". Planning contracts are common institutional arrangements to regulate relations between the State and territorial public authorities. French experiences and theorising produce a welcome complement (Perrot, 1992). One might say that French economic ideas and practices are a pioneering experience of institutional economics over a long period. In mainstream Anglo-American economic literature, it was quite common to discredit French theorising and practice for an excess of (juridical) institutionalism. One could mention historical French excesses in institutionalism, but there are Anglo-American excesses in short-sighted non-institutionalism also. Institutional economics can be seen as a belated reaction in Anglo-American economic literature to a development in which institutionalising is a crucial phenomenon. France was a pioneer in this field, so analysis of French literature and economic history reaps rewards. An interesting point of view is elaborated by the "École de la régulation" of R. Boyer (1986), M. Aglietta and others. In his "Régulation et crises du capitalisme" (1995) Aglietta argues that no economic phenomenon can be understood without taking historical evolution into account. He criticises theorising in which the actor is defined as rational by nature, and in which economic relations are defined as ways of co-ordinating the predetermined, invariable behaviour of economic actors. Aglietta prefers to study how capitalism is able to reproduce itself. A crucial role is given to institutional forms. The Marxist idea that institutions are passive "suprastructures" following dynamic processes of economic infrastructure, is rejected.

Since the Welfare State crisis, dominantly a financial, fiscal crisis, retrenchment policies have been needed. It is amazing that Anglo-American (new) institutional economics stresses the relevance of adequate organisation of property rights and contracts for the regulation of society, pre-eminently a juridical instrument (Rowley, 1993). The debate seems to be reduced to accentuating differences between self-regulating society (market and contracts) and a society more regulated by public authorities (public management of society). Even adherents of the market as dominant instrument of societal regulation have to admit that regulation by (national and international) public authorities has a crucial role in disciplining, conditioning and regulating market processes. Recent examples of fraudulent audits by chartered accountants in the US testified to this in 2002. Part of the spirit of French institutional-economic philosophy is that it is beneath civilised human intelligence and will empower (voluntarism) to abandon societal forces to the blind working of the market mechanism (an institution by itself). One might say that the development of French economic thought and historical experiences are especially relevant in re-institutionalising economics. The issue is not so much about more or less State, eventually in the disguised form of the catchall notion governance, but about the best ways of professional Public Management of Society. French economic performance is generally undervalued in mainstream literature (Maddison, 1995). Sneering comments about the losses of French public enterprises, rolled off upon taxpayers, are reiterated. Adequate accounting of these data often fails. Societal cost-benefit analyses could make these roll-on-roll-off games and their effects more transparent. What about losses in American hard rock capitalism, rolled off onto society (shareholders, buyers of products)? On closer investigation, a more balanced appreciation is appropriate in the French case.

More and more the European Union (EU) is becoming an internal market and an institutional set of binding arrangements for Member-States, corporations, and citizens. France, as an overactive actor, is in the midst of this extraordinary institutional phenomenon of the EU. In recent years, the accent has been upon European monetary integration with the common currency, the euro (Vanthoor, 1996). There are also sweeping, imposing juridical-institutional changes with far-reaching consequences. France and her EU partners have important challenges, with regard to expansion of the European Union with member-states from Central and Eastern Europe, and with renovation of the institutional construction of the European Union. Zecchini (1997) analysed experiences with economic transition in Central and Eastern Europe in the 1990s. Successes and failures in transition strategies are sketched. The success of quick liberalisation in trade, production and prices is underlined. In literature about transition economics, the crucial role of adequate institutionalising (property rights, contracts, courts, tax systems, etc.) is generally underrated. For restructuring of society and Public Management of Society in Central and Eastern Europe, French experiences with Public Management of Society are more relevant than most Anglo-American recipe-books suggest. A valid hypothesis is that the French contribution to institutional economics is more pronounced and rewarding than mainstream Anglo-American literature would admit. It is opportune to concentrate on the French approach, explicitly in comparative perspective. Economics has a prominent position in Public Management of Society, nationally and internationally. Co-disciplinary analyses are a necessary condition for effective Public Management of Society. Public authorities have important tasks in regulating, conditioning and institutionalising society and markets. At the start of the 21st century, the French way of Public Management of Society has important contributions to make. The next paragraphs are about the management of reconstruction since 1945; modernisation with the Fifth Republic; changed circumstances in a transformed France; a specific kind of French planning; sophisticated public management; and a sketch of some public policies. This chapter might fill the void in Barratt Brown's "Models in Political Economy" (1995), as that has no reference to the French model in political economy.

## 5.2. Managing reconstruction of devastated France since 1945

Reconstruction after 1945 needed all societal energies (Eichengreen, 1996) for the conditions of France in 1945 were utterly sorrowful. There were about 600,000 dead because of the war, and in addition to that about 530,000 dead as a consequence of the war situation. Due to a decline of births of about one million, there was a demographic retrogression of some two million in an ageing population. Material losses were hardly quantifiable (Berstein/Milza, 1995). In 74 departments, 50,000 agricultural enterprises, 50,000 industrial plants and 300,000 buildings were devastated, equivalent to 20% of real estate. Bombardments destroyed 115 railway stations, 9,000 bridges, and 80% of port quays, canals and rails. The economic infrastructure was a disaster. During the war, France lost a quarter of its locomotives, 3/4 of its oil tankers, 40% of its motorcars, 1/3 of its ships etc. Material losses were estimated at 85 billion gold-francs, equivalent with a quarter of the national wealth. Financial war losses can be quantified at 1,500 billion francs (about 1,100 billion paid to the Germans, and 460 billion for budget deficits in 1939/1944). This provoked enormous inflation. After Liberation, governments chose for a controlling approach, maintaining the economic regulation of the Vichy-regime (Paxton, 1972). Monnet went in February 1945 to the US, which gave France 1,600 million dollars and a 0.37% loan of 900 million dollars for reconstruction of infrastructure. Great Britain gave France a 0.5% loan of 1 billion dollars, to be repaid from 1950 on. This support was welcome. It gave France, in the grip of scarcities and hyper-galloping inflation, the needed relief.

French government had to devalue the franc on 25 December 1945, because the International Monetary Fund, limiting the possibilities for nations to alter exchange rates, had started. The franc had lost 3/5 of its value a year earlier. The American dollar was now 119 francs (against 49,60) and the pound sterling 480 francs (against 200). The franc was overvalued. On the parallel markets, the dollar made 213 francs and a pound sterling 809 francs. Minister Mendès France proposed a rigorous financial policy. He resigned in April 1945 when his proposals met nearly unanimous opposition. Premier De Gaulle decided to follow the easy method of inflation. To have economic take-off it was necessary for the French State to choose interventionist measures. The spirit of the time was interventionist, fed by ideas and practices during economic crisis and occupation (Andrieu, 1984). The ideas of J.M. Keynes played a crucial role for institutional macroeconomic policies (effective demand; the multiplier with its leverage for economic growth; etc.), exposed in his "General Theory" (1936). The "Comité générale d'études" of Courtin in 1943 argued for a return to economic liberalism. "Organisation civile et militaire", a resistance movement, argued for a technocrat system of State planning (Kuisel, 1984). A system of oriented economy with co-operation of social and professional organisations under the direction of the State had wide support. The majority of the Assembly wanted to nationalise large private enterprises, as in heavy industry, insurance companies, banks and other key sectors (Andrieu c.s, 1987). Nationalisations were effected shortly after Liberation. By nationalising economic key sectors such as energy, transports and credit, the French State had instruments to direct and modernise the French economy. This implied a social policy, laying foundations of the Welfare State. There were elements of social security legislation before. France had the social security system as established by Poincaré in 1928, and financial family-allocations, part of the "Code de la famille" (1939). The social security system, funded by employers and employees, benefited some 9 million workers. Following Beveridge, the concept of social security was changed. Workers were protected against a number of risks, instead of the existing system of individual insurance.

France, after the huge losses during the war, needed workers in all parts of its economy, and so immigrants were made welcome. In 1946, there were 1.74 million foreigners in

France, and 2.17 million in 1962. To enable more control over the influx of immigrants and further cultural assimilation, the "Office national d'immigration" (ONI) was created in 1945. In 1946 there were some 450,000 Italians in France, and 629,000 in 1962. Spanish immigrants increased from 302,000 to 441,000 in the same period. Italian and Spanish immigrants formed about half of the immigrant population. The number of Polish immigrants fell back from 423,000 in 1946 to 177,000 in 1962. Because Algerians had French nationality, the ONI did not check them. Their number rose from 22,114 in 1946 to 211,675 in 1954 and 350,484 in 1962. Immigration of Europeans was replaced by immigration of celibate inhabitants from the Maghreb, supplemented by family-reuniting. About 80% of immigration in 1965/1966 took place without any check by the ONI. The composition of the immigrant population changed. In 1975, the number of Algerians had risen from 473,000 (1968) to 710,000 (20.6%), while there were 260,000 Moroccans and 140,000 Tunisians. The number of Portuguese immigrants rose from 50,000 (1962) to 759,000 in 1975. This was due to the Salazar regime and its colonial wars, provoking massive desertion (Berstein/Milza, 1995). It was not an easy task to integrate these new immigrants into French society. Other developments also changed French society. While France had, up to the Second World War, a predominantly rural character, this had been changed by accelerated urbanisation. This provoked a number of problems, such as housing and education facilities. Urbanisation was dramatic in Paris. From 1954 to 1962, the population of Paris grew with one million inhabitants (one-third of the growth of French population). Paris had 8 million inhabitants in 1964. The "schéma directeur de la région parisienne" (1965) intended to create "villes nouvelles" like English satellite-cities. Most of these were of meagre quality, creating a series of social problems.

Principles and modalities of French social security were elaborated in 1945-1946 under Pierre Laroque, director-general of Social Security. Social security insurances became obligatory for all workers. Insurance against the costs of sickness included 80% of medical costs, costs for pharmaceuticals and hospital for the salaried person and his family. When their work was interrupted, workers received daily payments. A disability insurance guaranteed a pension for the invalid worker. A retirement insurance provided for 20% of the basic salary from 60 years on (plus 4% yearly up to 65 years). There was an insurance in case of death for relatives, and family-allocations as a supplement to the salary, equal for all salaried workers and variable according to the number of children. To finance costs, social premiums were deducted from salaries (6%) and paid by employers (10%). With amounts paid by employers for family-allocations, sickness insurance and paid holidays, social costs for employers were about 33-38% of paid salaries. The idea of social justice materialised in a system of social security in which the State, as manager of the French economy, was responsible for the well-being of the population. This was part of all-encompassing planning, "planification à la française". Mendès France, Minister of National Economy in 1944, created a "Direction du Plan" to stimulate planning of the economy (a Socialist idea of the thirties). Minister Pleven abolished this initiative, but Jean Monnet, back from his trip to the US, made a memo for Premier De Gaulle in December 1945 arguing for the necessity of planning to modernise the economy. De Gaulle was won over by this idea and in January 1946, the "Commissariat au Plan" started, under the direction of Monnet, with a team of technocrats (Hirsch, Marjolin, Uri, Delouvrier).

The "Plan de modernisation et d'équipement" was launched in January 1947 by government-Blum. It had as targets to return production in 1948 to its 1929 level, and to exceed this in 1950 by 25%. The State, having the tools since the nationalisations, gave priority to six key-sectors (electricity, steel, coal, cement, railways and agriculture). For the first time, the whole of the French economy was encompassed in a systematic development plan. It was not like the forced State planning in the Soviet-Union. The "planification à la française" had specific characteristics. After consultation with employers and trade unions the State, in an indicative planning process, decided priorities and subsidised incentives ("planification indicative"). Nationalised industries got 3/4 of credits voted in Parliament. Many problems had to be solved: a serious shortage of labour, enormous price rises. There was an insurmountable financing problem. In the years 1946/1949, imports were 9 billion dollars, and exports only 4 billion. France had a deficit of 6 billion dollars. France was forced to sell gold and to borrow abroad. The Byrnes-Blum Agreement (May 1946) was signed to settle the French debt to the US. The US rescheduled a large part of the French debt, which was reduced from 2,630 to 700 million dollars, repayable in 35 years with an interest of 2%. France got new loans, American donations and in 1948/1949 Marshal-Aid (1,300 million dollar). American aid, working as economic multiplier, was crucial for reconstruction, but a lot of economic, financial and social problems remained. The State debt grew to 2,845 billion francs (1951). The fiscal burden increased. There were harsh cuts in public expenditure. The franc was devalued by 80% in 1948; the dollar was 264 francs. After devaluation of the pound sterling, the franc devalued again in September 1949; the dollar had a value of 350 francs.

On 21 June 1950, the Korean War disturbed stability. This caused a rearmament wave and big price rises (about 40% for strategic raw materials). The Korean War provoked a rise in French exports, while inflation and consumer prices went up sharply. Social tensions became unbearable. Prices of agricultural products and salaries were raised. In 1952 the "Salaire minimum interprofessionnel garanti" (SMIG), a minimum salary indexed with the price level, was introduced. From March 1952 centre-right government-Pinay tried an orthodox financial policy. Pinay as "the new Poincaré" had the confidence of many. There was a big gap between the myth and the economic reality of the "expérience Pinay". The growth of the national product and exports dropped, the trade balance had a deficit (618 million dollar), and the public budget had a deficit too. The conjuncture of the world economy in 1952/1953 was in a recession. The policy of Pinay aggravated this for France. In 1951 the treaty was signed for the European Coal and Steel Community (ECSC), starting in 1953. Governments were in the mood for expansion, economic modernisation and financial stability. The period from 1945 on was a crucial period of three prosperous decades, the "Trente Glorieuses". Government-Faure launched the second "Plan de modernisation et d'équipement" (1954/1957). This Plan-Hirsch had ambitious targets. National income had to rise with 6% yearly. Construction industry had to grow its production with 60% during the period, industry with 30%, and agriculture with 20%. In 1953, the "Commissariat de la Productivité" was established to promote productivity in all sectors. To supplement State financing, other sources of finance were mobilised. Salary rises provoked growth of consumption, a stimulus for economic growth. Families restored the birth rate. On 1 January 1958, France had 44.3 million inhabitants, with 11.4 million below 15 years and 5.1 million above 60 years. Active population was 19.6 million (44% of total population). It was necessary to call on foreign workers.

Another problem was far more serious. After the dramatic decolonisation of French Indo-China, the Algerian question caused a deep crisis. The Algerian War cost huge sums of money, and many human lives. An adequate cost-benefit analysis of the Algerian War is not available. The public budget had a deficit for years, and inflation was galloping. Governments gave inflation-related subsidies to help the people to cope with the consequences of inflation. In 1957, the French State was forced twice to ask the "Banque de France" for advances (550 milliard francs). The financial crisis became ever more acute. The budget for 1958 included a tax rise of 32%. In August 1957 Minister Felix Gaillard did not dare to implement devaluation openly, so he invented the "operation 20%", a disguised devaluation. This de facto devaluation was formalised in June 1958: the dollar was 420 French francs (against 350 francs before). The balance of payments had a surplus in 1955 of 423 million dollars, but a deficit again in 1956 of 783 million dollars. In 1957, the deficit was 859 million dollars. At the beginning of 1958 France had exhausted its reserves of foreign exchange. The Fourth Republic regime came to an end on 13 May 1958, caused by a miscarried military putsch in Algiers. De Gaulle came back into power. He is said to have found the coffers of the State empty. De Gaulle needed huge expenditure to get control of the situation in France and Algeria, on the verge of civil war.

## 5.3. Construction of the Fifth Republic: modernisation

De Gaulle had as an impossible task, firstly, to restore public authority over the military and to solve the Algerian question. There was a serious public finance crisis in 1958, but it would be wrong to assert, as Gaullists did, that the French economy was then also a mess. The Fourth Republic had played an impressive part in economic reconstruction and recovery, which brought the "Trente Glorieuses" (1945-1975) as analysed by Fourastié (1979). For De Gaulle the important aspect of economics was that it was an instrument of the "grandeur de la France". This was his driving concept, not the party-political and ideological preferences of the political left (Socialists and Communists) for State interventionism (Jeanneney, 1992). He made use of economic instruments created before 1958 with a strong State apparatus. The sixties formed a crucial period with the opening up of the French economy to the Common Market. In 1970, 50% of French exports went to the five EEC member-states, and 10% to the French franc zone. In 1952, this was 16% and 42% respectively. De Gaulle had a decisive role in opening the French economy for international competition as part of a modernisation program to give French enterprises better chances. Especially in key-industries (nuclear energy, space, weaponry, aeronautics, informatics etc.). De Gaulle thought that the French State had to play a central role, to give France a prominent position in strategic industries. He intensified the instruments of French planning. He was convinced by Jacques Rueff that the French economy had to be liberalised, and on 30 September 1958 charged committee-Rueff to make a report about the needed economic policies. The "Plan Pinay-Rueff" (12 November 1958) proposed three key-issues: fighting inflation, stabilising the French franc and liberating external exchange rates. The Fifth Plan (1966-1970) accentuated modernisation to improve the competitiveness of French industry. A new physical-financial model ("FIFI") which encompassed quantifying the planning process in value, and not only in volume, supported this approach. Creating international companies with French capital was a key issue.

The coming to power of De Gaulle coincided with circumstances which had a positive impact on the economy (Prate, 1978). The (active) population was growing. International conjuncture was going upward, inter alia supported by declining prices of energy. France could realise an impressive economic growth in 1958/1974. There was a rise in energy consumption, doubling from 1960 to 1973. While the part of coal diminished from 75% in 1950 to 17% in 1973, the part of hydrocarbon energy rose sharply in this period from 18% to 75%. Because France produced hydrocarbon energy marginally, it was dependent on imports for some 3/4 of its needs. The "Plan Jeanneney" (1959) implied the closing-down of most coalmines, to allow industry to profit from cheap energy (imported oil). Implementing the "Plan Pinay-Rueff" meant the abolition of trade-barriers between countries of the Common Market, which gave the French economy an important push. France was cooperative in liberalising its economy for industrial products, but for agricultural products it claimed a protectionist policy. Since 1962, European agricultural policy had guaranteed prices and subsidies. A happy coincidence was that when the part of French exports to its (former) colonies dropped from 30% to 3.9%, French exports to the Common Market rose from 16% in 1952 to 50% in 1970. The first period of the Fifth Republic was for most inhabitants a prosperous period. Income per head rose by some 50%

in 1958/1969. The society of mass-consumption started, bringing domestic apparatus to all families. Differences between rich and poor were sharper. To soften the effects of economic growth, governments had redistribution policies. In 1970, about 20% of national income was involved in redistribution.

With hindsight, one can conclude that the period 1958-1973 (De Gaulle/Pompidou) was the longest period of robust economic growth in the history of France so far. The national product grew from an average 4.6% in 1949-1958 to 5.5% in 1958-1973. Exports, for 2/3 composed of industrial products and for 14% of agricultural products, rose spectacularly. It was a problem that coverage of industrial imports by French industrial exports fell back from 204% (1959) to 98% (1969). Although a devaluation of the franc was inevitable in 1968, De Gaulle stubbornly refused to give his consent, so French exports were burdened with an overvalued franc. French enterprises complained bitterly. When President De Gaulle retired, President Pompidou devaluated the franc in August 1969 by 11%. This stimulated economic growth, but also inflation. Spectacular modernisation was going on in French agriculture during the 1958-1973 period, after adaptations realised in the years 1945-1958. Minister Debré launched the "Loi d'orientation agricole" (1960), supplemented by rulings of Minister Pisani in 1962 and 1964. In 1972, farmers formed 12% of active population (25% in 1958). Productivity had grown, as agricultural production in 1974 had doubled since 1946. Coverage of agricultural imports by agricultural exports was 21% in 1959, and 104% in 1973. The part of agriculture in gross national product fell from 17% (1946) to 5% (1974). In 1954, 26.7% of the active population worked in agriculture, this was less than 10% in 1975. Society changed.

Modernisation was especially intensified in the industrial sector. The French State, using its prominent position in many enterprises, systematically furthered key-sectors, "branches-pilotes". The State gave huge subsidies when industries modernised: steel industry (1966), shipbuilding industry (1968) etc. Scientific-technological modernisation, nuclear energy and the weapons industry became top priorities (Gilpin, 1968). In other branches, State capital, subsidies and guarantees were used to strengthen the economy, making it independent from foreign dominance. About 80% of French "R and D" efforts were in favour of only four branches: aviation, energy, electronics and chemicals. Some 89% of the funds went to space travel and electronics. France realised important improvements by modernising its economy, but there were many examples of costly and miscarried projects. As French leadership wanted to prevent dependency on American enterprises, a "Plan Calcul" (1968-1970) for informatics was launched, and a Space-program (1969-1970). In 1963, the "Délégation à l'aménagement du territoire" (DATAR) was set up to co-ordinate regional developments, followed in 1963-1964 by "Commissions de développement économique régional" (CODER), responsible for economic development in 22 regions. The State made it its responsibility to modernise all parts of the economy. The Fifth Republic used the foundations of social security as laid by the Fourth Republic, which contributed to social stability in spite of fundamental changes. France had 38.45 million inhabitants in 1901 and 39.84 million in 1946, by 1954 this had become 42.78 million (a baby boom and immigrants). In the next 20 years, the population grew by 10 million to 52.6 million in 1975.

A number of factors changed the structure of economic production, with a series of social consequences. Technological developments changed the composition of labour forces with a sharp fall in handwork and increased mechanisation and automation. New technological qualifications were needed. It was not possible any more to speak about a working class, as the composition of the mass of workers was differentiated strongly. This had its impact upon the character of trade unions, based earlier on masses of industry-workers. Governments tried to regulate tensions between employers and employees by institutionalising their relation with contracts. Among the larger trade unions, the "Force

Ouvrière" (FO) seemed the sole syndicate prepared to institutionalise labour conflicts. FO, offshoot of the CGT since 1947, was anti-Communist. FO was seen by many as a syndicate, which was allied with employers and government (this was unfair and untrue). Large trade unions were CGT and "Confédération française des travailleurs chrétiens" (CFTC), since 1964 the "Confédération française démocratique du travail" (CFDT). CGT refused institutionalisation of employer/employee relations with contracts. It preferred mass strikes. The miners' strike in 1963 forced government to interfere. On the basis of the "rapport Massé" (made by Jacques Delors and trade unions) miners got higher salaries. It became a standard-method: tensions between organisations of employers and employees caused social tensions, forcing government to interfere with costly, subsidised arrangements. CGT preferred general strikes as the instrument of the class struggle. CFTC (later CFDT) wanted to bridge the gap between employers and employees by furthering workers' power in enterprises and improving the quality of labour conditions. The social explosion of May 1968 proved that trade unions were not adapted to new circumstances. The "68" crisis made salaries rise sharply. Devaluation of the franc of 1969 (11%) was inevitable.

Special attention must be given to the specific position of the leading class in French society. As was the case with the privileged position of nobility in the Ancien Régime, the same can be said more or less ("mutatis mutandis") about the privileged position of the élite in the second half of the 20th century. Leading positions in private and public management were mostly reserved for a small élite, sometimes supplemented by successful newcomers from the common people (Parodi, 1981). Leading positions in private enterprises were more and more in the hands of professional and politically appointed managers instead of owners. The career path was evidently preferential for the members of well-to-do families. There was a stiff selection process from the beginning of the education system to the highest positions of societal hierarchies. The best pupils were selected for "grandes écoles" with specific courses: "Polytechnique", "Mines", "ENA", "HEC", "ESSEC", and "Écoles normales supérieures" for those who wanted to go to university. This was so much in favour of members of well-to-do families that it was called a system of reproduction of the elite (Bourdieu/Passeron, 1970). Bourdieu (1989) characterised the élite as the State aristocracy, "La Noblesse d'État". The summits of political and administrative hierarchies and leading groups in private enterprises were ever more intertwined. Since the Fifth Republic this process had been intensified. During the Third and Fourth Republic politics and administration were more separate. Mobility of the leading élite (especially former students of "ENA", later working in the well paid private sector ("pantouflage") was growing (Birnbaum, 1977). Public enterprises and public-private hybrids (osmosis between public and private spheres), were an ideal playing field for capable and ambitious actors (Bauer/Bertin-Mourot, 1994).

The first oil crisis (1973) had severe effects as energy prices rose astronomically. This affected economic policy in France as elsewhere, but in 1974, another event was seen as more important. When Pompidou died in April 1974, France was in suspense over the question of who would succeed him. Above all the issue was whether the new institutions of the Fifth Republic would outlive its founder, De Gaulle, and his right-hand man, Pompidou. After the presidential elections Giscard d'Estaing became President of the Republic, for the first time not a Gaullist. It became apparent that the situation of continuous economic growth during the "Trente glorieuses" (1945-1975) had come to its end. France was more than before integrated in the world economy, which was then in recession. The first oil crisis of 1973 caused a break called "stagflation", a combination of stagnating production and inflation. The Yom Kippour war, started by Egypt and Syria attacking the territories occupied by Israel since 1967, ended on 22 October 1973. Oil exporting Arab countries decided to raise oil prices by 70% and to have an embargo on oil exports to countries which had friendly relations with Israel.

This caused fourfold price rises for crude oil between October and December 1973, and inflation stimulated by indexed salaries (Gauthier, 1989). The blow was heavy for France, which had based economic growth on cheap hydrocarbon energy, comprising 3/4 of the energy consumption. France had to import this energy. The balance of payments was disrupted and production fell. Unemployment was high, a new phenomenon. The foundations of the Welfare State, set up after 1945, were questioned because massive claims for payment of social benefits made the system unaffordable. The number of unemployed was 420,000 in 1974 and rose to one million in 1977. Criticisms against the unaffordable Welfare State grew, but economic liberalism sailed before the wind. The second oil crisis (1979), starting with the revolution against the Shah of Iran in Autumn 1978, gave another blow. Prices for crude oil had increased tenfold since 1973. Thatcher came to power in Great-Britain (1979) and Reagan in the US (November 1980). Following the advice of neo-liberal economists (deregulation) Anglo-American enterprises could export products more easily with a cheap dollar. European countries had high costs due to high social standards (Bourguinat, 1985) and unemployment in France increased to 1.5 million in 1980, and to 2 million in October 1981 (8.9% of active population unemployed). It was a structural phenomenon: 10% in 1985, 3 million in February 1993.

These social problems impaired confidence in neo-liberal governments under President Giscard d'Estaing (1974-1981). It was an earthquake when the Socialists won the presidential elections in 1981. For the first time since the start of the Fifth Republic the left could rule France after 23 years of governments of the right. Mitterrand was conscious of the fact that he could not rule properly with the support of only 200 deputies in the Assembly. He decided on 22 May 1981, now sailing before the political wind, to dissolve the Assembly. Legislative elections of 14/21 June 1981 were a brilliant victory for the Socialists: 285 seats in the Assembly. Gaullist RPR had only 66 seats, UDF 62 seats, and Communists 44 seats. At last the "alternance" was a fact. Socialists wanted to prove that they could solve the economic crisis. After the double Socialist victory, government-Mauroy tried to demonstrate that a Keynesian economic policy (expanding public expenditures, raising salaries and benefits) would give the French economy the needed push to stimulate economic growth and to reduce unemployment. Groups in the Socialist party were eager to ride their ideological hobbyhorses, proposing revolutionary reforms. Government decided in September 1981 to nationalise five industrial giants, two financial groups and 36 banks. Opposition used all its weapons, but the law for these nationalisations was adopted in February 1982. The government project to promote decentralisation was also popular. The "loi-Defferre", giving more policy room for municipalities, departments and regions, was adopted in 1982. Under leadership of Michel Rocard, Minister of the Plan, planning got a new impulse with more power for the State. An interim-plan (1982-1983) was launched to correct negative effects of Giscard d'Estaing's "septennat" (1974-1981). Work for the IXe Plan (1984-1988) started, Socialist planning.

While other countries, including the EEC partners of France, continued their restrictive economic policies, France did the opposite. This caused huge problems for France. In 1982 President Mitterrand had to change his economic policies drastically (repudiating his electoral promises). Since 1983-1984, there had been a worldwide economic recovery. Industrialised countries had more success in finding ways to cope with the energy problems since the second oil crisis by increasing oil production in non-OPEC-countries. Artificial reduction of crude oil production did not work without problems, so prices for crude oil fell to more normal levels and alternative energy production was promoted. France drastically expanded its nuclear power programme, so covering 2/3 of its energy requirements. Industrial production rose with 2% yearly in the 1980-1986 period. The imbalance in the worldwide financial system, in the grip of multi-national companies, switching "hot money" every hour over the whole world, was approaching a crash in 1987. On 19 October 1987, prices of shares on the New York Stock Exchange fell with 22.6% (on "Black Thursday" in 1929 with 12%). This caused a worldwide economic shock. On 12 November 1987 the index of the Paris Stock-Exchange, "CAC 40", lost 38% of its best value that year. To prevent a recession, the American Federal Reserve Board in 1988 put massive liquidities into monetary circulation (Bourguinat, 1987).

The world economy seemed to be on the path of stability, especially since the fall of the Berlin Wall (1989) and the collapse of the Communist bloc in Eastern Europe. Then all of a sudden there was a new shock. The troops of the Iraqi dictator Saddam Hussein invaded Kuwait in the summer of 1990, starting the Gulf War. Because he refused to comply with the UNO ultimatum demanding prompt withdrawal, an international army was set up which defeated the troops of Hussein quickly. In France economic growth was meagre. Changes in technology (automation etc.) and international competition forced a number of enterprises to close down and to fire masses of employees. Unemployment increased, up to 11% of the active population in February 1993 (3 million unemployed). In the 1980s and 1990s circumstances had changed, several conditions were different for the French economy (Berstein/Milza, 1995). The 1990 census revealed that the population of France had increased by 4 million since 1975 to 56,634,000 inhabitants, of which 51,248,000 were indigenous to France, 1,778,000 naturalised French and 3,608,000 foreigners. Diminishing economic growth had minor consequences for natural population growth, but it changed the influx of foreign workers. Since 1974, governments had closed the frontiers to foreign workers. The number of foreigners rose in spite of this, because of family reuniting and clandestine immigration. There were 1,765,000 foreigners in France in 1954, and 3,442,000 in 1975. Their number stabilised: 3,714,000 in 1982, and 3,608,000 in 1990. The composition of the group of foreigners changed, while more settled permanently (instead of a temporary stay). The Portuguese were still the largest group with 650,000 in 1990 (759,000 in 1975). For other groups it was as follows: some 614,000 Algerians in 1990 (in 1975 711,000), Moroccans rose to 573,000 in 1990 (was 260,000), Italians were 253,000 in 1990 (was 463,000), some 216,000 Spaniards in 1990 (497,000 in 1975), Tunisians were 206,000 in 1990 (in 1975 140,000), the Turks with 198,000 in 1990 (51,000 in 1975) and remaining groups with different nationalities.

Foreigners generally were hit harder by the economic recession than the indigenous population, with a percentage of unemployment which was twice as high, and a number of problems with societal integration. Foreigners mostly lived concentrated in a number of city quarters ("bidon-villes", or "cités-HLM") where living conditions were "less bright". As economic perspectives became worse (massive unemployment etc.) extreme-rightist Le Pen and his "Front National" fished in troubled waters, blaming foreigners for the economic crisis. The immigration of Algerians and other North-Africans, mostly adhering to Islam and having problems with integration into French society, was particularly blamed for taking 'French' jobs. Not only had this extreme-rightist movement problems with foreigners, but a large part of the French population as well. For most citizens there was a big difference between old immigration from European countries and new immigration from the Maghreb and Turkey. This is explained partially by the fact that the Catholic Church and their members had an important role in integrating immigrants adhering to the Catholic religion, and this integrating role of the Church had diminished. A large proportion of new immigrants (some 46%) adhered to Islam, which promised them a better life than the miserable circumstances they were in. The 3.5 million Muslims in 1990's France, the majority living normally with other citizens, provided a fertile soil for those propagating Muslim fundamentalism. Trouble with Islamic girls wearing head scarves at school were the top of the xenophobic iceberg. Adherents of a plural France started "SOS Racisme" in 1984 as a counter-movement.

Immigration of foreigners was not the sole migration which changed French society. There was a huge migration from countryside to towns and cities and between different regions. In the twenty years after 1947, France as agricultural country (45% of the population living in the countryside, and 35% living from agriculture) developed into an industrial country (Mendras, 1967). This process has continued since then (Mendras, 1984). In 1968, 4,100,000 people worked in agriculture, in 1990, this was 2,521,000: only 5% of the active population (in 1968 15%). Experts complained about "désertification des campagnes" (countryside as desert), devastating societal networks in wide areas of the countryside. In the 1960s, the "Délégation à l'aménagement du territoire et à l'action régionale" (DATAR) tried to redress disruption of society in these areas. The lifestyle of farmers and their families changed fundamentally. Life in the countryside was so different from before that for Mendras (1994) agrarian civilisation was dead with the last farmers. Urbanisation created many problems, especially in bigger cities, above all in Paris. The shortage of housing made it necessary to build more. With a series of measures (subsidising etc.), governments promoted the construction of houses for lower-income groups. In 54% of the households, houses were private property in 1990. The Paris region, for a number of reasons, worked as a magnet for new employment, supported by fast public transport facilities and newly created jobs. To reduce overstressed urbanisation in Paris, governments between 1988 and 1993 forced public organisations to leave Paris (ENA to Strasbourg, etc.). Urbanisation in the three decades since the Second World War was robust, but has diminished since then. Experts forecast that in the 21st century some 80% of the French would live in cities and towns. Between 1975 and 1990, French population grew by 3%; 7% in municipalities and 1% in cities. After thirty years of urbanisation, France was still the most agrarian of industrialised countries (Mendras, 1994).

More or less the same might be said about the end of the traditional working class as could be said about the end of farmers. In 1975, there were about 8.5 million workers in industry, forming nearly 40% of the active population (50% working in services). This had fallen to 28.5% in 1993; more than 65% was working in the tertiary sector. Between the two censuses of 1982 and 1990, industry had lost 798,000 workers. Since the beginning of the 20th century, the working class had been predominantly identified with industrial workers, putting their stamp upon trade unions. Since the 1970s this had changed, because of massive losses of jobs in industry (mines, steel industry, metal industry etc.). This provoked a crisis in the trade unions. The number of members fell to some 2,500,000. The largest trade union, CGT, had strong ties with the Communist party and when Communists lost political influence, this impaired the CGT. The CFDT, following the German model, had changed its policy from breaking with capitalism to fighting for social reforms since the 1980s. Trade union CGT-FO, trying to improve the position of workers by contracts, had been, since 1989, radicalising by using strikes as weapon. Since 1981 governments had tried to improve representation of workers in the management of enterprises with works councils (laws of Auroux, Roudy and Rigout).

Several factors caused structural problems of unemployment in France for a long period. There were about 450,000 unemployed at the beginning of the seventies, rising to 900,000 in 1975, and 1.5 million in 1980, the year before Socialists took over the government. It was 2.5 million in 1986. Unemployment diminished in the years 1987-1990, but after the autumn of 1990 it rose again. In 1991, there were 2.5 million unemployed, and in December 1993 3.4 million (12% of active population). The French situation had its own characteristics. Of the youngsters under 25 years, 22% were unemployed. A high percentage, 33%, of unemployment was of long duration (more than one year). It was said that France needed an economic growth of at least 3.5% yearly for 15 years to reach the

1974 level of employment. This high percentage of unemployment had serious effects in society. Social tensions were piling up, especially in poorer quarters with many unemployed and people living from meagre social benefits, contrasting with ostentatious consumption by many others. The split between the "haves" (having a job, a good house in a good quarter) and the "have-nots" (without job, living poorly), excluded from normal life ("l'exclusion"), caused growing problems (Mazel, 1996).

It became an urgent task for public authorities to create better conditions for millions, a fight against "exclusion" and "the new poverty" (Brisset, 1996). Public management of the economy in the French social model has to bring reasonable social and economic conditions for the whole population. Unlike the Anglo-American model, this means that, according to the still dominant conception in France, the solution of societal economic problems cannot be entrusted to the market as many Anglo-Americans believe. What can we expect from a country reducing itself to a market? France also has large numbers of poor people. Chassériaud (1993) estimated that in France the number of people in serious social trouble was about 1.5 million. It is difficult to compare conditions of the poor in different countries. In Great Britain it is estimated that 14 million inhabitants live below the poverty level (Vaïsse, 1996; Wilding, 1993). In 1942 the Beveridge-Report gave priority to fighting the four giant causes of misfortune: indigence, sickness, unhygienic housing, and unemployment. More than half a century later the country still suffers the same social and economic scourges. Although Member-States of the European Union spent 22-30% of national income on social provisions, some 53 million lived below the poverty line (half the modal income in the Member-States). In the United States (255 million inhabitants) it is reported (Marti, 1994) that 26 million people were badly nourished and 35 million living below the poverty line (14,000 dollars per year for a 4-persons family). France does not use the Anglo-American model, but social injustice permeates French society for Dejours (1998).

### 5.4. Original French planning, "planification à la française"

France has a long tradition of centralist management, which has its impact in contemporary practice. Minister Colbert, under the reign of King Louis XIV, organised State intervention in the economic process by founding public enterprises, regulating imports and exports (managed trade), and administering the national market. An important part of French interventionism is the systematic building up of professional schooling in a "corps d'état". To produce qualified engineers, the "École Nationale des Ponts-et-Chaussées" was founded in 1747. Now it is a training centre of excellence for electronics, aeronautics and space travel among other things. The famous "École Polytechnique" dates from 1794, so a series of prestigious institutions was formed to train candidates for leading positions in business and public organisations: "École Nationale d'Administration"; "École Nationale Supérieure des Mines de Paris"; "École Centrale des Arts et Manufactures"; etc. "Corps d'état" painstakingly plan the careers of their pupils: "Inspection des Finances"; "Conseil d'État"; "Cours des Comptes"; "Corps des Mines"; "Corps des Ponts et Chaussées", etc. These "Corps d'État" have a dominant influence in top positions of State and business (Birnbaum, 1978). Selection for the "grands corps" is done at the "École Nationale d'Administration" (ENA) and "École Polytechnique". ENA, training for superior positions in State, public organisations and public enterprises, allocates places for trainees at the highest levels of the State, only the best can hope for an interesting job in a prestigious institution. In the Fifth Republic it became normal to alternate bureaucratic and political functions. Politicians were sure of getting a good job in bureaucracy at the end of their political term. Political and bureaucratic positions were a springboard for lucrative jobs in business: "pantouflage" (Bauer/ Bertin Mourot, 1994). So France had its new aristocracy.

Before the Second World War, the idea of planned economy was very popular in leftist parties. The crisis in the 1930s enforced the expansion of State interventionism. The Popular Front government realised several nationalisations: armament industry, aircraft (1936) and railways (1937). During the Second World War there was more or less consensus within the resistance movement to expand the public sector drastically. The "Conseil National de la Résistance" (CNR), a forum composed of political parties and trade unions, was a unanimous supporter after the war of bringing the grand monopolised means of production into the hands of the State. The preamble of the Constitution of 1946 proclaimed: Each provision or enterprise having the character of a national public service or a factual monopoly has to become the property of the community, so there was a broad societal basis for reconstruction and nationalisations: mining industry; banking sector; insurance companies, aviation; motorcar industry. The decision was taken to start "planification" for the steering of the economy on the basis of quantitative medium-term targets for production. The Soviet Union with its 5-years plans was a model, but the French approach differed significantly (Petit, 1983). With a Decree of 3 January 1946, signed by Premier de Gaulle, the project to institutionalise an all-encompassing Plan for the French economy was set in motion. The "Commissariat général du Plan" (CGP), under the inspiring direction of Jean Monnet (Fontaine, 1988) and Pierre Massé, was charged with the elaboration of a Plan for future periods. The first three Plans had a coherent character in the framework of reconstruction after the war (Bauchet, 1964). The French State thus had an instrument with quantitative techniques for interventionist economic planning, especially after numerous nationalisations (Perroux, 1965). With successive plans disruptive economic circumstances forced adaptations. In the first Plan (1947-1953) reconstruction was the central issue. There were investment programs for coal, electricity, steel, cement, transport and agricultural machines, financed with Marshall-Aid. The crisis of the Korean War (1950-1953) had its impact and in 1953 a start was made with national accounting, since 1965 the task of the "Direction de la Prévision". The second Plan (1954-1957) accentuated quality and productivity. The third Plan (1957-1961) prepared adherence to the European Economic Community in 1958. The start of the Fifth Republic in 1958 had an imposing impact.

Bloch-Lainé (1959) argued for flexible, democratic planning, in which social-economic objectives had to be realised by means of contracts between public authorities and private enterprises. With the law of 4 August 1962, a new phase was started with an extended reach of planning in the framework of the 4th (1962/1965), 5th (1966/1970) and 6th (1971/-1975) Plans (Bauchet, 1973). Implementation of the 4th Plan was strongly influenced by the massive exodus from Algeria to France after the end of the Algerian War in 1962. The intended policies of the 5th Plan were shaken up by the political crisis in May 1968, which started with students' protests but then became a societal row ("'68") and the sixth Plan was upset by the first oil crisis (1973). Public authorities tried to steer the radical transformation of the social-economic structure of French society. Some regions with obsolete agrarian and industrial structures had serious problems. Therefore on 16 February 1963 the government decided to start with the "Délégation à l'aménagement du territoire et à l'action régionale" (DATAR). DATAR had a crucial role in the co-ordination of policies between State, regions and local authorities (Pouvoirs, 1967). In 1964, a "Commission de Développement Économique Régionale" was installed in all 22 regions. Circumstances changed, forcing authorities to take a new approach. Enterprises took over part of the planning, "déplanification" (Pierre/Praire, 1976). First priority was no longer to realise the targeted production, but to create the best conditions for economic and social development of the Nation. Planning got a more indicative character. The objective of the 5th Plan was to improve the competitiveness of French industry. The societal crisis of May 1968 prevented implementation of this Plan and French industry was confronted with fierce international competition. The accent was on economic growth (5.8-6% yearly), eliminating structural weaknesses, and priority for industrial development. In 1975, growth was for the first time in 15 years negative (- 0.3%).

With the 7th Plan (1976-1980), a third phase of French planning started: The Crisis. The usefulness of the planning was increasingly questioned because of growing uncertainties in development of the world market, the impact of economic crises, and discrepancy between targets and realisation (Cotta, 1978). In spite of progress made with national accounting and a new econometric model "FIFI", the second oil crisis (1979) reinforced doubts about the usefulness of planning. Budgetary programming was improved with 25 "programmes d'actions prioritaires" (PAP) involving 110 billion francs. The 8th Plan (1981/1985) was stillborn, as Socialists, after their long opposition, returned to government during a deep world economic crisis. The Socialist government had an intermediary Plan (1982). As authorities and experts knew that French planning was not adequate any more, government tried to revitalise planning with a reform (Law of 29 July 1982). Each plan treated macroeconomic policies, sector policies, programming of public outlays, and social policies. Planning was placed in the new institutional context of decentralisation ("contrats de plan État-Région"). The Plan was officially made a 5-year plan. It ruled that the Parliament had to adopt two laws regarding the Plan. One law had the strategies, objectives and actions while the second law formulated juridical, administrative and financial measures to implement objectives of the first law (CGP, 1983). A "Commission national de planification" (49 members) was established to institutionalise preliminary consultation.

The 9th Plan (1984/1988) chose, for a change, a strategic approach; ten great actions and 12 "programmes prioritaires d'exécution" (PPE). Implementation was hampered by the take-over of the political right after elections in 1986 ("cohabitation"). Neo-gaullist Premier Chirac dropped the idea of 5-year plans. When his government was followed in 1988 by the Socialist government-Rocard, there was not much time for preparing the next plan. The 10th Plan (1989/1993) was less ambitious, without financial programming and a strict macro-economic framework. Apart from such objectives as high levels of economic growth and employment, adaptation to the Common Market, etc., there were five priorities: education and development; research and furthering competition; solidarity; spatial planning and public service. The Socialist government did not adopt the 11th Plan (1993-1997) after the elections of March 1993, leaving the way free for the neo-gaullist government-Balladur (1993-1995). Meanwhile there remain three generations of rather successful "contrats de plan État-Région" for 1984-1988, 1989-1993 and 1994-1998. Generally, the "Commissariat général du Plan" (CGP) stimulated many outstanding studies about a broad spectre of relevant societal issues.

CGP (staff about 200), with a strongly changed character, still has a crucial role as a professional "think-tank" for the government in co-operation with several institutes. To name some: CEPII ("Centre d'Études Prospectives et d'Informations Internationales"); CERC ("Centre d'Études des Revenus et Coûts"); CREDOC ("Centre de Recherches et de Documentation sur la Consommation"); CEPREMAP ("Centre d'Études Prospectives d'Économie et Mathématiques Appliquées à la Planification"); BIPE ("Bureau d'Informations et de Prévisions Économiques"). CGP has wide network-relations with organisations inside and outside the public sector. INSEE produces economic analyses, statistical databases, and national accounts. "Direction de la Prévision", like INSEE part of the Ministry of Finance, makes long-term forecasts with macroeconomic models. In regional planning, CGP has a bond with DATAR ("Délégation à l'Aménagement du Territoire et à l'Action Régionale") and regional authorities. CGP is a think-tank, and participates with decision-making organs such as the yearly decision-making process about the budget, and inter-ministerial commissions. The first Plan (1947-1953) started with a government decree, the second Plan was approved by Parliament, but only two years after its start. Since the fourth Plan (1962-1965), Parliament decides about the Plan in two phases after hearing advice from the "Conseil économique et social" (Quinet, 1990). In the first phase general orientations are decided upon and in the second phase the law about the elaborated Plan is voted. The conjuncture made it necessary to adapt the formal Plan. Strategies were developed to deal with changes in economic conditions. Macroeconomic criteria with thresholds are used; the crossing of these requires intervention.

The coming to power of the Socialists in 1981 enabled them to reinforce the planning instrument more according to their ideology of State interventionism. This was formalised in the law of 29 July 1982 to reform the planning, making it more democratic, contractual and decentralised. Already the "Programmes d'Action Prioritaires" (PAP) were limited by financial commitments of the State (investments, exploitation outlays) and explicit targets. Now the "Programmes Prioritaires d'Exécution" (PPE) had to be programmed. Since the "Rapport Nora" (1968) there had been planning contracts between the State and public enterprises. The "contrats de Plan" were made part of the planning process more strictly. The system of planning contracts, signed by State and the (public) enterprises involved, was combined with a new arrangement of regional organisation of responsibilities, decentralisation (1982/1983). Regional Plans were made autonomous with regard to the National Plan, while coherence was realised with "contrats de Plan État-Régions". The tenth Plan (1989-1992) was not made according to formalised procedures, because in 1988 there was a Socialist President and a rightist Government, political cohabitation. In September 1988 7 committees were formed to formulate policy proposals, within six months, on: technological, industrial and commercial Europe; financial and monetary Europe; social relations and employment; social protection; education, formation, research; daily life; and efficacy of the State. Working-groups were formed, about macroeconomic perspectives, the year 2000; etc. This work, used for the tenth Plan (1989-1992), was condensed in "La France et l'Europe d'ici 2010" (Foucauld, 1993).

It seems useful to summarise the theoretical underpinning of the French indicative planning. The first three plans were realised without much theoretical conceptualisation. Pierre Massé, Plan manager from 1959, gave an impulse to the formulation of a theory of indicative planning, building on known ideas such as market failure, external effects and collective goods. He accentuated the defective capacity of the market to co-ordinate the future plans of economic actors. Stressing adequate information, he argued for an institutionalised structure to give economic actors the information they needed. The market was made more transparent with systematised information. Knowledge, expectations and plans were transformed into a coherent whole, to produce a common view about future economic developments. In a process of consultation, commissions of interested parties per sector (representatives of employers, employees, civil servants, consumers) were brought together to collect information. This information was systematised and used for medium-term indicative plans. Taking account of reservations due to fear of yielding confidential information to competitors, indications were presented on the meso-level (in between micro and macro) for further participation. With this indicative planning, giving relevant information, "économie orientée" was thought to be more efficient than a market without planning (with less relevant information). Incentives are used (subsidies, fiscal facilities) to further specific developments. When the economy was more open to international markets, macro-indications got a prominent place in planning.

Macro-indications have been the strong part of French indicative planning. They are based on macroeconomic models, representations of reality with mathematical equations. Exogenous variables from outside the model are confronted with endogenous variables in the model, of which one wants to know the values. Since Keynes had the view that government could influence the economic process with the volume of public outlays these form a crucial exogenous variable, influencing private investments as endogenous variable. In the course of time, macroeconomic modelling has been refined. Since the 5th Plan (1966-1970) the financial sector has been part of it with "TOF" ("Tableau des opérations financières"). In 1970 an elaborated model was used for the 6th Plan: the physical-financial "FIFI", differentiating between sectors with or without international competition. Since the 7th Plan (1976-1980) the model DMS ("Dynamique Multi-Sectoriel") has been used. This model, dividing the productive system into 13 sectors, had about 2,000 equations and 400 exogenous variables. With values for variables in a base year and with future values for exogenous variables, simulations are worked out for eight years into the future. This DMS model was flanked with other models for specific aspects such as "PROPAGE" (productive system with 36 sectors); "SPHYNX" (households); "SECUS" (social security) and "SPORE" (regional prospects for employment). The 10th Plan (1989-1992) had an innovation, with pluralist prospects of three different models. "HERMES-France" was made by the "Laboratoire d'Économie de l'École centrale de Paris". "ICARE" by "Ipecode" and a mini-DMS by INSEE (CGP, 1989). Forecasts were for the medium (5 years) and long term (10 years). In 1963 calculations of variables for 1985 were used for the 5th Plan. These were quite to the point (Dubois, 1985). For long term modelling, scenarios are used. Qualitative indications are prominent.

In indicative planning, macroeconomic data are complemented with adequate data about sectors. From the beginning sector data were collected in numerous commissions with representatives from sectors. Theoretical conceptions are available: orthodox neo-classical theory; "structure-conduct-performance paradigm" (SCPP); Anglo-Saxon principal-agent theory; and more recently new institutional economics. The neo-classical view holds that there are rational actors with given preferences (methodological individualism). The analysis is directed at a stable equilibrium (no historical time) with no information problem (no uncertainties). There is no problem of market organisation (exogenous, constant). In micro-economics the issue is optimising: the optimal combination of price and volume, when behaviour of actors and environment (market structure) are given. In the neo-classical concept, the market structure determines results, as the exogenous structure determines behaviour via causal relations (Chevallier, 1977). The SCPP asserts that performance in markets depends on the conduct of sellers and buyers, which depends on the structure of the relevant market. As SCPP was developed for industrial organisation, this paradigm seems less relevant for public enterprises in the sector of services. That is evident in policies of privatisation and deregulation (Bergeijk/Haffner, 1996).

Since the 1970s attempts have been made to develop another conceptualisation, better adapted to the specific French industrial structure, the dominant position of the State, and the intensive interpenetration of public and private sectors (Bellon/Chevallier, 1983). The "filière" concept (networks) was part of this, encompassing economic, technological, social-political and organisational aspects (Jacquemin/Rainelli, 1984). At the micro-level, it treats relations of the enterprise with its environment (strategies about product-market mix, integration forwards and backwards, co-operation). At meso-level, it is about the economic and socio-political structure and at macro-level, it is used for economic policies. The "filière" concept, with its multi-disciplinary and dynamical analysis based on the systems approach, is said to be more advanced than original new institutional economics (Laurent, 1986). Economic reality is structured with this "filière" concept as statistical instrument. Business units are linked with a nomenclature of activities ("secteur"), products ("branche": units making the same product), and "filière" (units related with each other by mutual transactions). Transactions between branches are worked up to "Tableaux d'Entrées et

Sorties" (TES), input-output models, so one can say which sectors are strategic for their key position (Montfort, 1985). Montfort/Dutailly (1983) transformed the 90 branches of TES to 19 "filières", with two methods of clustering. Since the eighties, BIPE ("Bureau d'Information et de Prévision Économique") has developed detailed yearly revised 5-years forecasts "Prévisions glissantes détaillées" (PGD) for some 300 sectors. Indicative planning was used to plan public outlays. For decision-making about tariffs and investments of public enterprises the "calcul économique" was used. Jules Dupuit, in 1848 "Ponts et Chaussées" engineer, in this way calculated the collective utility of public works.

With this "calcul économique", the significance of decisions was not quantified from the perspective of the economic actors themselves, but from the viewpoint of the interests of the community (Malinvaud, 1981; 1983), so it is a kind of societal cost-benefit analysis, while remaining a highly sophisticated tool. A less successful method was the French replica of the American PPBS (Planning Programming Budgeting System) called "Rationalisation des Choix Budgétaires" (RCB). The programming of public outlays, under the discipline of the budget and not of the market, took the form of programming of collective equipment and personnel (input) on the basis of reasoned calculations of collective wants. Originally the Plan concentrated on economic aspects but, with the 6th Plan, the social sector got a more prominent place with Jacques Delors as first manager of the social sector in indicative planning. This "planification sociale" was about health care, social security, employment, (urban) quality of life, education and professional development, justice, recreation and sports and culture. The character of the French system of indicative planning has been changed, becoming more medium-term regulation. In the beginning it was a rather interventionist planning, and although it got a legal status by the voting in Parliament, the Plan generally had no compulsory character and it lacked sanctions. With planning contracts it became possible to operationalise planning commitments for specific aspects and sectors. The Plan got its prominent place in society for its professionalised, influential information, excellent analyses, and psychological impact. The role of the Plan in society decreased, due largely to changed circumstances. The position of the State in the economy, with its traditional instruments of political economy (budget, monetary policy) declined, but public outlays (State, regional and local communities, social expenditures) still represent about 50% of national income.

The French economy is thoroughly intertwined with the European Union (EU) and with international and world markets. The EU by no means adopts the French approach to planning. Most other Member-States prefer more liberal economic policymaking though one might see some resemblances with the regular expert meetings for exchange of information. The whole institutional construction of the EU (juridical rulings etc.), with its ever more direct effects upon the national markets of Member-States, imposes itself prominently. A crucial part of this institutional interpenetration is the confrontation of common law and predominantly French continental law traditions. A plausible hypothesis is that French juridical philosophy, conceptualisation and operationalisation will be a decisive part of public management of European society. Some propositions were launched to reform the planning system (Bloch-Lainé, 1959). Ruault (1986) proposed to accentuate programming of public finances for three years, to organise a debate each year in Parliament, and separate counselling of government, based on participation in formalised consultations. The Economic and Social Council adopted the "Report-Velitchkovitch" (1987), arguing for the maintainance of planning for its information. It should encompass a document for social-economic strategy for the medium-term; prospective analyses with policy proposals; economically programmed lawmaking and medium-term programming of public outlays; contracts between State and public enterprises; and regional programming. A commission analysed French planning, and proposed renewal (De Gaulle, 1994). There is convergence with macroeconomic planning elsewhere though differences remain.

## 5.5. From centralist interventionism to sophisticated public management of society

Economic order, organisation of the economic process (production, exchange, consumption) in society, includes institutions that influence the behaviour of economic actors. Institutions are structures in which societal values and rules of the game are embedded. Traditions, informal interactions ("social capital"), customs, conventions and juridical rules (contracts, laws, treaties) structure institutions. A popular opinion opposes markets to institutions but markets are organised and institutionalised exchange (Hodgson, 1988). It is an empirical fact that the economic order in countries does differ significantly, as the whole cultural-historical context has its impact. There is an impressive variety of economic systems. Describing one specific economic system, qualitatively and/or quantitatively, runs the risk of producing an endless series of facts, but it is possible to structure relevant data by distinguishing some conceptual ideal-types. In economics it is common practice to distinguish two basic, extreme, types of economic order: totally managed national economy and free economy led by the market mechanism only. Most national economic systems are a mixture, combining market and some control by public authorities and/or private actors. In the theoretical model of the free economy all actors are absolutely free to make choices about production, investment, exchange, consumption or saving. Many individual choices, partly incompatible with each other, require co-ordination. This co-ordination problem is entrusted, in the free economy model, to the price mechanism of the market. Supply and demand of all kinds of products are confronted with each other, the prices are the decisive factor. At the opposite of the absolutely free economy, there is the theoretical conception of the absolutely planned economy. Instead of myriads decisions of economic actors, the State decides all. There are experiences with centralised economic planning as in the Soviet Union (1917-1990), but it proved impossible for a central authority to get a grip on all aspects of the economic process.

Hoffmann (1976) wrote that France, with a system of centralised decision-making, was becoming more like other nations. Others suggest that the French model of administration was specific and would continue to be so, for example Nizard (Baecque/Quermonne, 1982). Rouban (1990) had the rhetorical thesis that the specific French model of administration was coming to its end because of modernisation of the French State. A popular idea about French public management is that the French model is special due to the dominant position of the French State, reinforced yet again in the Fifth Republic. Realities of the French institutionalising are far more complicated than that. Institutionalisation of the Fifth Republic was intended to further centralisation (Quermonne, 1987). Different explanations for centralised French public management are available. The structure of public management and the decisive role of the "grands corps" are thought relevant (Bodiguel, 1978; Kessler, 1986). Crozier (1970) thought that the rigidity of historically built-up structures was a special feature of French public management, "le blocage". Rosanvallon (1990) mentioned specific intervention methods such as societal modernisation and indicative planning. The genius of legal thinking is a factor. Often the French approach in public management is criticised for its dominantly legalistic character, but the French approach is influenced by several philosophical movements that were dominant in different historical periods. Historical analyses of French public management show that history-inclusive thinking is a necessary condition for trying to understand the French way of public management. The modern system of public management has its fundaments in Antiquity and the Middle Ages (Strayer, 1979). In the historical framework, it is evident that public management is not an original American invention, but dates back to Antiquity. American public management has its specialities though. It is not possible to give an adequate survey of the abundant French literature but an analysis of literature shows that the French way of institutionalising is characteristic in many dimensions. The hypothesis of a specific French formula of institutional engineering is corroborated by the evidence as shown in literature. In spite of the economic-technological influences of international convergence and globalisation, French willpower intends to maintain the French identity (voluntarism).

As in Anglo-American literature, French authors emphasize that the way public authorities do their jobs (or fail to do so) has to be improved by using scientific methods and the approaches of a number of sciences. So "Science administrative", Political science, Public Law, Sociology, History, Economics, Social Psychology, Geography, and other disciplines are seen as relevant. Calling in the help of administrative science is controversial in France however, it is thought to be mostly the application of public law, neglecting strategic analyses and social sciences. This approach undervalues the contributions of administrative science. More than in Anglo-American literature and practice, public law has played a prominent role in French public management. American public administration profiled itself a century ago by opposing itself to the law-dominated conception of the European continent (Thorpe, 1901; Wilson, 1889). Taking business administration as a model for public administration, it could give an important impetus to the development of more business-like public administration. In the United States, with its dominating contractual culture in private and public spheres, they were mostly reserved about the use of public law. Later in American public management the relevance of public law was recognised, contributing to new institutionialism (March/ Olsen, 1989). In France, cradle of the Constitutional State, the "État de droit" (Rule of Law) was given priority above efficient fulfilment of tasks by public authorities. Law has always been a key variable of public management. Troubles in French society, due to adaptations of the all too benevolent Welfare State to conditions of the international market, can give the erroneous impression that French public intervention is obsolete. At the start of the 21st century, the French formula of institutional engineering holds many lessons, also for Anglo-Americans.

The debate about the needed modernisation of French public management placed the concept and position of the French State in the middle of the arena. It is not adequate to concentrate this debate on administrative questions or administrative reform (Kickert, 1997). On the contrary, the political-administrative system and the whole range of intervention methods are at stake. At the beginning of the 20th century American public administration was in the grip of the politics-administration dichotomy, seen as a method to professionalise public administration (not burdened by party-political passions). Empirical evidence undermined this normative rule of thumb, even though public administration was seen as wholly political in character. Comparable developments can be mentioned in France. In the framework of historical traditions, there are tendencies that continue to accentuate juridical dimensions of State intervention, but ever more State activities are seen as thoroughly impregnated by politics and power aspects. In the French context, one has to add that State activities have been predominantly in the party-political grip (leftist versus rightist politics). Political parties see power positions in institutions of public authorities as the spoils of elections. Elections are thought to give the winning party, or functionary, the democratic legitimacy to use the public apparatus to push through partisan opinions and policies. This party-political kidnapping of public authority positions and policies seriously erodes the legitimacy of public authorities based on their primary function of representing the general, non-partisan interest. Following on the 19th century of imperialism of the law (in the framework of the "État de droit") the 20th century has been an era of imperialism of party-politics and the market. France in the 21st century might develop more in the direction of law-based, professional public management for the general interest. In this context it is important to reject the popular American concept of "Public Affairs", encompassing all public organisations but also political parties, media, interest groups and non-governmental organisations. The essential failure of this concept is that it blurs the authentic, unique responsibilities of law-based public authorities. The heart of the matter is that public authorities have specific competencies and a specific societal function as the sole organs which represent society as a whole. Public Management of Society demands specialised professionalisation.

In practice all kinds of combinations between parts of public and private organisations have become popular in the framework of public-private partnerships (Jobert/Muller, - 1987). This might be part of a sound development, but only if some basic conditions are fulfilled. One of these conditions is that responsibilities have to be clear. A second condition is that public authorities have to claim a position of last resort, making it possible to act if necessary against the combined forces of private and public-private combinations when the general interest is at stake, also when there are other organisations claiming that they represent the general interest themselves. In reality, the structures of public authorities are very complex. Hundreds and even thousands of different organisations, administrations, offices, and all kinds of subsystems with different, specialised competencies together form what are normally indicated as public authorities. This fragmented system of public management requires measures to prevent it from falling apart into independent empires, "l'administration en miettes" (Dupuy/Thoenig, 1985), especially when public authority positions are used as vehicles for partisan policies, as Le Pen did in municipalities where the ultra-rightist Front National won municipal elections. To be fair, other political parties often did the same elsewhere.

The traumatic defeat by the Germans in 1940 made French leadership more conscious of the technological and industrial backwardness of its economy (Kuisel, 1984). Modernisation was a key issue in policies with an accent on State interventionism (Muller, 1994). A professionalised political-administrative elite, prompted by the modernisation movement, gave important impetus to reforms (Grémion, 1976). The prominent position of the higher echelons of bureaucracy in the French State has been analysed amply in political science and sociological studies about bureaucratic elites (Birnbaum, 1977; Thoenig, 1987). State functionaries promoted the development of ambitious programs and grand projects, meant to further the French prestige in the framework of "Colbertisme high tech" (Cohen, 1992). It was not always a success. In the 1980s and 1990s, the spectacular failure of technological projects undermined French public self-confidence. National technological independence was thought more important than commercial yields, as in the military-bureaucratic complex, related to French companies exporting weaponry (Cohendet /Lebeau, 1987).

Societal conditions have changed, and this has made it necessary for public authorities to adapt their methods of intervention, so technology is forcing adaptations (Bouvier, 1985). Globalisation in combination with information technologies and worldwide economic competition make national boundaries more relative frameworks in the global village, and European integration increasingly has a more intensive impact. For Muller (1992), the French model of public policymaking is in crisis, torn between Europe and the local sphere. The French model, built on national constructivist images of the world and specific methods, in his view can be characterised by three features: the central position of the French State in societal processes, dominating political agenda and monopolising of national constructivist images of the "espace public" (Rosanvallon, 1990), mechanisms for articulation of social interests, while corporatism in sectors reinforces the central position of the State, giving public management a key role in societal representation (Segrestin, 1985), and a specific relation between State and territorial public organisations (regions, departments, municipalities), giving the State a privileged position, while the power of local authorities is residual (Mabileau, 1991). One might say that the French model of public management developed a rather unique territorial dimension, as analysis of the "pouvoir périphérique" showed (Grémion, 1976). This has changed since the decentralisation of the 1980s. Public management is characterised by strong deconcentration. More than in other countries, the French State formed France: For De Gaulle, France existed thanks to the French State. During the "Trente glorieuses" especially (1945-1975) the Colbertist tradition was revitalised.

Up to the recent past, the obvious part of the French model of public management was the predominant role of the state. Since the 1990s, the picture has been more differentiated. The decentralisation movement gave an impetus to the transformation of local administration, under centralised control of the State, into a system of local self-government. This made regions, departments and municipalities more relatively autonomous partners of the State. The rules of the institutional game are changing, besides, territorial public authorities are increasingly recognised as actors in the framework of the European Union. The impact of the European Union upon the situation in the Member-States is growing steadily. In 1987, the European Council of Ministers had already adopted 458 regulations, 40 directives and 125 decisions, and the European Commission 3,655 regulations, 4,212 decisions and 23 directives. An important institutional fact is, that institutions of the European Union don't have external services for the preparation and implementation of communauty regulations, directives and decisions. This task devolves upon the public authorities of the Member-States. Instead of elimination of national public authorities by European institutions, this implies intensified integration of national public authorities. Administrations on all levels have to co-operate with European institutions and administrations of other Member-States: a new phenomenon of co-national work., French public authorities have slowly built up institutional arrangements to adapt to European challenges (Quermonne, 1991). As elsewhere, the functioning of public authorities in France is placed in the perspective of the aphorism: One has to manage public services like a private enterprise. At the end of the 19th century, the organisation of public authorities was seen as a model for improving the organisation of private enterprises (Max Weber). In the 20th century, it has been the other way round. Private management is seen as a model for public authorities also. From there it is an easy step to proclaim privatisation as the key to better government (Savas, 1987). Analysis makes it evident that management of (most) public organisations is, and should be, different. Some (parts of) public organisations can be run more or less like private organisations, but these are few.

Public management has specific rationalities. French public management is specific in many dimensions. It is an exaggeration to say that nothing in the institutional history of France, its culture or social organisation of its State has predisposed French public administration to turn to the private sector for inspiration (Santo/Verrier, 1993, p.3). At least five features characterise public organisations: pursuit of external objectives; no capitalist productivity; assured tasks with imperfect or no competition; complex, closed systems and the subordination of administration to politics. Private organisations, within the constraints of the market and conditions of the law, can have their internal, autonomous objectives but for most public organisations, these are set externally by the objectives of the general interest as formulated by the law, and they dispose of several specific means to implement their measures (law, police, justice, treasury etc.). For many Anglo-American authors there are only marginal differences between the management of private and public organisations. Starting with obvious examples where differences are marginal indeed (efficient organisation of offices, etc.) they often generalise about the characteristics of all organisations in all their dimensions. Inspired by the successes of industrial organisation, pioneers like Wilson (1887), Taylor (1911) and Fayol (1916) elaborated their ideas about scientific management. Wilson (1887) rightly put forward the idea that it was not necessary to take over the whole fabric of French monarchic administration to use useable concepts of French administration. Since their work, ideas about general administration have been developed to a rather sophisticated level (Ducan, 1990). In France, the idea was always that administration and management are not just easily transferable technologies. Management is a "mode finalisé de direction", depending fundamentally on the final objectives within the context of specific cultural circumstances. This is relevant as public management is exercising authority in the name of society (Laufer/Burlaud, 1980).

French public authorities encountered a new challenge with the integration of France into the institutionalising arrangements of the common market, EEC and European Union. The handling of European issues by public authorities in France is said to be based on two rules. Each public administration is thought to be competent for its own issues and there is centralised co-ordination by an organ directly responsible to the Prime Minister. The "Secretariat Général du Comité Interministériel pour les questions de coopération économique internationale" (SGCI), was originally created by a decree of 3 April 1948 concerning the OECE (later OECD). Two ministries, having a global and general approach, are involved in all European dossiers: the Ministry of Foreign Affairs (Quai d'Orsay), with the formal monopoly of diplomatic negotiations, and the Ministry of Economics and Finance (Quai de Bercy) which has to control all budgetary implications of communitarian policies. All directions and services of all ministries must take account of the European dimension of their policy areas, but there are offices specialising in European issues, such as the "Service de coopération économique", "Bureau du droit communautaire", "Direction des affaires politiques", "Bureau agriculture, affaires européennes", "Bureau organismes européennes" (monetary issues), etc. Professional cells were created in several ministries and SGCI, under the control of President and Premier responsible for co-ordination between ministries and permanent representation of France at the European Community, is the strategic centre of control for European politics (Matthiessen, 1981). The creation in 1983 of a Ministry of European Affairs seemed to interfere with SGCI functions. A circular of 22 September 1988 confirmed the central position of SGCI (about 120 functionaries), organising inter-ministerial meetings daily, in about 90% of dossiers realising consensus. In some cases President or Premier interfere (Lequesne, 1986). French permanent representation in the European Community, created in 1958, developed intense communications with the SGCI (Lequesne, 1993; Middlemas, 1995).

Functionaries are more conscious of the new European realities. Administrations of Member-States operate as external offices of the European Union. The new situation is qualified by "dédoublement fonctionnel" of national institutions, being national institutions and external offices of the European Union. They have to apply Community law with norms which are superior with regard to national legality. Citizens and corporations can invoke Community law above national jurisdictions, which act also as jurisdictions of Community law. Member-States must transpose Community law into national law so the public authorities of Member-States have to implement a growing body of Community law. The "Conseil d'État" was for a long time the exponent of national opposition against the penetration of superior Community law. At last it gave way to the new institutional reality and in its 20 October 1989 decision (Nicolo), it recognised its competence to apply Community law, instead of national law. The "Conseil d'État", in its report of 30 May 1990, showed that French legislation had to give way to international law, especially to Community law. Lack of confidence in politicians time and again seems to make the threat of an institutional crisis imminent. When about 10% of the active population is without work there is reason for concern, but, on the basis of some criteria, France is the fourth economic power in the world, and the third nuclear power. The country has a reasonable system of social security. A number of developments (immigration, international competition, etc.) does stir up society-wide pessimism: "Les Peurs françaises" (Duhamel, 1993). It is useful to compare the French model with other models. Suleiman (1995) stressed that most studies in mainstream literature don't adequately perceive the situation of France. Analyses often build a one-sided construction of French society, bypassing fundamental changes experienced in French society in the last half-century. Some studies signal changes in some aspect or part of French society.

It was a popular premise that France continued to be a monolithic, stagnating society, only marginally adapting to changing international developments, but France is a dynamic society on the move. Compared with other countries, France has its specific characteristics. The role of partisan (party) politics in Public Management of Society can be qualified as dominant. More than in mainstream literature, one has to differentiate between what France has in common with other countries in respect of crucial transformations, and what is specific for France: French specificity (Petot, 1998; Rouban, 1990). A popular bias about France is, that in comparison to the United States, it is a stagnating, State-dominated, blockaded society (Crozier, 1980). This idea became popular in publications like "Le Mal français" (Peyrefitte, 1976). Conservatism was seen as a structural characteristic of French society; French mentality was as it was. Overstressing the impact of some "affairs", France was even dismissed as a "banana Republic" (Coignard/Lacan, 1989). Often over-regulation and over-administration are accentuated. It cannot be denied that there have been blockades in a number of sectors but that is not enough to generalise about a "Société bloquée". How did it come about that many writers continually gave France this epithet? For Suleiman (1995) it is obvious that Tocqueville is responsible for this train of thought. Starting from two factors, the origins of the French Revolution, and the capacities of American people to develop real democracy, Tocqueville, in the years 1835-1840, developed the idea that France was a democratically and economically stagnating country. His conception inspired many followers, as it still does today. Tocqueville's analysis was largely to the point in his time, but is not adequate for contemporary France. Generally at least three factors are mentioned as components of stagnation and problems of governing in France: the State-centralised management of society ("étatisme"; "jacobinisme"); an anti-economic mentality; and a paralysing cultural heritage.

In "L'Ancien Régime et la Révolution" (1856), Tocqueville elaborated that State-centralisation was already strongly developed before the French Revolution. Since the Revolution, a dominant idea has been that the common good had to be imposed upon society, and public order realised by a strong State. This was quite different from America, where citizens participated more in local decision-making (Kaspi, 1986; Lacorne, 1991). It is asserted that most institutions of public management in France – in spite of different regimes in feudality, absolutism, constitutional monarchy, empires, and republics, have been largely the same. Popular comment has it that the overpowering presence of the State in French society provoked an anti-economic mentality, reducing risk-taking private initiatives. With regard to the dominantly Catholic France this has been related to the famous thesis of Max Weber (1990) in the years 1904-1905, that there was a direct relationship between the spirit of capitalism and Protestantism, and it was quite common to have a theory about France as a static society, while it is obvious that this theory was static, not society. The revisionist school of economic historians argued that the handicaps of the French economy were generally underlined, while its advantages were underrated. For J. Bouvier, France was never superior or inferior to comparable countries (Fridenson/Straus, 1987). France, while giving some observers the impression that it was a lazy country, was praised for its economic miracle at the time of reconstruction, which was no miracle at all. During its "Trente Glorieuses" (Fourastié, 1979) in the years 1945-1975, France used its capacities to overcome the disaster of the Second World War and its aftermath (Carré c.s., 1984). The Gross National Product (GNP) in 1945 was 54% of that in 1938 (Bonin, 1988). In 1949, GNP was at the 1938 level (Becker, 1988). Then followed a period of rapid expansion, with high growth rates (5-6%), up until the oil crises in the 1970s, which forced France to the decision to reduce its energy dependence. In 1973 it covered 22.5% of its energy needs. With nuclear energy it now covers about 45% of its needs.

All in all, the often criticised French State administration proved to be one of the most crucial instruments of reconstruction and modernisation of French society. France regained its lost wealth producing capacities, and could even realise a position as one of the first economic powers in the world (Mendras, 1994). It could become a technologically innovative country (Suleiman/Courty, 1996). Transformations took place in the system of production (OECD, 1988). The part of the population active in agriculture dropped from 29.2% in 1949 to 6.7% in 1988, and 5% later (Eck, 1990) and agriculture produced more with less workers, with modernisation and mechanisation bringing impressive rises in productivity (Tuppen, 1983). The future of French agriculture is not easy though (Fottorino/Benoit, 1989; Hervieu, 1993). In industry impressive changes took place, with an accent on technologically advanced sectors: nuclear energy; telecommunications; armament; aeronautics. "Colbertisme high-tech" (Cohen, 1992). The service sector expanded, its part of the population active there grew from 35.8% in 1949 to 64.4% in 1988. In the system of production and the social structure important transformations changed society. Women participate more in the labour market and France, as other countries, was conquered by all characteristics of the consumer society (Borne, 1988; - Fourastié, 1987). Massive immigration gave problems (Weil, 1992).

Traditionally, French economic interventionism has been imposing ("dirigisme"). The impact of the French system of planning ("planification") was often praised (Kuisel, 1984). It was effective in the reconstruction period (Bloch-Lainé/Bouvier, 1986) and later as an instrument of modernisation (Rousso, 1986). The French model of planning was spoken of with awe (Cohen, 1969), but international competition, regional developments (European Union), and globalisation had their influence (Adam/ Stoffaes, 1986). The role of the State in steering the economy had to be reviewed because of the failure of some projects financed with public funds among other things (Closets, 1992; Cohen/Bauer, 1985) and methods of interventionism were criticised. Socialists, coming to power at last in 1981 after decades in opposition, firstly expanded the nationalised sector (Machin/Wright, 1984). Inter alia 90% of financial activities and 11 out of 16 grand industrial conglomerates were nationalised. The public nationalised sector represented about half of investments and 85% of bank credits in 1982 (Suleiman, 1995, p.98). Soon Socialists had to admit that they could not resist international competition in an open economy. Nationalisation was out (in spite of election promises of Socialists) and privatisation was in (Wright, 1993). Although Mitterrand promised in 1988 that there would be no more nationalisations or privatisations ("ni, ni"), privatisation continued (it was called something else). Traditional methods of planning fell partially out of use as new instruments were developed to influence economic developments. This "New French Capitalism" is a complex phenomenon, with an important role for the State, in spite of huge privatisations (Albert, 1991). Thanks to benevolent social security, it is capitalism with a more human face. This social security is too costly: a new social question (Rosanvallon, 1995).

## 5.6. Some specific public policies

The Fifth Republic brought France the political stability and new institutions that it needed but it got a useful heritage from the Fourth Republic (1946-1958) in the field of socio-economic policies (Schor, 1993). From an economic point of view, the Fourth Republic was more important than Gaullists would normally admit. In 1958 they emphasised the enduring high inflation, and deficits of budget and trade balance. In the Fourth Republic, reconstruction of devastated France had been dynamically handled with the accent on State interventionism (rigid control of prices, salaries, etc.). This was a logical step. Who else could manage the superhuman task of reconstruction? Right from the start there were nationalisations in key sectors (credit, transport, energy), and of industries which had collaborated with the Nazis. The State also influenced private investments with rulings, fiscal measures and subsidies. Initiated by Jean Monnet, as the first commissioner of the Plan nominated by De Gaulle, a specific French kind of planning was launched, "planification". In this indicative and participative planning, "concertation" for the promotion of consensus played a central role. Economic actors determined priorities together. The State, in its budget and investment decisions, took account of the results of these consultations. The First Plan was published in January 1947, with the target of making French productivity 1950 25% higher than its 1939 level. Social calm was reasonably realised with a policy of social cohesion in a time of practically full employment. A law of 22 February 1945 brought works councils and a law of 16 April 1946 organised representation of the personnel. The 1946 Constitution recognised several social and economic rights and the foundations were laid for the social security system.

The big issue was whether the French economy was ready to open its frontiers to the international market. Weak points in economic policy of the Fourth Republic were monetary and financial policies. To finance reconstruction and modernisation flexibly, the franc was weakened. Government (budget deficit, negative trade balance) couldn't manage the monetary instruments adequately. The State tried to get some control, inter alia with a forced loan to finance its budget deficit. In July 1946, salaries were raised by 25% or more. Inflation rates between 1946 and 1948 were more than 50% a year. This hyperinflation caused a flight of capital from the French franc. And between 26 January 1948 and 20 September 1949 the French franc lost 66% of its value in relation to the American dollar. During the years 1948-1950 the economic situation was gradually normalised with a package of measures (reduction of subsidies, fiscal amnesty for flight capital, liberation of prices, etc.) and so price rises could be reduced from about 50% in 1948 to 10% in 1950. Since 1950, State control has been relaxed gradually. The normal market economy could develop within a specific French context of mixed economy. Collective contracts became an important instrument in the employer-employee relationship. Economic recovery was for an important part due to American "Marshall Aid" which enabled the deficit of the trade balance to be compensated for, but there was a reversal, due to the boom of prices for raw materials (Korea War). Budget deficits rose again. Minister Pinay pursued a rigid, restrictive policy (control of prices, cuts in expenditures). In May 1952, he launched the Pinay-loan with exceptional advantages (indexation; tax relief; etc.).

France had a pleasant surprise when the US paid French military costs in Indo-China almost completely. After 1954, the French economy recovered. The Algerian war intensified existing economic disequilibria however and the structure of foreign trade, with an excess of raw materials, agricultural and other products of a low added value, was not at all as it should be for a developed country. Government increasingly opened the closed French market to the world market, accentuating relations with economies in the European Economic Community (EEC) and former French colonies. The creation of a Common Market (about 200 million inhabitants) was an innovative challenge. The French Minister of Foreign Affairs, Schuman, in May 1950 proposed placing German and French coal and steel production under the control of a Common High Authority, inviting other countries to do the same. The ECSC, the first community institution for coal and steel, was created in 1951. The French Parliament ratified the ECSC treaty, Communists (against powers given to Germany) and Gaullists (against the loss of sovereignty) opposing. After the failure to set up a Common Defence Community, the Benelux-countries took the initiative to further institutionalising of the European Community. On 25 March 1957 treaties were signed for European Economic Community and Euratom (atomic energy) and in July 1957, these treaties were ratified by the Parliament (Gaullists and Communists opposing). In 1958, there was De Gaulle's comeback to power. He was seen as the only person able to manage the Algerian problem. Primarily concerned with this and a new Constitution, De Gaulle was not interested in economics, except when these furthered French independence (Bertrand, 1992).

With the perspective of opening the economic frontiers in the framework of the Common Market, the French government decided on a programme to cure the financial situation with a devaluation of the franc by 17.5% on 27 December 1958. De Gaulle accentuated the politics of independence for France as great power ("politique de grandeur") from 1958. He rejected the "American protectorate", promoting the idea of independent nations in Europe ("L'Europe des nations") and opposing a supranational European Community (La Gorce/Schor, 1992). After the (expected) US refusal to combine the nuclear potential of US, Great-Britain and France in a tripartite management, De Gaulle accelerated the development of an independent French nuclear weapon, begun under former governments. The first French atomic bomb was exploded in 1960. The French industries of arms and nuclear energy were furthered as key sectors. De Gaulle indefatigably questioned the American hegemony where he could (Paxton/Wahl, 1994). He criticised the international monetary system, based on the primacy of the American dollar. The Bretton-Woods Agreement (July 1944) had laid foundations for a gold-based international monetary system, with a prominent position for the American dollar. De Gaulle blocked the entrance of Great Britain into the European Community, in 1963 and in 1967. In 1962, the "Fonds européen d'orientation et de garantie agricole" was set up, a system to guarantee an income for farmers and to protect them against the vicissitudes of the world market. This system was questioned by commercial partners such as the US (Kennedy Round). Hallstein proposals (31 March 1965), giving EC institutions their own budgetary incomes, and extending powers of the European Parliament when the qualified majority rule would replace decision-making by unanimity, caused a crisis in the EC (30 June 1965). De Gaulle's France didn't accept proposals for financing agriculture (a politically sensitive dossier in France). France left her seat in the EC decision room empty, so no decisions could be taken. This empty-chair politics ended with the Luxemburg compromise (4 May 1966). The qualified majority rule was abandoned. Yearly negotiations about the prices of agricultural products ("Marathons of Brussels") continued (lobbying by farmers).

The student protests of May 1968 ("68") brought a severe political and societal crisis in France. Since the spectacular retirement of President De Gaulle after losing a referendum in 1969, there was some unrest about the chances of the Fifth Republic. This faded away, because De Gaulle's former right-hand as Premier, Pompidou, became President. As a prominent banker, he knew about economic problems. With his Minister of Finance, Giscard d'Estaing, he decided to devalue the franc again in August 1969. In January 1969 the Common Market was about to take effect with the abolition of national tariffs and the introduction of a common system of external tariffs. In 1960 37% of French exports went to countries of the "Union française" (former French colonies) and 22% to the European Community. This was in 1973 5% and 48% respectively. Before the start on 30 June 1970 of negotiations with Great Britain, Denmark, Ireland and Norway about their entry into the EC, France wanted to regulate the financing of the common agricultural policy more definitely. Otherwise than De Gaulle, Pompidou was positive about the entry Unlike De Gaulle, Pompidou was positive about the entry of Great Britain into the EC. He also initiated the Conference in The Hague (1-2 December 1969) which started the project of Economic and Monetary Union (EMU), but it took ten years before the EMU had its real take-off in 1979, replacing the "monetary serpent system" (since 1972). The objective was fixed rates of exchange between the Member-States of the EC, and in the long run a common money system. When Socialists took power in June 1981 President Mitterrand preferred to ride his hobbyhorses of old-fashioned Socialist policies (extending public outlays, nationalisations), so the working week was shortened to 39 hours, a fifth week of paid holiday was given without salary cuts, and the pension age was reduced to 60 years. Partners of France did the opposite in the changed economic circumstances with rigid retrenchment policies, but after a year, Mitterrand decided in June 1982 to follow suit to keep France in the EMU. Forgetting electoral promises, he cut public outlays and had rigid economic policies. Mitterrand chose for the perspective of France as a prominent partner within the European Community. The EC had to be not only a monetary and economic union, but also a social union. A Social Europe was an ambition, taking form in the Treaty of Maastricht (Great Britain opposing). In the EMU it was no longer possible to use devaluation as a competitive weapon. Devaluations of the French franc in October 1981, June 1982 and March 1983 were necessary though.

The question was, time and again, whether French enterprises would be modern and competitive enough to withstand competition in the European Common Market and the world market. Since 1974 more or less, there had been a situation of stagflation (stagnation and inflation). The oil crises of 1973 and 1979 had an important impact, because the price of energy was rising drastically, and so the already stagnating economy, in a dip again for the first time since the period of enduring economic growth during the "Trente Glorieuses" (1945-1975), had a serious problem because the costs of production rose steeply. In the 1960-1973 period the average yearly economic growth rate was above 5%, then it started to fall to 3% up to 1980 and to 1.5% in the period until 1987. From 1988 to 1990, it was 3% again, later falling to 2%. In the period 1973-1992, the number of unemployed had risen to five times higher, from 600,000 to 3 million. France was confronted with an economic crisis like other industrialised countries of the OECD. Inter alia because of much higher energy costs and the competition of newly developed countries. France had some negative factors which were specific. The active professional population grew in the 1971-1991 period by more than 2.5 million. Loss of employment in industry was, up to 1980, compensated by the growth of jobs in the service industries, but between 1980 and 1986 some 500,000 jobs were lost. It was evident that there was serious structural unemployment. Of the group of 2.4 million unemployed in March 1986, one million persons had no financial support, the "new poor". To meet the demands of employers, a law of 28 February 1986 made it easier to fire employees. After the Gaullist victory (March 1986), Government-Chirac had five objectives for the recovery of competitive abilities: less regulation, privatisation of nationalised enterprises, promotion of contractual policies in labour relations, elimination of the budget deficit; reduction of fiscal charges. In July 1986 a list was made of 65 enterprises which had to be privatised, with 10% of shares going to personnel (a Gaullist idea of participation). This privatisation brought the State some 50 billion francs.

Government-Chirac cancelled measures as taken by the Socialist Government: the taxing of large fortunes was cancelled, fiscal amnesty for flight capital and restoration of anonymity for gold transactions. Government-Chirac did not cancel the 39 hour working week, nor the fifth paid week of holidays. Unemployment figures remained dramatically high: 2,654,000 in February 1987. When the Socialists came back into government after the victory of Mitterrand in the presidential elections in 1988, Government-Rocard followed a moderate course. The years 1988 and 1989 were economically relatively favourable, but in 1991 and 1992, the economic situation worsened again, followed by an economic recession in 1993. Economic activity in the years up to 1996 grew on average by 2%. The unemployment situation remained very problematic (Boissonat, 2001; Fitoussi, 1994), not only in France, but in the whole of Europe (Muet, 1994). In 1996, economic growth was 1%, social tensions abounded with many unemployed and many excluded and poor people, "l'exclusion" (CERC, 1993). The "new social question" was prominent on the political agenda (Rosanvallon, 1995). After the coming to power of Government-Jospin in 1997, the number of unemployed diminished with one million. Good news; it fell from 12.6% (more than 3 million unemployed). In January 2001, 9% of the professional population was unemployed, higher than the 8.7% average in the Euro-zone. Some 2.3 million workers were unemployed. Officially the government target is full employment in 2010, based on the report of Jean Pisani-Ferry ("Plein emploi").

The year 2002 was a year of presidential and legislative elections. Neo-Gaullist Chirac won the presidential election (82.5% of the votes) against extreme-rightist Le Pen, who had beaten the Socialist Premier Jospin. Because Jospin resigned promptly, there was a Neo-Gaullist Government-Raffarin in power up to the legislative elections. These produced a victory for Chirac's newly formed electoral cartel, "Union pour la Majorité Présidentielle" (UMP), with 369 seats in the Assembly (total 577 seats). Government-Raffarin II was installed. Premier Raffarin had asked the "Cour des Comptes" to audit the performance of Government-Jospin. The report-Bonnet/Nasse (2002) was an eye-opener. The State budget was expected to have a deficit of 2.3% or 2.6% BNP at the end of 2002 instead of the official 1.4%: not 30, but 45 billion euro. The unfinanced debts of preceding years were some 2 billion euro. Social security had a deficit instead of the announced surplus. The real budget-devouring sectors in 1990 were salaries/pensions (41%), State debt (10%) and other expenses (49%). For 2002 it was: salaries/pensions (44%), State debt (14%) and other expenses (42%). If no drastic measures were taken the projected totals for 2040 were: salaries/pensions (90%), State budget (6%) and other expenses (4%). No easy task then for Government-Raffarin, especially not as Chirac promised cuts in the income tax, among other things, and according to the Maastricht criteria (euro), the State budget has to be balanced in 2004. A sketch follows of social security, health care, environmental, educational and cultural policies.

## 5.7. Social security

In France social security expenditures in 1995 required a budget of 2,300 billion francs (Montalembert, 1995). It was financed mainly by social premiums (paid by employers, employees and the State) and by taxes. Outlays for social security rose from 10% of GNP in 1950 to 30.1% of GNP in 1993. The social security system is seen in France generally as a dear "acquis social", threshold of civilisation, but the system is in crisis because of its costs (Rosanvallon, 1981; 1995). Social security encompasses a broad field: health insurance; insurances for unemployment, invalidity, professional accidents and sickness; pensions; guarantees for a minimal income; social help; maternity help and family assistance. Contemporary organisation of social security is based on new foundations as laid since 1945 (Collective, 1995), but historical developments have their impact. At the start of the 19th century, there was social security for those having landed property. Others had to save for difficult times to survive. Otherwise one had to invoke charity (mostly organised by the Church, or public charity). Public outlays for social affairs were about 0.5% of GNP, against about 30% now. In the 19th century, social security was coupled with having a job. Social security by property was generalised into social security by jobs and related social rights. The role of employment for social security made the plea for full employment popular (Louis Blanc, Proudhon), but the liberal spirit had it that everybody should care for himself. Thiers, in 1850, argued that a legally obligatory insurance was an attack on liberty and property rights.

The July Monarchy is reputed to have made a start with the first grand social law of 22 March 1841, forbidding children dangerous work or work at night, while the minimum age for working children was fixed at 8 years. After 1848, the number of mutual associations for social help grew, and a law of June 1850 brought a "Caisse nationale des retraites". There were "caisses de retraite" for which workers had to pay 6.6% of their salary for 36 years to get a pension of 150 francs a year. Many thought that they would do better to save for themselves: money saved in this way went to the family when one died. In the case of no income from work (unemployment, invalidity, old age), societal movements argued that social insurances had to be organised. A law of 11 July 1868 ruled a "Caisse nationale d'assurance contre les accidents du travail" to encourage employers and employees to organise social insurances. This had little effect. Gradually the difference between "justice commutative" (formal equality of rights) and "justice distributive" (real economic equality) crystallised. More economic equality in society needed the intervention of public authorities. In 1880 the turning point came, Nadaud initiated a parliamentary movement in France for obligatory social insurances. In 1886, a "direction de l'Assistance publique" was created, organising in 1889 a congress in Paris where principles for public assistance were formulated. Germany pioneered social insurances against several risks: sickness (1883), work accidents (1884), invalidity and old age (1889), and death (1891). Great Britain had social insurances early: unemployment (1906), old age (1908) and sickness (1911-1912). In France it took 18 years for the law of 9 April 1898 (accidents at work). There were a number of laws which became part of the "Code de l'aide sociale", such as laws for children (1889 and 1904), needy sick people (1893), indigent old persons and other distressed persons (1905), and big families (1913). The law of 5 April 1910 brought a pension for workers and farmers and laws of 5 April 1928 and 30 April 1930 introduced social insurance for workers (with the lowest salaries) against risks of sickness, invalidity, pregnancy, old age and death. A law of 11 March 1932 facilitated family allowances.

France nevertheless had arrears with regard to other West-European countries. Germany already had its unemployment insurance law in 1929. In France, Unedic ("Union pour l'emploi dans l'industrie et le commerce") was created in 1958 for a nation-wide system of unemployment benefits (paid with a social premium of 0.25% of salaries). In the sixties not more than 50,000 people got these benefits. In 1967, Anpe ("Agence nationale pour l'emploi") was created to further re-employment. These institutions could not handle the massive problems since the 1980s. The number of people getting unemployment benefits in 1990 was more than 1,200,000. For this facility, salaried persons had to pay 7.05% of their salaries. Unedic paid out some 90 billion francs yearly, its accumulated deficit was estimated at nearly 22 billion francs in 1992. To further the opportunities for newcomers in the labour market the victims of mass dismissals over the age of 60 got 70% of their last salary. In 1977 this was lowered to 55 years. Between 1973 and 1989, some 5.3 million persons were removed from the labour market with a package of measures. The pre-pension facility cost about 43 billion francs in 1992. After December 1988, the unemployed who had no right to unemployment benefit any more (estimated to be some 40%) could get the RMI ("Revenu minimum d'insertion"), a minimum benefit costing some 13 billion francs yearly. Expansion of social security in the framework of the welfare state ("L'État-Providence") was by no means uncontroversial. Opposition against legally obligatory sickness insurances was fierce. An often used quote was from a German medical doctor Liek (1929): "Sickness insurance furthers in sick persons a weak body, a weak mind and the perpetuation of sickness." Employers warned of loss of employment due to higher labour costs. Many argued for a free market, without State intervention. In leftist circles the expansion of social security rights was disputed. Social security was seen as a Trojan horse, as it would postpone the collapse of capitalism. Experts and politicians were divided about the principle of legal obligation; financing by pro rata apportionment or otherwise; limitation of rights to guarantee that these could be paid etc., and about the difference between social insurance ("I paid, I have rights.") and a tax-financed public facility (public assistance).

The preamble of the 1946 Constitution for the Fourth Republic (still in force now) was clear: "The Nation guarantees the individual and his family the necessary conditions for their development. It guarantees all, especially children, mothers and older workers, the protection of health and maternity care, tranquillity and recreation. Every human person, who by his or her age, physical or mental condition, or his or her economic situation is not able to work, has the right to obtain from the community reasonable means of subsistence." An ordinance of 4 October 1945 founded modern social security for workers and their families. A law of 22 May 1946 generalised social security, making social insurances obligatory for the whole population. A law of 11 February 1950 created SMIG ("Salaire minumum interprofessionnel garanti") as basic income, in 1970 replaced by SMIC ("Salaire minimum interprofessionnel de croissance"). To break the class struggle ideology Gaullists tried to further participation by workers to overcome the capital-labour controversy. In 1956, a third week of paid holidays was introduced, followed in 1968 by a fourth week. Since 1959 laws made the participation of workers in the profits of enterprises obligatory. A law of 11 November 1990 lowered the number of workers for which enterprises must have participation in profits to 50. Regulation made a section of public functionaries shareholders. An abundant literature about the technicalities of social security is available: Bertrand, 1987; Hirsch, 1994; Lamiot/ Lancry, 1989; Majnoni d'Intignano, 1993; Murard, 1988. As background there are manuals: Alfandari, 1989; Bichot, 1992; Dupeyroux, 1993; Fournier et al, 1989; Join-Lambert, 1994.

From the seventies on, the problem of financial deficits became more urgent. This was marked because the social security system had its own budget, distinct from the State budget. "Plans de sauvetage financier" were launched: plan Durafour (1975), plan Barre (1976), plans Veil (1977/1978), plan Barrot (1979), plan Questiaux (1981), plans Bérégovoy (1982/1983), plan Dufoix (1985), plans Séguin (1986/1987), plans Evin (1988, 1990), plan Bianco (1991), and plan Veil (1993). Between 1974 and the report-Soubi (1994) more than 30 reports were made about the social security system, with reform proposals (Oudin, 1992). Not only the economic legitimacy of social security was questioned ever more, but also its social legitimacy. The "Sécu" could not solve or lessen urgent social problems for the large mass of poor people in a neo-liberal climate (Jobert, 1994). The Report-Oheix (1981) came up with 60 proposals, as f. e. introduction of a minimum income. The "Revenu Minimum d'Insertion" (RMI), financed by taxes, was introduced with the law of 1988. In 1993, about 793,000 households received RMI, some 1,575 million persons (2.7% of population). This number has been rising. The guaranteed minimum income was about 2,400 francs per month in 1995. The social issue is that social rights are no longer based primarily upon having a job, but on being a citizen (social equity and justice as argued by Rawls and others). The State has a prominent impact on the working of the social security system. Inter alia with its juridical rules: "Code de la sécurité sociale"; "Code de la santé publique"; "Code de la famille"; "Code du travail"; "Code des assurances"; "Code de la famille et de l'aide social".

In its main principles, the French complex and differentiated model of social security can be positioned somewhere between the German, Bismarck-model and the English, Beveridge-model (Join-Lambert, 1994). It has been observed that the French system wants to realise the objectives of Beveridge with the instruments of Bismarck (Esping-Andersen, 1990; Palier/Bonoli, 1995). Bismarck (1815-1898) laid a foundation for German social insurances, with the guarantee of a minimum income for workers as the objective. It had the following features: socio-professional social insurances, a decentralised system ("Kassen"), funded by maximised amounts related to salaries, services in proportional relation to salaries (with a maximum), and guarantees for salaries lower than a fixed amount. This brought laws for social insurances against sickness (1883), work accidents (1884), and old age (1889). In 1942 W.H. Beveridge launched his Report to the Parliament of Great Britain, "Social insurance and allied services". The Beveridge-plan, with the fight against poverty as primary target ("freedom from want"), encompassed three proposals: family allowances, the introduction of a national health service, and full employment. Features of his idea for a social security system can be summarised: universal (with a condition about financial resources: means tested); organised by the State; funded from taxes, mostly with a flat rate and obligatory for all.

The French system of social security has some characteristics: social insurances tending to universality; decentralised organisation under State control; combination of taxes and social premiums; services are generally proportional to the social minima; destined for all citizens. Undoubtedly those who tried to give the French system of social security its form after 1945 knew the ideas of Beveridge, though no explicit reference is made to the Beveridge-report in documents about the French plan for social security (Kerschen, 1995). The "plan français de sécurité sociale" got its structure under P. Laroque, director-general of social security at the Ministry of Labour, the "French Beveridge" (Baldwin, 1990; Marshall, 1985). When the French system was developed, it kept its distance with regard to the Beveridge-plan (Baldwin, 1990; Galant, 1955). While Beveridge argued for the unity of the system, the French system adapted to the historical situation by allowing pluralism: autonomy for family allowances, and specific regimes for farmers and other categories. The French rejected State bureaucracy for administration of social security, preferring "gestion démocratique". To win a social and political basis, French leadership chose for participation by representatives of workers and mutual associations. Another difference was, in the beginning, the absence of the unemployment risk in the French system. The State gave support for unemployed, financed by taxes. Since 1958 France has had social insurance against unemployment. The most important difference is probably that there is a prominent role for representatives of workers in the functioning of the French social security system.

As in other Western countries (Lindbeck, 1993) there is an ongoing debate about the crisis of social security and welfare state (Castel, 1995; Meny/Thoenig, 1989; Rosanvallon, 1995). The crisis is a financial crisis in the first place, the "trou de la Sécu" (Foucauld, 1995). The crucial question is how to rescue this dear attainment (Chotard, 1989). About 80% of social security is financed by social premiums ("cotisations"), related to salaries and paid by employers and employees. Yields depend on the economic situation, as do outlays: when unemployment is high, there are many who claim their social security rights. Raising social premiums makes the costs of labour higher, with the risk that unemployment gets worse. It is logical that experts argue that the rights of the social security system have to be reduced. To create a broader basis for receipts of the "Sécu", a new proportional levy on all revenues was introduced in 1989, "Contribution Sociale Généralisé" (CSG). The CSG (tariff 2.4%) was good for 65.5 billion francs in 1994 (Join-Lambert, 1994, p.342), but pressures on the social security system cause problems continuously, especially because new societal problems, or old societal problems (poverty) with new names ("l'exclusion"), aggravate the social situation. In 1974 two eye-opening books were published: "Les exclus" (Lenoir, 1974) and "Vaincre la pauvreté" (Stoléru, 1974). Poverty was re-invented (Jobert, 1981). "Exclusion sociale" means: poverty; long term unemployment; bad living conditions; city problems; handicaps; racism; aids; and immigration. Policies to integrate problem-groups into society were elaborated by Schwartz (1981), Bonnemaison (1983) and Dubedout (1983). Some parts of these social inclusion policies dealt with: positive discrimination on behalf of socially weak persons (at variance with a tradition of universal, equal treatment); differentiated facilities and services, adapted to local, personal circumstances; decentralised organisation and project management (Castel/Laé, 1992; CERC, 1993; Donzelot, 1991; Fragonard, 1993; Merrien, 1994; Paugam, 1993). From 1985 on, urban policies got an impetus, with policies to further solidarity (co-operation of public authorities, social services, enterprises and groups in neighbourhoods).

A specific problem is related to the growing number of elderly people in the population (Creedy, 1995). This will become more acute than before, because from the year 2005 on the baby boom generation will become pensionable in France ("Rapport Charpin"). The French system of pensions is based upon the apportionment method. Social premiums of the active working population are used each year to pay for the pensions in that same year. It would be possible to build up a capitalisation method gradually: premiums of the active working population are used to save for its own pensions. The choices to be made about the "crise de Sécu" are difficult. Outlays related to old age pensions in 1994 were about 900 billion francs, forming 40% of social outlays. Recipients of a pension were estimated at 11 million in 1995. The "Livre blanc sur les retraites" (DF, 1991) said that the deficit of the "Caisse nationale d'assurance-vieillesse des travailleurs salariés" would be 68 billion francs in 2000, and about 100 billion francs in 2015. To cover the structural deficit, government used a 110 billion francs loan in 1994, so postponing the burden to the rising generation. Reform is urgent, but is nearly unworkable due to its painful effects. In January 2001 the French organisation of employers MEDEF advised its members to stop paying supplementary premiums for employees from their 60th (legal age of pension) to their 65th birthdays. Trade unions were upset, organising a general strike. MEDEF argued that the pension system was unaffordable, with more problems coming in the future. Now there are 4 inactive persons for every 10 workers, in 2040 this will become 7 inactive persons for each 10 workers. Workers pay three months salary towards the pension system yearly.

Government-Juppé dared to present the "Plan Juppé" (15-11-1995). Socialists, then in the opposition, didn't deny the necessity of a structural reform though they disputed that the extent of the accumulated deficit of the "Sécu" was 260 billion francs as the government said, they thought it to be 120 billion francs, not a small discrepancy. To cover the deficit, a levy of 0.5% on all incomes was introduced, "Remboursement de la dette sociale" (RDS), and an extended series of cuts in the outlays was planned. The "Plan Juppé" aroused storms of protest. In autumn 1995, enduring strikes (public transport and other public organisations) forced government to change reform proposals. The situation in 1996 and 1997 was also hectic for government-Juppé (unpopular for its retrenchment policies). This made President Chirac bring forward legislative elections from 1998 to 1997, with dramatic losses for the parties supporting government-Juppé, and a spectacular victory for Socialists who with Communists could form government-Jospin (1997-2002). Government-Jospin had now the unpopular task of cutting public outlays, but the economic situation has been better in recent years. The deficit for 1999 was not 4 billion francs as expected, but was transformed into a surplus of 200 billion, after 15 years of deficits. The expected surplus for 2000 was 5 billion francs. In "Economic perspectives" (2000) the OECD forecast improvements in Western Europe, and economic growth in France of 3.75% in 2000. At the end of 2000 there was a forecast surplus for the "Sécu" in 2001 of 4.4 billion francs. An Insee analysis (2001) concluded that poverty had stabilised. In 2000, 7.3% of households lived below the poverty line, some 4.2 million individuals. In 1997 government created a monitor of poverty. Lévy/Pelletier (Le Monde, 13-7-2001) wrote about its first report cynically: "Stay poor, you're being watched!"

## 5.8. Health care

The economics of health care demands a specific approach because of its specific characteristics (Culyer, 1991). Health care has a prominent role in French public social and economic policies (Duriez et al., 1996). The population is entitled to health care, a fundamental right as recognised since 1946 in France, and in the preamble of the World Health Organisation (WHO), "Déclaration universelle des droits de l'homme" (1948) and

"Convention européenne de sauvegarde des droits de l'homme et des libertés fondamentales." (1950). The Constitution of the Fifth Republic guarantees all, especially children, mothers and older workers, protection of their health. Formal recognition of the responsibility of public authorities for health care of the whole population was a historically important fact. Health care, up to the Second World War, was for a number of aspects not organised optimally. During the Middle Ages, there was no public policy in the field of health care. The struggle against sickness was a matter of private initiatives. Health care was seen as a matter of Christian charity. The Church had a dominant position in society and organised health care in dedicated institutions. "Hôtels de Dieu" were administered by parishes, until the French Revolution (Rochaix, 1959). Surgeon Renon said in 1760 that hospitals are a criterion of the level of civilisation. After the French Revolution (1789) the State organised public hospitals. After the suppression of trade unions by the "Loi Le Chapelier" (1791) chains of mutual assistance were built up, ruled by the "Loi sur la mutualité" (1898). The quality of health care improved markedly after the end of the 19th century, and from 1905 on there was medical care free of charge. After the deadly epidemic of Spanish influenza in 1920 France finally got a "Ministère de la Santé Publique". Priority was given to prevention. To implement effective health care, adequate information was needed. Epidemiology developed, to gather data about the health of the population (Harant/Delage, 1984). Up to the 19th century the health situation of the population was defined mainly by mortality figures (data of parishes). Public hospitals were accessible for the indigent, pregnant women and old people. These became organisations for all, later with advanced technologies and medical treatments. Charity was prominent in French society up to the time that social insurances became normal. Then health care became accessible at all levels of society.

Since 1945, health care has had several impulses. Unlike Great Britain, which chose in 1948 for a State-funded system of health care, the tax-based National Health Service (Rivett, 1998), France decided to build up a diversified system under State control. The State determines health care policies, and has a grip on public, private and public-private institutions producing or financing health care services. The State is responsible directly for the operational organisation of health care in military and national hospitals. Municipalities, departments and regions are generally the relevant public authorities for public health care establishments. With regard to the financing, the State (paying as an employer social premiums for public functionaries) contributes only about 1% to the costs of health care. Several ministries have responsibilities, especially the "Ministère de la Santé et de l'Assurance maladie" and "Ministère de l'Économie et des Finances". In the local field: "Directions régionales d'action sanitaire et sociale" and "Directions départementales d'action sanitaire et sociale". From December 1994 health care was reorganised, and since 1995 there has been only one regional tariff; the role of the region in the distribution of the budget became more prominent. Of course, there is a series of specific institutions, such as "Comité fr. d'éducation pour la santé" (1952), "Comité consultatif national d'éthique pour les sciences de la vie et de la santé" (1983), "Conseil national du syndrome immunodéficitaire acquis" (1989), "Agence nationale pour le développement de l'évaluation médicale" (1989), "Délégation générale pour la lutte contre la drogue et la toxicomanie" (1991), 'Agence fr. du sang" (1992), "Agence du médicament" (1993), "Établissement fr. des greffes" (1994), etc. Since 1991, the "Haut Comité de la Santé Publique" has been charged with defining objectives of health care policies, making proposals and evaluating policies. As adequate information about sickness, health and health risks is crucial, systematic gathering of data was organised: "Service des statistiques, des études et des systèmes d'information"; "Institut National de la Santé et de la Recherche Médicale"; Institut National des Statistiques et des Études Économiques"; "Institut National des Études Démographiques".

For an adequate sketch about the system of health care, it is not enough to accentuate the financial aspects. Health care is also an important part of the French productive system with some 1.7 million people working in this sector (Bocognano/Raffy-Pihan, 1995). About 7.4% of the total actively working population works in health care. To rationalise the supply side (hospitals) and to adapt it to the needs and planned norms, a law of 31 December 1970 introduced a "carte sanitaire". With this quantitative instrument ratios for capacities (number of beds per 1,000 inhabitants, etc.) and capacities per territory were calculated. The "Loi hospitalière" (31 July 1991) formalised a system of capacity planning with qualitative criteria. Planning targets were defined per region, the central framework for hospital policies, with "carte sanitaire" and "Schéma Régional d'Organisation Sanitaire" (SROS) as instruments. With the "carte sanitaire" operational capacities were fixed in relation to size of population, data about medical urgency etc. This is used to give subsidies, especially for expensive equipment. The SROS ensures that medical activities and equipment are distributed over a region, to realise such objectives as quality, accessibility and cost control. The SROS is also used to reduce the number of beds in hospitals. Public hospitals got more autonomy regarding their exploitation, but the budget and the creation of medical capacities were subject to preceding control. Public establishments in 1994 had about 348,000 hospital beds whilst private hospitals had about 35% of the total (546,423 beds, or 9.2 beds per 1,000 inhabitants). Public and private hospitals (commercial and non profit making establishments) differ in several dimensions. Apart from the juridical statute (public or private), the notion "service public hospitalier" is used. Introduction in 1984 of the "Financement par dotation globale" for all establishments working as "service public hospitalier", fulfilling preordained norms, made them different from commercial hospitals. In addition to medical doctors and other professionals working in hospitals, many professionals work in other units.

In 2001, statistical life expectancy in France was 83 years for women, and 75.5 years for men. Yearly about 526,000 people die (9.2 per 1,000 inhabitants). Important causes of death (accounting for some 2/3 of the total of deceased) are: heart and vascular diseases (169,000); tumours (142,000); trauma and accidents (48,000), of which some 10,000 in traffic, 1,000 accidents at work and 20,000 accidents at home; lung diseases (38,000); food canal disorders (26,000). Risk factors have an important impact, especially those due to the "social scourges" (aids, drugs, alcohol, tobacco). For France (highest consumption of alcohol worldwide), alcohol is an important risk factor (Malignac, 1992). About 99.8% of the French population is protected by health insurance, administered by "Régime général de la Sécu" (about 80% of the population), "Mutalité sociale agricole" (some 9%), "Caisse nationale d'assurance maladie des professions indépendantes" (about 6%), and smaller units. Prominent are organisations of social partners (employers/employees). "Caisse nationale d'assurance maladie des travailleurs salariés"; "Caisses régionales d'assurance maladie"; "Caisses primaires d'assurance maladie". To cover rising costs, the social premium has had to be raised repeatedly. Since 1 January 1992, the employer had to pay 12.8% and the employee 6.8% of gross salaries. The normal health insurance covers about 3/4 of medical costs. There are complementary arrangements: about 6,500 "mutuelles" (mutual associations) for more than 30 million persons (covering 6.6% of the costs of medical treatments); 20 "institutions de prévoyance" (covering some 1.3% of health care costs); and about 80 private insurance companies. According to the law of 29 July 1992, all persons and their dependents living in France have the right to medical aid. When they cannot pay the costs, the "Sécu" pays the bills.

From the viewpoint of social justice, French health care scored reasonably well in the 1990s, generally speaking, but socio-economic factors determining the health situation of the population cause pressures: living conditions; work circumstances; unemployment; life styles; inequalities of income and circumstances; environmental situation; etc. The French system of health care in the first years of the 21st century is confronted with many difficult choices (Soubié, 1993): rising costs; ageing population; problems of the "new poverty" ("exclusion"); developments in technology and medical treatments; environmental circumstances to name but a few. In the coming period the number of elderly people will rise, absolutely and relatively with regard to other groups of the population. This causes problems in the sphere of costs. Total costs of health care in France were about 748.8 billion francs in 1994; that is 10.2% of BNP, or 12,934 francs per person yearly. Medical consumption took the biggest part of it: 668.2 billion francs; 9.0% of BNP, or 11,540 francs per person yearly. Elderly people (multiple pathology) cost more than younger persons. Those of 65 years and older (now 14% of the population, and 16% in 2010) use medical care facilities two or three times more than other people on the average (CREDES, 1994). For 2015, calculations show, that persons of 65 years and older will realise 60% of total medical consumption (those older than 75 years one-third). An institutional renovation, as elaborated in "Santé 2010" (Soubié, 1993), is intended to further social justice and efficacy. Since the first of January 2000, the law about the "Couverture-Maladie Universelle" (CMU) has been in operation. It guarantees healthcare for low-income groups. Its costs are covered with a premium of 8% of incomes above 42,000 francs yearly. The report of the "Haut Comité de la Santé Publique" (2002) provides information. In health care, work must be done in impossible situations (Vallancien, Le Monde, 20-4-2001).

## 5.9. Environmental policies

Environmental policies are crucial for health. Environment encompasses all natural and other aspects affecting the living conditions of human beings, determining their biological and cultural situation. The economics of exhaustible resources (Heal, 1993) makes it evident that adequate management of the environment is essential for humanity. The "Living Planet Report" (1998) of the World Wildlife Fund is clear about this. Environmental issues are structurally underrated in the market (positive and negative externalities), so ecological policies to manage environmental conditions are a crucial part of Public Management of Society (Folmer c.s., 1995; Oates, 1996). Environmental economics became a top priority in public policy (Oates, 1996). Adequate cost-benefit analysis is useful to protect vital interests of sustainable development (Hanley/Spash, 1993; Tisdell, 1993). Braden c.s (1996) compared environmental policies in European Union and US. The French Ministry of Environment (1996) made a survey of economic data in relation to the environment for France. Mathieu (1994) wrote that the French don't bother about the risks of a deteriorating environment. Probably, it is in France much as it is in other developed countries, where the importance and consequences of environmental factors are undervalued, but public consciousness about environmental dimensions and public environmental policies have developed, especially since the Club of Rome Report about "Limits to Growth" (1966). It is a false idea that society is ungovernable with regard to environmental issues. Environmental deficiencies are due to deficient Public Management of Society (Dror, 1997). Protection of environment is not (yet) a formal, constitutional principle, as in other countries but article 1 of the law about the protection of nature (10 July 1976) defined the width of the task adequately. Other legal regulations are relevant too. French environmental circumstances and policies have to be positioned in an international, global perspective. The "Plan National pour l'Environnement" (PNE) of 1990 put the task into an international perspective. To manage these problems, public management on a local, national and global level is needed (Mathieu, 1994, p.4). France participates in international activities to further international quality of environmental aspects worldwide. The Intergovernmental Panel on Climate Change (IPCC) made evaluation reports in 1990 and 1995, and in 2001 was more pessimistic about warming up of the planet.

Public authorities, of course, had policies regarding aspects of the environment long before the notion environment was used. In 1971, a "Ministère de l'Environnement" was created to co-ordinate the activities of the State. Municipalities, departments and regions had their environmental policies too. A law of 7 January 1983 determined the competencies of the State and territorial public bodies with regard to environmental policies. Many organisations were built up to develop and implement environmental policies. Ministry of Environment. Interministerial structures: "Haut Comité de l'environnement", "Conseil pour les droits des générations futures", "Commission supérieure des sites, perspectives et paysages", and consultative organs like "Conseil national du bruit" and others. The State has its role via "établissements publics" like the "Agence de l'environnement et de la maîtrise de l'énergie". To organise information about the environment systematically, the "Institut français de l'environnement" was created in 1992. With regard to the territory of regions, departments and municipalities, the Ministry of the Environment has had direct representation since 1991. On the regional level with "Directions régionales de l'environnement". The prefect implements policies with regard to the environment. One of the most specific instruments for public authorities is the production and implementation of legal regulations. Generally speaking, a reasonably effective environmental legal system has not yet been realised in France (Prieur, 1991). The environmental law system is weak (Mathieu, 1994, p.23). Property rights are better protected in France than environmental rights. There is no legal text declaring that the right to an environment of reasonable quality is a "droit inviolable et sacré". It is often impossible to prove juridically that activities caused ecological damage in order that some individual organisation could be obliged to compensate for damages.

Ecological damage often has a definite character, as restoration is impossible. The general ecological interest is not adequately represented, ruled and implemented. To bring environmental and economical aspects more into balance in decision-making processes, it is advisable to calculate the costs and benefits of environmental aspects, especially those for which there is no market (Barde/Pearce, 1991). Environmental rulings impair economic interests, often more strongly than ecological interests. For some aspects repressive regulations to protect the environment have been made more effective: for water, "loi sur l'eau" (3 January 1992); for waste, "loi relative à l'élimination des déchets." (13 July 1992); for noise, "loi relative à la lutte contre le bruit" (31 December 1992). As regards urbanisation projects, their impact upon the environment has to be reckoned with. A report must make explicit the effects on the environment of the choices made in the "schémas directeurs" (SD). Public authorities are expected to prevent ecologically damaging projects. The massive disaster at the end of 1999 due to storms of huge force, showed that this kind of disaster cannot be prevented. Public authorities must prepare for natural disasters. "Plans d'Occupation des Sols" for building activities must report about measures to guarantee ecological values. To engage actors with policies for sustainable development, the Ministry of Environment makes ecological contracts with local authorities, and commits enterprises with a "Plan Environnement Entreprise". Recently, Deneux (2002) presented his rather alarming analysis of climatic changes in France for the years to come, up to 2025, 2050 and 2100. His report has about a hundred recommendations.

### 5.10. Educational and cultural policies

It is a truism that adequate education systems are important to structure society. The economic value of education is obvious (Blaug, 1992). Economics of education is a part of multidisciplinary analyses about education (Cohn/Johnes, 1994). The contemporary French education system is profoundly steeped in traditions, ideas and practices from the past (Leon, 1967; Minot, 1986; Ponteil, 1966; Prost, 1968; Vasconcellos, 1993). The 1881-1882 laws of Jules Ferry are seen as a decisive caesura. Developments from the Enlightenment, and even before that period are relevant. The program of alphabetisation started during the Ancien Régime (Furet/Ozouf, 1977). Up to the 17th century, there were "petites écoles paroissales" under the authority of bishops and monasteries. After the 16th century, printed texts furthered a generalised need to be able to read. The Reformation had its impact, because it appealed to its believers to read the Bible personally. The Contra-Reformation also wanted to ensure that children could read. The Roman-Catholic Church built up schools all over the country free of charge, run by religious brethren and female congregations. This system of education with lessons from a teacher and exercises was the model for later public schools. With the "Déclaration royale" (18 December 1698), the principle of education under control of the State and the Church was laid down. Since the Middle Ages there have been several universities. The oldest university is that of Paris (1208/1209), followed by other towns such as Montpellier (1220), Toulouse (1360) etc. Pupils with command of reading, writing and Latin could be registered at faculties, to get a grade: "baccalauréat", "licence", or "maîtrise ès arts". The last grade qualified for the three higher faculties leading to the doctorate in theology, law and medicine. From the 16th century on, universities deteriorated as a consequence of the rigid religious framework and formalism of theology in the grip of scholasticism. In 1530, King François I established the "Collège royal", since 1852 the "Collège de France".

At the beginning of the 16th century, there were no educational establishments between primary schools and universities (Chartier c.s., 1976). In some larger towns there were "écoles de grammaire", with training in Latin and preparation for higher education. Between 1556 and 1640 the Jesuits established a network of 70 colleges for boys. Congregations like the Dominicans did the same. Fénélon (1651-1715) after Bossuet the most important prelate under Louis XIV, argued for the education of girls in his "Traité de l'éducation des filles" (1687). Female congregations like the Ursulines started boarding schools for girls. From the second half of the 18th century, new insights were breaking through about the organisation of colleges. Schools of religious brethren gave lessons in technical subjects (printing trade, bookkeeping) and professional education. The "École des Ponts et Chaussées" (1747) was a model for the "Grandes Écoles" for which an entrance examination was needed. Then came schools preparing for this examination. In 1751, the "École militaire" started in Paris, followed by 12 other establishments. Suppression of the "Compagnie de Jésus" in 1762 and the expulsion of the Jesuits from France brought reorganisation of the colleges. "Concours d'agrégation" were obligatory from 1766 to guarantee the level of knowledge and good education of teachers. The idea of organising education in public schools under State control gained ground. At the end of the Ancien Régime, education as organised by the Church was criticised. Condorcet argued in "Tableau historique des progrès de l'esprit humain" for public schools for emancipation. The "Déclaration de Lamoignon" (1783) had it, that public schools were "d'utilité générale et pour le bien de l'État". The former Jesuit colleges came under State control.

Before the French Revolution, ideas of the Enlightenment concerning education had their impact (Lelièvre, 1991). During discussions in the revolutionary assemblies, the importance of education as an instrument to further national unity was emphasised. Condorcet produced his report on education in April 1792. Primary schools were seen as essential to transmit ideas of the Enlightenment to the population. Condorcet argued for free, non-religious primary schooling; equality of boys and girls; and an obligatory program of lessons (reading, writing, calculating, grammar, moral opinions). The proposal of Le Pelletier de Saint-Fargeau was for an obligatory boarding school for girls and boys (5-11 years), with citizenship formation and physical education. In 1792, religious congregations were forbidden, the religious had to take an oath of loyalty to the Republic. Military academies and universities disappeared. After 1794, compulsory primary schooling was abolished (lack of finances, opposition of families). Primary schooling was seen as a task for local authorities. From 1796 on, there were "écoles centrales départementales" for secondary education, with a different character from the former colleges, and following the ideas of Condorcet. The "Convention" decided to start establishments for training engineers and the "École centrale de travaux publics" (1794), later to become "École polytechnique". Its pupils finished their training in professional schools: "Mines", "Ponts et Chaussées", "Génie civil". Faculties of medicine were replaced by "écoles de santé". Institutions were established as "Muséum national d'histoire naturelle", "Institut nationals des sciences et des arts", "Conservatoire national des arts et métiers".

In 1802, the "écoles centrales départementales" were abolished. Colleges were established by municipalities or by private initiatives, and "lycées" under responsibility of the State. In 1806, the Imperial University was created with a monopoly for the whole university system. No educational institute could be created outside the competence of this prestigious Imperial University. All existing institutes came under its control, directed by the "grand maître", nominated by the Emperor himself. France was geographically divided up in 28 "académies" with a rector as manager and representative of the "grand maître" (Lelièvre, 1991). The educational system was militarily-hierarchically organised by the State. Although this model was abolished later, it had its influence upon the developing national educational system. Religiously based educational institutions campaigned against the State monopoly, by pleading for freedom of education. Return of religious congregations made it possible to build up schools by religious brethren and nuns again. The State tried to get some control. With regard to primary schools it handled such criteria as respect for the law, sovereignty of the State, and minimum requirements for teachers. In 1816, teachers had to have a "brevet de capacité". With the establishment of "lycées" after 1802, Latin became an important subject again. With the "Loi-Guizot" (1833), the State tried to regulate primary schools. Each municipality with more than 500 inhabitants had to have a public school, teaching: morals, religious development; reading; writing; French; and calculation. Each department should have an "école normale". Guizot promoted the editing of schoolbooks (harmonisation of the teaching program), and a corps of inspectors for primary schools. From the Second Republic (February 1848), teachers were expected to transmit the ideals of the Republic to the young.

Minister Falloux made Parliament adopt the "Loi-Falloux" (March 1850), governing the freedom of secondary education. In 1867 Minister Duruy decided to introduce secondary education for girls. Only some municipalities organised this kind of schooling. It was abolished again under the Second Empire (Mayeur, 1979). Roman-Catholic colleges were popular, due to the quality of education given there. Jesuits returned and beginning in 1870 opened 27 colleges. In the Third Republic a passionate debate about education was going on again. After the defeat against Prussia, there was a general call for better education. It was thought that French education was lagging behind. A law of 1879 obligated each department to have an "école normale" for girls, as this school existed already for boys (Delsaut, 1992). In Fonteney (1880) an "école normale supérieure" was created for female teachers at "écoles normales" for girls, and in Saint Cloud (1882) for teachers at boys schools. "Lois-Ferry" (1881/1882) introduced free education with a non religious character. Citizenship and moral development replaced religious education. Tensions between Republicans and adherents of religious education flared up after the Ferry-laws. The school was seen as an important institution to further national unity (but in an anticlerical mood). Religion and regional languages were banned from study programs. Families were free to give their own children a religious education. In the period 1880-1914, the religious question in education was at the centre of a passionate political debate. The Church claimed authority over schools due to its mission for spiritual development. The Church administered more than 90% of private education and demanded freedom of education. Republicans sharpened adherence to the 1789 principles by forcing conflicts with their anti-religious, anticlerical activism. The conflict had its apex in 1904, when Minister Combes formulated the rights of the State in an anticlerical animosity. The formalised split between State and Church (1905) was a blessing in disguise. This institutional arrangement was placed in a vindictive political atmosphere (anti-clericals versus Catholics).

After the First World War there was a relatively stable situation regarding religion and schooling. Leftist parties gave priority to economic questions. After 1929, the Church recognised that the State could interfere in education. A group for secularised education claimed a State monopoly for education whilst the Church claimed liberty of education. Between 1880 and 1900, primary schools served almost all children of school age, from 6 to 13 years (Furet/Ozouf, 1977). The certificate of primary education, "certificat d'études primaires" (CEP) had a societally important function. The structure of the educational system was based on the division into primary and secondary education. Primary education, obligatory and free for all children, was finished with the CEP. In the secondary education for "baccalauréat", which was not free, the number of children from less favoured families was limited. Good pupils went to "lycées" for general forming and preparation for university. In the years 1880-1902, there was debate about the choices to be made (classical versus modern education). In the years before 1914, reform of schooling was pleaded for constantly. The manifesto "L'Université nouvelle" (1918) argued for an equal basic education for all children. The project "l'école unique" aimed at bringing the pupils of municipal schools and "lycées" into one school. Controversies in teaching staff abounded.

Revolutionary workers launched the movement "Émancipation de l'instituteur" (1903) and the journal "L'école émancipée" (1910). During the war there was no time for activities to reform education. In September 1919, the reform movement of Léon Jouhaux (CGT) was transformed into a "Syndicat national des instituteurs" (SNI), which proposed obligatory schooling up to 14 years. Education in nursery schools ("maternelle") was mixed for boys and girls and in "écoles primaires supérieures" in smaller municipalities, from the start of the Third Republic in 1924, a circular ordained that girls could attend lessons in boys' schools if necessary. After 1926, "secondaires" with less than 150 pupils were mixed, but up to the end of the 1950s mixed schools were the exception. With "collèges d'enseignement secondaire" (CES) since 1963, mixed schools became the norm. A circular of 15 June 1965 made primary schools mixed. The "Loi Haby" (1975) formulated mixed schooling as an obligation, to further the equality of chances. In a circular of 22 July 1982 mixed schooling was seen as an objective of egalitarian schooling (Lelièvre, 1991). Around 1900 only 2.3% of university students were female, this was 26% in 1930, and also in the sixties. In 1975, girls formed half of the students, in 1987 53%. Girls lagged behind in university education, preparing classes for "grandes écoles" and industrial sections of the IUT. Girls were over-represented in female professions, health care and education (Baudelot/Establet, 1990).

After 1945 the schools question (public versus private, religious education) returned to the political agenda again. The "Lois Marie et Barangé" (1951) gave grants to students of private schools. Premier Debré wanted to solve the school question once and for all with a compromise acceptable to all. The "Loi Debré" (1959) created the "contrat d'association", on the basis of which the State paid the costs of teaching staff and other exploitation costs, when some conditions were fulfilled. So the staff of colleges could be modernised with personnel having the same professional background as public schools. Catholic schools, which organised themselves as a public service on a par with public schools, could sign a contract with the State, in two variants (with a program as determined by the State, or a limited program with freedom to set a curriculum). This had its price: the State would get control of private schools. The "Loi Guermeur" (1977) accentuated State financing, but autonomy of private schools was increased (Prost, 1992). The share of pupils in the total of private schools diminished from 20% (1925) to 15% in 1992. Up to the fifties, parents sent their children to private schools due to animosity against the non-religious public schools. Later this diminished markedly. Private schools left religious development to parishes. A school was chosen for pedagogical considerations and quality of education. The "querelle de l'école" was arousing political passions again in the years 1983-1984. Socialists, after a long period in the opposition, seized the momentum to promote their ideas about the reform of education. They stressed the symbolic, ideological meaning of their reform proposals, so activating opposition groups in society. Minister Savary came up with a proposal about higher education, giving more power to the already mighty trade unions in the field of national education. Opposition in parliament deposed 1,400 amendments, but could not stop adoption. Another project was more upsetting. It was about reforming the relations between public authorities and private, mainly Roman Catholic, education. The Socialist government had touched a very sensitive nerve, a consequence of a struggle between State and Church for more than a century. Since 1945, freedom of education outside public schools had not been the issue. Adherents of the Roman Catholic education system claimed financial aid for private schools as a right, and opposed the idea that only public schools should receive adequate support. Adherents of public schools claimed that the State should not subsidise private schools.

Pressure groups made themselves known. The APEL ("Associations de parents d'élèves de l'enseignement libre"), active since 1930 and representing some 800,000 families and teacher's trade unions. On the other side, the CNAL ("Comité national d'action laïque"), co-ordinating among others the "Fédération de l'Éducation nationale", "Ligue de l'enseignement" and "Fédération des conseils de parents d'élèves de l'école laïque". In the common government program of 1972 the "Parti Socialiste" (PS) proposed the nationalisation of private schools. The PS claimed that subsidies to private schools should be followed by nationalisation of these schools. Mitterrand, leading the PS in elections, came forward with 110 proposals. One of these was the creation of a "grand service unifié et laïque de l'enseignement public". A proposal of Savary (December 1982) was criticised by the "Comité national de l'enseignement catholique". His adapted proposal of October 1983 was unacceptable for adherents of the "école laïque". Minister Savary published his new proposal in March 1984. Both sides organised mass manifestations. The mass demonstration on 24 June 1984, in defence of the liberty of education, gathered more people than that in 1968. Confronted with this massive opposition, President Mitterrand decided to withdraw the Savary-project. In the Fifth Republic (1958-), the educational system has its structure for the time being (Charlot, 1987; Durand-Prinborgne, 1989; Gaulupeau, 1992). Reforms in 1959 and 1975 ("Loi Haby") were important. Education has an important position in French society. About 1 out of 18 persons in the active professional population works in education. There are some 63,000 primary schools, and more than 11,000 secondary schools. The Ministry of Education organised 28 geographically divided areas, "académies". Each academy has a seat in the capital of the region, under authority of a "recteur", nominated by the Council of Ministers.

Since the decentralisation law (2 March 1982) competencies were redistributed between State and local public authorities. The State is responsible for study programs; formation of the cadre; creation of educational institutes; provision of didactic materials and higher education. Local public authorities for evaluating needs; construction, maintenance and renovation of schools; formulating targets and pre-calculated personnel development, made by the regional council; transport of pupils and school canteens. The region is responsible for "lycées", the department for colleges, municipalities for schools. Almost 3/4 of the personnel of the Ministry of Education (in 1992 more than one million) belongs to the teaching staff. The proportion of women is high (62%), especially in primary schools (75%). Some 300,000 persons work in nursery schools and primary schools. About 400,000 teachers work for colleges, "lycées" and "lycées professionnels", training for CAP ("Certificat d'aptitude professionnelle"), BEP ("Brevet d'études professionnelles", or professional baccalaureate. The IUFM ("Instituts universitaires de formation des maîtres") with a two-year course play a prominent role in the development of teachers. Certified teachers and "professeurs agrégés", graduates in a specific subject, teach in "lycées", CPGE ("Classes préparatoires aux grandes écoles", IUT (Institut universitaire de technologie"), universities, and STS ("Sections de techniciens supérieures"). In 1992, there were some 3,200 "professeurs certifiés", and about 4,000 "professeurs agrégés". ATOS ("administratif, technique, ouvrier de service et de santé") personnel account for about 1/4 of total personnel.

To become "professeur agregé" one can go to university. The best testimonials after training come from one of the four ENS ("Écoles normales supérieures") in Sèvres-Jourdan, Ulm; Fontanay-Saint-Cloud; Lyon; and Cachan. To fulfil entry requirements one must prepare oneself, after the baccalaureate, for two years. Higher education is given in universities; IUT; grand "établissements publics" like "Collège de France"; "École des hautes études en sciences sociales", etc.; "Grandes Écoles" like ENS or ENA, institutes for training engineers etc. A law of 1989 created "Centres d'initiation à l'enseignement supérieur" to train university teachers and researchers. "Attachés temporaires et de recherche" have contracts on a temporary basis. The "dépense intérieure d'éducation", the total of education outlays, rose more than GNP: from 292.5 billion (price level 1992), 6.3% of GNP in 1974, to 460.6 billion francs in 1992 (6.6% of GNP; 28,100 francs per pupil, and 8,050 francs per inhabitant). About 58% is chargeable to the Ministry of Education, other ministries pay some 8%. Enterprises pay more than 6%, mainly with "taxe d'apprentissage" (0.5% of wages) and tax on professional training (1.2% of wages). Households pay more than 9%. Since the decentralisation law (1982), local authorities (regions, departments, municipalities) pay 18% (in 1980 14%).

The costs per category of education, per pupil, differ substantially, from 15,600 francs for nursery schools to 121,500 francs for engineers. The costs per pupil were 392,000 for the baccalaureate, and for the "brevet d'études professionnelles" 354,000 francs, for a "bachelier professionnel" 437,000 francs, for students of the "diplôme universitaire de technologie" 497,000 francs (Vasconcellos, 1993). The French educational system came under pressure in the last decades because of mass education, inadequate educational infrastructure and lack of adaptation to the needs of society and the labour market. Proposals for reforms were launched (Fauroux, 1996). The value of university certificates on the labour market was diminishing because of the great number of certified students seeking a job. Having a certificate was no longer a guarantee of getting a job as before. Nevertheless, it is expedient to work and to study for certificates. As a consequence of high levels of unemployment, it has become more difficult to get a job, especially for those without a certificate. Having a certificate is a necessary condition for getting a reasonable job but not a sufficient condition. In the eighties a political objective had it that 80% of those attending school should attain "BAC". For the generation up to 15 years, the proportion achieving the baccalaureate did rise from 34% (1980) to 70% (1994). In 1994, there were some 2.1 million students, of which 1.4 million were registered at universities. The level of schooling of the active population rose in France. At the beginning of the seventies some 60% had no certificate (apart from the "certificat d'études"). In 1995 this was less than one-third. One out of five of the active professional population has a certificate of higher education, as against one out of twenty in the late sixties (INSEE, 1996). Proposals to improve education are elaborated in the excellent Fauroux-report,

"Pour l'École" (1996). Minister of Education, Allègre, tried to reform secondary education, growing from 300,000 to 3 million pupils in 40 years. Trade union SNES (communist roots) opposed, claiming ever more personnel. Premier Jospin distanced himself from Allègre, who resigned (Allègre, 2000).

## 5.11. Cultural engineering and "Francophonie"

In important parts of Western Europe, including France, Latin was used as the official language during the Middle Ages and later (Waquet, 1998). For French public authorities it was already clear early that language is a prominent carrier of culture and community building. King François I signed the "Ordonnance de Villers-Cotterêts" (5 August 1539). This ordered that public acts had to be formulated in French, and that all tribunals had to use French, instead of the Latin which was common then. A decree of "2 thermidor an II" (20 July 1794) ordered public functionaries to use French on penalty of 6 months imprisonment. With regard to dialects as practised in France, the "Décret Lakanal du 27 Brumaire an III" (17 November 1794) ordered that French had to be the language in primary schools (dialects were tolerated as an auxiliary tool). In more recent times, the Law of 31 December 1975 is notable. French language was made obligatory in indications, offers, presentations, written or spoken publicity, and directions for the use of an article or product. With a constitutional law (26 June 1992) the 1958 Constitution was supplemented in article 2 with: "La langue de la République est le français.": The language of the Republic is French. In 1993 the "Conseil Constitutionnel" adapted the law of Minister Toubon about the use of French language. The State can oblige enterprises and private persons, involved in fulfilling a public service, to use French, but, referring to the freedom of communication as proclaimed by the "Déclaration des droits de l'homme" (1789), the use of foreign terms for which there is a French equivalent cannot be forbidden. Worldwide there are some 3,000 languages, but the position of the French language is impressive. Some 44 countries are part of "Francophonie institutionnelle" (Deniau, 1995; Dollot, 1992). In international relations and diplomacy, French is prominent. Many public and private organisations are active in the promotion of "Francophonie" (Chatton/ Mazuryk Bapst, - 1991). Since 1973, there is a yearly "Francophonie" conference of heads of state.

Several organisations are active, as "Agence de coopération culturelle et technique"; "Haut-Conseil de la francophonie"; "Conseil supérieur de la langue française"; "Délégation générale à la langue française"; "Agence pour l'Enseignement français à l'étranger". Private organisations like "Association francophone d'amitié et de liaison"; "Alliance française", with the objective "diffusion de la langue et de la civilisation française"; "Association des écrivains de langue française"; "Conseil international de la langue française". More than 100 million people speak French worldwide; in Europe 61 million, in Africa more than 22 million, and in Canada 6.5 million. Many citizens of the world speak French as a second language. In "L'invention de la France" (1981), Le Bras and Todd assert that France forms a single entity in cultural terms only, due to anthropological and ethnological divisions. France is of old a prominent pioneer in cultural policies and the public management of culture (Duby/ Mandrou, 1984). King Louis XIV, "Roi Soleil", made France the world cultural centre by his pompous "maecenate" (Brebisson, 1993). In the Third Republic the State was active in the cultural field (Genet-Delacroix, 1993). Farchy/Sagot-Duvauroux (1993) analysed the economics of French cultural policies and Mollard (1994, p.3) sketched French cultural policies in the framework of cultural engineering: "Cultural engineering is the capacity to find optimal solutions – in terms of quality, costs and delivery times – for the demands, as expressed by participants in cultural life, for objectives, implementation of programs, mobilisation of financing, and technical realisation of projects." Cultural engineering includes all activities to optimise energies in producing, preserving and distributing cultural products, by realising a synthesis between rationality and creativity. It is meant to professionalise activities. This cultural management approach tackles the money problem explicitly. This is different from the popular attitude: culture is all and don't bother about the money needed. According to Mollard, the "Centre Pompidou" is a marked innovation in the framework of cultural engineering. The French cultural system is a mixture of market and State intervention (Fumaroli, 1991). Democratisation of culture is a prominent task of the State, to be realised with a variety of instruments (subsidising, etc.). Mostly the multiplier effect of subsidies is used: by giving a subsidy of 20%, the State mobilises 80% to be paid by regions, departments and municipalities. The State budget is used for nearly 50% for conservation (museums, archives, cultural heritage); 30% for diffusion of culture; and the rest for cultural development and the promotion of creative activities. Educational establishments are often administered by the State, like "École du Louvre", "École nationale du patrimoine", "Conservatoire national de musique", and "Fondation européenne des métiers de l'image et du son" (FEMIS).

Since the decentralisation laws (1982/1983) cultural policies have a different character (Fumaroli, 1991; Rioux, 1991). Territorial public authorities are free to undertake cultural activities. Territorial public authorities (regions, departments, municipalities) that like to mobilise State subsidies, have to close contracts with the State (Latarjet, 1991). Drawbacks are the length of negotiations and multiple responsibilities. Municipalities form the base level for cultural activities. Departments have differing activities, they may or may not have departmental museums and music schools, subsidised theatres, etc. Regions mostly help municipal projects. There are also "Fonds régionaux d'art contemporaine", regional orchestra, etc. It would be wrong to reduce cultural activities to that which is organised by public authorities. In the sphere of culture, the market also plays an important role. The "marché de la Culture" is formed by all cultural products and services, delivered by private producers for market prices, and by public distributors often charging a fee, which does not cover the costs.

The boundaries of the cultural market are rather fluid, though. Although it is difficult to get adequate figures, the cultural market was estimated at some 180 billion francs in 1993 (audio-visual services 85 billion, television 40 billion, books 20 billion, modern and classical art 15 billion, cinema 5 billion). The impact of the intervention of public authorities varies. If the entrance fees for museums were to cover the costs, they would need to be 200 francs. If the "Opéra" in Paris were not subsidised, it would cost 2,000 francs per seat. All in all the total cultural consumption was estimated at 250 billion francs in 1990 (Donnat/Cogneau, 1990). It must not be forgotten that cultural activities create employment, some 500,000 people have jobs in this branch. Busson (1993) and Evrard (1993) show that the management of cultural activities is quite different from management in other branches. The wars over the French cultural identity continue, as in the period 1900-1945 (Lebovics, 1992). The trained common consciousness about the past and the "cult of the greatness of the fatherland" (Gildea, 1994) are a kind of substitute for a national religion. On the basis of several criteria, France can be seen as pioneering in the field of cultural economics. The extravagant exposure by the "Roi Soleil", Louis XIV, as Maecenas furthering arts and culture by all means, had a great impact worldwide. Since then French governments in different regimes have invested prominently in cultural capital goods. Not for nothing is there wide consensus in French society about the relevance of education, investment in human capital, as a prominent part of both public and private sector. After the Second World War the economics of art and culture has been presented internationally as a more or less specific branch of economics, especially since the seventies. Studies of Baumol/Bowen (1966), Schneider/Bonjean (1973), Throsby/Withers (1979), Herdon (1980), Galbraith (1983), and others laid some foundations. There is a full-blown field of cultural economics. Some studies are: Bourdieu (1993), Crane (1992), Frey/Pommerehne (1989), Grampp (1989), Heilbrun/Gray (1994), Klamer (1996). Several arguments are used to deal with arts and culture in cultural economics: positive externalities (not to realise via the market); merit goods; public goods. Cultural policies and politics are a topic (Djian, 1996; Moulinier, 1999; Poirrier, 2000; Saint-Pulgent, 1999).

## 5.12. Concluding remarks

The survey in this study shows that it is worthwhile to acquaint oneself with the specificity of French socio-economic history, ideas, policies and practices. In the framework of this study it is not possible to give a complete picture but the extensive list of literature can be consulted fruitfully. French history has a wide field of policy successes and policy fiascos. French traditions of Public Management of Society are an inspiring laboratory for institutional engineering. Mutatis mutandis, French experiences, ideas and practices present ample lessons for contemporary society worldwide. An important structural aspect of the French way of Public Management of Society is integration of socio-economic policies in a generalised institutional framework. France can be qualified as a pioneering nation in institutional engineering. There is an ongoing debate about the adequacy of its system of Public Management of Society, especially due to huge problems in contemporary France. To mention some of them: overburdening of the social security system; unemployment, poverty, "exclusion"; problems of old age; environmental challenges; European integration (expansion with new members); globalisation; problems of developing countries; worldwide financial crises. It is useful to give the floor to Crozier for some comments. The relative excess of socio-economic interventionism in France was a regular target for criticisms abroad, but also in France itself. Crozier (1970) made himself the mouthpiece of the critics with his diagnosis about the blocked society. The fundamental problem of French society was seen in the urgent need for modernisation in the style of human relations, models of authority, and methods of collective decision-making. His diagnosis, that a qualitative modernisation was needed, was confirmed later. President Pompidou reacted to the illusionism of May 1968 with his economic-quantitative strategy to further industry by entrusting economic future to technocratic elites. The results of French industries were impressive, at a high societal cost. Social unrest was redeemed with benevolent social security and rising wages, making inflation structural, with effects in the long run. After the Gaullist-Giscardian era (1958-1981), the Socialist take-over in 1981 promised changes.

Socialists could ride their ideological hobbyhorses, accentuating nationalisations. Enterprises should in their view be part of the community, because property gives real power. The international economic situation forced the Socialist government to comply with market forces and economic laws. Socialists, trying to change society with a mass of legislation, didn't have an adequate approach then. Indeed, it is not possible to change society with decrees (Crozier, 1982). Analysing public management in comparative perspective (Japan, Sweden, US), Crozier (1988) concluded that the crisis of public management was by no means a unique French phenomenon, it was universal. Each country has to counter this crisis with a specific approach, adapted to its specific cultural environment. For Crozier (1991) a modest State is modern. As in Britain it is about government versus market (Middleton, 1996). Meanwhile, a sophisticated box of instruments has replaced the older rigid planning for Public Management of Society. As others did, Crozier tried to articulate the French specificity. French society is different. Its system of public management is more centralised, more nationalised than in most other Western countries. It does play a more imposing role. With about the same number of public functionaries for the same sector and the same kind of levies and taxes as elsewhere, the French State intervenes more penetratingly. Each society has its institutions, practices and philosophy of public management. The significance of human interactions, characterised by social and psycho-sociological mechanisms structuring behaviour, has to be accentuated. By studying these social mechanisms, one may hope to discover the original character of the French way of Public Management of Society.

The French philosophy of Public Management of Society is based upon the unity and hierarchy of functions and levels. Not only everything public is subordinated to the national State, but even private activities are in a sense thought to be subordinate to public activities. A specific French conception of the common interest, with the State having its monopoly, legitimises this hierarchy. Only the national State is thought to incarnate the common interest. From this point of view all regional and local public authorities are seen as representing only the interests of specific groups, they have to give way to the common interest of the State (Crozier, 1991, pp. 74-75). Changed circumstances in society demand adaptations but not all renovations are improvements. Often "new" solutions are in fact new names for old practices. Especially with institutional engineering, it is evident that historical processes of ongoing experimentations produce crucial yardsticks and criteria for real improvements. The Fifth Republic, giving France new institutions, was positioned in a perspective of modernisation, but its institutions are steeped in aspects of institutional arrangements made centuries earlier. Probably nothing in human society is more difficult to change than culture. In France, pre-eminently an institutional laboratory, the institutionalising of Public management of Society is part of a very specific culture. Its role is based on the longest tradition in Europe. Generally institutions of Public Management of Society in France are simultaneously very old and very modern. France had to manage society during and after three imposing war experiences on its own territory (1870-1871; 1914-1918; 1940-1944). Between 1945 and 1975 ("Les Trente Glorieuses") French society changed more than in the entire century before. Agriculture was one of the most important economic sectors, now it has a more modest position. The rural exodus combined with urbanisation and technological innovations changed the socio-economic climate drastically. Socio-economic circumstances improved markedly. French economy became, more than before, part of the European and the world market. France, exploiting its competitive advantages as nation (Porter, 1990), realised a prominent economic position.

It would not be very intelligent to dismiss the French ways of institutionalising and economic organisation by saying that the too voluminous public sector has shown examples of inefficient and costly experiences. French leading circles are fully conscious of the fact that modernisation remains a top priority. Government-Jospin asked recognised experts to produce reports about reforms in all kinds of policy fields, Le Monde (15-9-1998) counted 50 reports. As in other Western democracies, partisan politicking often blocks modernisation in France. It remains one of the most intriguing aspects of modern pluralist democracies that the cockpit of Public Management of Society is entrusted to party-political elites or cliques, meaning that the real common good of all, the general interest, the objective of public authorities, is under the continuous pressure of private and partisan interests. It seems possible to develop objective norms about the way public authorities ought to behave to bring real democracy closer by, and to use norms to further the sense of responsibility in the public sector. In the contemporary world of advanced countries, public organisations, private and hybrid organisations need to adapt their management philosophy (Crozier, 1989). Public authorities fulfil a crucial role for the normal functioning of markets. Accentuation of the relevance of contracts in economic life, as in institutional economics, is a truism. Self-regulation in a contracting society where possible. Conditioning regulation (legislation, treaties) by public authorities where necessary. Crozier criticises mainstream economic theorising and practices for the predominance of the "logic de la quantité", thinking in quantities. This quantitative logic of economics had its merits. By improving productivity and raising economic growth, it enabled Western countries to break the vicious circle of misery (the law of Malthus). Industrial mass production was a decisive instrument to procure a wide range of products. In several phases of industrial society economics was mostly rigidly separated from the social. Western countries up to the seventies were dominated by this dichotomy between the economic domain of the rational and the social domain of values (social, distributive justice). There was debate about making production social (participation etc.), and about better redistribution of the results of production. In the Welfare State a more social society was realised. Its provisions asked huge sums of money, and so even endangered production in the post-industrial society (services, technology, information).

Ever more the qualitative logic proves to be decisive for performance. This implies investment in human capital, people in other words (education, professional development, knowledge and information). That applies specifically to the public sector in which other intellectual methods are needed for developing and implementing adequate strategies. Quantification of qualitative aspects (formulating indicators) is a recognised instrument: societal cost-benefit analyses. Three paths of professional reasoning are generally followed according to technical, financial and juridical rationalities. These are mostly overruled by party-political rationalities and interests. Apart from this party-political dominance, one might say that the Budget is often governing. Globalisation of society is a dominant feature at the start of the 21st century. France was always world-champion in diplomacy, an active participant, organising its environment beyond its national boundaries whenever possible. This country has an inexhaustible kit of tools for public management of national and international society. Public Management of Society requires broad, co-disciplinary rationalities. The ecological neglect and destruction of the world needs new approaches. This is obvious in the "Living Planet Report" (1998) of the World Wildlife Fund. On the basis of quantified indicators it concluded that since 1970 one-third of the nature in the world had been destroyed. At the UN Population Conference in The Hague (February 1999) it was stated as fact that the richest part of the world consumes 86% of world resources, and produces 83% of the $CO_2$ emissions. In October 1999, world population surpassed the 6 milliard mark for the first time in history. Public Management of Society with social justice and law is important, also on a global scale (Rischard, 2002): The Global Village of Law as perspective, in which the Idea of Public Authority is a reality.

**References**

French
Adam, G., La Refondation Sociale à Inventer. Le Renouveau du Dialogue Social au Coeur du Débat Public. (Paris, Éd. Liaisons, 2002).
Affichard, J., Foucauld, J.B. de, dir., Justice sociale et inégalité. (Paris, Esprit, 1992).
Aglietta, M., Régulation et crises du capitalisme. (Paris, Odile Jacob, 1995; 1997).
Aglietta, M., Orléan, A., La Monnaie entre Violence et Confiance. (Paris, Odile Jacob, 2002).
Albert, M., Capitalisme contre capitalisme. (Paris, Seuil, 1991).
Alfandari, E., L'Insertion. (Paris, Sirey, 1989).
Alfandari, E., Action et aide sociale. (Paris, Dalloz, 1995).
Allègre, C., Toute vérité est bonne à dire. (Paris, Laffont/Fayard, 2000).
Allemand, S., Borbalan, J.C.R., La Mondialisation. (Paris, Le Cavalier, 2002).
Andrieu, C., Le programme commun de la Résistance. Des idées dans la guerre. (Paris, Éd. de l'Érudit, 1984).
Andrieu, C., et al., dir., Les Nationalisations de la Libération. (Paris, FNSP, 1987).
Babès, L., Oubrou, T., Loi d'Allah, Loi des Hommes. (Paris, A.Michel, 2002).

Baecque, F. de, Quermonne, J.L., dir., Administration et politique sous la Cinquième République. (Paris, FNSP, 1982).
Barlow, M., Clarke, T., La Bataille de Seattle. (Paris, Fayard, 2002).
Barratt Brown, M., Models in Political Economy. (Harmondsworth, Penguin, 1995).
Bauchet, P., La Planification française. Du premier au sixième Plan. (Paris, Seuil, 1964; 1973).
Baudelot, C., Establet, R., Les filles et les garçons dans la compétition scolaire. Dans: Données sociales. (Paris, INSEE, 1990).
Bauer, M., Bertin-Mourot, B., Les Énarques en entreprise de 1960 à 1990: 30 ans de pantouflage. (Paris/London, Boyden Global Executive Search, 1994).
Beaumais, O., Economie de l'environnement. Méthodes et débats. (Paris, DF, 2002).
Becker, J.J., Histoire politique de la France depuis 1945. (Paris, A.Colin, 1988/1992; 1998).
Bellon, B., Chevallier, J.M., dir., L'Industrie en France. (Paris, Flammarion, 1983).
Bensidoun, I., Chevallier, A., dir., L'Économie mondiale 2003. (Paris, Découverte, 2002).
Béroud, S., dir., L'Année Sociale. (Paris, Syllepse, 2002).
Berstein, S., Milza, P., Histoire de la France au XXe siècle. (Bruxelles, Complexe, 1995).
Bertrand, A., Kalafatides, L., OMC. Le Pouvoir Invisible. (Paris, Fayard, 2002).
Bertrand, J., La Protection sociale. (Paris, PUF, 1987).
Bertrand, J., Politique économique et sociale, 1944-1969, les années de Gaulle. (Paris, Eyrolles, 1992).
Bichot, J., Économie de la protection sociale. (Paris, A.Colin, 1992).
Bichot, J., Les Politiques Sociales en France au XXe siècle. (Paris, A.Colin, 1997).
Bichot, J., Retraites en péril. (Paris, Presses de Sciences Po, 1999).
Birnbaum, Les Sommets de l'État. (Paris, Seuil, 1977).
Birnbaum, P., La Classe dirigeante française. (Paris, PUF, 1978).
Bloch, B.M., Code des Marchés Publics Annoté. (Paris, Berger-Levrault, 2001).
Bloch-Lainé, F., A la recherche d'une économie concertée. (Paris, Éd. de l'Europe, 1959).
Bloch-Lainé, F., Bouvier, J., La France restaurée 1944-1954. (Paris, Fayard, 1986).
Bocagnano, A., Raffy-Pihan, M., L'Emploi dans le secteur de la santé. (Paris, CREDES, 1995).
Bodiguel, J.L., Les anciens élèves de l'ENA. (Paris, FNSP, 1978).
Boissieu, C., dir., Les Mutations de l'Économie Mondiale. (Paris, Economica, 2000).
Boissieu, C., dir., Les Entreprises Françaises 2002. (Paris, Economica, 2002).
Boissonat, J., La Révolution de 1999. De l'Europe à l'euro, de l'euro à l'Europe. (Paris, France Loisirs, 1997).
Boissonat, J., La Fin du chômage? (Paris, Calmann-Lévy, 2001).
Boniface, P., dir., L'Année stratégique 2003. (Paris, IRIS, 2002).
Bonin, H., Histoire économique de la France depuis 1880. (Paris, Masson, 1988).
Bonnemaison, G., Prévention, répression, solidarité. (Paris, DF, 1983).
Bonnet, J., Nasse, P., Audit des Finances Publiques. (Paris, Cour des Comptes, juin 2002).
Borne, D., La Société française depuis 1945. (Paris, A.Colin, 1988).
Boubakeur, D., Les Défis de l'Islam. (Paris, Flammarion, 2002).
Bourdieu, P., La Noblesse d'État. Grandes écoles et esprit de corps. (Paris, Minuit, 1989).
Bourdieu, P., Passeron, J.C., La Réproduction. Éléments pour une système d'enseignement. (Paris, Minuit, 1970).
Bourguignon, F., Bureau, D., L'Architecture des Prélèvements en France. État des lieux et voies de réforme. (Paris, DF, 1999).
Bourguinat, H., L'Économie mondiale à découvert. (Paris, Calmann-Lévy, 1985).
Bourguinat, H., Les Vertiges de la finance internationale. (Paris, Economica, 1987).
Bourguinat, H., L'Économie morale. (Paris, Arléa, 1998).
Bourguinat, H., Finance internationale. Après l'euro et les crises. (Paris, PUF, 2000).
Bouvier, P., Technologie, travail, transports. (Paris, Librairie des Méridiens, 1985).
Boyer, R., La Croissance, début de siècle. De l'octet au gène. (Paris, A.Michel, 2002).
Boyer, R., dir., La Théorie de la régulation: une analyse critique. (Paris, Découverte, 1986).
Boyer, R., dir., Le Gouvernement économique de la zone euro. (Paris, DF/CGP, 1999).
Boyer, R., Saillard, Y., dir., Théorie de la régulation. L'État des savoirs. (Paris, Découverte, 1995).
Boyer, R., Souyri, P.F., dir., Mondialisation et régularisations. Europe et Japan face à la singularité américaine. (Paris, Découverte, 2001).
Braibant, G., Stirn, B., Le Droit Administratif Français. (Paris, FNSP/Dalloz, 1999).
Braudel, F., L'Identité de la France. (Paris, Flammarion, 1990).
Brébisson, G. de, Le Mécénat. (Paris, PUF, 1993).
Brisset, C., dir., Pauvretés. (Paris, Hachette, 1996).

Busson, A., Le Management des entreprises artistiques et culturelles. (Paris, Economica, 1993).
Cabanel, P., La République du certificat d'études. (Paris, Belin, 2002).
Cacheux, A., Le Logement locatif social. (Paris, DF, 2002).
Carré, J.J., et al., Abrégé de la croissance française. (Paris, Seuil, 1984).
Carroué, L., Géographie de la Mondialisation. (Paris, A.Colin, 2002).
Carsalade, Y., Les Grandes étapes de l'histoire économique. (Paris, Ellipses, 1998).
Castel, O., Le Sud dans la mondialisation. Quelles alternatives? (Paris, Découverte, 2002).
Castel, R., Les Métamorphoses de la Question Sociale. (Paris, Fayard, 1995).
Castel, R., Laé, J.F., Le RMI, une dette sociale. (Paris, Harmattan, 1992).
CERC, Précarité et risque d'exclusion en France. (Paris, Centre d'études des ressources et des coûts, 1993).
CGP, Rapport annexé à la première loi du Plan. (Paris, Commissariat général du Plan? DF, 1983).
CGP, La France, l'Europe. Xe Plan, 1989-1992. (Paris, DF, 1989).
Charlot, B., L'école en mutation, crise de l'école et mutations sociales. (Paris, Payot, 1987).
Chartier, R., et al., L'éducation en France du XVIe au XVIIIe siècle. (Paris, SEDES, 1976).
Chasseriaud, C., dir., Rapport sur la grande exclusion sociale. (Paris, Ministére des affaires sociales, 1993).
Chatton, P.F., Mazuryk Bapst, J., Le Défi francophone. (Bruxelles, Bruylant, 1991).
Chauchard, J.P., Droit de la Sécurité sociale. (Paris, LGDJ, 1994).
Chebel, M., Le Sujet en Islam. (Seuil, 2002).
Chevalier, J.M., Pastré, O., dir., Où va l'Économie Mondiale? Scénarios et Mesures d'Urgence. (Paris, Odile Jacob, 2002).
Chevallier, J., L'Économie industrielle en question. (Paris, Calmann-Lévy, 1977).
Chotard, Y., Comment sauver la Sécurité sociale. (Paris, Economica, 1989).
Clement, A., Nourrir le peuple, entre État et marché, XVIe-XIXe siècle. Contribution à l'histoire intellectuelle de l'approvisionnement alimentaire. (Paris, Harmattan, 1999).
Closets, F. de, Tant et plus: comment se gaspille notre argent. (Paris, Grasset/Seuil, 1992).
Club Ulysse, Le Politique saisie par l'Économie. Enjeux économiques et sociaux des élections de 2002. (Paris, Economica, 2002).
Cohen, E., Le Colbertisme "high tech". (Paris, Hachette, 1992).
Cohen, E., Bauer, M., Les grandes manoeuvres industrielles. (Paris, Belfond, 1985).
Cohendet, P., Lebeau, A., Choix stratégies et grands programmes civils. (Paris, Economica, 1987).
Coignard, S., Lacan, J.F., La République bananière. (Paris, Belfond, 1989).
Collective (Oeuvre), Cinquante ans de sécurité sociale. Espace social européen. (Paris, Observatoire européen de la protection sociale, 1995).
Conseil d'orientation des retraites, Age et Travail. Un axe de réflexion essentiel pour l'avenir des retraites. (Paris, DF, 2002).
Conseil d'orientation des retraites, Retraites: Renouveler le contrat social entre les générations. (Paris, DF, 2001).
Cotta, M., La France et l'impératif mondial. (Paris, PUF, 1978).
CREDES, L'Enquête Santé, Protection sociale. (Paris, 1994).
Crozier, M., La Société bloquée. (Paris, Seuil, 1970; 1980).
Crozier, M., On ne change pas la société par décret. (Paris, Grasset, 1979; 1982).
Crozier, M., Comment réformer l'État? (Paris, DF, 1988).
Crozier, M., L'Entreprise à l'écoute: apprendre le management postindustriel. (Paris, InterÉditions, 1989).
Crozier, M., État modeste, État moderne. (Paris, Fayard, 1991).
Dalloz (Éditions), Les Impôts en Europe. (Paris, Dallioz, 2002).
DATAR, Aménager la France de 2020. (Paris, DF, 2002).
Dayan, J.L., 35 Heures, des Ambitions aux Réalités. (Paris, Découverte, 2002).
Decreton, S., dir., Service Public et Lien Social. (Paris, Harmattan, 1999).
De Gaulle, J., L'Avenir du Plan et la place de la planification dans la société française. (Paris, DF, 1994).
Delfau, G., La Poste, un service public en danger. Constat et proposition. (Paris, Harmattan, 1999).
Delorme, C., Les Banlieues de Dieu. (Paris, Bayard, 1998).
Delorme, C., Begag, A., Quartiers Sensibles. (Paris, Seuil, 1994).
Delsaut, Y., La place du maître. Une chronique des écoles normales d'instituteurs. (Paris, Harmattan, 1992).
Dejours, C., Souffrance en France. La Banalisation de l'injustice sociale. (Paris, Seuil, 1998; 2000).
Deneux, M., L'Évaluation de l'ampleur des changements climatiques et leur impact prévisible sur la géographie de la France à l'horizon 20025, 2050 et 2100. (Paris, Sénat, 2002).
Deniau, X., La Francophonie. (Paris, PUF, 1995).
Documentation française (DF), Livre Blanc sur les retraites. (Paris, DF, 1991).
DF, Livre Blanc sur les retraites. (Paris, DF, 1991).

DF, Quele habitat pour les ménages à faibles revenues? (Paris, Caisse des dépôts, 2001).
DF, Durée, réduction et aménagement du temps de travail. (Paris, DF, 2002).
DF, Le Gouvernement Raffarin. L'Audit des finances publiques. (Paris, DF, 2002).
Djian, J.M., La Politique Culturelle. (Paris, Le Monde, 1996).
Djian, J.M., Ingénierie et management culturels. (Paris, DF, 1997).
Dollot, L., La France dans le monde actuel. (Paris, PUF, 1992).
Donnat, O., Cogneau, D., Les pratiques culturelles des Français, 1973-1989. (Paris, DF, 1990).
Donzelot, J., L'Invention du social. (Paris, Fayard, 1984).
Donzelot, J., dir., Face à l'Exclusion. Le Modèle français. (Paris, Ed. Esprit, 1991).
Dosière, R., Hoorens, D., La Commune et ses Finances. (Paris, Imprimerie nationale, 2001).
Dubedout, H., Ensemble. Refaire la ville. (Paris, DF, 1983).
Dubois, P., Vingt ans après. Les projections 1985 confrontées à la réalité. (Paris, Économie et Statistiques, 1985).
Duboist, M., Etre Chrétien Aujourd'hui. (Paris, Pygmalion, 2002).
Dubost, N., et al., Guide Pratique de l'Élu du Comité d'Entreprise. (Paris, Forma CE, 2002).
Duby, G., Mandrou, R., Histoire de la civilisation française. (Paris, A.Colin, 1984).
Ducan, J.W., Les grandes idées du management des classiques aux modernes. (Paris, AFNOR, 1990).
Duhamel, A., Les Peurs françaises. (Paris, Flammarion, 1993).
Dupeyroux, J.J., Droit de la Sécurité sociale. (Paris, Dalloz, 1993; 1995).
Duplat, C.A., Gérer sa Retraite. (Paris, Éd. d'organisation, 2002).
Dupré, D., dir., Éthique et Capitalisme. (Paris, Economica, 2002).
Dupuy, F., Thoenig, J.C., L'Administration en miettes. (Paris, Fayard, 1985).
Durand-Prinborne, C., L'Égalité scolaire par le coeur et par la raison. (Paris, Nathan, 1989).
Durand-Prinborne, C., L'Administration scolaire. (Paris, Sirey, 1989).
Durand-Prinborne, C., dir , Le Système Éducatif. (Paris, DF, 1991).
Duriez, M., et al., Le Système de santé en France. (Paris, PUF, 1996).
Eck, J.F., Histoire de l'économie française depuis 1945. (Paris, A.Colin, 1990; 1996).
Evrard, Y., dir., La Management des entreprises artistiques et culturelles. (Paris, PUF, 1993).
Ewald, F., L'État-Providence. (Paris, Grasset, 1986).
Fahmy, M., La Condition de la Femme dans l'Islam. (Paris, Éd. Allia, 2002).
Farchy, J., Sagot-Duvauroux, D., Economie des politiques culturelles. (Paris, PUF, 1993).
Fauroux, R., dir., Pour l'école. (Paris, Calmann-Lévy, 1996).
Fayol, H., Administration industrielle et générale. (Paris, Dunod, 1916).
Ferrières, M., Histoire des peurs alimentaires. Du Moyen Âge à l'aube du XXe siècle. (Paris, Seuil, 2002).
Fevre-Pelee de Saint Maurice, V., Élus et marchés publics. (Paris, DEMOS, 2001).
Filali-Ansary, A., L'Islam est-il Hostile à la Laïcité? (Paris, Sinbad/Actes Sud, 2002).
Fitoussi, J.P., dir., Pour l'emploi et la cohésion sociale. (Paris, OFCE, 1994).
Fondation Abbé Pierre, L'état du mal-logement en France. (Paris, Fondation Abbé Pierre pour le logement des défavorisés, 2002).
Fontaine, P., Jean Monnet, l'inspirateur. (Paris, Grancher, 1988).
Fottorino, E., Benoit, J.P., La France en friche. (Paris, Lieu commun, 1989).
Foucauld, J.B. de, Le Financement de la protection sociale. (Paris, DF, 1995).
Foucauld, J.B. de, Les Trois Cultures du Développement Humain. (Paris, Odile Jacob, 2002).
Foucauld, J.B. de, dir., La France et l'Europe d'ici 2010. (Paris, Facteurs et acteurs décisifs. (Paris, DF, 1993).
Fourastié, J., Les Trente Glorieuses ou la Révolution invisible de 1946 à 1975. (Paris, Fayard, 1979; Hachette, 1986).
Fourastié, J., La Productivité. (Paris, PUF, 1987).
Fournier, J., et al., Traité du social. (Paris, Dalloz, 1989).
Fournier, J., Mesnil de Buisson, M.A., Livre Blanc sur le Dialogue Social dans la Fonction Publique. (Paris, DF, 2002).
Fragonard, B., Propositions pour un plan de lutte contre la pauvreté. (Paris, CGP, 1995).
Fragonard, B., dir., Cohésion sociale et prévention de l'exclusion. (Paris, CGP, 1993).
Fridenson, P., Straus, A., dir., Le Capitalisme français, 19e-20$^e$ siècles. (Paris, Fayard, 1987).
Fumaroli, M., L'État Culturel. (Paris, Fallois, 1991).
Fumaroli, M., Quand l'Europe pralait français. (Paris, Fallois, 2001).
Furet, F., Ozouf, J., Lire et écrire. L'alphabetisation des Français, de Calvin à Jules Ferry. (Paris, Minuit, 1977).
Gabet, A., La Fracture Sociale. (Paris, Ellipses, 2002).

Galant, H.C., Histoire politique de la sécurité sociale française, 1945-1952. (Paris, FNSP, 1955).
Garnier, M., Trois Indicateurs de Performance des Lycées. (Paris, Ministère du L'Éducation Nationale, 1999).
Gaudin, J.P., Gouverner par Contrat. L'Action Publique en Question. (Paris, Presses de Sciences Po, 1999).
Gaulupean, Y., La France à l'école. (Paris, Gallimard, 1992).
Gauthier, Y., La Crise Mondiale de 1973 à nos jours. (Bruxelles, Complexe, 1989).
Genet-Delacroix, M.C., Art et État sous la Troisième République. Le système des Beaux-Arts, 1870-1940. (Paris, Sorbonne, 1993).
Génisson, C., La parité entre les femmes et les hommes: une avancée décisive pour la démocratie. (Paris, DF, 2002).
George, S., Wolf, M., La Mondialisation Libérale. (Paris, Grasset, 2002).
Gide, C., Rist, Histoire des Doctrines Économiques depuis les Physiocrates jusqu'à nos jours. (Paris, Dalloz, 2002).
Gordon, P.H., Meunier, S., Le Nouveau Défi Français. La France face à la Mondialisation. (Paris, Odile Jacob, 2002).
Greciano, P.A., Les Retraites en France. Quel Avenir? (Paris, DF, 2002).
Grémion, C., Profession: décideurs. Pouvoir des hauts fonctionnaires et réforme de l'État. (Paris, Gauthier-Villars, 1979).
Grémion, P., Le Pouvoir périphérique. Bureaucrates et notables dans le système politique français. (Paris, Seuil, 1976).
Gresh, A., Ramadan, T., L'Islam en Questions. (Paris, Actes Sud, 2002).
Groupe de Bruges, Agriculture, un Tournant Nécessaire. (Paris, Éd. de l'Aube, 2002).
Groux, G., L'Action Publique Négociée. Approches à partir des "35 heures". (Paris, Harmattan, 2002).
Hafsi, T., Entreprise publique et politique industrielle. (Paris, McGraw-Hill, 1984).
Harant, H., Delage, A., L'épidémiologie. (Paris, PUF, 1984).
Hatzfeld, H., Du paupérisme à la sécurité sociale. Essai sur les origines de la Securité Sociale en France, 1850-1940. (Paris, A.Colin, 1971; Nancy, PU, 1989).
Haut Comité de la Santé Publique, La Santé en France 2002. (Paris, DF, 2002).
Haut Conseil à l'intégration, Les parcours d'intégration. (Paris, DF, 2002).
Haut Conseil du secteur financier public, Un secteur financier public, pour quoi faire? (Paris, DF, 2002).
Hervieu, B., Les Champs du Futur. (Paris, Bourin, 1993).
Hirsch, M., Les Enjeux de la protection sociale. (Paris, Montchrestien, 1994).
Hoffmann, S., Sur la France. (Paris, Seuil, 1976).
INSEE, Données sociales. (Paris, INSEE, 1996).
INSEE, L'Économie française. (Paris, INSEE, 2002).
INSEE, Les Bas Salaires. (Paris, Liaisons sociales, 2002).
Jacquemin, A., Rainelli, M., Filières de la nation, filières d'entreprises. (Dans: Revue économique, pp.379-392, 1984).
Jacquet, P., et al., Gouvernance Mondiale. (Paris, DF, 2002).
Jacquillat, B., Désétatiser. (Paris, Laffont, 1985).
Jacquillat, B., Chevalier, M., Principes et Techniques du Gouvernement des Entreprises. (Paris, Éd. d'organisation, 1970).
Jeancourt-Galignani, A., La Finance Déboussolée. (Paris, Odile Jacob, 2002).
Jeanneney, J.N., dir., De Gaulle en son siècle. 3. Moderniser la France. (Paris, DF/Plon, 1992).
Jelloun, T.B., L'Islam Expliqué aux Enfants. (Paris, Seuil, 2002).
Jestin-Fleury, N., dir., Effet de serre: modélisation économique et décision publique. (Paris, DF, 2002).
Jetin, B., La Taxe Tobin et la Solidarité entre les Nations. (Paris, Éd. Descartes, 2002).
Jobert, B., Le Social en plan. (Paris, Éd. ouvrières, 1981).
Jobert, B., dir., Le tournant néo-libéral en Europe. (Paris, Harmattan, 1994).
Jobert, B., Muller, P., L'État en action. (Paris, PUF, 1987).
Join-Lambert, C., et al., Politiques sociales. (Paris, Dalloz, 1994; 1997).
Kaspi, A., Les Américains. Les États-Unis de 1607 à nos jours. (Paris, Seuil, 1986).
Kennedy, C., Toutes les Théories du Management. (Paris, Mesnil, trad., 2002).
Kerschen, N., L'Influence du Rapport beveridge sur le Plan français de Sécurité sociale. (Dans: Revue française de science politique, pp.570-595, 1995).
Kessler, M.C., Les grands corps de l'État. (Paris, FNSP, 1986).
Keynes, J.M., La Pauvreté dans l'Abondance. (Paris, Gallimard, trad., 2002).
Keynes, J.M., Les Conséquences économiques et politiques de la paix. Suivi de "Les Conséquences politiques de la paix" de J. Bainville. (Paris, Gallimard, 2002).

Kiss, A.C., Droit International de l'Environnement. (Paris, Pedone, 2000).
Kuisel, R., Le Capitalisme et l'État en Franxce. Modernisation et dirigisme au XXe siècle. (Paris, Gallimard, 1984).
Lacorne, D., L'Invention de la République: Le Modèle Américain. (Paris, Hachette, 1991).
La Gorce, P.M. de, Schor, A.D., La politique étrangère de la Ve République. (Paris, PUF, 1992).
Lamberterie, I. de, dir., Les actes authentiques électroniques. Réflexion juridique prospective. (Paris, DF, 2002).
Lamiot, D., Lancry, P.J., La Protection sociale, les enjeux de la solidarité. (Paris, Nathan, 1989).
Landry, C., Sevre, F., dir., École et Entreprise vers Quel Partenariat. (Quebec, Presses Universitaires, 1994).
Laroque, M., Politiques sociales dans la France contemporaine. (Paris, STH, 1991; 1993).
Latarjet, B., L'Aménagement culturel du territoire. (Paris, DF, 1991).
Laufer, R., Burlaud, A., Management public: gestion et légitimité. (Paris, Dalloz, 1980).
Laurent, P., Contribution pour l'étude des relations de pouvoir par l'analyse de filière. (Lyon, École supérieure de commerce, 1986).
Lebon, A., Migrations et nationalité en France en 2000. (Paris, DF, 2002).
Le Bras, H., Todd, E., L'Invention de la France. (Paris, 1981).
Le Cercle des Économistes, Espérances et Menaces de l'Élection Présidentielle. (Paris, Descartes, 2001).
Lefebvre (Éditions), Les Impôts en France 2001-2002. Traité de Fiscalité. (Paris, Lefebvre, 2001).
Le Galès, P., Du Gouvernement Local à la Gouvernance Urbaine. (Dans: Revu Française de Science Politique, pp. 57-95, 1995).
Legrand, A., Le Système F. L'École... de réformes en projets. (Paris, Denoël, 1994).
Lelièvre, C., Histoire des institutions scolaires (1789-1989). (Paris, Nathan, 1991).
Le Moigne, G., Lebon, A., L'Immigration en France. (Paris, PUF, 2002).
Lenoir, R., Les Exclus, un Français sur dix. (Paris, Seuil, 1974).
Lenoir, R., Les Exclus. (Paris, Seuil, 1989).
Léon, A., Histoire de l'Enseignement en France. (Paris, PUF, 1967).
Lequesne, C., Les instruments de la politique européenne de la France. (Paris, IEP, 1986).
Lequesne, C., Paris-Bruxelles. Comment se fait la politique européenne de la France. (Paris, FNSP, 1993).
Le Roy Ladurie, E., Histoire des paysans français. De la Peste noire à la Révolution. (Paris, Seuil, 2002).
Levet, J.L., dir., Les Pratiques de l'Intelligence Économique. Huit Cas d'Entreprises. (Paris, Economica, 2002).
Lojkine, J., Malétras, J.L., La Guerre du Temps, le Travail en quête de mesure. (Paris, Harmattan, 2002).
Loubes, O., L'École et la Patrie. (Paris, Belin, 2001).
Luethy, H., A l'heure de son clocher. Essai sur la France. (Paris, Calmann-Lévy, 1955).
Mabileau, A., Le système local en France. (Paris, Montchrestien, 1991).
Majnoni d'Intignano, B., La Protection sociale. (Paris, Livre de poche, 1993).
Malignac, G., L'Alcoholisme. (Paris, PUF, 1992).
Malinvaud, E., Choix des investissements publics décentralisés en période de croissance ralentie. (Paris, CGP, 1981).
Malinvaud, E., Calcul économique et résorption des déséquilibres. (Paris, CGP, 1983).
Marchand, O., Plein-emploi, l'Improbable Retour. (Paris, Gallimard, 2002).
Marcou, G., Costa, J.P., Durand-Prinborgne, C., dir., La Décision dans l'Éducation National. (Lille, PUL, 1992).
Marseille, J., Vive la Crise et l'Inflation. (Paris, Hachette, 1983).
Marseille, J., Empire Colonial et Capitalisme Français. Histoire d'un Divorce. (Paris, A.Michel, 1984).
Marseille, J., La France Travaille Trop. (Paris, A.Michel, 1989).
Marseille, J., Le Grand Gaspillage. (Paris, Plon, 2002).
Marseille, J., dir., 1900-2000. Un Siècle d'Économie. (Paris, Calmann-Lévy, 1999).
Marti, S., L'Économie des États-Unis. (Paris, Le Monde, 1994).
Massé, P., Le Plan ou l'Anti-Hasard. (Paris, Gallimard, 1965).
Mathieu, J.L., La défense de l'environnement en France. (Paris, PUF, 1994).
Matthiessen, M., Le SGCI. (Paris, IEP, 1981).
Maurin, E., L'Égalité des Possibles. (Paris, Seuil, 2002).
Maury, Y., Les HLM. L'État-Providence vu d'en bas. (Paris, Harmattan, 2001).
Mayeur, J.M., L'éducation des filles en France au XIXe siècle. (Paris, Hachette, 1979).
Mazel, O., L'Exclusion. Le Social à la Dérive. (Paris, Le Monde, 1996).
Mazoyer, M., Roudarit, L., Histoire des Agricultures du Monde. (Paris, Seuil, 2002).
Meddeb, A., La Maladie de l'Islam. (Paris, Seuil, 2002).
Mendras, H., La Fin des paysans. (Paris, A.Colin, 1967).

Mendras, H., La Fin des paysans suivi d'une réflexion sur la Fin des paysans vingt ans après. (Ales, Actes Sud, 1984).
Mendras, H., La Seconde Révolution française, 1965-1984. (Paris, Gallimard, 1994).
Mény, Y., dir., Les Politiques Décentralisées de l'Éducation: Analyse de quatre expériences régionales. (Paris, GRAL/CNRS, 1990).
Mény, Y., Thoenig, J.C., Politiques publiques. (Paris, PUF, 1989).
Merlin, P., L'Urbanisme. (Paris, PUF, 2002).
Merrien, F.X., dir., Face à la pauvreté. (Paris, Éd. ouvrières, 1994).
Michalet, C.A., Qu'est-ce que la mondialisation? (Paris, Découverte, 2002).
Michaud, Y., La Société et les Relations Sociales. (Paris, Odile Jacob, 2002).
Minard, P., La Fortune du Colbertisme. (Paris, Fayard, 1998).
Miné, M., Rose, H., Struillou, Y., Droit du Licenciement des Salariés Protégés. (Paris, Economica, 2002).
Ministère des Affaires Sociales, Guide pratique du droit du travail. (Paris, DF, 2002).
Ministère de la Culture, Les collectivités locales et la Culture. Les formes de l'institutionnalisation: XIXe-XXe siècles. (Paris, DF, 2002).
Ministère de la Culture, Chiffres Clés de la culture 2001. (Paris, DF, 2002).
Ministère de l'Écologie, Plans de prévention des risques naturels. (Paris, DF, 2002).
Ministère de l'Économie, Les Comptes des Communes 2000. (Paris, DF, 2002).
Ministère de l'Économie, Les Comptes des Régions 2000. (Paris, DF, 2002).
Ministère de l'Emploi, La Santé en France 2002. (Paris, DF, 2002).
Ministère de l'Environnement, Plan National pour l'Environnement. (Paris, 1990).
Ministère de l'Environnement, Données économiques de l'Environnement. (Paris, Economica, 1996).
Ministère de l'Environnement, L'Application Renforcée du Droit International de l'Environnement. (Paris, Frison-Roche, 1999).
Minot, J., L'Entreprise Éducation Nationale. (Paris, A.Colin, 1970).
Moïsi, D., Les Cartes de la France à l'heure de la mondialisation. (Paris, Fayard, 2000).
Mollard, C., L'Ingénierie culturelle. (Paris, PUF, 1994).
Monier, F., Le Front Populaire. (Paris, Découverte, 2002).
Montalembert, M. de, dir., La Protection sociale en France. (Paris, DF, 1995; 2001).
Montbrial, T. de, dir., Retraites, Santé, n'est-il pas trop tard? (Paris, Académie des sciences morales et politiques, 2002).
Montfort, M.J., L'Analyse des filières de production. (Paris, Economica, 1985).
Montfort, M.J., Dutailly, J.C., Les Filières de production. (Paris, INSEE, 1983).
Moriceau, J.M., Terres mouvantes. Les campagnes françaises du féodalisme à la mondialisation, XIIe-XIXe siècle. (Paris, Fayard, 2002).
Moulinier, P., Politique et décentralisation. (Paris, CNFPT, 1995).
Moulinier, P., Les Politiques publiques de la culture en France. (Paris, PUF, 1999).
Muet, P.A., dir., Le chômage persistant en Europe. (Paris, FNSP, 1994).
Muller, P., Les politiques publiques. (Paris, PUF, 1994).
Muller, P., L'Administration française est-elle en crise? (Paris, Harmattan, 1992).
Murard, N., La Protection sociale. (Paris, Découverte, 1988).
Mutin, G., De l'eau pour tous? (Paris, DF, 2002).
Nicollier, E., Le Travail sur Internet. (Paris, Grancher, 2002).
Nomides, P., La Fiscalité Écologique. (Paris, Fondation Robert Schuman, 2002).
Oudin, J., Rapport d'information sur les aspects financiers de la protection sociale. (Paris, Sénat, 29 octobre 1992).
Palier, B., Réformer la Sécurité sociale. (Paris, IEP, 1999).
Palier, B., Bonoli, G., Entre Bismarck et Beveridge. (Dans: Revue française de science politique, pp.668-699, 1995).
Parodi, M., L'économie et la Société française depuis 1880. (Paris, A.Colin, 1981).
Parodi, M., L'Économie et la Société française depuis 1945. (Paris, A.Colin, 1981).
Paugam, S., La Société française et ses pauvres. (Paris, PUF, 1993).
Paugam, S., La Disqualification Sociale. (Paris, PUF, 2002).
Pelletier, D., La Crise Catholique. Religion, Société, Politique en France (1965-1978). (Paris, Payot, 2002).
Perrot, J.C., Une Histoire intellectuelle de l'économie politique, XVIIe-XVIIIe siècle. (Paris, EHESS, 1992).
Perroux, F., Les Techniques quantitatives de la planification. (Paris, PUF, 1965).
Petit, P., Origine et originalité de la planification française. (Paris, Cepremap, 1983).
Peyrefitte, A., Le Mal français. (Paris, Plon, 1976).
Pierre, C., Praire, L., Plan et autogestion. (Paris, Flammarion, 1976).

Piketty, T., Les Hauts Revenus en France au XXe siècle. (Paris, Grasset, 2000).
Pisani-Ferry, J., Plein Emploi. Rapport du Conseil d'analyse économique. (Paris, DF, 2000).
Plihon, D., Ponssard, J.P., La Montée en Puissance des Fonds d'Investissement. (Paris, DF, 2002).
Poirrier, J., L'État et la Culture en France au XXe siècle. (Paris, Livre de poche, 2000).
Poirrier, P., Société et Culture en France depuis 1945. (Paris, Seuil, 1998).
Poirrier, P., Bibliographie de l'histoire des politiques culturelles. France, XIXe-XXe siècles. (Paris, DF, 1999).
Poirrier, P., Les politiques culturelles en France. (Paris, DF, 2002).
Ponteil, E., Histoire de l'Enseignement 1889-1965. (Paris, Sirey, 1966).
Pouvoirs, DATAR. (Paris, Seuil, 1967).
Pouyet, B., La Délégation à l'aménagement du territoire et à l'action régionale. (Paris, Cujas, 1967).
Prager, J.C., La Politique Économique aujourd'hui. (Paris, Ellipses, 2002).
Prate, A., Les Batailles économiques du Général de Gaulle. (Paris, Plon, 1978).
Prémare, A.L. de, Les Fondations de l'Islam. Entre Écriture et Histoire. (Paris, Seuil, 2002).
Prieur, M., Droit et l'environnement. (Paris, Dalloz, 1991).
Prost, A., Histoire de l'Enseignement en France (1800-1967). (Paris, A.Colin, 1968; 1979).
Prost, A., Éducation, societé et politiques. (Paris, Seuil, 1992).
Quermonne, J.L., Le Gouvernement de la France sous la Ve République. (Paris, Dalloz, 1987).
Quermonne, J.L., L'appareil administratif de l'État. (Paris, Seuil, 1991).
Quilichini, P., La Politique locale de l'habitat. (Paris, Imprimerie nationale, 2002).
Quinet, E., La Planification française. (Paris, PUF, 1990).
Rasera, M., La Démocratie Locale. (Paris, LGDJ, 2002).
Renaud-Coulon, A., Universités d'Entreprise. Vers une Mondialisation de l'Intelligence. (Paris, Éd. Village Mondial, 2002).
Renaudin, H., La Vie, Entrée Libre. (Paris, Bayard, 2002).
Rioux, J.P., et al., L'État et la Culture. (Paris, 1991).
Rioux, J.P., dir., Deux cents ans d'inspection générale, 1802-2002. (Paris, Fayard, 2002).
Rioux, J.P., Sirinelli, J.P., dir., La Culture de Masse en France de la Belle Époque à aujourd'hui. (Paris, Fayard, 2002).
Robineau, Y., Les mesures d'aide aux emplois du secteur non maerchand. (Paris, DF/CGP, 2002).
Rochaix, M., Essai sur l'évolution des questions hospitalières de la fin de l'Ancien Régime à nos jours. (Paris, Fédération hospitalière de France, 1959).
Rosanvallon, P., La Crise de l'État-Providence. (Paris, Seuil, 1981; 1992).
Rosanvallon, P., L'État en France, de 1789 à nos jours. (Paris, Seuil, 1990; 1993).
Rosanvallon, P., La Nouvelle Question Sociale. (Paris, Seuil, 1995).
Rouban, L., La modernisation de l'État et la fin de la spécificité française. (Dans: Revue française de science politique, pp.521-544, 1990).
Rouet, A., La Chance d'un Christianisme Fragile. (Paris, Bayard, 2002).
Rouillé d'Orfeuil, H., Économie. Le Réveil des Citoyens. (Paris, Découverte, 2002).
Rousso, H., dir., De Monnet à Massé. Enjeux politics et objectifs économiques dans le cadre des quatre premiers Plans (1946-1965). (Paris, CNRS, 1986).
Ruault, J.P., Rapport sur la planification française. (Paris, 1986).
Saez, G., et al., dir., Gouvernance Métropolitaine et Transfrontalière. (Paris, Harmattan, 1997).
Saint-Étienne, C., Appel à une génération citoyenne, 21 propositions pour construire notre avenir. (Paris, Economica, 2000).
Saint-Pulgent, M. de, Le Gouvernement de la culture. (Paris, Gallimard, 1999).
Santo, V.M., Verrier, P.E., Le Management Public. (Paris, PUF, 1993).
Schor, A.D., La politique économique et sociale de la Ve République. (Paris, PUF, 1993).
Schwartz, B., L'Insertion professionnelle et sociale des jeunes. (Paris, DF, 1981).
Sedjari, A., dir., La mise à niveau de l'administration face à a la mondialisation. (Paris, Harmattan, 1999).
Segrestin, D., Le phénomène corporatiste: essai sur l'avenir des systèmes professionnels fermés en France. (Paris, Fayard, 1985).
Sen, A., Un Nouveau Modèle Économique. (Paris, Odile Jacob, 2000).
Sen, A., Repenser l'Inégalité. (Paris, Seuil, 2000).
Simonnot, P., Vingt et Un Siècles d'Économie. (Paris, Belles Lettres, 2002).
Soubié, R., dir., Santé 2010. (Paris, CGP/DF, 1993).
Soubié, R., et al., Livre blanc sur le système de santé et d'assurance maladie. (Paris, DF, 1994).
Stébé, J.M., La Crise des Banlieues. (Paris, PUF, 2002).
Stébé, J.M., Le Logement social en France: 1789 à nos jours. (Paris, PUF, 2002).

Stoléru, L., Vaincre la pauvreté dans les pays riches. (Paris, Flammarion, 1974).
Stoléru, L., Economie, comprendre l'avenir. (Paris, Dunod, 1999).
Sudre, F., La Convention Européenne des Droits de l'Homme. (Paris, PUF, 2002).
Suleiman, E., Courty, G., L'Âge d'or de l'État. (Paris, Seuil, 1996).
Talbi, M., Penser Libre en Islam. (Paris, A.Michel, 2002).
Thélot, C., L'Évaluation du Système Éducatif Français. (Dans: Revue Française de Pédagogie, pp. 5-28, 1994).
Thevenet, A., L'Aide sociale aujourd'hui après la décentralisation. (Paris, ESF, 1990).
Thoenig, J.C., L'ère des technocrates. (Paris, Harmattan, 1987).
Tixier, P.E., dir., Du Monopole au Marché. Les Stratégies de Modernisation des Entreprises Publiques. (Paris, Découverte, 2002).
Tomaszewski, R., Les politiques audiovisuelles en France. (Paris, DF, 2002).
Toulemonde, B., Petit Histoire d'un Grand Ministère. (Paris, Seuil, 1994).
Tronquoy, P., dir., Enjeux et politiques de l'environnement. (Paris, DF, 2002).
Truche, P., et al., Administration électronique et protection des données personnelles. (Paris, DF, 2002).
Vaïsse, P., Le Royaume-Uni: économie et société. (Paris, Le Monde, 1996).
Vallemont, S., dir., Le débat public: une réforme dans l'État. (Paris, LGDJ, 2001).
Vasconcellos, M., Le Système Éducatif. (Paris, Découverte, 1993).
Velt, P., Des Lieux et des Liens. Politiques du Territoire à l'Heure de la Mondialisation. (Paris, 'Ed. de l'Aube, 2002).
Vernimmen, P., Quiry, P., Ceddaha, F., Finance d'Entreprise. (Paris, Dalloz, 2002).
Vesperini, J.P., dir., Les Problèmes Actuels de l'Économie Français. (Paris, PUF, 2002).
Waquet, F., Le Latin ou l'Empire d'un Signe, XVIe-XXe siècle. (Paris, A.Michel, 1998).
Weber, M., Éthique protestante et l'esprit du capitalisme. (Paris, Plon, 1990).
Weil, P., La France et ses étrangers. (Paris, Calmann-Lévy, 1992; Gallimard, 1995).
Wright, V., dir., Les Privatisations en Europe: programmes et problèmes. (Arles, Actes Sud, 1993).

English
Adam, W.J., Stoffaes, C., eds., French Industrial Policy. (Washington DC, Brookings Institution, 1986).
Archer, M.S., Social Origins of Educational Systems. (London, Sage, 1979).
Arestis, P., Sawyer, M., eds., The Economics of the Third Way. (Cheltenham, Elgar, 2001).
Bailey, E.E., Pack, J.R., The Political Economy of Privatization and Deregulation. (Cheltenham, Elgar, 1995).
Baldwin, P., The politics of social solidarity. Class bases of the European Welfare State 1875-1975. (Cambridge, CUP, 1990).
Barde, J.P., Pearce, D.W., Valuing the Environment. (London, Earthscan, 1991).
Barrat Brown, M., Models in Political Economy. (Harmondsworth, Penguin, 1995).
Baumol, W.J., Bowen, W.G., Performing Arts. The Economic Dilemma. (New York, Twentieth Century Fund, 1966).
Behn, R.D., Rethinking Democratic Accountability. (Washington DC, Brookings Institution, 2001).
Bennett, C., ed., Decentralisation Local Government and Markets: Towards a Post-Welfare Agenda. (Oxford, Clarendon, 1990).
Bergeijk, P.A.G. van, Haffner, R.C.G., Privatization, Deregulation and the Macroeconomy. (Cheltenham, Elgar, 1996).
Bjerke, B., Business Leadership and Culture. National Management Styles in the Global Economy. (Cheltenham, Elgar, 2000).
Blaug, M., The Economic Value of Education. (Cheltenham, Elgar, 1992).
Bourdieu, P., The Field of Cultural Production. (Cambridge, Polity, 1993).
Braden, J.B., et al, eds., Environmental Policy with Political and Economic Integration. The European Union and the United States. (Cheltenham, Elgar, 1996).
Buelens, F., ed., Globalisation and the Nation-State. (Antwerp, University of Antwerp, 1999).
Burlamaqui, L., et al., eds., Institutions and the Role of the State. (Cheltenham, Elgar, 2000).
Caiden, G.E., et al., eds., Where Corruption Lives. (Bloomfield, Kumarian Press, 2001).
Club of Rome, The Limits to Growth. (New York, Universe Books, 1966; 1972).
Cohen, S., Modern capitalist planning. The French model. (London, Weidenfeld & Nicolson, 1969; 1977).
Cohn, E., Johnes, G., Recent Developments in the Economics of Education. (Cheltenham, Elgar, 1994).
Cole, A., The New Governance of French Education? (In: Public Adminstration, pp. 707-724, 2001).
Cole, A., John, P., Local Governance in England and France. (London, Routledge, 2001).
Cooter, R.D., The Strategic Constitution. (Princeton, Princeton UP, 2001).

Corbett, A., Moon, B., eds., Education in France. Continuity and Change in the Mitterrand Years, 1981-1995. (London, Routledge, 1997).
Crane, D., The Production of Culture. (New York, Sage, 1992).
Creedy, J., The Economics of Ageing. (Cheltenham, Elgar, 1995).
Creedy, J., Pensions and Population Ageing. An Economic Analysis. (Cheltenham, Elgar, 1998).
Culyer, A.J., The Economics of Health. (Cheltenham, Elgar, 1991).
Davidson, P., ed., A Post Keynesian Perspective on Twenty-First Century Economic Problems. (Cheltenham, Elgar, 2001).
Dolzer, R., ed., Protecting Our Environment. (Sankt Augustin, Adenauer Stiftung, 2002).
Eichengreen, B., ed., The Reconstruction of the International Economy, 1945-1960. (Cheltenham, Elgar, 1996).
Dror, Y., The Capacity to Govern. Report to the Club of Rome. (New York, 1997).
Esping-Andersen, G., The Three Worlds of Welfare Capitalism. (Cambridge, Polity, 1990).
Farrazmand, A., ed., Handbook of Crisis and Emergency Management. (New York, Dekker, 2001).
Folmer, H., et al., eds., Principles of Environmental and Resource Economics. (Cheltenham, Elgar, 1995).
Frey, B.S., Pommerehne, W., Muses and Markets. Explorations in the Economics of the Arts. (Oxford, Blackwell, 1989).
Galbraith, J.K., Economics and the Arts. (London, Arts Council, 1983).
Garrouste, P., ed., Ioannides, S., eds., Evolution and Path Dependence in Economic Ideas. (Cheltenham, Elgar, 2001).
Gildea, R., The Past in French History. (New Haven, Yale UP, 1994).
Gilpin, R., France in the Age of the Scientific State. (Princeton, Princeton UP, 1968).
Gordon, P.H., Meunier, S., The French Challenge. Adapting to Globalization. (Washington DC, Brookings Institution, 2001).
Grampp, W.D., Pricing the Priceless. Art, Artists, and Economics. (New York, Basic Books, 1989).
Hanley, N., Spash, C.L., Cost-Benefit Analysis and the Environment. (Cheltenham, Elgar, 1993).
Hassenteufel, P., Marketization through the State. Health Insurance Reform in France. (In: Public Policy and Administration, 2001).
Heal, G., The Economics of Exhaustible Resources. (Cheltenham, Elgar, 1993).
Heilbrun, J., Gray, C.M., The Economics of Art and Culture. (Cambridge, CUP, 1994).
Hendon, W.S., ed., Economic Policy for the Arts. (Cambridge, MA, Harvard UP, 1980).
Hodgson, G.M., Economics and Institutions. (Oxford, Polity, 1988).
Hodgson, G.M., Evolution and Institutions. (Cheltenham, Elgar, 2000).
Hoppe, H.H., Democracy. The God that Failed. The Economics and Politics of Monarchy, Democracy and Natural Order. (New Brunswick, Transaction, 2002).
Keynes, J.M., The General Theory of Employment, Interest and Money. (London, Macmillan, 1936).
Kickert, W.J.M., ed., Public Management and Administrative Reform in Western Europe. (Cheltenham, Elgar, 1997).
Klamer, A., ed., The Value of Culture. (Amsterdam, Amsterdam UP, 1996).
Lebovics, H., True France. The Wars of Cultural Identity 1900-1945. (Ithaca, Corenell UP, 1992).
Lindbeck, A., The Welfare State. (Cheltenham, Elgar, 1993).
Lindblom, C.E., Inquiry and Change. The troubled Attempt to Understand and Shape Society. (New Haven, Yale UP, 1990).
Loughlin, J., Keating, M., eds., The Political Economy of Regionalism. (London, Cass, 1997).
Machin, H., Wright, V., Economic policy and policymaking under the Mitterrand presidency, 1981-1984. (New York, St.Martin's, 1984).
Maddison, A., Monitoring the World Economy, 1820-1992. (Paris, OECD, 1995).
March, J.G., Olsen, J.P., Rediscovering Institutions. (New York, Free Press, 1989).
Marshall, T.H., Social policy in the twentieth century. (London, Unwin Hyman, 1985).
Middlemas, K., Orchestrating Europe. (London, Fontana, 1995).
Middleton, R., Government Versus The Market. (Cheltenham, Elgar, 1996).
Ministry of National Education (France), The French University Libraries Directory in 2000. (Paris, DF, 2002).
Moïsi, D., France in an Age of Globalization. (Washinton DC, Brookings Institution, 2001).
Morrisson, F.L., ed., International, Regional and National Environmental Law. (The Hague, Kluwer, 2000).
Oates, W.E., The Economics of Environmental Regulation. (Cheltenham, Elgar, 1996).
OECD, Economic Perspectives. (Paris, OECD, 2000).
Ott, A.F., Hartley, K., eds., Privatization and Economic Efficiency. (Cheltenham, Elgar, 1991).

Pope, J., Confronting Corruption. The Elements of a National Integrity System. (Berlin, Transparency International, 2000).
Paxton, R.O., Vichy France: Old Guard and New Order, 1940-1944. (New York, Knopf, 1972; Columbia UP, 1982).
Paxton, R.O., Wahl, N., De Gaulle and the United States. (Oxford, Berg, 1994).
Porter, M.E., The Competitive Advantage of Nations. (New York, Free Press, 1990).
Pot, F., Employment Relations and National Culture. Continuity and Change in the Age of Globalization. (Cheltenham, Elgar, 2000).
Rifkin, J., The Hydrogen Economy. The Creation of the Worldwide Energy Web and the Redistribution of Power. (London, 2002).
Rischard, J.F., High Noon, 20 Global Issues, 29 Years to Solve Them. (New York, Basic Books, 2002).
Rivett, G., From Cradle to Grave. Fifty Years of the National Health Service. (London, 1998).
Rowley, C.K., ed., Property Rights and the Limits of Democracy. (Cheltenham, Elgar, 1993).
Savas, E.S., Privatization, the key to better government. (New York, Chatham, Chatham House, 1987).
Schneider, L., Bonjean, C.M., eds., The Idea of Culture in the Social Sciences. (New York, CUP, 1973).
Schokkaert, E., Ethics and Social Security Reform. (Aldershot, Ashgate, 2001).
Strayer, J.R., On the Medieval origins of the Modern State. (Princeton, Princeton UP, 1979).
Suleiman, E.N., France. The Transformation of a Society. (New York, 1995).
Susskind, L., ed., International Environmental Negotiation. An Integrative Approach. (Cambridge, MA, Pon, 1999).
Taylor, F.W., Principles and methods of scientific management. (New York, 1911).
Thorpe. F.N., The Constitutional History of the United States, 1765-1895. (New York, 1901; Da Capo Press, 1970).
Throsby, D., Withers, G.A., The Economics of Performing Arts. (London, Arnold, 1979).
Tisdell, C., Environmental Economics. (Cheltenham, Elgar, 1993).
Tuppen, J., The Economic Geography of France. (London, Croom Helm, 1983).
Vanthoor, W.F.V., European Monetary Union since 1848. (Aldershot, Elgar, 1996).
White, P., Hollingsworth, K., Audit, Accountability and Government. (Oxford, Clarendon, 1999).
Wilding, P., Talking Politics. (London, 1993).
Wilson, W., The Study of Administration. (In: Political science quarterly, pp. 198-222, 1987).
Wilson, W., The State. Elements of historical and practical politics. A sketch of institutional history and administration. (Boston, Heath, 1889).
World Bank, The State in a Changing World. (New York, OUP, 1997).
World Wildlife Fund, Living Planet Report. (London, 1998).
Zecchini, S., ed., Lessons from the Economic Transition: Central and Eastern Europe in the 1990s. (Dordrecht, Kluwer, 1997).

# 6. Politics and Public Management of Society

## 6.1. The two births of French political science

For Braud (1994, p.6) political sociology does not have an object of its own without the concepts "le pouvoir" (power), "l'État" (State) and "systèmes et régimes politiques" (political systems and regimes). In his view, political sociology is only one approach of the political object between others. Braud sees political sociology as a branch of political science. Political science might be seen as a branch of sociology as the broadest social science, however. At the end of the 1880s Émile Boutmy, founder in 1871 of the "École libre des Sciences Politiques" (Damamme, 1982) had a controversy with jurist Claude Bufnoir. The latter accentuated the relationship of political science to public law whilst Boutmy argued for autonomy of experimental and inductive "sciences politiques". More than elsewhere, public law was dominant in France as a sphere of knowledge about public authorities. This was due to the cherished invention of the "État de droit" (Rule of Law). Favre (1989) distinguished two birth-periods of French political science: the period 1871-1913, and 1943-1956, when it was definitely institutionalised. To determine the historical birth of a scientific discipline, a criterion of the scientific character of cognitive activities is needed in the first place. There is consensus about the statement that a proposal is scientific in so far as it is constructed and presented so that every competent other person can verify and falsify it adequately. This implies a logical criterion (procedures of reasoning, and confronting findings with reality) and a social criterion (formation of a group of competent others). The necessary possibility of reiterating what was done by others supposes a scientific community of experts, so there can be a scientific discipline only when there is an organised scientific community (institutions of debate, communication of results of research, and evaluation). Favre argues that social sciences change the object of study as social realities are dynamically changing realities. It is not clear what political science is about: politics, but what is politics? Up to the 1880s "politique" was more general than "social" (reduced to the labour movement). Later "social" was all-encompassing and "politique" had a reduced meaning.

In the 1880s the most common meaning of the term politics in France was "ce qui est relatif au gouvernement de l'État, ni plus ni moins" (what is relevant to the government of the State, no more no less). Thus more public management than political science. The term was extensively interpreted, and variously interpretable and so it was by no means easy to determine the object of political science. According to Favre (1989, pp. 12-13) it is unknown and even impossible to know what French political science was about in the 19th century. In his view, there is a discipline when the following criteria are fulfilled: it has a name as recognised by a community of scientists; a relative consensus that a number of study objects falls within the sphere of this discipline; institutions of education and research and a means of communication to spread the results of research. At the end of the 19th century, insiders (university) were of the opinion that scientific study of all political facts was possible, but at that time there was no university organisation which could materialise concentrated research. The nature of scientific activities was mostly not empirical. In about 1890 a key issue was the position of political sciences in the development of higher positions in public management (Tranchant, 1878). There were "wars" between adherents of different solutions. Three formulas were suggested (Favre, 1989, p.84). Formula 1: integration of political sciences in the normal program of faculties of law. Formula 2: creation of a new structure, "facultés politiques et administratives". And Formula 3: a special school outside university. Boutmy took the initiative in 1871 by creating a private

"École libre des sciences politiques". Hippolyte Carnot started an "École nationale d'administration", but this was a failure. A bill of June 1881 tried nationalisation with a "Faculté d'État de sciences politiques". This failed too when it was postponed for budget reasons. Organisation of "sciences politiques, économiques et administratives" in faculties of law was the least costly alternative. Quite a tactical move, after half a century of opposition by jurists, now adhering to this solution.

Bufnoir (1881) and most jurists then had the view that political science is the science of law by definition (disciplinary imperialism "avant la lettre"). Boutmy (1889) tried to counter this by defending the thesis that political sciences don't belong to the science of law, because they are based on history by principle. The proposed study program in the faculties of law (economics, constitutional law, administrative law, international public law, and public finance) included less than half of the "sciences politiques et administratives". He stressed that the science of law is deductive, while political science is experimental and inductive. Between 1890 and 1905, public law made the word "science politique" disappear from faculties of law for half a century, up to the reform of 1954, which introduced political science (Rev.int. d'histoire politique et constitutionnelle, 1957). A comparable issue was the question of if and how sociology would have to be integrated into the faculties of law, dominantly in the grip of Roman law and civil law. Some argued for transforming faculties of law into faculties of social sciences. Jurists answered the question by denying that sociology had to be instructed in the faculties of law. They thought they had done enough by organising courses and research in "sciences politiques, administratives et économiques". Since about 1890, social sciences have been more the vogue than political sciences. Favre (1989, p.98) gives the Duguit-Hauriou debate a central position. Duguit (1889) argued: "Social science or sociology is mainly composed of two parts, law and political economy." He said that sociology had a general part too. It studies the forming of social groups, determines laws about this, and classifies different social types. There are accessory sciences such as political science. For Duguit there is no distinct political science, as "political phenomena are about the origin and functioning of the State." They are in essence juridical phenomena. For Hauriou (1893) there is an important difference between law and sociology. Sociology is based on the hypothesis of universal determinism, with the ambition that it can predict exactly the destiny of societies. For law, however, there are responsible subjects, having an impact on social developments. After meeting Durkheim, Duguit changed his attitude, and he became "durkheimien". The Duguit-Hauriou debate changed after Hauriou's "Précis de droit administratif et de droit public" (1896), and Duguit's study, "L'État, le droit objectif et la loi positive" (1901-1903).

Political science at the end of the 19th century was called "science du gouvernement de l'État", or "science de l'État en général" in France: more Public Management of Society than Political science. That is evident already from the empirical fact that there were many books about the State. To enumerate some: "L'État, ses origines, sa nature et son but" (1885) by A. Régnard; "L'État moderne et ses fonctions" (1890) by P. Leroy-Beaulieu; "Le droit individuel et l'État" (1891) by C. Beudant; "L'Idée de l'État" (1894) by H. Michel; "État, politique et morale de classe" (1901) by J. Guesde; and L. Duguit's "L'État, le droit objectif et la loi positive" (1901-1903). The French scientific community was by no means introvert, or closed with regard to scientific developments abroad. Translations did abound, as with "Théorie générale de l'État" (1877) by M. Bluntschli; "L'État" (1902) by W.W. Wilson; "L'État moderne et son droit" (1911) by G. Jellinek; and "L'État, ses origines, son évolution et son avenir" (1913) by F. Oppenheimer. While there seems to be consensus about the non-existence of the State in the Middle Ages, this term has been used since then, with varying interpretations. Strayer (1979) is known for his assertion that constitutive elements of the modern state have been present in Western Europe since the period 1,000-1,300. The term State was used to denote central public authority (monarchy, republic), recognised internally within a specific territory, and externally by other states. Up to the French Revolution terms like nation, society, constitution, people, and public interest were also used. Tocqueville in his "Ancien Régime et la Révolution" (1856) prefered the notions "institutions politiques", "autorité publique", "pouvoir central" or "l'ordre social et politique". At the end of the 19th century, the notion "État" crystallised. Carré de Malberg gave a generally accepted definition: "a community of human beings, fixed on their own territory, with an organisation, which has a superior power of action, command and coercion with regard to members of this community". This shows the drawback of most definitions of the State: it denotes the people living together upon a specific territory with a common public authority, and/or public authority. This last interpretation is clear in Tilly's formulation (1975): 'the organization that controls the population on a specific territory, being differentiated from other organizations functioning in the same territory, being autonomous and centralized with co-ordinated subdivisions."

The notion of State soon got competition from notions such as "pouvoir", "système politique", "régime". Also in "The Process of Government" (1908) by A.F. Bentley. Many French jurists distanced themselves from the notion "État" by concentrating upon the public service concept: "service public, la pierre angulaire du droit administratif" (Jèze). Sociologists such as E. Durkheim in his "De la division du travail social" (1893) and even more pronouncedly in his courses (1898-1914, edited only in 1937 and 1950: "Leçons de sociologie") took "État" as the starting-point for elaborations on societal questions. He defined the political nature of a society with the division between (powerful) governors and (powerless) governed (Lacroix, 1981). This criterion was not a sufficient condition, though, as there are power phenomena elsewhere also (for example in families). Durkheim elaborated complementary characteristics. A society is called political when "formed by the collection of a number of social groups that are subdued to the same authority, which itself is not subdued to any regularly constituted authority". A second element was that "a certain group differentiated itself from the collective mass to form a specific organ, distinguished from the rest of society". Durkheim accentuated the need for a special word for denoting "the special group of functionaries charged to represent that authority, .the State". Durkheim even stated that individual rights were not given with the individual, but only by the work of the State. He had a rather exalted idea of the State with an unlimited range of tasks, such as bringing the individual gradually to moral existence, etc. Durkheim opposed the State and the mass of simple, thoughtless citizens: "The State is the seat of a higher, clear consciousness, with the highest level of consciousness and reflection.".  "Strictly speaking, the State is the organ of the social thinking as such...Its essential function is to think, it is the central nervous system, it is the social brain." The State, in his conception, is not there to receive what the mass thinks: "The role of the State is not to express or resume the unthoughtful assertions of the mass, but to add to their superficial reasoning a more sophisticated thought. The State cannot be otherwise than different." This could by no means be seen as political sociology. Durkheim's work is a mixture of sociology and loose, pre-scientific intellectualism and moralism. Prominent jurist L. Duguit explored "L'État" in two basic volumes (1901/1903): "L'État, le droit objectif et la loi positive" (I), and "L'État, les gouvernants et les agents" (II). The last volume started: "The State is the historical product of a social differentiation between strong and weak members of a given society." Being a jurist, Duguit started in the introduction to his first volume with a modern, sociological-empirical and realist approach. "The State is a human community, fixed on a given territory, where the most powerful impose their will upon the weaker members." (I, p.9). In his view, one must observe reality to treat State and law, it is a necessary condition for science.

Duguit distances himself from all fictions, metaphysical hypotheses and abstractions. He ridicules artificial products of juridical construction: "...Social organism? Observed by nobody (p.6). Does there exist a collective essence? Nobody knows (p.7). Is the human act free? Nobody knows. (p.17)." With his realism, Duguit criticised so-called "modern" theories of the State, founded on personification of the collectivity. In these theories, the State is seen as a person, an organism with a will, or as a titular of rights. Duguit asks rhetorically: When we observe reality, what do we see? Powerful persons imposing their will on weak persons. Instead of expecting the solution of societal conflicts from realist power relations, Duguit emphasizes the need for law to bind powerful persons also. "The Rule of Law, superior to individual and State, superior to governors and governed." (I, p.12). And where does this Rule of Law come from, so that it is accepted also by powerful persons? This is accepted due to its "objective character" (I, p. 16). According to Duguit, "the Rule of Law is a factual rule. An imposing rule for human beings, not on the basis of a superior principle (common good, general interest or happiness), but by the force of facts, because humans cannot do otherwise than live in society. This in a sense is the law of social life. People do feel or conceive this law. Scholars give it a definition. The legislator draws it up and guarantees its respect. The legislator himself is subject to this law, because his legislation is nothing, if it is not expression of this law of social life imposing itself upon all." (I, p.16). The science of law has to formulate the material contents of the Rule of Law. So, there is a narrow path to making the science of law the primary science of society, imperialism of law: "The notion of law is general. It encloses the notion of the whole society." (I, p.310). Duguit's work about the State is not political science proper, it is philosophy of law and perhaps political philosophy. If the State has power to impose itself, this power should only be in the service of the law (I, p.11), and: "The power of the State becomes legitimate if persons disposing of this power use it to accomplish commitments which are imposed upon them by the Rule of Law." (I, p.15). Duguit deduced the Rule of Law from "social solidarity". The role of the State is to establish that there already exists a Rule of Law, and that this Rule of Law is guaranteed in practice. Crucial in his conception is that the State has to be subject to law.

## 6.2. French institutionalist paradigm. Emergence of empirical social science

Another prominent jurist, A. Esmein, elaborated a fundamental contribution to the theory of the State and public law. In "Éléments de droit constitutionnel français et comparé" (1896), Esmein defined some key concepts for the law of the State within a coherent framework. In his view, there is a nation only if there is a superior authority with regard to individual wills (p.1), sovereignty (the competence to command over all citizens in a nation). The State is the juridical personification of the nation and permanent titular of sovereignty (identification of State and sovereign). The State is there as long as there is a nation: "Its juridical existence does not allow any discontinuity...By its personification of the nation, the State is destined to endure as long as the nation itself." (p.2). Esmein argued that the State is a corporate body, a juridical fiction. The State must be distinguished from physical persons who are exercising sovereignty, and citizens. So the State has no material existence, it is a construct to produce juridical effects. Its construction is meant to prevent any person or corporation expropriating sovereignty, because its objective is that it works for all: "Sovereignty may only be exercised in the interest of all." As the State is only a fiction, somebody has to exercise sovereignty, willing or acting for the State (p.3). Sovereign can be one person (monarch), an assembly or the people (directly or indirectly, via representatives).

Esmein jumps from State-as-sovereign to government-as-sovereign: "Government ... that's sovereignty in operation ... exercising sovereignty of public authority ... fulfilling the functions as they are genuine for the State' (p.9). He differentiated despotic government ("those who exercise sovereignty according to their own will") and legal government ("If those persons exercising sovereignty are doing this according to rules, known previously, which dictate the decision in concrete cases to the sovereign".). Law is crucial as imperative or prohibitive rule, which for the sake of the general interest is ruling for all, for the future, for always (p.10). Esmein emphasized, that the individual has rights, which are anterior and superior to those of the State, and that they have to be respected therefore by the State. This principle forbids the sovereign to make laws that affect individual rights, and forces him to issue laws that guarantee the full use of these rights." (pp. 19-20). Esmein elaborated object and method of the study of "droit constitutionnel et institutions politiques": constitutional law and political institutions. An overlapping borderland between public law science and political science. Esmein accentuated the importance of "L'État de droit" (Rule of Law) by developing constitutional principles. On this is based the usage in French political science of what was called "le paradigme institutionnaliste" (Favre, 1989, p.198). As in J.J. Chevallier's "Histoire des institutions politiques..." (1981), and publications about social and political questions in the framework of public law and political science (Fuzier-Herman, 1880; Lefebvre, 1882; Saint-Girons, 1881) and studying institutions, while making tasks of public authorities concrete (Desplaces, 1892; Hervieu, 1893; Lair, 1889). The term "political institutions" is confusing, often not properly defined and including institutions such as courts (public authorities) and political parties (private organisations not being public authorities). It is better to agree to reserve the notion of public institutions for institutions with a task as public authority.

Not only juridical, but also economic approaches to the activities of public authorities had their impact on the development of French political science and public management science. To make this clear, it is time to present a summary of "L'État moderne et ses fonctions" (1890) by P. Leroy-Beaulieu. In the framework of political economy and sociology of the State, he wrote about many issues in social sciences. He took the modern, representative State as object of study, characterised by the temporary delegation of public authority by those who elect their political leaders. This kind of State did run the risk of politics-for-the-short-run structurally. All decisions are taken with elections as the decisive perspective. In the spirit of the time, Leroy-Beaulieu (p.88) accentuated the liberal, limited-State approach: "Because the State is an organism of authority using or threatening to use coercion, the path of liberty has to be followed, whenever this realises results that are almost equivalent." The State has, as a monopolist, two crucial dimensions: it has the power to impose its will, even by legitimated use of violence; and it can levy taxes for an open-ended range of activities. For Leroy-Beaulieu, the State has three basic functions: guaranteeing social security of the nation and the rights and security of citizens; jurisdiction and application of law; and conservation of the national patrimony. He did add as a special function colonisation as mission for the greater States of the West. With regard to the rising popularity of economic State interventionism (railway industry), Leroy-Beaulieu (p.214) observed a tendency towards costless use for clients, funded by taxpayers. The State tended to apply interventionism in enterprises, for electoral considerations: unstoppable growth of public functionaries (bureaucratisation).

A fertile source for the development of political science and public management science was the emergence of empirical social sciences, especially sociology and social psychology. Studies in social psychology abounded in France in the period 1890-1910: Abbo (1910); Boutmy (1901); Fouillée (1898;1903); Le Bon (1898;1910); Marie (1909); Tarde (1890). When Le Bon wrote his "Psychologie politique" (1910), his political psychology was more or less the same as political science or public management science. Favre (1989, p. 211), in his interesting attempt to describe and explain the several births of French political science in the 1870-1914 period, argued: "The invention of a science such as political science was a factual process of a group of authors, of whom a minority realised work which by contemporary criteria could be qualified as scientific. All did collectively contribute to a new way of approaching political phenomena, so enabling the development of future political science. Before ranging these works in the category of ideological writings, it is necessary to search more thoroughly and analyse, case for case, what kind of intellectual method was used." Knowing the world was capable of reform, was a rule of thumb. This was an impulse for social sciences, with the level of positive sciences as perspective. Auguste Comte, in "Système de politique positive" (1854), used positivist knowledge to improve, so substituting the traditional "philosophise to judge". Changing society gave ample materials for social research (industrialisation, social question, colonisation, etc.). Social and political problems abounded, producing many studies about social and political questions (Deschanel, 1898; Desjardins, 1893; Faguet, 1898), particularly about the social question (Abzac, 1881; Barolin, 1902; Blondel, 1887; Brasseur, 1900; Charlier, 1894; Delory, 1893; Legay, 1891; Mannequin, 1894; Molinari, 1891; Stein, 1900). There was a certain obsession to search for facts (hyperfactuality). Not all the studies complied with scientific criteria. One tried to further the objective, scientific study of political phenomena. There was a confusion of "scientific socialism" (comparable with "scientific Marxism") and "sociologie". Durkheim (1970, p.242) wrote: "About socialism conceived as a theory of social facts, sociology has only this to say: Sociology, wanting to be true to itself and methodologically correct has to refuse to see this as a scientific enterprise."

The impact of the science of history is relevant (Bourdé/Martin, 1983; Carbonell, 1976). Up to the second half of the 19th century it was often thought that one could know the present through historical references going back to Antiquity, or a philosophy of the historical evolution of millennia, then it became the vogue to study the present only with reference to the immediate past. Of course, adequate studies about social phenomena should do both. With prominent forerunners like Michelet, Guizot, and Quinet, history became scientific in France from the first half of the 19th century. Two books about the classification of sciences were published, A. Comte (1830) and A. Ampère (1834; 1843). Ampère classified 128 sciences, with a prominent place for political science ("science ultime, science multiple"), for the development of which knowledge about all other sciences was thought necessary. It was seen to have a multiple character, encompassing 16 different sciences. Four economic sciences; four military sciences (armaments, tactics, strategy, "science de la victoire"); four juridical sciences (study of laws, jurisprudence, comparative legislation, theory of the laws) and four political sciences (public law, diplomacy, art of governing, theory of power).

After Ampère, A.A. Cournot (1851) made his own division for co-ordination of human sciences. Comte in his "Cours de philosophie positive" (1830-1842) had a rational classification of fundamental positive sciences: "la science mathématique, l'astronomie, la physique, la chimie, la physiologie, et physique sociale". The last was renamed "sociologie". In "Catéchisme positiviste" (1852), he classified: "1. mathématique, 2. physique, 3. biologie, 4. sociologie, 5. morale". The classification of Comte had ample success. At the end of the 19th century, "sciences de la société" were no longer called "sciences politiques", but "sociologie ou sciences sociales". This meant a change of paradigm: the social got priority with regard to the individual, and to politics as well. Political science was only one of the social sciences. For one of the founding fathers of social science, E. Durkheim, there were as many branches of sociology or specific social sciences as there are different social facts. He proclaimed that social facts had to be studied as material objects, as things. He differentiated in 1886 between general sociology and normal sociology encompassing three disciplines. One studying the State, the second studying the regulatory functions (law, moral, religion) and the third studying economic functions and pathological sociology (criminology). After 1888 however, Durkheim no longer gave a place to "sociologie de l'État" or "sociologie politique". Coste in "Principes d'une sociologie objective (1899) gave a prominent place to facts of political order or government. For Gumplowicz (1895) the primary object of sociology is "the State, a coercive organisation for the domination of one or more social groups over other groups." At the end of the 19th century, political sociology was seen as a branch of sociology, and political science as one of the social sciences. Gabriel Tarde's endeavour to give political sociology an impulse failed. The influence of Durkheimians faded after Durkheim's death and the First World War. Political sociology developed in "facultés des lettres" (Gurvitch, Aron).

At the start of the 20th century there were many studies about social and political questions, which might be qualified as scientific in the field of political phenomena. The official start of French political science is seen in A. Siegfried's "Tableau politique de la France de l'Ouest sous la Troisième République" (1913). This book of geographer Siegfried was pioneering in the scientific study of elections. It was based upon exemplary empirical observations, statistics and systematised scientific work, so this work did stand out from mainstream publications in his time about social and political themes. Later, aspects of his work were criticised though. Siegfried was criticised for simplifying the division of political groups to the left-right scale, while his methods of assembling data and methodological approach were commented, but generally the scientific status of his work was recognised. This study was seen as founding electoral geography, while it laid the foundations for the theory of electoral behaviour. Siegfried's book was tested according to the ideas of Popper (falsification) by P. Bois (1960), and partly falsified. The research of Siegfried was such that it could be falsified, and this marks its scientific standard (Favre, 1989, p. 254). More than the publication of a scientific book is needed to conclude that a scientific discipline has been born, including a community of scientists working in a field of science. The pioneering "Tableau politique de la France de l'Ouest" (1913) was ignored for about 30 years. In the period 1945-1950 only electoral sociology had a real start. Siegfried's own interests were mostly elsewhere. In Siegfried's footsteps, a team directed by Y. Lacoste did prominent work with "Géopolitiques des régions françaises" (1986). Siegfried did not succeed in realising official recognition by way of an independent discipline, where M. Duverger (1951) did, with a prominent university position, research, and students. This was due to circumstances, the First World War and its aftermath (Favre, 1989, p. 306).

The vicissitudes of Siegfried's "Tableau", according to Favre, is exemplary for the development of French political science between the two world wars. The "École libre des sciences politiques" was recognised for formation of the elite, but had no innovative potential (Rain, 1963). To the end of the 1930s, the Durkheimian school was dominant in sociology, with no interest in political sociology. Historians followed the innovative "Annales", created in 1929 by Lucien Febvre and Marc Bloch, with "l'exclusion du politique" as one of its features. In the faculties of law, the idea of developing political science within the framework of the science of law was put aside. There were exceptions, such as Carré de Malberg's "Contribution à la théorie générale de l'État" (1920). Its implications were rediscovered at the end of the 1950s. Favre compared the development of political science in France with that abroad (US, England, Germany). In these countries there was no such stagnation as in France, exhausted by the 1914-1918 war (Grawitz/Leca, 1985). From the second half of the thirties, the situation changed, as can be concluded from "La révolution nécessaire" (1933) by Aron and Dandieu, Marxist studies etc. Authors analysed societal developments: R. Pelloux with "Le parti national-socialiste et ses rapports avec l'État", and M. Prélot with "L'empire fasciste" (1936). Future political scientists such as G. Burdeau and J. Chevallier, defended theses in faculties of law.

## 6.3. The second birth of French political science

Favre (1989) elaborated the thesis that French political science was born for the second time in the period 1943-1956. J. Stoetzel, after creating the "Institut français d'opinion publique" (IFOP) in 1938, produced his thesis "Théorie des opinions" (1943). In 1943 Chevallier started his course about the history of political ideas at the "École libre" and B. de Jouvenel published his "Du pouvoir" (1943). Burdeau, after his "Cours de droit constitutionnel" (1942), published "Le droit public et l'État" (1943), which anticipated his magistral "Traité de science politique" (1949-1957). They started a privileged object of study in French political science according to the French institutionalist paradigm: "public law and political institutions". M. Duverger's "Les constitutions de la France" (1944), and F. Goguel's "Politique des partis sous la Troisème République" (1946) were relevant too. On 9 October 1945, the "École libre des sciences politiques" was nationalised. It was transformed into two institutions: "Institut d'études politiques" (IEP) of the University of Paris, and "Fondation nationale des sciences politiques", promoting progress and diffusion of political, economic and social sciences. IEP's were started in Aix-en-Provence, Bordeaux, Grenoble, Lyon, Strasbourg and Toulouse. In 1949 the "Association française de science politique" started, and in 1951, the "Revue française de science politique". French political science got impulses from prominent jurists, increasingly themselves becoming political scientists (Burdeau, Duverger, Vedel, etc). Some relevant factors have to be taken into account when one concludes that there is a new, specific scientific discipline (Favre, 1985). The methods used in this field of study should comply with standards of social sciences. The social determinants for social sciences are part of general history. Political science, a social science, has common ground in what binds social sciences together (culture of humanity). Political science does take a part of social reality as its object of study, politics, while this object is intensively interrelated with society and social phenomena. A choice of study object for a social science is always relative. Social science should be clear about the definition of its object. What is "political" in political science? Definitions abound, but don't give clear boundaries. In the search for the meaning of political in political science, it is evident that the word political is variously interpretable (political as semantically fluid term).

Often political is used as a catch-all-notion, encompassing all social phenomena and so becoming identical with social. Political is associated with many connotations, which make it less valuable for inter-subjectively acceptable propositions. Experiences in representative democracy show that what is commonly called politics is often largely an arena of partisan activities, but political science is claiming to study the functioning of public authorities adequately. To operationalise progress in the scientific study of social sciences, it is a good procedure to differentiate and to concentrate research in-depth upon a well-defined social phenomenon. So it seems a priori plausible to concentrate on an unique phenomenon in human history, public authorities. Political science studies of political public authorities (ministers, elected representatives) as part of political science are a relevant topic, but it is stretching the span-of-control of political science too far when political science claims more or less the whole field of activities of public authorities as its own. This is done by using the notion political system and then including almost everything in this political system (for example courts). It is a question of semantics too. Incorporation into political science of all public authorities and everything that they are (not) doing, causes structural underscoring of very relevant dimensions that are part of other social sciences (law, social anthropology, sociology, economics, geography, etc.). It produces only a political science model of public authorities.

A representative study about "Sociologie politique" (1994, pp. 12-16), by P. Braud, has it that political sociology is a branch of political science. Why not see political science as political sociology, and so as part of sociology? Apart from the influence of Tocqueville and Marx, the start of social sciences is placed in the period 1830-1900 with the work of Tönnies, Weber, Durkheim and Simmel. These four men are generally considered to have done the most to give modern sociological theory a systematic form (Nisbet, 1984, p.10). An important fact for European political sociology is the rise of Anglo-Saxon intellectual influence since the fifties of the 20th century, and especially in the sixties and seventies. In France, analysis of institutions seems to escape from Anglo-Saxonism. More or less jumping to conclusions, Braud states that, along with economics and sociology, political science has an object, making political science an independent social science, subdivided into political theory, international relations, "science administrative" and "sociologie politique". Political sociology is seen as a branch of political science, and as sociology. "Science administrative" is seen as an independent discipline and as a branch of political science. This is rather confusing. Formulating more precisely, it seems adequate to define political science analytically as social science studying politics, the power aspect of human life, and sociology as a social science about all social aspects of human life. Both sociology and political science study a part of the public authority phenomenon. The artificial, inconsistent demarcation of science of administration, the non-political part of the public authority phenomenon, as branch of political science can better be replaced by public management science, including the complete public authority phenomenon.

A further cleaning-up of notions and definitions is needed with regard to key-notions such as "pouvoir" (power) and "État" (State). For Braud (1994, pp. 21-66) it is obvious that the notion "pouvoir" is a heavily overstrained one. Without claiming completeness, one might mention some different meanings for "pouvoir". In the institutionalist approach as a synonym of "gouvernants" (governors) or "gouvernement" (government) or "l'État" (State); "instance politique" (political instance) versus "administration publique" (public administration) and "organe constitutionnel de l'État" (constitutional organ of the State). "Pouvoir" is used as a substantialist notion in having power (substantialist approach), and "pouvoir" can denote a relation between two or more individuals: having power over somebody else (interactionist approach). Jurists use "pouvoir" as juridical competence. A relevant item is execution of power by (a representative of) the State in relation to the liberty of the individual. B. Constant (1797), writing at the start of the 19th century, distinguished "liberté des Anciens" (liberty as participation in the making of law) and "liberté des Modernes' (liberty as autonomy). Max Weber is famed for saying: "Power is each chance of making one's own will triumph in a social relation, against all resistance; irrespective of which foundation this chance is based on." (1971, p.56). For John Stuart Mill (1863) and the English utilitarianist school (Hume, Bentham), the rationally calculating individual is guided by seeking a compromise between expected advantages and costs (in the broadest sense). H. Simon in "Administrative Behaviour" (1947) developed the idea of limited rationality as the normal case. Dahl (1973) said: A has power over B in so far as A gets something Y done by B, who would not have done this otherwise.

## 6.4. German influences, Marxism and Communism

In the history of political ideas, German philosophers Kant, Hegel, Schopenhauer and Nietzsche have a prominent place. Kant (1724-1804) in "Kritik der reinen Vernunft" (epistemology), "Kritik der praktischen Vernunft" (ethics) and "Kritik der Urteilskraft" (aesthetics) laid the basis of his criticism against all dogmatism (also that of Enlightenment). Hegel (1770-1831), inspired by Kant, Lessing and Herder, conceived an imposing philosophy of absolute idealism (Hyppolite, 1983). Schopenhauer (1788-1860) in "Die Welt als Wille und Vorstellung" (1819) had a pessimist philosophy: the world is only what the human subject is thinking; the irrational will is the driving force. Nietzsche (1844-1900) produced a broad oeuvre. He criticised Christianity, as its doctrine of humility and self-denial made men slaves (Andler, 1958). He opposed "Herrenmoral" against this "Sklavenmoral". Nietzsche elaborated his ideas in "Also sprach Zarathustra", "Jenseits von Gut und Böse", and "Der Wille zur Macht". He even made the will to power the highest principle. Hegel's dialectical method was adopted by Karl Marx. Hegel launched his theory of the historical necessity of the State, thereby replacing the basic position of natural law by history (Bourgeois, 1969). Instead of elaborating universal principles applicable in all circumstances, Hegel accentuated the primordial relevance of historical truth and circumstantial evidence. In his study about the Constitution of Germany (1799/1802), he transposed Machiavelli's idea to the contemporary situation in Germany, in the grip of many small independent lords, not being a State, but having to become one by historical necessity. Historical necessity replaced the dominant idea of natural law by means of positive law in the framework of the State. The philosopher was seen as "secretary of History". Hegel did not shrink from exalted terms, qualifying the State as the subject of history, a real God on earth, apex of the development of the human spirit (Taminiaux, 1984). After realising his "Phaenomenologie des Geistes" (1806-1807), Hegel elaborated his ideas about the State in "Grundlinien der Philosophie des Rechts" (1821). Hegel rejected theoretical constructions (universal abstractions) about the ideal State without relations with historical realities, and also the elaboration of positive law particularities (empiricism), as law theoreticians did, so the dialectics of universal and particular in the historical process were neglected (Rosenfield, 1984).

Hegel's complicated abstractions caused many different interpretations (Hondt, 1982; Weil, 1974). Soon a movement, called Young Hegelians, developed. They thought to read in Hegel's works that the history of the world was completing itself in the rational State, and the history of philosophy in that of Hegel. Heirs of Hegel were distinguished in Left, Centre and Right. Hegelian Left was given a profile by Feuerbach. For Feuerbach, human beings were alienated from their own essence because the essence of humanity was attributed to God. The time had come for humanity to take its existence in its own hands. Feuerbach criticised the idealism of Hegel to whom he attributed the thesis that human existence came from thinking. Feuerbach argued that thinking came from the human being, sensible to materialism. Karl Marx (1818-1883) in the years 1838-1844 was a Young Hegelian before following his own path of communism (Marxism). Marx criticised Hegel's Principles of the philosophy of law in "Critique de la philosophie du droit de Hegel" (1843). Marx was also deeply influenced by others: Proudhon, Saint-Simon and many others (Russ, 1973). Although there are other influences upon the development of the conception of Marx, it became custom to mention three sources for Marxism: German philosophy (Hegel), English political economy (Ricardo, Smith) and French socialism (Saint-Simon, Fourier). During his stay in Paris (1843-1845) Marx had contacts with groups of French and German communist workers.

Inspired by workers' activism, Marx became convinced that workers were the activists for the realisation of revolution and emancipation. In 1845, he elaborated his eleven "Theses about Feuerbach", inter alia about revolutionary praxis. In the 11th thesis, Marx stated that it was necessary to know and interpret the world, but especially to transform the world. Using Feuerbach's model of religious alienation, Marx argued that Hegel's universalist concept of the abstract and alienated State was not adequate in relation to the people as concrete reality. Marx took as starting-point French materialism, according to which principle it is necessary to change the external, material conditions first. The non-Cartesian branch of French materialism (Condillac, Helvétius) lead, in the view of Marx, by its theory about the influence of circumstances upon human beings, directly to socialism and communism. When man is formed by the circumstances, one has to form the circumstances humanely. Marx argued for the primacy of the circumstances, the material and the objective. Criticising the materialism of Feuerbach, Marx made the jump of a dialectical synthesis. The contradiction between French materialism and German idealism was solved by revolutionary praxis. His break with Hegel's concept of the State was manifest. Marx had a philosophy of historical materialism and revolutionary praxis. The class of workers as proletariat was the subject to realise a revolution against bourgeois society. Studying the doctrines of Smith and Ricardo, Marx (Mandel, 1982; 1983) criticised capitalism. He wrote several works with Friedrich Engels (1820-1895). They were active in the Internationale, founding "scientific socialism" (Cornu, 1955/1970).

Marx emphasized that human history has to be distinguished from natural history, because human beings made history, but not nature. Social relations are not natural facts, but are produced historically by human beings, and can be transformed by them: revolutionary praxis. Opposing Hegel, Marx gave the primacy to the real movement above the thinking. This real movement is primarily formed by material processes of production. The foundation of human history is related to human relations as determined by processes of production. Historical materialism analyses social reality as totality which has its material base in the modes of production ("infrastructure"), while many human activities ("suprastructure") often play an important role. Material production (or economic conditions) is conditioning (not necessarily determining) the whole of social life, dominantly influenced by factors such as religion or politics. Marx distinguished production forces (means of production, labour) and production relations (social relations, developing into productive processes). The contradiction between capitalist production forces and old production relations is the material basis for bourgeois revolutions in 17th and 18th centuries. The most important production relation is the division of society into classes. In the Communist Manifesto (1848), Marx and Engels argued that the history of society is the history of the class struggle. The class of oppressors is formed by all who own or control the means of production. The class of oppressed, proletarians, is composed of the labour force, producing social wealth. Exploitation is the vital relationship between the two. The dominant class takes the surplus, produced by the labour of the oppressed.

In the capitalist system of production, workers often have the illusion that they get a salary more or less equivalent to the value of their work, but capitalists appropriate part of the surplus value of their work in the form of profits, rent and interest. Consciousness of this unjust exploitation determines when oppressed classes rebel to limit or eliminate exploitation. Capitalism tends to simplify class struggle by dividing people in propertied and unpropertied persons. Industrialisation expands the number of unpropertied proletarians, local class struggles extend to the national level. The class of proletarians, becoming conscious of the exploitation, form a political party. Communists are seen as the most activist of workers' parties. They are said to distinguish themselves from other parties by promoting the common interests of all proletarians in the whole world, and by representing the interests of the whole proletarian movement in several phases of the struggle between proletarians and bourgeois. As Marx said during the First Internationale, emancipation of the workers has to be done by themselves. To give this a better chance against national bulwarks, workers had to combine their action internationally: "Proletariat of all countries, unite!" The First Internationale (1864-1876) did succumb, due to the conflict between Marx and Bakoenin. The Second Internationale (1889-1939) was a renewed attempt to co-ordinate the activities of national Socialist parties. The Third Internationale (1919-1943) was the club of Communist parties under the control of Moscow, "Komintern". Followers of Trotsky had a Fourth Internationale.

In the conception of Marx and Engels, dominant classes in capitalist societies have an institutional apparatus to control, neutralise or smooth the class struggle and to maintain social order: the State. The State, proceeding from civil society, places itself increasingly above this civil society, alienating itself from it. The State seems to be the representative of the whole society, but the State works as an instrument of the bourgeois dominant class, as feudal lords did in the Middle Ages and masters of slaves in Antiquity. Marx and Engels recognised that in some periods the State can have a degree of autonomy with regard to the classes, and can play a role as arbiter or mediator. In his study "Le 18-Brumaire de Louis Bonaparte" (1852), Marx accentuated the power of the State apparatus in France: Executive power with its bureaucratic and military organisation, its complex and artificial State mechanism, its army of about half a million functionaries, and its other army of 500,000 soldiers, terrible parasitical corps which encompasses the whole French society, as it was formed during the absolutist monarchy. It was necessary for the proletariat to destroy the State apparatus with the help of the farmers. Speaking about the "Commune" of Paris (18 March/29 May 1871) Marx praised "communards" for having ruined the military and bureaucratic apparatus. A proletarian revolution against the State as such, "that supernatural abortion of society". Lenin called the Commune of Paris a paradigmatic example of the "dictatorship of the proletariat". The proletarian revolution, in the vision of Marx and Engels, would bring communism by collectivising the means of production and abolishing the alienation of the State. When the final phase, communism, was realised, the State would languish, as Engels said. In "Origine de la famille, de la propriété privée et de l'État" (1884) he stated: Society, reorganising production with egalitarian association of producers, will put the State machine where it belongs: in the museum of antiquities. Marx and Engels derived much from utopian socialists. Their vision differs in method. A revolutionary struggle of the world proletariat is thought to produce a society without classes. Their ideas had a wide emanation.

## 6.5. From State to Public Management of Society

The term State is often used in political science studies to denote national, central public authority as a political phenomenon (State as political power), but the term State is an overburdened concept. It is often suggested that this term should be done away with in scientific projects (Lacroix, in Grawitz/Leca, 1985, I. p. 472). For Bergeron (1965) the State is not an important theoretical concept. In practice, the State-concept has its impact: as the national organ of public authority. In international relations, national countries, nation-states, are recognised as subjects of international law. Other interpretations are used in the opposition State/Society, and as representation of a collectivity. It is useful to follow Braud (1994, p.67) differentiating the concept of the State as "pouvoir politique" (government), juridical society and symbolic production. Max Weber (1922) is known for his definition of the State as institutional undertaking, which by implementation of its rules disposes of legitimate physical coercion. It seems impossible to define the State completely by circumscribing all its tasks. What differentiates the State from other institutions are its instruments, legitimised by its objective, the common good. In the course of time the notion State crystallised as having specific characteristics. To further insight about the State phenomenon (as public management), one can compare archaic societies without a specialised institution (State), with societies in which the State has crystallised (Balandier, 1984; Lowie, 1927). Lapierre (1968), on the basis of ethnological material, distinguished nine phases, reducible to three criteria: specialisation of public agents; centralisation of coercion; and institutionalisation. Braud (1994, p.70) about primitive societies: "Political activities (issuing norms, making them respected, defining the collective ends) were carried out by individuals with other roles (religious, economic, domestic)."

It is however necessary to distinguish between politics (as power relations in society) and specific public authorities (public management). In medieval Europe there was differentiation between governors (having competencies towards all inhabitants of a territory, the governed) and public officials working under the command of governors (monarchs). In modern States, with an enlarged scope of responsibilities, the number of public officials grew considerably (bureaucratisation and professionalisation). The second criterion, centralisation of coercion over all inhabitants of a territory, is a crucial factor in qualifying the specific character of public authorities as functioning in the name of the collectivity. The right to administer justice was often in private hands, or ruled by customs. In France, the "droit coutumier" (customary law) prevailed for centuries, with different rules for local communities, towns, regions and categories of people (aristocracy, clergy). Under the impact of military power-play against vassals (especially after Charles VII and Louis XI) French monarchs could impose their rule in the whole area of France. It took a long period, before juridical and administrative unification was realised. A crucial aspect of centralisation was its pyramidal character in law and administration. In modern states, the efficacy of pyramidal structures is guaranteed by making the legitimised use of violence, in case of infringements, a monopoly of public authorities. In a mature democracy, the competencies of public authorities, or as Jellinek said the "Kompetenz-Kompetenz", are determined by the Constitution. On the basis of this Constitution, laws rule the activities of public authorities and citizens. A Supreme Court decides in last resort on the interpretation of laws, binding for lower jurisdictions. Public administration has an in-built pyramidal hierarchy. Each public functionary is subordinate to a superior, self subordinate to another, and so on. Public officials are seen as an administrative machine, while top officials are subordinate to politicians.

The third criterion is the process of institutionalisation. Many systems of public management in historical times were characterised by powerful individuals having their power as personal prerogative. On the basis of previous military successes, members of a specific family were seen as entitled to the highest power position (throne). Mostly there was no differentiation between the private patrimony of the monarchical family and the public authority competencies. This personalised form of public authority was a weak guarantee for public management of a society. Gradually, a more sophisticated form of public authority developed in a process of institutionalisation (Burdeau, 1980). The person with public authority competence was differentiated from the office of public authority. In monarchies one distinguished between King and Crown. From the latter part of the Middle Ages, this idea was developed with the theory of the "two bodies of the King" (Kantorowitz, 1989). The physical body of the King was mortal, but his mythical body was thought to be immortal, so guaranteeing the continuity of the monarchical principal. Governors, fulfilling a public authority function, became "organs of the State", whose functions were not impaired by the death of human beings. This innovation was of the highest relevance, because on its basis regimes were not generally confronted any more with traumatic experiences, such as succession wars, when a monarch died. Often this innovation of "organ of the State" was limited to the most important functions. Other functions within the sphere of public administration, usually denoted as administrative functions, were not normally qualified as organs of the State, but a full-blown theory of institutionalisation implies that every person doing a job in the public authority sphere has to be qualified as an organ of the State.

In historical perspective, it was a crucial development that a differentiation arose between religious and non-religious authority. In undifferentiated societies, religious and public authority functions were indissolubly intertwined, and so were the roles of inhabitants of a territory and their adherence to a religion. In feudal times, there were many personal bonds of authority between a leader and his followers in Western Europe (Strayer, 1979) and quite an ongoing institutional warfare between Church and public authorities about their respective competencies and powers. Outcomes were possible other than a split-up between two autonomous spheres (Church and State). The dominance of the Pope over Christianity (theocracy) or dominance of the King or Emperor over all dimensions of society, religion included (caesaro-papism). After the 13th century an institution, called State, developed in Western Europe (England, France). All kinds of personal bonds between a lord and his vassals were gradually replaced by a direct relation between King and his subjects. John Lackland had to accept the Magna Carta (1215), reducing his policy freedom. In England, the "Petition of Rights" (1628) and "Bill of Rights" (1689) ruled citizens' rights against arbitrariness of monarchs and public authorities. A logical step was the development of democratising tendencies giving representative assemblies influence upon decision-making (parliamentarism). It took a long time before the bond between King and subjects in France was replaced by the concept of inhabitants being members of a nation, as citizens. This did happen with the French Revolution of 1789. Earlier the relation between governors and governed was gradually embedded in juridical norms. Ever more specialisation took place in public management tasks (military tasks, police, jurisdiction, etc). To give governors legitimacy, elections were organised, mostly for restricted groups (later on the basis of universal suffrage). Generally spoken, the military potential was a basic component of European States, being confronted with many rivalries. So the identity of States was formed.

In studies of political science, the concept "political system" is often used. D. Easton (1953, p.146) is reputed to have invented this concept as the object of political science: "Political science is the study of the authoritative allocation of values as influenced by the distribution and use of power." Easton defined political system as "the interactions through which values are authoritatively allocated for a society". He was not original with his concept of political system. Two years before, Talcott Parsons, for whom political theory was part of the theory of social systems, published "The Social System" (1951). Easton wanted to develop political systems theory as the basis for political science as a distinct discipline. He rejected Parsons' approach. Describing political science as the study of distribution and production of values in a society, was seen by Easton as too broad. In that way political science would coincide with social science. In prevailing literature about political science, Easton found two main notions: studying political life by analysing the State, or the distribution and use of power. He rejected both (State and power) as key object of political science. So Easton reduced the object of political science with the qualification "authoritative allocations or policies". H. Heller in his "Staatslehre" (1934) had already qualified the societal function of public authorities as realisation of binding decisions for a society. Amazing as it is, Easton used Heller's criterion, meant to qualify the specific function of public authorities, as the criterion to denote political phenomena. For Easton (1953, p.134) political science is not about "all authoritative policies found in a society", but about "the way in which values are authoritatively allocated, not for a group within society, but for the whole society". He made political phenomena depend on the existence and functioning of public authorities. Many used his notion "authoritative allocation of values" in an open-ended and variously interpretable sense. The success of Easton's formula is explained by the fact that prevailing political science coincided with government science or science of the State. This concept was handicapped by not being broad enough to embrace phenomena such as political parties, interest groups, etc., but one has to differentiate between the public authorities phenomenon and political phenomena (qualified by the power dimension). The public authorities phenomenon has political aspects, but also other dimensions. It is more consistent to qualify political aspects of social life by the power dimension and not half-heartedly or in disguised form with some relationship with the public authorities phenomenon.

Luhmann (1995) developed an authentic all-encompassing social systems theory of his own. In his view, differentiation between "Politik" (politics) and "Verwaltung" (public administration/management) is fundamental. This differentiation has nothing to do with the famous politics-administration dichotomy. Luhmann argued that there are two prominent ideas about the difference between politics and administration. The politics/administration relation is seen as "above/under" or as "end-means". Politics is placed hierarchically above subordinate public administration, or is seen as the end of public administration (instrument). For Max Weber, public bureaucracy as "Instrument rationaler Herrschaft" was superior as the most rational organisation. According to Weber, social systems are rational inasmuch as they succeed in finding instruments to fulfil any objective whatsoever. Weber didn't seek a clue in the specific character of objectives, but in an instrument, so generalised that it serves different, changing objectives: power, or authority as qualified power. Differentiating traditional, charismatic and legal-rational authority, Weber developed the conception of rationalising society with legal-rational authority by means of public bureaucracy. Luhmann, accentuating the open systems approach, criticised Weber's conception for its closed-system approach. He stressed that the capacity to manage societal problems can be enlarged by differentiating politics and public management, both with specific functions and roles. The institutional partition between political processes (processes to realise legitimate power) and public management processes (processes to use and implement legitimate power) is a crucial innovation. Public authorities can do their work, professional and reliable execution of public tasks (public management), better if they are not forced to continually take account of all possible political implications. Differentiation of politics and public management requires a splitting up of roles, offices, organisations, competencies and finances, and also specific criteria of rationality as basis for action. The trustworthiness of public authorities can be furthered, when citizens can be sure that they function according to the Rule of Law. This implies that realising of legitimacy (politics) is distinguished from the use of legitimacy (public management).

It seems useful to interpret politics as party-political, partisan activity with specific rationalities. Party-political processes are important to realise legitimacy, but party-political decisions don't have a binding character for society in a pluralist democracy. Citizens are not bound by them. In a one-party system it is different. A decisive criterion for differentiation of (party-) politics and public management is whether decisions can be supposed to be binding for everybody or not. This is so only for decisions which, according to prevailing formal rules and procedures, are taken by public authorities. This shows that parliament, often seen as a political organ, is part of the public management system. Parliament can produce formal decisions for all citizens, which can be seen as binding for all. For Luhmann, the public management system is an open system with several boundaries: especially with politics, public administration personnel and society (citizens, institutes, enterprises). In Luhmann's conception of the public management system, the public administration personnel are part of the environment. This is due to his idea that social systems are composed of acts (not human beings). Luhmann made it evident that reflections about the public management phenomenon from a political point of view give only a partial perspective upon the public authorities phenomenon. (Party)-politics and public management system are intensively intertwined in a kind of "osmosis", but have to be distinguished. Modern political systems in pluralist democracies are characterised by a primary differentiation between politics and public management systems. Politics is about the acquiring of power; recruiting of personnel for political functions; developing of legitimising ideologies; making party-political programs as frame of reference for government policies; and producing adherence for party-political movements. The public management system encompasses the executive apparatus, but also the tribunals/courts and more political organs like parliament and government. There is not a static boundary between politics and the public management system. This boundary is determined in a process of political planning of public management, by transformation of political rationalities into public management rationalities. Political planning of public management takes place dynamically by persons in parliament, government and the top of bureaucracies, who transform political programs into public management programs.

The controversy between two German theoreticians Habermas and Luhmann is interesting in general, and specifically with regard to the notion of power. Habermas is known for his conception about "Diskurs" (dialogue) as "Zwang-freie Kommunikation" (communication without coercion). According to Habermas, power is the capacity to hinder others to serve their interests. Power has to be reduced as much as possible, because power is contrary to free communication. For Luhmann, on the other hand, power is a medium of communication which can reduce ànd enlarge selection possibilities for others. For Luhmann, power has to increase, by giving those persons, who are confronted with the power of others, more freedom. The wielding of power must be disengaged from the personal characteristics of its agents: power has to be generalised. Habermas pleads for a situation whereby binding decisions of public authorities are recognised only if everybody sees these decisions as reasonable. Luhman shows that in a modern political system many decisions by public authorities are needed. It would be impossible to make all these decisions dependent on the approval of every citizen. Luhmann does not deny the relevance of personal recognition of binding decisions taken by public authorities, but he argues that in a society with citizens having different wants and interests a general climate is needed in which most binding decisions of public authorities are normally accepted. This asks for the confidence that public authorities are doing their job in accordance with regulations and procedures as prescribed by the Rule of Law, so trust and power are functionally equivalent in realising adequate societal processes (Luhmann, 1979).

The focus in this study is upon public authorities, so there should be some clarity provided about the notions authority, power, force, violence and influence in relation to each other. Braud (1985) developed some useful clarifications, distinguishing between power of command ("pouvoir d'injonction") and power of influence ("pouvoir d'influence"). In the case of power of command, the subject has a choice between submission and accepting behaviour as commanded, or risking the sanctions related to possible reactions of the commanding person. In the case of power of influence, the influenced actor can do what is asked (with material or symbolic advantages: positive sanction) or not, while not worsening his situation. When there is no risk of eventual force by the commanding person or organ, the injunction loses its plausibility as command, so the possibility of effective punishment is an essential part of public authority. Public authorities must dispose of (legitimised) means of coercion, and of persons authorised to execute that which public authorities are ordering (police). Braud (1994, p.38) distinguishes three categories of injunction: "injonction de facto" (factual), "injonction morale" (moral) and the most institutionalised form of injunction, "la norme juridique" (juridical). With de facto injunction there is no juridical justification for the use of power, only factual power causing inequality is at stake. In the case of moral injunction, moral values and ethics play a role. Without using force to support these values there is an impact upon behaviour, psychological coercion. Not living up to these moral values normally or often causes the subject an unbearable tension. Juridical norms are the most institutionalised form of injunction. Max Weber (1971) saw the essential prerogative of public authorities in their capacity to apply laws as organs of the State, disposing of the monopoly of legitimate coercion. With the Rule of Law, negative sanctions are possible as applied by tribunals or public administration, following legalised procedures including coercion, if necessary.

In the sphere of public authorities, it is relevant to know what is the character of the way in which they fulfill their functions. Max Weber gave a useful criterion by distinguishing between charismatic, traditional and legal-rational authority as "ideal types". Charismatic authority is based upon the extraordinary, charismatic character and personality of a leader who has a specific relation with all who like to identify themselves with this leader (Wilner, 1984). Traditional authority is based upon traditional sources such as belief systems and time-honoured mores. As Herodotus, living 484-424 BC, wrote: All peoples are convinced of the excellency of their customs. A monarchy which can claim its relation with a descent going back far into history, or to the will of God, can found its legitimacy in a rather invincible way. The most advanced form of authority is legal-rational authority, based upon the legality of a formal system of norms and competencies. Weber distinguished traditional, charismatic and legal-rational dominance. Traditional dominance is dominated by personal relations between lord and vassals, sovereign and subjects. Charismatic dominance is marked by an asymmetrical feature (charisma) giving the leader a tremendous control over his followers. In modern societies, the State is the most important system of legal-rational dominance. One can distinguish other categories of authority, as for example based upon professional competence (medical doctors, jurists, etc.) and values (belief systems, ideologies, etc.). Many authors accentuate that public functionaries, functioning under the control of politically chosen or nominated persons, have ample policy room. Although in mainstream publications it is seen as a more or less definite, not improvable stadium of democracy, that only political persons have legitimacy on the basis of regular elections, this is questioned here. This axiom often leads to the conclusion that public functionaries, working for the common good but not being elected, derive authority exclusively from their being an executor of the elected politician's will (public functionaries as politically sterilised executors). This overlooks a fundamental dimension of the functioning of non-elected public functionaries having authority "ex officio", derived directly (not indirectly via their elected political bosses) from the public good. The finality of their functioning is directly related to the common good underlying their office.

In mainstream literature it is seen as a normal model of public administration that public officials execute the orders of politicians, who, by a system of election, are thought to be formally legitimised to give orders to public officials, while democracy is thought to function adequately by this means. In this predominant model, the position and role of public functionaries is minimised and misjudged. Public functionaries, in mainstream democratic theory about governors and governed, are mostly non-existent as the uninteresting executors of politicians' wills. Even worse, public functionaries, because of their power and possibilities of misusing their power, are seen as enemies of the people or as non-elected, crypto-politicians with "bureau-power". Often an illusion is created that elected politicians represent the wishes of the common people, and so can control bureaucracies. The most authentic objective of public authorities, and all public functionaries, is that they have to function for the general interest. The top layers of public authorities such as government and parliament are composed exclusively of partisan, party-political persons. How can the general interest be adequately served? In spite of this party-political dominance over public authorities, public functionaries mostly do what they can to bring the general interest into practice. Public functionaries are generally "ex officio" driven by an "esprit de corps public" which takes its fundamental, principal task of serving the general interest as primary with regard to eventual party-political deviations. Public functionaries have to be praised for doing their jobs professionally, not least by preventing or correcting the practice of "kidnapping of public authority" by politicians for party-political or personal reasons. The position of elected politicians is generally overrated, even in scientific studies. This is due partly to the overstressed governors/governed dichotomy, in which there is no place for public functionaries. Democracy cannot function adequately, however, without a prominent role for professional public functionaries. In practice, public functionaries have (too) often no other choice than to compromise, sometimes by themselves becoming party-political public functionaries or practising administrative politicians. Therefore, institutional arrangements are needed to further structurally a more mature democracy in which the general interest is the real criterion of success. The popular slogan of party-political politicians about the primacy of politics (over bureaucracy as enemy) has to be interpreted with many pinches of salt. Democratic theory must be reformulated with due recognition of the real position of public functionaries (now mostly a black box).

It is evident that public authorities need professional, competent functionaries for their effective functioning. To recruit able men and women to do the job, public authorities have to compete with the, generally better paying, private sector. The financial side is an important matter, but perhaps more decisive are atmosphere and working conditions. Too often the work of public functionaries is demoralising due to all kinds of suffocating party-politicking. The loyalty of public functionaries is often overstressed by utterly annoying situations. It is not only about choosing between loyalty to the service of the general interest and loyalty to party-political options. In literature, the answer to this loyalty problem is mostly given by suggesting that there are only two solutions. One can apply to some "spoils system". Then the interesting appointments, promotions or job mutations are made on the basis of party-political criteria. This has the consequence that a change of the ruling party-political majority causes, of necessity, the firing of public functionaries recruited by the foregoing party-political majority, and that a permanent atmosphere of distrust, conflicts and the tricks of party-political networks poisons the heart of public authorities. Neutrality of public functionaries is presented as the alternative for this party-politically diseased system. Neutrality of public functionaries is preached in many States. Following this neutrality model, they should distance themselves from party-politics and interest groups, treating all citizens and organisations equally. When the ruling party-political majority changes, public functionaries continue to function, getting jobs on the basis of competencies (not party-political preferences). The ideal of neutrality is generally not realised. Public functionaries often don't conceal party-political adherence (party membership pays, when one chose the correct party). Membership of trade unions makes public functionaries all but neutral servants of the general interest. Functioning of public authorities is treated in the framework of "déontologie", codes of behaviour (Vigouroux, 1995).

One might say that the exercise of (political and non-political) power is going on within socially constructed situations. The social space for interactions characterised by the exercise of power is called "champ" by Bourdieu (1981, p.113), with a specific system of characteristic properties, issues, logics and rationalities. For Bourdieu, the issues are especially relevant on two levels, an economic (material goods) and a symbolic level. On the symbolic level, dominant groups are able to impose their definitions of what is legitimate in a specific field. Symbolic issues, for Bourdieu (1979, p.281) are: "all that in the social world is in the order of beliefs, credit or discredit, perception and appreciation, knowledge and recognition, name, fame, prestige, honour, glory, authority. In short, all that makes symbolic power a recognized power". According to Braud (1994,p.45) Bourdieu seems to underrate the genuinely coercive character of politics: "In fact, the specificity of this power is that it is supported by a commanding administration, a police and an army monopolising the use of legitimate force and by tribunals and prisons, guaranteeing in the last resort respect for the laws as issued." Symbolic battles are relevant in the field of politics. For Braud, "The political field is specifically structured by competition over control of the State apparatus, a control which does imply possibilities of intervention in the whole of society "en régie", in both the material sphere and the symbolic sphere. Making order reign, supporting the economy and further social income transfers. All this has a double dimension (material and symbolic), so the political field is extended. In a sense, it encompasses all other fields, whenever they are subdued to the laws of the State."

(o.c, p. 45). This viewpoint can be partially questioned, as the notion political is more or less made dependent upon another notion, public authority ("Kategorienverlagerung"). The State is a specific kind of political power. It would be more consistent to use the term political for all applications of power. The notion political is overburdened, it means, among other things, partisan, as with all political parties being factions and also as all that concerns society in a State, so becoming more or less identical with social.

In the framework of a naive, widespread empiricist tradition of scientific work, it is a dominant idea that scientific work is a kind of photography of reality as it is, ontological security as Giddens (1987) called it, but this view is inadequate. In the exact sciences and in social sciences especially, it is relevant to inquire into the conditions of science, as everybody or every intellectual seems to know about social life as it is. Even when observations are based upon accepted methods and techniques it is a must to be on the alert: epistemological alertness. In the last decades, consciousness developed about the fact that human beings construct social realities (constructivism). When one reads a book about elections or political parties, it is impossible to understand the issues adequately without knowing the relevant "champ" (Bourdieu), the frame of reference in which these phenomena get their sense (the universe of politics). A scientific theory about some phenomenon is the more relevant inasmuch as its information is adequate. It creates for those receiving this information maximal cognitive effects for minimal costs (Sperber/Wilson, 1989). Scientific research in social sciences is impossible without language and socially constructed representations. Social facts normally cannot be interpreted adequately without the use of means of social communication (script, mass media). One can even say that social facts don't exist without culturally determined codes. One has to be on the alert for reification. The term denoting an object is not necessarily the object denoted: "Le mot qui nomme n'est pas nécessairement celle de la chose nommée." A nasty problem with words, terms and concepts is that they are nearly always variously interpretable. Social scientists are seduced to use words current in everyday life, instead of especially constructed terms that define what they mean to describe. It is necessary to unveil subjective and ideological connotations ("l'espace idéologique") combined with the notions as used by social actors.

It would be interesting to know in what measure ideas within the French sphere of culture were used and adapted in Anglo-American culture, as if these ideas were authentically Anglo-American. This process is furthered by the fact that among French studies in the broad field of political history, public law and social-cultural developments, there is often a strong accent upon normative, juridical and institutional aspects. One might say that in comparative perspective, the French approach is often institutional in character. This is, implicitly or explicitly, used as an argument to dismiss these studies, although they have a rich scope. In the Anglo-American intellectual tradition, it seems to be beneath the dominantly empirically oriented political science to handle this sort of study. A hypothesis might be that more than once ideas from the rich French cultural history were renamed and propagated as genuinely American or English (marketing of "new ideas"). A sophisticated differentiation between politics and public management of society seems appropriate. Full account must be taken of historical practices and the context of political parties and politicians as in the following sketch in the French cultural context.

## 6.6. Political parties and politicians, trying to kidnap public authority

Politics is not what it once was in France (Rémond, 1993), but contemporary politics in France is steeped in historical developments, so historical insight is a necessary condition for a knowledge of politics in France. Circumstances, power-games, opportunities, disasters, personalities, ambitions, animosities, opposing opinions, the psychology of actors, and much more from former periods is relevant material for an analysis of politics now. The French Revolution realised a crucial institutional break by replacing arbitrary power of the monarchy to dictate the functioning of public authorities. From then on, the dominant idea was that institutions like government and legislative assembly had to be composed on the basis of elected persons, representing the people as such. Representative democracy, organising society by means of representatives of the people, is praised as an important part of progress in the development of civilisation. For more than a century, different political parties were active in France as vehicles of democratic movements trying to influence, via elections, the functioning of political institutions (government, legislative assembly). A political party is an association of a number of people having common ideas about the way the "Public Good" (common interests of the people, general interest) has to be served, and having influence via the number of their elected representatives. In the context of democratic institutions, especially on the basis of election systems, political parties, via their representatives, could get a grip on legislative and executive powers. Using and abusing the constitutionally recognised principle of the elected, and therefore legitimised, position of party-political and often purely partisan representatives, political parties and politicians replaced the "bonum commune" mostly with partisan interests and sectarian power politics. The basic flaw is that elected representatives behaved dominantly or exclusively as extension of their political party or voters. An example is former German chancellor Kohl, at the end of 1999, defending his party's illegall acceptance of money from business with the argument that he did it all for his party.

As unanimity is seldom possible, the majority rule is regarded as the next best formula in representative assemblies, but the majority rule is just only if the interests of minorities or not represented interests are taken into account in a reasonable way. By not satisfying this necessary condition of democracy, representatives denatured the essence of pluralist, representative democracy. According to the rule of the democratic game, representatives, once elected, have to behave primarily as representatives of the people as a whole. Party-political practices often degenerated however, into abuses of democratic principles by partisan ruling on the basis of a majority in parliament. The impact of this partisan abuse of majority rule in parliament has often been disproportionately intensified by the idea that (the majority of) the parliament is the sole representative of the people and can dictate the functioning of all public authorities. This looks like the old tradition in war: winner takes all. In French history there are many examples of abuses of the concept of representative democracy. In former Communist regimes of Eastern Europe (often calling themselves democratic!) the idea of democracy was violated completely by means of militarily extorted one-party systems (elections only being a sham), realising totalitarian dictatorships: People = Communist party = State. After the terrible experiences of the Second World War and the collaborationist Vichy Regime, France made it crystal clear in the Constitutions of 1946 and 1958, that France is a Republic as government of the people, on behalf of the people and by the people. After this constitutional recognition of the French people, the collectivity of all citizens as subject of a representative democracy, the crucial question was and remains how this representative democracy can be made operational as optimally as possible. In practice, it is impossible that all citizens together rule a democratic system. Especially in mass-democracies it is necessary, that a limited number of citizens fulfil functions on behalf of the public. They are directly or indirectly elected as representatives of the people, politicians with political functions, or appointed to fulfil a task as public servants or officials.

Worldwide there is a widespread conception, implicitly or explicitly accepted by many, that elected or appointed politicians have a kind of monopoly on the public cause, legitimised by elections as "carte blanche". In this misguided view, appointed public officials are seen and treated as purely executive servants of political bosses, responsible for public policies. In the first half of the 20th century, the "politics-administration dichotomy" was a dominant idea in institutionalising of the relationship between politicians and civil servants in the United States. This dichotomy proved to be unworkable, especially in its rigid interpretations (policy = politics; administration = pure execution). In practice, many public servants work in highly responsible, powerful and policy-laden functions. They are even accused of being politicians: "politics of bureaucracy". There are always public functionaries working on the basis of party-political criteria, favouritism etc., directly at variance with the principles of the Rule of Law, but it should be the exception, not the rule. A set of rules of behaviour for civil servants is generally operational (loyalty etc). Traditionally, politicians are seen as, via election or appointment, the legitimised bosses of civil functionaries, themselves having no legitimised authority whatever. In so far as civil functionaries are recognised as having responsibilities, they are seen to have only responsibilities as delegated by politicians. This idea is deduced from the axiom that all responsibilities in a representative democracy should be based on authorisation by elections. A more sophisticated conception is possible, accentuating responsibilities of several functionaries. A carefully balanced view implies, that there are public responsibilities of politicians, and genuine public responsibilities of civil servants directly deduced from the public tasks which they fulfil within the legal constraints. These public responsibilities of officials are not directly or indirectly deduced from some politician, as a frequent fiction has it. This implies that officials are completely responsible for what they are doing by fulfilling (or not) their public tasks. They cannot shield themselves behind the authority of politicians who are completely responsible for their own function (without hiding themselves behind officials, competent professionals).

Politics, of course, mirrors societal developments. At the beginning of the 20th century, France had a dominantly agrarian society (Berstein/Milza, 1995; Duby, 1985a). Since then urbanisation has transformed France (Duby, 1985b). French society has changed drastically since 1945 (Borne, 1988) becoming a mass consumption society (Baudrillard, 1974). There was an impressive economic take-off, one might call it the French Miracle (Guyard, 1970). The three decades after the Second World War became known therefore as "Les Trente Glorieuses" (Fourastié, 1979). International developments, the world market and technology had their impact upon the process of modernisation in France. Rural life in France was intensively modernised (Weber, 1983). In other Western countries, especially in Western Europe, comparable developments can be observed, but developments in France are in many dimensions specific (Mendras, 1997). Political passions are traditionally aroused by a number of societal questions: religion (Coutrot/Dreyfus, 1965), education (Prost, 1968), decolonisation, as with regard to Algeria (Rioux/Sirinelli, 1991), ethnic discrimination and immigration (Milza/Amar, 1990; Noiriel, 1988) and social and economic issues. The impact of the media (press, radio, TV) on mass opinion has been relatively strong, especially that of television as mass communicator (Albert/Tudesq, 1981; Miquel, 1984). The dynamics of political parties requires attention for its special features. Regularly political crises caused outbursts of the "French fever" (Winock, 1986). The position of trade unions was strong in the last century. In 1984, the start of French syndicalism in 1884 was commemorated (Regards, 1984). Economic circumstances have their impact on public policies and the positions taken by political parties, trade unions and other societal organisations. A summary sketch is given now of the historic development of French political parties (Berstein/Milza, 1995). The general conclusion is, that one of the causes of structural crises in French society is that political parties and politicians regularly kidnapped powers and competencies exclusively meant for public authorities, legitimised to serve the general interests of society.

## 6.7. Party-politics in the first half of the 20th century

Nowadays democracy is thought to be impossible without political parties as organisations for the representation of the people, so a key-issue is the question of whether political parties are fulfilling their role and mission adequately. Party-political or personal interests of politicians have often taken priority over the general interest. Ideological positions of French political parties were related to several interpretations of the Republican concept, which was idealised as inspired by the Revolution, human rights, rationality, science and progress, and by Republican values such as liberty, equality before the law and education without religious indoctrination. This Republican model had broad support in French society, and was systematically propagated by leading elites, press, in schools, etc. (Berstein/Rudelle, 1992). Catholics who wanted to be loyal to their Church and preferred schools with a religious atmosphere, were branded as anti-republicans so political conflicts were created. There were stubborn opponents of this reduced Republican model, which denied a fair position for some minorities. Rightist movements like monarchists and nationalists, and leftist movements like revolutionary syndicalists. Déroulède's "Ligue des patriotes" mobilised for the restoration of a strong state to prepare France for revenge against Germany.

On the eve of the First World War, the influence of this movement weakened. At that time, the "Action française", created in 1898, was a politically more important nationalist movement. In 1899 Charles Maurras was the leading personality of the "Action française", with a journal of the same name, promoting "nationalisme intégral", a synthesis of nationalism and monarchy. Hereditary monarchy had to be restored, as otherwise the Republic, offshoot of the Revolution, would be irreparable. The next step would have to be the elimination of all "foreigners" (Jews, Protestants, Freemasons, and "Métèques") and restoration of the powerful position of the Catholic Church in French society. Journal "Action française" (with Maurras, Daudet, Bainville) urged direct action against the Republic, supporting campaigns against Jews. The "Ligue d'Action française" (from 1905) was supported by "Camelots du Roi" (for direct action since 1908), and "L'Institut d'Action française" (after 1906). Revolutionary syndicalism, combining anarchism and trade unionism, posed a different threat. From 1892 anarchists organised criminal assaults, trying to disrupt the Republic. Anarchists were supported by trade unions for their target of changing society with general strikes. The CGT took over these ideas in its "Charte d'Amiens" (1906). In the years 1906-1910, strikes were disruptive, forcing police to answer violence with violence. Revolutionary syndicalism could mobilise only a minority. Governments repressed this anarchism. The majority of workers preferred improvement by policy rather than revolutionary anarchy.

In October 1879 the "Fédération du parti des travailleurs socialistes de France" was formed. In 1900, there were six socialist parties (Touchard, 1977). "Parti ouvrier français" of Jules Guesde, with a doctrinaire Marxism. "Parti socialiste révolutionnaire", or "Blanquistes" of Édouard Vaillant, trying to find some combination of Republican legality and rebellious direct action as proposed previously by Blanqui. The "Fédération des travailleurs socialistes" of Paul Brousse ("Broussistes"; "Possibilistes"), adherents of Socialism of the possible, with their idea of the local public service. The "Parti ouvrier socialiste révolutionnaire" of Jean Allemane (or "Allemanistes"), with strong sympathies for the spontaneous action of workers, militant anti-militarism and virulent anti-parliamentarism. The "Alliance communiste" of Arthur Groussin, and the "Socialistes indépendantes", adherents of the presence of socialists in government to improve conditions for workers, with personalities like Alexandre Millerand, Jean Jaurès, Réné Viviani and Aristide Briand. When Millerand entered the "gouvernement de Défense républicaine" of Waldeck-Rousseau, next to General Gallifet, who repressed the Commune of 1871, this was defended by Jaurès, but criticised by Guesde. It was branded as "ministérialisme" or "millerandisme". This caused the creation of two parties in 1901. The "Parti socialiste français" (PSF), combining independents, "Alemanistes" and "Possibilistes", with Jean Jaurès as leader and the "Parti socialiste de France" (PSDF), combining Marxists, "Blanquistes" and "Alliance communiste", with Jules Guesde as leader. Jaurès and Guesde, trying to unite the socialist movement, asked the international workers movement to take a decision. The Socialist Internationale of Amsterdam (1904) had to choose between doctrines (Marxism or Reformist Socialism) and practices ("ministérialisme" or refusing government participation). It chose for non-participation in bourgeois governments, and the class struggle. On 23-25 April 1905 the "Parti socialiste unifié" (PSU) was created as "Section française de l'Internationale Ouvrière" (SFIO). The elections of 1914 gave the "Parti socialiste" a hundred deputies, thanks to the charisma of Jaurès (Jaurès, 1996).

In June 1901, the "Parti républicain, radical et radical-socialiste" ("Parti républicain-socialiste" or "Parti radical"), was formed with the intention to unite all "républicains" (i.e. all "dreyfusards"). Its founding conference assembled 201 deputies, 78 senators, 476 committees, 155 Masonic lodges, 849 mayors and local authorities, and 215 journals. This political party was in fact the continuation of the radical movement, which had been coming up since the middle of the 19th century, with the idea of developing political and social democracy in France. At the start of the Third Republic this was an extreme-leftist movement. During the 20th century it was the party of leftist notables who wanted to govern France. With prominent personalities like Combes, Clemenceau, Caillaux, Herriot, Daladier, Pelletan, Chautemps, the brothers Sarraut, Bonnet, Delbos and Jeanneney, it had a rather vague program to attract as many groups as possible, and won the elections of 1902 and after overwhelmingly. To have some 200 deputies was seen as quite normal. It was impossible to govern France without this party in government. This party defined the republican concept by identifying it with militant anti-clericalism. Its program, settled in Nancy in 1907, had three foundations: the defence of republican institutions, with an overpowering parliament; a reformist social program, rejecting Marxist class-struggle and Liberalism, proposing nationalisations and State intervention to correct inequalities of income, trying to make everybody proprietor; and a foreign policy, based upon patriotism and national defence, trying to regulate international conflicts with international law. The "Parti radical" represented the middle classes quite well. This explains its success (Berstein, 1982). It claimed to follow principles of the Revolution, while improving conditions for the masses. It identified itself with the regime of the Republic.

Many of those who were considered by republicans in power as not being adherents of (their reduced model of) the Republic, and to be excluded from the advantages public authorities could give citizens, accepted the regime, for example the "antidreyfusards" and all who opposed the militant anti-clericalist politics of republicans. Catholics who supported the Republic, with the leadership of Jacques Piou and Albert de Mun, started the "Action libérale populaire" in 1902, with some 200,000 adherents and a network of about 1,500 committees. They asked for a liberal Republic, allowing decentralisation, liberty of religious cult and education, and a social policy based upon the voluntary organisation of professional workers. In 1903, the "Fédération républicaine" was created by moderate "antidreyfusards" and allied Catholics. At the beginning of the 20th century this "Fédération républicaine" was the party of rightist conservatives. They defended Catholic tradition, were opposed to the "politique laïque", nationalistic, and attached to the existing social order. At the start of the 20th century, three issues aroused political debate: the conflict with the Catholic Church, the battle against attempts to organise a revolution to overthrow the regime and the risk of an eventual war. Government-Waldeck-Rousseau (June 1899/May 1902) took measures against Catholic congregations which had been active "anti-dreyfusards". The "loi sur les associations" (1901) enabled government to control religious congregations. Civil associations were free, but religious congregations needed the authorisation of parliament. Pope Pius X deplored this discrimination against Catholic religious associations. He was reassured by Waldeck-Rousseau, that this law would be applied with tolerance. Some 460 religious congregations asked for authorisation. Elections of 1902 brought the "Bloc des catholiques" against the "Bloc des gauches" (Radicals, Socialists and Moderates). The socialist coalition won a victory with 368 seats against 222 seats for Conservatives and Catholics. The Radicals campaigned for strict application of the law of 1901, and now dominated the coalition with 250 seats. Waldeck-Rousseau (sick) was succeeded by Émile Combes (May 1902/January 1905). Combes, former student priest, made his name by making anticlericalism a political issue. His government was fanatical with "combisme". It implied militant anticlericalism, party-political favouritism and a rigorous purge of all functionaries suspected of anti-republicanism. Combes instructed prefects that favours of the Republic should be given only to persons and organisations loyal to the regime. Judges were succeeded by magistrates known as "republican". Minister of War, André, forced the dismissal of military officers with monarchist opinions.

Combes changed the law of associations (1901). Unauthorised schools of authorised religious congregations were closed. After June 1901, parliament refused all authorisations for religious congregations so that they were forced to close down. In 1904, parliament adopted a law forbidding all education by members of religious congregations, even when authorised. This was intended to break education by the Catholic Church. The police had to use force to expel members of religious congregations. This aroused Catholics and many functionaries resigned (moral dilemma). "Combisme" became, because of its Catholic-baiting, identical with persecution of the Catholic Church. The rigid anticlericalism of Combes made him break diplomatic relations with the Vatican in July 1904. This break caused a serious juridical problem. Since the Concordat of Napoleon with the Pope, the statute of the French Catholic Church ordained that the French government and Vatican had to agree about the nomination of bishops. Combes wanted to continue this system, this enabled government to control bishops, but because of the rift with the Vatican, he proposed a law for the separation of State and Church in November 1904. In autumn 1904, "l'affaire des fiches" poisoned public opinion, because it was revealed that minister André favoured the party-political nominations of officers, using "fiches" of Freemasonry about opinions of officers. The Law of Separation of December 1905 was not the war machine against the Catholic Church as intended. It made the Republic recognise liberty of conscience and religious cult, but it did not recognise salary or subsidise any religion as the religion of the Republic. Church properties were handed over to cultural associations, which could use public buildings free of charge. Pope Pius X condemned the Law of Separation in encyclical "Vehementer" (February 1906). Encyclical "Gravissimo Officii" (July 1906) forbade Catholics to form cultural associations with the new rules. Public order had to be restored by the police and army, as Catholics tried to block forced stocktaking of ecclesiastical properties. Clemenceau, premier since October 1906, stopped the stocktakings. After Combes' venomous anticlericalism, it took time before relations between Republic and Church normalised. Separation of State and Church was a fact, religion was a private matter.

## 6.8. Party-politics as a kind of "power-capitalism"

Especially on the political left, a nerve-racking fight was going on against a revolutionary movement which intended to overthrow the regime of the Republic (Touchard, 1977). In the period before the 1914-1918 war, the "Bloc des gauches", supporting the Republic, had an overwhelming majority. In the 1906 elections they won 60 seats, getting 411 deputies (247 Radicals, 90 "Républicains de gauche", 54 SFIO, 20 Independent Socialists) from the total of 585. In the 1910 elections this coalition held 449 seats (252 Radicals, 93 "Républicains de gauche", 74 SFIO, and 30 Independent Socialists) so the first decade of the 20th century was rightly called the "République radicale", although this dominating leftist coalition was already crumbling. Since 1906, when anticlerical fanatic Combes was succeeded by moderate Clemenceau, the social question was deposing the conflict with the Catholic Church from first place on the political agenda. Clemenceau announced social reforms, and decided to start a Ministry of Labour under René Viviant. To find financial resources for social reforms, he asked his Minister of Finance, Joseph Caillaux, to prepare a new tax: an income tax. Agitation, caused by revolutionary syndicalists, did not give Clemenceau enough time for his social reformist program however. Strikes and disturbances of public order forced the government to take action and to use violence. This split the unity of the left. Government-Clemenceau was overthrown in July 1909. He was succeeded by Briand (July 1909/February 1911). When Briand broke strikes, syndicalist friends remembered that Briand had supported earlier strikes as a revolutionary method. Briand pursued reconciliation of Republicans and Catholics. This brought approval of centre-rightists, but disapproval of Radicals. They forced reconstruction of his government in the autumn of 1910. He lost support for his reasonable secularism, tolerance and respect for all religions in 1911.

Foreign policy was increasingly pushing aside social reform programs from the political agenda, as a result of growing tensions with Germany. The Crisis of Tanger (1905), a military confrontation of Germany and France, raised public awareness of the possibility of war. The majority of the French were passionately patriotic. Socialists tried to reconcile pacifism with the conception of national defence. In the ranks of CGT, the anti-patriotic movement was confused, especially because the majority of the French were patently patriotic. SFIO continued its opposition to war. There were three different movements in the SFIO. Guesde and his comrades thought that it was in vain to try to prevent a war as long as capitalism was not defeated, so they supported the idea of inactivity, preparing for a revolution. An ultra-leftist wing of the SFIO, under the leadership of anti-patriotic and anti-militarist Gustave Hervé, supported a general uprising as the answer to military mobilisation. Jaurès tried to construct a synthesis by trying to prevent war with actions of the Socialist Internationale, but he was not clear about the methods, if this should fail. The Agadir Crisis (1911) showed that the efforts of Caillaux to prevent war by negotiations aroused indignation in the public. In January 1912, Caillaux was overthrown, he was succeeded by Poincaré, opponent of the militarist German Reich. Poincaré organised alliances with Russia and Great Britain ("Entente Cordiale"). The Assembly adopted a law for three years compulsory military service. This provoked a reaction from the Socialists and leftist Radicals who preferred a shorter term of conscription. They thought France could be defended by the "nation armée". This concept of an armed population was launched by Jaurès in "L'Armée nouvelle" (1913). In December 1913, the government of Barthou was overthrown. Poincaré asked Doumergue to form a government. After 1914, the split up of the political left was explicit. The moderate wing were with Poincaré in wanting military reinforcement and modest fiscal reforms. The leftist wing wanted to abolish the law of three years, and adoption of an income tax.

Barthou and Briand formed a "Fédération des gauches" (December 1913) supporting "politique laïque" and separation of State and Church. It accepted income tax and social reforms, supporting proportional representation and administrative reorganisations. The "Fédération des gauches" wanted to realign "dreyfusards" of "Alliance démocratique" and the right wing of Radicals who were opposed to a coalition with Socialists. At the 1914 elections, the left ("Radicaux unifiés", SFIO, "Socialistes Indépendantes") got 268 seats, 30 seats short of an absolute majority, but the political right was beaten. At the SFIO congress (14/16 July 1914) Jaurès had his vote for a general strike in all countries, preparing for war in case of an impending war, accepted, to force governments to settle their conflicts without war. In July 1914, the public was less upset by an impending war than by the process against Madame Caillaux, wife of the former Premier. She shot the editor of "Le Figaro" for his permanent attacks against her husband, and on 31 July 1914, nationalist Villain murdered Jaurès. At the funeral of Jaurès, the secretary-general of the CGT, Jouhaux, said that workers would defend France. The thin internationalist veneer of the workers movement was broken by patriotic nationalism (Becker, 1977). Abruptly, in July-August 1914, France was deeply involved in war, starting with an assault on Austrian Archduke Franz-Ferdinand on the Balkans, and becoming the First World War. An overwhelming majority of the working class rallied to national defence efforts. There was a stubborn minority with revolutionary opinions urging for the overthrow of the regime. Government had taken precautionary measures, making lists of potential revolutionaries ("Carnet B") but government did not use them in 1914. President Poincaré in the Assembly on 4 August 1914 branded aggression of Germany and Double-Monarchy. He was the representative of France, heroically defending itself in a "Union Sacrée". Two Socialists entered government on 26 August 1914, Guesde and Sembat. It was thought that the war would be short. This was an illusion. On 22 December 1914 Parliament resumed activities. "Parlementarisme à la française" was resumed with adaptations to the war situation. Government-Viviani resigned on 29 October 1915. Briand had his 5th, and on 12 December 1916 his 6th government. On 20 March 1917 the government fell again.

The massive loss of human life and bad material conditions for the French population provoked crises time and again. From 4 May 1917 mutinies upset the army. Pétain succeeded Nivelle as commander-in-chief, criticised sharply for his acceptance of massive losses of French soldiers trying in vain to defeat the German troops. The war situation was changed drastically by two crucial facts. The United States entered the war in April 1917 and in Russia there was a Bolshevik Revolution, paralysing the Russian military efforts against Germany. In France more and more strikes were organised as a protest against the war efforts. Since 1915, inside the SFIO a pacifist movement around Jean Longuet, grandson of Karl Marx, had become stronger, and since 1916 opposition against the war had grown in SFIO and CGT. In 1917, government refused passports for Socialists, attending a conference in Stockholm about a "white peace" so Socialists left the "Union Sacrée". After the fall of government-Ribot in September 1917, Socialists refused to participate in government-Painlevé. From July 1918 onwards SFIO had a pacifist majority. When at last the Armistice of 11 November 1918 ended the war, political parties could resume their quarrels. Social problems flooded the whole of France. A new phenomenon was the gigantic number of war victims. The "Anciens combattants et victimes de guerre" was a dominant pressure group (Prost, 1977). In 1920 there were 6,441,000 survivors between 20 and 50 years, 90% of this generation and 60% of the adult male population. Half of them were wounded during the war, and more than 1,100,000 had scanty invalidity pensions. War widows, aged persons and orphans with meagre incomes; about 9 million French were directly hit by the war. This had a dominant impact on French politics until 1939. For the political right, peace was the result of a strong France, which had to use its strength to intimidate Germany, preventing this aggressive nation from starting aggressions again. On the political left there was a strong belief in co-operation of the people in the framework of the League of Nations. The French population wanted nothing more than peace. While Clemenceau was busy winning the peace at Versailles, social tensions were abundant because of sharply rising price-levels. Workers demanded higher salaries. This was furthered by the fact that during the war salaries were raised in industries which were crucial for defence (but not in other sectors). Minister Thomas averted the strikes by negotiating with the CGT, This would be a costly precedent, often misused since then (up to massive strikes of truckers in 1996 and 1997, and of others since then).

In 1919, CGT had 2,400,000 members. CGT leadership was convinced of the advantages of a dialogue with government and employers to get higher salaries etc. Strikes were used to put pressure on this dialogue for changes in production structure (nationalisations, workers' control in enterprises etc.). For the revolutionaries in CGT, admiring Bolshevik Revolution, this reformist attitude was not enough. The Russian Revolution was an inspiration for them, more inspiring than strikes against a high cost of living. There was also a revolutionary atmosphere in Germany. At the beginning of 1919, Clemenceau, fearing that 1 May manifestations would be violent, arranged that on 23 April 1919, the law about the 8-hour working day was adopted. This did not satisfy militant workers. There was opposition against the French military intervention in Russia, to help "white armies" against revolutionaries. In 1919 France was in the grip of a panic that the Russian Revolution would provoke the overthrow of the French Republic. The 1919 elections were held in the framework of the "Bloc National", as continuation of the "Union Sacrée" (with all political parties except "Parti Socialiste") under the new conditions. "Parti Socialiste" was under pressure from a militant minority, planning to imitate the Communist revolution. Politicians examined a new electoral system with proportional representation, such as rightists and moderates had tried to introduce before the war. The Assembly adopted this in July 1919. It was thought the most effective weapon to break the "discipline républicaine" which in the system in effect since 1889 ("scrutin uninominal majoritaire à deux tours") brought Socialists and Radicals into a winning coalition. Radicals were now liberated from their traditional alliance. This system gave the winning majority an advantage with all seats (winner takes all). SFIO thought to win the elections, as it was the sole party which had chosen pacifism. At its congress of April 1919 it adopted the "motion Bracke", refusing any coalition with bourgeois parties (Radicals). So SFIO entered the elections alone.

Radicals accepted a "Cartel Républicain" with Independent Socialists and Moderates. The "Cartel Républicain" was centrist, "laïque", rejecting revolution and reaction, defending neutral education and standing for the extension of social reforms. The "Bloc National" was fiercely anti-communist, identifying communism with the German danger. It used social anxiety for a communist take-over, and branded all who organised social unrest with strikes as collaborationists. Elections of November 1919 gave the most rightist Assembly since February 1871. SFIO had more votes (1,700,000) than in 1914 (1,380,000), but it lost nearly half of its seats, a result of the new electoral system (from 102 to 68 seats). There was a massive number of ex-combatants, wearing a blue uniform in 1918. So it was the "Chambre bleu-horizon". "Bloc National" had an absolute majority with 319 of the 620 seats. This jerk to the right was relative. Elections in November and December 1919 and Senate elections of January 1920 produced a strong majority for the old coalition of Radicals and Moderates. The Senate had the same competencies as the Assembly for budget and laws, so government, with a "Bloc National" majority in the Assembly, had an opposing majority in the Senate. Until 1923 "Bloc National" policies were seen as a continuation of "Union Sacrée" policies during the war. The "Bloc National" changed religious policy. In spite of the "Combist" law, forbidding religious congregations, government tolerated the re-establishment of forbidden religious congregations. Government decided to maintain the religious statute of the Concordat of 1801 in Alsace-Lorraine, not French when the separation of State and Church was legally established, with the effect that even in 1997 bishops had to get the permission of government to become bishop. Government, against opposition of the Radicals, decided to restore the French embassy at the Vatican, closed since 1904. The Senate relaxed its decision about this restoration of the French embassy until December 1921. Public opinion was no longer concerned with anticlericalism. Strikes were often seen as part of a revolutionary movement, steered by Russian Communism, therefore repression of strikes was considered a patriotic action. Revolutionary activities came from "Comités syndicalistes révolutionnaires" (CSR), organised by a minority within CGT. Their leader announced a strike for the railways. At the commemorations of 1 May strikes were announced, starting with the railways and followed by strikes in harbours, the building industry and mines. Government reacted with repression. There were many conflicts in CGT and "Parti Socialiste" about the choices to be made.

### 6.9. Specifics of the French political system

The French political system has specific characteristics having deep historical roots and a unique cultural background (Duverger, 1996). Up to the 19th century there were political groups forming themselves around a leader or having some ideological conception. After the violent shocks of the French Revolution and the hectic period under Napoleon, the Restoration period seemed a time of relative stability, until Charles X tried to force a rigid comeback of the Ancien Régime. Experiences with the reactionary July Monarchy (1830-1848) and February Revolution (1848) caused a conservative reaction with wide support in the population longing for public order. After the 1851 coup of Napoleon III, his humiliating defeat in 1870 and the miscarried "Commune" (1871) it was obvious that dissenting opinions and organisations in society had to be channelled to make democracy work reasonably. The development of ideas about the creation of modern political parties in France dates back to the last quarter of the 19th century, as in the rest of Europe (Rials, 1986). There were pioneering forerunners. In the French Revolution "Girondins" and "Montagnards". The Jacobins in 1793 were the first to have built an organisation which can be compared with that of modern political parties. According to Benjamin Constant, a (political) party is an association of people having the same political doctrine. In Great Britain, two important political groups had developed since 1680: Tories and Whigs. As a consequence of the electoral reform of 1832 in Great Britain, the first modern political parties were formed, and thereafter Whigs called themselves Liberals. Robert Peel founded the Conservative party (still also known as the Tories). Electoral committees started in 1867 with the "caucus of Birmingham". In 1868, the Conservative party was established, in 1874, the Liberal party and the socialist Labour party was formed in 1900. In 1864 Marx created the First International Workers Union in London. In Germany, the party of the social democrats was established in 1875 as the first political party. Before the last part of the 19th century there were groups with different ideologies and opinions, all trying to get as much support as possible at elections.

After the debacle against the German troops at Sedan, the Third French Republic was proclaimed on 4 September 1870. After elections in February 1871, monarchists, in favour of the restoration of the French monarchy, had a majority in the Assembly, but the monarchists were deeply divided between Legitimists (who wanted to restore the Bourbon monarchy) and Orleanists (who wanted to give France a parliamentary monarchy with an Orleanist). Three constitutional laws of 1875 laid the foundation for the Third Republic with the Constitution of 1875. This was a semi-monarchist constitution, after negotiations between Orleanists and Republicans. Orleanists saw this constitution as a vehicle to easily transform the elected president into an Orleanist monarch when political circumstances would allow. On 16 May 1877 President Mac Mahon sent away a government, having the confidence of the majority in the Assembly. The President got the support of the senate to dissolve the Assembly when this organised a majority against the new government. The elections were a confrontation between the president of the republic, who wanted to have strong powers, and republicans, who preferred to give as much powers as possible to parliament. Republicans won the elections of October 1877. This had an important impact upon institutional engineering of France during the next century. Political parties were organised parallel to the development of democracy (Debbasch/Pontier, 1986). Democratisation of societal life made political parties a logical step but having political parties is not a sufficient condition for democracy; there are political parties or systems of a unique party in autocratic regimes. In a normative sense, democracy is about the functioning of several political parties in a pluralist society with respect for minorities and their values. International influences had an impact on political parties in Western Europe.

The First International Workers Union succumbed in 1876, after a conflict between adherents of Marx and the anarchists of Bakunin, expelled at the congress in The Hague (1872). The Second Internationale (1889-1939) was an association of national, socialist parties. Since October 1877 the equilibrium in France between public authorities, as formulated in the 1875 Constitution, was broken. Parliament, elected by the sovereign people, had preponderance. Executive power was subordinated to the legislative power of the Assembly. Since the eighties of the 19th century, "Radicaux" had claimed the inheritance of the Jacobins. When Mac Mahon resigned as president in 1879, Jules Grévy succeeded him. He promised that he would never challenge a parliamentary majority: the so-called "Constitution Grévy". President of the Republic, government and executive power became dependent on the parliamentary majority. Since 1887-1889, French society had been in the grip of a serious economic crisis and of a political crisis as well. Boulangism and the Dreyfus Affair shook society to its foundations. General Boulanger, former Minister of War, fed the frustrated feelings of many by speculations about revenge against Germans. Boulanger could make himself the leader of leftist republicans, radicals, "Blanquistes", nationalists, monarchists and Bonapartists. As Boulanger won the elections in Paris on 27 January 1889, his friends tried vainly to make him organise a coup to give France a strong government and powerful executive power. The French Republic escaped this Bonapartist caesarism by the narrowest margin. It reinforced many politicians in their opposition to powerful executive power, seen as impairing sovereignty of the parliament (as representatives of the people). The spirit of the times was interpreted quite well by "Le citoyen contre les pouvoirs" of Alain (1925). At the beginning of the 20th century, the republican concept was based on an overpowering parliament ("parlementarisme à la française") and weak executive power. In 1894 Jewish Alfred Dreyfus was condemned for espionage, indicted for passing secret military documents to Germans. He was sentenced to lifelong deportation to Devils' Island (Cayenne). In 1898 it became obvious that this had been a judicial error. An action to review the sentence started with Emile Zola's "J'Accuse!" A vitriolic political crisis split opinions deeply for a long time: "dreyfusards" (radicals, socialists, adherents to the "Ligue des droits de l'homme") against "anti-dreyfusards" (opponents of the Republic such as monarchists, Catholics, rightist republicans and nationalists), who opposed a review of the case (Birnbaum, 1994). They were activated by the "Ligue des Patriotes", created in 1882 by Paul Deroulède, "Ligue de la patrie française", the militantly anti-semitic Catholic journal "La Croix", and the "Ligue antisémitique". The guilty parties were nevertheless at last exposed: Major Esterhazy and Lieutenant-colonel Henry, participating in an anti-semitic, clerical and military atmosphere in the general staff, opposed to radical movements.

In 1899 Dreyfus was sentenced for 10 years instead. It was 1906 before Dreyfus was absolved and rehabilitated. This affair made republican politicians, hating the dominant position of the Catholic Church in French society, more anticlerical than ever. In June 1899, the "Gouvernement de défense républicaine" was formed under Waldeck-Rousseau with the support of the winning "Bloc des gauches" (supported by Socialists, Radicals, "dreyfusards" and moderates). "Dreyfusards" monopolised republican ideals, all their antagonists were seen as political opponents and also as adversaries of the regime. Being Republican was synonymous with anticlericalism and adherence to "laïcité". Political movements in France got real tools to organise political parties in the modern sense after the "Loi de 1901 sur les associations". The system of political parties developed between 1870 and 1914 (Goguel, 1958). At the start of the Third Republic there were three rightist, monarchist parties: "Légitimistes" (claiming a legitimate, Bourbon King in a monarchy as before 1789), "Orléanistes" (supporting Orleanists on the throne with a limited monarchy in a parliamentary regime) and "Bonapartistes" (supporting a Bonapartist in a populist, plebiscitary monarchy). A fourth, rightist movement rallied to the Republic. On the left, parties were adherents of the Republic. "Républicains modérés" and "Radicaux", forming a political party from 1902 on. "Radicaux" dominated the left side of the political sphere from 1905 to the Popular Front in 1936. After the Fourth Republic, their role was marginalised by the impact of Communists and Socialists. Socialists had been reformist since the second half of the 19th century (Proudhon, Saint-Simon, Fourier). They formed the "Parti Socialiste Unifié" (PSU), part of the Internationale: "Section française de l'Internationale ouvrière" (SFIO) since 1905. SFIO had wings: Marxist revolutionaries under Jules Guesde ("Guesdistes"), and moderate Socialists with Jean Jaurès as leader.

The Russian Revolution of 1917 had a decisive impact upon the organisation of the leftist parties. During the congress of SFIO at Tours (1920) the party split. The majority formed a Communist party, accepting the authority of the Third Internationale which was dominated by the Communist party in Moscow. Communists organised themselves in the "Parti Communiste" (PC) in 1920. After the Second World War, PC maintained its servile obedience to Soviets for a long period in the Fourth Republic. Several rightist political parties were established in the period between the two world wars: "Parti Social Français" (PSF) of Colonel De La Roque, and "Parti Populaire Français" (PPF) of Jacques Doriot. In the Fourth Republic (1946-1958) the Christian-Democrat party "Mouvement Républicain Populaire" (MRP) was established and the "Rassemblement du Peuple Français" (RPF), supporting De Gaulle. Originally, right referred to the group of parliamentarians sitting to the right of the president in the Assembly, and those sitting to his left were called left. Traditionally "right" describes that part of the population which is attached to the maintenance of established order, and "left" those who oppose this. There are several interpretations such as confrontation between conservatives and liberals, or between socialists and capitalists. Western societies developed from monarchist regimes to democracies, and from economic liberalism to social democracy. The conflict between conservatives and liberals had an outburst in the French Revolution (1789), dominating developments in the first half of the 19th century and beyond. The conflict was between the aristocracy (dominant in agrarian society) and the bourgeoisie. Bourgeois wanted to combine their growing economic power with political power, which was in the hands of aristocracy with privileges. When the French King chose the side of aristocrats, monarchy was disrupted. Aristocracy defended an authoritarian society full of inequality and hereditary privileges. Conservatives defended traditional society as if this was the natural order as desired by God. For a long time the Catholic Church supported this conception: alliance of throne and altar. The self-confident bourgeois claimed a position in society, in congruence with their economic position. A specific characteristic of the French system of political parties has been the weak discipline of political parties in parliament, causing structural governmental instability. This was stimulated by a concept, dating back to the French Revolution, that parliament had all the powers in the Republic. This governmental instability was evident in the Third and Fourth Republics. This caused a fundamental reorganisation of institutions on the basis of the new Constitution of 1958. De Gaulle started after Liberation as the first Premier of a provisional government and as the first

Premier of the Fourth Republic. Since 1946, he had retired because of the continuing games of the parties or "parlementarisme à la française". Since the Fifth Republic, governmental stability has been striking.

After 1945, the party-political landscape changed drastically. Radicals, dominant in the first half of the 20th century, were swept away. Communists, building upon their goodwill during Resistance against the Nazis, could in the beginning claim to be the first political party. New parties came up, like the Christian-Democrat "Mouvement Républicain Populaire" (MRP) since 1944. Adherents of De Gaulle, himself against the formation political parties, formed the "Rassemblement du Peuple Français". Later, Gaullists changed names several times. In the nineties they had the RPR, co-operating with UDF. After losing their majority following the electoral successes of Socialists in the double "septennat" of Mitterrand (1981-1995), the RPR/UDF had a majority in the Assembly again from 1993. Government-Balladur (1993-1995) had to live with a Socialist President ("cohabitation"). After the presidential elections of 1995, RPR/ UDF had control of all power positions (president, government, parliamentary majority). The party-political grip upon the organs of public authority was regularly criticised: "État-PS", and since 1995, "État-RPR/UDF" but it was difficult for the RPR/UDF coalition to gain acceptance of their policies, which were necessary for French participation in a common European currency (euro). In April 1997, President Chirac decided to voluntarily dissolve the Assembly one year before the normal term expired. Socialists and Communists answered this surprise attack with a counter-attack by forming a winning coalition. France had its "cohabitation" again, now with Neo-Gaullist Chirac as President, a Socialist Premier Jospin (with Communists in his government) and a leftist majority in parliament. Chirac's party paid dearly for his gamble, the RPR lost 119 of their previous 258 seats in the Assembly. Its ally, the UDF, lost nearly 100 seats and now had only 109 seats. The PS was the victorious party with 246 seats, 190 seats more than in 1993. This was only 42 seats short of absolute majority (288). That was no problem for the PS of Jospin, who could form a leftist government with the help of the Communists (37 seats), Radical Socialists (13 seats), Ecologists (8 seats), Citizens' Movement (7 seats) and various Leftist groupings (9 seats). As a result of the election-system, the extreme-rightist "Front National" with 15.24% of the votes, got only one seat in the Assembly, for the mayor of Toulon. The hangover was shocking for the political right. The elections in 2002 changed the political power positions. Neo-Gaullist Chirac won the presidential elections with 82.5% of the votes (huge abstention) against extreme-rightist Le Pen, and Chirac's newly formed "Union pour la Majorité Présidentielle" (UMP) got the absolute majority in the National Assembly. With all power positions in their hands (Presidency, government, and majorities in Assembly and Senate), the UMP has a decisive position for the period 2002-2007. It remains to be seen whether the UMP can refrain from becoming an "État-UMP". There is evidence for the hypothesis that politicians and political parties have often kidnapped public authority for more than a century.

## 6.10. Socialist and other leftist movements

The "Parti Socialiste" (PS) had rejected the Second Internationale in 1914 because SFIO and the German SPD supported war. PS refused to join the Third Internationale of Lenin (January 1919), the "Komintern" as an international union of Communist parties under Soviet leadership. After the debacle at the 1919 elections, two leaders of PS went to a meeting of the Communist Internationale in Moscow, in the summer of 1920, to investigate participation. Lenin imposed first 9 and then later 21 conditions, all opposed to democratic French traditions: absolute obedience to orders of the Kremlin; party organisation with "democratic centralism" and a quasi-military discipline; creation of a secret organisation;

absolute control of the press; purging of syndicates; support of nationalist movements in colonies; exclusion of reformists; etc. At the Tours congress in December 1920, the "Parti Socialiste" decided with a 3/4 majority to transform itself, accepting these dictates, into "Section Française de l'Internationale Communiste" (SFIC). A minority refused to accept the dictates of Lenin and the decision at Tours, and decided to maintain SFIO. This split of the Socialist party into a reduced SFIO and a Communist party was followed by the split of the CGT. When the congress of December 1921 refused to give revolutionaries the majority, they left CGT and created the "Confédération générale du travail unitaire" (CGTU). While leaders of the new "Parti Communiste" considered the 21 conditions of Tours originally as purely formal rules, leaders of the Communist Internationale were deadly serious about these conditions. National parties had to be an effective instrument for the worldwide revolutionary strategy as decided in Moscow. The Komintern demanded that French Communists should combine with Socialists in 1921 to form a unique proletarian front. The first major crisis broke out because French Communists refused (this would mean loss of face with regard to Socialists) only one year after Tours. This crisis was resolved at the beginning of 1923. The party was purged. When a "troika" in Moscow removed Trotsky in August 1924, in 1924-1926 "trotskyists" were also removed. Since 1924, a process of "bolchevisation" had been launched: replacement of geographic sections by cells in factories; ideological unity, and automatic obedience to the Communist Internationale and elimination of opponents. The Russian model of Communism was seen as the counter-model to capitalism. Since the end of 1927, the Communist Internationale, thinking that a confrontation with capitalism (in the grip of Fascism) was inevitable, had decreed a merciless battle against bourgeoisie and its accomplice, social-democracy, qualified as "social-fascisme". Socialists were a privileged target of Communist propaganda.

At the elections the Communists had to reject "republican discipline" and refused to support Socialist or Radical candidates in the second round. The French Communist Party looked for a leader, preferably one schooled in the International Leninist School of Moscow. After a new purge in 1929, Maurice Thorez (Sirot, 2000) became member of the Central Bureau, and from 1931 he became the secretary, responsible to the Communist Internationale. Amazing as it may seem, many intellectuals were attracted by this Soviet Communism, but the number of militant members of the "Parti Communiste" diminished from 120,000 in 1920 to 29,000 in 1933. After the elections of 1924, the first in which the Communists took part, they had 25 seats in the Assembly, in 1932 only 9 seats. SFIO, after the 1920 split of Tours, had only about 32,000 members. Most of its press and the majority of elected representatives were loyal to the traditions of the French workers' movement. Competition between SFIO and SFIC was heavy. Many members of SFIC, disappointed in its hard-line practices, regretted their unhappy choice and became members of SFIO again. SFIO had 60,000 members in 1924, and 137,000 in 1932, an impressive electorate. With the Radicals, SFIO got 103 seats in the Assembly in 1924. With the restoration of election per arrondissement in 1928 it had 18% of the votes, more than the Radicals, so SFIO became the first leftist party, but due to the election system (and the refusal of Communists to withdraw candidates in the second round) SFIO got 100 deputies. In 1932 SFIO got 20.5% of the votes and 131 deputies. SFIO had an identity crisis. Like the Communists, SFIO wanted to be proletarian with Marxist ideals. They had a common objective: realisation of a society without classes, and collective property for the means of production. The objective was the same, but the methods of the SFIO were absolutely different.

Socialists reproached Communists for confusing victory of Socialism with dictatorship of the Communist Party. They rejected Leninist methods as being contrary to Western democratic principles. Socialists wanted to take power by legal means on the basis of democratic elections and to transform society by laws, which would change the structures of property and distribution of incomes, so realising a real revolution. With a different concept of revolution SFIO had to compete with the Communists, who constantly outbid them. That was not the sole problem for SFIO. During its congresses, it emphasized its character as the party for workers, but its sociological basis was more a people's party with a prominent place for the middle class, not interested in overthrowing the regime. SFIO had a wing, loyal to strict Marxism as formulated by Guesde at the beginning of the 20th century, refusing all compromises of sharing power with bourgeois parties. A right wing of SFIO wanted to co-operate with Radicals, so realising legal improvements for workers. In between, the centre, under leadership of Léon Blum, tried to preserve the unity of SFIO, not knowing what choice to make between reform and revolution. The "Parti Radical" had its own identity problems (Berstein, 1982). During their 1914-1918 participation in the "Union Sacrée", Radicals refused to participate in the "Bloc National". While Herriot, party president since 1919, had tried to push Radicals to the left, the power was in the hands of deputies with divided opinions. The split in the CGT and the restoration of the French embassy at the Vatican caused passionate reactions. This was seen as an attack against the tacit "contrat de laïcité" which needed the participation of Radicals in government. In 1921, Radicals tried to negotiate an arrangement with "Républicains-Socialistes", "Syndicalistes Modérés" and others to form a "Ligue de la République" which could attract the moderate wing of SFIO. This failed, and from 1922 on the "Ligue de la République" was dormant. Following a new electoral law, Radicals had to form a coalition with SFIO to prevent a new defeat and after June 1923 Radicals opposed government-Poincaré more than before.

In February 1924, Radicals proposed the formation of a "Cartel électoral" with the Socialists on the basis of five issues: respect for social laws; strict implementation of income tax; support of the League of Nations; return to "laïcité de l'État et de l'école' and rejection of "décrets-lois" (decrees with the effect of laws, without the cumbersome procedure via Parliament). At the elections of 1924 the situation was the reverse of 1919, the political right was divided and the left was united. In the vote the right won narrowly but, due to the electoral system, the Leftist Cartel got a majority of seats thanks to the 40 seats of "Gauche Radical", opposed to SFIO policies in practically all issues. The new majority asked president Millerand (leader of the "Bloc National") to withdraw. He tried to hold power via Premier François-Marsal, who could not survive four days in office (9/13 June 1924). Millerand resigned and Doumergue became president (June 1924/ June 1931). Herriot was made Premier (June 1924/April 1925) and tried vainly to make SFIO participate in government. The "Cartel des gauches" formed a government with "Radicaux-Socialistes" (139 seats), "Républicains-Socialistes" (44 seats), and "Gauche Radicale" (40 seats). This government wanted to make the policies of the Left Cartel as different as possible from that of the "Bloc National". Innovations were obvious in foreign policy (ending the isolation of France), internal policy (restoring Republican values) and social policy (legal measures for social solidarity, employers/employees dialogue with the State as coach), but not regarding colonial policy (maintenance of the French colonial empire) and finance policy. In January 1925 the "Conseil national économique" was installed. Public servants got permission to strike. Opposed by employers, government made itself ever more the arbiter in conflicts between employers and employees. Stubborn opposition was provoked by the narrow-minded "retour à la politique laïque" of the Left Cartel. Socialists and Radicals agreed about restoring the situation before the "Bloc National" interfered in the sacrosanct field of "true Republicanism", They were also in accord about the implementation of Republican laws in Alsace-Lorraine, abolishing confessional schools, Concordat of 1801, and the embassy at the Vatican and the removal of religious congregations without official concessions, allowed again since the war.

From the end of 1924 the government implemented this narrow-minded anticlerical policy by disbanding congregations and cancelling the budget for the French embassy at the

Vatican. This reactivation of anticlericalism provoked emotional outbursts from the outraged masses and mobilised Catholics. The "Association catholique de la jeunesse française" organised mass demonstrations against "Néo-Combisme". The "Fédération nationale catholique", created by general de Castelnau as a resistance movement against persecution of the Catholic Church, was also active in this way. This massive pressure made Herriot shrink back and in January 1925, he announced that the Concordat continued in Alsace-Lorraine. He did not hurry to confirm the cancellation of the budget for the French embassy at the Vatican. After Herriot's fall in 1925 his successors abandoned this narrow-minded and politically stupid anticlericalism. The Left Cartel was overthrown on 10 April 1925 for its financial policy. Its anticlericalism played a major role in this event. Trying to survive, Herriot placed government under control of the bankers of the "Banque de France". In April 1925, Herriot had to choose between repaying State loans to this bank or forcing the Assembly to pass a law permitting enlarged advances. When the bank made public the extent of these advances, the Senate overthrew the government. Subsequent governments of the Left Cartel tried their best, but in July 1926 this coalition was forced out of government. To prove that this coalition could not govern, President Doumergue forced Herriot to form a government. This had just happened when the third crisis of exchange rates started. The "Banque de France" claimed that Herriot would inform the Assembly about the catastrophic situation of public finances and take adequate legal steps to control this. Financial panic broke out. People with exchequer bills asked for their money back en-masse. Herriot was overthrown on 21 July 1926. Poincaré formed a government. Governmment-Poincaré stabilised public finances, restoring confidence in the financial markets and, with the "Union Nationale", organising a majority which accepted reforms. At the 1928 elections Poincaré was so popular that all parties except the Socialists and Communists presented themselves as "poincaristes".

The era of Poincaré ended on 27 July 1929. New leaders were coming up: André Tardieu and Pierre Laval. Tardieu, three times premier in the period 1929/1932, adhered to neo-liberalism. He argued for institutional reforms to reinforce the position of the executive and to reduce powers of parliament. For him the real political divide is not between right and left, but between Marxism and the rest. Tardieu wanted to introduce a political party like the Conservatives in Great Britain. Laval, three times premier from January 1931 to February 1932, was quite another character. He began as a Socialist, having earned a lot of money in the press business, and acted as a pragmatic "parvenu". Leagues were politically active: "Ligue nationale républicaine" (created by Millerand); anti-communist "La Légion"; "Fédération nationale catholique" (FNC); "Action française". Italian Fascism was imitated by organisations forming nationalist, para-military leagues: "Jeunesses patriotes"; "Le Faisceau"; "Jeunesses patriotes" etc. In 1926, the "Action française" was condemned by the Pope. In 1930, Marcel Déat, writing the book "Perspectives socialistes", tried to renew ideological doctrine in the "Parti socialiste", actualising Marxism and formulating an ideology of "néo-socialisme". Instead of the Marxist idea, that the State is an instrument of dominant classes, he argued that the State is an institution above social classes. Class struggle was replaced by integration of classes and national solidarity. Déat made corporatism the central principle for society. He traversed the road from anti-Marxist Socialism, to authoritarian National-Socialism and Fascism. Tardieu tried in vain to form an anti-Communist coalition, but by making it explicit that the powers of the executive had to be enlarged at the cost of parliament, he made enemies in circles of "Républicains", cherishing a dominant parliament.

At the elections of 1932, the French could choose between Tardieu (rightist, anti-Communist, "antirépublicain", adherent of a strong executive), Blum (Socialist) or Herriot (in between). Herriot propagated the traditional radical program, accentuating "laïcité", values of the Republic (superiority of parliament), fighting economic crisis, and financial orthodoxy (budget equilibrium, maintaining the value of the franc). The Left won these elections with one million votes more than the right, and with 334 seats in the Assembly against 259 for the right. Herriot became premier, he postponed asking the SFIO to join the government until after their congress in the "salle Huyghens" in Paris. Herriot was sure that SFIO would demand unacceptable conditions for partnership in government. The Socialist congress adopted 9 conditions ("cahiers de Huyghens"): cuts in military expenditures; suppression of commerce in war weapons; nationalisation of the weapons industry; reduction of public expenditures must not hit social, agricultural or education outlays or salaries; control of banks; 40-hours working week without cuts in salaries; nationalisation of railways and insurance companies; general political amnesty. On 31 May, Radicals rejected this. Herriot formed a government of Radicals and Moderates without Socialists. Herriot made Socialists responsible for the failure of the Left Cartel (1924-1926), but his government in 1932 was a failure without them. Herriot needed Socialists (support without participation) for a parliamentary majority but they opposed his policies. Government-Herriot was overthrown in December 1932. Succeeding governments soon fell too, because Socialists refused to accept all the government proposals for financial policy. The economic crisis was doubled with a political crisis, paralysed by immobility. This caused defeatism, and the parliamentary system was discredited. Scandals undermined confidence in the parliamentary system. Tardieu, exasperated by his defeat at the 1932 elections, supported anti-parliamentarism. All political parties had their own crisis. Communists had their structural identity crisis, being a subordinate section of the Soviet-dominated Communist Internationale and a national party (Wolikow, 1990).

This meant that from 1928 the Communists practiced "class against class" politics, fighting Socialists and Radicals by not supporting them in the second round of elections. French Communists, by making themselves agents of the Soviet-Union in France, were accused of a planning a coup against the French Republic. "Parti Communiste" (PC) was branded as an anti-French party, ruled by foreigners and, according to public opinion, rightfully outlawed. PC, internally stressed by continuous purges, was inimical to Socialists of the SFIO, seen as traitors to true proletarian revolution for their reformist cooperation with bourgeois parties (Becker/Berstein, 1987). SFIO had its own identity problems, with internal controversies and militant wings striving for different policies. This party wanted to be Marxist and revolutionary, but rejected the Leninist methods and adhered to reforms of society. Blum tried to bring Socialists back into government. At the SFIO congress of July 1933, neo-Socialist revisionists and adherents of participation in government were criticised and in November 1933, revisionists were expelled from the SFIO. They started the "Parti socialiste français/Union Jean Jaurès", which was fused with the "Union socialiste républicaine" in November 1934. It seemed that the SFIO had controlled its problems, when it participated in government again in 1936. The "Parti radical" (PR) had its own problems. Since the debacle of the Left Cartel, a movement called "Jeunes Turcs" and "Jeunes Radicaux", had tried to renew ideological ideas of the PR. These Neo-Radicals wanted a State reform, reinforcing powers of the executive; representation of socio-economic forces in public decision-making and more State regulation of the economy; maintaining peace in Europe by a European federation with French-German reconciliation (Berstein, 1980/1982). When Herriot did not take up the ideas of "Jeunes Turcs", there were many disappointed members, a number of whom left the PR. Not only traditional parties of the left were in crisis, it was the same with traditional rightist parties. "Alliance républicaine démocratique", composed of Liberals, "Fédération républicaine" (Catholics supporting the Republic) and nationalists, were torn by animosities too. Mounier started the Catholic journal "Esprit" (Winock, 1975). His movement for a Christian-social order rejected restoration of the order before the French Revolution. It wanted to replace materialist, individualistic, productivist ideas of the 18th century with a society in which the dignity of the human individual was the basic principle, "Personnalisme" (Lacroix, 1981). This anti-capitalist, anti-liberal and anti-materialist movement rejected Marxism, capitalism, and false fascist spiritualism.

## 6.11. Conservative, rightist movements and leftist reactions

The ideas of Liberals did not provide enough confidence in their capacity to solve the problems of these times. Tardieu argued for a regime with a strong executive, giving the president of the Republic the power to dissolve parliament, reducing powers of parliament, and introducing the referendum. These ideas foreshadowed the Fifth Republic of 1958, but in the thirties, Tardieu was accused of Fascism, not least because he supported the movements of several leagues. The "Fédération républicaine", rallying the Republic, was criticised by members who blamed the French Revolution for the evils of French society. In journals they attacked the sicknesses of democracy, capitalism and the "État laïc". They wanted the restoration of old-time France with a dominant position for the Catholic religion (Loubet del Bayle, 1969). There was a fertile soil for rightist "ligues" (Sirinelli, 1992). Since the end of the 19th century movements had organised themselves as leagues. Up to 1932 their following was relatively reduced, although since the twenties it had been growing due to the return of the left into government and the Italian example of Fascism. When the left took power in 1932 in the midst of an economic crisis, leagues became more popular with their plea for direct action and anti-parliamentarism. The "Association d'anciens combattants" created in 1927 to organise actions on behalf of veterans and war victims, was reorganised in 1930 as a political organisation "Croix-de-Feu" by ex-colonel La Rocque. This had a para-military nature with "dispos", disposable for provocative military activities. Provocations of La Rocque, as the "French Mussolini", who wanted to replace the parliamentary regime with an authoritarian, effective regime, were alarming. These seemed to forestall civil war, especially when the Nazis in Germany got 6.5 million votes and 107 seats in parliament at the elections of September 1930.

On 11 December 1932, the German claim of equal rights for nations was recognised at an international conference. This meant that Germany could build up its military organisation again until it was more equal to that of France, then seen as militarily superior on the continent. Hitler was in power on 30 January 1933 as "Führer of the Third Reich" (Bloch, 1986). In the beginning he played his ruthless power-game with peaceful declarations, so winning time to build up his military apparatus. In France, Bucard created "Francisme" in September 1933, with Italian Fascism as his example. Also in 1933 Coty formed the paramilitary "Solidarité française", with regions and brigades, under direction of Jean Renaud, a former infantry commander. Comparisons can be made with German and Italian Fascism, but some dispute that this can be called French Fascism (Soucy, 1989). French leagues could not mobilise such massive organisations as in Germany or Italy, but there were phenomena furthering Fascism in France (anti-parliamentarism, longing for the strong man, enthusiasm for paramilitary exhibitions of direct power in the streets). Masses of discontented people, who had seen their way of life threatened by war and economic crisis eagerly devoured all information promising solutions for their problems by authoritarian government. Rémond (1982) accentuated the differences between Fascism and the French leagues, arguing for nationalist traditions and effective government without a totalitarian society. According to Milza (1991), public opinion in France was imbued with a long period of Republican values, which worked as an antidote against foreign fascist ideas. There were violent riots in January 1934, when "L'Action Française" intensified attempts to destabilise the regime, perplexed by the "Affaire-Stavisky" which compromised politicians. La Rocque used this to mobilise the "Croix-de-Feu" for actions on 6 February

1934. Government-Chautemps fell on 28 January 1934 because of another affair, the swindles by Sacazan which compromised the Minister of Justice and rightist politicians awaited their chance to take over when the leftist government was eventually worn-out by scandals. The decision of the Premier on 3 February 1934 to fire the Paris prefect of police, Jean Chiappe, for failing to act more effectively in the "Affaire-Stavisky", caused dismay among ministers of the centre-right and indignation of the leagues. They invited adherents to organise massive demonstrations on 6 February 1934. Communist organisations did the same. Violence was inevitable: 15 killed and 1,435 wounded.

What happened that day could be interpreted differently: a fascist coup which had to be countered; outrage at the murder of honourable veterans or a chance for the Communists to fish in troubled waters (Berstein, 1975). Government-Daladier fell on 7 February 1934, succeeded by government-Doumergue (February/November 1934). This government wanted to reform the State, reinforcing the executive and reducing the powers of parliament. As it postponed legislative actions until after summer, the chance to make parliament adopt the necessary laws faded away. The "Alliance Démocratique" decided to form a coalition with Radicals which overthrew the government. A new chance to reorganise the State had to wait until 1940 (Monnet, 1993). The political impasse became more manifest in the period 1934/1936. German Chancellor Brüning exploited the risk of a take-over by Hitler as a means to make France abandon its claims for German reparations. In the end Germans paid not the 132 billion Deutschmark, as the Treaty of Versailles had ordered, but 23 billion; 9 billion to France. In the summer of 1934 there was a Nazi-putsch in Vienna and on 25 July 1935 Austrian Chancellor Dolfuss was murdered. The risk of loss of independence for Austria prompted Mussolini, sending troops to the Brenner, talk about that "horrible sexual degenerate" Hitler. Minister Barthou saw his chance of bringing Italy into the anti-German coalition, while reinforcing the bond with the Soviet-Union and creating a "pacte de l'Est". Barthou was murdered on 9 October 1934. Laval succeeded him as Minister of foreign affairs, continuing his policy. Radicals were prominent in government, Laval (June 1935/January 1936) while participating in the opposing "Rassemblement Populaire", a coalition with Socialists and Communists for the 1936 elections. In March 1936, Hitler remilitarised the Rhineland, contrary to all treaties. France was weakened by political immobility and impotence. With hindsight we know that Hitler would have withdrawn his troops if French troops had intervened. French government did nothing. In May 1936, Laval and Stalin signed a French-Soviet Pact. Mussolini announced a German-Italian pact on 1 November 1936, creating the "Rome-Berlin Axis". All attempts to break the coalition of Hitler and Mussolini had failed.

Attempts since 6 February 1934 to form an anti-fascist coalition in France itself had initially failed. Communists, following orders of the Communist Internationale, accused Socialists and Radicals of being "social-fascistes". There seemed to be an insurmountable rift between Communists and Radicals, with the Communists accused of being a rebellious party and an instrument of the Soviet-Union, with the aim of overthrowing the French Republic. Bertrand de Jouvenel (1935), trying to find a third way in between Socialism and Liberalism, broke his relationship with the "Parti radical" and concluded that neither was able to solve the capitalist crisis. Together with Drieu La Rochelle in his "Socialisme fasciste" (1934), he argued for an authoritarian approach. The program of the Fascist party PPF ("Parti populaire français") was promoted by a former Communist, later a minister of Pétain, Marion (1938). Controversies between Socialists and Radicals were fierce. At the Ivry conference (June 1934) of the "Parti Communiste", Thorez (after consent of Moscow) called for an anti-fascist coalition of the three parties. On 27 July 1935 Socialists and Communists signed a pact for united action, made easier for Socialists by the Laval/Stalin Pact, which seemed to make French Communists patriots defending France against Nazi-Germany. Since 1935, a majority of committees in the "Parti Radicale" had argued for participation in a "Front Populaire". After demonstrations in favour of this, a "Comité national du Rassemblement populaire" was formed. In January 1936, a common program of the Popular Front was published, with the headlines: battle against the economic crisis (public works, raising purchasing power of the masses by "reflation"; peace; and defence of liberties). Workers unions CGT and CGTU decided to fuse in March 1936. The 1936 elections were a victory for the Popular Front, with 369 seats against 231 seats for the right (Dupeux, 1959). SFIO (146 seats) and Communists (72 seats) needed 10 seats of the "Parti d'unité prolétarienne" to break even with the right, so the majority of the Popular Front depended on "Parti radical" (115 seats) and its ally, the "Républicains-socialistes" (26 seats), to govern.

Blum (SFIO) formed a government of Socialists and Radicals. Communists chose for support without participation in government. The country was ravaged by general strikes, with the occupation of enterprises. Government-Blum tried to solve social conflicts by a series of measures. On the invitation of the government CGT and the "Confédération générale de la production française" signed the "Accords Matignon" (5 June 1936). These implied rises in salaries of 12%; collective conventions about working conditions; representation of employees in committees of the enterprises; and liberty of syndicalist activities. Parliament adopted two laws in July 1936, realising two weeks of paid holidays and making the working week a maximum of 40 hours (without reducing salaries). The Popular Front euphoria of the first months, with planned renovations in the sphere of culture and education (Ory, 1994), soon withered away. In the extreme-rightist press hate campaigns were launched, some of which were especially anti-Semitic. As premier Blum and other ministers were Jews, this gave them a special edge. Maurras in the "Action française" and Béraud in the "Gringoire" exploited this. Another theme was a fierce anti-Communism (Becker/Berstein, 1987). The pressure of continuous strikes was seen as an intrigue of the "Parti communiste", preparing to take over government. Government dissolved leagues after June 1936 and in December 1936, a law restrained the press for slander etc. Suppression of the "Croix-de-Feu" made La Rocque create the "Parti Social Français" (PSF), trying to reach its objectives by legal means. The PSF exploited the motto "Travail, Famille, Patrie", which had its appeal for the French, so between 1936 and 1940, tens of thousands became members of the PSF (probably the largest political party at the time). In 1936 former Communist Jacques Doriot (1938) created the "Parti Populaire Français" (PPF), and with his sharp criticism of government and anti-Communism, he mobilised 300,000 adherents (Brunet, 1986). When General Franco organised a military uprising against the legal government in Spain on 18 July 1936, government-Blum reacted with military support for the legal government (Hermet, 1989). This provoked a storm of protests. Then Blum proposed a non-intervention pact, which was signed by France, Great Britain, Italy and Germany in August 1936, while the 11th Olympiad was going on in Berlin. Only Great Britain stuck to its agreements, Italy and Germany sent massive support to Spain and France helped (passage of "Brigades internationales" via the Pyrenees, etc.).

Economic policy of the Popular Front failed due to fierce opposition by the business community and the consequences of government measures. Government-Blum, in "solving" the crisis with ongoing strikes by a series of costly measures, in fact made the "patronat" pay the costs. The level of salary costs was raised by about 30%. There was a huge outflow of capital abroad, inflation was galloping and in spite of the solemn promises of Blum, he was forced to devalue the franc in June 1936 by 25-35%. The franc-Poincaré (65.5 mg fine gold) was replaced by the franc-Auriol (42-49 mg fine gold). Devaluation was seen as a debacle of government policy. This monetary adjustment was not enough to close the gap between French prices and world market prices. In less than 8 months the Popular Front government recognised the failure of its economic policy. In February 1936 Blum announced a pause in social reforms (indexation of salaries, etc.) to give enterprises more time. He did return the budget to equilibrium. Rising expenditures for national defence would be financed with loans. While Blum thought to win back the confidence of the business community, he lost this in the world of the workers. Strikes and occupation of enterprises gave part of the public the impression that Communists were preparing to overthrow the Republic. Employers, organised in the "Confédération Générale du Patronat Français" (CGPF), had "Comités de salut économique" throughout France to fight government policy. Disappointment of the middle classes (basis of the Radicals), hit hard by the economic crisis, was growing. On 10 June 1937, the Minister of Finance asked the Assembly for full powers until 31 July 1937 to redress financial problems. Although the Assembly accepted this, the Senate refused and the government of the Popular Front had to resign. The troubled years from then on to the German invasion of 1940, and the nasty period of the Vichy-Regime (1940-1944), put all political movements and parties in a difficult position. Their true loyalties were put to a thorough test.

## 6.12. Political life after Liberation

France in 1945, happy after Liberation, was in a political and juridical void (Berstein/Milza, 1995). The Assembly, suspending the Constitution of the Third Republic, had given Pétain full powers on 10 July 1940 and he had been able to establish a quasi-personal dictatorship in the Vichy-regime, subordinate to Nazi-control. Since 1945, some collaborationist functionaries in key positions had been purged, while an unknown number of them were not. After four years of German occupation the pre-war political parties had lost their coherence and they all had leadership problems. The existing structures of traditional political parties were almost swept away. Only the clandestine "Parti communiste" had actively survived since 1939. Vichy-regime and Resistance alike branded traditional political parties as a nuisance. They were held responsible for the shameful defeat by the Nazis, with their partisan squabbling undermining national unity, but leading actors in the "Résistance" thought it necessary to revive political parties as a medium for representing the population. The idea was born for a "parti de la Résistance", which would occupy the political vacuum caused by the discrediting of political parties after Liberation. This was not viable and traditional parties tried in one way or another to revive their cadre and their following. They had problems with the values they had supported before the war, which had since then lost their inspiration. The US and the Soviet-Union had been proven to have the capacity to fight Nazi-terror, and were models that could possibly free France from its weaknesses. Just before Liberation, the CNR adopted the "Charte du Conseil national de la Résistance" (Andrieu, 1984). Its objectives were liberty, democracy and welfare, collective control of essential production sectors and social justice, guaranteed by a strong State.

Since June 1941, when the Germans invaded the Soviet-Union, the "Parti communiste" (PC) had participated actively in resistance. Members of resistance movements, till then not emphasizing their adherence to political parties, now had to make up their minds; Would they accept the PC presenting itself as party of resistance? Daniel Mayer, inspired by Blum, created a "Comité d'Action Socialiste" in 1941, which revived the SFIO in 1943. George Bidault had organised militant Christian-democrats in resistance since 1941, forming a structure which would become "Mouvement républicain populaire" (MRP) after Liberation. Since 1943, De Gaulle, wanting to make manifest to suspicious Anglo-Americans that the CNR was representative, had made political parties members of the CNR. Traditional political parties, dormant since 1940, had to reactivate themselves. At Liberation, PC, SFIO and MRP and some minor parties occupied the political field. This reduced any chance for a political party of the resistance. Former members of resistance and "Mouvement de

Libération nationale" (MLN) launched the "Union travailliste". They tried, with the help of SFIO, to establish a new party with the British Labour movement as example. This was a failure, as most Socialists wanted to maintain SFIO (Quilliot, 1982). A minority started the "Union démocratique et socialiste de la Résistance" (UDSR) in May 1945. The idea of making a party for Socialists and Christian-democrats stood no chance. Political parties could engage in their partisan games again as before the war.

Since the municipal elections of April/May 1944, it had become evident that the political situation had changed drastically. PC, SFIO and MRP were the largest political parties, while other political parties had lost an important part of their following. PC, without any appeal after its support of the Soviet-German Pact (August 1939), had won the hearts of many with its courageous resistance against the Nazis. It exploited this by profiling itself as a party of the resistance supporting the CNR program (Brunet, 1982). SFIO seemed to be better equipped to reap the spoils of resistance because of its humanistic Socialism (Michel, 1962). There were some factors which mitigated the appeal of SFIO (Ligou, 1967). Traditionalists opposed any reform which would take their party further away from orthodox Marxism. The popular idea of the resistance movement to form a breakthrough-party, bridging the gap between Socialists and Christian-democrats, was contrary to cherished opinions of those who were attached to "laïcité". At the congress of August 1945, militant Socialists won a majority for their idea to revive traditional anticlericalism, so SFIO decided to maintain its pre-war identity, alienating many social Christian-democrats. This reinforced the "Mouvement républicain populaire" (MRP), created in November 1944 which from the beginning had profiled itself as a new party of the Fourth Republic (Deschamps, 1981). It emphasized that this party bore no relation to the loathed pre-war parties with their "parlementarisme à la française", creating structural instability and a weak France. MRP placed its leadership in the hands of inspiring leaders of the resistance movement: Maurice Schumann, Georges Bidault, P.H. de Teitgen and F. de Menthon. MRP emphasized its adherence to De Gaulle, profiling itself as the sole party opposed to the Communists, now that the Socialists maintained their ambiguous adherence to Marxism. Pre-war rightist parties were compromised by the Vichy-regime, though Michel Clemenceau, son of the "Tiger", did lead the new, moderate and centrist "Parti républicain de la Liberté" (PRL). "Indépendants" and a "Parti paysan" tried to appeal to moderates and centrists. Radicals, according to public opinion largely responsible for the failing governments of the Third Republic, had big problems finding a new approach.

As promised by De Gaulle, there was a referendum on 21 October 1945, combined with legislative elections. These first national elections since the war would reveal political power relations. Since an ordinance of 1944, giving women the right to vote, the composition of the electorate was essentially changed. The institutional genius of De Gaulle had ensured that his provisional government asked two questions in the referendum. The first yes or no question was about the drafting of a new constitution, which after a positive response of the electorate would mean the abolition of the Third Republic. To this 96% of the electorate said yes, which meant that the Assembly, just elected that day, was a Constituent Assembly. The second question was about the proposal of a text limiting powers of the Assembly to seven months for the making of a new constitution. In spite of the campaigning of Communists and Radicals to vote no to the second question, 66% of the electorate did vote yes. PC became the first party with 26.2% of votes and 160 seats in the Assembly (in 1936 14.76% and 72). SFIO got 23.4% and 142 seats (in 1936 20.07% and 147 seats). The new MRP got 23.9% and 152 seats. Radicals and their allies got 10.5% and 59 seats (against 19.65% and 157), and centre-rightist Moderates got 15.6% and 61 seats (in 1936 42.56% and 220 seats). Elections revealed that Communists and Socialists had a majority (49.6%), with 302 of the 586 seats. The position of Radicals was greatly weakened, and also that of Moderates, who lost votes to the MRP. Nearly 3/4 of the electorate voted for three mass-parties: PC, SFIO and MRP.

Soon the conflict between the "Man of 18 June 1940" and the political parties would explode. De Gaulle, since 1944 recognised by the great powers, governed with the acclamation of the French and with two organs, wholly dependent upon himself: "Gouvernement provisoire de la République française" (GPRF) and "Assemblée consultative". Communists, since October 1945 the first party, were the most stubborn opponents of De Gaulle. De Gaulle adhered to constitutional concepts wholly opposed to most political parties, devoted to the dominant position of parliament with regard to government and the executive. According to De Gaulle, the institutional and political centre had to be in the hands of executive power under leadership of government, while the powers of parliament had to be reduced to voting on laws and the budget, while checking government. In view of the elections of October 1945, the Communists proposed to form a government with Socialists, disposing of a majority. SFIO, fearing they would become the hostages of PC in a project leading France into the position of a people's democracy as in Eastern Europe, rejected this. It suggested a coalition of the three (PC, SFIO and MRP). The new Christian-Democratic party MRP with 24.9% was the second party (Vaussard, 1956), and so on 13 November 1945, the Second GPRF under De Gaulle was supported unanimously in parliament. PC demanded one-third of portfolios and one of the key-departments (foreign affairs, national defence, internal affairs). After heavy negotiations, De Gaulle, threatening to retire, managed to control this pressure. PC got only 5 of the 21 ministries and none of the key-departments for important issues (armament, national economy, labour). The dominant idea was that in the case of opposing views between government and parliament, parliament would have the last word. Government-De Gaulle could bring about some important measures. De Gaulle appointed Jean Monnet in December 1945 "Commissaire au Plan", who made the "Plan de modernisation et d'équipement 1946-1950" as launched in January 1946. A number of nationalisations were adopted. In December 1945, the conflict of the parties with De Gaulle about the voting of the military budget was acute. Socialist Philip demanded a reduction of 20%. On 1 January 1946 De Gaulle asked: "Does one want to have a government which governs, or an almighty Assembly, delegating powers to government to accomplish what the Assembly wants?". He was irritated, as the commission charged with a draft for a new constitution refused to inform him. De Gaulle convoked his ministers on 20 January 1946, threatening to retire if they did not accept his proposals. He expected that they would accept but they did not (Charlot, 1983). MRP decided not to follow him. The field was free for political parties to play their games as before the war.

The retreat of Premier De Gaulle on 20 January 1946, who until then had dominated the governing coalition, forced the parties of this coalition to alter their attitudes. PC, SFIO and MRP could no longer hide behind the proclaimed national unity of government, in turn distancing themselves from specific political issues, sure that their majority was enough. De Gaulle, with all his legitimacy, cleared the way for the only other legitimised actors, politicians elected by universal suffrage. He himself enabled the "République des partis" to revive. As SFIO refused to form a two-party government with Communists, "tripartisme" was the prevailing formula. According to Charlot (1983), the leadership of MRP had decided not to risk a Marxist two-party government. Elgey (1993) put forward the idea that a letter from General Billotte, threatening American military intervention in the case of a PC-SFIO government, was decisive for the MRP attitude. On 23 January 1946, the "Charte du Tripartisme" was signed by the three parties. It was an armistice between PC, SFIO and MRP, establishing some rules of conduct. Felix Gouin (SFIO), behaving as the puppet of political parties, succeeded as Premier. Instead of initiating the formation of a government, he merely divided portfolios, giving coalition parties the power to designate ministers. The power to govern the country was in the hands of the leaders of three political parties. This government had as key task: the production of a draft for a new constitution in May 1946. The first draft of the committee for the constitution, dominated by PC and SFIO, was oriented towards a mono-cameral system. It proposed a one-house Assembly, elected for 5 years, disposing of all institutional powers and electing the president of the Republic and premier, and which could overthrow government at any moment. Representatives of MRP in the committee were able to get reduced amendments. François de Menthon, directing the committee, resigned and was succeeded by Radical Pierre Cot (adhering to Communist ideas). Radicals, at their congress (April 1946), rejected the draft and Pierre Cot was expelled. They formed the "Rassemblement des Gauches républicaines" (RGR) with the "Alliance démocratique", "Parti républicain et social de la Réconciliation française", "Parti socialiste-démocratique", "Parti républicain-socialiste" and "UDSR". On 19 April 1946 the Assembly adopted the draft for a new constitution, which would be presented to the population in a referendum, with 309 votes (PC, SFIO) against 249 (RGR, MRP). The referendum became a passionate issue between adherents and opponents of a people's democracy. On 5 May 1946 80% of the electorate voted, and the draft was rejected by 53% of the votes. Elections of 2 June 1946 made MRP the first party with 28.2% and 169 seats. PC maintained its position and had 25.9% and 153 seats. SFIO, as a consequence of its hesitating and ambivalence (Marxism or not) lost with 21.1% and 129 seats. RGR got 11.6% and 53 seats, while Moderates got 12.8% and 67 seats. This was a shift to the right, PC and SFIO had lost their majority.

In his famous speech at Bayeux (16 June 1946), De Gaulle broke his silence. He wanted to put maximum pressure on the Constituent Assembly working on its second draft (Julliard, 1968). Vituperating the loathed system of party-politics and the rejected draft for a new constitution, De Gaulle unfolded his own conception. In his view, the powers of parliament had to be reduced (only voting about laws and budget). A second house of parliament, like the Senate before, with elected members of municipal and departmental councils, representatives of overseas territories and societal organisations, would form a countervailing power against the Assembly. Executive power would not be dependent on the Assembly, but only on the President of the Republic as "clé de voûte", chosen for 7 years by an electoral college. Again MRP, exploiting its position as party of De Gaulle, disappointed him by not supporting the "Constitution de Bayeux". The Assembly adopted the second draft in September 1946 with 443 against 106 votes. In his "discours d'Épinal" (22 September 1946), De Gaulle gave his scathing criticism of this draft. The break between De Gaulle and MRP was complete. MRP lost an important part of its electorate. The referendum on the second draft in October 1946 adopted it with 53% (one-third abstentions). This Constitution of 1946 was commented on by De Gaulle with his 1/3-1/3-1/3 formula: One-third of the French acquiesced, one-third opposed, and one-third disregarded this Constitution.

## 6.13. The Fourth Republic (1946-1958)

The Fourth Republic started with a dominant position for the Assembly and the large political parties. The second house of parliament, the "Conseil de la République" (Senate), as advisory body had no real power. The president of the Republic, chosen for 7 years by Assembly and Senate, was in the reins of the Assembly. According to the 1946 Constitution, government had the direction of executive power. In party-political fact, the majority of the Assembly was more than a match. Parliamentary habits of the Third Republic survived, and were reactivated. Control of government by the Assembly took the form of more or less permanent participation of members of the Assembly in executive power (committees etc.). In a sense, the government-by-committees, as shortly after the French Revolution, seemed to revive. The first legislative elections of the Fourth Republic on 10 November 1946 confirmed the situation of three dominant parties. PC got 28.3% and 183 seats, SFIO had 17.8% and 105 seats, while MRP got 25.9% and 167 seats. RGR (70 seats), Moderates (71 seats) and others ("Union gaulliste") with 22 seats, had only a marginal role. As the position of SFIO was weakened, the frail equilibrium in tripartism was upset. Blum formed a government for the time until the presidential elections on 16 January 1947, which made Vincent Auriol the first president of the Fourth Republic. He appointed Paul Ramadier, an outspoken representative of pre-war "parlementarisme à la française", as premier (Berstein, 1990). Ramadier set the tone by creating precedents and making government dependent on parties in the Assembly. He dared to take up 7 ministers into his government from outside PC, SFIO or MRP: 3 Radicals, 2 Independents and 2 UDSR. This was an important break in the seeming monopoly of tripartism. Ramadier made Communist Billoux Minister of National Defence. To watch over him, he appointed three other Ministers: Michelet (MRP) Army; Maroselli (Radical) Air Force; and Jacquinot (Moderate) Navy. To make it a real "régime des partis", Ramadier made the leaders of political parties choose members of government.

Soon all sorts of tensions between political parties brought instability back as before the war. MRP refused to nationalise banks as demanded by the PC. Government was forced to reduce claims for higher salaries. Even the PC supported this policy for a time, but soon PC and CGT came under heavy pressure in the world of workers. In the sphere of colonial politics conflicts piled up. When there was an uprising in Madagascar in March 1947, the government reacted with repression and the arrest of parliamentarians. PC then rejected the military budget. When PC at the end of April 1947 tried to force its will on government with strikes in Renault plants, Ramadier was interpellated in the Assembly by the PC on 4 May 1947. All Communists and their Ministers voted against the government. That is what made Ramadier fire them, not because the US forced him to do so, as Lacroix-Riz (1986) asserted. After this the PC was out of government until 1981. The Cold War between two blocs was an explanation for this. After September 1947 Moscow forced the PC to distance itself from imperialist governments. PC profiled itself as party of abroad. PC branded American Marshall-aid as an imperialist trick, and intensified its action to provoke strikes. In the CGT, Communists forced others to leave CGT. They established the "CGT-Force Ouvrière". At the end of 1947, government-Ramadier fell. Civil war seemed imminent. Premier Schuman decided to call up more men to the armed forces. Soviet-troops occupied Prague (February 1948) and the PC was finished in public opinion.

The "Troisième Force" (1947-1952), composed of Socialists, Moderates and MRP, with Communists and Gaullists in opposition, succeeded tripartism. On 7 April 1947, De Gaulle announced establishment of the "Rassemblement du Peuple français" (RPF), founded on 14 April 1947. He presented himself as saviour of France against Soviet-Communism (at a distance of only two "étappes du Tour de France"). Communists were branded as enemies ("séparatistes"). Institutions of the Fourth Republic were criticised as causing the weakness of France. He made it clear that the State had to be reformed according to the conception in his Bayeux-speech (16 June 1946). De Gaulle did not want to create a new political party which would divide the French population. Instead, he argued for the forming of an association open to all the French (also for members of political parties). De Gaulle, visiting all parts of his country, actively promoted his ideas. His success was unprecedented, halfway through 1948 the RPF had about 400,000 members (Charlot, 1983). MRP and SFIO reacted promptly, forbidding members to combine their membership with adherence to the RPF. Others combined their membership of a political party with that of the RPF. Municipal elections of October 1947 were a Gaullist victory. The coalition with RPF had about 40% of the votes, while RPF alone had more than 28% of the votes. On 20

October 1947 RPF mayors were installed in the 13 largest cities. RPF got positions in 52 prefectures. The brother of General de Gaulle, Pierre de Gaulle, became mayor of Paris. On 27 October 1947 De Gaulle provoked the Assembly by arguing that it no longer represented the French nation. This was branded as "Boulangisme". De Gaulle had to wait four years until 1951 for the next legislative elections.

Immobility was characteristic for the party-political situation during the period of the "Troisième Force". Queuille, premier from September 1948 to October 1949, was recognised as the grandmaster of immobility, combining doing nothing with some tricks and so surviving (Le Béguec/Delivret, 1987). To counter the threat of a tidal wave of the RPF, he changed the electoral system and postponed the time of elections. The international situation was stressed. After the Soviet-coup in Prague (February 1948), blockade of Berlin (June 1948/May 1949), and start of the Korean War (1950-1953), the Cold War became rather a hot war. Successive Ministers of Foreign Affairs, Bidault and Schuman, asked the US to engage itself in military aid for Europe and on 4 April 1949 the US signed the Atlantic Pact, treaty for a military alliance between US, Canada and countries in Western Europe. The "North Atlantic Treaty Organisation" (NATO) was a defensive alliance against militarist Soviet-Communism. Schuman, leader of MRP, which since the launching of RPF could no longer present itself as the party of De Gaulle, found in the construction of West-European integration a new perspective for his electorate. This resulted firstly only in the creation of the consultative Council of Europe (May 1949). After the "Plan Schuman" (9 May 1950), inspired by Jean Monnet, the European Coal and Steel Community (ECSC) was a supranational construction, integrating German heavy industry under a High Authority. In October 1950, the "Plan Pleven" (October 1950) was brought forward to create a European Defence Community (EDC). This was meant to make the re-armament of West Germany acceptable. The US wanted to defend Western Europe against Soviet imperialism by integrating the German army into a European army.

In the legislative elections of 17 June 1951 the "Troisième Force" lost votes, but could maintain its majority with 51.2% (against 67.6% in 1946). PC had 26.9% and 101 seats. SFIO got 14.6% and 106 seats. MRP, losing half of its votes and seats, was the losing party with 12.6% and 88 seats. RPF with 21.6% and 117 seats robbed the MRP of an important part of its electorate, but RPF was disappointed, because it expected to get at least 200 seats. These elections could bring only a government of the "Troisième Force" again, because PC and RPF (refusing to play the games of the parties) could only be in opposition. Pleven (UDSR) in August 1951 was premier of a government with Radicals, MRP and Moderates, and with the support of Socialists in parliament (not in government). Pleven allowed the Assembly to adopt a law-proposal to give all families with a child in primary school a subsidy of 3,000 francs a year. Socialists overthrew the government in January 1952. Government-Faure did not last long either (40 days). Auriol tried to convince RPF to join government and nominated Pinay as premier. Government-Pinay (8 March 1952/23 December 1953) was accepted by a majority in the Assembly, so the centre-right came into power (1952-1954) with three objectives: economic recovery and financial stability; anti-Communism and soberness; and maintaining French sovereignty in colonial territories. In 1953, more than 27 members of RPF voted for government-Mayer (8 January 1953/21 March 1953) and government-Laniel (27 June 1953/12 June 1954). Integration of RPF-parliamentarians into the regime of the Fourth Republic was hitting the political Achilles' heel of De Gaulle hard. He decided to dissolve RPF in May 1953. Gaullist deputies formed "Union républicaine d'action sociale" (URAS), and "Républicains-Sociaux". The "Plan Pleven" to form a European Defence Community (EDC) was accepted by the Assembly in 1952, but soon it caused a passionate debate. This military integration seemed to involve a hidden political integration.

This political forest fire was stimulated by Gaullists and others, arguing that this would imply an irrevocable loss of French sovereignty in supranational Europe should it become a political union in the future. Between adherents of EDC in MRP and adversaries (Gaullists and Communists), other political parties were divided internally. Government-Pinay and other governments had signed the EDC-agreement in May 1952. Because Pinay, fearing opposition against it, postponed ratification by the Assembly, MRP forced him to resign in December 1952. Nomination of the President of the Republic by the "Congrès" (Assembly and Senate together) in December 1953 was also an issue which proved the weakness of the Fourth Republic. It took 13 rounds to nominate René Coty as second and last President (January 1954/January 1959), succeeding Auriol. A death blow for the Fourth Republic came from the colonial front. In 1953, the death of Stalin and the coming to power of Eisenhower caused some thaw in the Cold War. The armistice in the Korean War (June 1953) had its effect. Eisenhower and Churchill, at a meeting in Bermuda (December 1953), got the agreement of the French Premier Laniel to organise a 5-powers conference (US, Great Britain, France, Soviet-Union, Communist China), in Geneva in 1954, to settle conflicts, especially in Asia. French government wanted to enter this conference in a position of strength and ordered a spectacular military action in French Indo-China. The general staff devised a plot round Dien Bien Phu. This was meant to hit Vietminh troops, arriving en-masse to deliver a blow to the French. Instead the French army would strike the Vietminh. The French fell in their own plot, as the expected air support failed to arrive. On 7 May 1954, the Vietminh conquered Dien Bien Phu, a terrible blow for French prestige. Public opinion, indifferent about warfare in French Indo-China, was hostile. Government-Laniel was overthrown on 12 June 1954. Mendès France formed a government.

The experience of government-Mendès France (19 June 1954/5 February 1955) in collective memory generates mixed feelings about "mendésisme" (Bédarida/Rioux, 1985). Mendès France challenged the practices of political parties, and he had the courage to reduce their role (Lacouture, 1981; Pouvoirs, 1983). Unlike former governments, characterised by wait-and-see immobility, his government took initiatives. He formed a business-government with prominent figures of different parties (some without their consent): Radicals Faure (Finance) and Berthoin (Education); Mitterrand of the UDSR (Home Affairs); Social-Republicans Koenig (National Defence), Chaban-Delmas (Public Works) and Fouchet (Moroccan/Tunisian Affairs); and of MRP Buron (Overseas Territories). Socialists of the SFIO refused to participate, as the composition of the government was not in the hands of political parties. For the first time since the start of the Cold War, Communists decided to vote for the government-Mendès France, because he promised to make peace in French Indo-China. Mendès France even had the spirit to say that he would resign if he could only reach a majority in the Assembly with the votes of the PC. On 18 June 1954, he got 419 votes (of which 99 from the PC), against 47 votes, and 143 abstentions. Although Pierre Mendès France ("PMF") had a vulnerable position in the Assembly, he had great popularity with the public. He dared to bring political parties back to their proper role, and did not accept their meddling with the public management task of government. L' "Express", founded in 1953, became the official organ of "Mendésisme".

Mendès France did what he had promised. The Geneva Agreement (20 July 1954) brought the 7 year long war in French Indo-China to an end. It cost France the loss of about 100,000 men and of 3,000 billion francs. Vietnam was divided into two parts along the 17th degree of latitude. North Vietnam was for the Communist Vietminh. South Vietnam became an independent country. In both countries there were to be free elections within two years. In July 1954 Mendès France also went to Tunisia, and there he declared that negotiations would be started to give Tunisia internal sovereignty. On 1 November 1954 an uprising of the "Front de Libération nationale" (FLN) started in Algeria which was the beginning of the Algerian War (1954-1958). This Algerian movement for an independent

Algeria, FLN, with its "Armée de Libération nationale" (ALN), was not at all representative of this country. Mendès France and Mitterrand (Home Affairs) reacted with prompt declarations that Algeria was French and would remain so. The ethnologist Jacques Soustelle (Gaullist), former director of the secret services of "France libre", was appointed governor-general of Algeria in January 1955. Meanwhile another hot file had to be handled, that of the European Defence Community (EDC). Mendès France tried vainly to renegotiate the terms with European partners (less supra-nationality). On 30 August 1954, the National Assembly voted on a preliminary question, which caused the EDC to be rejected without a debate. "PMF" had "solved" this tricky problem. MRP accused "PMF" of the "crime of 30 August".

Because of the threat of Soviet aggression, the US wanted to restore the military potential of West Germany. "PMF" placed German rearmament within the context of general recognition of total sovereignty of the Federal Republic, which became a member of NATO and the West-European Union (WEU). The French National Assembly accepted this in December 1954. Politicians of all political parties manoeuvred against the dynamism of "PMF", pushing political parties from the centre of power. MRP did not forgive him the Agreement of Geneva (1954) and the debacle of the EDC. Social-Republicans ended their support, as did Communists and many Socialists in December 1954 when "PMF" proposed to accept German rearmament. Colonial policy especially alienated many Radicals (his own party) from "PMF". When Mendès France asked for a vote of confidence in the Assembly on 5 February 1955, he was overthrown with 379 against 273 votes. The policy of centre-right government-Faure (23 February 1955/24 January 1956) was not really different from its predecessor. More than Mendès France, Faure respected the primary role of political parties. "Mendésistes" argued against the regime of the Fourth Republic. Economic changes had hit many small shopkeepers, craftsmen and farmers, irritated by the rigid practices of tax collectors, trying to collect raised taxes. Pierre Poujade, a small merchant, protesting against taxes, founded the "Union de défense des commerçants et artisans" (UDCA) in November 1953. This movement, known as "Poujadisme", refused the tax system which forced those with small incomes to pay high taxes while sparing the rich. It denounced parliamentarism and regime, and argued for xenophobe nationalism (Borne, 1977; Hoffmann, 1956). Premier Faure disbanded the Assembly on 2 December 1955 for the first time since 16 May 1877.

A dominant issue for the elections of 2 January 1956 was "Mendésisme". There was a "Front républicain", a reconstructed "mendésiste" coalition, with SFIO and parts of Radicals, UDSR and Social-Republicans. The results were far from clear. "Front républicain" as such had the most votes, so it was entitled to form a government-Mendès France, which was what the public expected. President Coty, however, concluded that the left (Communists included) had 56% of the votes. Because SFIO was the largest in the "Front républicain", Socialist Guy Mollet was asked to form a government. This provoked deep public disappointment, alienating many more from the Fourth Republic. Government-Mollet (1 February 1956/21 May 1957) was the first leftist government since 1947. It brought France into Euratom and the European Economic Union (EEC) when, on 25 March 1957, the Treaty of Rome was signed. It launched a new development with the "loi-cadre Defferre", regulating gradual independence for French African colonies. In the election campaign "Front républicain" had demanded the end of the Algerian War ("guerre imbécile"). On 6 February 1956, Mollet, spat upon by "colons" in Algiers, wanted to install Catroux minister plenipotentiary in Algeria, so replacing Soustelle, adherent of a military solution of Algerian uprisings and terrorism. When Mollet encountered the opposition of "colons", he replaced Catroux and appointed Lacoste. Mollet formulated policy with regard to Algeria such as: end of fighting, elections, negotiations. In April 1956, Soustelle and Bidault created the "Union pour le Salut et le renouveau de l'Algérie française".

Maintenance of French Algeria had strong adherence. Government-Mollet reinforced French military potential in Algeria, trying to force pacification with military power. In October 1956, the government organised a military attack on Suez in Egypt, base of the Algerian FLN, in coalition with the British, enraged by Nasser, who annexed the Suez-canal, and Israelis, fearing a new Arabic war against Israel. This action was rapidly successful (Suez and Port-Said were taken; the regime-Nasser collapsing). On the diplomatic front it was a debacle. The UN, under pressure of the US and USSR, forced the evacuation of the Suez-canal (Ferro, 1983). The Algerian problem was internationalised.

The Algerian War, combined with social and economic problems, caused a financial, political and moral crisis for the Fourth Republic. The balance of payments had a surplus in 1955 (423 million dollars) but deficits in 1956 (783 million) and 1957 (859 million). At the beginning of 1958 France had no reserves of foreign exchange: De Gaulle said he had found the coffers of the State empty. The budget for 1958 implied a tax-rise of 32%. The disguised devaluation, effective since August 1957, was regularised in June 1958 with a devaluation, bringing the dollar from 350 to 420 French francs. Public opinion was increasingly aroused by scandals and by information about the torturing of Algerian freedom fighters, themselves using violent terrorist methods. French authorities primarily reacted with intensified repression, damaging the image of France. Within France itself this provoked a situation of an approaching civil war. Political parties began to withdraw support from government. In December 1956 PC voted against the Algerian policy, while most other political parties were deeply divided. Government-Mollet was overthrown in May 1957. Political parties were trapped in a bewildering confusion. Government was immobilised and the institutions with public authority were paralysed. On the right, nationalists were disappointed by the defeats of Indo-China and Suez, and wanted to defend at all cost "Algérie française". Several extreme-rightist movements, supported by Le Pen, tried to fish in troubled waters. Military leadership, frustrated by Dien Bien Phu, blamed French governments. It was thought that the battle had to be won in Paris, overthrowing the regime of weak cowards. On 26 April 1958, a mass demonstration in Algiers demanded the formation of a "Gouvernement de Salut Public" to rescue French Algeria. Increasingly the name of De Gaulle was mentioned as the only statesman who could give France the leadership it needed. President Coty phoned De Gaulle, asking his conditions for an eventual return to power. There were rumours of a putsch and several sorts of actions (Bromberger, 1959; Tournoux, 1960).

On 13 May 1958, Pierre Pflimlin would present himself to the National Assembly as the new Premier. That day there was a mass demonstration in Algiers, protesting against the murder of three captured French soldiers by the FLN. Pflimlin was seen as an adherent of "politics of abandoning Algeria". The buildings of public authorities in Algiers were occupied. General Massu made Salan, commander-in-chief in Algeria, president of a "Comité de Salut Public de l'Algérie française". Salan, combining legal authority and the power of the rebels, appealed to De Gaulle on 15 May 1958. On 24 May 1958, Corsica joined the uprising. There was talk of conquering France by parachutists on 27/28 May 1958 ("Opération Résurrection"). On 13 May 1958, government-Pflimlin got its majority in the Assembly. Government decided to use force against the putsch, but it did not have the tools for this. On 19 May 1958 De Gaulle declared that he respected democracy and he had friendly words for the leadership of the Fourth Republic. De Gaulle had some crucial consultations with Pflimlin, Chaban-Delmas, Pinay, Mollet. On the eve of the proclaimed "Résurrection" on 27 May 1958, De Gaulle made a declaration that he had started the regular process necessary to establish a Republican government. There was a general feeling of relief in France. The military sounded the retreat for this strategic bluff of the military grandmaster. Government-Pflimlin retired in the night of 27 May 1958. On 1 June 1958, government-De Gaulle was voted in with 329 votes against 250 votes of the

Communists, "Mendésistes" and a part of the Socialists. On 2 June 1958 the government got full powers for 6 months. On 3 June 1958 the Assembly voted through, with 351 against 161 (Communists, "Mendésistes") and 70 abstentions, a law giving government-De Gaulle the power to revise the Constitution, on 3 conditions: respect of fundamental principles of constitutional laws (separation of powers; responsibility of government before parliament); advice of "Comité consultatif constitutionnel" and "Conseil d'État"; and the draft for a constitution decided by referendum. This was the end of the Fourth Republic.

## 6.14. From "Gaullist Republic" to post-De Gaulle Fifth Republic

De Gaulle had, since 1 June 1958, made use of his authorisation to rule with "ordonnances", eliminating parliament. This would end 4 months after the proclamation of the Constitution, 4 February 1959. In this period some 70 regulations came into force by "ordonnance". The Constitution left it to organic laws to make rulings for the election system, competencies of "Conseil supérieur de la magistrature" (CSM) and "Conseil constitutionnel" (CC). This CC was a crucial innovation, because it could test constitutionality of laws (Avril/Gicquel, 1995). This was against French tradition, according to which no person or organ could be superior to the will of the majority in the Assembly (the Jacobin dogma). The institutional framework of the Fifth Republic in its first phase was completed with 21 organic laws. With "ordonnances", reorganisations were put to work in housing; transport; judiciary; national defence; social policy; financial and economic policy; etc. In June 1958, there was a large budget deficit, the balance of payments was out of order in spite of a devaluation of Summer 1957. Government-Mollet had arranged with EEC partners that France would implement the first lowering of customs tariffs on 1 January 1957, while the French economy was not prepared for this. At the end of 1958 measures were taken on the basis of the plan-Rueff to restore macro-economic equilibrium. The Constitution was adopted by referendum on 28 September 1958.

The franc was devalued by more than 17%. A new money unit was introduced, "le nouveau franc", equal to 100 old francs. De Gaulle decided to free customs tariffs for 90%. This financial-economic program provoked negative reactions. Socialists left government. To fulfil the condition of strict separation of powers, election of the president in the Constitution was not entrusted to Parliament. On the 2nd of December 1958, less than three weeks before presidential elections on 21 December 1958, De Gaulle told President Coty that he was a candidate for presidency. He got 77% of the votes of the "grands électeurs" (electoral college). On 8 January 1959 the former president received the new president in the "Élysée". On this formal date, the old regime (by way of 13 May, 1 June and 28 September 1958) was replaced by the new regime of the Fifth Republic. De Gaulle nominated Debré premier and other members of government. Although in compliance with the Constitution, it seemed to be a little coup. The centre of power was in the "Élysée". Designated by the President, the Premier had to organise a majority in the Assembly. SFIO did not participate in government-Debré (8 UNR; 4 MRP; 5 Independents). De Gaulle in the "Élysée", Debré in "Matignon" and Chaban-Delmas president of the Assembly. Gaullists had the power on the national level.

The successful build-up of the Constitution as the foundation of the Fifth Republic was not what the people had in mind when they said yes to the referendum for a new constitution. Solving the Algerian drama was the issue. Promptly after the debate in the Assembly on 4 June 1958, De Gaulle went to Algeria where he was received enthusiastically. Algerian French saw De Gaulle as their last bulwark against bargaining with rebels fighting for an independent Algeria. They expected that De Gaulle would realise integration of Algeria with France. De Gaulle did or said nothing to arouse their anxiety, and received applause when he said: "I do understand you!" With an eloquent speech, De Gaulle gave, in covert terms, some thoughts about the future of Algeria, with equal rights for all residents. After his speech ultras and the military had the idea that De Gaulle was on their side for "Algérie française". Later, when De Gaulle's policy was outspoken, they felt themselves to be victims of word breaking. The debate goes on over De Gaulle's vision for the Algerian question. Probably he thought it impossible to integrate Algeria with France. He thought that it was inevitable that aspirations of colonial areas for more autonomy had to be taken seriously but he sought a third way in between, more autonomy for Algerians and close relations with France.

De Gaulle announced that French Algerians could decide their future and elect their representatives in public bodies within three months: "With these elected representatives we will see how to arrange the rest." He had taken all measures needed to restore order, upset by the putsch of 13 May 1958 (Vaisse, 1983). After massive support for the referendum (28 September 1958) he used the opportunity to reinforce his grip. On 9 October 1958, as general and commander-in-chief, De Gaulle ordered all officers to end support for "comités de salut public", which caused confusion about their mixed nature as insurrectional organisations and public authorities. He recalled Salan, military commander and civilian governor of Algeria. His tasks were split up. A loyal military commander was appointed. Paul Delouvrier got ample powers as representative of France in Algeria. Civilian control over the armed forces was restored. De Gaulle was not hindering ongoing military activities to pacify the country by chasing rebels. Rebels had to be convinced that continuation of their activities was useless. France had to negotiate in a position of strength. De Gaulle appealed to rebels to accept a courageous peace. On 3 October 1958, he developed a plan for emancipation of the indiginous population at Constance, where he had launched a similar plan 15 years earlier. It included speeding up participation of Algerians in public organs; promotion of education; establishment of industries; reallocation of land; and 100 billion francs aid.

Elections did not bring for De Gaulle the expected composition of representation ("to arrange the rest"). Nearly all were members of "Algérie française". The Algerian question appeared even more insoluble but De Gaulle started to restore order. He hoped to win time for reaching national harmony in this highly delicate state of affairs but it took more time than he had foreseen, 45 months after his return on 13 May 1958. In 1962, he had to withdraw conditions, which had been declared not negotiable, as with the Sahara. The French were heavily divided about the Algerian question. The four years (1958-1962) were a series of crises, and during this time it seemed possible that civil war could break out anywhere in France. In May 1958, the majority of the French were in favour of integration of Algeria with France, so it took time to accept a situation with independence for Algeria. Each time De Gaulle came closer to this target, tensions grew. With his matchless management by speeches and his fine tuning of endless reinterpretations, he did increasingly mould the French to the acceptance of the inevitable. It started with De Gaulle's "discours de l'autodétermination" on 16 September 1959 for radio and TV. He presented three options for inhabitants of Algeria: independence, "francisation" (integration in France) or Algerian home-rule and close relations with France. It was obvious that De Gaulle had the third option in mind but this was not what adherents of "Algérie française" wanted. Chaban-Delmas (UNR), president of the Assembly, launched the theory of the "domaine réservé", the policy area reserved for the president. De Gaulle was thought to have free mandate to solve the Algerian question. General Massu, commander in Algeria, said that he was in favour of "Algérie française". De Gaulle called him back to Paris. Reactions were furious; mutineers occupied a part of Algeria. On 29 January 1960, De Gaulle said that nothing could stop him from doing what the nation had asked of him.

Mutineers surrendered on 31 January 1960. The Assembly authorised De Gaulle to rule with "ordinances". De Gaulle seemed to hesitate over how to proceed.

Opposition against continuation of the Algerian war became stronger. The student union UNEF, concerned because of the 27 months conscription, declared sympathy with the forbidden Algerian union of Muslim students. Circles around Jean-Paul Sartre and the review "Les Temps modernes" launched the "Manifeste des 121". This appealed for conscientious objection to military activities against a people fighting for independence. De Gaulle's endeavour in June 1960 to come to terms failed. After announcing a referendum about the future of Algeria, De Gaulle went for a visit to Algeria, from 13 to 19 December 1960, which degenerated into uprisings. The referendum was on 8 January 1961. De Gaulle now declared his choice: Algerian home-rule. He made it a vote of confidence, pro or contra his person as head of state. More than three-quarters of the electorate supported him. Of some 20 million votes, there were 15.2 million pro and less than 5 million against. In Algeria 70% were pro, a bitter unexpected disappointment for many adherents of French Algeria. They had a strong position in Algeria and could trust the army if they tried to overthrow government. Early in the morning of 22 April 1961, France got the news that a military putsch had taken over in Algeria. The commander was made prisoner, government was in the hands of four pensioned generals: Salan, Challe, Jouhaud and Zeller. De Gaulle, using article 16 of the Constitution, proclaimed a state of emergency, giving him sweeping powers.

Soon it was evident that an important part of the army did not support the mutinous ex-generals. Challe gave up, and the other three continued clandestinely, giving leadership to the O.A.S. ("Organisation armée secrète"), a terrorist organisation not eschewing violent means, trying to provoke civil war everywhere in France. Negotiations, started on 20 May 1961 at Évian, came to a deadlock as the GPRA ("Gouvernement provisoire de la République Algérienne") refused to keep the Sahara out of negotiations. France wished to keep the Sahara for the considerable reserves of oil and gas, and it was also a nuclear test area. In February 1960, the first French nuclear bomb was tested there. To get negotiations restarted, De Gaulle recognised on 5 September 1961 that the Sahara was part of Algeria. The Algerian war had lasted seven years already. On 17 October 1961 Algerian FLN organised a manifestation in Paris: a lot of violence, more than 11,500 arrests, many persons killed. OAS intensified terrorist intimidation, but this could not stop negotiations. On 18 March 1962 De Gaulle proclaimed an armistice next day, and two referenda on the "Accords d'Évian" (one in France on 8 April, and one in Algeria on 1 July 1962). The core of this arrangement was that Algeria became an independent state. UNR, SFIO and MRP proposed to give a positive vote, the PSU intended to abstain. More than 90% voted pro on the 8th of April 1962, out of some 20 million votes; less than 1.8 million votes were negative, so it was proved that Algerian independence was not the choice of De Gaulle alone, but also of the French. De Gaulle decided to replace Premier Debré. By doing this he wanted to accentuate the difference between the president as symbol of continuity and the Premier as replaceable. Although the Constitution is silent on this issue, De Gaulle used the interpretation that his explicit constitutional power to appoint the Premier includes the competence to dismiss him. Formally Debré resigned on 14 April 1962. De Gaulle appointed Georges Pompidou as Premier. De Gaulle wanted to accentuate the personal character of the presidential regime.

Preceding the referendum of 1 July 1962 in Algeria, a provisional government was established (9 Algerians, 3 Europeans, 6 members of the FLN). Fouchet represented France, having sovereignty in Algeria up to the first of July 1962. Signing of the "Accords d'Évian" meant that French soldiers were now foreign soldiers in Algeria. Soon, in reaction to a provocation, local order troops began shooting into a crowd on 26 March 1962: 46 dead and more than 200 wounded. The OAS tried to prevent implementation of the Evian

Accords, and organised a chaos of revenge. It tried to show that Europeans could not live with an Algerian government. OAS terrorists intensified violent attacks everywhere. At the referendum of 1 July 1962, with practically no participation of Europeans, a vast majority naturally chose for independence. On 3 July 1962, President De Gaulle formally recognised the new independent Algerian State. After 92 months, this terrible Algerian war, which began on 1 November 1954, finally came to an end, after the killing and wounding of innumerable victims. The complex and tricky relation between France and Algeria began a new phase. The loss of "Algérie française" after 132 years of French hegemony was more frustrating than the collapse of Dien Bien Phu. The Algerian war left deep scars in the French collective consciousness. Many French patriots could not excuse De Gaulle for giving away Algeria and for giving independence to Algeria against the expectations he himself created. OAS continued with horrifying terrorism, including attempts on the life of De Gaulle. De Gaulle had created more policy room for the president than was formalised in the Constitution. He thought an authoritarian power necessary to take control of the Algerian problem. By legitimising the notion "domaine réservé", the Algerian war influenced institutional relations between president and premier. De Gaulle's choice for Algerian independence can be explained by the fact that the international position of France was handicapped by this "colonial" war.

De Gaulle was always clear about his priority for foreign affairs over domestic policies. From June 1958 up to July 1968, with Couve de Murville minister of foreign affairs, he had a professional and loyal executor of the policies, which De Gaulle directed personally. In this way De Gaulle was able to leave his mark on French foreign policy, becoming irreversible in a number of dimensions. On 14 September 1958, he sent a memorandum to president Eisenhower and the British prime minister MacMillan, proposing to form a directorate of the US, Great-Britain and France to establish leadership of the Atlantic alliance. As he had expected, he did not get an answer. Then he systematically built up French independence in the sphere of defence. On 11 March 1959, he withdrew the French Mediterranean fleet from the Allied NATO command. De Gaulle was obsessed by the need for a French nuclear weapon as a necessary condition for a great power. Governments in the Fourth Republic created the possibility of military use of nuclear energy; De Gaulle pushed research and tests. The first French atomic bomb exploded on 13 February 1960 at Reggane (Sahara), so France could enter the restricted club of the nuclear elite. Political parties and the public protested; they did not believe France was able to develop a nuclear weapon with the capacity to scare potential enemies (costs etc.). Public opinion was sceptical about this "bombinette", but De Gaulle persevered. NAVO partners were uneasy about this selfish action. French Communists were opposed, especially because the Soviets were seen as virtual enemy.

In the debate over the 1960 budget, more than 150 centre-right deputies supported a motion of no-confidence, from the Communists and Socialists, against the "loi-programme sur la force de frappe" (nuclear weapon). Government had to use the specific procedure of article 49 of the Constitution. De Gaulle wanted to follow an independent course, not recognising the US as the leading power. Part of it was building up good relations with the Soviet Union, and so, by releasing rigid tensions between the two blocks, contributing to a détente. The Cold War had to be followed by a new relationship. Strategically, he saw geography as more important than ideology. In March 1960, De Gaulle received Soviet leader Kruschev with all honours in Paris. De Gaulle planned to play a crucial role in bringing Americans and Soviets closer to each other. His independent attitude with regard to the Atlantic alliance did not compromise his stubborn approach to Soviet aggression and provocations. When Soviets caused crises (Berlin Wall in August 1961, Cuban rocket-crisis in October 1962), De Gaulle was the first of US allies to support the US. The period from the coming to power of De Gaulle in 1958 to the death of President Pompidou in April

1974, marked important changes in France (Deutsch et al., 1966). In the "République gaullienne" (1958/1969), President De Gaulle could solve the Algerian drama in 1962, and also construct the institutional foundations of the Fifth Republic. Because of repeated abuses of power by political parties and their kidnapping of public authority in the Third Republic, it was thought necessary to institutionalise their position. The draft for the Constitution of 1946 stated, that a unique political party was prohibited as being against the principles of republican liberties, and that political parties had to be legal. This was not inserted into the Constitution of the Fourth Republic. The Constitution of 1958 did not create a statute for political parties. Article 4 ruled: "Political parties and groups compete at the elections. They can form themselves freely and organise activities, as they like. They have to respect the principles of national sovereignty and democracy."

When De Gaulle was followed by President Pompidou (1969/1974), his right hand man, it was possible to prove to French society that the institutions of the Fifth Republic could survive its creator. During this period it was very difficult for political parties opposing Gaullists to find their way. When Pompidou was President, the position of Gaullists, without De Gaulle in the midst of the political theatre, was strong. Many had thought that it would be otherwise. Since 1971, most Socialists had been united in the "Parti Socialiste" (PS) with the leadership of Mitterrand. In 1972, PS, Communists and Leftist Radicals had signed a common government program, but this could not bring them into government in 1973. When Pompidou died in 1974 and "pompidolisme" was history, political knives were sharpened, from left to right. Mitterrand seemed to have a real chance of becoming the next president. On the political right there were problems. Chaban-Delmas was appointed by the UDR, and Giscard d'Estaing proclaimed his candidacy on 8 April 1974. Premier Messmer made known on 9 April 1974 that he wanted to be a candidate of the political right, if Chaban-Delmas and Giscard d'Estaing would withdraw. As the first refused and the last accepted, Messmer was not a candidate any more (Bothorel, 1983). Giscard d'Estaing had a good campaign (Berne, 1981). In the first round (5 May 1974) Chaban-Delmas had 14.6% and Giscard d'Estaing 32.9%. Mitterrand beat them with 43.3%. The predicted neck-and-neck race for the second round on 19 May 1974 materialised: 50.8% for Giscard d'Estaing and 49.2% for Mitterrand. President Giscard d'Estaing proclaimed a new era for French politics: renewal and change (Petitfils, 1981). Giscard d'Estaing appointed Jacques Chirac as Premier, because of the overpowering position of Gaullists in the Assembly. This was seen as a reward for support given by Gaullist Chirac to Giscard d'Estaing in the presidential campaign, although Gaullists had Chaban-Delmas as a candidate. Government-Chirac had only 4 UDR Ministers, while all the Gaullist "barons" were passed over. Françoise Giroud, a declared opponent of Gaullism, was made a minister. The composition of the government was amazing, because there were 183 Gaullists in the Assembly, and only 55 Independent Republicans and 30 members of the allied centrist union.

Without the UDR, the President had no majority in the Assembly. He demanded, more or less, that Chirac organise a docile majority. Giscard d'Estaing presented himself with a new style (advanced liberalism, centrist, European), surrounding himself with technocrats (Petitfils, 1981). RPR chose Chirac as its secretary-general on 14 December 1974. Chirac, leader of the majority party in the Assembly, had a powerful position. There was a "dyarchie" of Giscard d'Estaing and Chirac. Giscard d'Estaing did his best to realise promised reforms. A constitutional law, enabling 60 deputies or 60 senators to ask the advice of the "Conseil Constitutionnel", was adopted on 29 October 1974. This meant that a minority could ask independent judges to evaluate if legal regulations, adopted by a majority, conformed to the Constitution. The voting age was lowered from 21 to 18 years in July 1974 and the electorate got some 2,400,000 new voters. France was, in the years 1974-1976, in the grip of an economic crisis. Government realised some redistribution by raising taxes and improving social benefits, but this did not stop growing opposition. Socialists, encouraged by a marginal loss at elections, reinforced their position. PSU of Michel Rocard and members of CFDT joined them. Opposition by "CERES" of Chevènement (more an ally of Communists) had been eliminated since the congress of Pau (1975). The PC had, since 1976, dropped the "dictatorship of the proletariat", while stressing its independence with regard to the Soviets. It now promoted "Eurocommunism". Forecasts had predicted a leftist majority since the end of 1974. Cantonal elections (7/14 March 1976) made this leftist majority a reality. While Premier Chirac demanded more room to profile himself, President Giscard d'Estaing did not yield. The two diverged even more. On 26 July 1976, Chirac wrote a letter to President Giscard d'Estaing, presenting his resignation. Chirac resigned on 25 August 1976, commenting: "I don't have the instruments to assure effectively my functions as Premier." Economist Raymond Barre was appointed as Premier. On 22 September 1976, the Council of Ministers adopted the "Plan Barre". Its major targets were control of price rises; recovery of the trade balance; and reducing of the budget deficit. Barre wanted to give priority to economic issues. For him the best way to solve economic problems was to give room to the market, making enterprises able to confront international competition. "Plan Barre" encompassed several measures: a price freeze until the end of 1976, and of public tariffs up to Spring 1977; temporary lowering of buying-power for well-to-do and stabilisation for others; a supplementary income tax; a rise in corporate tax; a rise of the price for petrol; adaptations in social benefits; etc. Because Socialists could not organise more than 181 votes against this plan in the Assembly (while 242 votes were needed to block it), it was adopted. Chirac used his time to transform the UDR into a more effective organisation, the Gaullist "Rassemblement pour la République" (RPR) which was created on 5 December 1976. The first test would be the municipal elections in March 1977. When Chirac was Minister of Home Affairs, he had made the Assembly adopt a law which made it possible for Paris to have a mayor like other cities (Paris had a special regime). Although Giscard d'Estaing had his own candidate for mayor of Paris, Chirac made himself a candidate too. Chirac won and was mayor of Paris, an ideal springboard. Prognoses for legislative elections of 1978 did not promise good results for Giscard d'Estaing and the political right. In May 1977, "Républicains-Indépendants" (Colliard, 1971) changed their name: "Parti Républicain" (PR). In February 1978, Giscard d'Estaing made an electoral cartel of "Parti Républicain", "Centre des démocrats sociaux" (Lecanuet) and "Parti radical" (Servan-Schreiber). "Union pour la démocratie française" (UDF) was formed as having a better chance to win the elections with RPR.

Tensions between Socialists and Communists piled up, as their coalition seemed to benefit only the Socialists, while marginalising Communists. In September 1977 there was a break between the two. On 12 March 1978, RPR got 154 seats, UDF 124 seats, Communists 86 seats and Socialists 114 seats. President Giscard d'Estaing and Premier Barre had not lost, although prospects for a victory of the left seemed realistic. The second government-Barre (1978-1981) was reshuffled a little. Monory became Minister of Economic Affairs. Former prefect Papon was now Minister of the Budget. Negative consequences of the economic crisis made themselves felt even more. Government could not convince people as unemployment rose alarmingly. A leftist majority seemed impossible due to the break between Socialists and Communists. Chirac profiled himself against Giscard d'Estaing and elections for the European Parliament in June 1979 made this controversy manifest. Chirac, in a hospital in Cochin after a motor-accident, opposed a common list, supported by Giscard d'Estaing. In a communiqué he criticised "Giscardiens" for their support of supranational Europe and its economic slavery ("Appel de Cochin"). The list of Madame Veil had 27.6% of the votes, and the RPR 16.2%. There was an open war between the two parties in the majority. The first round of presidential elections on 26 April 1981 brought Giscard d'Estaing 27.8%, Mitterrand 26% and Chirac 18%. The second round on 10 May 1981 brought Mitterrand the victory with 52.2% against 47.8% for Giscard d'Estaing. The "septennat"-Mitterrand (1981-1988) could begin.

## 6.15. "Double Septennat-Mitterrand" (1981-1995); Chirac Era (1995-2002; 2002-2007)

President Mitterrand, after 23 years in opposition, was gloriously installed on 21 May 1981 (Manceron/Pingaud, 1981). He knew that the majority in the Assembly wanted to end this first "cohabitation" (a President of one political party; an opposing majority in the Assembly) as soon as possible. On 22 May 1981, he decided to dissolve the Assembly. The legislative elections of 14/21 June 1981 proved his instincts correct. Socialists won 285 seats in the Assembly, the absolute majority with a "vague rose". For only the second time in more than 130 years (UDR did the same only in 1968), one party had the absolute majority in parliament. The "alternance" was complete. RPR had only 88 seats, UDF 62 seats, and PC 44 seats. After 23 years in the desert, Socialists could rule France (Portelli, 1980). The second government-Maurois, with four Communist Ministers, wanted to govern differently. Socialists had removed Communists from government 34 years ago in 1947. Now Socialists made PC, minimalised since their embrace by Mitterrand, partner in government. This was a reward from Mitterrand for the co-operation of the PC, who supported him at presidential elections. As PS had the absolute majority, it was not dependent on PC, and with PC in government Mitterrand could buy off social unrest. Government had politicians instead of technocrats more than before. In the Socialist party, movements wanted to realise ideological objectives. Government-Mauroy pushed its new priorities. Nationalisations, decentralisation, and Socialist planning giving the State more tools to manage the economy, and reforms in areas of justice, healthcare and human values. In February 1982, the law ruling the nationalisation of five industrial giants, two financial enterprises and 36 banks was adopted. The "loi-Defferre" (1982) decentralised power from State to regions, departments and municipalities. Minister Rocard gave a new impetus to planning, less ambitiously used in the neo-liberal period. The interim-plan (1982-1983) was meant to correct all effects of the "septennat" of Giscard d'Estaing (1974-1981). The IXe Plan (1984-1988) would be the real Socialist Plan.

There were reforms in other fields. Healthcare was made a public sector more than before, penal practices were humanised and the death penalty was abolished. "Lois-Auroux" (1982) gave workers in enterprises more rights (council of employees etc.) and "Loi-Quilliot" reinforced the position of tenants with regard to proprietors. The structure of social security was changed, giving representatives of workers more influence. A new career perspective was created with the third path for entering the ENA for functionaries or syndicalists. A law of 1982 ruled the "Haute Autorité de l'Audiovisuel", an independent organ to control media and there was the "Loi-Savary" (1983) about higher education. The most controversial of reforms was implementation of the 90th proposal of Mitterrand's electoral program, transforming National Education into a united and secular public service, including private organisations. Economic and social problems had priority. From June 1981, social benefits for families were raised by 25%, the old age pension was raised by 20%, and employees with the lowest salaries ("SMIC") got more. To pay for this generosity, taxes were raised, especially for higher earners. With ideological demagogy, a new tax upon large fortunes was introduced, hitting 1% of fiscal family units (200,000 households with a wealth of more than 3 million francs).

During the first weeks of 1982, several ordinances were adopted, with a fifth week of paid holidays, "Contrats de solidarity", a kind of pre-pensions, to create jobs for others and partial jobs, and professional training for youngsters (16-18 years old). The working week was shortened from 40 to 39 hours (without reducing salaries), with the prospect of a 35-

hours week coming later. The pension age was lowered to 60 years. This Socialist feast resembled the generosity of the Popular Front (1936). It would be a disaster as before. Inflation hit a record with 14.1% in 1981. On 4 October 1981, there was a readjustment of currencies in the "European Monetary System" and the French franc was devalued by 8.5%. Worst of all, unemployment rose to 2 million. The Minister of Economic Affairs proclaimed a pause with regard to reforms. Meanwhile opposition became fiercer, also in the ranks of Socialists. Cantonal elections of May 1982 revealed a loss for the Socialists, accentuated by a loss in municipal elections of March 1983: the left had 44.2% and the right 53.6% in the first round. The second round gave the right primacy in many municipalities and cities. Socialist leadership was fundamentally split about which policies to pursue. Delors wanted to restore the relation with the international market by a program of budget cuts and unpopular measures. Bérégovoy argued for leaving the European Monetary System. Mitterrand decided that there would have to be unpopular budget cuts. In June 1982, the franc was devalued (by 9.5%) for the second time since Socialists came to power. Socialist government policies proved to be a disaster. Consumption, stimulated by the increased buying-power of the masses, expanded imports, exporting companies were hit by raised taxes, the trade balance was disrupted and borrowing was needed to cover the rising budget deficit. At the end of 1983, public debt was about 40 billion francs.

The position of the Socialists was weakening in that period. Mitterrand was pondering on initiatives. On 12 July 1984, he made it known that there would be a referendum to enlarge the reach of the referendum. He decided that the unpopular law about the reform of education must be withdrawn, although the Parliament had adopted this law. A very undemocratic and anti-republican act by monarch Mitterrand. The Minister of Education retired, and Government-Mauroy followed. Communists refused to have ministers in the new government and the "Union de la gauche" was again shipwrecked. The tone of government-Fabius (1984-1986) was not ideological, but pragmatic. The Assembly adopted a law for a new electoral system in June 1985. Elections would take place in one round for 577 seats in the Assembly (instead of the existing 491 seats). For the first time in thirty years, a proportional system was used for the legislative elections of 16 March 1986. The left got no more than 44%. Right was disappointed, RPR and UDF had 44.7%, due to the 9.9% for extreme-rightist "Front National". RPR and UDF had now 277 of the 577 seats in the Assembly. PS had 216 seats. The right conquered nearly 3/4 of departmental and 2/3 of city councils. It could benefit from decentralisation. The "Cohabitation" of President Mitterrand and Premier Chirac had been an experience.

From then on, presidential elections in May 1988 were the crucial issue. The right could not overcome structural dissension; several candidates took their chance. President Mitterrand had given the electorate confidence. He painstakingly followed the Constitution, and he had taken measures on behalf of the country as needed. Mitterrand played the game coolly and adroitly by presenting himself as statesman-arbiter, standing above the partisan positions of political parties. Chirac, however, was demagogically fighting Socialism. At the first round on 24 April 1988, Mitterrand got more than 34% of the votes, Chirac nearly 20% and Barre 16.5% (so Chirac and Barre together had more than Mitterrand!). The second round on 8 May 1988 was a victory for Mitterrand with 54.02%, Chirac had only 45.98%. Chirac resigned. President Mitterrand appointed Rocard as Premier. Mitterrand felt his position to be strong enough to try new legislative elections again, as he had in 1981. He dissolved the Assembly with its rightist majority. PS was now, with 275 seats, only 12 seats short of an absolute majority, while it could not rely upon the weakened Communists (27 seats). Government-Rocard II (23 June 1988/15 May 1991) had only 26 Ministers of PS out of a total of 49 Ministers. Rocard tried to build bridges with the political centre, as he had no majority in Parliament.

Rocard did it very well. That was not what Mitterrand wanted (his favourites were Fabius and Jospin). The congress of Socialists (15/18 March 1990) was a disgusting scene of power-ambitious "elephants" fighting for positions in the post-Mitterrand period. Circles around Mitterrand were divided between "Fabiusiens" and "Jospinistes". The situation was becoming worse, personal ambitions and rivalries abounded. Giscard d'Estaing (UDF) and Chirac (RPR) both aimed for the presidency in 1995. This dissension frustrated the right for fifteen years. In March 1990, the co-ordination group of RPR, UDF and UDC adopted Pasqua's idea of organising primaries to designate the sole candidate for presidency. In June 1990, co-operation between these three parties of the rightist opposition resulted in the creation of the "Union pour la France" (UPF). In November 1990, this would be celebrated with a grand event. This was cancelled, as Giscard d'Estaing, knowing that this would make Chirac the sole candidate, did not agree to holding primaries but in 1991, the procedure of primaries was accepted. Paralysing left-right controversy, the weakened position of parliament, declining position of the trade-unions and the uninspiring activities of political parties caused a general feeling of malaise, "morosité". Societal debate was about the crisis of democracy.

The Fall of the Berlin Wall (1989), two centuries after the French Revolution (1789), was a European Revolution, because it symbolised the collapse of East-European Communist regimes. This was the end of a dominant ideological movement, which had deep imprints in France, but new controversies enflamed political passions. An incident in November 1988, concerning Moroccan girls who, refusing to drop the head-scarves which symbolised their Islamic faith, were not admitted to their school, provoked a row, which assumed more massive dimensions with discussions and demonstrations. There were controversies between adherents of "laïcité scolaire", forbidding any religious activity in a public school, and those who were attached to freedom of religion. The issue was not public school against Catholicism as for so long in French history, but different cultures and religions side by side on French soil. The religion of the majority of the French population had been Catholicism for more than 1,500 years. This had influenced French identity and society deeply. Festivities in 1996 to commemorate the baptism of Clovis in 496, with a ceremonial mass by Pope Jean-Paul II in Paris, made this obvious anew, and revived controversies about the separation of State and Church. Two conceptions were dominant: first that foreigners are welcome in hospitable France, if they become French like their compatriots, behaving with respect for French culture, second, that everybody is entitled to develop his or her own cultural identity, which means that France has to be multi-ethnic, multi-religious and multi-cultural. Although the "affaire des foulards" (head-scarves) was gradually losing its acuteness, time and again this controversy flares up. The growing adherence to Le Pen's "Front National", provocatively arguing against foreigners, made it difficult for other parties to assume a consistent attitude.

The Presidential elections of 1995 formed the crucial issue for political parties, especially since legislative elections of 1993 had given the political right the majority in the Assembly. Chirac, from his own experience as a former Premier, knowing that having this function brings a heavy risk for becoming unpopular, pushed for Balladur as Premier. Although Premier Balladur (1993-1995) had to take a number of unpopular measures, he was very popular. Because he was even more popular as a candidate for the presidency than Chirac himself as the year 1995 approached, animosities between Chirac and Balladur meant that their respective adherents were at each other's throats. Prospects for the right were bright but the right had one insuperable handicap, its structural dissension about issues and especially about candidates. At the first round of the presidential elections on 23 April 1995, Chirac and Balladur were candidates. Results were alarming for the right and encouraging for the left. Against all expectations, Socialist Jospin came first with 23.30% of the votes, before Chirac (20.84%), Balladur (18.58%), Le Pen (15%) and Communist

Hue (8.64%). The second round on 7 May 1995 brought the Jospin-Chirac duel that was won by Chirac (52.63% of the votes), beating Jospin (47.37%). The Socialist era of the double "septennat" of Mitterrand (1981-1995) was finished. President Chirac started his "septennat" (1995-2002) in a euphoria of the right. In 1995, Gaullists had all the powers in their own hands: presidency, government and majority in the Assembly. Since then, popularity polls for President Chirac and Premier Juppé had fallen drastically, giving new hopes for Socialist Jospin, especially for the legislative elections of 1998.

The problems for governments Juppé-I and Juppé-II were overwhelming, especially in the sphere of economic policies, because of high rates of unemployment, social exclusion and the need to cut expenses drastically. Convergence with the international market and the policies of the European Union required drastic, painful measures, provoking a series of strikes. There were many frustrations for the political left, as Socialists were involved in some nasty scandals, for example: illegal financing of party-political activities. During a long period there was no legal ruling about the financing of political parties, for the practical reason that this would not prevent secret financing (Campana, 1976). There was a draft for a bill about public financing of political parties adopted by the Council of Ministers on 19 September 1979, but Parliament did not discuss this draft. In 1986, the "Affaire Carrefour du développement" renewed this debate. This remained a weapon to brand other political parties. Although the political right had a large majority in the Assembly, Chirac surprised all with his 21 April 1997 decision to dissolve the Assembly. This meant new legislative elections for 25 May and 1 June 1997 (instead of a year later).

The rightist parties expected that they would win the elections, perhaps with a slightly smaller majority than they had. Problems for government, trying to implement unpopular policies and so bringing France into the first group of member-states in the European Union with a common currency ("euro"), would become more manageable. They feared legislative elections in 1998, as the rightist government would have been forced to implement unpopular policies in the midst of social crisis (12.5% unemployment). Part of the RPR/UDF scenario was that it would not be possible for Socialists and Communists to form an electoral coalition within a period of one month. PS (Jospin) and PCF (Hue) did present a common declaration on 29 April 1997, however. The situation as compared with the common program (1972) of these parties was quite different now. No common program, but a common declaration of intent to form a leftist government, respecting political positions of Socialists and Communists. The decision of President Chirac was seen as a manoeuvre to give the political right a blank cheque for cutting public expenses during the period 1997-2002 (Le Monde, 2 May 1997). The reaction of the French electorate did not fulfil either Chirac's or the rightist parties' expectations. Socialists won the elections on 25 May and 1 June 1997, and with Communists, Greens, a small PS-offshoot and Left-Radicals, Socialist Jospin became Premier of a slender, "plural" majority, thought impossible by Chirac The right was divided, licking its wounds after the miscarried bluff of Chirac. France had its "cohabitation" again with "L'État-PS".

Government-Jospin presented its ambitious program on 19 June 1997 (the day after the end of the Treaty of Amsterdam negotiations). This program, supported in the Assembly with 297 against 252 votes, tried to make it clear that government-Jospin would change public management. Some of the 45 measures did look like those of the Socialist government of 1981. Minimum wage raised by 4%; abolition of financial family support for those with a monthly income above 25,000 francs; family benefits made dependent upon incomes; revision of legislation about resignation of employed persons; equality between women and men in the Constitution. Re-examination of laws about nationality; restoring of the "droit du sol"; lowering of the VAT; a general social health insurance; spreading wage-levies for sickness over a broadened "CSG"; renewal of healthcare budget; pension before sixty for those employed for 40 years; restoring of one million social houses; revision of the individual housing subsidy; revision of the tax for "surloyer de solidarité"; rise of the school-subsidy from 420 to 1600 francs; extra subsidising for socially backward zones; 1% of the budget for culture. Limitation of the "cumul des mandats" (combination of several political functions); harmonisation of the terms of several elections to 5 years; automatic registration for all at the age of 18 on electoral lists. Guarantees for careers of jurisdictional functionaries by the "Conseil supérieur de la magistrature"; no interventions by the Minister of Justice in the work of the public prosecutor during the "instruction" any more; 35,000 more jobs for local police; an independent public authority to judge the "secret-défense"; abolition of all information-gathering about political life; a plan against violence in schools; creation of an "Agence de sécurité sanitaire", and adaptation of the subsidising of the press; maintenance of a public television service; reinforcing competencies of the "CSA"; revision of the procedure for declaring big projects to be a public utility; abolition of the "Superphénix" (nuclear energy); stopping the Rhine-Rhône canal project; revision of the law for city, town and country planning, and anticipated return of the Parliament halfway through September 1997; an audit of public finances in July 1997; a conference about employment, in the perspective of reducing the working-week from 39 to 35 hours; promotion of work for young people (700,000 more jobs promised); a social plan for students; no reduction of jobs in the public sector; stabilising or reducing of obligatory levies; maintenance of public services and adaptation of public enterprises (Le Monde, 21 June 1997).

Unsurprisingly, Government-Jospin (1997-2002) realised only a part of its promised policies. During these four years there were a lot of opposing movements in society, often coupled with massive demonstrations. Unemployment remained high, social unrest was intensive and a broad feeling of insecurity in society bred a negative atmosphere. Extreme-rightist Le Pen (Bresson/Lionet, 1994), with his xenophobic propaganda, could blame the foreigners for all society's miseries (stealing jobs from the French; causing criminality etc.). His pleas for a halt to immigration and even re-migration of immigrants fell on fertile soil. Le Pen formed the "Front National" in 1973, fighting the Fifth Republic. He had since 1983 had about 10-15% of the vote at elections. When, at the first round of the presidential elections of April 2002, Le Pen (16.95% of the votes) had 233,196 votes more than Prime-Minister Jospin (16.12%), French society was shocked. Rightists and leftists voted for neo-gaullist Chirac to stop Le Pen. When the results of the second round of the presidential elections on 5 May 2002 became known, Chirac 82.15% and Le Pen 17.85%, there was a general feeling of relief in French society. Prime-Minister Jospin resigned promptly (qualified as political blunder, giving the floor to rightists in elections). President Chirac nominated Jean-Pierre Raffarin as Prime-Minister for the period up to the second round of the parliamentary elections on 16 June 2002. Now that the shameful risk of Le Pen as President had been eliminated, political parties could concentrate the political battle on parliamentary elections. Leftists tried to get the most votes possible to organise a realistic leftist countervailing power, possibly by forcing a new "cohabitation". Rightists tried to stave off a new, immobilising cohabitation with a leftist government. Chirac's newly formed electoral cartel, "l'Union pour la Majorité Présidentielle" (UMP) had a sweeping victory (abstention 39.71%), with 369 members of the Assembly having the absolute majority (total 577). The rightist-leftist power balance in the Assembly changed from 314 leftists against 245 rightists in 1997, to 399 rightists against 178 leftists in 2002. For the coming five years, there are only 4 formal parliamentary groups (with all facilities, subsidies, etc.): UMP (369); UDF (22), Parti Socialiste (141) and Parti Communiste (21). Strange detail: the extreme-rightist party of Le Pen got not one seat in parliament. With all the trump cards in his hands (Presidency, government, majority in the Assembly) Chirac got his last chance to change the situation in France before the Fifth Republic has its 50th anniversary in 2008. He does not have an easy job in fulfilling electoral promises:

reforming the pension system; fighting criminality; controlling immigration; income-tax reductions; etc. Meanwhile, the "Convention pour la VIe République" (C6R) started an initiative in 2002 for a Sixth Republic with a manifesto "Pourquoi et comment une VIe République" (Allies, 2002).

Winock (1999) gives a good overview of political France in the 19th and 20th centuries, showing the relevance of history-based analyses but the French political system has changed significantly during the last two decades, as the special issue of the review "West European Politics" (1999) showed, and the French system of Public Management of Society has also been markedly transformed. Europeanisation has an imposing impact upon nearly all aspects and sectors of society, especially with European law (Guyomarch, 1998; Harding, 2000). A positive trend is that economic and state approaches in the process of European integration (Siedentop, 2000) are a countervailing correction of societal law (Karpik, 2000). Especially for France with its party-politically influenced, dominantly State-made law (legislation), this is a welcome improvement. National political parties experience a loss of power in the framework of globalisation and European integration. Economics contributes to societal transformations, and the euro, common currency in the Euro-land of the twelve from 2001 on, is a decisive step. Globalisation and Europeanisation enforce adaptations in society. Societal organisations must reorganise themselves. Workers' unions must form trans-national arrangements, "Eurostrike" (Imig/Tarrow, 1997). They have to familiarise themselves with the new situation, while the State is no longer able to arrange things as before under pressure of mass protests. The French State cannot be weak in the same way as before by repaying protests and pressures with favourable institutional arrangements for pressure groups. Euro-management in a co-national arena is becoming ever more crucial, for both private and public organisations. European integration transforms traditional State-society relations, it reduces State autonomy in policy formation and flexibility in policy implementation. "At the implementation stage, the French state has lost flexibility mainly because the European regulatory model, which demands that European laws apply equally to all and without exception, proscribes the administrative discretion that has been the state's way of responding to societal interests in the policy process." (Schmidt, 1999, p.146). This European regulatory model has reduced traditional interest accommodation in national implementation of public policies markedly. This contributes to the weakened position of political parties. France changed significantly due to processes of decentralisation, deregulation and privatisation. Although retreat of the State was not as drastic as it looked, because it "was accompanied by the colonization of business by the personnel of the state. Change in policies and processes was moderated by the lack of change in the players." (o.c., p.153). To get an adequate idea about French Public Management of Society, one has to deal with European integration.

A specific factor, neglected by political scientists, is the increased legalisation of institutions, public policies and even political processes. These developments have their special impact in a country like France, seen by the French as having an exemplary "État de droit". The State is seen as sole representative of the general interest, while legislation by parliament makes law dominant in all societal sectors. Wright (1999) made an overview of the process of legislation in the Fifth Republic. He summarised some features of the French judicial tradition: formal equality of individuals before the law; ubiquity of law; law established and policed by the "imperial state"; abiding disrespect for the current constitution; instrumental State-law; hostility towards jurisprudence as source of law, and towards judicial review; separate administrative jurisdiction; subordination and politicisation of the judiciary; judicial self-restraint. The increasing legalisation of public policy in the Fifth Republic is remarkable. Litigation in all parts of law grew, it became normal for the decisions of public authorities to be challenged in courts for being unconstitutional (judicial review of public policies). Intervention of courts and judges in the process of policymaking expanded at the expense of politicians and administrators. Courts are rendering policy issues justiciable (subject to law). Decision-making in policy areas regulated by government, legislature or public administration came into the hands of judges. Besides, activities, previously outside the scope of the law, are criminalised (juvenile delinquency, immigration policy, financial market malpractice). More than before political and administrative officials are made personally responsible for their acts, and subject to criminal proceedings. They can no longer hide behind principles of anonimity and political responsibility (Greilsamer/Schneidermann, 2002). Outside the judicial arena, judges play an increasing role as public policy makers and advisers on a scale unknown before (ad hoc commissions, self-regulating bodies, etc.).

Distinguishing in the process of growing legislation of French public policy between types of law (constitutional, administrative, civil and criminal), specific sectors, and types of legislation, Wright (1999) enumerated some factors as explanation for this growing legislation. There is judicial expansion, and State regulation increases despite privatisation, liberalisation and deregulation. The increasing recourse to judges and judicial processes is related to interrelated factors: Europeanisation, replacement of an ideological paradigm based on collective goods, public interest and citizenship, by a paradigm emphasising private goods, individual rights and consumerism. Several economic developments have their impact (creation of new modes of legally based regulation). The model of citizen integration with homogenising pressures of education is giving way to growing diversity and multiculturalism. Technological developments have their impact. State authority of a politico-bureaucratic nature is given to self-regulating agencies, functioning by informal and bargained quasi-legal processes ("soft law"). Administrative agencies with operational autonomy are tied to central State and local authorities by contracts with a quasi-legal character. Deliberate attempts of the legislator enlarge role and autonomy of the judiciary. Civil society demands greater consultation, participation and transparency. Growing demands for decentralisation gave local authorities more independence towards State authorities. In the sectors a transformation took place. When pressure groups could not satisfy their needs as before at the political level, courts were used as an arena to express grievances, seeking redress.

Public opinion, encouraged by investigative journalism, is positive about the activities of judges and the independence of judges. Revelation of cases of corruption and malpractice furthered the growth of investigations. "The pillars of the Jacobin temple of the 'imperial state' have been shaken by these processes, and in five essential ways: the acceptance of European law; the general support for 'government by constitution' and of the judicial review of political action which runs counter to the concepts of popular executive or parliamentary sovereignty; the growing role of courts as policy makers; the spread of diverse sources of 'soft law'; the criminalisation of public officials for negligence." (Wright, 1999, p.113). There are factors limiting the power of courts: rules explicitly restricting the power of courts; practices of politicians and administrators; continued politicisation of justice. For Wright these are manifestations of a profound phenomenon. The "lingering cultural aversion to the rule of law which affects many groups..." (o.c., p.116). Politicians interfere in appointments and processes of justice, but no democracy can be entirely ruled by judges. "All democratic polities are locked into the management of a set of trade-offs between market forces, social regulation and mobilisation, efficient processes of government, and judicial review. The construction of an "État de Droit" recognises this requirement." (o.c., p.119). This shows that for adequate realisation of the Idea of Public Authority in society it is useful to distinguish between politics and Public Management of Society. The Rule of Law is crucial for the Idea of Public Authority.

## References

French

Abbo, A., Les crimes des foules. (Paris, 1910).
Abzac, La question sociale, un projet de réforme. (Paris, Guillaumin, 1881).
Agacinsky, S. Journal interrompue, 24 janvier – 25 mai 2002. (Paris, Seuil, 2002).
Agulhon, M., Marianne au Pouvoir. (Paris, 1989).
Agulhon, M., La République. De Jules Ferry à François Mitterrand. (Paris, Hachette, 1990).
Agulhon, M., Les Métamorphoses de Marianne. (Paris, 2001).
Alain, Le citoyen contre les pouvoirs. (Paris, 1925).
Alain, Éléments d'une doctrine radicale. (Paris, 1925).
Alain, Propos de politique. (Paris, 1934).
Algalarrondo, H., Sécurité: La Gauche Contre le Peuple. (Paris, Laffont, 2002).
Albert, P., Tudesq, A., Histoire de la radio-télévision. (Paris, PUF, 1981; 1995).
Allies, P., Pourquoi et Comment une VIe République. (Paris, Climats, 2002).
Amar, C., Chemin, A., Jospin & Cie. Histoire de la Gauche Plurielle. (Paris, Seuil, 2002).
Ampère, A., Essai sur la philosophie des sciences, ou Exposition analytique d'une classification naturelle de toutes les connaissances humaines. (Paris, 1834-1843).
Andler, C., Les origines du socialisme d'État en Allemagne. (Paris, Alcan, 1911; 1958).
Andrieu, C., Le programme commun de la Résistance. (Paris, Éd. de l'Érudite, 1984).
Aron, R., Dimensions de la conscience historique. (Paris, Plon, 1961).
Aron, R., Démocratie et totalitarisme. (Paris, Gallimard, 1965).
Aron, R., Les étapes de la pensée sociologique. (Paris, Gallimard, 1967).
Aron, R., Études politiques. (Paris, Gallimard, 1972).
Aron, R., Dandieu, A., Décadence de la nation française. (Paris, Rieder, 1931).
Aron, R., Dandieu, A., La Révolution nécessaire. (Paris, Grasset, 1933).
Askolovitch, C., Lionel. (Paris, Grasset, 2002).
Avril, P., Gicquel, J., Droit constitutionnel. (Paris, PUF, 1995).
Babès, L., Oubrou, T., Loi d'Allah, Loi des Hommes. (Paris, A.Michel, 2002).
Bacot, P., Les Dirigeants du Parti Socialiste. (Lyon, PUL, 1979).
Bacqué, R., Chirac ou le Démon du Pouvoir. (Paris, A.Michel, 2002).
Badinter, R., L'Abolition. (Paris, Livre de poche, 2002).
Baecque, A. de, Pour ou Contre la Révolution. De Mirabeau à Mitterrand. (Paris, Bayard, 2002).
Baecque, A. de, La Cérémonie du Pouvoir. Les Duels Politiques de la Révolution à nos jours. (Paris, Grasset, 2002).
Baecque, F. de, Quermonne, J.L., dir., Administration et Politique sous la Cinquième République. (Paris, FNSP, 1981).
Balandier, G., Anthropologie politique. (Paris, PUF, 1984).
Bancaud, A., Une Exception Ordinaire. La Magistrature en France, 1930-1950. (Paris, Gallimard, 2002).
Barolin, J., La question sociale, sa solution pacifique. (Paris, Giard et Brière, 1902).
Baruch, M.O., Servir l'État Français. (Paris, Fayard, 1997).
Bascou-Bance, P., La Mémoire des Femmes. (Paris, Élytis, 2002).
Baudrillard, J., La Société de consommation: ses mythes, ses structures. (Paris, Gallimard, 1974).
Becker, J.J., Comment les Français sont entrés dans la guerre en août 1914. (Paris, FNSP, 1977).
Becker, J.J., Berstein, S., Histoire de l'anticommunisme en France. (Paris, Orban, 1987).
Bédarida, F., Rioux, J.P., Pierre Mendès France et le mendésisme. (Paris, Fayard, 1985).
Bedel, J., Zola assassiné. (Paris, Flammarion, 2002).
Benoit, J.M., et al., La Politique à l'Affiche. (Paris, Éd. du May, 1986).
Bergeron, S., Fonctionnement de l'État. (Paris, A.Colin, 1965).
Bernard, P., Immigration: Le Défi Mondial. (Paris, Gallimard, 2002).
Berne, J., La Campagne de Valéry Giscard d'Estaing en 1974. (Paris, PUF, 1981).
Berstein, S., Le 6 février 1934. (Paris, Gallimard, 1975).
Berstein, S., Histoire du parti radical. (Paris, FNSP, 1980-1982).
Berstein, S., dir., Paul Ramadier, le socialisme et la République. (Bruxelles, Complexe, 1990).
Berstein, S., dir., Les Cultures politiques en France. (Paris, Seuil, 2000).
Berstein, S., Milza, P., Histoire de la France au XXe siècle. (Paris, Complexe, 1995).
Berstein, S., Rudelle, O., dir., Le Modèle républicain. (Paris, PUF, 1992).
Beudant, C., Le droit individuel et l'État. (Paris, 1891).
Birnbaum, P., dir., L'Affaire Dreyfus. (Paris, Gallimard, 1994).

Bizot, J.F., Au Parti des Socialistes. (Paris, Grasset, 1975).
Bloch, C., Le IIIe Reich et le monde. (Paris, Imprimerie nationale, 1986).
Bloch-Lainé, F., Profession: Fonctionnaire. (Paris, Seuil, 1976).
Bloch-Lainé, F., La France en Mai 1981. (Paris, DF, 1981).
Blondel, J., La question sociale et sa solution scientifique. (Paris, Guillaumin, 1887).
Bluntschli, M., Théorie générale de l'État. (Paris, 1877).
Bodiguel, J.L., Les Anciens Élèves de l'ENA. (Paris, FNSP, 1978).
Bodiguel, J.L., Quermonne, J.L., La Haute Fonction Publique. (Paris, PUF, 1983).
Boia, L., Pour une Histoire de l'Imaginaire. (Paris, Belles Lettres, 1998).
Boia, L., Le Mythe de la Démocratie. (Paris, Belles Lettres, 2002).
Bois, P., Paysans de l'Ouest. (Paris, Mouton, 1960).
Bongrand, M., Splendeurs er Misères de la Politique. (Paris, Larousse, 1986).
Borloo, J.L., Un Homme en Colère. (Paris, Ramsay, 2002).
Borne, D., Petits bourgeois en révolte? Le mouvement Poujade. (Paris, Flammarion, 1977).
Borne, D., La Société française depuis 1945. (Paris, A.Colin, 1988).
Bothorel, J., Le Pharaon. Histoire de septennat giscardien, 19 mai 1974 – 22 mars 1978. (Paris, Grasset, 1983).
Boubakeur, D., Les Défis de l'Islam. (Paris, Flammarion, 2002).
Bourdé, G., Martin, H., Les écoles historiques. (Paris, Seuil, 1983).
Bourdieu, P., La distinction: critique sociale du jugement. (Paris, Minuit, 1979).
Bourdieu, P., La représentation politique. Éléments pour une théorie du champ politique. (Paris, Actes de la Recherche en sciences sociales, 1981).
Bourdon, J., Histoire de la Telévision sous De Gaulle. (Paris, Anthropos, 1990).
Bourdon, J., Haute Fidélité, Pouvoir et Télévision 1935-1994. (Paris, Seuil, 1994).
Bourgeois, B., La pensée politique de Hegel. (Paris, PUF, 1969).
Bourlanges, J.L., Droite année zéro. (Paris, Flammarion, 1988).
Boutmy, E., Observations sur l'enseignement des sciences politiques et administratives. (Paris, Martinet, 1876).
Boutmy, E., Des rapports et des limites des études juridiques et des études politiques. (Dans: Revue internationale de l'enseignement, pp.217-238, 1889).
Boutmy, E., Psychologie politique du peuple anglais au XIXe siècle. (Paris, 1901).
Boutmy, E., Éléments d'une psychologie politique du peuple américain. (Paris, 1902).
Boutros-Ghali, B., Démocratiser la Mondialisation. (Paris, Éd. du Rocher, 2002).
Brasseur, A., La question sociale, études sur les bases du collectivisme. (Paris, Alcan, 1900).
Braud, P., Sociologie politique. (Paris, LGDJ, 1994).
Bréchon, P., dir., Les Partis politiques français. (Paris, DF, 2002).
Bréchon, P., dir., Les Élections présidentielles en France. Quarante ans d'histoire politique. (Paris, DF, 2002).
Bresson, G., Lionet, C., Le Pen. (Paris, 1994).
Brizay, B., Le Patronat. (Paris, Seuil, 1975).
Bromberger, S. et M., Les treize complots du 13 mai. (Paris, Fayard, 1959).
Brunet, J.P., Histoire du PCF. (Paris, PUF, 1982).
Brunet, J.P., Jacques Doriot. (Paris, Balland, 1986).
Bufnoir, C., Rapport sur l'organisation de l'enseignement des sciences politiques et administratives. (Dans: Revue international de l'enseignement. Paris, 1881).
Bunel, J., Saglio, J., L'Action Patronale. (Paris, PUF, 1979).
Burdeau, G., Cours de droit constitutionnel. (Paris, 1942).
Burdeau, G., Le droit public et l'État. (Paris, 1943).
Burdeau, G., Traité de Science Politique. (Paris, 1949/1957; LGDJ, 1980).
Burrin, P., La France à l'Heure Allemande. (Paris, Seuil, 1995).
Campana, A., L'Argent secret. Le financement des partis politiques. (Paris, Arthaud, 1976).
Capdevieille, J., et al., France de Gauche Vote à Droite. (Paris, FNSP, 1981).
Carbonell, C.O., Histoire et historiens, une mutation idéologique des historiens français, 1865-1885. (Toulouse, Privat, 1976).
Carcassone, G., La Constitution. (Paris, Seuil, 2002).
Carré de Malberg, R., Contribution à la théorie générale de l'État. (Paris, 1920).
Cayrol, R., Mercier, A., dir., Télévision, Politique et Élections. (Paris, INA, 2002).
Cespedes, V., La Cerise sur le Béton. Violences Urbaines et Libéralisme Sauvage. (Paris, Flammarion, 2002).
Chagnollaud, D., Le Premier des Ordres. (Paris, Fayard, 1991).
Chagnollaud, D., La Vie Politique en France. (Paris, Seuil, 1993).

Chagnollaud, D., ed., Bilan Politique de la France 1991. (Paris, Hachette, 1991).
Chagnollaud, D., Quermonne, J.L., Le Gouvernement de la France sous la Ve République. (Paris, Fayard, 1996).
Chagnollaud, D., Quermonne, J.L., La Ve République. (Paris, Flammarion, 2000).
Chapsal, J., Lancelot, A., La Vie Politique en France depuis 1940. (Paris, PUF, 1979).
Charlier, J., La question sociale résolue. (Paris, Lecène et Oudin, 1894).
Charlot, J., Le Gaullisme d'opposition, 1946-1958., histoire du Gaullisme. (Paris, Fayard, 1983).
Chebel, M., Les Sujets en Islam. (Paris, Desclée de Brouwer, 2002).
Chenot, B., Les Entreprises Nationalisées. (Paris, PUF, 1959).
Chevallier, J.J., Histoire des institutions politiques et des régimes politiques de la France de 1789 à nos jours. (Paris, Dalloz, 1967; 1981; 2001).
Chirac, J., Une Nouvelle France. (Paris, Nil, 1994).
Club Ulysses, Le Politique saisie par l'Économie. Enjeux Économiques et Sociaux des Élections de 2002. (Paris, Economica, 2002).
Cohen, S., Les Conseillers du Président. De Charles de Gaulle à Valéry Giscard d'Estaing. (Paris, PUF, 1980).
Cole, G., Le Conseiller du Prince. (Paris, Lafon, 1999).
Colliard, J.C., Les Républicains-Indépendants. Valéry Giscard d'Estaing. (Paris, PUF, 1971).
Commission nationale consultative des Droits de l'Homme, Rapport 2001. La Lutte contre le Racisme et la Xénophobie. (Paris, DF, 2002).
Comte, A., Cours de philosophie positive. (Paris, 1830/1842; Hermann, 1975).
Comte, A., Catéchisme positiviste ou sommaire exposition de la religion universelle. (Paris, 1852).
Comte, A., Système de politique positive. (Paris, 1854; Aubier, 1970).
Constant, B., De la liberté des modernes. (Paris, 1797; Livre de poche, 1980).
Cornu, A., Karl Marx et Friedrich Engels. (Paris, PUF, 1955/1970).
Coste, A., Principes d'une sociologie objective. (Paris, 1899).
Cotta, M., Carnets Secrets de la Présidentielles. (Paris, Plon, 2002).
Cournot, A.A., Essai sur les fondements de nos connaissances et sur les caractères de la critique philosophique. (Paris, 1851).
Coutrot, A., Dreyfus, F.G., Les forces religieuses dans la société française. (Paris, A.Colin, 1965).
Couve de Murville, M., Une Politique Étrangère, 1958-1969. (Paris, Plon, 1971).
Crozier, M., et al., Où va l'Administration Française? (Paris, Éditions d'organisation, 1974).
Damamme, D., Histoire des sciences morales et politiques et de leur enseignement des lumières au scientisme. (Paris, Université, 1982).
Déat, M., Perspectives socialistes. (Paris, Valois, 1930).
Debbasch, C., L'Élysée Dévoilé. (Paris, A.Michel, 1982).
Debbasch, C., et al., La Ve République. (Paris, Economica, 1985).
Debbasch, C., Pontier, J.M., Introduction à la politique. (Paris, Dalloz, 1986).
Debray, R., L'Oeil Naïf. (Paris, Seuil, 1994).
Delannoy, P., Viard, J., La République du 5 Mai, vue de France et d'ailleurs. (Paris, L'Aube, 2002).
Delion, A.G., L'État et les Entreprises Publiques. (Paris, Sirey, 1958).
Delion, A.G., Durupty, M., Les Nationalisations 1982. (Paris, Economica, 1982).
Delmas-Marty, M., Leyssac, C.L. de, dir., Libertés et Droits Fondamentaux. (Paris, Découverte, 2002).
Delorme, C., Les Banlieues de Dieu. (Paris, Bayard, 1998).
Delorme, C., Begag, A., Quartiers Sensibles. (Paris, Seuil, 1994).
Delorey, M., La solution de la question sociale. (Paris, Charles, 1893).
Deschamps, H., La démocratie chrétienne et le MRP de 1946 à 1959. (Paris, LGDJ, 1981).
Deschanel, P., Question sociale. (Paris, Calmann-Lévy, 1898).
Desjardins, A., Questions sociales et politiques. (Paris, Plon, 1893).
Desplaces, H., De la légitimité des Chambres hautes et des principes qui président à leur recrutement. (Aix, 1892).
Desportes, G., Maudit, L., L'Adieu au Socialisme. (Paris, Grasset, 2002).
Deutsch, E., et al., Les familles politiques aujourd'hui en France. (Paris, Minuit, 1966).
Dieckhoff, A., La Nation dans tous les états. Les Identités nationales en mouvement. (Paris, Flammarion, 2002).
Documentation Française (DF), Institutions et Vie Politique. (Paris, DF, 1991).
DF, La Lutte contre le Racisme et la Xénophobie. (Paris, DF, 2002).
Doriot, J., Refaire la France. (Paris, Grasset, 1938).
Dreyfus, F., Arcy, F. d', Les Institutions Politiques et Administratives de la France. (Paris, Economica, 1989).

Drieu La Rochelle, P., Socialisme fasciste. (Paris, Gallimard, 1934).
Duby, G., dir., Histoire de la France rurale. (Paris, Seuil, 1985a).
Duby, G., dir., Histoire de la France urbaine. (Paris, Seuil, 1985b).
Duguit, L., Le droit constitutionnel et la sociologie. (Dans: Revue internationale de l'enseignement, 1889).
Duguit, L., L'État, le droit objectif et la loi positive (I). (Paris, Fontemoing, 1901).
Duguit, L., L'État, les gouvernants et les agents (II). (Paris, Fontemoing, 1903).
Duguit, L., Traité de droit constitutionnel. (Paris, Fontemoing, 1923; 1930).
Duhamel, O., La Gauche et la Cinquième République. (Paris, PUF, 1980).
Duhamel, O., Jeanneney, J.N., Présidentielles. Les Surprises de l'Histoire 1965-1995. (Paris, Seuil, 2002).
Duhamel, O., Weber, H., dir., Changer le PC? (Paris, PUF, 1979).
Dupeux, G., Le Front populaire et les élections de 1936. (Paris, A.Colin, 1959).
Dupin, E., Sortir la Gauche du Coma. (Paris, Flammarion, 2002).
Dupuy, F., Thoenig, J.C., L'Administration en Miettes. (Paris, Fayard, 1985).
Durkheim, E., De la division du travail social. (Paris, 1893; PUF, 1973).
Durkheim, E., Leçons de sociologie. (Paris, 1898/1900).
Durkheim, E., La science sociale et l'action. (Paris, PUF, 1970).
Duverger, M., Les constitutions de la France. (Paris, PUF, 1944; 1993).
Duverger, M., Introduction à la politique. (Paris, Gallimard, 1964).
Duverger, M., La Cohabitation des Français. (Paris, PUF, 1987).
Duverger, M., Le système politique français. (Paris, PUF, 1996).
Elgey, G., Histoire de la IVe République. (Paris, Fayard, 1993).
Emmanuelli, X., Frémontier, C. (Paris, PUF, 2002).
Esders, V., La Photographie du Président. (Paris, Hazan, 2002).
Esmein, A., Éléments de droit constitutionnel français et comparé. (Paris, 1896).
Essig, F., DATAR, des Régions et des Hommes. (Paris, Stanké, 1979).
Evin, K., Montpezar, E. de, A Table avec les Politiques. (Paris, Gallimard, 2002).
Fabre, C., Les Élections, Mode d'Emploi. (Paris, Librio, 2002).
Faguet, E., Questions politiques. (Paris, 1898).
Fahmy, M., La Condition de la Femme dans l'Islam. (Paris, Éd. Allia, 2002).
Favier, P., Martin-Roland, M., La Décennie Mitterrand. (Paris, Seuil, 1990/1991).
Favre, P., Histoire de la Science Politique. Dans: Grawitz, M., Leca, J., Traité de Science Politique. (Paris, PUF, 1985).
Favre, P., Naisssances de la science politique en France, 1870-1914. (Paris, Fayard, 1989).
Ferrières, M., Histoire des peurs alimentaires. Du Moyen Age à l'aube du XXe siècle. (Paris, Seuil, 2002).
Ferro, M., Suez. (Bruxelles, Complexe, 1983).
Feuerbach, I., Manifestes philosophiques. (Paris, PUF, 1973).
Filali-Ansary, A., L'Islam est-il Hostile à la Laïcité? (Paris, Sinbad/ Actes Sud, 2002).
Foll, O., L'Insécurité en France. Un Grand Flic Accuse. (Paris, Flammarion, 2002).
Fougères, L., Machelon, J.P., Monnier, F., Les Communes et le Pouvoir. (Paris, PUF, 2002).
Fouillée, A., Psychologie du peuple français. (Paris, 1898).
Fouillée, A., Esquisse d'une psychologie des peuples européens. (Paris, 1903).
Forni, R., Un Enfant de la République. (Paris, Stock, 2002).
Fourastié, J., Les Trente Glorieuses ou la Révolution invisible de 1946 à 1975. (Paris, Fayard, 1979).
Fournier, J., Le Travail Gouvernementale. (Paris, FNSP, 1987).
Fourrier, C., Oeuvres complètes, (Paris, Anthropos, 1971).
Freyssinet, J., et al., dir., Planification et Société. (Grenoble, Université de Grenoble, 1974).
Fuzier-Herman, E., La séparation des pouvoirs d'après l'histoire et le droit constitutionnel. (Paris, Maresq, 1880).
Gabet, A., La Fracture Sociale. (Paris, Ellipses, 2002).
Garrigou, A., Histoire Sociale du Suffrage Universel. En France. (Paris, Seuil, 2002).
Gélédan, A., Le Bilan Économique des Années Mitterrand, 1981-1994. (Paris, Le Monde, 1993).
Giddens, A., La constitution de la société (1984). (Paris, PUF, 1987).
Giddens, A., Blair, T., La Troisième Voie. Le Renouveau de la Social-Démocratie. (Paris, Seuil, 2002).
Giesbert, P., Jacques Chirac. (Paris, Seuil, 1987).
Giscard d'Estaing. V., Démocratie Française. (Paris, Fayard, 1976).
Giscard d'Estaing, V., Le Pouvoir et la Vie. (Paris, Cie 12, 1988/1991).
Goguel, F., La Politique des Partis sous la IIIe République. (Paris, Seuil, 1946; 1981).
Goguel, F., Le Régime politique français. (Paris, Seuil, 1958).
Gourévitch, J.P., L'Image du Président. (Paris, Tema, 1975).

Gourévitch, J.P., L'Image en Politique. (Paris, Hachette, 1998).
Gourévitch, J.P., Burnier, A., Mercadet, L., Comment devenir Président de la République en 90 minutes. (Paris, Plon, 1992).
Grawitz, M., Leca, J., dir., Traité de Science Politique. (Paris, PUF, 1985).
Greer, G., La Femme Entère. (Paris, Plon, trad., 2002).
Greilsamer, L., Schneidermann, D., Où vont les Juges? (Paris, Fayard, 2002).
Grémion, P., Le Pouvoir Périphérique. (Paris, Seuil, 1976).
Grémion, P., Profession: Décideurs. Pouvoir des Hauts Fonctionnaires et Réforme de l'État. (Paris, Gauthier-Villars, 1979).
Gresh, A., Ramadan, T., L'Islam en Questions. (Paris, Actes Sud, 2002).
Grosser, A., La Quatrième République et sa Politique Extérieure. (Paris, A.Colin, 1961).
Grossmann, R., Miclo, F., La République Minoritaire. Contre le Communautarisme. (Paris, Michalon, 2002).
Guénaire, M., Déclin et Renaissance du Pouvoir. (Paris, Gallimard, 2002).
Guesde, J., État, politique et morale de classe. (Paris, Giard et Brière, 1901).
Guizot, F., Histoire générale de la civilisation en Europe depuis la chute de l'Empire romain jusqu'à la Révolution française (1828). (Paris, Livre de poche, 1985).
Gumplowicz, L., Un programme de sociologie. (Dans: Annales de l'Institut de sociologie, 1895).
Gurvitch, G., L'Idée de droit social. (Paris, Sirey, 1932).
Gurvitch, G., Les fondateurs français de la sociologie contemporaine: Saint-Simon et Proudhon. (Paris, Sorbonne, 1955).
Guyard, J., Le Miracle français. (Paris, Seuil, 1970).
Hauriou, M., Les facultés de droit et la sociologie. (Dans: Revue générale du droit, pp.289-295, 1893).
Hauriou, M., Précis de droit adminstratif et de droit public. (Paris, 1896).
Hauriou, M., Principes de droit public. (Paris, Sirey, 1916; 1923).
Hauriou, M., Précis de droit constitutionnel. (Paris, Sirey, 1929; CNRS, 1965).
Haziza, F., Chirac ou la Victoire en pleurant. (Paris, Ramsay, 2002).
Hegel, G.W.F., Principes de la philosophie du droit (1821/1822). (Paris, Gallimard, 1940).
Hermet, G., Le Peuple contre la Démocratie. (Paris, Fayard, 1989).
Hervieu, H., Les ministres, leur rôle et leurs attributions dans les différents États organisés. (Paris, Larose, 1893).
Hoffmann, S., Le Mouvement Poujade. (Paris, A.Colin, 1956).
Hondt, J. d', De Hegel à Marx. (Paris, PUF, 1972).
Hondt, J. d', Hegel et l'hégelianisme. (Paris, PUF, 1982).
Huerre, P., Ni Anges Ni Sauvages. Les Jeunes et la Violence. (Paris, Carrière, 2002).
Hurtig, M.C., et al., Sexe et Genre, de la Hiérarchie entre les Sexes. (Paris, CNRS, 2002).
Hyppolite, J., Introduction à la philosophie de Hegel. (Paris, Seuil, 1983).
Jaurès, J., L'Oeuvre de Jean Jaurès. (Paris, Valesco, 1996).
Jellinek, G., L'État moderne et son droit ("Allgemeine Staatslehre"). (Paris, 1911).
Jelloun, R.B., L'Islam Expliqué aux Enfants. (Paris, Seuil, 2002).
Jobert, B., Muller, P., L'État en Action. (Paris, PUF, 1987).
Jospin, L., L'Invention du Possible. (Paris, Flammarion, 1991).
Jospin, L., Le Temps de Répondre. (Paris, Stock, 2002).
Jouvenel, B. de, Le Réveil de l'Europe. (Paris, Paris, Gallimard, 1935).
Jouvenel, B. de, Du Pouvoir (1943). (Genève, 1947; Paris, Hachette, 1972).
Julliard, J., La IVe République (1947-1958). (Paris, Calmann-Lévy, 1968).
Kabbas, M.Y., L'Islam. (Paris, Éd. Les 12, 2002).
Kantorowitz, E.H., Les deux corps du Roi (1957). (Paris, Gallimard, 1989).
Karli, P., Les Racines de la Violence. Réflexions d'un Neurobiologiste. (Paris, Odile Jacob, 2002).
Karpik, L., Les Avocats. Entre l'État, le public et le marché. (Paris, Gallimard, 1995).
Karpik, L., L'Avancée de la Justice menace-t-elle la République? (Dans: Le Débat, pp.238-257, 2000).
Kimmel, A., L'Assemblée Nationale sous la Ve République. (Paris, FNSP, 1991).
Laborie, P., Les Français des Années Troubles. (Paris, Desclée de Brouwer, 2001).
Lacoste, Y., Géopolitiques des régions françaises. (Paris, Fayard, 1986).
Lacouture, J., Pierre Mendès France. (Paris, Seuil, 1981).
Lacouture, J., De Gaulle. (Paris, Seuil, 1984/1986).
Lacouture, J., François Mitterrand. (Paris, Seuil, 1998).
Lacouture, J., Rotman, P., Mitterrand, le roman du pouvoir. (Paris, Seuil, 2000).
Lacroix, B., Durkheim et le politique. (Montréal, Presses universitaires, 1981).

Lacroix, B., Ordre politique et ordre social. Objectivisme, objectivation et analyse politique. (Dans: Grawitz, M., Leca, J., dir., Traité de Science Politique. Paris, PUF, 1985).
Lacroix-Riz, A., Le Choix de Marianne (les relations franco-américaines de la Libération aux débuts du Plan Marshall, 1944-1948). (Paris, Messidor, 1986).
La Gorce, P.M. de, Moschetto, B., La Cinquième République. (Paris, PUF, 1996).
Laguiller, A., Mon Communisme. (Paris, Plon, 2002).
Lair, A.E., Des Hauts Cours Politiques en France et à l'étranger et de la mise en accusation du président de la République et des ministres. (Paris, Thorin, 1889).
Lalumière, P., Les Finances Publiques. (Paris, A.Colin, 1970).
Lapierre, J.W., Essai sur le pouvoir politique. (Paris, Ophrys, 1968).
Laroche-Flavin, C., La Machine Judiciaire. (Paris, Seuil, 1968).
Larousse, Napoléon. (Paris, Éd. Mémoire du livre, 2002).
Lavau, G., A Quoi sert le Parti Communiste Français? (Paris, Fayard, 1981).
Le Béguec, Delirvet, P., dir., Henri Queuille et la République. (Limoges, Trames, 1987).
Le Bon, G., Psychologie du socialisme. (Paris, 1898).
Le Bon, G., La psychologie politique et la défense sociale. (Paris, Flammarion, 1910).
Lefebvre, C., Étude sur les lois constitutionnelles de 1875. (Paris, Maresq, 1882).
Legay, G., La question sociale, l'unique solution. (Paris, Guillaumin, 1891).
Legendre, P., Miroir d'une Nation. L'École Nationale d'Administration. (Paris, Mille et une nuits, 2000).
Le Moigne, G., Lebon, A., L'Immigration en France. (Paris, PUF, 2002).
Lénine, W.I., Origine de la famille, de la propriété privée et de l'État. (Paris, 1884).
Lénine, W.I., Que faire? (Paris, 1902; Seuil, 1966).
Lénine, W.I., La faillite de la Iie Internationale. (Paris, 1915; Editions sociales, 1953).
Lénine, W.I., La Révolution prolétarienne et le renégat Kautsky. (Paris, 1918; UGE, 1972).
Le Pen, J.M., Les Français d'abord. (Paris, Carrère-Lafon, 1984).
Le Pen, J.M., Pour la France. (Paris, Albatros, 1985).
Le Pen, J.M., Front National. Pour la France. Programme du Front National. (Paris, Albatros, 1985)
Le Pen, J.M., Les Priorités de Jean-Marie Le Pen. (Paris, 1995).
Le Roy Badurie, E., Histoire des Paysans Français. De la Peste noire à la Révolution. (Paris, Seuil, 2002).
Leroy-Beaulieu, P., L'État moderne et ses fonctions. (Paris, 1890; 1911).
Lienemann, M.N., Ma part de'inventaire. (Paris, 2002).
Ligou, D., Histoire du socialisme en France 1871-1961. (Paris, PUF, 1967).
Lochak, D., Chevallier, J., La Haute Administration et la Politique. (Paris, PUF, 1986).
Loubet del Bayle, J.L., Les non-conformistes des années 30. Une tentation de renouvellement de la pensée politique française. (Paris, Seuil, 1969).
Lowie, R., Traité de sociologie primitive (1927). (Paris, Payot, 1936).
Lumbroso, O., Mitterrand, H., Les Manuscrits et les dessins de Zola. (Paris, Ed. Textuel, 2002).
Maire, E., Julliard, J., La CFDT d'aujourd'hui. (Paris, Seuil, 1975).
Manceron, C., Pingaud, B., F. Mitterrand, l'homme, les idées, le programme. (Paris, Flammarion, 1981).
Mandel, E., La formation de la pensée économique. (Paris, Découverte, 1982).
Mandel, E., Introduction au marxisme. (Paris, La Brèche, 1983).
Mannequin, T., La question sociale et la science. (Paris, Guillaumin, 1894).
Marie, A., La psychologie collective, psychologie normale et morbide comparée. (Paris, 1910).
Marion, P., Programme du Parti populaire français. (Paris, Oeuvres français, 1938).
Marseille, J., Le Grand Gaspillage. Les Vrais Comptes de l'État. (Paris, Plon, 2002).
Martinet, G., Les Clés de la Ve République, suivi de Mendès-France: Le Contre-Exemple. (Paris, Seuil, 2002).
Marty, F., dir., Le Jeune Délinquant. (Paris, Payot, 2002).
Marx, K., Le 18-Brumaire de Louis Bonaparte. (Paris, 1852; Editions sociales, 1984).
Marx, K., Oeuvres. (Paris, Gallimard, 1963/1982).
Marx, K., Engels, F., Manifeste du parti communiste. (Paris, 1848; Editions sociales, 1986).
Marx, K., Engels, F., Critique des programmes de Gotha et d'Erfurt. (Paris, 1875; Editions sociales, 1950).
Maurras, C., Enquête sur la monarchie. (Paris, Nouvelle Librarie Nationale, 1900; Fayard, 1928).
Maurras, C., Mes idées politiques. (Paris, Fayard, 1937; Albatros, 1986).
Maurras, C., De la politique naturelle au nationalisme intégrale. (Paris, Vrin, 1972).
Maus, D., Les Grandes Textes de la Pratique Institutionnelle de la Ve République. (Paris, DF, 1995).
Mayer, N., Perrineau, P., dir., Le Front National à Découvert. (Paris, FNSP, 1989).
Meddeb, A., La Maladie de l'Islam. (Paris, Seuil, 2002).
Mendras, H., L'Europe des Européens. Sociologie de l'Europe occidentale. (Paris, Gallimard, 1997).

Mendras, H., La Seconde Révolution Française, 1965-1984. (Paris, Gallimard, 1994).
Mény, Y., Centralisation et Décentralisation dans le Débat Politique Français, 1945-1969. (Paris, LGDJ, 1974).
Merlin, P., L'Urbanisme. (Paris, PUF, 2002).
Meynaud, J., Les Groupes de Pression en France. (Paris, A.Colin, 1957).
Michaud, Y., Changements dans la Violence. Essai sur la Bienveillance Universelle et la Peur. (Paris, Odile Jacob, 2002).
Michaud, Y., La Société et les Relations Sociales. (Paris, Odile Jacob, 2002).
Michel, H., L'Ídée de l'État. (Paris, 1894).
Michel, H., Histoire de la Résistance en France. (Paris, PUF, 1962).
Michelet, J., Histoire de la Révolution française. (Paris, Gallimard, 1952).
Milza, P., Fascisme français. (Paris, Flammarion, 1991).
Milza, P., Amar, M., L'Immigration en France au XXe siècle. (Paris, A.Colin, 1990).
Minc, A., Le Fracas du Monde. Journal de l'Année 2001. (Paris, Seuil, 2002).
Miquel, P., Histoire de la radio et de la télévision. (Paris, Perrin, 1984).
Mital, C., Izraelewicz, E., Monsieur Ni-Ni. L'économie selon Jospin. (Paris, Laffont, 2002).
Mitterrand, H., Zola. (Paris, Fayard, 2002).
Molinari, G. de, Comment se résoudra la question sociale? (Paris, Guillaumin, 1891).
Momigliano, A., Contributions à l'Histoire du Judaïsme. (Paris, Éd. de l'Éclat, 2002).
Monier, F., Le Front Populaire. (Paris, Découverte, 2002).
Monnet, F., Refaire la République. André Tardieu, une dérive réactionnaire, 1876-1946. (Paris, Fayard, 1993).
Morel, C., Les Décisions Absurdes. Sociologie des Erreurs Radicales ert Persistants. (Paris, Gallimard, 2002).
Moriceau, J.M., Terres Mouvantes. Les campagnes françaises du féodalisme à la mondialisation, XIIe-XIXe siècle. (Paris, Fayard, 2002).
Mouriaux, R., La CGT. (Paris, Seuil, 1983).
Mucchielli, L., Robert, P., dir., Crime et Sécurité. L'État des Savoirs. (Paris, Découverte, 2002).
Muxel, A., Les Français et la politique. (Paris, DF, 2002).
Négrin, J.P., Le Conseil d'État et la Vie Publique en France depuis 1958. (Paris, PUF, 1968).
Nietzsche, F., Par delà le Bien et le Mal. (Paris, Hachette, 1987).
Nisbet, R., La tradition sociologique. (Paris, PUF, 1984).
Noel, L., De Gaulle et les Débuts de la Ve République, 1958-1965. (Paris, Plon, 1976).
Noiriel, G., Le Creuset français. Histoire de l'immigration, XIXe-XXe siècles. (Paris, Seuil, 1988).
Offerlé, M., Un Homme, Une Voix? Histoire du Suffrage Universel. (Paris, Gallimard, 2002).
Oppenheimer, F., L'État, ses origines, son évolution et son avenir. (Paris, 1913).
Ory, P., La Belle Illusion. Culture et politique sous le ligne du Front Populaire, 1935-1938. (Paris, Plon, 1994).
Pagé, J.P., dir., Profil Économique de la France. (Paris, DF, 1981).
Paugam, S., La Disqualification Sociale. (Paris, PUF, 2002).
Pelletier, D., La Crise Catholique. Religion, Société, Politique en France (1965-1978). (Paris, Payot, 2002).
Pelloux, R., Le parti national-socialiste et ses rapports avec l'État. (Paris, 1936).
Perrot, M., dir., Histoire des Femmes. (Paris, Perrin, 2000).
Petitfils, J.C., La Démocratie giscardienne. (Paris, PUF, 1981).
Peyrefitte, A., Le Mal Français. (Paris, Plon, 1976).
Pierret, C., Ministre à Gauche. (Paris, Le Pré aux Clercs, 2002).
Pilleul, G., dir., L'Entourage et de Gaulle. (Paris, Plon, 1979).
Pingaud, D., L'Impossible Défaite. (Paris, Seuil, 2002).
Popper, K., La Logique de la découverte scientifique (1934). (Paris, Payot, 1990).
Portelli, H., Le Socialisme français tel qu'il est. (Paris, PUF, 1980).
Portelli, H., La Politique en France sous la Ve République. (Paris, Grasset, 1990).
Pouvoirs (Revue), La Gauche au Pouvoir. (Paris, Seuil, 1982).
Pouvoirs, Le Mendésisme. (Paris, Seuil, 1983).
Pouvoirs, La République. (Paris, Seuil, 2002).
Pouyet, B., La Délégation à l'aménagement du twerritoire et l'action régionale. (Paris, Cujas, 1967).
Prager, J.C., La Politique Économique aujourd'hui. (Paris, Ellipses, 2002).
Prélot, M., L'Empire fasciste, les tendances et les institutions de la dictature et du corporatisme italiens. (Paris, Sirey, 1936).
Prémare, A.L. de, Les Fondations de l'Islam. Entre Écriture et Histoire. (Paris, Seuil, 2002).
Probst, J.F., Chirac & Dépendances. (Paris, Ramsay, 2002).

Prost, A., Histoire de l'enseignement en France (1800-1967). (Paris, A.Colin, 1968).
Prost, A., Les Anciens combattants et la société française. (Paris, FNSP, 1977).
Proudhon, P.J., Qu'est-ce que la propriété? (Paris, 1840).
Proudhon, P.J., Système de contradictions économiques ou Philosophie de la misère. (Paris, 1865).
Proudhon, P.J., De la capacité politique des classes ouvrières. (Paris, 1865).
Proudhon, P.J., Theorie de la propriété. (Paris, 1865).
Proudhon, P.J., Misère de la philosophie. (Paris, UGE, 1964).
Proudhon, P.J., Oeuvres complètes. (Genève, Stalkine, 1982).
Quermonne, J.L., Le Gouvernement de la France sous la Ve République. (Paris, Dalloz, 1980).
Quilliot, R., La SFIO et l'excercice du pouvoir (1944-1958). (Paris, Fayard, 1972; 1982).
Quinet, E., La Révolution. (Paris, Belin, 1987).
Raffarin, J.P., Pour une Nouvelle Gouvernance. (Paris, Archipel, 2002).
Raffy, S., Jospin, Secrets de Famille. (Paris, Fayard, 2002).
Rain, P., L'école libre des sciences politiques, 1871-1945. (Paris, FNSP, 1963).
Rasera, M., La Démocratie Locale. (Paris, LGDJ, 2002).
Regards sur l'actualité, 1984: le syndicalisme a 100 ans. (Paris, DF, mars 1984).
Régnard, A., L'État, ses origines, sa nature et son but. (Paris, Dervaux, 1885).
Rémond, B., Blanc, J., Les Collectivités Locales. (Paris, FNSP, 1989).
Rémond, R., Les Droites en France de 1815 à nos jours. (Paris, Aubier, 1982).
Rémond, R., La politique n'est plus ce qu'elle était. (Paris, Calmann-Lévy, 1993).
Rémond, R., La République Souveraine. La Vie Politique en France 1879-1939. (Paris, Fayard, 2002).
Revue internationale d'histoire politique et constitutionnelle, L'Entrée de la Science Politique dans l'Université française. (Paris, 1957).
Robert, J., Libertés Publiques. (Paris, Montchrestien, 1977).
Rials, S., Révolution et Contre-Révolution au XIXe siècle. (Paris, Albatros, 1986).
Riot-Sarcey, M., Histoire du Féminisme. (Paris, Découverte, 2002).
Rioux, J.P., La France et la Quatrième République. (Paris, Seuil, 1980).
Rioux, J.P., Sirinelli, J.F., La Guerre d'Algérie et les intellectuels français. (Bruxelles, Complexe, 1991).
Rioux, J.P., Sirinelli, J.F., La Culture de Masse en France de la Belle Époque à aujourd'hui. (Paris, Fayard, 2002).
Roché, S., Tolérance Zéro? Incivilités et Insécurité. (Paris, Odile Jacob, 2002).
Rondin, J., Le Sacre des Notables. (Paris, Fayard, 1985).
Rosenfield, D., Politique et liberté, structure logique de la philosophie du droit de Hegel. (Paris, Aubier, 1984).
Roussel, E., Georges Pompidou. (Paris, Lattès, 1984).
Roussel, E., Charles de Gaulle. (Paris, Gallimard, 2002).
Roussel, F., Les Femmes dans le Combat Politique en France, La République selon Marianne. (Paris, L'Hydre, 2002).
Ruhl, L., La Politique Militaire de la Ve République. (Paris, FNSP, 1976).
Russ, J., Pour connaître la pensée des précurseurs de Marx. (Paris, Bordas, 1973).
Saint-Girons, A. de, Essai sur la séparation des pouvoirs dans l'ordre politique, administratif et judiciaire. (Paris, Larose, 1881).
Saint-Simon, C.H., Oeuvres. (Paris, Anthropos, 1966).
Sander, A., Hommes du XXe Siècle. (Paris, Éd. de la Martinière, 2002).
Saussez, T., Politique- Séduction. (Paris, Lattès, 1986).
Schäppi, R., La Femme est le Propre de l'Homme, de l'Éthologie Animale à la Nature Humaine. (Paris, Odile Jacob, 2002).
Schifres, M., Sarazin, M., L'Élysée de Mitterrand. (Paris, Moreau, 1985).
Séguéla, J., Le Vertige des Urnes. (Paris, Flammarion, 2000).
Siegfried, A., Tableau politique de la France de l'Ouest sous la Troisième République. (Paris, A.Colin, 1913; Imprimerie nationale, 1995).
Sirinelli, J.F., dir., Histoire des Droites en France. (Paris, Gallimard, 1992).
Sirot, S., Maurice Thorez. (Paris, Presses de Sciences Po, 2000).
Souchard, M., Le Pen, Les Mots. Analyse d'un Discours d'Extrême Droite. (Paris, 2002).
Soucy, R., Le Fascisme français, 1924-1933. (Paris, PUF, 1989).
Soudais, M., Le Front National en face. (Paris, Flammarion, 1998).
Soulez Larivière, D., Dalle, H., Notre Justice. Le Livre Vérité de la Justice Française. (Paris, Laffont, 2002).
Sperber, D., Wilson, D., La pertinence. Communication et cognition. (Paris, Minuit, 1989).
Stebe, J.M., La Crise des Banlieues. (Paris, PUF, 2002).

Stein, L., La question sociale au point de vue philosophique. (Paris, Alcan, 1900).
Stoetzel, J., Théorie des opinions. (Paris, Université, 1943).
Strauss-Kahn, D., La Flamme et la Cendre. (Paris, Grasset, 2002).
Strayer, J.R., Les origines médiévales de l'État moderne. (Paris, Payot, 1979).
Stuart Mill, J., L'utilitarisme (1863). (Paris, Flammarion, 1988).
Sudre, F., La Convention Européenne des Droits de l'Homme. (Paris, PUF, 2002).
Taguieff, P.A., La Nouvelle Judéophobie. (Paris, Éd. Mille et Une Nuits, 2002).
Taguieff, P.A., L'Illusion Populiste. (Paris, Berg, 2002).
Talbi, M., Penser Libre en Islam. (Paris, A.Michel, 2002).
Taminiaux, J., Naissance de la philosophie hégélienne de l'État. (Paris, Payot, 1984).
Tarde, G., Les lois de l'imitation. (Paris, 1890).
Tarde, G., La logique sociale. (Paris, 1895).
Tardieu, A., Notes sur les États-Unis. (Paris, 1908).
Tardieu, A., L'Heure de la décision. (Paris, Flammarion, 1934).
Tardieu, A., La Révolution à refaire. (Paris, Flammarion, 1936/1937).
Terrazzoni, A., La Décentralisation à l'Épreuve des Faits. (Paris, LGDJ, 1987).
Thoenig, J.C., L'Ère des Technocrates. (Paris, Éditions d'organisation, 1973).
Tillinac, D., Chirac le Gaulois. (Paris, La Table Ronde, 2002).
Tocqueville, A. de, Ancien Régime et la Révolution. (Paris, 1856; Gallimard, 1987).
Touchard, J., La Gauche en France depuis 1900. (Paris, Seuil, 1977; 1981).
Touchard, J., Le Gaullisme, 1940-1969. (Paris, Seuil, 1978).
Tournoux, R., Secrets d'État. (Paris, Plon, 1960).
Tranchant, C., De la préparation aux services publics en France, améliorations dont l'enseignement politique et administratif serait susceptible sous sa forme générale. (Paris, Berger-Levrault, 1878).
Tronquoy, P., dir., La Ve République, permanance et mutations. (Paris, DF, 2002).
Trotski, L.D. (Bronstein), Nos tâches politiques. (Paris, 1904; Denoël, 1971).
Trotski, L.D., La Révolution trahie. (Paris, 1935; UGE, 1969).
Vaïsse, M., Alger, le putsch. (Bruxelles, Complexe, 1983).
Vaussard, M., Histoire de la démocratie chrétienne: France-Belgique-Italie. (Paris, Seuil, 1956).
Vigouroux, C., Déontologie des fonctions politiques. (Paris, Dalloz, 1995).
Villepin, D. de, Le Cri de la Gargouille. (Paris, A.Michel, 2002).
Weber, M., Le savant et le politique (1919). (Paris, Plon, 1959).
Wasserman, G., dir., À Gauche. (Paris, Découverte, 2002).
Weber, E., La fin des terroirs. La modernisation de la France rurale, 1870-1914. (Paris, Fayard, 1983).
Weber, H., Le Parti des Patrons. (Paris, Seuil, 1986).
Weber, M., Économie et société (1922). (Paris, Plon, 1971).
Weil, E., Hegel et l'État. (Paris, Vrin, 1950; 1974).
Wilson, W.W., L'État. (Paris, 1902).
Winock, M., Histoire politique de la revue "Esprit" (1930-1950). (Paris, Seuil, 1975).
Winock, M., Le Socialisme en France et en Europe (XIXe-XXe siècles). (Paris, Seuil, 1992).
Winock, M., La Fièvre hexagonale. Les grandes crises politiques, 1871-1968. (Paris, Calmann-Lévy, 1986; Seuil, 1995).
Winock, M., L'Affaire Dreyfus. (Paris, Seuil, 1998).
Winock, M., La France politique (XIXe-XXe siècles). (Paris, Seuil, 1999).
Winock, M., dir., Histoire de l'extrême droite en France. (Paris, Seuil, 1994).
Wolikow, S., Le parti communiste français et l'Internationale communiste (1926-1933). (Paris, Université de Paris-VIII, 1990).
Ysmal, C., Les Partis Politiques sous la Ve République. (Paris, Montchrestien, 1989).
Zola, E., Paris (1898). (Paris, Gallimard, 2002).

English
Acton, H.B., The Illusion of an Epoch: Marxism-Leninism as a Philosophical Creed. (London, Cohen and West, 1955.)
Adereth, M., The French Communist Party, a Critical History (1920-1984). (Manchester, Manchester UP, 1984).
Almond, G.A., ed., A Discipline Divided: Schools and Sects in Political Science. (Newbury Park, CA, Sage, 1990).
Ambler, J.S., Soldiers against the State. The French Army in Politics, 1945-1962. (Columbus, Ohio, Ohio State UP, 1966; New York, Doubleday, 1968).

Ambler, J.S., The Government and Politics of France. (Boston, Houghton Mifflin, 1971).
Ambler, J.S., ed., The French Socialist Experiment. (Philadelphia, Institute for the Study of Human Issues, 1985).
Aminzade, R., Ballots and Barricades. Class Formation and the Republican Politics in France, 1830-1871. (Princeton, Princeton UP, 1993).
Anderson, M., Government in France. (New York, Pergamon, 1970).
Anderson, M., Conservative Politics in France. (London, Allen & Unwin, 1974).
Anderson, R.D., France 1870-1914. Politics and Society. (London, Routledge & Kegan Paul, 1977; 1984).
Andrews, W.G., Presidential Government in Gaullist France: A Study of Executive-Legislative Relations, 1958-1974. (Albany, State University of New York Press, 1982).
Andrews, W.G., ed., Handbook of Contemporary World Political Science. (Westport, Greenwood, 1982).
Andrews, W.G., Hoffmann, S., eds., The Fifth Republic at Twenty. (Albany, State University of New York Press, 1981).
Ardagh, J., France in the 1980s. (Harmondsworth, Penguin, 1982).
Ardagh, J., France Today. (Harmondsworth, Penguin, 1988).
Ashford, D.E., Policy and Politics in France. (Philadelphia, Temple University Press, 1982).
Ashford, D.E., British Dogmatism and French Pragmatism. Central-Local Policymaking in the Welfare State. (London, Allen & Unwin, 1982).
Avril, P., Politics in France. (Harmondsworth, Penguin, 1969).
Beer, M., A History of British Socialism. (London, Allen and Unwin, 1948).
Beer, M., Patterns of Government. The Major Political Systems of Europe. (New York, McGraw-Hill, 1973).
Behn, R.D., Rethinking Democratic Accountability. (Washington DC, Brookings Institution, 2001).
Bekke, A.J.G.M., Perry, J.L., Toonen, T.A.J., eds., Civil Service Systems in Comparative Perspective. (Bloomington, IN, Indiana UP, 1996).
Bell, D., Contemporary French Political Parties. (New York, St.Martin's, 1982).
Bell, D., Criddle, B., The French Socialist Party. (Oxford, Clarendon, 1988).
Bell, D., Criddle, B., The French Communist Party in the Fifth Republic. (Oxford, Clarendon, 1994).
Bentham, J., The Principles of Morals and Legislation (1789). (New York, Macmillan, 1948).
Bentham, J., Works. (Edinburgh, University, 1838/1843).
Bentham, J., The Collected Works. (London, Athlone, 1968).
Bentley, A.F., The Process of Government. (Chicago, University of Chicago, 1908).
Bjerke, B., Business Leadership and Culture. National Management Styles in the Global Economy. (Cheltenham, Elgar, 2000).
Blanning, T.C.W., The Culture of Power and the Power of Culture. Old Regimes Europe 1660-1789. (Oxford, OUP, 2002).
Blondel, J., Godfrey, E.D., The Government of France. (London, Methuen, 1968).
Brown, B.E., Socialism of a Different Kind: Reshaping the Left in France. (Westport, Greenwood, 1982).
Burns, M., Rural Society and French Politics. Boulangism and Dreyfus Affair. (Princeton, Princeton UP, 1984).
Cahm, E., Politics and Society in Contemporary France, 1789-1971. (London, Harrap, 1972).
Campbell, P., French Electoral Systems and Elections since 1789. (London, Faber, 1966).
Carmoy, G. de, The Foreign Policies of France, 1944-1968. (Chicago, University of Chicago Press, 1970).
Caute, D., Communism and the French Intellectuals, 1914-1960. (New York, Macmillan, 1964).
Cerny, P., The Politics of Grandeur. Ideological Aspects of de Gaulle's Foreign Policy. (Cambridge, CUP, 1980).
Cerny, P., ed., Social Movements and Protest in France. (London, Pinter, 1982).
Cerny, P., Schain, M., French Politics and Public Policy. (London, Pinter, 1980).
Cerny, P., Schain, M., Socialism, the State and Public Policy in France. (London, Pinter, 1985).
Chandler, R.C., ed., A Centennial History of the American Administrative State. (New York, Free Press, 1987).
Chapman, B., Introduction to French Local Government. (London, Allen & Unwin, 1953).
Chapman, B., The Profession of Government. (London, Unwin, 1970).
Charlot, J., The Gaullist Phenomenon. (London, Allen & Unwin, 1970).
Clarke, J.M., Teachers and Politics in France: (A Pressure Group Study of the Fédération de l'Éducation Nationale. Syracuse, NY, Syracuse UP, 1967).
Cobban, A., A History of Modern France. (London, Penguin, 1965; 1990).
Cohen, S.S., Gourevitch, P.A., eds., France in the Troubled World Economy. (London, Butterworths, 1982).
Cole, A., ed., French Political Parties in Transition. (Aldershot, Dartmouth, 1990).
Cole, A., Campbell, P., eds., French Electoral Systems and Elections since 1789. (Aldershot, Gower, 1989).

Crozier, M., The Bureaucratic Phenomenon. (London, Tavistock, 1964).
Crozier, M., Friedberg, E., Actors and Systems. The Politics of Collective Action. (Chicago, University of Chicago Press, 1980).
Dahl, R., Regimes and oppositions. (New Haven, Yale UP, 1973).
Dahl, R., Power. In: International Encyclopaedia of the Social Sciences. (New York, Macmillan, 1985).
Daley, A., ed., The Mitterrand Era. (New York, New York UP, 1996).
De Gaulle, C., Memoirs of Hope. (London, Weidenfeld and Nicolson, 1971).
Derbyshire, I., Politics in France. From Giscard to Mitterrand. (Edinburgh, Chambers, 1990).
Deutsch, K.W., Politics and Government. How People Decide Their Fate. (Boston, Houghton Mifflin, 1980).
Documentation Française (DF), An Introduction to French Administration. (Paris, DF, 1996).
DF, The French Civil Service. (Paris, DF, 1998).
Dupeux, G., French Society 1789-1970. (London, Methuen, 1976).
Duverger, M., The French Political System. (Chicago, University of Chicago, 1974).
Duverger, M., Political Parties. (London, Methuen, 1964).
Dyson, K., The State Tradition in Western Europe. (Oxford, Robertson, 1980).
Easton, D., The Political System. (New York, Knopf, 1953; 1971).
Easton, D., A Systems Analysis of Political Life. (New York, Wiley, 1965).
Easton, D., A Framework for Political Analysis. (New York, 1965).
Ehrmann, H.W., Schain, M.A., Politics in France. (Boston, Little/Brown, 1992).
Einaudi, M., et al., Nationalization in France and Italy. (Ithaca, NY, Cornell UP, 1955).
Elgie, R., ed., The Changing French Political System. (London, Cass, 2000).
Evans, P.B., et al., eds., Bringing the State Back In. (Cambridge, CUP, 1985).
Feigenbaum, H.B., Henig, J.R., Shrinking the State: The Political Underpinnings of Privatization. (Cambridge, CUP, 1998).
Fields, A.B., Student Politics in France. (New York, Basic Books, 1970).
Finer, S.E., The History of Government from the Earliest Times. (Oxford, OUP, 1997).
Flockton, C., Kofman, E., France. (London, Chapman, 1989).
Flood, C, Bell, L., eds., Political Ideologies in Contemporary France. (London, Pinter, 1997).
Flower, J.E., ed., France Today. (London, Methuen, 1987).
Flynn, G., ed., Remaking the Hexagon. The New France in the New Europe. (Boulder, Westview, 1995).
Forse, M., et al., eds., Recent Social Trends in France, 1960-1990. (Montreal, McGill-Queen's UP, 1993).
Fraser, N., Bartky, S.L., eds., Revaluing French Feminism. (Bloomington, Indiana UP, 1992).
Fraser, W.R., Reforms and Restraints in Modern French Education. (London, Routledge, 1971).
Frears, J., Political Parties and Elections in the Fifth Republic. (London, Hurst, 1978).
Frears, J., France in the Giscard Presidency. (London, Allen & Unwin, 1981).
Frears, J., Parties and Voters in France. (London, Hurst, 1991).
Friedrich, C.J., Man and His Government. An Empirical Theory of Politics. (New York, McGraw-Hill, 1963).
Gaffney, J., The French Left and the Fifth Republic. The Discourse of Socialism and Communism. (London, Macmillan, 1989).
Gallie, D., In Search of the New Working Class. (Cambridge, CUP, 1978).
Giddens, A., The Third Way: The Renewal of Social Democracy. (Cambridge, Polity, 1998).
Gildea, R., France since 1945. (Oxford, OUP, 1996).
Girling, J., France, Political and Social Change. (London, Routledge, 1998).
Giscard d'Estaing, V., French Democracy. (London, Collins, 1977).
Gladden, E.N., A History of Public Administration. (London, Cass, 1972).
Godt, P., ed., Policy Making in France. (London, Pinter, 1989).
Goguel, F., France under the Fourth Republic. (Ithaca, Cornell UP, 1952).
Gordon, P.H., A Certain Idea of France. French Security Policy and the Gaullist Legacy. (Princeton, Princeton UP, 1993).
Gourevitch, P., Paris and the Provinces. The Politics of Local Government Reform in France. (London, Allen & Unwin, 1980).
Graham, B.D., Choice and Democratic Order: The French Socialist Party, 1937-1950. (Cambridge, CUP, 1994).
Grosser, A., French Foreign Policy under de Gaulle. (Boston, Little/Brown, 1967).
Guyomarch, A., Machin, H., Ritchie, E., France in the European Union. (New York, St. Martin's, 1998).
Hall, P., Hayward, J., Machin, H., Developments in French Politics. (London, Macmillan, 1994).
Halls, W.D., Education, Culture and Politics in Modern France. (Oxford, Pergamon, 1976).

Hamson, C.J., Executive Discretion and Judicial Control: An Aspect of the French Conseil d'État. (London, Stevens, 1954).
Hanley, D., Keeping Left? CERES and the French Socialist Party. (Manchester, Manchester UP, 1986).
Hanley, D., et al., Contemporary France. Politics and Society since 1945. (London, Routledge, 1984).
Harding, C., The Identity of European Law. Mapping Out the European Legal Space. (In: European Law Journal, pp.128-147, 2000).
Harrison, M.M., The Reluctant Ally: France and the Atlantic Security. (Baltimore, Johns Hopkins UP, 1981).
Hartley, A., Gaullism. The Rise and Fall of a Political Movement. (London, Routledge, 1972).
Hassenteufel, P., Marketization through the State. Health Insurance Reform in France. (In: Public Policy and Administration, 2001).
Hauss, C., The New Left in France. The Unified Socialist Party. (Westport, Greenwood, 1978).
Hayward, J., Governing France. The One and Indivisible Republic. (London, Norton, 1983).
Hayward, J., ed., De Gaulle to Mitterrand. (London, Hurst, 1993).
Hayward, J., Watson, M., eds., Planning, Politics and Public Policy: The British, French and Italian Experience. (Cambridge, CUP, 1975).
Hazareesingh, S., Political Traditions in Modern France. (Oxford, OUP, 1994).
Hewlett, N., Modern French Politics: Analysing Conflict and Consensus since 1945. (Cambridge, Polity, 1998).
Hirsch, A., The French New Left. An Intellectual History from Sartre to Gorz. (Boston, South End, 1981).
Hoffmann, S., ed., In Search of France. (New York, Harper and Row, 1963).
Hoffmann, S., Decline or Renewal? France since the 1930s. (New York, Viking Press, 1974).
Hoffmann, S., et al., France: Change and Tradition. (London, Gollancz, 1963).
Hollifield, J., Hall, P., eds., Searching for the New France. (London, Routledge, 1991).
Horne, A., Savage War of Peace: Algeria 1945-1962. (Harmondsworth, Penguin, 1979).
Horne, A., The French Army and Politics, 1870-1970. (New York, Longman, 1984).
Horovitz, I.L., Radicalism and the Revolt against Reason. The Social Theories of Georges Sorel. (London, Routledge, 1961).
Hume, D., An Enquiry concerning Human Understanding. (Oxford, Clarendon, 1739).
Imig, D., Tarrow, S., From Strike to Eurostrike. The Europeanisation of Social Movements and the Development of an Euro-Polity. (Cambridge, MA, Harvard UP, 1997).
Inglehart, R., Culture Shift. (Princeton, Princeton UP, 1990).
Ingraham, P.W., Romzek, B.S., eds., New Paradigms for Government: Issues for the Changing Public Service. (San Francisco, Jossey-Bass, 1994).
Irvine, W., The Boulanger Affair Reconsidered. Royalism, Boulangism and the Origins of the Radical Right in France. (New York, New York UP, 1988).
Irving, R.E.M., Christian Democracy in France. (London, Allen & Unwin, 1973).
Johnson, R.W., The Long March of the French Left. (London, Macmillan, 1988).
Jones, H.S., The French State in Question. Public Law and Political Argument in the Third Republic. (Cambridge, CUP, 1993).
Judt, T., Marxism and the French Left. Studies in Labour and Politics in France. (Oxford, OUP, 1986).
Kant, I., Political Writings. (Cambridge, CUP, 1991).
Keeler, J., The Politics of Neo-Corporatism in France. (Oxford, OUP, 1987).
Keeler, J.T.S., Schain, M.A., eds., Chirac's Challenge: Liberalization, Europeanization and Malaise. (New York, St.Martin's, 1996).
Kesselman, M., ed., The French Workers' Movement. (London, Allen & Unwin, 1984).
Kettl, D.F., The Global Public Management Revolution. (Washington DC, Brookings Institution, 2000).
Kley, D. van, ed., The French Idea of Freedom. The Old Regime and the Declaration of Rights of 1789. (Cambridge, CUP, 1997).
Klinck, D., The French Counter-Revolutionary Theorist, Louis de Bonald, 1754-1840. (New York, Lang, 1996).
Kohl, W.L., French Nuclear Diplomacy. (Princeton, Princeton UP, 1971).
Koldziej, E.A., French International Policy under de Gaulle and Pompidou. The Politics of Grandeur. (Ithaca, NY, Cornell UP, 1974).
Kriegel, A., The French Communists. Profile of a People. (Chicago, University of Chicago, 1972).
Kuisel, R., Capitalism and the State in Modern France. (Cambridge, CUP, 1979).
Kuisel, R., Seducing the French: The Dilemma of Americanization. (Berkeley, University of California Press, 1993).
Lacouture, J., De Gaulle. (New York, Norton, 1990/1992).
Lagroye, J., Wright, V., eds., Local Government in Britain and France. (London, Allen & Unwin, 1979).

Lamber, V., The Political Economy of France: From Pompidou to Mitterrand. (New York, Praeger, 1983).
Laqueur, W., ed., Fascism. (Harmondsworth, Penguin, 1979).
Larmour, P.J., The French Radical Party in the 1930s. (Stanford, Stanford UP, 1964).
Larkin, M., France since the Popular Front. Government and People, 1936-1986. (Oxford, Clarendon, 1988).
Lebovics, H., True France. The Wars over Cultural Identity, 1900-1945. (Ithaca, Cornell UP, 1992).
Levy, J.D., Tocqueville's Revenge: State, Society and Economy in Contemporary France. (Cambridge, MA, Harvard UP, 1993).
Light, P.C., The True Size of Government. (Washington DC, Brookings Institution, 1999).
Lipset, S.M., Marks, G., It Did'nt Happen Here. Why Socialism Failed in the United States. (New York, Norton, 2001).
Lord, G., The French Budgetary Process. (Berkeley, University of California Press, 1972).
Loughlin, J., Keating, M., eds., The Political Economy of Regionalism. (London, Cass, 1997).
Lucas, N.J.D., Energy in France. Planning, Politics and Policy. (London, Europa Publications, 1979).
Luhmann, N., Trust and Power. (Chichester, Wiley, 1979).
Luhmann, N., Political Theory in the Welfare State. (Berlin, De Gruyter, 1990).
Luhmann, N., Social Systems. (Stanford, Stanford UP, 1995).
Machin, H., The Prefect in French Public Administration. (London, Croom Helm, 1977).
Machin, H., Wright, V., eds., Economic Policy and Policy-Making under the Mitterrand Presidency, 1981-1984. (London, Pinter, 1985).
Macrae, D., Parliament, Parties and Society in France, 1946-1958. (New York, St.Martin's, 1967).
Macridis, R., French Politics in Transition. (Cambridge, CUP, 1975).
MacShane, D., François Mitterrand: A Political Odyssey. (London, Quartet, 1982).
Magrew, R., A History of the French Working Class. (London, Blackwell, 1992).
Marcus, J., The National Front and French Politics. (Basingstoke, Macmillan, 1995).
Marks, E., Courtivron, I., New French Feminisms. (Brighton, Harvester, 1985).
Martin, K., The Rise of French Liberal Thought. (Westport, Greenwood, 1980).
Marwick, A., The Sixties: Cultural Revolution in Britain, France, Italy and the United States, c.1958 – c.1974. (Oxford, OUP, 1998).
Marx, K., Engels, F., The Communist Manifesto. (London, Lawrence & Wishart, 1948).
Mazey, S., Newman, M., Mitterrand's France. (London, Croom Helm, 1987).
McArthur, J.H., Scott, B.R., Industrial Planning in France. (Cambridge, Harvard UP, 1969).
McCarthy, P., ed., The French Socialists in Power, 1981-1986. (New York, Greenwood, 1987).
McMillan, J., Dreyfus to De Gaulle: Politics and Society in France, 1889-1969. (London, Arnold, 1985).
McMillan, J., Twentieth Century France. (London, Arnold, 1992).
Mendl, W., Deterrence and Persuasion: French Nuclear Armament in the Context of National Policy, 1945-1969. (London, Faber, 1970).
Mendras, H., Cole, A., Social Change in Modern France. (Cambridge, CUP, 1991).
Mill, J.S., Considerations on Representative Government. (London, 1861; New York, Dutton, 1977).
Mill, J.S., Utilitarianism. (London, 1863).
Mitterrand, F., The Wheat and the Chaff: The Personal Diaries of the President of France, 1971-1978. (London, Weidenfeld and Nicolson, 1982).
Morris, P., French Politics Today. (Manchester, Manchester UP, 1995).
Moses, C., French Feminism in the Nineteenth Century. (Albany, NY, State University of New York Press, 1984).
Nugent, N., Lowe, D., eds., The Left in France. (London, Macmillan, 1982).
Parsons, T., The Social System. (New York, Free Press, 1951).
Paxton, R., Vichy France. Old Guard and New Order. (New York, Columbia UP, 1972).
Peters, B.G., The Future of Governing: Four Emerging Models. (Lawrence, University Press of Kansas, 1996).
Pickles, D., The Government and Politics of France. (London, Methuen, 1972).
Pickles, D., Problems of Contemporary French Politics. (London, Methuen, 1982).
Pierson, P., Dismantling the Welfare State? Reagan, Thatcher and the Politics of Retrenchment. (Cambridge, CUP, 1994).
Pollitt, C., Bouckaert, G., Public Management Reform. A Comparative Analysis. (Oxford, OUP, 2000).
Raadschelders, J.C.N., Government: A Public Administration Perspective. (Armonk, NY, Sharpe, 2003).
Remond, R., The Right Wing in France from 1815 to de Gaulle. (Philadelphia, University of Pennsylvania Press, 1966).
Rendel, M., The Administrative Functions of the Conseil d'Etat. (London, Weidenfeld and Nicolson, 1970).
Richardson, J., Policy Styles in Western Europe. (London, Allen & Unwin, 1982).

Ridley, F., Revolutionary Syndicalism in France. (Cambridge, CUP, 1970).
Ridley, F., Blondel, J., Public Administration in France. (London, Routledge, 1969).
Rioux, J.P., The Fourth Republic, 1944-1958. (Cambridge, CUP, 1987).
Ross, G., Workers and Communists in France. (Berkeley, Un. of California Press, 1981).
Ross, G., Hoffman, S., Malzbacher, S., eds., The Mitterrand Experiment. Continuity and Change in Modern France. (Cambridge, Polity, 1987).
Safran, W., The French Polity. (London, Longman, 1985; 1997).
Savas, E.S., Privatization and Public-Private Partnerships. (New York, Chatham House, 2000).
Scheinman, L., Atomic Energy Policy in France under the Fourth Republic. (Princeton, Princeton UP, 1965).
Schmidt, V.A., Democratising France. (Cambridge, CUP, 1991).
Schmidt, V.A., From State to Market? The Transformation of French Business and Government. (Cambridge, CUP, 1996).
Schmidt, V.A., The Changing Dynamics of State-Society Relations in the Fifth Republic. (In: West European Politics, pp.141-165, 1999).
Serfait, S., The Foreign Policies of the Left. (Boulder, Westview, 1979).
Shonfield, A., Modern Capitalism. The Changing Balance of Public and Private Power. (Oxford, OUP, 1965).
Siedentop, L., Democracy in Europe. (Oxford, OUP, 2000).
Simon, H., Administrative Behaviour. (New York, Macmillan, 1947).
Slater, M., Contemporary French Politics. (London, Macmillan, 1985).
Soucy, R., Fascism in France. (Berkeley, University of California Press, 1972).
Soucy, R., French Fascism: The First Wave, 1924-1933. (New Haven, Yale UP, 1986).
Stevens, A., The Government and Politics of France. (London, Macmillan, 1992; 1996).
Strayer, J.R., On the Medieval Origins of the Modern State. (Princeton, Princeton UP, 1970).
Strayer, J.R., Medieval Statecraft and the Perspectives of History. (Princeton, Princeton UP, 1970).
Suleiman, E., Politics, Power and Bureaucracy in France. (Princeton, Princeton UP, 1974).
Suleiman, E., Elites in French Society: The Politics of Survival. (Princeton, Princeton UP, 1978).
Tallet, F., Atkin, N., eds., Religion, Politics and Society in France since 1789. (London, Hambledon, 1991).
Tarr, F. de, The French Radical party from Herriot to Mendès-France. (Oxford, OUP, 1961).
Thompson, D., Democracy in France since 1870. (Oxford, OUP, 1969).
Tiersky, R., French Communism, 1920-1972. (New York, Columbia UP, 1974).
Tilly, C., ed., The Formation of National States in Western Europe. (Princeton, Princeton UP, 1975).
Tint, H., French Foreign Policy since the Second World War. (London, Weidenfeld and Nicolson, 1972).
Tocqueville, A. de, The Old Régime and the French Revolution (1856). (New York, Doubleday, 1955).
Tuppen, J., Chirac's France 1986-1988. (London, Macmillan, 1991).
Vaughan, M., et al., Social Change in France. (Oxford, Robertson, 1980).
Védrine, H., France in an Age of Globalization. (Washington, Brookings Institution, 2002).
Vinen, R., Bourgeois Politics in France, 1945-1951. (Cambridge, CUP, 1995).
Wadia, K., Williams, S., eds., France and Europe. (Wolverhampton, ASMCF, 1993).
Wallace-Hadrill, J.M., ed., France: Government and Society. (London, Methuen, 1970).
Ware, A., ed., Political Parties: Electoral Change and Structural Response. (Oxford, Blackwell, 1987).
Weber, E., Peasants into Frenchmen. The Modernisation of Rural France. (Stanford, Stanford UP, 1979).
Weber, E., My France. Politics, Culture, Myth. (Cambridge, MA, Belknap, 1991).
West European Politics (Review), The Changing French Political System. (October 1999).
White, P., Hollingsworth, K., Audit, Accountability and Government. (Oxford, Clarendon, 1999).
Williams, P., The French Parliament 1958-1967. (London, Allen & Unwin, 1968).
Williams, P., French Politicians and Elections, 1951-1969. (Cambridge, CUP, 1970).
Williams, P., Crisis and Compromise. Politics in the Fourth Republic. (London, Longmans, 1972).
Williams, P., Harrison, M., Politics and Society in de Gaulle's Republic. (London, Longmans, 1971).
Willis, F.R., The French Paradox. Understanding Contemporay France. (Stanford, Hoover Institution Press, 1982).
Wilner, A.R., The Spellbinders. Charismatic and Political Leadership. (New Haven, Yale UP, 1984).
Wilson, F.L., French Political Parties under the Fifth Republic. (New York, Praeger, 1982).
Wright, V., The Government and Politics of France. (London, Unwin Hyman, 1989).
Wright, V., The Fifth Republic: From the Droit de l'État to the État de droit? (In: West European Politics, pp.92-119, 1999).
Wright, V., ed., Conflict and Consensus in France. (London, Cass, 1979).
Wright, V., ed., Giscard and the Giscardians. (London, Allen & Unwin, 1983).
Wright, V., ed., Continuity and Change in France. (London, Allen & Unwin, 1984).

Zahariadis, N., Markets, States and Public Policy: Privatization in Britain and France. (Ann Arbor, University of Michigan Press, 1995).
Zeldin, T., The French. (London, Kodansha International, 1996).
Zysman, J., Political Strategies for Industrial Order. State, Market and Industry in France. (Berkeley, University of California Press, 1977).

# Part Four

# France in the International and Co-national Arena

# 7. International Relations: Military Management, Peace Management and Diplomacy

A national state is seen as an independent actor with competencies in a specific geographic territory. It is crucial that relations with other national states are dealt with. Of course, before the formation of national states there were already relations between public authorities in several areas. International relations have to be considered in a broad sense, including relations between national states, but also with non-governmental and international institutions. Even whole national societies, increasingly interconnected due to dynamic globalisation, have to be dealt with. In international relations, military management and peace management play a prominent role, as do all-encompassing activities in the sphere of diplomacy. Tacitus (55-118 AD) in "Historiae" wrote: "Nam neque quies gentium sine armis neque arma sine stipendiis neque stipendia sine tributis haberi queunt." Indeed, you can't have peace among peoples without armies, and no armies without paying them, and no paying of armies without taxes. International relations in the perspective of the 21st century have fundamentally different characteristics from earlier historical periods, but earlier periods (ideas, practices) have their impact upon contemporary and future international relations. An imposing fact is the development of demography. Paul Ehrlich in "The Population Bomb" (1971) predicted a Malthusian catastrophe. Some forecasts for world population had apocalyptic dimensions: 7 billion in 2000, 20 billion in 2050, and 55 billion in 2100. The UNO has lowered its forecasts for world population in the 21st century: 8 billion in 2025; 11 billion in 2100. While it took 120 years to grow from 1 to 2 billion world citizens, world population grew from 5 billion in 1987 to 6 billion in 1999. Statistics conclude that in 1999 world population reached 6,000,000,000 world citizens for the first time in history. Projections give the following data about the future expected population (Worldwatch Institute). China 1.25 billion in 1999, and 1.56 billion in 2025. India 0.987 billion in 1999, and 1.41 billion in 2025. The European Union (15 Member-States) 0.376 billion in 1999, and 0.380 billion in 2025. The United States 0.272 billion in 1999 and 0.335 billion in 2025. Geopolitical effects of demographic developments are important. One example: three neighbouring countries China, India and Pakistan (0.146 billion in 1999, and 0.224 billion in 2025) are all nuclear powers. Adequate Public Management of Society for this growing population will be one of the world's most crucial tasks.

## 7.1. Military management and peace management

*7.1.1 War and peace as institutions. French historical experiences*

It is amazing that military management is often underexposed in most studies about politics, public management and public policy, apart from super-specialised analyses. The more so, as this field has also been very fertile in producing innovative ideas, methods and techniques for civilian public management and private management. There are many examples where military models are used for analysing and solving problems of policy and administration. From the outset it must be recognised that military management is a very special part of the whole of management (sectoral logic, specific rationalities). Armed forces are not confronted with a market, customers or users of the "product defence" (the country as customer). War is their "market", while the enemy could be seen as a customer. Armed forces have a special task to guarantee the security of their country, and so they fulfil a distinctive public management task. Of course, there have often been private armies in historical times, and worldwide there are now private armies (and terrorist fighting networks). Generally spoken, armies in modern countries are part of public management. There is debate about the privatisation of (parts of) the armed forces, or some unit (catering, etc.). The main point is that armed forces in representative democracies are normally placed under the control of civilian public authorities within a legal framework. Armed forces, disposing of a terrible war-machine, do their job under the umbrella of the public authorities' responsibility for the legitimised use of violence. The military machine, especially in modern times with biological, chemical and nuclear weapons and sophisticated electronics for accurate long-distance rocket-systems, is very complex (Demchak, 1991). Considering the negative effects of the use of armed forces, one might conclude that warfare and military terrorism should be forbidden and eliminated (Levene/Roberts, 1999). On the basis of historical evidence, this ideal seems to be unattainable for mankind. If one wants to have peace, readiness for warfare seem to be necessary: "Si vis pacem para bellum!" So there is a task for public authorities, ordering national security from the armed forces operating normally within a legal framework. Even in peacetime they have to be on the alert for possible conflict. This fighting mission largely dictates the specific characteristics of armed forces. Military management can be seen as part of peace management (peacekeeping operations, etc.), but peace management encompasses more. A crucial task of public authorities is to do all possible in co-operation with public authorities of other nations and international organisations (and peace-movements, non-governmental organisations etc.) to maintain peace and prevent warfare (organised violence between groups of people). War is a complex, multi-faceted and puzzling phenomenon.

During the whole memorable history of mankind, war has been a nasty fact of life. To come to terms with the horrors of war and incomprehensible riddles of human beings killing each other massively (Pincus, 2001) one must distinguish several characteristics and levels of relations between human beings. In the case of aggression, one can differentiate individual behaviour, relations between individuals, interactions, groups, nations and societies. Communications and activities between human beings are influenced by socio-psychological factors and socio-cultural dimensions like belief-systems, values, norms, roles, symbols, codes and institutions. In interactions, historical dimensions and expectations about future circumstances are crucial factors. Several factors can predispose for aggression, but the act of aggression is also dependent on choices. Aggression between groups can be induced by (perceived) serious, structural problems, and by objectively trivial immediate causes. Inter-group relations are part of social psychology (Gilbert c.s., 1998). Individuals with unique personalities have their personal identity and social identity (members of one or more emotionally significant groups). In-group co-operation is furthered by contributing to the group, so gaining the respect of others, while promoting self-esteem. Co-operation of individuals is necessary for organised aggression between groups.

Part of the psychological process of aggression between groups is the spread of negative characteristics of the out-group as object of aggression. Specific leadership and management are needed in situations of crisis, as preparation for war and operational fighting are the order of the day and night. The complexity of warfare has increased considerably since the tribal conflicts in former times as opposed to more recent experiences of war like the Second World War (1940-1945), Gulf War (1990-1991), NATO intervention in Kosovo (1999), US fighting in Afghanistan (2001) and ongoing warlike circumstances in several regions of the globe. It is argued that war has become an institution (Hinde, 1991). Tribal conflicts do still play their role even in contemporary society, as the worldwide effects of recent fighting in Afghanistan shows (Alexander/Swetnam, 2001; Bodansky, 2001). Institutionalised war is qualified with some criteria. It involves conflict between complex societies, consisting of many groups. Interactions and negotiations are realised by complex bureaucracies. Furthering the integration of groups at each side of conflicting partners is a demanding challenge for leadership. Political, administrative and military leaders at every level have to be up to the task, for the chain of activities needed for effective management of warfare is as strong as the weakest link. Warfare requires extended division of labour and role differentiation, so war is an institution with a large number of constituent roles: politicians, civil public functionaries, generals, officers, soldiers, and all kinds of professionals (doctors, nurses, etc.). It is obvious that analyses about the causes of war have to deal with many aspects, including societal, socio-cultural, economic, social-psychological factors. "Rational appraisal, historical knowledge, and personal experience all testify to the horror of war, yet wars continue to happen. For reasons, which must surely be sought, wars remain an acceptable way of solving conflicts. This must be a result of powerful forces that support the institution of war." (Hinde, 1997).

Modern warfare is unthinkable without structured institutions. A popular slogan to denote the core-business of modern warfare is the military-industrial-scientific complex. If war is an institution, peace is an institution also. War is so imposing that, to a great extent, history is taught as the history of wars, so education for peace is crucial (Hinde/Parry, 1989), and building up institutions for peace management as well (peace as institution). Research to organise knowledge about causes, methods and consequences of warfare remains an important issue. Belief-systems play a crucial role in attitudes to warfare (Hinde/Watson, 1995). The Old Testament is largely a story about bloody strife in tribal conflicts. Nearly all religions talked peace, while often in fact contributing to an "us versus them" attitude. There were even "holy wars", such as the Muslim holy warfare and Christian crusades. Early Christians were largely pacifists, but, after the Roman Emperor Constantine was converted to Christianity, Christians partly profiled themselves as militarists from the fourth century onwards. Augustine tried to overcome this contradiction between a faith-based belief in non-violence and eventual participation in fighting with his concept of the "just war". A war was seen as just, if it was necessary to maintain or restore earthly justice and to revenge injury. This just war concept was used to legitimise wars. Its criteria were reinterpreted and adapted to circumstances (Teichman, 1986). Atheistic societies such as the USSR sanctified the communist system to the point where it effectively took the place of religion in a mass-psychological sense. Apart from individuals who are driven by religious zeal or similarly based fanaticism, the question is: why are so many individuals prepared to endure the horrors of warfare? One important way to make millions disposed to participate in warfare was the invention of patriotism and nationalism, in combination with some kind of enemy, real or imaginary (X as the Devil). A number of factors play a role in national consciousness of warfare. The people living in France generally have a high consciousness of what warfare means, due to experiences on French soil in recent times (Franco-Prussian War, two World Wars), and their historical consciousness of past centuries filled with experiences of warfare. French history of warfare and conceptualisation about warfare have a paradigmatic significance and the French have a specific contribution to make to the conceptualisation of military management (Carrias, 1960). An all-round picture of French military practices and concepts cannot be given, but only a sketch. With due respect for historical dimensions, and with the accent on the 20th century and the Fifth Republic (Gregory, 2000).

France has had experience of military activities through the millennia (Greigueuil, 1999). De Gaulle wrote in his "La France et son Armée" (1938, p.1): "France was made with the sword. The civilisation of the Romans brought their weapons also. Thanks to Clovis our fatherland confirmed its identity after the fall of the Roman Empire." Experiences go back to the Gallo-Roman period, Middle Ages and after. During the Hundred Years War (1328-1453) between France and England, which started because English King Edward III claimed the French throne, the French had about 10,000 soldiers out of a population of less than 20 million inhabitants. Around the year 1500, Europe, with some 50-55 million inhabitants, was an enfeebled area, invaded by various tribal hordes. At that time, China (100-130 million inhabitants) seemed to have a far better chance of playing a leading role in the world than Europe. The Ming-dynasty (1368-1644) united the Chinese Empire with a high civilisation. In 1453, Constantinople was in the hands of the Turks who, at the end of the 15th century, had conquered Greece, Bosnia, Albania and an important part of the Balkans. By about 1520, Turks stood at the gates of Budapest and Vienna, and the Ottoman Empire of the Turks during the first half of the 16th century encompassed Egypt, Syria, Arabia, Mesopotamia, Tripoli and a part of Hungary. Unlike the Chinese and Ottoman Empires, Europe was divided up into many kingdoms, principalities and city-states. The Muslim world was in dynamic development, due to the activities of Turks and Persians controlling old trading routes to China, while Muslims also had control of India. Turks were formidable opponents in the maritime sphere until their defeat at Lepanto on 7 October 1571. The Holy Roman Empire (962-1806) survived the Turkish siege of Vienna (1529 and again in 1683). The Ottoman Empire was weakened (military rebellions, religious conflicts between Sunnites and Shi'ites), losing its grip upon its extensive territory (Cook, 1976; Kortepeter, 1973).

The "European Miracle" has been analysed time and again (Jones, 1981; Kennedy, 1987; McNeill, 1967; Parry, 1966). Thanks to economic and technological developments, Western Europe began to play a dominant role in the world. The most probable explanation is that this was the result of a combination of factors such as economic and intellectual freedom, political-military pluralism and the use of the geographical situation. Western Europe was politically fragmented, although Christian faith and culture had a wide range and Charlemagne (768-814) realised centralised administration for a short period. Geographical variety (valleys, mountains, rivers, and seas) furthered decentralisation. Geographical circumstances fostered trade relations over land and water, with permanent challenges to improve techniques for transport, communications etc. Sea transport over long distances in heavy seas was a new challenge. Opening up of local closed economies to a wider market for trading surpluses was the result of activities by many individuals, while public authorities mostly had no real influence in this field. Gradually many independent power-centres developed in cities, city-states and states. The Spanish-Austrian Habsburg Empire was a prominent example of centralised public management on the European continent. In the period following 1450 the birth of national states or nation-states in Europe was closely related to their potency to survive by means of warfare to gain or maintain control of territory within militarily recognised frontiers. It is evident that military organisation was crucial for the formation and continuation of a political community with a regime and public authorities. Stability of political community and public authorities depended on the way armed forces were organised (paid or unpaid; permanent or ad hoc; nationals and/or foreigners). The structure of armed forces determined largely how and in what measure public authorities could extract resources from the people (taxation). Resources determined military potency. Finer (1997, pp. 15-16) called this interdependency the "coercion-extraction cycle". He observed that warfare (expenditures for armed forces) was generally the most important drain upon the resources of public authorities in history. He saw maintenance of military forces, particularly standing military forces, as the most important reason for the emergence of civil bureaucracy. Distribution of military power between social strata was related with technology of weapons (bronze weapons, cavalry).

For nomadic hordes and city-states, it was normal that all able-bodied men, mostly with their own weapons, helped in eventual military activities. The more lethal the weapons, the more costly they tended to be, so distribution of power tended to follow distribution of wealth. This was especially the case in feudal times and in the Middle Ages with a prominent role for aristocratic notables-in-arms ("baron-management"). Mail-clad cavalry prevailed, so military nobility could dominate politically as well. Long after military feudalism was withering away, "baron-management" played a role. In France, this was the case until after the "Fronde" (1648-1653). Circumstances changed when the population was disarmed and armed forces became a professionalised permanent public organisation. This monopolisation of weaponry threatened the power position of public authorities however, armed forces can sometimes be more loyal to their military leaders than to civil public authorities. It is possible for armed forces to have a more or less permanent hold over civil public authorities with their potent threat to take over. Civil-military relations are one of the trickiest problems in the sphere of Public Management of Society. The ever rising costs of warfare in expensive wars during the 14th century and after contributed to the tradition of convening assemblies of political elites as representatives of taxpayers, so the idea of representation was invented. As these assemblies did not enable rulers to extort the financial means they required, coercion was needed also. This contributed to the development of fiscal absolutism for which armed forces were a necessary condition. In France, King Louis VII during the traumatic Hundred Years War (1338-1453) levied taxes without asking approval of anybody. With this money, he created the first standing army in post-Roman Europe: the "Compagnies d'Ordonnance". French fiscal absolutism accompanied repressive activities of the standing army. Between the 15th and the 17th century, national states extended centralised administration, supported by a national army and a bureaucratic apparatus (Shennan, 1974; Tilly, 1975). In the 16th century, warfare was a test to see if a national state was viable, also financially, as the costs of warfare were astronomically high. The period 1450-1650 made it obvious that warfare was the basis for formation of national states (Kennedy, 1989). In this process, the monopolisation of military power by the state was crucial. Monarchs did everything to get finances for warfare, against opposition to taxation and soldiers claiming higher payments.

In 1557 the French monarchy was bankrupt because of the cost of warfare. Rivalry between several power-centres furthered a competitive arena. This rivalry got an extra dimension after Martin Luther, in 1517, precipitated the Reformation, ending the unity of Christendom. Habsburg monarchs and Spanish kings were militant adherents of Catholicism (Koenigsberger, 1971; Mamatey, 1978). Spaniards only managed to end the Dutch rebellion, after the Eighty Years War (1568-1648), with the Treaty of Munster (1648). Military conflicts of Habsburgers with several opposing coalitions in the Thirty Years War (1618-1648) were concluded with the Treaty of Westphalia. Whoever had the financial means could buy the newest military technologies. Competition between producers of weapons fostered an innovative climate in which the quality and efficacy of weapons was constantly improved. France had strong neighbours: Spain in the South and, along the northeast borders, the Holy Roman Empire (including Northern Italy, Switzerland, Germany, Low Countries). French kings, feeling encirclement by the Habsburg Vienna-Madrid axis, used mercenary armies to expand and control their territory. Habsburgers seemed to get control of Western Europe, but this was prevented by a coalition of States. Only after the Peace of the Pyrenees (1659) did Spain recognise its defeat. Political pluralism was accepted, no one of the greater powers was able to get absolute hegemony. France with 16 million inhabitants succeeded Spain as the most important military power (an army of 100,000 men). European hegemony worldwide developed after 1500. Well-armed ships which could cover long distances played a crucial role. Portugal (Boxer, 1969; Magalhaes-Godinho, 1969) and Spain (Gibson, 1966) benefited from conquered areas in South-America (gold and silver) and elsewhere. Science and technology had less hindrances in Europe than elsewhere to break through (Mendelsohn, 1976), and in the 17th century, the power-balance shifted from the Ottoman and Chinese Empires to Europe.

From 1500, the Spanish-Austrian Habsburg Dynasty was dominant on the European continent for 150 years, but Habsburgers lastly had an overloaded military superstructure and a weak economic infrastructure. In the period 1660-1815, there were five greater powers: France, England, Russia, Austria and Prussia. In changing coalitions they dominated warfare and diplomacy in Europe. England became the leading seafaring nation, and could maintain this position despite losing its colonies in North America in the American War of Independence (1775-1783). Armies and fleets were functioning permanently, and there was a high frequency of warfare (Childs, 1982). Between 1689 and 1815 France had to fight seven wars against its traditional rival, England. The economic basis of States and their capacity to raise the needed finances were crucial, especially for wars of attrition (Webber/Wildavsky, 1986). Since the Middle Ages, France had not been able to build up an adequate system of public finances. Gathering of revenues was farmed out to municipalities, provinces, clergy, and private tax farms, who demanded high commissions for this, and loans meant paying formidable interest-rates. The French monarchy, spending lavishly and often not able to pay its debts, had to pay heavy risk-premiums (especially in times of frequent warfare) because of its notoriously bad solvency, but France was, through the centuries, the most prominent military power on the European continent. Louis XIV (1667-1713), ruling over some 23 million inhabitants, had some 300,000 soldiers. France had several costly wars: Nine Years War (1688-1697); Spanish War of Succession (1701-1713); Austrian War of Succession (1740-1748); and the Seven Years War (1756-1763), which forced France to give up Canada and Nova Scotia. When the French monarchy supported the American colonists in their rebellious war against Great Britain, this caused, combined with the luxury of the court, the actual bankruptcy of France. Minister Calonne came up with proposals for financial reforms. These were rejected, as they would abolish privileges for the aristocracy. The French monarch convoked the "États Généraux" in 1789 (for the first time since 1614) with the intention to raise taxes. The meeting with the "États Généraux" (clergy, aristocracy, third order) was the prelude for the historic chain of events which culminated in the French Revolution exploding the Ancien Régime.

One would have expected this momentous event to hamper France's ability to organise warfare for a long period, but it was a relatively short time before French military adventures started again. In 1792, it was the First Coalition War (1792-1797) against Prussia and Austria, followed in 1793 against England, Spain and Holland. Bonaparte started his campaign in Italy (1796-1797) and Egypt (1798-1799), and then came the Second Coalition War (1799-1801). After its defeat, Austria accepted the conditions of the Treaty of Lunéville (1801) and Bonaparte concluded the Treaty of Amiens (1802) with England but war soon started again with the Third Coalition War (1805) and the Fourth Coalition War (1806-1807), and eventually the Fifth Coalition War (1809) against England and Austria. Napoleon Bonaparte, at the beginning of the 19th century, had command of more than one million soldiers. France had 25 million inhabitants in 1789. Due to the annexation of countries and territories, the number of French inhabitants in 1810 had risen to about 44 million. In 1812 Napoleon began his stupid military attack on Russia, which cost the deaths of some 270,000 soldiers and 200,000 prisoners. Napoleon then had to fight the Sixth Coalition War (1812-1814), and after losing the battle of Leipzig (1813) he was exiled to Elba (1814). Napoleon managed to escape and, during the Hundred Days Regime,

Emperor Napoleon could rule again. In the Seventh Coalition War (1815) against Russia, England, Prussia and Austria, Napoleon was finally defeated in 1815 at Waterloo (Lachouque, 1972). The Treaty of Paris (1815) brought France geographically back to its 1789 situation (Barnett, 1978; Chandler, 1966; Glover, 1979). The enormous loss of lives and material damage had won France no expansion of territory at all. Costs of warfare abroad were unloaded on countries where wars raged (Bergeron, 1981; Dowd, 1971; Lefebvre, 1969).

At the Congress of Vienna (1815), the European powers defined their relations after the defeat of Napoleon (Nicolson, 1946). The notion of territorial sovereignty, in international law, still recognised today, was defined then. Metternich (Austria), Wellington and Castleraegh (England), Hardenberg and Von Humboldt (Prussia), Nesselrode (Russia) and Talleyrand (France) were the representatives of the five powers. Following the domination of one State (France) the classic power-balance was restored (Gulick, 1967), but England was a superior seafaring power. England, Russia, Prussia and Austria did their best to place France under custody in the Metternich-system. Metternich used "European concert" as a metaphor for the intended co-operation between European nation-states. Since the end of the 18th century, England, favoured by its geographical situation, had gained a growing advantage from the Industrial Revolution. England could enlarge its world power militarily, industrially and commercially in a stable international climate. European States were competing with each other in their hunt for colonial territories. In the first half century after 1815, France (larger population, higher national income, large army and fleet) had the chance to surpass Prussia or the Habsburg Empire (Clough, 1939; Kemp, 1971), but other powers were allergic to French attempts to acquire hegemony over Europe (Kennedy, 1989). The industrial revolution promoted the economies of England and Prussia more than the economy in protectionist France (Cameron, 1971; Caron, 1979; Rowley, 1982). In the period 1815-1914, there were no long coalition-wars, the prevailing strategic equilibrium was maintained by the "European Concert" but in this period there was warfare: Crimean War (1853-1856); French-Austrian War (1859); wars about the unity of Germany; and the Franco-Prussian War (1870-1871), during which Napoleon III deployed about 2 million military men. After 1815 Russia (with an army of 800,000 men) was seen as an effective bulwark against eventual revolutionary and nationalistic movements which could change the territorial status quo (Bridge/Bullen, 1980; Seton-Watson, 1967). In the Crimean War between Russia and the coalition (France, England, Turkey), Russia was militarily debilitated. Napoleon III, dazzled by the French performance, was too self-confident about French military potency. He recklessly started a war against rival Prussia when the French army was not adequately prepared. After the second half of the 19th century, economics and technology in the industrial revolution began to weigh decisively in the military power-balance (Henderson, 1967; Kemp, 1969; Landes, 1969; Milward/Saul, 1973; Pollard, 1981; Trebilcock, 1981).

In the 19th century, the relationship between fiscal absolutism and standing armies changed markedly, in Europe first and later elsewhere. This was due to the invention of the ideology of nationalism. Individuals were prepared to fight and die in the name of their nation, on a scale unknown so far. People were disposed to pay taxes for warfare. This idea of nationalism was quite an invention, as coercion could be substantially diminished. The "Deutsche Zollverein", the German Common Market, had functioned since 1830 with Prussia as unchallenged leader of the 39 German States. The Prussian military revolution had, since 1860, caused a break in the power-balance between Prussia and France (Pflanze, 1963). Kaiser Wilhelm I (1861-1888) and his Premier Bismarck (1862-1890) introduced conscription for 3 years (later 4 years for reservists). Von Moltke reorganised armed forces with military professionalism. After beating the Austrians in 1866, the Prussians, with their superior organisation, defeated the French rapidly in 1870 (Howard, 1981). During the two decades following 1870, the centre of diplomacy shifted to the capital of the Second German Reich (1871-1918), the Berlin of Bismarck (Calleo, 1978). Shocked by the defeat against Germany, the French began to study German methods (Mitchell, 1979;1984). Military strategists thought that, with technologically advanced means, wars would be shorter ("Blitzkrieg") and different from the warfare of the 18th century. For France, Germany was the real enemy. England was also an opponent, but of a different character. France and England were especially rivals in the hunt for colonial territories. Since the English occupation of Egypt (1882), both countries had tried to get maritime control of the Mediterranean. There were several Franco-English conflicts: Congo (1884-1885); West Africa (1880-1900); Siam (1893); Nile-valley (1898). France expanded its colonies substantially between 1871 and 1900. It became the second colonial power after Great-Britain (Betts, 1978; Brunschwig, 1966; Ganiage, 1968; Girardet, 1968). The Habsburg Empire was a countervailing power against Russia and Prussia (Albrecht-Carrié, 1965; Bridge/Bullen, 1980).

The Habsburg Empire couldn't maintain the status quo, it collapsed, with decisive effects for the European power equilibrium, as proven in the First World War (1914-1918). At the start of the 20th century, the international system became less stable. The Europe-centric world-system, prevailing for three centuries, had changed, inter alia because of differences in economic growth and industrial capacity between States. New powers came to the fore: United States and Russia. At the end of the 19th century, the diplomatic world-centre seemed to be in the triangle London-Paris-Berlin. Since 1892 the European powers had re-valued their diplomatic representation in Washington by making them embassies. France organised its diplomacy shrewdly, having realised substantial progress with Delcassé, Minister of foreign affairs, and his diplomatic staff (Andrew, 1968). Relations with Russia were intensified, despite German obstruction. Alliance-diplomacy was a hectic and dynamic process. To form a countervailing power against Russia, Bismarck made an alliance with Austria-Hungary (1879). This obliged Bismarck to support Austria-Hungary if Russia should attack its territories. With a German-Italian Treaty (1882), Germany promised to support Italy, if attacked by France. Later France would loosen this "Triple Alliance" (Germany-Austria-Italy). In 1883, Germany, Austria and Romania had a secret alliance, to help Romania in the event of a Russian invasion. In 1897 Austria and Russia agreed to freeze the territorial situation in the Balkans. France and Russia felt isolated. This brought a French-Russian alliance in 1897 (Kennan, 1984). In the Russian-Japanese War (1904) due to conflicts over Manchuria and Korea, England and France were neutral.

*7.1.2 French position as dominant power lost in the First World War*

In 1904, the Franco-British "Entente Cordiale" was formed. England recognised that French security was of interest to England also, especially since Russia was weakened after the Russian-Japanese War (1904-1905). Russia could not be an adequate countervailing power against rising German militarism. After the Treaty of Algeciras (1906), Germans started provocations about Morocco again in the Agadir-crisis (1911). England supported the French. In Germany and France strong nationalistic movements arose. In November 1912, the English-French Fleet Treaty was signed. When Austria-Hungary annexed Bosnia-Herzegovina, this aroused the fury of Russia in the Balkans Crisis (1908-1909). Germany said that Russia had to accept this, otherwise it had to face the consequences (Lieven, 1983). Russia drew in its horns, but prepared itself for a military confrontation. Italy invaded Turkey (1911-1912) and conquered Tripoli. The Balkan Wars (1912-1913) broke out, which routed the Turks from Albania and Macedonia. Now that the Ottoman Empire was expelled from Europe, there was a conflict about the spoils. The rise of Serbia at the cost of Turkey and Bulgaria caused panic in Austria. The growing influence of Germany in

Turkish territories meant Russia was on the alert. The murder of Franz Ferdinand, Austrian successor to the throne, and his wife by a Serbian nationalist on 28 June 1914, put the spark to the tinder. This event brought a growing number of States into armed conflict with each other, causing the First World War (1914-1918). Austria made war on Serbia, Russia supported Serbia. This made Germany accelerate its "Schlieffen Plan" (Ritter, 1958): an invasion via neutral Belgium. So France and England were involved in the First World War (Steiner, 1977). In November 1914, Turkey joined the Germans. France prepared itself for a military confrontation in Alsace-Lorraine with the "Plan XVII" (Kennedy, 1979; Miller, 1985). It was thought that it would be a short war, but the military alliances made it a long drama.

France as a power had interests in all five continents of the world. Its foreign policy had as its primary target security (with regard to Germany) and expansion of its colonial empire. Both dominated French economic policy. Delcassé, foreign minister (June 1898/June 1905), laid the foundations for French foreign policy. His "grande politique" meant the build-up of a diplomatic system to make allies against Germany, which had realised a military encirclement of France since Bismarck. First came an alliance with Russia. A secret arrangement of 1891 was followed by a military convention (August 1892), ratified by the Russians in December 1893 and in January 1894 by the French. If France were attacked by German troops, Russia would help with 800,000 men. If Russia were to be attacked by Germany, French would help with 1,300,000 men. Even a partial military mobilisation by one of the Triple Alliance since 1882 (Germany, Austria-Hungary, Italy) would trigger a general mobilisation in France and Russia. Relations between France and Great-Britain were stressed, especially since the Fashoda-incident (1898), when French troops under Marchand had a military confrontation with British troops under Kitchener on the High-Nile. Delcassé decided to withdraw. He intensified attempts to have cordial relations with Great Britain. This produced the "Entente Cordiale" (April 1904). He tried to peel off Italy from the Triple Alliance. A customs war between France and Italy came to an end with a secret convention (December 1900) in which France promised not to hinder Italian interventions in Tripoli., and a further secret convention (June 1902) guaranteed for France that Italy would be neutral in the event of war between France and Germany. A German provocation over the Moroccan question forced Delcassé, who had not consulted Germany about French interventions in Morocco to make it a protectorate, to withdraw in 1905. Kaiser Wilhelm II was provocatively present at the end of March 1905 in Tanger, supporting the sovereignty of the Moroccan sultan and claiming the right of the Reich to expand its colonial possessions. Repeated rebellions against the sultan formed a pretext for French troops to intervene. After an international conference of Algeciras (January 1906), a convention between France and Germany of February 1909 recognised the specific position of France in Morocco. On 21 May 1911, France went further than the Algeciras convention allowed. Germany reacted. On 1 July 1911, the German submarine Panther was in Agadir (Allain, 1976): the second Moroccan crisis. France and Germany made an arrangement (4 November 1911). Germany would accept French activities in Morocco and in turn could occupy a part of the French Congo. War was averted, but the arms race was intensified.

"Germanophobie" (fear of Germans) had been strong since 1871. There was a feeling of revenge in the air when events gave an indication of German aggressiveness. Tensions in Alsace caused demonstrations claiming the "souvenir français". The real centre of tensions was elsewhere though. France had interests in Serbia and Romania, its ally Russia was extending its influence in the Balkans. Here three crises caused tensions. In October 1908, Austria-Hungary annexed Bosnia-Herzegovina, "provisionally" administered by the Double-monarchy since 1878. Russia asked France to support Serbia; France refused ('no vital interest of Russia"), a bitter pill for Russia. In the following Balkan crises of 1912 and 1913, France had to determine its position again. In the first, the Ottoman Empire was opposed to the Balkan League (Bulgaria, Greece, Montenegro, Serbia) supported by Russia. In the nick of time a general war was prevented by the diplomatic actions of Great Britain. In June 1913, there was a "Balkan war" about the division of territories of the Ottoman Empire between Bulgaria and other countries. France and Germany had to decide whether they would interfere, so causing a European war, or accept the crumbling of their alliances. They did not interfere. Then all of a sudden Austrian Archduke Franz-Ferdinand was murdered on 28 June 1914 by a Bosnian nationalist in Serajewo. Austria claimed that its functionaries could investigate the case on Serbian soil to determine the responsibility of the authorities in Belgrade. When this claim was refused, Austria declared war on Serbia on 28 July 1914. Russia decided on a general mobilisation on 30 July 1914, while on the same day, the French President Poincaré and Premier Viviani disembarked at Dunkirk, back from their visit to Russia. On 31 July 1914, Germany sent Russia and France an ultimatum. France, mobilising on 1 August 1914, did not answer. Germany mobilised on 1 August 1914 and declared war on Russia. On 2 August 1914, Germany demanded free passage for its troops through Belgium. On 3 August 1914, Germany started operations against France. Great Britain supported Belgium after the German occupation of this country and on 4 August 1914 Great Britain declared war on Germany. France was drawn into this war. France wanted to be loyal; pacifists were not strong enough (Becker, 1977). The First World War cost France 1,300,000 men, huge economic losses and its position as dominant European power.

In France, the "Parti Socialiste" had made the fight against war their highest priority. Antimilitarism was part of the Amiens program of the CGT, adopted in 1906. Government had prepared for a possible war situation by, among other things, making a list ("carnet B") of all possible opponents and revolutionaries, in order to incarcerate them all and so prevent agitation. On 29 July 1914, Jaurès was present at the meeting of the International Socialist Bureau in Brussels to discuss possible measures to prevent war. Nationalist Raoul Villain then murdered Jaurès on 31 July 1914. Workers were practically unanimous in their support of national defence, so "Carnet B" was not implemented. On 4 August 1914, President Poincaré organised the "Défense Nationale" (Keiger, 1997). He launched the "Union sacrée". On 26 August 1914, support of Socialists for government was made explicit when two Socialist ministers entered government: Guesde and Sembat. It was thought that war would take several weeks. Just before war broke out, the dominant military conception was that France would have a rapid victory after massive attacks in a mobile war. The attack in Lorraine failed. In the second half of August 1914 France lost the "fight at the boundaries", while Germans implemented the Schlieffen Plan, bringing German troops through Belgium and penetrating France from the north (Keiger, 1983). As Joffre ordered his troops to withdraw, to prevent encirclement, German troops penetrated French soil more easily than expected. This made the German command decide to send troops from the northern part of France to Prussia where the German army was in trouble under Russian attacks. From 30 August 1914 on, Germans bombed Paris. Government left Paris for Bordeaux. on 3 September 1914. French and British troops launched a counterattack at the battle of the Marne (6-13 September 1914) over a front of 250 kilometres. When no army was able to gain superiority (battle of the Somme, of Arras, in Flanders), the race to the sea was started from half September to half November 1914. So on 15 November 1914, the front was consolidated over 750 kilometres, from the Swiss boundary to the North Sea.

When the First World War broke out, France had an army of 4 million men (a population of 40 million inhabitants). France had enlarged its armed forces (80 divisions) by conscription. Germany had more troops (100 divisions) and better weapons. The French supreme command had repeatedly demanded reinforcement of its armed forces, but in vain (Mitchell, 1984). The First World War surprised French military leadership with their largely obsolete conceptions; in 1914 there was still excessive confidence in light infantry.

In the first half of the 20th century, France was seriously handicapped by its weakly developed industrialisation. It had a rigid protectionist policy, not favourable for the development of industry and the industrial capacity of France was only 40% of that of Germany (Trebilcock, 1981). The population of France grew in the period 1890-1914 by about one million, the German population grew by 18 million. French leadership was convinced that it would be a short war: the short-war illusion (Farrar, 1973). Losses of human lives and material damages were immense, but the decisive blow did not come during the first years. It was necessary to organise a totally different concept, because the two opposing armies had a long stalemate. Stationary warfare (1915-1917), with stubborn defence of occupied territories by fortified trenches, required improvised measures on both sides. During the trench-warfare, several miscarried and bloody attempts were organised to break the front. This cost the French about 350,000 men in 1915, and the German attack at Verdun in February 1916 cost some 700,000 men (from both sides). In July 1916, Joffre launched a heavy offensive at the Somme, which lasted until November 1916, and cost the French 200,000, the British 420,000, and the Germans 500,000 men. The target seemed to be to outdo one's own losses by enemy's losses, and to win by a war of attrition. From the summer of 1916, Hindenburg was German supreme commander. In December 1916 Nivelle succeeded Joffre. Nivelle did not believe in a war of attrition. From 16 April 1917 he organised a massive attack with 30 divisions. This attack failed within some hours, with 800,000 losses for the Allies. After three and a half years of war, no military solution seemed possible. Pétain succeeded Nivelle on 16 May 1917. In 4 May 1917 mutinies began to undermine morale. The red flag was used in demonstrations and the Internationale was sung. Generals thought this was part of a revolutionary conspiracy, organised by Germany to upset the French army. Pétain decided on 19 May 1917 to abandon the massive attacks. The United States joined the Allies against Germany in April 1917.

One setback was the Russian Revolution of 1917. In Tsarist Russia dissatisfaction about bad living conditions for the masses was a fertile soil for the Russian Revolution, which broke out in 1917, bringing Bolsheviks to power with the start of the Communist regime. Following the loss of 600,000 men in 1914, and of 1.5 million men in 1915, France was on the brink of total collapse since the miscarried Nivelle-offensive in 1917 and widespread mutinies. Germany had an advantage as aggressor, with its industrial and military potency, but was outflanked by the Allied coalition. Germany suffered losses of 850,000 men in 1915 and of 1.2 million men in 1916. It had to send large numbers of reservists home to maintain production of war materials. Germany was on the losing side, especially when the US, with its overpowering industrial production, joined the Allies. The US did this, inter alia, because of attacks by German submarines on ships in international waters. On 3 March 1918 Russia and Germany-Austria concluded the Treaty of Brest-Litovsk, so Germans could prepare themselves for an all-or-nothing attack on the Western Front. In June 1918 the German troops of Ludendorff came within a short distance of Paris, but they lost about 2 million men (dead, wounded, invalid) in July 1918. In October 1918 the Germans had 2.5 million men left and it was difficult to recruit new troops. From July 1918 onwards Allied troops were superior at the Western Front and in Syria, Bulgaria and Italy, and by October 1918 Germany was in complete disorder. Other countries on the continent were also ruined (Williams, 1972). Germany accepted unconditional surrender on 11 November 1918. The First World War ended with several treaties: Versailles (28 June 1919) with Germany; St. Germain (17 October 1919) with Austria; Neuilly (27 November 1917) with Bulgaria; Trianon (4 June 1920) with Hungary; Sèvres (10 August 1920) with Turkey. Many analyses are available of the First World War: Albertini (1952/1957); Becker (1977); Duroselle (1994); Falls (1989); Hardach (1977); Herwig (1996); Joll (1984); Keegan (1999); Stokesbury (1981).

*7.1.3 Versailles Treaty, crisis and collaborative Vichy Regime (1940-1944)*

A cost-benefit analysis of the "Grande Guerre" makes appalling reading. Those who were in political and economic control were not able to handle the problems adequately and the Second World War was, for an important part, a consequence of impotent management since 1918 (Asselain, 1984; Parker, 1969). France was hit more than other combatant countries, in human losses and material damage. Ruins were everywhere in a looted France. Between 1914 and 1918, 8,660,000 men were mobilised in France, and 5 million of them were active in combat. About 27% of the effectively committed men died: 1,350,000 men. This meant 15% of mobilised and 10.5% of the active male population. Some 100,000 individuals died prematurely after being wounded (out of a total of nearly 3 million wounded). There were about 1,100,000 war-invalids, and numerous civillian victims, but many survived this crazy massacre. Material losses were colossal, especially in regions where military operations destroyed practically everything (Northern and Eastern France). Before leaving, Germans flooded the mines, causing drastic production losses. Reconstruction required superhuman effort and huge financial means, while the French public debt was 219 billion francs at the end of 1919. Since 18 January 1919, negotiations for a peace treaty had been started in Versailles, with representatives of 27 nations and British Dominions. The French had one issue on their mind: Germany must pay (Miquel, - 1972). US president Wilson dominated the negotiations at Versailles, forming with Lloyd George (Great Britain), Clemenceau (France) and Orlando (Italy) the "Council of Four". France had security as a central issue, but Wilson had his 14 issues: recognition of the right of self-determination; rejection of secret diplomacy; liberty of the seas; disarmament; creation of the League of Nations; etc.

Clemenceau did not meet French expectations (Duroselle, 1988). "Action Française" demanded the dissolution of the Reich into pre-Bismarck territories. Clemenceau tried to convince Wilson and Lloyd George of the feasibility of the concept of Foch, but in vain. To implement the Rhine as a strategic, natural boundary, Rhineland would have to be permanently occupied and buffer-states would have to be created under the supervision of the League of Nations. Instead, Wilson and Lloyd George offered a treaty guaranteeing the security of France and its boundaries (this treaty was never ratified). The left-bank of the Rhine would be occupied by the Allies temporarily. This became a demilitarised zone (Germans were not allowed to bring in their troops). The unity of the Reich was maintained. The next issue was the return of Alsace-Lorraine, claimed by France (boundaries of 1814). Wilson and Lloyd George refused this. They came up with an a-historic construction. Mines in this area would be given to the French State, while the area would be part of the French customs union, and for 15 years it would be placed under control of the League of Nations. After this period, a plebiscite would decide the future of the area. In the event of a choice to return to Germany, this country must buy back the mines from the French State. In fact, this happened in 1935. The French negotiated about the "corridor de Dantzig" on behalf of Poland, and a clause in the Treaty of Versailles, prohibiting "Anschluss" of Austria with Germany. With the Treaty of Versailles, Germany lost 1/7th of its territory, 1/10th of its population, and all colonies. The German army was reduced to 100,000 land-forces, with limited armament.

Part IV of the Treaty of Versailles (15 chapters with 444 articles) was especially relevant from the economic and financial point of view. Article 297,b gave 31 countries the right to liquidate all German goods, rights and interests. Article 260 said the same for Russia, Austria, Hungary and Turkey. Rivers were internationalised (Rhine, Elbe, Oder). Article 231 ruled that Germany and her allies were responsible for losses and damages resulting from the war of allied governments and associated territories and of their national inhabitants. The German Reich had to pay reparations (in 1921 fixed at 132 billion gold-marks) in 30 annuities. J.M. Keynes, British representative at the Versailles negotiations, was opposed to huge German reparations. In "Economic consequences of the peace" (1920) Keynes argued that these would disrupt the international economy. About half of the reparations had to be paid to France, trying to exploit its right as victor. According to Soutou (1989) France tried to become the first steel-power on the European continent. There was a steel project, and the target was to rob Germany of half its energy potential. In the Treaty of Versailles, Germany lost 40% of its production of cast iron, 30% of its production of steel and it risked a paralysed steel-industry due to shortages of coal and cokes. The Treaty of Versailles was accepted by the Reichstag (237 against 138 votes) and on 28 June 1919 signed in Versailles. This "Friedensdiktat" was exploited by Germans: it was not a negotiated peace treaty. France was dominant on the continent for a decade, but its position was weakened. The demographic imbalance between France (40 million) and Germany (60 million) was alarming, it was an invitation to German revenge. French economic potential would be less than that of Germany once recovered. France had to exploit its temporary military superiority, pressing for implementation of the Versailles Treaty.

France had to play its role as policeman of Europe. This meant military intervention in Russia (end 1918) to support "white generals" against revolutionary troops, until French troops were withdrawn in spring 1919 following a mutiny on the Black Sea. Other military and diplomatic interventions followed, especially when the USA withdrew its military potential from Europe. France was repeatedly confronted with Great Britain, also aspiring to build up a dominant position. In the three years of war between Greece and Turkey (1919-1922), France supported Turkey, and Great-Britain Greece. In the Middle East, where distribution of remnants of the Ottoman Empire through mandates under the control of the League of Nations was at stake, demarcation of French and British spheres caused tensions. Observance of the Treaty of Versailles (politics of implementation) had the highest priority for France. It proved to be easier to win the war than to win the peace. A drawback was that the American Senate refused to ratify this treaty, winter 1919/1920. This implied that the US would sign a separate peace treaty with Germany. Anglo-American guarantees for the security of France, as promised by the USA in Versailles, became worthless. Clemenceau had given up the left-bank of the Rhine (physical guarantee against Germany) for nothing. J.M. Keynes argued that the collapse of the German economy would have enormous negative consequences for Europe. Anglo-Americans were won over to the idea that the Weimar Republic should be given the chance for rapid economic recovery, otherwise there was the risk of a kind of Bolshevik revolution in Germany. France used its influence in Central and Eastern Europe to build up friendly relations with several countries, trying to "contain" Germany. France made itself responsible for the boundaries between Poland and Germany, the corridor of Dantzig, and for the integrity of Czechoslovakia and Austria.

Meanwhile, Germany did everything possible to wreck the implementation of the Treaty of Versailles. In 1922, production in the German steel industry had returned to its 1913 level, while the French steel industry had troubles with its structural shortages of coke and sales potential. The Committee for Reparations had fixed German reparations at 132 billion gold-marks (about 150 billion gold-francs). This had to be paid in installments of 2 billion annually and more than 26% of the yearly exports. In July 1920, arrangements were made for the distribution of German reparations to its victims: France (52%), Great-Britain (22%), Italy (10%), Belgium (8%) and other countries the rest. France needed this money badly for its reconstruction. From July 1922 it was obvious that the US and Great Britain, though flexible with regard to German reparations to France, would be strict regarding repayment of the French war debt. France tried in vain to make repayment of these inter-allied debts dependent on the payment of German reparations. In summer 1922, the German chancellor declared that Germany could not fulfil its obligations to pay, and asked for a moratorium of 6 months. Poincaré decided on 27 November 1922 that he would occupy the Ruhr to get his reparations in kind if Germany refused to pay. On 26 December 1922 a committee declared Germany to be in default. On 11 January 1923, French troops occupied the Ruhr. Germany, asking for a 3-years moratorium, reacted with passive resistance with a general strike of two million workers (supported financially by government). The Republic of Weimar was on the brink of total collapse (colossal inflation, separatist movements, several attempts at a coup). On 26 September 1923, Stresemann stopped the official policy of passive resistance. In November 1923, Hitler and his Nazis organised their coup in Munich.

Management of the post-war situation in Europe was complex. New States were created, formerly part of the Habsburg, Romanov or Hohenzollern territories: Czechoslovakia, Austria, Poland, Hungary, Yugoslavia, Estonia, Latvia, Lithuania and Finland. Germany did not come off well: Alsace-Lorraine became French; border corrections with Belgium and Denmark; military occupation of Rhineland; French economic exploitation of Saarland; demilitarisation; and huge reparations. Besides, Germany lost its colonies. Not all questions could be settled, but it was expected that the newly created League of Nations would find solutions (Marks, 1976; Silverman, 1982). At the beginning of the 20th century, it was thought that the USA, Russia and Germany would become leading powers, but Germany had suffered a crushing defeat. The US in 1918 was the primary world power. As the US preferred isolationism and Russia was in the grip of the Communist take-over, England and France had a dominant role in the world-theatre of diplomacy: the League of Nations. For France, security against eventual German aggression was top priority. When the US did not ratify the Versailles Treaty, France lost the American guarantees for its security in case of German aggression. France tried to organise security guarantees otherwise; with the "Entente petite" (1920) with Romania, Czechoslovakia and Yugoslavia and bilateral treaties with several countries: Belgium (1920); Poland (1921); Czechoslovakia (1924); Romania (1926); and Yugoslavia (1927). France decided to have large armed forces on the alert, to intervene if Germany did not comply with its obligations for reparations. France invested in military infrastructure (Young, 1978). Under Minister of War, Maginot (1929-1932) a system of fortifications along French-German borders was constructed: "Ligne Maginot". Crisis and retrenchment policy impeded improvements (to foster capacities for a counter-attack). Government rejected De Gaulle's plea in 1934 for a regular, motorised army for quick assaults.

When Germany failed to honour its treaty obligations to pay reparations, the Allies had problems with repayment of their own war debts. Relations between the US and its European allies worsened (McDougall, 1978; Shuker, 1976; Trachtenberg, 1980). Inflation was high, especially in Germany. Nearly all European States had huge debts to England and France. Both were heavily indebted to the USA, claiming its money back in due time. France and England refused to pay unless Germany paid them its scheduled reparations. To force the US and Great Britain to take unpaid German reparations seriously, France decided obstinately to occupy the Ruhr (Artaud, 1968; Bariéty, 1977). After the Ruhr-Crisis (1923) the Dawes-Plan (1924) was launched, allowing Germany to pay substantially less. With the Locarno-Treaties (1925) Germany recognised existing borders, maintaining the status quo in the Rhineland. Some countries declared that they would guarantee German borders. With the Treaty of Paris (1928) some countries pledged that they would not solve conflicts with warfare. It was a time for reconciliation diplomacy, with Briand (France), Chamberlain (England) and Stresemann (Germany) playing leading roles. There was general euphoria that the enduring war and its violent aftermath (Eastern Europe, Poland, Armenia), with about 60 million victims in Europe, was over. Material damages were evaluated at some

260 billion dollars, as much as 6.5 times the total of all national debts in the world from the end of the 18th century up to the First World War (Aldcroft, 1978, p.19).

After the crash on the New York Stock Exchange (October 1929), a deep economic crisis had its impact worldwide (Kindleberger, 1973). The financial centre of the world had shifted from London to New York and the US had become the largest creditor (Rowland, 1976). Money was borrowed massively on short notice by European countries and enterprises, willing to pay high interest-rates to cover long-term financial commitments. When the financial world lost confidence in this artificial construction, the whole fabric collapsed. The Wall Street Crisis caused an uncontrollable chain-reaction: investments; consumption and economic activities fell dramatically. Several countries tried to roll off their problems (massive unemployment, social tensions) onto each other. "Beggar-my-neighbour-politics" was popular: abandoning the gold standard; devaluations; reducing imports; not paying scheduled repayments; etc. The hopeless situation in Germany and Italy was fertile soil for demagogues such as Hitler and Mussolini. They propagated authoritarian Fascism as alternative for weak party-political democracies that proved to be unable to solve societal problems (Hamilton, 1971; Hayes, 1973). Communism, with its biting criticism of capitalism as the root of all evils, had an appeal for the masses. In Europe, many ethnic groups lived on the wrong side of artificial new borders, creating tensions with minorities claiming their rights. "Nazionalsozialisten" (Nazis) exploited general dissatisfaction (massive unemployment, galloping inflation; rising prices; humiliating Treaty of Versailles; etc.) with brutish violence, and Hitler came to power in 1933. He increased tensions with outrageous demands (Stoakes, 1986). France wanted strict implementation of Versailles (payment of reparations; no territorial concessions; no German re-armament), but England and the US did not agree, and Germany got the Saarland back in 1935.

Hitler occupied the Rhineland in 1936. This blatant brutality produced no military reaction, so Hitler became ever more reckless in claiming more territories to get Germans "Heim ins Reich". Hitler demanded German rearmament to bring Germany onto an equal footing with France. The League of Nations proved to be unable to settle problems (Spanish civil war, 1936-1939; Japanese attack on China in 1937) and in November 1937 Germany and Japan signed a treaty for military co-operation against the Soviet Union. The violent "Anschluss" of Austria on 12 March 1938, making it part of the German Reich, was accepted by France and England. The later much maligned Munich Treaty (29 September 1938), signed by England (Chamberlain), France (Daladier), Italy (Mussolini) and Germany (Hitler) was celebrated as historical fact. It was presented as though it would prevent war (Taylor, 1979). England and France accepted that Germany would annex territory in Czechoslovakia, where Sudeten Germans lived, but although this treaty guaranteed new borders for Czechoslovakia, this country was brutishly occupied in March 1939. It was crystal clear that Poland would be the next victim of Hitler's voracity. Hitler, well informed about the anti-war atmosphere in France and England, prepared the conquest of Poland by playing false with the Soviet Union. On 20-21 August 1939, the Molotov/Von Ribbentrop Treaty was signed by Germany and the Soviet Union, giving Hitler free play to invade Poland. Fascist Germany, Italy and Japan chose to undertake military adventures causing the Second World War. In the Far East, Japanese troops invaded China in 1937, where they raised the devil on the poor Chinese population, causing vast numbers of dead, wounded and disabled, and enormous material damages (Storry, 1979, 1982). The Nazi-invasion of Poland on 1 September 1939 started the Second World War.

At the start of the Second World War (1940-1944) France had 5 million military men mobilised, but it was not well prepared. Political leadership did not dare to have a robust attitude to the brutish provocations of Nazi-Germany. The population was not willing to make heavy sacrifices again after 1914-1918, and the French economy was not yet recovered from that damaging war (Kemp, 1972). France had a rearmament program, but this was too meagre and came at too high a price (Frankenstein, 1939; Young, 1978). French society was deeply divided ideologically. Societal problems were beyond the capacity of weak government coalitions: 24 governments in the 1930-1940 period (Dubief, 1976; Duroselle, 1979; Joll, 1959). In the years 1936-1937 France was itself on the brink of civil war. Supreme command was in the hands of veterans (Gamelin, Georges, Weygand, Pétain) with obsolete ideas of warfare. They were in the grip of the non-strategy of the "Ligne Maginot" fortifications along the French-German border (underground bunkers, field-hospitals etc.). De Gaulle's idea to form small units with tanks was waved aside. Military leadership did not make use of the adequate information of French intelligence services about the German military build-up (Adamthwaite, 1977; Posen, 1984). The French supreme command shrank back from the eventual necessity to interfere militarily to support Czechoslovakia or Poland, as was laid down in treaties. It was the same with England. In spite of the biting criticisms of Churchill, Chamberlain remained confident of Hitler's reasonableness. His permissive "appeasement policy" did not contribute to security of Europe. Hitler was insatiable, concessions only furthered his territorial hunger (Mommsen/Kettenacher, 1983). Circumstances worsened. Spain had a Fascist regime, Belgium declared itself neutral. After the Munich-Treaty (1938) the Soviet Union was not any longer disposed to co-operate with the unreliable West and the French-Russian Treaty (1935) was not taken seriously any more. France trusted its alliance with England but the relationship was stubborn (Preston, 1978). England did not understand the renewed alliance of France with the USSR. The Anglo-German Fleet Treaty (June 1935) upset France, but England committed itself in 1939 with regard to France. With its seafaring potential, England gave priority to the Mediterranean at the cost of British interests in the Far East (so Japanese got free play). With its extensive British Empire, England had about 1/4 of the globe under its control, but militarily it was not a match for militarist Nazi-Germany. England in 1939 gave military guarantees to Poland, and later also to Greece, Romania and Turkey.

France and England, bound by their guarantees with regard to the Polish borders, could not do otherwise than declare war on Germany on 3 September 1939 after the brutish Nazi-invasion of Poland on 1 September 1939. Soviets, making common cause with the Nazis, invaded Poland on 17 September 1939 by attacking it in the rear. On 27 September 1939 Poland stopped fighting, and two days later it was divided up as spoils between bloodthirsty Nazis and Soviets (Bell, 1986; Taylor, 1964; Weinberg, 1994). Soviets attacked Finland on 30 November 1939 and Germany invaded Denmark and Norway (9 April 1940) and, in the next few months, the Netherlands (capitulation 14 May), Belgium (capitulation 26 May) and France (capitulation 22 June). While France was facing these enormous military problems, Italy also made a cowardly declaration of war on France (Knox, 1982). In 1939-1940 French military and civilian leadership trusted in the would-be security of the "Ligne Maginot", fortifications along the French-German boundary ("impenetrable by German tanks"). German generals solved this by invading France via neutral Belgium. In the period after Versailles (1919) De Gaulle had argued regularly for making the army more mobile, but he had no support. Problems of the thirties (economic crisis, rise of Communism and Fascism, governmental instability) caused immobility. Military organisation had sclerosis (retrenchment policy, pacifism, obsolete military conceptions, outdated material facilities).

After the invasion of Poland by Nazi-troops on 1 September 1939, Premier Daladier did not ask Parliament to ratify a declaration of war on Germany. On 2 September 1939 he asked to adopt the budget needed to counter the international situation (70 billion francs), accepted unanimously in the Assembly and by the Senate (only Laval voting against). So Daladier, on 3 September 1939, could declare war on Germany as Great Britain did. Unlike the calculations of French military strategists in 1914, based upon a short war (several weeks), in 1940 military strategy anticipated a long war. Therefore, the French planners started to concentrate on a defensive strategy, based upon the "Ligne Maginot". It was not thought necessary to construct fortifications in the Northern part of France along the boundary with Belgium, because Belgium had declared itself neutral since 1936. Military leadership had learned a lesson since 1914, when the German armies, violating Belgian territory, had invaded France. French planning anticipated a German military manoeuvre north from the Maginot-line (Plan Dyle) and via the Netherlands (Plan Breda). Although France was at war from 3 September 1939, it was May 1940 before military operations got under way in the French region. This was therefore called a "silly war" (Richer, 1990; Rossi-Landi, 1971). This caused irritation among the people, who did not understand measures like rationing, and it was demoralising for the French army. The Prime Minister was criticised by pacifists for having declared war on Germany, and by others waiting for a rapid offensive. On 19 March 1940, Daladier retired when he effectively lost a vote of confidence, with 239 against one, but with 300 abstentions. He was succeeded by Reynaud, striving for a more active military role for France. On 9 May 1940, Reynaud submitted his resignation. Hearing the next morning that Germans had invaded Belgium and the Netherlands, he withdrew this. Reynaud, on 18 May 1940 also Minister of National Defence, fired general Gamelin, and made General Weygand commander-in-chief. "Panzerdivisionen" passed the Ardennes, a feat which French military leadership had thought they could not perform and so the Germans were able to trap British and French troops between the Somme and the Netherlands.

Germans took Paris on 14 June 1940, and on 20 June 1940 reached Bordeaux. It was complete chaos, with about 6 million refugees on the roads (Vidalenc, 1957). The French had to experience a humiliating defeat, although the Allied forces were more or less on a par with German troops (Michel, 1980). Pétain blamed the Popular Front for this, always cutting the military expenditure the generals asked for, but he told only half the story (Frankenstein, 1982). French generals have to be blamed for not having an adequate strategy, preparing a static war, while Germans overcame all hindrances (also the Ardennes) for their "Blitzkrieg" (Addington, 1971; Azéma, 1990). In the circumstances of 1940 generals were able to burden politicians with the responsibility for the shameful defeat. On 16 June 1940 Reynaud resigned, because a majority of his ministers was in favour of accepting an armistice. Lebrun appointed Pétain. Pétain asked the Germans for an armistice that night. Without waiting for their answer he broadcast that an armistice was inevitable on 17 June 1940, so making himself totally dependent on the Nazis, who presented unbearable conditions on 22 June 1940. Pétain signed the Armistice at Rethondes, where Germans had signed their armistice on 11 November 1918. From 25 June 1940 on France was split up into two parts: the Occupied Zone and the Unoccupied Zone (with Vichy as centre). After the first of June 1940, government, parliament and administration were in Vichy.

On 10 July 1940 the National Assembly gave Pétain full powers to make a new constitution for the "État français". The terrible year 1940 (Azéma, 1990) cost France huge losses in human lives, wounded and handicapped people, and material losses. The Nazis made Pétain agree to pay all costs of the occupation. Germany forced France to pay 400 million francs daily in 1940, and 300 million francs in 1941. After the occupation of the unoccupied zone in the South of France from November 1942 on, France had to pay 500 million francs per day, then 700 million francs daily from June 1944 (Berstein/Milza, 1995). Nazis confiscated anything they fancied (gold, art-treasures, etc.). The economic burden of the occupation was very heavy. The total of German forced charges is estimated at about 700 billion francs. As the French State could not pay this, the pressing of bank notes was used, causing a galloping inflation. We must not forget the plundering and confiscation in kind. About 12-17% Of French agricultural production was transported to

Germany (without payment). To a large extent industry also worked for Germany. One has to reckon also with the seizure of French manpower. At the end of 1941, some 1,600,000 French worked for the German war-machine and by the summer of 1944, about 2,600,000 were working for Germany. French industrial production fell sharply. Nazis levied this production with 34%. There was unbearable Nazi-repression and meagre living conditions for millions, especially for Jews (Kaspi, 1991) and Gypsies (Peschanski, 1994). When the Nazis forced the French to capitulate, the First World War "hero" Pétain became collaborating head of state in the "Vichy-régime" (1940-1944). This regime condemned De Gaulle, who had been leading resistance against the Nazis from London since 18 June 1940, for high treason with the death penalty. De Gaulle's "Free French" got more adherents, especially after the Nazi-attack on the Soviet Union (June 1941), bringing French Communists onto the side of resistance against the Nazis. When British and American troops occupied French North Africa (November 1942), Nazis occupied the French unoccupied zone.

During 1942, French resistance became better organised, but it was not completely loyal to De Gaulle. In May Pétain said "I want the victory for Germany.". In September 1942 the hated "Service du Travail Obligatoire" (STO) for forced labour in Germany was set up. The movement for De Gaulle had growing success. The "red orchestra" of Communists reported directly to Moscow. In November 1942, their boss Trepper (1975) was arrested. On 24 September 1942 the "Comité National Français" (CNF) was formed to co-ordinate the activities of resistance movements. Not only De Gaulle, since July 1942 leader of "France combattante", but others claimed leadership for France. US President Roosevelt promoted Henri Giraud, leader in Algeria, as the successor of De Gaulle. Studies on the basis of Moscow archives show that the PCF tried to get control of the French resistance, apart from the Free French (Andrew/ Mitrokhin, 1999). French Communists proved to have the organisation of a national uprising in mind after Liberation, under the leadership of the armed forces of the resistance. Moulin frustrated these Communist plans: this refutes the assertion that Moulin would have been co-operating with a Communist take-over (Buton, 1994, pp. 19-20). In August 1942 Moulin started to build up the "Armée Secrète" (AS) to co-ordinate three para-military resistance movements. At first, Communists refused to integrate their FTP ("Franctireurs et Partisans") but, when Moulin stopped financial support from London for this FTP, they gave in. In January 1943, FTP, "Combat" and "Libération" were fused. On 21 February 1943 De Gaulle established the "Conseil National de la Résistance" (CNR) with Moulin as president. On 15 May 1943 Moulin proposed the formation of a provisional government under De Gaulle in Algeria. This was needed to give him legitimacy in the eyes of Anglo-Americans. Giraud invited De Gaulle to Algeria. On 27 May 1943, the CNR declared that France expected that De Gaulle would form a provisional government in North Africa. On 30 May 1943, there was a "spontaneous" demonstration in support of De Gaulle and on 3 June 1943 the "Comité Française de Libération Nationale" (CFLN) was formed under De Gaulle and Giraud and their troops were combined. But there was treachery in the ranks, a resistance leader in Marseilles gave information to Nazis under pressure. Moulin went to Lyon, and Klaus Barbie, chief of Himmler's SD, was informed of a secret meeting in the nearby village of Caluire on 21 June 1943. Barbie and his henchmen beat the group, until they discovered which was Moulin. He was transported to Germany in a coma, and he died before arriving there (Lacouture, 1984; Noguères, 1981).

The French had to discover by bitter years of war and occupation that a neglected system of national defence had far-reaching consequences. After the capitulation of France, Hitler attacked Britain with air raids. When the British won this air-battle, Germans concentrated their attack upon the Balkans. Yugoslavia and Greece were crushed by the Nazi jack-boot (6-27 April 1941). At the beginning of 1941, German troops under Rommel had even driven back the British in North Africa. In spite of a non-aggression pact (August 1939) between Germany and the Soviet Union, Hitler invaded the Soviet Union on 21 June 1941: Plan Barbarossa (Clark, 1965). Recently, research in archives has revealed that Hitler only just trumped Stalin who had prepared a massive attack on Germany (Andrew/Mitrokhin, 1999). Soviets became an ally who would repel German armies, and contributed considerably to the defeat of Nazi-Germany. German troops reached Moscow and Leningrad, conquered the Ukraine but had to capitulate after their miscarried attack upon Stalingrad (2 February 1943). Hitler's decision to invade the Soviet Union was probably fatal. German troops had to fight on many fronts simultaneously. It was a blunder to think that a "Blitzkrieg" of 3 months would be enough (Erickson, 1983). The German army could not withstand a long fight in the biting Russian winter (Clark, 1965; Seaton, 1971). Information about the German invasion of the Soviet Union contributed to the decision by Japan to start their surprise-attack on the American fleet at Pearl Harbour on 7 December 1941. This made the US declare war on Japan (Spector, 1985). On 11 December, Germany and Italy declared war on the US. At last, Montgomery defeated the Italians and Germans decisively in the Battle of El Alamein (23 October/2 November 1942). After the Allied disembarkation, on 8 November 1942, the Germans were chased from Morocco and Algeria (May 1943). When Sicily was conquered by the Allies in July 1943, Mussolini was overthrown on 25 July 1943. On 3 September 1943, American and English troops landed in Southern Italy. That same day Italy signed an armistice, but Germans continued fighting in Italy, until their own capitulation (29 April/1 May 1945). In 1944 Soviet troops came near to the German borders, conquered Romania and penetrated Poland and Hungary (Calvocoressi/Wint, 1989).

On 6 June 1944 ("D-Day") American and British troops landed in Normandy (Hastings, 1984). After breaking German counter-attacks, France was liberated with the help of French troops, followed by Belgium (August/September 1944). The rivers Meuse, Rhine and Scheldt proved to be a hindrance to the rapid thrust of the Allies. Germans tried a last, abortive, Ardennes-offensive (December 1944/January 1945). During the following months, the Western and Southern parts of Germany were conquered by American, English and French troops. Soviets had started a decisive offensive against the Germans on 12 January 1945, so by April 1945 they were in Berlin (Werth, 1964). Hitler could not bear it, and committed suicide on 1 May 1945. On 7 May 1945, German armed forces surrendered unconditionally. In the Far East, Japan continued armed resistance in an absolutely hopeless fight against superior American forces. Americans used two nuclear bombs (Hiroshima, Nagasaki), forcing a Japanese capitulation on 15 August 1945 (Feis, 1966; Giovanetti/ Freed, 1967). Soviet dictator Stalin sent troops to Manchuria before the Japanese capitulation, so he could profit from the collapse of the Japanese armed forces. Communists took over in China after beating Tsjiang-kai-Sjek. The Chinese Democratic People's Republic was proclaimed (1949); Tsjiang-kai-Sjek withdrew to Formosa (later Taiwan).

*7.1.4 After the Second World War, changing geopolitical conditions*

When hostilities ceased in Western Europe, French Communists intended a take-over in 1944. In May PCF got control of the "Comidac" with a grip on the "Forces Françaises de l'Intérieur" (FFI). De Gaulle, anticipating a coup, disbanded FFI and Comidac on 28 August 1944. Communists accepted this after fierce opposition, probably, because Stalin gave priority to defeating Germans (Buton, 1994, pp. 298-314). Communists continued to strive for a take-over by systematically penetrating public administration, armed forces, police and secret services. In 1946, the "Service de Documentation Extérieure et de Contre-espionage" (SDCE) was formed in the ministry of war. This SDCE had a strong Gaullist mark, especially in the "Service Action", which was extended in relation to the war in Indo-

China, and which would provide many men for the armed "service d'ordre" of the Gaullist RPF (Péan, 1990). PCF, obeying strict instructions from Moscow, got 1/4 of the votes after the war. For De Gaulle it was irritating that Roosevelt, Churchill and Stalin (Feis, 1967) divided the post-war spheres of influence in Europe, while France was not represented at the Yalta Pact of 4-11 February 1945 (Senarclens, 1990). Anglo-Americans made a gesture by giving France a role of co-victor in Berlin. The Second World War made the US and Soviet Union the two superpowers, Great Britain and France were relegated to the second division. France managed to have itself recognised as one of the greater powers though, obtaining a permanent seat in the UN Security Council from May/June 1945. One of the three Western occupation zones in Germany was French (American, British, French), the other being Russian. Later Germany was divided up between West Germany (Federal Republic) and Communist East Germany (DDR). On the European Continent the "Iron Curtain" separated Communist Eastern Europe from the Free West. Western European democracies were seriously weakened at the end of the war. American Marshall Aid (1948), which was offered to Communist countries also (but forbidden by Moscow as a trick of capitalism), prevented the total collapse of Western Europe.

Since 1945 the Soviet Union has been a superpower, although it had serious drawbacks. In a rigid State-dirigist economy, priority was given to heavy industry and the production of weapons. Via Communist parties in satellite-States in Eastern Europe, the Soviet Union had totalitarian control there (Warsaw Pact; Comecon; etc.). Opposing groups were ruthlessly eliminated; purges were the order of both day and night. Democratic movements in Poland and Czechoslovakia (Coup in 1948) were stamped out brutally as Soviets worked for Communist hegemony in the world, with Moscow as cockpit (Dibb, 1985; Holloway, 1984; Hosking, 1985). This was alarming, the Soviet Union supported uprisings in the Third World (Porter, 1987) and the "Cold War", bi-polar confrontation between West (US leadership) and Communist East (Soviet Union leadership) dominated the international situation up to the 1990s. After the "Fall of the Berlin Wall" (1989), Germany was re-united in 1990. At the end of the 20th century, the US was the dominant world power. Since the collapse of Communist Eastern Europe, the situation has changed completely. Communist China (largest population in the world), has behaved like a world-power.

After the Second World War, De Gaulle became the first (and later also the last) Prime Minister of the Fourth Republic (1944-1958). When Socialists, participating in his government, refused to raise the military budget, De Gaulle resigned in January 1946. The international situation was stressed, dominated by the conflict between the two superpowers, US and Soviet Union. A third world war was close to breaking out. In February 1948, there was a Communist coup in Prague. Fusion of the three Western zones in West Germany in 1947 was seen by the Soviets as being against the Yalta-agreement (1945). Stalin reacted with the blockade of Berlin (June 1948/May 1949). Americans did not give up, organising a massive air-bridge (Davison, 1958). After ending their occupation-regime in 1949, the Western Allies made the way free for the formation of West Germany. Soviets formed East Germany as a satellite. The "Cold War" made large military budgets a necessity (Grosser, 1984). To prevent an economic collapse in Western Europe, with the risk of Communist take-overs, Americans supported Western Europe financially with the Marshall Aid (1948). During the Second World War and after, De Gaulle stuck to the idea that France was still a major power. He made himself immortal by his continuous fight to make "les Anglo-Saxons" (Americans and the British) recognise French "grandeur" (Kersaudy, 1981; Paxton/Wahl, 1994). Since 1945, France had a most extensive colonial empire second only to Britain, but France and the UK were giants with feet of clay (Kennedy, 1989). In 1950, the US, with 1.38 million military men, spent 14.5 billion dollars a year on its military budget. The USSR spent 15.5 billion dollars (4.3 million military men). Britain spent 2.3 billion dollars (680,000 military men) while France spent

1.4 billion dollars (590,000 military men). Nuclear weapons were decisive (Brodie, 1946; Sherwin, 1975). It was a shock when the Soviet Union broke the American nuclear monopoly (Garthoff, 1958; Kahn, 1960). For Britain, not to be member of the nuclear club was unthinkable (Freedman, 1980; Groom, 1974; Pierce, 1972) and the same applied to France (Kohl, 1971). De Gaulle forced the US to decide on complete participation of the UK and France in the American nuclear secret. When the US rejected this, France chose for an independent nuclear weapons system.

In March 1948, France, the UK and the Benelux-countries signed the Treaty of Brussels for mutual military assistance and consultation, building on the British-French Dunkirk Treaty (1947). Italy and West Germany joined this settlement in 1954. The Brussels Treaty provided the basis for the Western European Union (WEU) and NATO. On 4 April 1949, the North Atlantic Treaty Organisation (NATO) was established with 12 member-states. France became a member with reservations. NATO was the military reaction to Soviet militarism (Kaplan, 1984). The Soviet Union reacted with the Warsaw Pact (1955). When Hungary decided to stay out of this military alliance, Soviets stamped out this sign of independence with an invasion of Hungary (1956). According to the Brezhnev-doctrine, once a country was Communist it was not allowed to break out. France needed troops in French Indo-China. It had a traumatic experience with ongoing warfare (1946-1954) up to the fall of Dien-Bien-Phu (1954). Since the Korea-War (1950-1953) Americans, fearing an expansion of world Communism (Heller, 1977), enabled the French to withdraw troops from Western Europe, as Americans had troops (350,000 men) stationed there. France and the US were deeply involved in attempts to keep Indo-China free from Communism. After the Korean War, China had her hands free to support North Vietnam in the Vietnam War (Irving, 1975). Americans wanted to promote the reconstruction of West Germany as a countervailing power against East-European Communism, but the French, with memories of three military confrontations with Germany (1870/1871; 1914/1918; 1940-1944), were not enthusiastic.

Fears for the recovery of the West-German economic-military complex and its dominance over France, gave Jean Monnet, "first statesman of interdependence" (Duchesne, 1994), the idea of overcoming the French-German controversy structurally by bringing their basic industries under common control. The Schuman-Plan (1950) incorporated the European Coal and Steel Community (ECSC) in 1951, and the European Community of the Six (France, West Germany, Benelux-countries) from 1957. In 1954, West Germany was a member of both NATO and WEU, promising to refrain from nuclear, biological and chemical weapons. West Germany agreed to station troops from the US, Canada, Great Britain and France. France did not guarantee the territory of West Germany with its nuclear "force de frappe", and the French National Assembly rejected plans for a European Defence Community in August 1954. Initiatives were started for an alternative. This brought the establishment of the WEU on 6 May 1955. In 1958, Khrushchev ("Berlin is a cancerous tumour for East-Germany") provoked the second Berlin-crisis. West Berlin (prosperous) was a thorn in the side of the shabby performance of the "Socialist paradise" in the D.D.R. Many thousands fled to the West until the "Berlin Wall" was built in August 1961 as part of the "Iron Curtain", dividing Communist Eastern Europe from free Western Europe. After the Marxist take-over by Fidel Castro in Cuba, the US tried vainly to disembark troops in the Bay of Pigs to fight Castro (April 1961). Khrushchev provocatively sent ships with nuclear material to Cuba, bringing the world to the brink of a third world war. President Kennedy, already on the alert because of a build-up of facilities in Cuba for the launching of missiles, reacted by ordering the interception of the Soviet ships. This "Cuban Missile Crisis" (October 1962) made it obvious to many Americans that they could also be hit by nuclear weapons (Allison, 1971).

After the humiliating defeat in the French Indo-China war (1946-1954) France was deeply involved in the Algerian war (1954-1962). Following the Dien-Bien-Phu disaster (7 May 1954) government decided to stop warfare and accept the Geneva Agreements (1954). Vietnam was split up into Communist North Vietnam and South Vietnam, where the French, with 80,000 military men, thought to maintain their influence. On 11 May 1955, Premier Faure decided to withdraw all troops from Indochina. The Algerian uprising required the transfer of these well-trained troops. On 10 October 1954, the Algerian independence movement "Organisation Spéciale" became "Front de Libération Nationale" (FLN). This organisation of Algerian Muslims tried to undermine the French will to remain in Algeria. To bring this about, its armed wing, "Armée de Libération Nationale" (ALN), organised terrorist outrages and uprisings. Weak governments proved to be impotent to solve the nasty problems of Algeria. When Egyptian President Nasser nationalised the Suez-canal in November 1956 Egypt was invaded by British and French armed forces. One reason for France to interfere was that Egypt supported Algerian rebels. The British, without consulting the French, pulled out of this adventure when the US threatened the position of the pound sterling. This experience and Soviet blackmail with the threat of nuclear weapons if the intervention in Egypt did not stop, contributed to the French decision to develop an independent military organisation with its own nuclear weapons.

In 1957, France had half a million men in Algeria; a quarter of the total national budget was needed for the military program. There was a strong movement to maintain French Algeria, against all attempts to make Algeria an independent country. France was on the brink of civil war, while an important part of the armed forces was passionately opposed to making Algeria independent. When adherents of "Algérie française" concluded that De Gaulle was not sticking to their objective, they formed a clandestine army, the "Organisation Armée Secrète" (OAS). This OAS organised terrorist activities in Algeria and in France (Rioux, 1990). When De Gaulle came back in power in May 1958, France was in a dangerous situation. At a commemoration of the dead on 13 May 1958 in Algeria, "Algérie française" was proclaimed. Lagaillarde appealed to some 20,000 "pieds noirs" (Algerian inhabitants with European origin) to start a rebellion. They stormed the office of the governor. With reference to 1793, a "Comité de Salut Public" was formed with Massu, Trinquier and Lagaillarde. On 24 May 1958, rebels occupied Corsica. Before their planned "Opération Résurrection" in France could go ahead, De Gaulle made known that he had started the procedure for forming a new government. Premier Pflimlin retired on 28 May 1958, and the next day, President Coty announced that he had asked De Gaulle to form a new government. On 30 May 1958 De Gaulle asked Parliament full powers. Parliament (with 329 against 224 votes) gave him full powers to rule by decree for six months and to establish a new constitution, and in this way the formally competent authorities decided to end the Fourth Republic.

Once De Gaulle was in charge again, the military leadership in Algeria originally thought that he would adhere to their favoured "Algérie française", but it became increasingly evident that, since September 1959, De Gaulle had been working in the direction of decolonisation and an independent Algeria. As an experienced general, De Gaulle knew that the restoration of military discipline was a top priority. It was evident to him that the grip of the public authorities on the army had to be restored. Using article 16 of the 1958 Constitution, De Gaulle could purge the corps of military officers. He reorganised the top structure by reinforcing political control upon military police and operational command structure with the "Secrétariat général de la défense nationale" (SGDN) under General Fourquet. After a referendum in January 1961 on independence for Algeria and the crushed general's putsch of 21/22 April 1961, negotiations for independence began. In the referendum of 8 April 1962, the Evian Agreements were adopted with 90%. After the positive referendum in Algeria (1 July 1962), the country became independent on 3 July

1962. De Gaulle had his hands free to build up a nuclear arsenal. Between 1962 and 1967 outlays for conventional armament were cut by 43%, in order to invest in the nuclear program.

A certain degree of détente developed internationally with intermittent periods of increased tensions in some regions. After the French defeat in Indo-China (1954), Communist pressure grew steadily in South East Asia. A new phenomenon was the split between the Soviet Union and Communist China. The Chinese XXth congress (1956) condemned Stalinism and Soviet imperialism and from 1959 relations with Communist China broke down when Khruschev ended aid to China's nuclear program. In 1964, it was known that China had exploded its first nuclear bomb and it had an ambitious program for advanced nuclear activities. The Sino-Soviet relations grew ever worse, with territorial claims and warfare (1969). Chinese dictator Mao claimed that a territory of some 1.5 million square kilometres had to be given back to China (Hoffman, 1978; Bartlett, 1984). The rising power of China made the Soviet Union willing to co-operate with the West (disarmament negotiations). Americans feared that, as in a game of dominoes, a series of countries would be conquered and the whole of South East Asia would be taken over by Communists (Gaddis, 1982). The Tonkin incident, when two US destroyers were attacked by Vietminh, made a reaction inevitable (Davidson, 1988). This started a growing US intervention in this region, escalating into the frustrating Vietnam War (1963-1975), a nightmare, because the Vietcong, supported by North Vietnam and China, forced the US to engage ever more men and means in this unending military operation (Kolko, 1986).

Because the US refused to start a total war against North Vietnam, negotiations ended with the Agreements of Paris (1973), but this was not the end, for Communists invaded South Vietnam in April 1975, and Laos and Cambodia as well. The security advisor to US President Nixon, Kissinger, argued for a new American diplomacy in the multi-polar world with five important areas: US, China, USSR, Japan and Western Europe (Bell, 1977). Carter, the US president from 1976, influenced Egypt and Israel to sign the Camp David Settlement (1978). Growing Muslim-fundamentalism in the Middle East (Iraq, Iran etc.) became a major security issue. In Europe, several developments had an impact on relations between the two superpowers. The Soviet Union was confronted with dissension in its satellites in Eastern Europe. Tito's Yugoslav road to Communism, the pro-China position of Albania, reformist Hungary, Romanian autonomy, and repetitious crises in Poland undermined Soviet superiority. The "Prague Spring" (1968) caused an invasion by Warsaw Pact troops on 21 August 1968. Tensions between the West and the Communist East in Europe were structural. Gradually there was normalisation of relations: the four-party-accord about Berlin (1971) and Helsinki-accords (1975). Circumstances brought Soviets to negotiations with the US and its partners. The nuclear arms race was alarming. The conquest of the space was a new dimension (Freedman, 1981).

There were contacts between the superpowers to restrain the arms race. Both knew that they could destroy each other and the whole world: Mutually Assured Destruction (MAD). Relations between the two Germanies were normalised ("Fundamental Treaty" of 21 December 1972) and both became member-states of the UN. The "Conference of Security and Co-operation in Europe" (CSCE) was organised (1973-1975), resulting in the "Helsinki Agreements" (1975). These recognised the frontiers as issued from the Second World War and had some declarations about furthering security in Europe. In the sphere of nuclear weapons, the SALT-1 Treaty (Strategic Arms Limitation Treaty) on arms control was signed on 26 May 1972. From 1975-1976 the USSR installed new nuclear missiles, SS-20, explicitly aimed at Western Europe. The SS-20 had a reach of 3,500 km., not falling under SALT-1 (intercontinental missiles). This caused a "Crisis of Euromissiles". Distrust about the effectiveness of controls on nuclear weapons, and the Soviet invasion of Afghanistan

(December 1979) meant that SALT-2 was not ratified in 1979 (Talbott, 1979). The USSR, with an enormous fleet, made its presence felt on the world's seas (Garthoff, 1985).

Next to the First World (the West) and the Second World (Soviet Bloc), a third cluster of countries without a bond with one of the blocs developed, the Third World (Mortimer, 1980; Rothstein, 1977; Stavrianos, 1981). The Soviet Union expanded its financial and military support for Third World countries, especially for Communist liberation movements. It adroitly exploited decolonisation processes. While there had been a certain rapprochement between the Soviet Union and Communist China since 1978, the US-USSR relations became ever more strained, especially when Reagan became President of the US in 1980 ("USSR is the Empire of Evil."). With its "Star Wars" concept, the US declared in 1986 that it considered itself no longer tied by SALT-2 (Ghebali, 1989). Thanks to the coming to power of Gorbachev in the USSR, the first agreement on nuclear disarmament in history was signed, the Treaty of Washington (December 1987). It concerned the total elimination of missiles for 1000-5,500 and 500-1000 kilometres in Europe (3-4% of the total arsenal of the two superpowers). This ameliorated chances for SALT with about a 50% reduction of offensive strategic nuclear weapons.

On 9 November 1989 the Berlin Wall came down, the symbolic and factual beginning of the collapse of East-European Communist regimes. The security situation then changed drastically. After the "2 + 4" negotiations (31 August 1990), the two Germanies were united on 3 October 1990, so the territory of the former Communist DDR came within the NATO-sphere. The international system, more or less in euphoria about the collapse of Communist regimes in East-Europe, was abruptly in the midst of crisis due to Saddam Hussein's invasion of Kuwait on 2 August 1990. The UN Security Council, for the first time since 1945 unanimously, condemned this aggression. When diplomatic activities failed, a coalition of 29 countries under leadership of the US reacted militarily: in the shortest possible time (17 January/28 February 1991) Iraq was crushed, but the US failed to finish the job by eliminating Saddam Hussein and he spent years reorganising his terrorist campaign. In 2002, there was serious debate about US warfare against Saddam Hussein's Iraq, believed to have nuclear biological and chemical weapons. The disintegration of the Soviet Union after 1991 was attended by numerous problems. Comecon was abolished on 27 June 1991 and the Warsaw Pact was disbanded on 1 July 1991. On 31 July 1991 the Start-I Treaty was signed by the US and Soviet Union about a reduction of strategic weapons with 30%. An abortive military coup took place on 19 August 1991. A series of new nation-states developed in Eastern Europe. Beginning in January 1992 the former Yugoslavia was torn apart by civil wars (a series of ethnic purges) between Croats, Serbs and Muslims (Bildt, 1998; Corwin, 1995; Owen, 1996; Ullman, 1996; Zimmerman, 1996). This drama caused a large scale military intervention by NATO in 1999, as Serbian dictator Milosevic persevered in a shameful program of massive ethnic cleansing (Thomas, 1999). It was NATO's first war, and NATO won this "humanitarian war" militarily. This war was called a new chapter in the history of European diplomacy. Diplomacy could not prevent actual warfare.

## 7.2. Nuclear weapon heart of French strategy for military independence

*7.2.1 Nuclear diplomacy: keeping up with the superpowers*

The use of nuclear weapons for the first time in Hiroshima and Nagasaki (1945) produced a shock, and forced capitulation by Japan's Emperor Hirohito. This new military technology was shocking, not only because of the victims of nuclear bombing, but also because it opened a new era in the history of military technology. American military hegemony has since then, inter alia, been based on its monopoly of nuclear weapons. The big question was how long it would take to break this monopoly. Soon the Russians proved to be a nuclear power. On 13 February 1960, France exploded its first nuclear bomb at Reggane in the Sahara desert. This caused chain-reactions. Preparations for an independent French nuclear program had been going on long before this, but had been a cherished secret (Mendl, 1970; Mongin, 1997). Government-Mendès France (1954-1955) gave a first push by approving a scientific project. This project was supported by succeeding centre-leftist governments. The gaffe of the failed military intervention in Suez (1956) showed France's weakness: Soviets threatened to use their nuclear weapon if this intervention did not stop. Several factors contributed to the decision to build up a French nuclear weapons system. During the Second World War, the US made the British partners in nuclear research, whilst excluding the French. The US "MacMahon-Act", forbidding the proliferation of nuclear know-how to other countries, was rigidly implemented. During the Cold War Americans did not trust their French allies due to the strong position of French Communists (25.9% of the votes, against 15.2% for Socialists) and their relationship with the Soviet Union. In 1952, government-Eisenhower had a new concept of defence policy, based on massive nuclear retaliation, and after the Korea War, with a reduction of land-forces. The new American concept implied that Western Europe (West Germany included) should be rearmed conventionally as a "shield" for the American nuclear "sword" (Huntington, 1961). After his 12 years outside active politics, but actively criticising government policies especially in the military field, De Gaulle came back into power in 1958. Primarily active in crushing a military putsch in Algeria and preventing a civil war in France itself, he did not forget to stimulate the rapid build-up of a French nuclear weapons system (Duval/Le Baut, 1992; Duval/Mongin, 1993). The situation worsened for France after the defeat in Indo-China and escalation of a colonial war in Algeria.

It was annoying that since amendments of the "MacMahon-Act" in 1954 and 1958, Great Britain could participate in nuclear secrets of the US, but this was forbidden for France. In September 1958, De Gaulle sent a memorandum to Eisenhower and Macmillan, proposing to form a tripartite directorate disposing of the military strategy, use of nuclear weapons included. After their negative reaction, De Gaulle decided to develop an independent French nuclear program. Presidents of the Republic succeeding De Gaulle since 1969, walked in the footsteps of the founder of the Fifth Republic, especially in the military field, including the build-up of a French nuclear weapons system. The common government program (27 June 1972) of Socialists and Communists had renouncement of nuclear armaments as a central issue. After 1978 Socialists changed their policies completely, accepting the "politique de dissuasion". Through the years, French peace-movements have been less active than elsewhere in Western Europe. France had, since 1966, withdrawn itself from the integrated command-structure of NATO, so it was not involved in the NATO-decision of December 1979 to place land-based nuclear rockets on European soil and there was relatively little debate about Pershings-2 and "Euromissiles" (1983). This French non-opposition can be explained by the fact that many did not believe in the efficacy of these nuclear weapons to defend their fatherland and sanctuary. The French believed in French nuclear weapons as a political tool to found their independence with regard to the US and USSR. Regularly the "force de frappe" was characterised as the weapon to prevent war, a weapon that would not actually be used. In the French societal debate, "le nucléaire" is primarily about nuclear energy, and only in the second place about nuclear weapons (Chafer, 1984). Under President Giscard d'Estaing (1974-1981) France had an ambitious program for nuclear energy: between 5 and 7 new nuclear energy plants were built yearly. Protests had their apex with demonstrations against the "Superphénix", a fast breeder reactor (Cerny, 1982). Ecologists against nuclear energy were thought to have allies in the PS (in the opposition) but were frustrated by the PS-government confronting them with "faits accomplis". Socialist Minister of Defence, Hernu, in his budget of 1982 gave priority to nuclear weapons: "Hernucléaire" and the outlay for nuclear weapons formed 32% of the military budget in 1983. By the end of the 20th century, France had a specific position with regard to nuclear energy; about 80% of its electricity had a nuclear source as against only 18% of electricity consumed worldwide. In 1997 Government-Jospin decided to close "Superphénix".

In the middle fifties, nuclear weapons were seen as an alternative to conventional weapons. Some pioneers of Gaullist, independent nuclear strategy questioned this: General C. Ailleret (1968) and colonel P.M. Gallois (1964). Military circumstances changed drastically, because defence against nuclear rockets seemed impossible. A new strategy of deterrents had to be developed. After the 1960 decision of De Gaulle to develop an independent nuclear "force de frappe", French strategists got their chance and when in 1962 Soviets proved to have thermonuclear warheads and intercontinental launching sites, the American monopoly was broken. A threat of nuclear annihilation of the Soviet Union was no longer an adequate stand for the USA to take when the USSR was militarily aggressive in Europe. Soviets could bomb American cities. The strategy of flexible response was developed, defence of US and Western Europe was uncoupled. There was no longer a nuclear umbrella above Western Europe and armed conflicts between the two superpowers on European territory were a real possibility. The threat of total destruction of Europe, over about 3,000 kilometres from the Atlantic Ocean to the borders of the Soviet Union, without necessarily involving the territories of the two superpowers themselves, was now a realistic scenario. Gallois (1964) argued for a strategy of proportional deterrents to enable France to inflict damage on a superpower in order to make it give up plans for a nuclear attack: "stratégie du faible au fort". How can the weak (David) beat the strong (Goliath)?

Another prominent French strategist, General Beaufre (1964), foresaw the spread of nuclear weapons to more countries, which would increase nuclear uncertainties. When the Soviet Union could see that the American nuclear umbrella above Western Europe was removed, it might be tempted to call the "NATO-bluff". France would then need the threat of a nuclear attack upon Moscow to bring the nuclear umbrella back. This made General Ailleret in 1967 conclude that his "défense tous azimuts" theory (deploying nuclear weapons in all directions, everywhere in the world) was an adequate strategy. The time seemed right. De Gaulle had withdrawn France from the integrated command-structure in NATO while he was making overtures to East-European countries, but this strategy was never used; the Soviets invaded Czechoslovakia (1968). By the time De Gaulle had finished his presidency in 1969 France was cooperating ever more with the NATO-approach and accepted "tactical nuclear weapons" for the flexible response. As Melandri (Vaïsse, 1995) proved, the US supported France secretly with its nuclear arsenal during the presidency of Pompidou (1969-1974). When Giscard d'Estaing was President of the French Republic in 1974 France was more co-operative with regard to NATO. In 1976, French nuclear strategy could no longer be distinguished from NATO-strategy. In 1977, Socialists and Communists gave up their opposition to nuclear weapons and when Socialist Mitterrand became President of the Republic in 1981 French nuclear strategy came very near to the original Gaullist vision. Most ideas for a nuclear strategy were developed in the "Centre de Prospective et d'Évaluation" of the Ministry of Defence, with political directives of the Presidential Élysée. General L. Poirier (1977; 1982) played a central role in this think-tank. Nuclear submarines became the heart of the French nuclear weapons system, with the accent upon political independence based on a technologically advanced and credible nuclear arsenal, sufficient to prevent war. Access to nuclear weapons meant that France could join the restricted club of nuclear diplomacy. The question is, whether the French President of the Republic, called a nuclear monarch (Cohen, 1985) as only he is competent to push the nuclear button, will ever do that (Theleri, 1997).

Strange as it may seem, there has been through the years an apparent consensus about the French nuclear weapons system. There were differing opinions between political parties about military affairs and nuclear weapons. A short historical retrospective view seems appropriate. In the 19th century, the most important way of recruiting men for the military was assignment by lot. Those assigned by lot were permitted to find a substitute, generally well paid. The average length of military service was 7 years. Laws of 1872, 1873 and 1875 introduced general conscription, exemptions were possible. A law of 1889 abolished these exemptions; conscription was reduced to 3 years. In 1905, it was further reduced to 2 years and in 1913 it was again raised to 3 years. Up to the end of the 19th century there was no opposition to the military activities of the State, but that later changed. An anti-militarist movement was active in the anarcho-syndicalist workers movement, "Confédération Générale du Travail" (CGT). The CGT branded the army as strike-breakers. Socialists were divided between adherents of Jacobinist nationalism and those who saw French Socialism as a branch of international Socialism. A minority thought that national defence was as senseless as antimilitarism, due to the international revolution. A majority under the leadership of Jaurès glorified the nation and argued for a reorganised army of civilian militia, adequate to defend their fatherland passionately but not equipped for aggression. In August 1914 the ranks closed for the national war effort, but in 1917, because of massive losses and bad conditions, there was a lot of mutiny during the trench-warfare. The success of the Bolshevik Revolution in Russia caused new divisions. The "Parti Communiste Français" (PCF) appealed to the masses and proletarian internationalism tried to undermine the credibility of national defence. Stalin, fearing the threat of Fascism, concluded a pact with France in 1935, so revolutionary internationalism could be combined with involvement in national defence in the name of the battle against Fascism. Socialists had problems embarking on a course (Bilis, 1979; Gombin, 1970). The "pacifist" majority included pacifists and revolutionary internationalists. Pacifists expected to guarantee collective security with international organisations; revolutionary internationalists adhered to a class struggle ideology, near to that of the PCF. They condemned a national defence under a bourgeois government.

After 1945, the situation changed with regard to national defence as leftist parties gave their support, and dissent played a marginal role. The Communists solved their dilemma, transforming their position into fierce anti-Americanism. Socialists remembered the trauma of the misguided pacifism of the thirties and supported the Atlantic approach in the framework of NATO. Gaullists were obsessed with the idea that French "grandeur" had to be restored. In opposition from 1946 to 1958, they did not oppose French military strategy at the time, but were against the hegemony of the US. That was exactly what appealed to the French majority. According to the Gaullist philosophy, in a world with two superpowers, only nuclear weapons could give other powers autonomy. The French nuclear weapon had to be used as a weapon of last resort to defend French territory as sacrosanct in the last instance. Adherents of disarmament argued for a third way, in between the superpowers. "Dissuasion" (discouraging), with a priority for avoiding war, became a popular policy option next to military deterrents. The French nuclear weapon became a mighty abstraction in French public opinion; war and military defeats could be prevented, not by using this weapon, but by not using it. It was not easy for the anti-nuclear lobby to find the key to fighting French nuclear strategy. When De Gaulle was back in power after 1958, he could give French nuclear weapons a boost. Nuclear weapons were seen as crucial for the politics of "grandeur" of independent France (Cerny, 1980). The "Force Nucléaire Stratégique" (FNS) became, from 1960 the nucleus of the French military concept on behalf of a second-range power, with a minimum nuclear potential, sufficient to be taken seriously internationally. When the US changed nuclear strategy from massive retaliation to the McNamara-idea of flexible response with tactical nuclear weapons from 1962 on, a reorientation was necessary. Before 1963, the ambition of Great Britain to build up an independent nuclear deterrent could be thought to have a chance, but this changed with the "Nassau-agreement" (1963). Great Britain ordered the American Polaris, giving up its ambitions for nuclear independence and accepting an Atlantic defence system. De Gaulle, knowing that it would be rejected, made a proposal for a directorate of US, Great Britain and France to decide about the use of nuclear weapons. De Gaulle did not get an answer, and decided to go his own way.

In 1966 De Gaulle surprised everybody, including his military advisers and European NATO-allies, by saying that France withdrew itself from the integrated command-structure in NATO, while continuing participation in NATO. To realise co-operation, the "Lemnitzer-Ailleret Agreement" (1966) was concluded. De Gaulle knew that French nuclear weapons could not provide a completely credible deterrent. In the 1970s, France complemented its arsenal of FNS with tactical nuclear weapons. In spite of doubts about the efficacy of FNS and opposition from French allies and within France itself, FNS was supported by a broad consensus. In preparation for legislative elections of 1973, PS and PCF had signed a common government program (June 1972), which promised that a common leftist government would abolish the nuclear arsenal, transform production centres for nuclear weapons into an industry for civilian uses of nuclear energy, and work for a nuclear-free Europe: the old Rapacki-plan revitalised (Klein, 1978). As the chance of participation in government came closer, PCF changed its policy. Since the mid seventies Socialists and Communists had supported FNS. PCF saw the "Méry"-declaration (1976) of the chief-of-staff, proposing to widen the area of the sanctuary to include territories outside France, as a move by President Giscard d'Estaing to please the US. It meant that French troops could be committed by an invasion of West Germany. This breach of the "Ailleret-doctrine" (all or nothing deterrents, for the French sanctuary alone) was for PCF a clandestine clustering with NATO. Before 1977, PCF emphasised its hostility to NATO as an instrument of American imperialism and the cause of war (Whetten, 1982), but in May 1977, PCF recognised the necessity of an independent French nuclear deterrent. The real explanation for this abrupt switch in PCF policy lies in the sphere of party-politics. PCF thought to profit most from co-operation with Socialists, and as public opinion was attached to the ideas of De Gaulle about the independence of France, PCF thought that this moderate standpoint on the supported military independence of France would have electoral advantages. The French nuclear weapon was seen as an instrument to bind the US to the defence of Western Europe: less risks that Americans would give away Western Europe to the Soviet Union, in exchange for Soviet concessions elsewhere in the world. Restrained anti-Americanism and a refusal to deal roughly with the Soviets characterised the French attitude. French distrust in American objectives is explained by expressions of Sonnenfeldt, asserting in 1976, that a Soviet-US condominium was in America's interest ("Sonnenfeldt Doctrine").

Socialists had a long history of ideas about national defence before the modern "Parti Socialiste" (PS) was formed in June 1971 (Buffotot, 1981). A pacifist, anti-militarist movement saw war as the inevitable result of capitalism, so it was not acceptable for workers. A Jacobinist-patriotic movement joined with adherence of many workers to their own culture and country, and thought national defence to be indispensable. PS had to take a standpoint about NATO. Fearing Soviet expansion, many Socialists saw NATO as an instrument to guarantee security for France. Official party documents argued for an alternative defence policy, based on ideas of Jaurès in "L'Armée nouvelle" (1913). This meant a decentralised army of citizens as in the Swiss model. In the seventies, another view came to the fore, after the military invasion of Prague in August 1968 by Warsaw Pact troops. Starting from Jacobin tradition, Minister of Defence Hernu (1975) and the "Centre d'Études, de Recherches et d'Éducation socialistes" (CERES) developed a military concept not far removed from that of De Gaulle. In May 1976, "Organisation générale de la défense" was published: PS accepted nuclear weapons. The PS congress in 1978 formulated a policy with these ideas which combined a multilateral disarmament approach with an independent nuclear weapons system. Disarmament was the target, but only if others did the same. France had to remain in NATO. After 1978 PS was the largest party of the left with 22.79% of the vote. PS was divided about the NATO-double decision (December 1979) to station Pershing-2 rockets in West-Europe (as reaction against the SS-20 of Soviets) and to negotiate with Soviets about the reduction of Euromissiles. CERES denounced Soviet military superiority in Europe and criticised the NATO-double decision, as this would increase dependency on the US. Modernisation of the French nuclear arsenal was seen as the sole method to prevent nuclear war. "Projet Socialiste pour la France des années 80" (1980) of Chevènement, directing CERES, was positive about the modernisation of the French nuclear deterrent and the idea of a citizen army (Jaurès). Mitterrand, in his 110 proposals for the 1981 campaign, was for ordering two new nuclear submarines. Elections of 14 June 1981 gave PS 36.05% of vote following on Mitterrand's election as president on 10 May 1981.

When Socialists came to power in 1981, they were more or less tied to a Gaullist defence concept. Mitterrand, while having a government with four Communist ministers in it, stressed the relationship of France with the US. The leftist wing in the PS (CERES, anti-American, sceptical about European defence, mistrusting Germany and England) stood against a rightist wing under Rocard, whose followers were active in movements against civilian uses of nuclear energy (Touraine, 1980). Mitterrand, forgetting electoral promises (disarmament), continued French defence policy with adaptations. Having denied that France had developed a neutron bomb, Mitterrand and Minister Hernu had to admit in June 1983 that France had carried out a test with a neutron bomb on the Mururoa atoll in the South Pacific. To prepare for the UN disarmament conference, PS produced a document in 1982 which combined disarmament with the maintenance of the French nuclear arsenal and included a plea for a European security conference to activate the "Helsinki-process" and a conference of the 5 nuclear powers (US, Great Britain, France, USSR, China) for worldwide disarmament. Mitterrand drove his following to despair by supporting US plans to install Pershing-2 rockets. Between 1972 and 1979 all three armed forces (land, air, sea) got their own nuclear unit, so the junction with the "Armement Nucléaire Tactique" (ANT) was guaranteed. For the use of these tactical nuclear weapons a decision of the President of the Republic is needed, as is the case for strategic nuclear weapons.

In the eighties, the French nuclear weapons system was small in comparison with the two superpowers: less than 1/40 of the American and about 1/25 of the Soviet arsenal. It was more varied and more extensive than the British system, and not much less than that of the Chinese. The Swedish SIPRI Yearbook gives actual data. The French nuclear arsenal was almost wholly of French making. This is due to the French policy of realising autonomy in production of weapons, seen as a necessary condition for independence and national security. This choice was also brought about by the refusal of the US to give France nuclear information. Possibilities for co-operation with Great Britain to develop nuclear projects were also limited. The British feared losing their special relationship with the US. French enterprises had built up a position in production of weapons: Dassault-Breguet (combat-planes), Aérospatiale/SNIAS (helicopters, nuclear weapons), SNECMA/Matra (air force motors and rockets), Thomson/CSF (electronics). "Délégation générale pour l'armement" (DGA), under responsibility of the Ministry of Defence, produced all kinds of weapons, also for export. The "Commissariat à l'énergie atomique" (CEA) is responsible for nuclear projects. The French weapons industry, highly dependent on export opportunities, is under rigid State control: CEA and DGA are public organisations, SNIAS and SNECMA are public corporations, and Dassault, Matra and Thomson are nationalised industries.

France refused to sign the non-proliferation treaty prohibiting the transfer of nuclear weapons technology to non-nuclear countries, operative since 1970. France declared that it would adhere to it voluntarily. It was June 1991 before President Mitterrand decided that France should accede to the nuclear Non-Proliferation Treaty (NPT). France became the most important exporter of conventional weapons (in relation to its population) and on average spent 15-20% of its defence budget on nuclear systems. It had structural financial problems following the launching of its independent nuclear program. The "Loi de programmation militaire 1984-1988" fixed the military budget at 830 billion francs. The technological gap between France and the superpowers is said to grow exponentially. Technological inferiority to the US was estimated in 2000 as a backlog of 20 years, as against 4 years in 1958. The French strategic nuclear weapon is disputed, but so are tactical strategic weapons. According to the official "doctrine de dissuasion", after using tactical nuclear weapons as a warning the use of the strategic nuclear weapon follows rather automatically. It was argued that it is not justifiable to send conventional battle-units into the theatre of war without tactical nuclear weapons (Haenel, 1982). Willis in "The French Paradox" (1982) wrote that the French independent nuclear strategy supported US interests. France did more for defence than other NATO-partners. It created the "wild card" in the nuclear poker game. French defence had only one potential enemy (Soviet Union), so the French nuclear arsenal could not remain outside negotiations about weapons reduction of the superpowers. Co-operation with NATO or on a European level was needed to update nuclear weapons (Chilton, 1984).

In the field of "dissuasion", the French nuclear strategic arsenal (FNS) was split into two units: "Forces Aériennes Stratégiques" (FAS) and "Force Océanique Stratégique" (FOST). At the end of the fifties Dassault developed a relatively small supersonic bomber. This Mirage IV A was used in 1964 for the first time. Historically, this was the first and for 7 years the only transport-plane for the French nuclear deterrent. It was the original "force de frappe", intended eventually to deposit nuclear bombs in the heartland of the Soviet Union. Mirages IV A were replaced by Mirages 2000N and SX rockets. In the eighties, the French fleet of "Sousmarins Nucléaires Lanceurs d'Engines" (SNLE), with Brest as operational harbour, was the kernel of the French nuclear arsenal. With the sixth nuclear submarine in 1985, this had 52 effective nuclear warheads at its disposal. Firepower and efficacy, "second-strike capability" and the ability to escape detection are relevant. Submarines are especially superior in this field. The first French nuclear submarine, "Le Redoutable", launched in 1967, was operational in 1971. Then came "Le Terrible" (1973), "Le Foudroyant" (1974), "L'Indomptable" (1976), and "Le Tonnant" (1980). These submarines had 16 two-phase rockets with a megaton nuclear warhead (with a power five times the Hiroshima-bomb of 1945), having a range of more than 3,000 kilometres. The sixth nuclear submarine, "L'Inflexible" (1985) had three-phase rockets (M4), able to hit an area of 350 and 150 kilometres with nuclear warheads of 150 kiloton. In 1999 the first two had to be taken out of service. The technological question is how it is possible to protect submarines against advanced detection systems. The FOST has "Sousmarins nucléaires d'attaque" (SNA) submarines of 2,500 tons armed with Exocet SM39 rockets, but not transporting nuclear weapons. Military planning foresaw that France in the year 2000 would have 36 SX (cruise missiles), 5 SNLE (with 80 M4), 112 Mirage 2000N (with "Air-Sol Moyenne Portée", ASMP), 42 Hades and 50 Super Étendards (with ASMP).

While units with strategic nuclear weapons (FNS) and tactical nuclear weapons (ANT) were rather autonomous, reorganisation of conventional forces was an important part of the defence program. This meant forming of "Forces d'Action Rapide" (FAR); reorganisation of local and civil defence, "Défense Opérationnelle du Territoire" (DOT); and development of C3I (command, control, communications and information systems). At the start of the Fifth Republic in 1958 armed forces had more than 1 million military men, of which nearly 450,000 were involved in the Algerian war. Military conscription was for 18 months, but most extended their military service (32 or 34 months). The choice to build up a French nuclear arsenal within inevitable budgetary constraints meant that there had to be cuts elsewhere. In the period of the presidency of De Gaulle (1958-1969), the number of military men was reduced from 1,200,000 to about 550,000 (gendarmerie excluded). After nasty affairs concerning French military involvment in attrocities during the French Indo-China War (1946-1954) and the Algerian War (1954-1962), there was a correction. From 1966 on military discipline was no longer accepted as an excuse to commit illegal acts. Every military person is thought to be responsible for his own actions, the hierarchical principle no longer provides an alibi. Other areas of the "crise de la condition militaire" needed attention also. A law of 13 July 1972 gave the military their own statute. The memoirs of general Aussaresses in "Services spéciaux, Algérie 1955-1957" (2001) caused a row in 2001, as he admitted to having used torture. In 1963, conscription was reduced to 15 months, and under President Pompidou (1969-1974) to 12 months. The defence program of President Giscard d'Estaing reduced the land army from 330,000 in 1977 to 314,000 in 1982. When Chirac became President in 1995 France had a half million military personnel (more than half of them conscripts, about 12,000 women). Land forces had 3/4, air force 1/5, and navy less. The gendarmerie had 83,000 trained troops. Conscripts formed about 2/3 of the army, 1/3 of the air force, and about 10% of the gendarmerie. Later conscription was abolished.

### 7.2.2 France attached to an independent role

After the Second World War France could not keep its former prominent position in the international sphere of military strength, when the US and Soviet Union (and its successor) became the two superpowers, but France was still an important player in the international theatre. France has been one of the five permanent members of the UN Security Council since the start, and a recalcitrant member of NATO. In 1988, before the collapse of Communist Eastern Europe, 16% of the French budget was needed for national defence with about 700,000 persons (military and civilian). Through the years, France had a relatively large defence budget, going from 12,384 billion francs in 1975 (constant 1992 francs) to 17,803 billion francs in 1992. With "Décrets Armées 2000", operational from 1 September 1991, the aim was to adapt the military arsenal to new circumstances. The number of armed forces in 1993 was 505,922 (half of that in 1962): land army 241,401; 90,649 air force; and 64,411 navy. When the Iraqi troops of Saddam Hussein invaded Kuwait on 2 August 1990, President Mitterrand decided that France would participate in the military operation of the coalition against this aggression. On 18 May 1989, Mitterrand boasted: France is the third military power in the world. The Gulf War was the largest overseas commitment of French forces since the Algerian War. The French, who did their military job very well, had only a minor part in operations of the "Desert Storm" coalition under the leadership of the US from January 1991. Of 114,000 offensive air sorties during the 43 days of the conflict (17 January/28 February 1991) French aircraft performed only 1,387: 1.2 per cent. France sent 2.5 times fewer troops and material than Great Britain (Yost, 1993). The short Gulf War made Iraq accept 12 UN Security Council resolutions unconditionally on 27 February 1991. After the Gulf War, France could learn its lesson. The US armed forces had advantages due to superior technologies. The Gulf War made manifest that the US were the world's sole superpower, and that French conventional forces had serious deficiencies (Buffotot, 1995).

In 1992, President Mitterrand decided to suspend nuclear tests. One of the first things President Chirac did on 13 June 1995 was to announce that French nuclear tests would be restarted. With this "fait accompli" Chirac surprised his NATO partners, and caused worldwide protests against this example of the arrogance of the nuclear monarch Chirac. Experts said that France could have gathered the information they needed by simulation instead of tests. Clearly Chirac wanted to (mis)use the last chance for nuclear tests in the traditional way, before it became prohibited. After the first test at the Mururoa atoll (August 1995) France said that it would suggest a total ban on nuclear tests in Geneva (zero-option). Since January 1994, experts from 38 nations have met in Geneva to formulate a "Comprehensive Test Ban Treaty" (CTBT). On 29 January 1996, Chirac announced that French nuclear tests would be reduced to six (less than planned) and he announced the end of French nuclear tests. On 22 February 1996, Chirac presented ideas to prepare French defence for the 21st century. They included the forming of a regular army, and abolition (for political reasons qualified as a reduction) of conscription (9 months in 1996). For the period 1997-2002 the annual military budget would be under 185 billion francs. Abolition of conscription (estimated to produce a reduction of outlay of 14 billion francs yearly) by no means produced enthusiasm in French society. There was fierce opposition to this idea, which would impair the cherished conception of the "nation-in-arms" as a foundation for real democracy. There was a passionate debate in French society. A strong movement in public opinion was for the maintaining of conscription (with a choice between military and civil work) but this proved to be too expensive. On 27 November 1997 the Council of Ministers approved the Millon bill for the reform of military service with a typically French solution. Conscription was not abolished, but maintained for one week, the "rendez-vous citoyen"; in cases of national emergency for a longer period. Youngsters born after 1 January 1997 would not be called up for military service, but the "rendez-vous citoyen" (5 days) would be obligatory for young men from 1997 on and for women from 2003 on (Buffotot, 1996).

The "Livre blanc sur la défense 1994", meant to cover the period up to 2010, was published 22 years after the "Livre blanc" (1972), where the main features of the defence policy had been set out by General De Gaulle himself. After the traumatic experience of two World Wars, the French Indo-China War (1946-1954) and Algerian War (1954-1962), De Gaulle had the ambition to protect France against humiliating experiences, which had in his view been due to the neglect of the military potency of France. The Presidents of the Republic who came after De Gaulle more or less continued the military policy as determined, but since the Fall of the Berlin Wall (1989), the collapse of East-European Communist regimes and the end of their military coalition in the framework of the Warsaw Pact, military strategy had changed fundamentally. There were also other factors which had made an impact upon the military reorganisation needed for security purposes in Europe in the 21st century (globalisation, technological innovations, etc.). The situation as prophesied by De Gaulle ("L'Europe des nations, de l'Atlantique à l'Oural") was more real than could have been forseen thirty years ago. The 1994 "Livre blanc", with the guaranty of national independence and the defence of vital national interests as objective, confirmed the choice of a credible, permanently adapted, "force nucléaire de dissuasion". It warned against the idea that it was possible to cut military outlays drastically to enjoy the "dividends of peace". The security of Western Europe had to be guaranteed by intensified co-operation in Western Europe. The Treaty of Maastricht (7 February 1992) gave the perspective of a common defence for the European Union. France also had to review its military strategy with regard to NATO, a military alliance that had made a fundamental contribution to European security since 1949. The rather unexpected "Fall of the Berlin Wall" (1989) was the start of the collapse of Communist regimes in Eastern Europe under leadership of the Soviet Union (Fejto, 1992). The military strategy of the West, operational in NATO, was based upon a one-enemy concept: the Soviet Union and its satellites. This military concept had to be changed radically. Now that there was no enemy as before, one might suggest NATO could be abolished.

NATO had however invested much energy in reviewing its role for the future, taking account of the changes in Eastern Europe. In the "North Atlantic Co-operation Council" (NACC), NATO is co-operating with former Warsaw-Pact countries. A "Partnership for Peace" (PFP) was established with 24 Eastern European countries. NATO provided for the "Combined Joint Task Forces (CJTF) to support the defence-part of the WEU. A new task was seen in the battle against the proliferation of nuclear weapons and in the organisation of peacekeeping missions. A new security structure, maintaining transatlantic relations and also implying a new relationship with Russia, was assiduously sought for. This was not easy though. Russia might see an enlargeed NATO including Eastern European countries as a kind of "containment" policy, a security belt against Russia. In December 1994 Russia abruptly refused to sign the PFP-agreements. Russia had its gigantic problems, inter alia its war to prevent Cheznian independence. Americans are generally of the opinion that Europeans themselves should take a much larger part of the responsibility for European security, also financially. At the end of the nineties, some 100,000 American troops were stationed permanently in Europe. Henry Kissinger, in his foreword to "European security and France" (1984) by F. de Rose, questioned the fact that the European continent is delegating its most important security decisions to an ally about 3,000 miles away. France had the idea of giving Europeans a more prominent role in the organisation of NATO. Since December 1990, France had argued for making WEU defence instrument of the European Community (Dumoulin, 1995). This was more or less part of the Maastricht Treaty, ratified in France after approval in the referendum of September 1992. In 1997, France suggested that the supreme command of NATO in the southern part of Europe should be given to a French general or admiral, but that was refused, the Americans wanted to continue their control in this area. At the end of the 1990s, NATO had difficulties in dealing with the question of which East-European countries (formerly Warsaw Pact members, fighting against NATO!) may become members of NATO. Problems, which have to be tackled as a result of the completely changed situation in Europe. Of course, a negative aspect is that NATO had not been able to prevent the ethnic warfare in former Yugoslavia, nor play a decisive role in ending it (Raufer, 1992; Ullman, 1996). The non-intervention principle with regard to internal, national affairs was used as a formal basis to refrain from military force (Damrosh, 1993). NATO lost credibility. The UN had only a peacekeeping, humanitarian role, coupled with diplomatic pressure.

More and more experts are convinced of the necessity to combine efforts in a West-European context. While it is not thought possible for France to maintain its position as an independent, adequate military power (cuts in the military budget, necessity to invest in modern technologies), it has been a fixed French idea that independence does imply procurement of defence material from French industries (as far as possible). Several arguments are used: domestic production is good for employment and the balance of payments, it creates technological spin-offs for civil production. French weapons can be tailored to the needs of the French armed forces and in 1988 the French arms industry directly employed some 261,000 people, about 5 per cent of the industrial workforce (DGA, 1990). Leading French high-tech firms are heavily dependent on arms sales and exports. The three armed forces, publicly lobbying for their part of the military budget, have an intensive network of contacts with the arms industries, in which the French State, and therefore party-politics, has a prominent role (Haenel/Pichon, 1989). Huge outlays for production, research and development in armaments do however reinforce co-operation in the military-industrial complex with other countries (Serfati, 1996) Such collaboration can reduce costs per unit of production, spread financial risks and enable a reasonable critical mass of technical expertise and R & D facilities (Brzoska/Lock, 1992). It was no surprise that on 9 December 1997 France, Great Britain and Germany announced that they would co-operate intensively in the field of military and civil aircraft. In March 1998, a more operational program would be produced. A European Aerospace, combining French Aérospatiale, British Aerospace and German Dasa (and national industries in other European countries), was seen as necessary to meet competition from the overpowering American position (Boeing, Lockheed). Authorities in Spain, Italy and Sweden made it known that they were interested in this initiative. It remains to be seen if France will relinquish national control to win a prominent say in a European context.

On 20 June 1996, Parliament adopted the "loi de programmation militaire 1997-2002", replacing the law for the period 1995-2000. Retrenchment policy made this necessary. The cumulated deficit of the total budget was 558 billion francs in the period 1987-1991, and it was 1,450 billion francs for the period 1992-1996. Public debt rose from 418 billion francs (15% of GNP) in 1980 to 3,500 billion francs (42% of GNP) end 1996. In 1996, interest payments on the public debt (226 billion francs) were higher than military outlays (190 billion francs, pensions excluded). The budget for the new military program was fixed at 185 billion francs a year (99 billion for equipment, 86 billion for operating costs), 20 billion francs less than the former military program budget. The (military and civil) personnel of National Defence were to be reduced in six years from 573,000 to about 440,000 (a cut of 24%). This was due to cancellation of 201,000 jobs for conscripts and 15,600 jobs for non-commissioned officers, and the creation of 27,000 jobs for volunteers, 48,000 jobs for professionals and 9,000 for civilians. The army was hit the most: a reduction from 236,000 to less than 139,000 military. Navy personnel were reduced from 63,000 to 44,800, and air force personnel from 88,000 to 64,000. The total of professionals could grow from 44,450 to 92,527 in 2002. Young volunteers got about 4,000 francs a month, professionals 6,000 francs (Tiroch, 1996). Reductions and retrenchments meant that most programs were impossible to implement adequately. Credits for the "dissuasion nucléaire" were reduced by 20%. A 1998 survey revealed that the fourth position for the French navy had been lost in 1997 (Prézelin, 1998). After the US, Russia and Great-Britain came Japan, overtaking France.

As had become increasingly evident, it was not easy to keep up with nuclear superpowers. The nuclear superpowers themselves are experiencing structural difficulties in keeping up with their own prominent position, especially since the disintegration of the former Soviet Union, there seems to be one super-super nuclear power left: the United States. There are then a number of second-order nuclear powers: France, Russia, China, India, Pakistan. Non-proliferation is by no means under control. In August 1999, preparations for a START-3 treaty between the US and Russia were started, to try to reduce nuclear weapon systems to some 2,500 on both sides. The international "Comprehensive Test Ban Treaty" (CTBT), prohibiting nuclear tests, was signed by five nuclear powers on 24 September 1996,: US, Great Britain, France, Russia, China. Not only the development of new nuclear weapon systems was banned, but also tests which are needed to check whether existing nuclear weapon systems are functioning adequately. The risk of obsolescence looms large for nuclear weapons. The US, sticking to its doctrine of nuclear deterrents, maintains the nuclear triad (nuclear systems located in the US, on submarines and transported by aircraft). To maintain its credibility as a nuclear superpower, US nuclear laboratories issued the "Stockpile Stewardship Plan", costing 45 billion dollars for ten years. All nuclear weapons must be tested yearly for a certificate of complete deployment. Money is needed for "everlasting" usefulness, for simulation projects, etc. It was frustrating that the US Senate, due to party-political games between Republicans and Democrats, refused ratification on 13 October 1999. American law requires a 2/3 majority in the Senate to make ratification possible. Republicans, with a majority in the Senate, used their position to thwart President Clinton (a Democrat). This was a bad example for those States which argue that the CTBT is favourable for the nuclear powers. In October 1999, 154 States had signed the CTBT, and 26 States had in fact ratified this treaty. For the CTBT to become operational it was necessary that the 44 States with nuclear installations also ratify this treaty, so superpower US itself is not bound, while expecting that other States refrain from nuclear testing. This is a risky gamble. India, Pakistan and North Korea, having nuclear capacity, are among the 44 States whose ratification is needed, and who did not sign the CTBT. China signed the treaty in September 1996, but has not yet ratified the CTBT, so the future looks grim, as the way is open for growing nuclear proliferation (Attali, 1995).

## 7.3. Secret services

### 7.3.1 A long tradition of French secret services

A specific part of diplomacy, military and peace management is the work of the secret services on behalf of external and internal security. History is a rich source of relevant information (Faligot/Kaufer, 1993/1994; Hitchcock, 1991; Neilson/McKercher, 1992). There are publications about the secret services in several countries, but about the French secret services there is little information, mostly fragmentary, with some exceptions (Deacon, 1990; Galtier-Boissière, 1938; Garder, 1967; Péan, 1986). French secret services have been analysed systematically in the excellent study by Douglas Porch (1995; 1997): From the discovery of the "bordereau" in the wastebasket of the German military attaché (1894), precipitating the "Dreyfus Affair", to the Gulf War (1990-1991). The "Dreyfus Affair" poisoned French politics for many years (Brédin, 1986; Paléologue, 1958). Secret services functioned under the umbrella of different codes: "BS", "deuxième bureau", "SDECE", "ST", "DST", "RG", "RGPP", "DGSE", "SR", etc. (Esclaibes, 1949/1950) The relationship between public authorities and secret services is ambivalent, often it is a missing dimension (Andrew/Dilks, 1984). Access to information about secret services is restricted, as the law allows the release of information only after 60 years. In the Second World War a lot of information about French secret services was lost. Interception of correspondence was a practise in France of old. In 1590 King Henry IV set up the "Poste aux Lettres" to get information about private matters in the nation. During the "Ancien Régime", the office with the task of opening letters was called the "cabinet noir", "bureau de secret" and "bureau de dedans" (Vaillé, 1959). When this became known, word and cipher codes were used. The Bourbons paid code-breakers well. In the "Cahiers de doléances", the list of complaints on the basis of which the "États Généraux" formulated their propositions for reform in 1789, violation of the privacy of letters was often mentioned. Revolutionaries used all techniques of espionage to trace the (supposed or fictitious) plots of emigrants and others. A "bureau de police générale" was set up to inspect the correspondence of private persons. At the "Quai d'Orsay", the French ministry of foreign affairs, a statistical bureau was formed as a disguise for the secret service. Later Napoleon made espionage an efficient bureaucracy (Savant, 1957). He gave control of national security to the disreputable Joseph Fouché as minister of police, with the "Sûreté" (secret police) as its most prominent part (Arnold, 1979; Madelin, 1903). But Napoleon did not trust Fouché and intriguer Talleyrand. He got daily confidential reports about their activities (Stead, 1957, p.78). When Fouché proved to have secret contacts with the English he was replaced in 1810. The most famous spy of Napoleon was Karl Schulmeister (Elmer, 1932; Savant, 1957). Opposition against "cabinets noirs" was growing from 1828. Government declared that they were abolished, but the work was continued, only more discretely. During the July Monarchy, French police used spies to eliminate opponents of the regime (Daudet, 1912).

With the February Revolution (1848), the "cabinets noirs" were abolished. Some secret agents who had spied upon Louis Bonaparte later worked for him as Napoleon III. During the Second Empire a permanent secret police was formed (Payne, 1966). The collection of information about the opinions and activities of citizens was traditionally a priority for intelligence services in France, this was due to the fear of subversive internal actions supported by external forces. Changes of regime contributed to the fact that police and secret services functionaries saw themselves as working more for the State than for the regime in power. Up to 1866 no foreign power was able to challenge the French armed forces, this partly explains why French military intelligence was less efficient than a century before (Hitchcock, 1991, p.18). "Section Statistique du Dépôt de la Guerre" collected military information about foreign countries, but there was practically no military espionage (Navarre, 1978, p.15). The disastrous decision to send an expeditionary army to Mexico in 1862, was based on distorted information which suggested that a French intervention would be advantageous. According to Stieber (1985), it was easy to get military information about France before the Franco-Prussian War (1870-1871). After 1871, a "Deuxième bureau" was formed, with a "Section de Statistiques et de Reconnaissances militaires" in Rue de Lille, near the German embassy. Shortly before the First World War, secret services were adequate. Throughout Europe governments were most interested in revolutionary movements. "Sûreté" collected information about politicians (Gambetta, Boulanger), former "Communards" (organising the 1871 "Commune" against government) and German spies. Frequent changes of government meant that ministries of defence, foreign affairs and interior built up isolated intelligence services. When Boulanger ("Général Revanche") was minister of war in 1886, counter-espionage received more attention. He ordered the making of a list of individuals who had to be interned in case of war ("Carnet A"). The "Carnet B" included all persons suspected of espionage, who had to be imprisoned in case of a crisis. In 1892, there were preparations for interning some 100,000 suspects in the event of war. Many people on this list were adherents of the anarchist and leftist movements. Before 1890, functionaries, working in the army or navy, had been caught handing over military information. The "Section de Statistiques" ("SS"), seeing spies and treason everywhere, was in the grip of a professional distortion. "SS" was suspicious of people from Alsace who had chosen for French nationality in 1871 when this area was assigned to Germany.

Since the invention of the telegraph, many messages had been sent by telegram, but because of its openness, it was necessary to use codes. In 1883, a new system of cryptography, adapted to telegraphy, became the vogue. This "St.Cyr" system of Kerckhoffs, combined with the tradition of intercepting diplomatic messages, encouraged the breaking of other countries codes. France had the lead in this field (Kahn, 1967). Mrs. Bastian, cleaner at the German embassy in Paris, handed over the contents of the wastebasket to Major Henry of the "Section de Statistiques". On the basis of this practice, Dreyfus, accused of high treason for giving military information to Germany, was arrested. This message leaked out on 1 November 1894 and, on 6 November, the boss of the "SS", Sandherr, found a decoded message on his desk with the addition "our sender is warned" This seemed to prove Dreyfus' guilt, and Sandherr stuck to this conclusion, even when he got the true decoding on 10 November 1894; admitting that a mistake had been made would mean a dramatic loss of prestige for the "SS" and general staff. Major du Paty de Clam concocted another version of the telegram, which was secretly added to the file against Dreyfus. In December 1894 Dreyfus was condemned to lifelong deportation to Devil's Island (Cayenne). The true version of the telegram was disclosed in April 1899 during the re-opening of the case. The sentence was reduced to 10 years and finally annulled in 1906 when Dreyfus was rehabilitated (Paléologue, 1958). This attempt at deceit, which began with not solving the problem of admitting a mistake, had far-reaching consequences. Government avoided thorough investigation, and covered it up (secret service as the honour of the army). Doise (1994) argued that not admitting to false accusations against Jewish officer Dreyfus had nothing to do with anti-Semitism, it was to protect Esterhazy, via whom the Germans were fed information to cheat them over the development of 75-mm artillery. For a long time after this the secret services were in complete disarray and not able to fulfil their genuine task: protection of France against rising German militarism. The "SS" was disbanded. "Sûreté Général" at the Interior got the task of counter-espionage. The French had their "Plan IVbis", based upon the idea that the Germans would attack via Belgium instead of at the French line of defence in Lorraine (Ritter, 1985). There were complaints in Parliament about the poor value for money from the one billion francs spent on intelligence by the Quai d'Orsay. From 1913 the rumours increased about the German army planning to invade via Belgium. According to Navarre (1978, p.18) French intelligence had the Ludendorff-mobilisation plan in its hands, then, shortly before hostilities started, there was a second plan for a rush via Belgium. Intelligence services were handicapped, there was no central point to coordinate the flood of messages and vital information was withheld from other parts of bureaucracy (Homberg, 1938; Navarre, 1978). This meant that in June 1909, armed forces were only informed about a secret treaty between France and Italy, and a large army was stationed in the Alps for nothing (Joffre, 1932).

Governmental instability (governments had an average term of 9 months) contributed to distrust between the fragmented and politicised intelligence services, abused for their political ambitions. In spite of a French lead in intelligence methods and information about German plans, the German offensive was a surprise for the French supreme command. This was probably not the fault of the French intelligence services, but was due to Joffre's reduced and predisposed mental framework (Navarre, 1978, p.18). French military leadership was so self-assured within its own prejudices about the plans of enemies that they did not adequately handle (sometimes confused) information from the intelligence services. In 1911 Michel, convinced that the Germans believed in a "Blitzkrieg" after a rush though Belgium, proposed to concentrate troops (500,000 men) near Lille, with a reserve of 200,000 men near Paris and a reduced army in Alsace-Lorraine (May, 1986), but Joffre's "Plan XVII" was accepted: concentration of troops in Alsace-Lorriane. In February 1912 Joffre asked the government for permission to penetrate Belgian territory if necessary. This was refused, with the argument that this violation of Belgian neutrality would risk the withdrawal of British support (Joffre, 1932; Poincaré, 1926). On 30 July 1914 the Quai d'Orsay received a telegram from the French ambassador in Moscow, Paléologue, informing them that Russian sources reported a general German mobilisation that day. Then Joffre got permission to move his troops, but only up to 10 kilometres from the German borders (Albertini, 1952/ 1957). On 5-6 August 1914 the German attack upon Liege (in neutral Belgium) began. French leadership, ruling by commissions, was divided. The Belgians asked for support from Joffre but he only sent a small army. The French suffered huge losses at the start of the fighting (Cruttwell, 1982), partly because of defective information about the hostile armies (Liddell Hart, 1970). Reports of 31 August 1914 said that German troops were moving Southeast, towards Paris. Tapping German information via radio was of great help (Flicke, 1977). The situation changed when Germans started to move troops to the eastern front, to tackle an unexpected Russian invasion in East Prussia. German troops withdrew to the Marne. German and Allied troops tried to encircle hostile forces. This caused the construction of fortifications and trenches from Switzerland to the North Sea. French code-breakers had successes about the movements of the German armies, greatly improving their prestige.

During the trench-war, circumstances changed for military intelligence services. New techniques became available (radio, telephone, air-reconnaissance) and there was a lot of information. Generally the professional expertise to process this material was scarce. In 1916 the French army had a new military intelligence system (Paquet, 1925). Georges Painvin, professor in palaeontology, was a successful code-breaker (Givierge, 1930) and plotting the location and frequency of radio-transmitters was a good indicator of troop movements. Growth in the number of radio-transmitters near Verdun was one of the first signs of an intended attack by the Germans in 1916 (Morin, 1959), but Joffre did not use this information (Horne, 1963; Krop, 1993). The "deuxième bureau" had already tipped Verdun in January as a potential location for a German attack (Morin, 1959). Later several more indications came in (deserters) but still the attack on 20 February 1916 was a complete surprise (Paquet, 1928). German soldiers approached via "Stollen" (underground passages). A decrease of radio traffic in 1918 was an indication of the retreat of German troops. Lack of information-discipline was an important source of information, combined with the amateurish games with self-fabricated codes (Flicke, 1977; Givierge, 1930). Troop movements behind the front were a clear signal for a planned attack. The interrogation of prisoners of war was a well-tried method of old and the French used language specialists for this work, so a lot of relevant military information was lost. Spies and secret agents were committed (Krop, 1993). Air reconnaissance was useful and the number of air photo's rose from 48,000 (1914) to 675,000 (1918).

A famous case of treachery was that of Mata Hari (Margaretha Zelle-MacLeod), or agent H-21 (Howe, 1986). Germans trained this courtesan-dancer for intelligence work in Paris (Kahn, 1978), where she contacted French intelligence services to work for the French also (Ladoux, 1932). She was arrested in December 1916, and after a spectacular trial (she had prominent clients), condemned and executed in October 1917 (Schirman, 2001; Wheelwright, 1992). This trial furthered the popular idea that France was full of spies, but the German coach of spies, Nicholai (1924, p.183) concluded that his spies did not produce much material. In 1918, Germans had 190 divisions in France. After 10 March 1918 they began to change their codes daily, a signal to their opponents that an attack was coming soon (Givierge, 1930). On the morning of 21 March 1918, some 6,000 pieces of artillery started a curtain-fire over a front of fifty miles between Arras and La Fère near the Somme. Within a week allied troops were driven back 38 miles to Amiens. Since March 1918, Germans had used the "ADFGX" code and messages had come in muddled combinations of these characters (Kahn, 1967, p.339). By 4 April 1918, top French code-breaker Painvin could already decipher this code. A message from German headquarters to the 8th Corps was intercepted on 3 June 1918: the "radiogramme de la Victoire". It meant that Ludendorff would attack near Compiègne. When this hypothesis was confirmed it became possible to drive the German troops back on 9 June 1918. The French knew from 8 July 1918 on that the Ludendorff operation "Friedensturm" (15 July 1918) would take place near Reims and Epernay. The German Michael-offensive bled to death on 8 August 1918 in Amiens. With the golden era of French intelligence (1914-1918) the French had reached the peak of professional intelligence expertise (Lastours, 1998; Porch, 1995, p.112).

*7.3.2 After the First World War*

After 1919 the well-organised French secret services had to cope with new challenges like the rise of Communism and Fascism, while France was in the grip of party-political machinations and governmental instability. Following the Russian Revolution (1917) some two million Russians emigrated to France (Voline, 1997). Paris was a centre of Soviet espionage (Andrew/Gordievsky, 1990). Establishment of the "Parti Communiste Français" (PCF) after the Congress of Tours (1920) increased the possibilities for Soviet intelligence activities. Soviets built up a network of intelligence cells and agents within sections of the armed forces and factories (Dallin, 1955; Faligot/Kauffer, 1993). Communist journal "L'Humanité" started a column "Tribune du Soldat", said to contain information given by soldiers and their families, to undermine the morale of the troops. A police-raid on the offices of PCF in 1923 produced many military documents, collected by comrades in uniform. When the capitalist encirclement theory became dominant in the Kremlin-ideology after 1926, Communist parties in other countries had to be completely Stalinist. France was one of the countries where this objective was substantially realised. Total submission to the Communist party in Moscow was a leading principle. This implied spying against the fatherland. Jean Cremet, member of the central committee of PCF, was the leading man in building up a network in France (Dallin, 1955; Robrieux, 1984). Cells were also formed in the armed forces and public offices, and in heavy industry and the weapons industry. A contact of Cremet, a Soviet-spy (false name Bernstein), disseminating questionnaires on issues of interest to Moscow, was arrested on 9 April 1927 in the act of handing over classified documents. PCF and the Soviet-embassy admitted to the questionnaires. These were qualified as legitimate to defend the interests of workers against warfare and capitalism, active in encirclement of the Soviet Union. Jacques Duclos was a prominent contact of PCF with the Soviets. The attitude of PCF changed drastically after the Nazi take-over in Germany (1933). The French government, with the memory of the Franco-Russian alliance of 1894-1917, concluded a Pact with the Soviets (May 1935). Catching Soviet spies was not a priority any more. In 1936, a Popular Front government was formed with the Communists. Espionage by Soviets was concentrated upon spying on Nazis. Successive governments tolerated the illegal activities of Soviets. Soviet agents could easily get key-positions in the troubled political circumstances of the inter-war period (Ducloux, 1958) and later several persons were exposed as Soviet agents when the Soviet code Venona was broken in 1948. Edouard Pfeiffer, first secretary of Daladier, Minister of war and Premier (1936/1940), was one of them.

The discovery of a Soviet web in the top of the air force (with Soviet agent André Labarthe and others) was alarming. Under responsibility of Pierre Cot, six times minister of the air force since the thirties and pleading passionately for an alliance with Soviets, Moulin, hero for his role in the French resistance, was permanent secretary to Cot. It has been a highly disputed thesis whether or not Moulin was a Soviet spy (Cordier, 1993; Frenay, 1973; Giraud, 1988; Wolton, 1993). According to Wolton (1993) the Air Ministry under Cot was comparable to Cambridge University as a breeding ground for Communist spies and sympathisers. In the inter-war period, intelligence services had to face the fact that governments did not listen to their warnings, even when the Second World War was imminent. The German threat was thought to be non-existent after the Armistice of 11 November 1918. With hindsight, Stehlin (1964) and Moravec (1975) criticised French intelligence services for doing nothing with the warnings about remilitarisation in Germany and the timing of the German attack, but Gauché (1953, p.101), leader of the "deuxième bureau" since 1935, argued that it was political and military leaders who had done nothing with the adequate reports from his office (Castellan, 1954; Garder, 1967; Stehlin, 1964). The methods of the 'Blitzkrieg", used in Poland in September 1939, were known by professional reports of French intelligence (Beaufre, 1968; Laqueur, 1988). Alexander (1992) listed the achievements of French intelligence services. They had warned in time of a German reoccupation of Rhineland (1936); "Anschluss" with Austria (1938); preparations for occupation of Czechoslovakia (1938); invasion of Poland (1939) and German-Russian Treaty (August 1939). Communications between the "Quai d'Orsay" and the "deuxième bureau" were good (Navarre, 1978). French "SR" played a decisive role in deciphering the "Enigma" codes, very useful for the Allies (Bertrand, 1973). The relationship between professional information-gathering and decision-making was the weak point. Political and military leaders did not use intelligence work. Supreme commander Gamelin (1946-1947), unwilling to fight for countries in Central-Eastern Europe, played games. Alarming messages about German combat capacity undermined the will to fight in an atmosphere of disarmament illusions.

When Pétain had accepted an armistice after the humiliatingly quick defeat of June 1940, without even knowing the conditions, France had its Vichy-regime (1940-1944). Intelligence officer Paillole (1975), who had a problem of loyalty with regard to the Vichy-regime because it collaborated with Nazis against the French resistance movement, escaped to London with Roger Rivet. By December 1942 he was at BCRA ("Bureau Central des Renseignements et d'Action") of the Free French, where he met Passy (André Dewavrin). Passy was a young officer to whom De Gaulle had entrusted the guidance of intelligence work (Passy, 1947;1951). Rivet was given charge of the "SR". In Autumn 1940 operation-Dakar of the Free French was a complete failure due to a lack of intelligence security. Churchill ordered the arrest of the supreme commander of the Free French, Muselier, on the basis of evidence from M15 that he was responsible for the leak. On 8 January 1941 De Gaulle demanded that Muselier be released, otherwise he would break relations with the British government. When Scotland Yard had found out that the documents were forged, Churchill apologised and Muselier was released. This incident contributed to structural suspicion between British and French intelligence services. The British had two separate intelligence services, one related with the Free French and one to the Vichy-regime. Gaullists viewed this as criminal (Foot, 1966; Porch, 1995, p.184). Jean Moulin, forging the unity of the French resistance, came to London (December 1941). He got the task of bringing France into the best position after the German defeat. When it seemed that an agent of the Vichy-regime had penetrated the BCRA, Passy ordered Roger Wybot (alias Warin) to organise counter-espionage (Bernert, 1975). Passy tried to persuade the French resistance to be loyal to De Gaulle, but the French were paralysed by their defeat (Ferro, 1987). On 3 June 1943 the "Comité Française de Libération Nationale" (CFLN) was formed, under leadership of De Gaulle and Giraud. Their troops were fused for the fight against the Nazis. De Gaulle made himself president of the provisional government and Giraud supreme commander. He later fired Giraud.

But there was an internal war between the secret services, some of whom feared party-political influences (Garder, 1967). On 27 November 1943, Soustelle was asked to lead the new "Direction Générale des Services Spéciaux" (DGSS), overarching existing secret services. De Gaulle formed a "Comité d'Action en France" (CAF), with himself as president and Soustelle as secretary. In this way De Gaulle ensured that the DGSS did not fall under military command, but reported directly to him (Soustelle, 1950). Secret services of the resistance made an important contribution, but their influence should not be exaggerated, any more than that of French resistance (Buton, 1994). Despite the loss of many lives, the "Résistance", as a major contribution to the defeat of Nazi-Germany, was a national myth, exploited especially by the Communists and Gaullists. Because of their activities in resistance Communists got prominent positions in the provisional government and first governments of the Fourth Republic. After the Second World War circumstances had also changed for the secret services. During and shortly after this war, De Gaulle, in his insatiable drive for French independence with regard to the Anglo-Americans, tried to build up relations with the Soviet Union (Paxton/Wahl, 1994). De Gaulle was criticised for his tolerance with regard to French Communists, allowing them to reach high positions in several public authority functions and sensitive sectors. Communist Joliot-Curie became chief of scientific research, inclusive of nuclear research. Peter Wright, formerly a member of the British intelligence service M15, made known that his office suspected that the inner circle around De Gaulle (Labarthe, Muselier) had been infiltrated by Communists. More became known about this after 1964 following the breaking of the Soviet Venona-code

(1948). Not only could Burgess and McLean be unmasked as spies but the French Labarthe and Cot proved to have given information to Soviets. One can understand why Anglo-American intelligence services kept their French colleagues at a distance. Much military information was given to the Soviets (Dallin, 1955). Communists, thanks to their role in resistance against Nazis, had the support of 1/4 of the electorate.

It was difficult for the secret services to concentrate work upon the USSR. This changed after the Cold War. It was a "mission impossible" to do their work impartially in a thoroughly party-political atmosphere. Quai d'Orsay was informed in February 1946 that, according to the American embassy in Paris, a Communist uprising was likely. In that same month, Socialist Ribière succeeded Passy as chief of "Direction Générale des Études et Recherches" (DGER). On 5 May 1946 Passy was arrested on the authority of his successor Ribière for fraud with bank accounts. This arrest, announced just before the 6 May 1946 referendum about the Constitution, was seen as damaging for De Gaulle, because Passy was one of his closest colleagues, but Passy was soon rehabilitated. When colonial wars (Indo-China) increasingly influenced politics, there were many rivalries between the fragmented secret services, poisoned by old settlements and party-political machinations (Williams, 1970). On 2 July 1954, Fouchet, Minister of Moroccan and Tunisian affairs in the Government-Mendès-France, got a report with regard to a meeting of the PCF politburo from an officer of the secret services, Dides. This gave a complete account of the meeting of the "Comité de Défense Nationale" (CDN) of 28 June 1954. Dides said that he could not give this document to his superiors, as he thought that the new Minister of the Interior, Mitterrand, was the source of the leak. Fouchet informed Mendès-France, ordering an investigation without informing Mitterrand. Shortly before a CDN meeting of 10 September 1954 the Prime Minister handed over the document to Mitterrand.

Mitterrand's "treason" was secretly-openly discussed in Paris. It was found that only two people made notes during CDN meetings, secretary Mons (with Mendès-France as friend) and one of his two assistants, Labrusse or Turpin. Labrusse admitted that Turpin made copies from Mons' notes for Baranès, giving them to his former boss in the "Libération" movement, d'Astier de la Vignerie. Labrusse got six years in prison, and Turpin four years. The case against Baranès was dropped (he did what Dides ordered him) and d'Astier was not prosecuted because of his parliamentary immunity. So this "affaire des fuites" (leakages), seemed to show that spies with good connections were immune from prosecution (Porch, 1995, pp. 289-291). For Wybot (Bernert, 1975), d'Astier was the centre of a spy network, which if revealed, would have equalled the unmasking of spies like Philby in Great Britain or Guillaume, assistant to German Chancellor Brandt, who had to resign in 1974. The atmosphere was troubled, as became obvious from Soviet defectors, who in the sixties declared that French secret services had been penetrated by Soviets (Brook-Sheperd, 1989). KGB-agent Golitsyn said, when he defected in December 1961, that there were "moles" inside NATO-headquarters, French ministries and the inner circle around De Gaulle and a KGB-network, "Saffier" seemed to have infiltrated the French SDECE (Faligot/Krop, 1989; Mangold, 1991). President Kennedy, via diplomatic channels, warned De Gaulle of this, who reacted by ordering his secret services to break all ties with the CIA. This Saffier-case would bring suspicion between US and France to its nadir. The CIA thought that Foccart, organising Gaullist secret services in the fifties, was leading Saffier from the Élysée itself (Péan, 1990). Colonial wars in Indochina (Francini, 1988) and Algeria (Jauffret, 1990), and the process of decolonisation were very demanding for the secret services. For Porch (1995, p.403), decolonisation wars in Indo-China and Algeria showed that French services had a unique intelligence culture.

After the Socialist victory at the elections in 1981, Socialist Belorgey presided over a parliamentary investigation into secret services. This committee concluded that intelligence services, throughout 23 years of conservative rule (1958-1981) under the umbrella of the "loi secret-défense", had accumulated a great number of failures, scandals and dubious operations (Guisnel/Violet, 1988, pp. 107-108). Marion (1991, pp. 115-116), chief of SDECE since 1981, said that secret services had been disparaged by the political leadership of the previous two decades. In 1981 SDECE was succeeded by the DGSE ("Direction Générale de la Sécurité Extérieure") for foreign intelligence. Rivalry between intelligence services was intense. DST ("Direction de la Surveillance du Territoire") was responsible for internal security. In the summer of 1985, during the "Rainbow Warrior affair", DST co-operated with the New Zealand police by informing them about operations of DGSE (Guisnel/Violet, 1988, p.215). It was normal to build up party-politically trustworthy intelligence networks, parallel to the official intelligence services. Hundred of thousands of dossiers were made on French individuals on the basis of tapping, opening of correspondence, infiltration in political parties, trade-unions etc. Tapping of telephones increased after 1962 with the "Groupement Interministériel de Contrôle" (GIC) during the struggle with the OAS (Delarue, 1981; Kauffer, 1986). Telephone tapping became a public non-secret, everybody took account of it (Moréas, 1990). Gaullist Pasqua, becoming Minister of the Interior in 1986 after Socialist Joxe, saw that his RG dossier contained notes about his private telephone calls. He criticised Joxe for transforming the RG into a political police force. The satirical journal "Le Canard Enchaîné" revealed in July 1994 that an RG agent had overheard a non-public meeting of the Socialist bureau, so Minister Pasqua knew that Rocard would end his position as party-leader. Pasqua ordered that RG should no longer report on political parties, although this was their mandate as long as Socialists were in government. Apart from officially authorised tapping, there was much "wild" tapping ("sauvage"). For several intelligence services, withholding of information and spying on each other was just a sport (Burdan, 1990, p.83).

President Mitterrand built his own Élysée-cell, as his predecessors had done before. Foccart, an active Gaullist after work in the colonies and resistance, formed the "Service d'Action Civique" (SAC), a Gaullist paramilitary organisation. Foccart arranged that everywhere in public administration there were officials who were absolutely loyal to De Gaulle. When De Gaulle retired in 1969, Foccart, with his SAC and import-export business Safiex, had an extensive network throughout former French colonies in Africa (McNamara, 1989). He could arrange anything (including violence). When Chirac was Premier in 1975, he had Foccart as his adviser for Africa. Later Foccart proved to be involved in a number of affairs (Péan, 1983). One of the suspect characters working for Foccart was Bob Denard, who was charged in 1993 for his part in the 1977 coup in Benin. Insiders told the court that Denard was acting with official authorisation. Denard remained active in organising coups etc. He moved to the Comoro Isles, where he organised a failed coup in 1995. When the Socialists came to power in 1981, they were very eager to start a parliamentary investigation about SAC (Report "Assemblée nationale", 1982). SAC, branded as a dangerous parallel police-organisation, was disbanded in July 1982. President Mitterrand was over-suspicious about official secret services after the "Affaire des fuites" (1954), in which he had been falsely accused. He charged his son to organise a parallel intelligence network for African matters. When terrorism became outrageous after 1985, Mitterrand, distrusting regular services, charged the GIGN ("Groupement d'Intervention de la Gendarmerie Nationale") under Prouteau with anti-terrorism. There was a bitter fight between DST, DGSE and "Élysée cellule", misinforming each other (Burdan, 1990, pp. 10-11). Mitterrand had to work with a conservative government after 1986. Feeling cut off from DST, he gave the Élysée cell a grand computer linked with the systems of DGSE, giving Prouteau full powers for anti-terrorist measures with his authority.

An absolute nadir for French secret services was the "Rainbow Warrior Affair" (Porch, 1995, ch. 19). The sinking of this ship, belonging to the international environmental movement Greenpeace, on 10 July 1985 in the harbour of Auckland (New Zealand) was a drama full of lessons about failing leadership (Mafart, 1999). During the night of 10 July 1985, two frogmen swam to the Rainbow Warrior to place time bombs. When two French secret agents, Mafart and Prieur (travelling with false Swiss passports as Alain and Sophie Turenge), approached the ship half an hour later, they were detected by guards who noted the registration number of their rented car. Near midnight, the first bomb exploded and the twelve people on board left the ship, as was intended in the planning, so that no one would be hurt by the second bomb. Things went wrong, however, because the Dutch photographer went back to the ship to collect his equipment and died in the second explosion. The operation was so amateurish that the New Zealand police had an easy job. The Turenges were detained when they returned their rental car. They were charged with murder. French authorities tried to cover it up and when the press got hold of some information, DGSE started a misinformation project: the dead photographer was a KGB-agent, it was an Anglo-Saxon plot! The clumsy attempts to hush up this nasty affair produced more explosive reactions, as the truth gradually became known. Minister of Defence Hernu and DGSE chief Lacoste tried to deny that they had ordered the sinking. Mitterrand asked Tricot to investigate the case. The report-Tricot (end August) exonerated DGSE: Hernu and Lacoste had told him that DGSE people were on an intelligence mission, and did not plant the bombs.

Although the public realised that this was a new hush-up trick, the lies and shuffling continued. On 19 September 1985 Mitterrand forced Hernu and Lacoste to take the blame. At last, too late, Hernu and Lacoste faced the consequences and resigned. It was evident that this sinking by the French secret service could never have happened without the explicit authorisation of President Mitterrand himself. Later it was proven that Mitterrand had authorised this operation. But Mitterrand continued to brazen it out. The sinking was not an accident, but part of long-term planning. Since 1970 SDECE had the sinking of ships of environmental groups, opposing the French nuclear tests, in its toolbox, though activities mostly had a limited character, such as wrecking etc. (Dyson, 1986; King, 1986). Tensions near the Mururoa atoll, centre of French nuclear testing, became ever more stressed (Danielsson, 1986). Governments and peoples of South Pacific countries sharply criticised the French nuclear tests. Faligot and Krop (1989) argued that an obsession had developed on the Mururoa atoll, fearing a bizarre conspiracy of Anglo-Saxons, environmentalist activists, and nationalist groups financed by Communists and Soviets. They were all seen as undermining French nuclear independence. When the time approached for tests in 1985, Admiral Fages, head of "Direction du Centre d'Expérimentations Nucléaires", feared that Greenpeace would blockade tests crucial for the nuclear warheads of the M4 submarine Hades and the tactical neutron bomb. The operation might have been successful, if only...

Once the operation had failed, the most appropriate procedure for the politicians involved would have been, for Mitterrand in the first place, to have taken responsibility as a professional. But the opposite happened. Premier Fabius did his best to discover who was ultimately responsible, but he could not break the secret Élysée kernel. This caused a rift between Mitterrand (blaming the secret services, "full of bandits", for this) and Fabius. Fabius put pressure on the New Zealand government to free the captured French secret agents, arguing that as they were only executing orders they were not guilty. Both agents (professionally) were willing to plead guilty to involuntary manslaughter, to spare the French government and DCSE. On 22 November 1985, they were sentenced to ten years in prison. The French government made things worse by retaliating against New Zealand in the sphere of customs tariffs. Canadian Premier Trudeau mediated for an agreement. France would pay 2.3 million francs to the family of the dead photographer, compensate Greenpeace for the lost boat and offer New Zealand a formal apology. For these concessions the captured French agents were released into French custody in July 1986. Mafart and Prieur would have to remain on the Hao atoll until July 1989, but Premier

Chirac had Mafart, who was suffering from gastro-enteritis, moved to France in December 1987. For Dominique Prieur a solution was concocted: her husband was sent to the Hao atoll to make his wife pregnant, and in May 1988 the mother-to-be was permitted to return to France. France had to pay New Zealand 2 million dollars to compensate for this "bad faith" in living up to its obligations. Porch (1995, p.468), rightly accentuating the specific French culture in which secret services have to function, concludes that intelligence might have been important for policy at significant moments in French history, but that it seldom functioned efficiently. Experts as Paillole (1975) and Navarre (1978) found that intelligence work was good but that politicians and generals did not care for it enough (Lacoste, 1998).

Relations between public authorities, responsible for decision-making about policy and for the interests of their nation, and secret services (guarding the interests of the nation) are complex. As a historical view shows, it is an impossible mission (Marion, 1991) to fulfil the functions of intelligence in a neutral, objective way, while circumstances and responsible persons change so often. A crucial factor is the mindset of decision-makers, responsible as public authorities. Intelligence can give public authorities the information they want to hear, filtering away that which contradicts their prejudices. Then intelligence is denying its professionalism (Handel, 1989). This professionalism has its price, because intelligence flying in the face of authority risks being disparaged. Political and military leadership normally has more impact upon the secret and intelligence services than the reverse. Secret services must be able to switch when circumstances change or responsible authorities are replaced by others. There is historical evidence for the thesis that excellent intelligence cannot prevent bad judgement. Fragmentation of intelligence services, with their rivalries and even wars, can be a patent medicine against "groupthink". Authorities can then dispose of various advices (multiple advocacy). In a party-politically distraught climate such as in the French Third and Fourth Republics, this fragmentation can be counterproductive, especially when information is used for the objectives of politicians. During the Fifth Republic, this dominant influence of party-politics has been continued so far. Keiger (2001, p.107) argued: "The French need to know themselves and the value of an intelligence community before they can realistically and effectively assess their place in the world. The abiding French belief that what France does or says is a permanent source of admiration or jealousy for the rest of the world is the kind of national complex that the intelligence services have tended to feed rather than overcome." As was made crystal clear during the Gulf War (1990-1991), the US military intelligence was far superior to that of the French (Cooke, 1993). Without any doubt, the French learned lessons. In the coming period new revelations will doubtless produce shocking material about the work of secret services and involvement of important politicians, unknown so far. Disclosure of the "Mitrokhin Archive" made this obvious (Andrew/ Mitrokhin, 1999). Codes are a necessary tool (Singh, 1999). There are new challenges, such as the fight against terrorism and criminality; scientific and technological espionage; etc. Secret services are professionally condemned to work amidst ambiguous claims, even in the 21st century (Baud, 1997; Codevilla, 1992; Waller, 1996). Espionage will always be with us. "Echelon" proves it (European Parliament, 1998; 2000).

## 7.4. International relations and diplomacy

### 7.4.1 Territorial obsession

Ubi societas, ibi ius. Lasting peace by making the Rule of Law dominant is crucial for the building of society. Creating a society for a group of people within a specific territory depends on the capacity to manage relations with other groups. Making the Rule of Law dominant in international relations has of old been the weak link in their management. International relations between Nation-States are a field in which physical, material, economic and military dimensions are relevant, but also cultural, ethical, psychological and spiritual aspects (Jouve, 1992; Zorgbibe, 1993). The study of international relations has been about diplomatic history, international law, political philosophy, and economics. Now it includes disciplines like anthropology, sociology, psychology, and ethnology among others. Many changes have transformed the field of international relations (Braillard/Djalli, 1994): universalisation of the Nation-State, multilateralisation of diplomacy, globalisation, decolonisation, new weapons systems (nuclear, biological, chemical), the worldwide impact of economic and financial markets, communications technology, consciousness of ecological problems as worldwide problems, migration flows and international terrorism. The discipline "International Relations" was named daughter of the Versaillles Conference (1919), with an accent on regulating international conflicts by law, but International relations are a phenomenon with roots in history from earliest times (Renouvin/Duroselle, 1970). For a long period, populations lived in isolated communities with little communication with the outside world. Of old groups had a "territorial obsession" (Scelle), an unquenchable drive for expansion of territory as power base. Peoples or groups living together in the neighbourhood of other peoples and groups had communications (warfare, economic relations). There were customs, which evolved the characteristics of law ("treaties", commercial contracts). In other parts of the world, extensive empires developed (China, Egypt etc.). The Roman Empire had its hegemony around Mediterranean and in Western Europe (Ferrill, 1985; Harmand, 1967; Harris, 1985; Keppie, 1984; Luttwak, 1987; Peddie, 1994; Richardot, 1998).

Touscoz (1993, p.30) distinguished three periods with regard to international law: the period up to the 16th century (international law under influence of Roman law and Christianity); "Europe-centric" international law, up to the First World War; and universalisation of international law since 1914-1918. Up to the fall of the West-Roman Empire (476), military force determined international relations, law had some influence. There were juridical rulings between Greek settlements around the Mediterranean. Romans, with their military power and legal system, established an institutional basis for control over a wide territory. The rule of war was dominant, foreigners were barbarians, forced to sign "treaties". Christianity, in the cultural footsteps of Jewish traditions, caused the most impressive transformation in the building up of international society (Touscoz). Without denying the impact of other religions, especially in other parts of the world, it can be said that Christianity had a special impact thanks to its combination with the organising genius of Roman institutions. After being persecuted systematically, Christianity became the official religion in the Roman Empire. Christianity taught that all human beings of all races, languages or nations are created by a loving God, and are therefore equal and free. Inevitably this had its influence on the origins of Western international law (humanising warfare, condemnation of aggression wars, "pacta sunt servanda", etc.). During the Middle Ages (5th-15th centuries) the impact of Roman and Christian institutions was different in Western Europe (fragmentation of public authorities in a feudal society) from that in the East-Roman Empire. In Western Europe, appalling societal uncertainty and insecurity were frustrating normal life, especially because of structural insecurity, and disastrous uncertainty about the existence of law and the question of which law was applicable. Throughout these ten centuries, international law was developed within a specific context. With the inspiration of Church fathers and theologians, the concept of law of nations ("ius gentium") was elaborated. Natural law was seen as law, which could be deduced by reason from human nature. Among the first authors about international law, theologians and pioneers of natural law like Francisco de Vitoria (1480-1546) and Francisco Suarez (1548-1617) were prominent. In "De potestate civili" and "De Indis et de iure belli", De Vitoria saw public authority as a necessary institution, coming from natural law (not from Church or a Prince). For him, the partition of territories was possible, but the sea has to be open for all.

Suarez differentiated between (variable) law of nations and (invariable) natural law. De Vitoria and Suarez were the intellectual heirs of Aristotle (384-322 BC), as interpreted by Thomas Aquinas (1225-1274) in his search for the "bonum commune". Natural law was seen as law according to the will of God, which could be discovered from human nature. This natural law was elaborated, systematised and stripped from its character as necessarily-given-by-God ("laïcisé", secularised) by Hugo Grotius (1583-1645). His publications "Mare liberum" (1609) and "De iure belli ac pacis" (1625) are famous. Grotius elaborated that natural law is composed of principles of the just reason, which give individuals and states criteria for good and evil. This idealistic natural law continued to inspire for a long time, until it was succeeded by legal positivism in the 1850s. In medieval times, there were numerous local wars between feudal war lords. The conflict between Christianity and Islam was an overarching phenomenon. In the West, Islam was held back after Charles Martel won the battle of Poitiers (732). To re-conquer the "Holy Land", Popes even asked civilian authorities to start Crusades against Islam (1096/1270). In spite of military confrontations, there were numerous contacts between Christian and Islamic worlds in cultural and economic-commercial fields. Venice and Genoa, with commercial networks in the Islamic world, formed a creative ambience for innovations (bills of exchange, arbitration, ambassadors and consuls, etc.). In 1453 the Turks conquered Constantinople, the fall of the East-Roman Empire. After 1492, Muslims were expelled from Spain.

When Columbus "discovered" America in 1492, a new period began with a new world order (1492-1648). The dominant position of the Church was apparent with the Bulla "Inter Caetera" (1493) of Pope Alexander VI. The Pope, acting as if he were supreme authority of the whole world, ruled that the territory left of a line 100 sea miles from the Cape Verde Islands was under the sovereignty of Spain. Portugal and Spain, on the basis of this papal partition, made settlements about new territories. The Treaty of Tordesillas (1494) moved the line some 270 sea miles further to the West, and the Treaty of Saragossa (1529) complemented this settlement. These treaties had regulations to prevent papal initiatives in the field of territorial division. The Reformation, following Luther's 95 theses to reform the Church (1517), ended the unity of Christianity. In the German Holy Roman Empire conflicts and wars between Protestants and Catholics had a grim character until the Religious Peace of Augsburg (1555). From then on the principle was that a Protestant or Catholic prince could determine the religion of the people in his territory: "cuius regio eius religio". Religious wars in France (1562-1594) were a terrible experience, also for Jean Bodin (1530-1596). He elaborated a concept of indivisible, perpetual and supreme sovereignty for the monarch or the State (Republic) as the best medicine for chaos as during the religious wars. Niccolo Machiavelli (1469-1527) in "Il Principe" (1513) argued that absolutist power of the monarch was necessary for the ruling of a State. The Thirty Years War (1618-1648) was traumatic for German Catholics and Protestants. Other countries became involved in this conflict also. It was a real blessing when the Peace of Westphalia (1648) ended this religious warfare. In negotiations leading to this Peace of Westphalia, the great majority of European countries were represented, the first Grand European Congress. The Peace of Westphalia formally ruled Europe for nearly a century, with guarantees for European order. Sovereignty and equality of the States were settled.

Since the 16th century, Europe, in spite of dissension and conflicts, had become more or less the centre of the world. International law had Europe-centric characteristics (Mauro, 1988). In Europe, sovereign Nation-States developed. This model of political organisation has been universal since then. The Nation-State was seen as the appropriate sphere to end the existing chaotic situation of several law systems, by organising national law. A new phenomenon was the creation of a continent-state with the independence of the United States since 1776. After the future shock of the French Revolution (1789) and the Napoleonic wars, the Congress of Vienna (1815) laid the foundations for the "European Concert" with an extended network of bilateral or multilateral treaties and conventions. European countries were active in colonising territories in other continents (Africa, Asia). After the 16th century, and especially in the century between the Congress of Vienna and the outbreak of the First World War, so-called classical international law was elaborated, largely inter-state law. Sovereign and formally equal States developed a system of treaties and alliances in the framework of diplomacy for a balance of power (diplomatic law). This was combined with customary rules and conventions, which partly continue to have validity up till now. The Vienna Congress (1815) prohibited slavery, but the transport of slaves was only combated effectively since the Convention of London (1841). In 1899 and 1907, two conferences were organised in The Hague, leading to treaties for settling international conflicts. Since the start of the 19th century, former colonies have become independent states in Latin America. Decolonisation accelerated after 1945. The First World War, with an impact on the whole world, made it obvious that international law was necessary for humanity: peace by law.

The League of Nations, formed in the aftermath of the 1914-1918 war, had a series of competencies, but this League of Nations functioned upon the principle of unanimity. This meant that when one totalitarian state or several states refused co-operation there was no possibility for the League of Nations to intervene. When it is said, at the end of the 20th century, that France would never agree to giving away part of its sovereign rights in exchange for international or supranational institutional arrangements, it has to be remembered that during the Versailles process France had a farsighted attitude. France tried in vain to persuade other countries to enable the League of Nations to dispose of armed forces to interfere against aggressors. The Permanent Court of International Justice (PCIJ) was established, the first court with limited competencies to decide upon conflicts between States. The weakness of the League of Nations was manifest when Germany and Japan caused the Second World War. After this war, the conquerors established a new international order with the United Nations Organization (UNO), having the General Assembly as the organ in which all member-states participate. Primary responsibility for maintenance of peace was entrusted to the Security Council, composed of five countries with veto-power: United States, Great Britain, France, USSR and China. After the Communist take-over, China was not adequately represented, as it was represented by Formosa (later Taiwan). The Cold War between US and USSR meant that all issues were blocked by a veto of one or other member of the Security Council. The conflict between East (Communist Eastern Europe, co-operating in the Warsaw Pact under leadership of the Soviet Union) and West (US with partners in NATO) dominated international relations up to 1989 (Fall of the Berlin Wall). Other conventions were more effective: World Bank, International Monetary Fund (IMF), General Agreement on Tariffs and Trade (GATT), and World Trade Organisation (WTO). Since the collapse of Communist Eastern Europe, there has been a new situation.

The process of decolonisation accelerated after the sixties and seventies. The new independent Nation-States, the "Group-77", had the majority in the General Assembly of the UN. Now this group consists of more than 120 Nation-States, causing a new international economic order. When Iraq invaded Kuwait in August 1990 the USSR did not use its veto in the Security Council, so a coalition under the leadership of the US was able to drive the Iraqi's back in the Gulf War (January-February 1991). International security is a permanently vulnerable issue, while in several parts of the world there are time and again new wars. A recent example were the civil "ethnic" wars in former Yugoslavia, ending formally (not really) with the Dayton Agreements (1995). UN peacekeeping forces had to prevent civil wars breaking out again. In 1999, NATO had to intervene militarily in Kosovo. The number of wars and armed conflicts in the world was 52 in 1992, a record since 1945. The Hamburg Institute for War Research concluded that there were 25 armed conflicts worldwide in 1997 (11 in Africa). Several factors causing real risks for the outbreak of armed conflicts can be enumerated: international trade in conventional weapons worth about 37 billion American dollars (2000), poverty and hunger for millions, ethnic conflicts, proliferation of nuclear weapons (Pakistan and India had nuclear weapons in 1999), massive debts for developing countries, territorial ambitions, international terrorism and criminality (Laqueur, 1987; Reich, 1990), environmental problems, shortage of primary raw materials, energy, water etc.: "Global 2001" (Earthscan London, 1999). Peace depends on people's goodwill more than on institutions and international law, important for a peaceful world.

*7.4.2 International law is broader than interstate law*

The growing influence of international relations in earlier times made it necessary for States (or their predecessors) to build up a professional diplomatic organisation. During the 5th and 4th centuries BC, there was a kind of diplomacy in Greece and Asia Minor (Anderson, 1970). Greek city-states used commercial, political and military networks for communications with other city-states and with the Persian Empire, sending special envoys (Watson, 1983). In the Byzantine Empire, trained professionals were sent abroad (Nicholson, 1954). The Carolingian Empire used "missi", following examples of the Roman Empire and the Church (Der Derian, 1987). Since the 14th century, Italian Republics (Venice, Genoa) had sent representatives abroad to organise their commercial interests. Soon international customs were developing which also had their influence upon the wider economic and political dimensions of international relations. Diplomacy was developing, especially after the Thirty Years War (1618-1648), but with reminiscences to the period before our era. Since the time that Nation-States were formed, diplomatic work has been extended and professionalised. By the end of the 17th century, most of institutionalised diplomacy was established in Europe: resident diplomatic missions, a "corps diplomatique" with professional diplomats, and diplomatic immunities. An important part of diplomacy took place secretly. In times when international communications for our ideas were rather primitive, it became common practice to have embassies abroad. The ambassador was the representative of his State, more or less the incarnation of the State. He had to protect the interests of his State and its nationals, and to build up good relations with public authorities in the other State. Diplomacy (organised dialogue between independent states), as the game of Nations, has a long history. French diplomacy for centuries (Droz, 1982) and recently (Duroselle, 1985) set its seal upon diplomatic management of international relations worldwide. The diplomatic envoy under Louis XIV, François de Callieres, wrote the first modern manual for diplomats (Watson, 1983). An apex of diplomacy was the Congress of Vienna (1815), when European powers pursued diplomacy with the European Concert to maintain the existing balance of powers (Albrecht-Carrié, 1965; Heeren, 1873). This European diplomacy kept Europe free from wars for a century, except for some partial wars such as the Franco-Prussian War in 1870-1871 (Watson, 1983). In a rush for colonies European powers shifted rivalries outside Europe.

Many authors identify international law and interstate law, and so States are considered to be the sole or principal subjects of international law. Touscoz (1993, p.22) does question this dominant French doctrine. He emphasizes that the State is neither the sole nor the principal subject of international law. In his conception, international law regulates international society, which is more diverse than interstate society. States have a prominent position in international society, and international public law is an important part of international law. But there are several other subjects of international law too. Worldwide there are more than 200 States. More than 200 international (intergovernmental) organisations can be enumerated. More than 3,000 non-governmental organisations (NGOs) are internationally active. Many private organisations and corporations play an important role also and, last but not least, all human beings have to be seen as subjects of international society (global village). Without underrating these actors, some aspects of the role of the Nation-States in the context of public international law are dealt with here. International private law is largely composed of national rules to solve conflicts between laws and jurisprudence from different Nation-States. There are a number of conventions between Nation-States, regulating relations between the individuals or corporations of various Nation-States. International customs law is important. The law system can be more knit up between some Nation-States in a region, as in the European Union.

The international juridical order is the whole body of rules and institutions regulating relations in international society. Although there are many partial, regional and local juridical orders, the international juridical order can be qualified as a specific order by its unity and its juridical character (binding rules, with sanctions upon violations). In international relations, the international juridical order is a reality, although far from satisfying, when one uses criteria such as justice and peace for all human beings. Many authors deny that there is a real international juridical order. So-called realists argue that international law is only an expression of existing power-relations. Others argue that international law is mostly nothing more than uncoercive ethics. Realists assert that treaties as concluded between Nation-States are violated as soon as the real power-equilibrium is disturbed and also that international law is stretched for a sovereign Nation-State if vital interests are at stake. It is said that international law is often invoked to legitimise the power politics of Nation-States. These views have their relevance for international relations as they are often in practice, but international law is a reality, and a protection for the weak against the powerful. Implementation of international law is often relative due to insufficient sanctions, but there is a generally respected body of international law. There are many international, regional, multilateral and bilateral conventions that have smoothed international relations. The UNO is reasonably effective for regulating international conflicts, but its competence is reduced by the non-intervention principle: it cannot interfere in the internal affairs of a State, even in case of genocide, ethnic cleansing and other brutalities.

In national law, the existence of the (Nation-) State is mostly taken for granted. This is different for international law, partly because the conditions under which a specific organisation upon a certain territory can be recognised as State are relevant (Charpentier, 1956). For the birth of a State (Jessup, 1974), two juridical questions are relevant in international law. The right of peoples to make their own choices, the principle of self-determination (Jouve, 1986), and under what conditions existing States will recognise a new State, and what the consequences of this will be. There are groups and minorities, with a specific culture, religion, race, history and/or language, which are oppressed or cannot develop their identity adequately within the territory of a State. Upon the same territory, one section of the population, claiming the right of self-determination, is often in conflict with another group which wants to maintain the status quo. Realisation of the right to self-determination depends on political circumstances (Pomerance, 1982). Difficulties can develop when the legitimate claim of an oppressed minority, longing for independence and using violence to achieve this end, disturbs international order and security. Since revolutions of 1848, it has been popular to claim the right to form an independent State. The nationality-principle was invoked within the Ottoman Empire and the Austrian-

Hungarian Donau Monarchy. After 1914-1918, the nationality-principle was applied for the creation of new States or the revitalisation of old States. That this nationality-principle can also be abused was demonstrated by Hitler claiming that all Germans (by race, culture, and language) should be reunited in one "Reich". Organisation of Eastern Europe after the Second World War was in a number of cases (annexation of the Baltic States by the USSR; division of Germany; dislocation of Polish borders; etc.) against the self-determination principle. Since the collapse of the Communist regimes in Eastern Europe, this principle gained a new actuality. This principle also played an important role with regard to the process of decolonisation, especially after 1945. Often there is a tension between the principle of self-determination and that of the integrity of the State territory. New States, resulting from the decolonisation process, are often multicultural and/or multi-ethnic, with artificial borders. As the sense of nationality is weak and controversies on the basis of tribes frequently strong, many new independent States were confronted with civil wars and secession movements. In older States, there are also secession movements, trying to form an independent State.

Mostly, three necessary elements or criteria are recognised for a State: a population, a territory and a public authority (government). As there are public authorities for territorial collectivities other than States (provinces etc.), a fourth necessary element is added: sovereignty. Sovereignty determines equality of States. In spite of important factual differences, States are juridically seen as equal. The population of a State is determined by a juridical criterion: adherence of people to a State on the basis of the bond of nationality as circumscribed by the State concerned. The State has the competence to decide upon the nationality of physical persons, and of corporations as well. International law determines if and when national rules can be invoked with regard to other States. Hauriou and Carré de Malberg defended the "théorie du territoire sujet" (territory as body of the State) against the "théorie du territoire objet" (territory as property of the State). It is accepted generally that the territory is the geographical space in which a State has specific competencies. Borders of the State are juridical lines recognised by neighbouring States (Foucher, 1987). A specific characteristic of the State is its sovereignty: the State within its borders has the highest powers. This is not, as in French absolute monarchy, an absolute power. The State has sovereignty (a bundle of exclusive competencies) in international law, constitution and national law. The State's sovereignty founds its independence, right of non-intervention in national affairs and formal equality of States. In international law, a State can use the presumption to be exclusively competent as public authority in its own territory.

At least four important conceptions of international law can be distinguished: naturalism, voluntarism, objectivism and positivism. Naturalism has probably the oldest testimonials: law, especially international law, has its foundation in human nature. Natural law is often considered to be valid universally, although human nature proves to be different in various cultural circumstances. The main conceptions of natural law are rationalistic naturalism based upon reason, and spiritual naturalism based upon a religious or spiritual inspiration. For rationalistic naturalism, human beings, with their reason, can rule their relations reasonably so that common life is possible with order, security, peace and justice. Since the golden era of rationalistic naturalism (16th-19th centuries), this approach has been criticised for its universalist pretensions. Cultural diversity is not adequately dealt with. For adherents of spiritual naturalism, it is evident that human beings base their activities not only upon reason, but also on their spiritual nature. There are religions stating that human beings, as created by God, have a relationship with God via their spirit. The monotheist religions (Judaism, Christianity, Islam) assume that their holy books (Thora, Bible, Koran) are inspired by God (revelation) and give indications for correct human behaviour. So-called fundamentalists assume that there must be a direct relation between revelation (of their own religion) and the ordering of society. Others assume that societal law must be developed without trying to base its legitimacy on religious instructions. Fundamentalists, as in the framework of Islam, divide the world into those who obey the revelation of Islam, and others. So they reject universal international law. Another criticism is that existing international law is too much in the grip of a Western bias, as formed in the framework of Western civilisation, neglecting values from other civilisations.

For voluntarism, the basis of the law is the will of its subjects and their conventions. According to the interstatist interpretation of international law, the will of the Nation-States is the only foundation of international law. This voluntarism has an Achilles' heel: treaties can be breached at any moment if they are solely dependent on the will of the States. To rescue a voluntarist approach it is necessary to invoke an external postulate. For adherents of the pure theory of law, this external postulate is the principle "pacta sunt servanda". This formal construction cannot really solve the problems, so long as it does not deal with the legitimacy of international norms. Without denying the relevance of the will of States for the development of international law in societal reality, it is obvious that more is needed. In the objectivist approach, international society and international law are submitted to more or less objective or intersubjective laws which scientific analysis and observation have to discover. This objectivist approach, in two variations (solidarism and Marxism), starts from presuppositions, however. For solidarist authors, the unity of the international community, with a superiority of international law with regard to national law, is an axiom. In each human society, law tends to further social solidarity, especially in international society. For the French jurist Georges Scelle (1984), a prominent solidarist in the beginning of the 19th century, social solidarity is based on ethics (what is good for society) and public authority having the task to further ethics and to transform this into juridical norms. As law is at the crossroads of ethics and power, law has to be legitimate and effective. In Marxism, society is basically determined by the class struggle in a materialist-dialectical process. In all periods of history, the class which owned the means of production exploited the have-nots. If the means of production were to be collectivised, the class struggle, in the conception of Marx and followers, could be ended and the communist society without classes could be realised. In Marxism, law in capitalist society is a superstructure phenomenon (result of determining forces in the productive infrastructure), serving the interests of the dominant classes. In Marxist doctrine, war between capitalist and communist States is inevitable until the victory of the proletarian revolution. Later coexistence was recognised and since the collapse of Eastern European Communism, Marxism has lost its dominant position and appeal.

Auguste Comte (1798-1857) was a pioneer of positivism. In "Cours de philosophie positive" (1830-1842), he elaborated a philosophical conception with the objective of realising a new society. In his view, this was possible by means of the human spirit which would deal exclusively with social phenomena and their immutable relations. For Comte, it was useless to try and discover the essence of phenomena (as ontology pretends to do). It was relevant to develop an epistemology only, a positivist method to know social phenomena. Therefore, scholars had to refrain from value judgements. They had to deal only with empirical realities, which can be observed, and had to concentrate themselves on the empirically verifiable. For jurists, positivism implied that value judgements about juridical norms were forbidden in a scientific context. Juridical positivism had adherents, especially because it was a sound reaction to prevailing dogma, but it was partly an overreaction. It paralysed the development of law as social discipline, which has an important function in society to further justice and peace. Were juridical positivism to be taken seriously, it would be impossible to investigate foundations of law, its legitimacy and its values. It would result in a complete value-free relativism. Without stressing the implications of juridical positivism, it is possible to recognise its relevance as a method for analysing juridical phenomena, complementary to other methods. When axiomatic values are made explicit, it is justified to deal with value-laden law phenomena. According to the law-positivist method, (international) law is an observable social phenomenon for which claims of reason are strictly applicable. Law, for juridical positivism, is the result of institutionalised procedures. It has to be distinguished by formal criteria (specific procedures etc.) from other social phenomena like ethics. Jurists have to analyse law with all available rational methods, and to interpret norms and institutions.

*7.4.3 French preference for law as tool of diplomacy*

Part of diplomatic management was and is the development of international law, in which French scholars and jurists played a considerable role (La Pradelle, 1950; Pillet, 1904). It has been asserted that the French approach to diplomatic management was and is too dominantly influenced by the juridical approach. Mostly this criticism is without adequate argumentation. In international law, there is a set of specific rules about embassies and consulates: inviolability, immunities etc. It took a period up to the 1960's for codification in two Conventions of Vienna for diplomatic relations (1961) and consular relations (1962). It was no surprise that the UN Security Council and the International Court of Justice (24 May 1980) condemned Iran, held responsible for the taking hostage of American diplomats in Teheran for more than a year. During the Cold War, a considerable part of energies was used for the "diplomatie de la détente" (Ghebali, 1989). Economic-commercial diplomacy and world trade diplomacy is coming increasingly to the fore (Carreau c.s, 1990; Mudec, 1990) and also "environmental diplomacy" (Kiss, 1989). "High diplomacy" (questions of national security) remains a top priority in the 21st century. France attaches great importance to maintaining or improving French cultural emanation worldwide in the framework of "Francophonie" to further the use of the French language. In this "language diplomacy" it is a trump card that the French have for centuries had a dominant impact on diplomacy and international relations. At the start of the 21st century, it remains to be seen how the French language can cope with the hegemonic Anglo-American language worldwide. Within the framework of international relations as object of study, three complementary conceptions are often distinguished: realistic paradigm, interdependency paradigm, and imperialism/dependency paradigm. The realistic view has old testimonials: Thucidides (460-400 BC) wrote a classic about the Peloponnesian War (431-404 BC) between Athens and Sparta. Hobbes (1588-1679) in Leviathan (1651) elaborated this realism. For Hobbes, the international setting was anarchy. Before and after the First World War, several authors had an idealist, sometimes rather naive conception of international relations.

Since 1918, great powers have tried to replace the traditional "European Concert" by a new international order (Bartlett, 1984). The idealist tendency, fed by Liberalism, utopian Socialism, Christianity and Pacifism, got a new impetus. Its idealism was based on the idea that building interstate relations on the mastery of law, moral considerations and democracy can prohibit violent conflicts between States. An international society composed of democratic States, would in this conception tend to arrange conflicts peacefully by applying law and by using international organisations to implement effective co-operation. The idealistic concept has collective security as primary objective, while States would have to abandon war as an instrument to settle conflicts. Disarmament and reorganisation of international relations were priorities. US President Wilson was the driving force for the creation of the League of Nations, built on these ideas (Ferrell, 1985). The Briand-Kellog Agreement (1928) endorsed abandoning wars to settle conflicts. With worldwide economic crisis, growing social tensions within States (massive unemployment and poverty) and between States, and weakening of the League of Nations, there was a world war again due to the militarism of Fascist Germany and Japan. The ridiculously naive and disastrous "diplomacy of accommodation" by Chamberlain (British) and Daladier (French) in Munich (1938) proved to be an illusion. The Second World War outdid the First World War in massive cruelty and violence. The Holocaust (systematic murdering of about 6 million Jews) was the most disgusting part. At last, the Nazi-terror was stopped with the defeat of the German troops by the coalition of the Western Allies and the USSR. For the capitulation of militarist Japan under Emperor Hirohito (Edgerton, 1997; Harries, 1991) the US used the terrible new nuclear weapons, bombing Hiroshima and Nagasaki. In Europe, soon after the end of the Second World War, the Cold war started between the two former allies against the Nazis: the Western Allies and Communist Eastern Europe. Several authors defended a realistic approach with regard to international relations: G. Kennan, G. Schwartzenberger, K. Thompson, A. Wolfers, E.H. Carr, H. Kissinger, H. Morgenthau and R. Aron.

For Morgenthau (1948), international conflicts are inevitable, because of the innate aggressive impulses in human nature and the lack of coercive authority in the international field. International society has only an ordering of sovereign national States, moved by self-interest, while international ordering is weak. Power relations between States are tipping the scale in a "zero sum game", in which every State attempts to enlarge its own power and reduce the power of other States, but for Morgenthau, it is possible to develop a realistic foreign policy and to realise international minimum ordering by diplomacy, international law and international organisations. For Aron (1962), legitimacy and legality of violence by States are specific for international relations. At the end of the 1970s, neo-realists emphasized the anarchist character of the international system (Keohane, 1986). Waltz (1979) saw horizontal relations of authority as the essential of the international, anarchist system (Bull, 1977). Each State has to count on itself to defend its interests, if necessary with violence. In the 1960s, some authors distanced themselves from the realistic paradigm, while accentuating growing interdependency between nations. In modern times, economic traffic and impressive achievements in the technological field have contributed to an intensively increased and accelerated network of communications and interdependencies between communities living all over the world. Next to the Nation-States, international, supra-national, transnational and sub-national organisations got a role in the international field, while reducing the policy room for Nation-States. Many other actors, like multinationals and non-governmental organisations, got a prominent position in international relations. International interdependency made national policy and foreign policy ever more integrated. The co-operation model would replace the conflict model. For Mitrany (1946), co-operation is needed as the foundation for a new integrated international system. Others elaborated this interdependency paradigm, like Haas (1964), and Burton (1972).

New developments in the 20th century had an impact on international relations: nuclear weapons and energy; technological developments; conquest of outer space (Lakes, 1972); informatics and its deterritorialisation effects; the impact of globalisation (Dollfus, 1997). These developments had effects for international law also. The growing number of newly independent States (mostly former colonies) in developing countries also influenced the character of international relations, and of international law. We live in the age of internationalising terrorism (11 September 2001 the Twin Towers of the World Trade Center in New York) and criminality (Laqueur, 1987). At the start of the 21st century, several developments ensure that the Fukuyama-hypothesis (1992) about the so-called end of history has no validity. Shortly after the Second World War, it was an illusion that mankind had learned a lesson: never war again Reality was totally different. Between 1945 and 1976 there were worldwide 120 wars, with 25 million people dead in the territories of 71 countries. In this period, there were only 26 days of peace (Kende, 1977). During the period since then the situation has not been better. So military management, peace management and diplomacy to further international security will be a top priority in the coming century. After the Cold War, the risks of the (ab)use of nuclear weapons are by no means negligible (Kegley/Schwab, 1991). There is a real, apocalyptic risk due to the proliferation of nuclear weapons (Attali, 1995). Recent experiences with India and Pakistan, playing their games of possible nuclear warfare, testify to this. Other problems also require adequate management by public authorities, despite all illusions of the market-mechanism as the decisive instrument. Massive migration over the borders of nations and continents will stress the nerves of many public authorities and others (Badie/Wihtol de Wenden, 1994). Terrorism on a world scale, barbarous acts, ethnic conflicts, ethnic cleansing, genocide, and a wide range of other atrocities show the need for public authorities with competencies to interfere. A lot of energy must be invested in actions to preserve the environmental habitat of mankind after the Kyoto-conference of 1997. There are many other urgent tasks for public authorities. Public authorities should never forget their specific responsibilities for the "damned on earth" (Fanon, 1961), the many millions living in inhuman conditions. Growing worldwide interdependence in the global village makes adequate common law for mankind an urgent issue (Jenks, 1968). In all dimensions of society, interdependence between national territory and the world is accelerated with intensified communication and the new technologies of communication and informatics. The notion of national and international has to be reconsidered.

The withering away of the State, as asserted by authors accentuating the loss of some competencies for the national State, is not the issue. The functions of public authorities have to be adapted to the new circumstances. The changing environment in contemporary society with its worldwide globalisation can be compared in a sense (mutatis mutandis) with radical transformations in the Middle Ages. Then self-sufficient town-economies were forced to adapt to a nation-wide system of commerce and communication. Intensified co-operation between national and international public authorities and organisations is now required. Let the world market arrange matters: that is too simplified an ideology. Instead of the former "Deus-ex-machina", the "State for all matters", there is now a rather naive belief in the world-market as the solution for all problems. As long as an adequate world-government is not possible, a complex of co-operating national and international public authorities is the next best alternative and a necessity. French President Chirac, at the yearly seminar for all French ambassadors on 26 August 1998 in the "Élysée", sketched some headlines of French foreign policy and diplomacy. Europe, in a globalising world, is seen as the best instrument for France to have an influence and to serve its own national interests. In his view the European Union doesn't want to be a United States of Europe, but a United Europe of the States. The euro as a common currency is welcomed, and European integration should be reinforced in the spheres of culture and common security. Chirac mentioned, as as second objective, the promotion of moving towards a multi-polar world. Organisation of good relations between established and developing powers, with respect for each individual, and the international law and organisations with competence to implement it. A third objective was seen in the management of the irreversible globalising process of technologies and markets. This would be better if it could be managed with common rules applied by international organisations, reducing the risks of crises and phenomena such as "social exclusion". Chirac argued that in the modern globalising world with communication technologies, forming alliances and strategies of negotiation cannot be the same as in traditional diplomacy. He argued that relations between nations are wider than relations between States. Societies are intensively in contact with each other. This explosion of human communications transforms role and tasks of ambassadors (Le Monde, 28-8-1998).

## 7.4.4 Collective security, common defence: NATO and NEO-NATO logics

After the Second World War, it was obvious that relations between the superpowers, US and USSR, formerly allied against Nazi-Germany, would be structurally overstressed. Soon the Cold War was permanent on the agenda, as was a set of measures to further security in Europe. The Security Council of the United Nations could not be an effective institution because of the veto power for the permanent members (US, Great Britain, France, USSR and China). The US and a number of West-European countries organised a common defence institution in 1949, creating NATO (North Atlantic Treaty Organisation) to counter military threats from the Soviet Union and its satellites (Gaddis, 1987; 1997). Article 5 of the Washington Treaty formulated a crucial obligation and guarantee simultaneously (an attack on one is an attack on all). Common defence has to be distinguished from collective security. Alliances of Nation-States for common defence organise their military potential in co-ordination with each other to counter the threat from a common enemy. Collective security encompasses more than that. It includes everything done to avoid or reduce threats of military aggression and includes activities to further peace, stability and well-being for the countries concerned. A whole range of activities can be seen as collective security: crisis management, conflict resolution, peacekeeping operations, organised communication between opponents, negotiations (Betts, 1992). After a series of East-West confrontations in Europe, the Conference on Security and Co-operation in Europe (CSCE) was started in 1973. Delegates from 35 Nation-States met to work on the Helsinki Accords (1975), and the "Helsinki Final Act" (Helsinki Final Document, 1992). Three "baskets of agreements" were adopted. The first basket had principles guiding relations between participating states, such as respect for human rights; equal rights; self-determination of peoples; territorial integrity of states; peaceful settlement of disputes; inviolability of frontiers; military security. The second basket had engagements for co-operation outside the specific sphere of security, and the third basket concerned family reunification and visits across the divide in Europe, as well as free flow of information, cultural co-operation, and educational exchanges.

All kinds of meetings were organised about specific topics. Up to the late 1980s, CSCE activities were in the grip of worsening US/USSR relations (CSCE Overview, 1992). CSCE was used by the West to fight human rights abuses under East-European communist regimes. The first CSCE follow-up sessions were confrontational: I. Belgrado (1977-1978) and II. Madrid (1980-1983). Following Gorbachev's "perestroika", real advance in collective security institutionalising was realised in the third follow-up session in Vienna (November 1986/ January 1989). The Vienna follow-up meeting expanded CSCE with conventional arms reductions and security-building measures (CSCE, From Vienna to Helsinki, 1992). It contributed to the disintegration of authoritarian Communism in Eastern Europe. According to Nelson (JSS, 1994), the Vienna follow-up meeting was "the beginning of a disastrous foreign policy blunder." The West missed an historic chance to transform CSCE into an imposing institution, more sweeping than later Helsinki II (1992). It would have been possible to institutionalise the Euro-Atlantic architecture for the 21st century. In 1989, this was quickly forgotten in the general euphoria about the Fall of the Berlin Wall and its aftermath. After the Fall of the Berlin Wall and the collapse of the Warsaw Pact and Communist regimes in Eastern Europe, the Cold War came to an end (Beschloss/Talbott, 1993). This did not mean that world order was assured. It was said that the post-Cold War situation was a kind of new world disorder. At the second CSCE summit in Paris (November 1990), the end of the Cold War was formalised: "Charter of Paris" (Lehne, 1991). The CFE treaty (conventional armed forces in Europe) was signed. The Charter of Paris (November 1990) committed States of the Euro-Atlantic region to reinforce democracy. The connection between regional security and the internal situation in the States concerned implied collective responsibility to guarantee democracy, Rule of Law and human rights. The Charter of Paris ruled the right of intervention in internal affairs: "...commitments undertaken in the field of the human dimension of the CSCE are matters of direct and legitimate concern to all participating States and do not belong exclusively to the internal affairs of the State concerned. Protection and promotion of human rights and fundamental freedoms and reinforcement of democratic institutions continue to be a vital basis for our comprehensive security." International security concerns concentrated upon the breaking out of the Gulf War (1990/1991) after Saddam Hussein's invasion of Kuwait.

In late 1991, the North Atlantic Cooperation Council (NACC) was formed, including former Warsaw Pact members and all NATO members, to further collective security. This low-profile NACC did not satisfy a number of East-European countries, striving for complete NATO membership. At the time of the Helsinki follow-up meeting (March 1992), warfare, ethnic cleansing and genocide in Bosnia and other parts of former Yugoslavia were raging (Cuthbertson, 1993). In April 1992 NATO agreed that it alone would decide if military forces would be committed in Europe for peacekeeping or peace-enforcement. It was announced that NATO would be prepared to consider a CSCE request for military assistance in peacekeeping activities. It was quite discouraging that NATO could only organise minimal activities in Bosnia and other areas where genocide and ethnic cleansing were going on. Far-reaching military intervention by the US did not materialise either (Damrosh, 1993). What were the national vital interests of the US? The Clinton Administration with its "Bottom Up Review" of military strategy was ambiguous. The end of the Cold War meant a formidable change for NATO, set up as military coalition of allied forces under US leadership to counter threats of the Soviet Union. There was a fundamental compatibility of interests between US and its European allies to set up NATO. The original rationale for NATO, defending Western Europe against militarist USSR, now dissolved, was gone for lack of an overpowering enemy. At a summit (January 1994), the "Partnership for Peace" (PFP) program was adopted. This enabled former members of the Warsaw Pact and neutral European countries to become members of NATO if they would comply with a number of conditions. Twenty-one countries signed the PFP, including Russia, thus committing themselves to transparent defence budgets and budget processes; democratic control of armed forces; capacity and willingness to contribute to NATO operations authorised by UN or CSCE; joint planning and training with NATO members to accomplish these tasks; and development of military forces that can operate side-by-side with those of NATO-members. In this way these countries could join some common projects within the NATO framework. For the time being, they can do so only without the NATO mutual security guarantee. The WEU, following the NATO initiative with the PFP, admitted 9 countries as associate partners in May 1994: Bulgaria, Czech Republic, Estonia, Hungary, Latvia, Lithuania, Poland, Romania, and Slovakia. The geopolitical change demanded new institutional creativity in the post-Cold War Debate about NATO.

The Journal of Strategic Studies (JSS) had a useful special issue on "The Future of NATO" (1994). Complex issues had to be dealt with. Some dilemmas and questions can be mentioned. Can NATO, successful vehicle for controlling the Cold War situation, be as effective for managing the Post-Cold War situation? Is it not a better choice to replace NATO with a new institutional arrangement, suited from the beginning to the fundamentally new circumstances? And, if so, how should the architecture of this new institution be built up? The tricky problem is in choosing which countries could become full members and when. There is the problem of the US hegemony in NATO, questioned for decades, especially by France. Are American taxpayers prepared to continue to pay huge sums of money to give Europe a security guarantee (transatlantic solidarity) while European taxpayers and governments talk of cuts in military outlays? A hypersensitive issue is whether the new NATO alliance can have an anti-Russian character (encirclement or containment issue). Russia itself is an unstable country, and will need many years to overcome post-communist crises. The financial crisis in 1998 was part of a more serious disruption of Russian society (uncontrolled powerful oligarchies; widespread poverty; lack of adequate public management; no adequate law; weak institutions for realisation of law; weak democratic institutions). Unsolvable problems of conflicts between NATO-members (Greece and Turkey about Cyprus) and between potential NATO-members were perplexing. As the situation in former Yugoslavia and Eastern Europe proved, military crisis-management required other strategies and activities in the sphere of conflict prevention and resolution. In many East- and Central-European countries there are serious ethnic and nationalistic conflicts, with minority groups striving for a more reasonable situation, and ethnic majorities opposing them. The tragedy of history is that most problems have their roots in arbitrary boundaries, ruled since the dissolution of the Ottoman, Austro-Hungarian and Russian empires after the First World War.

Lepgold (JSS, 1994) distinguished three options: 1. incrementally deepening NATO partnerships; 2. acceleration of NATO membership for "Visegrad countries" (Poland, Hungary, Czech Republic, Slovakia), and eventually Ukraine and Baltic States, while leaving out Russia; and 3. replacement of NATO by a post-Cold War Euro-American security system. The PFP formula meanwhile has provoked very different reactions. It would keep open all possible options, but according to some it is a bad compromise. For the time being, the PFP can be seen as a vehicle for furthering security in Europe. It prevents a new division of Europe, avoiding giving Moscow the feeling of being encircled. East European countries are stimulated to realise a take-off with internal reforms. Its objective is the creation of a pluralistic security community. Common projects between NATO members and PFP members can lessen mistrust and further a more democratic style in civil-military relations. Candidate NATO members are trained, preparing for membership. The transition period is used for joint exercises, peacekeeping activities with NATO members, exchanges of staff officers and building up relationships. Promotion of transparency by intensified communication is an important target, inter alia by regular exchange of information about military planning, but PFP is criticised by experts such as Kissinger and Brzezinski, who plead for rapid expansion of NATO. PFP would risk blurring NATO membership. Postponing decisions about expanded membership does not make them easier later on. East-Central European countries in the power vacuum are asking for protection with regard to Russia, which continues pretensions to intervene freely in neighbouring countries (IEDSS, 1993). Clear limits around Russia are needed ("cordon sanitaire") because of Russia's obviously expansionist tendencies. Recent Russian attempts to crush Chechen independence do not inspire trust, but this can be seen as an "internal" matter. Russia's activities depend on the power-equilibrium between powerful factions inside Russia. Fast NATO expansion with "Visegrad countries" could weaken moderates, while exacerbating hard-liners. A Russian military document in 1999 portrayed NATO as the enemy.

Anyhow, a gradual expansion of NATO to 19 members was probably the best option, but the complete change in geopolitical circumstances also asks for new institutionalising arrangements all the more so with countries in Central and Eastern Europe becoming members. Some authors argue that NATO is too much a Cold War instrument. They even suggest that it is searching for new tasks to prolong its existence. The Western alliance was at its best with a common enemy, which was a good medicine against discord, but with the lack of an obvious enemy and in a diffuse security situation, unity in institutionalising and operationalising security instruments is not an easy task. NATO is leaning heavily upon US military potential and financial resources. Europeans should take a much larger part of the burden, militarily and financially. US military spending equals roughly the global defence outlays of all other Nation-States. It is more than double the military spending of the four other permanent members of the UN Security Council (IISS, 1993). US military spending, with a very high proportion for West-European security, is questioned more in the US than before (Williams, 1985). In effect the US is subsidising the security costs of its major economic competitors. Meanwhile, American troop deployments diminished from 311,000 (1990) to 100,000, and might be reduced further to about 50,000. Since the end of the Cold War, the most important West-European countries reduced their military efforts drastically. By continuing the "addiction" of Europeans to US military security guarantees, they would structurally lose the habit of caring more for their security themselves, at the cost of US taxpayers. Western unity was branded as subordination to the US, especially by the political leadership of France, in the footsteps of De Gaulle. The position of France in the Atlantic alliance is ambiguous. It is loyal and performs its obligations in the NATO framework, but France continued to refuse to participate in the unified command structure. The French distance themselves from new forms of co-operation, like the "Combined Joint Task Forces" (CJTFs) enabling groups of countries to intervene together outside NATO's article 5 Treaty area. The argument used for this is that this gives (American) Supreme Allied Commander Europe too much power over the French armed forces.

The debate over the future of NATO is ongoing (Asmus c.s., 1993; Simon, 1993). For adherents of political realism ("Realpolitik"), it is obvious that Nation-States in the post-Cold War setting will return to the old game between powers, pursuing national interests, if necessary by military means (Kegley/Wittkopf, 1987, 1992; Mearsheimer, 1990). In the framework of this political realism, a Nation-State uses its power when its national interests are threatened. It would be a crucial policy failure to blur the objectives of a common defence institution (NATO) with those of a broader collective security institution (observer and peacekeeping missions, conflict resolution, confidence building, early warning, etc.). The European security situation is basically furthered by promoting common economic activities, possibly ending in membership of the European Union (EU) for several East- and Central-European countries after a difficult and costly process of "NATO-isation". Membership of the EU is certainly an advantage for countries applying for NATO membership. Expanding the EU's military scope would mean reinforcing the Western European Union (WEU), its defence arm, without US participation. A new European security institution could take several institutional forms (Lepgold, ISS, 1994). It is not realistic to expect that CSCE (preventive diplomacy), not a military institution, could replace NATO, as Russia was pleading for. A European Defence Organisation (EDO), guaranteeing existing borders against (threats of) violence, would be an option, with article 5 of the NATO Treaty as model. NATO remains the sole credible security institution. Whether a new institution or a reorganised old institution such as NATO, a kind "NEO-NATO", could guarantee collective security in Europe is an open question with no answers. Arguments pro and contra are discussed professionally (Lynn-Jones/Miller, 1992). Generally speaking, a common security institution works relatively well in democracies (normally not attacking each other). For several countries the path towards a really functioning democracy is full of problems. Major powers could make it a trustworthy institution. Lepgold (ISS, 1994, p.23) concluded: "If the Partnerships are deepened over the long run, and Russia does evolve into a relatively benign, democratic, Eurasian power, NATO will eventually be so broad as to effectively become another institution. At that time, it would have lost most of its identity as an alliance and become a genuine collective-security institution." A step-by-step approach has the advantage that NATO's identity as alliance could re-emerge quickly, if Russia should fall back into authoritarianism and aggression as a reaction to internal chaos.

War and peace as institutions will probably accompany humanity to the end of the world. Regulating conflicts by international law, to be enforced if necessary by regulated violence under the responsibility of public authorities, is the best alternative for warfare.

Preparing for peacekeeping, peace making and warfare, and, if necessary for operational warfare, remains a crucial task for Public Management of Society. Ubi ius, ibi societas. This means warfare, when the Rule of Law is violated, and the other instruments of public authorities do not provide the solutions. Actual warfare in Europe made this evident anew in 1999. From spring 1992 to September 1995, the international community (UN, EU and NATO) could have interfered earlier and more adequately in the ongoing warfare in Bosnia-Herzegovina (some 200,000 to 300,000 lost their lives). A combination of humanitarian aid, diplomatic initiatives and military selective strike actions could not prevent ethnic cleansing, genocide and criminal atrocities (Zimmermann, 1996). In August 1995, UN soldiers were made hostages. Fearing new hostage taking, UN commanders gave Bosnian Serbians free play. So-called "safe-havens" were all but safe (Bildt, 1998). The position of the UN peaceforce Unprofor was untenable (Corwin, 1995). Eventually bombardments against Bosnian Serbs in September 1995, and the activities of American diplomat Holbrooke produced negotiations leading to the Dayton Accords of 1995 (Holbrooke, 1999). Since June 1998 however, there has been another humanitarian disaster with all the characteristics which gave the Balkans its bad reputation (ethnic cleansing, murdering etc.). Balkan-experts like Robert Kaplan and David Owen have been arguing for a long time that in the multi-ethnical Balkans there is a very deep-rooted cultural need for "ethnic apartheid" (Owen, 1996). It is asserted that ethnic cleansing is an inevitable component of the Balkan-mindset. This could give the international community the idea that it had better have a hands-off policy. Especially as the prevailing non-intervention principle in international law does not give many clues for an effective approach.

After all the failed diplomatic activities to stop large-scale massacre by Serbians in Kosovo, NATO, in the last week of March 1999, started bombardment of targets in several parts of Yugoslavia (Serbia and Montenegro). The NATO decision to use this method of last resort was taken after the stubborn refusal of Serbian President Milosevic to sign the "Interim Agreement for Peace and Self-government in Kosovo", result of exhaustive negotiations in Rambouillet and Paris. Kosovo would get autonomy for three years under the control of NATO, while after this period the situation would get a more definite solution (with chances for independence after a positive referendum). Representatives of the Albanic community in Kosovo signed the Interim-Agreement on 18 March 1999. Negotiations for this Interim-Agreement implied that the Kosovo Albanians were seen as the subject of international law. Serbia would have to accept that – within its national boundaries (non-intervention principle). The province of the Kosovo-Albanians got a de facto recognition for international law. NATO in fact took a high-risk decision, because what could be achieved by bombing Serbia? Would Milosevic finally give way, and sign the "Interim-Agreement"? If so, it could be argued that his signature is not legally valid. Because an agreement, signed under pressure of military intervention, is not legally valid according to article 51 of the Vienna Convention about the law of treaties.

Ten years ago Milosevic illegally deprived Kosovo Albanians of their autonomy, contrary to the since 1974 prevailing constitution of Yugoslavia. Albanians proclaimed an independent republic, confirmed by a referendum in 1991 (Gow, 1997; Owen, 1996). The Yugoslav Federation (Serbia, Montenegro) was not recognised internationally as the successor State of former Yugoslavia (Bennet, 2000). From former Yugoslavia, four parts were declared independent, confirmed by international recognition and membership of the UN: Slovenia, Croatia, Bosnia and Macedonia. Former communist hard-liner Milosevic exploited a new track after the collapse of Communist regimes in Eastern Europe: nationalism. Dramatic developments in Kosovo proved again that history is relevant (Ullmann, 1996). For nationalist Serbians, Kosovo became a symbol of Serbian identity: in 1389 Ottoman Turks defeated Serbians in Kosovo (Judah, 2000). In spite of an Albanian majority in Kosovo, Milosevic forced them to leave. It was a nightmare for the Member-

States of NATO: the decision to attack Serbia, massive ethnic cleansing, and then the necessity to engage ground forces. How to get out of this mess? NATO operations, Allied Force and Allied Harbour (humanitarian aid) started on 24 March 1999 (Daalder/O'Hanlon, 2000). The strategic decision to reduce military intervention to air raids, without using ground troops, was criticised because it was thought impossible to win the war without the use of ground troops, but NATO won this war in 78 days. Serbian dictator Milosevic (Thomas, 1999) seemed unimpressed by the gigantic chaos he had created. He eventually accepted the NATO-conditions. NATO and Yugoslav authorities signed the Technical Accord on 9 June 1999. After the end of fighting the key-issue remains to trouble international and national public authorities: How to realise a reasonable society, also for all inhabitants in the Balkans? Ten years after the fall of the Berlin Wall (1989) three former Member-States of the Communist Bloc of Eastern Europe, Poland, Czech Republic and Hungary became member of NATO on 12 March 1999. Before 1 April 1999, when the 50th anniversary of NATO (since 1 April 1949) was celebrated, NATO had 19 members: U.S., Canada, U.K., France, Italy, the Netherlands, Belgium, Luxembourg, Germany, Denmark, Norway, Iceland, Greece, Turkey, Spain, Portugal, Poland, Czech Republic, Hungary. Since June 1997, with the decision to make these last three countries members of NATO and not (yet) other applicants, tensions about the future membership of other countries continue. Eastern European countries tried to become NATO members.

Several criteria are used to help decision-making about this sensitive issue. Meanwhile, preparations are finished for the New Strategic Concept of NATO. European countries try to develop a more European concept for its military strategic concept (Deighton, 1997). The WEU-Assembly in March 1999 adopted two reports in Paris, calling upon their governments to further that the EU will take over military competencies of WEU. WEU would have to be inserted completely into the EU (Rees, 1998). NATO-leadership was more concerned in April 1999 about military intervention against Serbian dictator Milosevic, who did not shrink back from massive ethnic cleansing in Kosovo. After its massive air raids NATO had this dictator on his knees, and the warfare could be stopped. The North-Atlantic Council issued its "Declaration of Washington" (23-24 April 1999) and the Member-States engaged themselves for a new century to defend their populations, territories and liberty on the basis of democracy, human rights and the Rule of Law. Collective defence remains the key task of NATO. The North-Atlantic Council adopted the "New Strategic Concept" (23-24 April 1999), enabling NATO to manage the security situation in the coming century. NATO is open for new candidates who are willing to accept their conditions. An "Action-plan for aspirant Member-States" (23-24 April 1999) was adopted. At the semi-annual NATO-meeting in Reykjavik (14/15 May 2002) it was decided to transform the "Permanent Joint Council NATO-Russia" (19 + 1) into the "Council NATO-Russia" (with limited competencies), in which all twenty are theoretically equal. This council does not give Russia a veto against NATO activities. When 19 NATO-Members want to decide something which Russia opposes, they have a meeting without representatives of Russia. A breakthrough was the Disarmament Treaty, signed in Moscow on 24 May 2002. Russia and the US agreed to reduce their nuclear armoury by 2/3 in the period 2002-2012. In November 2002 the following seven countries became NATO members: Estonia, Latvia, Lithuania, Slovakia, Slovenia, Romania and Bulgaria.

According to the SIPRI yearbook 2000, outlays for military purposes grew in 1999. With regard to 1998 it was a 2.1% rise. This growth was due especially to the activities of the United States, Japan, France and Germany. Overall, these countries together spent some 780 billion dollars on weaponry in 1999. The report "Conventional Arms Transfers to Developing Nations, 1993-2000" (US Congress, 2001) has a list of the most important suppliers of conventional weapons: US (18.6 billion dollars); Russia (7.7 billion dollars); France (4.1 billion dollars); Germany (1.1 billion dollars); Great Britain (600 million dollars); China (400 million dollars). Weapons will be with us, and wars also. Si vis pacem, para bellum. Secret services and espionage activities remain instruments in the toolbox of international management. This is evident from information about the worldwide electronic espionage system "Echelon" (Bamford, 2001; European Parliament, 1998/2000). With the world in the grip of globalisation, France has a marked ambition to play a role (Védrine, 2000), also in the European Union. The terrorist attack on the Twin Towers of the World Trade Center in New York and the Pentagon on 11 September 2001 showed that no country in the world is free from terrorism (Boniface, 2002; Heisbourg, 2002; Maisonneuve/Guellec. 2002). European countries had the dilemma of whether or not to join in with the US military actions in Afghanistan, fighting terrorism and the search for Ben Laden, thought to be responsible for this inhumane massacre in the name of Allah (Gozlan, 2002; Rinaldi, 2002; Lux-Wurm, 2002).

A new institution is the Permanent International Criminal Court, sitting since 1 July 2002 in The Hague. This Court is competent only for crimes committed after 1 July 2002. The crimes under the competency of the Court are: genocide (activities meant to exterminate national, ethnic or religious groups); crimes against humanity (murder, deportation, torture or rape as part of a systematic violation of a group); war crimes (crimes as the use of forbidden weapons, assaults of civilian targets, maltreatment of prisoners of war, hostage taking, sexual crimes); and aggression (not yet defined). This Court will start a trial only when national States are not in a position to handle a trial or are not disposed to do it. Meanwhile 139 countries signed the covenant of the International Criminal Court, and 73 countries have ratified it. The United States, refusing to sign the covenant, played a remarkable role with regard to this Court. The US has tried everything to reduce the competencies of this Court as much as possible, and in the Security Council of the United Nations, the US tried to shield American soldiers from prosecution by the International Criminal Law by presenting a resolution with this objective. The US, the sole superpower left in the world, has a more and more isolated position. It has already distanced itself from the Kyoto-protocol about the "greenhouse effect", and from the treaty which limits defence against aggression with rocket systems. The US chose to follow a hands-free policy (as Henry Cabot Lodge argued long ago), but the US signed the Genocide Treaty (1948) and the Treaty of Geneva against war crimes. In 1993 the United Nations installed an ad hoc Yugoslavia Tribunal, and in 1994 an ad hoc Rwanda Tribunal for the prosecution of criminals. It remains to be seen how the International Criminal Court can contribute to humanise the international community by fair trials of war crimes, genocide and other atrocities.

**References**

French
Abel, O., De l'Amour des Ennemis. (Paris, A. Michel, 2002).
Ailleret, C., L'Aventure atomique française. (Paris, Grasset, 1968).
Allain, J.C., Agadir 1911. Une crise impérialiste en Europe pour la conquête du Maroc. (Paris, Sorbonne, 1976).
Allain, J.C., dir., La Moyenne Puissance au XXe siècle. (Paris, FEDN/IHCC, 1989).
Aron, R., Paix et guerre entre les nations. (Paris, Calmann-Lévy, 1962; 1984).
Aron, R., Le Grand Débat. Initiation ~a la Stratégie atomique. (Paris, Calmann-Lévy, 1963).
Aron, R., Penser la Guerre. (Paris, Gallimard, 1976).
Artaud, D., La Question des dettes interalliés et la reconstruction de l'Europe 1917-1929. (Lille, Université, 1968).

Artaud, D., Kaplan, L., dir., Dien Bien Phu. (Paris, La Manufacture, 1989).
Asselain, J.C., Histoire économique de la France. (Paris, Seuil, 1984).
Asselain, J.C., Histoire économique. De la Révolution industrelle à la Première Guerre Mondiale. (Paris, FNSP, 1991).
Assidon, E., Les Théories économiques du développement. (Paris, Découverte, 2002).
Attali, J., Économie de l'Apocalypse. Trafic et prolifération nucléaires. (Paris, Fayard, 1995).
Aussaresses, P., Services spéciaux, Algérie 1953-1957. (Paris, Perrin, 2001).
Azéma, J.P., 1940. L'année terrible. (Paris, Orban, 1990).
Azéma, J.P., dir., Jean Moulin face à l'histoire. (Paris, Flammarion, 2000).
Azéma, J.P., Bédarida, F., dir., Le Régime de Vichy et les Français. (Paris, Fayard, 1992).
Azéma, J.P., Bédarida, F., dir., La France des années noires. De l'Occupation à la Libération. (Paris, Fayard, 1993).
Azni, B., Harkis, crime d'État. Généalogie d'un abandon. (Paris, Ramsay, 2002).
Badie, B., L'État importé. L'Occidentalisation de l'ordre politique. (Paris, Fayard, 1992).
Badie, B., La Fin des territoires. (Paris, Hachette, 1995).
Badie, B., Withol de Wenden, C., dir., Le Défi Migratoire. (Paris, FNSP, 1994).
Bariéty, J., Les relations franco-allemandes après la première guerre mondiale. (Paris, Pedone, 1977; 1986).
Barrea, J., Théories des relations internationales. (Louvain, 1978).
Baud, J., Encyclopédie des renseignements et des services secrets. (Paris, Lavauzelle, 1997).
Bayart, J.F., et al., dir., La Criminalisation de l'État en Afrique. (Paris, Complexe, 1997).
Beaufre, A., Dissuasion et Stratégie. (Paris, A.Colin, 1964).
Beaufre, A., Introduction à la Stratégie. (Paris, A.Colin, 1965; Hachette, 1998).
Becker, J.J., 1914: Comment les Français sont entrés dans la guerre. (Paris, FNSP, 1977).
Becker, J.J., Les Français dans la Grande Guerre. (Paris, Laffont, 1980).
Becker, J.J., Berstein, S., Victoire et frustrations 1914-1929. (Paris, Seuil, 1990).
Bédarida, F., L'Angleterre triomphante (1882-1914). (Paris, Hatier, 1974).
Bédarida, F., La Stratégie secrète de la drôle de guerre. (Paris, FNSP, 1977).
Bédarida, F., Churchill. (Paris, 1999).
Bensoussan, G., Une Histoire Intellectuelle et Politique du Sionisme (1860-1940). (Paris, Fayard, 2002).
Bergen, P.L., Guerre Sainte, Multinationale. (Paris, Gallimard, trad., 2002).
Berger, V., Jurisprudence de la Cour Européen des Droits de l'Homme. (Paris, Sirey, 2000).
Bernard, P., Immigration. Le Défi Mondial. (Paris, Gallimard, 2002).
Bernert, P., Roger Wybolt et la bataille por la DST. (Paris, Presses de la Cité, 1975).
Bernert, P., S.D.E.C.E. Service 7. (Paris, Presses de la Cité, 1980).
Bernis (commandant), Le Service de renseignements. (Paris, Berger-Levrault, 1934).
Berstein, S., Milza, P., Histoire du XXe siècle. (Paris, Hatier, 1995).
Bertaud, J.P., Guerres et société en France de Louis XIV à Napoléon Ier. (Paris, A.Colin, 1998).
Bertaud, J.P., Nouvelle histoire militaire de la France. (Paris, Fayard, 1998).
Berteil, L., De Clausewitz à la guerre froide. (Paris, Berger-Levrault, 1958).
Bertrand, G., Enigma ou la plus grande énigme de la guerre 1939-1945. (Paris, Plon, 1973).
Bertrand, M., La Stratégie suicidaire de l'Occident. (Bruxelles, Bruylant, 1993).
Bertrand, M., La Fin de l'Ordre Militaire. (Paris, FNSP, 1996).
Biarnès, P., Les États-Unis et le Reste du Monde, Les Chemins de la Haine. (Paris, Harmattan, 2002).
Bilis, M., Socialistes et Pacifistes, 1933-1939. (Paris, Syros, 1979).

Boniface, P., Repenser la Dissuasion Nucléaire. (Paris, Éd. De l'Aube, 1997).
Boniface, P., La France est-elle encore une Grande Puissance? (Paris, Presses de Sciences Po, 1998).
Boniface, P., Les Guerres de demain. (Paris, Seuil, 2002).
Boniface, P., dir., L'Année stratégique 2001. Analyse des enjeux stratégiques, démographiques et économiques. (Paris, Michalon, 2000).
Boniface, P., dir., Les Lens du 11 septemnbre. (Paris, PUF, 2002).
Boubakeur, D., Les Défis de l'Islam. (Paris, Flammarion, 2002).
Boustany, K., ed., Génocides. (Bruxelles, Bruylant, 1999).
Boutros-Gahli, B., Démocratiser la Mondialisation. (Paris, Rocher, 2002).
Braillard, P., Théorie des relations internationales. (Paris, PUF, 1977).
Braillard, P., Djalili, M.R., Les Relations Internationales. (Paris, PUF, 1994).
Brédin, J.D., L'Affaire. (Paris, Julliard, 1983; Fayard, 1986).
Brunel, S., Famines et Politique. (Paris, Presses de Sciences Po, 2002).
Bucaille, L., Générations Intifada. (Paris, Hachette, 2002).
Buffotot, P., Le Parti socialiste et la Défense ou la recherche de la fonction patriotique. (Paris, Université de Pais X, 1981).
Buffotot, P., De la Guerre du Golfe au Conflit Yougoslave. (Paris, DF, 1995).
Buffotot, P., La Réforme du service national. (Paris, DF, 1996).
Buffotot, P., dir., La Défense en Europe. Les adaptations de l'après-guerre froide. (Paris, DF, 1998).
Buffotot, P., dir., La Défense en Europe. Nouvelles réalités, nouvelles ambitions. (Paris, DF, 2001).
Burdan, D., DST. Neuf ans à la division antiterroriste. (Paris, Laffont, 1990).
Buron, R., Carnets politiques de la guerre d'Algérie. (Paris, Éd. Cana, 2002).
Buton, P., Les Lendemains qui déchantent. Le Parti communiste français à la Libération. (Paris, FNSP, 1994).
Cantier, J., L'Algérie sous le Régime de Vichy. (Paris, Odile Jacob, 2002).
Carreau, D., Droit International. (Paris, Pedone, 1997).
Carreau, D., et al., Droit international économique. (Paris, LGDJ, 1990).
Carrias, E., La Pensée militaire allemande. (Paris, PUF, 1948).
Carrias, E., La Pensée militaire française. (Paris, PUF, 1960).
Castellan, G., Histoire de l'Armée. (Paris, PUF, 1948).
Castellan, G., L Réarmement clandestin du Reich, 1930-1935, vu par le 2ème bureau de l'état-major français. (Paris, Plon, 1954).
Castellan, G., L'Allemagne de Weimar. (Paris, A.Colin, 1969).
Charpentier, J., La reconnaissace internationale et l'évolution du droit des gens. (Paris, Pedone, 1956).
Chebel, M., L'Imaginaire arabo-musulmane. (Paris, PUF, 2002).
Chemille-Gendreau, M., Humanité et souverainetés. (Paris, 1995).
Cohen, E., L'Ordre Économique Mondial. Essai sur les Autorités de Régulation. (Paris, Fayard, 2001).
Cohen, S., La Monarchie nucléaire. Les coulisses de la politique étrangère sous la Ve République. (Paris, Hachette, 1985).
Cohen, S., La Défaite des généraux: le pouvoir politique et l'armée sous la Ve République. (Paris, Fayard, 1994).
Colard, D., Les Relations internationales. (Paris, Masson, 1991).
Collectif, Le Mal. (Paris, Gallimard, 2002).
Collet, A., Histoire de la stratégie militaire depuis 1945. (Paris, PUF, 1994).
Colombani, J.M., Tous Américains? Le Monde après le 11 septembre 2001. (Paris, Fayard, 2002).

Cooley, J.K., CIA et Jihad, 1950-2001 (Contre l'URSS, une désastreuses alliance). (Paris, Autrement, trad., 2002).
Cordier, D., Jean Moulin. L'Inconnu du Panthéon. (Paris, Lattès, 1993).
Courrière, Y., La Guerre d'Algérie. (Paris, Fayard, 2002).
Daudet, E., La Police politique. Chronique des temps de la Restauration d'après des agents secrets et les papiers du cabinet noire, 1815-1820. (Paris, 1912).
David, D., Sécurité: L'Après-New York. (Paris, Presses de Sciences Po, 2002).
De Gaulle, C., Vers l'armée de métier. (Paris, Berger-Levrault, 1934; Presses Pocket, 1989).
De Gaulle, C., La France et son armée. (Paris, Plon, 1938).
Delarue, J., OAS contre De Gaulle. (Paris, Fayard, 1981).
Delpech, T., Politique du Chaos. L'Autre Face de la Mondialisation. (Paris, Seuil, 2002).
DF (Documentation française), Développement. (Paris, DF, 2000).
DGA (Délégation générale pour l'armement), L'Industrie française de défense. (Paris, DGA, 1990).
Doise, J., Histoire militaire de l'affaire Dreyfus ou un secret bien gardé. (Paris, Seuil, 1994).
Dollfus, O., La Mondialisation. (Paris, FNSP, 1997).
Droz, H., L'Oeil de Moscou à Paris. (Paris, Lulliard, 1964).
Droz, J., Histoire diplomatique de 1648 à 1919. (Paris, Dalloz, 1982).
Droz, J., Histoire de l'Allemagne. (Paris, PUF, 1994).
Droz, J., Bariéty, J., République de Weimar et Régime hitlérien, 1918-1945. (Paris, Hatier, 1973).
Droz, J., Rowley, A., Histoire générale du XXe siècle. (Paris, Seuil, 1986).
Dubief, H., Le Déclin de la IIIe République, 1929-1938. (Paris, Seuil, 1976).
Ducrey, P., Guerre et guerriers dans la Grèce antique. (Paris, Hachette, 1999).
Dumoulin, A., L'UEO et la politique européenne de la défense. (Paris, DF, 1995).
Dumoulin, A., L'Avenir du Nucléaire Militaire. (Paris, DF, 2001).
Dumouin, A., Remacle, E., L'Union de l'Europe Occidentale, Phénix de la défense européenne. (Bruxelles, Bruylant, 1998).
Dupuy, P.M., Droit International Public. (Paris, Dalloz, 2000).
Dupuy, P.M., dir., Les Grands Textes de Droit International Public. (Paris, Dalloz, 2000).
Dupuy, R.J., La clôture du système international. (Paris, PUF, 1989).
Duquesne, J., Pour comprendre la Guerre d'Algérie. (Paris, Perrin, 2002).
Duret, A., Conquête Spatiale: Du Rêve au Marché. (Paris, Gallinmard, 2002).
Duroselle, J.B., La Politique extérieure de la France de 1914 à 1945. (Paris, CDU, 1965).
Duroselle, J.B., L'Europe de 1815 à nos jours. (Paris, PUF, 1967; 1995).
Duroselle, J.B., La Décadence. (Paris, Imprimerie nationale, 1979).
Duroselle, J.B., Histoire diplomatique de 1919 à nos jours. (Paris, Dalloz, 1985; 1990).
Duroselle, J.B., L'Europe de 1895 à nos jours. (Paris, PUF, 1988).
Duroselle, J.B., La Grande Guerre des Français, 1914-1918. (Paris, Perrin, 1994).
Duval, M., Le Baut, Y., L'Arme Nucléaire française. Pourquoi et comment. (Paris, SPM, 1992).
Duval, M., Mongin, D., Histoire des forces nucléaires françaises depuis 1945. (Paris, PUF, 1993).
Elmer, A., L'Agent secret de Napoléon, Charles-Louis Schulmeister. (Paris, Payot, 1932).
Etienne, G., Imprévisible Afghanistan. (Paris, Presses de Sciences Po, 2002).
Fabre, M., Convention Européenne des Droits de l'Homme. Application par le Juge Français: 10 Ans de Jurisprudence. (Paris, Litec, 1998).
Faligot, R., Kaufer, R., Les Résistants: De la guerre de l'ombre aux allées du pouvoir, 1944-1984. (Paris, Fayard, 1990).

Faligot, R., Kaufer, R., Histoire mondiale du renseignement (Paris, Laffont, 1993-1994).
Faligot, R., Krop, P., La Piscine: Les Services Secrets français, 1944-1984. (Paris, Seuil, 1989).
Fanon, F., Les Damnés de la Terre. (Paris, Maspero, 1961).
Faure, C., Shalom, Salam. Dictionnaire pour une Meilleure Approche du Conflit Israélo-Palestinien. (Paris, Fayard, 2002).
Faure, J.C., Coopération pour le Développement. (Paris, OCDE, 2002).
Fejtö, F., Histoire des Démocraties populaires. (Paris, Seuil, 1992).
Fejtö, F., Kulesza-Mietkowski, E., La Fin des Démocraties populaires. Les chemins du post-communisme. (Paris, Seuil, 1997).
Ferro, M., La Doctrine de Gaulle d'indépendance nationale et les rapports franco-américains. (Nice, Université, 1973).
Ferro, M., De Gaulle et l'Amérique. Une amitié tumultueuse. (Paris, Plon, 1973).
Ferro, M., Pétain. (Paris, Fayard, 1987).
Ferro, M., Nazisme et Communisme. Deux régimes dans le siècle. (Paris, Hachette, 1999).
Ferro, M., Histoire de France. (Paris, Odile Jacob, 2001).
Ferro, M., Le Choc de l'Islam, XVIII-XXIe siècle. (Paris, Odile Jacob, 2002).
Foucher, M., L'Invention des frontières. (Paris, FEDN, 1987).
Foucher, M., Fronts et frontières. Un tour du monde géopolitique. (Paris, Fayard, 1991).
Foucher, M., La République Européenne. (Paris, Belin, 2001).
Foucher, M., Kieffer, J.P., Les Défis de sécurité en Europe médiane. (Paris, DF, 1996).
Francini, P., Les Guerres d'Indochine. (Paris, Pygmalion, 1988).
Frankenstein, R., Le prix du réarmement français, 1935-1939. (Paris, Sorbonne, 1939; 1982).
Frenay, H., La Nuit finira: Mémoires de Résistance 1940-1945. (Paris, Laffont, 1973).
Gallois, P.M., Stratégie de l'âge nucléaire. (Paris, Calmann-Lévy, 1964).
Gallois, P.M., L'Aventure de la bombe. (Paris, Plon, 1985).
Gallois, P.M., Géopolitique, les voies de la puissance. (Paris, Plon, 1990).
Gallois, P.M., Livre noir sur la Défense. (Paris, Payot, 1994).
Gallois, P.M., La France sort-elle de l'histoire? Superpuissance et déclin national. (Lausanne, L'Age d'Homme, 1998).
Ganiage, J., L'expansion coloniale de la France sous la Troisième République 1871-1914. (Paris, Payot, 1968).
Garcia, S., Des Sables du Désert aux Tours de Manhattan. (Paris, Dido, 2002).
Garder, M., La Guerre secrète des services spéciaux français, 1935-1945. (Paris, Plon, 1967).
Gauché, Général, Le Deuxième Bureau au travail (1935-1940). (Paris, Amiot-Dumont, 1953).
Geré, F., Pourquoi les Guerres? (Paris, Larousse, 2002).
Ghebali, U.Y., La Diplomatie multilatérale de la Détente. Le processus de la CSCE, d'Helsinki à Vienne (1973-1989). (Bruxelles, Bruylant, 1989).
Giesen, K.G., L'éthique des relations internationales. Les théories anglo-américaines contemporaines. (Bruxelles, Bruylant, 1992).
Girardet, R., La société militaire dans la France contemporaine (1815-1939). (Paris, Plon, 1953; Perrin, 1998).
Girardet, R., L'idée coloniale de la France, 1871-1914. (Paris, Table Ronde, 1968).
Girardet, R., L'idée coloniale de la France de 1871 à 1962. (Paris, Table Ronde, 1972).
Girardet, R., Problèmes militaires et stratégies contemporains. (Paris, Dalloz, 1989).
Giraud, H.C., De Gaulle et les Communistes. (Paris, A.Michel, 1988/1989).
Givierge, M., Au service du chiffre: 18 ans de souvenirs, 1907-1925. (Amiens, NAF, 1930).

Gombin, R., Les Socialistes et al Guerre. (Paris, Mouton, 1970).
Gorru, E., Le Procès Papon. Un Procès pour la Conscience Universelle. (Biarritz, Atlantica, 1999).
Gozlan, M., Pour comprendre l'intégrisme islamiste. (Paris, A.Michel, 2002).
Greigueuil, P. De, 2000 Ans d'Histoire de France. (Paris, Assouline, 1999).
Gresh, A., Israël, Palestine. Vérités sur un conflit. (Paris, Fayard, 2002).
Grosser, A., Les Occidentaux: les pays d'Europe et les États-Unis depuis la guerre. (Paris, Seuil, 1984).
Grove-Valdeyron, N., Hamdouni, S., Les Institutions Internationales et Communautaires. (Paris, Ellipses, 2002).
Guisnel, J., Violet, B., Services secrets. Le Pouvoir et les Services de Renseignements sous François Mitterrand. (Paris, Découverte, 1988).
Haenel, H., La Défense nationale. (Paris, PUF, 1982).
Haenel, H., Pichon, R., La marine nationale. (Paris, PUF, 1986).
Haenel, H., Pichon, R., L'armée de l'air. (Paris, PUF, 1987).
Haenel, H., Pichon, R., L'armée de la terre. (Paris, PUF, 1987).
Haenel, H., Pichon, R., La Défense nationale. (Paris, PUF, 1989).
Haffner, S., Histoire d'un Allemand. (Paris, Actes Sud, trad., 2002).
Haggenmacher, P., Grotius et la Doctrine de la Guerre Juste. (Paris, 1983).
Hamoumou, M., Et ils sont devenus harkis. (Paris, Fayard, 1993).
Harmand, L., L'Armée et le soldat à Rome de 107 à 50 avant notre ère. (Paris, Picard, 1967).
Heisbourg, F., Hyperterrorisme. La Nouvelle Guerre. (Paris, Odile Jacob, 2002).
Heller, M., Histoire de la Russie. (Paris, Flammarion, 1999).
Hernu, C., Soldat-Citoyen: essai sur la défense et la sécurité de la France. (Paris, Flammarion, 1975).
Homberg, O.M., Les Coulisses de l'histoire: Souvenirs 1898-1928. (Paris, Fayard, 1938).
Huntzinger, J., Introduction aux relations internationales. (Paris, Seuil, 1987).
Hureau, J., La Mémoire des pieds-noirs de 1830 à nos jours. (Paris, Orban, 1987).
Iannucci, U., Soldat dans les gorges de Palestro. Journal de guerre. (Lyon, Éd. Aléas, 2002).
Jauffret, J.C., La Guerre d'Algérie par les documents. (Vincennes, SHAT, 1990).
Jaurès, J., L'Armée nouvelle. (Paris, L'Humanité, 1913).
Jeanson, F., Notre guerre. (Paris, 1961; 2001).
Joffre, J., Mémoires. (Paris, Plon, 1932).
Jordi, J.J., Hamoumou, M., Les Harkis, une mémoire enfouie. (Paris, Autrement, 2002).
Jouve, E., Le droit des peuples. (Paris, PUF, 1986).
Jouve, E., Relations internationales. (Paris, PUF, 1992).
Joxe, A., Voyage aux Secrets de la Guerre. (Paris, PUF, 1991).
Joxe, A., L'Empire du Chaos. Les Républiques face à la Domination Américaine dans l'Après-Guerre Froide. (Paris, Découverte, 2002).
Julien, C.A., L'Afrique du Nord en marche. Algérie-Tunésie-Maroc, 1880-1952. (Paris, 1952; 2002).
Karam, P., Asie Centrale. Le Nouveau Grand Jeu. (Paris, Harmattan, 2002).
Kaspi, A., Les Juifs pendant l'Occupation. (Paris, Seuil, 1991).
Kaspi, A., Les États-Unis d'aujourd'hui. Mal connus, mal aimés, mal compris. (Paris, Plon, 1999).
Kateb, K., Européens, "indigènes" et juifs en Algérie 1830-1962. (Paris, PUF, 2002).
Kauffer, R., O.A.S.: Histoire d'une organisation secrète. (Paris, Fayard, 1986; Seuil, 2002).
Kepel, G., Chronique d'une Guerre d'Orient. (Paris, Gallimard, 2002).
Khoury, E., La Porte du Soleil. (Paris, Actes Sud, trad., 2002).

Khoury-Tadié, A., Palestine: La Perte de l'Innocence. (Paris, Maisonneuve et Larose, 2002).
Kiss, A.C., Répertoire de la pratique française en matière de droit internationale. (Paris, 1962/1970).
Kiss, A.C., Receuil de traités multilatéraux relatifs à la protection de l'environnement. (Nairobi, PNUE, 1982).
Kiss, A.C., Droit international de l'environnement. (Paris, Pedone, 1989; 2000).
Klein, J., La Gauche française et les problèmes de la défense. (Dans: Politique étrangère, pp.508-520, 1978).
Klein, J., Maîtrise des armements et désarmement. Les accords conclus depuis 1945. (Paris, DF, 1991).
Klein, J., Montbrial, T. de, dir., Dictionnaire de stratégie. (Paris, PUF, 2000).
Korany, B., et al., Analyse des relations internationales. (Québec, Gaëtan Morin, 1987).
Krop, P., Les secrets de l'espionage français de 1870 à nos jours. (Paris, Lattès, 1993).
Lachouque, H., Waterloo. (Paris, 1972).
Lacoste, P., dir., Le Renseignement à la française. (Paris, Economica, 1998).
Lacouture, J., De Gaulle. (Paris, Seuil, 1984/1992).
Lacouture, J., Algérie. la guerre est finie. (Bruxelles, Complexe, 1985; 2002).
Lacroix-Riz, A., Le Choix de Marianne. Les relations franco-américaines de la Libération au début du Plan Marshall (1944-1948). (Paris, Editions sociales, 1985).
Ladoux, G., Les chasseurs d'espions: Comment j'ai fait arrêter Mata-Hari. (Paris, Éd. du Masque, 1932).
Ladoux, G., Mes souvenirs. (Paris, Éd. de France, 1937).
La Gorce, P.M. de, La Guerre et l'atome. (Paris, Plon, 1985).
Laidi, Z., dir., L'Ordre mondial relâché. Sens et puissance après la Guerre froide. (Paris, FNSP, 1992).
La Pradelle, P. de, Maîtres et doctrines du droit des gens. (Paris, 1950).
La Pradelle, P. de, Politis, N., dir., Receuil des arbitrages internationaux. (Paris, 1905; 1932/1954).
Lastours, S. De, La France gagne la guerre des codes secrets. (Paris, Tallandier, 1998).
Laurens, H., La Question de Palestine. (Paris, Fayard, 2002).
Legohérel, H., Histoire du droit international public. (Paris, PUF, 1996).
Lellouche, P., Le nouveau désordre mondial. (Paris, Grasset, 1992).
Livet, G., L'équilibre européen de la fin du XVe à la fin du XVIIIe siècle. (Paris, 1976).
Livre Blanc sur la Défense. (Paris, UGE, 1994).
Livre Blanc de l'Armée française en Algérie. (Paris, Contretemps, 2002).
Luttwak, E.N., La Grande Stratégie de l'Empire Romain. (Paris, Economica, 1987).
Lux-Wurm, P.C., Les Drapeaux de l'Islam. (Paris, Buchet-Chastel, 2002).
Madelin, L., Fouché. (Paris, Plon, 1903).
Mafart, A., Carnets secrets d'un nageur de combat. Du Rainbow Warrior au glaces de l'Arctique. (Paris, A.Michel, 1999).
Magalhaes-Godinho, V., L'économie de l'Empire portugais aux XVe et XVIIe siècles. (Paris, 1969).
Maisonneuve, E. de la, Incitation à la réflexion stratégique. (Paris, Economica, 1998).
Maisonneuve, E. de la, Guellec, J., Un Monde à Repenser. (Paris, Economica, 2002).
Mansour, L.B., Frères Musulmanes, frères féroces. Voayage dans l'enfer du discours islamiste. (Paris, Ramsay, 2002).
Mardam-Bey, F., Sanbar, E., Le Droit au Retour. Le Problème des Refugiés Palestiniens. (Paris, Actes Sud, 2002).
Marion, P., La Mission impossible. A la tête des services secrets. (Paris, Calmann-Lévy, 1991).

Marseille, J., dir., France et Algérie. Journal d'une passion. (Paris, Larousse, 2002).
Mathieu, J.L., La Défense Nationale. (Paris, PUF, 1996).
Mauro, F., L'Expansion européenne: 1600-1870. (Paris, PUF, 1988).
Merle, M., Sociologie des relations internationales. (Paris, Dalloz, 1982).
Messadié, G., Mourir pour New York? (Paris, Max Milo, 2002).
Michel, B., La Chute de l'Empire Austro-Hongrois. (Paris, Laffont, 1991).
Michel, H., Les courants de pensée de la Résistance. (Paris, 1962).
Michel, H., Histoire de la France libre. (Paris, Haxchette, 1972).
Michel, H., La Défaite de la France. (Paris, PUF, 1980).
Michel, H., Histoire de la Résistance. (Paris, PUF, 1980).
Michel, H., Pétain et le Régime de Vichy. (Paris, PUF, 1993).
Michel, H., La Seconde Guerre Mondiale. (Paris, PUF, 1996).
Miller, J., Engelberg, S., Broad, W., Germes. Les Armes Biologiques et la Nouvelle Guerre Secrète. (Paris, Fayard, 2002).
Miquel, P., La Paix de Versailles et l'opinon publique française. (Paris, Flammarion, 1972).
Miquel, P., Les Guerres de religion. (Paris, 1980).
Miquel, P., La Seconde Guerre Mondiale. (Paris, Fayard, 1986).
Miquel, P., La Guerre d'Algérie. (Paris, Fayard, 1993).
Miquel, P., L'Affaire Dreyfus. (Paris, PUF, 1996).
Minc, A., Le Fracas du Monde. Journal de l'Année 2001. (Paris, Seuil, 2002).
Ministère de l'Environnement (France), L'Application Renforcée du Droit International de l'Environnement. (Paris, Frison-Roche, 1999).
Mink, G., Szurek, J.C., dir., Cet étrange post-communisme. (Paris, CNRS, 1992).
Mongin, D., La Bombe Atomique Française, 1945-1958. (Bruxelles, Bruylant, 1997).
Moravia, A., Histoires de Guerre et d'Intimité. (Paris, Flammarion, trad., 2002).
Moréas, G., Écoutes et espionnage. (Paris, Stock, 1990).
Moreau-Defarges, P., La Mondialisation. (Paris, PUF, 2002).
Morin, H., Service secret. A l'écoute devant Verdun. (Paris, Durasse, 1959).
Morin-Rotureau, E., 1939-1945: Combats de Femmes. Françaises et Allemandes, les Oubliées de la Guerre. (Paris, Autrement, 2002).
Mougel, F.C., Pacteau, S., Histoire des relations internationales. (Paris, PUF, 2002).
Navarre, H., L'Agonie de l'Indochine, 1953-1954. (Paris, Plon, 1956).
Navarre, H., Le Service de renseignements, 1871-1944. (Paris, Plon, 1978).
Navarre, H., Le Temps des vérités. (Paris, Plon, 1979).
Neher-Bernheim, R., Histore juive de la R'evolution à l'État d'Israël. (Paris, Seuil, 2002).
Nguyen Quoc, D., Daillier, P., Pellet, A., Droit international public. (Paris, LGDJ, 1994).
Noguères, H., Histoire de la Résistance en France. (Paris, Laffont, 1967/1981).
Nyss, E., Les Origines du Droit International. (Paris, Thorin, 1894).
OCDE, L'Endettement international. (Paris, OCDE, 1988).
OCDE, Perspectives économiques de l'Afrique. (Paris, OCDE, 2002).
Paillole, P., Services spéciaux (1935-1945). (Paris, Laffont, 1975).
Paillole, P., Notre espion chez Hitler. (Paris, Laffont, 1985).
Paléologue, M., Journal de l'affaire Dreyfus, 1894-1899. (Paris, Plon, 1958).
Paquet, C., La Défaite militaire de l'Allemagne en 1918. (Paris, Berger-Levrault, 1925).
Paquet, C., Dans l'attente de la ruée: Verdun (janvier – février 1916). (Paris, Berger-Levrault, 1928).
Parti Socialiste, Projet Socialiste pour la France des années 1980. (Paris, PS, 1980).
Parti Socialiste, Déclaration sur la paix, la sécurité et le désarmement. (Paris, PS, 1982).
Passy (pseudonyme de André Dewavrin), Souvenirs: Deuxième Bureau Londres. 10 Duke Street, Londres (Le BCRA). (Monte Carlo, Solar, 1947).

Passy, Missions secrètes en France. Souvenirs du BCRA. Novembre 1942 – juin 1943. (Paris, Plon, 1951).
Passy, Mémoires du chef des services secrets de la France Libre. (Paris, Odile Jacob, 2000).
Péan, P., Affaires africaines. (Paris, Fayard, 1983).
Péan, P., Secret d'État: La France du Secret. Les secrets de la France. (Paris, Fayard, 1986).
Péan, P., L'Homme de l'ombre. Éléments de l'enquête de Jacques Foccart, l'homme le plus mystérieux et le plus puissant de la Ve République. (Paris, Fayard, 1990).
Péan, P., Le Mystérieux Docteur Martin, 1895-1969. (Paris, Fayard, 1993).
Péan, P., La Diabolique de Caluire. (Paris, Fayard, 1999).
Péju, M., et al., Le Procès du Réseau Jeanson. (Paris, Découverte, 2002).
Pelissier, P., La Bataille d'Alger. (Paris, Perrin, 1995; 2002).
Pervillé, G., Pour une Histoire de la Guerre d'Algérie. (Paris, Picard, 2002).
Peschanski, D., Vichy 1940-1944. (Paris, CNRS, 1986; 1994).
Pillet, A., dir., Les fondateurs du droit international, leurs oeuvres, leurs doctrines. (Paris, Giard & Brière, 1904.
Poincaré, R., Au Service de la France: neuf années de souvenirs. (Paris, Plon, 1926/1928).
Poirier, L., Des Stratégies Nucléaires. (Paris, Hachette, 1977).
Poirier, L., Essais de Stratégie Théorique. (Paris, FEDN, 1982-1997).
Porch, D., Histoire des services secrets français. (Paris, A.Michel, 1997).
Pouillot, H., La Villa Susini. Tortures en Algérie. Un appelé parle, juin 1961-mars 1962. (Paris, Tirésias, 2002).
Prézelin, B., Flottes de combat 1998. (Paris, Éditions maritimes et d'outre-mer, 1998).
Puy-Montbrun, D., L'Honneur de la guerre. (Paris, A.Michel, 2002).
Rashid, A., Asie Centrale, Champ de Guerres. (Paris, Autrement, 2002).
Raufer, X., et al., Le Chaos Balkanique. (Paris, Table Ronde, 1992).
Ravenel, B., Kosovo. Une guerre de gauche? Pour la paix à travers le droit. (Paris, Golias, 1999).
Redslob, A., Histoire des grands principes du droit des gens. (Paris, 1923).
Reinhart, T., Détruire la Palestine ou Comment Terminer la Guerre de 1948. (Paris, La Fabrique, 2002).
Renouvin, P., La Question d'Extrême-Orient 1840-1940. (Paris, Hachette, 1946).
Renouvin, P., Histoire des relations internationales. (Paris, Hachette, 1954; 1996).
Renouvin, P., Le Traité de Versailles. (Paris, Flammarion, 1969).
Renouvin, P., Duroselle, J.B., Introduction á l'histoire des relations internationales. (Paris, A.Colin, 1970; 1991).
Reuter, P., Introduction au Droit des Traités. (Paris, 1972).
Reuter, P., Combacau, J., Institutions et relations internationales. (Paris, PUF, 1985).
Rey-Goldzeiger, A., Aux origines de la Guerre d'Algérie 1940-1945. (Paris, Découverte, 2002).
Richardot, P., La fin de l'armée romaine (284-476). (Paris, Economica, 1998).
Richer, P., La drôle de guerre des Français, 2 septembre 1939/10 mai 1940. (Paris, Orban, 1990).
Rinaldi, N., Dieu, guerre et autres paysages. (Paris, Harmattan, 2002).
Rioux, J.P., dir., La Guerre d'Algérie et les Français. (Paris, Fayard, 1990).
Ritter, J.C., L'Alsace. (Paris, PUF, 1985).
Rivet, D., Le Maghreb à l'épreuve de la colonisation. (Paris, Hachette, 2002).
Robrieux, P., Histoire intérieure du Parti Communiste. (Paris, Fayard, 1980-1984).
Rose, F. de, La France et la Défense de l'Europe. (Paris, Seuil, 1976).
Rose, F. de, Contre la Stratégie des Curiaces. (Paris, Julliard, 1983).
Rossi-Landi, G., La drôle de guerre, la vie politique en France, 2 septembre 1939/10 mai 1940. (Paris, A.Colin, 1971).

Rowley, A., Évolution économique de la France du milieu du XIXe siècle à 1914. (Paris, SEDES, 1982).
Roy, O., Généalogie de l'Islamisme. (Paris, Hachette, 2002).
Sabbah, M., Paix sur Jérusalem. Propos d'un Évêque Palestinien. (Paris, Éd. DDB, 2002).
Sala-Molins, L., Le Code Noir ou le Calvaire de Canaan. (Paris, PUF, 2002).
Savant, J., Les Espions de Napoléon. (Paris, Hachette, 1957).
Scelle, G., Manuel de droit international public. (Paris, 1948).
Scelle, G., Précis du droit des gens. Principes et systématiques. (Paris, 1932; 1984).
Schirmann, L., Mata Hari, Autopsie d'une Machination. (Paris, Éd. italiques, 2001).
Schirmann, L., Le Dossier Secret du Conseil de Guerre. (Paris, Éd. italiques, 2001).
Senarclens, P. de, Yalta. (Paris, PUF, 1990).
Senarclens, P., L'Humanitaire en catastrophe. (Paris, Presses de Sciences Po, 1999).
Senarclens, P., Maîtriser la Mondialisation. (Paris, FNSP, 2000).
Serfati, C., Production d'armes, croissance et innovation. (Paris, DF, 1996).
Soustelle, J., Envers en contre tout. I. De Londres à Alger (1940-1942). II. D'Alger à Paris (1942-1944). (Paris, Laffont, 1947/1950).
Soutou, G.H., L'or et le sang. Les buts de guerre économique de la Première Guerre Mondiale. (Paris, Fayard, 1989).
Soutou, G.H., L'Alliance incertaine, les rapports politico-stratégiques franco-allemandes 1954-1996. (Paris, Fayard, 1996).
Soutou, G.H., La Guerre de cinquante ans. Les relations Est-Ouest 1943-1990. (Paris, Fayard, 2001).
Stehlin, P., Témoignage pour l'histoire. (Paris, Laffont, 1964).
Stieber, W., Espion de Bismarck. (Paris, Pygmalion, 1985).
Stoltzfus, N., La Résistance des Coeurs. Berlin, 1943: La Révolte des Femmes Allemandes Mariée à des Juifs. (Paris, Phébus, trad., 2002).
Sun Zi, L'Art de la guerre. (Paris, Economica, 1990).
Theleri, M., Initiation à la Force de Frappe Française, 1945-2010. (Paris, Stock, 1997).
Tatu, M., Ben Laden et le XXIe siècle. (Paris, Éd. XXIe siècle, 2002).
Thomas, P.A., Les Désarrois d'un officier en Algérie. (Paris, Seuil, 2002).
Timsit, D., Algérie, récit anachronique. (Paris, Bouchène, 1998).
Timsit, D., Récits de la longue patience. (Paris, Flammarion, 2002).
Tiroch, B., La loi de programmation militaire 1997-2002: un grand bouleversement. (Dans: Regards sur l'actualité. Paris, DF, pp.3-16, juillet-août 1996).
Touraine, A., La prophétie antinucléaire. (Paris, Seuil, 1980).
Touscoz, J., Droit international. (Paris, PUF, 1993).
Trepper, L., Le Grand Jeu. (Paris, A.Michel, 1975).
Trigano, S., L'Ébranlement d'Israël. Philosophie de l'Histoire Juive. (Paris, Seuil, 2002).
Tucker, R.W., De l'inégalité des nations. (Paris, Economica, 1980).
Vaillé, E., Le Cabinet Noir. (Paris, PUF, 1959).
Vaïsse, M., La Grandeur. Politique étrangère du général de Gaulle, 1958-1969. (Paris, Fayard, 1998).
Vaïsse, M., dir., La France et l'Atome. (Bruxelles, Bruylant, 1995).
Vaïsse, M., dir., La France et l'Opération de Suez. (Paris, Addim, 1997).
Vaïsse, M., Doise, J., Dipomatie et outil militaire, 1871-1991. (Paris, Seuil, 1991).
Vaïsse, M., Dufour, J.L., La Guerre au XXe siècle. (Paris, Hachette, 1993).
Vaïsse, M., Melandri, P., Bozo, F., dir., La France et l'OTAN, 1949-1996. (Bruxelles, Complexe, 1996).
Van Creveld, M., Les Femmes et la guerre. (Paris, Rocher, 2002).
Vasak, K., Les Droits de l'Homme à l'Aube du XXIe Siècle. (Bruxelles, Bruylant, 1999).
Védrine, H., Les Cartes de la France à l'heure de la mondialisation. (Paris, Fayard, 2000).

Verdès-Leroux, J., Les Français d'Algérie de 1830 à nos jours. (Paris, Fayard, 2002).
Vernant, J., Les relations internationales à l'âge nucléaire. (Paris, Découverte, 1987).
Vidalenc, J., L'Exode de mai-juin 1940. (Paris, PUF, 1957).
Vidal-Naquet, P., La Raison d'État. (Paris, Découverte, 2002).
Voline, La Révolution inconnue. (Paris, Éd. Verticales, 1997).
Vilboux, N., Les Stratégies de Puissance Américaines. (Paris, Ellipses, 2002).
Warschawski, M., Sur la Frontière. (Paris, Stock, 2002).
Weil, P., Écrits de Droit International. (Paris, PUF, 2000).
Winterm J.P., Marin La Meslée, V., Stupeur dans la Civilisation. (Paris, Pauvert, 2002).
Wolton, T., Le KGB en France. (Paris, Grasset, 1986).
Wolton, T., Le Grand Recrutement. (Paris, Grasset, 1993).
Wolton, T., La France sous influence. Paris-Moscou: 30 ans de relations secrètes. (Paris Berger-Levrault, 1998).
Yost, D., La France et la Sécurité européenne. (Paris, PUF, 1985).
Zorgbibe, C., Textes de stratégie nucléaire. (Paris, PUF, 1993).
Zorgbibe, C., Les relations internationales. (Paris, PUF, 1993).
Zorgbibe, C., L'après-guerre froide dans le monde. (Paris, PUF, 1993).
Zorgbibe, C., Le droit d'ingérence. (Paris, PUF, 1994).
Zorgbibe, C., Géopolitique et histoire du Golfe. (Paris, PUF, 1995).
Zorgbibe, C., L'Impérialisme. (Paris, PUF, 1996).
Zunz, O., Le Siècle Américain. Essai sur l'essor d'une grande puissance. (Paris, Fayard, 2000).

English
Adamthwaite, A.P., The Making of the Second World War. (London, Cass, 1977).
Adamthwaite, A.P., France and the Coming of the Second World war. (London, Cass, 1977).
Adamthwaite, A.P., The Lost Peace: International Relations in Europe 1914-1940. (London, Cass, 1980).
Adamthwaite, A.P., Grandeur et Misery. France's Bid for Power in Europe 1914-1940. (London, Arnold, 1995).
Addington, L.H., The Blitzkrieg Era and the German General Staff, 1865-1941. (New Brunswick, Rutgers UP, 1971).
Alagappa, M., ed., Coercion and Governance. The Declining Political Role of the Military in Asia. (Stanford, Stanford UP, 2001).
Alagappa, M., ed., Military Professionalism in Asia. Conceptual and Empirical Perspectives. (New York, East West Center Publication, 2001).
Albert, M., et al., eds., Civilizing World Politics. Society and Community Beyond the State. (Boston, Rowman and Littlefield, 2000).
Albertine, L., The Origins of the War of 1914. (Oxford, OUP, 1952-1957).
Albrecht-Carrié, R., A Diplomatic History of Europe since the Congress of Vienna. (London, Macmillan, 1965).
Albrecht-Carrié, R., The Unity of Europe. A Historical Survey. (London, Macmillan, 1966).
Albrecht-Carrié, R., The Concert of Europe 1815-1914. (London, Macmillan, 1968).
Aldcroft, D.H., The European Economy 1914-1980. (London, 1978).
Aldcroft, D.H., From Versailles to Wall Street, 1919-1929. (London, 1997).
Alexander, M., The Republic in Danger. General Maurice Gamelin and the Politics of French Defence, 1933-1940. (Cambridge, CUP, 1992).
Alexander, M., ed., Knowing your Friends. Intelligence inside Alliances and Coalitions from 1914 to the Cold War. (London, Cass, 1998).

Alexander, Y., Swetman, M.S., Osama bin Laden's Al Qaida. (New York, Tirion, 2002).
Allensworth, W., The Russian Question. Nationalism, Modernization and Post-Communist Russia. (Lanham, Rowman & Littlefield, 1998).
Allison, G.T., Essence of Decision. Explaining the Cuban Missile Crisis. (Boston, Little-Brown, 1971).
Allison, G.T., Treverton, G.F., eds., Rethinking America's Security. (New York, Norton, 1992).
Anderson, P., Passages from Antiquity to Feudalism. (London, NLB, 1970; 1978).
Andrew, C., Théophile Delcassé and the making of the Entente Cordiale. (London, Macmillan, 1968).
Andrew, C., Secret Service. The Making of the British Intelligence Community. (London, Sceptre, 1992).
Andrew, C., Dilks, D., eds., The Missing Dimension. Governments and Intelligence Communities in the Twentieth Century. (Urbana, University of Illinois Press, 1984).
Andrew, C., Gordievski, O., KGB. The Inside Story. (New York, HarperCollins, 1990).
Andrew, C., Kanya-Forstner, A.S., The Climax of French Imperial Expansion 1914-1924. (Stanford, Stanford UP, 1981).
Andrew, C., Mitrokhin, V., The Mitrokhin Archive. The KGB in Europe and the West. (London, Penguin, 1999.
Arnold, E.A., Fouché, Napoleon and the General Police. (Washington, University Press of America, 1979).
Asmus, R.D., et al., Building a New NATO. (In: Foreign Affairs, pp.28-40, 1993).
Bacevich, A.J., Cohen, E.A., eds., War over Kosovo. (New York, Columbia UP, 2001).
Ball, H., Prosecuting War Crimes and Genocide. The Twentieth-Century Experience. (Lawrence, University of Kansas, 1999).
Ball, N., Pressing for Peace: Can Aid Induce Reform? (Washington DC, Overseas Development Council, 1992).
Barnett, C., The Collapse of British Power. (London, 1972).
Bamford, J., Body of Secrets. (New York, Doubleday, 2001).
Barnett, C., Britain and her Army, 1509-1970. (Harmondsworth, Penguin, 1974).
Barnett, C., Napoleon. (London, 1978).
Barnett, C., The Spirit of War. The Illusion on Reality of Britain as a Great Nation. (London, Macmillan, 1986).
Barkan, E., The Guilt of Nations. Restitution and Negotiating Historical Injustices. (New York, Norton, 2002).
Bartlett, C.J., The Global Conflict. The International Rivalry of the Great Powers, 1880-1970. (London, Longman, 1984).
Bartlett, R., The Making of Europe. Conquest, Colonization and Cultural Change, 960-1350. (Princeton, Princeton UP, 1993).
Bayoumi, M., Rubin, A., eds., The Edward Said Reader. (New York, Vintage. 2002).
Beaufre, A., 1940: The Fall of France. (New York, Knopf, 1968).
Beck, U., The Reinvention of Politics. Rethinking Modernity in the Global Social Order. (Cambridge, Polity, 1997).
Beitz, C.R., Political Theory and International Relations. (Princeton, Princeton UP, 1979).
Bell, C., The Diplomacy of Détente. The Kissinger Era. (New York, 1977).
Bell, P.M.H., The Origins of the Second World War in Europe. (London, 1986).
Bennett, C., Yugoslavia's Bloody Collapse. (New York, New York UP, 2000).
Bergen, P., Holy War Inc. Inside the Secret World of Osama bin Laden. (New York, Free Press, 2001).
Bergeron, L., France under Napoleon. (Princeton, Princeton UP, 1981).

Berton, P., ed., International Negotiation. Actors, Structure/Process, Values. (Basingstoke, Macmillan, 1999).
Beschloss, M.R., Talbott, S., At the Highest Levels. The Inside Story of the End of the Cold War. (Boston, Little/Brown, 1993).
Betts, R., Tricouleur. The French Colonial Empire. (London, 1978).
Betts, R., Systems for Peace or Causes of War? Collective Security, Arms Control and the New Europe. (In: International Security, pp.5-43, 1992).
Betts, R., ed., Cruise Missiles. Technology, Strategy, Politics. (Washington, Brookings, 1981).
Bildt, C., Peace Journey. The Struggle for Peace in Bosnia. (London, Weidenfeld & Nicolson, 1998).
Blackwell, O., Public International Law. (London, Cavendish, 1998).
Blanning, T.C.W., The Culture of Power and the Power of Culture. Old Regime Europe 1660-1789. (Oxford, OUP, 2002).
Bodansky, Y., Bin Laden. The Man Who Declared War on America. (New York, Forum, 1999).
Bosworth, R.J.B., Mussolini. (London, Arnold, 2002).
Boxer, C.R., The Portuguese Seaborne Empire 1415-1825. (London, 1969).
Boxer, C.R., The Dutch Seaborne Empire 1600-1800. (London, 1972).
Brédin, D., The Affair. The Case of Alfred Dreyfus. (New York, Brazilier, 1986).
Bridge, F.R., Bullen, R., The Great Powers and the European States System, 1815-1914. (London, Longman, 1980).
Brodie, B., A Guide to Naval Strategy. (Westport, Greenwood, 1977).
Brodie, B., ed., The Absolute Weapon. Atomic Power and World Order. (New York, Harcourt/Brace, 1946).
Brook-Sheperd, G., The Storm Birds. Soviet Postwar Defectors. (New York, Holt, 1989).
Brown, C.L., International Politics of the Middle East. Old Rules, Dangerous Game. (Princeton, Princeton UP, 1984).
Bruni, F., Ambling into History. The Unlikely Odyssey of George W.Bush. (New York, HarperCollins, 2002).
Brunschwig, H., French Colonialism, 1871-1916: myths and realities. (London, Praeger, 1966).
Brzezinski, Z., Out of Control. Global Turmoil on the Eve of the Twenty-first Century. (New York, Macmillan, 1993).
Brzoska, M., Lock, P., eds., Restructuring of Arms Production in Western Europe. (New York, OUP, 1992).
Bull, H., The Anarchical Society. A Study of Order in World Politi8cs. (London, Macmillan, 1977; New York, Columbia UP, 1997).
Bull, H., ed., Intervention in World Politics. (Oxford, Clarendon, 1984).
Bull, H., Watson, A., eds., The Expansion of International Society. (Oxford, OUP, 1984).
Burton, J.W., World Society. (Cambridge, CUP, 1972).
Butler, F., ed., Human Rights for the New Millennium. (The Hague, Kluwer, 2000).
Buzan, B., An Introduction to Strategic Studies. (London, Macmillan, 1987).
Calleo, D.P., The German problem reconsidered. Germany and the World Order, 1870 to the present. (Cambridge, CUP, 1978).
Calvocoressi, P., Wint, G., Total War. Causes and Course of the Second World War. (New York, 1989).
Cameron, I., National Security and the European Convention on Human Rights. (Uppsala, Iustus, 2000).
Cameron, R.E., France and the economic developments in Europe 1800-1914. (Princeton, Princeton UP, 1961; 1971).

Campbell, D., Why Fight: Humanitarianism, Principles and Post-Structuralism. (In: Millennium, 27-3, 1998).
Cannadine, D., Ornamentalism. How the British saw their Empire. (London, Penguin, 2002).
Caparoso, J., Across the Great Divide: Integrating Comparative and International Politics. (In: International Studies Quarterly, 41-4, 1997).
Caron, F., An Economic History of Modern France. (New York, Methuen, 1979).
Carlsnaes, W., Ideology and Foreign Policy. (Oxford, Blackwell, 1986).
Carr, E.H., What is History? (London, Penguin, 1990).
Castellino, J., International Law and Self-Determination. (The Hague, Kluwer, 2000).
Castles, S., The Age of Migration. International Population Movements in the Modern World. (New York, Guilford, 1998).
Cerny, P.G., The Politics of Grandeur. Ideological aspects of De Gaulle's foreign policy. (Cambridge, CUP, 1980).
Cerny, P.G., ed., Social movements and protest in France. (London, Pinter, 1982).
Chafer, T., Ecologists and the Bomb. (In: Howorth, J., Chilton, P., eds., Defence and Dissent in Contemporary France. London, Croom Helm, 1984).
Chandler, D.G., The Campaigns of Napoleon. (London, Weidenfeld & Nicolson, 1966).
Chandler, D.G., The Art of Warfare in the Age of Marlborough. (New York, Hippocrene, 1976).
Cheng, C.J., ed., The Utilization of the World's Air Space and the Outer Space in the 21st Century. (The Hague, Kluwer, 2000).
Chibundu, M.O., Globalizing the Rule Of Law. (In: Indiana Journal of Global Legal Studies, pp.79-116, 1999).
Childs, J., Armies and Warfare in Europe 1648-1789. (Manchester, Manchester UP, 1982).
Chilton, P., French Nuclear Weapons. (In: Howorth, J., Chilton, P., eds., Defence and Dissent in Contemporary France. (London, Croom Helm, 1984).
Chimini, B.S., ed., International Refugee Law. (New Dehli, Sage, 2000).
Clark, A., Barbarossa: The Russo-German Conflict 1941-1945. (London, 1965).
Clark, I., Beyond the Great Divide: Globalization and the Theory of International Relations. (In: Review of International Studies, 24-4, 1998).
Clark, I., Globalization and International Relations Theory. (Oxford, OUP, 1999).
Clausewitz, C. von, Principles of War. (Harrisburg, Military Service Publications, 1983).
Clausewitz, C. von, On War. (Princeton, Princeton UP, 1984).
Close, P., The Legacy of Supranationalism. (Basingstoke, Macmillan, 2000).
Clough, S.B., France. A history of national economics 1789-1939. (New York, 1939; 1970).
Cochran, M., Normative Theory in International Relations. (Cambridge, CUP, 1999).
Cockburn, P., Getting Russia Wrong. The End of Kremlinology. (London, Verso, 1989).
Codevilla, A., Informing Statecraft. Intelligence for a New Century. (New York, Free Press, 1992).
Conboy, K., Morrison, J., The CIA's Secret War in Tibet. (Lawrence, University Press of Kansas, 2002
Cook, M.A., ed., A History of the Ottoman Empire to 1730. (Cambridge, CUP, 1976).
Cooke, J.J., 100 Miles from Bagdad. With the French in Desert Storm. (Westport, Praeger, 1993).
Corwin, P., Dubious Mandate. A Memoir of the UN in Bosnia. (Duke University Press, 1995).
Crutwell, C., A History of the Great War, 1914-1918. (London, Paladin, 1982).
CSCE, From Vienna to Helsinki. (Washington DC, Commission on Security and Cooperation in Europe, 1992).

CSCE, Overview. The Conference on Security and Cooperation in Europe. (Washington DC, Commission on Security and Cooperation in Europe, 1992).
Cupitt, R.T., Reluctant Champions. Truman, Eisenhower, Bush and Clinton. US Presidential Policy and Strategic Export Controls. (London, Routledge, 2000).
Cuthbertson, I.M., ed., Redefining the CSCE. (New York, Institute for East West Studies, 1993).
Daalder, I., O'Hanlon, E., Winning Ugly. NATO's War to Save Kosovo. (New York, Brookings Institution, 2000).
Dallin, A., Lapidus, G., eds., The Soviet System. From Crisis to Collapse. (Boulder, Westview, 1995).
Dallin, D., Soviet Espionage. (New Haven, Yale UP, 1955).
Damrosh, L.F., ed., Enforcing Restraint. Collective Intervention in Internal Conflicts. (New York, Council on Foreign Relations Press, 1993).
Danielsson, B. and M.T., Poisoned Reign. French Nuclear Colonialism in the Pacific. (London, Penguin, 1986).
Davidson, P.B., Vietnam at War. The History, 1946-1975. (Novato, Presidio Press, 1988).
Davison, W.P., The Berlin Blockade. (Princeton, Princeton UP, 1958).
Deacon, R., The French Secret Service. (London, Grafton, 1990).
Deighton, A., ed., Western European Union, 1954-1997. (Oxford, St. Antony's College, 1997).
Demchak, C.C., Military Organizations, Complex Machines. Modernization in the US Armed Services. (Ithaca, Cornell UP, 1991).
Der Derian, J., On Diplomacy. (Oxford, Blackwell, 1987).
Der Derian, J., Anti-Dipomacy. (Oxford, Blackwell, 1992).
Dibb, P., The Soviet Union. The Incomplete Super-Power. (London, 1985; 1986).
Dolzer, R., ed., Protecting our Environment. (Sankt Augustin, Konrad Adenauer Stiftung, 2000).
Dowd, D.L., The Napoleonic Era in Europe. (New York, 1971).
Drucker, P.F., Post-Capitalist Society. (New York, Harper Business, 1993).
Duchesne, F., Jean Monnet. The First Statesman of Interdependence. (London, Norton, 1994).
Ducloux, L., From Blackmail to Treason: Political Crime and Corruption in France, 1920-1940. (London, Deutsch, 1958).
Dyson, J., Sink the Rainbow Warrior! An Enquiry into the "Greenpeace Affair". (London, Gollancz, 1986).
Earthscan, Global 2001. UN Envronment Program. (London, 1999).
East, M.A., et al., eds., Why Nations Act. (Beverley Hills, Sage, 1978).
Edgerton, R.B., Warriors of the Rising Sun. A History of the Japanese Military. (New York, Norton, 1997).
Ehrlich, P.R., The Population Bomb. (New York, Ballantine, 1971; 1978).
Elias, N., The Civilizing Process. The History of Manners and State Formation and Civilization. (Oxford, Blackwell, 1994).
Elman, C., Fendius Elman, M., eds., Bridges and Boundaries: Historians, Political Scientists and the Study of International Relations. (London, MIT Press, 2001).
Erickson, J., Stalin's War with Germany. The Road to Stalingrad. The Road to Berlin. (New York, 1975/1983).
European Parliament, An Appraisal of the Technologies of Political Control. (Strasbourg, STOA, 1998).
European Parliament, Second Report. (Strasbourg, STOA, 2000).
Faligot, R., Krop, P., La Piscine. The French Secret Services since 1944. (Oxford, Blackwell, 1989).

Falls, C., The First World War. (London, 1989).
Farazmand, A., Handbook of Comparative and Development Public Administration. (New York, Dekker, 2001).
Farrar, L.L., The Short-War Illusion. German Policy, Strategy and Domestic Affairs. (Santa Barbara, 1973).
Feis, H., The Atomic Bomb and the End of World War II. (Princeton, Princeton UP, 1966).
Feis, H., Churchill-Roosevelt-Stalin.The War they staged and the Peace they sought. (Princeton, Princeton UP, 1967).
Ferguson, Y.H., Mansbach, R.W., The Elusive Quest. Theory and International Politics. (Columbia, University of South California Press, 1988).
Ferrell, R., Woodrow Wilson and World War I. (New York, 1985).
Ferrell, R., American Diplomacy in the Twentieth Century. (New York, Norton, 1988).
Ferrill, A., The Origins of War. From the Stone Age to Alexander the Great. (London, Thames & Hudson, 1985).
Finer, S.E., State- and Nation-Building in Europe. The Role of the Military. (In: Tilly, C., ed., The Formation of National States in Europe. Princeton, Princeton UP, pp.84-163, 1975).
Finer, S.E., The History of Government from the Earliest Times. (Oxford, OUP, 1997).
Finney, P., ed., The Origins of the Second World War. (London, Arnold, 1997).
Flicke, W.F., War Secrets in the Ether. (Laguna Hills, CA, Aegean Park, 1977).
Foot, M.R.D., SOE in France. (London, HMSO, 1966).
Foot, M.R.D., Resistance. (London, Granada, 1978).
Frankel, J., Contemporary International Theory and the Behaviour of States. (London, OUP, 1981).
Freedman, L., Britain and Nuclear Weapons. (London, Macmillan, 1980).
Freedman, L., The Evolution of Nuclear Strategy. (London, Macmillan, 1981; 1989).
Freedman, L., The Revolution in Strategic Affairs. (London, IISS/OUP, 1998).
Freedman, L., ed., Europe Transformed. Documents on the End of the Cold War. (New York, St.Martin's, 1990).
Freidberg, A.L., In the Shadow of the Garrison State. America's Anti-Statism and its Cold War Grand Strategy. (Princeton, Princeton UP, 2000).
Fukuyama, F., The End of History and the Last Man. (New York, Free Press, 1992).
Gaddis, J.L., Strategies of Containment. (New York, OUP, 1982).
Gaddis, J.L., The Lomg Peace. Inquiries into the History of the Cold War. (Oxford, OUP, 1987).
Gaddis, J.L., The United States and the End of the Cold War. (Oxford, OUP, 1992).
Gaddis, J.L., We Know Now. Rethinking Cold War History. (Oxford, OUP, 1997).
Galtier-Boissière, J., Mysteries of the French Secret Police. (Plymouth, Stanley Paul, 1938).
Garthoff, R.L., Soviet Strategy in the Nuclear Age. (New York, Praeger, 1958).
Garthoff, R.L., Détente and Confrontation. American-Soviet Relations from Nixon to Reagan. (Washington DC, Brookings Institution, 1985; 1994).
Gellner, E., Nations and Nationalism. (Oxford, Blackwell, 1993).
Ghebali, V.Y., La Diplomatie multilatérale de la Détente. Le Processus de la CSCE, d'Helsinki à Vienne (1973-1989). (Bruxelles, Bruylant, 1989).
Gibson, R., Spain in America. (New York, 1966).
Gibson, R, Best of Enemies: Anglo-French Relations since the Norman Conquest. (London, Sinclair, 1995).
Gilbert, D., et al., eds., Handbook of Social Psychology. (New York, McGraw-Hill, 1998).
Gilpin, R.G., War and Change in World Politics. (Cambridge, CUP, 1981).
Giovanetti, L., Freed. F., The Decision to Drop the Bomb. (London, 1967).
Glover, M., The Napoleonic Wars. An illustrated history 1792-1815. (New York, 1979).

Gordon, M., et al., The Americas in Transition. The Contours of Regionalism. (Boulder, Rienner, 1999).
Gow, J., Triumph of the Lack of Will: International Diplomacy and the Yugloslav War. (London, Hurst, 1997).
Gray, C.S., Explorations in Strategy. (New York, Praeger, 1998).
Gray, C.S., The Second Nuclear Age. (London, Rienner, 1999).
Gray, C.S., Barnett, R.W., eds., Seapower and Strategy. (Annapolis, Naval Institute, 1989).
Gray, C.S., Sheldon, J.B., Spacepower and the Revolution in Military Affairs. (Hull, Centre for Security Studies, 1998).
Gregory, S., French Defence Policy into the Twenty-First Century. (London, Macmillan, 2000).
Grew, J.C., Turbulent Era. A Diplomatic Record of Forty Years, 1904-1945. (Boston, 1952).
Griffin, M., Reaping Whirlwind. The Taliban Movement in Afghanistan. (London, Pluto, 2001).
Griffith, P., The Military Thought in the French Army, 1815-1851. (Cambridge, Harvard UP, 1989).
Groom, A.J.R., Light, M., eds., Contemporary International Relations. A Guide to Theory. (London, Pinter, 1994).
Groom, J., British Thinking about Nuclear Weapons. (London, Pinter, 1974).
Grosser, A., French Foreign Policy under De Gaulle. (Boston, Little/Brown; Westport, Greenwood, 1977).
Grosser, A., The Western Alliance: European-American Relations since 1945. (London, Macmillan, 1980).
Grove, H.D., Banning Chemical Weapons. The Scientific Background. (Cambridge, CUP, 1992).
Guelke, A., The Age of Terrorism and the International Political System. (London, Tauris, 1998).
Gulick, E.V., Europe's Classical Balance of Power. (New York, Norton, 1967).
Haas, E.B., Beyond the Nation-State. Functionalism and International Organization. (Stanford, Stanford UP, 1964).
Haas, E.B., When Knowledge is Power. (Berkeley, University of California Press, 1990).
Hamilton, A., The Appeal of Fascism. (London, 1971).
Handel, M.I., ed., Clausewitz and Modern Strategy. (London, Cass, 1986).
Handel, M.I., ed., Leaders and Intelligence. (London, Cass, 1988).
Handel, M.I., ed., War, Strategy and Intelligence. (London, Cass, 1989).
Handel, M.I., ed., Intelligence and Military Operations. (London, Cass, 1990).
Hardach, G., The First World War 1914-1918. (London, 1977).
Harries, M.S., Soldiers of the Sun. The Rise and Fall of the Imperial Japanese Army. (New York, Random House, 1991).
Harris, S., et al., The Day the World Changed? Terrorism and World Order. (Canberra, Department of International Relations, 2001).
Hartley, K., Sandler, T., The Economics of Defence. (Cheltenham, Elgar, 2001).
Hastings, Overlord: D-Day and the Battle of Normandy. (London, 1984).
Hayes, P., Fascism. (London, 1973).
Heeren, A.H.L., A Manual of the History of the Political System of Europe and its Colonies. (London, Bohn, 1873).
Held, D., Democracy and the Global Order. From the Modern State to Cosmopolitan Governance. (London, Polity, 1995).
Heller, F.H., ed., The Korean War. A 25-years Perspective. (Lawrence, University of Kansas, 1977).

Helsinki Final Document, Final Document from the 1992 Helsinki Follow-Up Meeting. (Washington, US Congress, 1992).
Henderson, W.O., The industrial revolution on the continent: Germany, France, Russia 1800-1914. (London, 1967).
Herwig, H., The First World War. Germany and Austria-Hungary. (London, 1996).
Hinde, R.A., War: some psychological causes and consequences. (In: Interdisciplinary Reviews, pp.229-245, 1997).
Hinde, R.A., ed., The Institution of War. (London, Macmillan, 1991).
Hinde, R.A., Parry, D., eds., Education for Peace. (Nottingham, Spokesman, 1989).
Hinde, R.A., Watson, H., eds., War: a Cruel Necessity? (London, Tauris, 1995).
Hitchcock, W., France Restored. Cold War Diplomacy and the Quest for Leadership in Europe, 1944-1954. (Chapel Hill, University of North Carolina Press, 1998).
Hitchcock, W., ed., The Intelligence Revolution. A Historical Perspective. (Washington, DC, Air Force History, 1991).
Hobsbawm, E.J., Nationas and Nationalism since 1780. (Cambridge, CUP, 1990).
Hoffmann, S, Primacy or World Order. American Foreign Policy since the Cold War. (New York, McGraw-Hill, 1978).
Hoffmann, S., Duties Beyond Borders: On the Limits and Possibilities of Ethical International Politics. (Syracuse, Syracuse UP, 1981).
Hogan, M.J., The Marshall Plan: America, Britain and the Reconstruction of Western Europe, 1947-1952. (Cambridge, CUP, 1987).
Hogan, M.J., A Cross of Iron: Harry S. Truman and the Origins of the National Security State. (Cambridge, CUP, 1998).
Holbrooke, R., To End a War. (New York, Modern Library, 1998; 1999).
Hollis, M., Smith, S., Explaining and Understanding International Relations. (Oxford, OUP, 1991).
Holloway, D., The Soviet Union and the Arms Race. (New Haven, Yale UP, 1984).
Holloway, D., Stalin and the Bomb. The Soviet Union and Atomic Energy, 1939-1956. (New Haven, Yale UP, 1994).
Horne, A., The Price of Glory: Verdun 1916. (New York, St.Martin's, 1963).
Horne, A., The French Army and Politics 1870-1970. (London, Longman, 1984).
Hosking, G., A History of the Sovet Union. (London, Collins, 1985).
Hosking, A., The Awakening of the Soviet Union. (Cambridge, MA, Harvard UP, 1990).
Hosking, G., Russia and the Russians. (London, Allen Lange, 2001).
Hosking, G., Service, R., eds., Reinterpreting Russia. (London, Arnold, 1999).
Hosmer, S.T., Why Milosevic Decided to Settle When He Did. (Santa Monica, Rand, 2001).
Howard, M., The Franco-Prussian War. (Oxford, OUP, 1981).
Howard, M., The First World War. (Oxford, OUP, 2002).
Howard, M., ed., The Theory and Practice of War. (London, Cassell, 1965).
Howard, M., Paret, P., eds., On War. (Princeton, Princeton UP, 1984).
Howe, R.W., Mata Hari. The True Story. (New York, Dodd-Mead, 1986).
Howorth, J., Chilton, P., eds., Defence and Dissent in Contemporary France. (London, Croom Helm, 1984).
Human Rights Watch, World Report 2001. (New York, Human Rights Watch, 2000).
Huntington, S.P., The Common Defence. Strategic Programs in National Politics. (New York, Columbia UP, 1961).
Huntington, S.P., The Clash of Civilizations and the Remaking of World Order. (New York, Simon & Schuster, 1997; Touchstone, 1998).
Huntington, S.P., et al., The Clash of Civilizations? The Debate. (New York, Council on Foreign Relations, 1993).

IEDSS, NATO. The Case for Enlargement. (London, Institute for European Defence and Strategic Studies, 1993.
IISS (International Institute of Strategic Studies), The Military Balance 1993-1994. (London, Brassey's, 1993 and yearly).
IISS, Strategic Survey, annually. (Oxford, OUP, 1997)
Irving, E.M., The First Indochina War. French and American Policy, 1945-1954. (London, 1975).
Jacobson, D., Rights across Borders. Immigration and the Decline of Citizenship. (Baltimore, Johns Hopkins UP, 1996).
James, L., Warrior Race. A History of the British at War. (New York, Little/Brown, 2002).
Jenks, W., The Common Law of Mankind. (London, Stevens, 1968).
Jeong, H.W., ed., The New Agenda for Peace Research. (Aldershot, Ashgate, 2000).
Jessup, J.E., An Encyclopedic Dictionary of Conflict and Conflict Resolution, 1945-1996). Westport, Greenwood, 1998).
Jessup, J.E., Loakley, R.W., A Guide to the Study and Use of Military History. Washington DC, Center of Military History, 1982.
Jessup, P., The Birth of Nations. (New York, Columbia UP, 1974).
Joll, J., The Origins of the First World War. (New York, 1984).
Joll, J., ed., Britain and Europe: Pitt to Churchill, 1793-1940. (London, 1950).
Joll, J., ed., The Decline of the Third Republic. (New York, 1959).
Jomini, A.H., The Art of War. (Westport, Greenwood, 1977).
Jones, E.L., The European Miracle. (Cambridge, CUP, 1981).
JSS (Journal of Strategic Studies), The Future of NATO. (London, Cass, 1994).
Judah, T., The Serbs. History, Myth and Destruction of Yugoslavia. (New Haven, Yale UP, 1998).
Judah, T., Kosovo: War and Revenge. (New Haven, Yale UP, 2000).
Kahn, D., The Codebreakers. The Story of Secret Writing. (New York, Macmillan, 1967).
Kahn, D., Hitler's Spies. (New York, Macmillan, 1978).
Kahn, H., On Thermonuclear War. (Princeton, Princeton UP, 1960).
Kaldor, M., New and Old Wars. Organized Violence in a Global Era. (Cambridge, Polity, 1999).
Kaldor, M., ed., Global Insecurity. (London, Pinter, 2000).
Kaplan, L., The United States and NATO. (Lexington, University of Kentucky Press, 1984).
Kaplan, R.D., The Coming Anarchy. Shattering the Dreams of the Post Cold War. (New York, Random House, 2000).
Kaplan, R.D., Warrior Politics. Why Leadership demands a Pagan Ethos. (New York, Random House, 2002.
Kedourie, E., Nationalism. (Oxford, Blackwell, 1993).
Keegan, J., War and our World. (London, Hutchinson, 1990).
Keegan, J., The Second World War. (New York, Viking, 1990).
Keegan, J., The First World War. (London, Hutchinson, 1999).
Kegley, C.W., The New Global Order. The Power of Principle in a Pluralistic World. (In: Ethics & International Affairs, pp.21-40, 1992).
Kegley, C.W., Schwab, K.L., eds., After the Cold War. Questioning the Morality of Nuclear Deterrence. (Boulder, Westview, 1991).
Kegley, C.W., Wittkopf, E.R., eds., American Foreign Policy. (New York, St.Martin's, 1987).
Kegley, C.W., Wittkopf, E.R., eds., The Global Agenda. (New York, McGraw-Hill, 1992).
Keiger, J.F.V., France and the Origins of the First World War. (London, Macmillan, 1983).
Keiger, J.F.V., Raymond Poincaré. (Cambridge, CUP, 1997).

Keiger, J.F.V., France and the world since 1870. (London, Arnold, 2001).
Kemp, T., Industrialization in Nineteenth-century Europe. (London, 1969).
Kemp, T., Economic forces in French history. (London, 1971).
Kemp. T., The French economy 1913-1939: the history of a decline. (London, Longman, 1972).
Kende, I., Dynamism of war, of arms trade and of military expenditure in the Third World, 1945-1976. (In: Instant Research on Peace and Violence, pp.59-67, 1977).
Kennan, G., American Diplomacy, 1900-1950. (Chicago, University of Chicago Press, 1984).
Kennan, G., The Fatal Alliance. France, Russia and the coming of the First World War. (Manchester, Manchester UP, 1984).
Kennedy, P., The Rise and Fall of of the Great Powers. Economic Change and Military Conflict from 1500 to 2000. (New York, Random House, 1987; 1989).
Kennedy, P., Preparing for the Twenty-Fist Century. (New York, Vintage, 1994).
Kennedy, P., ed., The War Plans of the Great Powers 1880-1914. (London, Allen & Unwin, 1979).
Keohane, R.O., ed., Neorealism and its Critics. (New York, Columbia UP, 1986).
Keohane, R.O., ed., International Institutions and State Power. (Boulder, Westview, 1989).
Keohane, R.O., Milner, H.V., eds., Internationalization and Domestic Politics. (New York, CUP, 1996).
Keohane, R.O., Nye, J.S., eds., Transnational Relations and World Politics. (Cambridge, Harvard UP, 1972).
Keohane, R.O., Nye, J.S., eds., Power and Interdependence. World Politics in Transition. (Boston, Little/Brown; New York, HarperCollins, 1989).
Keohane, R.O., Nye, J.S., Hoffmann, S., eds., After the Cold War. (Cambridge, Harvard UP, 1993).
Kepel, G., Jihad. Expansion and Decline of the Islamist Movement. (Cambridge, Belknap, 2001).
Keppie, L., The Making of the Roman Army, from Republic to Empire. (London, Batsford, 1984).
Kersaudy, F., Churchill and De Gaulle. (London, 1981).
Kershaw, I., Hitler, 1889-1936. Hubris. (London, Penguin, 1998).
Kershaw, I., Hitler, 1936-1945. Nemesis. (London, Pengun, 2000).
Keynes, J.M.,The Economic Consequences of the Peace. (New York, Harcourt etc., 1920).
Kindleberger, C.P., The World in Depression, 1929-1939. (London, Penguin, 1973).
Kindleberger, C.P., Theory of International Politics. (Reading, Addison-Wesley, 1979).
Kindleberger, C.P., Realism after the Cold War. (Boston, ASPA meeting, 1998).
King, M., Death of the Rainbow Warrior. (Harmondsworth, Penguin, 1986).
Kissinger, H., The Troubled Partnership. A Re-Appraisal of the Atlantic Alliance. (Garden City, Doubleday, 1965).
Kissinger, H., The White House Years. (Boston, Little-Brown, 1979).
Kissinger, H., Diplomacy. (New York, Simon & Schuster, 1994).
Kissinger, H., The Kissinger Transcripts. (New York, 1999).
Klein, J., The Naturel. The Misunderstood Presidency of Bill Clinton. (New York, Doubleday, 2002).
Knippenberg, H., ed., Nationalising and Denationalising Border Regions, 1800-2000. (Dordrecht, Kluwer, 1999).
Knox, M., Mussolini unleashed 1939-1941. (London, 1982).
Koenigsberger, H.G., The Habsburgers and Europe 1516-1660. (Ithaca, Cornell UP, 1971).
Kohl, W.L., French Nuclear Diplomacy. (Princeton, Princeton UP, 1971).

Kolko, G., Anatomy of a War. Vietnam, the United States and the Modern Historical Experience. (New York, Free Press, 1986).
Kolko, G., Century of War. Politics, Conflict and Society since 1914. (New York, Free Press, 1994).
Kolko, G., Vietnam. Anatomy of Peace. (London, Routledge, 1997).
Kolodziej, E., French International Policy under De Gaulle and Pompidou. The Politics of Grandeur. (Ithaca, Cornell UP, 1974).
Kortepeter, C.M., Ottoman Imperialism during the Reformation. (London, 1973).
Kramer, M., Ivory Towers on Sand. The Failure of Middle Eastern Studies in America. (Washington DC, Institute for Near East Policy, 2002).
Layne, C., Schwartz, B., American Hegemony without an enemy. (In: Foreign Policy, 92, pp.5-23, 1993).
Lakes, M., The Law of Outer Space. (Leyde, Sijthoff, 1972).
Lambeth, B.S., NATO's Air War for Kosovo. (Santa Monica, Rand, 2001).
Landes, D.S., The Unbound Prometheus. Technological change and industrial development in Western Europe from 1750 to the present. (Cambridge, CUP, 1969).
Laqueur, W., The Age of Terrorism. (Boston, Little/Brown, 1987).
Laqueur, W., A World of Secrets. The Uses and Limits of Intelligence. (New York, Basic Books, 1988).
Laqueur, W., Europe in Our Time. (Harmondsworth, Penguin, 1993).
Laqueur, W., The Guerilla Reader. (New York, Meridian, 1997).
Laqueur, W., Guerilla Warfare. (New Brunswick, transaction, 1998).
Laqueur, W., The New Terrorism. Fanatism and the Arms of Mass Destruction. (New York, Phoenix, 2000).
Lefebvre, G., Napoleon from 18 Brumaire to Tilsit, 1799-1807. (London, Routledge, 1969).
Lehne, S., The CSCE in the 1990s. Common European House or Potemkin Village? (Vienna, Austrian Institute for International Affairs, 1991).
Lepgold, J., The Next Step toward a More Secure Europe. (In: JSS, pp.7-26, 1994).
Lepgold, J., NATO's Post-Cold War Collective Action Problem. (In: International Security, pp.78-106, 1998).
Lepgold, J., Weiss, T.G., eds., Collective Conflict Management and Changing World Politics. (Albany, State University of New York Press, 1998).
Levene, M., Roberts, P., The Massacre in History. (London, 1999).
Lewis, B., The Assassins. A Radical Sect in Islam. (London, Weidenfeld & Nicolson, 2001).
Lewis, B., What Went Wrong? Western Impact and Middle Eastern Response. (Oxford, OUP, 2001).
Lewis, J.P., Pro-Poor Aid Conditionality. (Washington DC, Overseas Development Council, 1993).
Liddell Hart, B.H., History of the Second World War. (London, Pan Books, 1970).
Light, M., Groom, A.J.R., eds., International Relations. A Handbook of Current Theory. (London, Pinter, 1985).
Lieven, D.C.B., Russia and the Origins of the First World War. (London, 1983).
Lourie, R., Sakharov. A Biography. (New York, Brandeis UP, 2002).
Lukacs, J., The End of the Twentieth Century. (New York, Tickner and Fields, 1993).
Lumsdaine, D.H., Moral Vision in International Politics. The Aid Regime, 1949-1989. (Princeton, Princeton UP, 1993).
Lynn-Jones, S.M., Miller, S.E., eds., America's Strategy in a Changing World. (Cambridge, MIT Press, 1992).

MacWhinney, E., The United Nations and the New World Order for a New Millennium. Self-Determination, State Succession and Humanitarian Intervention. (The Hague, Kluwer, 2000).
Maier, C.S., In Search of Stability: Explorations in Historical Political Economy. (Cambridge, CUP, 1987).
Mamatey, V.S., Rise of the Habsburg Empire 1526-1815. (Huntington, NY, 1978).
Mangold, T., Cold Warrior. James Jesus Angleton. The CIA's Master Spy Hunter. (New York, Simon & Schuster, 1991).
Marks, S., The Illusion of Peace. International Relations in Europe 1918-1933. (London, 1976).
Marks, S., The Riddle of All Constitutions. International Law, Democracy and the Critique of Ideology. (Oxford, OUP, 2000).
Marsh, I., et al., eds., Democracy, Governance and Economic Performance: East and Southeast Asia. (Tokyo, United Nations UP, 1999).
McDougall, W.A., France's Rhineland Dipomacy 1914-1924. (Princeton, Princeton UP, 1978).
McNamara, F.T., France in Black Africa. (Washington, National Defence University, 1989).
McNeill, W.H., The Rise of the West. A History of the Human Community. (Chicago, Chicago UP, 1967).
Mearsheimer, J.J., Back to the Future: Instability in Europe After the Cold War. (In: International Security, pp.5-56, 1990).
Mearsheimer, J.J., The Tragedy of Great Power Politics. (New York, 2001).
Melanson, R.A., American Foreign Policy since the Vietnma War. (New York, Sharpe, 2000).
Mendelsohn, K., Science and Western Domination. (London, 1976).
Mendl, W., Deterrence and Persuasion. French Nuclear Armament in the Context of National Policy, 1945-1969. (London, Faber and Faber, 1970).
Miller, D., The Cold War. A Military History. (New York, St.Martin's, 2000).
Miller, L.B., Smith, M.J., Ideas & Ideals: Essays on Politics in Honor of Stanley Hoffmann. (Boulder, Westview, 1993).
Miller, S.E., ed., Military Strategy and the Origins of the First World War. (Princeton, Princeton UP, 1985).
Milward, A.S., Saul, S.B., The economic development of continental Europe 1780-1870. (London, 1973).
Milward, A.S., Saul, S.B., The development of the economies of Continental Europe 1850-1914. (Cambridge, MA, 1977).
Mitchell, A., The German Influence in France after 1870. (Chapel Hill, University of North Carolina Press, 1979).
Mitchell, A., Victors and Vanquished. The German Influence on Army and Church in France after 1870. (Chapel Hill, University of North Carolina Press, 1984).
Mitrany, D., A Working Peace System. An argument for the functional development of international organization. (London, 1946; Chicago, Quadrangle, 1966).
Mommsen, W.J., Kettenacher, L., eds., The Fascist Challenge and the Policy of Appeasement. (London, 1983).
Moravec, F., Master of Spies. (Garden City NY, Doubleday, 1975).
Morgenthau, H.J., Politics among Nations. (New York, Knopf, 1948; 1985).
Morrisson, F.L., ed., International, Regional and National Environmental Law. (The Hague, Kluwer, 2000).
Mortimer, R.A., The Third World Coalition in International Politics. (New York, 1980).

Mudec, R.E., The Gatt Legal System and World Trade Diplomacy. (Salem, Butterworth, 1990).
Mylroie, L., Study of Revenge. Saddam Hussein's Unfinished War against America. (New York, 2001).
Naimark, N.M., Fires of Hatred. Ethnic Cleansing in Twentieth-Century Europe. (Cambridge, MA, Harvard UP, 2002).
Nardin, T., Mapel, D.R., eds., Traditions of International Ethics. (Cambridge, CUP, 1992).
Navari, C., Internationalism and the State in the Twentieth Century. (London, Routledge, 2000).
Neilson, K., McKercher, B.J.C., Go Spy the Land. Military Intelligence in History. (Westport, Greenwood, 1992; 1995).
Nelson, D.N., America and Collective Security in Europe. (In: JSS, pp.105-124, 1994).
Nelson, J.M., Eglinton, S.J., Encouraging Democracy: What Role for Conditioned Aid? (Washington DC, Overseas Development Council, 1992).
Nelson, J.M., Eglinton, S.J., Global Goals, Contentious Means: Issues of Multiple Aid Conditionality. (Washington DC, Overseas Development Council, 1993).
Neumann, I.B., Waever, O., eds., The Future of International Relations. (London, Routledge, 1997).
Nicholai, W., German Secret Service. (London, Stanley Paul, 1924).
Nicholson, H., Diplomacy. (Oxford, OUP, 1950; 1963).
Nicholson, H., The Evolution of Diplomatic Method. (London, Constable, 1954).
Nicholson, M., Formal Theories of International Relations. (Cambridge, CUP, 1989).
Nicolson, H., The Congress of Vienna. (London, 1946).
Nolan, C.J., Principles Diplomacy. Security and Rights in US Foreign Policy. (Westport, Greenwood, 1993).
Nussbaum, A., A Concise History of the Law of Nations. (New York, 1954).
Obote-Odora, A., The Judging of War Criminals. (Stockholm, University of Stockholm, 1997).
Ojo, B.A., Human Rights and the New World Order. Universality, Acceptability and Human Diversity. (Commack, Nova Science, 1997).
Okafor, O.C., Re-Defining Legitimate Statehood. International Law and State Fragmentation in Africa. (The Hague, Nijhoff, 2000).
Overy, R., Interrogations. The Nazi Elite in Allied Hands, 1945. (London, Penguin, 2002).
Owen, D., The Balkan Odyssey. (New York, Harcourt/Brace, 1995; 1996).
Parker, G., Western Geopolitical Thought in the Twentieth Century. (London, Croom Helm, 1985).
Parker, G., The Military Revolution. Military Innovation and the Rise of the West, 1500-1800. (Cambridge, CUP, 1988).
Parker, R.A.C., Europe, 1919-1945. (London, 1969).
Parry, J.H., The Establishment of the European Hegemony, 1415-1715. (New York, 1966).
Paxton, R.O., Wahl, N., eds., De Gaulle and the United States. (Oxford, Berg, 1994).
Payne, H.C., The Police-State of Louis-Napoléon Bonaparte, 1851-1860. (Seattle, University of Washington Press, 1966).
Payne, K.B., Missile Defence in the 21st Century. Protection against limited threats. Including lessons from the Gulf War. (Boulder, Westview, 1991).
Peddie, J., The Roman War Machine. (Gloucestershire, Alan Sutton, 1987).
Pfaff, W., The Wrath of Nations. Civilization and the Furies of Nationalism. (New York, Simon & Schuster, 1993).
Pflanze, O., Bismarck and the Development of Germany. The Period of Unification. (Princeton, Princeton UP, 1963).

Pierce, A., Nuclear Politics. The British Experience with an Independent Strategic Force, 1939-1970. (New York, OUP, 1972).
Pincus, J.H., Base Instincts. What Makes Killers Kill? (New York, 2001).
Pollard, S., Peaceful conquest: the industrialization of Europe 1760-1970. (Oxford, OUP, 1981).
Pomerance, M., Self determination in law and practice. The new doctrine in the UN. (The Hague, Nijhoff, 1982).
Porch, D., The French Secret Services. (New York, Farrar/Straus/Giroux, 1995).
Porte, A.W. de, Europe between the Superpowers. (New Haven, Yale UP, 1987).
Porter, A.N., European Imperialism, 1860-1914. (London, 1994).
Porter, B., The Lion's Share. A Short History of British Imperialism, 1850-1970. (London, 1976).
Porter, B., The USSR in Third World Conflicts. Soviet Arms and Diplomacy in Local Wars, 1945-1980. (Cambridge, CUP, 1987).
Porter, B., The Competitive Advantage of Nations. (New York, Free Press, 1990).
Posen, B.R., The Sources of Military Doctrine. France, Britain and Germany between the World Wars. (Ithaca, Cornell UP, 1984).
Potter, W.C., ed., International Nuclear Trade and Nonproliferation. The Challenge of the Emerging Suppliers. (Lexington, Lexington Books, 1990).
Powell, R., Nuclear Deterrence Theory. (Cambridge, CUP, 1990).
Powers, T., Thinking about Nuclear Weapons. (New York, 1983).
Pratt, M., ed., Borderlands under Stress. (The Hague, Kluwer, 2000).
Preston, A., ed., General Staffs and Diplomacy before the Second World War. (London, 1978).
Rashid, A., Jihad, the Rise of Militant Islam in Central Asia. (New Haven, Yale UP, 2002).
Rees, G.W., The Western European Union at the Crossroads. Between Trans-Atlantic Solidarity and European Integration. (Boulder, Westview, 1998).
Rehnquist, W., All the Laws But One: Civil Liberties in Wartime. (New York, 1998).
Reich, W., ed., The Origins of Terrorism. Psychologies, Ideologies, Theologies, States of Mind. (Cambridge, CUP, 1990).
Reiff, D., The Crusaders: Moral Principle, Strategic Interests and Military Force. (In: World Policy Journal, 17-2, 2000).
Richard, J., ed., State, Conflict and Democracy in Africa. (Boulder, Rienner, 1999).
Riemer, N., ed., Protection against Genocide: Mission Impossible? (Westport, Praeger, 2000).
Ritter, G., The Schlieffen Plan: Critique of a Myth. (London, Wolff, 1958).
Ritter, G., The Sword and the Sceptre. The Problem of Militarism in Germany. (Coral Gables, University of Miami Press, 1969/1973).
Rose, F. de, European Security and France. (Paris, Julliard, 1984).
Rosenau, J., Normative Considerations for Students of World Politics. Moral Education III. (New York, Carnegie Council on Ethics and International Affairs, 1993).
Rosenberg, J., The Empire of Civil Society. A Critique of the Realist Theory of International Relations. (London, Verso, 1994).
Rothstein, R.L., The Weak in the World of the Strong: The Developing Countries in the International System. (New York, 1977).
Rothstein, R.L., ed., The Evolution of Theory in International Relations. (Columbia, University of South Carolina Press, 1991).
Rowland, B.M., ed., Balance of Power or Hegemony. The Interwar Monetary System. (New York, 1976).
Said, E., Orientalism. (London, Routledge, 1978).
Said, E., The End of the Peace Process. (London, 2000).

Said, E., Reflections on Exile and other essays. (Cambridge, MA, Harvard UP, 2001).
Seaton, A., The Russo-German War 1941-1945. (London, 1971).
Seaton, A., German Army 1933-1945. (New York, St.Martin's, 1982).
Seton Watson, H., The Russian Empire 1801-1917. (Oxford, Clarendon, 1967).
Shennan, J.H., The Origins of the Modern European State, 1450-1725. (London, 1974).
Sherwin, M.J., A World Destroyed. The Atomic Bomb and the Grand Alliance. (New York, 1975).
Shuker, S.A., The End of French Predominance in Europe. (Chapel Hill, University of North Carolina Press, 1976).
Siedentop, L., Democracy in Europe. (Oxford, Penguin, 2000).
Silverman, D.P., Reconstructing Europe after the Great War. (Cambridge, MA, 1982).
Simes, D.K., After the Collapse. Russia seeks its place as a great power. (New York, Simon & Schuster, 1999).
Simon, J., Does Eastern Europe Belong in NATO? (In: Orbis, pp.21-35, 1993).
Singh, S., The Code Book. The Science of Secrecy from Ancient Egypt to Quantum Cryptography. (New York, Fourth Estate, 1999).
Smith, K.E., Light, M, eds., Ethics and Foreign Policy. (Cambridge, CUP, 2001).
Smith, M.J., Humanitarian Intervention: An Overview of the Ethical Issues. (In: Ethics and International Affairs, 12, 1998).
Smith, S., The Discipline of International Relations: Still an American Social Science? (In: British Journal of Politics and International Relations, October 2000).
Smith, S., ed., International Relations: British and American Perspectives. (Oxford, Blackwell, 1985).
Spears, E.L., The Fal of France. (London, Heinemann, 1954).
Spector, L.S., McDonough, M.G., Mapping Proliferation. (Washington, Cargenie Endowment for International Peace, 1995).
Spector, R., Professors of War. (Newport, Naval War College Press, 1977).
Spector, R., Eagle Against the Sun. The American War Against Japan. (New York, Free Press, 1985).
Spector, R., Advice and Support. The Early Years of the United States Army in Vietnam, 1941-1960. (New York, Free Press, 1985).
Stavrianos, L.S., Global Rift. The Third World Comes of Age. (New York, 1981).
Stead, P.J., The Police of Paris. (London, Staples, 1957).
Stead, P.J., Second Bureau. (London, Evans, 1959).
Steiner, Z.S., Britain and the Origins of the First World War. (London, 1977).
Stoakes, G., Hitler and the Quest for World Dominion. Nazi Ideology and Foreign Policy in the 1920s. (Leamington Spa, Wawickshire, 1986).
Stokesbury, J.L., A Short History of World War I. (New York, 1981).
Storry, R., Japan and the Decline of the West in Asia 1894-1943. (London, 1979).
Storry, R., A History of Modern Japan. (Harmondsworth, Penguin, 1982).
Strange, S., The Retreat of the State. The Diffusion of Power in the World Economy. (Cambridge, CUP, 1996).
Susskind, L., ed., International Environmental Negotiation. An Integrative Approach. (Cambridge, MA, Pon. 1999).
Symonides, J., ed., Human Rights: Concept and Standards. (Dartmouth, Ashgate, 2000).
Talbott, S., Endgame. The Inside Story of SALT II. (New York, Harper & Row, 1979).
Tapinos, G., Piothrow, P.T., Six Billion People. Demographic Dilemmas and World Politics. (New York, 1978).
Taylor, A.J.P., The Origins of the Second World War. (Harmondsworth, Penguin, 1964).
Taylor, T., Munich: The Price of Peace. (New York, 1979).
Teichman, J., Pacifism and the Just War. (Oxford, Blackwell, 1986).

Thomas, R., Serbia under Milosevic. (London, Hurst, 1999).
Thompson, K.W., The Literature of Decline. (In: Ethics & International Affairs, pp.303-315).
Thucydides, On Justice, Power and Human Nature. (Indianapolis, Hackett, translation, 1993).
Tilly, C., Coercion, Capital and European States, AD 990-1990. (Oxford, Blackwell, 1990).
Tilly, C., ed., The Formation of the National State in Europe. (Princeton, Princeton UP, 1975).
Todorova, M., Imagining the Balkans. (London, 1997).
Trachtenberg, M., Reparation in World Politics. France and European Diplomacy 1916-1923. (New York, 1980).
Trachtenberg, M., History and Strategy. (Princeton, Princeton UP, 1991).
Trebilcock, C., The Industrialization of the Continental Powers 1780-1914. (London, Longman, 1981).
Trepper, L., The Great Game. Memoirs of the Spy Hitler Couldn't Silence. (New York, McGraw-Hill, 1977).
Tuthail, G., Critical Geopolitics. (Minneapolis, University of Minnesota Press, 1996).
Ullmann, R.H., The World and Yugoslavia's Wars. (New York, 1996).
US Congress, Conventional Arms Transfers to Developing Nations, 1993-2000. (Washington DC, Library of Congress, 2001).
US Ministry of Foreign Affairs, Patterns of Global Terrorism. (New York, 2001).
Waller, J.H., The Unseen War in Europe. Espionage and Conspiracy in the Second World War. (New York, Tauris, 1996).
Waltz, K.N., Man, the State and War. (New York, Columbia UP, 1959).
Waltz, K.N., Theory of International Politics. (New York, McGraw-Hill, 1979).
Walzer, M., Just and Unjust Wars: A Moral Agreement with Historical Illustrations. (New York, Basic Books, 2000).
Watson, A., Diplomacy. The Dialogue between States. (Philadelphia, Institute for the Study of Human Issues, 1983).
Watson, A., The Evolution of International Society. (London, Routledge, 1993).
Watson, J.S., Theory and Reality in the International Protection of Human Rights. (Ardsley, Transnational, 1999).
Webber, C., Wildavsky, A., A History of taxation and expenditure in the Western world. (New York, 1986).
Weinberg, G.L., A World at Arms. A Global History of World War II. (Cambridge, CUP, 1994).
Weiss, T.G., Researching Humanitarian Intervention. (In: Journal of Peace Research, 38-4, 2001).
Welch, D.A., Justice and the Genesis of War. (New York, CUP, 1993).
Wendt, A., Social Theory of International Politics. (Cambridge, CUP, 1999).
Werth, A., Russia at War, 1914-1945. (New York, 1964).
Wheelwright, J., The Fatal Lover: Mata Hari and the Myth of Women in Espionage. (London, Collins & Brown, 1992).
Whetten, L., New International Communism. (Lexington, Heath, 1982).
Williams, E.N., The Ancien Regime in Europe. Government and Society in the Major States, 1648-1789. (Harmondsworth, Penguin, 1979).
Williams, J., The Home Fronts: Britain, France and Germany, 1914-1918. (London, 1972).
Williams, P., US Troops in Europe. (London, Routledge, 1984).
Williams, P., The Senate and US Troops in Europe. (London, Macmillan, 1985).
Williams, P.M., Wars, Plots and Scandals in Post-War France. (Cambridge, CUP, 1970).
Williams, W.A., The Tragedy of American Diplomacy. (New York, Dell, 1972).

Williamson, S.R., The Politics of Grand Strategy. France and Britain prepare for war, 1904-1914. (Cambridge, MA, Harvard UP, 1969).
Willis, F.R., The French Paradox. (Stanford, Hoover Institution, 1982).
Wohlgemuth, L., et al., eds., Institution Building and Leadership in Africa. (Uppsala, Nordiska Afrikainstitutet, 1998).
Wolff, L., Inventing Eastern Europe. (London, 1994).
Yost, D.S., France's deterrent posture and security in Europe. (London, IISS, 1984/1985).
Yost, D.S., France and the Gulf War 1990-1991. Political-military lessons learned. (In: Journal of Strategic Studies, pp.339-374, 1993).
Young, H., This Blessed Plot. Britain and Europe from Churchill to Blair. (London, Macmilllan, 1998).
Young, J., France, the Cold War and the Western Alliance 1944-1949. (Leicester, Leicester UP, 1990).
Young, J., Cold War Europe, 1945-1989. (London, Macmilan, 1991).
Young, J., Britain and European Unity, 1945-1992. (London, Macmillan, 1993).
Young, J., The Longman Companion to Cold War and Detente 1941-1991. (London, Longman, 1993).
Young, R.J., In Command of France. French Foreign Policy and Strategic Planning, 1933-1940. (Cambridge, Harvard UP, 1978).
Young, R.J., ed., French Foreign Policy, 1918-1945. A Guide to Research and Research Materials. (Wilmington, Scholarly Resources, 1981).
Ziegler, D.W., War, Peace and International Politics. (New York, Longman, 2000).
Zimmerman, W., Origins of a Catastrophe. Yugoslavia and its destroyers. (New York, Random House, 1996).

# 8. Public Management of Society in the European Union, in the Neo-European Age

## 8.1. A short history of European integration

It is not possible to analyse Public Management of Society in France without dealing with its environment, Europe. This is true for all periods in the history of France, especially for contemporary France, because France is indissolubly intertwined with Europe and with the European Union. In the year 2000, the European Union had 15 Member-States, while 13 States are recognised officially as candidates for membership. European integration is a very special institutional phenomenon, while France, for about half a century has played first fiddle. A structural feature is the tension between national public management of sovereign Nation-States and co-national public management in the framework of the European Union. Co-national public management is a central characteristic in Member-States of the European Union, so it is justified that this chapter deals more with the European Union than with France (Sauron, 2000). For the French, European integration is in the first place a French ambition (Duhamel, 1999). In the French consciousness, Europe is often experienced as France with other instruments. The whole institutional set-up of the European Union and its institutional arrangements is, to a high degree, of French making. Europe has deep roots in history (Carbonell, 2000). This is obvious from a sketch in broad outline. The European culture, open to assimilating aspects of other civilisations (for example Celtic), is especially marked by Jewish, Christian, Greek and Roman influences. One might say that the notion of Europe, for a geographically inaccurate territory, was invented in Antiquity, before the beginning of our era (Duroselle, 1965). The Roman Empire (31 BC – 476 AD) encompassed a part of Europe, stretching from the area of contemporary England through France, Spain, Italy, Greece, and the Balkans to the Middle East. Since the time of the Romans England has had a special relationship with the European continent because it is an island (Black, 1994). Charlemagne (768-814), king of the Franks, was crowned by the Pope in 800 as emperor of the West-European Empire ("tota occidentalis Europa").

This West-European Empire, seen also as "Respublica Christiana", enclosed a reduced territory in comparison with the Roman Empire of which it was seen as a continuation: France, the Low Countries, part of Germany (up to the Elbe), Austria, Switzerland, and Italy. This empire soon fell apart, it was divided up at the Treaty of Verdun (843). Charles the Bold (843-877) got more or less the territory which became France. The "Respublica Christiana" declined, public authorities in the feudal system of the Middle Ages were ever more fragmented. There was a conflict lasting centuries, intensified in the time of Pope Gregory VII (1073-1085), about who ruled the "Christian world", the Pope or the Emperor? At the beginning of the 9th century, militant Islam had conquered a huge territory in the southern part of the Mediterranean, extending from the Middle East up to Spain. The Christian world reacted to militant Islam ("Jihad") with the Crusades, 11th-13th centuries (Gabrieli, 1996). In Germany, the Holy Roman Empire (962-1806) claimed to be the continuation of the Roman Empire. In 1054, Orthodox-Christians split off from the Roman-Catholic Church (Evdokimov, 1990). This schism has had its impact on political relations in Eastern Europe since then, as seen in the Balkans at the end of the 20th century. After the 15th century, nation-states (permanent army, bureaucracy, taxes) in the more modern sense developed in France, Britain, Spain, Portugal, etc. In 1453, Turks conquered Constantinople, which meant the end of the East-Roman Empire (395-1453). International perspectives in Europe changed following the "discovery" of America by Columbus (1492) and the opening of the route to the East-Indies via the Cape by Vasco da Gama (1498). This marked the end of the Middle Ages (Brake, 1997). Luther gave a tremendous impulse to revitalise Christianity from 1517, followed by Calvin (Reformation). The medieval unity of Christian society fell apart. The victory at Lepanto (1571) brought a turnaround. The Turks retreated to the Middle East. European nation-states demarcated their spheres of influence, trying to arrange relations with treaties (European equilibrium). With "De jure belli ac pacis" (1625) of Grotius, the law of nations was developed (treaties).

Since the 17th century, a more scientific approach came to the fore, and since the 18th century the rationalistic ideas of the Enlightenment had a dominant impact. The French Revolution (1789) and Napoleonic wars shook Europe. The Vienna Congress (1814-1815) established the new territorial boundaries in Europe. Nationalist movements were trying to alter boundaries, especially in Eastern Europe. In September 1914, the First World War (1914-1918) started, a crime against Europe (Rolland). After this terrible trauma, Europe lost its prominent position in the world. The United States was taking the lead. The Russian Revolution (1917) was the start of Communist oppression in Eastern Europe. American president Wilson saw the League of Nations as a substitute for European equilibrium on the basis of treaties, the "European Concert" (Langhorne, 1980), but this League of Nations could not control Fascist imperialism and the militarism of Germany (Hitler), Italy (Mussolini) and Japan (Hirohito). The Second World War (1939-1945) was a terrible experience in Europe, not only for the "Holocaust" (some 6 million Jews murdered because of Hitler's obsession for the "final solution"), but also for all the millions of other victims of Nazi-terror. In Potsdam, decisions were taken about Allied administration of Germany (Feis, 1960). Countries with a West European culture were in the grip of Communist Eastern Europe (Brown, 1988), and the continent was split by the "Iron Curtain" (Harbutt, 1986). The Hungarian revolt (1956), the Prague Spring of 1968 followed by the Soviet occupation, and revolts in Poland (1956; 1968; 1970; and after) were examples of oppressed countries with a historic national culture. Since the Fall of the Berlin Wall (1989) and the collapse of the Soviet-Communist empire a new situation has developed for Central and Eastern Europe as "The Other Europe" (Rupnik, 1993), and for Western Europe as well.

With former historical periods as a frame of reference, several ideas for a united Europe were launched in the period between the two world wars. In 1849 Victor Hugo had already spoken about "Les États Unis de l'Europe". With the end of the First World War (1914-1918) the European idea had a new appeal (Brugmans, 1970). Austrian Richard Coudenhove-Kalergi, with his Pan-European movement, pleaded in 1923 in favour of a united Europe. Aristide Briand, French Foreign Minister (1925-1932) and his German colleague Gustav Stresemann (1923-1929) did the same, but these initiatives could not block militant Fascism. During the Second World War, resistance movements in West-European countries had ideas about a federal Europe after the war. A Draft Declaration of the European Resistance Movements (1944) proposed the formation of a Federal Union, with a supranational government, a federal army and a federal supreme court (Vaughan, 1979). In 1944 the Netherlands, Belgium and Luxemburg established a customs union, "Benelux". At the Yalta conference (February 1945) of the USA, Great Britain and the Soviet Union (France was absent) the continent of Europe was divided up (Anderson, 1981; Laloy, 1988). The Cold War between the Western Alliance and Soviet-dominated Communist Eastern Europe was the central issue (Fleming, 1961; Fontaine, 1967; Gaddis, 1987, 1997; Hertz, 1986; Thomas, 1986). Winston Churchill, in his Zurich speech on 19 September 1946, suggested a kind of United States of Europe, as a third power of the Western Alliance with the US and Great-Britain. Churchill then formulated a "reservatio Britannica" about the integration of Great Britain into Europe. In 1946 the Union of

European Federalists (UEF) was established. Christian Democratic parties in several Western countries pleaded for a supranational European federal state, while others preferred a looser confederation. On 5 June 1947 George Marshall, in a speech at Harvard University, offered financial aid for reconstruction in Europe on behalf of the US government. When 16 European countries accepted this offer on 15 July 1947, the Marshall Plan started (Hogan, 1987; Milward, 1984). The launching of this program for financial and material aid was very welcome in many European countries on the brink of collapse. It gave national efforts for recovery a chance (Hogan, 1987; Mee, 1984; Wexler, 1983).

Stalin refused American financial aid for East-European countries, because this was seen as a trick to prevent the collapse of capitalism (Dornbusch, 1991).The US made Marshall Aid dependent on the realisation of more co-operation between nation-states in Western Europe and the Organisation of European Economic Co-operation (OEEC) was set up in 1948. Security and economics dominated the political agenda, not the reconstruction of democracies and development of the constitutional state with guarantees for human rights and liberties. Due to opposing views at The Hague Congress on European co-operation (1948), the sole result was the Council of Europe (1949), a forum for voluntary co-operation between national governments. The Brussels Pact of 17 March 1948, forming the West European Union (WEU) was an agreement for military co-operation between France, Great Britain and the Benelux-countries. More important was the forming of NATO on 4 April 1949 (Ismay, 1954). For the French it was evident that after three bloody French-German military confrontations (1871; 1914-1918; 1939-1945) it was necesary to prevent renewed German militarism. The containment concept came to the fore (Deibel/Gaddis, 1986; Gaddis, 1982). If Germany could be bound in a supranational framework, France would have enough countervailing powers to control developments in this potentially dangerous country. On 9 May 1950, Robert Schuman, French Minister of foreign affairs, proposed in a official declaration to place French and West-German production of steel and coal under a common High Authority, to create factual solidarity, with a provision for other European countries to join (Schuman, 1963; Poidevin, 1986). His initiative was inspired by Jean Monnet (Fontaine, 1988; Monnet, 1976). The Monnet-conception was based on the development of a political union by the creation of factual solidarity in economic activities; preference for supranational integration above classical intergovernmental co-operation; and a central role for French-German co-operation. The Schuman/Monnet initiative had the result that France, Italy, West Germany and three Benelux-countries signed the ECSC-treaty on 18 April 1951 (Diebold, 1959; Gillingham, 1991; Schwabe, 1988). The French Assembly ratified it on 13 December 1951 (Communists and Gaullists opposing). ECSC, operational since 25 July 1952, was supranational with a High Authority, presided over by Monnet (Spierenburg/ Poidevin, 1994).

The Korean War (1950/1953) made the US change its strategic concept. The US wanted to reinforce defence of Western Europe by rearming West Germany. Chancellor Adenauer could not accept the integration of German military contingents in NATO, while giving up the possibility of rebuilding a national army (equality of rights for sovereign nations). France, fearing for a revival of German militarism, did not like the idea of a German national army. On 24 October 1950 Pleven suggested the formation of a European Defence Community (EDC). Then West-Germans could participate in the burden of military defence under a common command. The EDC treaty was signed on 27 May 1952. This caused a passionate debate between proponents and opponents for years (Aron/Lerner, 1956). Government-Mendès France, vainly trying to renegotiate the EDC treaty, brought the project before the Assembly. On 30 August 1954 the project was rejected (369 against 264 votes): Gaullists, Communists and half of the Socialists and Radicals opposed. The "Accords de Paris" (23 October 1954) realised restoration of German sovereignty and participation of West Germany in NATO. The Assembly accepted this on 30 December 1954. After the EDC failure, economic integration became the issue (Léonard, 1990).

## 8.2. Social and economic conditions of a Common Market

On 18 May 1955 the three Benelux-countries took the initiative with the Benelux-memorandum, proposing the establishment of a common market and common projects for energy (especially nuclear energy) and transport (Gerbet, 1994). Government-Faure, with Gaullist ministers, did not even reply to the Benelux-memorandum (Gerbet, 1987). The British government was invited to participate in negotiations about a common market, but this invitation was not accepted (Brivati/Jones, 1993; Heiser, 1959). During the Messina-conference (1/2 June 1955) and discussions about the report of the Spaak-committee (1956), France proved to be interested in forming a European Atomic Energy Community (Euratom), but France was not amused at the idea of a European Economic Community (EEC). The French thought that their protectionist economy could not stand open competition. To get Euratom, France had to accept the EEC, but it did so only under strict conditions: national export subsidies and import taxes had to be maintained for the time being; principles ruling the Common Agricultural Policy (CAP); affiliation to the EEC of French overseas territories; and no supranational organ in the EEC as existed in the ECSC, decision-making competencies would have to be given to the European Council of Ministers. The EEC treaty was signed in Rome on 25 March 1957. The French Assembly ratified the Euratom and EEC treaties on 10 July 1957 (with Communists, Gaullists and Poujadists opposing). So a six member EEC started on 1 January 1958. When De Gaulle came back into power on 1 June 1958, EEC-partners of France felt uneasy because of the continuing opposition of Gaullists to European integration. Soon De Gaulle, with the Algerian problem in mind, made it clear that he accepted the EEC as a means to revitalise the French economy (marriage of convenience). The Pinay/Rueff measures (December 1958) enabled the French economy to digest the first lowering of customs tariffs. Germans wanted a customs union for industrial products, and the same favourable conditions as the French for agricultural products. De Gaulle and Adenauer made a deal on 14 January 1962 about the application of the Treaty of Rome on agriculture, favourable for French farmers (some 23% of active professional population).

One of the most prominent concepts in the process of European integration was the development of a common market. When two or more states agree to remove all restrictions on mutual trade, and when these states make individual arrangements for their trade with other countries, they form a free trade area. A customs union is a free trade area plus a common set of arrangements about trade with other countries. A common market is a customs union with guaranteed free movement of goods, services, capital and labour. Since the "Single European Act" (SEA, 1986), the EEC has become a Single Market (Swann, 1992; Tsoukalis, 1993). The European Union forms a Common Market, it is also an "Uncommon Market" (Holland, 1980). The original Treaty of Rome said, in its article 2, that the European Community had to establish a common market (Goodman, 1993). Article 3 of the EEC Treaty looked for realisation of an internal market characterised by abolition of obstacles to the free movement of goods, persons, services and capital. The internal market is defined as an area without internal frontiers, where free movement of goods, persons, services and capital is guaranteed (article 7a). The four freedoms are seen in a broader context, considering the European common market as a contribution to worldwide mutually advantageous trading relations. Customs duties on imports and exports and all charges having equivalent effects are forbidden between Member-States (article 9). Quantitative restrictions are prohibited (articles 30/34). The EEC Treaty ruled that duties and quotas had to be abolished within a 12-year period. This could be realised earlier. From 1 July 1968 on, the common external tariff could be applied. Article 95 EEC did not allow discriminatory taxation, but governments could protect or favour domestic enterprises and markets (tax measures, product specifications). In several cases the European Court of Justice was asked to decide if national measures were conforming to the EEC Treaty. In its "Cassis de Dijon" decision (1979), the European Court of Justice stated that goods in free, legal circulation in one Member-State cannot be excluded from other Member-States.

The Cockfield-report (1985) identified some 300 concrete measures needed to transform the EEC market into a real single market. The non-tariff barriers were categorised in technical barriers (product specifications), physical barriers (customs formalities, frontier controls) and fiscal barriers (which had to be harmonised). Removal of these barriers proved to be a lingering process, as article 100 EEC asked for unanimous decision-making in the Council of Ministers. The Single European Act (SEA, 1986) came with article 100a EEC, allowing extension of qualified majority voting to this area. The Single Administrative Document (1988), which made the crossing of internal, national frontiers easier, abolished road haulage quotas, simplified transit procedures and removed animal and plant health controls from the point of entry to offices inside the Member-States. This made it possible to remove frontier controls affecting the free movement of goods from 1 January 1993 (El-Agraa, 1994; Emerson, 1992). The EEC Treaty ruled the free movement of persons also (articles 3, 8a, 48). The European passport is expected to make it easier to recognise citizens of the European Union at the frontiers. According to article 8a, every citizen of the Union shall have the right to move and reside freely within the territory of the Member-States. The principle of free movement of workers was recognised in article 8a. It is subject to limitations justified on the grounds of public policy, public security or public health. Employment in public service was excluded. Member-States have different definitions of public services. In a Belgian railways case the European Court of Justice (149/79) had as definition: "employment connected with specific activities of the public service in so far as it is entrusted with exercise of powers conferred by public law and with responsibility for safeguarding the general interests of the State, to which specific interests of local authorities ..must be assimilated." This definition excluded many public sector employees. The EEC Treaty in the ruling of the free movement of persons dealt with workers (a Regulation and a Directive of 1968). In preparations for the Single Market, the accent was on legislation of freedom of persons. After the Palma-document (1989) directives were issued for the right of residence for retired people, students and nationals of other Member-States, not covered by other provisions.

Article 1 of the Directive 90/364 ruled that any citizen of the European Union may reside anywhere in the Union as long as he or she is covered by sickness insurance and has welfare benefits or other income (sufficient to avoid becoming a burden on the social assistance system of the host Member-State). Removal or relaxation of controls at internal frontiers was brought in relation with strengthening of controls at external borders. Laborious discussions went on about immigration, the right of asylum, visas, treatment of nationals of non-member countries, control of criminality and drugs traffic, etc. Member-States that wanted to advance in the field of free movement of persons signed the Schengen Agreement (14 June 1985) and the Convention for application (19 June 1990). Great Britain, Ireland and Denmark did not sign, so it was again "Europe à la carte". As part of a People's Europe, the right of free movement is recognised in the European Economic Area (EEA). Controls were maintained at external frontiers, and some internal frontiers, to have more instruments for fighting terrorism, organised crime and drugs traffic. The Maastricht Treaty (title VI, article K 1.9) ruled for police co-operation in preventing and combating terrorism, drugs trafficking and international crimes, and Union-wide exchange of information within a European Police Office (Europol). The Europol Convention was agreed on the European Council at Cannes (June 1995). The right to practise a trade or profession, and the freedom of establishment, were guaranteed by articles 52-54 of the Treaty of Rome for nationals of Member-States (employed and self-employed persons). Article 55 EEC excluded activities connected, even occasionally, with the exercise of public authority. Freedom of establishment was facilitated by mutual recognition of qualifications (Weatherill/Beaumont, 1995). The freedom to provide services was concerned with performance of services anywhere within the European Union without the provider of the service having his or her place of business established in the country where the service is performed. According to article 59 EEC, Member-States have to remove all restrictions on freedom to provide services for citizens of the European Union. Article 61 EEC had special provisions for banking, insurance and transport. Member-States could impose restrictions on grounds of public policy and exclude services involving the exercise of public authority. Since mutual recognition of qualifications in the late 1980s, freedom to provide services has largely been realised. Since the Second Banking Directive (1989), progress has been realised for financial services. Credit institutions may establish branches in other Member-States and in the EEA, remaining subject to "home country control" (Usher, 1994).

A remarkable development in European integration is that public policies in Member-States are in a process of "Europeification" (Andersen/Eliassen, 1993). This brings some convergence and more uniformity, but also a revitalisation of national, regional and local consciousness, opportunities and perspectives. Arguments in defence of continuing diversity are available (Flynn/Strehl, 1996; Pollitt/Bouckaert, 2000). As Pollitt (2001) argued, convergence may be a useful myth, requiring more subtle conceptualisation. This implies an unique, creative and dynamic process of convergence, divergence and revitalisation of national, regional and local diversities (Knill, 2001). There are ever more norms for common action in the framework of the European Union. According to P. Muller (Pouvoirs, 1994), this process of European convergence has its specific impact upon the European agenda, representation of interests and operational methods of political actors. National governments have to take account of the agenda-setting in Brussels. This agenda-setting has a dynamism of its own. Community institutions, acting with their responsibilities for policy fields, are feeding the agenda continuously, but representatives of Member-States in a policy competition are also trying to get their favoured topics on the agenda, and to get their ideas about interventions accepted. Meanwhile, activities in the European policy arena can be exploited as assets in national politics (Europe as the devil, as inevitable development, as "Deus ex machina", etc.). The European process of decision-making is part of the public management strategy of European actors: Euro-management or co-national management. Factual evidence about infractions of Community norms is a flywheel to provoke European regulation. Realisation of the Single Market is seen as a take-off for intensifying more European public policies. Citizens, corporations, pressure groups and public authorities are forced to ongoing SWOT analyses (strengths, weaknesses, opportunities and threats). A double dynamism is working, caused by heavier competition in the quasi-national Common Market and the process of globalisation. The European Union (EU) became the strategic level for public policies. The EU as dominant frame of reference provoked different crises of national identity in Member-States. Not only in Great Britain is there strong opposition against the loss of national sovereignty. In France, there is debate about the crisis of the French model of public policies (Muller, 1992). Governments in France try to handle European matters along the Paris-Brussels axis (Lequesne, 1993). Member-States have representatives in Community institutions, and can influence agenda-setting, decision-making and public policy. Bargaining takes place in committees and in the "Comité de Représentants Permanents" (COREPER), Committee of Permanent Representatives. Pressure groups are active in Brussels, trying to influence decision-making

(Mazey/Richardson, 1993; Van Schendelen, 1994). Actors must make up their mind about new strategic alliances and strategies, in the sphere of Community institutions, and at the national and regional level (Europe of the regions).

Although from the beginning the accent was on the economic dimension of the common market, one must not forget that the original EEC Treaty (1957) also had a low profile chapter about social policy in Title III (articles 117-128). Article 2 of the EEC Treaty stated as objective a high level of employment and social protection, raising of the standard of living, a better quality of life, economic and social cohesion and solidarity among Member-States. Member-States recognised the need of improvement and mutual adaptation in standards of living and working conditions of workers (article 117). They thought that this development would follow the functioning of the common market, furthering approximation of social systems, procedures in the EEC Treaty, and harmonisation of legal and administrative rules. In article 118, the European Commission (EC) was given the task to promote co-operation between Member-States in the social field, explicitly mentioning employment; labour law and labour relations; vocational training and retraining; social security; protection against labour accidents and professional diseases; labour hygiene; the right to form labour unions, and collective bargaining between employers and employees. After consulting the Economic and Social Committee (ESC), the EC can give advice and arrange consultations. In article 119, the equal pay principle with regard to equal work was laid down for men and women, while Member-States declared to strive for maintaining existing equivalence of rulings about holidays (article 120). Article 121 ruled that the Council of Ministers (deciding unanimously) could ask the EC to implement common measures, especially about the social security of migrating workers. The EC must make a separate chapter on social policy in its annual report. The Council of Ministers can ask the EC to report on specific questions in the social field (article 122). Article 123 EEC created the European Social Funds (ESF). The Treaty of Maastricht revised this, stating that the ESF objective is to render employment of workers easier, and to facilitate adaptation, especially with vocational training and retraining. Since 1994, ESF amounted to about 6.5 billion ECU's.

The Social Chapter of the EU must not be confused with the European Social Charter, originally counterpart of the European Convention for the protection of human rights and fundamental freedoms (4 November 1950), signed by the States participating in the Council of Europe. This Convention, less ambitious than the "Universal Declaration of Human Rights" (10 December 1948) in the framework of the United Nations, came into force on 3 September 1953. It has been amended since then, having 66 articles and several protocols. The Council of Europe adopted the European Social Charter (1965). In view of the completion of the internal market, the EC issued a working paper on the Social Dimension of the Internal Market (1988). The European Council adopted the Community Charter of Fundamental Social Rights of Workers in 1989. In December 1991 Great Britain refused to accept amendments to the Social Chapter of the EEC Treaty. The other 11 Member-States, accepting the British opt-out, signed a separate Social Protocol to the Maastricht Treaty (1992). In this Social Protocol, the 11 Member-States committed themselves to promotion of employment, improved living and working conditions, proper social protection, dialogue between management and labour, development of human resources for lasting high employment and combating of exclusion. It took account of diverse forms of national practices and the need to maintain the competitiveness of the Community economy. Several items are subject to unanimity in the consultation procedure (social security, employment rights of nationals, dismissals, representation of workers' and employers' interests, financing promotion of employment). The Social Protocol made it possible to adopt legislation in the co-operation procedure, using qualified majority voting, QMV (adjusted for the UK), and to make social partners at their joint request responsible for implementing

European Directives. In September 1994, the British opt-out was exercised with regard to draft Directives about works councils and parental leave. The original proposals were withdrawn, resubmitted under the working of the Social Protocol, and adopted. The countries which joined the European Union in 1995, accepted the Social Protocol. The British opt-out from the Social Chapter is seen in other Member-States as vehicle for social dumping by the UK. With less restrictive labour laws and resultant lower labour costs, the UK is thought to export unemployment to other Member-States. A case in point was the decision of the European Court of Justice of 12 November 1996, obliging the UK to apply the 1993 Directive limiting the working week to 48 hours. The victory of Labour in May 1997 came just in time to make it possible for Premier Blair to ensure British acceptance of the incorporation of the Social Chapter into the Treaty of Amsterdam (1997).

The high rate of unemployment in the European Union is a heavy mortgage upon public policies. An EC White Paper (1993) made it evident that unemployment in the European Union had risen since the late 1980s. It set a target of 15 million new jobs by the year 2000. The main causes of unemployment were seen as: low rates of growth and investment; high labour costs; inflexible labour markets and an ageing population. The EC issued the White Paper "European Social Policy: "A way forward for the Union" (1994). In this document, the European social model was defined as a unique blend of economic well-being, social cohesiveness and high quality of life. This White Paper concluded that some 52 million people in the European Union live below the poverty line (expenditures less than half the national average). It signalled the growing acuteness of the problem of ageing, reducing the number of persons of working age as a percentage of the population. In 1995, some 18 million were unemployed, about 12%. Political and social tensions grew when national governments tried to comply with the five convergence criteria of the Maastricht Treaty and so become members of the European Monetary Union (EMU). The French government, opting for the EMU and so cutting public expenditures, had to face repeated political and social tensions and strikes. Experts saw this deflationary policy as one of the causes of high unemployment in France and argued for alternative policies. Former president Giscard d'Estaing asked for a devaluation of the overvalued franc on 21 November 1996, to prepare the way for the euro. Employment can be seen as the forgotten sixth criterion. In Autumn 1996, the Italian government decided to cut government expenditures drastically and to impose an extra tax, so that in national public opinion this tax was identified with Europe (Europe = extra taxation). On 25 November 1996 the Italian lire could again participate in the European Monetary System for the first time since 1992, at a rate of 990 lires to one German mark. The use of the euro as a common currency for 11 (later 12) Member-States is a really significant next step in the process of European integration (Marshall, 1999; Szasz, 1999).

From the start of the European Community, relations with other countries were an essential part of the construction of communitarian Europe (Gerbet, 1983), especially the relations with developing countries. The EC of the Six signed treaties of association with (former) colonies and overseas territories. Former colonies having an independent status mostly wanted to maintain relations with former colonising countries. The Lomé Convention (1975), signed in Togo, was an agreement about trade and aid between Member-States of the European Community and 70 developing countries in Africa, the Caribbean and the Pacific (the ACP states). It had the objective of promoting and expediting economic, cultural and social development of the ACP states, and ofconsolidating and diversifying their relations with the European Community and its Member-States in a spirit of solidarity and mutual interest (article 1). Fundamental principles underlying the Lomé Convention were mentioned: equality between partners, respect for their sovereignty, mutual interest and interdependence. The Convention has been reviewed several times. Under the Lomé Convention, all ACP industrial products and most ACP agricultural products have free access to the EEC. Lomé IV was about the period 1990-2000. It made 12 billion ECUs available for development projects for the period 1990/1995, in the framework of the European Development Fund. Later other arrangements followed.

### 8.3. French politicking as a structural phenomenon

De Gaulle was continuously trying to further a prominent position of France ("politique de la grandeur") on the basis of organised co-operation of sovereign nation-states (Rideau c.s., 1975). At the first summit of the European Community in Paris (10 February 1961), De Gaulle made heads of state and governments of other Member-States accept his idea to give a commission the task of proposing amendments to the Treaty of Rome, inter alia to further political co-operation (Committee-Fouchet). According to the "Plan Fouchet I", the sovereign nations in the "Union d'États" would have to adopt unanimously their common foreign policy and defence policy (Bloes, 1970). The same formula would have to be applied to the spheres of economy and culture ("Plan Fouchet II"). Meanwhile, De Gaulle opposed majority decision-making in the European Council of Ministers and a prominent position of the European Commission in this field, against the ideas of its chairman, Hallstein (Hallstein, 1972). Convinced that good relations with West Germany would be decisive in the future, De Gaulle intensified relations with Chancellor Adenauer. Both laid the foundations for the Franco-German co-operation with the Elysée Treaty (22 January 1963). When De Gaulle could not make EEC-partners accept a financial agricultural arrangement which was favourable for French farmers, he withdrew France from decision-making in the European Council of Ministers. To prevent automatic application of a draft for financing the Common Agricultural Policy (CAP) with qualified majority voting in 1966, De Gaulle coerced his partners with the empty chair crisis. This "Crisis of the empty chair" (July 1965/January 1966) ended with the "Compromise of Luxemburg" (30 January 1966). This confirmed that the other EEC-partners disagreed with France regarding the use of the majority vote. From then on, unanimity was sought for on the basis of de facto power of veto, if vital national interests were said to be at stake (against the spirit of the treaties).

Since then, complex package deals have been needed, allowing Member-States concessions in some policy areas such as compensation for concessions to other Member-States in other policy areas. EC partners of France distrusted De Gaulle's intentions, especially when he abruptly decided to withdraw France from the integrated command structure of NATO. De Gaulle also used his position to settle an old score with the British. In January 1963 and in November 1967, De Gaulle blocked the way for Great Britain, trying at last to become an EEC member (George, 1991, 1994; Kitzinger, 1973). He had several reasons for this. The relationship between the US and Great Britain (Nassau-agreement etc.) and the Commonwealth were invoked (La Serre, 1987). When Gaullist Pompidou became the next French President on 15 June 1969, he tried to release the EC from its deadlock. At the European Top in The Hague on 1/2 December 1969, he made the French position clear. Completion of the common market for agricultural products beyond the provisional period (1958/1969); deepening communitarian policies (especially monetary); and enlargement of the EC. On 22 December 1969 France made adoption of the financial agricultural regulation a precondition for opening negotiations with Great Britain, Ireland, Denmark and Norway. In France, their membership of the EC was seen as a counterbalance to the economic dominance of West Germany with its "Ostpolitik". The "Plan Werner" (1970) for creation of an economic and monetary union was not accepted in 1971, as the Six could not reach an agreement. At the European Top-conference in Paris (1972), the EC proposal for further European co-operation for technological research was adopted. It was decided to launch a European environmental program, and to develop European social policy. The European Regional Development Fund (ERDF) was formed, operational since 1975. The European Council decided in 1972 that the EC should be a European Union by the end of the 1970s. Great Britain, Ireland and Denmark joined the EC in 1973, the EC of the Nine (Kitzinger, 1973).

The first oil crisis of 1973 and the economic recession which followed then brought the so-called "Eurosclercsis". There were bitter conflicts about the Common Agricultural Policy (CAP) and the community budget. When, in 1975, Belgian Premier Tindemans presented his report on the European Union, enthusiasm was gone. Tindemans suggested eventually starting the European Monetary Union with a number of Member-States, so that other Member-States could follow later on (Europe of two speeds). Giscard d'Estaing, independent, liberal and pro-European, becoming French President on 19 May 1974, gave the French approach to the EC a new form. He saw the EC as a power multiplier for France (Cohen/Smouts, 1985). Since 9/10 December 1974 (Paris), top meetings of Heads of State and Governments were transformed into "European Councils". On 20 September 1976, Giscard d'Estaing signed "L'Acte de Bruxelles" which implied direct election of the European Parliament. In Copenhagen Giscard d'Estaing (7/8 April 1978) proposed the creation of a European Monetary System, to further convergence of monetary policies. In 1979 the second oil crisis provoked social and economic problems in the EC and elsewhere. At the first elections for the European Parliament on 10 June 1979 (38.8% abstentions), French Communists with an anti-European attitude put pressure on Socialists, while the Gaullist RPR of Chirac distanced itself from the "Liste giscardienne" (Veil). From 1 January 1981 on, Greece became a member of the EC (of the Ten). With the election of François Mitterrand as President on 10 May 1981 and the legislative elections, Socialists had the power positicns in their hands for the first time in the Fifth Republic (Ross et al, 1987). In October 1981, French government presented its European partners with a memo proposing the revitalisation of the European Community ("espace social européen" etc.). In November 1981 came a German-Italian proposal to prepare an European Act to form a European Union. Government-Maurois, following the Socialist election program, drove up government expenditures and consumption in a Keynesian way. This forced France to devalue the franc in October 1981, June 1982 and March 1983. President Mitterrand, disavowing all his electoral promises, decided to continue French participation in the EMS. This meant curtailing government expenses. Government worked hard to have a "Franc fort" to match the Deutsche Mark. The European Council of Stuttgart signed a declaration to establish a European Union (1983).

At the European Council of Fontainebleau (25/26 June 1984), decisions were reached on enlargement of the EC's own financial resources by raising the value-added tax (VAT), and about a special arrangement for Great-Britain (abatement of the British contribution to VAT-resources of the EC), and progression of the EC. Mitterrand's France was at last accepting the applications of Spain and Portugal, who became Member-States of the EC from 1 January 1986, the EC of the Twelve. Mitterrand proposed to form two committees. The Adonnio-committee for Europe of the citizens, and the Dooge-committee for institutional reforms. The Dooge-report (1985) was less far-reaching than the "Traité d'Union Européenne", as adopted by the European Parliament on 14 February 1984 and supported by Mitterrand in Strasbourg on 24 May 1985. It proposed Intergovernmental Conferences (IGC) to prepare institutional reforms. Just before the European Council at Milan (28/29 June 1985) where the IGC was accepted, France and West Germany made a draft for a treaty of the European Union. During the IGC in Luxemburg (September/December 1985) France accepted gradual realisation of the internal market on the basis of the "Livre blanc" of the EC (June 1985). The Cockfield-report (1985) elaborated some 300 concrete measures needed to realise the internal market. On 17

February 1986, the "Acte Unique Européen" was signed, obliging Member-States to realise an internal market before 31 December 1992. The new Assembly since the legislative elections which gave Gaullists a dominant position, ratified the Single European Act (SEA) on 20 November 1986. Greenland, in the EEC as part of Denmark since 1973, seceded from the EEC on 1 February 1985. In 1985, "Eurosclerosis" came to an end. The EC sent a White Paper, "Completing the Internal Market" (June 1985) to the European Council of Ministers, starting the "Operation 1992". The SEA, the first important modification of the Treaty of Rome, and the program for 1992 formed a breakthrough. The SEA – modifying the three basic treaties, ECSC Treaty (1951), Treaty of Rome (1957) and Euratom Treaty (1957) – was operational since 1 July 1987.

From then on, executive competencies were concentrated in the hands of the European Commission (EC). This EC presents legislative proposals to the European Council of Ministers, the legislative body of the European Union. Other EU institutions are European Parliament ("democratic deficit"), a European Court of Justice, and an Economic and Social Committee. From 1 January 1993 on, the Single European Market had to be realised. Preparations were made for European political co-operation. Realisation of the European Monetary Union (EMU) was set as an important policy target. At the Paris meeting in 1972, Member-States had already committed themselves. SEA changed regulations in the Treaty of Rome with regard to social policy. Propositions to bring social improvements needed only a majority decision. The SEA preamble was also the basis for the European Social Charter (1989). With EC memo "Towards a European Technology Community" (1985), the treaty of the EC got articles about furthering the scientific and technological position of European industries. The EC was also given competencies in the sphere of environmental policies. The 1992 program for realisation of complete freedom of circulation for persons, products, services and capital in the EC gave an important impetus to further European integration (Colchester/Buchan, 1990). Jacques Delors made himself an authoritative adherent of European integration (Delors, 1988). For four decades the EC was developed via gradual and incremental modifications, giving community institutions more competencies. As a consequence of the German reunification, former East Germany became part of the EU from October 1990, and with the addition of Sweden, Finland and Austria in January 1995, the European Community consisted of 15 Member-States. In the 1990s, intensification of European integration (political integration, EMU) and enlargement of the EC were prominent on the political agenda. The European Union of 15 had difficulty in defining its relationship with countries in Central and Eastern Europe, newly liberated from Communist and Soviet domination. This required a redefinition of Europe by deciding which candidates may become Member-States (Miall, 1994). In 1999, 13 countries were given the status of aspiring EU candidates.

### 8.4. Treaty of Maastricht: European Union

An important step in the institutional development of the European Community was the Treaty of European Union, the Maastricht Treaty, signed on 7 February 1992 and effective from 1 November 1993 (Cloos c.s., 1993; Corbett, 1993). The Maastricht Treaty is built upon three pillars: adaptation of existing treaties; a common policy for foreign affairs and security; and political co-operation in the fields of immigration and policy with regard to asylum, drugs and criminality. In broad outline, the Maastricht Treaty laid foundations for further European integration (Moravscik, 1998). The first title is about forming the European Union (EU) with objectives such as the establishment of economic and monetary union (EMU) with a single currency; a common foreign policy and security policy; EU citizenship; co-operation in the fields of justice and home affairs; maintenance of the "acquis communautaire" (respect for what was realised); respect for the subsidiarity principle. The position of the European Council, defining general political guidelines, was made more prominent in the decision-making process. A condition for becoming a Member-State is that the government of a Member-State must be based upon principles of democracy. Fundamental rights are seen as general principles of Community law. European integration in the field of monetary policy, with price stability as primary objective, forms a prominent target. The European System of Central Banks (ESCB) and European Central Bank (ECB) would become prominent institutions. Member-States agreed to reach the objectives in three stages (Marshall, 1999; Szasz, 1999). In the first stage (1 July 1990/31 December 1993), economic policies of the Member-States had to converge and be co-ordinated. In the second stage (1 January 1994/1 January 1999), the European Monetary Institute (EMI) would be set up and preparations would be made for introduction of the single European currency. The third stage would start, at the latest, on 1 January 1999. Then the single European currency would be functioning as the heart of the EMU. Criteria of convergence for becoming a member of the EMU were formulated: 1. In the year before the decisive year 1998, inflation was not allowed to be more than 1.5 percentage-point above the average of the three Member-States with the lowest rises in prices. 2. In the year before 1998, the long term interest rate had to be within the margin of two percentage-points with regard to the three Member-States with the lowest inflation. 3. The deficit of the national budget had to be less than 3% of BNP. 4. The national debt was not allowed to be higher than 60% of BNP. 5. The value of the national currency must have been within the bandwidth of the European mechanism of the EMS for two years, and may not have been devalued. These 5 criteria were refined, with an attendant ongoing "war of interpretation". The Maastricht Treaty has provisions about a Common Foreign and Security Policy (CFSP), and co-operation in the field of justice and home affairs (JHA). New community policy areas were added: culture, education, public health, consumer protection and trans-European networks.

As one of the founding Nation-States of the European Community, France, disposing of a rich historically based institutional culture and legal genius, had and has a dominant impact upon the process of institutionalising. Of course, it could not always get its position and preferences accepted by other Member-States. France used its influence in all phases and in all dimensions of the community decision-making process. Sometimes, it tried to force a decision, as with regard to the financing of the Common Agricultural Policy, when De Gaulle used the technique of the empty chair (1966). As with other Member-States who have specific attitudes towards applying Community norms, France often had problems with adapting its national law and practices, although the European treaties were obligatory. Expert reports were regularly made asking French public authorities to take into account more effectively that France was a Member-State of the European Community (Clausade, 1991). National law and public administration had to be adapted in different policy fields. When the French government thought that the European Commission went too far, it did not hesitate to present a case before the European Court of Justice. The "Conseil d'État", after stubborn resistance, finally accepted that the law of the European Community was superior to (French) national law. This was made evident in the decision of the French Council of State in 1989 ("arrêt Nicolo"), reconfirmed in its "arrêt Boisdet" (1990). Its "arrêt Rothmans" confirmed that EU directives are superior to national laws. Oberdorff (Pouvoirs, 1994) analysed implications of the Maastricht Treaty for the French institutional system. Participation of the French Republic in the European Union had to be constitutionalised. This was made explicit by the "Conseil constitutionnel" (9 April 1992), concluding that this treaty implied infractions of French sovereignty. In the Fourth Republic, France was able to be a Member-State without needing to revise its constitution.

The Constitution of the Fifth Republic, more prudent with regard to international engagements, made continuous participation in the European Community possible, but under the condition that this worked as an international organisation without supranational pretensions. In previous constitutional controls (1970, 1976 and 1991) the "Conseil constitutionnel" had no problems with European institutionalising. After revision of the Constitution (June 1992), a French referendum authorised ratification. So the French Constitution qualified France as a Member-State in the European Union, and accepted European specificity (Luchaire, 1992). Two institutional paths were made possible with regard to sovereignty. The classical path as followed in the sphere of international agreements, and the path within the European Union with co-sovereignty. Common public management has become a normal method of public management in the European Union. European common public management does not mean, however, that the European Union has the structure of a federal State. The European Union has to be understood as an original, institutional "sui generis" construction making its residents European citizens without making them a European nation (Tarrow, 1998). The French institutional unbalance between executive and legislative powers, as defined by the Constitution of the Fifth Republic, is accentuated in the European Community. European policy of France is pre-eminently in the hands of the executive. This is reinforced by the prominent position of the French President with regard to the Prime Minister, in the national field, but also in the European Council. French Parliament has a modest position with regard to Europe, due to rationalisation of parliamentarism by the Constitution of the Fifth Republic (Pezet, 1993). With regard to the democratic deficit in the European Union because of reduced competencies of the European Parliament, France can be said to have a double democratic deficit. French Parliament can interfere when community law is transformed into national law in the legislative process, but its margins are small. A constitutional revision of 1992 obliged government to inform Parliament about proposals for European acts with a legislative character. Parliament can issue resolutions about European questions.

## 8.5. Juridical institutionalising from Rome (1957) to Amsterdam (1997)

European law and institutions have a strong influence on national jurisdiction of Member-States (Gerbet, 1983; Labouz, 1988; Louis, 1993). So national courts have become jurisdictions for Community law, although there is no hierarchical relationship with the European Court of Justice (Dehoussse, 1994; Mouton/Soulard, 1999). It took some time, but now national jurisdictions such as "Cour de cassation" and "Conseil d'État", accept the primacy of Community law above national law (Conseil d'État, 1992). The European Union also has an impact upon public administration and public management. Contrary to that which the popular idea would have us believe, the European Commission (with about 16,000 employees), does not have a super-bureaucracy to rule the more than 360,000,000 residents of the European Union. The European Commission must co-operate with the public administrations of the 15 Member-States. The French administrative apparatus had to be adapted (Sauron, 2000). Administrations are supposed to handle European questions as part of their job. Specialised sector agencies were set up to handle European policy areas. Interministerial co-ordination has been organised. The "Comité interministériel pour les questions de coopération économique européenne", and especially the office of its secretary general ("Secrétariat Générale de Coordination Inter-Ministériel", SGCI), have a central role. The SGCI takes care of cohesion in management of relations between French public administrations and EU institutions. It is in direct communication with the permanent French representation in the "Comité de représentants permanents" (Coreper), a Community institution officially recognised in article 151 of the EEC treaty. This Coreper, preparing decision-making in the European Council of Ministers, has its place at the heart of European decision-making. Decentralised administrations of territorial public authorities organised their Brussels connection, in autonomy and in co-operation with national public authorities. Communitarian decisions are often the result of compromises between representatives of Member-States following communications between national and community administrations. European co-national management brought a new administrative culture and management style, with a structural impact on public administration, changing concepts and methods.

European co-national management is a creative process of administrative acculturation, in which the representatives of different Member-States get concrete and operational knowledge about political, juridical and administrative solutions in other Member-States. The French are keen on training their representatives professionally for the European political-administrative arena (not only at the ENA). With the French formula of institutional engineering, permeated by juridical institutionalising, professionalised functionaries of France, as post-modern diplomats, are able to win many battles in the complex construction of the European Union. "Orchestrating Europe" by Middlemas (1995) is very instructive about that. Juridical institutionalising is at the heart of European integration (Hartley, 1994; Mathijsen, 1995; Monjal, 2000; Sbragia, 2000; Toth, 1990). The foundation of the European Community was laid with ECSC Treaty (1951), EEC Treaty (1957) and Treaty of Euratom (1957). Of course, the pioneering Six Member-States made use of known instruments of international law, treaties etc. (Church/Phinnemore, 1994) but while international treaties normally form a normative framework for relations between Nation-States, European integrationalist institutionalising goes much further. An important dimension of its juridical institutionalising is the relation between national law and European Community Law (Louis, 1990; Oppenheimer, 1994). National legal systems are more or less convergent (Markesinis, 1994). The ECSC Treaty (1951) organised competencies for a supra-national organ, the High Authority. The EEC Treaty in article 3 formulated the four freedoms of a single market: free movement of goods, persons, capital and the freedom to provide services. The Treaty of Rome (1957) formed the basis for five different types of legal instruments in article 189: 1.Regulations. 2.Directives. 3.Decisions. 4.Recommendations. 5.Opinions.

A Regulation is of general application, and is binding in its entirety and directly applicable in all Member-States. A Directive is binding as to the result to be achieved, for each Member-State to which it is addressed, but it leaves to the national authorities the choice of form and methods. A framework Directive is a directive, identifying European Union objectives over a broad field, and so preparing the way for legislative action on specific points. The key difference between a Regulation and a Directive is that a Regulation is directly applicable and has direct effect. A Directive must be transposed into national law within a deadline. A Decision is binding in its entirety upon those to whom it is addressed. Recommendations and Opinions have no binding force, but have their impact in the symbolic political universe. Regulations, Directives and Decisions addressed to all Member-States have to be published in the Official Journal. The Maastricht Treaty (1992) has provisions about "decisions", "acts", "joint acts" and "common positions". In an annex to this treaty, Member-States committed themselves to review legal instruments at the Intergovernmental Conference (IGC) of 1996. The EU is at a stage of more mature European law development, but it is a long way yet to the European Rule of Law as institution for citizens, organisations and enterprises (Church/Phinnemore, 1994; Weatherill/Beaumont, 1995; Wyatt/Dashwood, 1993). In the everyday life of citizens (Arnull, 1990), organisations and enterprises (Harding, 1993; Usher, 1993), European law increasingly interferes intensively (Constantinesco et al., 1995; Dutheil de la Rochère, 1999; Gautron, 1998; Cavalda/Kovar, 1992; Louis, 1996; Sauron, 1998; Simon, 1998).

The IGC is a special committee of representatives of governments of Member-States, convening to consider amendments to the Treaties. According to article N of the Maastricht Treaty, they meet after a request of the Council of Ministers. Conclusions have to be reached unanimously, and must then be submitted for ratification (on the basis of national constitutional requirements) to national parliaments, or eventually electorates. Since the start, there have been six major revisions of the treaties: Merger Treaty (1965); Treaties on budgetary powers of the European Parliament in 1970 and 1975; Single European Act (SEA) in 1986; Maastricht Treaty (1992); and Amsterdam Treaty (1997). The following, disputed Treaty of Nice (2000) was rejected by the electorate of Ireland in 2001, but accepted in 2002. Originally, IGCs were procedural mechanisms for starting up treaty amendments in case of broad consensus among Member-States (secret diplomacy). The 1961/1962 IGC on the Fouchet Plan ended in failure due to a French veto. Since 1985, IGCs have been strategic arenas for negotiating about EU structure, a forum for European constitution-making. Starting an IGC requires only a simple majority. Once in procedure, an IGC has the presumption that a reform will be realised, putting opponents on the defensive and forming a strong pressure to compromise. The IGC procedure implies much secret diplomacy, but since 1991 the process has had a more open character. The conclusions of an IGC must be agreed upon unanimously and ratified. When the Maastricht Treaty did not include a substantial reform towards political union, governments of Germany and the Benelux initiated proposals for commitment to another IGC in 1996 to review the Maastricht Treaty (Corbett, 1993). Some Member-States saw this as a means to cancel provisions of the Maastricht deal. The repudiation of the Maastricht Treaty by the Danish electorate in the June 1992 referendum was a shock, but the Single European Market was built upon an impressive legal fundament already (Blumann, 1995; Boulouis, 1997; Green c.s., 1992; Issac, 1999; Joliet, 1986; Manin, 1999; Raepenbusch, 1998; Rideau, 1998; Rideau/Picod, 1994; Sauron, 1998; Simon, 1998; Vandersanden, 1996). Negotiations at the 1996 IGC were prolonged. Its agenda was inter alia about the review of qualified majority voting, a more acute problem if the EU incorporates more Member-States.

More and more, at least two fundamentally opposing views are made explicit about the European Community, federalism and intergovernmentalism. Federalism implies a European government, putting national governments in a secondary position. The intergovernmentalist concept accentuates national sovereignty of the Nation-States, trying to keep supranational institutions and majority decision-making at a minimum (national veto). Intergovernmentalism is dressed up with terms like "L'Europe des nations" and confederate Europe. The OECD and Council of Europe are intergovernmental institutions. World wars showed that intergovernmentalism was not enough. The Nation-State as basis for international relations was questioned. Treaties of the European Communities were imbued with federalist ideas; the European Council of Ministers, European Commission, European Court of Justice and European Parliament are institutions with a quasi-federal character. Federalism has many interpretations. Mostly, it means loss of national sovereignty due to institutional constructions in which Nation-States accept decision-making and/or ruling competencies of supranational or international organs. De Gaulle was an eloquent opponent of supranationalism. Thatcher took over this anti-federalist position (Thatcher, 1988). In discussions preceding the Maastricht Treaty, the subsidiarity principlehad a prominent position. Simply put, this means that in a federal structure there is a reasonable balance of power between centralised and decentralised authorities, when everything which can be ruled by decentralised authorities is ruled in a decentralised way (Millon-Delsol, 1993). Opponents of federalist institutionalising caricature the impact of European integration with terms like "European superstate", "the Brussels government" etc. The anti-Europe movement, accentuating national sovereignty and opposing the ceding of competencies to external authorities, is strong in Great Britain (Bulmer, 1992; Young, 1993) but there were many British enthusiasts for European integration at the time of Great Britain's joining (Brittan, 1994; Butler, 1986; Franklin, 1990).

It is important for the future of European integration to institutionalise and operationalise a reasonable European optimum of centralised, common decision-making and decentralised self-government of nations, regions and communities. In operationalising a European Judicial Area, with a Common European Rule of Law, the European Court of Justice has a crucial role (Bergères, 1994; Boulouis/Chevallier, 1994; Dehousse, 1994; Lasok, 1984; Pouvoirs, 2001; Rideau/Picod, 1994; Shapiro, 1992; Stone, 1995; Sauron, 1998). Alongside Council of Ministers (Bulmer/Wessels, 1987), European Commission (Edwards/ Spence, 1995), and European Parliament (Abélès, 1992; Jacobs c.s., 1995; Westlake, 1994). In discussions about European integration, the focus is on political issues like loss of national sovereignty and democratic deficit, or economic issues like common market and single currency. Far less attention is generally given to juridical institutionalising, but development of European Community law is of no less importance, and can be more important than political or economic issues. In 1977, the French President Giscard d'Estaing proposed establishing a European juridical area (EJA). It was his idea to form a common European framework for all legal rulings with a Community dimension. This EJA would contribute to a sense of European identity by giving the People's Europe more contents in guaranteeing citizens of Member-States a common corpus of legal rights. Realisation of this European Juridical Area (EJA) will, for the time being, remain a utopian ideal, but partial successes contribute to the gradual development of a common sphere of European Law. Meanwhile, the whole of principles, treaties, laws, policies, obligations, practices and objectives that have been adopted within the European Union is known as "acquis communautaire" or "Community patrimony". The EU "finalités politiques", political objectives, (f.e. objectives adopted by the European Council) are seen as part of this "Community patrimony". This includes legislation and judgements of the European Court of Justice (Boulouis/Chevallier, 1994), which implies that Member-States recognise the primacy of Community law and the principle of direct effect. This Community patrimony, recognised in successive Acts of Accession, is especially relevant with regard to potential new Member-States.

Candidate Member-States have to accept the legal obligations in the Treaties, legal decisions of the institutions of the European Union, agreements within and between these institutions about their operation, and international agreements concluded by the European Union. Article 3.3 of the Acts of Accession is specific in stating that new Member-States are in the same situation as actual Member-States in respect of declarations, resolutions and positions of the European Council, or adopted by common agreement of Member-States. They are required to observe the principles and guidelines derived from those declarations, resolutions and positions, and to take measures as may be necessary to ensure their implementation. One might say with V. Nicolas that the European Union can be seen as a normative disorder, and with J.P. Jacqué that the European Union has, due to its historical development, a decision-making labyrinth with a mixture of "Latin fantasy" and "Cartesian tradition" (Bertrand, 1998; Pouvoirs, 1994). Some twenty different procedures can be distinguished, older procedures being maintained, while new procedures are added (co-operation, co-decision etc.). Procedures are the result of complex negotiations with different majorities and reflect a subtle equilibrium between the competencies of the institutions. The Council of Ministers can normally only deviate from a Commission proposal unanimously. The construction of the European Union is built up around an ingenious institutional equilibrium between components of the decision-making triangle (Commission, Council, Parliament) on the basis of representation of interests. The Commission is thought to represent the general interest of the European Union, including common interests of Member-States. The European Council represents the interests of Member-States, including those of the peoples they represent. The European Parliament represents the interests of the peoples of all Member-States. Democratic legitimising of Council (national governments, formed after elections, controlled by national parliaments) and Parliament (elected, with limited competencies, causing a democratic deficit) falls short of the legitimacy of national institutions. The Council decides unanimously to prove that it represents the general interest better than the Commission. The Council cannot overrule a Commission proposal without unanimity, and so is refrained from imposing a decision on a minority by a qualified majority.

To realise the most optimal decisions, it is important to choose the most suitable procedure (the institutional agenda). The most important legislative procedures are consultation, co-operation and co-decision (Blumann, 1995). The consultation procedure has a key role for Commission and Council, while the Commission may or may not change its proposal after an advice from the European Parliament. The Council can change a Commission proposal unanimously. So the vote of one Member-State, supporting a Commission proposal, is enough to prevent the Council from changing this proposal. The co-operation procedure enables the European Parliament to reject or to amend decisions of the Council after consultation of the European Parliament by the Council. In that case, the Commission can adapt its original proposition, taking over amendments adopted by the European Parliament. The Council can then decide with a qualified majority, or unanimously, when it wants to change the Commission proposal. With article 189B of the Maastricht Treaty, the co-decision procedure was introduced. The European Parliament in the co-decision procedure is allowed to reject a proposal twice. When Council and European Parliament don't agree, a conciliation committee can change the Commission proposal. The co-decision procedure gives more competencies to the European Parliament, which can ultimately use its right to reject proposals. The Commission then partially loses its legislative initiative, the Council has the last word (under proviso of the right of the European Parliament to reject this). In addition to these legislative procedures, one has to take account of acts, of which it is unclear if, and in what measure, they are sources of law, or pseudo-law such as communications of the Commission and declarations, resolutions, recommendations and conclusions of the Council. The European Court of Justice has in some cases concluded that these were of minor importance juridically, but they might mean much politically.

One of the most relevant issues is the juridical basis of the competencies of the European institutions, which are given by the treaties. Generally spoken, every community act has to be based on the adequate article of the treaty, defining competencies of the institution concerned. The act has to pinpoint exactly which article is the juridical basis. Each Commission proposal, therefore, mentions the juridical basis and the decision procedure. Choices have to be made, because it is not always obvious which procedure must or can be followed. The choice made has its impact upon the institutional equilibrium between European institutions, jealous of their own competencies. When one institution decides to use a procedure, which ensures this institution a strong position, while other choices could be made, other institutions can put the question to the Court of Justice. According to this Court, the choice of the juridical basis is not at the free disposal of the institution. It has to be founded on objective elements of jurisdictional control (decision 26 March 1987). Crucial elements are the objective and contents of the act. When more articles of the treaty are relevant, these have to be mentioned in the act, so it is not a purely theoretical possibility that several procedures can be applicable for the same issue. In the case of the Commission against the Council regarding titanium dioxide, this problem came to the fore. The handling of waste from titanium dioxide was an issue of the internal market and of protection of the environment. This meant that the Council would have to decide simultaneously with unanimity after consulting the Parliament (environment), and with qualified majority in the co-operation procedure (internal market). The Court decided on 11 June 1991 that the procedures were incompatible, and the co-operation procedure had to be followed (internal market).

Meanwhile, there is a profusion of community norms, making the question of the hierarchy of norms more acute. The original law of the European communities is at the top of the hierarchy of juridical norms. This original law encompasses the three treaties establishing the three European Communities and also the treaties and conventions revising these treaties, such as the treaties of accession for new Member-States and the treaty establishing the European Union, the Treaty of Maastricht (7 February 1992) about structure and functioning of the European institutions, and the Treaty of Amsterdam (1997). To prevent these codifications from becoming too massive, these treaties often have annexes, such as the Treaty of Maastricht with its 17 protocols. Member-States have developed a habit of issuing common declarations, not having the force of law but relevant, because the Court of Justice has to take account of them. 33 declarations were added to the Treaty of Maastricht. Juridical norms as derived from the original law are also growing. The "Conseil d'État" in its report (1993), concluded that there were already 22,445 European Regulations, directly applicable in Member-States, and 1,675 Directives which must be transformed into national legislation by Member-States, at the end of 1992. There were in addition; 1,198 protocols or agreements; 185 recommendations of Commission or Council; 291 resolutions of the Council; and 678 communications of the Commission. Community norms are taking an ever more prominent position in the legal order of Member-States, with direct implications for national organs, corporations and citizens. This includes norms transforming European Directives into national law, in France one out of every two legal texts already has its origin in Brussels. In the sphere of derived norms, the distinction between Regulation and Directive is crucial, but differences between these two are blurring. Regulations resemble national laws. Article 189 EEC rules that a Regulation is of general application, entirely binding and directly applicable in all Member-States. A Directive is binding for the result to be achieved, for each Member-State to which it is addressed, leaving the choice of form and methods to national authorities.

In practice, the Directive, becoming the instrument of harmonising national legislation, executive regulation and administration, has often pushed aside the Regulation. Directives are often very detailed. For the internal market, technical norms are mostly formulated in over-detailed Directives, which contribute to the image of the Kafkaesque bureaucracy of the Commission in Brussels. Often these over-detailed rulings are the result of lobbying by national administrations and interest groups. Over-detailed Directives restrict the possibilities of Member-States to adapt community norms to the national situation, which fosters an anti-Europe attitude. Increasingly interpenetration of European law and national law in the Member-States is part of public debate in society, because the everyday life of citizens and corporations is influenced directly in very concrete situations. European Community Law has a specific character, inter alia while it is integrally a part of national law. Court of Justice decisions made this evident: Van Gend and Loos (5 February 1963), and Costa/Enel (15 July 1964). In the Van Gend and Loos case, the Court concluded that the EEC Treaty was more than an agreement binding national States, as is normally the case in international law: The European Community has established a new legal order of which not only States but also inhabitants are subjects. In the Costa/Enel case, the Court declared that the European Community had created a specific legal order with norms having a specific character, and integrated into the legal order of the Member-States. This principle of integration has as consequence that Community law is directly applicable in national law of the Member-States and that Community law is superior to national law. Inhabitants and corporations can invoke community rules when they have a case in national jurisdictions. Due to article 189 EEC, Regulations are directly applicable. Other community norms are not directly applicable, and don't have a direct effect. The Court of Justice has a crucial role in stating the contents of Community law in its jurisprudence. Articles of the treaties are directly applicable, when they are sufficiently clear and exact and don't need specific procedures or complementary measures (Boulouis, 1997). Private persons and corporations can invoke these articles in their relations with other private persons and corporations. As the Court confirmed in the Delhaize case with regard to article 34 EEC (9 June 1992). The Court of Justice stated that dispositions of the treaties, not (yet) integrated into national law, although the Member-States had the obligation to do this within a concrete term, have a direct effect (Reyners case, 1 June 1974).

As Directives, addressed to Member-States, are by definition not directly applicable, they cannot create rights or obligations for private persons or corporations (not being addressed). Member-States have to incorporate Directives into the national legal order by an act of application, but the Court of Justice, in the Van Duyn case (2 December 1974) stated that Directives can be invoked by private persons and corporations before national courts. Directives have a compelling effect upon Member-States. Later the Court of Justice confirmed that a Member-State, with regard to its residents, cannot invoke the non-execution of obligations of a Directive (Ratti case, 5 April 1979). Dispositions in Directives, which are sufficiently outspoken and unconditional, are recognised as having a direct effect (Van Cant case, 1 July 1993). Due to often prevailing uncertainties, national courts increasingly make use of the technique of prejudicial questions to be answered by the European Court of Justice. The "Conseil d'État" has more than once opposed the positions of this Court of Justice, as in the Cohn-Bendit case (22 December 1978), when it stated that a private person cannot invoke a Directive against an individual administrative act of a national authority. French justiciables are thought to have the right to contest each norm of a Directive by invoking its incompatibility with regard to the objectives of this Directive. The "Conseil d'État" recognised the right of private persons and corporations to invoke a Directive to compel national authorities to abolish incompatible national regulations, which may even be illegal after the expiration of the term for integrating a Directive into the national legal order (Alitalia case, 3 February 1989). The "Conseil d'État" recognised that derived Community law is superior to contrary posterior national law. Controversies remain between "Conseil d'État", court in the communautairian legal order, and the European Court of Justice.

Since the Costa/Enel case (15 July 1964), it has regularly been confirmed that Community norms are superior with regard to national laws, but institutions of the Community don't have the competence to annul or declare inapplicable a regulation of national law which is incompatible with Community law. In these cases institutions of the Community can use the procedure to declare a Member-State in default before the Court of Justice. If a Member-State is declared in default, the act concerned remains applicable, while the Member-State is obliged to change this in its national law. In the Simenthal case (9 March 1978), the Court of Justice decided that national courts, in situations where a national act is contrary to Community law, have to apply Community law integrally, leaving aside each contrary national regulation. In Member-States like Italy and France, recognition of the superiority of Community law with regard to posterior national law took time. The Italian Constitutional Court decided in 1964 that the rules of the European treaties had the same juridical position as national law (principle of dualism), but the European Court of Justice rejected this in the Costa/Enel decision. In the Granital case (8 June 1984), the Italian Constitutional Court recognised the supremacy of Community law. Although the French Constitution of 4 October 1958 stated, in article 55, that European treaties are superior with regard to a French (even posterior) law, judicial authorities were reticent in recognising this. Judicial courts have done so since the Vabre case (24 May

1975). The "Conseil d'État" maintained that posterior French law, contrary to Community law, was superior to Community law. Since the Nicolo case (20 October 1989), the "Conseil d'État" has recognised the primacy of Community law, now recognised by all French jurisdictions.

It is useful to distinguish European law stricto sensu, characterised by structures of international law with international agreements etc., and communitarian, Community law with specific characteristics. Specific features are inter alia: the distribution of competencies between Community and Member-States; primacy of communitarian norms over national norms; extension of the so-called direct effect; and interpenetration and integration of Community law and national law of Member-States. The juridical order in the European Union is more complex than the dichotomy between Community law and European law might suggest. One might say that there is a juridical triad of European law, Community law and national law with mutual interpenetration and variable national combinations. According to Gautron we have "une Europe à droits variables" (Pouvoirs, 1994). This variability is evident for transitional periods as allowed for new Member-States and for temporary derogations, but there are numerous other examples. Great Britain and Northern Ireland did not subscribe to new social policy as defined in protocol 14 annexed to the Maastricht Treaty (1992), and so introduced "Europe à la carte" (until the Treaty of Amsterdam in 1997). Protocol 14 is based upon the Community Charter of the Fundamental Social Rights of Workers, the Social Charter (1989), and is more outspoken about social protection of workers than the original Community treaties. The third phase for the EMU, creating a Single European currency (Euro), brought the "Europe à géométrie variable". Some Member-States preferred to opt out (Great Britain, Sweden) or to organise a referendum first (Denmark). Gautron (Pouvoirs, 1994) accentuates the double institutionalising in the Treaty of Maastricht, using communitarian integration and intergovernmental co-operation.

## 8.6. Institutionalising a new architecture of decision-making

At the start of the European Community, the six Member-States got a different number of votes, commensurate with the size of the population: France (4), Italy (4), West Germany (4), Belgium (2), Netherlands (2) and Luxemburg (1). A measure was adopted when there were 12 assenting votes. In the absence of a Commission proposal, they had to be cast by 4 Member-States. In the years from 1958 to 1965, decisions were mostly taken unanimously. Because of proposals to use the method of qualified majority voting more often, De Gaulle was able to cause the "empty chair crisis", withdrawing French representatives from decision-making when France rejected proposals for financing the Common Agricultural Policy, widening of budgetary powers for the European Parliament and introduction of resources for the Community itself. This crisis ended with the "Luxemburg Compromise" (France and its partners agreed that they disagreed). Since then, it has more or less been recognised that each Member-State had a right of veto, if vital national interests were at stake. Complex decision-making about package deals thus became an often-used procedure, trying to reach unanimity by simultaneous negotiating about several policy items. Majority voting was only used in a limited number of policy areas after 1966. Attempts to restore the normal procedure with majority voting in the Council failed. Institutional immobility was going on up to the early 1980s. In May 1982, the United Kingdom invoked the Compromise about an agricultural issue. The Genscher-Colombo Plan (1981) with a draft for a European Act encompassed proposals for changing the voting procedure. A Member-State would have the right to postpone decision-making twice, but then had to accept the vote. The European Council in Stuttgart came up with the Stuttgart Declaration (June

1983), stating that application of the decision-making procedures in the Treaties is of vital importance. In fact the Luxemburg Compromise died when the SEA came into force in July 1987. At every enlargement of the European Community the weightings had to be adapted.

In the European Union of 15 the European Council of Ministers has a prominent position in community decision-making (Bertrand, 1998; Doutriaux/Lequesne, 1995; Fontaine, 1994). Of course, it is not always possible to reach unanimity, and the method of Qualified Majority Voting (QMV) is generally used. Article 148 of the Treaty of Rome gives the basis for a system of weighted voting. Every Member-State has a weighting in relation to the size of its population. In 1995 the 15 Member-States of the European Union had the following votes within the total of 87: France (10), Germany (10), Italy (10), United Kingdom (10), Spain (8), Belgium (5), Greece (5), Netherlands (5), Portugal (5), Austria (4), Sweden (4), Denmark (3), Finland (3), Ireland (3), and Luxemburg (2). For a measure to be adopted on a proposal from the European Commission, 62 votes were needed (abstention was seen as a vote against). A small number of Treaty articles made it possible to take a decision by QMV without a proposal of the Commission. In this instance the 62 votes must come from at least 10 Member-States. QMV is applied to the first stage (the Council's "common position") of any measure brought forward under the co-decision procedure (article 189b EEC) or the co-operation procedure (article 189c EEC), and can apply at stages thereafter. QMV is applied to most stages of the budget procedure. The Single European Act (1986) extended policy areas for which QMV could be applied. The Maastricht Treaty (1992) extended QMV to Common Foreign and Security Policy and Justice and Home Affairs. The Council must generally act by unanimity, but may decide unanimously that implementing measures in an area agreed as subject to joint action, are decided by QMV.

The decision-making structure in the European Union is very complex (Quermonne, 1993). Trying to rationalise the existing institutional system implies that thepowers of European institutions will diminish or grow. Discussions are going on about the decisionmaking procedure and possible adjustments. Adjustments are more urgent in the case of enlargement of the EU. Before 1973, the three large Member-States could push through a proposal of the Commission opposed by the other Member-States. Since 1973, (with Denmark, Ireland and United Kingdom becoming Member-States), large Member-States did not have enough votes to try this even if they wanted to. When Spain became a Member-State in 1986, large States (representing about 80 percent of the population of the European Union) could only force a decision by QMV with the help of two other Member-States. The voting system was in favour of small States. For more than two decades, a blocking minority was more or less constant at about a third of available votes. Discussions about modifying the voting system intensified with regard to enlargement negotiations (1993/1994) with Austria, Finland, Norway and Sweden. In the Ioannina-meeting (March 1994), the decision was to examine QMV in the 1996 IGC, while qualified majority would be fixed at 64 out of 90 votes. From 1 January 1995 on, the qualified majority was 62 votes, and the blocking minority 23-25 votes (taking account of Norway's decision not to participate in the European Union). The problem of qualified majority voting in the Council became more acute, as the European Union of the 15 aspired to enlarge itself with countries in Central and Eastern Europe (Guilhaudis, 1998). Not only is the decision-making process questioned, but also the rotating presidency of the European Council of Ministers. Since 1993, the "troïka" (president, former president, and prospective president) has been introduced to give more stability to the Council of Ministers, with a president from a different Member-State every six months. This "troïka" is a second-best solution as compared to the presidency of the United States. Innovations are needed, as for the "institutional triad" between Council of Ministers, Commission and Parliament. What about a President of the European Union, chosen by the European Council (or the electorate) for a period of 4 years?

The Maastricht Treaty (1992) introduced a new principle for institutionalising of the European Union: the "subsidiarity principle" (La Serre, 1992; Manin, 1993; Quermonne, 1994). In the preamble, Member-States endorsed the view that they wanted to develop the process creating an ever-closer union between peoples of Europe. Decisions would be taken as close to the citizens as possible, in accordance with the "subsidiarity principle". According to article 3B (article G, title II), the European Community, within the competencies and objectives of the Treaty, does, in conformity with the "subsidiarity principle", interfere in policy spheres outside its exclusive competence only if, and in so far as the intended objectives of the action cannot be reached sufficiently by the Member-States. Objectives can then be reached better by measures of the Community, while the Community action does not go further than necessary to realise objectives of the Maastricht Treaty. It was intended to give a central guideline about the relation between autonomy of Member-States and competencies of institutions of the European Union. It should guarantee that the institutional equilibrium would be maintained, under control of the European Court of Justice. The "subsidiarity principle" was known already, inter alia developed in the framework of Roman-Catholic social doctrine and in post-war German political writings (IEAP, 1993; Millon-Delsol, 1993). The idea of subsidiarity is said to go back to Aristotle, who saw it as a vital bridle of despotism, and to Thomas Aquinas, who saw perfection of the people as the sole objective of public authorities. Later Althusius, Locke, Stuart Mill, Tocqueville and others developed the subsidiarity idea. Encyclical letter "Quadragesimo Anno" (1931), 40 years after "Rerum Novarum (1891) reacting to the generally bad social conditions of workers, elaborated the Christian-social doctrine. It tried to give a reasonable equilibrium between State and citizens with the fundamental recognition of the human personality, and also an equilibrium between liberalism and solidarity. The "subsidiarity principle" was seen as a means to establish a reasonable distribution of competencies between hierarchically superior and lower public authorities. The "subsidiarity principle" is thought to have at least a double guideline. For the relation of State and citizens, and for the relation between a federation of States and its Member-States (like the relation between German Federal Republic and "Länder").

The ambiguous "subsidiarity principle" was meant to open a new perspective in political negotiations because it had a different emotional value from the federal principle, a very sensitive subject for the British. When President Mitterrand and Chancellor Kohl in their joint declaration of 6 December 1990 had implied that the European Union had a federal vocation, British Premier John Major could not accept it. His Conservatives, in the grip of a strong anti-Europe movement since Thatcher, could not stand the idea of Great Britain being a State within a federal union (Barber, 1993). Multiple interpretation of subsidiarity solved this blockade. The European Commission was formally restrained from bureaucratically ruling everything. Member-States were thought to maintain their national sovereign competencies, but subsidiarity is more fundamental. It can be used to accentuate the federal character of the European Union instead of all pleas for a more supranational Community, or, as "Eurosceptics" say, a European "SuperState". In a crucial phase of its development, when there were options to enlarge competencies of the European Union in the spheres of defence, foreign policy and monetary policy, subsidiarity could give the needed reassurance. The Birmingham European Council (16 October 1992) operationalised the "subsidiarity principle". As a result the European Council of Edinburgh (12 December 1992) could adopt guidelines, procedures and practices which made the "subsidiarity principle" an integral part of the decision-making process of the European Union. To accentuate the significance of these procedures, European institutions confirmed their willingness to apply the "subsidiarity principle" in the "Interinstitutional Agreement" (25

October 1993). The Commission accepted the obligation to make an annual report about application of the "subsidiarity principle" for European Council and Parliament. More important is if, and in what way, the European Court of Justice is competent to control whether acts of European institutions are compatible with this principle. The Court of Justice can give advice about the constitutionality in advance for agreements, but not for acts of European institutions, but the Court of Justice can be invoked a posteriori.

Two central questions have become especially urgent on the political agenda of the European Union of the 1990s, enlargement with new Member-States and institutional deepening (Fitoussi, 1999; Telo, 1995; Vandamme c.s., 1995). The European Council at Lisbon (June 1992) subordinated negotiations with candidates as Member-States to ratification of the Treaty of the European Union. Negotiations with Austria, Sweden and Finland finally started in February 1993 and with Norway in April 1993. In 1972, the population of Norway had already rejected membership of the European Community, and in November 1994, the draft for the accession treaty was rejected by referendum. Austria, Sweden and Finland have been Member-States of the European Union of the Fifteen since January 1995. Further enlargement of the European Union with candidates from Central and Eastern Europe places the European Union in a difficult position (La Serre c.s., 1994). Turkey asked to join in April 1987, Cyprus and Malta in July 1980. The European Community and Member-States felt that formal negotiations were premature. Countries in Central and Eastern Europe have declared membership to be their ultimate objective: Bulgaria, Hungary, the Czech Republic, Slovakia, Romania, and the three Baltic countries. The European Council at Copenhagen (June 1993) decided that they could become Member-States when they fulfilled the required conditions. The French attitude with regard to enlargement was analysed in the report of Raimond (1993). The European Council at Essen (9-10 December 1994) recognised that countries, having signed treaties of association with the European Union, could become Member-States. Hungary and Poland asked to be candidates in April 1994, Romania and Slovakia in June 1995, and the Czech Republic in January 1996. Malta withdrew its request to become member of the European Union in November 1996 (later Malta was aspiring to candidacy again). A future European Union of 28 Member-States makes it necessary to analyse the effect this will have on the institutional system (Kirchner, 1992; TEPSA, 1992). Former enlargements caused some adaptations. The Maastricht Treaty in article N 2 ruled that in 1996 an Intergovernmental Conference (IGC) would revise the Maastricht Treaty to enable the institutional capacity of the EU to cope with more Member-States.

This IGC started on 29 March 1996 in Turin. The Westendorp team at the European Council of Corfu (24-24 June 1994) was given the task to prepare this IGC. Its report (Westendorp, 1995) made it crystal-clear that further development of the institutional construction of Europe is very complex. The European Commission (EC) presented its own report about the functioning of the European Union (10 May 1995). The EC, confirming its mission as interpreter of the general interest in the European Union, had as its first priority making Europe everybody's business, and bringing Europe closer to the people as a permanent criterion of its activities. With reference to the "subsidiarity principle", the EC confirmed its position in saying that for each problem the most appropriate level has to be chosen (local, regional, national, European, global). The welcoming of new Member-States, while maintaining the "Community patrimony" was the second priority. A new legal order was established with a Member-State and its residents as subjects of a European Community, based upon the Rule of Law. The European model established a fundamental bond between the social dimension, human rights, and the rights of citizens. To maintain and renew this "Community patrimony", the EC formulated a double objective: the European Union has to function democratically, comprehensibly, and transparently, and has to act efficiently, coherently, and with solidarity. The EC presented an ambitious program for institutional renewal. On 17 May 1995 the European Parliament adopted a resolution with regard to the IGC 1996, followed by a declaration of the European Union at Messina on 2 June 1995, decisions of the European Council at Madrid (16 December 1995), the advice of the European Commission (28 February 1996), and the resolution of 13 March 1996 of the European Parliament (FNSP, 1996). The European Council at Turin on 29 March 1996 had some conclusions, to finish the work of the IGC, preparing meetings of the European Council in Dublin (13-14 December 1996) and Amsterdam (16-17 June 1997).

At the European Council in Dublin decisions were taken about the so-called Stability Pact, formulating conditions to guarantee that Member-States will apply the rules of the EMU game (Bulletin EC, 12-1996). Member-States gave up their power to intervene with economic policies by manipulating the value of their currency, and handed it over to the independent European Central Bank. The Stability Pact was an important step to realise the EMU with one common currency (euro), but this project was criticised sharply (Crawford, 1996). The calendar to start the EMU on 1 January 1999 was confirmed, as were the convergence criteria for Member-States who wanted to participate in the EMU. The Dublin deal implied that a budget deficit of more than 3% is allowed, if the economy of a Member-State decreases with 0.75 to 2 percent. The European Council of Dublin reconfirmed its objective to improve decision-making capacity and find solutions for institutional problems by taking decisions at the European Council in June 1997 in Amsterdam. While President Chirac and Premier Juppé had repeated, since 26 October 1995, that there was no alternative for French economic policy, intended from the beginning to bring France into the EMU, experts questioned this (Le Monde, 17-12-1996).To facilitate the bookkeeping of the European Communities, the European Unit of Account (EUA) was introduced in conjunction with the budget. In 1979, the European Monetary System (EMS) was established, making use of the EUA, which was replaced by the European Currency Unit (ECU) in 1981 (Ludlow, 1982). As was the case with the EUA, the ECU was a basket of national currencies (Ernst and Young, 1990). The weighting of each currency within the basket was fixed as a percentage, related to each country's share of the GNP of European Union and internal trade. Because of the start of stage 2 of the Economic and Monetary Union (EMU), the composition of the ECU was frozen on 1 November 1993. The ECU, backed by the European Monetary Institute (EMI) to which participating countries had to make available 20 percent of their gold and dollar reserves, established itself in the international money markets, but was not legal tender. At the IGC of 1990, Great Britain proposed establishing a hard ECU (so that it could not be devalued) as a common European currency, which could be used alongside national currencies, and could then evolve into a single currency, but this idea was not adopted. With the Maastricht Treaty, the ECU got a pivotal role in the third stage of the process leading to EMU. Exchange rates between national currencies of the ECU would be fixed irrevocably, and then the ECU would become the single currency. In 1996, the decision was taken to name the single currency euro, issued by the European Central Bank (ECB), a supranational organ, independent of national governments. From January 1994, the precursor of ECB, the European Monetary Institute (EMI) in Frankfurt, came into operation (Kauffman, 1997; Marshall, 1999). Because, at the beginning of stage 3, the central banks of participating states had to be independent of national governments (articles 107/108 EEC), France has, since 1993, at last realised independence of its central bank, the Banque de France.

European monetary integration is a long story (Riché/Wyplosz, 1993; Steinherr, 1994). The European monetary system in the 1990s was rather complex (De Grauwe/Papademos, 1990). Realisation of the Economic and Monetary Union (EMU) has more implications than simply the popular idea that it means a single currency (euro) (Padoa-Schioppa, 1994). Article B of the Maastricht Treaty (1992) puts as one of the targets of the European Union in becoming an EMU: "to promote economic and social progress which is balanced and sustainable, in particular through the creation of an area without internal frontiers, reinforcement of economic and social cohesion and establishment of an economic and monetary union, ultimately including a single currency..". The EMU implies co-ordination and integration of monetary, economic, and social policies of Member-States (Barrell, 1992; Colchester/Buchan, 1990). A distinction has to be made between Member-States that for the time being do not wish to be a partner in the EMU, such as Denmark and Great-Britain, and Member-States who are eager to adhere to the EMU, but are not (yet) able to qualify for the convergence criteria. At the start of the 21st century, not all of the 15 Member-States adhered to the EMU. This means a Europe of variable geometry. Only 11 Member-States started using the euro in January 1999: "Euroland" (Great Britain, Denmark, Sweden and Greece not participating). Later, Greece also joined "Euroland". Development of the EU since the Fall of the Berlin Wall (1989), implosion of the Soviet regime (Dahrendorf, 1990) and Maastricht Treaty (1992) is a new stage in the process of European integration (Duff c.s, 1994). Fear for irreversibility of the European integration process, with loss of national sovereignty and the risk of technological bureaucracy, has been exploited by adversaries of the Treaty of Maastricht (Guigou, 1994). Member-States felt the stress imposed by the convergence criteria of the Maastricht Treaty (7 February 1992), which came into force in November 1993 (Johnson/Collignon, 1994). The 5 convergence criteria with regard to inflation, interest rate, national budget deficit, national debt and value of the national currency were preconditions for Member-States wanting to participate in the EMU with the single currency. Because the entrance examination for EMU with these stiff criteria demanded radical retrenchment policies, Member-States have been in a straight-jacket since the middle of the 1990s, not least due to political and social tensions in a Europe with high percentages of unemployment. There are strong arguments to continue with an ever-closer European Union (Thomas, 1991). United States of Europe is one of the possible, not the most probable, scenarios (Holland, 1994; Wistrich, 1994). United Europe of Nation-States is more likely.

## 8.7. Treaty of Amsterdam (1997)

It became increasingly evident that the institutional set-up of the European Union (EU) was not adequate any more. This would become more serious when more countries (from Central and Eastern Europe) wanted to become Member-States (Le Cacheux, 1996). The 15 EU Member-States agreed upon trying to realise an institutional renewal with the Treaty of Amsterdam. After the Turin Intergovernmental Conference (29 March 1996) the Treaty of Amsterdam was prepared with 15 months of negotiations. At the Summit of Dublin (December 1996), EU Member-States, in preparation for the Summit of Amsterdam (16-17 June 1997), adopted a "Pact of Stability" to stiffen budget discipline in the EMU. Some main points of this milestone on the road to the third EMU phase can be mentioned. Member-States participating in the Euro-zone have to draw up stability programs. The other Member-States will draft a comparable convergence program. These programs cover a couple of years, and are intended to realise a medium-term budget equilibrium or surplus. The road to adapt to this medium-term target is defined in these documents which are made public, while important assumptions are made explicit. European Commission and European Council of Ministers monitor implementation of these programs. When there are significant deviations, the European Council can ordain a Directive (binding for the result to be achieved, leaving to the Member-State the choice of form or methods) for a Member-State. When the limit of 3% of GNP is transgressed in the budget deficit, and when there is an excessive deficit, the Member-State has to take measures within four months to correct this in the next year. If this is not realised, after a numerical calculation of the excessive deficit, within ten months, sanctions are ordered, such as the obligation to remit an interest-free deposit. The extent of this sanctioned deposit is calculated according to the formula: $0.2 + 0,1$ (deficit -3.0), with a maximum of 0.5% of the GNP. The sanctioned deposit is transformed into a fine when the budget deficit is still excessive after two years. There is an escape, however. The budget deficit can exceed the 3%-limit in some degree, when there are exceptional circumstances. An economic recession is seen as exceptional, when real economy shrinks by more than 2%. Or if this decline is within the margin of 0.75 and 2%, and when there is an abrupt decline or a relatively large cumulative loss of production. The decision about the issue of which Member-States were participating in the first round of the euro, the common currency, was scheduled for May 1998. Member-States had to present their financial data about 1997 at the end of February 1998. This data would be analysed by the European Monetary Institute (the predecessor of the European Central Bank) and the EC.

On 16 and 17 June 1997, Heads of State and Prime Ministers of 15 Member-States of the EU decided upon what is called the Treaty of Amsterdam, a new treaty for the European Union. The Treaty of Amsterdam can be summarised under six headings: fundamental rights, non-discrimination; freedom, security and justice; European Union of the citizens; effective and coherent foreign policy; institutions of the European Union; and intensification of co-operation. Once the official texts were signed, there would be public debate in national parliaments of the EU. Persons who are entitled to vote could give their opinion, via referenda or national parliaments. After this procedure the treaty could be ratified. The Treaty of Amsterdam has four objectives. A more substantial contribution of the EU to employment policies and the rights of citizens. Elimination of the last hindrances to free traffic and movement of people and products, and furthering of security. Enabling the (enlarged) EU to play a more important role in the world, and making the institutional set-up of the EU more efficient, taking into account enlargement with more Member-States. The Treaty of Amsterdam reinforces the three "pillars" of the EU since the Treaty of Maastricht came into operation on 1 November 1993: European Communities (first pillar); common foreign and security policies (second pillar); and co-operation for justice and national internal affairs (third pillar). The EU, with 6% of world population, realises some 20% of world production. The EU was then the largest economic unit worldwide with regard to production capacities, but the EU had enormous problems: about 18 million unemployed. The Treaty of Amsterdam confirmed the responsibility of Member-States for the promotion of employment, but co-operation and co-ordination in this field are seen as important targets.Insertion of a chapter about employment in the Treaty of Amsterdam, and rulings about the Economic and Monetary Union, form a new phase in institutionalising. Member-States are pledging themselves to co-ordinate their employment policy with EU economic policy, and to further the building-up of an adequate number of skilled and schooled workers able to react flexibly to economic changes. A Committee for Employment supervises national policies. Every year Heads of State and Prime Ministers will evaluate the (un-) employment situation.

On proposal of the European Commission, after consultation of the European Parliament, Economic and Social Committee and Committee for the Regions, the European Council will decide with a qualified majority upon Directives for Member-States. At the end of the year, the European Council will investigate implementation of Directives, and can formulate Regulations for Member-States. European Council and European Commission present a common annual report to the Heads of State and Prime Ministers who will examine new policies. In the field of employment, there are also provisions for activating measures to finance pilot-projects. This EU employment policy is part of an overall social policy for Member-States. Social legislation for the EU is well developed in several policy-fields, as for example with regard to free movement of workers, equal chances for men and women, and protection of health and security of working conditions for workers. In the EU, workers have the right to visit each Member-State and to work and live there. They have the same rights and privileges as national citizens for health insurance, pensions, social security, family allowances etc. In the whole EU, common high minimum standards are operative for protection of health and security of workers. The EU has had a substantial impact upon realising equal chances for men and women.

There are numerous issues for which Member-States are exclusively competent: wages, the right to strike, etc. For several matters, they have to decide unanimously (dismissal of workers, social security, representation of workers, etc.). Generally speaking, the Treaty of Amsterdam has enlarged competencies and potentialities of the EU to promote activities in the social field. The Treaty of Maastricht (December 1991) encompassed a "social protocol" to further common social policies of the EU. This social protocol was about the establishment of European works councils, equal rights for full-time and part-time workers, and the right to parenthood leave. All Member-States, except the United Kingdom, signed this social protocol. Later the United Kingdom signed the social protocol in the framework of the Treaty of Amsterdam. This made it possible to include the social protocol in the text of the Treaty of Amsterdam, in the rulings about social policy, education, schooling and training, and youth matters. Issues about working hours, pay systems, social security, employment policy, schooling, equal chances and the needs of small and medium-sized enterprises are tackled by social partners and public authorities on the European, national and regional level. Competitiveness, creation of fuller employment, flexibility and guarantees for jobs are challenges which will determine if the European social model is viable. The fight against poverty and social exclusion, affecting millions of European citizens, is a necessary complement. The Treaty of Amsterdam gives some guarantees, although the decisions concerned have to be taken unanimously.

The Treaty of Maastricht gave every citizen with the nationality of a Member-State clearly defined European rights. One has the right to move freely on the territory of Member-States and to live there. In every Member-State in which one lives, one has active and passive suffrage for the election of municipal councils and the European Parliament. Individuals can get support from the diplomatic and consular authorities of each Member-State in other countries where their own Member-State is not represented. One can present petitions to the European Parliament, and one can apply to the ombudsman. The Treaty of Amsterdam extends these rights for citizens in the field of fundamental rights, consumer rights, and rights of information. This treaty proclaims: "The European Union is founded on principles of freedom, democracy, respect for human rights, fundamental liberties and principles of the constitutional state (Rule of Law), principles which are common to the Member-States." Each individual can put questions to the European Court of Justice whenever European institutions act against fundamental rights. When the European Council concludes that there is a serious and persistent violation of these principles by a Member-State, it can decide sanctions for this Member-State. The EU can take measures to fight against discrimination in relation to sex, racial or ethnic origin, religion and philosophy of life, handicap, age or sexual disposition. Regarding consumers' rights, the Treaty of Amsterdam states: To look after the interests of consumers and to guarantee a high standard of consumer protection, the EU contributes to protect health, security and the economic interests of consumers. Protection of the health of individuals is guaranteed in the sphere of policymaking, policy implementation and activities of the European Community. In relation to the rights of information is ruled: Each citizen of the EU, and every natural person or corporation with its stay or statutory seat in one of the Member-states, has access to documents of the European Parliament, Council and Commission, in accordance with prevailing conditions. When the European Council acts as legislator, it publishes the result of the voting and voting statements.

In the paragraph about the European Union of the citizens, there is firstly a chapter about employment. Promotion of co-ordination between Member-States of employment policies is given priority to improve efficacy by elaborating a co-ordinated strategy for employment. Every year, the European Council, deciding with a qualified majority, will elaborate guidelines for the employment policy of Member-States. This will be done on the basis of a common report of the European Commission and European Council. To further co-ordination between Member-States, a consultative "Committee for employment" has been formed. In the field of social policy, it was possible to integrate the text of the "Social Charter" (1989) into the Treaty of Amsterdam, because the UK no longer blocked this. This rules, inter alia, that the EU completes actions of Member-States in the field of work conditions; information and consultation of workers; integration of persons excluded from the market; and equality for men and women. In this paragraph, there are also chapters about environment, public health and protection of consumers. There is a long chapter about the "subsidiarity principle", and chapters about transparency and the quality of legislation. Distant regions are taken into account; France had pleaded in favour of a specific status for its "DOM-TOM" territories. One objective of the Treaty of Amsterdam is to bring the Europe of citizens closer. At the start of the common market, the right of free movement of persons was valid for workers only. Since 1993, this applies to tourists, students, self-employed, pensioners, persons seeking employment, and all citizens of the EU. The Treaty of Maastricht anticipated the consequences of complete free movement of persons, by prescribing more intensified co-operation between Member-States in the field of Justice and Police. The new freedom of movement was not meant to be misused by organised crime, drugs traffic, fraud, organised illegal immigration etc., but the EU was not given adequate instruments then to realise the free movement of persons, control the outer-borders of the EU, and fight against criminality. This brought the application of the intergovernmental method in this field. So the Treaty of Amsterdam is a basis to eliminate the last hindrances for free movement of persons, and to organise more means to guarantee security more adequately. A substantive part of the rules with regard to co-operation in the field of Justice and Internal (national) affairs is incorporated in the "first pillar". This implies that EU rulings are applicable: all EU institutions are involved, control of legality by the European Court, and effective law instruments. The EU gets new competencies regarding visas, conditions for delivery of residence permits to immigrants, procedures for allowing asylum and rulings for judicial co-operation in civil matters.

To guarantee a gradual introduction of a "Room of freedom, security and justice" in the EU, a transitional period of five years is taken. Following the coming into force of the Treaty of Amsterdam, decisions of the European Council will be taken unanimously in this transitional period, and thereafter with the common decision-making procedure. When after a period of five years, the measures taken are judged to be sufficient, Member-States could decide to pass from unanimity in decision-making to qualified majority. Member-States bound themselves to take parallel measures in the field of police co-operation and judiciary co-operation for penal law cases. The European Council is committing itself to co-operation via the intermediary of the European Police Office, Europol, with growing competencies. Co-operation between police offices and other instances responsible for criminal cases (directly or indirectly via Europol) remains within the sphere of intergovernmental competencies. The same holds for mutual judicial support in criminal cases, and for important fields of co-operation between Member-States: the fight against terrorism; organised crime; crimes against children and other persons; drugs and weapons traffic; fraud; and corruption on international level. To make this co-operation effective, more means and instruments will be used. On the initiative of Germany, France and the Benelux-countries, the Schengen Agreement (1990) was signed. In the framework of this Schengen Agreement, a number of common rulings were drawn up about visas, asylum, control at external borders, and co-operation between police and customs-offices, so the free movement of persons would not be realised at the cost of public order. Later all Member-States joined this Schengen Agreement, except the UK and Ireland, who prefer to maintain existing control of all persons (regardless of their origin) entering their territory. The Schengen Agreement is also signed by Iceland and Norway, neither being Member-States of the EU. The Treaty of Amsterdam integrates the Schengen Agreement in the institutional system of the EU. The results of Schengen so far are incorporated in an annexed protocol in the Treaty of Amsterdam. Co-operation as arranged by the Member-States having signed the Schengen Convention will be continued within the juridical and institutional EU framework. This "acquis" will have to be accepted automatically by new candidates for the EU. By applying the system of "reinforced co-operation" (flexibility), the 13 Schengen-countries continue co-operation within the new law order of the Treaty of Amsterdam. In this way the development of two separate systems is stopped and it becomes possible to determine, which questions fall within the sphere of "intensified co-operation". Ireland and the UK maintain their border controls, and for Denmark specific measures have been agreed.

The Treaty of Amsterdam modified the treaties on the basis of which the European Union was founded, but no changes were made with regard to the procedures to realise the EMU as fixed by the Treaty of Maastricht. The European Council in Amsterdam did not renew the institutions of the European Union as was the intention. The Amsterdam Summit continued into the 18th of June, but it failed to come up with an institutional renewal to prepare for the enlargement of the EU with more Member-States. A decision about institutional renewal was postponed. This was the bad news; the good news was that the EMU with its Euro was pursued. The European Council can unanimously take all measures necessary to fight discrimination. The text states that the EU has as its mission to further a high level of employment and social protection, equality between men and women, economic and social cohesion, and solidarity of Member-States. It took some time to make Member-States and parliaments ratify the Treaty of Amsterdam. The French "Conseil constitutionnel" in its advice of 31 December 1997 had some comments to make, but the Council of Ministers on 29 July 1998 approved the Treaty of Amsterdam. The Congress (National Assembly and Senate together) in Versailles had the final say. French deputies adopted the Treaty of Amsterdam on 3 March 1998 with 447 votes against 75. The Congress adopted this treaty on 18 January 1999 with 758 against 111 votes.

From the beginning, the European Community, on behalf of the Member-States, participated in international commercial negotiations. The accent used to be primarily on agriculture and industry, wheras now the prominent position of services is taken into account. With the Treaty of Maastricht, the EU assumed responsibilities for external policy (foreign policy) and security. The first experiences of the EU in the international field were a disappointment. Member-States could not realise a reasonable common attitude with regard to problems in former Yugoslavia, the Middle East, or Africa. With regard to foreign policy, it has been ruled that the European Council, assembling the Heads of State and Prime Ministers of the Member-States, determines the general orientations of foreign policy and common security, "Politique Étrangère et de Sécurité Commune" (PESC). This Council decides the common strategies as launched by the EU in the fields where the Member-States have important common interests. Decisions in this domain are taken unanimously. Each Member-State can use "constructive abstention", making non-participation possible for an action, without impeding implementation by other Member-States. Common strategies in this domain are decided upon by a qualified majority. France had claimed that there should be a "Monsieur PESC", a highly qualified political personality responsible for foreign policy and common security matters, to speak on behalf of the EU. The European Council finally decided to entrust this function to the secretary-general of the Council, who is present at the Council meetings, contributing to formulation, elaboration and implementation of decisions. At the request of the president of the European Council, he can engage in political dialogues with third parties as representative of this Council. He is assisted by a "unit for policy planning and rapid alert". The EU is represented by the president of the European Council (changing every 6 months), assisted by the secretary-general.

In the field of defence policy, the Treaty of Amsterdam states that PESC covers all questions regarding the common security of the EU, including the gradual formulation of a common defence policy, in the perspective of a common defence. The Treaty of Amsterdam takes account of the commitments of most Member-States in the framework of NATO. Consensus exists between Member-States that common foreign policy and security policy have to encompass all aspects with regard to the security of the EU, gradual realisation of a defence policy included. There was a heated debate about the relationship between the EU and WEU (Western European Union), the sole existing purely European defence organisation. Especially between the UK and its most important partners, including the six founding Member-States. The Six wanted to include in the Treaty of Amsterdam the engagement to integrate the WEU as an armed force in the EU. London opposed this proposal. So this could only be decided upon later unanimously. Most Member-States are members of the WEU, except Denmark and the traditionally neutral countries Austria, Finland, Ireland and Sweden. International circumstances proved that peace operations and humanitarian activities in areas of crisis are essential, tasks explicitly mentioned in the Treaty of Amsterdam. These can be done in the WEU framework, in co-operation with some or all Member-States. With regard to the institutions of the EU, the vital non-decision was that the European Council postponed decisions about the needed institutional reforms. The new European Commission (EC) would be reorganised. A protocol annexed to the treaty states that the EC will have one Commissioner per Member-State before the next enlargement with countries from Central and Eastern Europe. Then the weighting of votes in the European Council will be modified, taking account of the number of inhabitants of Member-States. One year before the situation with more than 20 Member-States, a new IGC is convoked about the functioning of EU institutions, weighting of votes in the Council and decision-making process. The European Council agreed upon extending the qualified majority rule for some cases. It was decided to simplify procedures for the European Parliament and to reinforce its power of co-decision, making this more or less the general rule: European Council and European Parliament are co-legislators. Since the Treaty of Maastricht (1992), it had co-decision competence for 15 policy areas, now for 23 new policy areas (such as social policy, combating fraud).

National parliaments will be more involved in community decision-making, and as far as the improved co-ordination is concerned, the Council has agreed upon giving Member-States, if they wish, the opportunity to go further with common policies without waiting until others want to do so. This is bound by very strict conditions. They can do this only when there is a qualified majority. Or when, according to the files, Member-States agree unanimously that a restricted group of Member-States may engage in more intensive co-operation. At the start of the 21st century the EU is confronted with one of its major challenges, because there are a number of countries who see themselves as candidates for membership of the EU. At the end of 1999 the European Commission proposed to regard 12 countries as candidates for membership: Poland, Czech Republic, Hungary, Slovenia, Romania, Estonia, Latvia, Lithuania, Bulgaria, Slovakia, Malta and Cyprus. Turkey was seen as an aspiring candidate. The Helsinki Top (1999) decided to see all 13 countries as candidates. Cohen-Tanugi (1992) and others urged a speedy enlargement with new Member-States in Central and Eastern Europe. The "Other Europe" needs access to Western markets, financial and technological support and integration in a common security system, but why make these countries Member-States of the EU? After the end of the war in Kosovo, a UNDP "Human Development Report for Central and Eastern Europe and the CIS" (1999) showed that the shock therapy for countries in Eastern Europe had failed. Making several of these countries EU members is a promising perspective, butthe EU will have to solve many problems. The Treaty of Amsterdam has been in force since the first of May 1999 (McDonagh, 1998; Moravcsik/Nicolaïdis, 1999). There is a lot to do institutionally for "European integration After Amsterdam" (Neunreither/Wiener, 2000).

## 8.8. Convergence between "Rule of Law" and "État de droit" in the European Union

Developments in the law in Great Britain are a very relevant dimension in the framework of the growing interpenetration of European law and English law. Since the Second World War, development of English law is no longer a near-monopoly for judges, legislation also plays a role. Only a few decades ago, it was not done to use argumentation in academic books to decide cases in jurisdiction, but this "non-citation rule" has been rendered inoperative. European Law has had an important influence, especially since 1973, when the United Kingdom (UK) became a Member State of the European Community, later European Union (EU). There seems to be more impact of EU-law upon English law than conversely, of English law upon EU-law. The UK had to accept the "acquis communautaire" as it was when the UK became a Member State. French legal tradition, in particular, had a dominant influence on the original development of the primary communitarian law (the founding treaties). Primary communitarian law started with the ECSC treaty (1951), followed by the Treaty of Rome (1957) for EEC and Euratom. EEC and Euratom has functioned since 1 January 1958. On 1 July 1967, the "Merger Treaty" was effective, establishing a single Council and a single Commission of European Communities. On 1 July 1987, the Single European Act (1986) came into force. Its objective was completion of the internal market: "an area without internal frontiers in which the free movement of goods, persons, services and capital is ensured" (Art.7a EC).

The Treaty of the European Union, signed on 7 February 1992 in Maastricht, came into force on 1 November 1993. This Maastricht Treaty has a number of objectives, inter alia: the establishment of an economic and monetary union including a single currency; a common foreign and security policy; introduction of EU citizenship; co-operation on justice and home affairs; maintenance of the "acquis communautaire"; and respect of the "subsidiarity principle". It ruled that to be a member of the Community, the government of a State must be founded on principles of democracy, and that fundamental rights are seen as general principles of Community Law. New Community fields of action were education, culture, public health, consumer protection and trans-European networks. A co-decision procedure gave the European Parliament legislative competencies. This primary communitarian law had its provisional conclusion in the Treaty of Amsterdam (1997). The influence of English law upon this primary EU law has been modest. This is due to the defensive British attitude (George, 1994). In Maastricht Great Britain opposed the reform proposals of other Member-States (Laursen/Vanhoonacker, 1992). The existing informal English constitutional law was not an adequate model for the European Union, but an important part of modern constitutional law has its roots in the English constitutional law tradition. Secondary communitarian law, important characteristics of juridical instruments (regulations, directives, ordinances, decrees), and culture, style and techniques of European law making had already been shaped, when the UK became Member-State.

English law has nevertheless had an impact upon the contents of European legislation. In the law harmonisation process, the legal systems of Member-States are the inspiration, providing a source for finding the best available law. Often this best available law proved to be English, more than once because it was defended with cogency by English negotiators (Rometsch/Wessels, 1996). Perhaps, this might be attributed partly also to the fact that English law contained solutions which were relatively unknown in communitarian law, dominantly influenced by continental law. Some fields were strongly influenced by the British policy style (Jowell/Oliver, 1994). Generally speaking, the different legal concepts as used in several national law systems are less crucial than the underlying societal values and objectives of those law systems (Bell, 1995). For all Member-States, the decisive fact is that a growing part of law originates from EU Law. The principle of parliamentary sovereignty was acknowledged of old in Great-Britain: "Parliament has the right to make or unmake any law whatsoever."; and "No person or body outside the legislature is recognised by the law of England as having the right to override or set aside the legislation of Parliament." (Dicey, 1959). This means that treaties are binding in the UK only after an "Act of Parliament". The principle of parliamentary sovereignty has a wider impact, as a treaty (even after having been incorporated with an Act of Parliament) can be cancelled by a later Act of Parliament. Treaty law is not superior to later national legislation because, due to the "theory of implied repeal", later national legislation is supposed to have cancelled earlier legislation (even when this has a treaty as source): "Parliament cannot bind its successors.", and testing of Acts of Parliament by judges was not allowed. When the UK became a Member State, some feared that the UK would raise difficulties with the "acquis communautaire". Community law was accepted with the "European Communities Act" (1972). In the Factortame decision (1991), the House of Lords accepted that Community Law was superior to English law. The constitutional situation changed, but there have been some rearguard actions.

English law is in a creative and innovative situation (Beatson/Tridimas, 1998). In the UK, administrative law ("French import") has been distinguished as a specific area of law for only two decades or so (Allison, 1996; Schwarze, 1996). The Labour government of Tony Blair planned a sweeping constitutional reform program. There is a controversy in England, between those wanting to reform English law with written law, and others who prefer the activities of judges. In EU Member-States, there are a number of law ideas, law principles and law techniques which mutually penetrate national law spheres in a cross-fertilisation process. Jurisprudence of the European Court of Justice often works as a catalyst (O'Neill, 1994). The European Court of Justice has a crucial role in creating Common European Law. This law encourages the EU to become an internal law sphere for Member-States: the EU as "juridical inland" with a specific EU law culture. In education and professionalisation of jurists, developing Common European Law requires the adaptation of national education programs (Witte c.s., 1992). In all relevant dimensions of societal life, EU law proves to be a crucial aspect (Mathijsen, 1995). Some authors deny that European legal systems are converging (Legrand, 1996). The intriguing question is, how the relationship will develop between the laws of Member-States and European Union law. This development was not always straightforward, but was ongoing. In spite of critical reserves about European integration, there is much respect for the developing European law culture.

Development of the "État de droit" in Western Europe after the Second World War terrors has been a multi-faceted phenomenon. Before this war, several ideas were launched about the formation of a pan-European confederation of States (federalism) to establish a basis for durable peace. After this war, Europe lay in ruins, split up between Western Europe and Communist Eastern Europe (Milward, 1984). In 1946, several national federalist groups established the European Union of Federalists. In his Zurich speech in September 1946, Winston Churchill called for a kind of United States of Europe. His son-in-law, Duncan Sandys, stimulated the foundation of the United Europe Movement, which held its Congress in The Hague in May 1948 (Brugmans, 1974; Lipgens, 1985). This

Congress created the Council of Europe, as a step-up to more federalism. The UK, in the footsteps of Churchill's "reservatio Britannica" about more integration with the European continent, obstructed attempts to bring more integration. The Statute of the Council of Europe (1949) stated in its article 3 that each Member-State "recognises the principle of the pre-eminence of law, and the principle that each person under its jurisdiction has to benefit from human rights and fundamental liberties." The Committee of Ministers and the consultative Parliamentary Assembly wanted to make this proclamation more precise in connection with the "Greek Affair" (regime of colonels) and demands for the affiliation of Spain and Portugal, when these countries did not yet have a democratic regime. The Assembly concluded, in Resolution 361 (1968), that article 3 demanded a parliamentary regime, guaranteed by a truly democratic constitution. Greece then withdrew. When the military dictatorship came to an end and Greece renewed its request for membership, Resolution 558 (1974) of the Assembly stated that explicit conditions had to be fulfilled (liberation of political prisoners; a really democratic constitution; normal functioning of institutions). The rules of the Statute were extended. The Assembly took the initiative to send "missions d'enquête" to control the situation in prisons, examine constitutional aspects of the Greek regime etc. This meant more interference by an international organisation in national matters than before. Spain and Portugal were confronted with conditions for membership. This attitude of the Assembly had an important influence on the development of European law. The Constitutions of Portugal (1976) and Spain (1978) were adapted to satisfy the Council of Europe. The Council of Europe saw a controversy of "federalists", arguing for constitutional arrangements for federalism, and "functionalists", adhering to arrangements, whenever surrender of some aspect of sovereignty was a functional necessity.

On 3 November 1953, the "Convention de sauvegarde des droits de l'homme" (4 November 1950) came into operation. A series of liberties and classical fundamental rights was included (right to live; security; freedom of thought, conscience and religion; peaceful meetings and associations). Several articles concerned the constitutional state. Article 13: "Each person whose rights and liberties have been violated, has the right to bring his or her case before a national instance, even when the violation has been committed by persons exercising official functions." For every person arrested or in detention, article 5 rules that he or she can ask a judge to decide its legality. When there is a legal accusation, articles 6 and 7 rule the rights of the defence and guarantee the proper administration of justice. The case has to be dealt with publicly, with equity, and within a reasonable time, by an independent and impartial tribunal as established by law. The accused has the right to be informed of the nature of the accusation; to be given a reasonable time to prepare his defence; to have the defence of his choice, appointed officially when he does not have the finances to pay him; to interrogate witnesses; and if necessary to have a translator free of charge. The "Convention" guarantees the essential principles of a constitutional state such as: presumption of innocence; no retroactive effect of penal laws; "nullum crimen et nulla poena sine lege"; appeal to a higher jurisdiction; the right of not being prosecuted or punished by jurisdictions of the same State for an infraction for which some person has already been acquitted or condemned; and to be indemnified in case of a judiciary fault.

The "Cour européenne des droits de l'homme" has enlarged the reach of this Convention with a jurisprudence of more than 300 decisions. On this basis, a series of general law principles can be established which are binding for Member-States. They might be categorised under five headings (Morin, 1996, p.207): The principle that rights and liberties are subdued to jurisdiction; the principle of equitable lawsuit; the principle of the rights of defence; the principle of compensation for infringements; and the fundamental principle of the pre-eminence of the law. One of the most essential elements of a constitutional state is that procedures for appealing against decisions are effective. This condition is fulfilled only when justiciables have open access to a competent tribunal for the protection of their rights and liberties. The right of access to justice encompasses the right to be heard and the appeal for "habeas corpus". Each person who is arrested or detained as suspected of having committed an infraction has the right (art.5) to be brought promptly before a judge or magistrate. This right comes under pressure when the law wants to protect the community against terrorism. Most European Court decisions concerning "habeas corpus" were related to admissions topsychiatric hospitals. The principle of an equitable lawsuit (art.6) has its application especially with regard to the behaviour of a tribunal or the public prosecutor. There has to be a reasonable time within which one must hear what the accusation is, and there should be a decision. Defendants should have a reasonable time to study the files. The principles of independence and impartiality of judges are relevant. Publicity of discussions before jurisdictions is also a fundamental principle, but it is possible to abandon this right, when no important public interest is at stake. Although the rule of reasoned judgement is not explicitly formulated in the Convention, the European Court has takendecisions to make clear that judges have to formulate the grounds on which they base their decisions. Protocol no.7, appendix to the Convention, ruled the right of appeal to a higher jurisdiction.

The principle of respect for rights of the defence, by which procedural rights are essential for the protection of substantial rights, partly overlap the principle of an equitable lawsuit. Although not formulated as such in the Convention, the European Court recognised the right to be present (or be represented), when a decision is taken about a measure which restricts somebody's liberty. The accused has the right to defend himself (art.6). Arbitrary arrest and detention are prohibited by article 5 in the framework of the right of liberty and procedures (the right to be heard; access to a judge; habeas corpus). Article 3 of the Convention prohibits torture, and other inhuman or humiliating punishments. The Council of Europe initiated the "Convention européenne pour la prévention de la torture et des peines ou traitements inhumains ou dégradants", signed in 1987 and operative since 1989. A committee was established with competencies to investigate and visit all places where public authorities detain persons. This committee was important with regard to the situation of human rights in Turkey (Conseil de l'Europe, 1992; Colloque Nancy, 1994). Article 8 of the European Convention (1950) limits the competencies of public authorities when performing investigations, in respect of the private sphere. Telephonic communications are thought to be part of it. Soon the question was, in what measure this respect for privacy restricted secret tapping as necessary for national security or prevention of penal infractions (Mélanges Levasseur, 1992, pp. 263-285). The European Court, in the decision Klass (1978), decided that interference was acceptable with effective control by judiciary authorities. The European Court has been reluctant to admit material collected by secret tapping as proof. It is maintained that no jurisdiction may use evidence obtained illegally.

Several other rights of the defence with regard to justice and police can be touched on. When a person arrested or detained is not judged within a reasonable time, he must be released if there are guarantees for his reappearance. The European Court developed rules with regard to conditions of detention and motives for detention (dangers of destruction of evidence, escape, continuation of infractions etc.). After a given time, suspicions are not sufficient to continue detention. Persons held in detention also have the right to hear clearly what the juridical and factual reasons for their detention are, and to be given comprehensible information about the whole procedure. The accused has the right to have enough time and necessary facilities to organise his defence, with the help of the counsel of his choice. Article 6 of the Convention recognises that the accused has a right to the help of an "avocat d'office", when he has no financial means to pay for counsel, and when "the interests of justice make it necessary". There has been much debate about the principle of the "débat contradictoire". There should be "equality of weapons" for process parties with regard to hearing witnesses, experts and access to the files. In the decision Asch (26 April

1991), the European Court defined components of this principle: evidence is presented to the accused in public to make contradictory discussion possible; witnesses à charge should be subjected to contest; each party has the right to be aware of all evidence and all information produced by the other party; the prosecutor must communicate to the defence important elements ("à charge et à décharge"). The European Court, since the decision Kostovski (20 November 1989), is vigilant about anonymous declarations, occult informers and infiltrated agents.

The presumption of innocence (art.6) is also a crucial principle of the constitutional state. Article 7 of the European Convention confirmed the principles of "nullum crimen, nulla poena sine lege" and no retroactive effect of penal laws. The "non-incrimination rule", inspired by the American "Bill of Rights", implying that nobody can be forced to bear witness against himself, is recognised by the European Court as part of an equitable lawsuit, although it was not included in the Convention. The Protocol no.7 includes the principle "ne bis in idem", prohibiting the start of a new prosecution or lawsuit for a tribunal in the same State, when an infraction has been the object of a definite judgement. This is a principle of the European public order as the principles in article 7 are. The principle of reparations for judiciary faults was recognised in article 50 of the European Convention. It authorises the European Court to give the impaired process party an equitable compensation, when the internal, national law of a Member-State, which did not live up to its obligations, does not take away the consequences of an act which is contrary to the Convention. As yet there is a hiatus between international law and national law. Decisions of the European Court in Strasbourg cannot be executed in the territories of Member-States, who have to modify their rulings or practices to comply with decisions of the Court, but national jurisdictions are more receptive to jurisprudence of the European Court, adapting their own jurisprudence (Sudre, 1995). This summary sketch shows that the European Convention applies the principle of the pre-eminence of law as stated in article 3 of the Statute of the Council of Europe.

The European Court wanted to go further by making the principle of the pre-eminence of law a kind of synthesis-principle from which principles can be deduced, binding for parties at the European Convention (teleological interpretation). In the decision Golder (21 February 1975) about the scope of the Rule of Law within the European Convention, the United Kingdom was confronted with a kind of Europeanised version of the Rule of Law. Some twenty decisions, three of them in 1994, of the European Court were based on principles of the constitutional state, reinforcing guarantees of the European Convention. In the decision about the Greek Refineries (9 December 1994), pre-eminence of law was explicitly opposed to the interference of legislative power in the organisation of justice to influence the judiciary process. From jurisprudence of the European Court in Strasbourg it is obvious that principles of the constitutional state impose themselves upon all public authorities and organs in Member-States. So the juridical and philosophical traditions of the European continent concerning "État de droit" and "Rechtsstaat" are incorporated in the European Convention. As judge Fitzmaurice made clear in the Golder decision (1975), the "Common Law" spirit could have given a more restrictive interpretation of the Rule of Law in the preamble. The European Convention penetrated deeply into jealously guarded areas of national sovereignty. The preamble refers to a common conception of human rights as can be derived from constitutions in Western Europe. The institutions of Strasbourg enforced norms as proclaimed by the European Convention. The principle of pre-eminence of law got a fundamental value enabled to fill eventual gaps between principles. Those charged with guarding the European Convention seemed to interpret this as the first chapter of a kind "European Constitution" (Morin, 1996, p.232). The European Court in decision "Loizidou" (23 March 1995) saw the European Convention as constitutional instrument of the European public order. With regard to European Communities and European Union, a notable point is that there is no explicit guarantee for fundamental rights in the basic treaties or conventions (Colliard, 1974). Only some economic rights were included, such as the liberties of free circulation and establishment. The treaties of the European Communities contrasted with the Statute of the Council of Europe (1949) and "Traité instituant l'Union de l'Europe occidentale" (UEO, 1948, jo.1954). The last in its preamble mentioned attachment of Member-States to "fundamental human rights, human dignity and the value of the human person." Communitarian treaties accentuated the pre-eminence of communitarian law or the national juridical order of the Member-States.

The principle of the direct applicability of communitarian law before administrative tribunals and national jurisdictions was made explicit by the "Cour de justice des Communautés européennes" in Luxemburg, in its decisions about "Van Gend & Loos" (5 February 1963) and "Costa v. Enel" (11 July 1964). The impact of communitarian institutions and law made itself felt. As for individual liberties about property rights, free exercise of professions and freedom of association. Acts and competencies of communitarian institutions conflicted with constitutional guarantees given by each Member-State to individuals. A strange phenomenon was that competencies subject to constitutional restrictions in Member-States, were not restricted when they became part of the communitarian law order. This problem manifested itself also with regard to aspects of the constitutional state (Morin, 1996, p.236). The European Court of Luxemburg in its Stauder decision (12 November 1969), recognised openly for the first time its responsibility for guarding respect for fundamental rights by communitarian institutions. The following year, it was able to lay the foundation for its subsequent jurisprudence in the "Internationale Handelsgesellschaft" case (17 December 1970): "respect of fundamental rights is an integral part of general principles of law which the Court guarantees; guaranteeing these rights, inspired by common constitutional traditions of the Member-States, has to be assured in the framework of structure and objectives of the Community." The solicitor-general made clear that the legality of an act by a community organ should be judged in the framework of common law, the principles of which "contribute to form that common philosophical, political and juridical substratum of Member-States, on the basis of which unwritten law develops, guaranteeing respect for the fundamental rights of individuals as one of its objectives". This "pretorian step" was followed by a new one with the "Nold decision" (14 Mai 1974) and the "Hauer decision" (13 December 1979). These defined the institutional mechanism to determine comparable norms which are transposable in the communitarian law order. The Court of Luxemburg decided to stick to the most advanced national protection. The most progressive, highest norm. It rejected simple accumulation of national rulings (least common multiple), and chose the maximum standard. For the first time, the Court of Luxemburg referred to international instruments (treaties etc.) as possible indications for the contents of communitarian law.

The European Convention on human rights provided a European minimum standard. As in the constitutional law of the Member-States, fundamental rights and liberties can be seen as absolute prerogatives in the communitarian law order. Some limits might be justified by "objectives of the general interest pursued by the Community, if the substance of these rights is not impaired" ("Hauer decision, 13 December 1979). These limits must fulfil certain conditions, such as proportionality of the intervention in relation to the intended objective, a principle inspired by German law. So it was possible to formulate the contours of a communitarian Rule of Law. This encompasses a number of rules and principles, concentrated around the economic dimensions of the European Community. They have common characteristics with principles of the European Convention: efficacy of adequate procedures; right of access to a judge; respect for the rights of the defence; principle of legal security; principle of proportionality; principle of protection against arbitrary or disproportionate interventions of public authorities (Morin, 1996, p.239). In the "Johnston case" (15 May 1986), a community directive was contradicted by national law depriving a person of his right to bring his case before a jurisdiction. The solicitor general argued that the right of access to a judge was inherent in the Rule of Law. Although necessities of public order might induce a State to modulate jurisdictional control, it could not, being a Member State of the CEE as Community of Law, impair this right of access to a judge.

The Court of Luxemburg soon accentuated the contradictory character of procedures for tribunals "de droit commun" and administrative organs as the CEEA Committee (Decision UNECTEP, 15 October 1961). Since the "Decision Hoffmann-LaRoche" (13 February 1979), it is obvious that the rights of the defence are valid as a fundamental principle of community law, applicable also to the European Commission itself. The same applies to the principle of legal security and its sub-principles. This principle asks for clear and precise texts, especially also in fiscal matters ("Decision Société Gondrand, 19 July 1981). The Luxemburg Court in its "Farranto Decision" (18 February 1975) stated that the decision of a public authority must be communicated in a language which is understood by the person for whom this decision is meant. The publicity of a decision has to be sufficient, otherwise it cannot be made operative ("Racke Decision", 1959). A community act cannot be operative at a date before its publication, exceptional cases excluded ("Decision Kent Kirk", 10 July 1984). Community institutions have to exercise their competencies within a reasonable time. Legal security implies that one has to be protected against all arbitrary modifications of community rulings without preceding warning and with direct effect (legitimate confidence). The proportionality principle was applied in communitarian law. The European Communities have to pursue objectives with the most favourable conditions and the least possible sacrifices for citizens ("Klockner/Hoesch Decision", 13 July 1962). Community institutions have to take care not to impose upon economic actors more than is necessary to realise objectives ("Balkan Decision", 24 October 1973). Economic fundamental rights in the EU are protected by characteristic principles of the Rule of Law. The rights of property and free exercise of commerce, labour or profession are "immanent barriers". For the Luxemburg Court these are part of communitarian law.

The principle of protection against arbitrary or disproportionate interventions by public authorities stands out. Structural principles of the European Communities such as primacy of the law and direct effect penetrate into the internal law of the Member-States, from which these are sometimes derived, so there is a dynamic process of reciprocal penetration of law principles between European Union and Member-States. This osmosis or convergence of law principles is a creative process absorbing the traditions of Member-States in Western Europe. The principles which can be deduced from the Treaties and the constitutional law of Member-States are imperative norms of communitarian law, so the "État de droit" is "ius cogens" for Member-States of the European Union. Adherence to the Council of Europe and European Convention of human rights is seen as an important condition for candidate-members in the European Union. Why should the European Union not adhere to the European Convention, so unifying European law? This would bring the European Union and the Court of Luxemburg under jurisdiction of the Court of Strasbourg for human rights. The Court of Luxemburg elaborated economic law, and by using principles such as juridical security, legitimate confidence and proportionality, has brought the level of protection to a higher level in this field. The Treaty of Maastricht effected a solution by conciliating the two systems, with integration of the European Convention into the communitarian law order.

Article F, par.2 states: "The Union respects fundamental rights, as they are guaranteed by the European Convention ... and as they come from the common constitutional traditions of Member-States, as general principles of communitarian law". When the European Union is enlarged with countries in Central or Eastern Europe, there will be problems, because of the difference in law traditions in these countries (Morin, 1996, p.245). The Fall of the

Berlin Wall in 1989 and the subsequent collapse of the Communist regimes in Central and Eastern Europe created a completely different situation. Some twenty countries knocked on the door of European organisations. An important step towards convergence was set with the Helsinki Accords (1975) and the creation of the Conference for Security and Co-operation in Europe (CSCE) of which USSR and its satellites were member from the beginning (Decaux, 1992). This habituated participants to investigation of their behaviour regarding fundamental rights, in spite of the principle of non-intervention in internal affairs. The CSCE-method implied that no country was excluded and that there was no juridically binding commitment. It was necessary for the climate which would enable a thaw between the two blocks. At the Vienna Conference (1988 and 1989), the humanitarian dimension was elaborated by preparations for legislation of human rights. This was accelerated by the Copenhagen Conference (June 1990).

Participating countries affirmed that protection of human rights and fundamental liberties are essential tasks of the State, and that they would support the principles of justice which are the fundament of a constitutional state. This implied that public authorities in these countries subjected themselves to constitution and laws; an effective system of appeal against administrative decisions; independence of judges and solicitors; impartial jurisdiction; the right of everybody to an equitable process and the defence counsel of his own choice; presumption of innocence, and other guarantees. France was always prominently active in this process of European law creation. In the "Charte de Paris pour une nouvelle Europe" (21 November 1990), participating States confirmed that they would accept engagements in the sphere of human rights, constitutional state and democracy. In Moscow (September 1991), one of the most elaborate documents about principles of the Rule of Law was produced. More detailed than the European Convention, explicitly giving operational indications as to how to organise independence of jurisdictions. All candidates to the CSCE (since 1995 OSCE) had to subscribe to the Final Helsinki Act, "Charte de Paris" and all other documents of the CSCE. Serious and repeated violations of these engagements can bring suspension of participation of a State. This was the case with former Yugoslavia when civil war took the form of "ethnic cleansing" in May 1992. Events of 1989 brought a series of new candidacies for the Council of Europe. Experiences with Greece, Spain and Portugal had brought about an elaborated system of conditions for candidates. A status as special invitee, less exacting than complete adherence, has been given to the Soviet Union, Poland, Hungary, Czechoslovakia and Yugoslavia since 1989. In 1995, the following countries had this status: Albania, Belorussia, Bosnia-Herzegovina, Croatia, Macedonia, Moldavia, Russia and the Ukraine. Membership was granted to Hungary, Poland, Bulgaria, Estonia, Latvia, Lithuania, the Czech Republic, Romania, Slovakia and Slovenia, all bound also by the European Convention.

Committees of the Council of Europe Assembly give decisive impact to reports about the juridical order in a given country and its conformity to norms of the Council of Europe. Some reports show that membership of the Council of Europe and adherence to the European Convention sometimes form only the first stage on the road to the Rule of Law. Resolution 1031 (1994) refers to sanctions as formulated in the Council of Europe Statute in case of persistent shortcomings to accepted engagements. One condition for adherence to the Council of Europe is that a country is European, but where does Europe end? At the Helsinki Top (July 1992), heads of state and OSCE proclaimed the formation of a community of free and democratic States from Vancouver to Vladivostok. OSCE never was exclusively European. The "Report about the enlargement of the Council of Europe" (10 June 1994) concluded that the time had come for the Council of Europe to put limits on its enlargement. Europe does not have boundaries formally fixed by international law in the East. In this Report the Committee concluded that the Europe of the Council of Europe extends as far as its principles (pluralist democracy, constitutional state, human rights) can be applied, but it is recognised that it is not possible to apply the criteria of the European tradition everywhere in the world. In this Report, it was proposed to use the summit of the Ural Mountains as a demarcation line between Europe and Asia (not as a boundary in the sense of international law). The idea was General de Gaulle's.

As has been argued before, the West based the value put upon the rights of the individual person on its Judaeo-Christian heritage and the natural law conception deriving from it. Later, rationalised under the influence of Roman law conceptions and Greek philosophy, the law conception was secularised during the 17th and 18th centuries. The English Rule of Law and the French "État de droit" were instruments in this process by which appeal to adequate jurisdiction was made possible, and which created institutions to control the power of public authorities and to hold these within limits which have become ever more restrictive. Although the movement to domesticate public power dates back to before the philosophy of individual rights, human rights and "État de droit" are indissolubly intertwined. Techniques and mechanisms of the constitutional state can be seen as the instrumental side of fundamental rights, necessary to habituate public authorities to an adequate discipline. Other, sometimes older, civilisations than the Western civilisation have developed their own criteria of justice for the exercise of public authority, but the spread of Western juridical systems all over the world as an accompanying phenomenon of colonisation and commercial activities had a dominant impact (Mommsen/de Moor, 1992). Development of more humane conceptions, based on the principle of the pre-eminence of law, had to be conquered against resistance of public authorities and conceptions about absolute sovereignty for the monarchy. It took a long time to make public authorities in power accept human rights, with terrible revolutions in England, the American colonies and France, and later in other countries.

It is true that in the West there are several versions of the "État de droit". The British Rule of Law, in so far as it is applied to executive and administrative power, is based only upon the conscience of parliamentarians with regard to the legislator. There is as yet no control of constitutionality in Great-Britain. In many countries, American and French models have been followed by constitutionalising "Bills of Rights". In France, proclamation of the "Déclaration des droits de l'homme et du citoyen" (1789) preceded the establishment of an "État de droit" by some decades. It lasted until 1970, when the "bloc de constitutionalité" was imposed. Although constitutionalism makes the "État de droit" more complete, when the fundamental law is effectively applied, it depends on the political culture of a country to bring about pre-eminence of law even without constitutionalism. There are other differences between the Western systems of law, as in administration and penal law (accusatory or inquisitory trial). Differences are tending to be reduced in Europe, due to the Court of Strasbourg. An essential part of the Western model is a jurisdictional authority which is independent from other public authorities (separation of powers). This independence is crucial for effective application of the principles of an "État de droit". Discussions about risks of a government of judges or "hégémonie judiciaire" are going on. In most modern States, separation of powers is not applied in the relations between legislative power and executive power as supposed in the conception of Montesquieu.

## 8.9. Beyond the Treaty of Amsterdam. Towards a European Constitution

In the ongoing European debate about European democratic culture, two organising principles often confront each other: federalism and confederalism. The EU has federalist features (direct effect of European law, autonomous European institutions) and confederalist characteristics (intergovernmental structures). When one takes a nationalistic principle as starting-point (one Nation-State, one people, and one culture), one might qualify Europe as a kind of European Nation-State as ideal (or ideal-type), but is that wholly consistent for a society as multicultural as the EU is? In a confederalist setting, the EU would be a collection of Nation-States, only accountable to their own national parliament as elected representatives of the nation. Then the European Parliament, being redundant, would seem a rather curious institution. The EU is a sui generis institutional construction for which a federalist principle was recognised, the "subsidiarity principle". The treaties of Maastricht and Amsterdam acknowledge subsidiarity as a crucial guideline. On reflection, the EU proves to be a federal construction based upon co-sovereignty. Reinforcement of the powers of the European Parliament is often seen as necessary to solve the problem of the democratic deficit. Probably a system of two houses would be an adequate improvement: a directly elected Assembly (representing the peoples of the EU), and a "Sénat" (representing national governments). The EU had a crisis, after celebrating the introduction of the euro in January 1999, and before preparing decision-making about institutional deepening and adherence of new Member-States. This was manifest with the collective resignation of the European Commission (EC). This had never happened before in the history of EEC or EU, and politicians and officials feared lack of control with regard to the near future. It happened in response to the promise of the EC in the European Parliament that it would act on the conclusions of an independent committee inquiring into accusations of fraud, nepotism and corruption inside the EC. The Middelhoek Committee made a devastating report, especially with regard to the French commissioner, Edith Cresson. There had been rumours about widespread corruption in the EC earlier. In the autumn of 1998 it was proven that Cresson had made serious mistakes, serious enough to be fired in a normal democratic procedure. Cresson, denying everything, refused to resign. She made use of the prevailing arrangement that only the EC as a whole (20 commissioners) could be fired. If Cresson had resigned to save face, as would be usual in a normal democracy, it would have been an unremarkable incident. Because she arrogantly stuck to her position, she caused a serious crisis. An important factor in the recent problems in the EC was exposed. The EC has engaged itself in too many new policy areas, without fulfilling conditions of sufficient expertise, budget and adequate control of the implementation carousel.

This EU crisis was grist to the mill of Euro-sceptics and serious critics of the European construction. The EU was dismissed as a corrupt institution. This institution, (mis)using taxpayers money, is not accountable in the last instance to taxpayers. Even the European Council is not really accountable. The European Parliament, with reduced competencies and powers (democratic deficit) can only fire the EC as a whole. So it was made manifest that the prevailing institutional set-up had drawbacks. One of the most crucial deficits is that there is no effective system of responsibility and accountability for those having a job in which public authority is at stake (politicians and civil servants). It is argued that the existing democratic deficit in the EU can be eliminated when the European Parliament has comparable powers to national parliaments in Member-States, but that is not enough. European democratic culture asks for an institutional structure, in which all functionaries representing public authority (politicians and officials) are made personally fully responsible and accountable for their activities. This can be seen as a challenging institutional innovation, needed as a remedy for the widespread irresponsibility virus. After long and acrimonious negotiations, the European Council at last agreed, at the Berlin Summit (24/26 March 1999), on a compromise package (budgetary, farm and regional policy reforms). This paved the way for expansion of the EU with new Member-States, giving the EU a clear financial framework. A budget of 4.14 billion euro was set aside for new members in 2002, rising to 14.21 billion in 2006. The EU "Agenda 2000" was amended significantly to make the package more acceptable for farmers. French President Chirac upheld their subsidised position. He saw to it that plans for far-reaching cuts in support for cereals and beef were dropped, and that reform of the milk market was postponed. The EU budget was fixed at 268.1 billion euro. There was a modest reform of EU revenues, linked more to GNP, less to value added tax (VAT). The UK rescued its huge subsidy (paid by the other 14 Member-States), the budget rebate won by Thatcher earlier (1984). This mechanism will remain until the new arrangements expire in 2006. In 2000, 16.1% of EU finances came from duties and levies; 35.4% from VAT; and 48.4% from the GNP base (Laffan, 1997).

The EU summit conference in Helsinki (10-11 December 1999) was seen as a crucial step. For the first time since the failure of the project for a European Defence Community in the fifties, the EU now decided to form a military intervention corps (50,000 to 60,000 men and women) able to take action in case of crisis. Undoubtedly, the recent drama in Kosovo brought Member-States of the EU to the conclusion that something had to be done. In comparison to the armed forces of US and NATO, this intervention corps is only a minor military tool. With regard to the number of recognised candidates for the status of Member-State, decisions were taken. As expected, the following 12 countries got this status: Poland; Estonia; Latvia; Lithuania; Czech Republic; Slovakia; Hungary; Slovenia; Romania; Bulgaria; Malta; and Cyprus. It was a surprise that Turkey was also acknowledged as candidate. Turkey has been trying to get this status for a long time. Since the activities of Kamal Atatürk (1880-1938), the first president of the Turkish Republic from 1923 on (Mango, 2000), a part of the Turkish leadership has been trying to make Turkey more European. The decision about Turkey's candidacy was by no means undisputed, for a number of reasons. Turkey is criticised severely for its violation of minority rights (Kurds, etc.) and of human rights in general. According to criteria as used in Western democracies, Turkey cannot be qualified as a democracy. To become a Member-State, Turkey has to comply with many criteria. Its constitution must be adapted fundamentally. This means meddling with the dominant position of the army. Islam is the sole recognised religion, and all inhabitants are seen as Turks. Reforms as claimed by the EU are seen as a dictate from the Christian West with regard to Orientalist-Islamic culture. Estimates by the government of Turkey about Turkey's complete status as EU Member-State in the year 2004 are optimistic. Making Turkey adapt itself to the EU criteria will take more time.

Difficulties with regard to the other 12 candidates for membership of the EU should not be underestimated either. Fulfilling the so-called "Copenhagen criteria", formulated by the EU for making candidates acceptable as Member-State, is no easy target for all of them. Expansion of the EU with all 13 candidates would mean that the number of EU inhabitants would grow by some 45%. The EU of 15 Member-States (375 million inhabitants) would grow to the EU of 28 Member-States with some 545 million inhabitants. Economic backwardness of these candidate states as compared to the current EU is formidable, especially as it is combined with backwardness in the sphere of democracy and social conditions. Huge sums of money are needed to help these countries to fulfil the criteria for entrance. A specific problem is the huge bill for EU agricultural subsidies. France still profits the most: 9.4 billion euro on a total budget of 43.6 billion euro. When France pays 100 euro to the EU common agricultural policy, the French farmers get about 130 euro. So the new neo-Gaullist Government-Raffarin II (2002-) is stubbornly opposing all proposals to reduce this subsidy (as De Gaulle did before). The European Commission proposed the reduction of EU agricultural subsidies first, before making candidates new Member-States, otherwise these subsidies could not be paid. The EU of the 15 has bound itself to pay a lot for making the EU grow. Huge sums of financial development aid to Central and Eastern European countries are not the sole question. The urgency of the EU's institutional deepening is increasingly acknowledged. There is quite a difference between an institutional set-up for six Member-States of the EC (basically the same as contemporary EU institutions) and the institutional architecture as needed for an EU of 28 Member-States.

The existing EU of 15 Member-States has to reorganise its institutional structures before new Member-States can be admitted. It is a huge task to enable the EU to accept new Member-States.

At the Intergovernmental Conference in Nice (8-11 December 2000) decisions were scheduled about institutional arrangements (weighting of votes for Member-States; composition and size of the European Commission; extension of qualified majority voting; weighting of votes for Member-States in the European Council). The left-overs from the Treaty of Amsterdam were handled unsatisfactorily. Decisions about the definite composition of the European Commission were postponed until after the extension of the EU towards 27 Member-States. Extension of qualified majority voting was meagre, and decision-making about weighting of votes in the European Council was disgusting for its narrow-minded nationalism. Power-play dominated this EU top. The EU top at Nice will not get an honourable mention in history. France was criticised for its poor preparation of this EU top. After the conference, the text of the Treaty of Nice as decided, had to be adapted because of a fault with regard to the blocking minority in the European Council. In the last hours of the marathon meeting, Lithuania got one and Romania two votes extra, but this was not adapted in the text. Before the turn of the year, the Member-States agreed to adapt the text. It took two years to ratify the adapted EU treaty. Entry of a Member-State after that will make ratification by national parliaments necessary. Probably the first new Member-State will enter the EU not earlier than 2004. Negotiations with Poland, the Czech Republic, Hungary, Estonia, Slovakia and Cyprus will be continued. Negotiations have already started with other candidates. Although disappointment prevails about the results of Nice, there were some results. After 30 years of debate, a decision was taken about the juridical statute for the European company. A "Charte des droits fondamentaux de l'Union européenne" was proclaimed, after adoption by national governments, European Commission and European Parliament. This Charter is no more than a declaration and not juridically binding. A lot of work has to be done. The relationship between the Convention for Protection of Human Rights and Fundamental Freedoms (Court of Strasbourg), and rulings of the EU (Court in Luxemburg) has to be regulated. The EU should be a party to the Convention.

It is said that after Nice, under French presidency of the European Council, a specific model of Europe disappeared. Henceforth, Europe will no longer be a "jardin à la francaise". Germany won the diplomatic war at Nice. It became formally the most prominent Member-State. Due to its number of inhabitants (82 million), some 22 million inhabitants more than the second, Great Britain, with France as the third Member-State. A majority in the European Council will be effective only if the populations of the Member-States involved represent at least 62% of the European population. So 38% of the representatives of the EU population is enough to block decision-making. There are 37 combinations of three Member-States that can block decision-making. And 33 of these 37 combinations are not possible without Germany. Four greater Member-States can organise 86 combinations, and 38 of them are not possible without Germany. So-called "Latin" Member-States, France, Spain and Italy, could block decision-making by combining their votes. The final decision on distribution of votes in the European Council is highly disputable. The Belgian premier Verhofstadt, threatening to use his veto against the Treaty of Nice, rightly argued that the method for distribution of votes logically, consistently and justifiable should be equal for all Member-States. Instead, the four greater Member-States (Germany, Great Britain, France and Italy) got an equal number of votes, in spite of a huge difference in the number of inhabitants between Germany and the others. As for the smaller Member-States, the number of inhabitants was used proportionally. This sacrifice was needed to suit arrogant France, sticking to its equality-obsession between France and Germany, but there is a possibility to restore this failure of Nice (Neunreither, 2001).

To further a genuine European democratic culture, many are arguing for a European Constitution. In fact, the EU is based upon treaties between governments of Nation-States, so the ideas of citizens are only indirectly, via very long lines of representation, represented in these basic institutional documents. Creating a Europe of the citizens needs renewed formal recognition of the human rights of all inhabitants in the EU and guarantees for adequate, democratically controlled functioning of public institutions. But it is also necessary that citizens are more personally involved, as Europeans. All inhabitants of the EU, being world-citizens, have to be considered as having a composite identity. Language is an essential of culture. Of course, the time when the elite of Europe spoke French is gone (Fumaroli, 2001). In the EU of 15 Member-States, there are 11 official languages, implying that rules and regulation have to be enacted in these languages. Extension of the EU with 13 new candidates for membership brings the total of official languages to 22. So the EU has to be considered as more than a common market with one currency and a confederacy of national States, the EU is also a multi-lingual entity. These languages are crucial for the development of the Rule of Law in the whole EU. Every individual has a local/regional, national and European identity. To further this European identity, every European citizen should have a book with the European Constitution, in his or her own language. The Napoleonic codes, pioneering codification two centuries ago, might be seen as paradigmatic example for popularising the idea that the Rule of Law is relevant for every citizen. Realising a European Constitution is one step to bring the Rule of Law closer by. A Universal Declaration of the Rule of Law is another step (Bouloukos/Dakin, 2001).

At the EU Top at Laeken in Belgium, the "Declaration of Laeken" (15 December 2001) was adopted by the Heads of State and Premiers of the 15 Member-States. This Declaration ascertained that the EU is a success, but that there is a lot of work to be done to enable the EU for the coming period. Some issues are enumerated as urgent points on the EU agenda. Reforming the EU is seen as top priority. This implies a better division of competencies of public institutions. The Declaration formulates a series of questions about how to further democratic legitimacy and transparency of EU institutions, efficacy of decision-making, and functioning of institutions in a EU with about thirty Nation-States. Then ideas are mentioned about renewing the constitutional base of the EU as laid down in existing treaties. This in view of the fundamental issue of possibly giving the EU and citizens of its Member-States a constitutional text, a European Constitution. To prepare this complicated institutional issue for the coming Intergovernmental Conference, the European Council decided to organise a Convention of the most important participants in the debate about the future of the EU. Former French President Giscard d'Estaing was appointed president of this Convention, and G. Amato and J.L. Dehaene as vice-presidents. To broaden the public debate as far as possible, and to involve all citizens, a Forum is opened for organisations that represent civil society. This might become the first treaty in the world that is concluded by governments and parliaments after preparing a Convention together with representatives of civil society in an open debate. In relation to renewing the institutionalising of the European Union, it is useful to unravel a popular misunderstanding about the loss of sovereignty of the Member-States of the European Union.

It has been asserted more than once that the process of European integration is bringing about the decline of the sovereign state, and promotes a European "SuperState". Indeed, Member-States have handed over powers to EU institutions to a degree which is without precedent in history, even in fields seen as essential for the sovereignty of the state. Community law is an "independent legal order", autonomously determining effects of European Community law in the legal orders of the Member-States (European Court of Justice in the Van Gend and Loos and Costa Enel cases). According to MacCormick (1999), sovereignty in the EU is something akin to virginity, a property lost by one but not gained by another. It is to be hoped that EU reform will not be saddled with improper reasoning about loss of sovereignty. Werner/De Wilde (2001, p.304): "The broad and far-reaching transfer of powers to the EU does not mean, however, that the EU itself has become a new sovereign state. The reason for this is clear and compelling – the EU does not claim a sovereign status and is not recognized as a sovereign state by other members of international society. …What about the member states? Have they lost their sovereignty during the process of integration? Is sovereignty indeed something akin to virginity, which is not gained by the EU, but still lost by the member states? …we should wonder whether relevant audiences accept their claims to sovereignty. As far as the status of the member states in international society is concerned, it is safe to conclude that the process of integration has not affected their sovereign status."

Suggestions have been made to install a European Constituent Assembly, adopting a draft for a European Constitution. Why not take the citizens of the Member-States seriously by subjecting such a draft to a referendum procedure first? And if a draft is not accepted by the necessary majority, for example because it is thought to be not democratic enough, why not try again with a new round of a referenda, until there is a draft legitimised with the necessary majority? This would bring constitutional democracy in the EU closer to its citizens. The European Constitution should have adequate contents, with guarantees for the human rights of all EU inhabitants, and for a democratic functioning of all institutions representing public authority. The European Rule of Law already has a growing impact upon the daily lives of citizens, organisations and corporations in EU Member-States, and upon the functioning of all working in the name of public authority, both politically elected officials and civil servants. So why not take the Idea of Public Authority more seriously? Developments in Europe, especially on the continent, are deeply influenced by the cultural emanation of France. The same holds for the institutional set-up of the European Union and its institutional arrangements, predominantly of French making. The European Union is a "sui generis" institutional phenomenon. "The ambiguity of political space in Europe has to do with the unusual nature of the European Union. The European Community makes binding decisions but the symbol of its enforcement powers is the judge rather than the police officer or the soldier." (Sbragia, 2000, p.220). As elaborated earlier, the specific character of public authorities is determined by the fact that public authorities can make and enforce binding decisions for society. It makes sense to stress this point. Sbragia (2000, p.221): "Although the literature on comparative policy studies largely ignores it, the national state employs a coercive apparatus which underlies much of its other activities. The state always enjoys the implicit threat of criminal and police sanctions; it is the ability to use those sanctions that differentiates it from other actors in any network." The foregoing analysis makes it plausible that French Public Management of Society is especially relevant for its contributions to universal knowledge and know-how. France has been a pioneer in societal regulation by means of law. It is appropriate to deal with two crucial dimensions of institutionalising Public Management of Society in chapter 10: The Rule of Law and the Idea of Public Authority.

**References**

French
Abélès, M., La vie quotidienne au Parlement Européen. (Paris, Hachette, 1992).
Aron, R., Lerner, D., dir., La Querelle de la CED. (Paris, A.Colin, 1956).
Barber, S., Le Principe de subsidiarité et son controle. (Nancy, Centre européen universitaire, 1993).
Baron, G., Évaluation, participation, apprentissage dans l'action publique. Étude de l'évaluation d'un programme européen. (Paris, Harmattan, 2001).
Berbiet-Solliec, M., Les Interventions décentralisées en Agriculture. (Essai sur la composante territoriale de la politique agricole. Paris, Harmattan, 1999).
Berger, V., Jurisprudence de la Cour Européen des Droits de l'Homme. (Paris, Sirey, 2000).

Bergères, M.C., Contentieux communautaire. (Paris, PUF, 1989; 1994).
Bertrand, G., La prise de décision dans l'Union Européenne. (Paris, DF, 1998).
Bloes, R., Le "Plan Fouché" et le problème de l'Europe politique. (Bruges, Collège d'Europe, 1970).
Blumann, C., La fonction législative communautaire. (Paris, LGDJ, 1995).
Boissieu, C. de, dir., Les Mutations de l'Économie Mondiale. (Paris, Economica, 2000).
Bouckaert, G., Timsit, G., Administrations et Globalisations. (Bruxelles, IISA, 2000).
Boulouis, J., Droit institutionnel de l'Union Européenne. (Paris, Montchrestien, 1997).
Boulouis, J., Chevallier, R.M., Grands arrêts de la Cour de Justice des Communautés européennes. (Paris, Dalloz, 1994).
Boulouis, J., Damon, M., Contentieux communuataire. (Paris, Dalloz, 1997).
Brugmans, H., L'Idée européenne, 1920-1970. (Bruges, De Tempel, 1970).
Brugmans, H., Prophètes et fondateurs de l'Europe. (Bruges, De Tempel, 1974).
Carbonell, C.O., dir., Une histoire européenne de l'Europe. (Paris, Privat, 1999; 2000).
Clausade, J. de, L'Adaptation de l'administration française à l'Europe. (Paris, DF, 1991).
Cloos, J., et al., Le Traité de Maastricht. (Bruxelles, Bruylant, 1993).
Cohen, E., L'Ordre Économique Mondial. Essai sur les Autorités de Régulation. (Paris, Fayard, 2001).
Cohen, S., Smouts, M.C., dir., La Politique extérieure de Valéry Giscard d'Estaing. (Paris, FNSP, 1985).
Cohen-Tanugi, L., L'Europe en danger. (Paris, Fayard, 1992).
Cohen-Tanugi, L., Le Choix de l'Europe. (Paris, Fayard, 1995).
Colliard, C.A., Institutions des relations internationales. (Paris, Dalloz, 1974).
Colloque Association Justice et Droit, Droits fondamentaux, Institutions, Constitution: Où en est l'Europe? Paris, 2000).
Colloque Nancy, L'État souverain à l'aube du XXIe siècle. (Nancy, Pedone, 1994).
Colloque Paris, Le Traité d'Amsterdam. (Paris, Pedone, 1999).
Colloque Paris, L'Euro, facteur d'avancée de l'Europe. (Paris, Economica, 1999).
Combacau, J., Le Droit des Traités. (Paris, PUF, 1991).
Combacau, J., Sur, S., Droit international public. (Paris, Montchrestien, 1995).
Comité d'histoire de la Sécurité sociale, Un Siècle de Protection Sociale en Europe. (Paris, 2001).
Conseil d'État, L'Adaptation du Droit français au Droit communautaire. (Paris, DF, 1992).
Conseil de l'Europe, Rapport sur la situation des droits de l'homme en Turquie. (Strasbourg, DF, 1992).
Conseil de l'Europe, Combattre la torture en Europe. (Strasbourg, DF, 2002).
Conseil de l'Europe, Quel rôle pour les associations nationales de pouvoirs locaux. (Strasbourg, DF, 2002).
Conseil de l'Europe, Une Europe en évolution. Les flux migratoires au XXe siècle. (Strasbourg, DF, 2002).
Conseil de l'Europe, Droits de l'homme en droit international. (Strasbourg, DF, 2002).
Conseil de l'Europe, Charte sociale européenne. (Strasbourg, DF, 2002).
Conseil de l'Europe, Le Code Européen d'Éthique de la Police. (Strabourg, DF, 2002).
Constantinesco, V., Le Traité d'Amsterdam, réalités et perspectives. (Paris, Pedone, 1999).
Constantinesco, V., et al., dir., Traité instituant la CEE. Commentaire article par article. (Paris, Economica, 1992).
Constantinesco, V., et al., dir., Traité sur l'Union Européenne, signé à Maastricht le 7 février 1992. Commentaire article par article. (Paris, Economica, 1995).
Dalloz (Éditions), Les Impôts en Europe. (Paris, Dalloz, 2002).
Decaux, E., La Conférence sur la Sécurité et la Coopération en Europe. (Paris, PUF, 1992).
Decaux, E., Droit international public. (Paris, Dalloz, 1997).
Decaux, E., dir., Sécurité et coopération en Europe. (Paris, DF, 1992).
De Grauwe, P., Économie de l'intégration monétaire. (Bruxelles, De Boeck Université, 1999).
Dehousse, R., La Cour de Justice des Communautés européennes. (Paris, Montchrestien, 1998).
Delors, J., La France par l'Europe. (Paris, Grasset, 1988).
Delors, J., Le Principe de subsidiarité. (Maastricht, EIPA, 1991).
Delors, J., L'unité d'un homme. (Paris, Odile Jacob, 1994).
Delort, R., Walter, F., Histoire de l'environnement européen. (Paris, PUF, 2001).
DF, Le droit communautaire de la consommation. Colloque Boulogne-sur-Mer, 14 et 15 janvier 2000. (Paris, CEDECE/DF, 2002).
DF, Démarche communautaire et construction européenne Colloque Poitiers. (Paris, CEDECE/DF, 2002).
DF, L'outil économique en droit international et européen de l'environnement. (Paris, CEDECE/DF, 2002).
Doutriaux, Y., Le Traité sur l'Union Européenne. (Paris, A.Colin, 1992).
Doutriaux, Y., Lequesne, C., Les institutions de l'Union Européenne. (Paris, DF, 1995; 1998; 2000).
Duhamel, A., Une ambition française. (Paris, Plon, 1999).
Duroselle, J.B., L'idée de l'Europe dans l'histoire. (Paris, Denoël, 1965).
Dutheil de la Rochère, J., Introduction au droit de l'Union Européenne. (Paris, Hachette, 1999).
Dutheil de la Rochère, J., Droit au juge, accès à la justice européenne. (Dans: Pouvoirs, pp.123-141, 2001).
Dutheil de la Rochère, J., Colas, B., dir., Organisations internationales à vocation régionale. (Paris, DF, 1995).

Evdokimov, P., L'Orthodoxie. (Paris, Desclée de Brouwer, 1990).
Fitoussi, J.P., dir., Rapport sur l'état de l'Union Européenne. (Paris, FNSP, 1999; 2000; 2001).
FNSP, La Conférence Intergouvernementale. Enjeux et documents. (Paris, 1996).
Fontaine, A., Histoire de la Guerre froide. (Paris, 1967).
Fontaine, P., Jean Monnet, l'inspirateur. (Paris, Grancher, 1988).
Fontaine, P., L'Union Européenne. (Paris, Seuil, 1994).
Fumaroli, M., Quand l'Europe parlait français. (Paris, Éd. de Fallois, 2001).
Gabrieli, F., Europe musulmane. (Paris, Zodiaque, 1983).
Gabrieli, F., Histoire et civilisation de l'Islam en Europe. Arabes et Turcs en Occident du VIIe au XVe siècle. (Paris, Bordas, 1983).
Gabrieli, F., dir., Chroniques arabes des croisades. (Paris, Sindbad, 1996).
Gautron, J.C., Droit européen. (Paris, Dalloz, 1994; 1998).
Gavalda, C., Parléani, G., Traité de droit communautaire des affaires. (Paris, Litec, 1992).
Gavalda, C., Kovar, R., dir., Répertoire de droit communautaire. (Paris, Dalloz, 1992).
Georgel, J., République portugaise, 1974-1995. (Paris, Apogée, 1998).
Georgel, J., L'Italie au XXe siècle (1919-1999). (Paris, DF, 1999).
Georgeon, F., Des Ottomans aux Turcs, naissance d'une nation. (Istanbul, Isis, 1995).
Gerbet, P., La Construction de l'Europe. (Paris, Imprimerie nationale, 1983; 1994).
Gerbet, P., La Naissance du Marché Commun. (Bruxelles, Complexe, 1987).
Gerkrath, J., L'émergence d'un droit constitutionnel pour l'Europe. (Bruxelles, Université, 1997).
Guigou, E., Pour les Européens. (Paris, Flammarion, 1994).
Guilhaudis, J.F., L'Europe en transition. (Paris, Montchrestien, 1995; 1998).
Hérisson, P., Les Télécommunications, la Réforme cinq ans après, la Concurrence, la France et l'Europe. (Paris, Sénat, 2002).
Herzog, P., L'Europe Après L'Europe: Les Voies d'une Métamorphose. (Paris, De Boeck Université, 2002).
IEAP, Subsidiarité, défi du changement. (Maastricht, IEAP, 1991; 1993).
IFRI, La stratégie d'influence de l'Union Européenne. (Strasbourg, Institut français des relations internationales, 2002).
Isaac, G., Droit communautaire général. (Paris, Masson, 1994; A.Colin, 1999).
Joliet, R., Le droit institutionnel des Communautés européennes. (Liège, PU, 1986).
Kauffmann, P., L'Euro. (Paris, Dunod/Topos, 1997).
Labouz, M.F., Le Système communautaire européen. (Paris, Berger-Levrault, 1988).
Labouz, M.F., dir., Les Accords de Maastricht et la Construction de l'Union Européenne. (Paris, Montchrestien, 1992).
Lamy, P., L'Europe en Première Ligne. (Paris, Seuil, 2002).
La Serre, F. de, La Grande-Bretagne et la Communauté européenne. (Paris, PUF, 1987).
La Serre, F. de, De la coopération politique européenne à la politique étrangère et le sécurité commune. (Paris, DF, 1992).
La Serre, F. de, Le Traité d'Union Européenne. Spécial Maastricht. (Paris, DF, 1992).
La Serre, F. de, Lequesne, C., Rupnik, J., L'Union Européenne: ouverture à l'Est? (Paris, PUF, 1994).
La Serre, F. de, Leruez, J., Wallace, H., dir., Les Politiques étrangères de la France et de la Grande Bretagne depuis 1945, l'inévitable ajustement. (Paris, FNSP, 1990).
Le Cacheux, J.E., dir., Europe: la nouvelle vague. Perspectives économiques de l'élargissement. (Paris, FNSP, 1996).
Léonard, Y., dir., La France et l'Europe. (Paris, DF, 1990).
Lequesne, C., L'appareil politico-administratif central de la France et la Communauté européenne 1981-1991. (Paris, IEP, 1992).
Lequesne, C., Paris-Bruxelles. Comment se fait la politique européenne de la France. (Paris, FNSP, 1993).
Louis, J.V., L'Ordre Juridique Communautaire. (Luxembourg, CE, 1993; OPOCE, 1996).
Louis, J.V., L'Union Européenne et l'Avenir des Institutions. (Bruxelles, Presses interuniversitaires européennes, 1996).
Loussouarn, Y., L'Internationalisation du droit. (Paris, Dalloz, 1994).
Luchaire, F., dir., La Constitution de l'Europe. (Paris, Montchrestien, 1992).
Manin, P., Les Communautés européennes. L'Union Européenne. (Paris, Pedone, 1993; 1999).
Mélanges G., Levasseur, Droit pénal, droit européen. (Paris, Litec, 1992).
Mendras, H., L'Europe des Européens. Sociologie de l'Europe occidentale. (Paris, Gallimard, 1997).
Miall, H., dir., Les Droits des minorités en Europe. Vers un régime transnational. (Paris, Harmattan, 1997).
Millon-Delsol, C., Le Principe de subsidiarité. (Paris, PUF, 1993).
Monjal, P.Y., Les normes de droit communautaire. (Paris, PUF, 2000).
Monnet, J., Mémoires. (Paris, Fayard, 1976).
Morin, E., Penser l'Europe. (Paris, Gallimard, 1987; 1990).
Morin, J.Y., L'État de droit. Emergence d'un principe de droit international. (La Haye, Nijhoff, 1996).

Mouton, J.D., Soulard, C., La Cour de Justice des Communautés européennes. (Paris, PUF, 1999).
Muller, P., Entre le Local et l'Europe. La Crise du Modèle français de politiques publiques. (Dans: Revue française de science politique, avril 1992).
Nembot, M., Le Glas de la Fonction Publique dans les États d'Afrique Francophone. (Paris, Harmattan, 2000).
Nougayrede, D., Construire l'Impôt en Russie. Réformes Fiscales en URSS et dans la Fédération de Russie de 1987 à 2000. (Paris, Harmattan, 2001).
Pezet, M., Le suivi des affaires communautaires par la délégation: bilan de la neuvième législature et perspectives d'avenir. (Paris, Assemblée nationale, 1993).
Poidevin, R., dir., Histoire des débuts de la construction européenne (mars 1948 – mai 1950). (Bruxelles, Bruylant, 1986).
Poidevin, R., Bariéty, J., Les Relations franco-allemandes (1815-1975). (Paris, A.Colin, 1977).
Pouvoirs, Europe. De la Communauté à l'Union. (Paris, Seuil, 1994).
Pouvoirs, Le Royaume-Uni de Tony Blair. (Paris, DF, 2000).
Pouvoirs, Les Cours Européennes, Luxembourg et Strasbourg. (Paris, Seuil, 2001).
Quermonne, J.L., Le Système politique européen. (Paris, Montchrestien, 1993).
Quermonne, J.L., Le Système politique de l'Union Européenne. (Paris, LGDJ, 1994, 2001).
Quermonne, J.L., La Présidence de l'Union Européenne. (Grenoble, PUG, 1995).
Quermonne, J.L., Le Système de l'Union Européenne. (Paris, Montchrestien, 1998).
Quermonne, J.L., L'Europe en quête de légitimité. (Paris, Presses de Sciences Po, 2001).
Quermonne, J.L., dir., L'Union Européenne en quête d'institutions légitimes et efficaces. (Paris, CGP, 1999).
Raepenbusch, S.V., Droit institutionnel de l'Union et des Communautés. (Bruxelles, De Boeck Université, 1998).
Raimond, J.B., L'état d'avancement des négociations en vue d'élargissement. (Rapport. Paris, Assemblée nationale, 23 juin 1993).
Revol, H., dir., Le Marché Européen de l'Énergie. Enjeux et Conséquences de l'Ouverture. (Paris, Rapport du Sénat, 2001/2002).
Riché, P., Wyplosz, C., L'Union monétaire de l'Europe. (Paris, Seuil, 1993).
Rideau, J., Le Droit des Communautés européennes. (Paris, PUF, 1995).
Rideau, J., Droit institutionnel de l'Union et des Communautés européennes. (Paris, LGDJ, 1996, 1998).
Rideau, J., dir., Les États Membres de l'Union Européenne. (Paris, LGDH, 1997).
Rideau, J., dir., De la Communauté de droit à l'Union de droit. Colloque Nice. (Paris, 2001).
Rideau, J., et al., La France et les Communautés européennes. (Paris, Litec, 1975).
Rideau, J., Charnier, J.L., Code de procédures européennes. (Paris, Litec, 1990).
Rideau, J., Picod, F., Code de procédures communautaires. (Paris, Litec, 1994).
Rouban, L., dir., Le Service Public en Devenir. (Paris, Harmattan, 2000).
Rupnik, J., L'Autre Europe: Crise et Fin du Communisme. (Paris, Seuil, 1993).
Sauron, J.L., L'application du droit de l'Union européenne en France. (Paris, DF, 1995; 2000).
Sauron, J.L., Droit et pratique du contentieux communautaire. (Paris, DF, 1998).
Sauron, J.L., Droit communautaire et décision nationale. (Paris, LGDJ, 1998).
Sauron, J.L., L'administration française et l'Union européenne. (Paris, DF, 2000).
Schuman, R., Pour l'Europe. (Paris, Nagel, 1963).
Simon, D., Le système juridique communautaire. (Paris, PUF, 1997; 1998).
Spaak, P.H., Rapport du Comité intergouvernemental. (Bruxelles, 1956).
Strömholm, S., L'Europe et le Droit. (Paris, PUF, 2002).
Sudre, F., Droit international et européen des droits de l'homme. (Paris, PUF, 1995; 1999).
Sudre, F., Les grands arrêts de la Cour européenne des droits de l'homme. (Paris, PUF, 1997).
Sudre, F., dir., L'Interprétation de la Convention européenne des droits de l'homme. (Bruxelles, Bruylant, 1999).
Sudre, F. et al., Droit communautaire des droits fondamentaux. Receuil des décisions de la CJCE. (Bruxelles, Bruylant, 1999).
Telo, M., dir., Vers une nouvelle Europe? (Bruxelles, Université, 1992).
Telo, M., dir., Démocratie et Construction européenne. (Bruxelles, Université, 1995).
Telo, M., dir., L'Union européenne et les défis de l'élargissement. (Bruxelles, Université, 1995).
Telo, M., Magnette, P., dir., De Maastricht à Amsterdam. (Bruxelles, Complexe, 1998).
TEPSA, L'élargissement de la Communauté: adaptations institutionnelles. (Luxembourg, 1992).
Vandamme, J., Mouton, J.D., dir., L'Avenir de l'Union Européenne. Élargir et approfondir. (Bruxelles, Presses interuniversitaires européennes, 1995).
Van der Eyden, T., Futurs profiles pour le Delta du Rhin aux Pays-Bas et alternatives. (Dans: Les communes et le développement économique et social. La Haye, International Union of Local Authorities, 1971).
Vandersanden, G., Droit des Communautés européennes. (Bruxelles, PU, 1992; 1996).
Vandersanden, G., dir., L'Europe et les Régions. Aspects Juridiques. (Bruxelles, PU, 1997).

Vandersanden, G., Dony, M., dir., La Responsabilité des États Membres en cas de violation du droit communautaire. (Bruxelles, Bruylant, 1997).
Vavakova, B., La Science de la Nation? Les Paradoxes Politiques de la Logique Économique. (Paris, Harmattan, 2001).
Visscher, C. de, Varone, F., Évaluation des Politiques Publiques. Regards Croisés sur la belgique. (Louvain-la-Neuve, Academia-Bruylant, 2001).
Westendorp, C., dir. Rapport (pour le IGC 1996), 1995. (In: La Conférence Inter-gouvernementale. Paris, FNSP, 1996).
Withol de Wenden, C., La Citoyenneté européenne. (Paris, Presses de Sciences Po, 1997).
Withol de Wenden, C., L'Immigration en Europe. (Paris, DF, 1999).

English
Aage, H., ed., Environmental Transition in Nordic and Baltic Countries. (Cheltenham, Elgar, 1998).
Abel, I., et al., Money and Finance in the Transition to a Market Economy. (Cheltenham, Elgar, 1998).
Agh, A., Emerging Democracies in East Central Europe and the Balkans. (Cheltenham, Elgar, 1998).
Ahonen, P., et al., Public Administration in the New Millennium. Some European Scenarios. (Maastricht, EIPA, 2000).
Ahrens, J., Governance and Economic Development. A Comparative Institutional Approach. (Cheltenham, Elgar, 2002).
Aldcroft, D.H., Morewood, S., Economic Change in Eastern Europe since 1918. (Cheltenham, Elgar, 1995).
Aldcroft, D.H., Sutcliffe, A., eds., Europe in the International Economy 1500 to 2000. (Cheltenham, Elgar, 1999).
Allison, J.W.F., A Continental Distinction in the Common Law. A Historical and Comparative Perspective on English Public Law. (Oxford, Clarendon, 1996).
Allott, P., The Crisis of European Constitutionalism. Reflections on the Revolution in Europe. (In: Common Market Law Review, pp.439-490, 1997).
Alter, K.J., Establishing the Supremacy of European Law. The Making of an International Rule of Law in Europe. (Oxford, OUP, 2001).
Alter, K.J., Dehousse, R., Vanberg, G., Law, Political Science and EU Legal Studies. (In: European Union Politics, pp.113-136, 2002).
Amin, A., Hausner, J., eds., Beyond Market and Hierarchy. (Cheltenham, Elgar, 1997).
Andersen, S.S., Eliassen, K.A., eds., Making Policy in Europe. Europeification of National Policymaking. (London, Sage, 1993).
Andersen, S.S., Eliassen, K.A., eds., The European Union. How Democratic is It? (London, Sage, 1995).
Anderson, B., Imagined Communities. Reflections on the Origin and Spread of Nationalism. (London, Verso, 1991).
Anderson, J., German Unification and the Union of Europe. (Cambridge, CUP, 1999).
Anderson, M., Boer, M. den, eds., European Police Co-operation. (Edinburgh, University, 1992).
Anderson, M., Boer, M. den, eds., Policing Across National Boundaries. (London, Pinter, 1994).
Anderson, P., Passages from Antiquity to Feudalism. (London, Verso, 1974).
Anderson, T.H., The United States, Great Britain and the Cold War 1944-1947. (New York, 1981).
Antola, E., The Finnish Integration Strategy: Adaptation with Restrictions. (In: Möttölä, K., Patomäki, H., eds., Facing the Change in Europe: EFTA Countries' Integration Strategies. (Helsinki, Ulkopoliittinen Instituutti, 1989.
Arnull, A., The General Principles of EEC Law and the Individual. (Leicester, Leicester UP, 1990.
Auer, A., Demmke, C., Polet, R., Civil Service in the Europe of Fifteen. (Maastricht, EIPA, 1996).
Backhaus, J.G., Krause, G., eds., Issues in Transformation Theory. (Marburg, Metropolis Verlag, 1997).
Baer, W., Love, J.L., eds., Liberalization and its Consequences. A Comparative Perspective on Latin America and Eastern Europe. (Cheltenham, Elgar, 2000).
Baimbridge, M., Whyman, P., eds., Economic and Monetary Union in Europe. (Cheltenham, Elgar, 2001).
Banaian, K., The Ukrainian Economy since Independence. (Cheltenham, Elgar, 1999).
Barrell, R., ed., Economic Convergence and Monetary Union in Europe. (London, 1992).
Barry, D., Toward the Rule of Law in Russia? (New York, Sharpe, 1992).
Bartelson, J., Three Concepts of Globalization. (In: International Sociology, pp.180-196, 2000).
Bartelson, J., The Critique of the State. (Cambridge, CUP, 2001).
Beatson, J., Tridimas, T., New Directions in European Public Law. (Oxford, Hart, 1998).
Bell, J., English Law and French Law, not so different? (In: Current Legal Problems, vol.48, 1995).
Bell, J., The Political Economy of Reform in Post-Communist Poland. (Cheltenham, Elgar, 2001).
Bergeijck, P.A.G. van, et al., eds., The Economics of the Euro Area. (Cheltenham, Elgar, 2000).
Berglund, S., Aarebrot, F.H., The Political History of Eastern Europe in the 20th Century. (Cheltenham, Elgar, 1997).
Berglund, S., Dellenbrant, J.A., eds., The New Democracies in Eastern Europe. (Cheltenham, Elgar, 1994).

Berglund, S., et al., The Handbook of Political Change in Eastern Europe. (Cheltenham, Elgar, 1996).
Berglund, S., et al., Challenges to Democracy. Eastern Europe Ten Years After the Collapse of Communism. (Cheltenham, Elgar, 2001).
Bertrand, G., et al., European Futures. Five Possible Scenarios for 2010. (Cheltenham, Elgar, 2000).
Bird, G., ed., Economic Reform in Eastern Europe. (Cheltenham, Elgar, 1992).
Biro, A.M., Kovacs, P., eds., Diversity in Action. Local Public Management of Multi-Ethnic Communities in Central and Eastern Europe. (Budapest, Local Government and Public Service Reform initiative, 2001).
Bjerke, B., Business Leadership and Culture. National Management Styles in the Global Economy. (Cheltenham, Elgar, 2000).
Black, J., European Warfare, 1660-1815. (New Haven, Yale UP, 1994).
Black, J., Convergence or Divergence? Britain and the Continent. (London, 1994).
Black, J., A New History of England. (Gloucestershire, Sutton, 2000).
Blazyca, G., Rapacki, R., eds., Poland into the New Millennium. (Cheltenham, Elgar, 2001).
Blejes, M.I., Coricelli, F., The Making of Economic Reform in Eastern Europe. (Cheltenham, Elgar, 1995).
Bloom, W., Personal Identity, National Identity and International Relations. (Cambridge, CUP, 1990).
Bluffstone, R., Larson, B.A., eds., Controlling Pollution in Transition Economies. (Cheltenham, Elgar, 1997).
Bonin, J.P., et al., Banking in Transition Economies. (Cheltenham, Elgar, 1998).
Bonin, J.P., Székely, I.P., eds., The Development and Reform of Financial Systems in Central and Eastern Europe. (Cheltenham, Elgar, 1994).
Bouckaert, G., et al., A Potential Governance Agenda for Finland. (Helsinki, Minixstry of Finance, 2000).
Boulokos, A.C., Dakin, B., Toward a Universal Declaration of the Rule of Law: Implications for Criminal Justice and Sustainable Development. (In: International Journal of Contemporary Sociology, pp.145-162, 2001).
Brake, W. te, Making History. Ordinary People in European Politics, 1500-1700. (Berkeley, University of California Press, 1997).
Brezinski, H., Fritsch, M., eds., The Economic Impact of New Firms in Post-Socialist Countries. (Cheltenham, Elgar, 1996).
Brezinski, H., Fritsch, M., eds., The Emergence and Evolution of Markets. (Cheltenham, Elgar, 1997).
Brezinski, H., et al., eds., The Microeconomics of Transformation and Growth. (Cheltenham, Elgar, 1998).
Bridges, B., Europe and the Challenge of the Asia Pacific. (Cheltenham, Elgar, 1999).
Bristow, J.A., The Bulgarian Economy in Transition. (Cheltenham, Elgar, 1996).
Brittan, L., The Europe We Need. (London, 1994).
Brivati, B., Jones, H., eds., From Reconstruction to Integration. Britain and Europe since 1945. (Leicester, University, 1993).
Brown, J.F., Eastern Europe and Communist Rule. (Durham, N.C., 1988).
Bukowski, C., Racz, B., eds., The Return of the Left in Post-Communist States. (Cheltenham, Elgar, 1999).
Bull, H., The Anarchical Society. A Study of Order in World Politics. (London, Macmillan, 1977).
Bulmer, S., et al., eds., The United Kingdom and EC Membership Evaluated. (London, Pinter, 1992).
Bulmer, S., Wessels, W., The European Council. Decision-making in European Politics. (London, Macmillan, 1987; 1988).
Burlamaqui, L., et al., eds., Institutions and the Role of the State. (Cheltenham, Elgar, 2000).
Burley, A.M., Mattli, W., Europe before the Court. (In: International Organization, pp.41-76, 1993).
Buti, M., et al., eds., Taxation, Welfare and the Crisis of Unemployment in Europe. (Cheltenham, Elgar, 2001).
Butler, M., Europe: More than a Continent. (London, Heinemann, 1986).
Carlsnaes, W., Smith, S., eds., European Foreign Policy. The EC and Changing Perspectives in Europe. (London, Sage, 1995).
Carpenter, M., Jefferys, S., Management, Work and Welfare in Western Europe. (Cheltenham, Elgar, 2000).
Carr, F., Massey, A., eds., Public Policy in the New Europe. Eurogovernance in Theory and Practice. (Cheltenham, Elgar, 1999).
Casey, B., Gold, M., Social Partnership and Economic Performance. The Case of Europe. (Cheltenham, Elgar, 2000).
Christensen, T., Laegreid, P., Administrative Reform Policy: The Case of Norway. (In: International Review of Administrative Sciences, pp.457-484, 1998).
Church, C.H., Hendriks, G., Continuity and Change in Contemporary Europe. (Cheltenham, Elgar, 1995).
Church, C.H., Pinnemore, D., European Union and European Community. (London, 1994).
Clarke, S., The Formation of a Labour Market in Russia. (Cheltenham, Elgar, 1999).
Clarke, S., ed., Management and Industry in Russia. (Cheltenham, Elgar, 1995).
Clarke, S., ed., Conflict and Change in the Russian Industrial Enterprise. (Cheltenham, Elgar, 1996).
Clarke, S., ed., The Russian Enterprise in Transition. Case Studies. (Cheltenham, Elgar, 1996).
Clarke, S., ed., Labour Relations in Transition. Wages, Employment and Industrial Conflict in Russia. (Cheltenham, Elgar, 1996).

Clarke, S., ed., Structural Adjustment without Mass Unemployment? Lessons from Russia. (Cheltenham, Elgar, 1998).
Cockfield Report. (Brussels, EC, 1985).
Coffey, P., The EC and the United States. (London, Pinter, 1993).
Colchester, N., Buchan, D., Europe Relaunched. Truths and Illusions on the Way to 1992. (London, Hutchinson, 1990).
Considine, J.I., Kerr, W.A., The Russian Oil Economy. (Cheltenham, Elgar, 2002).
Cook, P., et al., eds., Privatization, Enterprise Development and Economic Reform. (Cheltenham, Elgar, 1998).
Coombes, D., Verheijen, T., eds., Public Management Reform. Comparative Experiences from East and West. (Brussels, European Commission, 1997).
Cooper, R.N., Gacs, J., eds., Trade Growth in Transition Economies. Export Impediments for Central and Eastern Europe. (Cheltenham, Elgar, 1997).
Cooter, R.D., The Strategic Constitution. (Princeton, Princeton UP, 2001).
Corbett, R., The Treaty of Maastricht. A Comprehensive Reference Guide. (London, Longmans, 1993).
Corte-Real, I., et al., Administrations in Transition. Modernisation of Public Administration in Four Countries: Portugal, the Netherlands, Ireland and France. (Maastricht, EIPA, 2000).
Coulson, A., ed., Local Government in Eastern Europe. (Cheltenham, Elgar, 1995).
Cox, T., Mason, B., Social and Economic Transformation in East Central Europe. Institutions, Property Relations and Social Interests. (Cheltenham, Elgar, 1999).
Craig, L.A., Fisher, D., The European Macroeconomy. Growth, Integration and Cycles, 1500-1913. (Cheltenham, Elgar, 2000).
Crawford, M., One Money for Europe? The Economics and Politics of Maastricht. (London, Macmillan, 1996).
Csaba, L., The Capitalist Revolution in Eastern Europe. (Cheltenham, Elgar, 1995).
Csanadi, M., Party-States and their Legacies in Post-Communist Transformation. (Cheltenham, Elgar, 1997).
Dahrendorf, R., Reflections on the Revolution in Europe. (London, 1990).
Dallago, B., Mittone, L., eds., Economic Institutions, Markets and Competition. Centralization and Decentralization in the Transformation of Economic Systems. (Cheltenham, Elgar, 1996).
Dangerfield, M., Subregional Economic Cooperation in Central and Eastern Europe. The Political Economy of the Central European Free Trade Agreement (CEFTA). (Cheltenham, Elgar, 2000).
Darmer, M., Kuyper, L., Industry and the European Union. (Cheltenham, Elgar, 2000).
Davis, M.J., ed., Security Issues in the Post-Cold War World. (Cheltenham, Elgar, 1996).
Deibel, T.L., Gaddis, J.L., eds., Containment: Concept and Policy. (Washington DC, National Defence UP, 1986).
Dehousse, R., Comparing National and EC Law. The Problem of the Level of Analysis. (EUI Working Paper. Florence, European University Institute, 1994).
Dehousse, R., The European Court of Justice: The Politics of Judicial Integration. (London, Macmillan, 1998).
Devlin, J., The Rise of the Russian Democrats. The Causes and Consequences of the Elite Revolution. (Cheltenham, Elgar, 1995).
Dicey, A.V., An Introduction to the Study of the Law of the Constitution. (Basingstoke, Macmillan, 1959).
Dicey, A.V., et al., The Conflict of Laws. (London, 1993).
Dickinson, D.G., Mullineux, A.W., eds., Financial and Monetary Integration in the New Europe. Convergence between the EU and Central and Eastern Europe. (Cheltenham, Elgar, 2002).
Diebold, W., The Schuman Plan. A Study in Economic Cooperation, 1950-1959. (New York, 1959).
Dillon, P., Wykoff, F.C., Creating Capitalism. Transitions and Growth in Post-Soviet Europe. (Cheltenham, Elgar, 2002).
Disney, R., Johnson, P., eds., Pension Systems and Retirement Incomes. An Analysis Across OECD Countries. (Cheltenham, Elgar, 2001).
Dobrinsky, R., Landesmann, M., eds., Transforming Economies and European Integration. (Cheltenham, Elgar, 1995).
Dooge Report. (Brussels, EC, March 1985).
Dornbusch, R., et al., Postwar Economic Reconstruction and Lessons for the East Today. (Cambridge, 1991).
Doty, R.L., Immigration and National Identity. Constructing the Nation. (In: Review of International Studies, pp.235-255, 1996).
Duff, A., Reforming the European Union. (London, Federal Trust, 1997).
Duff, A., ed., Subsidiarity within the European Community. (London, Federal Trust, 1993).
Duff, A., ed., The Treaty of Amsterdam. Text and Commentary. (London, Sweet & Maxwell, 1997).
Duff, A., et al., eds., Maastricht and Beyond. Building the European Union. (London, Routledge, 1994).
Dyker, D.A., ed., Foreign Direct Investment and Technology Transfer in the Former Soviet Union. (Cheltenham, Elgar, 1999).

Edwards, G., Pijpers, A., eds., The Politics of European Treaty Reform. (London, Pinter, 1997).
Edwards, G., Spence, D., The European Commission. (Harlow, Longman, 1995).
Ekengren, M., Time and European Governance. The Empirical Value of Three Reflective Approaches. (Stockholm, University of Stockholm, 1998).
Ekengren, M., The Time of European Governance. (Manchester, Manchester UP, 2002).
El-Agraa, A.N., ed., The Economics of the European Community. (London, 1994).
Emerson, M., et al., The Economics of 1992. The EC Commission's Assession of the Economic Effects of Completing the Internal Market. (Oxford, OUP, 1988).
Emerson, M., et al., One Market, One Money. (Oxford, OUP, 1992).
Eriksen, O., Fossum, J.E., eds., Democracy in the European Union. Integration through Deliberation? (London, Routledge, 2000).
European Commission (EC), Towards a European Technology Community. (Brussels, EC, 1985).
EC, Evaluating Public Expenditure Programmes. (Brussels, EC, 1997).
EC, Portugal in the Transition to EMU. (Brussels, EC, 1997).
Ernst and Young, A Strategy for the ECU. (London, 1990).
Feis, H., Between War and Peace. The Potsdam Conference. (New York, 1960).
Ferguson, Y.H., Mannsbach, R.W., The State, Conceptual Chaos and the Future of Intermational Relations Theory. (Boulder, Rienner, 1989).
Fleming, J., D.F., The Cold War and its Origins. (Garden City, NY, 1961).
Flynn, N., Strehl, F., eds., Public Sector Management in Europe. (Hemel Hempstead, Harvester Wheatsheaf, 1996).
Fontaine, A., History of the Cold War. (London, Secker & Warburg, 1970).
Forsberg, T., ed., Contested Territory. Border Disputes at the Edge of the Former Soviet Empire. (Cheltenham, Elgar, 1995).
Fournier, J., Governance and European Integration. Reliable Public Administration. (In: Sigma, Preparing Public Administrations for the European Administrative Space. (Paris, OECD/Sigma, pp.119-135, 1998).
Franklin, M., Britain's Future in Europe. (London, 1990).
Fritsch, M., Brezinski, H., eds., Innovation and Technological Change in Eastern Europe. (Cheltenham, Elgar, 1999).
Fulbrook, M., German National Identity After the Holocaust. (Cambridge, Polity, 1999).
Gacs, J., et al., eds., The Mixed Blessing of Financial Inflows. Transition Countries in Comparative Perspective. (Cheltenham, Elgar, 1999).
Gaddis, J., Strategies of Containment. (New York, OUP, 1982; 1992).
Gaddis, J., The Long Peace. Inquiries into the History of Cold War. (Oxford, OUP, 1987).
Gaddis, J., We Now Know: Rethinking Cold War History. (Oxford, OUP, 1997).
Galli, G., Pelkmans, J., eds., Regulatory Reform and Competitiveness in Europe. (Cheltenham, Elgar, 2000).
Garrett, G., The Politics of Legal Integration in the European Union. (In: International Organization, pp.171-181, 1995).
George, S., Politics and Policy in the European Community. (Oxford, OUP, 1991).
George, S., An Awkward Partner: Britain in the EC. (Oxford, OUP, 1994).
Gibson, J., Hanson, P., eds., Transformation from Below. Local Power and the Political Economy of Post-Communist Transitions. (Cheltenham, Elgar, 1996).
Gillingham, J., Coal, Steel and the Rebirth of Europe, 1945-1955. (Cambridge, CUP, 1991).
Glendon, M.A., et al., Comparative Legal Traditions. (St. Paul, West Publishing, 1985).
Goldmann, K., Transforming the European Nation-State. Dynamics of Internationalization. (London, Sage, 2001).
Goldmann, K., Internationalisation and the Nation-State. Four Issues and Three Non-Issues. (In: European Journal of Political Research, pp.281-305, 2002).
Goldmann, K., Gilland, K., eds., Nationality and Internationalisation. The National View of the Nation in Four EU Countries. (Stockholm, Stockholm University, 2001).
Goldmann, K., Hannerz, U., Westin, C., eds., Nationalism and Internationalism in the Post-Cold War Era. (London, Routledge, 2000).
Goldstein, J., Keohane, R., eds., Ideas and Foreiogn Policy. (Ithaca, Cornell UP, 1993).
Goodman, J., Monetary Sovereignty. The Politics of Central Banking in Western Europe. (Ithaca, Cornell UP, 1992).
Goodman, S.F., The European Union. (London, Macmillan, 1993; 1996).
Grauwe, P. de, Papademos, L., eds., The European Monetary System in the 1990s. (London, 1990).
Green, D.M.A., Petrick, K., eds., Banking and Financial Stability in Central Europe. Integrating Transition Economics into the European Union. (Cheltenham, Elgar, 2002).
Green, N., et al., The Legal Foundations of the Single European Market. (Oxford, 1992).
Greenwood, J., Representing Interests in the European Union. (London, Macmillan, 1997).

Grosveld, H., The Leading Cities of the World and their Competitive Advantages. The Perception of Citymakers. (Amsterdam, Thela Thesis, 2002).
Gustavsson, J., The Politics of Foreign Policy Change: Explaining the Swedish Reorientation on EC Membership. (Lund, Lund UP, 1998).
Haav, K., European Integration and Public Administration Reform in Estonia. (In: Jak, J., ed., Ten Years of Transition. Budapest, Hungarian Institute of Public Administration, pp.313-330, 2001).
Haavisto, T., ed., The Transition to a Market Economy. Transformation and Reform in the Baltic States. (Cheltenham, Elgar, 1997).
Hakovirta, H., East-West Conflict and European Neutrality. (Oxford, Clarendon, 1988).
Hallstein, W., Europe in the Making. (London, 1972).
Hansen, P., European Only? Essays on Identity Politics and the European Union. (Umea, University, 2000).
Hanson, P., Bradshaw, M., eds., Regional Economic Change in Russia. (Cheltenham, Elgar, 2000).
Harbutt, F.J., The Iron Curtain. (Oxford, OUP, 1986).
Harding, C., European Community Investigations and Sanctions. (Leicester, Leicester UP, 1993).
Harding, C., The Identity of European Law. Mapping Out the European Legal Space. (In: European Law Journal, pp.128-147, 2000).
Harrop, J., The Political Economy of Integration in the European Union. (Cheltenham, Elgar, 2000).
Hartley, T.C., The Foundations of Community Law. (Oxford, Clarendon, 1994).
Harvey, B., Networking in Europe. A Guide to European Voluntary Organizations. (London, NCVO, 1995).
Hausner, J., et al., eds., Strategic Choice and Path-Dependency in Post-Socialism. (Cheltenham, Elgar, 1995).
Hayward, J., Page, E., eds., Governing the New Europe. (Cambridge, Polity, 1995).
Hedetoft, U., National Identity and Mentalities of War in Three EU Countries. (In: Journal of Peace Research, pp.281-300, 1993).
Hedetoft, U., Signs of Nations. Studies in the Political Semiotics of Self and Other in Contemporary European Nationalism. (Aldershot, Dartmouth, 1995).
Heeks, R., ed., Reinventing Government in the Information Age. International Practice in IT-enabled Public Sector Reform. (London, Routledge, 1999).
Heiser, H.J., British policy with regard to the unification efforts on the European Continent. (Leyden, University, 1959).
Heisler, M.O., ed., Politics in Western Europe. (New York, McKay, 1974).
Helmenstein, C., ed., Capital Markets in Central and Eastern Europe. (Cheltenham, Elgar, 1999).
Herolf, G., EU Enlargement and Flexibility. (Stockholm, Utrikespolitiska Institutet, 1998).
Hertz, M.F., Beginnings of the Cold War. (Bloomington, Indiana UP, 1986).
Hesse, J.J., Rebuilding the State. Administrative Reform in Central and Eastern Europe. (In: Sigma, Preparing Public Administrations for the European Administrative Space. (Paris, OECD/Sigma, pp.168-179, 1998).
Heyen, E.V., There are many paths leading to Administrative History, and some lead through Europe. (In: Administrative Theory & Praxis, pp.719-731, 2000).
Hill, M.R., Environment and Technology in the Former USSR. The Case of Acid Rain and Power Generation. (Cheltenham, Elgar, 1997).
Hinshaw, R., ed., The World Economy in Transition. What Leading Economists Think. (Cheltenham, Elgar, 1996).
Hirschhausen, C. von, Modernizing Infrastructure in Transformation Economies. Paving the Way to European Enlargement. (Cheltenham, Elgar, 2002).
Hirschhausen, C. von, Bitzer, J., eds., The Globalization of Industry and Innovation in Eastern Europe. From Post-Socialist Restructuring to International Competitiveness. (Cheltenham, Elgar, 2000).
Hoen, H.W., The Transformation of Economic Systems in Central Europe. (Cheltenham, Elgar, 1998).
Hoen, H.W., ed., Good Governance in Central and Eastern Europe. (Cheltenham, Elgar, 2001).
Hoffmann, S., Obstinate or Obsolete? The Fate of the Nation-State and the Case of Western Europe. (In: Nye, J.S., ed., International Regionalism. Boston, Little/Brown, 1968).
Hofstede, G., Cultures and Organisations. Intercultural Co-operation and its Importance for Survival. (London, HarperCollins, 1994).
Hofstede, G., Culture's Consequences: International Differences in Work-Related Values. (Beverley Hills, Sage, 1997).
Hogan, M., The Marshall Plan. America, Britain and the Reconstruction of Western Europe, 1947-1952. (Cambridge, 1987).
Holland, M., European Integration. (London, Pinter, 1994).
Holland, M., European Union Common Foreign Policy. (London, Macmillan, 1995).
Holland, M., ed., The Future of European Political Co-operation. (New York, St.Martin's, 1991).
Holland, M., ed., Common Foreign and Security Policy of the European Union. (London, Pinter, 1997).
Holland, R.F., European Decolonization, 1918-1981. (London, 1985).
Holland, S., The Uncommon Market. (London, Macmillan, 1980).
Holland, S., The European Imperative. (Nottingham, Spokesman, 1993).

Hollis, G., Plokker, K., Towards Democratic Decentralisation. Transforming Regional and Local Government in the New Europe. (Brussels, Tacis, 1995).
Hosking, G., Russia and the Russians. (London, Lane, 2001).
Huldt, B., et al., Finnish and Swedish Security. Comparing National Policies. (Stockholm, Swedish National Defence College, 2001).
Hunya, G., ed., Integration through Foreign Direct Investment. Making Central European Industries Competitive. (Cheltenham, Elgar, 2000).
Hutchinson, J., Smith, A.D., eds., Nationalism. (Oxford, OUP, 1994).
Ingham, H. and M., eds., EU Expansion to the East. (Cheltenham, Elgar, 2002).
Ismay, Lord, NATO: The First Five Years. (London, 1954).
Jackson, D., The New National Accounts. An Introduction to the System of National Accounts 1993 and the European Systems of Accounts 1995. (Cheltenham, Elgar, 2000).
Jacob, H., et al., Courts, Law and Politics in Comparative Perspective. (New Haven, Yale UP, 1996).
Jacobs, F., European Community Law and Public International Law. Two Different Legal Orders? (Kiel, 1983).
Jacobs, F., The Effect of Treaties in Domestic Law. (London, Sweet & Maxwell, 1987).
Jacobs, F., Legislatice co-decision: a real step forward? (European Community Studies Association, 1997).
Jacobs, F., ed., Western European Political Parties. (Harlow, Longman, 1989).
Jacobs, F., et al., The European Parliament. (Harlow, Longman, 1995).
Jak, J., ed., Ten Years of Transition. Prospects and Challenges for the Future of Public Administration. (Budapest, Hungarian Institute of Public Administration, 2001).
Jak, J., Mirko, V., eds., Public Administration in Transition. (Bled, University of Ljubljana, 1995).
Jefferys, S., et al., eds., European Working Lives. (Cheltenham, Elgar, 2001).
Jenei, G., Establishment of an independent, neutral civil service in the former socialist countries of Central and Eastern Europe. (In: Simai, M., ed., The Democratic Process and the Market. New York, United Nations UP, pp.60-74, 1999).
Jenei, G., Leloup, L.T., East-West Co-operation in Public Administration. An Agenda for the Second Stage. (Paper EGPA Conference, Cape Sounion, Greece, 1999).
Jenei, G., Zupko, G., Public Sector Performance in a New Democratic State: The Hungarian Case. (In: International Review of Administrative Sciences, pp.77-98, 2001).
Jenkins, B., Copsey, N., Nation, Nationalism and National Identity in France. (In: Jenkins, B., Sofos, S.A., eds., Nation and Identity in Contemporary Europe. London, Routledge, 1996).
Jenkins, B., Sofos, S.A., eds., Nation and Identity in Contemporary Europe. (London, Routledge, 1996).
Jenkins, R., et al., Environmental Regulation in the New Global Economy. (Cheltenham, Elgar, 2002).
Joerges, C., Taking the Law Seriously: On Political Science and the Role of Law in the Process of European Integration. (In: European Law Journal, pp.105-135, 1996).
Johansson, A.W., Neutrality and Modernity. The Second World War and Sweden's National Identity. (In: Ekman, S., Edling, N., eds., War Experience, Self Image and National Identity. The Second World War as Myth and History. Stockholm, Gidlunds Förlag, pp.163-185, 1997.
Johnson, C., Collignon, S., eds., eds., The Monetary Economics of Europe. (London, 1994).
Jopp, M., Warjovaara, R., Approaching the Northern Dimension of the CFSP. Challenges and Opportunities for the EU in the Emerging European Security Order. (Bonn, Institut für Europäische Politik, 1998).
Jordan, B., Düvell, F., Irregular Migration. The Dilemmas of Transnational Mobility. (Cheltenham, Elgar, 2002).
Jorgensen, K.E., ed., Reflective Approaches to European Governance. (London, Macmillan, 1997).
Jossa, B., Cuomo, G., The Economic Theory of Socialism and the Labour-Managed Firm. (Cheltenham, Elgar, 1997).
Jowell, J., Oliver, D., eds., The Changing Constitution. (Oxford, Clarendon, 1994).
Jyränki, A., ed., National Constitutions in the Era of Integration. (The Hague, 1999).
Kaderjak, P., Powell, J., eds., Economics for Environmental Policy in Transition Economies. An Analysis of the Hungarian Experience. (Cheltenham, Elgar, 1997).
Kagarlitsky, B., Russia under Yeltsin and Putin. (New York, Pluto, 2002).
Karlsson, C., Democracy, Legitimacy and the European Union. (Uppsala, University, 2001).
Katzenstein, P., Small States in World Markets. Industrial Policy in Europe. (Ithaca, Cornell UP, 1985).
Katzenstein, P., The Culture of National Security. Norms and Identity in World Politics. (New York, Columbia UP, 1995).
Kirchner, E.J., The Role of Interest Groups in the European Community. (Aldershot, Gower, 1981).
Kirchner, E.J., Decision Making in the European Community. (The Council Presidency and European Integration, Manchester, Manchester UP, 1992).
Kitzinger, U., Diplomacy and Persuasion. How Britain joined the Common Market. (London, Thames & Hudson, 1973).
Kliksberg, B., Towards an Intelligent State. (Amsterdam, IOS Press, 2001).

Knell, M., ed., Economics of Transition. Structural Adjustments and Growth Prospects in Eastern Europe. (Cheltenham, Elgar, 1996).
Knell, M., Rider, C., eds., Socialist Economies in Transition. (Cheltenham, Elgar, 1992).
Knill, C., Europeanization of National Administrations. (Cambridge, CUP, 2001).
Knippenberg, H., ed., Nationalising and Denationalising European Border Regions, 1800-2000. (Dordrecht, Kluwer, 1999).
Kornai, J., Struggle and Hope. Essays on Stabilization and Reform in a Post-Socialist Economy. (Cheltenham, Elgar, 1997).
Knudsen, O.F., ed., Stability and Security in the Baltic Sea Region. (London, Cass, 1999).
Kolarska-Bobonska, L., ed., The Second Wave of Polish Reforms. (Warsaw, Institute of Public Affairs, 2000).
Kolodko, G.W., From Shock to Therapy: The Political Economy of Postsocialist Transformation. (Oxford, OUP, 2000).
Kratochwill, F., Rules, Norms and Decisions on the Conditions of Practical and Legal Reasoning in International Relations and Domestic Affairs. (Cambridge, CUP, 1989).
Kristinsson, G.H., Iceland. (In: Wallace, H., ed., The Wider Western Europe. Reshaping the EC/EFTA Relationship. London, Pinter, 1991).
Laffan, B., The Finances of the European Union. (London, Macmillan, 1997).
Laffan, B. et al., Europe's Experimental Union. Rethinking Integration. (London, Routledge, 1999).
Laloy, J., Yalta Yesterday. Today, Tomorrow. (New York, 1988).
Lane, D., ed., Russian Banking. (Cheltenham, Elgar, 2002).
Lange, T., Pugh, G., The Economics of German Unification. (Cheltenham, Elgar, 1998).
Langhorne, R., The Collapse of the Concert of Europe. International Politics 1890-1914. (London, 1980).
Lapidus, G., ed., The New Russia. Troubled Transformation. (Boulder, Westview, 1995).
Larsen, A., et al., EC Agricultural Policy for the 21st Century. (London, European Economy, 1994).
Lasok, D., Bridge, J.W., An Introduction to the Law and Institutions of the European Communities. (London, Butterworths, 1973).
Lasok, D., Lasok, K.P.E., Law and Institutions of the European Union. (London, Butterworths, 1994).
Lasok, D., Stone, P., Conflict of Laws in the European Community. (Abington, Professional Books, 1987).
Lasok, D., Vanhoonacker, S., eds., The Intergovernmental Conference on Political Union. (The Hague, 1992).
Lasok, K.P.E., The European Court of Justice. (London, Butterworths, 1984, 1994).
Laurent, P.H., ed., The European Community. To Maastricht and Beyond. (London, Sage, 1994).
Laurent, P.H., Maresceau, M., eds., The State of the European Union. (Boulder, Rienner, 1998).
Laursen, F., Pappas, S.A., eds., The Changing Role of Parliaments in the European Union. (Maastricht, EIPA, 1995).
Laursen, F., Vanhoonacker, S., eds., The Intergovernmental Conference on Political Union. (Maastricht, EIPA, 1992).
Laursen, F., Vanhoonacker, S. eds., The Ratification of the Maastricht Treaty. (Dordrecht, Nijhoff, 1995).
Leach, R., British Political Ideologies. (London, Allan, 1991).
Legrand, P., European legal systems are not converging. (In: International and Comparative Law Quarterly, 1996).
Lembke, J., Defining the New Economy in Europe. (Stockholm, University of Stockholm, 2002).
Lembke, J., Competition for Technological Leadership: EU Policy for High Technology. (Cheltenham, Elgar, 2002).
Lewis, M.K., Algaoud, L.M., Islamic Banking. (Cheltenham, Elgar, 2001).
Lewis, P.G., ed., Party Structure and Organization in East-Central Europe. (Cheltenham, Elgar, 1996).
Lima, M.A., Portugal in the European Union: What Can We Tell the Central and Eastern European Contries. (In: The World Economy, pp.1395-1408, 2000).
Lipgens, W., A History of European Integration 1945-1947. The Formation of the European Unity Movement. (Oxford, OUP, 1982).
Lipgens, W., ed., Documents on the History of European Integration. (London, 1985/1991).
Lister, F.K., The European Union, the United Nations and the Revival of Confederal Governance. (Westport, Greenwood, 1996).
Louis, J.V., The Community Legal Order. (Brussels, EC, 1990).
Ludlow, P., The Making of the European Monetary System. (London, Butterworths, 1982).
Lukauskas, A.J., Regulating Finance. The Political Economy of Spanish Financial Policy from Franco to Democracy. (Michigan, University of Michigan Press, 1997).
MacCormick, D.N., On Sovereignty and Post-Sovereignty. (Oxford, OUP, 1999).
Major, I., ed., Privatization and Economic Performance in Central and Eastern Europe. Lessons to be Learnt from Western Europe. (Cheltenham, Elgar, 1999).
Mango, A., Atatürk. The Biography of the Founder of Modern Turkey. (London, Penguin, 2000).
Markesinis, B., ed., The Gradual Convergence. (Oxford, 1994).

Marks, G., et al., eds., Governance in the European Union. (London, Sage, 1996).
Marks, G., Hooghe, I., Blank, K., European Integration from the 1980s: State-Centric v. Multi-Level Governance. (In: Journal of Common Market Studies, pp.341-378, 1996).
Marquand, D., After Whig Imperialism. Can there be a new British Identity? (In: New Community, pp.183-193, 1995).
Marsh, P.T., Bargaining on Europe. Britain and the First Common Market 1860-1892. (New Haven, Yale UP, 1999).
Marshall, M., The Bank. The Birth of Europe's Central Bank and the Rebirth of Europe's Power. (New York, Random House, 1999).
Mathijsen, P., A Guide to European Union Law. (London, Sweet & Maxwell, 1972; 1995).
Mazey, S., Richardson, J., eds., Lobbying in the European Community. (Boulder, Westview, 1993).
McCarthy, P., France looks at Germany, or How to become German (and European) while remaining French. (In: McCarthy, P., ed., France-Germany, 1983-1993. The Struggle to Cooperate. Besingstoke, Macmillan, pp.51-72, 1993).
McCarthy, P., ed., France-Germany, 1983-1993. The Struggle to Cooperate. (Basingstoke, Macmillan, 1993,
McCourt, W., Minogue, M., The Internationalization of Public Management. Reinventing the Third World State. (Cheltenham, Elgar, 2001).
McDonagh, B., Original Sin in a Brave New World. An Account of the Negotiation of the Treaty of Amsterdam. (Dublin, Institute of European Affairs, 1998).
McFaul, M., Russia's Unfinished Revolution. Political Change from Gorbachev to Putin. (Ithaca, Cornell UP, 2002).
McKim, R., McMahan, J., eds., The Morality of Nationalism. (Oxford, OUP, 1997).
Mee, C.L., The Marshall Plan: The Launching of the Pax Americana. (New York, 1984).
Meeusen, W., ed., Economic Policy in the European Union. (Cheltenham, Elgar, 1999).
Meunier, S., Nocolaidis, K., Who Speaks for Europe? The delegation of trade authority in the European Union. (Cambridge, MA, Kennedy School of Government, 1998).
Meyer, K., Direct Investment in Economies in Transition. (Cheltenham, Elgar, 1998).
Miall, H., Shaping the New Europe. (London, Pinter, 1993).
Miall, H., ed., Redefining Europe. New Patterns of Conflict and Cooperation. (London, Pinter, 1994).
Middlemas, K., Orchestrating Europe. The Informal Politics of the European Union. (London, Fontana, 1995).
Miles, L., ed., Sweden and the European Union Evaluated. (London, Continuum, 2000).
Miles, L., Mörth, U., Nordic Political Science and the Study of European Integration. (In: Journal of European Public Policy, pp.488-495, 2002).
Millard, F., The Anatomy of the New Poland. Post-Communist Politics in its First Phase. (Cheltenham, Elgar, 1994).
Miller, D., On Nationality. (Oxford, Clarendon, 1995).
Milward, A.S., The Reconstruction of Western Europe, 1945-1951. (London, Methuen, 1984; 1994).
Milward, A.S., The European Rescue of the Nation-State. (Berkeley, University of California Press, 1992; 1999).
Milward, A.S., et al., eds., The Frontier of National Sovereignty. (New York, Routledge, 1993).
Mommsen, W.J., Moor, J.A, de, eds., European Expansion and Law. (Oxford, Berg, 1992).
Moravcsik, A., The Choice for Europe: Social Purpose and State Power from Messina to Maastricht. (London, UCL, 1998).
Moravcsik, A., Nicolaïdis, K., Explaining the Treaty of Amsterdam. Interests, Influence, Institutions. (In: Journal of Common Market Studies, pp.59-85, 1999).
Morgenthau, H.J., Politics among Nations. The Struggle for Power and Peace. (New York, Knopf, 1961).
Morris, J., et al., Rural Planning and Management. (Cheltenham, Elgar, 2001).
Mouritzen, H., Waever, O., Wiberg, H., eds., European Integration and National Adaptations. A Theoretical Inquiry. (Commack, NY, Nova Science, 1996).
Müller, K., The Political Economy of Pension Reform in Central-Eastern Europe. (Cheltenham, Elgar, 1999).
Mullineux, A.W., Green, C.J., eds., Economic Performance and Financial Sector Reform in Central and Eastern Europe. (Cheltenham, Elgar, 1999).
Murray, J., The Russian Press from Brezhnev to Yeltsin. Behind the Paper Curtain. (Cheltenham, Elgar, 1994).
Myant, M., ed., Industrial Competitiveness in East-Central Europe. (Cheltenham, Elgar, 1999).
Myant, M., et al., Succesful Transformations? The Creation of Market Economies in Eastern Germany and the Czech Republic. (Cheltenham, Elgar, 1996).
Nagy, P.M., The Meltdown of the Russian State. The Deformation and Collapse of the State in Russia. (Cheltenham, Elgar, 2000).
Neumann, I., Uses of the Other: The 'East' in European Identity Formation. (Manchester, Manchester UP, 1999).

Neunreither, K.H., The European Union in Nice: A Minimalist Approach to a Historic Challenge (In: Government and Opposition, pp.184-208, 2001).
Neunreither, K.H., Wiener, A., eds., Amsterdam and Beyond. Institutional Dynamics and Prospects for Democracy. (Oxford, OUP, 1999).
Newland, C., Jenei, G., Suchorzewski, L., Transition in the Czech Republic, Hungary and Poland. Autonomy and Community among Nation-States. (In: Kickert, W., Stillman, R., eds., The Modern State and Its Study. Cambridge, CUP, pp.217-244, 1999).
Nixson, F., et al., The Mongolian Economy. A Manual of Applied Economics for a Country in Transition. (Cheltenham, Elgar, 2000).
Nørgaard, O., Economic Institutions and Democratic Reform. A Comparative Analysis of Post-Communist Countries. (Cheltenham, Elgar, 2000).
Nørgaard, O., et al., The Baltic States After Independence. (Cheltenham, Elgar, 1999).
OECD, Putting Citizens First. Portuguese Experience in Public Management Reform. (Paris, OECD, 1995).
OECD, Government for the Future. (Paris, OECD, 2000).
Ojanen, H., ed., The Northern Dimension: Fuel for the EU? (Bonn, Institut für Europäische Politik, 2001).
Ojanen, H., Herolf, G., Lindahl, R., Non-Alignment and European Security Policy: Ambiguity at Work. (Bonn, Institut für Europäische Politik, 2000).
Olsen, J.P., Organising European Institutions of Governance. A Prelude to an Institutional Account of Political Integration. (Oslo, ARENA Paper, 2000).
Olson, M., Power and Prosperity. Outgrowing Communist and Capitalist Dictatorships. (New York, Basic Books, 2000).
O'Neill, A., Decisions of the European Court of Justice and their Constitutioal Implications. (London, Butterworths, 1994).
O'Neill, P.H., Revolution from Within. The Hungarian Socialist Workers' Party and the Collapse of Communism. (Cheltenham, Elgar, 1998).
Oppenheimer, A., ed., The Relationship between European Community Law and Natural Law. The Cases. (Cambridge, CUP, 1994).
Orlowski, L.T., ed., Transition and Growth in Post-Communist Countries. The Ten-Year Experience. (Cheltenham, Elgar, 2001).
Padoa-Schioppa, T., The Road to Monetary Union in Europe: The Emperor, the Kings and the Genesis. (Oxford, OUP, 1994).
Pedersen, T., European Union and the EFTA Countries. (London, Pinter, 1994).
Pentecost, E.J., Van Poeck, A., eds., European Monetary Integration. (Cheltenham, Elgar, 2001).
Petrick, K., Green, D.M.A., eds., Banking and Financial Stability in Central Europe. Integrating Transition Economies into the European Union. (Cheltenham, Elgar, 2000).
Pogany, I., ed., Human Rights in Eastern Europe. (Cheltenham, Elgar, 1995).
Pollitt, C., Institutional Amnesia: A Paradox of the "Information Age"? (Rotterdam, Erasmus University, 1999).
Pollitt, C., Convergence: The Useful Myth? (In: Public Management, pp.933-947, 2001).
Pollitt, C., Clarifying Convergence. Striking Similarities and Durable Differences in Public Management Reform. (In: Public Management Review, pp.471-492, 2002).
Pollitt, C., Bouckaert, G., Public Management Reform. A Comparative Analysis. (Oxford, OUP, 2000).
Pollitt, C., Bouckaert, G., Evaluating Public Management Reforms. An International Perspective. (In: International Journal of Political Studies, pp.167-192, 2002).
Pomfret, R., Constructing a Market Economy. Diverse Paths from Central Planning in Asia and Europe. (Cheltenham, Elgar, 2002).
Posusney, M.P., Cook, L., eds., Privatization and Labor. Responses and Consequences in Global Perspective. (Cheltenham, Elgar, 2002).
Preston, P.W., Gilson, J., eds., The European Union and Pacific Asia. (Cheltenham, Elgar, 2001).
Prychitko, D.L., Markets, Planning and Democracy. Essays after the Collapse of Socialism. (Cheltenham, Elgar, 2002).
Puffer, S.M., Business and Management in Russia. (Cheltenham, Elgar, 1996).
Puffer, S.M., et al., The Russian Capitalist Experiment. From State-Owned Organizations to Entrepreneurships. (Cheltenham, Elgar, 2000).
Rasmussen, H., On Law and Policy in the European Court of Justice. (Dordrecht, Nijhoff, 1986).
Ray, L., Social Theory and the Crisis of State Socialism. (Cheltenham, Elgar, 1996).
Rifkin, J., The Hydrogen Economy. The Creation of the Worldwide Energy Web and the Redistribution of Power. (London, 2002).
Risse, T., et al., The Power of Human Rights. International Norms and Domestic Change. (Cambridge, CUP, 1999).
Roberts, K., et al., Surviving Post-Communism. Young People in the Former Soviet Union. (Cheltenham, Elgar, 2000).

Robinson, C., ed., Regulating Utilities. New Issues, New Solutions. (Cheltenham, Elgar, 2001).
Robinson, N., Ideology and the Collapse of the Soviet System. A Critical History of Soviet Ideological Discourse. (Cheltenham, Elgar, 1995).
Rometsch, D., Wessels, W., eds., The European Union and Member States. Towards Institutional Fusion? (Manchester, Manchester UP, 1996).
Rosenau, J.N., Along the Domestic-Foreign Frontier: Exploring Governace in a Turbulent World. (Cambridge, CUP, 1997).
Rosenau, J.N., Czempiel, E.O., eds., Governance without Government. Order and Change in World Politics. (Cambridge, CUP, 1992).
Ross, G., Jacques Delors and European Integration. (Oxford, OUP, 1995).
Ross, G., et al., eds., The Mitterrand Experiment. (Oxford, OUP, 1987).
Saeter, M., Norway and the European Union. Domestic Debate versus External Reality. (In: Miles, L., ed., The European Union and the Nordic Countries. London, Routledge, 1996).
Safran, W., State, Nation, National Identity and Citizenship: France as a Test Case. (In: International Political Science Review, pp.219-238, 1991).
Salverda, W., et al., eds., Policy Measures for Low-Wage Employment in Europe. (Cheltenham, Elgar, 2000).
Sbragia, A.M., The European Union as Coxswain: Governance by Steering. (In: Pierre, J., ed., Debating Governance. (Oxford, OUP, pp.219-240, 2000).
Sbragia, A.M., ed., Euro-politics: Institutions and Policymaking in the "New" European Community. (Washington DC, Brookings Institution, 1992).
Scharpf, F.W., Governing in Europe: Effective and Democratic? (Oxford, OUP, 1999).
Schermers, H.G., Waelbroeck, D., Judicial Protection in the European Communities. (Boston, Kluwer, 1992).
Schmähl, W., Hortsmann, S., eds., Transformation of Pension Systems in Central and Eastern Europe. (Cheltenham, Elgar, 2001).
Schnapper, D., The Debate on Immigration and the Crisis of National Identity. (In: West European Politics, pp.127-139, 1994).
Scholtes, P.R., ed., Industrial Economics from Countries in Transition. (Cheltenham, Elgar, 1996).
Schor, J., You, J.I., eds., Capital, the State and Labour. (Cheltenham, Elgar, 1995).
Schütte, C., Privatization and Corporate Control in the Czech Republic. (Cheltenham, Elgar, 2000).
Schwabe, K., ed., The Beginnings of the Schuman Plan. (Brussels, 1988).
Schwarze, J., European Administrative Law. (London, Sweet & Maxwell, 1992; 1996).
Schwarze, J., ed., Tendencies towards European Standards in National Administrative Law. (Baden-Baden, Nomos, 1996).
Selovuori, J., ed., Power and Bureaucracy in Finland 1809-1998. (Helsinki, Edita, 1999).
Sergeyev, V., Biryukov, N., Russia's Road to Democracy. (Cheltenham, Elgar, 1993).
Sevic, Z., Banking Reforms in South-East Europe. (Cheltenham, Elgar, 2002).
Shapiro, M., The European Court of Justice. (In: Sbragia, A.M., ed., Euro-politics. (Washington DC, Brookings Institution, pp.123-151, 1992).
Shapiro, M., Stone, A., The New Institutional Politics in Europe. (In: Comparative Political Studies, 1994).
Sharma, S., ed., Restructuring Eastern Europe. (Cheltenham, Elgar, 1997).
Sigma, Preparing Public Administrations for the European Administrative Space. (Paris, OECD/Sigma, 1998).
Sigma, European Principles for Public Administration. (Paris, OECD/Sigma, 1999).
Simoneti, M., et al., eds., The Governance of Privatization Funds. Experiences of the Czech Republic, Poland and Slovenia. (Cheltenham, Elgar, 1999.
Sinn, H.W., The German State Banks. (Cheltenham, Elgar, 1999).
Sjursen, H., New Forms of Security Policy in Europe. (Oslo, ARENA Paper, 2000).
Smith, A., Reconstructing the Regional Economy. Industrial Transformation and Regional Development in Slovakia. (Cheltenham, Elgar, 1998).
Söderström, H.T., ed., One Global Market. (Stockholm, SNS, 1989).
Spierenburg, D., Poidevin, R., The History of the High Authority of the European Coals and Steel Community. (London, 1994).
Spiliotopoulos, E.P., Makrydemetres, A., eds., Public Administration in Greece. (Athens, Sakkoulas, 2001).
Staab, A., National Identity in Eastern Germany. Inner Unification or Continued Separation? (New York, Praeger, 1998).
Stälvant, C.E., How a Non-EC Member copes with the Internal Market: The Case of Sweden. (In: Möttölä, K., Patomäki, H., eds., Facing the Change in Europe: EFTA Countries' Integration Strategies. Helsinki, Ulkopoliittinen Instituutti, 1989).
Stein, E., Lawyers, Judges and the Making of a Transnational Constitution. (In: American Journal of International Law, pp.1-27, 1981).
Steinherr, A., ed., Thirty Years of European Monetary Integration. (London, 1994).

Stewart, K., Fiscal Federalism in Russia. Intergovernmental Transfers and the Financing of Education. (Cheltenham, Elgar, 2000).
Stone, A., Constitutional Dialogue in the European Community. (EUI Working Paper, RSC, 1995).
Stone, A., Governing with Judges: The New Constitutionalism in Europe. (In: Hayward, J., Page, E. eds., Governing the New Europe. (Cambridge, Polity, pp.286-314, 1995).
Stone Sweet, A., Governing with Judges. (Oxford, OUP, 2000).
Stone Sweet, A., Brunell, T., Constructing a Supranational Constitution. Dispute Resolution and Governance in the European Community. (In: American Political Science Review, pp.63-80, 1998).
Stone Sweet, A., Slaughter, A.M., eds., The European Court of Justice and National Courts. Doctrine and Jurisprudence. (Oxford, Hart, 1998).
Svensson, A.C., In the Service of the European Union. The Role of the Presidency in Negotiating the Amsterdam Treaty 1995-1997. (Uppsala, University, 2000).
Sverdrup, U., Ambiguity and Adaptation. Europeanisation of Administrative Institutions as Loosely Coupled Processes. (Oslo, Department of Political Science, 2000).
Swann, D., The Economics of the Common Market. Integration in the European Union. (London, Penguin, 1995).
Swann, D., ed., The Single European Market and Beyond. (London, Routledge, 1992).
Szasz, A., The Road to European Monetary Union. (London, Macmillan, 1999).
Tamir, Y., Liberal Nationalism. (Princeton, Princeton UP, 1993).
Tamir, Y., The Enigma of Nationalism. (In: World Politics, pp.418-440, 1995).
Tarrow, S., Building a Composite Polity. Popular Contention in the European Union. (Ithaca, Cornell UP, 1998).
Teague, P., Reshaping Employment Regimes in Europe. Policy Shifts alongside Boundary Change. (In: Journal of Public Policy, pp.33-62, 1999).
Temmes, M., State Transformation and Transition Theory. (In: International Review of Administrative Sciences, pp.258-268, 2000).
Thatcher, I.D., ed., Alec Nove on Communist and Postcommunist Countries. (Cheltenham, Elgar, 1998).
Thatcher, M., Britain and Europe. (London, Conservative Political Centre, 1988).
Thomas, H., Armed Truce. The Beginnings of the Cold War. (London, 1986).
Thomas, H., Ever Closer Union. (London, 1991).
Thorhallsson, B., The Role of Small States in the European Union. (Aldershot, Ashgate, 2000).
Tiilikainen, T., Damgaard Petersen, I., The Nordic Countries and the EC. (Copenhagen, Copenhagen Political Studies Press, 1993).
Todorova, R., EU Integration and Public Administration Reform. The Bulgarian Case. (In: Jak, J., ed., Ten Years of Transition. Budapest, Hungarian Institute of Public Administration, pp.393-405, 2001).
Torremans, P., ed., Legal Convergence in the Enlarged Europe of the New Millennium. (The Hague, 2000).
Toth, A.G., The Oxford Encyclopaedia of European Community Law. (Oxford, Clarendon, 1990).
Toth, A.G., The Principle of Subsidiarity in the Treaty of Maastricht. (In: Common Market Law Review, 1992).
Trompenaars, F., Riding the Waves of Culture. Understanding Cultural Diversity in Business. (London, Brealey, 1997).
Trondal, J., Multiple Institutional Embeddedness in Europe: The Case of Danish, Norwegian and Swedish Government Officials. (In: Scandinavian Political Studies, pp.311-341, 2000).
Tsoukalis, L., The European Economy. The Politics and Economics of Integration. (Oxford, OUP, 1993).
Tsoukalis, L., The New European Economy Revisited. (Oxford, OUP, 1997).
Tsoukalis, L., ed., The European Community. Past, Present and Future. (Oxford, Blackwell, 1984).
Turnock, D., ed., Privatization in Rural Eastern Europe. (Cheltenham, Elgar, 1998).
UNDP, Human Development Report for Central and Eastern Europe and the CIS. (New York, UNDP, 1999).
Usher, J.A., European Community Law and National Law. (London, Allen & Unwin, 1981).
Usher, J.A., Cases and Materials on the Law of the European Communities. (London, 1993).
Usher, J.A., The Law of Money and Financial Services in the European Community. (Oxford, 1994).
Uvalic, M., Vaughan-Whitehead, D., eds., Privatization Surprises in Transition Economies. Employee-Ownership in Central and Eastern Europe. (Cheltenham, Elgar, 1997).
Van den Berg, F., Jenei, G., Leloup, L.T., eds., East-West Co-operation in Public Sector Reform. Cases and Results in Central and Eastern Europe. (Amsterdam, IOS Press, 2002).
Vanthoor, W.F.V., A Chronological History of the European Union 1946-1998. (Cheltenham, 1999).
Van Schendelen, M., National Public and Private EC Lobbying. (Aldershot, Dartmouth, 1994).
Vaughan, D., ed., Law of the European Communities Service. (London, Butterworths, 1990).
Vaughan, R., Twentieth-Century Europe. (London, Croom Helm, 1979).
Vaughan-Whitehead, D., Albania in Crisis. The Predictable Fall of the Shining Star. (Cheltenham, Elgar, 1999).

Verheijen, T., Nemec, J., Building Higher Education Programmes in Public Administration in CEE Countries. (Brussels, NISPAcee/EPAN, 2000).
Voigt, S., Wagener, H.J., eds., Constitutions, Markets and Law. Recent Experiences in Transition Economies. (Cheltenham, Elgar, 2002).
Waever, O., et al., Identity, Migration and the New Security Agenda in Europe. (London, Pinter, 1993).
Walker, R.B.J., Inside/Outside: International Relations as Political Theory. (Cambridge, CUP, 1992).
Waltz, K.N., Theory of International Politics. (Reading, MA, Addison-Wesley, 1979).
Watts, M., Walstad, W.B., Reforming Economics and Economics Teaching in the Transition Economies. (Cheltenham, Elgar, 2002).
Weatherill, S., Law and Integration in the European Union. (Oxford, Clarendon, 1995).
Weatherill, S., Beaumont, P., EC Law. The Essential Guide to the Legal Workings of the European Community. (London, Penguin, 1995).
Wedel, J.R., Collision and Collusion. The Strange Case of Western Aid to Eastern Europe, 1989-1998. (New York, St.Martin's, 1998).
Weiler, J., The Transformation of Europe. (In: Yale Law Journal, pp.2403-2483, 1991).
Weiler, J., The Constitution of Europe. (Cambridge, CUP, 1999).
Weiss, L., The Myth of the Powerless State. Governing the Economy in a Global Era. (Cambridge, Polity, 1998).
Weiss, L., Globalization and National Governance. Antinomies or Interdependence? (In: Review of International Studies, pp.59-88, 1999).
Wendt, A., Social Theory of International Politics. (Cambridge, CUP, 1999).
Werner Report, Realization by stages of economic and monetary union in the Community. (Luxembourg, OOPEC, 1970).
Werner, W.G., Wilde, J.H. de, The Endurance of Sovereignty. (In: European Journal of International Relations, pp.283-313, 2001).
Westlake, M., A Modern Guide to European Parliament. (London, Pinter, 1994).
Westlake, M., The Commission and the Parliament. Partners and Rivals in the European Policy-making System. (London, Butterworths, 1994).
Westlake, M., ed., The Council of the European Union. (London, Cartemill, 1995).
Westlake, M., ed., The European Union Beyond Amsterdam. New Concepts of European Integration. (London, Routledge, 1998).
Westlund, H., et al., Regional Development in Russia. (Cheltenham, Elgar, 2000).
Wexler, I., The Marshall Plan Revisited. (Westport, 1983).
Wightman, G., ed., Party Formation in East-Central Europe. Post-Communist Politics in Czechoslovakia, Hungary, Poland and Bulgaria. (Cheltenham, Elgar, 1995).
Wincott, D., Institutional Interaction and European Integration. Towards an Everyday Critique of Liberal Intergovernmentalism. (In: Journal of Common Market Studies, pp.597-610, 1995).
Wistrich, E., The United States of Europe. (London, Routledge, 1993; 1994).
White Paper, UK and European Communities. (London, 1971).
Whitley, R., ed., European Business Systems. Firms and Markets in their National Contexts. (London, Sage, 1992).
Wildavsky, A., ed., Beyond Containment. Alternative American Policies Toward the Soviet Union. (San Francisco, ICS, 1983).
Williams, P.R., International Law and the Resolution of Central and East European Transboundary Environmental Disputes. (Basingstoke, Macmillan, 2000).
Witte, B. de, International Agreement on European Constitution. Report for the Asser Conference on European Law (The Treaty on a European Union. Suggestions for Revision). (Leyde, 1995).
Witte, B. de, et al., eds., The Common Law of Europe and the Future of Legal Education. (Deventer, Kluwer, 1992).
Wollmann, H., Modernization of the Public Sector and Public Administration in the Federal Republic of Germany. (In: Muramatsu, M., Naschold, F., eds., State and Administration in Japan and Germany. Berlin, De Gruyter, 1997).
Wollmann, H., Germany's trajectory of public sector modernisation. Continuities and Discontinuities. (In: Policy & Politics, pp.151-169, 2001).
World Bank, Hungary. Structural Reforms for Sustainable Growth. (Washington DC, World Bank, 1995).
Wright, V., The Development of Public Administration in Britain and France. Fundamental Similarities Making Basic Differences. (In: Yearbook of European Administrative History, pp.305-319, 1999).
Wyatt, D., Dashwood, A., European Community Law. (London, Sweet & Maxwell, 1993).
Wyman, M., et al., eds., Elections and Voters in Post-Communist Russia. (Cheltenham, Elgar, 1998).
Young, H., The Blessed Plot. Britain and Europe from Churchill to Blair. (London, Macmillan, 1998).
Young, J.W., Britain and European Unity, 1945-1992. (London, Macmillan, 1993).

Ziller, J., EU Integration and Civil Service Reform. (In: Sigma, Preparing Public Administrations for the European Administrative Space. OECD/Sigma, pp.136-154, 1998).
Zloch-Christy, I., ed., Eastern Europe and the World Economy. (Cheltenham, Elgar, 1998).
Zürn, M., Democratic Governance Beyond the Nation-State. (In: European Journal of International Relations, pp.183-221, 2000).
Zylicz, T., Costing Nature in a Transition Economy. Case Studies in Poland. (Cheltenham, Elgar, 2000).

# Part Five

# A Dialogue in the Framework of Theoretical Perspectives

# 9. Public Management of Society in Co-disciplinary Perspective

## 9.1. Cultural specificity of French Public Management of Society

Public Management of Society by public authorities (or government) is timeless as Finer observed in "The History of Government from the Earliest Times" (1997): It is co-eval with history, and might even have antedated writing. Good public management, making citizens feel good, is one of the first necessities of life (Heater, 1990). In mainstream writings, it is normal to elaborate above all on the activities of public authorities as part of the political system, as politics, or as subordinate activities (public administration) in relation to the sphere of power politics and policymaking. This is questioned in this study. The crux of the matter is seen in a sophisticated differentiation: politics versus (professional) public management. Not in the sense of a politics-administration dichotomy. On the contrary, Public Management of Society has to be analysed, while taking full account of political dimensions. As shown in this research project, Public Management of Society (PMS) in the broadest sense is a relevant object of scientific research. Political Science is not the proper framework to study the PMS phenomenon-as-such. Neither is Public Administration. It is obvious that Public Management of Society has more dimensions than political dimensions. Political science cannot treat the Public Management of Society phenomenon completely or adequately. Political science is crucial for handling political aspects in society. It is relevant for the production of raw materials for analysis of Public Management of Society, but, is this the adequate frame of reference? No, other disciplines are crucial too, and not only via Political Science: philosophy, law, economics, geography, cultural anthropology, sociology, social psychology, history, etc.: problems of disciplinary specificity (specific approaches and data). Public Management of Society is object of many disciplines. Co-disciplinary work is a must.

The challenge is to develop the study of PMS as an object of research: the Public Management of Society phenomenon as such in co-disciplinary perspective. Public Management of Society is defined as a primary social system that regulates processes of society with specific instruments to fulfil this task (legislation, jurisdiction, taking care of the 'general interest', legal monopoly of the legitimised use of force). Public Management of Society is about the activities of public authorities. As historical developments are crucial for an adequate analysis of Public Management of Society, ample room must be given to historical aspects, as done in this study. Ongoing interpenetration of circumstances, ideas and practices in the dynamics of the specific cultural-existential context is a crucial aspect of Public Management of Society. In mainstream American Public Administration literature there is a certain bias, due to its specific historical development: keep American Public Administration at a distance from French and European law-based institutionalising. French institutional engineering since the French Revolution (Idea of Law, codification, etc.) was presented as part of universalist knowledge valid for the whole world. Many French ideas were seen as having a universalist character: the French legacy to humanity. There is a tendency to consider Anglo-American Public Administration literature as dominantly relevant for the whole globe, especially since the Second World War. Without adequately taking account of fundamental cultural differences in countries, nations and regions, as sophisticated comparative analysis should do. In an adequate approach, the specificity of culture(s) has to be recognised. This is shown when so-called universalist ideas (also French ideas) are confronted with specific cultures all over the world. It is a mixture of universalism and cultural specificity, which is at stake.

Studies in the framework of a more elaborated world-systems theory, since Wallerstein's first suggestion in 1974, prove that one has to concentrate on particular historical circumstances of specific cultures (Kardulias, 1999). France could not and cannot escape from its cultural path dependence. No nation, region or community can. France is devoted passionately to maintaining and developing its specific culture. Cultural mapping, analysis of relevant cultural data, is a necessary condition for adequate theorising about and practising of Public Management of Society. In the light of contemporary myopia with its "the market is all" approach and globalisation euphoria, it is well timed to accentuate the relevance of the Idea of Public Authority, making adequate Public Management of Society necessary also in the 21st century. Since Wilson's "Declaration of Independence" for the Study of Public Administration in 1887, there has been an American Era of Public Administration. The French approach to the PMS phenomenon was rightly criticised for its too juridical, formalist character (legalism), neglecting the relevance of the impact of social sciences for analysis of processes of human interaction as they are in empirical reality. Especially in Anglo-American literature, arguing for an empiricist approach in a "institutionloose" conceptualising, and regarding institutions as given. Institutionalism has recently the vogue. The impact of old time French institutionalism is forgotten or marginalised (Broderick, 1970). As shown in this study, the PMS phenomenon cannot be handled adequately in the artificial demarcation of Public Administration (a Procrustean bed). There is an ongoing debate about the "Crisis of Public Administration". This crisis of identity can be solved with the PMS concept.

For many reasons, the French contribution to development of PMS is especially relevant. France can be seen as the world-champion in developing arrangements for institutional engineering with regard to Public Management of Society for a period of about two thousand years (Greigueuil, 1999). In all historical periods in France, institutional innovations abounded. One might assert, that those historical aspects are interesting, but not so relevant to our knowledge-based network-society with drastically different features (globalisation, informatics, technology). Thàt is a serious blunder, in the same way as it is a blunder to look at an eclipse of the sun without eclipse-glasses. Without knowledge about historical aspects of contemporary Public Management of Society, the risks of blinding by the, superficially seen, dominant aspects of actuality are serious (a-historical myopy). The French contribution in institutionalising arrangements for Public Management of Society is paradigmatic. As elaborated in this research project, France, with its wide range of cultural accomplishments, proves to be a unique laboratory for Public Management of Society. This is due to ample potentialities of the French cultural legacy, with lessons for other countries, in search of their own optimum between universalism and cultural specificity, even in the 21st century. Lessons can be deduced from preceding chapters and literature. Studies in "Science politique" (political science), "Sociologie politique" (political sociology), "Science administrative" (public administration, administrative science), "Droit publique" (public law), "Droit administrative" (administrative law), "Psychologie sociale" (social psychology) and "Histoire" (history), as presented in mainstream literature, are taken as starting-point. Generally, these disciplines treat only partial aspects of the public authority phenomenon. Against a broad, co-disciplinary background, with a taste of history, this study attempts to make it plausible that the public authorities phenomenon, Public Management of Society, can be analysed more completely and consistently. Living together in society requires management to tackle strategic problems. Public Management of Society is the crucial formula ("formule vedette"), demanding a co-disciplinary approach, studying the PMS phenomenon-as-such.

In France, there were, in a sense, forerunners for this idea, although in earlier times there were differences in the interpretation of crucial concepts, and about what constitute rational behaviour and science. The notion "police" was used to denote what now is known as public administration and management, as in the "Traité de la police" (1705-1710) by De la Mare. In higher education, the accent was placed upon public law and history. Charles-Jean Bonnin is known as the first in France to have argued for a more scientific study of public administration (management) by developing general principles. D. Diderot in his "Essai sur les études en Russie" (1775-1776) put an "École de politique ou des affaires publiques" after the Faculty of Law. In 1820, Cuvier proposed creation of a "faculté des sciences administratives et politiques" with the program: public and administrative law; political economy; finance; agriculture; technology; public hygiene. H. Carnot created the "École d'administration", functioning for only a few months in 1848. The "École libre des sciences politiques", created in 1871 by É. Boutmy (1876), had more success. Characteristics for the study curriculum were: variety of courses (multiple disciplines); more State sciences than political sciences; preparation for high public functionaries: political, administrative, diplomatic, economic and financial knowledge needed for practitioners to become professionals. It had a positivist approach, professionalism was accentuated. In the latter part of the 19th century, a more positivist and empirical approach was breaking through in the so-called political sciences in France. Although the time-honoured philosophical and dogmatic approach had its stubborn adherents too. It was common practice to elaborate intellectually about the just society on the basis of subjective values (deduction). Most of these studies worked on the concepts of classical authors (Aristotle, Plato, etc.), treating political liberty, sovereignty, natural rights, forms of government, etc. (Janet, 1858; Parieu, 1870; Vacherot, 1860). At the turn of the 19th-20th centuries, social sciences were the mode of the time, everybody taking himself seriously as an intellectual was a sociologist (Hauser, 1903). Studies in the philosophy of political science were popular, often starting with a pretended scientific approach to develop political (partisan) programs (Acollas, 1877; Régnard, 1885).

The birth of administrative law, with the "Traité de la juridiction administrative et des recours contentieux" (1887) by E. Laferrière, marked a new phase. No longer was it thought adequate to assemble and comment on the texts of laws, decrees and judicial decisions. Administrative law had to be organised with systematic coherence. The years 1895-1905 were productive. Hauriou wrote "Précis de droit administratif et droit public" (1896), Berthélemy "Traité élémentaire de droit administratif" (1900), Duguit "L'État" (1901/1903), Jèze "Les principes généraux du droit administratif" (1904). Gény's "Méthode d'interprétation et sources en droit privé positif" (1899) made the study of law more scientific. The French science of public law was so sophisticated and influential that it annexed political science, even becoming political science (or sociology). In a battle between disciplinary imperialisms, the time-honoured faculty of law tried to claim exclusive rights to such new fields as "sciences politiques" and "sciences camérales", which were mostly identical with "sciences d'État". Political science and public law were seen as complementary. Favre (1989, p.61): "..in those years that public law mobilised its energies to impose itself as a major juridical science, it was done in such a way that public law became political science." Duguit defined constitutional law in 1889 as "the systematic study of facts about the origins of the State, its development in older societies and its organisation in contemporary societies. With the objective to determine the organisation in future societies. ..Political phenomena are those related to the origin and the functioning of the State, but, these are essentially juridical phenomena. That pretended political science is just constitutional law, a branch of the general science of law." For Laferrière, administrative law is based on three principles: the principle of irresponsibility of the State as sovereign, the principle of distinction between acts of authority coming from the public, sovereign power, and acts of execution and the principle of independence of public institutions towards jurisdiction. These were questioned by jurisprudence and doctrine.

Gradually, the "Conseil d'État" recognised that the State was responsible for its activities, and that public administration was subject to jurisdictional decisions. In decision "Prince Napoléon" (18 February 1875), the "Conseil d'État" declared itself competent with regard to acts of government. The most prominent authors (Duguit, Hauriou, Jèze, Carré de Malberg) developed fundamental, differing conceptions, in between two basic positions. According to the first, the State had to be seen from the viewpoint of its specific responsibilities to guarantee public services. This justified application of specific law, "droit administratif". In the other approach, the State was thought to have exorbitant competencies not under the control of common law. It has public power, limited by a principle of reduced powers (Chevallier, 1979). A theory of the State was necessary to found public law, becoming a theory of politics, within the framework of the philosophy of law. In a process of "desecration of the State", the State could not shelter behind political arbitrariness to escape its responsibilities (de-politicisation of public administration). Public law was seen as science, independent from political science. Esmein (1906) laid the foundations for constitutional law and the history of public law.

On the basis of this study, the hypothesis about a specific French model of Public Management of Society seems to have a reasonable plausibility: French specificity. French attitudes toward authority are quite special (Schonfeld, 1976). In France, there is a tendency to consider France as having a vocation as a consequence of the universality of its ideas about the organisation of society, due to the French Revolution and French culture. The French legacy to humanity is unique, but it has to be recognised that other countries and cultures have made their contributions too. There has always been an exchange of ideas between countries and cultures all over the world. Countries adapted imported ideas to their own specific culture. One might speak about a cultural import-export balance. Some universalist idea, when adapted to a specific national cultural tradition, is specific in its cultural context. Therefore, it is appropriate to take account of a mixture of universalism and cultural specificity. This study presents ample argument for the conclusion that the idea that management is a genuine American invention might be questioned (Godfrey, 1998). This conclusion applies with greater force to Public Management of Society. French Public Management of Society proves to be the ancestor of American Public Management, which has its own specifics, though. French Public Management of Society is prominent in European institutionalising. Genius and "esprit" of the French PMS have much to offer for other countries, as in former historical circumstances. Attention must be given to the modernisation and professionalisation of Public Management of Society. Against the background of a broad survey of French Public Management of Society, some contributions to the philosophy of Public Management of Society are sketched. Interpenetration of philosophy, social sciences and professionalisation in a co-disciplinary focus is accentuated here.

Of course, the conclusion of this research project about the specificity of French Public Management of Society does not mean that France is the sole Nation-State with a specific character. On the contrary, the conclusion is that every Nation-State has to find its own optimal mixture between universalism and cultural specificity. There is an ongoing, passionate debate between French authors about the risks of losing the French specificity in several dimensions of society, also in the sphere of Public Management of Society (Badie, 1994). Barreau wrote in 1997 questioning whether France is disappearing. For Hoffmann (1976), France has become more like the others. Several authors argue that France is in the grip of global culture (King, 1991; Robertson, 1992) and "Americanisation". Examples of this encroaching of the American way of life into French society are mostly taken from a few areas: dominance of the American film industry; American consumerism; American capitalism; American way of doing business; the supposed efficiency of the smaller American public sector as compared with the proliferation of the French public sector, but it was shown that the French who have work are efficient; labour productivity (output per hour worked) in France is reasonable. It is by no means so that the American public sector is more efficient than the French public sector. France is ridiculed for the 54% of its GNP needed to pay for public outlays, but a sizeable part of it is for education (in US financed privately) and high public outlays for social security are due to a cherished French model of social civilisation (Commaille, 1996). Several authors have accentuated French specificity with regard to Public Management of Society. Rouban (1990) argued that the French administrative system was increasingly losing its French specificity. Both are partly right. There is convergence in the field of institutional arrangements for Public Management of Society, but cultural specificity is much more relevant than commonly understood. The Cartesian approach maintains its position, as other French contributions do.

Generally, the heavy impact of historical developments on contemporary French Public Management of Society is recognised. Several aspects are accentuated for their contribution to its specificity. There has of old been a centralist tendency in French society (monarchy, colbertism, jacobinism). In a sense France can be seen as a creation of the French State, as De Gaulle saw it. In the 20th century State-dirigism was a structural feature. A specific way of State-planning was developed after the Second World War, "planification". The "Plan" was a decisive tool of Public Management of Society. Now the "Commissariat général du Plan" is a think-tank for public policies. The centrality of the State is still a dominant characteristic, as is obvious from the overpowering position of the French State in processes of societal mediation. Sectors and professions have their own networks in which representatives of the State play a crucial role. There is a French model of corporatism. Professional groups try hard to defend their interests independently (non-intervention between sectors), often succeeding by organising a monopoly of representation, guaranteed by the State: a structure of an exclusive dialogue with competent representatives of public authorities (Segrestin, 1984). The political-administrative elite has a crucial task to co-ordinate policies for sector-specific networks on the basis of overall public policy.

French corporatism differs from the model of Schmitter/Lehmbruch (1979), in a more fragmented system of interest groups and a missing framework of overall negotiation. A symbiosis of interests between parts of the State apparatus and specific interest groups and sectors is a structural feature. It is always possible to make the State responsible for nearly everything. As in September 2000, when truckers blocked the roads, protesting against high oil prices. In a sense, French society experiences its relation to the world through the action of the State. Often social tensions (street riots, etc.) are redeemed with inflationary solutions (Lévy-Leboyer/Casanova, 1991). The political-administrative elite has intensified informal networks with colleagues trained at "ENA" ("énarchie") or other "grandes écoles" (Bodiguel, 1978; Bodiguel/Quermonne, 1983; Kessler, 1986). This elite controls the societal agenda (Bourdieu, 1989; Grémion, 1979). Functionaries are public entrepreneurs organising networks in politically/economically sensitive sectors (Birnbaum, 1977; Cohendet/Lebeau, 1987). Processes of politicising of bureaucracy, and politicians becoming functionaries, make responsibilities rather diffuse (Thoenig, 1987). The boundaries between the public sphere and some private sectors are unclear (hybrids). Preponderance of the State apparatus is seen as decisive for French specificity (Quermonne, 1987,1991; Timsit, 1987).

The Fifth Republic is a modernised form of Public Management of Society, but there is also an ongoing debate about the crisis of the French PMS model. In a sense, constitutional arrangements are liable to a process of institutional sclerosis. In relation to fundamental changes in the system of Public Management of Society, Rouban (1994) even speaks about the French State as anonymous power. Fragmentation of State power and rising influence of powerful actors in a process of crumbling public management are blamed: "administration en miettes" (Dupuy/Thoenig, 1985). The slogan "more-market-and-less-State" became popular too, as in the plea by Crozier (1987). The French model of the Welfare State is time and again on the verge of financial collapse, due to its overwhelming success. The overall situation of Public Management of Society changed fundamentally in the last decades (Baumgartner, 1989; West European Politics, 1999). Often adaptations were realised in the framework of modernisation (evaluation procedures, quality circles, participative management, etc.). Time-honoured structures of French Public Management of Society had to be adapted to new institutional realities. This meant reshuffling of competencies, locally, regionally and in the framework of European integration (de-territorialisation; de-nationalisation). Because of the great variety of institutional structures and arrangements, and the autonomy sought for in all fragmented parts of the system of Public Management of Society, there is an abundance of case-knowledge. As elsewhere, representatives of public authorities have a different role in all kinds of public-private partnerships between public services and clients (March/Olsen, 1989).

In a number of cases, France imported institutional arrangements from abroad, as with the introduction of the "Médiateur" (Ombudsman) and establishment of independent administrative authorities, following the model of American "regulatory agencies". Anglo-American methods of accountability have made their way through French institutions (Riley, 1987). American "managerialism" was a challenge for all who wanted to modernise the French system in the private sphere, and in the public sphere as well. Often one was not fully aware of the American context of this way of doing things. The French even imported the American "spoils system" (Baecque/Quermonne, 1982). In the framework of European integration there is an intensified exchange with other Member-States. Creative competition of institutional arrangements and public policies are manifest in a continuous institutional game. French judges, with the prestigious "Conseil d'État" at their apex, persistently resisted the dominant impact of law from the European Community on practically all dimensions and sectors of French society. At last, they complied with European law, also in the national legal sphere. After some time lag, the French organised themselves professionally with regard to the new dynamics of the lobbying phenomenon in the European Union. The French are using models from abroad if they think these will suit them, "à la française", with due respect for their cultural tradition, rationalities and intelligence.

All in all, French Public Management of Society is much more sophisticated than most literature has it. It is unsatisfactory that, in France and in Anglo-American literature, many relevant issues and dimensions of the PMS phenomenon are not fully or adequately handled within the boundaries of administrative science and political science, due to an artificial demarcation between these two frames of reference for scientific analyses. In both disciplines, the important role of law for the functioning of public authorities is structurally underrated. Too often examples of bad law, inadequate formalism and wrong uses of juridical regulations are mentioned to argue for less law and more social-psychological methods of regulation. The mainstream French approach to law, interpreting law practically as almost exclusively State-law, is to criticise, as Cohen-Tanugi (1985) did so well, accentuating that a more creative approach to law and its potencies and capabilities would be beneficial. Rouban (1994) argued that the French State is in search of a new normative identity. Common sense ideas about management (making individuals responsible, evaluating and sanctioning their activities, de-concentrating decision-making) are relevant for the public sector, but Public Management of Society requires more. The concept of the State as strategic actor, guarantor of the general interest, can be revitalised (CGP, 1993).

Definitions are relevant. Often a restricted definition "administration publique" (public administration) or "appareil administratif" (administrative apparatus) is opposed to "système politique" (political system). "Institutions administratives" (administrative institutions) are distinguished from "institutions politiques" (political institutions). Mostly, authors make it crystal clear that these distinctions are very relative indeed, but they stick to their habit of using them. The phenomenon of Public Management of Society is the key issue in this study, with the general interest of society as criterion. From that perspective, it is not useful to use restricted notions of public administration. It is not adequate either to interpret politics as an all-encompassing concept. In the 19th century, the "Rule of Law" was such a breakthrough with regard to the former "Police State", that law became more or less the dominant criterion for organisation of public authorities (legalism). Due to this legalistic approach, dimensions of politics and sociological realities were neglected. In American Public Administration, the politics-administration dichotomy was used as distinguishing notion, but this endeavour failed. It is more useful to distinguish "Public Management of Society" (PMS) from politics. "Public Management of Society" is preferable to "political-administrative system" also. The suggestion is not to analyse activities of public authorities in an a-political way. Because of intensified interpenetration of intervention by public authorities and political processes, due attention must be given to political dimensions, but the specificity of activities of public authorities as public authorities has to be recognised.

During the 19th century, the formation of political parties was a rather innovative phenomenon, thought to be a necessary carrier for realisation of representative democracy. In the 20th century, the party-political approach has generally been too dominant with regard to the organisation of public authorities, neglecting crucial authentic features of the function of public authorities. True democracy is more than dominant political parties, preferring partisan interests above the general interest. There is a black spot in mainstream democratic theory, concentrated on giving politicians, on the basis of elections, full mandate for authority over the many officials who are the professionals for realising the tasks of public authorities. Minimising the role of these professionals in the field of Public Management of Society is often seen as a contribution to democracy. It is time to recognise the specific function and role of public officials in the realisation of true democracy. As with the plea for a separation between State and Church, now a separation between (political and official) functionaries working on behalf of public authorities and political parties has to be institutionalised according to transparent criteria and norms. Combination of the function of (prime) minister, representing the general interest of the Nation-State, and leader of a political party, representing partisan interests of one group only (as in Germany), in one person is fundamentally wrong. An adequate professional code for public authorities is needed. A balanced, co-disciplinary approach is required, with a due place for law and other dimensions. As the study of public authorities in many countries shows, public authority is often hi-jacked by party-political manoeuvring. The specific nature and function of public authorities has to be a distinguishing criterion.

The search for more mature theorising demands a framework that includes and goes beyond all kinds of approaches in mainstream literature. An improvement is realised when one frees oneself from the worn out notion of Public Administration and its rigidities. Mostly, it is developed by distinguishing public administration from political science, law, business administration, etc. and by using dichotomies: politics/administration; facts/values; equity/efficiency; rational/irrational; positive/normative; modern/post-modern, etc. It proved to be an illusion to maintain the existing politics-administration dichotomy to demarcate the field of public administration. Simon (1945), building upon insights in social psychology, presented logical positivism and behaviourism as an adequate approach. Although he elaborated useful contributions (limited rationality, satisfying behaviour, etc.), his rigid facts-values dichotomy was questioned. Waldo (1955) showed that it was not possible to exclude values from so-called "factual decisions". In American Public

Administration literature, the Minnowbrook Conference (1968) is known for its endeavour to question traditional scientific and practical work by promoting the New Public Administration (Marini, 1971). It was about "relevance, anti-positivism, dissatisfaction with the state of the discipline, personal morality and ethics, innovation, improved human relations, reconciling public administration and democracy, client-centred responsiveness, and social equity." (Frederickson, 1989, p.100). Harmon used existentialism, Maslow's concept of self-actualisation and other materials to elaborate his ideas about administrative responsibility (Marini, 1971). The New Public Administration realised much less than its pretensions. The same conclusion holds for the "New Public Management" wave. Mostly, it is not more than an emphasis on more market orientation and use of business methods in public organisations (Osborne/Gaebler, 1992). Instead of using lessons from the best private companies for businesslike government (Gore, 1997), it is common sense to use lessons from the best public management actors in the first place (Pollitt/Bouckaert, 2000).

The Blacksburg Manifesto can also be mentioned as an attempt to renew American Public Administration (Wamsley et al., 1990; Wamsley/Wolf, 1996). It argued that there is a reflexive relationship between an individual's emotional substructure and the conscious processes monitored by government. In the second Minnowbrook Conference (1988), the normative and anti-positivist approach was renewed with the idea of interconnection (Bailey/ Mayer, 1992). Accentuating the interconnectedness of several dimensions (social, economic, technological, informational), adherents argued for an inclusive inter-connectional approach. Public decision-making should include externalities (not included in the market mechanism) and intergenerational costs. Recently, the rationalist tradition in Public Administration has been questioned, inter alia by postmodernists and others. Postmodernists often replace existing dichotomies with a new dichotomy. For Fish (1989) anti-foundationalism "teaches that questions of fact, truth, correctness, validity, and clarity can neither be posed nor answered in reference to some extra-contextual, a-historical, non-situational reality, or rule, or law, or value; rather, anti-foundationalism asserts, all of these matters are intelligible and debatable only within the precincts of the contexts or situations or paradigms or communities that give them their local and changeable shape." Fox/Miller (1995) present their post-modern Public Administration theory by opposing postmodernist relativism and orthodox foundationalism. Following Habermas, they suggest public discourse as an alternative for the traditional myth of the "loop model of democracy": People elect representatives whose alternative packages best meet their preferences. Representatives enact laws, which reflect the choices of the people, while a vigilant populace monitors representatives and votes to replace them. Public administration officials, blindly carrying out what politically elected functionaries ask them to do, fail in their responsibilities to realise justice and fair public management for all.

Literature about Public Administration and Public Management is increasingly confronted with theoretical perspectives that became popular during the last decades. It might be useful to sketch briefly some aspects of the internationally available intellectual legacy. Constructivism as social construction of reality is indicated (Berger/Luckmann, 1966), and aspects of (New) Institutionalism (North, 1981; Williamson, 1998), insights of French Institutionalists (Broderick, 1970), modernism/ postmodernism debate (Bogason, 2001; Farmer, 1998; Fox/Miller, 1995; Rivera/Woller, 2000; Rosenau, 1992) are dealt with. The popular, ambiguous catchall term governance (Rosenau/Czempiel, 1992; World Bank, 1992) is handled, to clear the floor for the more adequate notion of professional Public Management of Society. Aspects of professionalism in Public Management of Society are treated. In the last paragraph, the seven thought-provoking working-hypotheses for an integrated science of Public Management of Society, as developed by Niklas Luhmann (1927-1998 ),are sketched. French scholar Langrod, after a thorough analysis of French and world literature, had already concluded more than three decades ago, that Luhmann's conception was the most advanced of all. This situation has not changed. Due to language problems and the complexity of Luhmann's theorising, he has not had the recognition he deserves. It seems appropriate to deal with a sketch of some theoretical developments in social sciences and thoughts about the Rule of Law and the Idea of Public Authority, before formulating a supplying working-hypothesis about cultural intelligence as a necessary condition for adequate Public Management of Society.

## 9.2. Construction of social reality, (new) institutionalism and French institutionalists

Several authors have made us more conscious of the fact that human beings construct social reality, constructivism (Berger/Luckman, 1986; Searle, 1995; Surel, 2000). Searle elaborated a theoretical explanation of social facts. This is based on four assertions: attribution of a social fact rests on collective "intentionality"; institutional facts have the form of "as-if validity"; the validity of institutional facts implies power or authorisation; and the pursuit of intended action is possible only on the basis of "background abilities" (Corsten, 1998). For Hund (1998, pp. 130-131) Searle's argument is an original invention, but there are precursors, such as Durkheim (1915, p.228): "There is one division of nature where the formula of idealism is applicable almost to the letter: this is the social kingdom. Here more than anywhere else the idea is the reality." We follow the constructivism path, developed by Searle (1995, p.1): "there are portions of the real world, objective facts in the world that are only facts by human agreement. In a sense there are things that exist only because we believe them to exist. I am thinking of things like money, property, governments, and marriages. Yet many facts regarding these things are 'objective' facts in the sense that they are not a matter of your or my preferences, evaluations, or moral attitudes." Brute facts don't need institutions for their existence. Institutional facts require human institutions for their existence. There are rules, which regulate existing activities (regulative). Other rules regulate, but also create the very possibility of certain activities (constitutive). How is it possible that there is an objective reality that exists in part by human agreement? It is an objective fact that some pieces of paper are money, while something is money only if we believe it is money. It is an objective fact that some activities (legislation, police) are government activities, because we believe that they are government activities. For Sørensen (Jackson, 1999) applying Searle's formula "X counts as Y in context C": X stands for "states with territory, people and government"; Y for constitutional independence "which is a legal, absolute, and unitary condition"; and C for "the international society of states". Werner/De Wilde (2001, p.292): "..a claim to sovereignty attempts to establish a relation as an institutional fact (the 'fact' of being the supreme or ultimate authority and the 'fact' of being an independent authority) and a set of rights and responsibilities. Sovereignty, therefore, is more than a set of norms and principles; it is 'fact' and 'norm' at the same time. The institutional nature of sovereignty helps to explain the discrepancy between the socially constructed nature of sovereignty and its appearance as a matter of fact."

Searle describes his investigation as ontological (about how social facts exist) in the framework of overall ontology (how does the existence of social facts relate to other things that exist?). We live in a world in which there are systems. Some systems are living systems, while some living systems have evolved consciousness. There are physical objects with intrinsic features that exist independently of our attitudes towards them, but there are physical objects, like a screwdriver, that have ("observer relative") features which exist only relative to the "intentionality" of human agents. These are ontologically subjective. It is a fact that this ontologically subjective feature is epistemologically objective. In the ontology of socially created reality: for an observer-relative feature F seeming to be F is logically prior to being F, as seeming to be F is a necessary condition of being F. To account for social reality requires a cognitive apparatus with the elements: assignment of function; collective "intentionality"; and constitutive rules. Functions are assigned from outside by conscious observers and users, and are not intrinsic to the physics of any phenomenon. According to Searle (1995, p.16), there are intrinsically no functional facts beyond causal facts as far as nature is concerned. The further assignment of function is observer relative. Several definitions of function are used. So function can be defined in terms of causes. Then there is nothing intrinsically functional about functions, they are just causes. Functions can be defined in terms of fostering values, and then they are observer relative. To create social facts, human beings have to assign functions to objects and other phenomena. Functions are assigned relative to interests of users and observers, so functions are never intrinsic. Human beings have a capacity for collective "intentionality": they can engage in co-operative behaviour and share intentional states such as beliefs, desires and intentions. It is not correct to reduce collective "intentionality" to individual "intentionality", as "intentionality" is thought to exist only in the heads of individual human beings. It is inadequate to reduce collective "intentionality" to individual "intentionality" as with methodological individualism. Any fact involving collective "intentionality" is a social fact. Institutional facts, involving human institutions, form a subclass of social facts.

A relatively new concept in social sciences is self-reference. It is recognised that self-referential concepts are needed to denote social facts. Self-reference can be indicated by referring to the notion money. To function as money, something must be thought to be money. When people don't believe that it is money, it will cease to function as money. To realise that something is considered and used as money, it has to be treated as money. What is appropriate for money, is appropriate also for institutions such as property and government. When something is money, if it is believed to be money, it seems to produce a vicious circle. This only seems to be so. Money denotes a nucleus in a network encompassing paying for products or paying off debts, buying, selling, owning, etc. The term money is not needed in the definition of money, so there is no circularity. Money is a "pars-pro-toto" concept for several practices. Social concepts are different from natural concepts like rivers or mountains. Even if nobody believes something to be a mountain, it can be a mountain. For social facts, however, the attitude with regard to a phenomenon is partly constitutive of the phenomenon. Part of being a government is being thought by the people to be a government. Many institutional facts can be created by pre-formatted utterances, "performatives" as a subclass of the class of speech acts (declarations). With declarations, a state of affairs, as represented by the content of the speech act, is brought into existence by the performance of the speech act. A declaration of war creates the state of affairs, which is intended. Institutional facts seem to be possible only when associated with some brute physical facts, some physical realisation.

Institutional facts can only exist within a framework of systematic relations to other facts. To arrange that everybody in a society could have money, there must be a system of exchanging goods for money, for which a system of property is needed. To have policemen, handling criminals, there have to be criminal laws and prisons according to laws as organised by government after a process of legislation. Social objects are constituted by social acts. According to Searle (1995, p.40), the radical break with other forms of life comes when humans, through collective "intentionality", impose functions on phenomena, where the function requires continued human co-operation in specific forms of recognition, acceptance and recognition of a new status to which a function is assigned. This is the starting point of all institutional forms of human culture. It must always have the structure X counts as Y in C. The term Y must assign a new status that the object does not already have in virtue of satisfying the term X. There must be continued collective agreement or acceptance with regard to the imposition of the status and the function that goes with that status. Creation of institutional facts takes place in a structure C where X things are counted as Y things. Collective intentional imposition of functions on entities, which cannot perform those functions without that imposition is crucial for the creation of social reality. A key element in the creation of institutional facts is imposition of a collectively recognised status to which a function is attached (status function). Material objects as involved in institutional phenomena (bits of paper, etc.) are objects like any other. Imposition of status-functions on these objects creates a specific level of description of the object, when it is an institutional object. Institutions are not worn out by continued use (as with cars). Use of the institution is renewal of that institution. Each use of an institution is a renewed commitment of users to the institution.

The recent development of linguistic sciences ("linguistic turn") is relevant for social sciences (Saussure, 1966). Language proves to be essentially constitutive of institutional reality. It is seen as impossible to have institutional structures such as governments without a form of language, because words and other symbols are partly constitutive of the facts. A society must have at least a primitive form of language to have institutional facts. Each institution requires linguistic elements of the facts within that very institution. An essential feature of language for the constitution of institutional facts is the existence of symbolic devices (words, etc.) which by convention mean, represent or symbolise something beyond themselves. Language is partly constitutive of institutional facts. Institutional facts contain some symbolic elements: words, symbols or other devices that mean, express or symbolise something beyond themselves, so that it is publicly understandable. Language contains entities that symbolise. These intentional capacities are not intrinsic to the entities, but are imposed by or derived from the intrinsic "intentionality" of human beings. It is useful to distinguish between language-independent facts (the fact that there was snow in Amsterdam yesterday) and language-dependent facts (such as the fact that "yesterday there was snow in Amsterdam" is a sentence in English). Take away language in the last case, and there is no fact. Language-dependent and language-independent thoughts (such as non-institutional, primitive cognitions not requiring linguistic devices) can be distinguished. For Searle (1995, p.62), a fact is language-dependent, if two conditions can be met. Mental representations (thoughts) have to be partly constitutive of the fact; and representations in question must be language-dependent. From the structure of constitutive rules it is possible to deduce that institutional facts fulfil the first condition. The status function as specified by the Y term can be fulfilled, if it is recognised or believed in. An institutional fact can exist, if it is represented as existing. Institutional facts are ontologically subjective, and generally, epistemologically objective.

Many thoughts are so complex that it would be empirically impossible to think them without having symbols. The thought that this acreage is my property requires a language as a matter of conceptual necessity. When we use stones for counting points in a game, these are linguistic symbols with essential features. They symbolise something beyond themselves, they do so by convention, and they are public. The desire to score points has no content independently of a socially accepted system of representing and counting points. Points in games are not "out there" as planets, men or lines are out there. The shift from the X to the Y in the move that creates institutional facts is a move from a brute level to an institutional level. This shift can exist only, if it is represented as existing. Without language, we see a man with a ball crossing a line. We cannot see the man score points, without language. Points cannot be thought of independently of words or symbols. What is true for points in games is true for property, government, and other institutional phenomena. Status-functions are partly constituted by thoughts, while pre-linguistic forms of thought are inadequate to do this, because they exist only by way of collective agreement. The Y term creates a status, which is additional to physical features of the X term. The status only exists if people believe it to exist and accept the reasons for its functioning. Status-functions, due to their language dependency, differ from causal agentive functions. Physically X and Y are the same thing, but it makes all the difference that we imposed a status on the X element, and this new status needs markers. The status cannot exist without markers, which are partly constitutive of the status.

We need words or other symbols to perform the shift from the X to the Y status. Institutional phenomena have a "deontic" status. About markings for boundaries of a territory there is nothing "deontic", when a tribe is not inclined to cross these boundaries: then there is no institutional fact. When members of the tribe recognise that a line of stones creates rights and obligations (they are forbidden to cross the line), there is symbolisation. The move from brute to institutional status is a linguistic move, because the X term symbolises something beyond itself. To think the thought that constitutes the move from X term to Y status, there must be a vehicle of the thought: words or other devices. From preliterate societies to the present there have been conventional markers that function like words. The capacity to attach a sense, a symbolic function, to an object not having that sense intrinsically, is pre-condition of all institutional reality. Pre-institutional capacity to symbolise is the possibility condition of creation for all human institutions (Searle, 1995, p.75). Institutional facts require language. Language is epistemologically indispensable. Institutional facts, inherently social, must be communicable. Institutional facts persist normally relatively independently from duration of actions of participants in the institution.

Governments have their origin in a number of primitive biological phenomena: the tendency to form groups with hierarchical structures; leadership patterns; power relations. What follows beyond that is a series of institutional structures by collective imposition and acceptance of status-functions, imposed on people, objects and events. One might think that acceptance of State power is compelled by military power and armed police, but in a more fundamental sense, the armed power of the State is based upon acceptance of constitutive rules. The terror based Soviet system collapsed after 1989, when the prevailing system of status-functions was no longer accepted. For Searle (1995, p.94) "everything we value in civilisation requires the creation and maintenance of institutional power relations through collectively imposed status-functions." In his view, there are few general formal properties of institutional facts. With the creation of a status-function, a new power is conferred, because then a status and a function are imposed on some entity. By collective agreement, we can create forms of power, where collective acceptance of this power is constitutive of having it. Status-functions can be divided into four categories: symbolic, "deontic", honorific and procedural. Institutions permit creation of institutional facts from social and brute facts. These institutions, consisting in constitutive rules, have the form X counts as Y in context C (Searle, 1995, p.114). Collective "intentionality" imposes a specific status (Y) on phenomenon X, and a function. Searle (1995, p.228): "What is special about culture is the manifestation of collective intentionality and, in particular, the collective assignment of functions to phenomena where the function cannot be performed solely by virtue of the sheer physical features of the phenomena." Institutional structures have a special feature, symbolism. Searle's study is more than a dead-end street, as Wetterstein (1998) suggests.

According to constructivism, actors and structures are mutually constituted. In the neo-realist conceptualisation of international structure, structure is seen as a set of relatively unchangeable constraints on behaviour of States (Waltz, 1979). In the constructivist approach, the relevant question is, how an action reproduces both actor and structure. All kinds of notions are seen as social constructs (Biersteker/Weber, 1996). The identity of a State in world politics is partly a product of social practices that constitute its identity at home (Katzenstein, 1996). Action, meaningful behaviour, is possible within an inter-subjective social context. Data must be placed in a social context to acquire meaning. Actors develop their relations and communications with others by means of norms and practices. Actions in the absence of norms would be devoid of meaning. Constitutive norms define an identity by specifying the actions, causing others to acknowledge that identity, and to respond to it. In a constructivist view, structure is meaningless without some inter-subjective set of norms and practices. Culture, norms, institutions, rules, procedures and social practices are the relevant sphere of action and communication for actors and structure alike. Hopf (1998, p.175): "..the producer of identity is not in control of what it ultimately means to others; the inter-subjective structure is the final arbiter of meaning." A State understands actors according to the identity it attributes to them, reproducing its own identity through social practices. Traditional realism assumes the self-interest of States. For constructivism, identities of States, depending on a historical, cultural, political and social context, are variables. Neorealism and neoliberalism assume, that material power (military and/or economic) is the single most important source of influence in global politics (Baldwin, 1993). For constructivism, understanding the world requires material and "discursive" power. Hopf (1998, p.177) emphasises material and "discursive" power (the power of knowledge, ideas, culture, ideology). As Foucault and others argued (Gordon, 1980), language is crucial. The capacity to reproduce order and predictability in understandings and expectations is a component of "discursive" power.

Recently, so-called institutional economics in Anglo-American literature gave more attention to the significance of institutions for economics (Williamson, 1975). In classical and neo-classical economic thought, it was a normal procedure to consider institutions as part of the data from which economic theorising could be developed. New institutional economics can be seen as belated reaction to "institution-loose" theorising in economics. This was a reaction against historical-institutional literature with the dominantly juridical impact. France can be seen as the paradigmatic prototype of an institutional approach (Broderick, 1970). The use of institutional instruments, especially juridical instruments (law, contracts) for societal regulation was emphasized (Ellul, 1993). Since the invention of the "État de droit" (19th century), legislative law was seen as the primary instrument for societal regulation. Economic thought was dependent on juridical institutionalising: juridical theoretical imperialism. In Anglo-American tradition, liberal ideas dominated with regard to economics, the market was thought to be the best instrument for co-ordinating decisions in society. The Welfare State, with huge programs of State intervention, was a correction. Since "The Years of High Theory" (Shackle, 1967) and the Second World War, economic science treated a wide range of fields, from microeconomics to macroeconomics (Keynes). Price theory, value theory, money theory, income theory, welfare theory; economic order, economic policy, business economics, public finance, international economic relations; economic geography, economic history. "..the general characteristic of economic efficacy is seen to lie in the fact that the decisions are taken on the basis of ..insight into the economic phenomena and their interrelationships." (Hennipman, 1995, p.29). Since the 1970s, there have been many studies of institutional economics and governance. Earlier, economic research was dominantly about (industrial) organisation (Bain, 1968) and the theory of the firm (Cyert/March, 1963), more as production function than as management structure. "Market failure literature", stimulated "government failure literature". Institutional economics (Samuels, 1990) was criticised.

So-called new institutional economics (Furubotn/Richter, 1991) is said to have started with Coase's "The nature of the firm" (1937) and "The problem of social cost" (1960). It got a more sophisticated allure with publications by Davis/North (1971), Williamson (1971), North (1981), Williamson (1985,1996) and others. Williamson (1998) constructed a framework with four levels for the economics of institutions: 1. social theory; 2. economics of the institutional environment; 3. governance, transaction cost economics; 4. neo-classical economics/ agency theory. On the first level, informal institutions, customs, traditions, norms, religion (taken as a given by most economists). The second level, with first-order-economising, covers more formalised organisations (polity, judiciary, bureaucracy of government), providing the rules of the game (laws) for economic activities. Here the issue is: Get the institutional environment right. At the third level, with second-order economising, transaction cost economics takes the institutional environment and its rules of the game as shift parameters, concentrating upon the play of the game (governance). Here the issue is getting the governance structures right (markets, hybrids, firms, bureaux). The fourth level, with third-order-economising, is about getting the marginal conditions right (prices, output, efficient allocation). Institutions can be defined as "the humanely devised constraints that structure political, economic, and social interactions. They consist of both informal constraints (sanctions, taboos, customs, traditions, and codes of conduct), and formal rules (constitutions, laws, property rights)." (North, 1991, p.97). Important stimuli for the analysis of organisations were given by Taylor (1911), Fayol (1916), Barnard (1938), Simon (1945) and others. Simon corrected theorising about rational economic man by emphasizing bounded rationality: behaviour that is rational by intention but only limitedly so. The study of organisations within an interdisciplinary framework of the social sciences was an important breakthrough (March/ Simon, 1978). Transaction cost economics, taking the firm as one of several modes of governance, tries to go further than market-firm dichotomies, accentuating adaptive management. The term governance gets a rather broad meaning: "governance is the means by which order is accomplished in a relation in which potential conflict threatens to undo or upset opportunities to realise mutual gains." (Williamson, 1998, p.37). Modes of governance are: firm, market, hybrid contracting, and public bureau modes of governance. Each is said to be supported by a distinctive form of contract law (Williamson, 1996).

In transaction cost economics, the exchange transaction is the starting-point, not the firm. What organisational structure has to be chosen to co-ordinate transactions? Choices are needed, as each organisational structure has its transaction costs. Markets and organisations are seen as alternatives to solve co-ordination problems (Williamson, 1975). Taking the transaction as the basic unit of analysis is seen as moving economics in the direction of a science of contract, instead of a science of choice. In the economics of property rights, defining and enforcing property rights is seen as a central issue of economic organisation. In developed economies, property rights might be assumed to be reasonably institutionalised. So the central issue becomes aligning of transactions with governance structures to further performance results. Transaction cost economics, standing upon law, economics and organisation, has analysed a wide range of issues like industrial organisation and market structures, corporate governance, strategic management, contracting and public policies with regard to business, non-profit organisations and public bureaucracies. A popular item is reform of public bureaux and privatisation. In public finance literature, the public bureau (government) was often seen as an omnipotent, omniscient and benevolent actor (Dixit, 1996, p.8). Transaction costs economics treats the public bureau as an alternative mode of governance, replaceable by other modes of governance. The public bureau is a kind of organisation of last resort: "try markets, try hybrids, try firms, try regulation, and resort to public bureaux only when all else fails (comparatively)." (Williamson, 1998, p.47). Public sector governance is a topic, but in institutional economics, the specific role of public authorities is mostly undervalued.

Several authors proclaim their adherence to New Institutionalism, while others ask what is really new about this approach (DiMaggio/Powell, 1991). Several disciplines are affected by this (reputedly New) Institutionalism. Setting aside institutionalism in economics, several approaches claim institutionalism to be their brand: organisation theory, rational choice and historical institutionalism. In historical and juridical literature, it has long been part of practical and more scientific work to give ample attention to formal rulings and institutional arrangements. Even though this kind of work was branded as formalistic, especially in social sciences in the grip of empiricism and behaviourism. In traditional economics, it was, until the aftermath of the Second World War, normal to take institutions as given (data). There were some forerunners, who accentuated the necessity to deepen our insight by analysing institutional constructions more thoroughly, also in economics. In sociology and political science, seeking to qualify as empirical sciences, behaviourism was, for decades a dominant approach (observable behaviour). For behaviourists, expressed preferences are the real preferences of any individual. Institutionalists could show that there are differences between expressed preferences and real preferences. In institutionalism, behaviourists' summation of preferences, aggregation of individual behaviours into collective phenomena, was questioned as problematic. Mechanisms to aggregate interests in fact reshape interests. Historians continued to deal with historical developments with regard to institutions. Historical institutionalists, in a macro-sociological and power-related framework, accentuated relations between State or politics and society in the context of historical periods. They could build up conceptualisations on a varied intellectual supply of materials (Durkheim, Comte, Weber, Parsons and many others).

In the field of democratic theory, ample attention was given to articulation of individual preferences of citizens by means of representation. General suffrage, supported by a system of political parties and interest groups, was seen as efficient carrier to transform individual preferences of citizens into policy formation by elected politicians. So pluralist representative democracy was thought to take form. This pluralist view was corrected by so-called structuralists. They emphasized that representation of interests and political processes are structured by such institutions as constitutions, State structures, and all kinds of collective arrangements and processes. Political demands, expressed in the political process, are not a complete or adequate reflection of the preferences of citizens. Institutional factors have an important impact upon agenda, procedures and outcomes of political decision-making processes. In the last decades social sciences were influenced by the interpretative approach, postmodernism and social constructivism. Historical institutionalism might be divided into two orientations: rational choice versus interpretation, or a "calculus" versus a "cultural" approach (Hall/Taylor, 1996, pp. 955-956). Questioning rationality in scholarly work is a plea for alternative rationalities, not for irrationality. Steinmo (1993, p.7): "any rational actor will behave differently in different institutional contexts."

Recently, three historicist themes, emphasising limits on human rationality and knowledge that can be redressed only by examining history, have come to the fore in the work of historical institutionalism (Immergut, 1998). Firstly, instrumental rationality is seen as a product of specific historical developments, constructed and supported by particular sets of institutions and beliefs. It is reductionist, to call alternative rationalities "norms", while forgetting that Western instrumental rationality is itself a norm. Secondly, causality has to be interpreted as contextual (contextual logics of causality). Historical-comparative analysis shows that it is not easy to break models down to casually independent variables. Many factors (mental constructs, political, social and economic circumstances) have an impact in an inextricable process of interaction. Thirdly, contingencies of history are accentuated. While actors have influence, our understanding of events and developments is constrained by the role of chance, so contributing to unexpected developments. Contingent developments are partly beyond logic, and can be grasped only by means of historical analysis. History is not only seen as method, but as theory and philosophy as well. Historians, examining materials left behind from earlier times, interrogate these data as artefacts. Their work is interpretation of available evidence. "The history of thought, and therefore all history, is the re-enactment of past thought in the historian's own mind." (Collingwood, 1993, p.215).

To demonstrate that so-called New Institutionalism is less original than generally supposed, due attention is now given to the French Institutionalists. In Anglo-American literature their work is relatively unknown. Broderick (1970) summarised their work: Hauriou (1925), Delos (1929) and Renard (1930), pioneers of "the theory of the institution". Societal problems "..require for their solution the sort of knowledge and skills that transcend specialization and technical proficiency. They call for a competence that is grounded in a wide perspective, one that represents an integration of the practitioner's technical skills with a knowledge of the various disciplines that bear directly on the wise solution of present day problems;.." (oc, p.vii). The fundamental aim of law for the "personalist" philosophers Hauriou (and the thomists) Renard and Delos is to constitute society as a "social whole of personalities". Hauriou's work is characterised in three phases: objectivist in the first phase (1907-1910); objectivist and subjectivist in the second phase (1916-1925); and personalist in the last phase (since 1925). Hauriou (1925) revised his "objectivist" version of institutional theory, as it did not account for the creative force in society, which is not pure reaction to externalised "conscience collective" (Durkheim) or "masse des consciences" (Duguit). After 1915, Hauriou emphasized individual initiative or creative ideas, starting and guiding institutions. In his "personalist" theory of law and institutions, the fully developed human person is central. Personification is the way in which social organisms with collective powers are instituted. Rejecting the "will" theory of law, Hauriou took "directing ideas" as an integral part of his theory of the institution. Hauriou (o.c., p. xvii) "..at any moment in a group's history, it was possible through investigation of objective data, primarily of institutional phenomena, and through reflection, to ascertain the central ideas of a given society."

For Hauriou, the function of law is to organise society, protecting it against abuses of power by forming objective situations, institutions, but he is fully aware of the impact of psychological factors (social science data dealing with conduct). In his conceptualisation, both "objective" and "subjective" factors are seen as relevant. According to Hauriou, there is in every organised society "a perpetual dialogue between the power of command and that of subjection", constituting its essential function. Hauriou's central insight was that an "institution" is a leading idea or set of ideas guiding organisations established to secure its achievement. Later Delos and Renard developed Hauriou's analysis of the "institution" into an "institutional" theory of law. French institutionalists, shifting the focus in law from concepts to observations, rejected exclusive conceptualism. In knowledge acquisition, existence of the world comes first, awareness of that world comes next (perception of phenomena, data of human existence), and then man's thoughts about the world become important. "I think, therefore I am.", Descartes said. In fact, human beings can say: "I am a human being, therefore I think." Nothing is in the mind that is not first in the senses. The human mind gives shape to matter for purposes of comprehension, putting special emphasis on the concept in the learning process. The human mind is thought capable of formulating an objective, also called an idea. In Hauriou's theory, "idea" is an important element, while the balance between concepts and observations is restored in comparison with approaches stressing either pure conceptualism or pure empiricism. Hauriou's conceptualisation is innovative about law, society, constitution of government and its administration. Delos (1931) argued that every juridical act (contract, law, or foundation of an institution) has the same structure: a will in service of an idea. Renard (1930) proposed to expand Hauriou's theory of the institution to an institutional theory of law. Hauriou gave the first place to the rights of the individual, while he saw the institution as only the second element of social order. Hauriou's synthesis built law on social institutions and individual rights. Only gradually did the insights of French institutionalists become known to some Anglo-American scholars (Coase could have known of the work of the French Institutionalists).

Predominant tendencies in French juristic thought before Hauriou were aptly summarised by Brèthe de la Gressaye (Broderick, 1970, pp. 15-24), qualifying Hauriou's conception of the institution as intellectual and psychological. In Hauriou's conception, the fundamental element is not the will, but the directing idea which explains the foundation of the institution and the juridical powers of its organs. The will has a role subordinate to the idea, as manifested by the power to act of the founders and organs in service of the idea. Thanks to the phenomenon of consciousness, the idea as assumed by the organs passes into a subjective state in the individual minds of the members, through a process of manifestations of communication between members and organs. So the cohesion of the group is furthered. In Hauriou's view, parties to a contract are equal, while members of an institution submitted themselves to the authority of the organs. In the 19th century, the ideas of the French Revolution made jurists conceive social relationships as a collection of autonomous individuals, forming a political society. Individuals were seen as born free and equal in law, invested with natural rights (liberty, property). These rights were considered as subjective rights attributed to the individual, connected with his/her juridical personality and consisting in power of will with effects that are sanctioned by the State.

Relationships among individuals constitute private law, relationships of individuals with the State public law (rooted in inequality because of the sovereignty of the State). Private law is founded upon contract, because man as a free person can be bound only by his will. The State can limit the autonomy of the individual will for reasons of public order. Public law is grounded largely upon the same individualist bases. The State is seen as a moral person, like physical persons endowed with subjective rights and powers of will. These powers of will are deduced from the sovereignty of the people as expressed in the constitution and laws of parliament. Constitution and laws are expressions of the general will of the people to which each individual has adhered in advance by virtue of the social contract, so the law is still seen as binding citizens by contract. This sovereignty is limited by the rights of man, public liberties and civic rights, and in international relations, the sovereignty of the State is limited only by obligations that the State has voluntarily contracted in international agreements. This subjectivist conception of law implied that the notion of moral personality for associations, corporations and the State is only a legal fiction, as there is no collective will. For Hauriou, agreeing that there are only individual wills, the moral personality is a reality, because the idea that animates it passes in the conscious minds of organs and members.

The subjectivist conception of law was severely disputed by Duguit (1901,1927). He argued that the State has no personality or will. In his view, nobody has subjective rights or powers of will. There are only objective situations determined by the juridical rule. All law is objective; the juridical rule has its source in society. For Duguit, using the sociology of Comte and Durkheim, social solidarity is the primordial social fact in juridical matters. Rules of custom become juridical rules, obligatory under social constraint, when observation of rules is indispensable for development of social solidarity. Durkheim argued that juridical rules are conceived by the collective conscience of society. Duguit, rejecting this myth, stated that it is the mass of individual consciences, which determines what social solidarity requires in a given country at a given time. Human wills express this imperative of society with juridical acts. A law as juridical act is thought to have no more value than a contract. A law is distinguished from contract by its form only. It is a collective act, a multitude of unilateral declarations of will converging to the same object. By its effects, law is an act-rule, creating a juridical situation that is general, abstract and permanent. A contract is a subjective act, creating a juridical situation that is concrete, particular to contracting parties and temporary. Hauriou called his theory of the institution a study in social vitalism. He argued against objectivism and subjectivism. In reaction to Duguit, he said that juridical rules are secondary, limiting the powers of individuals and institutions, which are sources of life and action. With regard to Durkheim, he wrote that the social milieu is inert without creative force.

Some jurists in the first decades of the twentieth century quite convincingly criticised several movements in the philosophy of law prevailing in 18th century (rationalism) and 19th century (positivism). Authors defending current doctrines, giving positive law a rational and moral explanation, did not consider its objective reality and refused to use findings of sociology. Philosophical abstraction and universal reason were substituted for history and experience. Sociological insights were not considered as relevant. Philosophical and juridical rationalism brought "voluntarist" positivism. The will of the legislator or the State was canonised. Positive law was the work of the commanding reason, the reason of the State. Geny (1899; 1914) showed that juridical activity works on four levels: real, rational, historical and ideal. Le Fur (1931) argued that general principles of natural law could be transposed to positive law and concrete applications only if reason worked upon diverse historical and economic data of law. An essential part of legal theory had to be constructed. So, the institutional theory of law, using insights from social sciences, had a crucial function by providing a principle of synthesis. Hauriou (1925) argued that the juridical theory of the institution could develop once controversies over the social contract and between the objective and the subjective were settled. Rousseau supposed that institutions existing in his time were corrupt, because they were founded on sheer force. They had to be revitalised by the social contract as an instrument of free consent, but Rousseau confused force with power. Institutions are founded on power, but this power leaves room for a form of consent ("coactus volui", meaning that I agreed although compelled). The theory of the institution reached maturity during the subjective/objective debate. Jurists by "droit subjectif" mean everything in law that depends on the conscious will of subjects (such as contracts), and by "droit objectif" everything in law that does not depend on the conscious will of particular subjects (such as self-sustaining juridical rules deriving from custom ). Seemingly self-sustaining juridical situations are bound to ideas remaining subconsciously in the minds of an indeterminate number of individuals. The subjective depends on conscious acts of will, the objective on subconscious ideas. Jurists have admitted the coexistence of the subjective and the objective for a long time.

Toward the middle of the nineteenth century however, this dualism was replaced by an ultra-subjectivist system, which was followed by an ultra-objectivist system fifty years later. The subjectivist system was based upon juridical personality. It assimilated corporate moral persons, notably the personified State, to individual persons, and claimed that these persons and their wills were the basis of all lasting juridical situations. German authors like Gerber, Laband and Jellinek, trying to force "regulation" within the subjectivist system, fancied that they could assimilate juridical rules to acts of will of the personified State. The attempt of "droit subjectif" adherents to monopolise all regulation failed (it was impossible to attribute customary rules to the will of the State). Besides, the State has not always existed. The State is a formation of a highly developed civilisation. As Hauriou said, human societies have lived very much longer under the regime of clans, tribes and feudal seigniories than under State regimes. In these primitive formations, law was customary or came directly from the power of the ruler. The new, objectivist thesis of Duguit was as absolute as the subjectivist thesis. The objective juridical rule, considered as something existing in itself, became the basis of all juridical existence (instead of the juridical person). Subjective rights lost their subjective centre. All juridical efficacy was concentrated in the objective juridical rule. The juridical rule was a product of the social milieu, a rule accepted as obligatory by "the mass of consciences". Hauriou argued that we must know where in society the creative power is: create juridical rules institutions, or produce institutions juridical rules owing to the power of government they contain? "The subjective elements are the creative forces in society; they furnish the action. The objective elements, the juridical rule, the social milieu, public policy, are merely elements of reaction, duration and continuity." (Hauriou, 1970, p.98).

Hauriou argued that the theory of the institution and the foundation, historically succeeding the subjectivist and objectivist systems, quite naturally took root in this matter of the foundation of institutions, which the two antagonistic systems had equally disclaimed. According to Hauriou (1970, p. 99) the main points of the new theory of the institution are: "an institution is an idea of a work or enterprise that is realised and endures juridically in a social milieu; for the realisation of this idea, a power is organised that equips it with organs; on the other hand, among the members of the social group interested in the realisation of the idea, manifestations of communion occur that are directed by the organs of the power and regulated by procedures." Elements of every corporate institution are: 1. the idea of the work or enterprise to be realised in a social group; 2. the organised power put at the service of this idea for its realisation; 3. the manifestations of communion that occur within the social group with respect to the idea and its realisation. In Hauriou's conceptualisation, each person under jurisdiction of a State has an idea of the State and is the subject of this idea. The subject of a State is like a shareholder in the enterprise of the State. For Hauriou, corporate institutions undergo the phenomenon of incorporation, which leads them to the phenomenon of personification. Incorporation and personification depend on "interiorisation", bringing organs of government, with their power of will and manifestations of communion of the members of the group, into the framework of the directing idea of the enterprise. The triple movement of "interiorisation", incorporation and personification is seen as crucial for the theory of personality. Hauriou postulated that society is a psychological work. In this psychological work, reciprocal action between the human mind and certain objective ideas are the basis of institutions.

According to Hauriou, the State is incorporated when it has reached the stage of representative government. At this stage, the first task of "interiorisation" has been accomplished: the organs of government, with their powers of will, act for the common good within the framework of the directing idea of the State. The State then has an objective individuality. In international law, it becomes a Power that is all the more distinctive as the nation adheres to its government. The State is personified, when it has reached the stage of political liberty, with citizens participating in government. In the framework of the directing idea, manifestations of communion among members of the group occur that intermingle with decisions of organs of representative government. In the formulation of Hauricu, the corporate institution at the stage of personification adds to the continuity of the idea in its objective state (realised at the stage of incorporation) the continuity of the same idea in its subjective state. The directing idea from this new form of continuity derives the threefold advantage of being able to express itself, to assume obligations, and to be responsible. The subjective continuity of the idea and moral personality bring the corporate institution into the domain of subjective responsibility, which is the counterpart of liberty. The subjective continuity of moral personality enriches effects of the objective continuity of a constituted body. Personality perfects incorporation, assuring realisation of the objective idea in the social milieu. The true objective element of the juridical system is the institution, with a subjective seed developed by personification. The objective element subsists in the institution, with its directing idea and organised power superior to the juridical rule. Institutions make juridical rules. Directing ideas are the vital principle of social institutions.

In Jacobin doctrine, there is nothing between individual and State. The State is all-powerful, producing juridical subjects at will. Against this doctrine, Renard (1930) opposes the theory of the institution, ascertaining that there is a multitude of institutions between individual and State. These institutions have their own reality independent of the State that recognises them. Institutions have an objective reality. True personality is reserved to man.

This marks a limit towards which institutions tend but never reach. Application of personality to anything other than the human individual implies a fiction for Renard. But Delos argued that moral personality of institutions is a social reality. He extended the theory of the institution in the light of sociological observation. "..the object always lies between the individuals involved, and this is what gives the social relationship its exterior, objective character. The societal relationship goes from an individual to an object that establishes the bond with other individuals, and this is why the social relationship takes on an 'objectivity', an externality. This characteristic objectivity is what distinguishes it from inter-individual relationships... but all the elements that integrate a social body – substantial subjects, common ideas, mutual relations – are realities, and thus a social body constitutes a reality that is objective and one." (Delos, 1970, pp. 233-234). "The social body has a personality of its own, distinct from the personalities of its members." (Delos, 1970, p.235). For Delos, social action of one of the members of the social body is simply the act by which this body moves itself, organises itself, administers itself, rules itself internally and regulates its relationships with others. It is the exercise of one of the functions of the social body. "This act is in the strict sense attributed to the group, because the one who performs it acts only in the capacity of organ, member, or minister. Since an act performed by the individual for the ends of the society is only a function, it is in its very essence an act of the group. ...An act is social when it is performed in view of the ends of a society by one of its members. ..since the life of the social body is a totality specifically distinct from individuals' lives, the social body is truly a person, a being conscious of its destiny and responsible for the realization of this destiny." (Delos, 1970, p.237). Recognition of the 'reality' of a moral person, without fiction or metaphor, is effect of the recognition of the 'reality' of social bodies, for personality is a manner of being that is proper to certain of these bodies and verified in them. In international order, the State is the juridical subject par excellence. Within the State, the citizen is the juridical subject par excellence. Delos emphasized that institutions are the ensemble of organising forms that constitute a society. Delos believes less in a 'theory of the institution' than in an 'institutional conception of law'.

For Renard (1930), the theory of the institution raises a problem of juridical ontology, it poses the whole problem of law. His suggestion was to understand moral personality ("crux iuris peritorum") as one of the degrees of institutional existence. Renard (1939) saw ontology and sociology as the two key pieces of the philosophy of the institution. The institution extends its influence beyond the juridical order. The 'social' or the 'institutional' is between the 'human' conceived as a nature and the 'interindividual' conceived as relation ad alterum. There are rights that man has as man: the right to life, and the right of property as expansion of personality. For the benefit of the 'common good', these rights may suffer restrictions, but juridical situations of the individual within an institution derive from that institution. Every title of membership in an institution has prerogatives and obligations accruing to the particular state that it qualifies (citizen, elector, magistrate); these words do not designate 'rights' but 'states' or 'statuses'. The term 'institution' evokes the mode of being that is founded upon the juridical act called constitution. Every institution has its charter, which gives it being ('institutional being') while determining its manner of being and behaving. Institutional dimensions have their institutional being from the external connection with an institution (analogy of attribution). For Renard, law is an analogical reason: "ratio entis, ratio juris". The 'reason' of institution is juridical organisation of the 'common good'.

A central problem in sociology is the relationship between the individual and the social, between personality and society. There is a fundamental difference between human societies and animal societies: reason, liberty, responsibility, in one word, personality. On the human level, there is a break in the hierarchy of beings and a reversal of values between the individual and the social. According to Renard, beneath humanity, the good of the individual is ordered to the good of the species. In the human order, society is ordered to the good of the person. Society is a collective manner of acting and being by the individuals who compose it. For adherents of sociological positivism in the footsteps of Comte, society is a natural product, so its origin is thought to be independent of the will of men. Renard argued that man is ever present at the origin of societies. Man acts everywhere and ever under pressure of his social nature and his historical and cultural environment. With liberty, reason is everywhere. Reason is its code, and the natural energy of the human species. "The higher you go up the scale of the sciences, and the higher you go within each science, the more the reality you are pursuing escapes the grasp of concepts." (Renard, 1970, p.315). In positive law, institution is a fragment of the juridical order. For Renard, of all juridical notions, the institution resists conceptual abstraction the most.

Disregarding the varieties of juridical positivism, Renard (1970, p.319) asserts that there are two essential juridical philosophies. The old Jacobin philosophy, and institutional philosophy, both based on two metaphysics of personality: 1. the personality of man as it would be if it could exist outside social interdependencies and if these interdependencies had no other origin than the juridical acts to which it seemed expedient to commit himself; and 2. the personality of man as it is. For Renard (1970, p.321) "..the jacobin conception envisages only external relationships among men; the institutional conception sees an interpenetration of human activities in the harmony of the common good; ..This fundamental unification ...that has overriden the antagonism between the 'individual' and the 'social' is a victory of juridical pluralism...". The institutional conception makes law a means of communication among peoples. Renard accentuates that the institution features three juridical truths which taken together constitute the institutional conception of law. The institutional conception of law is a reaction against voluntarism. The juridical order is the basis of power, and the juridical order is differentiated (pluralism). Every social power is ordered to a common good of a social character. In reality, law is a synthesis of rights and power. The institutional conception corrects Jacobin individualism putting them in separate camps, power in sovereignty and rights in the relations of private life. For Jacobin individualism, all power is in the State or comes from the State, but law is the 'informing' principle of society: every society, therefore, must have its law. (Renard, 1970, p.327). Ubi societas, ibi ius. Ubi ius, ibi societas.

## 9.3. Public Management of Society beyond the modernism/postmodernism debate

In Public Administration theorising and social sciences, the modernism/postmodernism debate has become popular, so it seems appropriate to sketch some aspects. Sorman (1989) proposed as criterion for genuine thinkers, that after their work it is not possible to think as before. In the course of time, France had many genuine thinkers (Daval, 1965). French philosophy, profoundly influenced by the philosophy of Antiquity and the Middle Ages, is indissolubly intertwined with European philosophy, and with German (Folscheid, 1994) and Anglo-Saxon philosophy (Locke, Bentham, Hume, Mill, Smith and others). French philosophers had a significant position in the development of Western philosophy and science (Brun, 1988; Jerphagnon, 1987). French philosophy, a "universum sui generis", is an inexhaustible source of inspiration (Lacroix, 1966) even in recent times (Trotignon, 1985; Wahl, 1962). It cannot be adequately summarised here. French philosophy should be taken as a structural frame of reference for all who attempt to get a glimpse of French culture or aspects like Public Management of Society. Up to the 16th century, French society seemed to be dependent on the Church, dominated by the ideas of St. Augustine and Thomas Aquinas. In the 16th century France was in the grip of the Renaissance,

Reformation and Humanism. Luther's reform proposals for the Church in 1517, and Calvin's alternative worldview transformed Christian unity into a divided Christianity. Michel de Montaigne (1533-1592), a bewildered observer of religious wars between Catholics and Protestants, was an exponent of Humanism with his "Essais". The appearance of Calvin's book, "Institution de la religion chrétienne" (1541) was a national event in France. Pascal (1632-1662), was a genial philosopher (Attali, 2000; Brun, 1994), and Descartes, a pioneer of modern philosophy ("Discours de la méthode", 1637), gave French philosophy its specific position (Rodis-Lewis, 1992). He used methodical doubt as basic scientific attitude, proclaiming the metaphysical sovereignty of the individual, thinking subject: "Cogito, ergo sum!" Cartesian rationalism became dominant in European thought (Leibniz, Spinoza, etc.). For Malebranche (1638-1715), using Cartesian metaphysics in "La Recherche de la Vérité" (1674/1675), God was the sole real cause of everything, the rest was "occasion": "occasionalisme" (Alquié, 1974).

Pierre Bayle's "Dictionnaire historique et critique" (1697) was an encyclopaedia (Dibon, 1959; Labrousse, 1963/1964). In the 18th century, there was a reaction to empiricism. Condillac (1715-1780) criticised rational apriorism, accentuating experience as the source of all knowledge in "Essai sur l'origine des connaissances humaines" (1748). The "Encyclopédie" (1751/1780), an overview of available knowledge, was a zenith. Ideas of philosophers contributed to a societal process of fermentation, exploding in the French Revolution of 1789. During the 19th century, several philosophical movements came to the fore. Positivism (Faure, 1988; Kremer-Marietti, 1980, 1993; Macherey, 1989). Spiritualism (Janicaud, 1969). And Neo-Thomism, later elaborated by Maritain (1932, 1936). Auguste Comte, fighting metaphysical thought and stressing facts, with "Cours de philosophie positive" (1830) and "Système de politique positive" (1842), founded positivism (Macherey, 1989). Spiritualism of Maine de Biran ("Oeuvres complètes", 1820) and Victor Cousin ("Oeuvres, 1840) argued for subjectivity and spiritual liberty as a reaction to materialist empiricism (Lacroze, 1970). Following "De la contingence des lois de la nature" (1874) by Émile Boutroux, contingency was a topic. At the end of the 19th century, Karl Marx made people speak of his ideas about the necessity of the proletarian revolution as reaction to exploitative capitalism. Property was sacrosanct for the French in the 19th century. Proudhon shocked them with his slogan: "Property is theft". In "L'Action", Blondel (1893) argued for a science of practice, to close the circle from thinking to practice and from practice to thinking. At the turn of the 19th and 20th century, spiritualism was making room for Kant's inspiration. For Renouvier, Kant advanced the Cartesian revolution in an original way. Consciousness and intellectual judgement were central issues. Anatole France wrote "L'Histoire contemporaine" (1896-1901).

The positivism of Comte (1830) and Durkheim (1895) had many adherents. The ideas of historian Taine (1828-1893) in "Les origines de la France contemporaine" (1875/ 1893) had a wide circulation. He rejected the French Revolution as the foundation of the French Republic, and tried to explain history with natural science methods. In his view, characters of human beings and nations are determined by race, environment and conjuncture. Le Roy (1912) promoted the work of Henri Bergson (1859-1941), trying to realise the unity of science and metaphysics, and giving intuition a central place. With his book "L'Évolution créatrice" (1907), Bergson launched an original theory of evolution. In this theory, the "élan vital" as inspiring source of all life has a crucial role. After the 19th century, French philosophy was thoroughly imbued by German philosophy. Kant made an impressive inquiry into the limits of analytical reason. Hegel and Marx searched for the dialectical reason to learn the laws which dominate history. In the historical materialism of Marx, historical reality had to be explained dialectically. German idealism and French rationalism made contributions. Jean Hippolyte (1909-1968) made Hegel accessible in France. Phenomenology caused a breakthrough in France, dominated by neo-Kantian and Hegelian ideas. The slogan of Edmund Husserl (1859-1938), "back to the matter itself" was popular, so was Heidegger's philosophy.

With "La transcerdance de l'égo" (1934), Jean-Paul Sartre (1905-1980) reacted to the ideas of Husserl. Husserl saw consciousness as "intentionality", while the transcendental ego was supposed to realise an ordering in the acts of consciousness. Sartre, however, argued that it was not the ego that realised coherence, but that the objects, upon which the activity of consciousness was directed, realised this. For Sartre, there is no ego in pre-reflexive consciousness. Ego and objects are outside consciousness, being consciousness-transcendent. In Sartre's view, human beings exist in spontaneous, natural, pre-reflexive life. Ego is not in the consciousness, but in the world. The ego-in-the-world has to be studied. Knowledge of the self is as uncertain as knowledge of the other. Sartre saw human beings as designing themselves for the future, and so responsible for their actions. In his "Critique de la raison dialectique" (1962), Sartre tried to combine existentialism (everybody makes his life in freedom in a unique way) and the Marxist concept of man (human beings are determined by socio-economic factors). Sartre supported French Communism, but after the Russian invasion in Hungary (1956) he broke with Communism. For Sartre, Marx's historical materialism was a scientific theory, lacking an epistemological and anthropological foundation. Sartre argued that dialectical laws get their validity from individual dialectical experience. As Descartes and Husserl, Sartre tried to prove self-consciousness as evidence, not using methodical doubt, but a regressive method. Reflecting his position in social reality, the human individual experiences himself as a historical personality. Existentialism has been a popular philosophy in France since 1945.

Maurice Merleau-Ponty (1908-1961) was a prominent representative of existential phenomenology. He rejected the transcendental phenomenology of Husserl, for whom the world constitutes itself in pure consciousness. Merleau-Ponty wanted to analyse the lived space and time, the situation as it was in real human existence. The world is the natural environment for scientific reflection about the world. Merleau-Ponty rejected the "eidetic reduction" of Husserl, reducing the world to a whole of notions about the "eidos" (essence). Human consciousness functions in the human existential world. In "Phénoménologie de la perception" (1945), Merleau-Ponty argued that the world is never totally knowable (mystery of the world of being). For this philosophy of ambiguity, our observation is ambiguous. The world of being, with its interconnectedness of human beings and world, precedes the world of knowing. The relationship between subject and object is not primarily one of knowledge, but of being, in which subject and object influence each other (perceptive relation). Observation takes place on the level of the pre-conscious. The "foi perceptive", referring to basic notions as given with human life, is important. Researchers using scientific methods for knowledge production and proof, often by-pass the essence of observation. Human beings are humans-in-the-world. Observation is determined by the notion of being-in-the-world. Merleau-Ponty distanced himself from the mechanistic worldview of Descartes, seeing the mind as a separate, higher substance, which would direct the body. Rejecting this dualistic mind-body scheme, he argued that there is a mutual relationship between mind and body.

Structuralism, in a sense pursuing Cartesian rationalism, is another approach. Claude Lévi-Strauss, pioneer in cultural anthropology, is seen as the father of structuralism (Bénoist, 1980; Clément, 1985). For him, the notion of structure, used by others before him, is crucial: a whole of enduring relations between mutually inter-changeable elements of a limited repertoire. Scientific inquiry has to analyse social relations as raw material for the construction of models, which have to make the hidden structure manifest. Structural analysis must expose the underlying structure, of which those involved often are unconscious. Structure refers to a part of reality which is mostly underneath the surface of the directly observable world, notions and knowledge-directing ideas in the cultural setting in which humans live. Structures exist due to structuring activities of the human mind, itself part of structured nature. Cultural anthropology inquires into different cultures, also so-called primitive cultures, so the bias of Westernised cultural attitudes, practices and concepts is made explicit. Cultural anthropology produces knowledge about other cultures, and necessary insights into one's own culture (Lévi-Strauss, 1973). A basic epistemological problem is the need for mutual communication between different cultures to translate and understand cultural basics. According to Lévi-Strauss, a combination of scientific distance and identification with others is needed. The collectively unconscious is seen as a bridge. The relationship between Westernised thought and world-views in non-Western societies is made explicit in his "La pensée sauvage" (1962). Lévi-Strauss rejects utilitarianism, dominant in Western cultures. In his view thinking in "primitive" societies, is not irrational as often thought. "Wild thinking" is not pre-rational, preceding modern, rational thought, but is only differently rational. Studying societies with other cultures makes comparison a necessity. Relativising progress in historical science, Lévi-Strauss had a non-Europe centred worldview.

Toynbee (1939) is reputed to have used the term postmodernism for the first time to denote the period after the First World War (Docherty, 1993). Postmodernism later became the name for a philosophy, which challenges the fundamental assumptions of modernism on which we order our thinking about values, world, government, society, social institutions, organisations, and the individual. Modernism is associated with the Enlightenment, viewing positivist epistemology for science as basis for establishing causality in explaining human behaviour and for regulating social interactions. Max Weber, differentiating traditional and modern conceptions of authority and social relations, is known for his social theory and his theory of bureaucracy. Weber (1971) accentuated rationality in the Protestant ethic and its impact upon rational-bureaucratic institutionalising in modern Western societies. Instrumental rationality, to realise goals by efficiently using available means, became the norm. For modernism, science as development of reason is, or should be, a technical, neutral form of knowledge. For Habermas (1972) the subordination of life to the demands of industrial production furthered rationality about the means of action, and produced irrationality with regard to the ends of human existence.

Jun/Rivera (1997, p.134): "Whereas modernism emphasises the utility of tradition (as proven practice), as well as legitimacy, identity, achievement, and rationality, postmodernism stresses detachment from tradition, pluralisation of identity, autonomy, and irrationality or at least counter-rationality, that is, a very different conception of rationality and agency." Bogason (2001) confronted American Public Administration with postmodernism. Postmodernist philosophers like Lyotard (1979; 1984) and Baudrillard (1973) relativised science. Woller (1997, p.9): "Just what is postmodernism? ..In general, postmodernism implies a questioning of the beliefs of modernism.. Modernism, comprising the "seat" on which the majority of the academy rests, can be described as having four legs (or beliefs): a. words, ideas, and things are distinct entities; b. the real world is objective – a fixed object separate from our way of talking about it or representing it; c. the priority of nature over culture; and d. the priority of the individual over society. ..Ultimately, postmodernism is about deposing the trinity of the Enlightenment – reason, nature, and progress – which presumably triumphed over the earlier Trinity." Prominent French postmodernists are: Jacques Derrida, Michel Foucault, and Jacques Lacan.

Derrida's deconstruction, according to D.J. Farmer, is an important practical resource for the public management theorist and practitioner. "..bureaucratic deconstruction is an important public administration resource" (Farmer, 1997, pp. 12-27). Farmer's analysis about Derrida's conceptualisation is followed here. The world (documents, institutional practices, events) is interpreted by Derrida as a text. Rejecting post-modern as a description of his philosophy, he does not identify himself with deconstruction (Derrida, 1995). He uses insights from linguistics (Saussure, 1966). That language is a closed system of signs and meaning as developed from differences between elements of that system. Modernist epistemology produced a logo-centric view of the world, in which conscious thought is valued as the dominant mode of interpretation. Specific terms are privileged over others, meaning is based on underlying oppositions or categories (mind/body, good/bad etc.). In the deconstruction approach, one of the opposing terms is valued at the cost of the other term. Deconstruction is thought to enrich insights by restoring the balance while repositioning the marginalised term, the "logic of the supplement" (Sturrock, 1979). Beyond the labels, Derrida is a postmodernist, just as he is rightly associated with deconstruction. Postmodernism, at its philosophical core, is scepticism about human capacity to grasp or define what is ultimately and totally real. Varieties of postmodernism can be characterised as attempts to explore the consequences and implications of understandings of this scepticism. It is an illusion to suppose that language is transparent. We cannot grasp reality directly without language, but language distorts. "For Derrida, there is no world of the signified independent of the signifier. The term signifier designates a symbol (e.g., a word like manager), and the term signified designates that to which the signifier refers (the person signified as manager). Language helps to construct reality rather than simply recording reality. ...deconstruction shows how the text is distorted by the text's inescapable reliance on binary oppositions and irreducible metaphors. It shows that there are multiple varieties of meanings in the text and that the text constrains the meaning that the writer can express. ...Derrida wants to break down binary opposites like inside-outside, true-false, private-public, masculine-feminine, politician-civil servant, subject-object, health-disease, and good-evil." (Farmer, 1997, p.14).

A metaphor has a distorting effect, as it not only disguises and shifts a text's meaning, but also yields multiple meanings. The reading, in Derrida's view, is necessarily multiple, because understanding a metaphor requires the reader to create. Derrida holds that even the most apparently literal text – for example those in physics – involves metaphor. The Newtonian view rests on the metaphor of the mechanical universe. For Sarap (1993), we think of theories as buildings, with foundations and superstructures. We think of organisations "spatially, in terms of up and down". Derrida opposes logo-centrism, the attitude that rational language can represent the essence of things – the attitude that signifiers, or words and sentences, are labels that refer clearly to items in the world. He holds that there is no immediately available area of certainty. Signs also refer to what is absent and to the relationship between signs. It is impossible to know the meaning of "I" without knowing relationships with other signs like "you, she, he, it, we, and they". Meaning emerges at the end of sentences and passages, and is not invariant between contexts. For Derrida, reason tyrannises by excluding the uncertain and marginal. In his view, there is no direct and unmediated knowledge of the world. His view is placed in perspectives: all that is available to us is thought and perception from a perspective (Farmer, 1997, p.15).

The clearing away of delusions in public administration thinking is seen as one of the benefits of deconstruction and postmodernism. "Liberating public administration thinking from entrapment in the efficiency metaphor. ...the failure to conceptualise government as the focus of business and financial pressures but also to the misguided attempt to structure, to judge, and to manage government activity "on business lines". ...Beyond the clearing of these and other delusions, deconstruction raises the prospect of anti-administration. Deconstruction, as an element in a post-modern attitude, suggests the possibility of a juxtaposition of "administration and anti-administration" that can provide significant change in public administration practice." (Farmer, 1997, pp. 16-17). The efficiency metaphor is a powerful modernist metaphor that is seen to require repeated deconstruction. An outline for a three-step deconstruction is summarised by Farmer (1997, pp. 18-19). The first step might be that it is false that the efficiency concept signifies an inevitable feature of any possible world. Efficiency is a social construct, not a given. A second step can point to the culture-specific and modernist character of the efficiency concept. Efficiency is part of the language of social control. The third step is to show that the opposition between efficient and inefficient is ambiguous. As a normative criterion, efficient is perverse. Regardless of whether it is defined in purely instrumental public administration terms or in the sense of Pareto efficiency or maximising social utility, it is perverse in the sense that efficiency does not guarantee a just outcome. Results can be unjust. "The government is responsible for the health and prosperity of the entire economy; by contrast, even the largest private corporation, is responsible only for its own profits. It is no wonder that because of this social construction, private sector activities appear more efficient." (oc, p.19).

"Any such deconstruction of the efficiency ethic in public administration is important because it opens up the prospect of a liberation ethic and anti-administration ..It clears the way for a liberation ethic that seeks to free public administration thinking from the conceptual constraints, prejudices, and stereotypes that public administration theory has inherited from the hierarchical view of bureaucracy." (Farmer, 1997, p.19). "Anti-administration ..is a method of administering that is opposed to the Weberian, hierarchical approach. Anti-administration suggests an outlook that favours anarchism, agnostic multiculturalism, and diversity. Rejecting cultural hierarchy, for example, anti-administration is radically multicultural... It is a form of managing that reflects the philosophical scepticism of postmodernism, a scepticism that rejects the certainties and context-free truths of modernity and the bold "take-charge" administrative style that sets out to control nature, events, and people. A non-hierarchical bureaucracy, constituting anti-administration, would lead to different sets of accepted "truths" than hierarchical bureaucracy. This is suggested by analyses like Foucault's accounts of normalising and power." (Farmer, 1997, p.20). For Foucault, knowledge is not primarily power, but power is primarily knowledge. Farmer (1997, pp. 20-21): "What counts as accepted knowledge within bureaucracies reflects the power relations in that bureaucracy and in that subculture. ..A non-hierarchical bureaucracy, expressing anti-administration, is a feasible concept. Various literatures, such as those on anarchism and on feminism, suggest this. ..Anarchists typically understand the nation-state to be a passing phenomenon.. Typically, they favour loose, non-compulsory, and decentralised organisation. For them, society should be non-coercive and non-hierarchical. Any post-modern turn in public administration involves more than merely deconstruction; deconstruction is only one suit in the post-modern deck of cards.". Elsewhere, Farmer (1995) argued that deconstruction is part of a post-modern attitude that must stand beside – and that is involved in – emphases like imagination, de-territorialisation, and "alterity". "Alterity is the relationship with the moral other.." (Farmer, 1997, p.21).

Attacks on deconstruction are widespread and strong, (Ellis, 1989)...Defences can be offered against such charges, however (Atkins, 1983). "Derrida's deconstructive conclusion that the meaning of texts is undecidable does tend, at first sight, to undermine the claim that deconstruction is an important resource for public administration thinking. Deconstruction does not appear to meet what might be considered minimal conditions for determining a right administrative act, that is what ought to be done. ..Deconstruction also makes problematic Derrida's claim (1992) that 'deconstruction is justice'." (Farmer, 1997, p.21). For Derrida (1976), deconstruction is a strategy without finality. So "Deconstruction represents a loss of confidence in the availability of objective criteria that allows texts to have distinct and transparent meanings. In Derrida's view, all texts are writings that refer to other texts. Meaning is deferred...The upshot of deconstruction is radical indeterminacy. Is a strategy without finality – or writing that leads to more writing, and more, and still more –

the required ticket for determining a right administrative act – or for justice?" (Farmer, 1997, pp. 22-23). For Farmer (1997, p.25) post-modernity is scepticism about the capability of human reason.

Michel Foucault (1926-1984), branded as "cryptonormativist", is a prominent representative of postmodernism or post-structuralism. "What we need ...is a political philosophy that isn't erected around the problem of sovereignty, nor therefore around the problems of law and prohibition." (Foucault, 1980, p.121). He introduced "governmentality" about a new arrangement, making the art of governing thinkable and practicable. His ideas have been aptly assembled by Burchell and others (1991): "Government resides in the things it manages and in the pursuit of the perfection and intensification of the processes which it directs; and the instruments of government, instead of being laws, now come to be a range of multiform tactics. Within the perspective of government, law is not what is important. ...the State can only be understood on the basis of the general tactics of governmentality" (p. ix). The Foucault perspective is more sophisticated than this assertion would make us believe. "I don't want to say that the State isn't important; what I want to say is that relations of power necessarily extend beyond the limits of the State." (Foucault, 1980, p.95). "The problem of government finally came to be thought, reflected and calculated outside of the juridical framework of sovereignty." (Burchell c.s., 1991, p. ix). "Methods of elaborating, defending, and inculcating discipline became more important 'when it became important to manage a population' (p.ix). The result is 'a triangle sovereignty-discipline-government, which has as its primary target the population and as its essential mechanism the apparatus of security' (p.ix). That is governmentality." Cawley/Chaloupka (1997, p.34) add that securing sovereign rights for a population makes necessary acts of discipline and governance that also keep government in power. They underline the shift from law to regulation, as elaborated by Hunt/Wickham (1994): "If law is the stipulation of general rules then regulation is more task oriented and less prohibitive, in that it is employed to define detailed goals and targets for training and other forms of intervention directed at the behaviour of individuals." (p.22).

Foucault, realising historical studies, which were characterised as philosophical exercises, tried to develop an "archaeology of knowledge" as historical method. About his way of critical reflection he said: "..criticism is no longer going to be practised in the search for formal structures with universal value, but rather as a historical investigation into the events that have led us to constitute ourselves and to recognise ourselves as subjects of what we are doing, thinking, saying...Archaeological – and not transcendental – in that it will not seek to identify the universal structures of all knowledge or all possible moral action, but will seek to treat the instances of discourse that articulate what we think, say and do as so many historical events." (Foucault, 1984, pp. 45-46). Foucault's analysis according to Owen (1996, p.127) is articulated along three axes: knowledge (reflection on oneself and others), power (action on the action of others), and ethics (action on the actions of oneself). While Habermas tried to provide an analytics of truth, Foucault is concerned with investigating the politics of truth: "..the types of discourse which (a society) accepts and makes function as true; the mechanisms and instances which enable one to distinguish true and false statements, the means by which each is sanctioned; the techniques and procedures accorded value in the acquisition of truth; the status of those who are charged with saying what counts as true." (Foucault, 1984, p.73). The relationship between power and knowledge is in the centre of his philosophy. For Owen (1996, p.132), "the interest which guides Foucault's reflection on the past concerns how we have become what we are in the present and how what we are acts to constrain what we may become in the future, which may seem to 'instrumentalise the past in terms of the needs of the present'."

While it is a matter of course that social-psychological dimensions are a crucial aspect of power, authority and management in human interaction and communication, it is not so obvious that psychoanalysis has a specific contribution to make in public management theorising. Since the work of Jacques Lacan (1981,1991), forerunner of the psychoanalytical study of culture, this has changed. According to McSwite (1997), trying to show why public administration needs Lacan, public administration scholars have been reluctant to discuss or establish a philosophical foundation for their theorising. Their assumptions about people and knowledge are said to be grounded in a common-sense grasp of experience. People are assumed to be rational, intentional and goal directed, and in doing so to calculate the costs and benefits of their actions. For McSwite, the question of ontology, a philosophical position on the nature of human beings, was almost entirely implicit in public administration theorising. McSwite (1997, p.45): "the grounding paradigm of public administration is congruent at virtually every point with the outline of satisfaction-oriented economic man and power-oriented political man. Public administration, in other words, has one of its paradigmatic feet planted in political science and the other in economics..". So, the crucial role of law is forgotten. Authors like Wildavsky consider economics as the best frame of reference for government and public administration. Market theory, seen as an alternative to governance through policy and administrative institutions, even enjoys pre-eminence worldwide in our society of globalisation. "The field of public administration has... legitimated the perspective of its worst intellectual enemy, economics." (McSwite,1997, p.46).

Public administration needs a way of understanding social life, including the importance of government for social order and the role of administration in government. Psychoanalytic theory is thought to help give public administration a perspective by exposing the insufficiency of methodological individualism of the economic model (Lane, 1991). Human nature transcends limits of the economic model (Rhoads, 1985). Relevant contributions were realised by Parsons (1951) and recent efforts to use the work of Carl Jung (1958) in developing social theory (Bernstein, 1989; Denhardt, 1981; Okajnyk, 1976; Progroff, 1973). Jungian theory had difficulty in demonstrating how the structure of human nature articulates with social order so that this social order is based on more than market transactions. This is what, according to McSwite (1997, p.47, Lacanian theory does so well: "It provides a powerful, detailed understanding of the social dimension of the self, the connection of all individual identity through the common medium of language ...Lacan thus provides public administration with an ontology that shows the importance of a stable symbolic order to social well-being." Lacan stressed human subjectivity in a world full of symbols: "the subject resides within and has its fate set by the world of language. This sense, ...that consciousness itself is located outside the individual in the symbolic process...In the Lacanian world, the organic body is not the body of the subject; the subject has no body until it has been given one through the symbolic process. ..life is lived in an imaginary realm, one that is configured by the play of signifiers in the symbolic system of signification." (McSwite, 1997, pp. 55-56). McSwite (1997, p.59): "Understanding social process as emanating from the symbolic level may indicate that a completely different approach to policy and program be adopted, one that aims not at effects on behaviour but on identity."

According to McSwite (1997, p.57), the prevailing epistemology of public administration sees the economic subject as a subject who only wants satisfaction: the idea of the human person as a utility maximiser. Public administration's role is the instrumentally, efficiently carrying out of satisfaction-producing programs. Administration becomes a policy design and implementation science, with a positive, rationalist and realist epistemology. McSwite (1997, p.57): "It can hardly allow for the existence of an unconscious dimension of mind, at least an unconscious dimension that is independent of the control and apprehension of the conscious mind. However, this is precisely the central emphasis of Lacan's model of the human subject. The subject, as conscious mind, is irretrievably cut off from not only the Real but from itself. The subject is barred from understanding itself, in the sense that consciousness means this. The subject, in other words, is a cipher that is operated on by the process of signification, the discourse of the Other, the unconscious. It means that truth is found by admitting the unconscious into the realm of consciousness.". McSwite (1997, p.58): "..it is precisely public administration's rationalism, grounded in its realist epistemology and its identification of itself as the technical aspect of government that has become its central problem. To escape the trap that this issue represents, we must find an alternative ontology and epistemology that point to a different identity. This is precisely what the Lacanian concept of the subject does." Lacan invites a "search for the enjoyment of acting in accord with the law of the symbolic. ..ethical action – action in accord with the law of the symbolic." (McSwite, 1997, p.60). "It gives us good reason for limiting the trust we place in our rational minds and thereby opening ourselves to an alliance with the unconscious Other and its personal, tacit, and intuitive way of approaching our experience and our action in the world." (McSwite, 1997, p.61). Postmodernism had its ascent as a philosophical movement in the 1960s. Since the 1990s, postmodernist Public Administration theorising has been a trend with the ideas of Wittgenstein, Foucault, Lyotard and others. Wittgenstein (1922, p.189), using the metaphor of language-games, accentuated the limits of language and said: "Whereof one cannot speak, thereof one must be silent.". Lyotard argued for knowledge as narrative. White (1992), inspired by Wittgenstein and Lyotard, questions that scientific work is different from the "stories, myths, fables, legends, and tales" that served as the foundation for social behaviour in pre-modern times.

For White, all knowledge systems, science included, are stories or narratives, telling people how to behave and to establish social relations, defining criteria for making judgements, and legitimising institutions that promulgate them. These narratives, based on playing language games, are composed of rules that allow utterances to have meaning for a community. They are not meaningful in a universal sense. Habermas (1990) inspired Fox/Miller (1995), arguing for societal discourse (open, societal communication) for decision-making on public policies. They see ideals such as justice and equality as self-validating foundational universals. So consistently, they should reject Habermas' idea of universal principles. As Scott (1997) elaborated, Habermas in his later work on the moral dimensions of public discourse was inspired by Kohlberg's theorising about moral development and by Rawls' theory of justice. Kohlberg (1984) divided the moral development of individuals into three levels, each with two stages (Kohlberg/Ryncarz, 1990). The pre-conventional level of moral reasoning is characteristic of children up to about the age of 11 or 12. The focus of the good is the individual; morality is seen in terms of personal rewards and punishments. At the second stage, individuals begin to recognise the needs of other individuals (agreements for mutual benefit). The conventional stage of moral reasoning can start at the age of 11 and is ordinarily achieved by the end of adolescence. At this level, morality is defined in social terms of conformity to role expectations, conventions and rules of society. At the second stage of the conventional level, individuals develop awareness of the general good of the group, institution or society; and concern for making a contribution. The post-conventional or principled stage of moral development is achieved by a small number of adolescents by the age of 16, but most adolescents and adults do not reach this level of moral development, characterised by differentiation of self from rules and expectations of others, and by recognition of a variety of moral beliefs held by others, and a moral system, which recognises that laws and rules derive from more general moral principles, a universal principle of justice. At the second level of post-conventional moral development (stage 6), individuals can understand and integrate moral conflicts, such as those between rules and principles.

Kohlberg's theorising about moral development was integrated by Habermas (1990) into his concept of discourse as a rational process of argumentation. He accentuates that engaging oneself in ethical discourse requires a thought process in which validity rather than the social currency of a norm is the basis of action. A concept of justice cannot be understood as such from a pre-conventional perspective of authority relations and external influence, but only after achieving the conventional stage. Only at the post-conventional stage is the truth about the world of pre-conventional conceptions revealed. The idea of justice can be gleaned only from the idealised form of reciprocity that underlies discourse (p.165). Habermas, rejecting moral relativism, argues for the grounding of discourse-based ethics in universal principles of justice. Habermas (1990, p.165): "Thus the orientation to principles of justice and ultimately to the procedure of norm-justifying discourse is the outcome of the inevitable moralisation of a social world become problematic.", and: "The discourse-centred approach to ethics does not limit itself to the claim that it can derive a general principle of morality from the normative content of the indispensable pragmatic preconditions of all rational debate. Rather this principle itself refers to the discursive redemption of normative validity claims, for it anchors the validity of norms in the possibility of a rationally founded agreement on the part of all those who might be affected, insofar as they take on the role of participants in a rational debate. In this view, settling of political questions, as far as their moral core is concerned, depends on the institutionalisation of practices of rational public debate." (Habermas, 1992, pp. 447-448).

Harmon (1995) criticises rational discourse on government, while elaborating on responsibility as paradox. For Harmon (1995, pp. 76-77), "schismogenic" paradoxes result from lapses or failures to see situations as unavoidably involving opposition or contradictory aspects: "The adjective schismogenic, then, may be used to describe sets of opposing or contradictory virtues, values and principles, whose individual elements have become split off from one another, and in which one side or element has been comprehended or chosen to the exclusion of the other, ostensibly in the interest of logical consistency and the pursuit of a purpose. Schismogenic thinking is a rational process characteristic especially of Western societies, and it reflects many of both the virtues and liabilities that rationality and rationalism exhibit." Traditional dichotomies in Public Administration (politics/ administration; facts/ values) are due to this schismogenic thinking as inherent in the rational model. Contradiction and opposition are not aberrations in an otherwise rational world, but "defining features, both empirically and morally, of the individual's inner experience and of the outer world of social and institutional relations." (Harmon, 1995, p.204). To tackle the problems with paradoxes, he argues for rejection of any strict distinction between factual and moral, and for unification of moral and factual polarities. For White (1990, p.144), rationalisation of administration and society resulted in a a failure to make necessary normative, political and moral judgements. He argues for practical discourse: "Practical discourse involves dialogue among decision makers about the rightness of the ends to be sought and the means to achieve them. Dialogue involves communication, argumentation, deliberation, persuasion and choice. The goal of practical discourse is the attainment of a mutual understanding of people's beliefs and values." So, a climate of moral maturity can be furthered.

For Rorty (1989, p.86), common vocabularies and common hopes bind societies together. Members of society need to share the same vocabularies in a measure that is sufficient to make peaceful coexistence possible. Society is not bound together by universal principles of rightness, but by adherence to similar vocabularies. Rorty sees science as a forum for unforced agreement. "Science is rational not because it has a foundation, but because it is a self-correcting enterprise which can put any claim in jeopardy, though not all at once." (Rorty, 1979, p.180). For Rorty, rationality becomes solidarity with an accepted set of beliefs. Tennert (1998, p.237): "Hence, his notion of knowledge is necessarily ethnocentric, not in the ideologically narrow sense that our culture provides the right answers to our questions, but in the broader sense that we are bound to our language and our own web of beliefs." Tennert (1998, p.239) concludes about the theory of public administration: "The question on knowing what to do cannot be solved by appeal to theory. Theory cannot tell us what to do. It can only be solved by dialogue. Moreover, the answers will vary from context to context, and will vary in similar contexts at different times.". Ethnocentrism implies recognition of the contingent nature of values. Whether others' values are reasonable depends on possibilities to integrate them into our existential-cultural mindset. This mindset includes the emotional intelligence of human beings in communications and interactions (Goleman, 1997). For Public Management of Society, this means: all its dimensions are context- and situation-dependent aspects with different meanings in specific cultures. Under the influence of positivism, an important part of scientific work has been abstract, logo-centric, empirically derived, generalisable, and hypo-deductive (King, 1998, p.163). Popper (1959) influenced post-positivistic social science. He argued that the role of science is to separate facts from fiction with scientific inquiry, while using not proof, but falsification as a basis for testing and experimentation. Instrumental rationality does play a role in theoretical writings with a Western bias, but: "..the empiricist and positivist citadels of English-speaking social philosophy have been threatened and undermined by successive waves of hermeneuticists, structuralists, post-empiricists, deconstructionists, and other invading hordes." (Skinner, 1985, p.6). They made conceptualising differ from what Popper prescribed. King (1998, p.164): "While foundationalist social science epistemology is concerned with certainty and how knowledge is possible, these new perspectives are concerned with the local and contingent and how understanding is possible...The focus is on meaning, whether seen in behaviours, intent, language, signs, signifiers, metaphors or hyperreality."

Many contemporary philosophers, accentuating understanding as the core business, might be called hermeneuticists. White (1998) invites us to go beyond reliance on technical rationality by using a broader conception of theoretical reflection, incorporating interpretative and critical reasoning. Interpretation and critique, usually associated with cultural and human sciences, are normally not seen as part of science. Yet, these are essential to development of professional identity and mature, cultivated persons. Technical or instrumental rationality dominated Western society. The post-modern condition of our society is characterised by a breakdown of the grand narratives that gave meaning to life. A broader conception than the over-accentuated rationality model might create opportunities to serve the needs of citizens by taking the public general interest more seriously. Dualistic thinking along the theory-practice demarcation, a socially constructed approach, impeded a broader conception. Scientific theory is not always practical in practice (Hummel, 1991). Practical theory, placed in a context, and focused on meaning, is theory that goes beyond knowledge on the way to understanding (Miller/ King, 1998). Scientists and practitioners (thinking about their activities) are engaged in theory. Schön (1983) focused on thinking professionals as reflective practitioners. The structuration theory of Giddens (1984) shows a pathway beyond the gap between theory and practice. Structuration theory makes explicit how deconstructed categories are reproduced in actions and other recursive practices, while actors constitute meaning through relationships. Harmon (1995) put forward that good relationships ask for self-reflexivity, a context of personal relation in which commitment to the other is central, and unity and separation are balanced. In the Western rationality model, underlying theory and practice, rationality is overvalued, while emotionality, feeling and intuition were undervalued. For Jung (1958, p.13), "rational argument can be conducted with some prospect of success only so long as the emotionality of a given situation does not exceed a certain critical level."

Both thinking (cognition, analysis) and feeling (intuition, evaluation) have their function in human communication, action and interaction. Not only intellectual intelligence is relevant, but especially also emotional intelligence (Goleman, 1997). Recent feminist literature is a welcome qualitative addition and correction with regard to all too masculine writings (Fonow/Cook, 1991; Lather, 1991), but it is too easy to argue for making scientific and practical work more feminist (Shepard, 1993). Above all, when this argumentation is, implicitly or explicitly, based on the supposition that feelings and emotions are the more or less exclusive domain of women. A more mature view holds that there is an overarching way of looking at the way human beings (women and men) are communicating and interacting as human beings. Complementary intelligence, based on adequate combination of feminine and masculine capacities and rationalities, is the real issue. The whole range of human capacities is needed for a reasonable society and adequate Public Management of Society. Some authors invoke hermeneutic imagination (Bleicher, 1982) with its emphasis on interpretative analysis of meaningful phenomena in a general meaning-context. This interpretative approach is developed in the philosophical hermeneutics of Heidegger (1962), Gadamer (1975), Ricoeur (1978, 1992), Taylor (1985, 1989) and others. The interpretative, hermeneutic approach is an alternative to approaches to social inquiry like naturalistic or explanatory; descriptivist; critical social science; and post-modern or social constructionist approaches (Richardson/ Fowers, 1998). In naturalistic inquiry, social phenomena are analysed by methods which are analogous to those of the natural sciences. This approach is based on the ideal of knowledge as empirical theory, with explanation (and eventually prediction) as objective. That kind of theory consists of universal, a-historical laws derived from some assumptions and confirmed empirically by carefully controlled experimentation.

Because values are seen as subjective, scientific knowledge with its pretension to objectivity is thought to be about facts, not values. In former times and cultures outside the modern West, this separation between social reality and morality was not the prevailing worldview. In the 16th and 17th centuries, a new kind of scientific inquiry developed. Descartes led the way into a rationalistic approach to science by emphasizing that knowledge does not come from authority, custom or tradition, but results from correct inner representations of reality. His method of systematic doubt as criterion of true science had a dominant impact. Scholars refined the naturalistic method of science. Mainstream social science in the 20th century was qualified as naturalistic and empiricist-positivist. This dominant approach is questioned time and again. Alternatives to this mainstream social science like descriptivism, critical social science, postmodernism and hermeneutics are worthwhile as a correction to the dominant view on knowledge and understanding in theory and practice. The critical theory of the German "Frankfurt School" made its fame by thoroughly criticising mainstream theorising, built on instrumental rationality (Held, 1980). For Habermas (1970, 1991), an imposing producer of critical theory, modern society is negatively influenced by confusion of "praxis" (cultural meaningful actions) with "techne" (technical capacity). Cultural and moral dimensions of human life are mostly reduced to technical and instrumental considerations. Many technical recommendations in the sphere of means-ends rationality don't give adequate answers to practical or moral questions. The positivistic approach, contrary to what its pretended value-neutral status would have us believe, contains a tacit system of values. In the framework of Enlightenment, positivism positions itself as doing away with ignorance, superstition, dogmatism and arbitrary authority, treating all values as subjective and reducing knowledge to findings of objective science. According to Habermas, we must restore the normal functioning of human action and social life as praxis. Not purposive-rational or instrumental actions, but communicative action or interaction, should be taken as the kernel of social life. Communicative action is not instrumental activity, governed by technical rules, but symbolic interaction governed by consensual norms defining reciprocal obligations for behaviour (Habermas, 1991, p.92). Habermas, arguing for an ethics of discourse, held emancipation as a primary value.

With open discussion and argumentation, a kind of "ideal speech situation" ("Diskurs") should be organised. Human beings as social, communicative beings should communicate about and discuss what they see as relevant and worthwhile. So a consensus might be created about fundamental issues such as social justice. "A major difficulty with Habermas's critical theory concerns its claim that the kind of moral reasoning defined by the ideal speech situation is both universally valid and sufficient for moral purposes. In the end, his approach seems to be a rich, dialogical version of liberal individualism and encounters some of the difficulties of that moral outlook. ..Liberal individualists or formalists try to legislate the how but not the what of ethical reasoning or debate." (Richardson/Fowers, 1998, p.478). Formalists in the liberal tradition try to legislate over how we engage in ethical reasoning. They claim neutrality because they don't dictate the content of discussions. Kant's "categorical imperative" (treat others as ends, not as means to one's own ends) and Kohlberg's theory of moral development are examples of this kind of formalism. The Rule of Law in liberal democracies, providing citizens with an abstract or procedural kind of justice, is another example. The critical theory of Habermas with his ideal speech situation seems to boil down to formalism. Taylor (1985) argued that such ethical principles reflect substantive moral beliefs and commitment of our civilisation to fundamental equality and dignity of all individuals. The procedural universalism of Habermas had an element of "Enlightenment dogmatism" for Warnke (1987, p.174).

The ideal speech situation forms a bias in favour of limiting moral discussion to broad, formal issues of justice. Post-modern thinkers reject the attempt of Habermas to define a universal standard or procedure for critically evaluating our values and practices. "They see that sort of critical theory as just another example of modern Western society's absolutising its own way of life and arbitrarily insisting that all cultures and peoples be judged in terms of its own ethnocentric point of view." (Richardson/Fowers, 1998, p.480). Habermas clarified the concept of communicative rationality, while distinguishing between three types of validity claims: claims of truth, claims of normative rightness (both redeemed discursively) and claims of truthfulness (redeemed by ongoing interaction). Discursive redemption of validity claims to truth and normative rightness entails that participants must presuppose three principles (Benhabib/Dallmayr, 1990, p.337): "1. The principle of universal moral respect (all beings capable of speech and action are entitled to participate in the argumentation process); 2. The principle of egalitarian reciprocity (participants have an equal right to introduce and question claims, to put forward reasons, to express needs, interests, and desires, etc.); 3. The principle of non-coercion (no participants should be prevented from exercising these rights to, and of, participation). Habermas (1987, p.322), recognising the context-dependence of idealising presuppositions of communicative action, claims that validity of these presuppositions is not context-bound: "The transcendental moment of universal validity bursts every provinciality asunder." In his view, a contested norm cannot meet with consent of participants in practical discourse, unless the principle of "universalisability" holds: "Unless all affected can freely accept the consequences and the side effects that the general observance of a controversial norm can be expected to have for the satisfaction of the interests of each individual. ..Only those norms can claim to be valid that meet (or could meet) with the approval of all affected in their capacity as participants in a practical discourse." (Habermas, 1990, p.93).

Objectivism, underlying a huge part of modern thought, can be defined as the "basic conviction that there is or must be some permanent, a-historical matrix or framework to which we can ultimately appeal in determining the nature of rationality, knowledge, truth, reality, goodness, or rightness." (Bernstein, 1983, p.8). Inquiry in natural sciences, and also in naturalistic social sciences, was dominantly objectivist in character. This objectivist nature was questioned by Kuhn (1970) with his paradigm shifts or theory-choices. Paradigms can be compared with each other, but it is often not possible to decide which paradigm has the preference, as there is no independent ground or criterion. "..theory-choice is a judgmental activity requiring imagination, interpretation, the weighing of alternatives, and application of criteria that are essentially open." (Bernstein, 1983, p.56). It is said that objective rationality is to be found not in rule following, but in rule transcending, in knowing how and when to put rules and principles to work and when not (Bernstein, 1983,p.57). In a post-positivist view, scientific inquiry is a judgmental activity, not making ourselves the victims of facts. Richardson and Fowers (1998, p.487) in a debate about natural science inquiry: "It seems to be part of the reality and risk of both scientific inquiry and the moral life that to act appropriately means different things in different situations and that one's understanding of what this involves can grow with experience." For Slife/Williams (1995, pp. 180 ff), this holds for social sciences.

For hermeneutic thinkers such as Taylor (1989) and Weinsheimer (1985) knowledge is historically conditioned, interpretative and creative. They show that there are differences between natural science and social science. It remains an ambition to develop knowledge as a correct representation of an independent reality. "Of course, this representational view leads to insoluble puzzles concerning, among other things, how we can gain indubitable access to realities through our mental representations that are at the same time independent of them." (Richardson/Fowers, 1998, p.488). For hermeneuticists, it is obvious that objectivism had to be corrected. Hermeneutics tries to go beyond approaches like scientism, constructionism, individualism and postmodernism (Gadamer, 1975, 1981; Guignon, 1991; Ricoeur, 1992). "Hermeneutic thinkers are committed to rethinking this representational view of knowledge, including its associated moral ideals, in a fundamental way. They agree with critics of foundationalism and subject-object ontology that we have no direct or immediate access to a real world or transcendent norms independent of our interpretation of things. Claims that we do are really just additional interpretations that need to be grounded as well, producing an infinite regress from which there is no escape. Our understanding today of the ways in which knowledge claims are the products of historical development and shaped by social processes makes the view of knowing as simply forming accurate inner pictures of an outer reality seem absurd." (Richardson/Fowers, 1998, p.489). Human beings interpret the existential situations they are in. "Historical experience changes the meaning events can have for us, not because it alters our view of an independent object, but because history is a dialectical process in which both the object and our knowledge of it are continually transformed." (Richardson/Fowers, 1998, p.490). For hermeneuticists, the hermeneutic dialogue (Richardson, et al., 1998) must replace the modernist quest for certainty, and the anti-foundationalism of postmodernism.

## 9.4. From governance to professional Public Management of Society

Recently, it has become customary to shy away from terms such as government and public administration, and to use governance instead. Is this really a productive step? No, particularly because this term is a multi-interpretable container-notion to suit all tastes (Pierre, 2000) although its blurring of responsibilities for public and private actors and sectors is propagated as an asset. From a democratic viewpoint, and from a professional perspective, it is a nuisance that actors are bereft of their responsibilities for their actions in specific roles. The term governance is associated by many with wishful objectives such as a new approach to co-operation between public and private sectors and actors, and new patterns of interaction between government and society. Therefore, a summary discussion of governance might be useful. In the framework of development politics, it seemed old-fashioned or even part of a Western bias to write about State, government and public administration. In a liberalising world market, the State was "out". Later "bringing the State back in" became popular. A new term was coined by the World Bank (1992): governance. Governance became popular as governing without government (Rosenau/Czempiel, 1992). Stoker (ISSJ, 1998) qualified the somewhat anti-authoritarian character of governance: "The essence of governance is its focus on governing mechanisms which do not rest on recourse to the authority and sanctions of government." Rosenau (2000, p.171) "..governance is conceived as systems of rule, as the purposive activities of any collectivity that sustain mechanisms designed to insure its safety, prosperity, coherence, stability, and continuance. Governments specialize in such mechanisms, but they are also to be found in a variety of other types of collectivities...I use the label 'collectivity' to refer to any group of people – be it a state, a corporation, a non-profit organization, a social movement, etc. – who have a common affiliation but who are so numerous that they cannot interact on a face-to-face basis." and: "..governance, however defined, is centrally concerned with the management of change and the reduction of complexity." (oc, p.174).

Kooiman (2000, pp. 138-139): "looks at governance as societal, with public as well as private 'governors' participating...social-political governance will be considered to be arrangements in which public as well private actors aim at solving societal problems or create societal opportunities, and aim at the care for the societal institutions within which these governing activities take place." and: "..not only the locus of boundaries between state and society change, but also that the boundaries themselves change in character and become increasingly permeable. Where government begins and society ends, becomes more diffuse." (oc, p.142). Quite a strange way of making theoretical problems, because society does not end (only at the end of time), and includes government. Kooiman (2000, p.144-145): "Since governance theory emphasizes interactions and, particularly, governing-as-interaction(s), it is essential not to lose sight of the actors. In fact they cannot be separated from the interactions among them. Actors and interactions mutually determine each other. ...Taking a closer view, the actors themselves consist of interactions and the boundaries from which they derive their identities are relative and often fuzzy." What to do with this high degree of hocus-pocus theorising? Actors don't consist of interactions, they are just human beings, teams of human beings or organisations run by human beings, that's all. In governance literature, the bad side of government is ascribed to "traditional government" and the good side is attributed to governance. Rhodes (2000, p.55) diagnosed: "..the term 'governance' has an unfortunately large number of meanings...There are at least seven separate uses of governance relevant to the study of Public Administration: corporate governance; the new public management; 'good governance'; international interdependence; socio-cybernetic systems; the new political economy; and networks. ..The word can be used as a blanket term to signify a change in the meaning of government."

Governance is often used in the framework of economic theorising about the relationship between the state and the economy. "..although the economy is governed it is not necessarily governed by the state. There are different modes of governance, many of them non-state. There is some disagreement about how many, but the list includes markets, hierarchies, networks/associations and clans/communities " (Gamble, 2000, p.111). Due especially to the impact of globalisation and "footloose global capital", the nation state has been described as becoming less relevant or even irrelevant. Public authorities are not footloose, but intensively interconnected with their local, regional and national contexts and cultural environments. Of course, the decline of the state has been exaggerated. While governance as corporate governance is explicitly about co-ordination in the field of capitalism and business, governance as networks is popular for all kinds of activities. Rhodes (2000, pp. 60-61): "Networks are the analytical heart of the notion of governance in the study of Public Administration. ...Networks are a common form of social co-ordination

...governance also suggests that networks are self-organizing. At its simplest, self-organizing means a network is autonomous and self-governing. Networks resist government steering, develop their own policies and mould their environments. So, Rhodes defines governance as self-organizing, interorganizational networks. ...Networks are not accountable to the state; they are self-organizing. Although the state does not occupy a privileged, sovereign position, it can indirectly and imperfectly steer networks." Rhodes (2000, p.77): "But networks are an example of private government." In the gospel of governance however, all that glitters is not gold. Rhodes (2000, p.81): "..networks, like all other resource allocation mechanisms, are not cost free. They are: closed to outsiders and unrepresentative; unaccountable for their actions; serve private interests, not the public interest; are difficult to steer; inefficient because co-operation causes delay; immobilized by conflicts of interest; and difficult to combine with other governing structures."

It is quite amazing that networks are so popular in serious theorising, which tries in vain to make the use of state, government, or public management concepts superfluous. Apart from that, networks are very useful, in theory and in practice. Hirst (2000, p.22), "The various conceptions of 'governance' thus do us a service: they point out that government in the classical liberal sense is less and less a reality..". He wrote: "Governance can be generally defined as the means by which an activity or ensemble of activities is controlled or directed, such that it delivers an acceptable range of outcomes according to some established social standard." (oc, p.24). Transformations of public authority are imputed to the container-notion governance. Public functionaries, doing what they always did, proudly boast that they are active in "modern governance". Governance seems to be only a marketed envelope for familiar things. Government is seen as a badly selling product in a market-orientated society, while the vague term governance is used in a less-governmental approach to cut government spending. In marketing, it is common practice to use new names for old, or slightly different products. A serious drawback of governance is that it seems to be used as an excuse for not employing history in theoretical explorations. The ambiguous term governance is sold as something new. Especially during the last two decades of the 20th century, as if something totally new has befallen humanity in post-modern society. Everybody can convince himself or herself by re-reading S.E. Finer's excellent book, "The History of Government from Earliest Times" (1997), that the public authorities phenomenon is very old indeed. Circumstances at the start of the 21st century are in many aspects different from circumstances in earlier historical periods, but not so different that historical experiences can be seen as obsolete and without relevance for contemporary practice and theorising. Governance can be seen as a stealthy way of giving public authorities the status of package for whatever actors may wish to do under the cover of "governance". Practitioners and theoreticians alike can be advised to work with Public Management of Society instead of wasting their time trying to find out what governance is all about.

In Anglo-American theorising, "government" usually refers to the formal institutions of the State (legislative, executive, judicial powers), although in practice, government simply means the political leadership of a country. Besides, it is confusing that Americans call "Administration" what in England is called "Government". The word governance is increasingly substituted for government, because the existing way of governing is criticised. Instead of improving practices of government, a new way of governing is associated with governance. The best contribution of the governance concept seems to be that it focuses upon the perspectives of co-operative interaction between public authorities and other societal actors. Kooiman (1993, p.2), accentuating the importance that public and private actors do not act separately but in 'co' arrangements, defines: "..by governing we mean all those activities of social, political and administrative actors that can be seen as purposeful efforts to guide, steer, control or manage (sectors or facets of) societies. ..By 'governance' we mean the patterns that emerge from governing activities of social, political and administrative actors." but governance cannot replace the need for the specific roles of public authorities. Public authorities have a very specific position and a unique legitimacy. They act on behalf and in the name of society: specific rationality of public authorities. Public authority was always a socio-psychological phenomenon of interaction between a number of social actors. Public management, – not as imitative application of business management methods in the field of government (Gore, 1997), but as a collection of activities of public authorities -, will do quite well. The term Public Management of Society is preferable to governance. It is not adequate to make the same faults in blurring responsibilities of public and private actors as for example in French history, when the jobs of public authorities were sold. Historical evidence can be used to argue for as clear-cut a differentiation as possible between the activities of public authorities (public management) and private actors (private management). Public-private arrangements can and must be organised with due respect for the specific responsibilities of public authorities.

Oakeshott (1975, 1991, 1993) developed a conception about government, which can be discussed in the framework of governance literature. For him, the State should not be seen as a structure of government, but as the way individuals understand their actions to be related to each other and to those of their government in a political community. For Oakeshott (1975, 114), the State as purposive association is "a relationship in terms of the pursuit of some common purpose, some substantive condition of things to be jointly procured, or some common interest to be continuously satisfied." Government is teleocratic, management of a purposive concern. Spicer (1997, pp. 90-91), arguing that a vision of the State as purposive association is inappropriate, summarises Oakeshott's position: "The role of government in a purposive state is to identify the common ends of the community and to manage the actions of various individuals and other resources toward the attainment of those ends." A citation: "to determine, to choose the pattern of activities, the condition of human circumstance to be imposed upon its subjects, to choose the 'common good' ", and to organise "the activities of its subjects so that each shall make a specific contribution to the achievement of the condition of human circumstance believed to be 'good'." (Oakeshott, 1993, p.91). For Spicer (1995) this concept of the State as a purposive association is part of a rationalist worldview, in which government is seen as an instrument for the collective exercise of reason by a community. In the post-modern condition there are a multiplicity of heterogeneous language games, and the social is atomised into flexible networks of language games (Lyotard, 1984, p.17). According to Spicer (1997, p.94) this means that in a State organised around a particular set of substantive purposes, meaningful political discourse can only take place within the context of particular language games. Spicer (1997, p.97): "..the idea of the state as a civil association seems to fit quite well with the post-modern idea of a multiplicity and diversity of political subcultures and language games." "Civil association and constitutionalism provide an important reminder that public administration, as a part of government, should serve no particular substantive ends or purposes but rather should serve to provide ways of resolving the inevitable collisions that arise between different interests and different visions of the public good." (Spicer, 1997, p.101). So the role of public authorities to realise the common good is minimised.

The trend to use the governance concept, also in France ("gouvernabilité"), is related to the perceived crisis of "governability" which is imputed to the limits of traditional forms of government intervention in the perspective of complex developments in contemporary society (CURAPP, 1996). New forms of regulation are seen as the answer. In governance, less powerful and less extended State institutions have to co-operate in networks of several societal actors on an equal basis with a sharing of responsibilities, and no specific prerogatives related to the public authority status of public functionaries (ISSJ, 1998). The current fashion is for slimming of the State apparatus, which is seen as part of good governance. Even the abolition of differentiation between public and private sectors is promoted as a good medicine. Concerning the use of governance in international relations, Smouts (ISSJ, 1998, p.81) remarked: "After all, there is nothing in the fact of ungovernability, which is its point of departure, to upset the internationalist who, indeed, works in an area whose hallmark has always been not to be governed." Often governance, associated with participation, negotiation and co-ordination, is used for a minimum-state policy. The World Bank used governance as a less confrontational concept than government. Governance and government became synonymous.

"Good governance implies: 1. that the safety of citizens is ensured and that respect for the law is guaranteed, especially through the independence of judges: this is called the rule of law; 2. that public agencies correctly and fairly manage public spending: this is called good administration; 3. that political leaders are answerable to the people for their actions: this is called responsibility and accountability; 4. that information is available and easily accessible to all citizens: this is called transparency." (Daudet, 1994, pp. 80-81). The Commission on Global Governance in "Our Common Neighbourhood" (1995): "Governance is the sum of the many ways individuals and institutions, public and private, manage their common affairs. It is a continuing process through which conflicting or diverse interests may be accommodated and co-operative action taken. It includes formal institutions and regimes empowered to enforce compliance, as well as informal arrangements that people and institutions either have agreed to or perceive to be in their interest." Governance is identified with common human activities, even absorbing the market: "At the global level, governance has been viewed primarily as an intergovernmental relationship, but it must now be understood as also involving non-governmental organisations (NGOs), citizens movements, multinational corporations, and the global capital market. Interacting with these are global mass media of dramatically enlarged influence." (oc, pp. 2-3). Rosecrance: "the only international civilisation worthy of the name is the governing economic culture of the world market." (Foreign Affairs, 1996, p.45).

The governance trend dated from the time when the market was 'in' and the State was 'out'. Neo-liberalism seemed to have reached a position of monopoly. For Fukuyama (1992) this meant the end of history since the superiority of capitalism. That was not a good hypothesis. Historical answers to different challenges maintain their relevance as frames of reference for contemporary and future circumstances. In the perspective of worldwide globalisation, the Nation-State, with the monopoly of legitimate political power within a specific geographical area, seems to be increasingly obsolete, but Nation-States are crucial institutions and will remain so in the future. "Thus the expansion of markets and communications does not prevent governments from continuing to be the main centres of political power, purveyors of standards and regimes, and prime sources of political allegiances. They take on an essential role in implementing a stable legal framework, maintaining internal security, . ..They continue to claim to exercise authority over people entitled to live within their borders, whether temporarily or permanently." (Senarclens, 1998, pp. 101-102). Genuine Public Management of Society by public authorities remains actual in contemporary and future society, whatever claims of governing without government might mean. White (1926) defined public administration as the management of men and materials in the accomplishment of the purposes of the State. The focus in Public Administration theorising is moving to a genuine Public Management of Society perspective (Kirlin, 1996; Lynn, 1996).

Conceptions about public functionaries have varied through the centuries. Thousands of years ago rulers employed professional servants, as Eisenstadt (1963), Finer (1997) and others have demonstrated. The idea that a public functionary is comparable with a person in the Roman period, who had lost in a military fight and therefore could be treated as a slave, still persists (slave model). It was common practice to see the vanquished as objects or property. The contemporary mentality of some politicians is not much different to this idea, or from the idea that they are the bosses of public functionaries, who simply have to obey whatever instruction they are given (servant model). The concept of political primacy over bureaucracy makes them neglect or even deny the public functionary due respect as a person with authentic rights and competencies. A popular idea is that an elected politician is more or less the absolutist master of public functionaries. The relation between politician and public functionary is often comparable with the hierarchical situation in the army, with the politician as superior and the public functionary as subordinate (military model). French kings were exemplary as exponents of the conception that the kingdom or the state was the personal property of the monarch. They made it common practice to give land and offices to aristocrats as compensation for military or other services. Public offices became hereditary and were the private property of those entitled, they became merchandise, privatisation "avant la lettre" (market model). The disadvantages were obvious. Progress was made when sale of public offices was abolished. It is strange that the privatisation of public offices is so popular in contemporary society, even for offices which have a genuine public authority character. Without adequately differentiating between the roles of public and private sectors, the efficiency of the private sector is often taken as a decisive criterion. That is a serious failure, because the public sector, with its specific legitimacy and cluster of tasks, has to be evaluated by its own efficiency criteria. Napoleon with the military model in mind, is said to have laid the foundations for the modern idea of the civil service as a permanent, professional organisation dedicated to the public interest (Grégoire, 1954). The "Grandes Écoles" realised an important contribution to the forming of an administrative elite in France. In the early 1800s, "Kameralwissenschaften" were taught in Prussia, preparing civil servants with a broad package of pragmatic knowledge about State affairs.

In the 19th century, this idea of forming a bureaucracy with expertise, specialised knowledge, integrity and professionalism was gaining ground in France, England and elsewhere. The English Northcote-Trevelyan Committee (1854) argued for the building up of a public body of permanent officers with sufficient independence, character, ability and experience, subordinate to Ministers who were themselves directly responsible to the Crown and to Parliament. In the US, the spoils system of giving public offices to partisan friends as a reward for party-political services, was replaced by a system of entry-conditions (examinations). The Pendleton Act (1883) made the idea of the neutrality of public functionaries operational. Since the end of the 19th century, a culture of professionalism has developed (Bledstein, 1976). For Gargan (1989), professional public administrators are professionals of government rather than professionals in government. In the first half of the 20th century, the politics-administration dichotomy was intended to protect professional administration from party-politics. The idea of the neutrality of civil servants is based on the possibility of separating administrative from political careers. Caiden (1996) proposed some conditions for this model. Administration is separated from politics and policy. Public servants have the task of executing the decisions made by politicians. They are appointed on the basis of merit rather than party affiliation. Public servants are not expected to engage in party-politics. Political executives accept responsibility for decisions, while protecting the anonymity of public servants. Public servants execute policy decisions loyally, irrespective of their personal opinions of the policies of the party in power.

This approach reduced the relationship between politics and administration into: the power and competence of politics to determine public policies, versus the a-political, neutral and professional execution of public policies as determined by politicians. Although this approach had wide acceptance, in reality public affairs proved to be less simple than this dichotomy would lead one to believe. The policy-influencing and power aspects of bureaucracy came more to the fore, the politics of bureaucracy (Peters, 1995). From the 1880s a new phenomenon broke through: political parties and trade union movement (class struggle), also within the civil service. In the 1920s and 1930s the idea of neutrality of the civil service was interpreted quite rigidly in Great Britain. Trade union affiliations and party-political activities were forbidden to public functionaries who must be exclusively loyal to the State. A specific British view about the civil service had its impact: a preference for government by amateurs, learning by experience (Laski, 1938). Civil services in Western Europe and the US grew steadily as more tasks were assigned to government. In France an interventionist State tradition, "l'étatisme", continued. This quantitative change by bureaucratisation caused a qualitative leap, the character of the civil service changed fundamentally. Hayek's "The Road to Serfdom" (1944) was an example of the fear of strangling bureaucracy causing collectivisation of society and threatening democracy. The public-private dichotomy played its role. Public organisations are seen as specific for several reasons. The ambiguity of their goals is the result of the nature, scope and impact of their tasks. The emphasis is placed on equity. In the public sector, there is no indicator equivalent to profit in the private sector and it is difficult to measure performance. In the public sector, legitimacy of performed acts is the parameter for success (Kogood/Caulfield, 1984). The public sector is permeated with legal, managerial and political constraints on discretionary scope for public functionaries (Gordon, 1982; Gortner, 1977; Starling, 1982). Some authors belittle differences between public and private organisations. The distinction between public and private organisations is blurred by the "privatisation" of public, and "publicisation" of private organisations (Cassell, 1983). Qualifying public organisations as political organisations is inadequate, especially when business organisations, due to their power dimensions, are seen as political systems (Long, 1962).

Authors demonstrated that the simple idea of the neutrality of public functionaries ignored realities of bureaucratic power in the modern Administrative State, but the norm is used that elected politicians should rule over a neutral or depoliticised public service. This norm is probably a bridge too far for human beings, especially when differing values, opinions, ideologies, interests and loyalties are at stake. All kinds of loyalties have their impact: ideology, religion, nation, language, ethnic origin, family, regime, profession; class, and political party. The relationship between politics and bureaucracy is too multi-varied to be neutral. "The public bureaucracy that runs the administrative state is too valuable a prize in contemporary society to be left to bloodless administrators. It has amassed so much power that it can make or break other social institutions. The fortunes of political elites are tied too closely to bureaucratic performance. The growing pressures for increased politicisation are almost irresistible and public administration is subject to greater external influence. In any event, the balance within government has shifted greatly in favour of the professional administrators over the professional politicians (and hence the need for strengthening constitutional and legal means by which the possible misuse of bureaucratic power can be checked and controlled)." (Caiden, 1996, p.30).

"Public administration ethics today is dominated by two distinct ethical frameworks: the bureaucratic ethos, which stresses efficiency and strict obedience to elected officials, and the democratic ethos, which stresses adherence to certain higher order moral principles embedded in the notion of democratic government." (Woller/Patterson, 1997, p.103). Woller and Patterson qualify ethical frameworks as foundational, because they are said to be based on the search for certain universal or quasi-universal principles, implying moral obligations from which ethical behaviour might be deduced or judged. They use a dialogic approach to administrative ethics. According to bureaucratic ethos, public administrators in a democracy are legally and morally bound to enforce the laws, and to implement policies enacted by the people's democratically elected representatives, believed to give authoritative voice to the public will. "The bureaucratic ethos presumes a direct line of communication from the people to their elected representatives, to bureau heads, and then down the hierarchical ladder to those responsible for administering and implementing public policies." (Woller/Patterson, 1997, p.103). According to traditional opinions about the people's sovereignty in a democracy, public administrators are supposed to do what elected representatives want them to do. Public administrators are thought not to have the right or moral standing to resist the representatives' will. When bureaucratic objectives are formulated they have to implement them efficiently and effectively in a morally neutral (not-partisan) way, so, administrative legitimacy was identified with efficiency, expertise, and professionalism. A neutral and efficient civil service was the norm for administrative legitimacy, even for legitimisation of democracy.

In reaction to the bureaucratic ethos model, adherents of the democratic ethos model presented an alternative view. They accept that public administrators, when implementing public policies concretely, should reflect the will of the governed, but they reject the overhead democracy model of democratic government, which is used as a basis for the bureaucratic ethos approach (Redford, 1969). In their view, there is no unambiguous line of communication from the governed (the people) to their representatives, and down through the bureaucratic hierarchy. Bureaucratic objectives are rarely unambiguously determined and deduced from the political process. Politicians often don't have effective control over bureaucracy. Public administrators are normally not the neutral servants of the public as supposed in the bureaucratic ethos model. They have ample policy room, administrative discretion and "ethical space" (Fox, 1989). An ethos, based upon hierarchical control and obedience to political superiors, cannot produce adequate guidelines for decision-making and implementation of public policies. Adherents of the democratic ethos model argue for an alternative set of values, deduced from higher order moral principles of democratic government. They correct overstressing of instrumental rationality (efficiency, effectiveness, expertise, scientific rationality, and hierarchical accountability), accentuating the application of democratic values in the implementation of public policies.

The relation between political representatives and (higher echelons of) public administrators is full of tensions in pluralist democracies, making the place of bureaucracy within the democratic political order a crucial issue in democratic theory and public administration theory (Burke, 1994). Controversies between political (wishful) thinking and bureaucratic expertise are a normal concomitant phenomenon of democracy, with aspects of party-political politicking and technocracy. It is too simple to assert that these controversies can be solved by the application of the primacy of politics principle. In popular argument, the decisive criterion is seen in the will of the people, but what is the will of the people? Mostly the practice of democracy is based upon second best (or third best, etc.) solutions. Even in well-organised pluralist democracies with a constitution, regular elections, a good balance between legislative, executive and jurisdictional powers, and reasonable practices for the implementation of public policies, it is not at all easy to realise the principles for good Public Management of Society concretely in dynamically changing circumstances. In the context of American Public Administration, a neutral, efficient civil service was seen as an essential part of democracy in the first decades after the Second World War. This had implications for the responsibilities and roles of public administrators. In Public Administration, scientific knowledge and techniques were used to determine the most efficient and effective means to achieve (arbitrary) political ends. As primary values or ends cannot be determined by rational analysis, they have to be accepted as given by the political process. Public administrators were thought to provide the technical means for accomplishing the ends as determined by their political superiors. They should not usurp the authority of democratically elected superiors. Bureaucracy would maintain its democratic legitimacy as long as it stuck to this way of implementing the will of the people, as ushered via the democratic process by democratically elected representatives (Woller/Patterson, 1997, p.106).

In the New Public Administration movement, this model of bureaucratic ethos has been questioned since the last years of the 1960s. Scholars tried to elaborate principles which could be used as guidelines for public administration beyond the rational model (neutral, efficient, effective). A number of principles were seen as relevant to fulfil this function: social equity (Marini, 1971); regime values (Hart, 1984); justice (Cooper, 1987); honour and benevolence (Denhardt, 1991); humanism (Dvorin/Simmons, 1972); and Judeo-Christian values (Golembiewski, 1973). The search for universal ethical principles is typical of Western ethical thought. According to Woller and Patterson (1997, p.108), no other distinction has been so important for Western ethical theory during the past 200 years than the distinction between deontology and teleology. Teleology, the ethic of purpose, goes beyond any act to assess its contribution to the achievement of one's purposes. Acts promoting these purposes are seen as moral, and acts that impede these purposes as immoral. Bentham and Mill developed utilitarianism, a branch of teleological reasoning. For utilitarianism, moral behaviour consists in doing what realises the greatest good for the greatest number of people. Deontology is an ethic of duty: ethical behaviour is determined by higher order moral principles from which other rules and one's moral duty may be deduced logically. The authors of democratic ethos, seeking an alternative to bureaucratic ethos as a foundation for administrative ethics, can be categorised as deontological, because they try to ground administrative behaviour in a higher order, core democratic principles, binding in a moral sense, whatever their imputed consequences.

"Bureaucratic ethos is teleological, employs instrumental rationality and is predicated on the values of capitalism and a market society. Democratic ethos, in contrast, is deontological, based on substantive rationality and emanates from classical values of the state and higher law." (Pugh, 1991, p.26). In spite of this supposed decisive distinction, attempts were made to reconcile them (Fox, 1994). Notions of internal and external ethical accountability are combined, implying that it is seen as the administrator's duty to follow his inner ethical principles when these would be offended by following externally determined organisational dictates (Thompson, 1987). In mainstream literature it is more or less taken for granted that democratic theory is only about the relation between governors and governed (Pactet, 1994) and not about public functionaries also. The idea is that everything has been done for democracy if the governed can elect governors regularly, as they are thereby thought to be democratically legitimised. Governors are thought to direct bureaucracy, as a driver does his motor car (machine model). Apparently the democratic circle is closed: citizens elect governors who instruct bureaucracy what must be done on behalf of citizens, so giving citizens what they need, but one of the most crucial links in the chain, realisation of what citizens need by professional public functionaries, is relatively underexposed. Insofar as public functionaries are dealt with the neutrality norm is mostly stressed (Kondylis, 1994). The norm of neutrality is put forward as a protection against misuses by party-political, partisan public functionaries, Politicisation of public functionaries has generally not improved the quality of public services (partisan model). Corruption is branded worldwide as one of the most persistent diseases of bureaucracy (Gould, in: Farazmand, 1991).

Development of the idea of a professional bureaucracy took time. Not neutrality, but professionalism is the issue (professional model). Argyriades (1996, p.69): "A measure of autonomy is not only compatible with the subordination of civil servants to the political leadership, but also a sine qua non condition of sustaining a climate of opinion in which professional values and personal integrity can flourish. It does not signify the absence of control, but neither should it mean subservience and servility to the political leaders.

Surely, what is required is strengthening the capacity of the political superstructure for control and accountability, not weakening the effectiveness of the administrative system.". Public sector jobs are often misused for party-political favouritism. It is obvious that this practice undermines the trustworthiness of the civil services. Civil services have a long tradition of hierarchically functioning organisations. We live in a world of bureaucracies. Friedberg (1993) concluded that most organisations (public or private) evolve to a situation in which organisation members are given more freedom in the way they do their jobs (policy discretion). The hierarchical command model is adapted to incorporate more participative practices. Often this is a pragmatic and rational approach in the context of growing complexities, which have to be tackled. According to P. Pactet (1994, p.25): "The danger is that those techno-structures become autonomous systems upon which political power has relatively little grip. Because the personnel of the bureaucratic apparatus is protected by its competencies and its statute. This on the margins of democratic theory, because these techno-structures are not representative for public opinion and because, these technostructures, working secretly, can do so practically without being called to account. It is odd that the personalisation of political power is accompanied by anonymity of techno-structures. Therefore control of these techno-structures is one of the most important problems for contemporary societies." Indeed, but not so much by exclusively stressing the reinforcement of (party-)political primacy. More important are adequate systems of accountability for all public functionaries (Kernaghan, 2000; Romzek, 2000). The popular idea that the quality of services in the private sector is superior to the public sector services proves to be a myth.

The situation for public functionaries might be compared with the position of medical doctors and other professionals in hospitals: they are professionally responsible and accountable for what they are doing or not doing (professional functional responsibilities). Control of professionals by other (independent) professionals or institutions is a good instrument. A more mature idea of fulfilling jobs by public functionaries can be developed. They should have the opportunity to report faulty developments in the functioning of public institutions without being sanctioned for this ("whistleblowers"). The idea has to be that each public functionary is personally an organ, with professional responsibilities for which he or she is personally accountable: responsibilities "ex officio". Instead of seeing neutrality, political sterilisation, and anonymity as the highest virtues of public functionaries, they must be seen as personal representatives of public authority. They must be personally accountable for the way they do their jobs. Institutional arrangements can be organised to realise a kind of "conditioned personalism" for public functionaries as the answer to the irresponsible anonymity of functionaries. Networks of professionals seem to work in impenetrable bastions of professional knowledge. To give the activities of public functionaries adequate legitimacy, conditioning of professional networks within the Rule of Law is the operational answer. Personal professionalism asks for a spirit of responsibility (Bovens, 1998).

In the last decades more attention has been given to measurement of performance and accountability (Romzek/Dubnick, 1998). It is not easy to make accountability work in practice (Seldon, 1999). The processes of accountability are influenced by relations to authority, while legitimate demands for high quality of performance can come from hierarchical superiors, elected or nominated politicians, the public, professional associations, law makers, pressure groups, colleagues and clients (Campbell/Wilson, 1995). Professionals have to make choices about changing demands that are preferably answered (multiple strategies). Romzek (2000) distinguishes four types of accountability: hierarchical (efficacy), legal (authority of the law), political (susceptibility to political opinions) and professional (expertise). Professional actors have more policy room in the case of political or professional accountability than when hierarchical or legal accountability is dominant.

Professionals are especially amenable to legal norms, professional norms and protocols: best practices. The character of the policy issue is also a relevant criterion. An example of professional accountability is the traditional Whitehall model (ministers are dependent on not partisan professionals with expertise). Adequate control of bureaucracy is a professional activity (West, 1995)

Part of professionalism is continuous, effective and comprehensive evaluation of policymaking and policy implementation. In the last decades it has been common practice to imitate business methods in the public sector, including this field. Often this has taken place without adequate reckoning with the specifics of the public sector, so creating problems. Guba/Lincoln (1989) differentiated four generations in the development of evaluation: 1. Measuring (first generation); 2. Description (second generation); 3. Assessment (third generation); and 4. Negotiation (fourth generation). According to Guba/Lincoln, the three first generations are largely obsolete due to several factors including a "management-bias", objectives and intentions of policymakers are used as success parameters. As consensus about these is supposed, there is often a one-sided perspective (not very realistic in pluralistic society). Besides, the findings of evaluations are hardly used in decision-making and so these are not very relevant. Often interested parties in the process of policymaking are approached as persons providing information only. There is no discussion with them about their viewpoints and interests, their expertise and experience is frequently not valued. Guba/Lincoln think to obviate these shortcomings with their fourth generation method of evaluation in the perspective of negotiation with all actors involved. They use interesting concepts for their approach, with a preference for qualitative methods. Criteria for evaluation are deduced from the claims, concerns and issues (CCI) of all actors concerned. Guba/Lincoln differentiate between groups of "stakeholders" (actors whose interests are at stake): "agents" (policymakers, professionals), "beneficiaries" (who benefit from policies) and "victims" (who are damaged).

They make themselves adherents of interactive policymaking in an open, inductive dialogue (limiting conditions: willingness to participate, change and share power) to realise an emergent design. This dialogue is furthered with hermeneutic-dialectical circles, with an agenda for negotiations. The fourth generation evaluation authors base their approach upon a social-constructivist theory, with some basic assumptions: A. Human beings are active producers of meaning, who construct their reality in interaction with others (different backgrounds). So reality is diversified and multiple. B. To know this diversified reality, not objectivity and detachment are asked for, but involvement and interaction between subject and object. C. For a deeper understanding, it is necessary to interpret issues in the framework of many factors and perspectives, not reducible to simple cause-effect relations. D. Knowledge is a function of time and geographical place, so generalisation of special knowledge is problematical. E. Evaluation is dependent on values. Traditional criteria for scientific research are not sufficient to judge the quality of fourth generation evaluation. Evaluators have to act in a disciplined and imitable way, reporting their sources, data and arguments for their interpretations. These are checked for credibility by respondents. The approach of Guba/Lincoln is promising. It would be jumping to conclusions, though, when it is asserted that in this perspective the role of public authorities will inevitably shift from central conductor to process facilitator (Chelimsky/Shadish, 1995).

It is interesting to draw attention to the French culture of public service, crucial in the framework of the French philosophy of public management. "The notion of public service came up in France as the essential key for the whole construction of the State. With this notion, it was possible to demarcate the public sphere from the private sphere. And also to integrate several components of the theory of the State, by combining them in a coherent and unified concept. This notion of public service became the obligatory door to penetrate into the heart of the State institution." (Chevallier, 1987, p.4). The public service is the outstanding instrument of French Statist dirigism and sophisticated public management. In the 19th century and before, the dominant conception about the State in France was related to sovereignty and "puissance", by which the State found its legitimacy in itself. The State was seen as unconditional, unlimited power. Therefore, the invention of the French public service, as an institutional structure answering the needs of citizens, was an innovative breakthrough. Up to the 20th century, State power was a basic juridical principle defining the tasks of the State, centred around its authority to organise public order. This State power conception provoked a specific way of societal intervention, while liberalism caused a restrictive idea about the "regalian" tasks of the State (army, justice, taxation, police).

This exaltation of State power was a common feature of German and French public law doctrine in the 19th and early 20th centuries. German authors like Gerber, Laband, Ihering and Jellinek had the thesis that the State disposed of "Herrschaft", absolute power and competence to force obedience. This State issued law rules on the basis of an absolutist will power, not restricted by external rules of law. Insofar as the State was limited by law, this was based upon self-restriction. Hegel was bringing the exaltation of the State to its theoretical apex. In French doctrine, this exalted view of the State found its echo. While German doctrine put the State in a prioritised position with regard to the nation, French doctrine was accentuating the combination Nation-State. In this view, the State is essentially the juridical personification of the Nation. Because public administration was seen as the instrument of this Nation-State, it had privileged means of action. It was thought necessary to treat "Administration", generally interpreted as State administration, with privileged law: "droit administratif". The "Édit de Saint-German" (1641) already forbade the "parlements" to acquaint themselves with everything concerning State, administration or government. The "Assemblée Constituante" prohibited all interference of judiciary tribunals in the administrative activities of the State in the law of 16-24 August 1790. After 1806, a subtler criterion of public power was gradually recognised. No longer was the fullness of State power present in all administrative acts. It was necessary to examine which law was applicable and which tribunal was competent. Jurisprudence and doctrine tried to formulate an adequate criterion of public power. This was found in the two forms of State activity. As proprietor or civil party, the State was treated as equal to private persons by the "tribunal judiciaire"; as public person, it was judged by the "juridiction administrative".

E. Laferrière (1887) enriched the doctrine with the best distinction between "actes d'autorité" (acts of authority) and "actes de gestion" (administration). When activities of public administration could be seen as resulting from delegated authority as an attribute of executive power, its acts of authority are manifestations of sovereignty. These had to be judged by administrative tribunals. When public administration was just executing the activities of public services, the activities should be judged equally with the activities of private persons. This distinction became insufficient when public interventionism changed drastically as a consequence of ideological, political and economic transformations. The industrialisation process made more intensive public intervention necessary, to guarantee a socially more acceptable equilibrium. Meanwhile, societal consciousness had furthered the idea of the "État de droit" as the adequate instrument to limit State interventionism within conditions of the law. Hauriou, qualifying the State as the institution of institutions, said: "The State presents itself as an institution to serve an idea." The character of administrative law changed from an instrument to protect the State, into a means to subject public administration to law. In jurisprudence, the creative process of law finding produced law principles to protect citizens against the arbitrariness of public organs. Activities of public organs were not seen as legitimate as such, but only in relation to the legitimate objectives pursued. The check on public administration activities by jurisdictional control of "excès de pouvoir" (excess of power) became normal practice. The State encroached on activities hitherto reserved for the private sector. The traditional concept of State power was not adequate for new fields of public activities. Some fields of public interference escaped from the traditionalist approach. "État-puissance" became the Welfare State, making the public service doctrine appropriate.

The primary objective of the public service philosophy was to organise, as objectively as possible, limits to State activities by law. Duguit, a pioneering theoretician of the public service, in his demystification of State power, indefatigably fought the myth of the almighty State. For him, the concept of the State as sovereign was a pure abstraction ("metaphysics") behind the social reality of governors claiming obedience from the governed. The powerful competencies of governors are based only upon legal rules. The actions of governors impose themselves on the governed not as a subjective right to command, but only in so far as they conform to objective law, forthcoming from social conscience. The idea of the public service is at the heart of this objective law: "The role of governors is to develop and realise social solidarity, especially by taking care of activities on behalf of the general interest as necessary for collective life. Their competencies are just the other side of this obligation. The public service is the foundation and limit of the competencies of governors. The power of governors is justified by the necessity to satisfy the collective wants of the public, but this should not go beyond what the social conscience admits and asks." (Chevallier, 1987, p.20). The most important task of public functionaries was seen as fulfilling their function, their part in the realisation of public services. The competencies they got are no more than the instruments to realise this objective. Instead of the abstract, superior and transcendental State, now the State is administrator of daily affairs. The analysis of Duguit implies that the growing number of public services, due to the process of civilisation organising social solidarity, do not necessarily produce more etatism. Discretionary competencies can be given to decentralised units under the control of governors.

The character of administrative law was also changing. G. Teissier (1906) defended public service as the basis for defining rules of competence. By making the notion of public service the basic principle for the administrative legal regime, it became the keystone of administrative law (G. Jèze). The competence of the administrative judge was no longer based on the privilege of public administration, but on the specific character of the public service involved. P. Weil qualified public service as the alpha and omega of administrative law. Evolution seemed to go in the direction of extending competencies of the "juge judiciaire" at the cost of the administrative judge, when the State interfered more in the market sector. With the notion of public service, it was the other way around. Nearly all activities of public administration could be dealt with as public services. Citizens in the "puissance publique" regime were submissive subjects. In the public service regime, they became subjects of rights. The public service idea accentuated the limited power of public administration and the prerogatives of governors on the basis of the public service as general interest of the collectivity. Duguit and Jèze tried to replace the "puissance" concept with the public service concept. There is a parallel development in the concept of governance, by which an attempt is made to strip it of notions of public authority and power. Hauriou in his institution theory combined "puissance" and "service public" in a new synthesis.

According to Chevallier (1987, p.30), the originality of the French administrative system is due to the idea of service combined with executive power within an extended institutional organisation. Jurisprudence played an important role in the development of applicable law. The term public service lost part of its clear-cut definition. The State was traditionally qualified above all by its monopoly of legitimised violence, but the "arrêt Blanco" (1873) made a break, by declaring for the first time, that public responsibility was based on the criterion of public service. In the "arrêt Bac d'Eloka" (1921), the "Tribunal des conflits" decided that a public organ can exploit a public service in the same way as a private enterprise, and so the "juge judiciaire" was made competent. This was quite a change. From now on the public service as a whole would be judged by the "juge judiciaire", not only in some aspects. The administrative regime was only applicable when public services were thought to be part of the State by nature. The public service school could not maintain its claim for an exclusive criterion of administrative law. The "arrêt Caisse primaire Aide et Protection" (1938) decided that social insurance companies, in spite of a private statute, must be seen as public services. Since 1938, some private organisations have been seen as public services due to explicit delegation by a public service, or to the nature of their activities.

After the Second World War many public enterprises and corporations were formed. The distinction between "service public" (with an objective of the general interest) and "secteur public", or "service à gestion publique" versus "service à gestion privé" was used. French State theory and administrative law are based upon the two fundamental notions "puissance publique" and "service public". The public service concept gave the State a new legitimacy while accentuating the tasks of governors and functionaries in fostering the well-being of citizens. According to Chevallier (1987, p.36) public authority is not a sinecure or property, but an imposing duty, service and task which one accepts for the greatest well-being of all. The next step is to recognise that the functional State is justified only by its activities on behalf of the common good, its performance for the public in a democratic perspective. The public service ideology was an stimulus for expanding State activities as the most adequate method of guaranteeing liberty, equality and social justice. Jurisprudence connected the public service concept with a number of juridical effects, so all public services are thought to be bound by common, specific obligations derived from the principles of continuity, equality and flexibility: continuity, daily 24-hour State functioning; equality for the public services, no discrimination or favouritism (differentiation between groups of clients is allowed); flexibility, public services should adapt themselves to changing circumstances. According to the law, when there is a public service, rules are applicable that differ from common law, but general principles valid for all public services are only a part of the rules applicable to them. The automatic identification of public organ and public service was loosened by jurisprudence using conceptually vague terms. A double presumption is used, activities of public organs are presumed to be a public service working for the general interest, and activities of private persons and organisations are presumed to be private. Apart from private activities within the public domain, explicit delegation to a private organisation for a specific mission is needed to make it a public service (formal condition). This qualification depends only on the explicit intention of the public authority creating it (subjective criterion). When this is absent, the nature of the activities has to be analysed (material indications).

The concept of public service was not only built up on the basis of purely juridical ideas. Economic aspects played a role (Stoffaës, 1995). Especially in the field of natural monopolies, economists contributed to the furthering of public services by arguing that there were good economic reasons for giving the control of natural monopolies to public authorities (Stoffaës, 1994). Economists argued that there are several circumstances in which the market does not function adequately, so that public authorities should interfere. This is the case when there are externalities (aspects not dealt with in the market mechanism), when there are pure collective goods: goods which consumers can use without diminishing the consumption of others, and when the market cannot guarantee optimal results (market failure). There are also several socio-political reasons to organise sectors of the economy as public services, as in the sphere of redistribution policies. The traditionalist French dirigism in the economic field ("Colbertisme") got an important revitalising impulse after the Second World War. Planning the economy was seen as a normal task for the State ("planification"). Nationalising a series of sectors became a normal pattern for political left and political right. Following the failed attempt of the Socialists to expand the public sector by new nationalisations since the beginning of the 1980s, the trend has been to diminish the public sector in the economic field, but in 1995, some 880,000 persons worked in national enterprises with a total debt of about 500 billion francs (nearly 1/6 of national debt). Several techniques of regulating national enterprises are used: "tutelle économique" (economic measures like tariffs etc.), "tutelle technique" (administrative regulation in the field of technologies), and "tutelle politique" (political control). Since the "Rapport Nora" (1968), "contrats de Plan" have been created, giving nationalised industries contractual certainties lasting years, instead of the yearly budget-gamble. Local public authorities created public services, while using contractual instruments (Offner, 1990).

In social reality, public services, although they might be partly seen as organisations like others, have a specific character, rationality and logic. Their ultimate object is the satisfaction of a need of the general interest and therefore they are ruled by a public authority. Part of the French specificity is the ideology of the general interest as public interest, transcending private interests and not as a common denominator of the private interests (Rangeon, 1986). Since the start of the 20th century, interventionism has grown significantly, not only at the level of central government, but also in the local sphere with municipal socialism. The notion of general interest has increasingly been interpreted more extensively to encompass the most diverse activities of national and local interventionism. Up to 1958 the principle was that the creation of a public service necessitated the passing of a law, although the law of 11 July 1938 authorised government to create services in time of war. Since the Constitution of 1958, creation of public services has been possible by the "pouvoir réglementaire" (government). Only in matters falling under article 34 (nationalisation, etc.) is a law required. After the Second World War the Welfare State expanded ever more in Western Europe, creating public services for all kinds of societal needs. The French "État-providence" had an open-ended program, stimulating a proliferation of public services and exploding the budget. Solutions, which had seemed adequate, have proved to be problematical since the 1970s. The State had no answer for the worldwide trend of giving market forces free play. Protectionism was not an adequate remedy for massive unemployment and the growing numbers of citizens using social security provisions made it impossible to continue along traditional paths. The position of the State as the solver-of-all-problems was undermined. This created the Crisis of the Welfare State. In the framework of European integration it remains to be seen in what way a European concept of public service will develop (Bauby/Boual, 1994). The European Union can develop a certain synthesis between "État régalien" and "Common Law tradition" (Colloque Bruxelles, 1993).

Marshall/Choudhury (1997), in the framework of the history of American Public Administration, drew attention to an old concept, thrown away in empiricist-positivist writings: the public interest. This concept is analysed in the context of the Federalist/Anti-Federalist tradition debate. For Federalists and Anti-Federalists, the public interest was related to accountability of the executive branch of government. Federalists, emphasising accountability to the legislature and adhering to a strong central government, interpreted public interest as efficient administration within the boundaries of legal accountability. For Anti-Federalists, adhering to accountability through a decentralised process, public interest meant effective public administration, informed by continuing interaction with the public. In the course of time, agencies of public administration, serving the public interest, were normally seen as legitimate institutions. They were established by an act of law (constitutional authority), had a political base, were recognised for their expertise, and had a normative view of the public interest. During the first part of the 20th century public administration was in the grip of rationalism and science. With the expansion of the Administrative State the normative meaning of the public interest was accentuated. In the

1940s and 1950s, some writers, qualified by White/McSwain (1990) as traditionalists, had common ideas about public administration. They adhered to the idea of the public interest as guiding administrative action. Later, knowledge in terms of empirical evidence and scientific technique was preferred as a guiding principle. Simon (1957) took the lead in developing the rational model of organisation during the heyday of modernism. This model (logical positivism; facts/values; administration/policy dichotomy) became dominant, though it had no real place for the public interest concept, because it is difficult to make it an operational concept. But is representation, a dominant concept in democratic theory, an operational concept beyond the number of votes at elections? There is a crisis of representation. The public interest concept is crucial (Flathman, 1966). Goodsell reinvented its relevance with six central values for the public interest concept: legality-morality; political responsiveness; political consensus; concern for logic; concern for effects; agenda awareness (Wamsley, 1990). Public services are carriers of the public interest, working for realisation of the common good.

## 9.5. Working-hypotheses for a co-disciplinary focus on public management of society

Since 1946, American Public Administration has had a strong impact upon Western European theorising, because in Western Europe the law-based public administration conception, lacking adequate digestion of performances in social sciences, was dominant. Following the "Posdcorb" formula and failure of the politics-administration dichotomy, American Public Administration has been in disarray. It took some comfort in psychological-behavioural studies (Simon), general administrative science, or political systems theory (Easton) and Ostrom, in "The Intellectual Crisis in American Public Administration" (1974), thought to overcome the crisis, caused by insufficiency of the paradigm in traditional Public Administration theory, by presenting an alternative from political economy: public choice. This alternative paradigm is seen in the criterion of efficiency to assess performance in provision of public goods and services (public choice economics). So Public Administration would be only a sub-discipline of economics. This is no solution at all. Waldo (1980, p.60) convincingly rejected the idea of Public Administration as a sub-discipline of Political Science: "..the attitude of political scientists generally toward Public Administration is likely to be one of indifference, at worst one of contempt or hostility. .the component that Political Science should provide is..after all but one component.". Stillman (1991, p.134; p.125) saw American Public Administration after 1945 as a loose heterodoxy of various multidisciplinary university studies, without any viable, broad-ranging paradigm.

Mainzer (1994) qualified Public Administration as a study in disarray, without an integrating theory, neither a discipline nor a component of a discipline. He challenged the character of (American) Public Administration as interdisciplinary study and saw politics as an appropriate discourse for Public Administration, but his arguments are not convincing. Each social discipline is a way of thinking, while inquiring a specific aspect of social life. Political science, law, social anthropology, economics, history and other disciplines are all relevant for the study of Public Management of Society, political Science does not have the monopoly. Public Management of Society is more an object of monopolistic competition between a number of social sciences, all having relevance for the object of study. Mainzer (1994, p.376) disqualifies a managerial conception of public administration with an old-fashioned idea of public management, without the dominance of the idea of the public good and without government as a central institution. He rightly criticised generic schools of administration or organisation for this absence in their theorising, but he is wrong in reducing the notion management and magnifying the notion politics out of all proportion. In democracies public authorities do not function in a political vacuum, but neither in a law vacuum or an economic vacuum. One can use an all-encompassing definition of politics, made identical to social, but, differentiating the contributions of several social sciences, one has to recognise that analytical political science studies one aspect, the power aspect. In theory and in practice, a broad notion of Public Management of Society is useful, encompassing political, economic, social and other aspects.

Many scientific disciplines, sub-disciplines and specialisations have studied specific aspects or parts of the multi-faceted phenomenon of Public Management of Society, the activity of public authorities. Since philosophy, mother of all sciences, could not encompass all available knowledge, new scientific disciplines have been created again and again. Control of knowledge made specialisation and abstraction necessary. In the framework of division of scientific work, it is effective to excise a restricted, analytical perspective, while abstracting away other aspects. The next step is to attempt an integration of the results of several analytical sciences having their specific perspectives upon the object of study. If one seeks to build up an integrated science, it is a mistake to bypass disciplined theoretical explorations and empirical results about the object of study. The products of research are mostly complex and based upon divergent substantive and methodological premises, so integration is not at all easy, even when possible. Proliferation of knowledge from many disciplines can be seen as a reaction to the extreme complexity of the world. Re-integration of divergent research with an integrating theory makes sense only when the potency for complexity is correspondingly extended. There are two basic approaches to the study Public Management of Society: normative-prescriptive and empirical-explanatory. It is not possible to choose between them, as the object is factual rationalisation, actual behaviour within rationally organised systems.

After research of available knowledge, German social scientist Niklas Luhmann concluded that so far no integrated science of Public Management has been realised. Luhmann formulated seven working-hypotheses for an integrative science of Public Management in his "Theorie der Verwaltungswissenschaft" (1966). This work has to be interpreted in combination with the whole of Luhmann's conception as elaborated over more than 30 years since then. No other conceptual frameworks to equal his have so far been developed. French scholar Langrod concluded this in 1968, and the situation has not changed since then. The lack of a complete English version has meant that Luhmann's conceptualisation of an integrative theory for Public Management is practically unknown in Anglo-American literature, though parts of Luhmann's work are easily accessible thanks to English translations (Luhmann, 1979; 1982; 1985; 1989; 1995). It is nearly impossible to give an overview of Luhmann's over-productive work. He started his publications in 1958, wrote a great many books and articles, and was still writing up until his death in 1998. Luhmann was able to elaborate his conception in four decades. His working-hypotheses are: 1. social systems theory; 2. realisation of binding decisions; 3. public management system and environment; 4. juridical structure of public management; 5. rationalising public management by systems rationality; 6. functional-comparative method; 7. bridging the gap between rationalising-normative and empirical-explanatory scientific disciplines. Luhmann produced an impressive theoretical work which seems to corroborate his thesis about the possibility of an integrative public management science. Luhmann's conceptual framework is used here. This has been put to the test by a long-term analysis of French Public Management of Society.

Social systems theory does present itself as the integrating nucleus of a general theory of administration or management. Luhmann's concept of social systems refers to the real world of experience, not to conceptions in theory (as in Parsons' theory). To ascertain the relation with the reality of empirical processes, social systems are conceptualised as systems of factual activity, treated by actors themselves as distinct units. A system of human actions, and specifically a system of public management, is a sense-directed coherence which is held constant with regard to an utterly complex and changing environment. Human activities are possible by reducing the complexity and changeability of the environment while structuring social systems. Relations between system and environment depend on causal processes, but are also managed by internal processes. Social systems therefore have a relative autonomy. The system structure realises selective processing of information and can maintain also the relative invariance of system boundaries. This system structure is composed of generalised expectations of behaviour. Actors in system roles expect certain events, reactions of themselves and of others, consequences, etc. These expectations are generalised when they are typologically presupposed and are not dropped if there are opposing experiences, but maintained as such (Schutz, 1962). In this sense, each structure of a system of human actions is normatively institutionalised. Strategic dimensions are analytically distinguished: social dimension, object-related dimension, and time dimension. In the social dimension, several environments are discerned which are handled differently by the system. In the object-related dimension several levels of the traffic with the environment are separated. In the time dimension past and future are differentiated. The system is partly determined by the past, and partly by pursued effects in the future. This shows that the system is relatively autonomous in deciding which orientation it follows, with regard to what environment, and at what level. Expectations generalised in three dimensions (social, object-related, time), are congruently generalised. The congruently generalised expectations are called the law of the social system.

What differentiates the public management system from other systems is its specific function: specialisation upon realisation of binding decisions for society. Public management systems are specific, as they bind their environment and themselves, and by doing this fulfil a specific function in society. With this characteristic of realising binding decisions for society, the public management system is not defined on the level of human actions, but on the system level. This implies a decision to define public management systems not with a substantive, exhaustive enumeration of all that these systems include, but by accentuating its specific function, its "raison d'être". Public management systems are based on the postulate that acceptance of their decisions can be supposed as implementation of their decisions can normally be guaranteed, if necessary by the legitimised use of violence. Parsons developed a systems approach for the social sciences in "The social system" (1951). In the history of American political science, research was originally concentrated upon institutions of public management, but it became increasingly evident that the influences of pressure groups and political parties had also to be considered to gain an insight into political processes. To prevent political science from coinciding with social science Easton (1953) developed a notion to distinguish a political system. He defined a political system with the criterion "interactions through which values are authoritatively allocated for a society". Since then, this concept of political system has generally been used in political science.

German author H. Heller had already suggested that the specific societal function of public authorities is that they realise binding decisions for a society in his "Staatslehre" (1934). Easton used the characteristic which Heller discovered as specific for public authorities to denote political phenomena. Authors in mainstream literature repeatedly switch easily between the notions of government and politics, and for them "authoritative allocation of values for a society" seems to be an adequate framework for political science, but it is not. Political parties, trade unions and other pressure groups are political actors, trying to further their partisan interests in the political power processes, but they are not legitimised to allocate values for a society and surely don't have the legitimacy or authority to allocate them as binding for all in society. Only public authorities, and actors working on behalf of them, are legitimised to issue and implement their decisions as binding for all, when the procedures as needed in a constitutional State are followed and laws are respected. Public authorities, as a political power phenomenon, should be studied by political science, but it is incorrect to study public authorities exclusively or dominantly within political science. Differentiation between Politics and Public Management of Society is essential. In studies of public authorities within Political Science the internal differentiation of the political system is at stake. Considering the political system, Luhmann differentiates between subsystems primarily politically oriented, and subsystems primarily oriented to the implementation of decisions. The relationship between politics and public management or administration is interpreted as superior/inferior or ends/means. Politics is seen as superior to subordinate administration, as decision-making about ends which have to be realised by implementation of the means as determined by politics. In this conception, empirical processes are presupposed, combining a hierarchy as command structure and the ends/means scheme as causal process.

Luhmann criticised these hierarchy and ends/ means models for their reduced capacity to process complexity. Often politics is seen as inevitably irrational, when compared to the possibilities of rational public management. This is correct if decision-making models for rational public management are used as criteria for judging the rationality and rightness of political activities. It is tautological to suppose that politics is by definition irrational. Political rationality and the rationality of public management must be distinguished. Max Weber saw bureaucracy an an instrument of rational ruling. For him, public bureaucracy was an example of the most efficient, rational organisation. In his conception, social systems are rational inasmuch as they organise the means to realise objectives. He did not seek a starting-point in the specific character of objectives, but in a means so generalised that it could serve several changing objectives: power, or authority as qualified power. Rationalising of society in Weber's view is legalised authority over and by means of public bureaucracy. Luhmann, explicitly adhering to an open systems approach, criticised Weber's conception for its closed system character. By differentiating between politics and public management it is possible to enlarge the complexity and capacity of political systems. Politics and public management fulfil more or less differentiated roles and functions in subsystems, narrowly intertwined in a process of continuous exchange of information and communication. Institutional separation between politics and public management enables us to distinguish between processes for realising legitimate power (political processes) and processes to use legitimised power (processes of public management). These can be specialised to fulfil their specific function. So the traditional concept of public administration is seen in a new perspective. The notion of public administration should be replaced by the notion of Public Management of Society, encompassing all public authorities.

Public Management of Society is able to adequately fulfil its task; the professional and reliable implementation of all that public authorities have to do, when it is not forced to think constantly about all the political implications of its actions. Differentiation between politics and public management requires a bifurcation in roles, organisations, offices, competencies, finances and other institutional arrangements, and the use of different criteria of rationality as a basis of activities. The feeling of confidence that public authorities are functioning according to the Rule of Law can be intensified when realisation of legitimacy (politics) is clearly distinguished from the use of legitimacy (public management). Politics is in fact mostly partisan party politics. Party politics has an important function in a pluralist democracy for the realisation of legitimacy via the legislative process after elections and for its potency to position representatives in the cockpit of the national society, but party politics doesn't have binding force for society, and doesn't have legitimacy, because citizens are not bound by its decisions. Decisions are binding for all citizens only when made within the constitutionally recognised framework and procedures of the Rule of Law. The decisive criterion is whether the binding force for all citizens can be assumed, and this is the case only with the formal decisions of public authorities according to prevailing procedures. The parliament is explicitly seen as part of public authorities (public management). Parliament is constitutionally competent and enabled to realise formal decisions, binding for all citizens. Parliamentary decisions are binding for all citizens. The public management system is an open system with several system boundaries, and with citizenry (citizens, organisations, enterprises), politics, and personnel of the public authorities. In mainstream literature this personnel is seen as part of the system, not of the system environment. Luhmann sees social systems as made up of human actions and communications, not of human beings. When the functioning of public authorities is seen from the viewpoint of political science, only a partial dimension of public management is handled.

Law has a crucial function for the structure and functioning of public authorities in a pluralistic democracy where the Rule of Law prevails (Minc, 1998). The public management system has to function in a differentiated environment (citizenry, public officials, politicians) Public officials (politicians and functionaries), on the basis of information from the environment, process this into decisions and activities for the population. There is a special relationship with the sphere of politics. To realise the activities of public authorities there is an internal structure of decision-premises that program decision-making. The individual case is decided on the basis of these programs which have the function of generally binding norms that keep their validity even when circumstances are changing. Generally, neither politicians nor public functionaries or citizens can render these programs inoperative for the individual case. The whole set of normative programming is called the program-structure of public management. This program-structure of modern public management, determined according to prevailing procedures, is valid as norm. In the European history of institutions, replacement of natural law by positive law was decisive. According to the natural law conception, the activities of public authorities are bound to norms, directly deduced from natural law. These norms were seen as external, coming from the environment, and binding for public authorities. The situation changed drastically due to growing societal differentiation.

The public management system, charged with ever more tasks, had to process more complexity and needed a larger societal autonomy. Public authorities enlarged the domain for which they could realise binding decisions for all citizens. This can be seen as a transfer of complexity from the environment into the public management system. External problems were processed into internal decision-premises on the basis of which objectives and juridical rules were programmed. Luhmann called this self-programming of public authorities by realising positive law. In the process of complexity reduction through programming, it is possible to have a starting-point for activities in specific information from the environment (inputs). Actions are then conditionally programmed: when A, then B. A program can also be started from certain effects of actions (outputs): target programming. A specific effect is chosen as preferred target. This target is the basis for choice and the justification of appropriate means. A conditional program neutralises other inducements for actions, only the chosen fact A causes decision B. A target program neutralises effects other than the selected effect. The chosen target justifies the application of means, whatever the additional effects. Luhmann argued that following principles of the Rule of Law, only conditional programs should be juridified. Conditional programs can be used to justify decision-making juridically. Conditionally defined factual circumstances bind decision-makers differently from target programs. Juridical norms formulated in the when/then scheme can be processed better with the specific juridical techniques of argumentation than target programs. Conditional programming has more scope to give decision-making a non-personal character than target programming. Target programming gives decision-makers more policy room. This explains why target programming is popular with politicians. With conditional programming programs are indifferent about the question of who decides. When one has the information needed for conditional programs, one knows what the decision is or should be. The person who decides cannot influence the individual case. Conditional programming and target programming are also found in mixtures.

One of the barriers to a more integrated scientific handling of the phenomenon of Public Management of Society is that mono-disciplines use different conceptions of rationality. In his prominent "Zweckbegriff und Systemrationalität" (1968), Luhmann analysed the conceptions of rationality in several disciplines. According to ends-means rationality, the dominant rationality conception in economics, the most complex organisations have to be rationalised in the same way as the individual action: as the best choice of means for the chosen end. One concentrated more on the rationality of the coherence of a social system in the other social sciences. According to Luhmann, it is possible to make the ends-means model of economics and the systems model of social science converge with social systems-rationality. A social system is rational insofar as it can solve its problems. This conception of systems-rationality has the advantage that the whole range of problems in social interaction between human beings is encompassed. Systems rationality is a social systems category, not based on a certain value or a specific effect of actions, but aimed at the realisation of a certain ordering of an over-complicated world. Social systems, enclosing human interactions and communications, are adapted to the reduced capacity of human beings in a complex world, making human actions possible. In social sciences a specific notion of function is developed: a social phenomenon has significance for another phenomenon. This function can be consciously aimed at (manifest function), or is a not-intended effect of actions (latent function). Latent functions can be rational, contributing to the solution of social problems. Latent and manifest functions are functionally equivalent.

A specific functional-comparing method was developed by Luhmann. During the first two decades after the Second World War Parsons had a dominant influence upon sociological theory and social sciences in general. His theory is known as the structural-functional systems theory. In this causal-scientific functionalism, function was seen as each contribution to the maintenance of the structure of a social system. When the structural-functional systems theory was confronted with conditions of causal methodology, this theory couldn't stand the test, so the functional method was also discredited. Luhmann sought the reason for failure with structural-functional theory. According to Luhmann, he found the weak point in the causal-scientific character of the notion of function in this theory. Function was seen as a causal relation: A does cause B. Luhmann demonstrated the solution, developing the functional method as an independent method by disengaging it from causal-scientific presuppositions. Turning the sequence from structure-function to function-structure, he radicalised functionalism. Functionalism became a genuine functionalism by taking function as the starting-point of analysis. Luhmann made functional equivalents the decisive criterion of the functional method. Function is not an effect of some cause, but a scheme for comparing equivalent contributions to a specific function. Usually similarities are compared with each other in comparative analyses of mainstream literature. With the method of functional equivalents, different factors are compared from an abstract point of view, to analyse whether they are equivalent for some function. With functional equivalents, as such not (directly) comparable factors, phenomena and aspects are compared with each other. From the viewpoint of if and how they fulfil an equivalent function for solving problems.

The real problem in organising an integrative theory for the study of Public Management of Society seems to be the gap between empirical disciplines and normative disciplines. Empirical disciplines, like sociology and social psychology, are often seen as proper scientific disciplines because these are based upon the empirical method, as is usual also in natural science. Empirical social sciences analyse the factual processes of human activities. They try to explain behaviour and to formulate predictions. Normative disciplines are different, and concentrate on the rationality and rightness of human activities. According to Luhmann, there is no choice between the status of normative or empirical discipline for the study of Public Management of Society, it is by its very character factual rationalising. With purely normative methods one can construct, on the basis of certain premises about values, a simplified model of the object of study, neglecting the facts. With empirical methods, one can inquire analytically into certain aspects of reality.

In fact the social reality of human beings is a mixture of the factual and the normative, therefore social sciences have to take account of this. A more appropriate way of disciplining knowledge about social reality is to recognise the relevance of several methods for all disciplines concerning social reality: empirical method, normative method, functional method. Specialised knowledge can be achieved by putting an object of study within the limited, analytical perspective of an aspect-discipline: political science (power aspect); law science (law aspect); economics (economical aspect); psychology (psychological aspect); etc. In all disciplines different methods (empirical, normative, functional) can be used, provided that these methods are used properly (consistency etc.). Pluralism of methods, within a sound competition between researchers, produces differently conditioned knowledge. It is a challenge to enrich mono-disciplined knowledge with disciplined forms of co-disciplinary research to understand social reality better. The object of study (locus) must be taken as the starting-point, and then the adequate tool box of methods has to be applied in the framework of a disciplined approach (focus). So, the traditional naming of disciplines as normative or empirical sciences is inadequate. In general, mono-disciplinary approaches dominate. Interdisciplinary work is often dismissed as impossible, with remarks like: it demands too much knowledge; or it lacks focus or discipline. Mainzer (1994), trying (vainly) to annexe Public Administration to Political Science, branded interdisciplinary work with regard to public administration as "interdisciplinary delusion". Disciplined co-disciplinary research in social sciences is possible more often than is supposed, and needed more than practised; with due respect to the contributions of different mono-disciplines, sub-disciplines and specialisations and their conditioned rationalities. Disciplines have the potential for co-disciplinary co-operation, scholars are the problem for not trying hard enough (Burdeau, 1959, p.95). Luhmann's conception for Public Management of Society seems especially appropriate, as it explicitly integrates law in an adequate social science perspective. His ideas seem much more adequate than the loquacious writing about governance, qualifying law as some old-fashioned phenomenon. In the next chapter, the crucial role of the Rule of Law and Idea of Public Authority is dealt with. Cultural intelligence, a necessary condition for adequate Public Administration of Society, is proposed as the eighth working-hypothesis for Public Management of Society.

**References**

French
Acollas, E., Philosophie de la science politique. (Paris, 1877).
Alquié, F., Le Cartésianisme de Malebranche. (Paris, Vrin, 1974).
Alquié, F., Plans de Philosophie Générale. (Paris, Table Ronde, 2001).
Attali, J., Blaise Pascal ou le Génie Français. (Paris, Fayard, 2000).
Badie, B., Le Développement politique. (Paris, Economica, 1994).

Baecque, F. de, Quermonne, J.L., dir., L'Administration et la police sous la Cinquième République. (Paris, FNSP, 1981, 1982).
Barreau, J.C., La France va-t-elle disparaître? (Paris, Grasset, 1997).
Bauby, P., L'État-Stratège. Le Retour de l'État. (Paris, Éditions ouvrières, 1991).
Bauby, P., Boual, J.C., dir., Pour une citoyenneté européenne. Quels services publics? (Paris, Éd. de l'Atelier, 1994).
Baudrillard, J., Le miroir de la production. (Paris, Tournail, 1973).
Bayle, P., Dictionnaire historique et critique. (Paris, 1697).
Bénoist, J.M., La Révolution Structurale. (Paris, Grasset, 1975/1980).
Bergson, H., L'Évolution créatrice. (Paris, 1907).
Berthélemy, H., Traité élémentaire de droit adminstratif. (Paris, 1900).
Birnbaum, P., La Classe dirigeante française. (Paris, Seuil, 1977).
Birnbaum, P., Les Sommets de l'État. Essai sur l'élite du pouvoir en France. (Paris, Seuil, 1977).
Birnbaum, P., Badie, B., Sociologie de l'État. (Paris, Grasset, 1982).
Blondel, M., L'Action (1893). (Paris, PUF, 1950).
Bodiguel, J.L., Les anciens élèves de l'E.N.A. (Paris, FNSP, 1978).
Bodiguel, J.L., Quermonne, J.L., La Haute Fonction Publique sous la Ve République. (Paris, PUF, 1983).
Bonnin, C.J., Principe d'administration publique. (Paris, Renaudière, 1812).
Bourdieu, P., La Noblesse de l'État. Grandes écoles et esprit de corps. (Paris, Minuit, 1989).
Bourdieu, P., Esquisse d'une théorie de la pratique. (Paris, Seuil, 2000).
Boutroux, E., De la Contingence des Lois de la Nature. (Paris, 1874).
Braudel, F., L'Identité de la France. (Paris, Flammarion, 1986).
Brèthe de la Gressaye, J., Institution. (Dans: Encyclopédie Dalloz, pp.29f., 1960).
Brun, J., L'Europe Philosophe: 25 siècles de Pensée Occidentale. (Paris, Stock, 1988).
Brun, J., La Philosophie de Pascal. (Paris, PUF, 1994).
Burdeau, G., Méthode de la science politique. (Paris, Dalloz, 1959).
Burdeau, G., Traité de science politique. (Paris, LGDJ, 1971/1986).
Burnier, M.A., L'adieu à Sartre. Suivi du testament de Sartre. (Paris, Plon, 2000).
Calvin, J., Institution de la religion chrétienne. (Genève, 1541; Belles Lettres, 1939).
Chevallier, J., Le service public. (Paris, PUF, 1987).
Chevallier, J., dir., Variations autour de l'idéologie de l'intérêt général. (Paris, PUF, 1979).
Cohendet, P., Lebeau, A., Choix stratégiques et grands programmes civils. (Paris, CPE, 1987).
Clément, C., Lévi-Strauss ou la structure et le malheur. (Paris, Seghers, 1985).
Cohen-Tanugi, L., Le Droit sans l'État. (Paris, PUF, 1985; 1992).
Cohen-Tanugi, L., La métamorphose de la démocratie française. De l'État Jacobin à l'État de Droit. (Paris, Gallimard, 1993).
Colloque Bruxelles, Vers un service public européen? (Bruxelles, 1993).
Commaille, J., Misères de la famille, question d'État. (Paris, FNSP, 1996).
Commaille, J., Les nouveaux enjeux de la question sociale. (Paris, Hachette, 1997).
Commaille, J., Nalletamby, S., Le Modèle français de production de la loi. (Dans: Cahiers de CEVIPOF, 1993).
Commissariat Général du Plan (CGP), Pour un État stratège, garant de l'intérêt général. (Paris, DF, 1993).
Comte, A., Cours de philosophie positive. (Paris, 1830/1842; Hermann/Mouton, 1975).
Comte, A., Système de politique positive. (Paris, 1842).
Condillac, É., Essai sur l'origine des connaissances humaines. (Paris, 1748).
Cousin, V., Oeuvres. (Paris, 1840).
Crozier, M., État moderne, État modeste. (Paris, Fayard, 1987; 1991).
CURAPP, La Gouvernabilité. (Paris, PUF, 1996).
Daudet, Y., dir., Les Nations Unies et la Restauration de l'État. (Paris, Pedone, 1994).
Daval, R., Histoire des idées en France. (Paris, PUF, 1965).
Debbasch, R., Science Administrative. Administration Publique. (Paris, Dalloz, 1989).
De la Mare, N., Traité de la Police. (Paris, 1705/1738).
Delos, J.T., La Société International et le Principes du Droit Public. (Paris, 1929; 1950).
Delos, J.T., La Théorie de l'Institution. (Dans: Archives de Philosophie du Droit et du Sociologie Juridique, pp. 87-153, 1931).
Derrida, J., La voix et le phénomène. Introduction au problème de signe dans la phénoménologie de Husserl. (Paris, PUF, 1967).
Derrida, J., L'écriture et la différence. (Paris, Seuil, 1967).
Derrida, J., De la grammatologie. (Paris, Minuit, 1967).

Derrida, J., Marges de la philosophie. (Paris, Minuit, 1972).
Derrida, J., Foi et Savoir. (Paris, Seuil, 2001).
Descartes, R., Discours de la méthode. (Paris, 1637).
Dibon, P., et al., Pierre Bayle, le philosophe de Rotterdam. (Paris, Vrin, 1959).
Duguit, L., L'État. Le droit objectif et la loi positive. (Paris, Fontemoing, 1901/1903).
Duguit, L., Traité de droit constitutionnel. (Paris, Fontemoing, 1923; 1927/1930).
Dumas, J.L., Histoire de la Pensée, I. II. Renaissance et Siècle des Lumières. (Paris, Tallandier, 1990).
Dumas, J.L., Histoire de la Pensée, I. III. Temps modernes. (Paris, Tallandier, 1990).
Dupuy, F., Thoenig, J.C., L'Administration en miettes. (Paris, Fayard, 1985).
Dupuy, F., Thoenig, J.C., Les mutations de l'administration locale en Europe occidentale. (Paris, CEPEL, 1986).
Durkheim, E., Règles de la méthode sociologique. (Paris, 1895; PUF, 1977).
Ellul, J., Histoire des Institutions. (Paris, PUF, 1992/1993).
Encyclopédie. (Paris, 1751/1780).
Esmein, A., Éléments de droit constitutionnel. (Paris, Sirey, 1906; 1929).
Faure, E., et al., Auguste Comte, qui êtes-vous? (Paris, Manufacture, 1988).
Favre, P., Naissances de la science politique en France, 1870-1914. (Paris, Fayard, 1989).
Fayol, H., Administration industrielle et générale. (Paris, Dunod, 1916).
Folscheid, D., Les Grandes Philosophies. (Paris, PUF, 1994).
Foucault, M., Les mots et les choses. (Paris, 1966).
Foucault, M., L'Archéologie du savoir. (Paris, Gallimard, 1969).
Foucault, M., L'ordre du discours. (Paris, 1971).
Foucault, M., Il faut défendre la société, (Paris, Gallimard, 1997).
Foucault, M., L'Herméneutique du sujet. (Paris, Gallimard, 2001).
France, A., L'Histoire contemporaine. (Paris, 1896-1901).
Friedberg, E., Le pouvoir et la règle. Dynamiques de l'action organisée. (Paris, Seuil, 1993; 1997).
Gény, F., Méthodes d'interprétation et sources en droit privé positif. (Paris, 1899).
Grégoire, R., La Fonction publique. (Paris, A.Colin, 1954).
Greigueuil, P., 2000 Ans d'Histoire de France. (Paris, Assouline, 1999).
Grémion, C., Profession: Décideur. Pouvoir des hauts fonctionnaires et réform de l'État. (Paris, Gauthier-Villars, 1979).
Hauriou, M., Précis de droit administratif et droit public. (Paris, 1896).
Hauriou, M., La théorie de l'institution et de la fondation. (Dans: Cahiers de la nouvelle journée, pp. 2-45, 1925).
Hauser, H., L'Enseignement des sciences sociales, état actuel de cet enseignement dans les divers pays du monde. (Paris, Chevalier/Maresq, 1903).
Heidegger, M., Qu'est-ce que la métaphysique? (Paris, 1937).
Hoffmann, S., Sur la France. (Paris, Seuil, 1976).
Husserl, E., Méditations cartésiennes: introduction à la phénoménologie (1931). (Paris, Vrin, 1969).
Janet, P., Histoire de la science politique dans ses rapports avec la morale. (Paris, Alcan, 1858; 1924).
Janet, P., Histoire de la science politique. (Paris, 1872).
Janicaud, D., Une généalogie du spiritualisme français. Aux sources du bergsonisme. Ravaisson et la métaphysique. (La Haye, Nijhoff, 1969).
Janicaud, D., Heidegger en France. (Paris, A.Michel, 2001).
Jerphagnon, L., Histoire de la Pensée. T.I. Antiquité et Moyen Age. (Paris, Tallandier, 1990).
Jerphagnon, L., dir., Histoire des grandes philosophies. (Paris, Privat, 1987).
Jèze, G., Les principes généraux du droit administratif. (Paris, Giard et Brière, 1904; 1914).
Kant, E., Oeuvres philosophiques. (Paris, Gallimard, 1986).
Kant, E., Critique de la raison pure. (Paris, Flammarion, 2001).
Kessler, M.C., Les Grands Corps de l'État. (Paris, FNSP, 1986; 1994).
Kondylis, V., Le principe de neutralité dans la fonction publique. (Paris, LGDJ, 1994).
Kremer-Marietti, A., Le Positivisme. (Paris, PUF, 1980; 1993).
Labrousse, E., Pierre Bayle. (La Haye, Nijhoff, 1963/1964).
Lacroix, J., Panorama de la philosophie française contemporaine. (Paris, PUF, 1966).
Lacroix, J., Kant et le kantisme. (Paris, PUF, 1993).
Lacroze, R., Maine de Biran. (Paris, PUF, 1970).
Laferrière, E., Traité de la juridiction administrative et des recours contentieux. (Paris, Berger-Levrault, 1887).
Laferrière, J., Manuel de droit constitutionnel. (Paris, 1947).

Langrod, G., La science administrative et sa place parmi les sciences voisines. (Dans: Auby, J.M., dir., Traité de Science Administrative. Paris, Mouton, pp.92-123, 1966).
Le Fur, L., Le droit naturel et la théorie de l'institution. (Dans: Vie intellectuelle, pp.76-102, 1931).
Le Roy, E., Une philosophie nouvelle: Henri Bergson. (Paris, 1912).
Lévi-Strauss, C., Anthropologie structurale. (Paris, Plon, 1973).
Lévi-Strauss, C., La Pensée sauvage. (Paris, Plon, 1962).
Lévi-Strauss, C., L'Identité. (Paris, PUF, 2000).
Lévy-Leboyer, M., Casanova, J.C., dir., Entre l'État et le marché, l'économie française de 1800 à nos jours. (Paris, Gallimard, 1991).
Lyotard, J.F., La Condition postmoderne. (Paris, 1979).
Lyotard, J.F., Le Tombeau de l'intellectuel. (Paris, 1984).
Macherey, P., Comte, la philosophie des sciences. (Paris, PUF, 1989).
Maine de Biran, F., Oeuvres complets. (Paris, 1820).
Malebranche, N., La Recherche de la Vérité. (Paris, 1674/1675).
Maritain, J., Distinguer pour unir, ou les degrés du savoir. (Paris, 1932).
Maritain, J., Humanisme intégral. (Paris, 1936).
Martin, M.M., Histoire de l'unité française, l'idée de patrie en France des origines à nos jours. (Paris, PUF, 1982).
Marx, K., Oeuvres. (Paris, Gallimard, 1965/1982).
Merleau-Ponty, M., Phénomènologie de la Perception. (Paris, Gallimard, 1945).
Merleau-Ponty, M., Le Primat de la Perception et ses Consequences Philosophiques. (Paris, Verdier, 2000).
Minc, A., Au nom de la loi. (Paris, Gallimard, 1998).
Montaigne, M. de, Essais. (Paris, 1580).
Offner, J.M., Performances de services publics locaux. (Paris, Litec, 1990).
Pactet, P., Droit constitutionnel. Institutions politiques. (Paris, Masson, 1994).
Parieu, E. de, Principes de la science politique. (Paris, 1870).
Proudhon, P.J., Qu'est-ce que la propriété? (Paris, 1840).
Proudhon, P.J., Philosophie de la misère. (Paris, 1846).
Quermonne, J.L., Le Gouvernement de la France sous la Ve République. (Paris, Dalloz, 1987).
Quermonne, J.L., L'appareil administratif de l'État. (Paris, Seuil, 1991).
Rangeon, F., L'Idéologie de l'Intérêt Général. (Paris, Economica, 1986).
Régnard, A., L'État: ses origines, sa nature et son but. Études de politique scientifique. (Paris, Dervaux, 1885).
Renard, G., La théorie de l'institution. (Paris, 1930).
Renard, G., La philosophie de l'institution. (Paris, 1939).
Rodis-Lewis, G., Descartes et le Rationalisme. (Paris, PUF, 1992).
Rouban, L., La modernisation de l'État et la fin de la spécificité française. (Dans: Revue française de science politique, pp.521-544, 1990).
Rouban, L., Le Pouvoir Anonyme. Les Mutations de l'État à la française. (Paris, FNSP, 1994).
Sartre, J.P., La transcendance de l'ego. (Paris, Vrin, 1934; 1965).
Sartre, J.P., Critique de la raison dialectique. (Paris, Gallimard, 1960; 1962).
Saussure, F. de, Cours de linguistique générale. (Paris, 1962; 1966).
Segrestin, D., Le phénomène corporatiste. (Paris, Fayard, 1984).
Senarclens, P. de, L'Humanitaire en catastrophe. (Paris, Presses de Sciences Po, 1999).
Senarclens, P. de, Maîtriser la mondialisation. (Paris, FNSP, 2000).
Sorman, G., Les vraies penseurs de notre temps. (Paris, Fayard, 1989).
Stoffaës, C., dir., Entre monopole et concurrence. (Pau, 1994).
Stoffaës, C., dir., Services publics. Question d'avenir. (CGP. Paris, DF, 1995).
Stoffaës, C., dir., L'Europe à l'épreuve de l'intérêt général. (Paris, ASPE, 1995).
Taine, H., Les origines de la France contemporaine. (Paris, 1875/1893).
Teissier, G., La responsabilité de la puissance publique. (Paris, 1906).
Thoenig, J.C., L'ère des technocrates. (Paris, Ed. d' Organisation, 1973; 1987).
Timsit, G., Administrations et États. Étude comparée. (Paris, PUF, 1987).
Timsit, G., Gouverner ou juger. Blasons de la légalité. (Paris, PUF, 1995).
Trotignon, P., Les philosophes français aujourd'hui. (Paris, PUF, 1985).
Vacherot, E., L Démocratie. (Paris, Chamerot, 1860).
Wahl, J., Tableau de la philosophie française contemporaine. (Paris, Gallimard, 1962/1969).
Weil, P., Mission d'étude des législations de la nationalité et de l'immigration. (Paris, DF, 1998).
Weil, P. Pouyaud, D., Le Droit Administratif. (Paris, PUF, 2001).

English
Abramowitz, M., Stegun, I.A., Handbook of mathematical functions. (New York, Dover, 1972).
Adams, G.B., Balfour, D.L., Unmasking Administrative Evil. (London, Sage, 1998).
Ahonen, P., ed., Tracing the Semiotic Boundaries of Politics. (Berlin, De Gruyter, 1993).
Alexander, C.N., Langer, E.J., eds., Higher Stages of Human Development. (New York, OUP, 1990).
Alexander, J.C., The Parsons Revival in German Sociology. (In: Collins, R., ed., Sociological Theory, pp.394-412, 1984).
Archer, M.S., Culture and Agency. The Place of Culture in Social Theory. (Cambridge, CUP, 1996).
Atkins, G.D., Reading Deconstruction. Deconstructive Reading. (Lexington, University of Kentucky Press, 1983).
Bailey, M.T., Mayer, R.T., eds., Public Management in an interconnected world. (New York, Greenwood, 1992).
Bain, J., Industrial Organization. (New York, Wiley, 1968).
Baldwin, D.A., ed., Neorealism and Neoliberalism. (New York, Columbia UP, 1993).
Barnard, C.I., The Functions of the Executive (1938). (Cambridge, MA, Harvard UP, 1958).
Baumgartner, F., Conflict and Rhetoric in French Policymaking. (Pittsburgh, University of Pittsburgh Press, 1989).
Bekke, H., Toonen, T., etcs., Civil Service Systems in Comparative Perspective. (Bloomington, Indiana UP, 1996).
Bemelmans-Videc, M.L., et al., eds., Carrots, Sticks and Sermons. (London, Transaction, 1998).
Benhabib, S., Dallmayer, F., eds., The Communicative Ethics Controversy. (Cambridge, MIT, 1990).
Berger, P., Luckmann, T.. The Social Construction of Reality. A Treatise on the Sociology of Knowledge. (New York, Anchor, 1966).
Bernstein, J.S., Power and Politics. (Boston, Shambhala, 1989).
Bernstein, R., The Reconstruction of Social and Political Theory. (Philadelphia, University of Pennsylvania Press, 1983).
Biersteker, T.J., Weber, C., eds., State Sovereignty as Social Construct. (Cambridge, CUP, 1996).
Bledstein, B.J., The Culture of Professionalism. (New York, Norton, 1976).
Bleicher, J., The Hermeneutic Imagination. (Boston, Routledge, 1982).
Bogason, P., Public Administration and the Unspeakable. Postmodernism as an academic trail of the 1990s. (Roskilde, Denmark, Roskilde University, 1999).
Bogason, P., Public Policy and Local Governance. Institutions in Postmodern Society. (London, Elgar, 2000).
Bogason, P., Postmodernism and American Public Administration in the 1990s. (In: Administration & Society, pp.165-193, 2001).
Boorstin, D.J., The Discoverers. A History of Man's Search to Know his World and Himself. (New York, Vintage, 1985).
Boston, J., et al., Public Management: The New Zealand Model. (Auckland, OUP, 1996).
Bovens, M., Bureaucratic Responsibility as a Virtue. (Leuven, Belgium, European Group of Public Administration, 1997).
Bovens, M., The Quest for Responsibility: Accountability and Citizenship in Complex Organizations. (Cambridge, CUP, 1998).
Bowman, J.S., ed., Ethical Frontiers in Public Management. The Case for Justice. (San Francisco, Jossey-Bass, 1991).
Braybrooke, D., Philosophy of Social Science. (Englewood Cliffs, Prentice-Hall, 1987).
Brèthe de la Gressaye, J., The Sociological Theory of the institution and French Juristic Thought. (In: Broderick, A., ed., The French Instiotutionalists. Maurice Hauriou, Georges Renard, Joseph T. Delos. Cambridge, MA, Harvard UP, pp.15-24, 1970).
Breton, A., Competitve Governments. An Economic Theory of Politics and Public Finance. (Cambridge, CUP, 1996).
Brzezinsky, Z., Out of Control. Global Turmoil on the Eve of the Twenty-first Century. (New York, Macmillan, 1993).
Broderick, A., Evolving Due Process and the French Institutionalists. (In: The Catholic University of America Law Review, pp. 99-135, 1964).
Broderick, A., ed., The French Institutionalists. Maurice Hauriou, Georges Renard, Joseph T. Delos. (Cambridge, MA, Harvard UP, 1970).
Brunsson, N., The Organisation of Hypocrisy. Talk, Decisions and Actions in Organisations. (Chichester, Wiley, 1989).
Burchell, G., Gordon, C., Miller, P., eds., The Foucault Effect. Studies in Governmentality. (Chicago, University of Chicago Press, 1991).

Burke, J.P., Bureaucratic Responsibility. (Baltimore, Johns Hopkins UP, 1986).
Burke, J.P., Administrative Ethics and Democratic Theory. (In: Cooper, T.L., ed., Handbook of Administrative Ethics. New York, Dekker, pp.147-156, 1994).
Caiden, G.E., Administrative Reform comes of age. (New York, De Gruyter, 1991).
Caiden, G.E., The Concept of Neutrality. (In: Asmeron, H.K., Reiss, E.P., eds., Democratization and Bureaucratic Neutrality. New York, St.Martin's, pp.20-44, 1996).
Calhoun, C., Habermas and the Public Sphere. (Cambridge, MIT, 1992).
Calhoun, C., ed., From Persons to Nations: The Social Constitution of Identities. (London, Blackwell, 1995).
Campbell, C., Wilson, G.K., The End of Whitehall. A Comparative Perspective. (Oxford, Blackwell, 1995).
Carrithers, M., Why Humans have Cultures. Explaining Anthropology and Social Diversity. (Oxford, OUP, 1992).
Cassell, F.H., The politics of public-private management. (In: Perry, J.L., Kraemer, K.L., eds., Public Management: Public and Private Perspectives. Palo Alto, Mayfield, pp.142-157, 1983).
Cawley, M.R., Chaloupka, W., American Governmentality. Michel Foucault and Public Administration. (In: Woller, G.M., ed., Public Administration and Postmodernism. In: American Behavioral Scientist, pp.28-42, September 1997).
Chelimsky, E., Shadish, W., eds., Evaluation for the 21st Century. A Handbook. (New York, 1995).
Christensen, T., Laegreid, P., New Public Management. Design, Resistance of Transformation? (In: Public Productivity & Management Review, pp.169-193, 1999).
Clarke, J., Newman, J., The Managerial State. (London, Sage, 1997).
Coase, R.H., The Nature of the Firm. (In: Economica, pp.386-405, 1937; Oxford, OUP, 1993).
Coase, R.H., The Problem of Social Cost. (In: Journal of Law and Economics, pp.1-44, 1960).
Collingwood, R.G., The Idea of History. (Oxford, Clarendon, 1993).
Collins, D., Management Fads and BuzzWords. Critical-Practical Perspectives. (London, Routledge, 2000).
Collins, R., The Sociology of Philosophies. A Global Theory of Intellectual Change. (Cambridge, Harvard UP, 1998).
Commission on Global Governance. Our Global Neighbourhood. (Oxford, OUP, 1995).
Cooper, C.L., Who's Who in Management Sciences. (Cheltenham, Elgar, 2000).
Cooper, T.L., Hierarchy, virtue and the practice of public administration. A perspective for normative ethics. (In: Public Administration, pp.320-328, 1987).
Cooper, T.L., ed., Handbook of Administrative Ethics. (New York, Dekker, 1994).
Corkey, J., et al., eds., Management of Public Service Reform. (Amsterdam, IOS Press, 1998).
Corsten, M., Between Constructivism and Realism. Searle's Theory of the Construction of Social Reality. (In: Philosophy of the Social Sciences, pp.102-121, 1998).
Crane, D., ed., The Sociology of Culture. Emerging Theoretical Perspectives. (New York, Blackwell, 1994).
Cyert, R., March, J., A Behavioral Theory of the Firm. (Englewood Cliffs, Prentice-Hall, 1963).
Davis, L., North, D., Institutional Change and American Economic Growth. (Cambridge, CUP, 1971).
Delos, J.T., The Theory of the Institution. (In: Broderick, A., ed., The French Institutionalists. Maurice Hauriou, Georges Renard, Joseph T. Delos. Cambridge, MA, Harvard UP, pp. 222-265, 1970.
Denhardt, K.G., Unearthing the moral foundations of public administration. Honor, benevolence and justice. (In: Bowman, J.S., ed., Ethical Frontiers in Public Management. The Case For Justice. San Francisco, Jossey-Bass, pp.91-113, 1991).
Denhardt, R.B., In the Shadow of Organizations. (Lawrence, KS, Regents, 1981).
Denhardt, R.B., Theories of Public Organization. (Monterey, Brooks-Cole, 1984).
Denhardt, R.B., The Ethics of Public Service. (London, Greenwood, 1988).
Denhardt, R.B., The Pursuit of Significance. Strategies for Managerial Success in Public Organizations. (Belmont, Wadsworth, 1993).
Denhardt, R.B. and J.V., The New Public Service: Serving Rather than Steering. (In: Public Administration Review, pp.549-559, 2000).
Derlien, H.U., From Administrative Reform to Administrative Modernization. (Bamberg, Verwaltungswissenschaftliche Beiträge, 1998).
Derrida, J., On Grammatology. (Baltimore, Johns Hopkins UP, 1976).
Derrida, J., Margins of Philosphy. (Chicago, University of Chicago Press, 1981).
Derrida, J., Force of Law. The Mystical Foundation of Authority. (In: Cornell, D., et al., eds., Deconstruction and the Possibility of Justice. New York, Routledge, 1992).
Derrida, J., The time is out of joint. (In: Haferkamp, A., ed., Deconstruction is/in America. A new sense of the political. New York, New York UP, pp.14-38, 1995).
Desch, M.C., Culture Clash. Assessing the Importance of Ideas in Security Studies. (In: International Security, pp.141-170, 1998).

DiMaggio, P.J., Powell, W.W., eds., The New Institutionalism in Organizational Analysis. (Chicago, University of Chicago Press, 1991).
Dixit, A., The Making of Economic Policy. A Transaction Cost Politics Perspective. (Cambridge, MA, MIT Press, 1996).
Docherty, T., After Theory: Postmodernism/Post-Marxism. (Lodnon, Routledge, 1990).
Docherty, T., ed., Postmodernism. A Reader. (New York, 1993).
Donaldson, L., In Defence of Organization Theory. (Cambridge, CUP, 1985).
Donaldson, L., American Anti-Management Theories of Organization. A Critique of Paradigm Proliferation. (Cambridge, CUP, 1995).
Dunleavy, Democracy, Bureaucracy and Public Choice. Economic Explanations in Political Science. (Hemel Hempstead, Harvester Wheatsheaf, 1991).
Durkheim, E., The elementary forms of religious life. (London, Allen & Unwin, 1915).
Durkheim, E., The Rules of Sociological Method. (Glencoe, Free Press, 1938; 1950).
Durkheim, E., The Division of Labour in Society. (New York, Free Press, 1964; 1970).
Dvorin, E., Simmons, R.H., From Amoral to Humane Bureaucracy. (San Francisco, Canfield, 1972).
Easton, D., The Political System. (New York, Knopf, 1953).
Egeberg, M., Laefreid, P., eds., Organizing Political Institutions. (Oslo, Scandinavian UP, 1999).
Eichner, A.S., Toward a New Economics. (London, Macmillan, 1985).
Eisenstadt, S., The Political System of Empires. (New York, Free Press, 1963).
Ellis, J.M., Against Deconstruction. (Princeton, Princeton UP, 1989).
Farazmand, A., Administrative Ethics and Professional Competence. Accountability and Performance. (Sunningdale, IIAS Conference, 1999).
Farazmand, A., ed., Handbook of Comparative and Development Administration. (New York, Dekker, 1991).
Farazmand, A., ed., Handbook of Bureaucracy. (New York, Dekker, 1994).
Farazmand, A., ed., Modern Systems of Government. Exploring the Role of Bureaucrats and Politicians. (London, Sage, 1997).
Farmer, D.J., The Language of Public Administration. Bureaucracy, Modernity and Postmodernity. (Tuscaloosa, University of Alabama Press, 1995).
Farmer, D.J., Derrida, Deconstruction and Public Administration. (In: Woller, G.M., ed., Public Administration and Postmodernism. In American Behavioral Scientist, pp.12-27, 1997).
Farmer, D.J., Public Administration Discourse. A Matter of Style? (In: Administration & Society, pp.229-320, 1999).
Farmer, D.J., ed., Papers on the Art of Anti-Administration. (Burke, Chatelaine Press, 1998).
Faulkner, D.O., Rond, M. de, eds., Cooperative Strategy. (Oxford, OUP, 2000).
Fay, B., Social Theory and Political Practice. (London, Allen & Unwin, 1975/1980).
Featherstone, M., ed., Global Culture. Nationalism, Globalization and Modernity. (London, Sage, 1990).
Featherstone, M., et al., eds., Global Modernities. (Newbury Park, Sage, 1995).
Felts, A., Philip, J., Time and Space. The Origins and Implications of the New Public Management. (In: Administrative Theory & Praxis, pp.519-533, 2000).
Ferlie, E., et al., The New Public Management in Action. (Oxford, OUP, 1996).
Finer, S.E., The History of Government from the Earliest Times. (Oxford, OUP, 1997).
Fish, S., Doing what comes naturally. Change, rhetoric and the practice of theory in literature and legal studies. (Durham, Duke UP, 1989).
Flathman, R.E., The Public Interest. An Essay Concerning the Normative Discourse of Politics. (New York, Wiley, 1966).
Flynn, N., Strehl, F., eds., Public Sector Management in Europe. (London, Prentice Hall, 1996).
Fonow, M.M., Cook, J.A., eds., Beyond Methodology. Feminist Scholarship as Lived Research. (Bloomington, University of Indiana Press, 1991).
Foucault, M., The Archaeology of Knowledge and the Discourse on Language. (New York, Pantheon, 1972).
Foucault, M., Power/Knowledge. (New York, Pantheon, 1980).
Foucault, M., The Foucault Reader. (Harmondsworth, Penguin, 1984).
Foucault, M., Governmentality. (In: Burchell, et al., eds., The Foucault Effect. Studies in Governmentality. Chicago, University of Chicago Press, pp.87-104, 1991).
Fox, C.J., Free to Choose, Free to Win, Free to Lose. The Phenomenology of Ethical Space. (In: International Journal of Public Administration, pp.913-930, 1989).
Fox, C.J., The Use of Philosophy in Adminstrative Ethics. (In: Cooper, T.L., ed., Handbook of Administrative Ethics. New York, Dekker, pp.83-105, 1994).
Fox, C.J., Miller, H.T., Postmodern Public Adminstration. (Thousand Oaks, Sage, 1995).

Frederickson, H.G., Minnowbrook II. Changing Epochs of Public Administration. (In: Public Administration Review, pp.95-100, 1989).
Frederickson, H.G., The Spirit of Public Administration. (San Francisco, Josey-Bass, 1997).
Frederickson, H.G., ed., Ethics and Public Administration. (Armonk, NY, Sharpe, 1993).
Frederickson, J.W., ed., Perspective on Strategic Management. (Grand Rapids, Harper, 1990).
Fukuyama, F., The End of History and the Last Man. (London, Penguin, 1991; 1992).
Furobotn, E., Richter, R., eds., The New Institutional Economics. (College Station, Texas A & M UP, 1991).
Gadamer, H.G., Truth and Method. (New York, Continnum, 1975).
Gamble, A., An Introduction to Modern Social and Political Thought. (London, Macmillan, 1981).
Gamble, A., Economic Governance. (In: Pierre, J., ed., Debating Governance. Oxford, OUP, pp.110-137, 2000).
Garcia-Zamor, J.C., Khator, R., eds., Public Administration in the Global Village. (Westport, Praeger, 1994).
Gargan, J.J., The Public Administration Community and the Search for Professionalism. (In: Rabin, J., et al., eds., Handbook of Public Administration. New York, Dekker, pp.965-1025, 1989).
Gargan, J.J., Handbook of State Government Administration. (New York, Dekker, 1999).
Geertz, C., The Interpretation of Cultures. (New York, Basic Books, 1974).
Giddens, A., The Constitution of Society. Outline of the Theory of Structuration. (Cambridge, Polity, 1984).
Giddens, A., Politics, Sociology and Social Theory. (Cambridge, Polity, 1995).
Godfrey, P.C., ed., The Philosophical Roots of Management Thought. (In: International Journal of Public Administration, 1998).
Goleman, D., Emotional Intelligence. (New York, Bantam Books, 1997).
Golembiewski, R.T., Organization as a Moral Problem. (In: Public Administration Review, pp.63-74, 1973).
Golembiewski, R.T., Practical Public Management. (New York, Dekker, 1995).
Goodsell, C.T., The Case for Bureaucracy. A Public Administration Polemic. (Charham, Chatham House, 1985; 1994).
Goodsell, C.T., Balancing competing values. (In: Perry, J.A., ed., Handbook of Public Administration, San Francisco, Jossey-Bass, 1977).
Gordon, C., ed., Power/Knowledge. Selected interviews and other writings, 1972-1997, by Michel Foucault. (Brighton, Harvester, 1980).
Gordon, G.J., Public Administration in America. (New York, St.Martin's, 1982; 1986).
Gore, A., Common Sense Government: Works Better and Costs Less. (Washington DC, US Government Printing Office, 1995).
Gore, A., Businesslike Government: lessons learned from America's best companies. (Pittsburgh, National Performance Review, 1997).
Gortner, H., Administration in the Public Sector. (New York, Wiley, 1977).
Gortner, H., Ethics for Public Managers. (Westport, Greenwood, 1991).
Greenstein, F.I., Polsby, N.W., eds., Handbook of Political Science. (Reading, Addison-Wesley, 1975).
Guba, E., Lincoln, Y., Effective Evaluation. (San Francisco, 1981).
Guba, E., Lincoln, Y., Naturalistic Inquiry. (Beverley Hills, Sage, 1985).
Guba, E., Lincoln, Y., Fourth Generation Evaluation. (Beverley Hills, Sage, 1989).
Guignon, C., Pragmatism or Hermeneutics? Epistemology after Foundationalism. (In: Bohman, et al., eds., The Interpretative Turn. Ithaca, Cornell UP, 1991).
Guignon, C., Overcoming Dualism. A Hermeneutic Approach to Understanding Humans. (University of Vermont, 1993).
Gunnell, J.G., Realizing Theory. The Philosophy of Science Revisited. (In: Journal of Politics, pp.923-940, 1995).
Gutting, G., ed., Paradigms and Revolutions. Appraisals and Applications of Thomas Kuhn's Philosophy of Science. (Notre Dame, University of Notre Dame Press, 1980).
Habermas, J., Toward a Rational Society. (Boston, Beacon, 1970; 1972).
Habermas, J., Legitimation Crisis. (Boston, Beacon, 1975).
Habermas, J., The Theory of Communicative Action. (Boston, Beacon, 1984/1987).
Habermas, J., Moral Consciousness and Communicative Action. (Cambridge, MIT, 1990).
Habermas, J., Justification and Application. (Oxford, Polity, 1990).
Habermas, J., The Philosophical Discourse of Modernity. (Cambridge, MA, MIT Press, 1991).
Habermas, J., Further Reflections on the Public Sphere. (In: Calhoun, C., ed., Habermas and the Public Sphere. (Cambridge, MIT, pp.421-461, 1992).
Habermas, J., The Structural Transformation of the Public Sphere. (Cambridge, MIT, 1989; 1994).
Hall, E. and M., Understanding Cultural Differences. (Yarmouth, Intercultural Press, 1990).

Hall, P., Taylor, R.C.R., Political Science and the Three New Institutionalisms. (In: Political Studies, pp.936-957; 1996).
Hampden-Turner, C., Trompenaars, F., The Seven Cultures of Capitalism. (New York, Doubleday, 1993).
Harden, I., The Contracting State. (Buckingham, Open University Press, 1992).
Harmon, M.M., Responsibility as Paradox. A Critique of Rational Discourse on Government. (Thousand Oaks, Sage, 1995).
Harmon, M.M., On the Futility of Universalism. (In: Administrative Theory & Praxis, pp.3-18, 1997).
Hart, D.K., The virtuous citizen, the honorable bureaucrat and public administration. (In: Public Administration Review, pp.111-120, 1984).
Hauriou, M., The Theory of the Institution and the Foundation. (In: Broderick, A., ed., The French Institutionalists. Maurice Hauriou, Georges Renard, Joseph T. Delos. Cambridge, MA, Harvard UP, pp. 93-124, 1970).
Hayek, F.A., The Road to Serfdom. (London, Routledge, 1944).
Heater, D., Citizenship. The Civic Ideal in World History, Politics and Education. (London, Longman, 1990).
Hegel, G., The Philosophy of Right. (London, 1942).
Hegel, G., The Philosophy of History. (Oxford, OUP, 1956).
Hegel, G., The Phenomenology of Mind. (New York, Harper & Row, 1967).
Heidegger, M., Being and Time. (New York, Harper, 1962; Oxford, Blackwell, 1988).
Held, D., Introduction to Critical Theory. (Berkeley, University of California Press, 1980).
Held, D., Political Theory and the Modern State. (Cambridge, Polity, 1989).
Held, D., et al., Global Transformations. (Cambridge, Polity, 1999).
Heller, A., Fehèr, F., The Postmodern Political Condition. (New York, Columbia UP, 1988).
Hennipman, P., Welfare Economics and the Theory of Economic Policy. (Brookfield, Elgar, 1995).
Hirst, P., Representative Democracy and its Limits. (Cambridge, Polity, 1990).
Hirst, P., Associative Democracy. (Oxford, Polity, 1994).
Hirst, P., The Global Economy. Myths and Realities. (In: Foreign Affairs, pp.490-425, 1997).
Hirst, P., From Statism to Pluralism. (London, UCL, 1997).
Hirst, P., Democracy and Governance. (In: Pierre, J., ed., Debating Governance. Oxford, OUP, pp.13-35, 2000).
Hirst, P., Khilnani, S., eds., Reinventing Democracy. (London, Blackwell, 1996).
Hirst, P., Thompson, G., Globalisation and the Future of the Nation-State. (In: Economy and Society, pp.408-422, 1995).
Hirst, P., Thompson, G., Globalization in Question. The international Economy and the Possibilities of Governance. (Cambridge, Polity, 1996).
Hofstede, G., Culture's Consequences. International Differences in Work-Related Values. (Beverley Hills, Sage, 1984).
Hofstede, G., Cultures and Organisations. Intercultural Co-operation and its Importance for Survival. (London, harperCollins, 1994).
Hofstede, G., Culture and Organizations. Software of the Mind. (New York, McGraw-Hill, 1997).
Hondeghem, A., ed., Ethics and Accountability in a Context of Governance and New Public management. (Brussels, EGPA/IIAS, 1998).
Hood, C., The Art of the State. Culture, Rhetoric and Public Management. (Oxford, OUP, 1998).
Hood, C., Jackson, M., Administrative Argument. (Aldershot, Dartmouth, 1991).
Hopf, T., The Promise of Constructivism in International Relations Theory. (In: International Security, pp.171-200, 1998).
Hughes, O., Public Management and Administration. (Basingstoke, Macmillan, 1998).
Hummel, R., Stories Managers Tell. Why they are as valid as science. (In: Public Administration Review, pp.31-41, 1991).
Hund, J., Searle's "The Construction of Social Reality". (In: Philosophy of the Social Sciences, pp.122-131, 1998).
Hunt, A., Wickham, G., Foucault and Law. Towards a Sociology of Law as Governance. (London, Pluto, 1994).
Huntington, S.P., The Clash of Civilizations and the Remaking of World Order. (New York, Simon & Schuster, 1996).
Huntington, S.P., et al., The Clash of Civilizations? The Debate. (New York, Council on Foreign Relations, 1993).
Hupe, P.L., Meijs, L., Hybrid Governance. (The Hague, Social and Cultural Planning Office, 2000).
Immergut, E.M., The Theoretical Core of the New Institutionalism. (In: Politics & Society, pp.5-34, 1998).
ISSJ ( International Social Science Journal), Governance. (Oxford, Unesco/Blackwell, 1998).

Jackson, R,H., ed., Sovereignty at the Millenium. (Oxford, Blackwell, 1999).
Jun, J.S., Philosophy of Administration. (Seoul, Daeyoung Moonhwa International, 1994).
Jun, J.S., Rivera, M.A., The Paradox of Transforming Public Administration. Modernity versus Postmodernity Arguments. (In: Woller, G.M., ed., Public Administration and Postmodernism. In: American Behavioral Scientist, pp.132-147, September 1997).
Jung, C.G., The Undiscovered Self. (New York, Penguin, 1958).
Kardulias, P.N., ed., World-Systems Theory in Practice. (Lanham, Rowman & Littlefield, 1999).
Kass, H.D., Catron, B.L., eds., Images and Identities in Public Administration. Discourse on Governance. (Newbury Park, Sage, 1990).
Katzenstein, P.J., Cultural Norms and National Security. (Ithaca, Cornell UP, 1996).
Kennedy, P., Preparing for the Twenty-first Century. (New York, Random House, 1993).
Kernaghan, K., The Ethics Era in Canadian Public Administration. (Ottawa, Canadian Centre for Management Development, 1996).
Kernaghan, K., The Post-Bureaucratic Organization and Public Sector Values. (Sunningdale, UK, IIAS Conference, 1999).
Kernaghan, K., The Post-Bureaucratic Organization and Public Service Values. (In: International Review of Administrative Science, pp.91-104, 2000).
Kernaghan, K., ed., For a Responsable Public Administration: Reconciliation of democray, efficacy and ethics. (In: International Review of Administrative Sciences, vol.66, no.1, March 2000).
Kettl, D., The Global Public Management Revolution. A Report on the Transformation of Governance. (Washington DC, Brookings Institution, 2000).
Kier, E., Imagining War. British and French Military Doctrine Between the Wars. (Princeton, Princeton UP, 1997).
King, A., ed., Culture, Globalization and the World System. (Houndmills, Basingstoke, Macmillan, 1991).
King, C.S., The Legacy of Public Administration Theory. Practising Postmodern Theory in a Modernist World. (Savannah, Paper for the Public Administration Theory Network, 1996).
King, C.S., Stivers, C. et al., Government is Us: Public Administration in an Anti-Government Era. (Thousand Oaks, Sage, 1998).
King, G., et al., Designing Social Inquiry. Scientific Inference in Qualitative Research. (Princeton, Princeton UP, 1994).
Kirlin, J.J., The Big Questions for the a Significant Public Administration. (In: Public Administration Review, pp.140-143, 1996).
Kirlin, J.J., The Big Questions of Public Administration in a Democracy. (In: Public Administration Review, pp.416-423, 1996).
Kogood, R.P., Caulfield, S., Beyond Corporate Responsibility. Toward a fundamental redefinition of the roles of public and private sectors. (In: Bozeman, B., Straussman, J., eds., New Directions in Public Adminstration. Montery, Brooks/Cole, pp.63-68, 1984).
Kohlberg, L., The Philosophy of Moral Development. (San Francisco, 1981).
Kohlberg, J., Essays on Moral Development. (New York, Harper and Row, 1984).
Kohlberg, L., Ryncarz, R.A., Beyond Justice Reasoning. Moral Development and Consideration of a Seventh Stage. (In: Alexander, C.N., Langer, E.J., eds., Higher Stages of Human Development. New York, OUP, pp.191-207, 1990).
Kooiman, J., ed., Modern Governance. (London, Sage, 1993).
Kooiman, J., et al., Social-political Governance and Management. (Rotterdam, Erasmus University, 1997).
Kooiman, J., Vliet, M. van, Governance and Public Management. (In: Eliassen, K., Kooiman, J., eds., Managging Public Organisations. London, Sage, 1993).
Krueger, A.O., Economists' Changing Perceptions of Government. (In: Weltwirtschaftliches Archiv, pp.417-431, 1990).
Kuhn, T., The Structure of Scientific Revolutions. (Chicago, University of Chicago Press, 1970).
Lacan, J., The Four Fundamental Concepts of Psycho-Analysis. (New York, Norton, 1981).
Lacan, J., The Seminar of Jacques Lacan. (New York, Norton, 1991).
Lakatos, I., Musgrave, A., eds., Criticism and the Growth of Knowledge. (Cambridge, CUP, 1970).
Lane, J.R., New Public Management. (London, Routledge, 2000).
Lane, R., The Market Experience. (New York, CUP, 1991).
Laski, H.J., A Grammar of Politics. (London, 1925; Allen and Unwin, 1938).
Lather, P., Getting Smart. Feminist Research and Pedagogy With/in the Postmodern. (New York, Routledge, 1991).
Liddell Hart, B.H., The British Way in Warfare. (London, Faber, 1932).
Long, N., The Polity. (Chicago, Rand McNally, 1962).

Luhmann, N., Trust and Power. (Chichester, Wiley, 1979).
Luhmann, N., The Differentiation of Society. (New York, Columbia UP, 1982).
Luhmann, N., A Sociological Theory of Law. (London, Routledge, 1985).
Luhmann, N., The Autopoiesis of Social Systems. (In: Geyer, F., Zouwen, J. van der, eds., Sociocybernetic Paradoxes. Observation, Control and Evolution of Self-Steering Systems. London, Sage, pp.172-192, 1986).
Luhmann, N., Ecological Communication. (Cambridge, Polity, 1989).
Luhmann, N., Essays on Self-Reference. (New York, Columbia UP, 1990).
Luhmann, N., Political Theory in the Welfare State. (New York, W. de Gruyter, 1990).
Luhmann, N., Sociology of Risk. (Berlin, W. de gruyter, 1993).
Luhmann, N., Social Systems. (Stanford, Stanford UP, 1995).
Lynn, L.E., Public Management as Art, Science and Profession. (Chatham, Chatham House, 1996).
Lynn, L.E., The Myth of the Bureaucratic Paradigm. What Traditional Public Administration Really Stood For. (In: Public Administration Review, pp.144-160, 2001).
Lyotard, J.F., The Postmodern Condition. (Minneapolis, University of Minnesota Press, 1984).
Macdonald, G., Pettit, P., Semantics and Social Science. (London, Routledge & Kegan Paul, 1981).
Mainzer, L.C., Public Administration in Search of a Theory. The Interdisciplinary Delusion. (In: Administration & Society, pp.359-394, 1994).
March, J.G., Olsen, J.P., Rediscovering Institutions. (New York, Free Press, 1989).
March, J.G., Simon, H.A., Organizations. (New York, Wiley, 1958).
Marini, F., ed., Toward a New Public Administration. The Minnowbrook Perspective. (Scranton, Chandler, 1971).
Marshall, G., Choudbury, E., Public Administration and the Public Interest. Re-Presenting a Lost Concept. (In: Woller, G.M., ed., Public Administration and Postmodernism. In: American Behavioral Scientist, pp.119-131, 1997).
Maturana, H., Varela, F.J., Autopoiesis and Cognition, the Realisation of the Living. (Boston, Riedel, 1980).
McCourt, W., Minogue, M., The Internationalization of Public Management. Reinventing the Third World State. (Cheltenham, Elgar, 2001).
McSwite, O.C., Postmodernism and the Public Interest. (In: Wamsley, G.J., Wolf, J.F., eds., Refounding Democratic Public Administration. Thousand Oaks, Sage, 1996).
McSwite, O.C., Jacques Lacan and the Theory of the Human Subject. How Psychoanalysis Can Help Public Administration. (In: Woller, G.M., ed., Public Administration and Postmodernism. In: American Behavioral Scientist, pp.43-63, September 1997).
McSwite, O.C., Legitimacy in Public Administration. A Discourse Analysis. (Thousand Oaks, Sage, 1997).
Miller, H.T., King, C.S., Practical Theory. (In: American Review of Public Administration, pp.23-60, 1998).
Mintzberg, H., Managerial Work. (New York, Harper and Row, 1973).
Mintzberg, H., Structure in Fives. Designing Organisational Effectiveness. (London, Prentice-Hall, 1983).
Mintzberg, H., Mintzberg on Management. (New York, Free Press, 1989).
Mintzberg, H., The Rise and Fall of Strategic Planning. (New York, Free Press, 1994).
Mintzberg, H., Managing Government, Governing Management. (In: Harvard Business Review, pp.75-83, 1996).
Moustakas, C., Phenomenological Research Methods. (London, Sage, 1994).
Murphy, J.W., Talcott Parsons and Niklas Luhmann. Two Versions of the Social System. (In: International Review of Modern Sociology, pp.291-301, 1982).
Murphy, W.T., The Oldest Social Science? Configurations of Law and Modernity. (Oxford, Clarendon, 1997).
Nagel, S., The Encyclopedia of Policy Sciences. (New York, Marcel Dekker, 1994).
Nisbet, R., The Making of Modern Society. (Brighton, Wheatsheaf, 1986).
North, D.C., Structure and Change in Economic History. (New York, Norton, 1981).
North, D.C., Institutions, Institutional Change and Economic Performance. (Cambridge, CUP, 1990; 1991).
Northcote and Trevelyan, Report of the Committee on the Organization of the Permanent Civil Service. (London, HMSO, 1854).
Oakeshott, M., Rationalism in Politics. (London, Methuen, 1962; Indianapolis, Liberty Press, 1991).
Oakeshott, M., On Human Conduct. (Oxford, Clarendon, 1975).
Oakeshott, M., On History and Other Essays. (Oxford, Blackwell, 1983).
Oakeshott, M., Morality and Politics in Modern Europe: The Harvard Lectures. (New Haven, Yale UP, 1993).
OECD, Managing with Market-Type Mechanisms. (Paris, OECD, 1993).
OECD, In Search of Results. Performance Management Practices. (Paris, OECD, 1997).
OECD, Government of the Future. (Paris, OECD, 2000).

Okajnyk, V.W., Jung and Politics. (New York, New York UP, 1976).
Olsen, J., Peters, G., eds., Lessons from Experience. Experiental Learning in Administrative Reform in Eight Democracies. (Oslo, Scandinavian UP, 1996).
Osborne, D., Gaebler, T., Reinventing Government. How the Entrepreneurial Spirit is Transforming the Public Sector. (Reading, Addison-Wesley, 1992).
Ostenberg, D., Luhmann's General Sociology. (In: Acta Sociologica, pp.15-25, 2000).
Ostrom, V., The Intellectual Crisis in American Public Administration. (Tuscaloosa, University of Alabama Pres, 1974; 1989).
Ostrom, V., The Meaning of Democracy and the Vulnerability of Democracies. (Ann Arbor, University of Michigan Press, 1997).
Owen, D., Maturity and Modernity. Nietzsche, Weber, Foucault and the Ambivalence of Reason. (London, Routledge, 1994).
Owen, D., Foucault, Habermas and the Claims of Reason. (In: History of the Human Sciences, pp.119-138, 1996).
Parsons, T., The Social System. (New York, Free Press, 1951).
Pawson, R., Tilley, N., Realistic Evaluation. (London, Sage, 1997).
Peters, B.G., Comparing Public Bureaucracies. (Tuscaloosa, University of Alabama, 1988).
Peters, B.G., The Politics of Bureaucracy. (London, Longman, 1995).
Peters, B.G., The Future of Governing. Four Emerging Models. (Lawrence, University of Kansas Press, 1996).
Peters, B.G., Institutional Theory in Political Science. The "New Institutionalism". (New York, Pinter, 1999).
Peters, B.G., Governance and Comparative Politics. (In: Pierre, J., ed., Debating Governance. Oxford, OUP, pp.36-53, 2000).
Peters, B.G., Pierre, J., Governance without Government? Rethinking Public Administration. (In: Journal of Public Administration, Research and Theory, pp.223-243, 1998).
Peters, B.G., Rhodes, R.A.W., Wright, V., eds., Administering the Summit. (London, Macmillan, 2000).
Peters, B.G., Savoie, D.J., eds., Governance in a Changing Environment. (Montreal, McGill-Queen's UP, 1995).
Peters, B.G., Waterman, R., In Search of Excellence. Lessons from America's Best-Run Companies. (New York, Warner, 1982).
Pierre, J., ed., Debating Governance. (Oxford, OUP, 2000).
Polanyi, M., Personal Knowledge. Towards a Post-Critical Philosophy. (Chicago, University of Chicago Press, 1958).
Pollitt, C., Justification by Works or by Faith? Evaluating the New Public Management. (In: Evaluation, pp.133-154, 1995).
Pollitt, C., Institutional Amnesia. A Paradox of the "Information Age"? (Rotterdam, Erasmus University, 1999).
Pollitt, C., Clarifying Convergence. Striking Similarities and Durable Differences in Public Management Reform. (In: Public Management Review, pp.471-492, 2002).
Pollitt, C., Bouckaert, G., Public Management Reform. A Comparative Analysis. (Oxford, OUP, 2000).
Pollitt, C., Bouckaert, G., Evaluating Public Management Reforms. An International Perspective. (In: International Journal of Political Studies, pp.167-192, 2002).
Pollitt, C., et al., Performance or Compliance? Performance Audit and Public Management in Five Countries. (Oxford, OUP, 1999).
Pollitt, C., et al., Agency Fever? Analysis of an International Policy Fashion. (In: Journal of Comparative Policy Analysis, 2002).
Popper, K.R., The Logic of Scientific Inquiry. (New York, Basic Books, 1959; 1968).
Powell, W., DiMaggio, P., eds., The New Institutionalism in Organisational Analysis. (Chicago, University of Chicago Press, 1991).
Price, D.K., The Scientific State. (Cambridge, M., Belknap, 1965).
Progroff, I., Jung's Psychology and its Social Meaning. (Garden City NY, Anchor Books, 1973).
Pugh, D.L., Looking Back, Moving Forward. A Half-Century Celebration of Public Administration and ASPA. (Washington DC, American Society for Public Administration, 1988).
Pugh, D.L., The Origins of Ethical Frameworks in Public Administration. (In: Bowman, J.S., ed., Ethical Frontiers in Public Management. San Francisco, Jossey-Bass, pp.9-33, 1991).
Rabin, J., et al., eds., Handbook of Public Administration. (New York, Dekker, 1989).
Raadschelders, J.C.N., Handbook of Administrative History. (New Brunswick, Transaction, 1998).
Raadschelders, J.C.N., A Coherent Framework for the Study of Public Administration. (In: Journal of Public Administration Research and Theory, pp.281-303, 1999).

Raadschelders, J.C.N., Understanding Government in Society. We see the trees, but could we see the forest? (In: Administrative Theory & Praxis, pp.192-225, 2000).
Raadschelders, J.C.N., Government. A Public Administration Perspective. (Armonk, NY, Sharpe, 2003).
Rainey, H.G., Understanding and Managing Public Organizations. (San Francisco, Jossey Bass, 1997).
Redford, E., Democracy in the Administrative State. (New York, OUP, 1969).
Renard, G., The Degrees of Institutional Existence. Broderick, A., ed., The French Institutionalists. Maurice Hauriou, Georges Renard, Joseph T. Delos. (Cambridge, MA, Harvard UP, pp. 163-190, 1970).
Renard, G., The Interior Life of the Institution. (In: Broderick, A., ed., The French Institutionalists. Maurice Hauriou, Georges Renard, Joseph T. Delos. Cambridge, MA, Harvard UP, pp. 191-218, 1970).
Renard, G., The Philosophy of the Institution. (In: Broderick, A., ed., The French Institutionalists. Maurice Hauriou, Georges Renard, Joseph T. Delos. Cambridge, MA, Harvard UP, pp. 283-333, 1970).
Rhoads, S.E., The Economist's View of the World. Governments, Markets and Public Policy. (Cambridge, CUP, 1985).
Rhodes, R.A.W., Control and Power in Central-Local Government Relations. (London, Gower, 1981; 1999).
Rhodes, R.A.W., The Institutional Approach. (In: Marsh, D., Stoker, G., eds., Theory and Methods in Political Science. (London, Macmillan, 1995).
Rhodes, R.A.W., The New Governance: Governing Without Government. (In: Political Studies, pp.652-667, 1996).
Rhodes, R.A.W., Understanding Governance. Policy Networks, Governance, Reflexivity and Accountability. (Buckingham, Open University Press, 1997).
Rhodes, R.A.W., It's the Mix that Matters. From Marketisation to Diplomcay. (In: Australian Journal of Public Administration, pp.4053, 1997).
Rhodes, R.A.W., Goverance and Public Administration. (In: Pierre, J., ed., Debating Governance. Oxford, OUP, pP.54-90, 2000).
Rhodes, R.A.W., ed., British Public Administration: the State of the Discipline. (London, Blackwell, 1995).
Rhodes, R.A.W., et al., The State of Public Administration. A Professional History, 1970-1995. (In: Public Administration, pp.1-16, 1995).
Rhodes, R.A.W., Weller, P., Bakvis, H., eds., The Hollow Crown. (London, 1997).
Richardson, Fowers, B., eds., Beyond Scientism and Constructionism. (Los Angeles, Americam Psychological Association, 1994).
Richardson, F., Fowers, B., eds., Social Inquiry. A Hermeneutic Reconceptualization. (In: American Behavioral Scientist, January 1998).
Ricoeur, P., The Philosophy of Paul Ricoeur. (Boston, Beacon, 1978).
Ricoeur, P., Oneself as another. (Chicago, University of Chicago Press, 1992).
Riggs, F.W., Administration in Developing Countries. The Theory of Prismatic Society. (Boston, Houghton Mifflin, 1964).
Riley, D.D., Controlling the Federal Bureaucracy. (Philadelphia, Temple UP, 1987).
Rivera, M.A., Woller, G.M., eds., Public Administration in a New Era. Postmodern and Critical. (Burke, CA, Chatelaine, 2000).
Robertson, R., Globalization: Social Theory and Global Culture. (London, Sage, 1992).
Robertson, R., Glocalization. Time-Space and Homogeneity-Heterogeneity. (In: Featherstone, M. et al., eds., Global Modernities. Newbury Park, Sage, 1995).
Romzek, B.S., Dynamincs of Public Accountability in an Era of Reform. (In: International Review of Administrative Sciences, pp.21-44, 2000).
Romzek, B.S., Dubnick, M.J., Accountability. (In: International Encyclopedia of Public Policy and Administration. Boulder, Westview, 1998).
Rorty, R., Philosophy and the Mirror of Nature. (Princeton, Princeton UP, 1979).
Rorty, R., Contingency, Irony and Solidarity. (Cambridge, CUP, 1989).
Rorty, R., Philosophical Papers. (Cambridge, CUP, 1991).
Rose, R., Lesson-Drawing in Public Policy. (Chatham, Chatham House, 1993).
Rosecrance, R., Srein, A.A., eds., The Domestic Bases of Grand Strategy. (Ithaca, Cornell UP, 1993).
Rosenau, J., Governance in the 21st Century. (In: Global Governance, pp.13-43, 1995).
Rosenau, J., Along the Domestic-Foreign Frontier. Exploring Governance in a Turbulent World. (Cambridge, CUP, 1997).
Rosenau, J., Change, Complexity and Governance in Globalizing Space. (In: Pierre, J., ed., Debating Governance. Oxford, OUP, pp.167-200, 2000).
Rosenau, J., Czempiel, O., eds., Governance without Government. (Cambridge, CUP, 1992).
Rosenau, P.M., Postmodernism and the Social Sciences. (Princeton, Princeton UP, 1992).

Rouban, L., The Civil Service Culture and Administrative Reform. (In: Peters, B.G., Savoie, D., eds., Governance in a Changing Environment. Montreal, McGill-Queen's UP, 1995).
Rutgers, M.R., Beyond Woodrow Wilson. The Identity of the Study of Public Administration in Historical Perspective. (In: Administration & Society, pp.276-300, 1997).
Rutgers, M.R., Paradigm Lost. Crisis as Identity of the Study of Public Administration. (In: International Review of Administrative Sciences, pp.553-564, 1998).
Rutgers, M.R., Public Administration and the Separation of Powers in a Cross-Atlantic Perspective. (In: Administrative Theory & Praxis, pp.287-308, 2000).
Samuels, W.J., ed., Institutional Economics. (Aldershot. Elgar, 1990).
Sanderson, S.K., ed., Civilizations and World-Systems. (Walnut Creek, Atlamira Press, 1995).
Sarap, M., An Introductory Guide to Post-Structuralism and Postmodernism. (Athens, University of Georgia Press, 1993).
Sartori, G., Concept Misformation in Comparative Politics. (In: American Political Science Review, pp.1033-1053, 1970).
Sarup, M., Jacques Lacan. (Toronto, University of Toronto Press, 1992).
Saunders, R.M., In Search of Woodrow Wilson. (Westport, Greenwood, 1998).
Saussure, F. de, Course in General Linguistics. (New York, McGraw-Hill, 1966).
Savoie, D., Thatcher, Reagan and Mulroney. In Search of a New Bureaucracy. (Toronto, University of Toronto Press, 1994).
Schmitter, P.C., Lehmbruch, G., eds., Trends towards corporatist intermediation. (London, Sage, 1979).
Schön, D.A., The Reflective Practioner. How Professionals Think in Action. (New York, Basic Books, 1983).
Schonfeld, W., Obedience and Revolt. French behaviour toward authority. (Beverley Hills, Sage, 1976).
Schutz, A., Collected Papers. (The Hague, Nijhoff, 1962/1964).
Scott, J., Seeing like the State. (New Haven, Yale UP, 1997).
Searle, J., The Construction of Social Reality. (New York, Free Press, 1995).
Seldon, S. et al., Reconciling Competing Values in Public Administration. Understanding the Administrative Role Concept. (In: Administration and Society, pp.171-204, 1999).
Shackle, G., The Years of High Theory. Invention and Tradition in Economic Thought. (London, 1967).
Shepard, L.J., Lifting the Veil. The Feminine Face of Science. (Boston, Shambala, 1993).
Shughart, W.F., Razzolini, L., eds., The Elgar Companion to Public Choice. (Cheltenham, Elgar, 2001).
Simon, H., Administrative Behavior. (New York, Macmillan, 1945; 1957; Free Press, 1976).
Simon, H., Models of Man. Social and rational. (New York, Wiley, 1957).
Skinner, Q., ed., The Return of Grand Theory in the Human Sciences. (Cambridge, CUP, 1985).
Slife, B., Williams, R., What's behind the research? Discovering hidden assumptions in the behavioral sciences. (Thousand Oaks, CA, Sage, 1995).
Snow, C.P., Public Affairs. (New York, Scribners, 1971).
Sörenson, G., Sovereignty: Change and Continuity in a Fundamental Institution. (In: Jackson, R.H., ed., Sovereignty at the Millenium. (Oxford, Blackwell, pp.168-182, 1999).
Spicer, M.W., The Founders, the Constitution and Public Administration. (Washington DC, Georgetown UP, 1995).
Spicer, M.W., Public Administration, the State and the Postmodern Condition. A Constitutional Perspective. (In: Woller, G.M., ed., Public Administration and Postmodernism. In: American Behavioral Scientist, pp.90-102, September 1997)
Starling, G., Managing the Public Sector. (Homewood, Ill., Dorsey, 1982).
Steinmo, S., Taxation and Democracy. Swedish, British and American Approaches to Financing the Modern State. (New Haven, Yale UP, 1993).
Stillman, R.J., Preface to Public Administration. A Search for Themes and Direction. (New York, St.Martin's, 1991).
Stillman, R.J., Public Administration. Concepts and Cases. (Boston, Houghton Mifflin, 1992).
Stoker, G., Governance as Theory. Five Propositions. (In: International Social Science Journal, pp.17-28, 1998).
Sturrock, J., ed., Introduction in Structuralism and Since. From Lévi-Strauss to Derrida. (Oxford, OUP, 1979).
Swartz, D., Culture and Power. The Sociology of Pierre Bourdieu. (Chicago, University of Chicago Press, 1997).
Talbot, C., Ministers and Agencies. Control, Performance and Accountability. (London, CIPFA, 1996).
Taylor, C., Philosophical Papers. (Cambridge, CUP, 1985).
Taylor, C., Sources of the Self. The Making of the Modern Identity. (Cambridge, MA, Harvard UP, 1989).
Taylor, C., Philosophical Arguments. (Cambridge, MA, Harvard UP, 1995).

Taylor, C., The Politics of Multiculturalism. (New York, Basic Books, 1995).
Taylor, F.W., The Principles of Scientific Management. (New York, Norton, 1911; 1967).
Tennert, J.R., Who Cares about Big Questions? The Search for the Holy Grail in Public Administration. (In: Administrative Theory & Praxis, pp.231-243, 1998).
Thompson, D.F., Political Ethics and Public Office. (Cambridge, MA, Harvard UP, 1987).
Toynbee, A., A Study of History. (Oxford, OUP, 1939; 1957).
Trompenaars, F., Riding the Waves of Culture. Understanding Cultural Diversity in Business. (London, Brealey, 1997).
Van der Eyden, T., Public Choice + public decisionmaking + public policymaking + public problemsolving +public organization = public administration. (In: Public Administration Review, pp.689-191, 1971).
Van der Eyden, T., Creative Management in Government. (In: Klinkers, L., ed., Life in Public Administration. Amsterdam, Kobra, 1985, pp.112-119.).
Van Parijs, P., Evolutionary Explanation in the Social Sciences. An Emerging Paradigm. (Totowa, Rowman & Littlefield, 1981).
Wagner, G., The End of Luhmann's Social Systems Theory. (In: Philosophy of the Social Sciences, pp.387-409, 1997).
Waldo, D., The Administrative State. (New York, Holmes & Meier, 1948; 1984).
Waldo, D., The Study of Public Administration. (New York, Random House, 1955).
Waldo, D., The Enterprise of Public Administration. (Novato, Chandler & Sharp, 1980).
Wallerstein, I., The Modern World System. (New York, Academic Press, 1974/1989).
Wallerstein, I., Culture as Ideological Battleground of the Modern World-System. (In: Featherstone, M., ed., Global Culture. Newbury Park, Sage, 1990).
Wallerstein, I., Unthinking Social Science: The Limits of Nineteenth-Century Paradigms. (Oxford, Polity, 1991).
Wallerstein, I., The National and the Universal. Can there be such a thing as World Culture? (In: King, A.D., Culture, Globalization and the World-System. Contemporary Conditions for the Representation of Identity. Binghampton, SUNY, 1991).
Walsh, K., Public Services go to the Market. Competition, Contracting and the New Public Management. (Basingstoke, Macmillan, 1995).
Waltz, K.N., Theory of International Politics. (Reading, Addison-Wesley, 1979).
Wamsley, G.L., et al., Refounding Public Administration. (Newbury Park, Sage, 1990).
Wamsley, G.L., Wolf, J.F., eds., Refounding Democratic Public Administration. Modern Paradoxes, Postmodern Challenges. (Thousand Oaks, CA, Sage, 1996).
Wamsley, G.L., Wolf, J.F., eds., On Governance and Reinventing Government. (London, Sage, 1997).
Warnke, G., Gadamer. Hermeneutics, Tradition and Reason. (Palo Alto, Stanford UP, 1987).
Warnke, G., Justice and interpretation. (Cambridge, MIT, 1993).
Warnke, G., Communicative Rationality and Cultural Values. (In: White, S., ed., The Cambridge Companion to Habermas. Cambridge, CUP, 1995).
Weber, M., The Protestant Ethic and the Spirit of Capitalism. (New York, Scribner, 1958; London, Unwin, 1971).
Weighley, R.F., The American Way of War. A History of United States Military Strategy and Policy. (Bloomington, IndianaUP, 1973).
Weinsheimer, J., Gadamer's Hermeneutics. (New Haven, Yale UP, 1985).
Werner, L., A Note about Bentham on Equality and about the Greatest Happiness Principle. (In: Journal of the History of Philosophy, 237, 1973).
Werner, W.G., Securitization and Legal Theory. (Copenhagen, Peace Research Institute, 1999).
Werner, W.G., Wilde, J.H. de, The Endurance of Sovereignty. (In: European Journal of International Relations, pp.283-313, 2001).
West, W.F., Controlling the Bureaucracy. Institutional Constraints in Theory and Practice. (Armonk, NY, Sharpe, 1995).
West European Politics (Review), The Changing French Political System. (1999).
White, J.D., Images of Administrative Rationality. (In: Kass, H.D., Catron, B.L., eds., Images and Identities in Public Administration. Discourse on Governance. Thousand Oaks, Sage, 1990).
White, J.D., Knowledge development and use in Public Administration. Views from Postpositivism, Poststructuralism and Postmodernism. (In: Bailey, M.T., Mayer, R.T., eds., Public Management in an Interconnected World. Westport, Greenwood, 1992).
White, J.D., The Place of Theory in Public Administration Education. A Critique. (In: Administrative Theory & Praxis, pp.179-186, 1998).
White, L.D., Introduction to the Study of Public Administration. (New York, Macmillan, 1926; 1972).

White, O.F., McSwain, C.J., The Phoenix Project. Raising a New Image of Public Administration from the Ashes of the Past. (In: Kass, H.D., Catron, B.L., eds., Images and Identities in Public Administration. Newbury Park, Sage, pp.23-59, 1990).
White, S., ed., The Cambridge Companion to Habermas. (Cambridge, CUP, 1995).
Williamson, O.E., The Vertical Integration of Production. Market Failure Considerations. (In: American Economic Review, pp.112-123, 1971).
Williamson, O.E., Markets and Hierarchies. (New York, Free Press, 1975).
Williamson, O.E., The Economic Institutions of Capitalism. Firms, Markets, Relational Contracting. (New York, Free Press, 1985).
Williamson, O.E., The Mechanisms of Governance. (New York, OUP, 1996).
Williamson, O.E., Transaction Cost Economics. How it works; where it is headed. (In: De Economist, pp.23-58, April 1998).
Wilson, E.O., Consilence. The Unity of Knowledge. (New York, Knopf, 1998).
Wilson, W., The Study of Administration (1887). (In: Stillman, R.J., ed., Public Administration. Concepts and Cases. Boston, Houghton Mifflin, pp.6-17, 1992).
Wilson, W., The State. (Boston, Heath, 1889/1918).
Winch, P., The Idea of a Social Science. And its Relation to Philosophy. (London, Routledge & Kegan Paul, 1958; 1986).
Witgenstein, L., Tractatus Logico-Philosophicus. (London, Routledge, 1922).
Wittgenstein, L., Philosophical Investigations. (Englewood Cliffs, Prentice-Hall, 1958; 1968).
Woller, G.M., ed., Public Administration and Postmodernism. (In: American Behavioral Scientist, September 1997).
Woller, G.M., Patterson, K.D., Public Administration Ethics. A Postmodern Perspective. (In: Woller, G.M., ed., Public Administration and Postmodernism. In: American Behavioral Scientist, September 1997).
World Bank, Governance and Development. (Washington DC, World Bank, 1992).
World Bank, Governance: The World Bank's Experience. (Washington DC, World Bank, 1994).
World Bank, The Privatization Challenge: A Strategic, Legal and Institutional Analysis of International Experience. (Washington DC, World Bank, 1997).
World Bank, The State in a Changing World. (Washington DC, World Bank, 1997).
Wright, V., The Paradoxes of Administrative Reform. (In: Kickert, W., ed., Public Management and Administrative Reform in Western Europe. Cheltenham, Elgar, 1997).
Yankelovich, D., Coming to Public Judgment. Making Democracy Work in a Complex World. (Syracuse, Syracuse UP, 1991).
Zeldin, T., The French. (London, Harvill, 1997).
Zifcak, S., New Managerialism. Administrative Reform in Whitehall and Canberra. (Buckingham, Open University Press, 1994).

# 10. Rule of Law, Idea of Public Authority and Cultural Intelligence

As has been shown in the preceding chapters, France is especially relevant, when historical developments and universal ideation with regard to Public Management of Society are being considered. France has a rich experience of building a society with the instruments of law, besides, in the process of emancipation of the Idea of Public Authority in France, the accent was placed on the central role of public authorities, the State. French thinking regarding law, State and public authority has throughout the centuries been characterised by specific circumstances and societal developments. Theoretical explorations of law, State and public authority are often dealt with in an abstract, even a-historical way, detracting from the fundamental interconnectedness of ideation and its cultural, historical environment. It is one of the axioms of this study that theoretical analyses about Public Management of Society have to deal with this fundamental interconnectedness of intellectual ideation and cultural-historical developments in the existential environment of human beings living together in their society. Cultural intelligence is a must for all who try to get a grip on the complexities of Public Management of Society, in theory and in practice. France had and has original solutions for societal problems, while its institutional genius has produced institutional arrangements which have had a worldwide influence (Farcy, 1996; Greigueuil, 1999). Often French institutional ideas were presented as if these were valid as universally the best possible, for all countries in the world, as with contemporary tendencies in the American intellectual world. Americans often present the American way of life as a universal model (democracy, market, reduced State). Americans made an important contribution during the last century to Public Administration as a study of government. They distanced themselves from the overly juridical approach of continental Europe, which followed the French model. The crucial role of juridical and other institutional arrangements for effective Public Management of Society is now recognised more. In contemporary France, a less State-dominated law develops, while American Public Administration is dominantly presented as Public Administration, not adequately recognising its cultural roots.

An adequate approach to Public Management of Society must recognise that each country has to find its own optimum between universal values and possibilities, and its cultural-historical environment. Against this background, the Rule of Law and the Idea of Public Authority are dealt with. Some main points of the theory of law and the theory of the State are sketched. Ubi societas ibi ius. In the perspective of the coming 21st century, many societies all over the world are ruled according to a seemingly universalist conception of the State as has been developed, especially in France, since the 18th century. It is a historical fact that Western, primarily European, countries have exported the institutional form of public authority, which has been developed since the Middle Ages and has been called the sovereign state, to all continents. The Nation-State, a brilliant combination of power and law for a Nation, was not always a blessing, as the 20th century ("Century of Genocide") has shown (Levene, 2000). When the State breaks away from the Rule of Law it can be an instrument of massive disaster. A crucial issue is, how to organise effective discipline for powerful ruling persons and organs in their relations with subordinates. Due to excessive abuses of public authority, appalling mismanagement and violation of elementary human rights by the French monarchy, the French Revolution was an overreaction of the too long pent-up rage of common people, who lived in misery while the aristocracy flaunted its extravagance. Doubtless one of the most vital energies of the people was activated by the widespread conviction that representatives of public authority systematically violated the Rule of Law. These public authorities outraged the Idea of Public Authority, as present in the consciousness and subconsciousness of the people. The Rule of Law implies the Idea of Public Authority, meaning that public authorities have to realise and guarantee the Rule of Law for all citizens. Before elaborating on some ideas about the theory of the State and the Idea of Public Authority, a summary sketch is given of the origins of the Rule of Law.

### 10.1. From the vicious circle of vengeance to Roman law

Law is a normative order, it organises standards for human conduct in a prescriptive way. The notion law is also used in literature to denote rules of behaviour in private organisations. Here law is explicitly meant in the sense of law as ruled or conditioned by public authorities. State law has a specific character, often recognised as supported by coerciveness, a consequence of the State's monopoly of legitimised use of violence, applied if necessary to force implementation of the law. Hart (1961) distinguished a primary level of law and a secondary level of law. The primary level of law is about the regulation of what persons must and must not do. It includes requirements for acceptable interpersonal conduct. The secondary level of law establishes institutions for regulation at the primary level of law. What makes State law special is the specific form of institutions at the secondary level for the enactment and enforcement of law, for judicial decision-making about its meaning and consequences in general and individual cases, and for implementation of public policies to further the general interest (interest of the people). Public authorities have a specific responsibility to make the Rule of Law prevail. Modern Western constitutionalism, emphasising individual's rights, is a variant, a system of restraints upon governmental action. Other forms are Greek, Roman and medieval constitutionalism. Plato made "nomos" (prevalent communal notions about what is right and just) the criterion to distinguish good regimes from bad. For Plato, observance of this "nomos" could be guaranteed only by concentrating the power of public authority in the hands of the wise (philosopher-king model). Aristotle argued for a mixed constitution, a mean between monarchy, aristocracy and democracy. Roman constitutionalism, developed through centuries, accentuated public order and stability, with a complicated system of interrelated restraints on public authorities. Public offices, from consuls down to functionaries at lower levels of the hierarchy, were subject to elaborated rules of law, supported by religious beliefs. Polybius, stressing the importance of stability and the strength of public authorities, produced an authoritative sketch of the Roman constitutional system as working around 200 B.C. Polybius and Cicero argued for mixed government by allocation of governmental functions to different organs.

Roman constitutionalism (people are the source of all law) provided stability for a city-state, but the power of Rome declined, because this system was not equal to its tasks for a wider territory. Later, Thomas Aquinas argued that the best form of constitution would be a judicious mixture of kingdom, aristocracy and democracy. Via his intermediary, ideas about public authority in Old Testament and Roman Corpus Iuris (Justinian) were spreading. Medieval constitutionalism took the form of balancing the public authority of "the one, the few and the many". The Church, arguing that all authority should be subjected to legal restraints, played a dominant role. Medieval constitutionalism was also applied to the Church, as "conciliarism": participation of lower clergy and laity in the councils called upon to formulate the law. William of Ockham and Nicholas of Cusa promoted consent as a vital, necessary condition of law. The movement for democracy in the Church failed, but some of its ideas were used for the organisation of public authority. One medieval idea was that legitimate public authority is public authority according to law. Medieval constitutionalism developed in the struggle of aristocracy, trying to prevent monarchical rulers from becoming tyrants. The Church developed the doctrine of natural law as elaborated by the Stoics and Cicero, and as found in the Corpus Iuris. The conception of Thomas Aquinas had a direct impact upon English seventeenth-century constitutionalism. Because of religious dissension and related civil wars, the cry was for political stability. Society was made ripe for a concentration of power in the hands of a ruler, as argued by Hobbes in "Leviathan" (1651). He radicalised ideas elaborated by Bodin (1576) about sovereignty. Locke, forestalling ideas as realised in the "Glorious Revolution" (1689), in " Second Treatise on Civil Government" (1690) developed the idea of a threefold division of governmental powers, but his three branches were all but equivalent. His "executive", combined with the judiciary, was thoroughly dependent on the supreme legislative branch. His third branch, the "federative", had a wide authority for conducting foreign relations. For him constitutional government was a government in which the decisive power to make laws was divided between King, Lords, and Commons. The other two powers, executive and federative, were attributed to the King, along with his share of legislative power.

As argued by Montesquieu in "L'Esprit des lois" (1748), the liberties of citizens are guaranteed most in a system of checks and balances, with several independent public authorities. Legislative, executive and judicial authorities should be independent (functional differentiation). His doctrine for the differentiation of the powers of public authority got universal support as "trias politica", better renamed as Public Authority trias. The Rule of Law accentuates the crucial three functions for public authority. Law making (legislation). Law administering (execution). And Law interpretation (judicial function). The Rule of Law needs public authorities to make law a societal reality. This makes it evident that the crucial institutional axis is that between the Rule of Law and the Idea of Public Authority. Up to the contemporary period, the Roman conception of law has had an imposing impact upon the Western approach to institutionalism. Romans distinguished between public law and private law: "Huius studii duae sunt positiones, publicum et privatum, publicum ius est quod ad statum rei Romanae spectat, privatum quod ad singulorum utilitatem sunt enim quaedam publice utilia, quaedam privatim." (Digesta, 1.1.1.2). This differentiation has been elaborated since then. Public law is law about establishment and regulation of public authorities. It includes rulings about the formal competencies of public authorities and limits on their powers and the duties of public authorities towards the political community and individuals in the country. Recognised fundamental rights of individuals, human rights, are very important. Public authorities are responsible for ensuring that fundamental rights are guaranteed. To guarantee these rights, a constitution is thought necessary as a basis for constitutional government. Ubi ius ibi societas et auctoritas publica. The Idea of Public Authority is crucial for reasonable life in each culturally specific society, to realise with culturally intelligent Public Management of Society.

In prehistoric times and after, jurisdiction and the solution of serious conflicts mostly took the form of private acts of vengeance (Guilaine/Zammit, 2001). According to the rules of private vengeance, anybody who had been damaged by a person, family, tribe or group, had the right to retaliate by damaging the other(s) unrestrictedly (private war). The existence of group life or society is fundamentally endangered when conflicts cause an unending series of retaliations. The sole satisfactory vengeance for bloodshed was seen as the bloodshed of the (perceived) offender, suspected of murdering somebody, himself: blood feud. This could provoke an unending process of murdering, a vicious circle of vengeance. Breaking this process of vengeance was a crucial task in primitive society (Lowie, 1947). Religion often fulfilled an important part of this task by organising ritual sacrifices of men or animals (Girard, 1972). These sacrifices could not cure the sickness of vengeance, but had a function in the sphere of prevention. Gradually, jurisdiction by private persons became a more advanced arrangement. Sacrifices fell out of use, especially where a system of jurisdiction was introduced, as in Greece and Rome. The need for vengeance had to be eliminated. This was done effectively by the recognition of some independent judiciary authority that had to decide about conflicts. By this means members of a social group or society were freed from that terrible duty of repeating vengeance endlessly for conscience' sake. The practice of vengeance was rationalised by creating, on behalf of all members of a social group or society, an institution having the monopoly of the eventual use of vengeance or violence. A higher level of civilisation was reached when a public authority organising jurisdiction developed, charged with decisions over juridical conflicts between private persons. The phenomenon of some individuals having recognised authority in a group dates back to the most ancient times (Amiet, 1995). Mostly, leaders in primitive society sought support for their position by reference to the gods. With the coming of urban civilisation in the 4th century BC work became more difficult for public authorities. The invention of writing at that time makes it clear to us that the support of the gods was sought, anticipating theories of divine law in the Judaeo-Christian tradition (Morin, 1996). Sumerian monarchs did not accept debate about their rules, they claimed to be executing the orders of the gods (Parrot, 1960). Innovations took place in conceptualisation of the phenomenon of public authority and law by Greek philosophers like Plato (428-347 BC) and Aristotle (384-322 BC).

Aristotle asked: is it better to be governed by the best person, or by the best laws? Plato, in his "Republic", developed the ideal concept of the philosopher-king, who has true knowledge concerning the common good (virtue). In his later work, "The Laws", Plato made law the basis of virtue. Aristotle, in a more empirical way, preferred to deal with human beings as they are. His research in some 158 Greek towns, mostly ruled by several forms of oligarchy or democracy, made him adhere to a moderate, participating democracy with the support of laws. Aristotle preferred the rule of law to the rule of some citizen. About a millennium later, Thomas Aquinas (1225-1274), grandmaster of scholasticism, in his epoch-making work, constructed a synthesis between Aristotle's philosophy and the Christian doctrine of realisation of the "bonum commune" as objective of society, emanation of divine law. The controversy between rule by men and the rule of law has been a structural element of Western philosophy. Developments in France before and after the French Revolution have specific relevance. France was ruled by Roman law in the Gallo-Roman period. After this the Middle Ages were characterised by the dominant influence of the Church. Later, French monarchy had France in its grasp, legitimising its public authority by claiming to represent God and acting on the basis of divine law.

Before dealing with modern developments, it has to be underlined that contemporary ideas and practices in France with regard to law, jurisdiction and justice have been deeply influenced by Roman Law from the beginning of our era (Mommsen, 1892). When "Gallia" (more or less the area of contemporary France) was conquered by Roman legions the Roman system of law and administration was introduced there. After defeating Carthage in 201 BC, Rome became master of the Mediterranean world. From 150 BC the Roman culture became partly Greek, a more refined civilisation. Rome preserved its public law structures of a state-town, with a few magistrates governing extensive areas. During civil wars an autocratic regime was installed. Around the beginning of our era, customs played an important role in Roman law ("mos maiorum"). The Roman Empire was universalist in character ("dominium mundi). Its law sanctioned inequality between freemen, slaves and women. The restrictive granting of Roman civic rights to citizens was a juridical technique to acculturate vanquished people. Emperor Caracalla in 212 AD extended civil rights to all inhabitants of the Roman Empire. Romans were flexible in giving vanquished peoples the choice between Roman law and their local law and customs, with juridical pluralism as a result. In the middle of the third century AD, the Roman Empire began to disintegrate, and the Roman structure of public authority became authoritarian. In 476 AD, the last western Roman Emperor was deposed. The northern part of France lived under the rule of customs for centuries. Classical Roman law had a strong centralised system of public authority, so French monarchs had a logical and pragmatic frame of reference. We should not forget that in the late third century BC, the Chinese Han Fei Tzu argued for good public management by strict adherence to the law (Watson, 1996).

The Merovingian period (481-751), with its reduced or even absent control by public authorities, was followed by the Carolingian Empire (757-987). Then came the feudal system, which disappeared at the end of the Middle Ages. From the 11th century, a central state slowly developed. Barbarian heads of clans such as Merovingian Clovis (481-511) acted as if their customs originated from the Eastern Roman Empire, not giving up sovereignty over the West for centuries. In 800 AD Charlemagne broke this allegiance by establishing the Holy Western Roman Empire. Practices of the Carolingian Emperor followed those of the Roman emperors. Some barbarian peoples were brought under Roman control before the fall of the Roman Empire, while other tribes were hostile to the Romans. Cultural and social diversity was a dominant characteristic. Roman provinces were not brought under control equally. Several groups in the same territory were judged in accordance with the law of their own people: personality of laws; different codifications of laws. Roman law for Romans, barbarian laws for barbarians. The Church tried to impose the unification of Christianity upon pagan peoples, so ethnic juridical pluralism weakened. In the Middle Ages, administration and law were fragmented in the area of contemporary France. There were many jurisdictional colleges and ecclesiastical jurisdictions, largely functioning up to the French Revolution. Jurisdiction in the name of the French king increasingly had an impact ("Curia Regis"). Legists, professional jurists, developed jurisdictional doctrine using ideas and concepts from Roman Law, elaborated in the "Corpus Iuris Civilis", the codification made by order of the East-Roman Emperor Justinian (527-565). Fragmentation of administration and law was a serious nuisance in the Middle Ages, therefore legists, with memories of the centralised system of Roman law, elaborated arguments, tools and techniques for justice in the name of the French king as the sovereign: "all justice is coming from the King" (Lebigre, 1988). In the eighth century territoriality of law replaced personality of law. Whatever their origins inhabitants of the same area obeyed the same law. Later jurisdictional pluralism was the vogue: noble, ecclesiastical and royal tribunals. This changed from the eleventh century on. Capetian kings asserted sovereignty over rival forces (Church, feudalists and cities). The Hundred Years War (1337-1453) provoked ideas of autonomy, heralding the advent of the nation. Kings were the most powerful lords, sovereigns of all inhabitants. Juridical pluralism gave way to unifying tendencies due to political will, using an abstract ideology. Law was more or less unified.

Roman law as expression of a centrally controlled system was consistent with the designs of the French monarchs. It was better suited to an urbanised economy, and developed as customs receded. The Church was in favour of Roman law, which influenced canonical law. Roman law was accepted more rapidly in the south (12th century), more directly under the influence of Roman colonisation. In the north, its influence remained limited until the end of the 14th century. Roman law did not penetrate all sectors equally. Custom was confronted with the impact of the centrally controlled law of public authorities. In the Middle Ages, the territorial field of application of royal enactments expanded and became compulsory for all. In 1454, Charles VII ordered the writing of customs by the Montils-les-Tours enactment, which remained in effect until 1789, and later prepared the Civil Code. Written customs became the principal source of customary law as instrument of a centralised organisation of public authorities. Royal jurists elaborated an absolutist doctrine, while royal power intervened directly in private law. As the writing down of customs contributed to unifying them, the codification of law was synthesising customs. During the reign of Louis XIV, Colbert made enactments to unify maritime law, commercial law and civil and criminal procedure. D'Aguesseau under Louis XV planned the writing of a unique code, but shrank back from the enormity of this task. Napoleonic Codes often reproduced integral texts of Colbert and D'Aguesseau. Napoleon, heir of absolute monarchy, was influenced by the same will to centralise and reduce diversities in the name of abstract principles. After the Gallo-Roman period, Roman law and administration had lasting impact upon institutional traditions in medieval France, Ancien Régime and after. A reasonable hypothesis is that the concepts of Roman law have continued up till now in the French conception of law more than elsewhere, certainly more than in Anglo-Saxon tradition.

## 10.2. Rule of law in gestation

The birth of the idea of prominence of law with regard to public authorities goes back in history far before the time that the modern State developed (beginning of the 14th century). Morin (1996, p.47) accentuates the influence of the Church in this sphere by the "papal revolution" (end of the 11th century). This made the Roman institution of the Church the first Western state, later imitated by most nation-states on the European continent. Canonic law was renovated, "ius novum", with reforms of Pope Gregorius VII (1073-1085) and the Investiture Conflict, ruled by the Worms Concordat (1122). This "ius novum" proclaimed that all powers, also the power of the pope, should be submitted to the principle of legality. Ecclesiastical judges had specific competencies, inter alia as jurisdiction of appeal against decisions of feudal monarchies (Berman, 1983; Haarscher, 1993). Ecclesiastical jurisdiction was given competencies especially with regard to "personae miserabiles" (widows etc.). There was resistance to this extension of competencies for ecclesiastical jurisdiction, but it had its impact on royal jurisdictions. According to Morin (1996, p.48), this first "modern" juridical system is a crucial source of the Western tradition of limitation and control of power. At the end of the Middle Ages, the battle between papacy and monarchies, both claiming supremacy, frustrated jurists in their search for the rule of law. At the beginning of the 14th century, the decisive confrontation between Pope Boniface VIII (1294-1303), issuing the bulls "Clericis Laicos" and "Unam Sanctam", claiming absolute papal supremacy, and Philippe le Bel (1285-1314) came to its apex. Gilles de Rome, in "De ecclesiastica potestate" (1302) asserted that public authority is subordinated to the salvation of souls and so to the Church (Dyson, 1986). Jean de Paris, in "De potestate regia et papali" (1302) working with the conception of Aquinas, argued differently. Secular power is necessary for the "bonum commune", it does not need ecclesiastical authorisation to be legitimate. The Church is autonomous in the spiritual order. Political authorities do not have universal competence. Both pope and monarch are subordinated to law. After Pope Boniface VIII, papal power declined, while kings proclaimed absolute monarchy, as elaborated in Bodin's "Six livres de la République" (1576).

The conception of the two swords was developed to argue that spiritual power and secular power should not be in one hand (spiritual sword and secular sword). The doctrine of Pope Gregorius VII and his successors had its risks, because prominence of the law was invoked to support political supremacy of the papacy. Popes interpreted their doctrine as to imply the competence of the papacy to interfere in worldly affairs. Especially during the zenith of the "Civitas Christiana" under Pope Innocentius III (1198-1216). He ordered a crusade against Albigenses and used the Inquisition against them (a heresy was seen as disobedience to secular public authority). Extensive interpretation of their powers over worldly affairs brought the popes into conflict with national States, causing fragmentation of the Christian world. The most known theoretician of the 12th century was Jean de Salisbury, bishop of Chartres. In "Policraticus" (1159), he developed the idea of the superiority of spiritual power over worldly powers. In his opinion the pope was competent to interpret the will of God, and could interfere in the worldly affairs of monarchs. He sketched a Christian conception of the rule of law: politically autonomous communities are under superior authority of the Church. "Canonists", papal jurists, invoked this conception for papal "plenitudo potestatis", sovereignty. Their conception provoked reactions from legists defending the autonomy of monarchs. They argued for the supreme power ("imperium") of monarchs: "Rex est imperator in regni suo." (Touchard, 1993).

It took centuries before the monarchs accepted limitations to their powers, so bringing the Rule of Law closer. This process manifested itself early in Great Britain and the Netherlands. Great Britain has played a significant role in developing Western ideas of law and democracy. The conquest of the British Isles by Normans in 1066 made the king, in theory, the unique source of law (Davies, 1999). This royal prerogative contradicted prevailing customs and unwritten laws of the country. Successors of William the Conqueror (1027-1087) gradually centralised jurisdiction and taxes as on the European continent. They founded their legitimacy on a respect for prevailing customs, trying to unify them by decisions of tribunals ("common law"). Under Henry II Plantagenet (1154-1189), a great reformer of the law, the first book (1187/1189) about common law was written by Glanvill (Hall, 1965). Reinforcing of law in relation to the royal prerogative was due to the influences of Church, barons, Parliament and tribunals. The Church had a role as counter-power. In June 1215, John Lackland was forced to accept the "Magna Carta" (Davis, 1971). Jurisdiction had deteriorated dramatically. The Magna Carta prohibited the King's agents from accusing somebody without reliable witnesses, replacing competent judges arbitrarily, and requisitioning goods or land without the consent of proprietors. Jurisdiction could not be sold or obstructed, so jurisdiction could function fully. Fines had to be proportional to the gravity of infractions. Professionals, who knew the law and were prepared to apply it appropriately, had to be appointed as judges or public prosecutors. According to the law of the country no free man could be arrested, imprisoned or bereft of possessions or rights without being judged by his fellows (peers).

This Magna Carta was a model for what was called a "pactum subjectionis", remote predecessor of the "contrat social", on which basis the "droit subjectif" was later developed. People on the British Isles did not accept arbitrary power, as was obvious in the 13th and 14th centuries. There was a series of civil wars (1216, 1263, 1326, 1381, 1455-1485). Henry de Bracton in "De legibus et consuetudinibus Angliae" (1268) asserted that the king was not subordinate to any other human being, but only to God and the law, because law makes the king ("quia lex facit regem"). Bracton argued: there is no king where the will dominates and not law (Thorne, 1977). The Rule of Law was more a plea then, a grand design. Gradually, it became the program of English parliamentarism. During the reign of Edward I (1272-1307), the "English Justinian", there was progress in the sphere of jurisdiction. Parliament emerged as a crucial institution, originally a mixture of judiciary and legislative powers. Edward I recognised older charters, responded seriously to petitions and furthered participation of rising social classes in the extension of the Rule of Law. In the 14th and 15th centuries the role of Parliament became more prominent. The War of the Roses (1455-1485) enabled Parliament to entrust monarchy to new dynasties like the Houses of York and Tudor. Fortescue, in "De laudibus legum Angliae" (1468/1470), argued for governing by kings on the basis of consent (Lodge/Thornton, 1935). Weakening of the political power of the Church, Nation-States profiling themselves, the impact of the Reformation and socio-economic developments changed the situation. Absolutism became the vogue in England, as on the European continent. The Church was nationalised (Durant, 1957, p.457): "Protestantism was nationalism extended to religion". Under Queen Elizabeth

(1558-1603) Calvinism penetrated England, diminishing the authority of the Anglican Church. J.T. Knox made Calvinism the leading religion in Scotland from 1560. The controversy between power and law was acute under the absolutism of the Stuarts, who did not accept the resistance of tribunals and Parliament.

The issue was: could the royal prerogative ("fountain of justice") overrule "common law" and statutes? Francis Bacon stated that judges had to refrain from interfering in affairs of State. During the first years of the Stuart period Chief Justice Edward Coke made himself the protagonist of "common law". He claimed that common law enabled tribunals to control laws of Parliament and to invalidate laws that were against common sense or reason (Thorne, 1985, p.224). According to the "Prohibitions del Roy" (1607) royal jurisdiction could only be fulfilled by duly selected judges. While the king could not interfere with the definition of new crimes by legislation, or by giving his opinion about cases at trial. Parliament proved to be the winner in this controversy, which started in 1610 and provoked a civil war thirty years later. The Chamber of the Commons adopted the "Petition of Grievances" (1610). Parliamentarians proclaimed for the first time that they wanted to be governed by "the certain rule of law" and not by some uncertain and arbitrary government (Cahen/Braure, 1960). They proclaimed common law and statutes adopted by Parliament to be the only valid laws. The Grand Remonstrance (1621) proclaimed fundamental civil liberties and the "Petition of Rights" (1629) referred to the Magna Carta (1215), the standard for parliamentarians. From 1629 to 1640 Charles I ruled without Parliament. Between 1642 and 1646, there was a civil war between the King and Parliament. Charles I was beheaded in 1649. England became a Republic with the dictatorship of Cromwell, and later a monarchy again.

English law and American law belong to a specific law family, Common Law. Law on the European continent generally belongs to the civil law family, heavily indebted to Roman law. In Great Britain Roman law was received differently to the reception elsewhere in Europe and judge-made English law was not codified. Countries on the European continent had their laws codified after the model of Napoleonic France. In the course of time, dynamics of law developments adapted law to changing circumstances, but crucial differences in law traditions survived. It will be interesting to see how law develops in the European Union, where both law families meet each other with increasing frequency. The development of law could be left to a great extent to social actors in society, but it is a crucial responsibility of public authorities to manage law development. The beginning of Common Law tradition dates back to 1066 when William the Conqueror ascended the throne of England (Hudson, 1996). Maitland/Pollock (1968) argued that lawmaking was dominated by the work of King Henry II (1154-1189) and his advisers, and later synthesised by chief justice Glanville between 1180 and 1189 in "Tractatus de legibus et consuetudinibus regni Angliae". For Caenegem (1988) the reforms of the Plantagenets are only understandable in the feudal context, consolidated by the monarchy since Anglo-Saxon times (Milsom, 1976). The notion of Common Law is by no means unambiguous. It is used in a general sense to denote the Anglo-Saxon, or Anglo-American law family tradition. It can also mean the oldest part of this law family tradition (law), to distinguish it from the later developed equity law (equity). Often Common Law as jurisprudence law, case law, is demarcated from law which is based upon legislation, statutory law. A fundamental characteristic of Common Law tradition is that it was developed in the practice of decision-making by judges and not by pre-ordained general rulemaking with abstract systematisation or codification. There are mixed systems with Common Law and codification: in Scotland, Louisiana and Quebec.

In the Common Law tradition there is some animosity with regard to codification. An important anvil for criticising codification is the "Code Napoléon", a consequence of the French Revolution which was not needed in Great Britain. The French Revolution is thought to have made tabula rasa of the past, while Common Law incorporated historical developments, but there was some form of codification, a compilation of existing law with mini-codes and codes. With a simplified parliamentary procedure, laws could be consolidated, "Consolidation of Enactment " of 1949. "Law Commissions" for England and Scotland, created by a law of 1965, wanted to use codification as a method of modernising reform. The English Law Commission proposed four codes (contract law, family law, penal law, real property law). For contract law, see McGregor (1993). But this plan for four codes was soon abolished in preference for piecemeal reform. Law is seen mostly as a series of texts to solve conflicts with sentences of judges (David, 1980). William Blackstone (1723-1780) was the first incumbent of the Viner chair for English law at the University of Oxford. In his "Commentaries on the Laws of England" (1767) he argued that it was not necessary to codify English law, asserting that English customary law was superior to any possible codification. As "English Gaius", Blackstone gave Common Law its systematisation which made codification superfluous. Francis Bacon had already proposed the codification of English laws to James I in 1614. With the "Institutes" (1628-1644) by E. Coke there were compilations of English jurisprudential law. "The Institutions of the Law of Scotland" by Lord Stair (1681) and the book with the same title by George Mackenzie (1684) used the model of the Institutiones by Justinian. Blackstone argued that Common Law was better due to its specific historicity (with no indication of its date of creation), its intrinsic reasonable nature, and its capacity to guarantee justice and to protect individual liberties better. Codifying would solidify law in rigid rules without the possibility to adapt to changing circumstances. Old time customary law had a function which is comparable to divine law in the French Ancien Régime, with the myth of the immemorial and having authority by this fact. Blackstone distinguished "lex non scripta" (customary law) and "lex scripta" (statutory law, law of Parliament).

Common Law was developed over a long period and adapted to circumstances. It resisted the temptations of the Roman law tradition. For Blackstone there is a crucial difference between Roman law (placing the Prince above the law) and Common Law (law applicable for all, also for monarchs). Bracton (1268): "Rex debet esse sub lege, quia lex facit regem." Blackstone's "Commentaries on the Laws of England" (1767) had a decisive impact on the establishment of the United States (Boorstin, 1958; Glendon, 1991). Jeremy Bentham, (1748-1832) with "Pannomium" (1811), wanted to realise a complete body of laws and norms (Bowring, 1962). The Bentham Code deserves a prominent place in the framework of the European science of law. Bentham criticised the classical natural law tradition. For him, nature as such cannot be directly normative. Rights follow the law. References to nature or equity as a foundation for the solutions of Common Law were questioned. When nature is silent it is possible to impute all to this silence and to deduce all. In a sense Bentham himself is a natural law adept, though criticising the way others elaborated the relation between nature and law. Bentham's theory of law is not purely positivist (Postema, 1986). Bentham used a logic of the will as theory of practical reason, with utility as criterion (like the criterion of truth in the logic of knowledge). Utility determines the objectives (the greatest happiness for the greatest number) and instruments of law. Bentham adhered to the idea that law could regulate society best. His positivist-utilitarian idea of law supposed a society without politics. He substituted the State as political reality by law. The link between nature and law, between naturalism and positivism, is realised by utility. For Bentham, law not directed by utility lacks rationality. His ambition was a complete body of laws, but he left room for adaptation (Kelly, 1990). For him, it was crucial that it was possible for the individual to know the contents of the law (Hart, 1982). In "Papers relating to codification", he qualified Common Law as "material without soul, work without author". His proposals were not transformed into codification, but Bentham's influence on English law is obvious, as is his influence on the development of bureaucracy and representative democracy (Hume, 1981; Rosen, 1983). Bentham's juridical thinking has actual relevance (Gérard c.s., 1987).

With regard to codification Americans have a different attitude to the English. Common Law does not have the same prestige for pragmatic Americans, who rate the Napoleonic codes at their true value. In his 1837 report, Judge Story argued for codification. Field initiated the movement for codification, which formulated five codes. A majority of States in the US and the Federation accepted the Code for civil procedure (1846), valid until the "Federal Rules of Civil Procedure" (1938) were adopted. The American Bar Institute, created in 1878, tried to further uniform legislation in the US for the States. The "Committee on Uniform State Laws" was installed in 1889, to prepare the "National Conference of Commissioners on Uniform State Laws", to which each State was invited every year. In 1912, all American States were represented. This conference made recommendations: "Uniform Acts", or "Model Acts". The American Law Institute, created in 1923, has since the twenties presented "Restatements of the Law", which were used by tribunals (Farnsworth, 1986). This American Law Institute saw the growing number of jurisdictional decisions as a structural threat to the vitality of law. Reasoned analysis of decisions of judges was seen as a necessary element of professionalism in the framework of American realism and sociological jurisprudence. Restatements were based on the science of law conception of Langdell at Harvard, originally developed with the case law method. Holmes (1881), arguing for experience, opposed this conception. American legal realism made school with codification activities, like those of K.N. Llewellyn (Kalman, 1986; Twining, 1985). Roscoe Pound had his sociological jurisprudence movement.

The impact of the Common Law tradition can be traced worldwide in countries which were formerly English colonies, such as the United States. For the Dominions there were summary codes of English law. Recognising differences between law in Great Britain and the US, one can conclude that their law systems have a structural congeniality. The US as former English colonies inherited the English Common Law tradition. Next to the new legislation, Common Law was applied, adapted to circumstances (Mommsen/Moor, 1992). In most English colonies, statutes of direct application and Common Law were declared applicable in so far as the colonial situation made this possible. Colonial laws of the British Crown and Parliament reduced the impact of Common Law. In a long period of English colonisation from the 15th century on, situations in several colonies differed. In the European context, the developing nation-states, enmeshed in intensive mutual competition, were changing from feudal regimes to autocratic monarchies and parliamentary democracies. Colonies had a feudal structure for much longer. There was more legislation in the colonies than in England. English "indirect rule" mostly suited very well. The Colonial Office in England produced laws tailored especially for the colonies. Since the 19th-20th centuries, there has been convergence in the Commonwealth, so that colonial law systems increasingly resembled the English system (Hooker, 1975). For centuries English case law developed along two paths, "in law", and "in equity", while legislation could not be invoked. With the "Judicare Act" (1873-1875) both kinds of jurisdiction were combined. Legislation had a marginal influence. Precedents traditionally have a prominent place ("stare decisis") and the search for precedents is important. When a precedent seems to be available an attempt is made, with the technique of "distinction", to find differences which prove that a new case cannot be ruled by this precedent. In this way law developed gradually.

In the time of Cromwell rebelling army officers formulated the first and only formal constitution of Great Britain: "Instrument of Government" (1653). Thomas Hobbes (1588-1679), observing civil war in England and the end of the Thirty Years War (1618-1648) on the European continent with the Peace of Westphalia (1648), wrote his "Leviathan" (1651). For Hobbes, the worst tribulation for humanity is war, which takes men back to the natural state of violence of all against all: violence as sole criterion. To escape from this misery, men conclude a pact, abandoning their liberties in favour of somebody with power to protect all against others. The power of this leader can only be absolute, so a "Commonwealth" or State is created (Hobbes, 1651). In his conception, public authority is based only upon force, not law. In 1660 monarchy was restored (Holdsworth, 1903). In 1679 the "Habeas Corpus" act proclaimed that no English subject could be arrested without a preceding sentence of a judge. The last Stuart king, James II (1685-1688) flew in 1688. Then the supremacy of Parliament was recognised. The Declaration of the Bill of Rights (1689) of the Parliament proclaimed fundamental democratic rights, which were accepted by William III of Holland who became King of England in 1689. The Bill of Rights recognised the fundamental rights of Parliament. Free elections, free debate, approval of taxes, limitation of the royal prerogative. It was more "Rule of Parliament" than "Rule of Law". Parliament held supreme power.

John Locke (1632-1704) defended this "Glorious Revolution" (1687-1689). His work, especially the "Second Treatise on Civil Government" (1690), was one of the most prominent conceptions in the West about the Rule of Law. Locke stood on the intersection between two conceptions. From Hooker (1597), representing medieval Christian tradition, he borrowed the primacy of the "bonum commune". This implied subjection of public authorities to superior rules, and the right to rebel against a sovereign who fails to fulfil his trusteeship (Keble, 1977). From Hobbes he derived individualism and the political rights of the middle classes. According to Locke, men in the natural state do not live in a situation of perennial war but are able to create peace. They need juridical order and public authorities, but do not give up their natural liberties. With these inalienable natural rights they can resist public authorities. In the last resort the rights of the individual have priority with regard to the common good. After the civil war Locke was so imbued with the idea of the supremacy of Parliament that he could not imagine some instance controlling Parliament. In his conception judges could only apply laws. When public authorities abuse powers citizens can only fall back upon their fundamental rights of resistance (Polin, 1960). This idea inspired American revolutionaries, supported in their rebellion against the English monarchy by the French monarchy. In Great Britain, undivided sovereignty of Parliament was a structural constitutional dogma for centuries, up until today. This did not mean that the Rule of Law was always positive for civil liberties. Parliament restrained the rights of citizens in several fields (Radzinowicz, 1968). Once the monarchy was disarmed with regard to the almighty Parliament political power came into the hands of Whigs, representing the landed gentry and the property-owning classes. Tribunals extended the rights of citizens against executive power. The liberal idea of the Rule of Law prevailed according to which all was allowed that was not forbidden by law

The conception of Grotius (1583-1645) was thought-provoking. With regard to the end of the unity in Christianity, he analysed the fundaments on which the law of nations had to be built. He elaborated the idea that the place previously given to faith must now be given to reason. Human nature and natural law replaced the divine order of the Scholastics. All power and public authority are seen as based on the social nature of man, the common will to establish order and a "pactum societatis" between monarch and subjects recognising liberties and the rights of each individual. From the basis of this secularised natural law, subjective rights are derived. These subjective rights are based on the human person as such and his consent, not on some objective superior order as the medieval conception had it. The natural law doctrine of Grotius, S. Pufendorf (1672), C. Wolf, J. de Barbeyrac and others spread all over Europe. With discussions between Hobbes and Locke (England), Burlamaqui and Rousseau (France) and E. Kant (Prussia), we are at the heart of the conception of human rights as elaborated in Europe (Morin, 1996, p.75). Europe exported it all over the world in the 19th and 20th centuries. The liberal philosophy of Locke (1632-

1704) and Montesquieu (1689-1755) extended tasks of the constitutional state in protecting the liberties and rights of individuals. Primacy of the individual required primacy of law. In the Middle Ages and later, the right of resistance against arbitrary uses of public authority was defended. Attempts to oppose the principles of natural law against the arbitrariness of monarchs mostly failed to be effective. In the Western tradition of law, going back to Judaeo-Christian and Greek-Roman civilisations, several notions were used to denote the prominence of law with regard to public authorities: Rule of Law; "Rechtsstaat" (German); "État de droit" (French). In the 18th and 19th centuries, these notions of the Rule of Law were developed mostly within the national context. With regard to relations between nation-states there were many references to the ideas of Grotius (1583-1645) in "De iure belli ac pacis" (1625). Grotius founded modern international law and secularised natural law. He defended the liberty of the individual with regard to public authorities. The French Revolution gave a vital impulse for the development of the Rule of Law, while building upon previously developed ideas, also in Great Britain and the American colonies, especially with the "Déclaration de droits de l'homme et du citoyen" (1789). Understanding the historical context of this major event means going back in history.

### 10.3. French Revolution, impact of revolutions in Great-Britain and Northern America

The intellectual sources of the French Revolution go far back in history. Western Europe, assimilating ideas of the period before our era, especially those from Greek, Roman and Judaeo-Christian civilisations, developed ideas about the primacy of law in social and societal relations throughout a period of two millennia. Plato (428-347 BC) had his original, idealist concept of the philosopher-king and a council of wise men to guard fundamental laws, and a mixed system of public authorities, combining the liberty of democratic government by many with the efficacy and wisdom of government by few (Luccioni, 1958). Aristotle (348-322 BC) later developed his ideas about a moderate constitution (Prélot, 1959). Greek conceptions penetrated Western Europe in the Gallo-Roman period and during the Middle Ages. Thomas Aquinas (1225-1274) built a bridge between Aristotelian philosophy and Christian doctrine with his ideas about the "bonum commune" as task for public authorities, deriving authority from divine law. French kings exploited the idea of monarchy based on divine law to its utmost, while forgetting the interests of the people, the "bonum commune" (general interest). Due to the anarchy in the 16th century and the "Fronde", France took the road to absolute monarchy. The hypothesis might be formulated that one of the most driving forces to vitalise powers of the people in the French Revolution (1789) was that fundamental rights were violated, with the masses living in misery while the royal court lived in disgusting luxury.

French monarchy developed, especially after the decline of the medieval "civitas christiana", by profiling itself with regard to the Church and competing powers inside and outside its territory. Legists derived their notion of absolute power from the "plenitudo potestatis" of former Roman emperors and proclaimed: "rex est imperator in regni suo". In the territory of France monarchs had to share authority with others for jurisdiction. They gradually extended their power as citizens asked for their legislation against feudal seigneurs for the common good of all (Olivier-Martin, 1992, p.351). In the 15$^{th}$ and 16th centuries there was debate between the adherents of absolute power for the monarchy (Ferrault, 1520) and with adherents of moderate monarchy, bound by fundamental customary laws of the kingdom (Seyssel, 1519) and the obligation to consult the "états généraux" for important matters (Ellul, 1964). The Hundred Years War (1338-1453) and religious wars (1562-1590) had an important impact. Insecurity and the miseries of warfare made one thing predominantly important: a power able to defend the people. A choice had to be made between a strong power and anarchy. In the "Fronde" (1648-1653) crisis, Joly (1652) argued that the power of monarchs was limited and that they could not dispose of their subjects arbitrarily. The English civil war had its impact on the "Fronde" in France (Knachel, 1967; Wicquefort, 1978). The basis was laid for absolute monarchy, seen as a necessary protection against anarchy. According to Bossuet (1709), the authority of the monarch could not be restrained by any other power while he should give an example in obeying reason and justice. For Fénélon (1699), people have the right to choose a monarch, maintaining fundamental laws and taking account of the opinions of "parlements" claiming to speak in the name of the people (Basse, 1973).

The Reformation created a new situation, because the unity of Christianity was explicitly questioned. In the beginning, Luther and Calvin (1541) argued for submitting to public authorities. The orders of kings had to be obeyed unless they ordered something against divine law. In Germany, Lutheran princes imposed Protestantism. They protected their States against the Empire, which remained true to the Roman-Catholic Church. In France the persecution of Calvinists forced them to resist the monarchy, which defended the religious unity of the country on the basis of Catholicism. After "Saint-Barthélemy" (1572) the debate about political conceptions concentrated on the issue of legitimacy. "Monarchomaques" like Hotman (1573) elaborated the idea of approval by the people and a monarchy moderated by law. Brutus (1579) argued for the murder of tyrants if the monarch violated the pact with his subjects. Some countries such as the Netherlands (Calvinist since 1581) and England (Puritanic in 1640) revolted against what they saw as tyranny. Liberal ideas transcended borders but it took a century for these to find a fertile soil in France. Louis XIV (1643-1715) ruled as an absolute monarch oppressing liberal ideas. In his youth, his mother, as regent, had been forced in 1648 by the "Cours" to agree to the young king making a proclamation of personal liberties for his subjects. Once adult, he annulled this in 1652. Louis XIV never forgot this "Fronde" anarchy, as is shown in his memoirs (1661).

Absolutism manifested itself with legislative power and "justice retenue". It enabled the French monarch to overrule the judgement of a court or to decide a case himself. This contrasted with the position of the English monarch, who was bound by the "Prohibitions del Roy" (1607). A component of absolutism was the practice of imprisonments on the basis of arbitrary "raison d'État" with "lettres de cachet" (Bluche, 1990, p.868). Louis XIV showed a more liberal attitude with his decision to incorporate in the "Ordonnance criminelle" (1670) the "lettres de justice" by which the monarch, invited by private persons, could intervene in the cases of tribunals. French criminal procedure was made inquisitory and secret in the 13th century, where before it had been accusatory, contradictory and public (Esmein, 1882). This was a reaction to a rise in criminality. The inquisitory procedure could include torture as a method of obtaining proof on the basis of which it was possible to get a confession. Beccaria in his "Des délits and des peines" (1765), criticised this criterion of truth by means of torture and condemned the death penalty. Voltaire, inspired by this, argued that the "Ordonnance criminelle" (1670) had to be reformed, making it as favourable for the innocent as it was terrible for the guilty. Diderot and d'Alembert joined in the criticisms. Louis XVI reacted with "Ordonnances" (1780 and 1788). The "Constituante" reduced the number of crimes to which the death penalty could be applied from 115 to 32.

In the course of time, ideas about the best way to organise public authority developed, as in the conceptualisation of the constitutional state. Public authorities have to act differently in a constitutional state where the Rule of Law prevails. A crucial characteristic ruling structure and the behaviour of all who act to fulfil tasks in the framework of public management. The conception of sovereignty of Jean Bodin (1530-1596) in his "Les six livres de la République" (1576) was famous. Gradually, the royal system of jurisdiction was extended in a hierarchical structure with "cours souveraines" (as the "Parlements") at the top, and the possibility of appeal to the King. At the end of the Ancien Régime the "Parlement de Paris" could register "actes royaux" before these were given validity as laws. The King had to follow the procedure of the "lit de justice", where grievances ("rémonstrances") could be ushered in the presence of the King. Following this procedure was enough. The King could proclaim his laws, even when "Parlement" was opposed to them. "Parlements" increasingly challenged the authority of the King. One of the abuses of the Ancien Régime was that judiciary offices could be purchased. Since 1604 the privatisation of jurisdiction had been hereditary, if a yearly amount of money was paid ("paulette"). Another bad institutional arrangement was that magistrates, who had to judge, were paid by advocates: bribery and corruption were normal. The procedure in criminal trials was rough and inhumane; torture was used often to extract confessions. At the end of the Ancien Régime there were enough occasions and arguments to change jurisdiction. There were stimuli from Montesquieu's "De l'Esprit des Lois" (1748) and the American War of Independence demonstrated that it was possible to challenge absolutist monarchy. Although there were some attempts to reform jurisdiction, the French Revolution was needed to put an end to flagrant injustice, abuses and privileges.

The "Déclaration des droits de l'homme et du citoyen" (1789) was a breakthrough. The dominant conception before that was that the State or monarchy was there on behalf of the common good, as Scholastic philosophy had it, and not to assure individual liberties. Customary laws and the conscience of the monarch were the limits to monarchical power. According to the Treaty of Westphalia (1648), there was no freedom of religion. Two revolutions and Locke's ideas about tolerance were necessary in Great Britain to bring recognition of Protestantism (1688). In contrast, the revocation in 1685 of the "Édit de Nantes" (1598) had abolished the modest religious liberties given to French Protestants nearly a century before. Liberty of expression developed in Great Britain and the Netherlands, but was tightly restricted in France. Enlightenment revitalised ideas about the value of the individual as previously elaborated. Guilleaume d'Ockham (1347) accentuated the position of the human individual in relation to the universalia, an intellectual concept then in vogue. Individualism and ideas about human rights were brought to the fore by Epicurism and Stoicism in Antiquity, and in Jewish and Christian traditions with emphasis on the dignity of man and the equality of all human beings before God. Ockham argued that freedom of thought should be practised in the Church and that the authority of the pope had to be limited when he was behaving as a tyrant. Reformation reactivated the debate about religious liberty when Protestants were persecuted as in France.

For Montesquieu, in his "De l'Esprit des Lois" (1748), the liberty of citizens was a key-issue of government. He defined this liberty as the certainty of each individual that the arbitrary whim of some governor cannot rob him of his life or possessions. Asking how this could be brought about, he referred to the Constitution of England and the past of France itself. To prevent abuses of power, it is necessary that power thwarts power (countervailing powers). With innovative creativity, he combined the ideas of Locke and a somewhat changed situation in England to present his conception of the separation of powers to realise an institutional equilibrium. What is remarkable is that Montesquieu did not give a crucial role to judges for the protection of individual liberties (as in the English system). This is due to the fact that there are two different jurisdictional models in his conception. In a monarchy like France, only one person governs, while in the English model the laws (legislative power) give the orders. For Montesquieu, judges should not be more than the mouthpiece of the law. They did not get a specific function in protecting individual liberties. In France, resistance of the "parlements" against the monarch, in the name of fundamental laws or the traditional rights of corporations, was mostly meant to obstruct reforms which impaired their personal rights. This heritage of the Ancien Régime had an important impact on the development of the Rule of Law in France. No matter how seductive Montesquieu's conception of the separation of powers might be, American revolutionaries implemented this basic idea more effectively than their French colleagues. Montesquieu, in his "Lettres persanes" (1721), stressed that there is no one ideal model of government for all countries. The most appropriate model is that which is adapted to the conditions of each country. Customs of a country are specifically relevant, because customs are more effective in making better citizens than laws.

For Rousseau liberty is the most essential objective for the individual person. It is a paradox that his reasoning leads to the conclusion that man has to subordinate himself completely to collectivity. Rousseau (1765) saw the masses in society bereft of their liberties and natural equality, everywhere they were "in chains". How to restore the liberty and equality that prevailed in the original natural state? Rousseau thought to remake society on the basis of a "contrat social" creating a "corps moral et collectif, sorte de 'moi commun' expressing la 'volonté générale'." (1762). Rousseau's constructions implied that each member of society would submit to this new monarch ("volonté générale"), but not to the individuals establishing this general will. So, the primacy of law as the expression of the general will, and not of the will of one person or a group, was theoretically realised. Rousseau handled the question of how individual liberties could be protected, if this general will became despotic. He argued that law based upon the general will is just by definition (just and for the benefit of the people). Rousseau was thinking about direct democracy as practised in Geneva. Narrow reading of the "Contrat Social" makes "État de droit" and human rights an unreal mystification. In the revolutionary euphoria, problems were solved by identifying the politics of representatives in the Assembly with the general will as propagated by Rousseau. Sovereignty of the law and juridically unlimited power of the legislator was the norm. American revolutionaries freed themselves from this rigid idea.

Revolutions in Great Britain and North America preceded the French Revolution, and had their impact on the overheated "bouillon des idées" in the French kitchen of political concepts (Morin, 1996). Enlightenment furthered the influence of rationalistic ideas. The enterprise of Diderot and d'Alembert to collect all available knowledge in the "Encyclopédie, ou dictionnaire raisonné des sciences, des arts et des métiers" (1751/1772; 1776/1780) in this context was a remarkable exhibition of rationalistic self-confidence. The French Revolution has attracted attention again and again, mostly for its violent character, but also for its ideas and impact upon democratic rule in a constitutional state. In 1789 the French wanted reforms in the governmental machinery, but not the overthrow of the regime. The regime of absolute monarchy was overthrown due to mismanagement of the country by the corrupt leading elite around the French King. Coupled with social and economic misery for millions of the French population, appalling violation of elementary human rights was a mighty driving-force. The Pilgrim Fathers sailed their boat Mayflower from Plymouth in England to Plymouth Massachusetts to create the first colony in New England. The "Mayflower Compact" (1620) based government on the agreement of settlers, not on the English Crown. English colonies in North America were created formally with adoption by the English Parliament of the "Petition of Rights" (1628), and when the New England Company got a Royal Charter in 1629, guaranteeing inhabitants of Massachusetts all the liberties and immunities of free and natural subjects of the king (Grimm, 1964), Governor Wintrop confirmed that nobody could be deprived of life or goods without a law as adopted by a general assembly. When civil war broke out (in Great Britain 1642-1646) Williams, as founder of the Rhode Island colony, said that the basis of civil government was the people. The wide open spaces of America made men naturally free (Tocqueville). Locke, Montesquieu, Rousseau and "encyclopedists" inspired American colonists. Their rebellion was a natural sequel to revolutions in England a century before. Benjamin

Franklin proposed to represent colonies in the British Parliament (Bigelow, 1904). Ending the authority of Parliament over American colonies got priority from 1765.

The American Declaration of Independence of 4 July 1776 marked a new departure. It proclaimed that all human beings are born equal, with inalienable rights, and that governments are established to guarantee these rights, while public authority is based on the agreement of the governed. If a government violates this fundamental objective people have the right to change or abolish it and establish a new government. The problem was how to assure that the colonies would implement the principles of the Declaration of Independence. This was a crucial question making constitutionalism the key-issue, repeated since then all over the world. Experiences with legal relations of subordination between Great Britain and her colonies made a hierarchy of legal rulings familiar. Some colonies had written principles of government earlier than the Cromwellian "Instrument of Government" (1653), such as the "Fundamental Orders of Connecticut" (1639). In May 1776 the intercolonial congress invited the colonies to adopt their own declaration of rights. Colonies did this over the next 4 years, except Rhode Island and Connecticut, who maintained their charters. It was a combination of allegiance to tradition ("English liberty") and invariable laws of nature, which according to the colonies had been violated by Great Britain. In these declarations human rights, elements of the Rule of Law and democracy were related. Natural rights were prominent: liberties of conscience, religious cult, press; the right to live; liberty, equality; the right to happiness and security; the right of property. The States were thought to implement them, guaranteed by recognition of the Rule of Law. The constitution of Massachusetts declared public authorities subject to these principles: government of laws, not government of men.

Constituents of the American federation affirmed the principle of constitutionalism. The Constitution of the United States of 17 September 1787, in operation the following year, declared that it was "the supreme law of the land". This meant that this Constitution was superior with regard to ordinary laws and had to be implemented by judges of the member States of the Union. The first Congress of the United States adopted the Bill of Rights in March 1789, operative in 1791. Constitution and Bill of Rights together form a complete framework for a constitutional state. The American Constitution marks the watershed between centuries of strife against absolutism, and constitutionalism, but it did not explicitly state that its rulings had to be implemented despite eventual federal laws which did not conform to the Constitution. This was a controversial topic until the Supreme Court, in the Marbury vs Madison case (1803), made itself competent to invalidate any federal act which was contrary to the Constitution. This authority of the Supreme Court is based on Common Law, and judicial review of acts of the English Crown and its agents. American Constitution and Bill of Rights had an influence all over the world. Also in France, where the monarchy joined the side of American revolutionaries against Great Britain.

A distinguished adherent of the English legal system, A.V. Dicey (1885) skillfully analysed the relationship between the traditional sovereignty of the Parliament and the Rule of Law. For Dicey government and its agents should be subordinate to the control of ordinary courts, while laws of Parliament should remain outside their jurisdictional control. Judges should quite naturally be subject to the legislator, defending their independence and authority with regard to the executive power. So, the "common law" of the tribunals was able to protect the liberties of English subjects. According to Dicey, the legal spirit of the legislator would preclude that the legislator, by a kind of despotism of Parliament, would abuse his supremacy. For Dicey, there was nothing more strange for the supremacy of law in the English tradition than French administrative law. Later Dicey admitted that the French "Conseil d'État" had developed a system of rules which made this organ a real court. Its jurisprudence had largely taken away the arbitrary character of administrative law. Essential differences with the English Rule of Law remained, while for Hewart (1929), the Rule of Law became second nature in England. For Allen (1931) French administrative law is defamed in Great Britain. On the basis of some principles, England could be given a genuine administrative law in harmony with English law. The parliamentary "Donoughmore Committee" (1932), following Dicey, concluded that ministers should not be withdrawn from the jurisdiction of the tribunals of Common Law. The "Franks Committee" (1957) concluded that administrative tribunals are essential for the good functioning of the State, and that ordinary tribunals should rule law questions. The plea by Robson (1951) for the idea of both committees to introduce in Great Britain a system like the "Conseil d'État", was rejected as contrary to the coherence of English law and tradition. The Parliament of Great Britain reorganised control of the legality of administrative acts by courts of justice. Between 1958 and 1981 appeals to Common Law were replaced by judicial review by a judge of the Supreme Court. The judiciary authority, following the French, established an administrative division within the Supreme Court.

Generally speaking, the important rules that have been elaborated by British tribunals for the control of public authorities more or less resemble those in other Western countries. The Rule of Law claims that delegated legislation and decisions conform to the law, otherwise these are declared "ultra vires" and annulled. When an administrative organ has a (quasi-) judiciary function, courts of justice, asked to judge them, investigate whether the procedure followed complies with "natural justice". Each party in the lawsuit has the right to be heard ("audi et alteram partem") in an equitable way (fair hearing). Nobody can be judge and litigant simultaneously. The criterion of natural justice gives judges a margin for appreciating the circumstances of each case. Although the judge generally does not give his opinion about the basis of an administrative decision, he comes near to this when examining whether a discretionary decision is reasonable (Jowell/Oliver, 1994). Therefore it is suggested that judiciary control should be entrusted to judges specialising in administrative questions. Lord Denning in the Gouriet case (1977) wanted to deduce from the Rule of Law as a general principle of English law that tribunals can control discretionary competences of the attorney general given him by law. In this case, the judge held that the decision of the attorney general was unreasonable. The Chamber of the House of Lords pronounced itself contrarily, concluding that one could go too far in extending the power of judges. There is an important difference between the British tradition and that of the majority of countries on the European continent. This is obvious in the jurisprudence of the European Court of Human Rights.

## 10.4. Institutional outburst of the French Revolution

Probably one of the decisive causes of the French Revolution (1789) was that the appalling injustice of existing institutions and practices piled up the fury of the masses, living in misery, while the royal court demonstrated a disgusting and degenerate extravagance (Soboul, 1950). The conviction was widespread that the country was managed badly and worse, in open violation of the most elementary rules of justice (class justice). Relations in society were deeply poisoned by the prevalence of injustice (Robin, 1970). The "parlements" demanded that the "États Généraux" (representatives of clergy, aristocracy and third order) must be convoked, then they could justify their refusal to register tax measures. At last, King Louis XVI, seen as source of justice in the Ancien Régime, gave way and convoked the "États Généraux". When he refused to decide the crucial issue in front of these "États Généraux" – voting by three orders, or, as claimed by the third order, voting in one assembly – the fury of the representatives of the common people was further inflamed. Representatives of the third order and their supporters decided to form the "National Assembly" as representation of the people. The French Revolution started by accident, with the violent storming of the "Bastille" on 14 July 1789 ("Quatorze Juillet"). On 4 August 1789 the National Assembly abrogated all privileges, also those in the sphere of jurisdiction. On 26 August 1789 the National Assembly voted the "Déclaration des droits de l'homme et du citoyen", founding the "État de droit". This Declaration of Human Rights also had a fundamental impact upon the spirit and organisation of jurisdiction, so the laws could not have retroactive effect. Primacy was given to public jurisdiction instead of private jurisdiction for all citizens. One could not be judged twice on the same evidence. To end the endless protraction of juridical procedures in the Ancien Régime it was ruled that justiciables had the right to appeal for a complete judging once. Several rulings were instituted to prevent arbitrariness in jurisdiction. Setting aside a number of cases (family law matters; public order) sessions of courts and tribunals were made public. Normally there had to be three judges to preclude subjectivity of one judge. The procedure before courts and tribunals was based upon a contradictory debate between representatives of the two parties. Mostly it had to be an oral procedure (no judging upon files only). Decisions of judges had to be motivated. Sentences had to explain the reasons on which the decision was based. Justiciables, given the right to counsel, were protected. Institutional arrangements for procedures before courts and tribunals were changed drastically.

The French Revolution brought about the abolition of all feudal and ecclesiastical jurisdictions, the hated privileges and the sale of jurisdictional offices. The law of 16/24 August 1790 proclaimed some essential principles such as: separation of powers; equality of all citizens before jurisdictions; jurisdiction for free. It was ruled that judges could not control the State (made competent to judge its own eventual excesses). Revolutionaries wanted to end the system of the Ancien Régime in which functions of administration and jurisdiction were not split up, and magistrates permanently tried to enlarge their competencies in the field of administration and politics, so a "juridiction judiciaire" was set up, competent for deciding conflicts between citizens (civil law) and infringments of the laws (penal law). And a "juridiction administrative" to handle conflicts between citizens and public administration. These rulings could not prevent the development of the "Terreur" (1793) during which a revolutionary tribunal could condemn anybody arbitrarily, especially those who qualified as enemies of the people. These excesses were corrected during "Consulate" (1799-1804) and First Empire (1804-1814/1815). Napoleon knew that stability in society can be promoted by institutions based on a solid codification. Differing from Anglo-Saxon tradition, which based jurisdiction on the earlier decisions of judges in comparable cases (precedents). The influence of American constitutionalism and ruling of human rights made itself felt in attempts to build up a constitutional monarchy in France. Due to clumsy and incompetent manoeuvring of the first French constitutional monarch, Louis XVI (1774-1792), France became a Republic after his execution by the guillotine. The Constitution of 3 September 1791 was followed by a new "Constitution montagnarde" of June 1793. These constitutions and proclamation of the "Déclaration des droits de l'homme et du citoyen" (1789) could not prevent the restoration of methods as practised during absolutist monarchy. For this Declaration it was possible to draw on the American "Bill of Rights", published a year before the French Revolution (Rials, 1988). A crucial difference between North America and France was that the French could not trust judges. Article 16 of the "Déclaration" (1789) said that any society without guaranteed rights or separation of powers has no constitution. By this criterion, revolutionary France, claiming to have a model for other countries, had no Constitution: no effective procedures or institutions for control over public authorities.

There has been discussion over the juridical status of the "Déclaration" (1789), which was made a preamble to the Constitution of 1791 by the "Assemblée Constituante". For Esmein (1906) the Declaration of 1789 proclaimed philosophical and moral principles without juridical potency, only relevant as inspirational directives for the legislator. For

Bastid (1985) it was meant to have a constitutional status. Duguit (1927) was very explicit in stating that the Declaration of 1789, with its supra-constitutional value, bound the constituents. It took nearly two centuries to place the Declaration of 1789 unquestionably in positive law, as was done in the 1970s. The French Revolution did not equip its theoretically proclaimed "État de droit" with the necessary tools for effective control, especially with regard to legislation. The most prominent reason for this was the deep distrust of jurisdictional and parliamentarian powers. In the last years before the French Revolution jurisdictional power had obstructed and frustrated all reforms, mostly to defend personal privileges. Therefore, the Constitution of 1791 forbade tribunals to meddle with the exercise of legislative power. The Declaration of 1789 influenced legislation, but the effective constitutional guarantee for realisation of the "État de droit" was missing. The sovereignty of the law became the sole fundamental norm. Several authoritarian regimes in France used this, confusing executive power and legislative power. The "Constitution de l'an VIII" (1799), creating the "Conseil d'État", which played a huge role in building the French constitutional state, did not prevent unlimited personification of power by Napoleon Bonaparte. After the Napoleonic wars all over Europe the constitutional state entered a new phase. Industrial revolution, changes in society and processes of democratisation provoked a debate between French, English and German philosophers and jurists about their institutions in a comparative perspective. This debate about "État de droit", "Rule of Law" and "Rechtsstaat" continues nowadays.

After 1789 revolutionaries tried to renew juridical institutions. Superceding all institutionalised rulings they saw the natural, inalienable and holy human rights, which were recognised and proclaimed by the National Assembly, sole representative of the whole population. The "Déclaration des droits de l'homme et du citoyen" (1789) was seen as fundamental law. The Constitution came directly under this Declaration of Human Rights in the hierarchy of norms, and had to guarantee these human rights, transforming them thereby into civil rights, and the separation of powers. On the third level in the hierarchy of norms came the laws, which had a superior authority provided that they were not in defiance of proclaimed human rights and Constitution. On the fourth level there were the decisions and rulings of organs of executive power. Executive power could issue these decisions and rulings only so far as it represented the Nation, charged with the issuing and implementation of laws. In the conception of the revolutionaries executive power had no genuine normative power whatsoever, but could only implement normative rulings made on a higher level. Public functionaries were thought to have no representative function, so they could not pretend to will for the nation and to express the "volonté générale". This was a complete "politics-administration dichotomy". Public functionaries had to execute the norms as established by others, without any room for interpretation or policy discretion. The judges were seen as pure mouthpieces of the laws, they could not interfere with the activities and rulings of legislative power, or suspend application of laws; a rather rigid system.

Revolutionaries had a mystical Rousseauesque obsession ("volonté générale") with regard to the meaning of laws. Once a law was voted for by representatives of the Nation it was seen as an expression of the general will of the people as such. Sovereignty of the Nation, the sole source of sovereignty, was transferred to the representatives in the National Assembly. The complex institutional arrangements for public authorities were simplified and reduced to the supremacy of the law (principle of legality). Due to the fixed texts of the Constitution in the 19th century the main point in the hierarchy of norms was laid ever more in the almighty position of parliamentarians. Revolutionaries wanted to restrict the power of the King as much as possible, so they refused to recognise that executive power had any normative power. In the course of time, the position of executive power changed. Authentic normative competence of executive power as "pouvoir réglementaire" was formally recognised in the first decade after the French Revolution (Verpeaux, 1991). The "pouvoir réglementaire" has been confirmed since then. Regulations from organs of executive power were split into regulations for the implementation of legal rulings, and regulations on the basis of legislative delegation after a mandate by the legislator. These last regulations were even given a quasi-legal character, bringing them onto the same normative level as laws. This lasted until 1907 when the "Conseil d'État" decided that appeal was possible against these regulations on the basis of "excès de pouvoir" (abuse of power). Regulations were recognised as a source for minor legal rulings. From the beginning of the 20th century the "Conseil d'État" recognised autonomous "pouvoir réglementaire" for the organisation of public services and "police administrative". The institutional arrangements of the revolutionaries gave no guarantees for the realisation of the hierarchy of norms. In the 19th century some corrections were made.

Although the supremacy of the Constitution was recognised there were no sanctions against trespasses. Laws were seen as unlimited discretionary acts and parliamentarians had free play to rule whatever they liked. This was reinforced by the prevailing idea that government and administration had to respect legality painstakingly, controlled by jurisdictions. On the basis of the idea that judging administration is administration, common jurisdictions were prohibited to judge administration itself. Revolutionaries ordained a separation of jurisdiction and administration. Common jurisdiction could not judge the activities of administration. Liberals tried to abolish this privilege for public administration after the July Monarchy (1830-1848) but it was maintained. So a rather specific institutional arrangement was organised in France; the constitutional state was not developed by subjecting public administration to controls of external jurisdictions, but with a jurisdiction within public administration itself. It took a century before separation was effected between "juridiction administrative" and "administration active", by giving administrative judges guarantees for independence. In prehistory of administrative law (P.Weil) 1799-1872, administrative jurisdiction developed in the public administration structure. Macarel, Cormenin and Vivien (1859) argued for administrative jurisdictions. Jurisprudence meant that public administration had to be submitted to jurisdictional control. The "Conseil d'État", guarantee of administrative legality, extended the scope of appeal against abuse of power to make the administration recognise the hierarchy of norms.

French judges had and have to work on the basis of written laws. Later jurisprudence had a supplementary role. Therefore, codification was crucial in France. Emperor Napoleon, who liked to be compared to the Roman Emperor Justinian as a prominent codifier, ensured that France got its modern codification elaborated by top-jurists (Tronchet, Portalis, Bigot de Préameneu, Malleville): "Code civil" (1800/1804); "Code de procédure civile" (1807); "Code de commerce" (1808); "Code d'instruction criminelle" (1808); "Code pénal" (1810). After this codification, the dominant notion was that the sole valid laws were those decided upon by the parliament as representing the Nation. This furthered a legalistic approach. Formal laws were seen as the only source of juridical norms. Jurisprudence was not recognised as a source of juridical norms. Judges had to apply what the laws ordained. Jurisdiction was a real State monopoly as "fonction publique", judges became professionals, officials paid by the State. Gradually French jurisprudence was recognised as a supplementary source of law. This solution was different from that in England, where the tradition is that most magistrates are citizens. Fundamental sources of law in England were "Magna Carta" (1215) and "Habeas Corpus Act" (1679). The "Common Law" tradition prevails there, accentuating jurisprudence instead of written laws (David, 1987; Kinder-Gest, 1993). "Common Law" is basically a collection of customary rulings, valid during the 12th century and adapted since then (Bouscaren, 1988; Scarman, 1974). The concept of law in the US is influenced by English "Common Law", but has authentic features (Levasseur, 1990; Tunc, 1989).

## 10.5. Confrontation of French doctrine with German ideas

In Germany, Kant (1724-1804), heir of Enlightenment and the natural law school, had great expectations of the French Revolution. He inspired jurists with his "Rechtsstaat" conception in the second quarter of the 19th century. "Rechtsstaat" was translated in France as "État de droit" at the end of the 19th century. Carré de Malberg (1920-1922) constructed a bridge between German and French intellectual climates and doctrines. German jurists were interested in conceptualisation and practices in Great Britain. British juridical doctrine (Dicey, 1885) had problems with the growing intervention of the State in social and economic life. In Germany the idea of subordination of public authorities to law was known in the Middle Ages, but in the 18th century the authority of monarchs was absolute ("Polizeistaat"). Citizens could complain to a higher level of the administrative hierarchy. According to Kant (1988), philosopher of Königsberg, from imperatives of our moral conscience and reason the obligation can be derived to leave the natural state, in which nobody is secure against violence, and enter the juridical state. In this juridical state with subordination to public, legal authority, the rights of the individual can be legally determined and guaranteed by adequate public authority. The contract by which people constitute a State is also binding for the monarch. While in Hobbes' Leviathan the monarch was the sole judge of his acts, the State, according to Kant is subordinate to the Idea of Law. Kant stressed the universal equality of subjects in the State, binding themselves reciprocally only by the authority of law. Before full realisation of the juridical state Kant accepted a temporary autocracy, provided that laws are such that a reasonable population could have made them (Ponton, 1990). Kant's conception of the State, although not elaborating democracy and the techniques for controlling public authorities, formulated the preliminary conditions of the constitutional State: civil liberty and subordination of governors to law (Lacroix, 1989). Development from legalist "État des lois" to "État de droit" took place in France from the second half of the 19th century (Redor, 1992). The notion "État de droit" was borrowed from "Rechtsstaat" in German doctrine.

This doctrine was developed by R. von Mohl ("Die Polizeiwissenschaft nach den Grundsätzen des Rechtsstaates", 1832), and F.J. Stahl ("Die Philosophie des Rechts", 1856). L. von Stein in "Die Verwaltungslehre" (1865) argued that the "Rechtsstaat" had to be a "sozialer Staat" also by correcting social inequalities. After elaboration of this doctrine (Gerber, Ihering, Laband, and Jellinek), it was introduced in France by Carré de Malberg and others. Before this import there was a specific development of juridical thinking in France itself on the basis of legislation since Ancien Régime, French Revolution, Napoleonic codes and jurisprudence. The accent of the concept of constitutional state was upon the framing and limiting of State power by law. There are several interpretations of the crucial and complex relation between State and law. Formal: a constitutional state is a State working by means of laws as instrument. Hierarchical: a constitutional state is a State, submitted to law. Material: a constitutional state is a State with several specific intrinsic characteristics. The confrontation of French doctrine with German doctrine is interesting (Chevallier, 1994). In France and Germany the administrative dimension of the "État de droit" prevailed up to the First World War. From the 1920s on the constitutional dimension, prominent since the 18th century in the United States, came to the fore in discussions in Europe. The issue was whether human rights and "État de droit" had to be part of constitutional guarantees against the power of parliaments. The Constitution of the Weimar Republic(1919) included the protection of civil and political rights, and of economic and social rights. This was allied with discussions about the character of the "Rechtsstaat". Formally protecting individuals by applying law without reference to justice or natural law, was seen by positivists as metaphysics. Or material, as proposed by H. Heller, arguing that the State had to interfere, to bridge the gap between individual liberties and inequalities

(Karpen, 1988, p.187). Others such as Kelsen (1927) in his pure theory of law had a formal conception. He argued that a State in which the validity of juridical norms depends on a strict hierarchy would be a "Rechtsstaat", whatever its material standard of justice. Kelsen used the disputed logic of a mathematically monistic hierarchy of norms. Sovereignty did not belong to the legislator, a constituted organ, but to the order of the State. Parliament could only be restricted in powers by an independent organ with a different public authority, a special court.

Discussions in France about the constitutionalisation of human rights and "État de droit" concentrated on the necessity of controlling the constitutionality of laws, and about the incumbent of this power of control. Prominent jurists like L. Duguit and M. Hauriou argued that the "Déclaration des droits de l'homme et du citoyen" (1789) had a juridically binding constitutional character. For Duguit (1923), the State is bound by pre-existing juridical norms like this Declaration, arising from social solidarity. Hauriou (1929) founded the superiority of fundamental norms in the "social constitution" of the country, arguing that the Declaration of 1789 must be imposed on legislative power, more dangerous for human rights than executive power. The question was how to change the Republican tradition of absolute superiority into legislative power. Hauriou wrote that constitutional control as practised in the United States should be introduced as an essential part of a constitutional regime. Sovereignty of parliament for him was a second "Bastille" to demolish. For Duguit, constitutionality of laws is a necessary effect of the hierarchy of laws. A country not recognising this authority of judges is not a true "État de droit". Some did not follow the reasoning of Duguit and Hauriou. G. Jèze (1924) argued that constant jurisprudence had a different conception. If constitutional control of laws were adopted in France it would be with an "exception d'inconstitutionalité", the American model. Lambert (1921), opponent of "government by judges" as introduced in the American Constitution and the "Marbury v. Madison Arrest" (1803), accentuated the difference between sovereign law in France and controlled, "humiliated" law in the US. He criticised U.S. judges for using the clause "due process of law" to impose their own ideas of justice and equity, saying this would have inhibited social reforms introduced since the end of the 19th century in European countries. Lambert decried pressures from the American Senate to make the President nominate favourites to the Supreme Court. This politicising of the jurisdictional function was thought inevitable due to limitless judiciary hegemony (Kagan, 2000; Peretti, 1999).

Before sketching the French conception of the Rule of Law, it is useful to summarise the German doctrine of the "Rechtsstaat". Two conceptions came to the fore. Von Mohl, in reaction to the development of the authoritarian State ("Obrigkeitsstaat"), worked out a liberal conception. He thought it was essential to limit the range of action of the State and to protect individual liberties. This opposed the rigid application of the idea of the superiority of law as voted by parliament. He questioned the fact that the contribution of citizens to lawmaking was reduced to their electing representatives to parliament. For F.J. Stahl, rules of law were less a means of limiting the powers of the State than an instrument to organise the State rationally by regulating relations between State and citizens. A substantial concept, based on the contents of rules of law, was opposed to a formalist conception, which accentuated formal juridical organisation of the State. In the formalist conception "Rechtsstaat" is a State in which public authorities are subordinate to law. Jurisdictions have the competence to eventually decide against organs of the State. In this formalist conception, "Selbstbindung" was prominent: as the State formulated laws it had also to restrain itself. In the "Polizeistaat", the State ruled arbitrarily. In the "Rechtsstaat" public authorities are committed to pre-existing and superior rules of law. The "Rechtsstaat" is a more emancipated State, in which rules of law are instrumental, but also restrict the power of public authorities, adhering themselves to the principles of written and unwritten rules of law. Public authorities must abstain from "contra legem" activities, act "secundum legem" and follow unwritten principles of law. In German doctrine, the substantial conception of the constitutional state was more prominent than in French doctrine, based on the formalist conception. Laband (1876) argued for the limitation of mutual rights and obligations between citizens. Public authorities with executive power had to apply general legislative rules in individual cases, and should not create rules. Public authorities organised their structure: a prerogative of executive power (Barret-Kriegel, 1992).

In the metaphysical approach of Kant the sole true law is rational natural law, the "Rechtsidee", preceding political activities. This was founded a priori upon Reason, creating a juridical order to realise freedom. Kant made the State a necessary condition of operationalising the "Rechtstsidee", laying some foundations for juridical positivism (Barreau, 1997). For Fichte and Hegel however, there was only law by and within the State. Fichte argued that there were juridical relations between human beings only within a community with a number of positive laws. According to Hegel the State was not subordinate to external norms or limits, because the State realised the unity and synthesis of general interest and private interests. Since 1848 and the rise of Bismarck public law had been the positive law of the State. Earlier the patrimonial conception had prevailed, but since then the State had been seen as a juridical person having subjective rights, the sole holder of sovereignty. The State was made an autonomous person, not coinciding with a governing elite or the collective unity of the nation. The State was seen as different from the Nation. This was in contradiction with French doctrine which argued that the State is the juridical personification of the Nation. In the German doctrine (Ihering, Laband, Jellinek) the State has "Herrschaft", dominant power to enforce its will over all other powers, and entitled to use violence. The logical result of this construction is that the State is seen as the sole source of law. Only the State can give the law its obligatory character, and so cannot be subordinate to any former or superior power. Even when admitting that law rules originate from the "Volksgeist", many German theoreticians saw the State as an existential condition of law. Because the State has the privilege of binding itself to self-made rules, it has a specific domain of rules (administrative law), different from that of private persons. For adherents of the State's self-binding character, law rules are binding for the State also. The State could not abolish the juridical order without blowing up the essence of its institution. The State would respect law rules, as that is in the interest of the State itself. By conforming itself to law, the State would further the acceptance of law by private persons. Social pressures, fed by a sense of justice, would promote this. Law rules are external rules for the State and intrinsic rules in a legal order characterised by coherence and stability.

A constitutional state normally exists when the rule of law prevails and when the State, in its relationship with citizens, is also bound by the rules of law. In a constitutional state, the State is allowed to use powers only when these are authorised within juridical order and procedures. Citizens have the right to defend their position against supposed abuses of the State before jurisdictions that are independent of government. This means that public authorities are allowed to act only on the basis of juridical norms, which frame their powers as competencies in a hierarchy of norms. Public authorities with executive powers are subordinate to the norms of law, while these norms form foundation, framework and limits of their range of action. Their law abiding behaviour has to be checked by jurisdictional control. Law is subordinate to a higher order legal ruling, a constitution, so specific jurisdiction is indispensable, constitutional jurisdiction. The United States have their own development with regard to the relationship between law and public authorities. The rules of due process of law, procedural due process and substantive due process were important developments. The idea that State and public authorities have to be subordinate to rules of law is as basic as it is simple, but the juridical order as created by the State, while the State itself must be subordinate to law, seems to be a rather artificial construction. The question is, how a circular or tautological reasoning can be prevented. French theoreticians argued against the idea of self-binding by supporting hetero-limitation of the State, placing the source of law outside the State. Kelsen (1927), with his pure formal theory of law, argued that State and law were identical.

German theorising about the "Rechtsstaat" was only expounded in France from 1911, by L. Duguit and A. Esmein. They argued that German doctrine was too specifically related to the political context in Germany to be useful for France, but this changed with Carré de Malberg, who succeeded German scholar Laband in the chair for public law at the Faculty of Law in Strasbourg after the First World War. Carré de Malberg constructed a creative synthesis of German and French components and formulated his theory of the constitutional state. French tradition had several elements that were also more or less present in German theorising, although in a different political context. The idea of a hierarchical juridical order had a long tradition in France. This was part of a passionate struggle against the almighty powers of absolute monarchy, and was intended to subordinate the arbitrary power of Kings to superior norms. Legists working for Kings elaborated the conception of absolute monarchy as superior and later as the sole source of law. The scope of monarchs was limited by customary laws, and fundamental laws of the kingdom, a kind of pre-constitutional constitution of the monarchy. These were not a constitution in the modern sense. The French Revolution gave France its constitution. In 1789, the monarch was replaced by the sovereign nation as the power to frame activities of all public authorities. In the intellectual atmosphere of imperial Germany the idea of power was central for the doctrine of the constitutional state. In republican France the accent was more upon legalism. It was the logical conclusion of the theory of nation-state and superiority of law, seen as the victory of the French Revolution. The theory of the constitutional state is contextually related to the political situation in the nation-state. The French Revolution created the idea that parliament (representative of the people) had to be the sole power in the nation-state. Rigid application of this idea in France, with the implication that judges only had to apply laws as voted in parliament, caused a creative impulse for the development of jurisprudence as a source of law. In France the German theory of the "Rechtsstaat" was criticised. It was seen as a doctrine which could be used to legitimise the German political regime. It was opposed to ideas about the Nation-State which were dear to the French Revolution. The German conception of self-binding of the State was criticised because it would prevent any real limitation of the State by law, so undermining any foundation of public law, but German doctrine influenced French theorising, albeit with a time-lag, especially with the work of Carré de Malberg (1920-1922) and his Strasbourg school.

In 1925, the German Supreme Court decided that its judges could declare a law invalid when it did not conform to the Constitution (Béguin, 1982). This "formalism" was unable to stop the Nazis with their brutish violence. On 27 February 1933, fundamental rights were suspended, and soon Hitler got full powers. The Hitler regime was characterised by a one party system, the Nazi Party, with its own police and armed forces; sub-ordination of the State to this Nazi Party; the near-monopoly of legislation for government; discriminatory racial laws (especially against Jews); complete reorganisation of jurisdiction; massive arbitrary executions and concentration camps. " In its last session the "Reichstag" decided that the "Führer" was not bound by existing laws ("Führer-staat"). After the Allied victory over this terrible regime, Federal Republic constituents wanted to proclaim "Rechtsstaat" principles. "Das Bonner Grundgesetz" (23 May 1949) of the "Bundesrepublik" proclaimed "Rechtsstaat" and fundamental rights directly applicable by State organs and tribunals (Karpen, 1988). Legislation was subordinated to constitutional order, executive power and jurisdictional tribunals were subject to law and justice. The juridical order of "Länder" had to conform to "sozialer Rechtsstaat" principles. The constitutional Fundamental Law determined that principles and fundamental rights could not be changed. All Germans had the right to resist anybody who tried to abolish the constitutional order if there was no other way to appeal. State organs had to ensure respect for constitutional order and "Rechtsstaatsprinzip". The "Bundesverfassungsgericht" could interpret the Fundamental Law and decide in the last resort on constitutional conflicts, including those of individuals complaining about a violation of fundamental rights on the basis of art. 93, paragraph 4a. Before taking a decision tribunals have to ask this Constitutional Court to decide whether a law is unconstitutional. This conception of constitutional state, inspired by the philosophy of natural law, making fundamental human rights supra-constitutional norms, was more extended than that before 1914. Supremacy of Constitution and law was valid for the whole of the German State. The "Bundesverfassungsgericht" even deduced non-written principles of law from the principle of the constitutional state (Karpen, 1988).

Inspiration for the control of constitutionality came from Austria and Germany. In France the ideas of Kelsen about a high constitutional court were propagated by Eisenmann (1928). In 1935 a parliamentary committee proposed to establish a supreme court with Austrian and American features. A crucial idea was to prevent superiority of legislative power by making the intervention of an independent, supreme jurisdiction possible, but parliament did not approve this idea. In 1946 the constituent Assembly refused citizens the right to invoke the "exception d'inconstitutionnalité" to be judged by "Cour de Cassation" (for laws) and "Conseil d'État" (for decrees and other decisions). Constituents of the Fourth Republic decided to establish a constitutional committee. Its competence did not involve the eventual annulment of laws declared unconstitutional. It could only investigate whether laws required a revision of the Constitution, if so the law had to be amended before promulgation (Duguit, c.s., 1952). The modesty of this change prepared the ground for the decisive transformation by the Fifth Republic. The Constitution of 4 October 1958 had the "Conseil Constitutionnel" (CC), a kind of watchdog for rules with which constituents wanted to restrict legislative power (Rials, 1989), and to protect the "pouvoir réglementaire" (competence to make rules with a general reach as laws) of executive power. The question of whether the 1789 Declaration of human rights was part of the Constitution and was obligatory remained unsolved in 1958.

The preamble to the 1958 Constitution said that the French were committed to the human rights as formulated in 1789 and 1946 (social and economic rights). On 16 July 1971 the "Conseil constitutionnel" (CC) took a decision recognising these fundamental rights as having constitutional value. Rivéro (1987, p.154) rightfully prophesied that the CC would come to this decision. Since 1974 sixty members of the National Assembly or Senate have been able to invoke the CC. Constitutional control as introduced in France in 1958 differed from that in the US. Disputed laws have to be presented to the CC before promulgation. In some decisions the CC has extended constitutional principles. "Principes fondamentaux reconnus par les lois de la République" (PFRLR) were thought to impose themselves upon the legislator as non-written principles with constitutional value. This provoked debate between adherents of the literal juridical text of the Constitution and those who emphasize the "esprit" of the Constitution. It is even said that the CC abuses the PFRLR and does what it likes with them, stretching interpretation of the constitutional text. It is seen as a risk that the "État de droit", founded upon these constitutional rulings, could be transformed into a government of judges (Turpin, 1992, p.96). Others point out that the CC has done a good job of reconciling controversies, so stabilising the basis of the French State (Colloque Paris, 1988; Lenoble, 1990). The president of the CC, M.R. Badinter suggested in "Le Monde" (3 mars 1989) giving all citizens the right to invoke an "exception d'inconstitutionnalité" against any law for which the CC had not had the opportunity to rule on its constitutionality, because public authorities or parliamentarians had not taken the initiative for it to do so. To prevent abuses of this instrument, Badinter proposed that "Cour de Cassation" and "Conseil d'État" could check the seriousness of this "saisine directe". President Mitterrand supported this proposition as progress for democracy, but the majority of the Senate opposed it. President of the Senate Poher said: the best guarantee for public liberties are properly functioning public institutions, especially Parliament, and nobody wants a government of judges (Le Monde, 26 May 1990).

The relationship between the power of judges and the sovereignty of the people (or parliament) is a problematical issue, not easily solved. In recent years the debate about this issue has continued. In all probability this will remain the case in France, Europe and elsewhere. Judges are not elected, and cannot be made responsible, as guardians of constitutionality, to parliament, the elected representative of the people (Favoreu, 1990; Pound, 1947). Judges could take decisions and so obstruct the democratic will of the people (or of their representatives) by declaring laws to be invalid. Is it possible to found the primacy of law upon the will of a few human beings, even when absolutely incorruptible? As Plato was already aware the pyramid of norms has to be complemented by a hierarchy of institutions. The constitutional judge has a place in the hierarchy subordinate to the constituent, but not subordinate to legislative or executive powers. The function of the judge, essential for a well-functioning constitutional state, is compatible with the democratic principle, especially in a "polyarchical system" (Morin, 1996, pp. 118/119). France did not always fully live up to its high standards of the constitutional state, but it has all the potential to do so. On 28 July 1999 France was condemned for torture by the European Court of Human Rights in Strasbourg: that was a shock. The constitutional judge participates in the creation of law. Constitutionalism of the West distanced itself from the ideas of the Greeks (Plato and Aristotle) and the conceptions of Locke and Montesquieu concerning individual liberty as the final objective of laws. As Dahl (1956) wrote, there is a narrow relationship between liberties, limitation of power by law and pluralism. Guarantees for a constitutional state and fundamental liberties are based on a moderate system of public authorities restrained by countervailing powers. A culture of well-balanced public authorities, with modesty and "esprit de service public" is a necessary condition for civilised countries.

## 10.6. Important French theoreticians of law

Originally, French scholars were cautious with regard to the German idea of "Rechtsstaat", seen as too much impregnated by political circumstances in Germany. Carré de Malberg tried to purge German doctrine before combining some elements of it with components of the French tradition. He argued that France had a system of "État légal", not of an "État de droit". Law not only limited the range of action for administration, but also determined the conditions of administration. The administrative function was interpreted as execution of laws. Carré de Malberg saw "État de droit" as the normative ideal for France with a legal State and nearly unlimited parliamentary sovereignty. The constitutional laws of 1875 did not subordinate legislative power to these constitutional laws. Parliament, supreme organ of the State and the sovereign, could at any moment change these constitutional laws without any real hindrance. Formal constitutional guarantees for individual rights had a marginal impact. For Hauriou (1929) this unlimited power of parliament was not compatible with the prevailing foundations of the juridical order. The hierarchy of norms and the supremacy of the constitutional laws were undermined. This almighty position of parliament was favoured by an idealised conception of law, legacy of Rousseau's ideals at the time of the Revolution. Law as holy and unquestionable act, which had to be accepted as such. Sovereignty of the Nation degenerated into the sovereignty of parliament, or sovereignty of (a majority of) parliamentarians. Carré de Malberg opposed this. Institutionalised power or public authority is not fully sovereign. Sovereignty implies that the Constitution includes rulings determining and limiting the power of the assemblies.

So the theory of the "État de droit" seemed to be a war machine against the system of the legal State (Chevallier, 1994). The privilege of inaccesibility in the prevailing conception of law was disputed. Introduction of controls on the constitutionality of laws was seen more as a necessary condition, but Duguit and others saw it as a development which risked government by judges (Mélanges Duverger, 1987). Although the idea of the "État de droit" had been penetrating more into French doctrine law was seen basically from the formal, not the material point of view. Doctrine held fast to this part of the conception of the legal State and the French conception of the State maintained its specific features. Carré de Malberg saw the juridical personality of the State as a condition of the modern system of the constitutional state. Sovereignty of the State was also seen as a crucial element of the "État de droit" conception. Legislative supremacy was made relative by the idea of sovereignty of the Nation. State and Nation were combined in the indissoluble Nation-State. Scholarly debate elaborated the relationship between this Nation-State and law. Duguit and Hauriou argued that the "Déclaration de l'homme et du citoyen" (1789) was superior to the Nation-State. The State has to be subordinate to an objective order, which it did not create. Based on "solidarité sociale" (Duguit) or the pre-existing "constitution sociale" (Hauriou). Carré de Malberg and Esmein argued that the sovereign State can only be limited by rulings it creates itself. For Carré de Malberg, observation had demonstrated that only the State has the power to provide rules with the special executive force, which characterises law, to regulate human behaviour. The State was seen as the sole creator of law, there was no source of positive law outside the State. This fundamental relation between State and law was deduced from integration of the sanction in the definition of law itself.

For Carré de Malberg, a rule of conduct can become a rule of law only in so far as it has a material sanction. Its implementation is guaranteed and its non-application repressed by intervention of the State. Because the State is the sole institution competent to compel implementation (monopoly of legitimised violence) the State is the sole source of positive law. There is no power, superior to the State, which can limit the State juridically. The State is the source of law, which limits its power. The whole juridical order is produced by the State and is based on the will of the State (its representatives). Carré de Malberg stressed the point that, in so far as the State and its order are juridical in nature, the power of the State is subordinate to law. Every power, existing by establishment and application of a juridical ruling, is by nature a power limited by law. The State communicates itself with juridical norms and so is a power regulated by law, functioning according to norms and conditions as fixed by the juridical order. This juridical order binds citizens and State, which by its essence and nature is limited by law. The scholar of the institution, Hauriou (Broderick, 1970), said that at the very moment that the State institutionalises itself as a lasting organisation the State is limited by juridical principles. The idea of self-limitation was criticised by French scholars, who saw law as a reality outside the State (Duguit, Michoud, Hauriou, Jèze, Berthélemy). As the idea of self-limitation of the State confirms the almighty character of the State, it would limit the power of the State formally. The juridical norm is thought to be born not from the State itself, but from a principle, which is anterior and superior: God, Nature, Man, Society. The juridical norm is based on an anterior order (divine, natural, human, or social). The State is only a secretary writing down what the law is, or at best an interpreter. Juridical norms exist independently of any intervention by the State, the source of law is outside the State itself.

After a period in which divine law fulfilled the function of basic source of law, natural law was seen as having this role. Proclamation in 1789 of the natural, inalienable and holy rights was placed in this perspective. The French Declaration of Human Rights, with its universalistic pretensions, was made a categorical imperative for all powers and public authorities. Later, after the beginning of the 20th century, the position of natural law was undermined, inter alia by the development of sociology. More and more the accent was placed on objective law. The idea of invariable norms based upon nature was thought to be unsatisfactory and not compatible with social dynamics. Social consciousness was put forward as the true source of juridical obligations. Duguit (1927/1930) elaborated the most advanced conception that genuine law is present already, and only has to be made explicit. Before building up his conception, Duguit had drastically deconstructed the German theory of self-limitation of the State. He criticised the notion of sovereignty as non-existent. The sole existing reality, in his view, is belief in sovereignty, and Duguit criticised this as preventing the construction of public law as it should be. Sovereignty gives the State "imperium", the competence to give orders, which can be implemented by the use of force, and control over the process of creating law. According to Duguit, there could only be public law if the State is bound by juridical norms. In Duguit's view the idea that the State disposes of public power as "droit subjectif" (property right) is based on a double fiction, that of the "droit subjectif" and that of "personnalité morale" (corporate capacity), as collective corporations don't have a juridical existence independent of their constituent elements. The State is for Duguit only an empty shell, an abstraction to legitimise the use of violence by physical governing persons. Imputing acts to the State is only a disguise for the individual will of governing functionaries. Their use of powers has to be limited by law.

The realistic conception of Duguit was intended to eliminate all metaphysical dimensions which gave a false idea of the power of the State. Powers and competencies of governing functionaries have their sole base and limits in objective law, which derives its existence from social reality. The conscience of human beings forming a social group or society is according to Duguit the creative source of law. Creation of law takes place when the mass in society understands that a reaction against those who violate the rules can be organised socially. At this very moment, the social norm, based upon solidarity and interdependence, becomes a juridical norm. Law is not a creation of the State as expression of its superiority, but a social fact. Duguit elaborated the idea that this social fact was formed spontaneously in the minds of the people, influenced by two feelings. "Sociabilité", forming the conviction that all attacks against social solidarity have to be sanctioned, and "Justice", on the basis of which all should be treated equally in mutual relations and relations with the group. This social consciousness, that rules of law are needed for social solidarity and that it is just that these are sanctioned, make juridical rules binding for all objectively, independent of State intervention. Governing functionaries have an important role in the production of juridical norms. They deduce, from normative rules of law as existing in social consciousness, juridical norms, which make the adequate application of law possible. These law rules do not have binding force because they are issued by the State, but because they are based on objective law.

Another concept was elaborated by Hauriou (1929), rejecting the idea of objectivist systems, in which the role of the subjective will in creating law was practically eliminated. Hauriou saw the State as a responsible continuous corporation with public power. One does not obey governing functionaries as persons, but only in their capacity and role as representatives of the State. Their powers and competencies are legitimate, as these are exercised on behalf of this abstract institution, incarnation of the unity of the social group and determining the whole of authority relations. In Hauriou's view the State, as with every institution, is based on customary consensus. The Nation needs an enforcing power. This power cannot survive for long without the permanent adherence of members of society. The principle of political and juridical limitation of the State was part of this conception. Citizens never give all their liberties into the hands of public authorities. When social consensus about the role of the State has disappeared, the State is illegitimate, so the State cannot be the exclusive source of law. The State forms a large part of law (internal, disciplinary law), but there is law outside the reach of the State, coming from "sociabilité humaine". For Hauricu the German idea of self-limitation of the State only takes account of internal, disciplinary law of the State. Next to this subjective self-limitation there is objective self-limitation, created by the institutionalisation and operationalised in the concept of the "service public". Hauriou's institution theory is based on the notion of institution as organisation subdued to an idea. Through institutionalisation, executive power takes its place in a structured organisation, submitting itself to the objective by self-limitation.

Other theoreticians also accentuated that rules of law are in fact an expression of pre-existing normative facts, which have to be established, either by previously developed technical procedures (formal positive law), or by direct and immediate intuition (intuitive positive law). Absorbing the ideas of others, G. Burdeau (1949) put forward that the State is limited by law in so far as its power is juridically conditioned by the Idea of Law which legitimises it. As is any institution, the State is an enterprise to serve an idea. Its formation is based upon a certain image of the collective future, and the will to form a community with others. The Idea of Law translates the representation of the desired order, formed within the context of a whole of rules destined to be applied, so the State is not the foundation of law. The State does not limit itself, it is born limited. Governing functionaries are not allowed to act against this Idea of Law, which is the frame of reference for the social group. These conceptions, seeing law as an external reality for the State, have their appeal, but are not satisfactory. Pisier (1972) argued that Duguit did not analyse conditions in which social norms are generated, or processes in which these are transformed into juridical norms. For Duguit, these were spontaneous phenomena; their structure was not elaborated. The social consciousness on which he pretended to build juridical norms, was only an aspect of individual consciousness. Subjection of the State to law is more appearance than reality. Acts of governing functionaries would have to be verified for conformity with objective law. Duguit did not accept this effect which would provoke anarchy. Obedience to acts of public authority is the normal procedure as they are assumed to be in conformity with objective law (presumption of correctness). Only a posteriori acts of public authorities can be questioned. It is a paradox that theories of hetero-limitation of the State ultimately reinforce the State by giving it new legitimacy. French doctrine could not escape the problem of limiting the State by law. Subjection of State organs to a hierarchical order contributes to a State, ruled by law.

The crucial relationship between State and law continues to be a difficult one. With his purely formal theory, German theoretician Kelsen (1927), identifying juridical order and "Rechtsstaat", placed this discussion on a historical summit. He and the Austrian Adolf Merkl ("Allgemeines Verwaltungsrecht", 1927) developed the conception of the constitutional state as hierarchical juridical order. Each juridical norm, being simultaneously application of a superior norm and creation of a subordinate norm, derives its validity from a hierarchically superior norm. This interconnected cascade of norms has a supreme positive norm, defining conditions for the production of norms, the Constitution. In the course of time, the juridical order of the State replaced the pre-existing juridical order(s), and became the sole juridical frame of reference within a specific territory. The State as sole legitimate juridical order is thought to have a monopoly. All juridical norms are considered to emanate directly or indirectly from the State and have to observe its conditions. The production process and implementation of juridical norms are rationalised by charging specialised organs with these tasks. The State is the total juridical order; its juridical norms are the sole valid law. This conceptual approach is at odds with more pluralist conceptions. The viewpoint of Romano (1946) is that there are as many juridical orders as there are institutions. For Gurvitch (1932) there is a pluralism of different, independent juridical orders limiting each other, co-operating on an equal footing. For Kelsen international law is co-ordination law, deriving its forcing character from the will of States and having a deficiency in coercion, although there are sanctions. This international law, merely valid for States recognising it, is only a part of the juridical order of a State, having its primacy within its territory. Kelsen saw international law as law which is superior with regard to the laws of the States (primacy of international law). For Kelsen, State and law form the same coercive order. A distinctive feature of law is that it can use force when its prescriptions are not followed up. The State has a specific character in that organs and persons acting on behalf of the State have competencies and are legitimised to use force. For Kelsen law is the same order of force as the State, which has to be thought of as juridical order. The power of the State is the efficacy of the juridical order. The State is seen as personification of the juridical order to which activities of its functionaries are imputed.

For Kelsen, the contents of juridical norms was not the most important issue, but the existence of a formal juridical order with an efficient force to guarantee implementation of norms. When the validity of the whole juridical order depends on the supreme norm as laid down in the Constitution the question is on what foundations is this Constitution built? The supreme norm can only be a positive norm. It has to be brought to the juridical order by an extra-juridical authority, a will external to this juridical order. This was brought to the fore by Carl Schmitt (1922), who distinguished between normal and exceptional situations. The authority competent to decide, if there is an exceptional situation, on the basis of its right to self-preservation can decide that the normal situation of the juridical order is suspended. The State, having at its disposal sovereignty, is then liberated from normative obligations, and can decide absolutely. So the juridical order does not base itself on a superior norm, but on a political will, a constituent power which can found the validity of the Constitution (Schmitt, 1927). The failure of the theory of the "Rechtsstaat", according to the "decisionist" conception of Schmitt, is that it reduced the State by stressing juridical guarantees while disregarding its political component, which is not reducible to law. This idea can also be found in the work of the Italian theoretician Evola (Boutin, 1992). When one takes this approach as premise, the whole juridical order becomes a product of contingent decisionmaking by public authorities that dispose of power. The supreme norm is then only the will of those who have political power. Kelsen wanted to build foundations for a science of law. He tried to break the vicious circle by postulating a basic principle, a "Grundnorm", as hypothesis to found the validity of the positive juridical order, but it is not convincing epistemologically to base the validity of the juridical order upon a hypothetical norm only.

There are several fundamental objections to be made with regard to Kelsen's formalist conception. It has the merit of having made the indissoluble coherence of State (a juridical entity governed by law) and law (founded and supported by the State) explicit, but it does not seem to be a valuable exercise to reduce the State to law or juridical order. He neglected the social and political dynamics of society, which are decisive for the State. The juridical order is only one of the elements of the State. Issuing juridical norms is important, but the State is characterised especially by its legitimate use of force to implement its norms in practice. Max Weber stressed the monopoly of legitimate force as the most prominent distinguishing feature of the State. Other than Kelsen seems to suggest, law cannot be reduced to the State, nor the State to law. In spite of its totalising character and its legitimate monopoly of force, the State can never encompass all juridical phenomena. A conception suggesting this forgets that social life is complex, while the diversity of law is overwhelming. Many juridical norms function in society without the mediation of the State. Kelsen argued that in his conception every State is a constitutional State. He recognised that the constitutional State is combined with material postulates such as democracy and legal security. Government administration and jurisdiction are regulated by laws. Governing actors are responsible for their acts. Jurisdictions can judge independently, and rights to liberty are guaranteed for citizens. Juridical positivism tends to obscure the fact that the conception of the Constitutional State is indissolubly interconnected with a wide collection of values, related to history and culture.

## 10.7. Ongoing debate about the state

Nobody has ever seen the State. From an empiricist point of view one might conclude that it is useless to digress on this seemingly unreal phenomenon. Nevertheless, great powers are imputed to the State. The role of the State is generally seen as crucial for life in society on the basis of law and order. There are concrete phenomena that refer to the State. We observe human beings playing a role in government, public services, and territorial boundaries for the scope of competencies for national governments. Legal rules are made by persons who, on the basis of their competencies within a specific State, act in the name of the people (legislation). Rules of law are maintained by public organisations acting in the name of the State and/or the law (police). Specific organs and persons have competencies in the field of interpreting the law and deciding conflicts (jurisdiction). A common conception is that jurisdiction is part of the political system in a State, as with Duverger (1996). One would not normally see the jurisdictional system as part of the political system. Political science literature does not generally digress on the organisation and functioning of jurisdictional instances. Duverger does. Rightly so, as jurisdiction is one of the most important tasks of public authorities, but the activities of judges ought not to be seen as political activities, on the contrary. It is useful to differentiate between politics and public management as management by public authorities. It all depends upon the definition of politics. When one uses an all-encompassing definition of politics as power-laden relations, political phenomena become nearly synonymous with social phenomena. Then political science would encompass social science and vice versa, as might be the conclusion of the work of Burdeau (1986). Burdeau does however differentiate between State and politics. There is a huge body of literature about the State, so it is impossible to give a complete sketch, but it is useful to elaborate on some parts of this bewildering richness of literature. Especially when French conceptualisation, narrowly related to universal ideas about Public Management of Society, is concerned (Badie/Birnbaum, 1982). The vague concept State was only thought to be of interest to jurists, or was dressed in all kinds of a-historical abstractions. Authors working in the social sciences, after neglecting historical dimensions, rediscovered the crucial relevance of historical aspects.

Karl Marx had the idea that the economic structure of society (infrastructure) is the basis for the juridical and political suprastructure. Marx (1948), criticising the idealist State conception of Hegel, had a materialist conception of the State. For him the State, in concrete historical circumstances, had been denatured as an instrument of exploitation for the capitalist class who owned the means of production. The State became a parasitical outgrowth. Instead of functioning as an instrument to make the State autonomous and independent from particularist interests, bureaucracy became a parasitical phenomenon. The original system for making use of the advantages of a functional division of labour, and to have an organisation to pursue the general interests of society, was being misused by a capitalist clique. The exploited proletarian class of workers and have-nots should make revolution to bring the means of production into the hands of the proletariat. Marx's conception of the State is more sophisticated than is commonly understood, as shown by Maguire (1978). Friedrich Engels (1966) argued that the State would eventually become redundant and could be placed in a museum of antiquities. Government by persons would be replaced by an administration of things (Engels, 1973). Communists in Russia, (mis)using the conception of Marx, took power in a violent revolution (1917) in the name of the proletariat. The brutish Soviet system of State-capitalism in the hands of one dictatorial communist party collapsed with the Fall of the Berlin Wall (1989).

Durkheim (1858-1917) was one of the pioneers of division of labour (Durkheim, 1960). In his evolutionary view of societies, division of labour necessarily induces the appearance of organisations of public authorities. The more societies develop in a historical process, the more the State must develop. For Durkheim, this was due to an ongoing process of functional differentiation. When one compares public authorities in modern States with those of the Middle Ages, the historical process of a continually growing system of public authorities is evident. Perhaps there is no better-established historical law than this (Durkheim, 1975, p.170). He claimed that the essential function of the State (a sui generis group of functionaries bound by authority and hierarchy) is to think. Its role is not to express the unreflected thoughts of the masses, but to add a sophisticated rationality, which is different (Durkheim, 1950, pp. 111-113). For Durkheim, individuals will be more respected in a strong State. The State is seen as an institution for the emancipation of citizens. In a developed society, the State is a specific organ of society, above all kinds of castes, classes and coteries. Writings of Marx and Durkheim about the State phenomenon are interesting, but Max Weber, accentuating the specificity of the State, was far ahead.

Weber (1971), herald of rationality in Western civilisation, distinguished three types of legitimate domination: charismatic, traditional and rational. He elaborated his typologies on the basis of broad and systematic historical analyses of the development of societies. Weber was a pioneering historical social scientist. His analyses of legitimacy, domination, subordination, authority, power and administration or bureaucracy are relevant. For Weber, it was evident that there is an ongoing process of growing rationalisation, with the legal form of legitimate domination by the State (working for the general interests of society) as apex. Not only in the sphere of the State, but in all societal domains (business, church, army, social organisations, etc.), Weber showed ongoing progression of bureaucracy. Modern States depended increasingly on bureaucratic organisation (Gerth/Wright Mills, 1958). Charismatic leadership is also a factor in contemporary democracies. More than Weber could foresee, the working of the State is made dependent on the charisma of elected, party-political politicians, who need media-charisma to gain and maintain popularity (regular polls). Weber saw the State as a political enterprise with an institutional character, successfully claiming the monopoly of legitimate physical coercion for the implementation of its rulings. For him, legitimate violence and bureaucracy are the two crucial instruments of public management, making the legitimate, rational and just action of public authorities possible. In a process of differentiation and institutionalising the State develops as a relatively independent institution. Weber's view on the pathologies of bureaucracy is interesting. He criticised prefects in France for being political functionaries. Since Bismarck, Germany had a kind of fusion between the roles of functionaries and politicians. Transforming of public functionaries into party-political partisans was for Weber (1959, p.129) an aberration from adequate functional differentiation.

At the beginning of the 20th century political sociology was not interested in the State (Badie/Birnbaum, 1982, p.49). Authors in the field of political sociology followed Weber, above all with regard to bureaucracy and political parties. In the inter-war period up to the fifties, Anglo-Saxon work about political phenomena was influenced by group theory (from Bentley to Truman). The State was nothing more than a group along with other groups, without any specific prerogative. Although since the studies of David Easton, the State had been seen as the centre of the political system, political systems theory became popular, trying to detach political science from its dominant status as science of the State. The State was not an issue in political science research (Birnbaum, 1975; Poggi, 1978), but since the sixties, the State in a sense had been partially rediscovered as Welfare State, or as synonym for bureaucracy (rational structure, neutral). Badie/Birnbaum (1982, pp. 51-86) elaborated a useful overview of the new approach to the State in social science. The sociological model built its analysis upon the progressive loosening of public authority from private social relations. The elements which had traditionally characterised the State, were reintroduced. Four processes, crucial in functionalist sociology, were related to the State phenomenon: progressive differentiation of social structures; their growing autonomy; their universalisation and the institutionalisation of procedures conditioning realisation of State activities. The concept of differentiation affecting all parts of society, as developed in sociological functionalism, is relevant for the State. Structures of public authority are in a process of division of labour, becoming ever more detached from other social structures. After neglecting the State, Parsons (1960) gave the State prominence in his conception. Parsons (1973) claimed that modern society requires strong government, not a reduced role of the State. Recognising the Welfare State as reality, Parsons elaborated a sociological Keynesianism (Gouldner, 1970). Growth of bureaucracy, advance of the legal system, market economy and democratic associations are features of modern societies: evolutionary universals (Parsons, 1964).

Parsons (1973) analysed and interpreted historical processes with regard to the development of the State. With a deterministic, cybernetic model, he saw differentiation of social systems as conditioned by necessities to mobilise economic resources. This process is controlled and made possible by capacities of the cultural system to realise and institutionalise the transformation. For Parsons, development of the State in Western Europe was possible, because of the cultural context, which was favourable for this crucial innovation. He saw Christianity as a cultural code, which made differentiation of the State, its autonomy and empowerment possible. As Weber before him, he saw the Protestant Reformation as a decisive factor in contributing to autonomy of the political system. The State is seen as the most complete part of the political system: State of the Rule of Law, and Democratic State, institutionalising a new consensus. Elites losing power changed strategies and replaced their resistance to the State with taking control of the State. Several authors pointed out the amazing difference between the U.S. and Great Britain (no strong State) on the one side, and France with its well-developed centralisation of public authority on the other. In France the division of labour with regard to public authority structures had developed in confrontation with a relatively strong but divided opposition of conflicting elites (feudal system). According to Elias (1975) the State in Renaissance France was above all a coalition of feudal lords, an association of private interests. In Great Britain the political centre could not build up a strong position because of a relatively united front of elites. This proves that making public authorities autonomous is more a response to historical circumstances than to general principles of modernisation (Badie/Birnbaum, 1982, p.63).

The State could not have a prominent position despite all kinds of opposition without adequate instruments. The State was a function of the institutional instruments necessary to realise its activities: army, judiciary system, civil bureaucracy (Tilly, 1975). A crucial dimension of public authorities is their universalist orientation, they have to function for all citizens in an egalitarian way: no privileges, particularism or partisan favouritism. The State organises a monopoly of public authority, guaranteeing equal rights for all. This process of universalisation can be considered on the basis of the paradigm of Hirschman (1970). In his view, people in a Nation-State have a choice between defection (emigration), protest and loyalty. When a State within a specific territory realises its monopoly of public authority, it is confronting inhabitants with an inevitable yes or no decision. Transformation of the feudal system into the more modern systems of public authority takes place when the

State is coercing its new, universalist order. This kind of domination has to earn its legitimacy. Invention of the concepts of citizen and nationality were crucial to create a basis for legitimacy. By creating and developing the idea of citizens as nationals, it was possible to mobilise feelings of community and togetherness, which were formerly bound to traditional circles (families, classes, and coteries). A process of institutionalising of the social-political process furthered development of the State. With its unique instruments (monopoly of legitimised use of violence; law; civil bureaucracy) the State is enabled to have a central position in the arena of social and political conflicts. Social actors have to take a position with regard to the State with its monopoly of public authority. Social demands can be regulated (Eisenstadt, 1973). For Huntington (1968) the more a society is differentiated the more it depends on institutions (adaptability, complexity, autonomy, and coherence).

It seems appropriate to position the development of the State concept in a historical perspective, especially because, in contemporary society, a predominant movement is preaching the gospel of globalisation, market forces and worldwide informatics as the sole relevant phenomenon (Giddens, 1999). It is by no means paradise when corporations rule the world (Korten, 1995). Often globalisation is preached with the implication that historical knowledge has become useless, due to totally different circumstances nowadays (Held et al., 1999). That is a real trap for many. In contemporary and future society public authorities will have a prominent position, at least in the role of universal legatee of unresolved societal problems. There is a fundamental path-dependence of the way public authorities are functioning, also in contemporary societies. There are several concepts of the State. For Lowie (1927) and others, in all societies, even in the most primitive communities, there was already the germ of a State The term State is used to denote a form of public authority. This is often the case in evolutionary conceptions of the State. The analysis of Eisenstadt (1963) of traditional empires uses an evolutionary perspective, in between traditional societies and modern States. In Roman times not all inhabitants were recognised as citizens with rights (Nicolet, 1976). The position of families was strong in the "res publica". In Antiquity there was mostly no differentiation between the political and religious domains (Fustel de Coulanges, 1879). In France autonomy of the political domain had to be fought for against the overpowering position of the Church. In Islamic societies there seemed to be no differentiation at all between political and religious domains (Arnold, 1924; Holt, c.s., 1970; Rosenthal, 1958). Wallerstein (1974) initially asserted that the beginning of the State as a more mature form of public authority more or less coincided with the development of capitalism, but he agreed with Perroy et al. (1955) who asserted that the State got its form in the 13th century. Another aspect of the State is its capacity to organise enough financial means for military tasks and the build-up of civil bureaucracy.

Nef (1967) reported that the yearly income of the relatively strong State in France in the first half of the 17th century was 80 million "livres tournois", and only 9 million in Great Britain in the same period. The French State is known for its early activities of intervention in the economy before, during and after Colbert (Cole, 1939). The relatively strong State in France, according to Badie/Birnbaum (1982, p.129), provoked a powerful party-political socialism. It was thought that a proletarian victory could be more successfully achieved against the powerful capitalist State (politics) than in confrontation with capitalist enterprises (corporatism). There were two basic strategies in the socialist movement: "Guesdistes" preferred an almighty political party (Willard, 1965), revolutionary syndicalists chose for the general political strike to force their claims (Badie, 1976; Brecy, 1966). When the general strike did not have the desired effect, the French workers' movement organised itself on the basis of partisan party-politics. Syndicates were made dependent on political parties (Adam/ Reynaud, 1978). French syndicalism could follow the example of Germany, where there was a political organisation of workers around a political party earlier, and the syndicalist organisation was made subsidiary to the parliamentary game (Perrot/Kriegel, 1966). In Great Britain, with a relatively less strong State structure, the workers' movement was more syndicalist than political, more corporatist than revolutionary. The workers' party was an extension of the trade unions (Pelling, 1963; Robertson/Thomas, 1968). National cultures, environments and circumstances created different forms of syndicalism (Abendroth, 1967; Crouch/Pizzorno, 1978).

The modern State (legal, secular, democratic), as developed in Western Europe, is seen as a universal model, to be exported all over the world (Bendix, 1964; Pye, 1967). Development of the State in the West European context, according to Badie/Birnbaum (1982, p.104), is heavily indebted to the specific West European cultural code, with an impact from the Christian religion, Roman Law and Greek philosophy. The West European State is considered as a model, which can be generalised as the modern State in the framework of modernisation (Western bias), but as a consequence of the dominant cultural code in most Islamic societies, adaptations to modern times could not fully follow the Western code (Binder, 1964). Many so-called developing countries in the Third World have their own path-dependence, showing a mixture of imported Western institutionalising and their own culturally and historically determined customs and institutions (Almond/ Powell, 1966; Badie, 1978, 1992; Geertz, 1963; Shils, 1960). Simply copying the Western State model as rationalistic formula in other (African, Asian, South American) cultures will not do. Their specific cultural, historical and traditional contexts have to be reckoned with.

For a number of authors in the 19th century "science de la politique" was more or less the same as "science de l'État". Even in the fifties M. Prélot defined "science politique" as "science de l'État". A number of notions are used in political science and social sciences which cannot be understood adequately without the underlying concept of the State: sovereignty, organ, representation etc. Troper (1994) shows that a juridical theory of the State makes sense. A prominent representative of the "Allgemeine Staatslehre", H. Kelsen (1927), had the thesis that the State coincides with the juridical order. He was criticised for this thesis, but each sociological concept of the State presupposes a juridical concept, the juridical order. It is possible to analyse objects sociologically which are juridically defined. Kelsen argued that it was not possible to conceive simultaneously a State as creator of law and as amenable to the law. Others "solved" this dilemma with their theory of the self-limitation of the State. Later the problem was solved by recognising, that the State is born juridically limited. Troper (1994, p.159): "It is not the State which defines the law, but the law, the juridical form, which definines and constitutes the State." G. Jellinek said that the State can be analysed from the point of view of the social sciences, and from that of juridical science. As a science defines its object, methodological dualism would mean that one is not examining the same object from different scopes (as Jellinek thought), but two different objects. It was R. Carré de Malberg (1920), familiar with the "Allgemeine Staatslehre", who laid the foundation of the general theory of the State in France. He is auctor intellectualis for the majority of the constitutive concepts of the State as used for the Fifth Republic.

There are fundamental differences between the German conception, in which the State is seen as juridically separate from the Nation, and the French conception of "Nation-État". Carré de Malberg criticised the method of authors writing about French public law, while taking the general theory of the State as the preliminary foundation for public law He accentuated that the general theory of the State was a consequence of the analysis of (possibly implicit) principles in prevailing institutions of public law. So a relation was realised between the general theory of the State on the basis of the French positive law, and the principles of the French Revolution. Carré de Malberg (1920, I, p.13) said that German ideas about the State were "contradicted by the principle of national sovereignty as proclaimed by the French Revolution. By proclaiming that sovereignty, the characteristic power of the State, resides essentially in the Nation, the French Revolution implicitly established as the basis of French law that the competencies and rights, of which the French State is the subject, are fundamentally competencies and rights of the Nation itself. So the French State is not a juridical subject, opposed to the Nation... One has to recognise that there is identity between State and Nation." To counter the concepts of German authors, defining the law by some material character, he brought "the true notion of law according to the French positive law" to the fore as a formal notion. The French Revolution was for Carré de Malberg what Roman law was for the German Pandectists, for whom the science of law was the science of Roman law. While French revolutionaries localised the centre of public authority in legislative power composed of elected representatives, Carré de Malberg preferred the German concept of organ to that of representation. This theory of organ tried to answer questions like: in what quality persons exercise the power of the State; and where does this quality come from?

Mostly one sees the State as national community, which in its history became a national unity. The organisation directing the State has the right to issue rules of law and to use violence to force the implementation of law. Often the State is conceived as State apparatus. In the French history of ideas the State was conceptualised in a philosophical-juridical, theoretical, if not transcendental way: the myth of the State. In reaction to this approach, L. Duguit (1927) developed the sociological idea that the State is nothing more than a differentiation between governors (having political power, power to force irresistibly) and governed, based upon a "fact of social solidarity". For Carré de Malberg (1920) the State (union of all members) is established as a juridical order by a constitution, ending previous disorder. M. Hauriou (1929) characterised the State ("community of interests") as the outstanding institution and the social cohesion of the group was accentuated. For the sake of solidarity, "volonté générale" has predominance politically, and general interest juridically. The State, organised to satisfy collective needs and interests, is everybody's business in a democracy. It has to work on the basis of collective adhesion. It is generally accepted that there are three basic conditions which have to be fulfilled in a State: a territory which determines the reach of its competencies, a population inhabiting this territory and thus forming a nation, and a political-juridical organisation to manage this nation. An essential characteristic of the State is that it forms a collectivity, which cannot be reduced to another collectivity. Two crucial State criteria are the juridical personality of the State, and the sovereignty of the State.

The State as institution is juridically a corporation, detached from governors. It becomes complicated when the notions of "État" and "pouvoir politique" are differentiated in French conceptualisation. Pactet (1994, p.45): "The progress marking the evolution of societies consisted in institutionalisation of the 'pouvoir politique'. This loosened the bond between this 'pouvoir politique" and the people in command. Governors receive competencies from the State, exercising their competencies in the name of the State. Competence is related to their office, not to their own being. The State, symbol of the national community and holder of 'pouvoir politique' (governors are provisional depositories and executing agents) is necessarily a corporate body of public law." In the mainstream literature of constitutional law, differentiation between governors and governed is mostly accentuated, while the position of public functionaries is neglected or marginalised. They are thought to be charged with administration or execution. It has to be emphasized that public functionaries have a specific function and role, directly derived from their position as representative of public authority, as with governors. Conceptualisation about institutionalisation has not been reflected fully when governors are seen as the sole responsible individuals with delegated State power. In the process of institutionalisation it is crucial to discern that public functionaries are not pure executors of the will of (party-)political elected subjects.

Public functionaries have an authentic responsibility, derived directly (and not indirectly via politicians) from the State, within constraints of law and instructions of political and/or bureaucratic masters. This institutionalising of public functionaries on the basis of their function ("ex officio") has important consequences. Public functionaries have a strong position in ensuring that public authorities are functioning in accordance with laws and the Rule of Law. This applies also when political masters are trying to force them to do things in conformity with party-political priorities, but against the law. Public functionaries have an important role in pluralist democracies. They have a specific responsibility of their own. It is part of their specific responsibility that they denounce illegal practices, malpractice, fraud and other wrong phenomena, counter to the principles of democracy and the Rule of Law. Public functionaries who do this as "bellringers" or "whistleblowers" to alert public authorities and public opinion, should get legal protection. The assertion of Pactet (1994, p.20) and others that democratic theory only knows governors and governed is incorrect.

While in Anglo-American texts, the "pars-pro-toto" notion of government is often used to denote public authorities, in French literature the notion "pouvoir politique" is generally customary. Pactet (1994, p.18): " 'pouvoir politique' might be defined as the power of prevision, impulsion, decision and co-ordination which belongs to the leading apparatus of the country, in principle of the State. This means, in a broad view, the governors who are able to determine and manage national politics, with all that this implies in the internal and the international order." It is confusing that Pactet adds: ".. in totalitarian regimes the 'pouvoir politique' resides more in the leading structures of the sole political party than in those of the State apparatus." There is a world of difference between public authorities, functioning in a pluralist democracy under the Rule of Law, and the puppet organs in totalitarian, so-called people's democracies, which are totally dependent on one political party. The relationship between State, public authorities and law is described in a complicated jargon by Pactet (1994, pp. 38-39): "The important thing is that power, incarnated in the State, and endowed with a constitution, is made juridical, and transformed from power of fact into power of law..One cannot dissociate State and political power, being its brain." A problem with the notion "pouvoir politique" is that the work of all public functionaries, realising implementation of public policies, is seen as an a-political, neutral, anonymous machinery, which can be used arbitrarily by politicians. Mostly public functionaries are covered by in the collective noun administration, interpreted as a-political, neutral execution.

But as Caiden (Asmerom/Reis, 1996, pp. 20-44) demonstrated, because of the reality of bureaucratic power, there is a problem with neutrality. The conclusion might be that the activities of public functionaries, because of the power-laden relations in their work, have to be analysed only by political science. This would overstretch and misinterpret the work of public functionaries as political, while the work of most public functionaries is generally better qualified as professionally doing the work of public authorities. This is where the handicap of the notion "pouvoir politique" to denote public authorities generally comes to the fore. Without denying that public functionaries are partly involved in (party-)political activities, it is more reasonable to use the term public management instead of "pouvoir politique" to denote the work of public authorities which cannot be reduced to the framework of the political system. Pactet (1994, p.36) uses "institutions politiques" for organs charged with the execution of "pouvoir politique" and application of its norms. Others, like F. Dreyfus and F. d'Arcy (1989) accentuate the difference between "institutions politiques" and "institutions administratives". It is a nuisance that the term "pouvoir politique" accentuates the political power dimension, neglecting other important dimensions and differentiating public authorities from other societal actors only by its (partly wrongly denoted) political character. This term runs the risk of underrating the unique character of public authorities as public authorities.

Of course, there are multi-varied relations between public authorities and society, itself composed of different social groups (classes; professions; regions; political, ethnic and religious groups). It is obvious therefore that many (ideological, economic, psychological, historical, international) factors have their impact upon these relations. Without taking these relations for granted, it is useful to treat the relation between public authorities, law and institutions first. Public authorities play an important role in the process of law creation and the build-up of institutions. The contemporary State is the most elaborate form of social organisation, with an intricate relation with law. Rules of law or juridical norms are general, obligatory rules, issued by recognised, official, public authorities, eventually sanctioned indirectly by courts of justice or directly by executive organs authorised for this. Positive law, as law issued and sanctioned by recognised public authorities, is set against natural law. Natural law is the idealistic collection of rules which are considered to be derived from nature by reason, as propagated by natural law school authors. Law about the State and other public collectivities, public law, has in France a more prominent and specific character than in Anglo-American law systems. French public law is differentiated from civil law (conflict resolution about private interests): "On the one hand public law is dominated by the search for the general interest, constituting the necessary and exclusive objective of the State and other public organisations, on the other hand public law is a law of inequality, because the general interest has to override private interests. State and other public organisations have specific juridical competencies, enabling them to make their will prevail over that of private persons. Private law is law of equality." (Pactet, 1994, p.35). But there has been a convergence of public and civil law during the last decades.

### 10.8. The principle of sovereignty

To qualify the State juridically, it is not enough to consider the State as a corporation, because there are other corporate bodies in the sphere of public law (regions, departments, municipalities, public corporations) and civil law. The decisive criterion of the State is seen in its sovereignty. According to the doctrine about the sovereignty of the State, the State is the sole institution with final competencies within its territory (but subordinated to the rules of international law). The concept of sovereignty as decisive criterion of the State is criticised though, because the State, limited by international public law, is not sovereign absolutely. Pactet (1994, p.47) wrote that each State which, with respect for rules of international law, disposes of the management of its external and internal policies, can be qualified as sovereign. This is thought to imply proclamation of juridical norms. The State has a commanding power within its territory with regard to its nationals. This power implies competence to limit itself, and even transfer the exercise of its competencies partly to an external organ. Some authors defend that the State determines its own competencies and fundamental rules as laid down in the constitution, and that the State, with its monopoly of legitimate use of armed forces, has armed forces or police to force implementation of laws. The State is considered to found and delimit the national juridical order. As G. Jellinek said, the State is the sole institution with "Kompetenz-Kompetenz", the competence to determine competencies of all other organs within its territory. State sovereignty is defined as power of the law, founding the national juridical order and having unconditional and supreme powers. In absolutist doctrines of State sovereignty there are no limits to the absolute sovereignty of the State. These doctrines are unsatisfactory. Constructions of self-limitation are rather artificial. It is reasonable to see the State as being born limited by law. In democratic conceptions, the State has the common good of the people as final objective. State sovereignty is seen as relative: the State, sovereign in the context of law, is subject to (international and national) law.

It seems useful, to deal more extensively with the principle of sovereignty, as sovereignty is seen as the decisive criterion of the State. Not for nothing did Werner/De Wilde (2001), stressing that sovereignty seems to be rather unimportant when the state's ability to rule and its external freedom are not at stake, write about the endurance of sovereignty. From the later part of the Middle Ages on, the concept of sovereignty was used to legitimise the power of princes with regard to Pope, Emperor and higher nobility, so it could play a crucial role when the medieval Respublica Christiana broke down (Jackson, 1999). Since the 16th century, public management has organised itself, in a number of European countries, around the principle of sovereignty. On the basis of a profane foundation as organised in the historical State. After terrible religious wars and the Thirty Years War (1618-1648), powers in Western Europe adopted a system of international relations known as the Westphalian system. It implied independent sovereign rulers mutually agreeing to accept their independence and differences. "The Westphalian system is easily misunderstood as resting on a belief in de facto isolation and the autarky of resulting entities, most of which were territorially defined and called states. In fact however, the Westphalian system is quite the opposite. It takes as its starting point the inevitable permeability of borders and the inevitable international interdependence of states, including both their governments and their societies." (Werner/De Wilde, 2001, p.287). In the conception of Mairet (1997), sovereignty is the principle of modern politics. Sovereignty (or profane political power) makes the freedom of human beings their own responsibility. Profane politics in the historical State is seen as a condition for the free actions of human beings. God or Nature were no longer seen as founding framework for law or authority. The principle of sovereignty appeared to be the principle for giving historical peoples their own identity. With the State, peoples and nations developed their identity, while using violence to make themselves recognised. For Mairet (1997, p 13), construction of political territoriality as materialisation of the principle of sovereignty constitutes the tissue of modern history. Mairet suggests as hypothesis that the period of sovereignty came to an end in the 20th century, that being the most violent century in human history (Levene, 2000). He did not foresee ethnic cleansing and murder in Europe, in Kosovo and elsewhere. "Res publica" has to be invented anew, also internationally.

N. Machiavelli (1469-1527), with his books "Il Principe" (1513) and "Discorsi", is seen as the first who made the theorising of sovereignty possible, without developing a theory of sovereignty himself. He stressed that politics as an activity to organise a new societal order was a purely human activity. Some decades later, the French jurist Jean Bodin (1530-1596), in his "Six livres de la République" (1576) defended the unlimited power of the State, "souveraineté". Machiavelli and Bodin in their conceptualisation liquidated the theological-philosophical tradition dominant in Antiquity and the Middle Ages by creating an innovative concept. Politics as autonomous field of human activity, not founded upon God or Nature, but upon the free will of human beings. Politics is power, and power is sovereignty. In Antiquity, philosophers speculated about how the "res publica" should be functioning. Modernisers concentrated on politics as it actually was. Machiavelli stressed historical "necessity" as a crucial element of politics and asserted that power was conquered to establish a State by law. He dismissed the Platonic idea of the philosopher-king who knows what is the best for the common good. For Machiavelli, it was essential to observe human passions and build up knowledge about human conditions in order to do what is politically opportune. He wanted to free politics from its theological-philosophical custody, since the Platonic idea was reproduced by the Christian Middle Ages. Then politics was seen as a divine or spiritual affair (in theory). For Machiavelli, a political theory is not successful because it is right, but because it has effect. He was innovative in preparing the ground for the modern conception to build the historical State on two human foundations, law and force.

Bodin, complementing the Machiavellian conception, had a conception of the State on the basis of sovereignty as profane, superior power over all other powers: "République est un droit gouvernement de plusieurs ménages et de ce qui leur est commun, avec puissance souveraine". This "droit gouvernement" meant government with sovereign power and based upon law: The State of sovereignty is a State of justice. Bodin made human will the key of the organising power in the republic (or state). Each non-human foundation of the state, either God or Nature, was disqualified. So it was a real historical state, produced by human will and the result of force. This historical state was qualified by autonomy, sovereignty as profane foundation. In so far as the sovereign referred to natural and divine law, the sovereign was the sole person competent for interpreting its meaning. The sovereign was uniquely competent for making a custom valid. Sovereignty is often reduced to the ultimate decision power of the sovereign, but then the quintessence is missed. The sovereign has the foundation of the state as objective. A sovereign, acting as his function requires, exercises competencies and powers to direct the State. There is a State only when there is sovereignty, the founding principle of the State. What is just is determined by the free will of the sovereign: "The law is the command of the sovereign using his power." The Bodin principle of sovereignty is the principle of the contingency of the just. Sovereignty is seen as the answer to the key problem of politics, civil war. Bodin was witness to the terrible religious wars (1562-1629) in France (Holt, 1995). Bodin got what he sought: Henri IV, a Protestant, was converted to Catholicism and established absolute monarchy in 1589. This lasted for two centuries until the French Revolution (Russell Major, 1994).

In a political perspective one might say that modern history is often about the world of States. Hobbes (1588-1679) in his "De cive" (1642) developed a new approach with his philosophy of the State. There are several dimensions in his work. The human foundation of law which produces justice and peace in the State. Public security is what people seek, and for this reason they are disposed to submit themselves. The law is what the sovereign is willing, and what he wills is just. Inhabitants of a territory give their rights of peace and war to one person or a council. According to Hobbes, both the sword of war and the sword of justice have to be in the hands of the person with sovereign power. Only the sovereign has to be competent to determine what is just. When it is given to the public to debate what is just, then everybody will follow his own ideas and the existence of the State runs the risk of dissolving. The construction of the myth of sovereignty is seen as profane sequence of the foundation of law. The myth of sovereignty (after the sequence: state of nature, a pact, society) is founding myth of the historical base of law. No longer is God seen as the basis, he does not guarantee contracts any longer. The sovereign is the sole foundation of law in the State, only the State can guarantee this foundation. Hobbes deduced the State from human nature. In the natural state, a situation without law, there is a state of war. Fear of violent death plays a crucial role. To escape this people arrange to entrust their defence to one person (or a council) as sovereign. The state of nature becomes a societal state, a constitutional state. Justice comes from the sovereign who determines the contents of norms. The sovereign gets his legitimacy from the people. Choosing a sovereign, giving up natural rights and liberties, citizens free themselves from anarchy and the war of all against all, by creating a State, "Leviathan" as a mortal God.

B. Spinoza (1632-1677) in his "Traité politique" (1677) opposed the view of Hobbes by accentuating human freedom as the crucial principle. For Spinoza freedom of the human individual is the basic axiom. Human beings should be freed from all fear, but not by transforming these reasonable men into animals or automatons. The objective of human society is liberty. Living in freedom means having a reasonable life. Living according to reason is having a life on the basis of natural law. The formation of a State should not have as its consequence that human beings have to abandon their natural rights. Spinoza's principle accentuates that every individual should maintain his natural rights. A sovereign has authority in so far as he has the power to make his will dominant. Subjects of a sovereign are only subordinate if, and so far as they don't want to resist. For Spinoza, sovereignty is a question of utility. When a sovereign has lost his utility he no longer has legitimacy. When somebody pledged himself not to resist a sovereign this bound him only as long as it served his interests. The same holds for a group. Hobbes (politics as submission) and Spinoza (politics as development of freedom) can be placed in the tradition of natural law, but their approaches are different. Hobbes makes the State dependent upon a pact, a contract. Spinoza argued that personal natural rights are not alienable at all; human association proceeds from nature; and political liberty is a necessity of nature.

For John Locke (1632-1704), two constitutive elements of human nature are essential for the constitution of civil society. The need for property and the human capacity to follow reason. The passage from natural property to civil property in society, in his view, coincides with the formation of the State (civil government). In Locke's vision, the proprietor is the incarnation of human nature. He concluded that non-proprietors should not participate in decision-making about laws. Locke saw sovereignty as a power forthcoming from property ("estate is state"). The proprietor was seen as subject of law, while non-proprietors were considered as subdued to law. On the basis of the connection property-state, Locke developed a modern theory of sovereignty in the form of the constitutional state. Unlike Hobbes, Locke saw sovereignty as a principle to establish a liberal regime, while taking landed property as the basis of civil liberty. For Locke, the origin of political relations is that which has been common to all (land) and became the property of some. So inequality was created in a situation of equality (state of nature). The crucial question is how private appropriation of what was common to all can be legitimate. Locke argued that every human being needs means of subsistence and that the result of what he does to survive is his personal property. For Locke, the law of nature itself created property rights, because the earth is given to all human beings, it is reasonable that one can appropriate a piece of land. The process of private appropriation from what is common is a material process, work. It is reasonable that one can consider the result of this work as personal property. Although the water in the common fountain is for all, the water in the jar is personal property. This process of appropriation creates inequalities. For Locke the introduction of money caused inequality, war and sovereignty, because money made it possible to acquire more than work produced and more than was needed for subsistence. Some could enrich themselves with what others needed for survival. The State was necessary to prevent civil war from breaking out and to defend private property. For Locke the theory of the constitutional state provides a basis by giving proprietors the right to vote laws in parliament. Law so preserved the existing order of property. The revolution of 1688 brought Great-Britain the "Bill of Rights" (1689), which had rulings that Locke could have endorsed. He developed a conception for distinguishing power of the executive (the King) and power of the legislative body (parliament). This inspired Montesquieu to accentuate the meaning of distribution of powers to preserve civil liberties when France had an absolute monarchy.

Modern constitutionalism as developed by Locke, got its theoretical foundation from Montesquieu (1689-1755). Montesquieu elaborated the idea that the powers of the State should be distributed to further the political liberties of citizens (separation of powers). In "De l'esprit des lois" (1748) he took Great Britain as example, as France, with its monarchy since 1589, had no parliamentary tradition. The origin of English parliamentarism goes back to the "Magna Carta" (1215) which ruled that an assembly representing the people voted on the laws. Since the 14th century the English parliament has had two houses: House of Commons, and House of Lords. The "Bill of Rights" (1689) ruled that the three competencies of State sovereignty should not be concentrated in one organ. The monarch had executive power within constraints as set by parliament. When executive power and legislative power were in one hand there were serious risks that it would produce despotism and that civil liberties would be impaired. Montesquieu developed the idea that the democratic principle penetrated into the concept of sovereignty by way of the constitution, a legal ruling which guarantees its spirit (political liberties). The constitutional principle presupposes representation, the people or the nation as the source of laws. The constitution has to rule power relations between institutions of the State. By moderating the competencies of several powers, civil liberties are furthered. The constitution, necessary condition for a free State, is not a sufficient condition. A constitution can only produce civil liberties when a nation lives up to democratic conditions due to its "esprit général" (book XIX). Concrete political liberties of a nation depend on its history, culture, customs, experiences and laws. It cannot be imposed from outside. For France, Montesquieu recommended taking account of its "humeur": "The legislator has to follow the spirit of the nation if this is not contrary to the principles of government. We do nothing better than what we do freely, following our natural genius." Montesquieu, with his conception, thought to rescue French monarchy while respecting the legitimate rights of the people and the interests of the nobility.

Jean-Jacques Rousseau (1712-1778), in his "Contrat social" (1762) rejected the conception of Montesquieu, among other things because he had considered only established regimes and had a specific idea of sovereignty. If one takes the point of view that law, as declaration of the "volonté générale", is the starting-point, then the civil state was not established everywhere at that time. Rousseau concluded that very few countries in his time had laws in this sense, so according to Rousseau, Europe was as yet in a state of nature. He rejected representation of the people, while in his view the "volonté générale" was being perverted by the will of an elite. Rousseau made a distinction between power and the will of the people (which never could be alienated): "Power can be transmitted, but not the will." His notion "volonté générale" was not seen as identical to the will of all. For Rousseau, with his logic "peuple-volonté générale-loi", the people as such were a "moi moral collectif", having a will of its own, and formulating this will in laws. When his "Contrat social" was published France discussed the issue of representation. "Parlements" (being courts, not representative organs) tried to confiscate legislative competencies, challenging the King. These were only competent for registering laws as issued by the King. Rousseau, seeing what "parlements" were (feudal representatives of private interests) and what they pretended to be (representatives of the people), rejected representation in this form. Louis XV at the "séance de flagellation" (3 March 1766) in the "parlement de Paris" combatted attempts to unite "parlements". This would corroborate their claim to be a legislative body, representing the nation.

Louis XV saw the whole of the public order as emanating from himself as the sole representative of the nation. What the "parlements" tried to realise was lese-majesty, separating the nation from the King. Rousseau had a revolutionary idea with his sovereignty of the people, as opposed to royal and parliamentary sovereignty. He prepared the ground for Sieyès, pleading for national sovereignty and adapting his conception by using the notion "nation", borrowed from the Ancien Régime. It was possible to realise continuity by a revolution. The sovereignty of the French monarchy was transposed to the sovereignty of the people as a nation. Sieyès was pragmatic in stating: "The Nation is constituent", meaning by this that all other powers were derived from it. Government has power, when constitutional, and it is legal when it is implementing the laws as imposed. The "volonté nationale" is legal by its origin: the nation only needs to be a reality to be legal. In confrontation with the established system of three orders (clergy, nobility, third order), Sieyès asked: "Who dares to assert that the third order does not have all that is needed to form a complete nation? .. When the privileged orders are taken away, the nation would not be less, but more." Each individual became a citizen; no individual (even the King himself) could appropriate sovereignty, because sovereignty resides in the nation. This was recognised in the "Déclaration des droits de l'homme et du citoyen" (1789): "The principle of all sovereignty in essence resides in the nation. No corporation and no individual may exercise authority unless forthcoming from it explicitly." The Constitution of 3 September 1791 said: "Sovereignty is one, indivisible, everlasting and inextinguishable. It belongs to the Nation." It took the violence of the French Revolution before this was recognised.

The era of nations started with the invention of the principle of national sovereignty (Mairet, 1997). Europe became a territory of nation-states and sovereignty was made territorial. War was the instrument to confirm sovereignty. Nation-States were organisations responsible for war and peace. Kant (1724-1804) published ideas about perpetual peace in his "Zum ewigen Frieden" (1795). He elaborated peace as a situation of freedom in a State based on the Rule of Law when three conditions were fulfilled: the constitution of States should be republican, so that civil legality is prevailing for its citizens; Public law should be based on a federation of free States; the law of nations ("ius gentium") founds the possibility of peace between Nation-States; and cosmopolitan law has to rule the conditions of universal hospitality. Fichte (1762-1814), a follower of Kant, in his "Reden an die deutsche Nation" (1807), elaborated ideas about conditions for formation of a German nation when Napoleonic armies dominated central Europe. He wanted to further German consciousness in its confrontation with the Napoleonic project to establish a kind of universal monarchy. Fichte, Germany's answer to Rousseau, accentuated the importance of national patriotism. Another author whose ideas were relevant for theorising about Nation-States was K. von Clausewitz (1780-1831), an admirer of Bonaparte. In "Vom Kriege", he developed advanced ideas about military strategy. He made the modern idea of warfare by Nation-States explicit as application of violence to realise political targets: war as an act of sovereignty. The modern State is said to find its legitimacy in force. Revolutionary war was seen as a passage from the sovereignty of a monarchy to sovereignty of a nation.

In the century between the English Revolution with its "Bill of Rights" (1689), and the French Revolution with the "Déclaration des droits de l'homme et du citoyen" (1789), the debate was about the legitimacy of royal sovereignty and constitutional monarchy versus absolute monarchy. In the two centuries from 1789 to the European Revolution of 1989 (Fall of the Berlin Wall), the discussion with regard to sovereignty was concentrated upon the influence of the people. When the people are sovereign and their will is law as the source of the constitutional state, the issue becomes how this will can express itself. There was always someone or some organ speaking in the name of the people: monarch-people-party. After the French Revolution De Bonald (1796) argued for a national revolution on the basis of absolute power, restored Catholicism and social hierarchies. Guizot (1821) was opposed to this reactionary doctrine, and tried to develop a concept with a representative principle based upon justice and reason. His idea of sovereignty on the basis of reason was narrowly interpreted. Only those who paid taxes were thought to be capable of exercising sovereignty. Tocqueville (1805-1859) had more impact. He wanted to analyse democracy, where it was already functioning, America. He took the compelling drive of peoples for equality as the basic principle.

In the United States democracy was the result of political experience (customs and habits), not of a prefixed conception. This was different from the situation in France, where the idea of sovereignty of the people had to be developed against the factual situation in the Ancien Régime. In the United States, the democratic movement came from the grass-roots (towns and provinces); here democracy provoked a revolution. One could say that the United States were democratic from the beginning, due to the fact that this was a new territory without history. Because there was no King the people had to be the basis of sovereignty. Tocqueville accentuated quite originally that democracy presupposes democratic customs, an immanent democratic consciousness in society. In France, a revolution was necessary to bring about more democracy because there was no recognised people as basis for democracy. There were only three orders (clergy, nobility and third order) and absolute monarchy.

After the French Revolution and Empire it was Karl Marx who proclaimed in his "Manifesto of the communist party" (1848): "proletarians don't have a fatherland" and "the law is only the will of the dominating bourgeois class transformed into law." For Marx, stressing the importance of productive forces for social conditions, the people were a fiction, and the State was an enforcing instrument for a dominant class, not for the people. He replaced one fiction (people) by another: the universal class of proletarians had to revolutionise existing power relations. At last the State could be abolished. Powers had to be concentrated in one political party for the time being. On the basis of the ideas of Marx and Lenin a fusion was realised between the State and the sole recognised party in the Soviet-system. With Lenin, dictatorship of the communist party became the target. After the debacle of the Soviet-system and the European Revolution of 1989 a new situation prevailed. For Mairet (1997, p.185) "politics is human activity to organise and maintain a community, the common being of human beings, as it developed historically. ..Policies are the public affairs of a community which modern authors call State. ..Studying politics is to question the metaphysical foundations of the modern State. The State is the historical form which the human community chooses in modern times." Mairet (o.c., p.211) saw that the 20th century changed political anthropology for the modern world. No longer can the question be answered positively that politics is about the common being of human beings. Systematic elimination of Jews and Gypsies by the Nazi-State annihilated the anthropological basis of the State in Germany. Human beings are equal, and humanity is unity, but the Nazi-State annihilated a minority in a civil war against humanity; not in a war against an enemy, but because a specific race was excluded from the right to live as other human beings. Max Weber founded the modern State on the monopoly of legitimised use of violence while denying the legitimacy of violence for private objectives. The State is only legitimised to use violence to realise justice. Elimination of violence is the sole raison d'être of a just State (Mairet, 1997, p.232). A historical State can define the rules of justice in a constitution. A constitution is not only a text, but mutual recognition of natural individual rights. The most constitutional State, Great Britain, has no formal constitution (Mairet, 1997, p.254).

Unlike Mairet (1997, p.13) Werner/De Wilde (2001, p.297) rightly argued that the period of sovereignty did not end in the 20th century but that sovereignty is enduring: "Sovereignty is not merely a bundle of rights, but consists in a status (being sovereign) and in the use of this status to legitimize certain rights, duties and competences (the sovereign rights). Only if one takes the existence of states for granted and treats their existence as an unproblematic matter of fact is it possible to argue that sovereignty boils down to merely a bundle of rights." The existence of quasi-states and the development of the European Union make the issue of sovereignty an actual issue. In view of the phenomenon of quasi-states Jackson (1990, pp. 27-29) distinguishes negative and positive sovereignty. Negative sovereignty is defined as the legally protected freedom from outside interference and "a positively sovereign government is one which not only enjoys rights of non-intervention and other international immunities but also possesses the wherewithal to provide political goods for its citizens." The concepts empirical sovereign statehood and juridical sovereign statehood are also used: "Empirical statehood or sovereignty denotes the material capabilities of a state to enforce, by means of its government, its claim to supreme authority over a population living on a given territory. Juridical statehood denotes the international recognition of a state under international law and the external rights and responsibilities attached to that international recognition." (Werner/De Wilde, 2001, p.301). Several authors endorse the popular view that the Member-States of the European Union lost their sovereign status as independent States. The Westphalian system of sovereign states would have been replaced by overlapping networks of competing power structures. Werner/De Wilde (2001, p.303) argues that one has to keep the nature of sovereignty in mind to override popular loss-of-sovereignty narratives: "..a successful claim to sovereignty establishes a relation between a status (being the highest authority, being independent) and a bundle of rights, powers and responsibilities related to that status (the 'sovereign rights', like the power to conclude treaties, right to immunity, etc.). The claimed status as such is something that cannot be partly handed over or pooled; it is an indivisible quality. The rights and powers linked to that status, however, can be handed over to other states or international organizations."

### 10.9. "All-is-politics" thesis. Institutionalising of the state (Burdeau)

The thought-provoking work of G. Burdeau (1971/1986) has been underexposed. His complicated conception deserves a more prominent place in scholarly discussions. Although nobody ever met the State, everybody has many confrontations and encounters with persons and organisations that function as part of the State. With judges, policemen, customs-officers, and other public functionaries who act with the public authority of the State. The State is neither territory, population, public organisation nor a system of obligatory rules, but is related to all of them. Burdeau (1970, p.14) said: "The existence of the State belongs not to the tangible phenomenology, it is part of the order of the mindset. The State, in its full meaning, is an idea. With no other reality than conceptual, the State exists only, because it is thought." A modern constructivist view. Burdeau stressed the point that the Idea of the State is not like other mental constructions as often used by jurists for a synthetic representation of some reality. The Idea of the State is not a mental construction to denote a pre-existing reality. The State is itself the whole reality which it is denoting, because this reality resides wholly in the spirit of the human beings who conceive it. French language has no adequate term for the whole collection of all public authorities except "L'État". So, Burdeau identifies "État" and "Pouvoir politique": "When thinking of the State, citizens do this to have an explanation for all phenomena that characterise the existence and activities of the "Pouvoir politique." He accentuated the crucial significance of the Idea of the State. The State was invented to make it possible that human beings need not obey other human beings as such, when public authorities do their jobs. The State is a form of Public Power ennobling the process of obedience. "Its primary raison d'être is to give the human mind a representation of the seat of Power, which authorises foundation of the differentiation between governors and governed upon another basis than relations of force." (p.15).

Traditionally, differentiation between governing elite and governed people is seen as a power-relation between persons who command and others who obey. Who has the power to govern? The use of the State might seem purely symbolic, but the whole political universe is full of symbols. One might say that the State is only an idea and not a concrete phenomenon, but it is an objective reality. It is not (only) the will of the policeman which makes me obey, but the power of the State. Public functionaries are not the owners of their jobs (as was the case during the Ancien Régime), because only the State is the real holder of the functions of public authorities. The Idea of the State represents a more mature stage of civilisation when a society has organised itself in a more sophisticated way. The State is institutionalised by loosening Public Power from human beings acting on behalf of this

Public Power, incarnated in the State. The State, unique instrument to act upon society with the monopoly of public authority legitimised to issue rules of law, becomes a key-issue of political strife. It is very interesting to win positions in the steering cockpits of the State. This gives specific and powerful possibilities to influence societal developments. It gives a huge legitimacy, especially on the basis of elections in a representative democracy, so that political rivals have normally no other choice than to accept or rebel. The State risks becoming an alibi for the governing elite when working not for the general interest but for partisan or particularistic interests. Karl Marx denounced the State as the instrument of the governing class to oppress the proletarian class. The State might function as such, but only when its most essential function is violated. According to Engels, this State must disappear. The same applies to abuses of the State in the form of party government. Communist States in Eastern Europe, with all powers for the Communist Party, did not work in conformity with the ideals of Karl Marx himself.

Burdeau found that the State ("État") in a qualified sense is the basic frame of reference for public authorities ("Pouvoir politique"). The State cannot be identified with differentiation between governors and governed, which is possible also when there is no State. The phenomenon of public authorities is universal. There is widespread confusion, as the term State is used to denote all kinds of political organisations in historic societies (Babylonians etc.). In each society there are social relations between its members in relation with societal objectives. Public authorities derive their significance, "raison d'être" and "finalité" from their functional, instrumental role with regard to these societal objectives. By its existential nature society has its own "finalité". It forms the necessary basis of values, relevant for relations between public authorities and members of society. Public authorities derive their authority from societal objectives, not from their own power. Society is not the simple sum of all its members. Common consciousness of forming a society (partially as subconsciousness) is crucial. To become a political society, a group is needed, conscious of its "raison d'être" and common objectives. Social consciousness is formed around a common project, conservation of the existing order or renewal of society. In the group of human beings forming society there are dominant concepts about the desired future. For Burdeau (1970, p.24) public authorities are an incarnation of the energy in the group provoked by the idea of a desired social order: "It is a force born from collective consciousness, destined to assure the enduring existence of the group, to lead the group in its search for its common good, and to be able to impose eventually the attitude required for this search."

A key problem in formation of the "Pouvoir", is its dual character of two interrelated components, willpower of a leader (or leading group) and power of a fundamental idea. The State conception can be seen as the vulnerable answer to this problem since the end of the 15th century. For millennia, the sole raison d'être for human groups was survival (food, defence against other groups, and satisfying the gods). At some point public authorities evolve as an extension of family authorities or representation of the gods. Social control in primitive society was predominantly active: no real differentiation with formation of specific public authorities (anonymity of public authority). When a certain degree of civilisation had been reached, specific public authorities are formed. Public authority is entrusted to some person(s) with special features ("Pouvoir individualisé"). In feudal times the personal bond between leader and vassals was crucial for the functioning of public authorities (Bloch, 1960; Boutruche, 1959; Calmette, 1934; Ganshof, 1957). It was important for acceptance of authority that there was a charismatic leader. Practical experiences showed that this personalised leadership was very vulnerable. All depended on the life of a leader, the incarnation of public authority. When he died there were often wars about leadership. A logical step was that ideas about a less personal leadership developed. This created the invention of institutionalised public authority. The idea of an institution was the solution: as enterprise to serve an idea, and organised so that this idea as incorporated in the enterprise, disposes of power and duration in a way that is superior with regard to the mortal persons involved. The institution as power in service of an idea, realisation of the desired future. At some point in societies the personal characteristics of a leader were no longer enough to justify authority. Instability and discontinuity in functioning of public authorities, totally dependent on the will of a mortal being, became intolerable.

In this way the idea was born to differentiate between public authority and the individual person having public authority, but public authority, no longer incarnated in the life of a mortal human being, needs an incumbent to function effectively. This is the institution of the State, exclusive seat of public power. Burdeau (1970, p.31) wrote: "In the State, public authority is institutionalised in the sense that it is transferred from the person of governors, who only exercise competencies given them, to the State, from then on the sole owner." In mainstream literature one can find the opinion that there is a State when there is a territory, a population and a commanding authority. This saw Burdeau's theory as an error. These three conditions can be fulfilled while there is still only individualised power. It is also necessary that the group is conscious about the territory as collective heritage, and not as property of a leader. Only the State can give this heritage an incumbent with continuity. The population has to develop into a nation as a community of dreams (Malraux). According to Burdeau (1970, p.36), "The Nation asks for the State, because only the State has the kind of power, of which it is the seat, that is commensurate to the durable data which are constituting the national community." In Western Europe, the rise of the State in the 16th century coincided with a weakening of societal control by the Church. The idea of an autonomous sphere for the temporal "bonum commune" broke through. In medieval times public authorities were seen as prefiguration of the Empire of God. Secularisation of the role of public authorities made spirits ripe for acceptance of the State without a relation with the Church. In feudal times, the personal bond between leader and followers was real. Physical distances in large territories removed governors from the governed by way of a series of delegated authorities. The idea was that one obeyed rules, rather than delegated authorities. For the acceptance of rules it was crucial that authorities making and implementing them had legitimacy.

Public authority based upon the Rule of Law has legitimacy. The problem of legitimacy can be solved only by institutionalising public authorities. Legitimacy cannot be seen as dependent on personal qualities of governors. " when legitimate power is related to law as recognised in the community, only those, who act in conformity with the dominant idea of law in the group, can claim this legitimacy" (Burdeau, 1970, p.46). The legitimacy of public authorities makes competencies of governors legitimate. For Burdeau, "once loosened from the persons who are exercising it, public authority becomes an entity which asks for another basis, also being abstract. This basis is the State. ..When one is asking how the Idea of the State was introduced in France, the conclusion is that this came about with this split-up of the power of public authority." In France, Kings had connected their kingdom so strongly with the nation that the monarchy developed as the natural political organ. The power of the French King became "Power of the Crown" which founded the legitimacy of the monarchy. The authority of governors was based on an external idea. The Crown was the incumbent of public authority. The will of governors has legitimacy and juridical value in so far as it can be ascribed to the State. As governors fulfil their function correctly, they act legitimately, if not their actions lack legitimacy. To overcome the vicissitudes of private wars between families claiming the rights of the kingdom, a dynasty was recognised as coinciding with the State institution: "the King does not die in France". Continuity of the State was a guarantee of the durability of laws, also after the death of the King. Legitimacy, continuity and sovereignty are seen as crucial features of the State.

Burdeau (1970, p.49) qualified the State: "It is Power, so its acts are obligatory. It is abstract Power, it is not affected by the vicissitudes of its agents. The State endures, over all historical contingencies, because the State incarnates an idea. Image of the desirable future order, which is the foundation of Power and Law."

In the case of an individualised Power, the factual leader can impose his will in the face of resistance only by using violence. His decisions as such don't have a superior character. These decisions are mandatory only because of the personal position of the leader. This means a vulnerable position (why he?) because at any moment his power can be wiped out by a person with more power. To assure a monopoly in decision-making the source of power has to be found elsewhere, not in the personal characteristics of a leader. The Idea of the State is the solution. When the Power is commensurate with dominant ideas in the group in relation to the Common Good, the governors, as agents exercising competencies in name of this Power, benefit from the authority which is related to that image of a desirable order." (Burdeau, 1970, p.50). Public authorities can claim to represent the common good of society (the general interest). Others can bring to the fore only private interests which may be against the general interest. For this reason French revolutionaries stressed the indivisibility of national sovereignty. They used the modern idea of sovereignty based upon the collectivity. After the French Revolution, the monarchy, basis for sovereignty, had to be replaced by the State. The State, representative of the Rule of Law and at the heart of all political passions, has an ambiguous character. The State seems to be an artificial construction. The will of governors becomes the will of the State, that's all. The State is not a natural phenomenon, and has to be conceived by the human mind. Burdeau (1970, p.55): "When the State is artificial, it is not conceptualised once and for all as a complete artefact. The State is a continuous creation. This asks for an effort from individual human beings to give its mechanisms and activities its true sense. They must associate external manifestations of the Power with the idea of a collective project, which the group forms to manage its destiny. A daily plebiscite."

The State is a mental phenomenon. The State exists only in so far as it is represented in the minds of members of society. What are we thinking when we think about the State? We associate the State with many phenomena in social life, all modalities of a central idea. "In the centre of all reflection about the State, at the origin and realisation of all efforts of human will to conceptualise the State, there is the idea of a discipline of life. The State is the form by which the group unites by submitting to law." (Burdeau, 1970, p.56). Consciousness about a discipline is combined with "Power" (public authority with power) as it responds to conditions of a definition of the State. In the complex jargon of Burdeau (1970, p.57): "the phenomenon of Power, expressing the State externally, corresponds with the idea of a discipline, determining in individual minds the forming of the notion of the State. The existence of the State depends on an intellectual attitude of all of us about the concrete phenomenon, which is constituted by public authority. The State concept is purifying the power of public authorities by detaching it from the governors' will, combining it with the idea, formed by the collectivity about its future and its management of society. This idea is the foundation of public authority and law." Burdeau (1970, p.58) had conditions. There is no society without an objective of a mental alliance of coexistence of individuals. Without consciousness about this objective there is a mass or a gathering, but no society. Perception of a common objective gives consensus, arising from the convergence of individual images into an image of the collective future. This consensus, criterion of sociability, is not the result of completed social unity. It develops around a unity created permanently with regard to a representation of the desirable order. It is not contemplation, but implies concern about the desired future order. This produces rules to direct the behaviour of individuals towards the desired future. These rules are rules of law. The Idea of Law is "the representation of the desirable order which in a given society constitutes a basic part of the collective mindset, crystallising the dominant consensus." (Burdeau, 1970, p.58).

The Idea of Law is not a philosophical conception about higher principles like justice or solidarity. It is a type of organisation of societal life according to prefixed rules (rights and obligations). The desired order is realised by observance of the rules of law. What distinguishes a rule of law from other rules of behaviour is that it emanates not directly from the principle, but from the fact that the desired order or collective good supposes that the rule has to be respected. Respect of the juridical rule is thought to be so crucial for social order that it asks for an intelligence to formulate it, a will to impose it and a force to sanction it." Public authority is simultaneously that intelligence, that will and that force. No other power realises this solidarity between the Idea of Law and Public Authority than the State (o.c., p.60), so the Rule of Law and the State regime coincide. This might sound alarming for those who remember the theory of Bismarckian theoreticians, for whom law was a creation of the State. Because the State was thought to incarnate force, at last force was seen to create law. Some German scholars thought to solve this problem with their idea of a self-limiting State. The State is incumbent of commanding power, but this is not absolute power. The institution absorbs power with all its characteristics, but these are conditioned by service to the Idea of Law. The State is subordinate to the Rule of Law. This removes the serious objection to making the State the incumbent of dominant power. "The State is limited by the law, because its power is juridically conditioned by the Idea of Law which legitimises it. The State does not limit itself, the State is born limited." (Burdeau, 1970, p.61). This formula of the State as born with limitations set by the Rule of Law opens perspectives. The role of governors is not restricted to transforming Rule of Law principles into operational juridical rules. The Rule of Law is not so precisely formulated that it binds public authorities exhaustively. Governors can have their impact on the Rule of Law, taking the measures needed to realise the common good as circumstances dictate. In the State, one has to distinguish sovereign public authority, governors implementing this power and State power making their decisions effective. Authors like Duguit reject this as useless metaphysics, claiming to write about the real State phenomenon, the differentiation between powerful governors and governed. This so-called realism is less realistic than it might seem. Governors come and go, but there is an enduring institution. The totality of public authority is not concentrated in governors.

A tricky part of public law doctrine concerns the notion of sovereignty, the collection of competencies giving the person or organ superior power. Burdeau (1970, p.63): ".the sovereign, that's the person, group or organisation deciding what Idea of Law prevails in a collectivity." This can be a person, like the King in the Ancien Régime, who had absolute decision-making powers with regard to collective life, or a class of the nation, or the nation as a whole as proclaimed in 18th century political philosophy. In all cases the sovereign has primary influence upon the Rule of Law. This Rule of Law can be effective only when it is accepted. Sovereignty is force, growing from the whole of historic national circumstances for a political community in a nation. A crucial criterion of sovereignty is the constituent power. The French Constitution of 1791 declared that the nation had sovereignty, so that all powers come from the nation. The Rule of Law has to be narrowly combined with the spiritual and material priorities of the national community. Only public authorities with the support of the dominant political power can be institutionalised at the formation of the State. Others might be opposed to this, but they can be factual powers only. The sovereign can see the decisions of governors as decisions taken in the name of the State if they conform to claims of the Rule of Law. One of the most concrete phenomena related to public authority is the existence of governors, competent for the management of public affairs and taking primary decisions with regard to national life. They can legally order the use of force. Within the framework of their constitutional statute they can do what they want. We must not forget that it is not always those with the formal competencies of governors who have real power. The position of governors, being organs of the State (so having delegated public authority) and representatives of the sovereign (the recognised political will-power) has a juridical and a political character. Decisions of governors, as organs of the State, are juridically founded, mobilising the power of the State. Governors are agents of the sovereign (monarch, dominant class, or nation). By their mediation public authorities are dynamically enriched with the societal influences of sovereign political forces. The power of the State has to be distinguished from the powers of governors and sovereign, deciding about the validity of the Idea of Law. By virtue of their political position governors dispose of powers of their own, dependent on the confidence of the sovereign in them. State power, related to the Idea of Law, is primarily juridical.

For Burdeau (1970, p.70), sovereignty and State power don't have the same nature. Sovereignty is a political quality emanating from a series of historical circumstances, which created a certain equilibrium of powers in society, and State power, directly related to the Idea of Law, is the juridical form of its energies. Sovereignty and State power do not have the same incumbent either. Sovereignty can belong to individuals who can lose this quality, as in revolutionary France, when the sovereignty of the King was replaced by the sovereignty of the Nation. State power is inseparable from the State however. Sovereignty and State power do not have the same object. Sovereignty concerns the contents of the Idea of Law, while State power is related to the behaviour of the group, and making this group accept the demands of the Idea of Law. Burdeau (1970, p.71) himself admits that these distinctions between sovereign, governors and State power seem rather subtle to denote the situation in societies where some give commands and others obey, but he claims that these distinctions are not artificial, but form elements of the State institution. From the dynamics of their relations, the specific and original form of public authority is deduced, the State. It is important that State agents don't appropriate its power, because otherwise the institutionalising has failed. "The State, that is primarily institutionalised public authority, and the institution in which public authority has its seat. ..This institution is an enterprise to serve an idea, with duration and power, superior with regard to those of the individuals by which it is functioning." (Burdeau, 1970, p.71).

The State incorporates an idea, which proceeds from conceptions about the desired order. A crucial aspect of the institutionalising of Power is that governors do not exercise competencies owing to a personal prerogative. There is only one incumbent of the right to command and to implement force, the State, but human will and human activities are needed to make the State operational. Governors and administrative functionaries are subordinate to the law of service, the public good, the general interest. Before the institutionalising of the State, they could combine the realisation of the Idea of Law and promotion of personal interests. This is different:since the existence of the State, "governors cannot do otherwise than serve the Idea of Law, incarnated in the institution, because they have competencies and authority only to do this. Disconnected from this idea, their orders and activities lose all legitimacy and juridical quality." (Burdeau, 1970, p.74). The principle is that public authority ends outside its legitimate function. Differentiation between public authority and governors reinforces legitimacy for public authorities. Governors have legitimacy, when designated according to prevailing procedures. It is not due to their choice or power to have positions in the name of public authority: "The continuity of public authority does not exist in their persons, but has its seat in the institution. So public authority never has a vacancy." (Burdeau, 1970, p.75). Continuity of the institution makes it possible to change governors in a rational way. The Constitution as statute of the institution regulates the regular transfer of competencies for persons acting as organs of the State. The Idea of the State forms a phase in a process of rationalisation. In Antiquity and after, a form of deification of leaders was normal to overcome the limitations of their personal characteristics. In France Kings used mystifications to support their position by claiming that they governed on the basis of divine law. In a more advanced, more intelligent society, a more rational conception is needed. "..the concept of the State has rescued public authority by rationalising it." (Burdeau, 1970, p.78).

Burdeau (1970, p.87) makes it difficult to understand his conceptualisation fully because of shifts in terminology: "The State is Power, but it is not the sole existing Power in the collectivity. There is a plurality of representations of the desired order, and therefore a multitude of Powers. Their rivalry forms the motor of political life, having as its objective the conquest of State Power. State Power will sanction the pretension of the victorious Power so that this will be recognised as the sole organ authorised to impute its wills to the State." Political parties and workers unions are mentioned as factual powers. In a normal democratic system these organisations do not function as public authorities. The specific position of the State has to be accentuated as sole institution legitimised to fulfil functions in the sphere of public authority. In the Soviet one-party system, one could say that the Communist Party was identical to the State, or that the State was an instrument of one political party, but in pluralist democracies it is a necessary condition for democracy that there are free elections for a diversity of political parties, all having the chance to influence the composition of parliament and government. A crucial aspect of institutionalising of the State is differentiation with public authorities legitimised to act for the general interest. In pluralist democracies there is always a risk of political parties or factions, particularist interest groups and/or bureaucratic cliques colonising the State. Often political parties do not want to support unpopular measures when governors try to persuade the governed to accept sacrifices or when they must tackle a crisis for the collectivity. Then governors can invoke the authority of the State, the "raison d'État".

The collectivity is accepting measures taken on behalf of the State which would not be accepted when taken by political parties. It is logical that political parties are opposing each other, trying to get a grip on powers of the State and so realising their ideas about running the State. Winning elections enables a political party to get control of legitimate powers and tools of the State via their representatives, and to produce rules that are binding for all members of the collectivity (law) and bring the desired order closer by. Governors have to make the Idea of Law operational. Often they try to do this, while giving priority to party-political conceptions of the Idea of Law, or to pure personal or party-political whims. The State has to play a role to regularise the strife between political parties according to the rules set in the Constitution. To establish the rules of the institutional game, the State needs an energy, power, which is autonomous with regard to political parties. Political parties have to accept this power of public authorities as representatives of the general interest, competent to limit their activities and to direct their energies for the common good. In a variant of liberalism, a plea is held for a State-without-power: "One asks for public administration, but without politics. Public services, but without Power. A waiter, but not a boss. One eliminates State-Power to have only a State-servant." (Burdeau, 1970, p.122). On the other side of the spectrum Marxism fights the position of the State in capitalism as the instrument of the dominant class. To overcome capitalism the communist party saw its task as the realisation of a one-party State. For Engels, there would be convergence of the State and the general will of the collectivity. At last the State would be redundant. Contemporary Western democracies chose a third way in between: pluralism of political parties, free elections to designate persons in parliament and government, and independent public authorities.

## 10.10. "Zero-State" thesis (De Bodinat)

Henri de Bodinat (1995) developed an interesting thesis about the "zero-State" in his analysis of the historical development of the State as Idea. As is usual in French literature, he uses the term "État" when dealing with public management by public authorities. His central, disputable thesis is, that it is possible to replace the organisation of a society with a modern State by a society without a State. His argument is: humanity lived for a long period without a State, which in the perspective of the history of mankind, is a recent innovation. "Homini erecti" are said to have lived as groups two million years ago. About 250,000 to 300,000 years ago, "homini sapientes" joined the theatre of mankind. They communicated by means of language, buried their dead, lived in groups, had utensils and lived from hunting and gathering food in nature. They lived without a State, laws, a constituted power or a leader, and did relatively well (Sahlins, 1976). This kind of society was possible due to direct social control in groups and the prevailing values of solidarity (Clastres, 1974). De Bodinat distinguishes three periods. Firstly, the time of hunters and collectors of food (150,000/50,000 BC, Stone Age), then from 50,000 to 20,000 BC it was normal to have domestic animals and from 20,000 to 15,000 BC agriculture was developed. In the Neolithic period, from about 15,000 BC, productivity in agriculture rose spectacularly (irrigation, plough) as in the fertile delta's of the Nile (Egyptian empire); Tigris and Euphrates (Sumerian empire); Indus and Ganges (Indian empire); and Yellow River (Chinese empire). This rise in agricultural productivity produced huge surpluses, more than needed to feed the people and these surpluses stirred up passions. One caste appropriated a large part of surpluses. This caste created an institution, a mechanism to seize a part of what farmers produced. A forced levy, without something offered in return: the State was born, a new organisation of society. Men guarded cultivated land against animals and robbers, a class of soldiers developed. Farmers, vulnerable to climate, natural catastrophes and diseases, had medical men, priests and faith healers: specialists in staving off misfortunes.

According to De Bodinat the State developed when these priests and soldiers became a class, claiming a substantial part of surpluses (compulsory levies). Taxation was invented when soldiers, priests and leaders no longer wanted to be dependent on farmers for their living. Not paying taxes became a crime combated with violence. The State was born when a class obtained a monopoly on the use of violence. This process took place about 3,000 BC in the delta's of Nile and Tigris; about 2,500 BC in China and India; and about 1,000 BC in Europe with the States of the Etruscans and Romans. For Kramer (1986), history began with the empire of the Sumerians. In the delta's of the Tigris and Euphrates the first traces of a State were found upon clay-tablets. Sumerian city-states invented a State: sovereigns legitimised by priests could dispose of soldiers, they had the leadership over a caste living from surpluses wrung from farmers. War was invented as an instrument to retain and extend power, within the cult of power, money and violence. To reinforce the power base scripts were used, meant to determine the possessions of taxable persons and to make laws with coercive rules. Scribes became top functionaries and written laws replaced customary rulings. In the Sumerian State the idea arose that the State was proprietor of the land, not the farmers, who could rent the land. The law of the strongest was clothed with the power of the State. The magnitude of agricultural surpluses made it possible to have a larger army. The basis was laid for expanding empires. As remuneration soldiers were given pieces of land in property. Around the monarch, a group of soldiers, aristocrats and bureaucrats developed as an aristocracy. Sargon I, conquering Sumerian city-states between 2,400 BC and 2,350 BC, created a large empire. Assyrians were able to take control of an extensive area with the use of ruthless violence (Roberts, 1990). Massive deportations of peoples forced to slavery were common practice. The deportation of the ten tribes of Israel is an example, as told in the Bible.

At the dawn of Greek civilisation in about the 8th century BC the organisation of society in the form of a State was still an exception. An overwhelming part of humanity lived as nomads travelling around in groups. Greek civilisation spread around the Aegean and Mediterranean Seas. Greeks with armies of citizens-soldiers managed to withstand violence from the Persian Empire. The Greek conception of city-states ("poleis"), in which citizens had a say in public affairs, was a pragmatic alternative to states with a huge bureaucracy. During the 7th century BC, the Greeks, starting from the individual citizen, invented democracy. In the last centuries before our era, the Romans conquered areas around the Mediterranean, which becomes "Mare Nostrum". Romans, influenced by Greek ideas and practices, started in a democratic way with ample competencies for citizens and limited power for aristocracy. With Octavianus (Augustus after 27 BC) the emperor was thought to get his power not from the people but from God. Emperor Caligula (37-41 AD) borrowed the idea of theocracy and bureaucracy from Egypt, under Roman control since the 2nd century BC. The idea of concentrating military and civilian power came from Egypt too (Gibbon, 1994). The Persian Empire under the Sassanides (226-651 AD) was a strong empire with a bureaucracy directed by governors (satraps). Arabs adopted this idea when they conquered the Persian Empire. The future seemed bright for large empires about 2,000 years ago. The Western Roman Empire, after centuries of undisputed hegemony, imploded in the third century. This was imputed to excessive taxation, many exempted parasites, and a huge bureaucracy; the same bureaucratic virus which demolished the Byzantine Empire in the 11th century. Following the collapse of the West European Roman Empire in 476, public authorities were weak for nearly a century. Barbarians, living along frontiers of the Roman Empire, penetrated its area.

According to De Bodinat, the Franks, before penetrating Gaul (1995, p.59), were a people without a State: Clovis was a tribal chief and war lord, a kind of small Genghis Kahn, but not a head of State. Despite those uncertain times however, the Franks had more or less effective public management. De Bodinat argues that in the time of Clovis and his followers, public authority and State taxation did not exist. The budget of the King of France was what his own domain, "L'Ile de France", gave him. Feudalism meant a decentralised system of levies on behalf of feudal lords (20% of national income). In spite of the efforts of Charlemagne to create a central State with a regular army and "missi dominici" France was a society with a relatively weak State until the 15th century. Since the 10th century, the Kings of France and England had been able to make their function gradually hereditary, so stabilising the position of public authorities. King Louis IX (1226-1270) could build up an orderly system of jurisdiction. Philip the Fair (1285-1314) reinforced the position of the monarchy, and introduced a permanent tax. In 1302, he enlarged the "États-généraux", composed of aristocracy and clergy, with representatives of the third estate. Driven by greed for the huge riches of the Templars, he abolished their order. Philip the Fair also contested the power pretensions of the Popes. This caused the Babylonic Captivity of the Popes in Avignon (1309-1377), and gave the French monarchy great influence over the Church. When Philip the Fair died, absolute monarchy was weakened. Louis XI (1461-1483) was able to intensify the grip of public management upon French society. During his rule, the tax burden quadrupled and the army was doubled. Monarchical public management after Louis XI was centralised ever more. The number of public "officiers" was enlarged from 10,000 to 50,000. These "officiers" had bought their public office. They paid mostly to make their function hereditary ("la Paulette"). The number of public functionaries rose from 20,000 to 100,000. The armed forces were enlarged to 400,000 men.

At the end of the Louis XIV regime, France was ruled by an absolute monarchy. The right of the monarchy to regulate France was based upon religious grounds. The monarch was thought to be the direct representative of God. The reaction against monarchy came with the French Revolution and its aftermath. During the French Revolution and the Napoleonic regime centralisation became ever more intensified. New ideas (human rights, democracy, the right to form a nation) also caused revolutions in Europe and elsewhere. At the end of the 19th century the French model of the Nation-State was dominant. The number of the State personnel was steadily growing, exploding in the 20th century due to the new concept of the Welfare State. De Bodinat stresses the point that the modern top-heavy State has too rigid a grip upon society. Public expenditures get out of control and cause irreparable damage to the economy. The French State budget in 1994 was about 1,700 billion francs, the deficit was more than 300 billion francs, and the public debt about 3,000 billion francs. Opposition to the lowering of public expenditures was fierce, especially from all who live on the redistributed "State manna". The stability of the State in the West is threatened by State obesity, appropriation of public power by a political caste, a fundamental democratic deficit, and its incapacity to solve serious problems like exclusion, poverty and global ecological exhaustion. Western countries with about 20% of world population (10% in 2025) use some 80% of global natural resources. With more countries developing this can only get worse. De Bodinat (1995,p.112): "The impasse of developed countries spreads to the whole planet."

Some 2/3 of the world's population live in the grip of powerful States, controlled by a small oligarchy. Often for them democracy does not exist or is only a façade, with a poor standard of living tending to become worse, and very low morale. The modern State holds society hostage, while failing to solve important issues. Because State-societies as invented some 5,000 years ago have become unworkable, it is, according to De Bodinat, necessary to think about an alternative. The State is sick, our modern societies are sick because of the State. Four scenarios are mentioned: progressive decadence; leadership for demagogues, accelerating decadence; totalitarianism; or a regulated transformation. De Bodinat thinks it should be possible for France to reduce the budget by 50%, or even by 80% within 20 years. Modern society can do without a State if two conditions are fulfilled. The values that made human life possible without a State should be restored and technological progress should be used to realise a society without a State. People without a State can elect representatives without much power. Direct, interactive democracy, made possible by technology, can be used. Everybody can take his destiny in his own hands, as L. Scheer elaborated in "La démocratie virtuelle" (1994). This zero-State hypothesis sounds like melodious music to all who are preaching the gospel of a globalising free market, but it is unrealistic. It can function as a model to improve the quality of the public authorities necessary for social life in society.

### 10.11. "Law-without-the-State" thesis (Cohen-Tanugi)

Woodrow Wilson in his "The Study of Administration" (1887), comparing administration in Europe and the US, argued for the importation of some European ideas about administration, without adopting un-American political concepts like monarchy. A century later, Laurent Cohen-Tanugi in "Le droit sans l'État" (1987), realised a thought-provoking analysis of the American law-system and contractual society as a mirror for France. He pleads in favour of adopting parts of the American way of law-based regulation in France, loosening the traditional French State/law combination which implies that the law is seen as almost exclusively coming from the State. It is popular now to argue for less State and less legal regulation because of over-juridification. In the actual debate about less State and more market the decisive meaning of law should be stressed, however: if less State, then more law. This is familiar for Americans and their self-regulated contractual society, law is more than law-by-the-State. Cohen-Tanugi criticises the French system of State-dominated law. He accentuates the advantages of the American self-regulating and contractual society. Many French authors criticise American society, such as M. Crozier in "Le mal Américain" (1980) or M.F.Toinet (1990). The fuss over the influence of judges on the result of the polls for election of the American President in the Bush-Gore controversy (November 2000) was not an exhortation to follow the American "government by judges" (Kaplan, 2001; Peretti, 1999). Cohen-Tanugi argues for the surplus value of self-regulation in a contractual society. He shows that France has disadvantages in growing international competition due to the French model of dominant, politicised State-law regulation. His advice is: less (politicised) State, and more law in a law culture, which subordinates politics to law in societal regulation. The impact of European Union law on national law seems to work in the direction of what he thinks necessary.

Cohen-Tanugi confronts two different conceptions of societal regulation with each other, in the perspective of their potential for democracy and modernity, while growing internationalisation and interdependency of national systems are dominant developments (globalisation). A model of State-regulation (State-law) versus a model of self-regulating society (contractual society). In the framework of an underdeveloped "Idea of Law", law in France is seen above all as the production of norms by the State, determining the contents of prevailing law. So creation of law by civil society itself is obstructed. The private sector, excluded from responsibility for contributing to the general interest (seen as a monopoly of the State), is not made responsible for fulfilling its authentic role in realising reasonable societal relations. Partners in French society lost the habit of making mutual arrangements. It is seen as normal that these should be organised under control of the State ("tutelle"). Cohen-Tanugi (oc, p.134): "The tutelage has caused apathy, and a systematic appeal to the State as saviour or arbiter, sometimes outside the established juridical framework. Government is thought to be responsible for all the social diseases of the country." This societal apathy is regularly converted into street-riots as an instrument to solve social conflicts. "The juridical apathy of French society is a signal that this society has put its destiny wholly in the hands of the State and its representatives. It abandons possibilities to solve its own conflicts, and to resist the expansion of powers of the State. The real substitute for the former Roman praetor is finally the street. The street is the escape, now that normal consultation is absent or fails." (oc, p.159). France is known for its well-developed culture of negotiation (Koetz/Ottenhof, 1983). This negotiation is not what it might be. Too much State-centred, party-political dominated manoeuvring, and not enough juridical arrangements. With many laws, life is under control of the State.

It is recognised that France lives still under the yoke of a rigid-dirigist model of State-regulation as developed since the French Revolution. This regulation model becomes ever more obsolete in a process of wear and tear and in the perspective of societal dynamics. State ideology robbed French society of fundamental law, hindering a normal development of democracy with a lot of self-regulation. Mainstream literature about comparisons between American and French societal regulation accentuates the economic dimensions (State versus market). Cohen-Tanugi stresses the importance of societal regulation by law. Scholars of American Public Administration blamed the French approach for its predominantly law-based character. Cohen-Tanugi pleads for more law-based regulation in France, but of a different character. The alternative for State-regulation is not wild capitalism or the law of the jungle, but more sophisticated self-regulation in society with adequately functioning public authorities. As with the function of the market in the economic order, the prominent instrument of a self-regulating society is the juridical system. Cohen-Tanugi questions that discussions about the dominant State in France practically ignore the juridical dimension. With a kind of juridical myopia, criticisms were reduced mostly to economic-financial and ideological aspects. France seems to develop into a more contractual society (Cannac, 1983; Prévost, 1983; Minc, 1984). Socio-cultural and technological factors are decisive in this evolution, with individualism, consumerism, recognition of private enterprises, decentralisation, and claims for participative democracy: "a certain bankruptcy of politics, or at the least a crisis in traditional political representation by political parties and workers unions...Technology, transnational by nature, weakens means of control by States, and reinforces societal centres of power." (p.16).

Jumping from dominant State-control to dominant market-control, as it is popular in the less-State movement (Jacquillat, 1985), will not do. Market forces have to be regulated. Law-based societal regulation is needed. Not less law, on the contrary, a "return of the juridical" (p.18). There is opposition to the juridification of society, especially from those who fear that this will mean more of the same old-fashioned State-law (legislation). So the traditional French distrust of law and legal quibbling has been exploited. It is important to recognise that a different kind of law is meant here. When one is arguing for deregulation and against the reinforcement of the juridical system, then one is mostly confusing bureaucratic administrative regulation and rules of law. Cohen-Tanugi (p.20) suggests that France is handicapped not only nationally, but also internationally by a specific juridical culture. The French often stick to the idea that international conflicts about commercial, technostrategic and industrial policies should be dealt with using diplomacy and political negotiations rather than with juridical arbitrages or judicial procedures. The concept of "external juridical policy" came to the fore (Lacharrière, 1983). In the European Union, France might be hindered by juridical deficiencies. The "Conseil d'État" in its report "Droit communautaire et droit français" (1982) feared with a Gallic reflex for the penetration of community law into French law, as it would lose the final grip on the French development of law. Due to some "horror of the juridical void" French philosophy of law might be qualified as "what is not explicitly allowed in legislation by the State is forbidden". On the other side stands "everything is allowed which is not explicitly forbidden". Cohen-Tanugi accentuates the prominent position of lawyers, law schools and law firms having societal power in the US. In France without a "grande école de droit" there is no comparable juridical establishment. Jurists from the "École nationale d'Administration" (ENA) as "énarques" have prestige for more than their professionalism. Marginalisation of law in recruiting elites is obvious.

Law is not really accepted in the social sciences, although it has the best possible title for this. Law is a poor parent of philosophy in the chapter of the philosophy of law and oscillates between the statute of a scientific discipline, with a purely academic prestige, and that of technique. "Procedure, formalism, paperwork, and lawsuits: that is the traditional sphere for the French jurist. A producer of formal documents and the custodian of a reality which escapes him, appearing as a notary at the very moment of the outcome in the comedies of Molière (oc, p.38). Cohen-Tanugi (p.42) denounces the too subordinate position of jurists in relation to managers and politicians: The French seem to take law less seriously than they might. This is due to a certain conception of the relationship between the juridical and the political, and to the obvious pre-eminence of the State with regard to law. Contrary to a deeply rooted myth about itself, France is said to be not really a very juridical country. The French, while often seeing law as packing (form) or the result of power processes, often have a too exclusive obsession for power and politics. The rigid way of dealing with law in France as "société bloquée" (Crozier) could explain that law is scarcely seen as an instrument of societal change and too often as the means to fix existing order only. Legislation, abstract and general, is seen as the primary source of law, not jurisprudence of law-courts or contracts. Legal rules are usually formulated in France in general terms so that many factual situations can be encompassed. When there is a new factual situation, the techniques of juridical hermeneutics are used to try to formulate a preexisting rule, thought to be implicitly ruled already in the general ruling. When this method does not apply legislation is extended with a new law, contributing to a proliferation of laws. Teaching of law in faculties of law in the Cartesian tradition is characterised more or less by repeating law as circumscribed in codes of law or manuals. Departing from the Cartesian axiom of legal security, legislation is systematised. There is not enough attention for the creative process as a method of finding law rules. Systematic abuses of jurisdiction in the Ancien Régime brought the prohibition of judges making "arrêts de règlement" and finding law. No creative interpretation, no government of judges. Judges had to apply law. Later jurisprudence did become a second source of law though.

There is a deficient consciousness about the specific nature of the juridical (Cohen-Tanugi, 1987, p.54). In France, people are apt to consider law as a simple external envelope, a model of politics. To give it the seal of authority, this has to be transformed into legislation and decrees, that is the law. But law is not only this form of authority. Law is above all a way of regulation with its own dimensions, internal dynamics and specific contents. French jurists are not happy with the consequences of the confrontation of French law with European Union law. Symptomatic for widespread fear for penetration of French law by EU law is the advice of the "Conseil d'État" in its 1982 report: "Each French functionary, each citizen who for one reason or another is consulted formally or informally in Brussels, should be impressed by their responsibility with regard to elaboration of juridical rules destined to take a place in the French juridical order." Hayek (1980) saw the fundamental transformation of the Idea of Law in the West, in transition from law made by judges and jurists (law of liberty: "nomos") into law enacted by a legislator ("thesis"). This applies especially to France as compared with Anglo-Saxon countries where jurisprudence and the rule of judiciary precedent are primary sources of law. Jurisprudence law is made by working with universal principles applied to specific cases. Legislation pretends to draw up ever more specific rulings for general application. An interesting question is whether it would be better, with regard to challenges by new technologies, to organise more legislation or more jurisprudence. For Cohen-Tanugi (1987, p.57) there is an alliance between technology and self-regulation: "The technological revolution necessarily increases responsibilities of judges and jurists. This will cause a juridical mini-revolution in France." Cohen-Tanugi (1987, p.59) confronts the political and juridical in their relation to "Pouvoir" (public authorities). As "pouvoir politique" (political power), and "pouvoir juridique" (juridical power): " the power of tribunals (judiciary power), the influence of law and the juridical as method of socio-political regulation, and the power of all jurists in society and State." The struggle of royal power with parliament in the English Glorious Revolution (1688) realised the triumph of parliament and an independent judiciary. Competencies of public authorities were precisely circumscribed in the "Bill of Rights" (1689). In France national unity was not yet realised by monarchy, while the struggle with societal powers (aristocracy, "parlements") continued. Revolutionaries, totally averse to the judiciary (government by judges), diseased as it was with the privileges of the Ancien Régime, subordinated the judiciary to political power. French Republics continued this tradition after the French Revolution. To cite the conclusion of Cohen-Tanugi (1987, p.62): "In France, the construction of absolutist monarchy and the heritage of conflicts in the Ancien Régime; revolutionary theories of law and 'volonté générale'; and the Napoleonic enterprise of codification. These developments, contrary to popular belief, did not exalt law. They contributed to subordination of the juridical to the political, in a way that persists in contemporary France. The method used for this subordination was control of the juridical by the political, integration of law into the State. The conception of law as prevailing since the French Revolution made it fundamentally an instrument for tutelage of the State over civil society. Law became an emanation of the State with the concept of sovereignty of law. Justice as a public service was integrated in the State apparatus. Parallel with this de-juridification of society and this Statist lawmaking the French Revolution developed theories of public service and general interest. It constructed the ideology of dialogue, solidarity and social justice, still pillars of State power today, but not sufficiently compatible with the Idea of Law."

In the Constitution of the Fifth Republic a modest place is given to the judiciary (art.64), not as "pouvoir" (power) but as "autorité" (authority). Its independence has to be guaranteed by the President of the Republic, head of executive power. President De Gaulle said in a press conference of 31 January 1964: "All State powers, a fortiori the judiciary authority, come from the President of the Republic, as elected by universal suffrage." For De Gaulle, all powers of the State, also the judiciary, are under the control of the Head of State, elected with a system of universal suffrage. The judiciary is placed directly under executive power. The judiciary is dependent on the Ministry of Justice for advancement, salary and transfers. The judiciary by its jurisprudence has a limited role for the production of norms. In an overreaction to the "parlementarisme à la française" in the Third Republic (parliament as sole power, governmental instability) executive power is given a preponderant position with regard to legislative power. This is made operational by the innovating distinction between the limited domain of legislative law (limitatively enumerated subjects in art.34) and the domain of the "règlement", general rules enacted by executive power (all other subjects, art.36). Legislative power for the executive is reinforced by giving executive power a preponderant position in initiating legislation, and by giving executive power control over the legislative procedure. The primacy of executive power is also reinforced with ruling by the party-political majority, making opposition in parliament quite impossible. When there is a serious movement in parliament which stands in the way of executive power, there are several techniques for containment ("rationalisation du parlementarisme"). Control of constitutionality by the "Conseil Constitutionnel" (CC), another innovation of the Fifth Republic, forms a certain, but limited, countervailing power. This is especially so since 1974, as adopted laws can be presented to the CC by a minority (60 members of National Assembly, or 60 members of Senate) before promulgation, with the question of whether they can stand the test of constitutionality. This instrument has drawbacks. Citizens cannot start a CC procedure, which is possible only for a short period of time.

After promulgation of a law, this law is invulnerable to any test of constitutionality. In the French Republican tradition "..the Rousseau fiction, by way of making law sacred, caused paradoxically a reduction of law and of the supreme law of the State, the Constitution. The idea that independence and competency of a professional corps could be a better guarantee than election seems profoundly strange to the French public ideology." (Cohen-Tanugi, 1987, p.70). The Constitution is generally recognised as supreme national law, but its contents do not always make effective control of laws possible. Since the seventies, the constitutional character of the Preamble to the Constitution of 1958, with references to the "Déclaration des droits de l'homme" and the newly recognised economic and social rights, has been ruled ("bloc de constitutionnalité"). So the whole of fundamental values and principles of the French Republic now has a recognised status as constitutional. Due to self-censure by constitutional judges, the use of constitutional norms is still less than it might be. A specific application of Rousseau's fiction about "volonté générale" has made the political majority the source of juridical power. The juridical was made a derivate of politics, and was often what the party-political majority decided. The notion of democracy is reduced to a sequential participation in power, when a majority is succeeded by another majority ("alternance"). One might say that the dominant French conception of law is inspired more by power than by juridical considerations. It is seen as normal that a party-political majority can push through a certain solution for societal problems by the dictatorship of the majority, disguised as law. With regard to fundamental juridical norms, Cohen-Tanugi (1987, p.77) argues: ".. a judiciary power and a juridical culture with which to make its norms triumphant with regard to politics does not exist in France. So, as long as the problem of social consensus remains unsolved in France, it will be impossible to constitute a true "état de droit", due to the non-existence of law external to the State, and imposing itself upon the State." The French solution is "law within the State (and State within society) instead of law external to and above the State." (Cohen-Tanugi, p.110).

The French juridical system also has a specific character, because State and civil society are submitted to two different systems of law: "droit administratif" (State and other public organs) and "droit privé" (civil law). This distinction is more than a differentiation between two domains of law. It is intended to create two different systems of law, with their specific fundamental conceptions, argumentations, and procedures. There are also two different jurisdictional systems: "judiciaire" and "administratif". Public authorities and societal actors are judged by different courts and according to different juridical norms. The principles of French administrative law are based upon the axiom that public authorities have to represent and to look after the general interest which has to be preferred against private interests (Laubadère, 1994). Tocqueville (1835) discerned about the judiciary in most European countries that in former times it had a quite independent position and broad competencies and that the post-revolutionary French State could escape from jurisdiction of the weakened judiciary by expropriation of judiciary power on behalf of the State apparatus. Administrative jurisprudence partially improved the institutional unbalance, thanks to creative activities of the "Conseil d'État" and administrative courts. In the field of the rights of citizens with regard to the State, French administrative jurisprudence got a reputation. The State could be tackled for "abus de pouvoir" (abuse of power), but the State still has exorbitant competencies with regard to the judiciary. Lacunae in the realisation of "État de droit" remain. Procedures against the State do not cause suspension. Administrative courts cannot give the State apparatus sanctions or instructions. Independence of the State apparatus (discretionary power) with regard to the judiciary is strong. Administrative courts have an ambivalent position: guaranteeing the good functioning of the State apparatus, and solving conflicts arising from society. A mentality of independence is not furthered. The career path of administrative judges goes from jurisdictional positions to executive jobs in the State apparatus and vice versa.

The crucial notion in French administrative law is general interest, from which the notions "puissance publique" (public power) and "service public" (public service) are derived. This notion of general interest runs the risk of functioning in the juridical system like the fiction of the "volonté générale", founding sovereignty of law in the political system. According to an unwritten, seemingly constitutional rule, a conception prevails that what the French State does is by definition in the general interest (a circular argument). It seems to be impossible to differentiate between the general interest and the interest of the State itself. While there is more or less a myth of the general interest, the interests as articulated by society are branded as categorical or corporatist. It is amazing that in France, where the State incarnates the general interest institutionally, politicians, when elected or nominated to positions which represent the State, often follow party-political interests instead, and are not called to account for this. This party-political abuse of State prerogatives is often seen as inevitable in a democracy. Setting aside the authentic responsibilities of public authorities (regalia like defence, jurisdiction, police) the crucial role of private sector and societal forces in realisation of the general interest should be recognised, especially in the social and economic field. General interest as a result of private and societal interests is mostly not recognised in French society; worse, State power is often abused by pressure groups and particularistic interests: ..occupation of the State by pressure groups and private interests.. The wheels of national education structure present an image of a universe in which administrative hierarchy and syndicalist corporatism (State in the State) live in perfect symbiosis, forming two components of the same complex. Certain private interests have made investments in the State and colonised the 'general interest' in such a way that all lobbying became redundant (Cohen-Tanugi, 1987, p.116). The general interest is even colonised. The Idea of Public Authority asks for realisation of the Rule of Law and for guarantees that the general interest will be effected by all who are exercising functions on behalf of public authorities. Ubi societas, ibi ius et auctoritas publica.

## 10.12. Cultural mindset base for constitutional government

As Montesquieu (1748) elaborated, adequate institutions for public authority in a country depend upon several factors such as climate, geographical situation, customs and history. So there can be no single ideal constitution for all countries in the world. With some exceptions, such as the United Kingdom, most countries have a written constitution, a collection of written and unwritten principles and rules about human rights and duties and the functioning of public authorities. It is not enough to analyse these documents, it is necessary to examine constitutional practices, traditions, customs and judicial interpretations, all in the framework of the specific cultural setting in which public authorities are functioning. A constitution is not only the supreme law of a country, it contains fundamental principles and the institutional build-up of the structures of public authorities. Mostly, the "trias politica" is used, differentiating legislative, executive and judicial institutions. Often a cabinet system is followed, in which the top of the executive branch of the public management system proceeds from an elected house of the national legislature, to which it is accountable and by which it can be fired. A crucial part of a constitution are legal constraints on the uses of powers and competencies given to public authorities. A fundamental criterion is used to assess whether a nation with a constitution complies with the norm of constitutional government (Friedrich, 1950). There is a constitutional government if a nation has a limited, accountable and responsive system of public authority that takes the implementation of participatory and civil rights seriously. A crucial part of constitutional government, based upon constitutional law, is a constitutional court, the highest appellate court in the judicial system of a nation. Constitutional government is broadly related to pluralist democracy. Both presuppose freedom of thought, speech, press, assembly; the right to impartial justice and free access of citizens to political processes with elections, political parties and interest groups. It is crucial that citizens and public authorities are subject to constitution and law. There is a gap between constitutional text and actual practice. Usually government is authorised by the constitution to suspend, for the limited period of an emergency, rulings about basic rights. In the 18th century, the accent in constitutions was laid on restraints on government, to guarantee civil rights and liberties. Later these rulings were supplemented with guarantees of economic, social and cultural rights, necessitating more government (outlays). In Welfare States rights of education, health care, work, income and clean environment were guaranteed. These guarantees depend on government resources.

Federalism is a specific way of organising the structure of public authority as laid down in a constitution (Wheare, 1961). A federal system divides the exercising of public authority in a territory between a government (federal or national) and territorial public authorities. Each of them is independent within its own sphere of jurisdiction, as ordained in the constitution. But having two or more levels of public authority in the same national territory inevitably causes conflicts about competencies and powers. In federal-state relations, it proved to be essential to have a final arbiter, as in the United States. Genuine federalism asks for democratic participatory processes. Federalism is a form of territorial institutional organisation of public authority to accommodate unity and regional diversity within a single system of public authority. Powers and competencies are distributed among two or more layers of public authority, so that the authority of each is constitutionally guaranteed. In spite of these notions, there is much debate about the definition and characteristics of federalism. Is its essence to be found in concepts of constitutionalism and covenant, in legal structures with distributed public authority, in pluralist ideology, in non-centralised political processes, or in social, economic and political phenomena that give pluralism a territorial dimension? One can use a broad definition to encompass a great variety of federations, as Duchacek (1986) and Riker (1975) do. Sawer (1976) and Wheare (1961) argue for a restricted definition, to denote typical federations like the United States, Canada and Switzerland. Federal systems are contrasted with unitary systems in which other public authorities in a territory are subordinate to central government. Federal systems are distinguished from confederacies in which central institutions, composed of delegates from constituent state governments, are subordinate.

The function of a constitution is to give a system of public authorities a basic law. Such a system needs an institutional framework, with a recognised division of powers, competencies and responsibilities among several public institutions, and an elaborated whole of individual rights for citizens that have to be guaranteed by public authorities. In the last part of the eighteenth century American and French constitutions set the tone by codifying basic rules in a document with a status superior to ordinary statute law, while this document can be amended only by a specific legislative procedure. England proved that it is possible to have a constitutional system without having a written constitution. England has fundamental statutory laws and tradition as its constitution: constitutional law, not having a superior legal authority, cannot be distinguished from other public law. Any constitutional practice can be overridden or revised by an act of Parliament. Most countries have a written constitution. Principles of constitutional law are determined by interpretation of the constitutional text, but this text leaves room for different interpretations. So who has the responsibility to interpret the constitution authoritatively? The executive branch interprets the constitution continually by making decisions about the use of executive power (policy room). The legislature has to interpret the constitution, while seeking creative innovations for solving societal problems in the legislative process (constitutional practices), and judicial institutions have the task of interpreting constitutional texts and practices in the light of the constitution. One might conclude that each branch of the public authority system is a recognised authoritative interpreter of all rulings about its own status and powers. In the early years of the American republic this tripartite theory of constitutional interpretation had supporters. In the Marbury v. Madison case (1803) this was challenged by Justice Marshall arguing for the primacy of judicial interpretation of the constitution. The Supreme Court declined to enforce a statute enacted by Congress, as it was thought to be contrary to the constitution. This was done, although the judicial power to declare acts of Congress unconstitutional was not stated explicitly in the constitution. Since then the Supreme Court's position as superior interpreter of the constitution has been accepted, while opposition to this innovation dwindled, due to self-restraint of the Supreme Court, accepting constitutional interpretations by President and Congress.

A constitution is meant to produce institutional order, stable constitutionally functioning public authorities and legal security, so adequate constitutional interpretation is crucial. It is asserted that the constitution does or should mean what its framers meant it to mean, but it is not always at all easy to determine what the original intention was of those who agreed the constitutional text. Another historical approach concentrates on the word meanings, and we have logical analysis as an approach. In the American context, the Supreme Court has taken an oath to uphold the constitution, while it is recognised that the constitution is the supreme law. It is a logical conclusion that the Supreme Court cannot enforce an act of

Congress that conflicts with the constitution, but has to declare it null and void. The problem is, logic alone is not enough. It is a matter of informed opinion and judgement whether a law is incompatible with the constitution. How a constitution is interpreted depends on the persons who are interpreting. There is no one best approach to constitutional interpretation. As Holmes (1963, p.5) said in "The Common Law" (1881): "The life of the law has not been logic: it has been experience. The perceived necessities of the time, prevalent moral and political theories, intuitions of public policy – avowed or unconscious, even prejudices which judges share with their fellows, have had a good deal more to do with determining the rules by which men should be governed. than the syllogism". It is a crucial challenge to adapt constitutional law to changing circumstances, while preserving basic values of the prevailing constitutional system. One can replace the old text by a new text, as France has done 15 times since the Revolution. Constitutional adaptation is often realised by amendment, interpretation and custom. Sometimes, there is a trend-setting institutional breach. Article 89 of the French constitution provides for amendment of the constitution by a vote of parliament. In 1962, President de Gaulle ignored this method. He submitted to popular referendum an amendment providing for election of the president by popular vote instead of limited suffrage. The referendum accepted this innovative but disputed method, so the system of electing the president was changed..

During the nineteenth century and after the study of constitutional law was predominantly juridical-historical, while accentuating rulings as they are and should be. Gradually attention was also given to empirical questions of how rulings functioned in reality. The study of constitutional law was influenced by behavioural trends in the social sciences. The Anglo-American school of legal realists, headed by Jerome Frank (1930), emphasised the influence of judicial personality on constitutional interpretation. Judicial behaviour has often been analysed in a sophisticated way by using the whole armoury of sociological, psychological and other tools (Schubert, 1963). Halpin (1997) analysed utilitarianism and the conceptions of authors who acquired pre-eminence in discussing rights from the perspective of general legal theory: Dworkin, Rawls and Nozick. Natural rights as elaborated in the natural law tradition were a target for Bentham (Finnis, 1980). Bentham's utilitarianism was declared to have won the battle in the moral arena. Utilitarianism was the object of intellectual attacks by Rawls, Nozick and Dworkin. Reconciliation was tried (Freeden, 1991; Glover, 1990; Raz, 1986). Halpin (1997, p.202): "the approach taken by all four theorists to the common problems that they face unites them far more than it divides them." Halpin (1997, p.205): "1. Moral theory justifies a practical moral approach – it provides a compelling reason for those subject to it to abide by that approach. 2. The moral approach thus justified is capable of determining what is and what is not required, permitted, or otherwise encouraged by that practical moral approach – and what lies wholly outside its provenance. 3. In both the above respects moral theory is sufficient, without recourse to an alternative or deeper theory, to provide full justification for a complete practical moral approach that it is capable of delivering. In short, we look for 1. Justification, 2. Practicality, and 3. Sufficiency."

Halpin (1997, p.206ff) identifies the three basic aspects of morality as M1, M2 and M3. M1 morality involves respect for the other, this respect is mutual and reciprocal: do as you would be done by (equal status as human beings). M2 morality requires denial of self-interest, in order to respect the other's interests. It is not a scheme expressing how people behave in order to achieve mutual satisfaction of their wholly compatible interests then, it is about co-ordination. "The point is that the moral agent is faced with a choice as to whether to behave in a way that respects the other by furthering his interests or whether to further his own interests, and morality places an obligation upon him to deny his own interests for the sake of the other." (Halpin, 1997, p.207). M3 morality promotes the interests of the moral agent and the other whose interests he serves. If this aspect of morality were not present there would be fulfilment of the one at the cost of depriving the other of fulfilment (this is oppression). Rawls, Dworkin and Nozick comply with M1 morality by insisting that every individual should be given proper respect through enforcement of his rights. "Since these rights are in each case available to every individual, it follows that M3 is satisfied. Compliance with M2 is usually more obliquely put in that the potential source of conflict for the rights of the individual is expressed as the interest of the state or general welfare. But even in such formulations it must follow that for the respect for others to be manifested in the enforcement of rights, those whose interests would be enhanced by the promotion of the contrary pull of general welfare (quite possibly the majority of the people) must deny such self-interest." (Halpin, 1997, p.232). Halpin (1997, p.235) concludes that Dworkin failed to satisfy criteria for successful moral theory: "His theory that is constructed on the 'axiomatic', 'fundamental' right to equal concern and respect turns out to have been built on an abstraction which provides no justification, practicality, or sufficiency for his theory as a moral theory, and his adherence to the premise that each is to count as one far from satisfying the aspects of morality is reduced to the proposition that everyone is to enjoy equal status as a member of society – a society that is capable of denying the practical aspects of morality in just the same way as a society determined by Bentham's utilitarianism."

Rawls, complaining that utilitarianism fails to respect persons, is seen as a hero for establishing the need for rights to protect the individual against the calculations of utility. Rawls (like Bentham, establishing his theory on the 'scientific' observation of the human desire for pleasure) provides a combined justification and motivation in his use of rational self-interest through his device of the "veil of ignorance" in "A Theory of Justice" (1971). In a sense for Halpin (1997, p.236), "Rawls' motivating force of rational self-interest is a more sophisticated version of Bentham's pleasure motive, but it fails for precisely the same reasons." Rawls (1993) in "Political Liberalism" limits the scope of his theory of justice to a society that accepts the liberal values on which it is founded. Halpin (1997, p.237): "Even in this more restricted habitat, Rawls' theory of rights suffers from a number of flaws. Assuming for the moment the liberal premises required by Rawls, the principles of justice he derives are still sufficiently abstract as to cause problems in deducing particular individual rights. Is there anything within the principle of maximum equal liberty, or within the principle of distributing resources to favour the position of the least well off "the difference principle", to ensure that the aspects of morality are complied with and that individuals are respected in concrete situations?" Rawls' theory proves to apply to a society that is already just, because there is already a sufficient level of welfare (Kymlicka, 1989).

In Nozick's minimalist state (1974) "it is the exclusive attention paid to property rights that is capable of marking out the separateness of persons required to fully respect others morally, which guards against the excesses of utilitarianism and at the same time stands against liberal welfarism. An obvious rejoinder to Nozick is that he has simply failed to consider other types of rights that might be equally as important as property rights. I will suggest that Nozick does in fact fail to provide a moral theory, in accordance with the criteria we have established." (Halpin, 1997, pp. 241-242). His argument to restrict the state to enforcement of property rights (to ensure the distinctness of individuals in permitting them the practical possibility of choosing a life plan and making their lives meaningful) is obviously weak. It would require a permanent redistribution of property rights to give all citizens a meaningful life. There is a circularity of argument: institutional structures of society determine the extent of property rights, and property rights determine the extent of institutional structures of society. Liberties which we possess over our property are constituted by correlative duties in others. Once we recognise these correlative duties as determining our liberty, it is evident that a society is needed with Public Management of

Society imposing duties on others. Halpin (1997, p.250) concludes his examination of Nozick's theory of rights with the finding that he fails to produce a moral theory. "The conclusion we have reached with regard to all four theorists is that they have failed to provide a justification for a practical moral approach, and further, that they have failed to work out in practice a moral approach that retains respect for each individual." (Halpin, 1997, p.252).

Realisation of social justice is the kernel of constitutional government. Fitzmaurice (1997) analysed available theoretical models about justice: neo-Hobbesian (Gauthier), Kantian (Rawls, 1972), "Kantian" with an empirical motivational base (Rawls, 1980; 1985), and neo-Aristotelian or communitarian (MacIntyre, 1981; Sandel, 1982; Walzer, 1984). They assume that principles of justice are principles for organising social life to which rational persons can or would assent. "For the purposes of mapping theories of justice onto theories of practical reason, the latter can be usefully divided into two categories: those which take all reasons for action as internal and those which take it that there are external reasons. This distinction corresponds roughly to that between hypothetical and categorical imperatives." (Fitzmaurice, 1997, p.16). A theory of justice incorporates a theory of practical reason and motivation, showing that acting justly can be rational and that persons can be motivated to do so. Fitzmaurice (1997, p.18): "The two classical models for reasoning about justice, those of Hobbes and Kant, represent opposite poles of the spectrum of theories of practical reasoning. Hobbesians are internal reason theorists of a pure and paradigmatic sort. ..Laws and institutions are rationally vindicable to those whose private ends they serve: universally rationally vindicable if the end, which they serve, is universally desired."

"Kantians argue that some principles for public institutions can be shown to conform to the requirements of non-instrumental reason. Just institutions are those which would be acceptable to agents thinking in conformity with the principles of pure practical reason, hence their legitimacy is quite independent of the contingent and varied desires of the actual agents who live under them. Some theorists who offer apparently formal or procedural vindications of principles of justice are not Kantian in any deep sense, for their superficially procedural vindications are properly understood as articulations of some fundamental value of fairness or equal respect, or a fundamental ideal of a person. The resulting principles of justice are then justifiable only to those who desire to realise the ideal. Rawls, who was once (at least arguably) strongly Kantian, and convinced of choice in the original position as a procedural equivalent of the categorical imperative, now acknowledges that his principles presuppose a contingently shared ideal of a person as rational, equal and free. His theory is super-structurally 'Kantian', but has an empirical motivational base." (o.c., p.18). Originally, Rawls was Kantian, because he stuck to his basic position: the provision of a purely rational ground for principles of justice. Fitzmaurice (1997, p.19): "theory of justice…of the later Rawls, which is plausibly thought of as a sort of communitarian liberalism, since the principles of reason rest ultimately not on a-historical principles of reason, but on a shared cultural ideal, for the realisation of which there is a widespread 'highest-order desire'. "

For Fitzmaurice (1997, p.18) a clear-cut theory of justice is harder to discern in work of theorists who may be called communitarian or neo-Aristotelian: "This is partly because these theories lack the sharp discontinuity between reason and value .. Neo-Aristotelians regard rational action as necessarily conforming to an order of value. Rational action is intelligible action, and intelligibility demands that the end to which action is oriented falls under a value-concept, or desirability description. ..What provides the order of value to which action, in order to be intelligible, must be appropriately oriented, is a given tradition or culture. " Fitmaurice (1997, p.19) concludes: "The neo-Aristotelians, I suggest, should also be placed in the internal reasons camp, since they eschew transcendental moral argument and treat the demands of morality, including political morality, as historically and culturally specific. Since there are no unconditional requirements of rationality, whether or not I ought to do such-and-such depends on the moral ideals I actually have, which in turn depends on the culture I inhabit." Principles of justice bind those who share an ideal. They apply universally but within constraints of the specific cultural-existential context. The Idea of Public Authority makes it plausible that culturally adapted Public Management of Society is a necessary condition for reasonable realisation of the principles of justice.

The conception of the Constitutional State as it was elaborated, was not a product of juridical reasoning as such, but influenced by the societal environment (socially, politically, ideologically, economically, culturally). The conception of the Constitutional State supposes a State as a collective entity, distinguished from civil society and from law, which has to represent the ideal of justice. In France, it was based upon ideas about the powers of public authorities and individual liberties of citizens as elaborated before and with the Revolution. Besides, in France as in other democratic countries, this conception was developed in the 19th century by adapting it to new insights of democracy. The idea of the constitutional State was elaborated to give society a political and social organisation which could meet the norms of liberal democracy (Cohen-Tanugi, 1989). This liberalising movement was a reaction to an overstressed accent upon State intervention. In the Ancien Régime, there were forerunners with conceptions about social consensus ("contrat social") as reaction against one-sided conceptions of absolutism. Law, on the basis of nature as source, was thought to have as its objective guaranteeing the collective security and protection of all citizens (Barret-Kriegel, 1992). French revolutionaries, who wanted to make excesses of absolutist monarchy impossible in the future, fulfilled their decisive historical role by proclaiming inalienable human rights which also had to be guaranteed against oppressive public authorities. Executive power had to be subjected to the Nation. In the 19th century, the conception of the constitutional State was elaborated in relation to the ongoing strife between movements trying to restore a more absolutist regime and others accentuating a more liberal regime. In the name of the primacy given to individuals and natural order, liberal-democratic foundations were given to the conception of the Constitutional State. A key issue was limitation of the powers of public authorities: protection of individual liberties; submission to the Nation; and strictly limited competencies. The juridical order was seen as instrument to operationalise and guarantee limitation of State powers. Renewed accentuation of the rights of the individual had its roots in natural law conceptualisation as dominant in the 18th and 19th centuries (Arnaud, 1991). It was argued that the individual was there already before the State. The State was due to a social contract between individuals, with general interest and the interests of citizens as objectives.

The American Revolution (1776-1783) and French Revolution (1789) were necessary events to give an impetus to a more liberal-democratic operation of the constitutional State. It was not so much in Nature but more in Reason that these new conceptions were founded (Gauchet, 1989). With the "Déclaration des droits de l'homme et du citoyen" (1789) the French conception of the constitutional State got a fundamental substantial basis. This gave French legal doctrine a strong position in its resistance to Kelsen's formalistic conceptualisation. Another part of the Constitutional State conception is its underlying democratic character. Democracy, defined by the will of the Nation as expressed via its representatives, has to fulfil many norms. Replacement of "Polizeistaat" by "Rechtsstaat" implied democratisation of institutions. In the French conception of the constitutional State, the State is a continuation of the Nation: Nation-State. As formulated in the 1791 Constitution, sovereignty belongs to the Nation. For Rousseau, the sovereign could only be "le peuple en corps". In the footsteps of Sieyès, sovereignty was thought to be delegated to representatives having to "will for the Nation". Setting aside a period in which Jacobins branded the despotism of representatives in overstressed ideas of popular sovereignty, national sovereignty is the foundation of the French constitutional State conception. For scholars in Germany, the nation is only one of the constituent elements of the State.

The French doctrine has structurally conceived the State as emanation of the Nation, its juridical personification. Without any will of its own or any objective for itself the State transforms the collective power of the Nation (foundation of sovereignty) into juridical terms (Pouvoirs, 1993). The Nation is seen as a subject, having rights (sovereignty) that can be opposed to the State. With the theory of the general will, building up from individuals to the collective, the Nation, having subjective rights, is an extension of the individuals. The idea that law is an expression of the general will is a fundament of the Constitutional State. Most French theoreticians of the Constitutional State agree that representative democracy emerged with the Revolution. Redor (1992) criticised the French representative system. Assemblies, made omnipotent in the Third Republic, are thought incapable of fulfilling their responsibilities. Representative logic is thought to be perverted by democratisation of suffrage. Universal suffrage would have falsified representation by introducing "gouvernment d'opinion", exposing elected representatives to the pressures of particularist interests. Independence of elected representatives, transformed into mandataries, was eliminated. In this approach, universal suffrage, instead of being a true representation of opinions, causes a tyranny of minorities, damaging individual liberties (Rosanvallon, 1992). Development of a constitutional State had to be realised by reducing the powers of Parliament and reinforcing powers of executive power. The importance of juridical controls instead of political controls was accentuated. A more mature theory of democracy developed. Democracy was no longer identified with law of the parliamentary majority, but was said to also encompass respect for superior rules and norms. The role of the State and the scale of State intervention were redefined, distinguishing more strictly between public and private domains (Leroy-Beaulieu, 1911). In the conception of liberal democracy, the focus was upon reducing State intervention to its minimum ("État minimal"). Independently from this liberal democracy movement, several features of a more mature constitutional State were elaborated. From a more or less idealised position, the production of ever more juridical norms was seen as promoting the Constitutional State ("fétichisme de la règle"). Juridical norms were often seen as reality itself. One could even speak about the "mystique de l'État de droit". The "culte de droit" in France has roots in medieval times (Legendre, 1974). Juridical rules were used to effect authority, and to defend individuals against absolutism. In capitalist activities, juridical rules were used to make exploitation effective. In Western civilisation juridical instruments were in this way continually extended. All spheres of society came into the grip of juridical rules. When the Constitutional State is pursued, it has to spread its reach everywhere, legality as totalising notion. A Constitutional State tends to lead to integral juridification of social order. An important feature is the strict demarcation between the domain of law and the domain of politics. Law was even sacrosanct. The objectivity of juridical norms, freed from political dimensions, is seen as guarantee for their real normative value. The juridical debate tends thus to be placed in the hands of judges (with independence and competencies) and jurists as professionals of juridical reason. Law during the 19th century was often seen as the sole true knowledge of the State, especially in the sphere of administrative law (Chevallier, 1993a). Up to 1870 administrative law was a component of knowledge to organise public administration.

From 1870 on, this situation changed. On the basis of the work of pioneering scholars like Laferrière (1854) a body of logic and coherent rules was built up, narrowly interconnected with administrative science. In this creative process, the needs of the constitutional State, as opposed to the police State (no limits to powers of public authorities), were stressed: administrative law was the dominant knowledge of public administration. This brought French administrative law science to the forefront worldwide, thanks to the "quatre mousquetaires" at the beginning of the 20th century: Esmein, Duguit, Hauriou and Carré de Malberg. Ongoing juridification of social life is said to tend to the elimination of the public power phenomenon, as all powers of public authorities are transformed into competencies ruled by law. The Constitutional State not as government by persons, but by ruling of juridical norms. The power of public authorities is not more than the execution of what has to be done according to norms. The ideal of the Constitutional State is thought to be brought closer with the elimination of discretionary powers. This elimination of discretionary powers was explicitly pursued with regard to the role of the judge, key-figure of the Constitutional State. He has to guarantee respect for laws. If this task were to be fulfilled "objectively" the judge would have no discretionary power whatever. Jurisdictional work is seen as purely deductive: the judge is thought to apply the law, nothing less, nothing more. The judge is thought to have no power at all, he is a pure law mechanic using syllogisms to apply legal texts to particular situations. This conception of the role of judges was seen as a method to eliminate the risk of government by judges. To accentuate that law is superior to politics, independence of judges was proclaimed. To eliminate abuses of the "Parlements de l'Ancien Régime" revolutionaries claimed that judges had to stick to the legal texts literally and so follow the will of legislative power. This is a fundamental cause for the structural feature of the French institutional arrangement which hindered the building of a genuine judiciary power. Some revolutionaries thought that law was more the result of reason than of will. That elimination of power was meant to make the issuing of norms a process ruled by law. This juridical formalisation could not eliminate the power phenomenon, however, of course not.

These conceptions about the constitutional State, while accentuating that law was anterior and superior to the State itself, contributed to promoting the legitimacy of the State. Effacing themselves behind the law, governing functionaries could use the competencies given to them by law more freely. This legal-rational legitimisation (Weber) enabled public authorities to further efficient fulfilment of their tasks. The conception of the Constitutional State was made an integral part of French juridical institutionalising. Because of the crucial function of the Constitutional State as an effective instrument of legitimising the activities of public authorities, it was given a central position. It also became a means to accentuate the autonomy of public law with regard to private law and social sciences. This was an important issue, as before civil law jurists could claim that the mother of all law was civil law. It was also possible to prevent the extended sphere of public law (and public administration) from being swallowed by sociology or political science. Since the last part of the 19th century, the accent had been laid more upon legality: executive power could do what it wanted, as there was a law for this. In the 20th century, the French conception of the Constitutional State was elaborated further, and was also given new dimensions as well. One innovation was that, more than before, the contents of juridical norms was stressed. It was not only a hierarchical juridical order, but also a series of rules which had to guarantee individual rights and liberties. By becoming more substantial in this way the French conception converged more with the British Rule of Law. Circumstances changed drastically with the First World War. Competencies for executive power had to be enlarged, a series of emergency acts was needed, often "à l'improviste". As public authorities had to encounter new, urgent problems the notion of legality was stretched to encompass new competencies. Legal authorisation of executive authorities got the form of a general, open-ended legal form, if any. After the First World War, public authorities needed enlarged competencies to take control of the post-war crisis. The depression of the thirties was a challenge for public authorities which were given enlarged competencies. "Lois-décrets" made public authorities rule with regulations-like-laws; the legislative process was avoided.

The weaknesses of the French idea of parliamentarism, putting all power in the hands of the majority in the National Assembly, and making government and executive power totally dependent on parliament (and party-political majorities), were apparent. Following the terrible experiences of the defeat in June 1940, Nazi-occupation and the collaborating Vichy-regime, it was possible to build up a constitutional State after Liberation. Formally, there was a new Constitution in 1946 for the Fourth Republic, but the "parlementarisme à la française" of the Third Republic continued. A climax in the Algerian crisis (Heymann, 1972) brought De Gaulle to power in 1958. He changed the institutional setting of the regime drastically. The Constitution of 1958, birth certificate of the Fifth Republic, at last gave France what it had needed for so long; a stronger executive power, while competencies of the parliament were restrained. A crucial development was that France became, since the fifties, one of the six pioneering Member-States of the European Community who signed the Treaty of Rome (1957). Although the accent was on forming a common market, it was the start of a comprehensive process of institutionalising architecture with a prominent role for French institutional philosophy. Since then, more countries have become Member-States. The 15 Member-States of the European Union prepared to take decisions about renewal of institutional arrangements with the Treaty of Amsterdam (1997). One issue which became more important in the last decade of the 20th century was the development of the "European law sphere". The European Court of Justice has actively applied juridical norms, based on the founding treaties and other juridical arrangements between Member-States of the European Union (Pouvoirs, 2001). The European Court of Justice uses its competencies to "find" European law rules (also outside explicit legislation) which are binding for Member-States and/or inhabitants and corporations. EU law increasingly has an impact upon daily life in the national law traditions. A new challenge for public authorities with their crucial task to make the Rule of Law prevail. The Rule of Law needs institutions to realise its rulings: public authorities.

## 10.13. Cultural mapping of public authority

The Idea of Public Authority, a vital component of civilisation, has gone through a process of emancipation in the history of mankind. The concept of authority is related to concepts like power, leadership and influence, often used to denote a social-psychological phenomenon in human relations, whereby some can make others do what they would not normally do. All societies have persons with a recognised position of authority, with competencies to issue, implement and maintain rules of behaviour in the relevant group. A crucial characteristic of public authority is its historical roots in the cultural environment, which makes its institutionalising fundamentally specific. Therefore cultural mapping of public authority is a necessary condition. In pre-society circumstances, positions of authority were indissolubly intertwined with other roles of persons with authority (familial, religious, economic, social, cultural). The key issue then was the question of where the final authority rested to define jurisdictions. This is still a key issue. From a certain point in the historical development, positions of authority became more differentiated, so that there were genuine, specific public authorities, having competencies to issue laws according to some recognised procedure and to cause them to be implemented. Freeman (1999) stressed the Greek Achievement as a foundation of the Western World. Some Greek philosophers were pioneers in developing the Idea of Public Authority in Antiquity. Socrates (469-399 BC) never stopped asking crucial questions. Is a person with public authority legitimised to issue a law reducing the liberties of citizens? Is a citizen obliged to obey an unjust law? Practising his method of criticising conceptions and practices of persons with positions in the polis (town), he paid with his life for sticking to his principles by drinking a cup of poison. In his dialogues "Apology" and "Crito" (428-347 BC) his disciple Plato elaborated on the obligations of citizens with regard to the polis, and persons having specific responsibilities for the polis as public authorities. Plato had a normative conception about ideal public authorities (philosopher king). Plato's disciple Aristotle (384-322 BC) innovated by accentuating empirical knowledge about the way public authorities functioned in reality. The normative and the empirical approach are relevant.

The Romans had a crucial impact upon institutional engineering of the process of organising differentiated structures of public authority in Europe. The term authority is derived from "auctoritas". A Roman father had "auctoritas" in the family. Romulus, the notional founder of Rome, was seen as supreme "auctor". This quality was thought to pass on to the Senate, originally composed of elders from the patrician class, later of experienced office-holders. The Senate managed the Roman (city) state on the basis of their "auctoritas" and not primarily by virtue of the power of the offices they held. In medieval Europe the Idea of Public Authority was developed in relation to the dominant position of the Church, and to Judeo-Christian ideas about public authority. Authority was thought to emanate from special competencies given to specific persons by divine law. This laid the basis for monarchies, claiming that Kings were issuing laws in the name of God: they had sovereignty. The person having sovereignty, able to define jurisdictions in the last resort, was recognised as a superior public authority. When the unity of Christian Europe fell to pieces, due to the attempts of Luther and Calvin to renew the Church, a new situation developed. Following the principle "cuius regio eius religio", the monarch, having power, could determine which religion his followers had to recognise. There was a difference between persons having a legitimised position of public authority and others who had the power in fact, but did not have the recognised position as public authority. Hobbes, in his Leviathan (1651), argued that public authority did not come from God but from the people. For him sovereignty was the consequence of an authorisation of those who have submitted to a sovereign. They have a vital interest in peace, and authorise a sovereign to organise situations of peace and war, and to make laws. Later, a more mature conception was developed going beyond formal authorisation of the holder of the position of public authority. This implied that policies of public authorities should get legitimacy with authorisation by (representatives of) the people. The dominant conception of public authority was that public authority emanates from the people by election (democracy).

A form of organisation of society emerged from the fifteenth century onwards in Europe, the State. This was an epoch-making institutional innovation, because the heart of public authority was made independent of mortal persons, furthering stability. In the complex power struggle between rulers, Church, nobility, cities and bourgeoisie, the term State came into use as a collective noun for public authority. Machiavelli developed the idea that the State had to be seen as an autonomous, secular realm, in which a specific morality was dominant, "reason of state". Bodin elaborated its specific attribute as sovereignty: absolute and unique authority involving the ability to make, apply and guarantee law. In historical fact State-building was accompanied with all kinds of conflict and war. The power of the State seemed the decisive dimension. Prominent in State conceptualisation was always the conception of the State as legal institution. Political science accentuated the power of the State. The science of law elaborated the idea of the State as legal institution. Experiences with autocracies of monarchs ruling with absolute arbitrariness furthered argument for the idea of the abstract, impersonal State. This State is seen as controlling a consolidated territory with a system of public offices, differentiated from that of other organisations operating in the same territory. Max Weber elaborated this idea by arguing for rational legal authority as a type of authority in the modern world, displacing traditional and charismatic authority. He made public bureaucracy the prominent instrument for realising rational legal authority. Many studies of the State are available. An analytical distinction between State conceptions distinguishes between State-as-might, State-as-law, and State-as-legitimacy. In the State-as-might approach, the power dimension is accentuated. As in Machiavelli's "reason of State", German ideas about "Machtsstaat" (Clausewitz, Treitschke, Schmitt), ideas of elite theorists (Mosca, Pareto) and Marxist analyses about the State as coercive instrument of the capitalist class. For the State-as-law approach, the crucial dimension of the State is not its power, but its legal powers and competencies. The State is seen as a set of offices, of which rights and duties are circumscribed in law or constitution. The "Rechtsstaat", in which the Rule of Law is the dominant, superior dimension, was a crucial innovation. In the State-as-legitimacy approach, fundamental principles, underlying State and public authorities, and giving their activities legitimacy, are stressed. A key assumption of State theory is the distinction between State and civil society. This is pre-condition of the State's claim to embody a unique public authority, and the capacity to take a disinterested view of the public interest.

In the twentieth century, one of the most imposing conceptions of public authority has been that of Max Weber (1922). He distinguished, ideally and typically, three types of authority: traditional, charismatic and legal-rational. The criterion he used was the kind of legitimacy each type produced. Traditional authority is based on factual circumstances (persons having power in fact). Charismatic authority is due to specific personal capacities of a leader. The most sophisticated type of public authority is legal-rational authority. Public authority can reach a more rational, more civilised level when its legitimacy is not dependent on factual power or personal charisma, but on laws. The next question is, what kind of laws give public authorities genuine legitimacy. Against a sizeable part of literature accentuating that the State is not distinguishable from other associations merely because it uses a specific kind of power, Max Weber characterised the State as follows: "A compulsory political association with continuous organisation will be called a "State" if and in so far as its administrative staff successfully upholds a claim to the monopoly of the legitimate use of physical force in the enforcement of its order." Social scientists do not agree on the definition and the concept of (public) authority. According to Bierstedt (1954, pp. 79-80), "authority becomes a power phenomenon .. it is sanctioned power, institutionalised power." Lasswell and Kaplan (1950, p.133), considering power as a form of influence, defined authority as "formal power". Friedrich (1963, p.207), seeing influence as a kind of power, rejected this definition. He defined authority instead as "the quality of a communication", which is "capable of reasoned elaboration" (pp. 218; 224). More convincing is the conception of Max Weber, seeing the State as a specific kind of power, legitimate power because it is acting as public authority. Public authority is a specific form of social control.

Trying to break the dominant conceptualisation in the prevailing political science of his time, Easton (1953) developed a new conception. Societal reality showed that societal actors other than State and public organisations played an important role in political decision-making: political parties, business, interest-groups etc. In a kind of overreaction with regard to the dominantly juridical approach, which neglected empirical facts while accentuating normative and formal aspects, social sciences presented the empirical approach more or less as the sole adequate scientific approach. To broaden the theoretical framework so that political science could encompass all political phenomena, he proposed to use the concept of a political system. Easton used "authoritative allocation of values" as the criterion to demarcate political phenomena from other social phenomena. Only persons and organs recognised as legitimate public authorities can legitimately and authoritatively allocate values for a society. Other social actors trying to do the same are usurping public authority, and don't have the legitimacy for it. The political system encloses all political phenomena, but the public authority phenomenon, although having political dimensions, cannot be analysed fully or adequately within the framework of political science. Political science is seen as conceptual framework for all political phenomena, for which power relations can be viewed as causal relations of a particular kind: analysis in terms of independent and dependent variables. An imposing distinction can be made between typically continental European societies, and other societies where the State was not so central in institutionalising and discourse (typically English-speaking countries).

In continental European countries the idea of the State as central, society-steering institution, combining public authority and political power, has deep roots in the cultural-historical setting (Roman institutionalising). In English-speaking countries with a remarkable continuity of medieval ideas and institutions (tradition as institutional sanctuary) there is far less reception of Roman law. In a sizeable part of literature it is normal to use terms that obscure the differences between authority (or power, or influence) and public authority In empirical analyses, this difference seems to be a pure formal distinction, but it is not a negligible formality. In mainstream literature, differences between public authority and other kinds of authority, influence or power are often marginalised. It is seen as more relevant to determine who has the real (political) power. A crucial characteristic of public authority is that unlike force, coercion or political power, it has specific legitimacy. Authority is a relational concept concerning human relations, where someone or some persons have influence over other persons. While there are relations of authority in all kinds of human interaction, the public authority phenomenon is specific due to a process of institutionalising, giving persons acting on behalf of public authority a specific position. This position is related to specific dimensions, characteristics, roles, competencies, and rationalities. Even empiricist scholars would eventually, at second thought, admit that the public authority phenomenon has empirical relevance. There is sufficient evidence to make this assertion more than plausible. As often in the context of social interaction the public authority phenomenon is interrelated with the whole of human interaction. It is necessary to analyse, in concrete situations, where and in what way the public authority phenomenon plays a role. It is often not easy to demarcate the boundaries of the public authority phenomenon. Mixed conceptions are mostly the vogue, mixing political power (political parties) with public authority (the State), or mixing social-psychological processes in organisations (public or private organisations), and confusing public-private arrangements (hybrids) within the unresolved notion of governance.

Although there are a number of comparative studies covering aspects of the public authority phenomenon in several countries, it has to be accentuated that frequently not enough attention is given to the specific cultural mapping of the public authority phenomenon. The cultural context is a primary factor having a crucial impact upon the way public authorities function and are experienced by other actors in societies concerned. Seen in a view as developed in social-cultural anthropology, there is a broad and multi-varied set of relevant cultural maps about specific identities of peoples, nations, regions and local communities. Often these fundamental dimensions are not taken into account seriously enough because one tries to elaborate universalist generalisations about some aspect of the public authority phenomenon. Abstracting away the specifics of cultural mapping of public authority is not admissible in an adequate approach. In Western literature it is recognised that Chinese culture is so specific that this has to be reckoned with in scholarly work. This basic cultural approach holds true for other peoples, countries or nations. The public authority phenomenon varies from culture to culture. Public authority is indissolubly intertwined with its cultural context. The way public authority functions in a country or nation (cultural styles of public authority) is part of the cultural identity that cannot be abstracted away in cross-cultural comparisons without seriously damaging the public authority phenomenon.

## 10.14. Cultural intelligence necessary condition for adequate Public Management of Society

After sketching the crucial role of Rule of Law and Idea of Public Authority in Public Management of Society in its cultural-existential environment some concluding remarks can be made. Mostly this crucial role is underexposed in scholarly works of political science and social sciences. A striking characteristic of social sciences is the fragmentation of social knowledge into so-called epistemological communities. "The social disciplines are greatly isolated from one another and enormously fragmented within their own borders. Hundreds, even thousands, of little islands of theory and research within each discipline are pursued independently, with no apparent prospect of their being linked up in any coherent, overall picture of human activity." (Richardson/Fowers, 1998, p.465). Probably the most advanced theoretical conceptualisation with regard to Public Management of Society was realised by Luhmann. In "Theorie der Verwaltungswissenschaft" (1966) he formulated seven working-hypotheses for development of an integrated theory of public management: social systems theory; binding decisions for society as specific function of public authorities; public management of society and its environment; law as structure of public management of society; rationalising public management of society; functional-comparing method; and bridging the gap between empirical and normative sciences. It seems possible to abstract away the cultural factor in universalised conceptualisation but social reality and social inquiry are intensely interconnected with cultural and moral values (Archer, 1996).

This makes it appropriate to formulate a complementary working-hypothesis about the cultural-existential dimension of Public Management of Society, taking account of Luhmann's work during more than three decades since his draft for an integrated theory for public management. The inclusive and common sense concept of Public Management of Society offers an adequate approach not by inadequate exclusion, but by the inclusion of relevant dimensions, as is normal in common sense practice. Confronted with our claim for an eighth working-hypothesis, Luhmann would probably agree. Historical and cultural-existential dimensions of Public Management of Society are decisive, determining the identity and mindset of Public Management of Society in each nation (Martin, 1982). Ideas, activities, mentalities and characteristics of actors in specific historical, cultural-existential circumstances do matter (Zeldin, 1997). France is a paradigmatic example of their relevance: "l'exception française" (Braudel, 1986). Often aspects of this crucial component are taken for granted, only formally recognised, or abstracted away in theoretical conceptions. "The human condition involves a gathering together of the past into the present as a projection of possibility into the future. Cultural and historical contexts provide a range of possibilities that become appropriated through the intentionality of the actors. Public administration cannot expect to create and control social action without understanding the relationships between the contexts and intentions of social actors or without reflecting on its own situatedness in these relationships." (Woller/Patterson, 1997, p.111).

Co-disciplinary dialogue over boundaries of existing epistemological communities is required, overcoming rigidities and reductions of disciplinary specificity with all the variety of approaches and data. The problem is that not only specialists but also well read scholars familiar with crossing disciplinary-boundaries meet the problem of not having read relevant studies. Since 1974 world-systems theory has developed as an important tool for comparative study of cultures (Kardulias, 1999). In the framework of world-systems theory, due attention is given to particularities of historical circumstances in specific cultural contexts. These are a welcome complement to mainstream literature, providing for ample cross-fertilisation between approaches of a wide range of disciplines and super-specialised knowledge. Another trend is the seemingly overpowering concept of globalisation

(Featherstone et al., 1995; Robertson, 1992; Sanderson, 1995), often presented as deterministically forcing a kind of global culture (Featherstone, 1990). Robertson (1995) rightly suggested the concept of glocalisation, to reckon with crucial cultural variety of local (regional, national) situations and circumstances, deeply rooted in specific cultural and historical settings.

Interregional and intercultural interactions are also important. Due attention must be given to all kinds of interregional and intercultural osmosis with interpenetration of ideas, values and practices. Cultural mapping, analysis of cultural dimensions, is needed for adequate understanding of Public Management of Society. We must be keen on these dimensions, correcting ourselves continually in our mindset. An adequate approach to theory and practice of Public Management of Society has cultural intelligence as a necessary condition. Luhmann quite rightly took freedom of action for (groups of) human beings as a basic premise in his conception of social system (defined as all actions, interactions and communications between human beings). This is especially relevant with regard to those critics who unjustly blame Luhmann for his conception as systems theory. Luhmann's conception is fundamentally different from mainstream systems theory conceptualisations, interpreting the notion system as a determinist structure imposing itself on social actors. A. Schütz, inspired by Max Weber's idea of the social world as the whole of sense-related social interactions, in "Der sinnhafte Aufbau der sozialen Welt" (1932) reinterpreted society. Society is the whole of social reality interpretations of groups and individuals. Luhmann, assimilating this, developed his conception of social system as fundamentally sense-related social interaction and communication. "Sinn" (sense, meaning), a combination of selection from possibilities and reference to not-selected possibilities, is the crucial heart of all human social interaction. It enables human capacities to reduce and maintain social complexity simultaneously by means of social systems. Social systems by specific ways of selection make human life in society possible.

The profiled conception of Luhmann soon provoked reactions. One of the most interesting discussions took place in the Habermas/Luhmann debate from 1971. According to Habermas, Luhmann gave the notion "Sinn" cognitively richer contents than systems theory allows. This is not adequate, but can be explained by a specific, idealised presupposition of Habermas that social interaction has to be based upon an ideal situation of perfect power-free communication ("Diskurs"). Only on the basis of this "Diskurs" (discourse), it would be possible to form consensus, and to formulate "true" judgements. When there is dissension, there is according to Habermas (1984) no "communicative action" oriented upon cultural values, but only "strategic action" oriented upon interests. So Habermas was able to criticise other conceptions, disqualified as interest-ruled knowledge. The Habermas/Luhmann is full of talking at cross-purposes with different terms and notions. Habermas defines power as capacity to hinder other actors from serving their own interests. For him, power as opposed to to power-free communication, should be reduced as far as possible. Luhmann has a realistic concept of power: as medium of communication which can reduce and enlarge the selection possibilities of others. Power should not be reduced or eliminated altogether, but widened by giving all who are confronted with power wielded by others more freedom. This can be realised by generalisation of power through loosening the bond with the personal characteristics of individuals. Habermas emphasized that each binding decision should be based on personal recognition by each individual as right. Luhmann shows that modern political systems need many binding decisions for which it is impossible to ask for personal approval by each citizen.

Habermas recognises the progress by Luhmann's social systems theory with regard to Parsons' structural-functionalist social systems theory. Habermas values the contribution of Luhmann to a theory of societal evolution, especially with his series of evolutionary universals: technique of generalisation; method of differentiation; reflexive mechanisms (application of processes upon themselves); media of communication to guarantee transfer of selections. These evolutionary universals are especially relevant for the analysis of a world-historical process of enlargement of the capacity of social systems for control and self-steering. According to Habermas, three dimensions must be distinguished in an evolutionary theory of societal systems. Scientific-technological progress, based on cumulative processes of learning about reality, determined by instrumentalism (development of productive capabilities: technical knowledge). Secondly, enlargement of steering capacities of societal systems, based on learning processes for strategic actions and social-technological planning (strategies, organisations, and management techniques: functional knowledge). Thirdly, emancipating transformation of institutional systems, based on learning processes about ideologies (legitimacy, renewal of justifications, criticism with practical consequences: practical knowledge). Habermas, referring to the four universalia of Marx (production, form of societal traffic, communication, ideology), defied Luhmann's claim to have developed a universalist theory. It would, according to Habermas, be adequate only for the second level. Agreeing with Marx, Habermas argued that the central conflict between productive forces and production relations (the institutional set built-up in a former phase of development) determines all other societal conflicts as far as these are relevant for structural changes of society. Luhmann argues that one has to use a higher level of abstraction than is done in the evolution theories of Marx and others who use a nature-causal process notion. Luhmann argues that his social systems theory encloses all three levels as distinguished by Habermas. He claims to have developed an universalist social theory in which all social phenomena can be interpreted adequately. He qualifies his own social systems theory even as a super theory: it not only encompasses the whole object (all social phenomena) but also makes room for all other theoretical conceptions, even those opposing his own conception.

Scholar Langrod worked during a long period to make the study of Public Management of Society an autonomous discipline in France. Langrod (Verwaltungsarchiv, 1968, p.85) concluded that Luhmann was the first to have laid a consistent and logically well considered basis for the modern science of Public Management of Society. This is still the case nowadays. Without making explicit that he knows Luhmann's conception, Gunnell (1995) asserts: "Political theory and political science continue to be held captive by philosophical images of science and the discursive fate of those images. Nowhere is this more evident than in the persistent influence of the instrumentalist image of scientific theory and the deductive or covering-law model of explanation." A misunderstanding in some literature is that Luhmann's social systems theory is more or less identical with Parsons's social systems theory (Murphy, 1982), so Luhmann's work could be seen as merely a Parsons revival in German sociology (Alexander, 1984). Since Parsons' theorising is criticised severely, this could give the impression that one could omit Luhmann's work unread, as it only repeats Parsons' conception. There is ample research available demonstrating that this is incorrect. The so-called "End of Luhmann's Social Systems Theory" (Wagner, 1997) is a misnomer, just as Fukuyama's "End of History" (1992) is. This does not mean that one has to interpret Luhmann's work dogmatically or uncritically. Luhmann's theorising semantics about the notion of politics is criticised in this study. He rightly differentiates economy, law and political system as functional systems but, as is elaborated in this study, Luhmann does not follow his own innovative path of differentiation enough. The potential of his conception can be enlarged by consistently differentiating politics and (professional) public management of society. Luhmann (1989, pp. 85-86): "In reality even the political system is differentiated by means of a special code through which it attains the closure of its own mode of operation and an openness to the environment and change of political programs. The code is commensurate with the centralization of political power in the state. Power is political only in so far as it can be used to cover collectively binding decisions ...The structure of state offices serves as the political code, indeed as the unified code of all of politics." So politics is differentiated on the basis of the notion "public authorities", the sole organs legitimised in a pluralist democracy with the Rule of Law to realise collectively binding decisions. Luhmann seems to follow mainstream literature here, using politics as a more or less all-encompassing notion.

It is rather odd to qualify politics by the "public authorities" phenomenon, especially because an important part of public authorities is explicitly seen as non-political (judiciary, public officials, the military). Politics does encompass public authorities and other spheres of society in which power aspects are relevant (business, society at large). Public authorities function in a political system (political science), an economic system (economic science), a law system (law science), etc., as business organisations do. Differentiation between politics and Public Management of Society is needed. Differentiation of society is crucial for Luhmann (1982), who characterises this as an inevitable part of modernisation in the perspective of the overwhelming complexity of society. In the course of socio-cultural evolution, segmentation, stratification and functional differentiation are distinguished. Functional differentiation is relevant for modern society: it organises communication processes with regard to specialised functions, which have to be performed at the societal level (and below that level). So functional subsystems, with specific roles, are formed which select relevant communications. On the basis of their self-reference they organise their activities and communications towards their specific environment. A number of functional subsystems can be distinguished: politics, economic system, legal system, etc. These functionally differentiated subsystems are characterised by specific semantics, roles, codes, professional skills, and rationalities. Each functional subsystem reconstructs society as a whole and forms specific communications. The economic subsystem represents the whole society as far as the economical aspects are concerned. In a long-term development with division of labour and functions, it was efficient to differentiate functionally. By concentrating on its specific function, it is possible for a functional subsystem to ignore all except selected aspects of its environment. Functional subsystems can further their self-reference and relative independence while they remain dependent on the functioning of other subsystems (interdependency).

Luhmann developed concepts, which are relevant for societal steering. Neurobiologists Maturana and Varela (1980) developed "autopopiesis" for living systems and they did not think this concept was usable for social systems. Luhmann (1986) however, specifically re-designed the "autopoiesis" concept for social systems. He distinguished between meaning and life as different kinds of "autopoietic" organisation. Meaning-using systems are psychic systems (based on consciousness) or social systems (based on communication). Psychic systems (minds) are "autopoietic" systems reproducing consciousness by a succession of thoughts, consciousness. Social systems (Luhmann, 1995) use communication as a specific mode of meaning-based reproduction, but in this conceptualisation communication is a specific notion. Mostly communication is defined as transmission of information (a sender is giving away something which is received by a receiver). This notion is inadequate for a richer social phenomenon denoted as communication, involving selections: information, utterance and understanding. For Luhmann not (communicative) action or people, but communication is the elementary unit of self-referential social systems. Action does not include the understanding of the (eventual) listener to the utterance of messages. Social systems do not consist of people or psychic systems. Others see the individual as unit of analysis of social systems. Luhmann, recognising that communication is impossible without people or individuals, does not see it that way. For him, individuals are crucial, but are part of the environment. The environment of a social system is internally reconstructed by means of communication. In a process of self-reference a social system determines whether events in the environment are relevant or not.

Studies show that culture is very relevant as a primary factor with regard to social and societal phenomena (Archer, 1996). "In other words humans do not have a transhistorical or transcultural nature. Rather, culture 'completes' humans by explaining and interpreting the world. Culture does not differently clothe the universal human. Rather, it infuses individuals, fundamentally shaping their natures and identities." (Richardson/Fowers, 1998, p.480). In mainstream literature it is normal to analyse aspects of social phenomena in a comparative perspective. Comparing those aspects in culturally different countries deepens our insight, also into our own specific cultural climate. Differences in national policy styles and bureaucratic attitudes matter, as a comparison of using policy instruments in different national contexts proves (Bemelmans-Videc c.s, 1998). When an attempt is made to formulate more general, universal conceptions and concepts, a common technique in overcoming culturally different situations is to abstract away differences in an overarching conceptualisation. For the conceptualisation of the phenomenon of Public Management of Society, thoroughly interconnected with culturally imbued processes of social-psychological communication, it is a crucial question whether abstracting away cultural differences is possible or allowable. After fulfilling this research project about the sui generis character of French Public Management of Society, one conclusion is that cultural differences may not be abstracted away in the search for universalist conceptualisations. In modernist conceptualisations, it is quite normal to develop universalist concepts in an implicit or explicit supposition that it is possible to go beyond cultural differences. The post-modern political condition is premised on the acceptance of the plurality of cultures and discourses (Heller/Fehér, 1988, p.5). This plurality of cultures takes place in language games and cultural games, in which cultural rationalities are crucial. Cultural rationalities are specific rationalities, to be distinguished from other rationalities, which are relevant in the sphere of human behaviour. Culture does matter (Huntington, 1996; Katzenstein, 1996).

In the study of international relations it has already been common practice for a long period to reckon with cultural differences between peoples and nations. These cultural differences have their impact upon a variety of practices, such as for example warfare. There is a British way of warfare (Liddell Hart, 1932), an American way of warfare (Weighley, 1973) and a French way of warfare (Kier, 1997). To know more about other peoples, "national character" studies have been made by cultural anthropologists and others. Culture had become the key issue for cultural anthropologists (Geertz, 1974), but culture proved to be an ambiguous concept, while it was difficult to define culture in a more operational way (Carrithers, 1992). In the field of international security there has even recently been an upsurge of cultural theories which are useful as complementary to the existing body of knowledge (Desch, 1998). Geertz (1974, p.22): "The great natural variation of cultural forms is, of course, not only anthropology's great (and wasting) resource, but the ground of its deepest theoretical dilemma: How is such variation to be squared with the biological unity of the human species?" Human beings share similarities, so formulation of generalised theories about human behaviour in different cultural environments is possible. In social science inquiries the "unit homogeneity assumption" holds that cases have enough meaningful similarities to be comparable (King, et al., 1994, - p.116). Studies accentuating the difference of cultural variables might be only configurative-ideographic studies, marking the limits of comparative studies. Cultural theories might possibly not be formulated about behaviour of all Nation-States, but could be relevant conceptualisations about a particular Nation-State over time (Desch, 1998, p.155).

There are ample reasons to reckon with specific cultural dimensions, and to go further than would-be shortcuts like "the French are like that". This research project about French

Public Management of Society shows that it is a good idea to see the cultural factor as a specific factor. French authors play a significant role in theorising about culture, as f.e. Bourdieu (Swartz, 1997). On the basis of material about French Public Management of Society an eighth working-hypothesis is formulated here for the development of a more integrated theory of Public Management of Society. This eighth working-hypothesis accentuates the relevance of the specific cultural-existential environment and inter-subjective cultural-existential mindset for the deployment of Public Management of Society. It is about cultural intelligence as a necessary condition for an adequate approach to the theory and practice of Public Management of Society. Sophisticated comparative analysis has to reckon with fundamental cultural differences in countries, nations and regions, and with the dimensions of multi-cultural society: cultural pluralism (Crane, 1994), so adequate cultural mapping is required. A crucial aspect of the Public Management of Society phenomenon is the ongoing interpenetration of circumstances, ideas, mentalities and practices in the specific cultural context, in historical perspective. The specificity of culture(s) has to be reckoned with more than is generally done in mainstream literature. This comes to the fore when so-called universalist ideas are confronted with specific cultures all over the world. Luhmann's social systems theory, based upon the existential reality of human beings and phenomenological "Sinn" related communication, seems especially suited to incorporate culture in his all-encompassing conceptualisation. During the last decades of the 20th century there was a notable return of culture as a dominant dimension of social sciences.

In comparative management literature the work of Mintzberg (1973) is seen as crucial for the "universality hypothesis": Western management theories are thought to be applicable worldwide regardless of culture or historic experience of a society. The issue is not whether Western management styles are transferable (Farazmand, 1994, p.253), it is more important to answer the question of whether cultural differences can be neglected in a rigid universality approach. Making human activities adequate in different cultural settings is the real challenge. The "universality hypothesis" is opposed by authors who stress the many-sided character of culture with an impact on all societal dimensions: the "cultural differences" hypothesis. In this study ample argument is given for the thesis that cultural specificity is a relevant criterion for making management effective, especially Public Management of Society. French Public Management of Society is culturally specific. In a global theory of intellectual change (Collins, 1998) French Public Management of Society has a unique position. There are developments making some aspects less specific in a seemingly irreversible process of convergence, as with regard to French law in the European Union or economic globalisation ("Americanisation"). The "convergence hypothesis" looks like being decisive in the long run, but another approach is to be seen as more mature. There is convergence and divergence in a dynamic, creative process. It is not adequate to accentuate either universality or cultural differences or convergence, neglecting or abstracting away crucial dimensions. This study has produced material for the "universality and cultural specificity hypothesis".

Cultural intelligence and common sense ask for the optimal combining of universalism and cultural specificity when one seeks adequate answers to the dynamic challenges of ever changing circumstances. This approach is a welcome complement to the valuable "global method", developed by the International Institute of Administrative Sciences for the 21st century (Vilella, in: Kernaghan, 2000). This global method, meant to improve public administration worldwide, includes a multidisciplinary, a comparative and a multicultural approach. Too much stressing of a multicultural approach runs the risk of bypassing the fundamental dimensions of each specific culture. As with the transplantation of human organs from one person to another person (risks of rejection) one has to take care with institutional transplantation from one country or culture to other countries or cultures.

Studying Public Management of Society in multicultural perspectives is useful and necessary, but Public Management of Society needs to be adequate in the specific cultural environment, it must be culturally intelligent. Let us be wise, let us be culturally intelligent, trying to realise a better world for all with adequate, fair and responsible Public Management of Society based on the fundamental axis of Rule of Law and Idea of Public Authority.

## References

French
Abéles, M., Un ethnologue à l'Assemblée. Comment se font nos lois. (Paris, Odile Jacob, 2000).
Abendroth, W., Histoire du mouvement ouvrier en Europe. (Paris, Maspero, 1967).
Adam, G., Reynaud, J.D., Conflits du travail et changement social. (Paris, PUF, 1978).
Amiet, P., L'Antiquité orientale. (Paris, PUF, 1995).
Arnaud, A.J., Les Juristes face à la Société (du XIXe siècle à nos jours). (Paris, PUF, 1975).
Arnaud, A.J., Critique de la raison juridique. (Paris, LGDJ, 1981).
Arnaud, A.J., Pour une pensée juridique européenne. (Paris, PUF, 1991).
Badie, B., Stratégie de la grève. Pour une approche functionnaliste du PCF. (Paris, FNSP, 1976).
Badie, B., Le Développement politique. (Paris, Economica, 1978).
Badie, B., L'État Importé. L'occidentialisation de l'ordre politique. (Paris, Fayard, 1992).
Badie, B., Un monde sans souveraineté. (Paris, Fayard, 1999).
Badie, B., Birnbaum, P., Sociologie de l'État. (Paris, Grasset, 1982).
Barreau, J.C., La France va-t-elle disparaître? (Paris, Grasset, 1997).
Barret-Kriegel, B., L'État et ses esclaves. (Paris, Calmann-Lévy, 1979).
Barret-Kriegel, B., L'État et la démocratie. (Paris, DF, 1986).
Barret-Kriegel, B., Les Chemins de l'État. (Paris, Calmann-Lévy, 1986).
Barret-Kriegel, B., Les droits de l'homme et le droit naturel. (Paris, PUF, 1989).
Barret-Kriegel, B., État de droit. (Dans: Dictionnaire constitutionnel. Paris, PUF, 1992).
Basse, B., La Constitution de l'ancienne France. (Paris, 1973).
Bastid, P., L'Idée de Constitution. (Paris, Economica, 1985).
Beccaria, C., Des délits et des peines. (Milan, 1765; Paris, Droz, 1965).
Béguin, J.C., Le controle constitutionnel de la constitutionnalité des lois en République fédérale allemande. (Paris, 1982).
Birnbaum, P., Le Pouvoir Politique. (Paris, Dalloz, 1975).
Bloch, M, La société féodale, les classes et et le gouvernement des hommes. (Paris, 1960).
Bluche, F., dir., Dictionnaire du Grande Siècle. (Paris, Fayard, 1990).
Bodin, J., Les Six livres de la République. (Paris, Éd du Puys, 1576).
Bodineau, P., Verpeaux, M., Histoire constitutionnelle de la France. (Paris, PUF, 2000).
Bossuet, J.B., Politique tirée des propres paroles de l'Écriture sainte. (Paris, 1709; Genève, Droz, 1967).
Bouscaren, C., et al., Les bases du droit anglais. (Paris, Ophrys, 1988).
Boutin, C., Politique et transition dans l'oeuvre de Julius Evola. (Paris, Kimé, 1992).
Boutruche, A., Seigneurie et féodalité. (Paris, 1959).
Braudel, F., L'Identité de la France. Espace et Histoire. (Paris, Flammarion, 1986).
Brecy, R., La Grève générale. (Paris, EDI, 1966).
Brutus, J., Vindiciae contra tyrannos. (Paris, 1579).
Burdeau, F., Histoire du droit administratif. (Paris, PUF, 1995).
Burdeau, G., Traité de Science Politique. (Paris, LGDJ, 1949/1957; 1971/1986).
Burdeau, G., L'État. (Paris, Seuil, 1970).
Burdeau, G., Droit constitutionnel et institutions politiques. (Paris, LGDJ, 1980).
Burdeau, G., Hamon, F., Troper, M., Droit constitutionnel. (Paris, LGDJ, 1993).
Cahen, L., Braure, M., L'Évolution Politique de l'Angleterre Moderne (1485-1660). (Paris, A.Michel, 1960).
Calvin, J., Institution de la religion chrétienne. (Genève, 1541; Paris, Belles Lettres, 1939).
Calmette, J., Le monde féodal. (Paris, 1934).
Cannac, Y., Le Juste Pouvoir. (Paris, Lattès, 1983).
Carbonnier, J., Flexible droit. (Paris, LGDJ, 1979).
Carré de Malberg, R., Contribution à la théorie générale de l'État. (Paris, Sirey, 1920/1922).

Chesnais, J.C., Histoire de la violence en Occident de 1800 à nos jours. (Paris, Laffont, 1981).
Chevallier, J., L'État propulsif. (Paris, Publisud, 1991).
Chevallier, J., Le droit administratif en mutation. (Dans: Le droit administratif entre science administrative et droit constitutionnel. Paris, PUF, 1993a).
Chevallier, J., Les interprètes du droit. (Dans: La Doctrine juridique. Paris, PUF, 1993b).
Chevallier, J., L'État de droit. (Paris, Montchrestien, 1994).
Chevallier, J., et al., La Gouvernabilité. (Paris, PUF, 1996).
Chevallier, J.J., Histoire des institutions et des régimes politiques de la France de 1789 à nos jours. (Paris, Dalloz, 1986; A. Colin, 2001).
Clastres, P., La Société contre l'État. (Paris, Minuit, 1974).
Clastres, P., Recherches d'anthropologie politique. (Paris, Seuil, 1980).
Clausewitz, K. von, De la Guerre. (Paris, Minuit, 1955).
Cohen-Tanugi, L., Le Droit sans l'État. (Paris, PUF, 1985; 1987; 1992).
Cohen-Tanugi, L., Les Métamorphoses de la démocratie. (Paris, Odile Jacob, 1989; 1993).
Cohen-Tanugi, L., L'Europe en danger. (Paris, Fayard, 1992).
Colloque Paris, Conseil Constitutionnel et Conseil d'État. (Paris, LGDJ, 1988).
Conseil d'État, Droit communautaire et droit français. (Paris, Conseil d'État, 1982).
Crozier, M., Le Mal américain. (Paris, Fayard, 1980).
David, R., Le Droit anglais. (Paris, PUF, 1987).
David, R., Les Grands Systèmes de Droit Contemporains. (Paris, Dalloz, 1992).
De Bodinat, H., L'État parenthèse de l'histoire? (Paris, Éditions P.A.U., 1995).
De Bonald, L.A., Théorie du pouvoir politique et religieux (1796). (Paris, Capitan, 1965).
Diderot, D'Alembert, Encyclopédie, ou dictionnaire raisonné des sciences, des arts et des métiers. (Paris, 1751/1772; 1776/1780).
Dreyfus, F., L'Invention de la Bureaucratie. Servir l'État en France, en Grande-Bretagne et aux États-Unis (XVIII-XX siècle). (Paris, Découverte, 2000).
Dreyfus, F., Arcy, F. d', Les institutions politiques et administratives de la France. (Paris, Economica, 1989).
Duguit, L., Manuel de droit constitutionnel. (Paris, Boccard, 1911).
Duguit, L., Traité de droit constitutionnel. (Paris, Fontemoing, 1923; 1927/1930).
Duguit, L., et al., Les Constitutions et les principales lois politiques de la France depuis 1789. (Paris, LGDJ, 1952).
Durkheim, E., Leçons de sociologie. (Paris, PUF, 1950).
Durkheim, E., De la division du travail. (Paris, PUF, 1960).
Durkheim, E., Textes. (Paris, Minuit, 1975; 1980).
Duverger, M., Constitutions et documents politiques. (Paris, PUF, 1996).
Duverger, M., Le système politique français. (Paris, PUF, 1996).
Dworkin, R., Prendre les droits au sérieux. (Paris, PUF, 1995).
Eisenmann, C., La justice constitutionnelle et la Haute Cour constitutionnelle d'Autriche. (Paris, Economica, 1928).
Elias, N., La Dynamique de l'Occident. (Paris, Calmann-Lévy, 1939; 1975).
Ellul, J., Histoire des institutions de l'époque franque à la République. (Paris, PUF, 1964).
Ellul, J., Histoire des institutions. (Paris, PUF, 1961; 1993).
Engels, F., L'Origine de la famille, de la propriété privée et de l'État. (Paris, Ed. sociales, 1966).
Engels, F., Anti-Dühring. (Paris, Éd. sociales, 1973).
Esmein, A., Histoire de la procédure criminelle en France. (Paris, 1882).
Esmein, A., Éléments de droit constitutionnel. (Paris, Sirey, 1906; 1929).
Farcy, J.C., Deux Siècles d'Histoire de la Justice (1789-1999). (Paris, CNRS, 1996).
Favoreu, L., La politique saisie par le droit. (Paris, Economica, 1988).
Favoreu, L., Droit constitutionnel. (Paris, Dalloz, 1998).
Favoreu, L., dir., Le Pouvoir des Juges. (Paris, Economica, 1990).
Favoreu, L., Philip, L., Les grandes décisions du Conseil constitutionnel. (Paris, Sirey, 1986).
Fénélon, F., Les aventures de Télémaque. (Paris, 1699; Nizot, 1993).
Ferrault, J., Insignia pecularia christianissimi Francorum regni. (Paris, 1520).
Fichte, J.G., Discours à la nation allemande (1807). (Paris, Aubier, 1975).
Fichte, J.G., Fondement du droit naturel selon les principes de la doctrine de la science. (Paris, PUF, 1998).
Fortescue, De laudibus legum Angliae. (London, 1468/1470).
Fustel de Coulanges, N.D., La Cité antique. (Paris, Hachette, 1879).
Ganshof, F.L., Qu'est-ce que la féodalité? (Paris, 1957).
Gauchet, M., La Révolution des droits de l'homme. (Paris, Gallimard, 1989).

Gauchet, M., La Révolution des pouvoirs. La souveraineté, le peuple et la représentation 1789-1799. (Paris, Gallimard, 1995).
Gérard, P., Ost, F., Kerchove, M. van de, Actualité de la pensée juridique de Jeremy Bentham. (Bruxelles, Facultés universitaires Saint-Louis, 1987).
Girard, R., La Violence et le Sacré. (Paris, Grasset, 1972).
Greigueuil, P. de., 2000 Ans d'Histoire de France. (Paris, Assouline, 1999).
Grotius, De iure belli ac pacis. (Paris, 1625.
Guilaine, J., Zammit, J., Le Sentier de la Guerre. Visages de la Violence Préhistorique. (Paris, Seuil, 2001).
Guizot, F., Histoire de la Civilisation en Europe (1821). (Paris, Hachette, 1985).
Gurvitch, G., L'idée de droit social. (Paris, 1932).
Haarscher, G., Philosophie des droits de l'homme. (Paris, 1993).
Habermas, J., Après l'État-Nation. (Paris, Fayard, 2000).
Harouel, J.L., et al., Histoire des institutions de l'époque franque à la Révolution. (Paris, PUF, 1994).
Harouel, V., Grands textes du droit humanitaire. (Paris, PUF, 2001).
Hauriou, M., Précis de droit administratif. (Paris, 1892; 1927).
Hauriou, M., Principes du droit public. (Paris, Sirey, 1916; 1923; 1929).
Hauriou, M., Précis de droit constitutionnel. (Paris, Sirey, 1923; CNRS, 1965).
Hayek, F., Droit, législation et liberté. (Paris, PUF, 1980; 1992).
Héritier, P., Gouverner sans le peuple. (Paris, Éd. de l'Atelier, 2002).
Heymann, A., Les libertés publiques et la guerre d'Algérie. (Paris, LGDJ, 1972).
Heymann-Doat, A., Libertés publiques et droits de l'homme. (Paris, LGDJ, 1997).
Hotman, J.F., La Gaule française. (Paris, 1573; Fayard, 1991).
Ihering, R. von, L'évolution du droit. (Paris, trad. de " Der Zweck im Recht", 1877; 1901).
Jacquillat, Désétatiser. (Paris, Laffont, 1985).
Jellinek, G., Létat moderne et son droit. (Paris, trad. de "Allgemeine Staatslehre", 1900; 1911.
Jèze, G., Notes de jurisprudence. Le controle constitutionnel des lois. (Dans: Revue de droit public, 1924).
Joffrin, L., Tesson, P., Où est passée l'Autorité? (Paris, Nil Éditions, 2000).
Joly, C., Receuil de maximes véritables et importantes pour l'institution du Roy. (Paris, 1652).
Kaftani, C., La formation de la fonction publique en France. (Paris, LGDJ, 1998).
Kant, E., Oeuvres philosophiques. (Paris, Gallimard, 1986).
Kant, E., Doctrine du droit. (Paris, Vrin, 1988).
Karpik, L., Les Avocats. Entre l'État, le public et le marché: XIIIe-XXe siècle. (Paris, Gallimard, 1995).
Karpik, L., L'Avancée de la Justice menace-t-elle la République? (Dans: Le Débat, pp.238-257, 2000).
Kinder-Gest, P.J., Droit anglais. Institutions politiques et judiciaires. (Paris, LGDJ, 1993).
Kinder-Gest, P.J., Les Institutions britanniques. (Paris, PUF, 1995).
Koetz/Ottenhoff, Les Conciliateurs. La Concilation. (Paris, Economica, 1983).
Kolm, S.C., Justice et équité. (Paris, CNRS, 1971).
Krynen, J., dir., Droit romain, ius civile et droit français. (Toulouse, PU, 1999).
Laband, P., Le droit public de L'Empire allemand (1876). (Paris, 1900/1904).
Lacharrière, G. de, La Politique Juridique Extérieure. (Paris, Economica, 1983).
Lacroix, J., Kant et le kantisme. (Paris, PUF, 1989).
Laferrière, J., Manuel de droit constitutionnel. (Paris, Montchrestien, 1947).
Laferrière, M.F., Cours théorique et pratique de droit public et adminstratif. (Paris, 1854).
Lambert, E., Le Gouvernement des Juges et la Lutte contre la législation sociale aux États-Unis. (Paris, 1921).
Langrod, G., La science administrative et sa place parmi les sciences voisines. (Dans: Auby, J.M., et al., Traité de science administrative. Paris, pp. 92-123, 1966).
Langrod, G., Niklas Luhmann: Theorie der Verwaltungswissenschaft. Bestandsaufnahme und Entwurf. (In: Verwaltungsarchiv, pp.85-88, 1968).
Laubadère, A. de, Traité de droit administratif. (Paris, LGDJ, 1994).
Laubadère, A. de, et al., Droit administratif. (Paris, LGDJ, 1994).
Lazzeri, C., Droit, pouvoir et liberté. Spinoza critique de Hobbes. (Paris, PUF, 1998).
Lebigre, A., La Justice du Roi. (Paris, A.Michel, 1988).
Legendre, P., Histoire de l'Administration de 1750 à nos jours. (Paris, PUF, 1968).
Legendre, P., L'amour de censeur. Essai sur l'ordre dogmatique. (Paris, Seuil, 1974).
Legendre, P., Sur la Question Dogmatique en Occident. Aspects théoriques. (Paris, Fayard, 1999).
Legoherel, H., Histoire du droit international public. (Paris, PUF, 1996).
Lenoble, J., dir., La Crise du Juge. (Paris, LGDJ, 1990).
Leroy-Beaulieu, P., L'État moderne et ses fonctions. (Paris, Guillaumin, 1911).

Levasseur, A.A., Le Droit des États-Unis. (Paris, Dalloz, 1990).
Louis XIV, Mémoires pour l'instruction du dauphin. (Paris, 1661; Didier, 1860).
Luccioni, J., La Pensée politique de Platon. (Paris, PUF, 1958).
Machiavel, N., Oeuvres complètes. (Paris, Gallimard, 1952).
Mahiou, A., dir., L'État de droit dans le monde arabe. (Paris, CNRS, 1997).
Mairet, G., Discours d'Europe. Citoyenneté, souveraineté, démocratie. (Paris, Découverte, 1989).
Mairet, G, Le Maître et la Multitude. L'État moderne entre Shakespeare, Machiavel et Gorbachev. (Paris, Félin, 1991).
Mairet, G., Les Principes de la Souveraineté. Histoires et fondements du pouvoir moderne. (Paris, Galliamrd, 1997).
Marx, K., Manifeste du parti communiste. (Paris, 1848).
Marx, K., Critique de la philosophie de l'État de Hegel. (Paris, Costes, 1948).
Marx, K., Préface à la contribution à la critique de l'économie politique. (Paris, Ed. sociales, 1957).
Mélanges M. Duverger. (Paris, PUF, 1987).
Mélanges G.J. Wiarda, Protection des droits de l'homme: la dimension européenne. (Paris, 1990).
Minc, A., L'Avenir en face. (Paris, Seuil, 1984).
Minc, A., Le Nouveau Moyen Age. (Paris, Gallimard, 1993).
Minc, A., Au nom de la loi. (Paris, Gallimard, 1998).
Mommsen, T., Le droit public romain. (Paris, Boccard, 1892; 1894).
Montesquieu, C. de Sécondat, baron de la Brède et de, Lettres persanes. (Paris, 1721; LGF, 1984).
Montesquieu, C., De l'Esprit des Lois. (Paris, 1748; Garnier, 1956; 1973).
Montesquieu, C., Oeuvres complètes. (Paris, Seuil, 1964).
Morin, J.Y., L'État de Droit. Émergence d'un principe du droit international. (The Hague, Nijhoff, 1996).
Nicolet, C., Le Métier du citoyen dans la République romaine. (Paris, Gallimard, 1976).
Ockham, G. d', Breviloquium de principatu tyrannica. (Paris, 1347).
Ockham, G. d', Court Traité du Pouvoir Tyrannique. (Paris, PUF, 2000).
Olivier-Martin, F., Précis d'histoire du droit français. (Paris, Dalloz, 1945).
Olivier-Martin, F., Histoire du droit français des origines à la Révolution. (Paris, CNRS, 1992).
Pactet, P., Institutions politiques. Droit constitutionnel. (Paris, Masson, 1994).
Pactet, P., Les Institutions françaises. (Paris, PUF, 2001).
Pansier, F.J., Guellaty, K., Le Droit musulman. (Paris, PUF, 2000).
Parrot, A., Sumer. (Paris, Gallimard, 1960).
Parsons, T., Sociétés. (Paris, Dunod, 1966; 1973).
Parsons, T., Le Système des sociétés modernes. (Paris, Dunod, 1973).
Pautrat, B., Éthique de Spinoza. (Paris, Seuil, 1999).
Perrot, M., Kriegel, A., Le Socialisme français et le Pouvoir. (Paris, EDI, 1966).
Perroy, E., et al., Le Moyen Age. (Paris, PUF, 1955).
Peyrefitte, A., La Société de confiance. (Paris, Odile Jacob, 1995).
Pisier, E., Les fondements de la notion de service public dans l'oeuvre de Léon Duguit. (Paris, LGDJ, 1972).
Polin, R., La politique morale de John Locke. (Paris, PUF, 1960).
Ponton, L., Philosophie et droits de l'homme. (Paris, 1990).
Pouvoirs (Revue), La Justice. (Paris, Seuil, 1981).
Pouvoirs, 1789-1989, histoire constitutionnelle. (Paris, Seuil, 1989).
Pouvoirs, Le Conseil Constitutionnel. (Paris, Seuil, 1991).
Pouvoirs, Morale et politique. (Paris, Seuil, 1993).
Pouvoirs, La souveraineté. (Paris, Seuil, 1993).
Pouvoirs, Qui gouverne la France? (Paris, Seuil, 1994).
Pouvoirs, Europe, de la Communauté à l'Union. (Paris, Seuil, 1994).
Pouvoirs, Les Cours Européennes, Luxembourg et Strasbourg. (Paris, Seuil, 2001).
Prélot, M., Histoire des idées politiques. (Paris, Dalloz, 1959).
Prévost, J.F., Le peuple et son maître. (Paris, Plon, 1983).
Pufendorf, S., Le droit de la nature et des gens. (Paris, 1672).
Rawls, J., Théorie de la justice. (Paris, Seuil, 1987; 1997).
Rawls, J., Libéralisme politique. (Paris, PUF, 1995; 2001).
Rawls, J., Le droit des gens. (Paris, Esprit, 1998).
Redor, M.J., De l'État légal à l'État de droit. L'évolution des conceptions de la doctrine française 1879-1914. (Paris, Economica, 1992).
Rials, S., La Déclaration des droits de l'homme et du citoyen. (Paris, Hachette, 1988).
Rials, S., Textes constitutionnels français. (Paris, PUF, 1989; 2001).

Rivéro, J., Le Conseil Constitutionnel et les Libertés. (Paris, Economica, 1987).
Robin, R., La Société française à la veille de la Révolution. (Paris, Plon, 1970).
Romano, S. L'ordre juridique (1946). (Paris, Dalloz, 1975).
Rosanvallon, P., Le Sacre du citoyen. Histoire du suffrage universel en France. (Paris, Gallimard, 1992).
Rosanvallon, P., dir., France. Les Révolutions invisibles. (Paris, Calmann-Lévy, 1998).
Rosenfeld, M., Les interprérations justes. (Paris, LGDJ, 2001).
Rousseau, J.J., Politique du contrat social ou principes du droit politique. (Paris, 1762; UGE, 1966).
Rousseau, J.J., Discours sur l'origine et les fondements de l'inégalité parmi les hommes. (Paris, 1765; UGE, 1966).
Sahlins, P., Age de pierre, âge d'abondance. (Paris, Gallimard, 1976).
Scheer, L., La démocratie virtuelle. (Paris, Flammarion, 1994).
Schmitt, C., Théologie politique (1922; 1934). (Paris, Gallimard, 1988).
Schmitt, C., Théorie de la Constitution (1927). (Paris, PUF, 1993).
Seyssel, C, de, La Grande Monarchie de France (1519). (Paris, Pujol, 1961).
Soboul, A., La Révolution française. (Paris, Éd. sociales, 1950).
Soboul, A., La Civilisation de la Révolution française. (Paris, Arthaud, 1970).
Soulez-Larivière, Les Juges dans la balance. (Paris, Ramsay, 1987).
Spinoza, B., Traité politique (1677). (Paris, Gallimard, 1954).
Tocqueville, A. de, De la démocratie en Amérique (1835-1840). (Paris, Flammarion, 1981).
Toinet, M.F., Le Système Politique des États-Unis. (Paris, PUF, 1990).
Troper, M., Pour une théorie juridique de l'État. (Paris, PUF, 1994).
Touchard, J., Histoire des idées politiques. (Paris, PUF, 1993).
Touscoz, J., Droit international. (Paris, PUF, 1993).
Tunc, A., Le Droit des États-Unis. (Paris, PUF, 1989).
Turpin, D., Droit constitutionnel. (Paris, PUF, 1992).
Verpeaux, M., La naissance du pouvoir réglementaire: 1789-1799. (Paris, PUF, 1991).
Vivien, A.F., Études administratives. (Paris, Guillaumin, 1859; Cujas, 1974).
Voltaire (F.M. Arouet), Oeuvres complètes de Voltaire. (Paris, 1785-1799; 1977-1985).
Weber, M., Le Savant et le Politique. (Paris, Plon, 1959).
Weber, M., Économie et Société. (Paris, Plon, 1971).
Weil, E., Hegel et l'État. (Paris, Vrin, 1950).
Weil, P., Pouyaud, D., Le Droit Administratif. (Paris, PUF, 2001).
Wicquefort, A., Chronique discontinue de la Fronde (1648-1652). (Paris, Fayard, 1978).
Willard, C., Les Guesdistes. (Paris, Ed. sociales, 1965).

English
Adams, G.B., Balfour, D.L., Unmasking Administrative Evil. (London, Sage, 1998).
Alexander, J.C., The Parsons Revival in German Sociology. (In: Collins, R., ed., Sociological Theory, pp.394-412, 1984).
Allen, C.K., Bureaucracy Triumphant. (London, 1931).
Almond, G.A., Powell, G.B., Comparative Politics. (Boston, Little-Brown, 1966).
Anderson, E., Value in Ethics and Economics. (Cambridge, MA, Harvard UP, 1993).
Archer, M.S., Culture and Agency. The Place of Culture in Social Theory. (Cambridge, CUP, 1996).
Arnold, T.W., The Caliphate. (Oxford, OUP, 1924).
Asmeron, H.K., Reis, E.P., eds., Democratization and Bureaucratic Neutrality. (London, Macmillan, 1996).
Backhaus, J.G., ed., The Elgar Companion to Law and Economics. (Cheltenham, Elgar, 1999).
Bacon, F., Francis Bacon's Essays. (London, 1906).
Barbard, F.M., ed., J.G. Herder on Social and Political Culture. (Cambridge, CUP, 1969).
Barzelay, M., Breaking through Democracy. A New Vision for Managing in Government. (Berkeley, University of California Press, 1992).
Bell, D.A., The Limits of Liberal Justice. (In: Political Theory, pp.557-582, 1998).
Bell, D.A., Which Rights are Universal? (In: Political Theory, pp.849-956, 1999).
Bemelmans-Videc, M.L., Rist, R.C., Vedung, E., eds., Carrots, Sticks and Sermons. (New Brunswick, Transaction, 1998).
Bendix, R., Nation-Building and Citizenship. (New York, Wiley, 1964).
Bentham, J., A Fragment on Government (1776). (Cambridge, CUP, 1988).
Bentham, J., An Introduction to the Principles of Morals and Legislation. (London, 1781; Athlone, 1977).
Bentham, J., Pannomium. (London, 1811).
Bentham, J., A Treatise on Judicial Evidence. (London, 1825).

Bentham, J., The Works of Jeremy Bentham. (Edinburgh, Tait, 1838/1843).
Bentham, J., The Theory of Legislation. (London, Routledge, 1931).
Bentham, J., Of Laws in General. (London, Athlone, 1970).
Bentham, J., Collected Works. (London, Athlone, 1970).
Bentham, J., On the influence of place and time in matters of legislation and of indirect legislation. (Oxford, 1986).
Bentley, A.F., The Process of Government. (New York, 1949).
Berger, R., Government by Judiciary. (Cambridge, MA, Harvard UP, 1977).
Berman, H.J., Law and Revolution. The Formation of the Western Legal Tradition. (Boston, Harvard UP, 1983).
Bielefeldt, H., "Western" versus "Islamic" Human Rights Conceptions? A Critique of Cultural Essentialism in the Discussion on Human Rights. (In: Political Theory, pp.90-121, 2000).
Bierstedt, R., The Problem of Authority. (In: Berger, M., et al., eds., Freedom and Control in Modern Society. New York, 1954; Octagon, pp.67-81, 1964).
Bigelow, J., ed., The Works of Benjamin Franklin. (New York, 1904).
Binder, L., The Ideological Revolution in the Middle East. (New York, Wiley, 1964).
Blackstone, W., Commentaries on the Laws of England. (Oxford, 1767).
Bonney, R., ed., The Rise of the Fiscal State in Europe. (Oxford, OUP, 1999).
Boorstin, D., The Mysterious Science of the Law. (Boston, Beacon, 1958).
Bouckaert, B., De Geest, G., eds., Encyclopedia of Law and Economics. (Cheltenham, Elgar, 2000).
Bowring, J., ed., The Works of Jeremy Bentham. (Edinburgh, Tait, 1838/1843; New York, Russell/Russell, 1962).
Bracton, H. de, De Legibus ac Consuetudinibus Angliae. (London, 1268).
Broderick, A., ed., The French Institutionalists. Maurice Hauriou, Georges Renard, Joseph T. Delos. (Cambridge, MA, Harvard UP, 1970).
Butler, F., ed., Human Rights for the New Millennium. (The Hague, Kluwer, 2000).
Caenegem, R. van, The Birth of the English Common Law. (Cambridge, CUP, 1988).
Carrithers, M., Why Humans Have Cultures. Explaining Anthropology and Social Diversity. (Oxford, OUP, 1992).
Chibundu, M.O., Globalizing the Rule of Law. (In: Indiana Journal of Global Legal Studies, pp.79-116, 1999).
Coke, E., Institutes of the Laws of England. (London, 1628/1644).
Cole, C.W., Colbert and a Century of French Mercantilism. (London, Cass, 1939).
Collins, R., The Sociology of Philosophies. A Global Theory of Intellectual Change. (Cambridge, MA, Harvard UP, 1998).
Confino, A., The Nation as a Local Metaphor: Würthemberg, Imperial Germany and National Memory, 1871-1918. (Chapel Hill, University of North Carolina Press, 1997).
Cooter, R.D., The Strategic Constitution. (Princeton, Princeton UP, 2001).
Crane, D., ed., The Sociology of Culture. Emerging Theoretical Perspectives. (New York, Blackwell, 1994).
Crough, C., Pizzorno, A., The Resurgence of Class Conflict in Europe. (London, Macmilan, 1978).
Dahl, R.A., A Preface to Democratic Theory. (New York, 1956).
David, R., English Law and French Law. (London, Stevens, 1980; 1987).
Davies, N., The Isles. A History. (London, Macmillan, 1999).
Davis, G.R.C., Magna Carta. (London, British Museum, 1971).
Desch, M.C., Culture Clash. Assessing the Importance of Ideas in Security Studies. (In: International Security, pp.141-170, 1998).
Dicey, A.V., Introduction to the Study of the Law of the Constitution. (London, Macmillan, 1885; 1960).
Dicey, A.V. et al., The Conflict of Laws. (London, 1993).
Donoughmore Committee, Committee on Ministers' Powers. (London, 1932).
Duchacek, I.D., Comparative Federalism. The Territorial Dimension of Politics. (New York, Holt-Rinehart-Winston, 1970).
Duchacek, I.D., Rights and Liberties in the World Today. (Santa Barbara, ABC-Clio, 1973).
Duchacek, I.D., The Territorial Dimension of Politics within, among and across Nations. (Boulder, Westview, 1986).
Dunbar, R., Knight, C., Power, C., eds., The Evolution of Culture. (Edinburgh, Edinburgh UP, 1999).
Durant, W., The Reformation. (London, 1957).
Dworkin, R., Taking Rights Seriously. (London, Duckworth, 1974).
Dworkin, R., Law's Empire. (Cambridge, MA, Harvard UP, 1986).
Dworkin, R., Freedom's Law. The Moral reading of the American Constitution. (Oxford, OUP, 1996).

Dworkin, R., Sovereign Virtue. The Theory and Practice of Equality. (Cambridge, MA, Harvard UP, 2001).
Dyson, R.W., Giles of Rome on Ecclesiastical Power (De ecclesiastica potestate, 1302). (Douvre, Bogdell, 1986).
Easton, D., The Political System. (New York, Knopf, 1953).
Eisenstadt, S., The Political Systems of Empires. (New York, Free Press, 1963).
Eisenstadt, S., Tradition, Change and Modernity. (New York, Wiley, 1973).
Eisenstadt, S., Rokkan, S., Building States and Nations. (Beverley Hills, Sage, 1973).
Ertmann, T., Birth of the Leviathan: Building States and Regimes in Medieval and Early Modern Europe, 1350-1750. (Cambridge, CUP, 1997).
Euben, R.L., Killing (for) Politics. Jihad, Martyrdom and Political Action. (In: Political Theory, pp.4-35, 2002).
Farazmand, A., Administrative Ethics and Professional Competence. Accountability and Performance. (Sunningdale, UK, IIAS Conference, 1999).
Farazmand, A., ed., Handbook of Bureaucracy. (New York, Marcel Dekker, 1994).
Farazmand, A., ed., Modern Systems of Government. Exploring the Role of Bureaucrats and Politicians. (London, Sage, 1997).
Farnsworth, E.A., An Introduction to the Legal System of the United States. (New York, Oceana, 1963; 1986).
Featherstone, M., ed., Global Culture. Nationalism, Globalization and Modernity. (London, Sage, 1990).
Featherstone, M., et al., eds., Global Modernities. (Newbury Park, Sage, 1995).
Feigenbaum, H.B., Henig, J.R., Shrinking the State. The Political Underpinnings of Privatization. (Cambridge, CUP, 1998).
Finnis, J.M., Natural Law and Natural Rights. (Oxford, OUP, 1980).
Fitzmaurice, D., Justice, practical reason and boundaries. (In: Lehning, P.B., Weale, A., eds., Citizenship, democracy and justice in the New Europe. (London, Routledge, pp.15-33, 1997).
Fletcher, J., Violence and Civilization. (Oxford, Polity, 1997).
Frank, J., Law and the Modern Mind (1930). (New York, Coward-McCann, 1949).
Franks Committee, Committee on Administrative Tribunals and Enquiries. (London, 1957).
Freeden, M., Rights. (Buckingham Open University Press, 1991).
Freeman, C., The Greek Achievement. The Foundation of the Western World. (London, Penguin, 1999).
Friedrich, C.J., Constitutional Government and Democracy. Theory and Practice in Europe and America (1937). (Boston, Ginn, 1950).
Friedrich, C.J., Constitutional Reason of State. The Survival of the Constitutional Order. (Providence, Brown UP, 1957).
Friedrich, C.J., The Philosophy of Law in Historical Perspective. (Chicago, University of Chicago Press, 1958).
Friedrich, C.J., Man and His Government. An Empirical Theory of Politics. (New York, McGraw-Hill, 1963).
Friedrich, C.J., Tradition and Authority. (New York, Praeger, 1972).
Friedrich, C.J., ed., Authority. (Cambridge, MA, Harvard UP, 1958).
Friedrich, C.J., ed., The Public Interest. (New York, Atherton, 1962).
Fukuyama, F., The End of History and the Last Man. (London, Penguin, 1992).
Garcia-Zamor, J.C., Khator, R., eds., Public Administration in the Global Village. (Westport, Praeger, 1994).
Gauthier, D., The Logic of Leviathan. (Oxford, Clarendon, 1969).
Gauthier, D., Morals by Agreement. (Oxford, Clarendon, 1986).
Gauthier, D., ed., Morality and Rational Self-Interest. (Englewood Cliffs, Prentice-Hall, 1970).
Geertz, C., The Interpretation of Cultures. (New York, Basic Books, 1973; 1974).
Geertz, C., ed., Old Societies and New States. (New York, Free Press, 1963).
Gerth, H., Wright Mills, C., From Max Weber. (New York, OUP, 1958).
Gibbon, E., The Decline and Fall of the Roman Empire. (London, Campbell, 1993/1994).
Giddens, A., The Constitution of Society. (Cambridge, Polity, 1984).
Giddens, A., Runaway World. How Globalisation is Reshaping our Lives. (London, Profile Books, 1999).
Glendon, M.A., Rights Talk. The Impoverishment of our Political Discourse. (New York, Free Press, 1991).
Glover, J., ed., Utilitarianism and its critics. (New York, Macmillan, 1990).
Goldworth, A., ed., Deontology in the Collected Works of Jeremy Bentham. (Oxford, Clarendon, 1983).
Gouldner, A., The Coming Crisis of Western Sociology. (London, Heinemann, 1970).
Gray, J., Berlin. (London, Fontana, 1995).
Grimm, A.P., American Politcal Thought. (New York, 1964).

Gunnell, J.G., Realizing Theory. The Philosophy of Science Revisited. (In: Journal of Politics, pp.923-940, 1995).
Guyer, P., Critique of the Power of Judgement (1790). (Cambridge, CUP, 2000).
Habermas, J., The Theory of Communicative Action. (Boston, Beacon, transl., 1984).
Habermas, J., Moral Consciousness and Communicative Action. (Cambridge, MA, MIT, 1990).
Habermas, J., The Structural Transformation of the Public Sphere. (Cambridge, MA, MIT, 1994).
Hall, E. and M., Understanding Cultural Differences. (Yarmouth, Intercultural Press, 1990).
Hall, G.D.G., The Treatise on the Laws and Customs of the Realm of England Commonly Called Glanvill. (London, 1965).
Hall, J.A., Powers & Liberties. The Causes and Consequences of the Rise of the West. (Oxford, OUP, 1985).
Hall, J.A., ed., States in History. (Oxford, OUP, 1986).
Halpin, A., Rights and Law Analysis and Theory. (Oxford, Hart, 1997).
Hardy, H., ed., The Crooked Timber of Humanity. Chapters in the History of Ideas. (New York, Knopf, 1991).
Hart, H.L.A., The Concept of Law. (Oxford, Clarendon, 1961; 1994).
Hart, H.L.A., Essays on Bentham. Studies in jurisprudence and political theory. (Oxford, Clarendon, 1982).
Hart, H.L.A., Essays in Jurisprudence and Philosophy. (Oxford, Clarendon, 1983; 1993).
Hart, H.L.A., ed., Of Laws in General. (Cambridge, 1970).
Hart, H.M., Sacks, A.M., The Legal Process. Basic Problems in the Making and Application of Law. (Cambridge, Harvard Law School, 1958).
Hegel, G.W.F., Philosophy of Right. (Oxford, OUP, transl., 1967).
Held, D., et al., Global Transformations. Politics, Economics and Culture. (Cambridge, Polity, 1999).
Heller, A., Beyond Justice. (Oxford, Blackwell, 1987).
Heller, A., Fehér, F., The Postmodern Political Condition. (New York, Columbia UP, 1988).
Hewart, Lord, The New Despotism. (London, 1929).
Hirschman, A.O., Exit, Voice and Loyalty. (Cambridge, MA., Harvard UP, 1970).
Hirst, P., Representative Democracy and its Limits. (Cambridge, Polity, 1990).
Hirst, P., From Statism to Pluralism. (London, UCL, 1997).
Hobbes, T., De Cive. (London, 1642).
Hobbes, T., Leviathan. (London, 1651; Cambridge, CUP, 1991).
Hobbes, T., The English Works of Thomas Hobbes. (London, Bohn, 1840).
Hobbes, T., A Dialogue between a pholosopher and a student of the common laws. (Chicago, 1971).
Hofstede, G., Cultures and Organizations. Software of the Mind. (London, McGraw-Hill, 1991).
Holdsworth, W.S., A History of English Law. (London, Methuen, 1903; 1956).
Holt, M.P., The French Wars of Religion 1562-1629. (Cambridge, CUP, 1995).
Holmes, O.W., The Common Law (1881). (Cambridge, MA, Harvard UP, 1963, 1973).
Holt, P.M., et al., The Cambridge History of Islam. (Cambridge, CUP, 1970; 1977).
Hood, C., The Art of the State. Culture, Rhetoric and Public Management. (Oxford, Clarendon, 1998; 2000).
Hooker, M.B., Legal pluralism: An Introduction to colonial and neo-colonial law. (Oxford, Clarendon, 1975).
Hooker, R., Of the Laws of Ecclesiastical Polity. (London, 1597).
Hudson, J., The Formation of the English Common Law. Law and Society in England from the Norman Conquest to Magna Carta. (London, Longman, 1996).
Hudson, J., ed., The History of English Law. (Oxford, OUP, 1996).
Hume, L.J., Bentham and Bureaucracy. (Cambridge, CUP, 1981).
Hunt, A., ed., Reading Dworkin Critically. (Oxford, Berg, 1992).
Huntington, S.P., Political Order in Changing Societies. (New Haven, Yale UP, 1968).
Huntington, S.P., The Clash of Civilizations and the Remaking of World Order. (New York, Simon and Schuster, 1996).
Inglehart, R., Culture Shift. (Princeton, UP, 1990).
Ingraham, P.W., Romzek, B.S., eds., New Paradigms for Government: Issues for the Changing Public Service. (San Francisco, Jossey-Bass, 1994).
Jackson, R.H., Quasi-States. Sovereignty, International Relations and the Third World. (Cambridge, CUP, 1990).
Jackson, R.H., ed., Sovereignty at the Millennium. (Oxford, Blackwell, 1999).
Jahanbegloo, R., Conversations with Isaiah Berlin. (London, Phoenix, 2000).
Jowell, J., Law and Bureaucracy. Adminstrative Discretion and the Limits of Legal Action. (Port Washington, Dunellen, 1975).
Jowell, J., Oliver, D., eds., The Changing Constitution. (Oxford, Clarendon, 1994).
Kagan, R., Adversial Legalism. The American Way of Law. (Harvard, Harvard UP, 2000).

Kahn, P.W., Legitimacy and History. Self-Government in American Constitutional Theory. (New Haven, Yale UP, 1992).
Kairys, D., The Politics of Law. A Progressive Critique. (New York, Pantheon, 1982).
Kalman, L., Legal Realism at Yale, 1927-1960. (Chapel Hill, University of North Carolina Press, 1986).
Kandiyoti, D., ed., Women, Islam and the State. (London, Macmillan, 1991).
Kant, I., Fundamental Principles of the Metaphysics of Ethics (1785). (London, Longmans, 1969).
Kant, I., Philosophy of Law. (London, 1887).
Kant, I., The Metaphysical Elements of Justice. (Indianapolis, Bobbs-Merrill, 1965).
Kant, I., Perpetual Peace and Other Essays (1795). (London, 1983).
Kantorowicz, E.H., The King's Two Bodies. (Princeton, Princeton UP, 1957).
Kaplan, R., The Coming Anarchy. (New York, 2001).
Kardulias, P.N., ed., World-Systems Theory in Practice. Leadership, Production and Exchange. (Lanham, Rowman & Littelfield, 1999).
Karpen, U., ed., The Constitution of the Federal Republic of Germany. (London, 1988).
Kateb, G., Can Cultures be Judged? Two Defenses of Cultural Pluralism in Isaiah Berlin's Work. (In: Social Research, pp.1009-1038, 1999).
Katzenstein, P.J., Cultural Norms and National Security. (Ithaca, Cornell UP, 1996).
Keble, J., dir., Richard Hooker. The Works. (New York, Olms, 1977).
Kelly, P.J., Utilitarianism and distributive justice. Jeremy Bentham and the Civil Law. (Oxford, 1990).
Kelsen, H., The General Theory of Law and State. (London, 1927; New York, Russell & Russell, 1961).
Kelsen, H., The Pure Theory of Law. (Berkeley, University of California Press, 1967).
Kelsen, H., General Theory of Norms. (Oxford, Clarendon, 1991).
Kelsen, H., Introduction to the Problems of Legal Theory. (Oxford, Clarendon, 1992).
Kernaghan, K., ed., For a Responsable Public Administration. Reconciliation of Democracy, Efficacy and Ethics. (In: International Review of Administrative Sciences, vol.66 no.1, March 2000).
Kettle, D., The Global Public Management Revolution. (Washington DC, Brookings Institution, 2000).
Kier, E., Imagining War: British and French Military Doctrine Between the Wars. (Princeton, Princeton UP, 1997).
King, A.D., ed., Culture, Globalization and the World System. (Houndmills, Basingstoke, Macmillan, 1991).
King, G., Keohane, R., Verba, S., Designing Social Inquiry. Scientific Inference in Qualitative Research. (Princeton, Princeton UP, 1994).
Knachel, P.H., England and the Fronde. The Impact of the English War and Revolution on France. (Ithaca, Cornell UP, 1967).
Kolakowski, L., Modernity on Endless Trial. (Chicago, University of Chicago Press, 1990).
Korten, D.C., When Corporations Rule the World. (London, Earthscan Publications, 1995).
Kramer, S.N., History begins in Sumer. (London, 1986).
Kymlicka, W., Liberalism, Community and Culture. (Oxford, Clarendon, 1989).
Kymlicka, W., Contemporary Political Philosophy. (Oxford, Clarendon, 1990).
Kymlicka, W., Multicultural Citizenship. A Liberal Theory of Minority Rights. (Oxford, Clarendon, 1995).
Larmore, C., The Morals of Modernity. (Cambridge, CUP, 1996).
Lasswell, H.D., Kaplan, A., Power and Society. A Framework for Political Inquiry. (New Haven, Yale UP, 1950; 1963).
Levene, M., Why is the Twentieth Century the Century of Genocide? (In: Journal of World History, pp.305-336, 2000).
Levene, M., Roberts, P., eds., The Massacre in History. (Oxford, 1999).
Liddell Hart, B.H., The British Way in Warfare. (London, Faber, 1932).
Light, P.C., The True Size of Government. (Washington DC, Brookings Institution, 1999).
Locke, J., Two Treatises of Government. (London, 1689; Cambridge, CUP, 1988).
Locke, J., Second Treatise on Civil Government. (London, 1690; New York, Nostrand, 1947).
Locke, J., A Letter concerning human understanding. (Indianapolis, Bobbs-Merrill, 1950).
Locke, J., An Essay concerning human understanding. (London, Dent, 1961).
Lodge, E.C., Thornton, G.A., English Constitutional Documents, 1307-1496. (London, 1935).
Lowie, R., Primitive Society. (New York, 1947).
Luhmann, N., Trust and Power. (Chichester, Wiley, 1979).
Luhmann, N., The Differentiation of Society. (New York, Columbia UP, 1982).
Luhmann, N., A Sociological Theory of Law. (London, Routledge/Kegan Paul, 1985).
Luhmann, N., The Autopoiesis of Social Systems. (In: Geyer, F., Zouwen, J. van der, eds., Sociocybernetic Paradoxes. Observation, Control and Evolution of Self-Steering Systems. London, Sage, pp.172-192, 1986).
Luhmann, N., Ecological Communication. (Cambridge, Polity, 1989).

Luhmann, N., Essays in Self-Reference. (New York, Columbia UP, 1990).
Luhmann, N., Political Theory in the Welfare State. (New York, W. de Gruyter, 1990).
Luhmann, N., Sociology of Risk. (Berlin, W. de Gruyter, 1993).
Luhmann, N., Social Systems. (Stanford, Stanford UP, 1995).
Lynn, L., Public Management as Art, Science and Profession. (Chatham, Chatham House, 1996).
MacIntyre, A., After Virtue. A Study in Moral Theory. (Notre Dame, University of Notre Dame Press, 1981; 1984).
MacIntyre, A., Whose Justice? Whch Rationality? (Notre Dame, University of Notre Dame Press, 1988).
Mackenzie, G., The Institutions of the Law of Scotland. (Edinburgh, 1684).
Maitland, V.F.W., Pollock, F., The History of English Law. (Cambridge, CUP, 1968).
Maguire, J., Marx's Theory of Politics. (Cambridge, CUP, 1978).
Marks, S., The Riddle of All Constitutions. International Law, Democracy and the Critique of Ideology. (Oxford, OUP, 2000).
Martin, M.M., Histoire de l'unité française, l'idée de patrie en France des origines à nos jours. (Paris, PUF, 1982).
Martin, O., Sociologie des sciences. (Paris, Nathan, 2000).
Maturana, H.R., Varela, F.J., Autopoiesis and Cognition, the Realisation of the Living. (Boston, Riedel, 1980).
McGregor, H., Contract Code, drawn up on behalf of the English Law Commission. (Milan, 1993).
McSwite, O.C., Legitimacy in Public Administration. A Discourse Analysis. (London, Sage, 1997).
Miller, D., Principles of Social Justice. (Cambridge, MA, Harvard UP, 1999).
Milsom, S.F.C., Historical Foundations of the Common Law. (London, 1969).
Milsom, S.F.C., Legal Framework of English Feudalism. (Cambridge, CUP, 1976).
Milsom, S.F.C., The Nature of Blackstone's Achievement. (London, Selden Society, 1981).
Mintzberg, H., Managerial Work. (New York, Harper and Row, 1973).
Mommsen, W.J., Moor, J.A. de, eds., European Expansion and Law. The encounters of European and indigenous law in 19th and 20th-century Africa and Asia. (Oxford, Berg, 1992).
Montesquieu, C. de Secondat, The Persian Letters (1721). (Harmondsworth, Penguin, 1973).
Montesquieu, C. de Secondat, The Spirit of the Laws (1748). (New York, Hafner, 1949).
Montesquieu, C. de Secondat, Considerations on the Causes of the Greatness of the Romans and Their Decline. (Ithaca, Cornell UP, 1968).
Murphy, J.W., Talcott Parsons and Niklas Luhmann. Two Versions of the Social System. (In: International Review of Modern Sociology, pp.291-301, 1982).
Navari, C., Internationalism and the State in the Twentieth Century. (London, Routledge, 2000).
Nef, J.U., Industry and Government in France and England, 1540-1640. (Ithaca, Cornell UP, 1967).
Nisbet, R., Twilight of Authority. (Oxford, OUP, 1975).
NOMOS, Authority. (Cambridge, MA, Harvard UP; Greenwood, 1982).
NOMOS, The Public Interest. (New York, Atherton, 1962).
NOMOS, Justice. (New York, Atherton, 1963; 1974).
NOMOS, The Limits of Law. (New York, New York UP, 1973).
NOMOS, Constitutionalism. (New York, New York UP, 1979).
NOMOS, Human Rights. (New York, New York UP, 1981).
NOMOS, Authority Revisited. (New York, New York UP, 1987).
NOMOS, Markets and Justice. (New York, New York UP, 1989).
NOMOS, The Rule of Law. (New York, New York UP, 1994).
NOMOS, Political Order. (New York, New York UP, 1996).
NOMOS, Integrity and Conscience. (New York, New York UP, 1998).
Nozick, R., Anarchy, State and Utopia. (Oxford, Blackwell, 1974).
Ojo, B.A., Human Rights and the New World Order. Universality, Acceptability and Human Diversity. (Commack, Nova Science, 1997).
Parisi, R.A., ed., The Economic Structure of the Law. The Collected Essays of Richard A. Posner. (Cheltenham, Elgar, 2000).
Parisi, R.A., ed., The Economics of Private Law. The Collected Essays of Richard A. Posner. (Cheltenham, Elgar, 2001).
Parisi, R.A., ed., The Economics of Public Law. The Collected Essays of Richard A. Posner. (Cheltenham, Elgar, 2001).
Parsons, T., The Structure of Social Action. (New York, McGraw-Hill, 1937).
Parsons, T., The Social System. (New York, Free Press, 1951).
Parsons, T., Structure and Process in Modern Societies. (New York, Free Press, 1960; 1964).

Parsons, T., Sociological Theory and Modern Society. (New York, Free Press, 1967).
Pelling, H., A History of British Trade Unionism. (London, Penguin, 1963).
Peretti, T., In Defense of a Political Court. (Princeton, Princeton UP, 1999).
Perry, M.J., The Idea of Human Rights. Four Inquiries. (Oxford, OUP, 1998).
Peters, B.G., Comparing Public Bureaucracies. (Tuscaloosa, University of Alabama, 1988).
Peters, B.G., The Future of Governing. Four Emerging Models. (Lawrence, University Press of Kansas, 1996).
Pogge, T.W., Realizing Rawls. (Ithaca, Cornell UP, 1989).
Poggi, G., The Development of the Modern State. (Stanford, Stanford UP, 1978).
Postema, G., Bentham and the Common Law Tradition. (Oxford, Clarendon, 1986).
Pound, R., Justice according to the law. (In: Columbia Law Review, pp.1-26, 1914).
Pound, R., Administrative Law. (Pittsburgh, University of Pittsburgh, 1942).
Pound, R., Jurisprudence. (St. Paul, West Publishing Company, 1959).
Pound, (Essays in honor of Roscoe), Interpretation of modern legal philosophies. (New York, OUP, 1947).
Pye, L., Aspects of Political Development. (Boston, Little-Brown, 1967).
Raadschelders, J.C.N., Understanding Government in Society. We see the trees, but could we see the forest? (In: Administrative Theory & Praxis, pp.192-225, 2000).
Raadschelders, J.C.N., Government. A Public Administration Perspective. (Armonk, NY, Sharpe, 2003).
Radin, M.J., Contested Commodities. (Cambridge, MA, Harvard UP, 1996).
Radzinowicz, L., A History of English Criminal Law and its Administration from 1750. (New York, Macmillan, 1948/1968).
Rakowski, E., Equal Justice. (New York, OUP, 1991).
Rawls, J., A Theory of Justice. (Oxford, OUP, 1971; 1972).
Rawls, J., Kantian Constructivism in Moral Theory. (In: Journal of Philosophy, pp.515-572, 1980).
Rawls, J., Justice as Fairness. Political not Metaphysical. (In: Philosophy and Public Affairs, pp.223-251, 1985).
Rawls, J., The Idea of an Overlapping Consensus. (In: Oxford Journal of Legal Studies, pp.1-25, 1987).
Rawls, J., Political Liberalism. (New York, Columbia UP, 1993).
Rawls, J., Collected Papers. (Cambridge, MA, Harvard UP, 1999).
Raz, J., The Authority of Law. (Oxford, Clarendon, 1979).
Raz, J., The Concept of a Legal System. (Oxford, Clarendon, 1980).
Raz, J., The Morality of Freedom. (Oxford, Clarendon, 1986).
Raz, J., Practical Reason and Norms. (Princeton, Princeton UP, 1990).
Raz, J., Ethics in the Public Domain. (Oxford, Clarendon, 1994; OUP, 1995).
Raz, J., ed., Authority. (Oxford, Blackwell, 1990).
Richardson, F., Fowers, B., eds., Social Inquiry. A Hermeneutic Reconceptualization. (In: American Behavioral Scientist, January 1998).
Riker, W.H., Federalism. (In: Greenstein, F.I., Polsby, N.W., eds., The Handbook of Political Science. Reading, MA, Addison-Wesley, 1975).
Riley, J., Defending Cultural Pluralism. Within Liberal Limits. (In: Political Theory, pp.68-96, 2002).
Riley, J., Mills's Radical Liberalism. London, Routledge, 2002).
Ripstein, A., Equality, Responsibility and the Law. (New York, CUP, 1999).
Roberts, J.M., The Penguin History of the World. (London, Penguin, 1990; 1992).
Robertson, N., Thomas, J.L., Trade Union and Industrial Relations. (London, Business Books, 1968).
Robertson, R., Mapping the Global Condition. Globalization as the Central Concept. (In: Featherstone, M., ed., Global Culture. London, Sage, pp.15-30, 1990).
Robertson, R., After Nostalgia? Willful Nostalgia and the Phases of Globalization. (In: Turrner, B.S., ed., Theories of Modernity and Postmodernity. London, Sage, pp.45-61, 1990).
Robertson, R., Globalization. Social Theory and Global Culture. (Newbury Park, Sage, 1992).
Robertson, R., Glocalization. Time-Space and Homogeneity-Heterogeneity. (In: Featherstone, M., et al., eds., Global Modernities. Newbury Park, Sage, 1995).
Robson, W.A., Justice and Administrative Law. (London, 1951).
Roemer, J.E., Theories of Distributive Justice. (Cambridge, MA, Harvard UP, 1996).
Rohr, J.A., To Run a Constitution. The Legitimacy of the Administrative State. (Lawrence, University Press of Kansas, 1986).
Rohr, J.A., Ethics for Bureaucrats. An Essay on Law and Values. (New York, Dekker, 1989).
Rohr, J.A., Public Service, Ethics and Constitutional Practice. (New York, 1998).
Rohr, J.A., The Ethical Aftermath of Privatization and Contracting Out. (In: Public Integrity, pp.1-12, 2002).
Rohr, J.A., Civil Servants and Their Constitutions. (New York, 2002).

Rosen, F., Jeremy Bentham and Representative Democracy. A Study of the Constitutional Code. (Oxford, Clarendon, 1983).
Rosenbloom, D.H., et al., Constitutional Competence for Public Managers. (Ithaca, Peacock, 2000).
Rosenthal, E.I.J., Political Thought in Medieval Islam. (Cambridge, CUP, 1958).
Russell Major, J., From Renaissance Monarchy to Absolute Monarchy. (Baltimore, Johns Hopkins UP, 1994).
Sandel, M., Liberalism and the Limits of Justice. (Cambridge, CUP, 1982).
Sandel, M., Democracy's Discontent: America in Search of a Public Philosophy. (New York, Belknap, 1999).
Sanderson, S.K., ed., Civilizations and World-Systems. Two Approaches to the Study of World-Historical Change. (Walnut Creek, CA, Altamira Press, 1995).
Sartori, G., Comparative Constitutional Engineering. (New York, New York UP, 1997).
Sawer, G., Modern Federalism. (London, Watts, 1976).
Scarman, L., English Law, the New Dimensions. (London, Stevens, 1974).
Schubert, G., "The Public Interest" in Administrative Decisionmaking. (In: American Political Science Review, pp.346-368, 1957).
Schubert, G., The Public Interest. A Critique of the Theory of a Political Concept. (New York, 1961).
Schubert, G., ed., Judicial Decisionmaking. (New York, Free Press, 1963).
Schubert, G., ed., Judicial Behavior. (Chicago, Rand McNally, 1964).
Schütz, A., Collected Papers. (The Hague, Nijhoff, 1962/1964).
Schütz, A., The Phenomenology of the Social World. (London, Heinemann, 1980).
Shils, E., Political Development in the New States. (The Hague, Mouton, 1960).
Spicer, M.W., Herder on Cultural Pluralism and the State. (In: Administrative Theory & Praxis, pp.309-325, 2000).
Stair, Lord, The Institutions of Law of Scotland. (Edinburgh, 1681).
Stark, A., Conflict of Interest in American Public Life. (Cambridge, MA, Harvard UP, 2000).
Stark, A., Beyond Choice. Rethinking the Post-Rawlsian Debate over Egalitarian Justice. (In: Political Theory, pp.36-67, 2002).
Swartz, D., Culture and Power. The Sociology of Pierre Bourdieu. (Chicago, University of Chicago Press, 1997).
Symonides, J., ed., Human Rights. Concept and Standards. (Dartmouth, Ashgate, 2000).
Thorne, S., Bracton and the Laws and Customs of England. (London, 1977).
Thorne, S., Essays in English History. (London, Ambledon, 1985).
Tierney, B., Religion, Law and the Growth of Constitutional Thought, 1150-1650. (Cambridge, CUP, 1982).
Tierney, B., Origins of Natural Rights Language. Texts and Contexts, 1150-1250. (In: History of Political Thought, pp.615-646, 1989).
Tilly, C., ed., The Formation of National States in Western Europe. (Princeton, Princeton UP, 1975).
Torremans, P., ed., Legal Convergence in the Enlarged Europe of the New Millennium. (The Hague, 2000).
Tribe, L., American Constitutional Law. (New York, Foundation Press, 1978).
Truman, D.B., The Governmental Process. Political Interests and Public Opinion. (New York, 1951).
Twining, W., Karl N. Llewellyn and the Realist Movement. (London, Weidenfeld & Nicolson, 1973; 1985).
Twining, W., W., Law in Context. Enlarging the Discipline. (Oxford, Clarendon, 1997).
Twining, W., Miers, D., How to do things with rules. (London, Weidenfeld & Nicolson, 1991).
Van Creveld, M., The Rise and Decline of the State. (Cambridge, CUP, 1999).
Van Parijs, P., Real Freedom for All. (Oxford, Clarendon, 1995).
Villela, G., The Administrative Sciences on the Wave of Transition. (Brussels, IIAS, 2000).
Volcansek, M.L., Lafon, J.L., The Cross-Evolution of French and American Practices. (Westport, Greenwood, 1987).
Vries, P.H.H., Governing Growth: Comparative Analysis of the Role of the State in the Rise of the West. (In: Journal of World History, pp. 67-129, 2002).
Wagner, G., The End of Luhmann's Social Systems Theory. (In: Philosophy of the Social Sciences, pp.387-409, 1997).
Wallerstein, I., The Modern World System I. (New York, Academic Press, 1974).
Wallerstein, I., The Modern World System II. (New York, 1980).
Wallerstein, I., The Modern World System III. (San Diego, 1989).
Walzer, M., The Spheres of Justice. (New York, Basic Books, 1983; 1984).
Walzer, M., Interpretation and Social Criticism. (Cambridge, MA, Harvard UP, 1987).
Walzer, M., The Legal Codes of Ancient Israel. (In: NOMOS, New York UP, pp.101-119, 1994).
Watson, B., Han Fei Tzu. Translations from the Asian Classics. (New York, Columbia UP, 1996).
Watson, M., An English Reader's Guide to the French Legal System. (Oxford, Berg, 1991).

Weber, M., The Theory of Social and Economic Organization (1922). (Oxford, OUP, 1957).
Weighley, R.F., The American Way of War. A History of United States Military Strategy and Policy. (Bloomington, Indiana UP, 1973).
Werner, W.G., Wilde, J.H. de, The Endurance of Sovereignty. (In: European Journal of International Relations, pp.283-313, 2001).
Wheare, K.C., Modern Constitutions. (Oxford, OUP, 1951).
Wheare, K.C., Federal Government. (Oxford, OUP, 1961).
Wilson, W., The Study of Administration. (In: Political Science Quarterly, pp.197-222, 1887).
Woller, G.M., Patterson, K.D., Public Administration Ethics. A Postmodern Perspective. (In: Woller, G.M., ed., Public Administration and Postmodernism. In: American Behavioral Scientist, pp.103-118, 1997).
Zeldin, T., The French. (London, Harvill, 1997).
Zerbe, R.O., Economic Efficiency in Law and Economics. (Cheltenham, Elgar, 2001).

# Epilogue

It is like opening an open door to write that the French legacy to the Western world is imposing. Indeed, French cultural emanation in the European context and worldwide is impressive. Starting from this axiom, research in the sphere of politics, public administration, law, economics, history and social sciences makes one wonder why the French contribution to ideas about the activities of public authorities is relatively underexposed in Anglo-American literature. Stimulated by this astonishment, a research project into the Public Management of Society phenomenon (PMS) has been accomplished, specifically about PMS in the historical-cultural circumstances in France throughout some 2,000 years, in comparative perspective. This has resulted in a convincing rediscovery of the relevance of French institutional engineering in its multi-various forms. There is a French way of Public Management of Society. Public Management of Society, defined as knowledge about the activities of public authorities, is a specific social phenomenon that has to be analysed with a co-disciplinary approach. This phenomenon is currently studied in several disciplines and sub-disciplines, but often in a partial way: only some aspects of this complex phenomenon are dealt with in mono-disciplinary studies. The challenge has been to analyse the PMS phenomenon as completely as possible, studying the object of PMS as such. PMS ("formule vedette") is chosen as the object instead of alternatives such as politics, state, government, public administration or governance (all having their constraints). Disciplined crossing of disciplinary boundaries is inevitable when PMS as such is the object of research. In this research project this has been attempted in the perspective of work done by many social scientists, "standing on their shoulders". Recognising their contributions one can conclude that this study makes sense. Intellectual travelling by transgressing the boundaries of scientific disciplines is challenging, feeding dynamic wonderment and fresh insights. Especially with its cultural dimensions along the English-French language frontier this book enables readers to make themselves familiar with PMS in the French environment, in historical perspective (I-XX centuries). Some aspects, ideas and conclusions are summarised here.

PMS can be studied adequately in the framework of the co-disciplinary social science conception of Luhmann, generally underexposed in mainstream literature. His advanced theoretical conception encompasses seven working-hypotheses for the analysis of the PMS phenomenon. The present study reached the conclusion that an eighth working-hypothesis can be added: Adequate analysis of PMS makes study of specific cultural dimensions in nations, countries, regions and communities a necessity. Analysis of cultural dimensions, cultural mapping, is a necessary condition for adequate theorising about PMS. Besides, practitioners need a thorough idea about the cultural context of their activities to be effective. Best practices are optimal only, if culturally intelligent. The French legacy in the sphere of PMS is quite impressive. France is a cultural superpower with a very positive surplus on its cultural import-export balance. France was and is a creative institutional laboratory for PMS, with useful insights and lessons, for the Anglo-Americans and the rest of the world. Lessons learned from experiences with failures, and lessons about the way to improve and to innovate. Up till now these have not been fully assimilated due to mental rigidities on both sides (Anglo-American and French). Former Communist countries in Eastern Europe can benefit especially from French experiences to transform their countries. Of course, France can also learn from other countries in several dimensions. The extended bibliography connected with this study can function as eye-opener for the checking of literature consumption by authors in mainstream literature. It can further critical awareness about selective reading, writing and thinking on both sides of the French-English language dichotomy. French institutional engineering has multi-various forms. Institutionalism is a structural character of French ideation, policies and practices, also in its negative aspects, as it caused rigidities when adaptations to societal dynamism were needed. Partly this can be explained by the fact that one of the functions of institutions is to give human activities some certainties in an uncertain world. Normally these don't change with the whims of fashion in societal regulation.

Law, organised by public authorities, has been prominent in the French context as an instrument for societal regulation. In the process of the emancipation of public authorities, law proved to be vital for the development of the Idea of Public Authority. As elaborated earlier, the axis between the Rule of Law and the Idea of Public Authority is crucial. France worked in the right direction by always stressing the relevance of a prominent position for law. The French way of institutionalising law had a drawback though. Always overstressing law as State law, it underexposed the relevance of law between societal actors as made by themselves. One of the lessons of this study is that the tendency in mainstream literature is to accentuate Public Administration as a total of technicalities, usable worldwide without adequate cultural mapping of relevant cultural dimensions. This is not correct. Societal regulation by public authorities always has to take account of the specifics of the cultural-historical context. The imposing role of the French institutional paradigm, pioneering in the overlapping spheres of public law and politics, is interesting. French authors had shown the relevance of institutionalism long before Anglo-American authors started to write about aspects of the subject. Probably this came about because several French authors developed a rigid-formalist approach, without sufficiently taking empirical realities into account.

Part of the French legacy is the development of the human rights movement. In his book "The Greek Achievement. The Foundation of the Western World", C. Freeman (1999, p.443) wrote: "The flaw of the Greek political system was that it never developed a theory of human rights." Following the French Revolution France pretended to formulate human rights as universal rights worldwide. Proclaiming human rights is one thing, implementation of human rights is more important, if necessary with intervention by public authorities. Human rights demand Public Management of Society, as public duties for public authorities. While it is popular in the euphoria over globalisation to make society dependent on the market, the primary role of law has to be stressed. Ubi societas, ibi ius. Society does not ask for the primacy of the market or the primacy of politics, but for the primacy of law, also in the international field. Long ago Georges Bernanos said that France for him continued to be an enigma in a number of aspects. Perhaps this study is useful in unveiling somewhat the enigma of French Public Management of Society. As is made clear in this study, for Public Management of Society to be effective it must be applied with cultural intelligence, reckoning with specific cultural dimensions. It might be useful to undertake a study like this about Public Management of Society in other countries of the European Union and in the countries that aspire to become member-states of the European Union. Ubi ius, ibi societas. Ubi societas, ibi ius et auctoritas publica.

RENEWALS 458-4574